Operating Systems

Third Edition

H. M. Deitel
Deitel & Associates, Inc.

P. J. Deitel
Deitel & Associates, Inc.

D. R. Choffnes
Deitel & Associates, Inc.

PEARSON
Prentice Hall

Upper Saddle River, NJ 07458

Deitel® Books, Cyber Classrooms, Complete Training Courses and Web-Based Training Courses published by Prentice Hall

Computer Science Series
Operating Systems, 3/E

How To Program Series
Advanced Java™ 2 Platform How to Program
C How to Program, 4/E
C++ How to Program, 4/E
C#® How to Program
e-Business and e-Commerce How to Program
Internet and World Wide Web How to Program, 3/E
Java™ How to Program, 5/E
Perl How to Program
Python How to Program
Visual Basic® 6 How to Program
Visual Basic® .NET How to Program, 2/E
Visual C++® .NET How to Program
Wireless Internet & Mobile Business How to Program
XML How to Program

Simply Series
Simply C#®: An Application-Driven Tutorial Approach
Simply Java™ Programming: An Application-Driven Tutorial Approach
Simply Visual Basic® .NET: An Application-Driven Tutorial Approach (Visual Studio .NET 2002 Edition)
Simply Visual Basic® .NET: An Application-Driven Tutorial Approach (Visual Studio .NET 2003 Edition)

CS1 Programming Series
Java™ Software Design

.NET How to Program Series
C#® How to Program
Visual Basic® .NET How to Program, 2/E
Visual C++® .NET How to Program

Visual Studio® Series
C#® How to Program
Getting Started with Microsoft® Visual C++® 6 with an Introduction to MFC
Simply C#®: An Application-Driven Tutorial Approach
Simply Visual Basic® .NET: An Application-Driven Tutorial Approach (Visual Studio .NET 2002 Edition)
Simply Visual Basic® .NET: An Application-Driven Tutorial Approach (Visual Studio .NET 2003 Edition)
Visual Basic® 6 How to Program
Visual Basic® .NET How to Program, 2/E
Visual C++® .NET How to Program

Deitel® Developer Series
Java™ Web Services for Experienced Programmers
Web Services A Technical Introduction

For Managers Series
e-Business and e-Commerce for Managers

Interactive Web-Based Training Series
Premium CourseCompass Version of Visual Basic® .NET Multimedia Cyber Classroom, 2/E
Premium CourseCompass Version of Java™ 2 Multimedia Cyber Classroom, 5/E
Premium CourseCompass Version of C++ Multimedia Cyber Classroom, 4/E

The Complete Training Course Series
The Complete C++ Training Course, 4/E
The Complete C#® Training Course
The Complete e-Business and e-Commerce Programming Training Course
The Complete Internet and World Wide Web Programming Training Course, 2/E
The Complete Java™ 2 Training Course, 5/E
The Complete Perl Training Course
The Complete Python Training Course
The Complete Visual Basic® 6 Training Course
The Complete Visual Basic® .NET Training Course, 2/E
The Complete Wireless Internet & Mobile Business Programming Training Course
The Complete XML Programming Training Course

Interactive Multimedia Cyber Classroom Series
C++ Multimedia Cyber Classroom, 4/E
C#® Multimedia Cyber Classroom
e-Business and e-Commerce Multimedia Cyber Classroom
Internet and World Wide Web Multimedia Cyber Classroom, 2/E
Java™ 2 Multimedia Cyber Classroom, 5/E
Perl Multimedia Cyber Classroom
Python Multimedia Cyber Classroom
Visual Basic® 6 Multimedia Cyber Classroom
Visual Basic® .NET Multimedia Cyber Classroom, 2/E
Wireless Internet & Mobile Business Programming Multimedia Cyber Classroom
XML Multimedia Cyber Classroom

To follow the Deitel publishing program, please subscribe to the free
Deitel® Buzz Online e-mail newsletter at:

www.deitel.com/newsletter/subscribe.html

To communicate with the authors, send e-mail to:

deitel@deitel.com

For information on Deitel instructor-led, corporate training seminars offered worldwide visit:

www.deitel.com

For continuing updates on Prentice Hall and Deitel publications visit:

www.deitel.com,
www.prenhall.com/deitel or
www.InformIT.com/deitel

Vice President and Editorial Director, ECS: *Marcia J. Horton*
Senior Acquisitions Editor: *Kate Hargett*
Associate Editor: *Jennifer Cappello*
Assistant Editor: *Sarah Parker*
Editorial Assistant: *Michael Giacobbe*
Vice President and Director of Production and Manufacturing, ESM: *David W. Riccardi*
Executive Managing Editor: *Vince O'Brien*
Managing Editor: *Tom Manshreck*
Production Editors: *Chirag Thakkar, John F. Lovell*
Production Editor, Media: *Bob Engelhardt*
Production Assistant: *Daniela Petrilli*
Director of Creative Services: *Paul Belfanti*
A/V Production Editor: *Xiaohong Zhu*
Art Studio: *Artworks, York, PA*
Creative Director: *Carole Anson*
Art Director: *Geoffrey Cassar*
Cover Design: *Harvey M. Deitel, David R. Choffnes, Suzanne Behnke*
Interior Design: *Harvey M. Deitel, David R. Choffnes, Geoffrey Cassar, Anne DeMarinis*
Manufacturing Manager: *Trudy Pisciotti*
Manufacturing Buyer: *Lisa McDowell*
Marketing Manager: *Pamela Hersperger*
Marketing Assistant: *Barrie Reinhold*

In memory of Edsger W. Dijkstra.

Harvey M. Deitel
Paul J. Deitel
David R. Choffnes

To my grandparents, Beverly and Jay Peddy:
For your love, generosity and inspiration.

David

Contents

13 File and Database Systems 583

Illustrations

4   Thread Concepts

5   Asynchronous Concurrent Execution

6 Concurrent Programming

7 Deadlock and Indefinite Postponement

8 Processor Scheduling

Part 3 *Physical and Virtual Memory* *374*

9 *Real Memory Organization and Management*

10 *Virtual Memory Organization*

11 Virtual Memory Management

Part 5 Performance, Processors and Multiprocessor Management 638

14 Performance and Processor Design

15 Multiprocessor Management

Part 6 Networking and Distributed Computing 746

16 Introduction to Networking

17 Introduction to Distributed Systems

18 Distributed Systems and Web Services

19 Security

Preface

Live in fragments no longer. Only connect.
Edward Morgan Forster

Welcome to the world of operating systems. This text is intended primarily for use in the one-semester and two-semester operating systems courses (as defined in the most recent ACM/IEEE curriculum) that universities offer to juniors, seniors and graduate students in computer science. Operating systems designers and systems programmers will find the text useful as a reference as well.

The text features extensive case studies on two of today's most important operating systems—Linux (94 pages) and Microsoft® Windows® XP (106 pages)—that represent two different operating system design paradigms—free, open-source development and licensed, corporate development, respectively. The Linux case study follows the development of the kernel through version 2.6. The Windows XP case study highlights the internals of the current version of the most widely used personal computer operating system. These case studies enable you to compare and contrast the design and implementation philosophies used in real-world operating systems.

Both Linux and Windows XP are massive, complex operating systems containing millions of lines of source code. We survey the major components of each operating system. The case studies present issues in personal computer, workstation, multiprocessor, distributed and embedded environments, including a detailed discussion on why Linux and other UNIX-like operating systems have become prominent in the open-source and open-systems philosophies of major corporations.

This preface introduces our teaching approach in *Operating Systems, 3/e* and the book's key content and design elements. We also discuss the ancillary support available with the text. The section entitled "Tour of the Book" overviews the rich coverage of operating systems this book provides.

Operating Systems, 3/e, was reviewed by a team of distinguished academics and industry professionals; their names and affiliations are listed in the Acknowledgements section.

As you read this book, if you have any questions, please send us an e-mail at **deitel@deitel.com**; we will respond promptly. Please visit our Web site, **www.deitel.com**, regularly and sign up for the *Deitel*® *Buzz Online* e-mail newsletter at **www.deitel.com/newsletter/subscribe.html**. We use the Web site and the newsletter to keep our readers current on all Deitel publications and services. The site **www.deitel.com/books/os3e** is dedicated to *Operating Systems, 3/e*. At that site, we will post various ancillary materials for students and instructors, including dependency charts, content updates, errata, suggested student research projects (term projects, directed studies and theses), sample syllabi and the bibliography of research materials from the prior edition of the book. Prentice Hall provides a Companion Website for the book at **www.prenhall.com/deitel**.

Book Design

Operating Systems, 3/e features a completely new, two-color design inspired by the work of Leonardo DaVinci. The two-color design is visually appealing and allows us to use color to improve the pedagogy of the book. For example, defining occurrences of key terms appear in **bold and color** so they stand out to you.

Operating Systems, 3/e Features

Operating Systems, 3/e includes extensive new content. We also revised and updated much of the material from the second edition. The focus on current technologies and issues in distributed computing makes this book unique from its competition. Several new sections have been added to address embedded, real-time and distributed systems. Some key features of this edition are:

- Conforms to all core requirements of the ACM/IEEE CC2001 Operating Systems course requirements.

- Discusses all the CC2001 elective operating systems topics except shell scripting.

- Provides an updated hardware introduction that includes leading-edge technologies and their impact on operating systems design.

- Presents process, thread, memory and disk management solutions that reflect the needs of current applications.

- Supplements the extensive coverage of general-purpose systems with concepts relevant to real-time, embedded and superscalar architectures.

- Highlights key evaluation techniques that enable effective comparative analyses of operating system components.

- Includes a richer treatment of networking concepts.

- Enhances the security treatment to include current trends in authentication mechanisms, security protocols, anti-virus research, access control methods and wireless security.

- Enhances the distributed computing coverage to acknowledge the tremendous influence of the Internet and the World Wide Web on computing and operating systems.

- Provides details of the ubiquitous Intel® architecture.

- Provides many diagrams, tables, working code examples, pseudocode examples and algorithms.

- Includes a new chapter on threads.

- Pseudocode is presented in Java-like syntax to capitalize on C/C++/Java literacy—virtually all computer-science students know one or more of these languages.

- Provides multithreading treatments in both pseudocode and Java that demonstrate issues in concurrent programming—enabling instructors to cover the material the way they prefer. The Java treatment is new to this edition and is optional. Visit `java.sun.com/j2se/downloads.html` to obtain the latest version of Java. The download page contains a link to the installation instructions.

- Enhances the multiprocessor management treatment.

- Provides new sections on thread scheduling and real-time scheduling.

- Includes a RAID discussion.

- Provides a case study on UNIX processes.

- Includes up-to-the-minute sections on memory-management and disk-scheduling strategies.

- Covers the important topic of I/O systems in many chapters—most notably Chapters 2, 12, 13 and the case study chapters (20 and 21).

- Provides 730 self-review questions and answers (approximately two per section) for immediate feedback.

- Includes extensive research with citations listed in the Works Cited section at the end of each chapter.

Teaching Approach

This book is divided into eight parts, each containing a set of related chapters. The parts are:

1. Introduction to Hardware, Software and Operating Systems
2. Processes and Threads
3. Real and Virtual Memory
4. Secondary Storage, Files and Databases
5. Performance, Processors and Multiprocessor Management
6. Networking and Distributed Computing

7. Security

8. Case Studies

The book's pedagogic features are described below.

Quotations

Each chapter begins with quotations—some are humorous, some are philosophical and some offer interesting insights. Many readers have told us that they enjoy relating the quotations to the chapter material. You might appreciate some of the quotations more *after* reading the chapters.

Objectives

Next, objectives tell you what to expect and give you an opportunity, after reading the chapter, to determine whether you have met these objectives.

Outline

The chapter outline helps you approach the material in a top-down fashion, so you can anticipate the concepts that will be presented in each chapter and set a comfortable learning pace.

Sections and Self-Review Exercises

Each chapter contains small sections that address important operating systems concepts. Most sections end with two self-review exercises and answers. These exercises enable you to test your knowledge, get immediate feedback and gauge your understanding of the material. These exercises also help prepare you for the end-of-chapter exercises and for quizzes and exams. Some of the self-review exercises cannot be answered only from the material presented in their corresponding sections; these are additional teaching and learning opportunities.

Key Terms

The defining occurrence of each term appears in **bold and color**. In addition, all chapters include a Key Terms section containing the terms defined in the chapter and their definitions (1800+ key terms in the text). A cumulative alphabetized glossary appears at the end of the book. The Key Terms sections and the Glossary are wonderful pedagogic devices for review and reference.

Figures

The text contains over 300 charts, diagrams, examples and illustrations that support the concepts presented in the text.

Web Resources

Each chapter contains Web resources that direct you to sites where you can locate valuable additional research materials.

Summary

Detailed end-of-chapter summary sections help you review the key concepts presented in each chapter.

Exercises, Suggested Projects and Suggested Simulations

Each chapter includes many exercises that vary in difficulty from review of basic operating systems principles to complex reasoning and research projects (900+ exercises in the text). Many OS instructors like to assign term projects, so we have included Suggested Projects and Suggested Simulations sections at the end of each chapter's exercises.

Recommended Readings

Each chapter lists recommended books and articles, and provides a brief review of the most important sources for the chapter content so you can do additional research on your own.

Works Cited

This book required an extraordinary research effort. The entire book is thoroughly cited (2300+ citations). Each citation appears as a superscript in the text and corresponds to an entry in the Works Cited section at the end of the chapter. Many of these citations are to Web sites. Prior editions of this text used only standard book and literature citations; those books and papers were often difficult for readers to locate for further research. Now you can access these citations directly via the Web. Also, it is easy to use search engines to locate additional articles on subjects of interest. Many research journals are accessible online—some are free and others are available through personal or organizational memberships in professional societies. The Web is truly a research bonanza that leverages your learning experience.

Index

We provide a two-level index to help you locate any term or concept quickly. For example, each operating system mentioned in the text appears in the index both alphabetically and indented under the term "Operating Systems."

Feature Boxes

The second edition of *Operating Systems* included a full chapter on analytic modeling with queuing theory and Markov processes. This edition omits that material, recognizing that operating systems is for the most part not a mathematical field. Rather it has a basis in what we call "systems thinking"—operating systems is largely a field of empirical results. To illuminate these issues, we have included in this edition four types of feature boxes, presenting material to challenge, entertain and enrich you.

Biographical Notes

Eighteen Biographical Notes provide interesting details about people who have made significant contributions to the field of operating systems—*Edsger Dijkstra, Linus Torvalds, David Cutler, Ken Thompson, Dennis Ritchie, Doug Engelbart, Tim Berners-Lee, Richard Stallman, Gordon Moore, Fernando J. Corbató, Leslie Lamport, Per Brinch Hansen, Peter Denning, Seymour Cray, Bill Gates, Ronald Rivest, Adi Shamir* and *Leonard Adleman*. Please do not attach any particular significance to our choices; these are only a few among thousands of important contributors. Please let us know of other people you feel deserve mention.

Mini Case Studies

In addition to the detailed case studies on the Linux and Windows XP operating systems, 14 Mini Case Studies focus on other important operating systems of historical research or commercial interest. These Mini Case Studies include *Mach, CTSS and Multics, UNIX Systems, Real-Time Operating Systems, Atlas, IBM Mainframe Operating Systems, Early History of the VM Operating System, MS-DOS, Supercomputers, Symbian OS, OpenBSD, Macintosh, User-Mode Linux (UML)* and *OS/2*.

Anecdotes

One of the authors, HMD, accumulated many anecdotes over decades of teaching operating systems in academia and industry. We have included 16 of these anecdotes. Some are humorous; others are thought provoking—raising deep philosophical issues. Each is a (hopefully) pleasant diversion from the book's technical discussions and concludes with a *Lesson to operating systems designers.*

Operating Systems Thinking

Academics enjoy the luxury of being able to study what is interesting about operating systems, especially clever algorithms, data structures and occasionally, areas that lend themselves nicely to mathematical analysis. Industry professionals must build real systems that work and meet the demanding cost, performance and reliability requirements of customers. Both kinds of thinking are rich with interesting issues. There are considerable overlaps as well as significant differences in what academics and industry professionals think about. This book aims to present a balanced treatment of both the academic and industry sides of operating systems theory and practice.

What is "operating systems thinking?" Forty-three Operating Systems Thinking features explore that question. Indeed, some aspects of operating systems lend themselves to sophisticated mathematical analysis. But the author's (HMD's) extended experience in the computer industry—42 years, including working (as a very junior person) on major operating systems research and development efforts at IBM and MIT, writing two earlier editions of this book and teaching operating systems in academia and industry dozens of times—has shown that these systems are far too complex for a significant mathematical treatment at the undergraduate or early graduate level. Even at the advanced graduate level, except for narrow areas of interest, operating systems defy mathematical analysis.

If there is not a mathematical basis for evaluating aspects of operating systems, how can we think about them productively? The answer is what we call "systems thinking," and the text certainly covers this. However, the Operating Systems Thinking features are our effort to capture key concepts that are prevalent in operating systems design and implementation.

The Operating Systems Thinking features are: *Innovation*; *Relative Value of Human and Computer Resources*; *Performance*; *Keep It Simple (KIS)*; *Architecture*; *Caching*; *Legacy Hardware and Software*; *Principle of Least Privilege*; *Protection*; *Heuristics*; *Customers Ultimately Want Applications*; *Data Structures in Operating Systems*; *Asynchronism vs. Synchronism*; *Concurrency*; *Parallelism*; *Standards Conformance*; *Scalability*; *Information Hiding*; *Waiting, Deadlock and Indefinite Postponement*; *Overhead*; *Predictability*; *Fairness*; *Intensity of Resource Management vs. Relative Resource Value*; *There Are No Upper Limits to Processing Power, Memory, Storage and Bandwidth*; *Change Is the Rule Rather Than the Exception*; *Spatial Resources and Fragmentation*; *Virtualization*; *Empirical Results and Locality-Based Heuristics*; *Lazy Allocation*; *Computer Theory in Operating Systems*; *Space–Time Trade-offs*; *Saturation and Bottlenecks*; *Compression and Decompression*; *Redundancy*; *Fault Tolerance*; *Mission-Critical Systems*; *Encryption and Decryption*; *Security*; *Backup and Recovery*; *Murphy's Law and Robust Systems*; *Graceful Degradation*; *Data Replication and Coherency* and *Ethical Systems Design*

Case Studies

Chapters 20 and 21 cover in depth the Linux and Windows XP operating systems, respectively. These thorough case studies were carefully reviewed by key Linux and Windows XP operating systems developers. The outlines for each of these case studies mimic the text's table of contents. The case studies truly reinforce the text's key concepts—the text presents the principles; the case studies show how these principles are applied in building today's two most widely used operating systems. The Linux case study follows the development of the latest kernel release (v. 2.6) and contains 262 citations. The Windows XP case study reflects the latest Windows operating system features and contains 485 citations.

Tour of the Book

This section provides an overview of the eight parts and 21 chapters of *Operating Systems, 3/e.*

Part 1—Introduction to Hardware, Software and Operating Systems— includes two chapters that introduce the notion of operating systems, present a history of operating systems and lay the groundwork of hardware and software concepts the reader will use throughout the book.

Chapter 1—Introduction to Operating Systems—defines the term "operating system" and explains the need for such systems. The chapter provides a historical perspective on operating systems, tracing their development decade by decade through the second half of the 20th century. The batch-processing systems of the 1950s are considered. We see the 1960s trend towards parallelism with the advent of mutiprogramming—both batch mutiprogramnming and interactive timesharing systems. We follow the development of key operating systems including CTSS, Multics, CP/CMS and Unix. The chapter considers the kinds of thinking that operating systems designers did in an era when computing resources were far more expensive than people resources (today the reverse is true). We follow the 1970s evolution of computer networking, the Internet and the TCP/IP protocol suite, and see the beginnings of the personal computing revolution. Personal computing matures in the 1980s with the release of the IBM personal computer and the Apple Macintosh, the latter popularizing the graphical user interface (GUI). We see the beginnings of distributed computing and the development of the client/server model. In the 1990s, Internet usage literally explodes with the availability of the World Wide Web. Microsoft becomes the world's dominant software maker and releases its Windows NT operating system (the ancestor of today's Windows XP operating system—the focus of Chapter 21). Object technology becomes the dominant development paradigm with languages like C++ and Java becoming popular. The rapid rise of the open-source-software movement leads to the phenomenal success of the Linux operating system—the focus of Chapter 20. We discuss how operating systems provide a platform for applications development. Embedded systems are considered with an emphasis on how crucial it is that mission-critical and business-critical systems be extraordinarily reliable. We consider the core components of operating systems and key operating systems goals. (The book maintains a focus on performance issues in virtually every aspect of operating systems.) Operating system architectures are introduced, including monolithic architecture, layered architecture, microkernel architecture and networked and distributed operating systems.

Chapter 2—Hardware and Software Concepts—summarizes the hardware and software resources operating systems manage. The chapter covers how trends in hardware design—most notably phenomenal increases in processing power, memory capacity and communications bandwidth—have affected operating system design and vice versa. Hardware components including mainboards, processors, clocks, main memory, secondary storage devices, buses, direct memory access (DMA), peripheral devices and more are discussed. We present recent and emerging hardware technologies, and discuss hardware support for operating systems, including processor execution modes, privileged instructions, timers, clocks, bootstrapping and plug-and-play. Performance enhancement techniques like caching and buffering are considered. Software concepts are examined including compiling, linking, loading, machine languages, assembly languages, interpreters, compilers, high-level languages, structured programming, object-oriented programming and application programming interfaces (APIs). The chapter also explains firmware and middleware.

Part 2—Processes and Threads—includes six chapters that present the notions of processes, threads, process- and thread-state transitions, interrupts, context switching, asynchronism, mutual exclusion, monitors, deadlock and indefinite postponement, and processor scheduling of processes and threads.

Chapter 3—Process Concepts—begins our discussion of operating system primitives by defining the fundamental notion of process. We consider the life cycle of a process as it transitions between process states. The representation of a process as a process-control block or process descriptor is discussed with an emphasis on the importance of data structures in operating systems. The chapter motivates the need for process structures in an operating system and describes operations that can be performed on them, such as suspend and resume. Multiprogramming considerations, including suspending process execution and context switching, are introduced. The chapter discusses interrupts—a key to the successful implementation of any multiprogrammed environment. We consider interrupt processing and interrupt classes, interprocess communication with signals and message passing. We conclude with a case study of UNIX processes.

Chapter 4—Thread Concepts—extends our discussion of process concepts to a smaller unit of concurrent program execution: the thread. The chapter defines what threads are and explains their relationship to processes. The life cycle of a thread and how threads transition among various thread states is discussed. We consider various threading architectural models, including user-level threads, kernel-level threads and combining user- and kernel-level threads. The chapter presents thread implementation considerations, including thread signal delivery and thread termination. We discuss the POSIX standard and its threading specification, Pthreads. The chapter concludes with a presentation of the Linux, Windows XP and Java threading implementations. The Java presentation is accompanied by a complete, working Java program with sample outputs. [*Note:* The Java source code for all of the Java programs in the book is available for download at `www.deitel.com/books/os3e`.]

Chapter 5—Asynchronous Concurrent Execution—discusses the issues of concurrency encountered in multiprogrammed systems. The chapter introduces the problem of mutual exclusion and how threads must manage access to shared resources. A feature of the chapter is the Java Multithreading Case Study: A Producer/Consumer Relationship in Java—which uses a complete, working Java program and several sample outputs to clearly illustrate what happens when concurrent threads access shared data without synchronization. This example clearly shows that sometimes such a concurrent program will work fine and sometimes it will produce erroneous results. We show how to solve this problem with a multithreaded Java program in Chapter 6. The concept of the critical section in program code is introduced. Several software mechanisms that protect access to critical sections are presented as solutions to the mutual exclusion problem; these include Dekker's Algorithm, Peterson's Algorithm and *N*-thread mutual exclusion with Lamport's Bakery Algorithm. The chapter also discusses hardware mechanisms that facilitate the implementation of mutual exclusion algorithms; these include disabling interrupts, the test-and-set instruction and the swap instruction. Finally, semaphores are presented as a high-level mechanism for implementing mutual exclusion and thread synchronization; both binary semaphores and counting semaphores are considered.

Chapter 6—Concurrent Programming—explains the notion of monitors (a high-level mutual exclusion construct) then proceeds to solve several classic problems in concurrent programming, using first pseudocode monitors then complete working Java programs with sample outputs. The monitor solutions are provided in a C/C++/Java-like pseudocode syntax. We explain how monitors enforce information hiding and discuss how monitor condition variables differ from "conventional" variables. The chapter illustrates how a simple monitor may be used to control access to a resource that requires exclusive use. We then discuss two classic problems in concurrent programming—the circular buffer and the readers-and-writers problem; we implement solutions to each of these with pseudocode monitors. Java monitors are explained and the differences between Java monitors and the ones described by the classic literature are discussed. The chapter continues our optional Java Multithreading Case Study by implementing a producer/consumer relationship and a circular buffer in Java. The student can use this latter program as a basis for implementing a solution to the readers-and-writers problem in Java.

Chapter 7—Deadlock and Indefinite Postponement—introduces two potentially disastrous consequences of waiting: deadlock and indefinite postponement. The key concern is that systems that manage waiting entities must be carefully designed to avoid these problems. Several examples of deadlock are presented, including a traffic deadlock, the classic one-lane bridge, a simple resource deadlock, deadlock in spooling systems and deadlock in Dijkstra's charming Dining Philosophers problem. Key resource concepts are considered, including preemptibility, sharing, reentrancy and serial reusability. The chapter formally defines deadlock and discusses deadlock prevention, avoidance, detection and recovery (almost invariably painful). The four necessary conditions for deadlock are explained, namely the "mutual-exclusion," "wait-for," "no-preemption" and "circular-wait" conditions. We examine Havender's methods for preventing deadlock by denying, individually, any of the last three conditions. Deadlock avoidance enables more flexible resource allocation than deadlock prevention. The chapter explains deadlock avoidance with Dijkstra's Banker's Algorithm, showing examples of a safe state, an unsafe state and a safe-state-to-unsafe-state transition. Weaknesses in the Banker's Algorithm are discussed. We explain deadlock detection with the resource-allocation graph reduction technique. The chapter concludes with a discussion of deadlock strategies in current and future systems.

Chapter 8—Processor Scheduling—discusses concepts and algorithms related to allocating processor time to processes and threads. Scheduling levels, objectives and criteria are considered. Preemptive and nonpreemptive scheduling approaches are compared. We explain how to carefully set priorities and quanta (finite-sized allocations of processor time) in scheduling algorithms. Several classic and current scheduling algorithms are considered, including first-in-first-out (FIFO), round-robin (RR), shortest-process-first (SPF), highest-response-ratio-next (HRRN), shortest-remaining-time (SRT), multilevel feedback queues and fair-share scheduling. Each algorithm is evaluated using metrics such as throughput, average response time and the variance of response times. We discuss Java thread scheduling, soft real-time scheduling, hard real-time scheduling and deadline scheduling.

Part 3—Real and Virtual Memory—includes three chapters that discuss memory organization and memory management in real and virtual memory systems.

Chapter 9—Real Memory Management and Organization—presents a historical discussion of how real memory operating systems have organized and managed physical memory resources. The schemes have gone from the simple to the complex, ultimately seeking optimal usage of the relatively precious main memory resource. We review the memory hierarchy consisting of cache(s), primary memory and secondary storage. Then, three types of memory management strategies are discussed, namely fetch, placement and replacement. We present contiguous and noncontiguous memory allocation schemes. Single-user contiguous memory allocation is considered with a discussion of overlays, protection and single-stream batch processing. We trace the evolution of multiprogramming memory organizations from fixed-partition multiprogramming to variable-partition multiprogramming, considering issues including internal and external memory fragmentation, and presenting memory compaction and coalescing as means of reducing fragmentation. The chapter discusses the first-fit, best-fit and worst-fit memory placement strategies, and concludes with a discussion of multiprogramming with memory swapping.

Chapter 10—Virtual Memory Organization—describes fundamental virtual memory concepts and the hardware capabilities that support virtual memory. The chapter motivates the need for virtual memory and describes typical implementations. The key approaches to virtual memory organization—paging and segmentation—are explained and their relative merits are analyzed. We discuss paging systems, focusing on paging address translation by direct mapping, paging address translation by associative mapping, paging address translation with direct/associative mapping, multilevel page tables, inverted page tables and sharing in paging systems. The chapter investigates segmentation systems, focusing on segmentation address translation by direct mapping, sharing in a segmentation system, protection and access control in segmentation systems. We also examine hybridized segmentation/paging systems, considering dynamic address translation, sharing and protection in these systems. The chapter concludes by examining the popular IA-32 Intel architecture virtual-memory implementation.

Chapter 11—Virtual Memory Management—continues the discussion of virtual memory by analyzing how operating systems attempt to optimize virtual memory performance. Because paging systems have become dominant, we focus on page management in detail, most notably on page-replacement strategies. The chapter considers one of the most important empirical results in the field of operating systems, namely the locality phenomenon, and we consider the results from both the temporal and spatial perspectives. We discuss when pages should be brought into memory, examining both demand paging and anticipatory paging.

When available memory becomes scarce, incoming pages must replace pages already in memory—an operating system's page-replacement strategy can have an enormous impact on performance. Many page-replacement strategies are examined, including random, first-in-first-out (FIFO and Belady's Anomaly), least-recently-used (LRU), least-frequently-used (LFU), not-used-recently (NUR), second-chance, clock and segmented queue (SEGQ), far page and page-fault-frequency (PFF). Denning's classic working set model of program behavior is considered as well as how various page-replacement strategies attempt to achieve its goals. The chapter discusses the possibility of voluntary page release. We carefully examine the arguments for small pages and large pages, and how programs behave under paging. The chapter discusses Linux page replacement and concludes with a discussion of global vs. local page-replacement strategies.

Part 4—Secondary Storage, Files and Databases—includes two chapters that present techniques which operating systems employ to manage data on secondary storage. Hard-disk performance optimization, and file and database systems are discussed. Our treatment of I/O systems is distributed throughout the book, most notably in Chapters 2, 12 and 13 and in the case studies on Linux and Windows XP (Chapters 20 and 21, respectively).

Chapter 12—Disk Performance Optimization—focuses on the characteristics of moving-head disk storage and how the operating system can optimize its performance. The chapter discusses the evolution of secondary-storage devices and examines the characteristics of moving-head disk storage. During a half century of explosive technological development, moving-head disk storage devices continue to endure. We define why disk scheduling is necessary and demonstrate why it is needed to achieve high-performance from moving-head disk devices. The evolution of disk-scheduling strategies is presented, including seek-optimization strategies, including first-come-first-served (FCFS), shortest-seek-time-first (SSTF), SCAN, C-SCAN, FSCAN, N-Step SCAN, LOOK, C-LOOK and VSCAN (introduced in the exercises), and rotational-optimization strategies, including SLTF, SPTF and SATF. Other popular disk-system performance techniques are discussed, including caching, buffering, defragmentation, data compression and blocking. One of the most important additions to this third edition is the extensive treatment of RAID systems in this chapter. RAID (Redundant Arrays of Independent Disks) is a set of technologies that enable disk systems to achieve higher performance and fault tolerance. The chapter presents various key RAID "levels," including level 0 (striping), level 1 (mirroring), level 2 (bit-level Hamming ECC parity), level 3 (bit-level XOR ECC parity), level 4 (block-level XOR ECC parity) and level 5 (block-level distributed XOR ECC parity).

Chapter 13—File and Database Systems—discusses how operating systems organize and manage collections of data called files and databases. We explain key concepts, including the data hierarchy, files, file systems, directories, links, metadata and mounting. The chapter presents various file organizations, including sequential, direct, index sequential and partitioned. File allocation techniques are examined, including contiguous file allocation, linked-list noncontiguous file allocation, tabular noncontiguous file allocation and indexed noncontiguous file allocation. We explain file access control by user classes and access control matrices. Data access techniques are discussed in the context of basic access methods, queued access methods, anticipatory buffering and memory-mapped files. We explain techniques for ensuring data integrity, including protection, backup, recovery, logging, atomic transactions, rollback, commitment, checkpointing, shadow paging and using log-structured file systems. The chapter considers file servers and distributed systems and points the reader to the extensive treatment of these topics and others in Chapters 16–18. The chapter also introduces database systems, and analyzes their advantages, data access, the relational database model and operating system services that support database systems.

Part 5—Performance, Processors and Multiprocessor Management—includes two chapters that discuss performance monitoring, measurement and evaluation techniques, and focus on the extraordinary performance that can be achieved with systems that employ multiple processors.

Chapter 14—Performance and Processor Design—focuses on one of operating systems designers' most preeminent goals—system performance—and discusses the important role of specific processor types in achieving that goal. The chapter surveys performance measures, considering issues including absolute performance measures, ease of use, turnaround time, response time, system reaction time, variance in response times, throughput, workload, capacity and utilization. We discuss performance evaluation techniques, including tracing and profiling, timings, microbenchmarks, application-specific evaluation, analytic models, benchmarks, synthetic programs, simulation and performance monitoring. Bottlenecks and saturation are considered. We demonstrate how systems dynamically adjust to positive and negative feedback. A system's performance depends heavily on the performance of its processor(s), which is, in turn, heavily influenced by its instruction set architecture. The chapter examines key architectures, including complex instruction set computing (CISC), reduced instruction set computing (RISC) and various kinds of post-RISC processors. The chapter concludes with a discussion of explicitly parallel instruction computing (EPIC).

Chapter 15—Multiprocessor Management—provides an in-depth introduction to the hardware and software aspects of multiprocessing. One way to build ever more powerful computing systems is to employ multiple processors and possibly massive numbers of them. The discussion begins with a Mini Case Study on supercomputers followed by a Biographical Note on Seymour Cray, the father of supercomputing. We investigate multiprocessor architecture, considering issues including the classification of sequential and parallel architectures, processor interconnection schemes and loosely coupled vs. tightly coupled systems. Multiprocessor operating system organizations are examined, including master/slave, separate kernels and symmetrical organization. We explain memory access architectures, including uniform memory access (UMA), nonuniform memory access (NUMA), cache-only memory architecture (COMA) and no remote memory access (NORMA).

The chapter discusses multiprocessor memory sharing, considering issues of cache coherence, page replication and migration and shared virtual memory. We continue the discussion on processor scheduling which we began in Chapter 8, presenting job-blind multiprocessor scheduling and job-aware multiprocessor scheduling. Process migration is considered and issues of flow of process migration and process migration strategies are examined. We discuss multiprocessor load balancing, examining both static and dynamic load balancing strategies. The chapter explains how to enforce multiprocessor mutual exclusion with spin locks, sleep/wakeup locks and read/write locks.

Part 6—Networking and Distributed Computing—includes three chapters that present networks, networked systems and distributed systems.

Chapter 16—Introduction to Networking—introduces computer networking to lay the foundation for the following two chapters on distributed computing. The chapter discusses network topologies, including buses, rings, meshes, fully connected meshes, stars and trees and we explain the unique challenges posed by wireless networks. We consider local-area networks (LANs) and wide-area networks (WANs), and present a major treatment of the TCP/IP protocol stack. Application layer protocols including the Hypertext Transfer protocol (HTTP) and the File Transfer Protocol (FTP) are examined. We explain transport layer protocols including the Transmission Control Protocol (TCP) and the User Datagram Protocol (UDP). At the network layer the chapter explores the Internet Protocol (IP) and its latest version—Internet Protocol version 6 (IPv6). The chapter discusses link layer protocols, including Ethernet, Token Ring, Fiber Distributed Data Interface (FDDI) and IEEE 802.11 (wireless). The chapter concludes with a discussion of the client/server model and *n*-tier systems.

Chapter 17—Introduction to Distributed Systems—introduces distributed operating systems and discusses the attributes of distributed systems, including performance, scalability, connectivity, security, reliability, fault tolerance and transparency. We compare and contrast network operating systems and distributed operating systems. Communication in distributed systems and the crucial role played by "middleware" technologies are discussed, including remote procedure call (RPC), Remote Method Invocation (RMI), CORBA (Common Object Request Broker Architecture), and Microsoft's DCOM (Distributed Component Object Model). The chapter considers process migration, synchronization and mutual exclusion in distributed systems, examining mutual exclusion without shared memory, and Agrawala and Ricart's distributed mutual exclusion algorithm. We discuss deadlock in distributed systems, focusing on deadlock prevention and deadlock detection. The chapter concludes with case studies on the Sprite and Amoeba distributed operating systems.

Chapter 18—Distributed Systems and Web Services—continues the study of distributed systems, focusing on distributed file systems, clustering, peer-to-peer computing, grid computing, Java distributed computing and Web services. The chapter begins by considering some characteristics and concerns of distributed systems, including transparency, scalability, security, fault tolerance and consistency and we present case studies on key distributed file systems, including the Network File System (NFS), Andrew File System (AFS), Coda File System and Sprite File System. We discuss clustering, considering high-performance clusters, high-availability clusters and load-balancing clusters; we investigate various examples of clusters including Linux-based Beowulf clusters Windows-based clusters. Peer-to-peer (P2P) distributed computing is explored considering the relationship between P2P and client/server applications, centralized vs. decentralized P2P applications, peer discovery and searching. We examine Sun Microsystems' Project JXTA and we consider how JXTA creates a framework for building P2P applications. The chapter considers grid computing and how it makes possible solutions to problems that require a truly massive amount of computation by using available unused processing power on personal and business computers worldwide. We discuss key Java distributed computing technologies, including Java servlets and JavaServer Pages (JSP), Jini, JavaSpaces and Java Management Extensions (JMX). The chapter concludes by surveying the exciting new technology of Web services and exploring two key Web services platforms—Microsoft's .NET Platform and Sun Microsystems' Sun ONE platform.

Part 7—Security—includes one chapter.

Chapter 19—Security—presents a general introduction to computer and network security techniques that operating systems can use to provide secure computing environments. The chapter discusses secret-key and public-key cryptography and the popular RSA and PGP (Pretty Good Privacy) public key schemes. Authentication is considered: password protection, password salting, biometrics, smart cards. Kerberos and single sign-on. We discuss access control, exploring issues of access rights, protection domains, access control models, access control policies and access control mechanisms, including access control matrices, access control lists and capability lists. The chapter presents the great variety of security attacks that have been attempted, including cryptanalysis, viruses, worms, denial-of-service (DoS) attacks, software exploitation and system penetration. We survey attack prevention and security solutions, including firewalls and intrusion detection systems (IDSs), antivirus software, security patches and secure file systems. We discuss the federal government's Orange Book Security classification system and present a Mini Case Study on OpenBSD, arguably the most secure operating system available. The chapter explores secure communication and consider the requirements for a successful, secure transaction—privacy, integrity, authentication, authorization and nonrepudiation. Key agreement protocols—the process by which two parties exchange secret keys over an unsecure medium—are discussed. We explain digital signatures—a technology that is enormously crucial to the future of electronic commerce—and their implementation. The chapter presents an in-depth treatment of public-key infrastructure, including digital certificates and certificate authorities. Various secure communication protocols are considered including Secure Sockets Layer (SSL), Virtual Private Networks (VPNs), IP Security (IPSec) and wireless security. We discuss the intriguing technology of steganography—the practice of hiding information within other information. This can hide secret messages in publicly transmitted messages; it can also protect intellectual property rights, with digital watermarks for example. The chapter compares and contrasts proprietary and open-source security solutions and concludes with a case study on UNIX Security.

Part 8—Operating Systems Case Studies—includes two chapters that provide in-depth case studies on the Linux 2.6 kernel and the Microsoft Windows XP operating system,. The case studies follow the book's outline to make it convenient for the student to comprehend topics discussed earlier in the book.

Chapter 20—Case Study: Linux—provides an in-depth study of Linux 2.6. This extensive (94 pages) case study was written and updated throughout the development of the release (by following the version 2.5 development kernel and having the material carefully reviewed by key Linux kernel developers). The chapter discusses the history, community and software distributions that have created the most popular open-source operating system in the world. The chapter examines the core components of the Linux operating system, with particular attention to their implementation in the context of concepts studied in previous chapters. Kernel architecture, process management (processes, threads, scheduling), memory organization and management, file systems (virtual file system, virtual file system caches, ext2fs and proc fs), I/O management (device drivers, character device I/O, block device I/O, network device I/O, unified device model, interrupts), synchronization (spin locks, reader/writer locks, seqlocks and kernel semaphores), IPC (signals, pipes, sockets, message queues, shared memory and System V semaphores), networking (packet processing, netfilter framework and hooks), scalability (symmetric multiprocessing, nonuniform memory access, other scalability features, embedded Linux) and security are all analyzed and explained.

Chapter 21—Case Study: Windows XP—complements the Linux case study by examining the internals of the most popular commercial operating system—Windows XP. This case study (106 pages) examines the core components of the Windows XP operating system and how they interact to provide services to users. We discuss the history of Windows operating systems, including Biographical notes on Bill Gates and David Cutler. The chapter presents the design goals of Windows XP and overviews its system architecture, considering topics including the Hardware Abstraction Layer (HAL), the microkernel, the executive, the environment subsystems, dynamic link libraries (DLLs) and system services. We discuss system management mechanisms, including the registry, Object Manager, interrupt request levels (IRQLs), asynchronous procedure calls (APCs), deferred procedure calls (DPCs) and system threads. We examine process and thread organization, considering control blocks, thread local storage (TLS), creating and terminating processes, jobs, fibers and thread pools. Thread scheduling is explained, and thread states, the thread scheduling algorithm, determining thread priorities and multiprocessor scheduling are considered. We investigate thread synchronization, examining dispatcher objects, event objects, mutex objects, semaphore objects, waitable timer objects, kernel mode locks and other synchronization tools. Memory management, and the concepts of memory organization, memory allocation and page replacement are explained. We explore file systems management, discussing file system drivers and NTFS topics including the Master File Table (MFT), data streams, file compression, file encryption, sparse files, reparse points and mounted volumes. We study input/output management, explaining device drivers, Plug-and-Play, power management, the Windows Driver Model (WDM), input/output processing, I/O request packets (IORPs), synchronous I/O, asynchronous I/O, data transfer techniques, interrupt handling and file cache management. We consider interprocess communication mechanisms including pipes (anonymous and named), mailslots, shared memory, and local and remote procedure calls. Microsoft's Component Object Model (COM) is overviewed. We explain drag-and-drop and compound documents. We discuss networking capabilities, including network input/output, network driver architecture, network protocols (IPX, SPX, NetBEUI, NetBIOS over TCP/IP, WinHTTP, WinINet and Winsock 2. Network services topics including Active Directory, Lightweight Directory Access Protocol (LDAP) and Remote Access Service (RAS) are discussed. We overview Microsoft's new .NET technology which is replacing DCOM. We examine scalability, considering both symmetric multiprocessing (SMP) and Windows XP Embedded. The chapter concludes with a discussion of security topics, including authentication, authorization, Internet Connection Firewall (ICF) and other security features.

Whew! Well, that completes the Tour of the Book. There is much here for operating systems students and professionals.

Ancillary Package for Operating Systems, 3/e

Operating Systems, 3/e has extensive ancillary materials for instructors. The Instructor's Resource CD (IRCD) contains solutions to the vast majority of the end-of-chapter exercises. This CD is available only to instructors through their Prentice Hall representatives. Visit **vig.prenhall.com/replocator** to locate your Prentice Hall representative. [*NOTE:* **Please do not write to us requesting the instructor's CD. Distribution of this CD is limited strictly to college professors teaching from the book. Instructors may obtain the solutions manual only from their Prentice Hall representatives.**] The ancillaries for the book also include a Test Item File of multiple-choice questions. In addition, we provide PowerPoint® lecture notes containing all figures, illustrations, diagrams and code in the text and bullet points that summarize key portions of the text. Instructors can customize the slides. The PowerPoint® slides are downloadable from **www.deitel.com** and as part of Prentice Hall's companion Web site (**www.prenhall.com/deitel**) for *Operating Systems, 3/e*, which offers resources for both instructors and students. For instructors, the Companion Web site includes a Syllabus Manager, which helps instructors plan courses interactively and create online syllabi.

Students also benefit from the functionality of the Companion Web site. Book-specific resources for students include:

- Customizable PowerPoint® lecture notes
- Source code for the Java programs

Chapter-specific resources available for students include:

- Chapter objectives
- Outline
- Highlights (e.g., chapter summary)
- Web links

Acknowledgments

One of the great pleasures of writing a textbook is acknowledging the efforts of many people whose names may not appear on the cover, but whose hard work, cooperation, friendship and understanding were crucial to the production of the book. Many of our colleagues at Deitel & Associates, Inc. devoted long hours to this book and its ancillaries: Jeff Listfield, Su Zhang, Abbey Deitel, Barbara Deitel and Christi Kelsey.

We would like to include a special note of thanks to Ben Wiedermann for organizing the effort to revise the material in the second edition of this book. He reviewed and updated much of the existing writing and diagrams. He also organized and directed a team of Deitel interns who researched the latest developments in Operating Systems for inclusion in this new edition. Ben currently is pursuing a Ph.D. in Computer Science at the University of Texas, Austin.

We would also like to thank the participants in the Deitel & Associates, Inc., College Internship Program who worked on the content of this book and its ancillary package: Jonathan Goldstein (Cornell University), Lucas Ballard (Johns Hopkins University), Tim Christensen (Boston College), John Paul Casiello (Northeastern University), Mira Meyerovich (Ph.D. candidate at Brown University), Andrew Yang (Carnegie Mellon University), Kathryn Ruigh (Boston College), Chris Gould (University of Massachusetts at Lowell), Marc Manara (Harvard University), Jim O'Leary (Rensselaer Polytechnic Institute), Gene Pang (Cornell University) and Randy Xu (Harvard University).

We would like to acknowledge Howard Berkowitz (formerly of the Corporation for Open Systems International) for co-authoring Chapter 16, Distributed Computing, in the second edition of this text. His work was the basis for our expanded, enhanced and updated treatment of networking and distributed computing in Chapters 16 through 18 of *Operating Systems, 3/e.*

We are fortunate to have worked on this project with the talented and dedicated team of publishing professionals at Prentice Hall. We especially appreciate the extraordinary efforts of our Computer Science Editor, Kate Hargett and her boss and our mentor in publishing—Marcia Horton, Editorial Director of Prentice-Hall's Engineering and Computer Science Division. Vince O'Brien, Tom Manshreck, John Lovell and Chirag Thakkar did a marvelous job managing the production of the book. Sarah Parker managed the publication of the book's ancillary package.

We would like to thank the design team that created a completely new look and feel for *Operating Systems, 3/e*—Carole Anson, Paul Belfanti, Geoffrey Cassar and John Root. We would also like to thank the talented creative team at Artworks, including Kathryn Anderson, Jay McElroy, Ronda Whitson, Patricia Burns, Matt Haas, Xiaohong Zhu, Dan Missildine, Chad Baker, Sean Hogan, Audrey Simonetti, Mark Landis, Royce Copenheaver, Stacy Smith, Scott Wieber, Pam Taylor, Anna Whalen, Cathy, Shelly, Ken Mooney, Tim Nguyen, Carl Smith, Jo Thompson, Helenita Zeigler and Russ Crenshaw.

The most important acknowledgment is to the thousands of authors represented in the Recommended Readings and Works Cited sections in the chapters; their research papers, articles and books have provided the diversity of interesting material that makes operating systems such a fascinating area.

We wish to acknowledge the efforts of our *Third Edition* reviewers and to give a special note of thanks to Carole Snyder and Jennifer Cappello of Prentice Hall who managed this extraordinary review effort. Adhering to a tight time schedule, these reviewers scrutinized the text, providing countless suggestions for improving the accuracy and completeness of the presentation. It is a privilege to have the guidance of such talented and busy professionals.

Third Edition reviewers:
Tigran Aivazian, Veritas Software, Ltd.
Jens Axboe, SUSE Labs
Dibyendu Baksi, Scientific Technologies Corporation
Columbus Brown, IBM
Fabian Bustamante, Northwestern University
Brian Catlin, Azius Developer Training
Stuart Cedrone, Hewlett-Packard
Randy Chow, University of Florida
Alan Cox, Red Hat UK
Matthew Dobson, Independent Consultant
Ulrich Drepper, Red Hat, Inc.
Alessio Gaspar, University of South Florida, Lakeland Campus
Allison Gehrke, Colorado Technical University
Michael Green, Central Texas College
Rob Green, Columbia Data Products, Inc.
James Huddleston, Independent Consultant
Scott Kaplan, Amherst College
Salahuddin Khan, Microsoft
Robert Love, MontaVista Software, Inc.
Barry Margolin, Level 3 Communications
Cliff Mather, Hewlett-Packard
Jeanna Matthews, Cornell University/Clarkson University
Manish Mehta, Syntel, India, Ltd.
Dejan Milojicic, Hewlett-Packard

Euripides Montagne, University of Central Florida
Andrew Morton, Diego, Inc.
Gary Newell, Northern Kentucky University
Bill O'Farrell, IBM
Mike Panetta, Robotic Sciences, Inc./Netplanner Systems, Inc.
Rohan Phillips, Microsoft
Atul Prakash, University of Michigan
Bina Ramamurthy, SUNY Buffalo
Eric Raymond, Thyrsus Enterprises
Jeffrey Richter, Wintellect
Sven Schreiber, Platon Data Technology
Wennie Wei Shu, University of New Mexico
David Solomon, David Solomon Expert Seminars
Brandon Taylor, Sun Microsystems
Bob Toxen, Fly-By-Day Consulting, Inc.
Joshua Uziel, Sun Microsystems
Carlos Valcarcel, EinTech, Inc.
Melinda Ward, Hewlett-Packard
Gerard Weatherby, Charles Consulting, LLC. /Rensselaer at Hartford
Xiang Xu, RSA Security, Inc.

***First and Second Edition reviewers and contributors
(and their affiliations at that time):***
Howard Berkowitz, Corporation for Open Systems
Dale A. Brown, The College of Wooster
Steven J. Buroff, AT&T Bell Laboratories
David D. Busch
John H. Carson, George Washington University
Ronald Curtis, Canisius College
Larry K. Flanigan, University of Michigan
Jon Forrest, Sybase
Jay Gadre, Corporation for Open Systems
Carlos M. Gonzalez, George Mason University
Mike Halvorson, Microsoft Press
Wayne Hathaway, Ultra Network Technologies
Christopher T. Haynes, Indiana University
Lee Hollaar, University of Utah
William Horst, Corporation for Open Systems
James Johannes, University of Alabama
Ralph Johnson, University of Illinois
Dennis Kafura, Virginia Polytechnical Institute
Herb Klein, Corporation for Open Systems
Michael S. Kogan, IBM
Thomas LeBlanc, University of Rochester

T. F. Leibfried, University of Houston, Clear Lake
David Litwack, Corporation for Open Systems
Mark Measures, Baylor University
Charles Oualline, Jr., East Texas State University
Ravi Sandhu, Ohio State University
Richard Schlichting, University of Arizona
Alan Southerton
John J. Zenor, California State University
James Peterson, University of Texas at Austin
Richard Wexelblatt, Sperry Univac
Paul Ross, Millersville State University
Anthony Lucido, Intercomp
Steve Paris, Prime Computer
Bart Guerreri, DSD Laboratories
Nathan Tobol, Codex Corporation and Chairman, IEEE 802 Local-Area
    Networking Subcommittee
Larry Nelson, AVCO Services
Barry Shein, Harvard University
Eliezer Gafni, MIT
Anat Gafni, Boston University
Josefina Bondoc, Boston University

Contacting Deitel & Associates

We would sincerely appreciate your comments, criticisms, corrections and suggestions for improving the text. Please address all correspondence to:

> deitel@deitel.com

We will respond promptly.

Deitel Buzz® Online E-mail Newsletter

Our free e-mail newsletter, the *DEITEL® Buzz Online*, includes updates to *Operating Systems 3/e*, commentary on industry trends and developments, links to free articles and resources from our published books and upcoming publications, product-release schedules, errata, challenges, anecdotes, information on our corporate instructor-led training courses and more. To subscribe, visit

> www.deitel.com/newsletter/subscribe.html

About Deitel & Associates, Inc.

Deitel & Associates, Inc., is an internationally recognized corporate training and content-creation organization specializing in Internet/World Wide Web software technology, e-business/e-commerce software technology, object technology, operating systems and computer programming languages education. The company provides instructor-led courses on Internet and Web programming, wireless Internet programming, object technology, and major programming languages and platforms, including C, C++, Visual C++® .NET, Visual Basic® .NET, C#, Java, J2EE, XML, Perl, Python and more. The founders of Deitel & Associates, Inc., are Dr. Harvey M. Deitel and Paul J. Deitel. The company's clients include many of the world's largest computer companies, government agencies, branches of the military and business organizations. Through its 27-year publishing partnership with Prentice Hall, Deitel & Associates, Inc., publishes leading-edge programming textbooks, professional books, interactive CD-based multimedia *Cyber Classrooms*, *Complete Training Courses*, Web-based training courses and course management systems e-content for popular CMSs such as WebCT™, Blackboard™ and CourseCompass℠.

To learn more about Deitel & Associates, Inc., its publications and its corporate on-site training curriculum, see the last few pages of this book or visit:

    www.deitel.com

Individuals wishing to purchase Deitel® books, *Cyber Classrooms*, *Complete Training Courses* and Web-based training courses can do so through bookstores, online booksellers and the following Web sites:

    www.deitel.com
    www.prenhall.com/deitel
    www.InformIT.com/deitel
    www.InformIT.com/cyberclassrooms

Bulk orders by corporations and academic institutions should be placed directly with Prentice Hall. See www.prenhall.com/deitel for worldwide ordering instructions and to find your local Prentice Hall sales representative.

Welcome to the exciting world of operating systems. We sincerely hope you enjoy learning with this book.

Dr. Harvey M. Deitel
Paul J. Deitel
David R. Choffnes

About the Authors

Dr. Harvey M. Deitel, Chairman and Chief Strategy Officer of Deitel & Associates, Inc., has 42 years experience in the computing field, including extensive industry and academic experience. Dr. Deitel studied operating systems at the Massachusetts Institute of Technology where he earned B.S. and M.S. degrees. Dr. Deitel earned his Ph.D. from Boston University. While an undergraduate and master's candidate at MIT, he worked on the pioneering virtual-memory operating-systems projects at IBM (OS/360 and TSS/360) and MIT (Multics) that developed techniques now widely implemented in systems including UNIX, Linux and Windows

XP. He taught operating systems for 20 years in academia and industry. He earned tenure and served as the Chairman of the Computer Science Department at Boston College before founding Deitel & Associates, Inc., with his son, Paul J. Deitel. He and Paul are the co-authors of several dozen books and multimedia packages and they are writing many more. With translations published in Japanese, German, Russian, Spanish, Traditional Chinese, Simplified Chinese, Korean, French, Polish, Italian, Portuguese, Greek, Urdu and Turkish, the Deitels' texts have earned international recognition. Dr. Deitel has delivered professional seminars to major corporations, government organizations and the military.

Paul J. Deitel, CEO and Chief Technical Officer of Deitel & Associates, Inc., is a graduate of the Massachusetts Institute of Technology's Sloan School of Management, where he studied information technology and operating systems. Through Deitel & Associates, Inc., he has delivered hundreds of courses to Fortune 500, academic, government and military clients, and many other organizations. He has lectured for the Boston Chapter of the Association for Computing Machinery. He and his father, Dr. Harvey M. Deitel, are the world's best-selling computer science textbook authors.

David R. Choffnes is a graduate of Amherst College, where he earned degrees in Physics and French while pursuing advanced topics in Computer Science. His research interests include the fields of operating systems, computer architecture, computational biology and molecular computing. David has contributed to other Deitel publications including *Simply Java™ Programming* and *Simply Visual Basic*® *.NET*.

Introduction to Hardware, Software and Operating Systems

Intelligence ... is the faculty of making artificial objects, especially tools to make tools.
—Henri Bergson—

Part 1

The following chapters define the term operating system, present a history of operating systems and lay a foundation of hardware and software concepts. As you study the history of operating systems you will see a constant emphasis on performance improvement and on increasing the intensity of resource management to achieve that improvement. You will see hardware power increasing dramatically as costs decline equally dramatically. You will see the emergence of two dominant operating systems, Linux and Windows XP, built with the open-source approach (Linux) vs. the proprietary approach (Windows XP). You will study key operating system architectures. You will study hardware that operating systems manage for users and hardware that supports operating systems functions. You will study your first performance enhancement techniques—a process that you will continue throughout the book.

Every tool carries with it the spirit by which it has been created.
—Werner Karl Heisenberg—

Live in fragments no longer. Only connect...
—Edward Morgan Forster—

Efficiency is getting the job done right. Effectiveness is getting the right job done.
—Zig Ziglar—

Nothing endures but change.
—Heraclitus—

Open sesame!
—The History of Ali Baba—

Chapter 1

Introduction to Operating Systems

Objectives

After reading this chapter, you should understand:

- what an operating system is.
- a brief history of operating systems.
- a brief history of the Internet and the World Wide Web.
- core operating system components.
- goals of operating systems.
- operating system architectures.

Chapter Outline

1.1 Introduction

Welcome to the world of operating systems. During the past several decades, computing has evolved at an unprecedented pace. Computer power continues to increase at phenomenal rates as costs decline dramatically. Today, computer users have desktop workstations that execute billions of instructions per second (BIPS), and supercomputers that execute over a trillion instructions per second have been built,[1, 2] numbers that just a few years ago were inconceivable.

Processors are becoming so inexpensive and powerful that computers can be employed in almost every aspect of our lives. On personal computers, users can edit documents, play games, listen to music, watch videos and manage their personal finances. Portable devices, including laptop computers, personal digital assistants (PDAs), cell phones, and MP3 players all have computers as key components. Wired and wireless network architectures are increasing our interconnectivity—allowing users to communicate instantly over vast distances. The Internet and World Wide Web have revolutionized business, creating demand for networks of large, powerful computers that service vast numbers of transactions per second. Networks of computers have become so powerful that they are used to conduct complex research and simulation projects, such as modeling the Earth's climate, emulating human intelligence and constructing lifelike 3D animations. Such pervasive and powerful computing is reshaping the roles and responsibilities of operating systems.

In this book, we review operating system principles and discuss cutting-edge advances in computing that are redefining operating systems. We investigate the structure and responsibilities of operating systems. Design considerations, such as performance, fault tolerance, security, modularity and cost, are explored in detail. We also address more recent operating system design issues arising from the rapid growth in distributed computing, made possible by the Internet and the World Wide Web.

We have worked hard to create what we hope will be an informative, entertaining and challenging experience for you. As you read this book, you may want to refer to our Web site at www.deitel.com for updates and additional information on each topic. You can reach us at deitel@deitel.com.

1.2 What Is an Operating System?

In the 1960s, the definition of an operating system might have been *the software that controls the hardware*. But the landscape of computer systems has evolved significantly since then, requiring a richer definition.

Today's hardware executes a great variety of software applications. To increase hardware utilization, applications are designed to execute concurrently. If these applications are not carefully programmed, they might interfere with one another. As a result, a layer of software called an **operating system** separates applications from the hardware they access and provides services that allow each application to execute safely and effectively.

An operating system is software that enables applications to interact with a computer's hardware. The software that contains the core components of the operating system is called the **kernel**. Operating systems can be found in devices ranging from cell phones and automobiles to personal and mainframe computers. In most computer systems, a user requests that the computer perform an action (e.g., execute an application or print a document) and the operating system manages the software and hardware to produce the desired result.

To most users, the operating system is a "black box" between the applications and the hardware they run on that ensures the proper result, given appropriate inputs. Operating systems are primarily resource managers—they manage hardware, including processors, memory, input/output devices and communication devices. They must also manage applications and other software abstractions that, unlike hardware, are not physical objects.

In the next several sections we present a brief history of operating systems from the simple, single-user batch systems of the 1950s to the complex, multiprocessor, distributed, multiuser platforms of today.

Self Review

1. (T/F) Operating systems manage only hardware.
2. What are the primary purposes of an operating system?

Ans: **1)** False. Operating systems manage applications and other software abstractions, such as virtual machines. **2)** The primary purposes of an operating system are to enable applications to interact with a computer's hardware and to manage a system's hardware and software resources.

1.3 Early History: The 1940s and 1950s

Operating systems have evolved over the last 60 years through several distinct phases or generations that correspond roughly to the decades (see the Operating Systems Thinking feature, Innovation).[3] In the 1940s, the earliest electronic digital computers did not include operating systems.[4,5,6] Machines of the time were so primitive that programmers often entered their machine-language programs one bit at a time on rows of mechanical switches. Eventually, programmers entered their machine-language programs on punched cards. Then, assembly languages—which used English-like abbreviations to represent the basic operations of the computer— were developed to speed the programming process.

General Motors Research Laboratories implemented the first operating system in the early 1950s for its IBM 701 computer.[7] The systems of the 1950s generally executed only one job at a time, using techniques that smoothed the transition between jobs to obtain maximum utilization of the computer system.[8] A **job** constituted the set of program instructions corresponding to a particular computational task, such as payroll or inventory. Jobs typically executed without user input for minutes, hours or days. These early computers were called **single-stream batch-pro-**

cessing systems, because programs and data were submitted in groups or batches by loading them consecutively onto tape or disk. A job stream processor read the job control language statements (that defined each job) and facilitated the setup of the next job. When the current job terminated, the job stream reader read in the control-language statements for the next job and performed appropriate housekeeping chores to ease the transition to the next job. Although operating systems of the 1950s reduced interjob transition times, programmers often were required to directly control system resources such as memory and input/output devices. This was slow, difficult and tedious work. Further, these early systems required that an entire program be loaded into memory for the program to run. This limited programmers to creating small programs with limited capabilities.[9]

Self Review

1. Why were assembly languages developed?
2. What limited the size and capabilities of programs in the 1950s?

Ans: **1)** Assembly languages were developed to speed the programming process. They enabled programmers to specify instructions as English-like abbreviations that were easier for humans to work with than machine-language instructions. **2)** The entire program had to be loaded into memory to execute. Because memory was relatively expensive, the amount of memory available to those computers was small.

Operating Systems Thinking

Innovation

Innovation is a fundamental challenge for operating systems designers. If we are going to make the massive investment required to produce new operating systems or new versions of existing operating systems, we must constantly be evaluating new technologies, new applications of computing and communications and new thinking about how systems should be built. We have provided thousands of citations and hundreds of Web resources for you to do additional readings on topics that are of interest to you. You should consider belonging to professional organizations like the ACM (www.acm.org), the IEEE (www.ieee.org) and USENIX (www.usenix.org) that publish journals on the latest research and development efforts in the computer field. You should access the Web frequently to follow important developments in the field. There is always a high degree of risk when innovating, but the rewards can be substantial.

1.4 The 1960s

The systems of the 1960s were also batch-processing systems, but they used the computer's resources more efficiently by running several jobs at once. Systems included many peripheral devices such as card readers, card punches, printers, tape drives and disk drives. Any one job rarely used all the system's resources efficiently. A typical job would use the processor for a certain period of time before performing an input/output (I/O) operation on one of the system's peripheral devices. At this point, the processor would remain idle while the job waited for the I/O operation to complete.

The systems of the 1960s improved resource utilization by allowing one job to use the processor while other jobs used peripheral devices. In fact, running a mixture of diverse jobs—some jobs that mainly used the processor (called **processor-bound jobs** or **compute-bound jobs**) and some jobs that mainly used peripheral devices (called **I/O-bound jobs**)—appeared to be the best way to optimize resource utilization. With these observations in mind, operating systems designers developed **multiprogramming** systems that managed several jobs at once.[10, 11, 12] In a multiprogramming environment, the operating system rapidly switches the processor from job to job, keeping several jobs advancing while also keeping peripheral devices in use. A system's **degree of multiprogramming** (also called its **level of multiprogramming**) indicates how many jobs can be managed at once. Thus, operating systems evolved from managing one job to managing several jobs at a time.

In multiprogrammed computing systems, resource sharing is one of the primary goals. When resources are shared among a set of processes, each process maintaining exclusive control over particular resources allocated to it, a process may be made to wait for a resource that never becomes available. If this occurs, that process will be unable to complete its task, perhaps requiring the user to restart it, losing all work that the process had accomplished to that point. In Chapter 7, Deadlock and Indefinite Postponement, we discuss how operating systems can deal with such problems.

Normally, users of the 1960s were not present at the computing facility when their jobs were run. Jobs were submitted on punched cards or computer tapes and remained on input tables until the system's human operator could load them into the computer for execution. Often, a user's job would sit for hours or even days before it could be processed. The slightest error in a program, even a missing period or comma, would "bomb" the job, at which point the (often frustrated) user would correct the error, resubmit the job and once again wait hours or days for the next attempt at execution. Software development in that environment was painstakingly slow.

In 1964, IBM announced its System/360 family of computers ("360" refers to all points on a compass to denote universal applicability).[13, 14, 15, 16] The various 360 computer models were designed to be hardware compatible, to use the OS/360 operating system and to offer greater computer power as the user moved upward in the series.[17] Over the years, IBM evolved its 360 architecture to the 370 series[18, 19] and, more recently, the 390 series[20] and the zSeries.[21]

More advanced operating systems were developed to service multiple **interactive users** at once. Interactive users communicate with their jobs during execution. In the 1960s, users interacted with the computer via "dumb terminals" (i.e., devices that supplied a user interface but no processor power) which were **online** (i.e., directly attached to the computer via an active connection). Because the user was present and interacting with it, the computer system needed to respond quickly to user requests; otherwise, user productivity could suffer. As we discuss in the Operating Systems Thinking feature, Relative Value of Human and Computer Resources, increased productivity has become an important goal for computers because human resources are extremely expensive compared to computer resources. **Timesharing** systems were developed to support simultaneous interactive users.[22]

Many of the timesharing systems of the 1960s were multimode systems that supported batch-processing as well as real-time applications (such as industrial process control systems).[23] **Real-time systems** attempt to supply a response within a certain bounded time period. For example, a measurement from a petroleum refinery indicating that temperatures are too high might demand immediate attention to

Operating Systems Thinking

Relative Value of Human and Computer Resources

In 1965, reasonably experienced programmers were earning about $4 per hour. Computer time on mainframe computers (which were far less powerful than today's desktop machines) was commonly rented for $500 or more per hour—and that was in 1965 dollars which, because of inflation, would be comparable to thousands of dollars in today's currency! Today, you can buy a top-of-the-line, enormously powerful desktop computer for what it cost to rent a far less powerful mainframe computer for one hour 40 years ago! As the cost of

computing has plummeted, the cost of man-hours has risen to the point that today human resources are far more expensive than computing resources.

Computer hardware, operating systems and software applications are all designed to leverage people's time, to help improve efficiency and productivity. A classic example of this was the advent of timesharing systems in the 1960s in which these interactive systems (with almost immediate response times) often enabled programmers to become far more productive than was possible with

the batch-processing systems response times of hours or even days. Another classic example was the advent of the graphical user interface (GUI) originally developed at the Xerox Palo Alto Research Center (PARC) in the 1970s. With cheaper and more powerful computing, and with the relative cost of people-time rising rapidly compared to that of computing, operating systems designers must provide capabilities that favor the human over the machine, exactly the opposite of what early operating systems did.

avert an explosion. The resources of a real-time system are often heavily underutilized—it is more important for such systems to respond quickly than it is for them to use their resources efficiently. Servicing both batch and real-time jobs meant that operating systems had to distinguish between types of users and provide each with an appropriate level of service. Batch-processing jobs could suffer reasonable delays, whereas interactive applications demanded a higher level of service and real-time systems demanded extremely high levels of service.

The key timesharing systems development efforts of this period included the **CTSS (Compatible Time-Sharing System)**[24, 25] developed by MIT, the **TSS (Time Sharing System)**[26] developed by IBM, the **Multics** system[27] developed at MIT, GE and Bell Laboratories as the successor to CTSS and the **CP/CMS (Control Program/Conversational Monitor System)**—which eventually evolved into IBM's **VM (Virtual Machine)** operating system—developed by IBM's Cambridge Scientific Center.[28, 29] These systems were designed to perform basic interactive computing tasks for individuals, but their real value proved to be the manner in which they shared programs and data and demonstrated the value of interactive computing in program development environments.

The designers of the Multics system were the first to use the term **process** to describe a program in execution in the context of operating systems. In many cases, users submitted jobs containing multiple processes that could execute concurrently. In Chapter 3, Process Concepts, we discuss how multiprogrammed operating systems manage multiple processes at once.

In general, concurrent processes execute independently, but multiprogrammed systems enable multiple processes to cooperate to perform a common task. In Chapter 5, Asynchronous Concurrent Execution, and Chapter 6, Concurrent Programming, we discuss how processes coordinate and synchronize activities and how operating systems support this capability. We show many examples of concurrent programs, some expressed generally in pseudocode and some in the popular Java™ programming language.

Turnaround time—the time between submission of a job and the return of its results—was reduced to minutes or even seconds. The programmer no longer needed to wait hours or days to correct even the simplest errors. The programmer could enter a program, compile it, receive a list of syntax errors, correct them immediately, recompile and continue this cycle until the program was free of syntax errors. Then the program could be executed, debugged, corrected and completed with similar time savings.

The value of timesharing systems in support of program development was demonstrated when MIT, GE and Bell Laboratories used the CTSS system to develop its own successor, Multics. Multics was notable for being the first major operating system written primarily in a high-level language (EPL—modeled after IBM's PL/1) instead of an assembly language. The designers of **UNIX** learned from this experience; they created the high-level language **C** specifically to implement UNIX. A family of UNIX-based operating systems, including Linux and Berkeley

Software Distribution (BSD) UNIX, have evolved from the original system created by Dennis Ritchie and Ken Thompson at Bell Laboratories in the late 1960s (see the Biographical Note, Ken Thompson and Dennis Ritchie).

TSS, Multics and CP/CMS all incorporated **virtual memory**, which we discuss in detail in Chapter 10, Virtual Memory Organization, and Chapter 11, Virtual Memory Management. In systems with virtual memory, programs are able to address more memory locations than are actually provided in main memory, also called real memory or physical memory.[30, 31] (Real memory is discussed in Chapter 9, Real Memory Organization and Management.) Virtual memory systems help remove much of the burden of memory management from programmers, freeing them to concentrate on application development.

Biographical Note

Ken Thompson and Dennis Ritchie

Ken Thompson and Dennis Ritchie are well known in the field of operating systems for their development of the UNIX operating system and the C programming language. They have received several awards and recognition for their accomplishments, including the ACM Turing Award, the National Medal of Technology, the NEC C&C Prize, the IEEE Emmanuel Piore Award, the IEEE Hamming Medal, induction into the United States National Academy of Engineering and the Bell Labs National Fellowship.[32]

Ken Thompson attended the University of California at Berkeley, where he earned a B.S. and M.S. in Computer Science, graduating in 1966.[33] After college Thompson worked at Bell Labs, where he eventually joined Den-

nis Ritchie on the Multics project.[34] While working on that project, Thompson created the B language that led to Ritchie's C language.[35] The Multics project eventually led to the creation of the UNIX operating system in 1969. Thompson continued to develop UNIX through the early 1970s, rewriting it in Ritchie's C programming language.[36] After Thompson completed UNIX, he made news again in 1980 with Belle. Belle was a chess-playing computer designed by Thompson and Joe Condon that won the World Computing Chess Championship. Thompson worked as a professor at the University of California at Berkeley and at the University of Sydney, Australia. He continued to work at Bell Labs until he retired in 2000.[37]

Dennis Ritchie attended Harvard University, earning a Bachelor's degree in Physics and a Ph.D. in Mathematics. Ritchie went on to work at Bell Labs, where he joined Thompson on the Multics project in 1968. Ritchie is most recognized for his C language, which he completed in 1972.[38] Ritchie added some extra capabilities to Thompson's B language and changed the syntax to make it easier to use. Ritchie still works for Bell Labs and continues to work with operating systems.[39] Within the past 10 years he has created two new operating systems, Plan 9 and Inferno.[40] The Plan 9 system is designed for communication and production quality.[41] Inferno is a system intended for advanced networking.[42]

Once loaded into main memory, programs could execute quickly; however, main memory was far too expensive to contain large numbers of programs at once. Before the 1960s, jobs were largely loaded into memory using punched cards or tape, a tedious and time-consuming task, during which the system could not be used to execute jobs. The systems of the 1960s incorporated devices that reduced system idle time by storing large amounts of rewritable data on relatively inexpensive magnetic storage media such as tapes, disks and drums. Although hard disks enabled relatively fast access to programs and data compared to tape, they were significantly slower than main memory. In Chapter 12, Disk Performance Optimization, we discuss how operating systems can manage disk input/output requests to improve performance. In Chapter 13, File and Database Systems, we discuss how operating systems organize data into named collections called files and manage space on storage devices such as disks. We also discuss how operating systems protect data from access by unauthorized users and prevent data from being lost when system failures or other catastrophic events occur.

Self Review

1. How did interactive computing and its improvement in turnaround time increase programmer productivity?
2. What new concept did TSS, Multics and CP/CMS all incorporate? Why was it so helpful for programmers?

Ans: **1)** The time between submission of a job and the return of its results was reduced from hours or days to minutes or even seconds. This enabled programmers to interactively enter, compile and edit programs until their syntax errors were eliminated, then use a similar cycle to test and debug their programs. **2)** TSS, Multics, and CP/CMS all incorporated virtual memory. Virtual memory allows applications access to more memory than is physically available on the system. This allows programmers to develop larger, more powerful applications. Also, virtual memory systems remove much of the memory management burden from the programmer.

1.5 The 1970s

The systems of the 1970s were primarily multimode multiprogramming systems that supported batch processing, timesharing and real-time applications. Personal computing was in its incipient stages, fostered by early and continuing developments in microprocessor technology.[43] The experimental timesharing systems of the 1960s evolved into solid commercial products in the 1970s. Communications between computer systems throughout the United States increased as the Department of Defense's TCP/IP communications standards became widely used—especially in military and university computing environments.[44, 45, 46] Communication in local area networks (LANs) was made practical and economical by the Ethernet standard developed at Xerox's Palo Alto Research Center (PARC).[47, 48] In Chapter 16, Introduction to Networking, we discuss TCP/IP, Ethernet and fundamental networking concepts.

Security problems increased with the growing volumes of information passing over vulnerable communications lines (see the Anecdote, Abraham Lincoln's Technology Caution). Encryption received much attention—it became necessary to encode proprietary or private data so that, even if the data was compromised, it was of no value to anyone other than the intended receivers. In Chapter 19, Security, we discuss how operating systems secure sensitive information from unauthorized access. During the 1970s, operating systems grew to encompass networking and security capabilities and continued to improve in performance to meet commercial demands.

The personal computing revolution began in the late 1970s with such systems as the Apple II, and exploded in the 1980s.

Self Review

1. What developments in the 1970s improved communication between computer systems?
2. What new problem was introduced by the increased communication between computers? How was this problem addressed?

Ans: **1)** The DoD's TCP/IP standards became widely used in network communications—primarily in university and military computing environments. Also, Xerox's PARC developed the Ethernet standard, which made relatively high-speed local area networks (LANs) practical and economical. **2)** Communication between computers introduced security problems because data was sent over vulnerable communication lines. Encryption was employed to make data unreadable to anyone other than the intended recipient.

Abraham Lincoln's Technology Caution

The story goes that during the Civil War one of President Lincoln's young lieutenants came running up to him eager to speak with the President. "What is it, lieutenant?" "Mr. President, Mr. President, we are wiring the bat-tlefields for this wonderful new technology called the telegraph. Do you know what that means, Mr. President?" "No lieutenant, what does it mean?" "Mr. President, it means we'll be able to make decisions at the speed of light!" The older and wiser President Lincoln looked down at the lieutenant and said calmly, "Yes, lieutenant, but we'll also be able to make wrong decisions at the speed of light!"

Lessons to operating systems designers: Every new technology you will evaluate has its pros and cons. You will inevitably spend a great deal of your time concerned with performance issues. But, making things happen faster may have unpleasant consequences.

1.6 The 1980s

The 1980s was the decade of the personal computer and the workstation.[49] Microprocessor technology evolved to the point where high-end desktop computers called workstations could be built that were as powerful as the mainframes of a decade earlier. The IBM Personal Computer released in 1981 and the Apple Macintosh personal computer released in 1984 made it possible for individuals and small businesses to have their own dedicated computers. Communication facilities could be used to transmit data quickly and economically between systems. Rather than bringing data to a central, large-scale computer installation for processing, computing was distributed to the sites at which it was needed. Software such as spreadsheet programs, word processors, database packages and graphics packages helped drive the personal computing revolution by creating demand from businesses that could use these products to increase their productivity.

Personal computers proved to be relatively easy to learn and use, partially because of **graphical user interfaces (GUI)** that used graphical symbols such as windows, icons and menus to facilitate user interaction with programs. Xerox's Palo Alto Research Center (PARC) developed the mouse and GUI (for more on the origins of the mouse, see the Biographical Note, Doug Engelbart); Apple's release of the Macintosh personal computer in 1984 popularized their use. In Macintosh computers, the GUI was embedded in the operating system so that all applications would have a similar look and feel.[50] Once familiar with the Macintosh GUI, the user could learn to use new applications faster.

As technology costs declined, transferring information between computers in computer networks became more economical and practical. Electronic mail, file transfer and remote database access applications proliferated. **Distributed computing** (i.e., using multiple independent computers to perform a common task) became widespread under the client/server model. **Clients** are user computers that request various services; **servers** are computers that perform the requested services. Servers often are dedicated to one type of task, such as rendering graphics, managing databases or serving Web pages.

The software engineering field continued to evolve, a major thrust coming from the United States government aimed at providing tighter control of Department of Defense software projects.[51] Some goals of the initiative included realized code reusability and the early construction of prototypes so developers and users could suggest modifications early in the software design process.[52]

Self Review

1. What aspect of personal computers, popularized by the Apple Macintosh, made them especially easy to learn and use?
2. (T/F) A server cannot be a client.

Ans: 1) Graphical User Interfaces (GUIs) facilitated personal computer use by providing an easy-to-use, uniform interface to every application. This enabled users to learn new applications faster. 2) False. A computer can be a client and server. For example, a Web server can be both a client and server. When users request a Web page, it is a server; if the server then requests information from a database system, it becomes a client of the database system.

1.7 History of the Internet and World Wide Web

In the late 1960s **ARPA**—the **Advanced Research Projects Agency** of the Department of Defense rolled out the blueprints for networking the main computer systems of about a dozen ARPA-funded universities and research institutions. They were to be connected with communications lines operating at a then-stunning 56 kilobits per second (Kbps)—1 Kbps is equal to 1,000 bits per second—at a time when most people (of the few who could be) were connecting over telephone lines to computers at a rate of 110 bits per second. HMD vividly recalls the excitement at

Biographical Note

Doug Engelbart

Doug Engelbart invented the computer mouse and was one of the primary designers of the original graphical displays and windows.

Engelbart's background was in electronics. During World War II he worked as an electronics technician on a variety of systems including RADAR and SONAR.[53] After leaving the military, he went back to Oregon State to complete a degree in Electrical Engineering in 1948.[54] He went on to receive his Ph.D. from the University of California at Berkeley, then took a job at the Stanford Research Institute (SRI), where he gained his first experience with computers.[55] In 1968, at the Joint Computer Conference in San Francisco, Engelbart and his coworkers displayed their computer system, NLS (oNLine System) which featured Engelbart's computer mouse and a graphical interface with windows.[56] This original mouse, called an X-Y Position Indicator for a Display System, had only one button.[57] The mouse had two wheels on the bottom, one horizontal and one vertical, to detect movement.[58] The mouse and the graphical windows were interdependent. The mouse made it significantly easier to switch between windows, and without windows the mouse was not as useful.

Engelbart has dedicated his life to augmenting human intellect. His original idea behind the NLS system was to create a system that could help people solve problems faster and enhance intelligence. Engelbart founded the Bootstrap Institute to foster worldwide awareness of his mission. Bootstrapping, according to Engelbart, is the idea of improving one's methods of improvement. He believes this is the best way to improve human intelligence.[59]

Today, Engelbart is still working with the Bootstrap Institute. He has received recognition for his work including the Lemelson-MIT Prize, the National Medal of Technology and induction into the National Inventors Hall of Fame.[60]

that conference. Researchers at Harvard talked about communicating with the Univac 1108 "supercomputer" across the country at the University of Utah to handle the massive computations related to their computer graphics research. Academic research was about to take a giant leap forward. Shortly after this conference, ARPA proceeded to implement what quickly became called the **ARPAnet**—the grandparent of today's **Internet**.

Although the ARPAnet did enable researchers to network their computers, its chief benefit proved to be its capability for quick and easy communication via what came to be known as electronic mail (e-mail). This is true even on the Internet today, with e-mail, instant messaging and file transfer facilitating communications among hundreds of millions of people worldwide and growing rapidly.

The ARPAnet was designed to operate without centralized control. This meant that if a portion of the network should fail, the remaining working portions would still be able to route data packets from senders to receivers over alternative paths.

The protocols (i.e., sets of rules) for communicating over the ARPAnet became known as the **Transmission Control Protocol/Internet Protocol (TCP/IP)**. TCP/IP was used to manage communication between applications. The protocols ensured that messages were routed properly from sender to receiver and that those messages arrived intact. The advent of TCP/IP promoted worldwide computing growth. Initially, Internet use was limited to universities and research institutions; later, the military adopted the technology.

Eventually, the government decided to allow access to the Internet for commercial purposes. This decision led to some concern among the research and military communities—it was felt that response times would suffer as "the Net" became saturated with users. In fact, the opposite occurred. Businesses rapidly realized that they could use the Internet to tune their operations and to offer new and better services to their clients. Companies spent vast amounts of money to develop and enhance their Internet presence. This generated intense competition among communications carriers, hardware suppliers and software suppliers to meet the increased infrastructure demand. The result is that **bandwidth** (i.e., the information-carrying capacity of communications lines) on the Internet has increased tremendously, and hardware and communications costs have plummeted.

The **World Wide Web (WWW)** allows computer users to locate and view multimedia-based documents (i.e., documents with text, graphics, animation, audio or video) on almost any subject. Although the Internet was developed more than three decades ago, the introduction of the World Wide Web (WWW) was a relatively recent event. In 1989, Tim Berners-Lee of CERN (the European Center for Nuclear Research) began to develop a technology for sharing information via hyperlinked text documents (see the Biographical Note, Tim Berners-Lee). To implement this new technology, Berners-Lee created the **HyperText Markup Language (HTML)**. Berners-Lee also implemented the **Hypertext Transfer Protocol (HTTP)** to form the communications backbone of his new hypertext information system, which he called the World Wide Web.

Surely, historians will list the Internet and the World Wide Web among the most important and profound creations of humankind. In the past, most computer applications ran on "stand-alone" computers (computers that were not connected to one another). Today's applications can be written to communicate among the world's hundreds of millions of computers. The Internet and World Wide Web merge computing and communications technologies, expediting and simplifying our work. They make information instantly and conveniently accessible to large numbers of people. They enable individuals and small businesses to achieve worldwide exposure. They are changing the way we do business and conduct our personal lives. And they are changing the way we think of building operating systems. Today's operating systems provide GUIs that enable users to "access the world" over the Internet and the Web as seamlessly as accessing the local system. The operating systems of the 1980s were concerned primarily with managing resources on the local computer. Today's distributed operating systems may utilize resources on computers worldwide. This creates many interesting challenges that we discuss throughout the book, especially in Chapters 16–19, which examine networking, distributed computing and security.

Biographical Note

Tim Berners-Lee

The World Wide Web was invented by Tim Berners-Lee in 1990. The Web allows computer users to locate and view multimedia-based documents (i.e., documents with text, graphics, animation, audio or video) on almost any subject.

Berners-Lee graduated from Queen's College at Oxford University with a degree in Physics in 1976. In 1980 he wrote a program called Enquire, which used hypertext links to help him quickly navigate the numerous documents in a large project. He entered into a fellowship at the European Center for Nuclear Research (CERN) in 1984, where he gained experience in communication software for real-time networked systems.[61, 62, 63]

Berners-Lee invented HTTP (the HyperText Transfer Protocol), HTML (Hypertext Markup Language) and the first World Wide Web server and browser in 1989, while working at CERN.[64, 65] He intended the Web to be a mechanism for open, available access to all shared knowledge and experience.[66]

Until 1993, Berners-Lee individually managed changes and suggestions for HTTP and HTML, sent from the early Web users. By 1994 the Web community had grown large enough that he started the World Wide Web Consortium (W3C; www.w3.org) to monitor and establish Web technology standards.[67] As director of the organization, he actively promotes the principle of freely available information accessed by open technologies.[68]

Self Review

1. How did the ARPAnet differ from traditional computer networks? What was its primary benefit?
2. What creations did Berners-Lee develop to facilitate data sharing over the Internet?

Ans: **1)** The ARPAnet was decentralized, so the network continued to be able to pass information even if portions of the network failed. The primary benefit of the ARPAnet was its capability for quick and easy communication via e-mail. **2)** Berners-Lee developed the HyperText Markup Language (HTML) and the Hypertext Transfer Protocol (HTTP), making possible the World Wide Web.

1.8 The 1990s

Hardware performance continued to improve exponentially in the 1990s.[69] By the end of the decade, a typical personal computer could execute several hundred million instructions per second (MIPS) and store over a gigabyte of information on a hard disk; some supercomputers could execute over a trillion operations per second.[70] Inexpensive processing power and storage enabled users to execute large, complex programs on personal computers and enabled small- to mid-size companies to use these economical machines for the extensive database and processing jobs that were once delegated to mainframe systems. Falling technology costs also led to an increase in the number of home computers, which were used both for work and for entertainment.

In the 1990s, the creation of the World Wide Web led to an explosion in the popularity of distributed computing. Originally, operating systems performed isolated resource management inside a single computer. With the creation of the World Wide Web and increasingly fast Internet connections, distributed computing became commonplace among personal computers. Users could request data stored at remote locations or request that programs run on distant processors. Large organizations could use distributed multiprocessors (i.e., networks of computers containing more than one processor) to scale resources and increase efficiency.[71] Distributed applications, however, were still limited by the fact that communication over a network occurred at relatively slow speeds compared to the internal processing speeds of individual computers. Distributed computing is discussed in detail in Chapter 17, Introduction to Distributed Systems, and Chapter 18, Distributed Systems and Web Services.

As demand for Internet connections grew, operating system support for networking tasks became standard. Users at home and in organizations increased productivity by accessing the resources on networks of computers. However, increased connectivity led to a proliferation of computer security threats. Operating system designers developed techniques to protect computers from these malicious attacks. Ever more sophisticated security threats continued to challenge the computer industry's ability to counter such attacks.

Microsoft Corporation became dominant in the 1990s. In 1981, Microsoft released the first version of its DOS operating system for the IBM personal computer. In the mid-1980s, Microsoft developed the Windows operating system, a graphical user interface built on top of the DOS operating system. Microsoft released Windows 3.0 in 1990; this new version featured a user-friendly interface and rich functionality. The Windows operating system became incredibly popular after the 1993 release of Windows 3.1, whose successors, Windows 95 and Windows 98, virtually cornered the desktop operating system market by the late 90s. These operating systems, which borrowed from many concepts (such as icons, menus and windows) popularized by early Macintosh operating systems, enabled users to navigate multiple concurrent applications with ease. Microsoft also entered the corporate operating system market with the 1993 release of Windows NT, which quickly became the operating system of choice for corporate workstations.[72] Windows XP, which is based on the Windows NT operating system, is discussed in Chapter 21, Case Study: Windows XP.

Object Technology

Object technology became popular in many areas of computing, as the number of applications written in object-oriented programming languages, such as C++ or Java, increased steadily. Object concepts also facilitated new approaches to computing. Each software object encapsulates a set of attributes and a set of actions. This allows applications to be built with components that can be reused in many applications, reducing software development time. In **object-oriented operating systems (OOOS)**, objects represent components of the operating system and system resources.[73] Object-oriented concepts such as inheritance and interfaces were exploited to create modular operating systems that were easier to maintain and extend than operating systems built with previous techniques. Modularity facilitates operating system support to new and different architectures. The demand for object integration across multiple platforms and languages led to support for objects in programming languages such as Sun's Java and Microsoft's .NET languages (e.g., Visual Basic .NET, Visual C++ .NET and C#).

Open-Source Movement

Another development in the computing community (particularly in the area of operating systems) during the 1990s was the movement toward **open-source software**. Most software is created by writing source code in a high-level programming language. However, most commercial software is sold as object code (also called machine code or binaries)—the compiled source code that computers can understand. The source code is not included, enabling vendors to hide proprietary information and programming techniques. However, free and open-source software became increasingly common in the 1990s. Open-source software is distributed with the source code, allowing individuals to examine and modify the software before compiling and executing it. For example, the Linux operating system and the Apache Web server, both of which are free and open source, were downloaded and installed by millions of users during the 1990s, and the number of downloads is increasing rapidly in the new millennium.[74] Linux, created by Linus Torvalds (see the Biographical Note, Linus Torvalds), is discussed in Chapter 20, Case Study: Linux.

In the 1980s, Richard Stallman, a software developer at MIT, launched a project to recreate and extend most of the tools for AT&T's UNIX operating system and to make the code available at no charge. Stallman (see the Biographical Note, Richard Stallman) founded the Free Software Foundation and created the **GNU** project—which is a recursive name that stands for "*GNU's Not UNIX*"— because he disagreed with the concept of selling the permission to use software.[75] He believed that granting users the freedom to modify and distribute software would lead to better software, driven by user needs instead of personal or corporate profit. When Linus Torvalds created the original version of the Linux operating system, he employed many of the tools published by GNU for free under the **General Public License (GPL)**. The GPL, published online at `www.gnu.org/licenses/gpl.html`, specifies that anyone can freely modify and redistribute software under its license, provided that the modifications are clearly indicated and any derivative of the software is also distributed under the GPL.[76] Although most GPL-licensed software is available free of charge, the GPL requires only that its software be free in the sense that users can freely modify and redistribute it. Therefore, vendors can charge a fee for providing GPL-licensed software and its source code, but cannot

Biographical Note

Linus Torvalds

Linus Torvalds was born in 1969 in Helsinki, Finland. As a child he taught himself how to program by playing with a Commodore VIC-20. In 1988 he entered the University of Helsinki to study computer science. While there, he wrote a UNIX clone based on Professor Andrew Tanenbaum's Minix to run on his new PC.[77, 78] In 1991 he completed the first version of the basic Linux kernel, which ran on the Intel 80386 processor.[79] He distributed Linux under the GNU Public License (GPL)[80] as open-source code and gladly accepted additions, corrections and free programs from other programmers.[81,82] By 1994 Linux had accrued enough applications to be a complete, usable operating system, and version 1.0 was released.[83] Programmers and professors using UNIX on large systems liked Linux because it brought the features and power of UNIX to inexpensive desktop systems for free.[84, 85]

Torvalds is currently a fellow of the Open Source Development Labs (OSDL), which funds his full-time work on the kernel. He continues to lead the open-source Linux project, managing changes and releasing new versions of the kernel.[86, 87] Linux has become one of the largest and best-known open-source developments in computing history and has become particularly successful in the server market. Linux is discussed in Chapter 20, Case Study: Linux.

prevent end users from modifying and redistributing them. In the late 90s, the **Open Source Initiative (OSI)** was founded to protect open-source software and promote the benefits of open-source programming (see www.opensource.org).

Open-source software facilitates enhancements to software products by permitting anyone in the developer community to test, debug and enhance applications. This increases the chance that subtle bugs, which could otherwise be security risks or logic errors, are caught and fixed. Also, individuals and corporations can modify the source to create custom software that meets the needs of a particular environment. Many open-source software vendors remain profitable by charging individuals and organizations for technical support and customizing software.[88] Though most systems in the 1990s still ran proprietary operating systems, such as IBM mainframe operating systems, UNIX systems, Apple's Macintosh and

Biographical Note

Richard Stallman

Richard Stallman was the original developer of the GNU project, started in the 1980s to create free software. Stallman graduated from Harvard in 1974 with a degree in Physics.[89] While at Harvard, he worked at the MIT Artificial Intelligence Lab. After graduating, he continued at the lab, where he and his colleagues worked with shared software.[90] The idea was that someone receiving someone else's executable program would also receive its source code. This was advantageous because a programmer could add more functionality to someone else's program.[91] Stallman's specific job was to modify and improve the ITS operating system the lab used. However, as the 1980s arrived, there was little

shared software.[92] The lab's new operating system was not shared. Stallman became frustrated with operating systems, drivers, and the like, that he could no longer modify.[93] In 1984 he left the MIT Artificial Intelligence Lab to work on a new shared operating system, which he called GNU (GNU's Not UNIX).[94]

As interest in Stallman's GNU project grew, he created the Free Software Foundation (FSF) in 1985 to promote free software and continue to develop the GNU operating system.[95] Stallman and his associates at FSF created a number of GNU programs, including GNU Emacs (a text editor), GCC (a C compiler) and GDB (a debugger), to name a few.[96] In 1992 Stallman used the Linux ker-

nel to complete his system. The system, known as GNU/Linux, is a fully functional operating system and includes a variety of programs.[97]

Stallman has received numerous awards and recognition for his work, including the Grace Hopper Award, MacArthur Foundation Fellowship, the Electric Frontier Foundation Pioneer Award, the Yuri Rubinksi Award, the Takeda Award, election to the National Academy of Engineering and two honorary doctorates from the Institute of Technology in Sweden and the University of Glasgow. Stallman continues to promote the free software cause and speaks about free software all over the world.[98]

Microsoft's Windows, open-source operating systems, such as Linux, FreeBSD and OpenBSD, became viable competition. In the future, they will undoubtedly continue to gain ground on proprietary solutions as a result of product improvement, industry standardization, interoperability, product customization and cost savings.

In the 1990s, operating systems became increasingly user friendly. The GUI features that Apple built into its Macintosh operating system in the 1980s became more sophisticated in the 1990s. "Plug-and-play" capabilities were built into operating systems, enabling users to add and remove hardware components dynamically without manually reconfiguring the operating system. Operating systems also maintained user profiles—serving authentication needs and enabling per-user customization of the operating system interface.

Self Review

1. How did object-oriented technology affect operating systems?
2. What are some of the benefits of open-source development?

Ans: **1)** Operating systems designers could reuse objects when developing new components. Increased modularity due to object-oriented technology facilitated operating system support for new and different architectures. **2)** Open-source software can be viewed and modified by anyone in the software development community. Because these people constantly test, debug and use the software, there is a greater chance that bugs will be found and fixed. Also, open-source software enables users and organizations to modify a program to meet their particular needs.

1.9 2000 and Beyond

In the current decade, **middleware**, which is software that links two separate applications (often over a network), has become vital as applications are published on the World Wide Web and consumers use them via affordable, high-speed Internet connections over cable television lines and digital subscriber lines (DSL). Middleware is common in Web applications, in which a Web server (the application that sends data to the user's Web browser) must generate content to satisfy a user's request with the help of a database. The middleware acts as a courier to pass messages between the Web server and the database, simplifying communication between multiple different architectures. **Web services** encompass a set of related standards that can enable any two computer applications to communicate and exchange data via the Internet. A Web service communicates over a network to supply a specific set of operations that other applications can invoke. The data is passed back and forth using standard protocols such as HTTP, the same protocol used to transfer ordinary Web pages. Web services operate using open, text-based standards that enable components written in different languages and on different platforms to communicate. They are ready-to-use pieces of software on the Internet.

Web services will help drive the shift toward true distributed computing. For example, the online retailer Amazon.com allows developers to build online stores that search Amazon's product databases and display detailed product information via Amazon.com Web Services (www.amazon.com/gp/aws/landing.html). The Google search engine also can be integrated with other functionality through the Google Web APIs (www.google.com/apis), which connect to Google's indices of Web sites using Web services. We discuss Web services in more detail in Chapter 18, Distributed Systems and Web Services.

Multiprocessor and network architectures are creating numerous opportunities for research and development of new hardware and software design techniques. Sequential programming languages that specify one computation at a time are now complemented by concurrent programming languages, such as Java, that enable the specification of parallel computations; in Java the units of parallel computing are specified via threads. We discuss threads and the technique of multithreading in Chapter 4, Thread Concepts.

An increasing number of systems exhibit **massive parallelism**; they have large numbers of processors so that many independent parts of computations can be performed in parallel. This is dramatically different in concept from the sequential computing of the past 60 years; there are significant and challenging problems in developing the software appropriate for dealing with such parallelism. We discuss parallel computing architectures in Chapter 15, Multiprocessor Management.

Operating systems are standardizing user and application interfaces so that they are easier to use and support a greater number of programs. Microsoft has already merged the consumer and professional lines of its Windows operating system into Windows XP. In its next operating system (code-named Longhorn), Microsoft plans to integrate the formats of different types of files. This will, for example, allow users to search their systems for all files (documents, spreadsheets, e-mails, etc.) containing certain keywords. Longhorn will also include an enhanced 3D user interface, improved security and support for recordable digital versatile discs (DVDs).[99, 100] Open-source operating systems, such as Linux, will become more widely used and will employ standard application programming interfaces (APIs) such as the **Portable Operating System Interface (POSIX)** to improve compatibility with other UNIX-based operating systems.

Computing on mobile devices, such as cell phones and PDAs, will become more common as mobile devices are equipped with increasingly powerful processors. Today, these devices are used for such functions as e-mail, Web browsing and digital imaging. Resource-intensive applications, such as full-motion video, will proliferate on these devices. Because mobile device resources are limited by the devices' small size, distributed computing will play an even larger role, as PDAs and cell phones will request increasing amounts of data and processing power from remote computers.

Self Review

1. What technologies can be used to bridge the gap between different operating systems? How would these technologies make it possible to execute the same application on multiple platforms?
2. Why is distributed computing useful for computations performed by mobile devices?

Ans: **1)** Virtual machines and operating system emulators bridge the gap between different operating systems. Applications can be written once to use the functionality of the virtual machine or emulator. The virtual machines or emulators can be implemented to hide the representation of the underlying platform from the applications. **2)** Distributed computing allows a mobile device to delegate jobs to other machines with more resources. The mobile device, having limited resources and battery life, can request data and processing power from larger computers across a network.

1.10 Application Bases

When the IBM Personal Computer (often called simply "the PC") appeared in 1981, it immediately spawned a huge software industry in which **independent software vendors (ISVs)** were able to market packages for the IBM PC to run under the MS-DOS operating system (IBM's version was called DOS). Operating systems free applications software developers from having to deal with the messy details of manipulating computer hardware to manage memory, perform input/output, deal with communication lines, and so on. The operating system provides a series of **application programming interface (API)** calls which applications programmers use to accomplish detailed hardware manipulations and other operations. The API provides **system calls** by which a user program instructs the operating system to do the work; the application developer simply has to know what routines to call to accomplish specific tasks (Fig. 1.1). Note that in Fig. 1.1, the area above the dashed line, user space, indicates software components that are not part of the operating system and cannot directly access the system's physical resources. The area below the dashed line, kernel space, indicates software components that are part of the operating system and have unrestricted access to system resources. We frequently use this convention in our diagrams to indicate the privilege with which software components execute. If an application attempts to misuse system resources, or if the

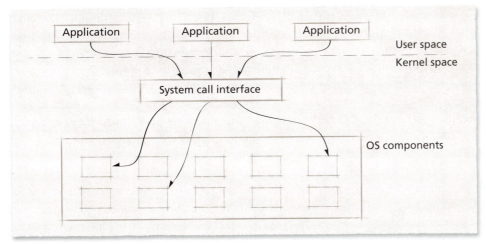

Figure 1.1 | *Interaction between applications and the operating system.*

application attempts to use resources that it has not been granted, the operating system must intervene to prevent the application from damaging the system or interfering with other user applications.

If an operating system presents an environment conducive to developing applications quickly and easily, the operating system and the hardware are more likely to be successful in the marketplace. The applications development environment created by MS-DOS encouraged the development of tens of thousands of application software packages. This in turn encouraged users to buy IBM PCs and compatibles. Windows could well have an application base of a hundred thousand applications.

Once an **application base** (i.e., the combination of the hardware and the operating system environment in which applications are developed) is widely established, it becomes extremely difficult to ask users and software developers to convert to a completely new application development environment provided by a dramatically different operating system. Thus, it is likely that new architectures evolving over the next several years will make every effort to support the existing major application bases.

1.11 Operating System Environments

This book focuses on operating system concepts related to general-purpose computers with a range of resources, including sizable amounts of main memory, high processor speeds, high-capacity disks, various peripheral devices, and so on. Such computers are typically used as personal computers or as workstations.

Many of the concepts that apply to general-purpose computers also apply to high-end Web and database servers, which contain high-performance hardware. Operating systems intended for high-end environments must be designed to support large main memories, special-purpose hardware, and large numbers of processes. We discuss these considerations in Chapter 15, Multiprocessor Management.

Embedded systems provide a different operating system design challenge. They are characterized by a small set of specialized resources that provide functionality to devices such as cell phones and PDAs. In embedded environments, efficient resource management is the key to building a successful operating system. Storage is often limited, so the operating system must provide services using a minimal amount of code. Considerations such as power management and the need for user-friendly interfaces create other challenges in embedded operating system design.

Real-time systems require that tasks be performed within a particular (often short) time frame. For example, the autopilot feature of an aircraft must constantly adjust speed, altitude and direction. Such actions cannot wait indefinitely—and sometimes cannot wait at all—for other nonessential tasks to complete. Real-time operating systems must enable processes to respond immediately to critical events. Soft real-time systems ensure that real-time tasks execute with high priority, but do not guarantee which, if any, of these tasks will complete on time. Hard real-time systems guarantee that all of their tasks complete on time. We discuss how Linux and Windows XP handle real-time applications in Chapters 20 and 21, respectively. These systems are found in many settings including robotics, avionics and other system control applications. Often, they are used in **mission-critical systems**, where the system fails to meet its objectives (i.e., mission) if any of its tasks are not successfully completed on time. In mission-critical systems such as those for air traffic control, nuclear reactor monitoring and military command and control, people's lives could be at risk.

Business-critical systems, such as Web servers and databases, must consistently meet their objectives. In e-business, this could mean guaranteeing fast response times to users purchasing products over the Internet; in large corporations, it could mean enabling employees to share information efficiently and ensuring that important information is protected from problems such as power failures and disk failures. Unlike mission-critical systems, the business does not necessarily fail if a business-critical system does not always meet its objectives.

Some operating systems must manage hardware that may or may not physically exist in the machine. A **virtual machine (VM)** is a software abstraction of a computer that often executes as a user application on top of the native operating system.[101] A virtual machine operating system manages the resources provided by the virtual machine. One application of virtual machines is to allow multiple instances of an operating system to execute concurrently. Another is emulation—using software or hardware that mimics the functionality of hardware or software not present in the system.

Virtual machines interface with the hardware in a system via the underlying operating system; other user programs can interact with VMs. A VM can create software components that represent the contents of physical systems—such as processors, memory, communication channels, disks and clocks (Fig. 1.2).[102] This allows multiple users to share hardware under the illusion of being serviced by a dedicated machine. By providing this illusion, virtual machines promote **portability**, the ability for software to run on multiple platforms.

The **Java Virtual Machine (JVM)** is one of the most widely used virtual machines. The JVM is the foundation of the Java platform and allows Java applications to execute on any JVM of the correct version, regardless of the platform on which the JVM is installed. The company VMware Software also provides virtual machines, particularly for the Intel architecture, enabling owners of Intel x86-based computers to run operating systems such as Linux and Windows concurrently on one computer (each virtual machine appears in its own window).[103]

Virtual machines tend to be less efficient than real machines because they access the hardware indirectly (or simulate hardware that is not actually connected to the computer). Indirect or simulated hardware access increases the number of software instructions required to perform each hardware action.[104]

Self Review

1. What type of system would a temperature monitor in a nuclear power plant probably be described as? Why?
2. Describe the advantages and disadvantage of virtual machines.

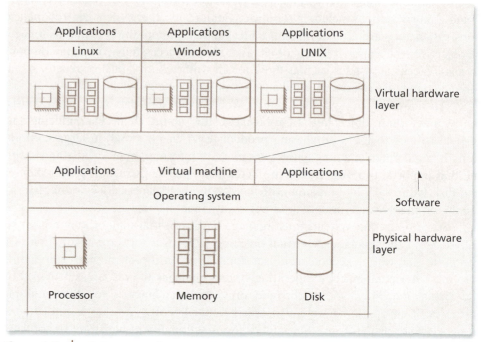

Figure 1.2 | Schematic of a virtual machine.

Ans: **1)** A hard real-time system would monitor the temperature in a nuclear power plant to ensure that it is always in an appropriate range, and would notify operators in real time (i.e., instantly) if there was a problem. **2)** Virtual machines promote portability by enabling software to run on multiple platforms, but they tend to be less efficient than real machines, because virtual machines must execute software instructions that simulate hardware operations.

1.12 Operating System Components and Goals

Computer systems have evolved from early systems containing no operating system, to multiprogramming machines, to timesharing machines, to personal computers and finally to truly distributed systems. As the demand for new features and improved efficiency grew and hardware changed, operating systems evolved to fill new roles. This section describes various core operating system components and explains several goals of operating systems.

1.12.1 Core Operating System Components

A user interacts with the operating system via one or more user applications. and often through a special application called a **shell**, or command interpreter.[105] Most of today's shells are implemented as text-based interfaces that enable the user to issue commands from a keyboard or as GUIs that allow the user to point and click and drag and drop icons to request services from the operating system (e.g., to open an application). For example, Microsoft Windows XP provides a GUI through which users can issue commands; alternatively, the user can open a command prompt window that accepts typed commands.

The software that contains the core components of the operating system is referred to as the kernel. Typical operating system core components include:

- the **process scheduler**, which determines when and for how long a process executes on a processor.

- the **memory manager**, which determines when and how memory is allocated to processes and what to do when main memory becomes full.

- the **I/O manager**, which services input and output requests from and to hardware devices, respectively.

- the **interprocess communication (IPC) manager**, which allows processes to communicate with one another.

- the **file system manager**, which organizes named collections of data on storage devices and provides an interface for accessing data on those devices.

Almost all modern operating systems support a multiprogrammed environment in which multiple applications can execute concurrently. One of the most fundamental responsibilities of an operating system is to determine which processor executes a process and for how long that process executes.

A program may contain several elements that share data and that can be executed concurrently. For example, a Web browser may contain separate components to read a Web page's HTML, retrieve the page's media (e.g., images, text and video) and render the page by laying out its content in the browser window. Such program components, which execute independently but perform their work in a common memory space, are called **threads**. Threads are discussed in Chapter 4, Thread Concepts.

Typically, many processes compete to use the processor. The process scheduler can base its decisions on several criteria, such as importance of a process, its estimated running time, or how long it has waited to obtain the processor. We discuss processor scheduling in Chapter 8, Processor Scheduling.

The memory manager allocates memory to the operating system and to processes. To ensure that processes to do not interfere with the operating system or with one another, the memory manager prevents each process from accessing memory that has not been allocated to it. Almost all of today's operating systems support virtual memory, as discussed in Chapters 10 and 11.

Another core function of the operating system is to manage the computer's input/output (I/O) devices. Input devices include keyboards, mice, microphones and scanners; output devices include monitors, printers and speakers. Storage devices (e.g., hard disks, rewritable optical discs and tape) and network cards function as both input and output devices. When a process wishes to access an I/O device, it must issue a system call to the operating system. That system call is subsequently handled by a **device driver**, which is a software component that interacts directly with hardware, often containing device-specific commands and other instructions to perform the requested input/output operations.

Most computer systems can store data persistently (i.e., after the computer is turned off). Because main memory is often relatively small and loses its data when the power is turned off, persistent secondary storage devices are used, most commonly hard disks. Disk I/O—one of the most common forms of I/O—occurs when a process requests access to information on a disk device.

Secondary storage, however, is much slower than processors and main memory. The **disk scheduler** component of an operating system is responsible for reordering disk I/O requests to maximize performance and minimize the amount of time a process waits for disk I/O. Redundant Array of Independent Disks (RAID) systems attempt to reduce the time a process waits for disk I/O by using multiple disks at once to service I/O requests. We discuss disk scheduling algorithms and RAID systems in Chapter 12, Disk Performance Optimization.

Operating systems use file systems to organize and efficiently access named collections of data called files located on storage devices. File system concepts are addressed in Chapter 13, File and Database Systems.

Often, processes (or threads) cooperate to accomplish a common goal. Thus, many operating systems provide interprocess communication (IPC) and synchronization mechanisms to simplify such concurrent programming. Interprocess communication enables processes to communicate via messages sent between the processes (and threads); synchronization provides structures that can be used to ensure that processes (and threads) share data properly. Processes and threads are discussed in Chapters 3 through 8.

Self Review

1. Which operating system components perform each of the following operations?
    a. Write to disk.
    b. Determine which process will run next.
    c. Determine where in memory a new process should be placed.
    d. Organize files on disk.
    e. Enable one process to send data to another.
2. Why is it dangerous to allow users to perform read or write operations to any region of disk at will?

Ans: **1)** a) I/O manager; b) processor scheduler; c) memory manager; d) file system manager; e) interprocess communication (IPC) manager. **2)** It is dangerous because users could accidentally or maliciously overwrite critical data (such as operating system files) or read sensitive information (such as confidential documents) without authorization.

1.12.2 Operating System Goals

Users have come to expect certain characteristics of operating systems, such as:

- efficiency
- robustness

- scalability
- extensibility
- portability
- security
- interactivity
- usability

An **efficient operating system** achieves high **throughput** and low average turn-around time. Throughput measures the amount of work a processor can complete within a certain time period. Recall that one role of an operating system is to provide services to many applications. An efficient operating system minimizes the time spent providing these services (see the Operating Systems Thinking feature, Performance).

A **robust operating system** is fault tolerant and reliable—the system will not fail due to isolated application or hardware errors, and if it fails, it does so gracefully (i.e., by minimizing loss of work and by preventing damage to the system's hard-

Operating Systems Thinking

Performance

One of the most important goals of an operating system is to maximize system performance. We are performance conscious in our everyday lives. We measure our cars' gasoline mileage, we record various speed records, professors assign grades to students, employees receive performance evaluations from their employers, a corporate executive's performance is measured by company profits, politicians' performance is measured in frequent polls of their constituents and so on.

High performance is essential to successful operating systems.

However, performance is often "in the eye of the beholder"—there are many ways to classify operating system performance. For batch-processing systems, throughput is an important measure; for interactive timesharing systems, fast response times are more important.

Throughout the book we present many performance improvement techniques. For example, Chapter 8, Processor Scheduling, discusses allocating processor time to processes to improve system performance as measured by interactivity and

throughput. Chapter 11, Virtual Memory Management, discusses allocating memory to processes to reduce their execution times. Chapter 12, Disk Performance Optimization, focuses on improving disk performance by reordering I/O requests. In Chapter 14, Performance and Processor Design, we discuss evaluating systems according to several important performance criteria. Chapters 20, and 21 discuss performance issues in the Linux and Windows XP operating systems, respectively.

ware). Such an operating system will provide services to each application unless the hardware it relies on fails.

A **scalable operating system** is able to use resources as they are added. If an operating system is not scalable, then it will quickly reach a point where additional resources will not be fully utilized. A scalable operating system can readily adjust its degree of multiprogramming. Scalability is a particularly important attribute of multiprocessor systems—as more processors are added to a system, ideally the processing capacity should increase in proportion to the number of processes, though, in practice, that does not happen. Multiprocessing is discussed in Chapter 15, Multiprocessor Management.

An **extensible operating system** will adapt well to new technologies and provide capabilities to extend the operating system to perform tasks beyond its original design.

A **portable operating system** is designed such that it can operate on many hardware configurations. Application portability is also important, because it is costly to develop applications, so the same application should run on a variety of hardware configurations to reduce development costs. The operating system is crucial to achieving this kind of portability.

A **secure operating system** prevents users and software from accessing services and resources without authorization. **Protection** refers to the mechanisms that implement the system's security policy.

An **interactive operating system** allows applications to respond quickly to user actions, or events. A **usable operating system** is one that has the potential to serve a significant user base. These operating systems generally provide an easy-to-use user interface. Operating systems such as Linux, Windows XP and MacOS X are characterized as usable operating systems, because each supports a large set of applications and provides standard user interfaces. Many experimental and academic operating systems do not support a large number of applications or provide user-friendly interfaces and therefore are not considered to be usable.

Self Review

1. Which operating system goals correspond to each of the following characteristics?
   a. Users cannot access services or information without proper authorization.
   b. The operating system runs on a variety of hardware configurations.
   c. System performance increases steadily when additional memory and processors are added.
   d. The operating system supports devices that were not available at the time of its design.
   e. Hardware failure does not necessarily cause the system to fail.
2. How does device driver support contribute to an operating system's extensibility?

Ans: **1)** a) security; b) portability; c) scalability; d) extensibility; e) robustness. **2)** Device drivers enable developers to add support for hardware that did not exist when the operating system was designed. With each new type of device that is added to a system a corresponding device driver must be installed.

1.13 Operating System Architectures

Today's operating systems tend to be complex because they provide many services and support a variety of hardware and software resources (see the Operating Systems Thinking feature, Keep It Simple (KIS) and the Anecdote,). Operating system architectures can help designers manage this complexity by organizing operating system components and specifying the privilege with which each component executes. In the monolithic design, every component of the operating system is contained in the kernel; in the microkernel design, only the essential components are included. In the sections that follow, we survey several important architectures (see the Operating Systems Thinking feature, Architecture).

1.13.1 Monolithic Architecture

The **monolithic operating system** is the earliest and most common operating system architecture. Every component of the operating system is contained in the kernel and can directly communicate with any other (i.e., simply by using function calls). The kernel typically executes with unrestricted access to the computer system (Fig. 1.3). OS/360, VMS and Linux are broadly characterized as monolithic operating systems.[106] Direct intercommunication between components makes monolithic operating systems highly efficient. Because monolithic kernels group components together,

Operating Systems Thinking

Keep It Simple (KIS)

Complex systems are costly to design, implement, test, debug and maintain. Often, operating systems designers will choose the simplest of several approaches to solving a particular problem. Sometimes, though, a more complex approach can yield performance benefits or other improvements that make such an approach worthwhile. Such trade-offs are common in computing. A simple linear search of an array is trivial to program, but runs slowly compared to a more elegant and complicated binary search. Tree data structures can be more complex to work with than arrays, but make it easier and faster to perform certain types of insertions and deletions. We typically consider alternate approaches to solving operating systems problems and developing resource management strategies. As you read these discussions, you will see the trade-offs between simplicity and complexity. As you read these solutions, you might be inclined to favor certain approaches. The systems you work with in the future may demand different approaches. Our philosophy is to present the pros and cons of the popular approaches to help you prepare to make your own best judgment calls in industry.

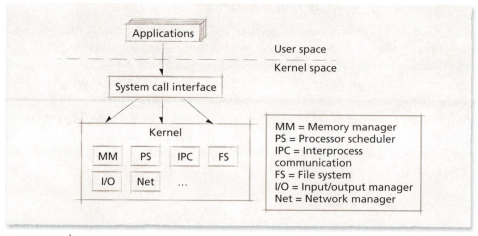

Figure 1.3 | *Monolithic operating system kernel architecture.*

however it is difficult to isolate the source of bugs and other errors. Further, because all code executes with unrestricted access to the system, systems with monolithic kernels are particularly susceptible to damage from errant or malicious code.

Self Review

1. What is the defining characteristic of a monolithic operating system?
2. Why do monolithic operating systems tend to be efficient? What is a key weakness of monolithic kernels?

Anecdote

System Architect vs. System Engineer

If you enter the field of operating systems development and you become more senior, you may be given a title like systems architect or systems engineer. A professional software colleague was a guest speaker at a conference some years ago. He was introduced as a systems architect. He said: "You may wonder how that differs from being a systems engineer." He humbly explained the difference with a building analogy: "When an engineer builds a building, it's very well built, but it's so ugly that the people tear it down; when an architect builds a building, it's very beautiful, but it falls down!"

Lesson to operating systems designers: You need to combine aspects of both architecture and engineering to insure that your systems are both well built and elegant. The latter goal is less important.

Ans: **1)** In a monolithic operating system every component of the operating system is contained in the kernel. **2)** Monolithic kernels tend to be efficient because few calls cross from user space to kernel space. Because all OS code in monolithic kernels operates with unrestricted access to the computer's hardware and software, these systems are particularly susceptible to damage from errant code.

1.13.2 Layered Architecture

As operating systems became larger and more complex, purely monolithic designs became unwieldy. The **layered** approach to operating systems attempts to address this issue by grouping components that perform similar functions into layers. Each layer communicates exclusively with those immediately above and below it. Lower-level layers provide services to higher-level ones using an interface that hides their implementation.

Layered operating systems are more modular than monolithic operating systems, because the implementation of each layer can be modified without requiring any modification to other layers. A modular system has self-contained componen that can be reused throughout the system. Each component hides how it performs

Operating Systems Thinking

Architecture

Just as architects use different approaches to designing buildings, operating systems designers employ different architectural approaches to designing operating systems. Sometimes these approaches are pure in that one architectural approach is used throughout the system. Sometimes hybridized approaches are used, mixing the advantages of several architectural styles. The approach the designer chooses will have monumental consequences on the initial implementation and the evolution of the operating system. It becomes increasingly difficult to change approaches the further into the development you proceed, so it is important to choose the proper architecture early in system development. More generally, it is much easier to build the building correctly in the first place than it is to modify the building after it has been built.

One of the most common architectural approaches employed in software systems such as operating systems is called layering. This software is divided into modules called layers that each perform certain tasks. Each layer calls the services provided by the layer below it, while the implementation of that layer is hidden from the layer above. Layering combines the virtues of the software engineering techniques of modularity and information hiding to provide a solid basis for building quality systems. We discuss layered software approaches throughout the book, starting with a historic mention of Dijkstra's THE system (see Section 1.13.2, Layered Architecture) and continuing to explanations of how layering is used in Linux and Windows XP in Chapters 20, and 21, respectively.

its job and presents a standard interface that other components can use to request its services. Modularity imposes structure and consistency on the operating system—often simplifying validation, debugging and modification. However, in a layered approach, a user process's request may need to pass through many layers before it is serviced. Because additional methods must be invoked to pass data from one layer to the next, performance degrades compared to that of a monolithic kernel, which may require only a single call to service a similar request. Also, because all layers have unrestricted access to the system, layered kernels are also susceptible to damage from errant or malicious code. The THE operating system is an early example of a layered operating system (Fig. 1.4).[107] Many of today's operating systems, including Windows XP and Linux, implement some level of layering.

Self Review

1. How are layered operating systems more modular than monolithic operating systems?
2. Why do layered operating systems tend to be less efficient than monolithic operating systems?

Ans: **1)** In layered operating systems, the implementation and interface are separate for each layer. This allows each layer to be tested and debugged separately. It also enables designers to change each layer's implementation without needing to modify the other layers. **2)** In layered operating systems, several calls may be required to communicate between the layers, whereas this overhead does not exist in monolithic kernels.

1.13.3 Microkernel Architecture

A **microkernel operating system** architecture provides only a small number of services in an attempt to keep the kernel small and scalable. These services typically include low-level memory management, interprocess communication and basic pro-

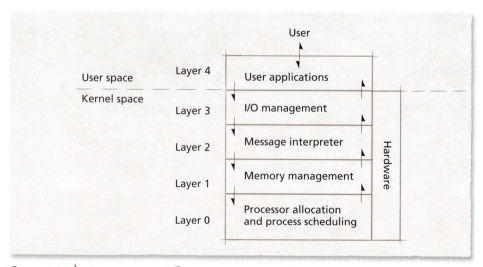

Figure 1.4 | *Layers of the THE operating system.*

cess synchronization to enable processes to cooperate. In microkernel designs, most operating system components—such as process management, networking, file system interaction and device management—execute outside the kernel with a lower privilege level (Fig. 1.5).[108, 109, 110, 111]

Microkernels exhibit a high degree of modularity, making them extensible, portable and scalable.[112] Further, because the microkernel does not rely on each component to execute, one or more components can fail, without causing the operating system to fail. However, such modularity comes at the cost of an increased level of intermodule communication, which can degrade system performance. Although few of today's popular operating systems fully embrace the microkernel design, Linux and Windows XP, for example, contain modular components.[113]

Self Review

1. What is the difference between a purely layered architecture and a microkernel architecture?
2. How do microkernels promote portability?

Ans: **1)** A layered architecture enables communication exclusively between operating system components in adjacent layers. A microkernel architecture enables communication between all operating system components via the microkernel. **2)** The microkernel does not depend on a particular hardware platform; support for new hardware can be provided by loading a new module.

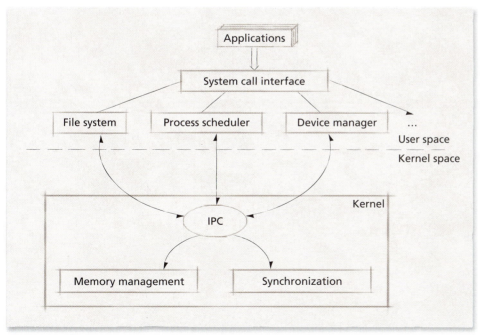

Figure 1.5 | *Microkernel operating system architecture.*

1.13.4 Networked and Distributed Operating Systems

Advances in telecommunications technology have profoundly affected operating systems. A **network operating system** enables its processes to access resources (e.g., files) that reside on other independent computers on a network.[114] The structure of many networked and distributed operating systems is often based on the client/server model (Fig. 1.6). The client computers in such a network request resources—such as files and processor time—via the appropriate network protocol. The servers respond with the appropriate resources. In such networks, operating system designers must carefully consider how to manage data and communication among computers.

Some operating systems are more "networked" than others. In a networked environment, a process can execute on the computer on which it is created or on another computer on the network. In some network operating systems, users can specify exactly where their processes run; in others, the operating system determines where processes are executed. For example, the system may determine that a process can be more efficiently executed on a computer experiencing a light load.[115]

Networked file systems are an important component of networked operating systems. At the lowest level, users acquire resources on another machine by explicitly connecting to that machine and retrieving files. Higher-level network file systems enable users to access remote files as if they were on the local system. Examples of network file systems include Sun's Network File System (NFS) and

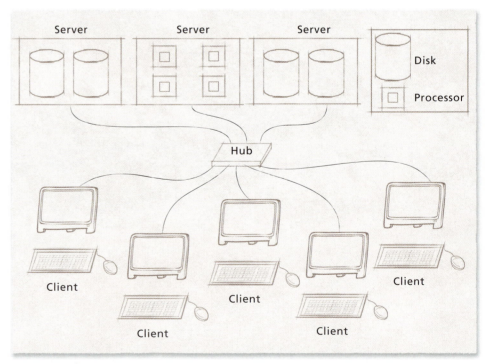

Figure 1.6 | *Client/server networked operating system model.*

CMU's Andrew and Coda file systems. Networked file systems are discussed in detail in Chapter 18, Distributed Systems and Web Services.

A **distributed operating system** is a single operating system that manages resources on more than one computer system. **Distributed systems** provide the illusion that multiple computers are a single powerful computer, so that a process can access all of the system's resources regardless of the process's location within the distributed system's network of computers.[116] Distributed operating systems are often difficult to implement and require complicated algorithms to enable processes to communicate and share data. Examples of distributed operating systems are MIT's Chord operating system and the Amoeba operating system from the Vrije Universiteit (VU) in Amsterdam.[117, 118] We discuss distributed systems in Chapter 17, Introduction to Distributed Systems.

Now that we have presented a seemingly endless stream of facts, issues, and acronyms, we proceed with a discussion of the basic principles of computer hardware and software in Chapter 2, Hardware and Software Concepts.

Self Review

1. What is the major difference between networked and distributed operating systems?
2. What is the primary advantage of a distributed operating system? What is the primary challenge of designing one?

Ans: **1)** A networked operating system controls one computer but cooperates with other computers on the network. In a distributed operating system, one operating system controls many computers in a network. **2)** The primary advantage is that processes do not need to know the locations of the resources they use, which simplifies applications programming. This comes at the expense of the systems programmer, who must implement complicated algorithms to enable processes to communicate and share data among many computers, creating the illusion of there being only a single larger computer.

Web Resources

www.bell-labs.com/history/unix/
Provides a history of the UNIX operating system, from its origins in the Multics system to the mature UNIX operating systems of today. Discusses many of the design and architectural considerations in the evolution of UNIX.

www.softpanorama.org/History/os_history.shtml
Provides a wealth of information on open-source software from a historical perspective.

www.microsoft.com/windows/WinHistoryIntro.mspx
Provides a history of the Microsoft Windows family of operating systems.

www.viewz.com/shoppingguide/os.shtml
Compares several popular operating systems, including Windows, Linux and MacOS, and provides a historical perspective.

developer.apple.com/darwin/history.html
Covers the evolution of Darwin, the core of Apple's OS X operating system.

www.cryptonomicon.com/beginning.html
Contains a link to the article, "In the Beginning Was the Command Line," by Neal Stephenson. This text is a narrative account of the recent history of operating systems, making colorful use of anecdote and metaphor.

www.acm.org/sigcse/cc2001/225.html
Lists the operating systems course curriculum recommendation from the ACM/IEEE Joint Task Force that completed the Computing Curricula 2001 (CC2001) project. The curriculum indicates key areas of coverage for a typical operating systems course.

whatis.techtarget.com/
Provides definitions for computer-related terms.

www.webopedia.com/
Provides an online dictionary and a search engine for computer- and Internet-related terms.

www.wikipedia.org/
Wikipedia is a project aimed at creating a free, open and accurate encyclopedia online. Any user may modify the entries in the encyclopedia, and all entries are licensed under the GNU Free Documentation License (GNUFDL).

Summary

Some years ago an operating system was defined as the software that controls the hardware, but the landscape of computer systems has evolved significantly since then, requiring a more complicated description. To increase hardware utilization, applications are designed to execute concurrently. However, if these applications are not carefully programmed, they might interfere with one another. As a result, a layer of software called an operating system separates applications (the software layer) from the hardware they access.

When a user requests that the computer perform an action (e.g., execute an application or print a document), the operating system manages the software and hardware to produce the desired result. Operating systems are primarily resource managers—they manage hardware, including processors, memory, input/output devices and communication devices. The operating system must also manage applications and other software abstractions that, unlike hardware, are not physical objects.

Operating systems have evolved over the last 60 years through several distinct phases or generations that correspond roughly to the decades. In the 1940s, the earliest electronic digital computers did not include operating systems. The systems of the 1950s generally executed only one job at a time, but used techniques that smoothed the transition between jobs to obtain maximum utilization of the computer system. A job constituted the set of instructions that a program would execute. These early computers were called single-stream batch-processing systems, because programs and data were submitted in groups or batches by loading them consecutively onto tape or disk.

The systems of the 1960s were also batch-processing systems, but they used the computer's resources more efficiently by running several jobs at once. The systems of the 1960s improved resource utilization by allowing one job to use the processor while other jobs used peripheral devices. With these observations in mind, operating systems designers developed multiprogramming systems that managed a number of jobs at once, that number being indicated by the system's degree of multiprogramming.

In 1964, IBM announced its System/360 family of computers. The various 360 computer models were designed to be hardware compatible, to use the OS/360 operating system and to offer greater computer power as the user moved upward in the series. More advanced operating systems were developed to service multiple interactive users at once. Timesharing systems were developed to support large numbers of simultaneous interactive users.

Real-time systems attempt to supply a response within a certain bounded time period. The resources of a real-time system are often heavily under-utilized. It is more important for real-time systems to respond quickly when needed than to use their resources efficiently.

Turnaround time—the time between submission of a job and the return of its results—was reduced to minutes or even seconds. The value of timesharing systems in support of program development was demonstrated when MIT used the CTSS system to develop its own successor, Multics. TSS, Multics and CP/CMS all incorporated virtual memory, which enables programs to address more memory locations than are actually provided in main memory, which is also called real memory or physical memory.

The systems of the 1970s were primarily multimode timesharing systems that supported batch processing, timesharing and real-time applications. Personal computing was in its incipient stages, fostered by early and continuing developments in microprocessor technology. Communications between computer systems throughout the United States increased as the Department of Defense's TCP/IP communications standards became widely used—especially in military and university computing environments. Security problems increased as growing volumes of information passed over vulnerable communications lines.

The 1980s was the decade of the personal computer and the workstation. Rather than data being brought to a central, large-scale computer installation for processing, computing was distributed to the sites at which it was needed. Personal computers proved to be relatively easy to learn and use, partially because of graphical user interfaces (GUI), which used graphical symbols such as windows, icons and menus to facilitate user interaction with programs. As technology costs declined, transferring information between computers in computer networks became more economical and practical. The client/server distributed computing model became widespread. Clients are user computers that request various services; servers are computers that perform the requested services.

The software engineering field continued to evolve, a major thrust by the United States government being aimed especially at providing tighter control of Department of Defense software projects. Some goals of the initiative included realizing code reusability and a greater degree of abstraction in programming languages. Another software engineering development was the implementation of processes containing multiple threads of instructions that could execute independently.

In the late 1960s, ARPA, the Advanced Research Projects Agency of the Department of Defense, rolled out the blueprints for networking the main computer systems of about a dozen ARPA-funded universities and research institutions. ARPA proceeded to implement what was dubbed the ARPAnet—the grandparent of today's Internet. ARPAnet's chief benefit proved to be its capability for quick and easy communication via what came to be known as electronic mail (e-mail). This is true even on today's Internet, with e-mail, instant messaging and file transfer facilitating communications among hundreds of millions of people worldwide.

The ARPAnet was designed to operate without centralized control. The protocols (i.e., set of rules) for communicating over the ARPAnet became known as the Transmission Control Protocol/Internet Protocol (TCP/IP). TCP/IP was used to manage communication between applications. The protocols ensured that messages were routed properly from sender to receiver and arrived intact. Eventually, the government decided to allow access to the Internet for commercial purposes.

The World Wide Web allows computer users to locate and view multimedia-based documents (i.e., documents with text, graphics, animations, audios or videos) on almost any subject. Even though the Internet was developed more than three decades ago, the introduction of the World Wide Web (WWW) was a relatively recent event. In 1989, Tim Berners-Lee of CERN (the European Center for Nuclear Research) began to develop a technology for sharing information via hyperlinked text documents. To implement this new technology, He created the HyperText Markup Language (HTML). Berners-Lee also implemented the Hypertext Transfer Protocol (HTTP) to form the communications backbone of his new hypertext information system, which he called the World Wide Web.

Hardware performance continued to improve exponentially in the 1990s. Inexpensive processing power and storage allowed users to execute large, complex programs on personal computers and enabled small to mid-size companies to use these economical machines for the extensive database and processing jobs that earlier had been delegated to mainframe systems. In the 1990s, the shift toward distributed computing (i.e., using multiple independent computers to perform a common task) rapidly accelerated. As demand for Internet connections grew, operating system support for networking tasks became standard. Users at home and in large corporations increased productivity by accessing the resources on networks of computers.

Microsoft Corporation became dominant in the 1990s. Its Windows operating systems, which borrowed from many concepts popularized by early Macintosh operating systems (such as icons, menus and windows), enabled users to navigate multiple concurrent applications with ease.

Object technology became popular in many areas of computing. Many applications were written in object-oriented programming languages, such as C++ or Java. In object-oriented operating systems (OOOS), objects represent components of the operating system. Object-oriented concepts such as inheritance and interfaces were exploited to create modular operating systems that were easier to maintain and extend than operating systems built with previous techniques.

Most commercial software is sold as object code. The source code is not included, enabling vendors to hide proprietary information and programming techniques. Free and open-source software became increasingly common in the 1990s. Open-source software is distributed with the source code, allowing individuals to examine and modify the software before compiling and executing it. The Linux operating system and the Apache Web server are both free and open source.

In the 1980s, Richard Stallman, a developer at MIT, launched the GNU project to recreate and extend most of the tools for AT&T's UNIX operating system. Stallman created the GNU project because he disagreed with the concept of paying for permission to use software. The Open Source Initiative (OSI) was founded to further the benefits of open-source programming. Open-source software facilitates enhancements to software products by permitting anyone in the developer community to test, debug and enhance applications. This increases the chance that subtle bugs, which could otherwise be security risks or logic errors, will be caught and fixed. Also, individuals and corporations can modify the source to create custom software that meets the needs of a particular environment.

In the 1990s, operating systems became increasingly user friendly. The GUI features that Apple had built into its Macintosh operating system in the 1980s were widely used in many operating systems and became more sophisticated. "Plug-and-play" capabilities were built into operating systems, enabling users to add and remove hardware components dynamically without manually reconfiguring the operating system.

Middleware is software that links two separate applications, often over a network and often between incompatible machines. It is particularly important for Web services because it simplifies communication across multiple architectures. Web services encompass a set of related standards that can enable any two computer applications to communicate and exchange data via the Internet. They are ready-to-use pieces of software on the Internet.

When the IBM PC appeared, it immediately spawned a huge software industry in which independent software vendors (ISVs) were able to market software packages for the IBM PC to run under the MS-DOS operating system. If an operating system presents an environment conducive to developing applications quickly and easily, the operating system and the hardware are more likely to be successful in the marketplace. Once an application base (i.e., the combination of the hardware and the operating system environment in which applications are developed) is widely established, it becomes extremely difficult to ask users and software developers to convert to a completely new applications development environment provided by a dramatically different operating system.

Operating systems intended for high-end environments must be designed to support large main memories, special-purpose hardware, and large numbers of processes. Embedded systems are characterized by a small set of specialized resources that provide functionality to devices such as cell phones and PDAs. In these environments, efficient resource management is the key to building a successful operating system.

Real-time systems require that tasks be performed within a particular (often short) time frame. For example, the autopilot feature of an aircraft must constantly adjust speed, altitude and direction. Such actions cannot wait indefinitely—and sometimes cannot wait at all—for other nonessential tasks to complete.

Some operating systems must manage hardware that may or may not physically exist in the machine. A virtual machine (VM) is a software abstraction of a computer that often executes as a user application on top of the native operating system. A virtual machine operating system manages the resources provided by the virtual machine. One application of virtual machines is to allow multiple instances of an operating system to execute concurrently. Another use for virtual machines is emulation—the ability to use software or hardware that mimics the functionality of hardware or software not present in the system. By providing the illusion that applications are running on different hardware or operating systems, virtual machines promote portability—the ability for software to run on multiple platforms—and many other benefits.

A user interacts with the operating system via one or more user applications. Often, the user interacts with an operating system through a special application called a shell. The software that contains the core components of the operating system is referred to as the kernel. Typical operating system components include the processor scheduler, memory manager, I/O manager, interprocess communication (IPC) manager, and file system manager.

Almost all modern operating systems support a multiprogrammed environment in which multiple applications can execute concurrently. The kernel manages the execution of processes. Program components, which execute independently but use a single memory space to share data, are called threads.

When a process wishes to access an I/O device, it must issue a system call to the operating system. That system call is subsequently handled by a device driver—a software component that interacts directly with hardware—often containing device-specific commands and other instructions to perform the requested input and output operations.

Users have come to expect certain characteristics of operating systems, such as efficiency, robustness, scalability, extensibility, portability, security and protection, interactivity and usability.

In a monolithic operating system, every component is contained in the kernel. As a result, any component can directly communicate with any other. Monolithic operating systems tend to be highly efficient. A disadvantage of monolithic designs is that it is difficult to determine the source of subtle errors.

The layered approach to operating systems attempts to address this issue by grouping components that perform similar functions into layers. Each layer communicates exclusively with the layers immediately above and below it.

In a layered approach, a user process's request may need to pass through many layers before completion. Because additional methods must be invoked to pass data and control from one layer to the next, system throughput decreases compared to that with a monolithic kernel, which may require only a single call to service a similar request.

A microkernel operating system architecture provides only a small number of services in an attempt to keep the kernel small and scalable. Microkernels exhibit a high degree of modularity, making them extensible, portable and scalable. However, such modularity comes at the cost of an increased level of intermodule communication, which can degrade system performance.

A network operating system runs on one computer and allows its processes to access resources such as files and processors on a remote computer. A distributed operating system is a single operating system that manages resources on more than one computer system. The goals of a distributed operating system include transparent performance, scalability, fault tolerance and consistency.

Key Terms

Advanced Research Projects Agency (ARPA)—Government agency under the Department of Defense that laid the groundwork for the Internet; it is now called the Defense Advanced Research Projects Agency (DARPA).

application base—Combination of the hardware and the operating system environment in which applications are developed. It is difficult for users and application developers to convert from an established application base to another.

application programming interface (API)—Specification that allows applications to request services from the kernel by making system calls.

ARPAnet—Predecessor to the Internet that enabled researchers to network their computers. ARPAnet's chief benefit proved to be quick and easy communication via what came to be known as electronic mail (e-mail).

bandwidth—Information-carrying capacity of a communications line.

business-critical system—System that must function properly, but whose failure of which leads to reduced productivity and profitability; not as crucial as a mission-critical system, where failure could put human lives could be at risk.

C—High-level programming language that was designed and used to implement the UNIX operating system.

client—Process that requests a service from another process (a server). The machine on which the client process runs is also called a client.

compute-bound—See processor-bound.

CP/CMS—Timesharing operating system developed by IBM in the 1960s.

CTSS—Timesharing operating system developed at MIT in the 1960s.

degree of multiprogramming—Number of programs a system can manage at a time.

device driver—Software through which the kernel interacts with hardware devices. Device drivers are intimately familiar with the specifics of the devices they manage—such as the arrangement of data on those devices—and they deal with device-specific operations such as reading data, writing data and opening and closing a DVD drive's tray. Drivers are modular, so they can be added and removed as a system's hardware changes, enabling users to add new types of devices easily; in this way they contribute to a system's extensibility.

disk scheduler—Operating system component that determines the order in which disk I/O requests are serviced to improve performance.

distributed computing—Using multiple independent computers to perform a common task.

distributed operating system—Single operating system that provides transparent access to resources spread over multiple computers.

distributed system—Collection of computers that cooperate to perform a common task.

efficient operating system—Operating system that exhibits high throughput and small turnaround time.

embedded system—Small computer containing limited resources and specialized hardware to run devices such as PDAs or cellular phones.

extensible operating system—An operating system that can incorporate new features easily.

fault tolerance—Operating system's ability to handle software or hardware errors.

file system manager—Operating system component that organizes named collections of data on storage devices and provides an interface for accessing data on those devices.

General Public License (GPL)—Open-source software license which specifies that software distributed under it must contain the complete source code, must clearly indicate any modifications to the original code and must be accompanied by the GPL. End users are free to modify and redistribute any software under the GPL.

GNU—Project initiated by Stallman in the 1980s aimed at producing an open-source operating system with the features and utilities of UNIX.

graphical user interface (GUI)—User-friendly point of access to an operating system that uses graphical symbols such as windows, icons and menus to facilitate program and file manipulation.

HyperText Markup Language (HTML)—Language that specifies the content and arrangement of information on a Web page and provides hyperlinks to access other pages.

Hypertext Transfer Protocol (HTTP)—Network protocol used for transferring HTML documents and other data formats between a client and a server. This is the key protocol of the World Wide Web.

I/O-bound—Process (or job) that tends to use a processor for a short time before generating an I/O request and relinquishing a processor.

I/O manager—Operating system component that receives, interprets and performs I/O requests.

independent software vendor (ISV)—Organization that develops and sells software. ISVs prospered after the release of the IBM PC.

interactive operating system—Operating system that allows applications to respond quickly to user input.

interactive users—Users that are present when the system processes their jobs. Interactive users communicate with their jobs during execution.

Internet—Network of communication channels that provides the backbone for telecommunication and the World Wide Web. Each computer on the Internet determines which services it uses and which it makes available to other computers connected to the Internet.

interprocess communication (IPC) manager—Operating system component that governs communication between processes.

Java Virtual Machine (JVM)—Virtual machine that enables Java programs to execute on many different architectures without recompiling Java programs into the native machine language of the computer on which they execute. The JVM promotes application portability and simplifies programming by freeing the programmer from architecture-specific considerations.

job—Set of work to be done by a computer.

kernel—Software that contains the core components of an operating system.

layered operating system—Modular operating system that places similar components in isolated layers. Each layer accesses the services of the layer below and returns results to the layer above.

level of multiprogramming—See degree of multiprogramming.

massive parallelism—Property of a system containing large numbers of processors so that many parts of computations can be performed in parallel.

memory manager—Operating system component that controls physical and virtual memory.

microkernel operating system—Scalable operating system that puts a minimal number of services in the kernel and requires user-level programs to implement services generally delegated to the kernel in other types of operating systems.

middleware—Layer of software that enables communication between different applications. Middleware simplifies application programming by performing work such as network communication and translation between different data formats.

mission-critical system—System that must function properly; its failure could lead to loss of property, money or even human life.

monolithic operating system—Operating system whose kernel contains every component of the operating system. The kernel typically operates with unrestricted access to the computer system.

Multics—One of the first operating systems to implement virtual memory. Developed by MIT, GE and Bell Laboratories as the successor to MIT's CTSS.

multiprogramming—Ability to store multiple programs in memory at once so that they can be executed concurrently.

network operating system—Operating system that can manipulate resources at remote locations but does not hide the location of these resources from applications (as distributed systems can).

object-oriented operating system (OOOS)—Operating system in which components and resources are represented as objects. Object-oriented concepts such as inheritance and interfaces help create modular operating systems that are easier to maintain and extend than operating systems built with previous techniques. Many operating systems use objects, but few are written entirely using object-oriented languages.

online—State describing a computer that is turned on (i.e., active) and directly connected to a network.

open-source software—Software that includes the application's source code and is often distributed under the General Public License (GPL) or a similar license. Open-source software is typically developed by teams of independent programmers worldwide.

open-source initiative (OSI)—Group that supports and promotes open-source software (see www.opensource.com).

operating system—Software that manages system resources to provide services that allow applications to execute properly. An operating system may manage both hardware and software resources. Operating systems provide an application programming interface to facilitate application development. They also help make system resources conveniently available to users while providing a reliable, secure and responsive environment to applications and users.

portability—Property of software that can run on different platforms.

portable operating system—Operating system that is designed to operate on many hardware configurations.

Portable Operating Systems Interface (POSIX)—API based on early UNIX operating systems.

priority of a process—Importance or urgency of a process relative to other processes.

process scheduler—Operating system component that determines which process can gain access to a processor and for how long.

process—An executing program.

processor-bound—Process (or job) that consumes its quantum when executing. These processes (or jobs) tend to be calculation intensive and issue few, if any, I/O requests.

protection—Mechanism that implements a system's security policy by preventing applications from accessing resources and services without authorization.

real-time system—System that attempts to service requests within a specified (usually short) time period. In mission-critical real-time systems (e.g., air traffic control and petroleum refinery monitors), money, property or even human life could be lost if requests are not serviced on time.

robust operating system—Operating system that is fault tolerant and reliable—the system will not fail due to unexpected application or hardware errors (but if it must fail, it does so gracefully). Such an operating system will provide services to each application unless the hardware those services requires fails to function.

scalable operating system—Operating system that is able to employ resources as they are added to the system. It can readily adapt its degree of multiprogramming to meet the needs of its users.

secure operating system—Operating system that prevents users and software from gaining unauthorized access to services and data.

server—Process that provides services to other processes (called clients). The machine on which these processes run is also called a server.

shell—Application (typically GUI or text based) that enables a user to interact with an operating system

single-stream batch-processing system—Early computer system that executed a series of noninteractive jobs sequentially, one at a time.

system call—Call from a user process that invokes a service of the kernel.

thread—Entity that describes an independently executable stream of program instructions (also called a thread of execution or thread of control). Threads facilitate parallel execution of concurrent activities within a process.

throughput—Amount of work performed per unit time.

timesharing system—Operating system that enables multiple simultaneous interactive users.

Transmission Control Protocol/Internet Protocol (TCP/IP)—Family of protocols that provide a framework for networking on the Internet.

TSS—Operating system designed by IBM in the 1960s that offered timesharing and virtual memory capabilities. Although it was never released commercially, many of its capabilities appeared in later IBM systems.

turnaround time—Time it takes from the submission of a request until the system returns the result.

UNIX—Operating system developed at Bell Laboratories that was written using the C high-level programming language.

usable operating system—Operating system that has the potential to serve a significant user base by providing an easy-to-use interface and supporting a large set of user-oriented applications.

virtual machine—Application that emulates the functionality of a computer system. A virtual machine can execute applications that are not directly compatible with the physical system that runs the virtual machine. The user "sees" the computer not as the virtual machine, but as the underlying physical machine.

virtual memory—Capability of operating systems that enables programs to address more memory locations than are actually provided in main memory. Virtual memory systems help remove much of the burden of memory management from programmers, freeing them to concentrate on application development.

VM operating system—One of the first virtual machine operating systems; developed at IBM in the 1960s and still used widely today; its latest version is the z/VM.

Web services—Set of services and related standards that can allow any two computer applications to communicate and exchange data over the Internet. Web services operate using open, text-based standards that enable components written in different languages and on different platforms to communicate. They are ready-to-use pieces of software on the Internet.

World Wide Web (WWW)—Collection of hyperlinked documents accessible via the Internet using the Hypertext Transfer Protocol (HTTP). Web documents are typically written in languages such as HyperText Markup Language (HTML) and Extensible Markup Language (XML).

Exercises

1.1 Distinguish between multiprogramming and multiprocessing. What were the key motivations for the development of each?

1.2 Briefly discuss the significance of each of the following systems mentioned in this chapter:

    a. MS-DOS

    b. CTSS

    c. Multics

    d. OS/360

    e. TSS

    f. UNIX

    g. Macintosh

1.3 What developments made personal computing feasible?

1.4 Why is it impractical to use a virtual machine for a hard real-time system?

1.5 What role did the development of graphical user interfaces play in the personal computer revolution?

1.6 The GNU Public License (GPL) promotes software that is free, as in "freedom." How does the GPL provide such freedom?

1.7 How has distributed computing affected operating system design?

1.8 What are the advantages and disadvantages of communication between computers?

1.9 Define, compare, and contrast each of the following terms:

    a. online

    b. real time

    c. interactive computing

    d. timesharing

1.10 How do middleware and Web services promote interoperability?

1.11 Evaluate monolithic, layered and microkernel architectures according to

    a. efficiency.

    b. robustness.

    c. extensibility.

    d. security.

Suggested Projects

1.12 Prepare a research paper on the Linux operating system. In what ways does it support Stallman's "free as in freedom" doctrine for software? In what ways does Linux conflict with this philosophy?

1.13 Prepare a research paper on the Internet and how its pervasive use affects operating system design.

1.14 Prepare a research paper on the open-source software movement. Discuss whether all open-source software is free, as in both "freedom" and "price." How do the GPL and similar licenses promote open-source software?

1.15 Prepare a research paper on the evolution of operating systems. Be sure to mention the key hardware, software and communications technologies that encouraged each new operating system innovation.

1.16 Prepare a research paper on the future of operating systems.

1.17 Prepare a research paper giving a thorough taxonomy of past and present operating systems.

1.18 Prepare a research paper on Web services. Discuss the key technologies on which the Web services infrastructure is being built. How will the availability of Web services affect applications development?

1.19 Prepare a research paper on business-critical and mission-critical applications. Discuss the key attributes of hardware, communications software and operating systems that are essential to building systems to support these types of applications.

1.20 Prepare a research paper on virtual machine systems. Be sure to investigate IBM's VM operating system and Sun's Java Virtual Machine (JVM).

1.21 Prepare a research paper on operating systems and the law. Survey legislation related to operating systems.

1.22 Prepare a research paper on the impact of operating systems on business and the economy.

1.23 Prepare a research paper on operating systems and security and privacy. Be sure to consider the issues of worms and viruses.

1.24 Prepare a research paper on the ethical issues with which operating systems designers must be concerned. Be sure to deal with issues such as the use of computer systems in warfare and in life-threatening situations, viruses and worms, and other important topics you discover as you do your research for your paper.

1.25 List several trends leading the way to future operating systems designs. How will each affect the nature of future systems?

1.26 Prepare a research paper discussing the design of massively parallel systems. Be sure to compare large-scale multiprocessor systems (e.g., the Hewlitt-Packard Superdome supercomputer, which contains up to 64 processors; www.hp.com/products1/servers/scalableservers/superdome/) to clustered systems and server farms that contain hundreds or thousands of low-end computers that cooperate to perform common tasks (see, for example, www.beowulf.org). Use www.top500.org, a listing of the world's most powerful supercomputers, to determine the type of tasks that each of these massively parallel systems performs.

1.27 What trends are leading the way to dramatic increases in parallel computation? What challenges must be addressed by hardware designers and software designers before parallel computation will become widely used?

1.28 Prepare a research paper that compares MIT's Exokernel (www.pdos.lcs.mit.edu/exo.html) and CMU's Mach microkernel (www-2.cs.cmu.edu/afs/cs.cmu.edu/project/mach/public/www/mach.html) research operating systems.[119] What is the primary focus of each operating system? Be sure to mention how the researchers organized components such as memory management, disk scheduling and process management. Has either or both of these systems become commercially successful? Has either or both of these systems influenced the designs of commercially successful operating systems?

1.29 Why have UNIX and UNIX-based systems continued to be popular in recent decades? How does Linux impact the future of UNIX systems?

Recommended Reading

This section will be used throughout the book to provide the reader with references to seminal books and papers and current research on the topic of each chapter. Many of the papers that are cited in each chapter can be found in one of several journals associated with either the Association of Computing Machinery (ACM) or the Institute of Electrical and Electronics Engineers (IEEE). *Communications of the ACM* is the ACM's flagship journal, containing research papers, editorials and features about contemporary topics in computer science. The ACM also sponsors several special-interest groups (SIGs), each dedicated to particular fields of computer science. SIGOPS, the SIG for the field of operating systems (www.acm.org/sigops/), holds annual conferences and publishes the *Operating Systems Review*. The IEEE Computer Society (www.computer.org), the largest IEEE society, publishes several journals related to computer science, including the popular *IEEE Computer* (www.computer.org/computer/). The reader is encouraged to join the ACM, SIGOPS and the IEEE Computer Society. In the Web Resources section, we have listed several links to sites that recount the history of operating systems. An enlightening account of the design and development of the OS/360 operating system can be found in Frederick P. Brooks, Jr.'s *The Mythical Man-Month*.[120] Per Brinch Hansen's *Classic Operating Systems: From Batch to Distributed Systems* provides an anthology of papers describing the design and development of innovative and pioneering operating systems.[121] The bibliography for this chapter is located on our Web site at www.deitel.com/books/os3e/Bibliography.pdf.

Works Cited

1. "Evolution of the Intel Microprocessor: 1971–2007," <www.berghell.com/whitepapers/Evolution%20 of%20Intel%20Microprocessors%201971%202007.pdf>.

2. "Top 500 List for November 2002," <www.top500.org/list/ 2002/11/>.

3. Weizer, N., "A History of Operating Systems," *Datamation*, January 1981, pp. 119–126.

4. Goldstein, H., *The Computer from Pascal to von Neumann*, Princeton: Princeton University Press, 1972.

5. Stern, N., *From ENIAC to UNIVAC: An Appraisal of the Eckert-Mauchly Computers* Bedford: Digital Press, 1981.

6. Bashe, C., et al., *IBM's Early Computers* (Cambridge: MIT Press, 1986).

7. Weizer, N., "A History of Operating Systems," *Datamation*, January 1981, pp. 119–126.

8. Grosch, H., "The Way It Was in 1957," *Datamation*, September 1977.

9. Denning, P., "Virtual Memory," *ACM CSUR*, Vol. 2, No. 3, September 1970, pp. 153–189.

10. Codd, E.; E. Lowry; E. McDonough; and C. Scalzi, "Multiprogramming STRETCH: Feasibility Considerations," *Communications of the ACM*, Vol. 2, 1959, pp. 13–17.

11. Critchlow, A., "Generalized Multiprocessor and Multiprogramming Systems," *Proc. AFIPS, FJCC*, Vol. 24, 1963, pp. 107–125.

12. Belady, L., et al., "The IBM History of Memory Management Technology," *IBM Journal of Research and Development*, Vol. 25, No. 5, September 1981, pp. 491–503.

13. "The Evolution of S/390," <www-ti.informatik.uni-tuebingen.de/os390/arch/history.pdf>.

14. Amdahl, G.; G. Blaauw; and F. Brooks, "Architecture of the IBM System/360," *IBM Journal of Research and Development*, Vol. 8, No. 2, April 1964, pp. 87–101.

15. Weizer, N., "A History of Operating Systems," *Datamation*, January 1981, pp. 119–126.

16. Evans, B., "System/360: A Retrospective View," *Annals of the History of Computing*, Vol. 8, No. 2, April 1986, pp. 155–179.

17. Mealy, G.; B. Witt; and W. Clark, "The Functional Structure of OS/360," *IBM Systems Journal*, Vol. 5, No. 1, 1966, pp. 3–51.

18. Case, R., and A. Padeges, "Architecture of the IBM System/370," *Communications of the ACM*, Vol. 21, No. 1, January 1978, pp. 73–96.

19. Gifford, D., and A. Spector, "Case Study: IBM's System/360–370 Architecture," *Communications of the ACM*, Vol. 30, No. 4, April 1987, pp. 291–307.

20. "The Evolution of S/390," <www-ti.informatik.uni-tuebingen.de/os390/arch/history.pdf>.

21. Berlind, D., "Mainframe Linux Advocates Explain It All," *ZDNet*, April 12, 2002, <techupdate.zdnet.com/techupdate/ stories/main/0,14179,2860720,00.html>.

22. Frenkel, K., "Allan L. Scherr: Big Blue's Time-Sharing Pioneer," *Communications of the ACM*, Vol. 30, No. 10, October 1987, pp. 824–829.

23. Harrison, T., et al, "Evolution of Small Real-Time IBM Computer Systems," *IBM Journal of Research and Development*, Vol. 25, No. 5, September 1981, pp. 441–451.

24. Corbato, F., et al., *The Compatible Time-Sharing System, A Programmer's Guide*, Cambridge: MIT Press, 1964.

25. Crisman, P., et al., eds., *The Compatible Time-Sharing System*, Cambridge: MIT Press, 1964.

26. Lett, A., and W. Konigsford, "TSS/360: A Time-Shared Operating System," *Proceedings of the Fall Joint Computer Conference, AFIPS*, Vol. 33, Part 1, 1968, pp. 15-28.

27. Bensoussan, A.; C. Clingen; and R. Daley, "The Multics Virtual Memory: Concepts and Designs," *Communications of the ACM*, Vol. 15, No. 5, May 1972, pp. 308–318.

28. Creasy, R., "The Origins of the VM/370 Time-Sharing System," *IBM Journal of Research and Development*, Vol. 25, No. 5, pp. 483–490.

29. Conrow, K., "The CMS Cookbook," *Computing and Networking Services*, Kansas State University, June 29, 1994, <www.ksu.edu/ cns/pubs/cms/cms-cook/cms-cook.pdf>.

30. Denning, P., "Virtual Memory," *ACM Computing Surveys*, Vol. 2, No. 3, September 1970, pp. 153–189.

31. Parmelee, R., et al., "Virtual Storage and Virtual Machine Concepts," *IBM Systems Journal*, Vol. 11, No. 2, 1972.

32. Ritchie, D., "Dennis M. Ritchie," <cm.bell-labs.com/cm/cs/ who/dmr/bigbio1st.html>.

33. Bell Labs Lucent Technologies, "Ken Thompson," 2002, <www.bell-labs.com/history/unix/thompsonbio.html>.

34. Mackenzie, R., "A Brief History of UNIX," <www.stanford.edu/~rachelm/cs1u-197/unix.html>.

35. Cook, D.; J. Urban, and S. Hamilton, "UNIX and Beyond: An Interview with Ken Thompson," *Computer*, May 1999, pp. 58–64.

36. Cook, D.; J. Urban, and S. Hamilton, "UNIX and Beyond: An Interview with Ken Thompson," *Computer*, May 1999, pp. 58–64.

37. Bell Labs Lucent Technologies, "Ken Thompson," 2002, <www.bell-labs.com/history/unix/thompsonbio.html>.

38. Bell Labs Lucent Technologies, "Dennis Ritchie," 2002, <www.bell-labs.com/about/history/unix/ritchie-bio.html>.

39. Bell Labs Lucent Technologies, "Dennis Ritchie," 2002, <www.bell-labs.com/about/history/unix/ritchie-bio.html>.

40. Ritchie, D., "Dennis M. Ritchie," <cm.bell-labs.com/cm/cs/ who/dmr/bigbio1st.html>.

41. Reagan, P., and D. Cunningham, "Bell Labs Unveils Open Source Release of Plan 9 Operating System," June 7, 2000, <www.bell-labs.com/news/2000/june/7/2.html>.

42. Bell Labs, "Vita Nuova Publishes Source Code for Inferno Operating System, Moving Network Computing into the 21st Century," <www.cs.bell-labs.com/inferno/>.

43. Kildall, G., "CP/M: A Family of 8- and 16-bit Operating Systems," *Byte,* Vol. 6, No. 6, June 1981, pp. 216–232.

44. Quarterman, J. S., and J. C. Hoskins, "Notable Computer Networks," *Communications of the ACM,* Vol. 29, No. 10, October 1986, pp. 932–971.

45. Stefik, M., "Strategic Computing at DARPA: Overview and Assessment," *Communications of the ACM,* Vol. 28, No. 7, July 1985, pp. 690–707.

46. Comer, D., *Internetworking with TCP/IP: Principles, Protocols, and Architecture*, Englewood Cliffs, NJ: Prentice Hall, 1988.

47. Martin, J., and K. K. Chapman, *Local Area Networks: Architectures and Implementations*, Englewood Cliffs, NJ: Prentice Hall, 1989.

48. Metcalfe, R., and D. Boggs, "Ethernet: Distributed Packet Switching for Local Computer Networks," *Communications of the ACM,* Vol. 19, No. 7, July 1976.

49. Balkovich, E.; S. Lerman; and R. Parmelee, "Computing in Higher Education: The Athena Experience," *Computer,* Vol. 18, No. 11, November 1985, pp. 112–127.

50. Zmoelnig, Christine, "The Graphical User Interface. Time for a Paradigm Shift?" August 30, 2001, <www.sensomatic.com/chz/gui/history.html>.

51. Engelbart, D., "Who we are. How we think. What we do." June 24, 2003, <www.bootstrap.org/index.html>.

52. Martin, E., "The Context of STARS," *Computer,* Vol. 16, No. 11, November 1983, pp. 14–20.

53. Ecklund, J., "Interview with Douglas Engelbart," May 4, 1994, <americanhistory.si.edu/csr/comphist/englebar.htm>.

54. Stauth, D., "Prominent Oregon State Alum Receives Leading Prize for Inventors," April 9, 1997, <oregonstate.edu/dept/ncs/newsarch/1997/April97/engelbart.htm>.

55. "Douglas Engelbart Inventor Profile," 2002, <www.invent.org/hall_of_fame/53.html>.

56. "Engelbart's Unfinished Revolution," December 9, 1998, <stanford-online.stanford.edu/engelbart/>.

57. "Douglas Engelbart Inventor Profile," 2002, <www.invent.org/hall_of_fame/53.html>.

58. World Wide Web Consortium, "Longer Bio for Tim Berners-Lee," <www.w3.org/People/Berners-Lee/Longer.html>.

59. "Engelbart's Unfinished Revolution," December 9, 1998, <stanford-online.stanford.edu/engelbart/>.

60. "Douglas Engelbart Inventor Profile," 2002, <www.invent.org/hall_of_fame/53.html>.

61. World Wide Web Consortium, "Longer Bio for Tim Berners-Lee," <www.w3.org/People/Berners-Lee/Longer.html>.

62. Quittner, J., "Tim Berners-Lee," March 29, 1999, <www.time.com/time/time100/scientist/profile/bernerslee.html>.

63. Berners-Lee, T., et al, "The World-Wide Web," *Communications of the ACM*, Vol. 37, No. 8, August 1994, pp. 76-82.

64. World Wide Web Consortium, "Longer Bio for Tim Berners-Lee," <www.w3.org/People/Berners-Lee/Longer.html>.

65. Quittner, J., "Tim Berners-Lee," March 29, 1999, <www.time.com/time/time100/scientist/profile/bernerslee.html>.

66. Berners-Lee, T., et al, "The World-Wide Web," *Communications of the ACM*, Vol. 37, No. 8, August 1994, pp. 76-82.

67. World Wide Web Consortium, "Longer Bio for Tim Berners-Lee," <www.w3.org/People/Berners-Lee/Longer.html>.

68. Quittner, J., "Tim Berners-Lee," March 29, 1999, <www.time.com/time/time100/scientist/profile/bernerslee.html>.

69. Moore, G., "Cramming More Components onto Integrated Circuits," *Electronics*, Vol. 38, No. 8, April 19, 1965.

70. "One Trillion-Operations-Per-Second," *Intel Press Release*, December 17, 1996, <www.intel.com/pressroom/archive/releases/cn121796.htm>.

71. Mukherjee, B.; K. Schwan; and P. Gopinath, "A Survey of Multiprocessor Operating Systems," Georgia Institute of Technology, November 5, 1993, p. 2.

72. "Microsoft Timeline," <www.microsoft.com/museum/mustimeline.mspx>.

73. Lea, R.; P. Armaral; and C. Jacquemot, "COOL-2: An Object-oriented Support Platform Built Above the CHORUS Micro-kernel," *Proceedings of the International Workshop on Object Orientation in Operating Systems 1991*, October, 1991.

74. Weiss, A., "The Politics of Free (Software)," *netWorker*, September 2001, p. 26.

75. "The GNU Manifesto," <www.delorie.com/gnu/docs/GNU/GNU>.

76. Weiss, A., "The Politics of Free (Software)," *netWorker*, September 2001, p. 27.

77. de Brouwer, C., eds, "Linus Torvalds," October 19, 2002, <www.thocp.net/biographies/torvalds_linus.html>.

78. Learmonth, M., "Giving It All Away," May 8, 1997, <www.metroactive.com/papers/metro/05.08.97/cover/linus-9719.html>.

79. Torvalds, L., "Linux History," July 31, 1992, <www.li.org/linuxhistory.php>.

80. Free Software Foundation, "GNU General Public License," May 26, 2003, <www.gnu.org/copyleft/gpl.html>.

81. Torvalds, L., "Linux History," July 31, 1992, <www.li.org/linuxhistory.php>.

82. Ghosh, R., "What Motivates Free Software Developers?" 1998, <www.firstmonday.dk/issues/issue3_3/torvalds/>.

83. Wirzenius, L., "Linux: The Big Picture," April 28, 2003, <liw.iki.fi/liw/texts/linux-the-big-picture.html>.

84. Learmonth, M., "Giving It All Away," May 8, 1997, <www.metro-active.com/papers/metro/05.08.97/cover/linus-9719.html>.

85. Wirzenius, L., "Linux: The Big Picture," April 28, 2003, <liw.iki.fi/liw/texts/linux-the-big-picture.html>.

86. "Linux Creator Linus Torvalds Joins OSDL," June 17, 2003, <www.osdl.org/newsroom/press_releases/2003/2003_06_17_beaverton.html>.

87. de Brouwer, C., eds, "Linus Torvalds," October 19, 2002, <www.thocp.net/biographies/torvalds_linus.html>.

88. Weiss, A., "The Politics of Free (Software)," *netWorker*, September 2001, pp. 27–28.

89. Stallman, R., "A Serious Bio," <www.stallman.org/#serious>.

90. Stallman, R., "Overview of the GNU Project," June 7, 2003, <www.gnu.org/gnu/gnu-history.html>.

91. DiBona, C.; S. Ockman; and M. Stone, eds., *Open Sources: Voices from the Open Source Revolution*, Boston, MA: O'Reilly, 1999.

92. R. Stallman, "Overview of the GNU Project," June 7, 2003, <www.gnu.org/gnu/gnu-history.html>.

93. DiBona, C.; S. Ockman; and M. Stone, eds., *Open Sources: Voices from the Open Source Revolution*, Boston, MA: O'Reilly, 1999.

94. Stallman, R., "A Serious Bio," <www.stallman.org/#serious>.

95. "Free Software Foundation," June 12, 2002, <www.gnu.org/fsf/fsf.html>.

96. DiBona, C.; S. Ockman; and M. Stone, eds., *Open Sources: Voices from the Open Source Revolution*, Boston, MA: O'Reilly, 1999.

97. Leon, M., "Richard Stallman, GNU/Linux," October 6, 2000, <archive.infoworld.com/articles/hn/xml/00/10/09/001009hnrs.xml>.

98. Stallman, R., "A Serious Bio," <www.stallman.org/#serious>.

99. Ricciuti, M., "New Windows Could Solve Age Old Format Puzzle—at a Price," *CNet*, March 13, 2002, <news.com.com/2009-1017-857509.html>.

100. Thurrott, P., "Windows 'Longhorn' FAQ," *Paul Thurrott's SuperSite for Windows*, modified October 6, 2003, <www.winsupersite.com/faq/longhorn.asp>.

101. Cannon, M. D., et al., "A Virtual Machine Emulator for Performance Evaluation," *Communications of the ACM*, Vol. 23, No. 2, February 1980, p. 72.

102. Cannon, M. D., et. al., "A Virtual Machine Emulator for Performance Evaluation," *Communications of the ACM*, Vol. 23, No. 2, February 1980, p. 72.

103. "VMware: Simplifying Computer Infrastructure and Expanding Possibilities", <www.vmware.com/company/>.

104. Cannon, M. D., et. al., "A Virtual Machine Emulator for Performance Evaluation," *Communications of the ACM*, Vol. 23, No. 2, February 1980, p. 73.

105. "Shell," *whatis.com*, <www.searchsolaris.techtarget.com/sDefinition/0,,sid12_gci212978,00.html>.

106. Mukherjee, B.; K. Schwan; and P. Gopinath, "A Survey of Multiprocessor Operating Systems," *Georgia Institute of Technology (GIT-CC-92/0)*, November 5, 1993, p. 4.

107. Dijkstra, E. W., "The Structure of the 'THE'-Multiprogramming System," *Communications of the ACM*, Vol. 11, No. 5, May 1968, pp. 341–346.

108. Karnik, N. M., and A. R. Tripathi, "Trends in Multiprocessor and Distributed Operating Systems," *Journal of Supercomputing*, Vol. 9, No. 1/2, 1995, pp. 4–5.

109. Mukherjee, B.; K. Schwan; and P. Gopinath, "A Survey of Multiprocessor Operating System Kernels," *Georgia Institute of Technology (GIT-CC-92/0)*, November 5, 1993, p. 10.

110. Miljocic, D. S.; F. Douglis; Y. Paindaveine; R. Wheeler; and S. Zhou, "Process Migration," *ACM Computing Surveys*, Vol. 32, No. 3, September, 2000, p. 263.

111. Liedtke, J., "Toward Real Microkernels," *Communications of the ACM*, Vol. 39, No. 9, September 1996, p. 75. Camp, T., and G. Oberhsause, "Microkernels: A Submodule for a Traditional Operating Systems Course," *Communications of the ACM*, 1995, p. 155.

112. Liedtke, J., "Toward Real Microkernels," *Communications of the ACM*, Vol. 39, No. 9, September 1996, p. 75. Camp, T., and G. Oberhsause, "Microkernels: A Submodule for a Traditional Operating Systems Course," *Communications of the ACM*, 1995, p. 155.

113. Miljocic, D. S.; F. Douglis; Y. Paindaveine; R. Wheeler; and S. Zhou, "Process Migration," *ACM Computing Surveys*, Vol. 32, No. 3, September 2000, p. 263.

114. Tanenbaum, A. S., and R. V. Renesse, "Distributed Operating Systems," *Computing Surveys*, Vol. 17, No. 4, December 1985, p. 424.

115. Tanenbaum, A. S., and R. V. Renesse, "Distributed Operating Systems," *Computing Surveys*, Vol. 17, No. 4, December 1985, p. 424.

116. Blair, G. S.; J. Malik; J. R. Nicol; and J. Walpole, "Design Issues for the COSMOS Distributed Operating System," *Proceedings from the 1988 ACM SIGOPS European Workshop*, 1988, pp. 1–2.

117. "MIT LCS Parallel and Distributed Operating Systems," June 2, 2003, <www.pdos.lcs.mit.edu>.

118. "Amoeba WWW Home Page," April 1998, <www.cs.vu.nl/pub/amoeba/>.

119. Engler, D. R.; M. F. Kaashoek; and J. O'Toole, Jr., "Exokernel: An Operating System Architecture for Application-Level Resource Management," *SIGOPS '95*, December 1995, p. 252.

120. Brooks, Jr., F. P., *The Mythical Man-Month: Essays on Software Engineering*, Anniversary edition, Reading, MA: Addison-Wesley, 1995.

121. Brinch Hansen, P., *Classic Operating Systems: From Batch to Distributed Systems*, Springer-Verlag, 2001.

"Now! Now!" cried the Queen. "Faster! Faster!"
—Lewis Carroll—

To conquer without risk is to triumph without glory.
—Pierre Corneille—

Our life is frittered away by detail ...Simplify, simplify.
—Henry Thoreau—

O holy simplicity!
—John Huss—
(Last words, at the stake)

Chapter 2

Hardware and Software Concepts

Objectives

After reading this chapter, you should understand:

- *hardware components that must be managed by an operating system.*
- *how hardware has evolved to support operating system functions.*
- *how to optimize performance of various hardware devices.*
- *the notion of an application programming interface (API).*
- *the process of compilation, linking and loading.*

Chapter Outline

2.1 Introduction

Today's computers allow users to access the Internet, browse Web pages, display graphics and video, play music and games—and more. Personal and office computers increase productivity by managing large amounts of data, providing application-development tools and presenting an intuitive interface for authoring content. Networks of computers coordinate to perform vast numbers of calculations and transactions per second. In the mobile computing market, cell phones store phone numbers, send and receive text messages and even capture photos and video. All of these computers contain various types of hardware and software, and they are all managed by operating systems.

Because the operating system is primarily a resource manager, its design must be intimately tied to the hardware and software resources that it manages. These resources include processors, memory, secondary storage (such as hard disks), other I/O devices, processes, threads, files, databases and so on. As computers evolve, operating systems must adapt to emerging hardware and software technologies and maintain compatibility with an installed base of older hardware and software. In this chapter, we introduce hardware and software concepts.

Self Review

1. List some common hardware and software resources managed by operating systems.
2. List the types of data referenced in the preceding introduction.

Ans: **1)** Processors, memory, secondary storage and other devices, processes, threads, files and databases. **2)** Web pages, graphics, video, music, game data, office data, content, transaction data, cell phone numbers, text messages, photos, data in memory, data in secondary storage, data input or output by I/O devices and data processed by processors.

2.2 Evolution of Hardware Devices

Every time technological development has allowed for increased computing speeds, the new capabilities have immediately been absorbed by demands placed on computing resources by more ambitious applications. Computing appears to be an inexhaustible resource. Ever more interesting problems await the availability of increasingly powerful computing systems, as predicted by Moore's law (see the Biographical Note, Gordon Moore and Moore's Law). We have a "chicken or the egg" situation. Is it increasing applications demands that force computing technology to evolve, or is it improvements in technology that tempt us to think about new and innovative applications?

Initially, **systems programming**, which entailed writing code to perform hardware management and provide services to programs, was relatively straightforward because the operating system managed a small number of programs and hardware resources. Operating systems facilitate **applications programming**, because developers can write software that requests services and resources from the operating system to perform tasks (e.g., text editing, loading Web pages or payroll processing) without needing to write code to perform device management. As the number of hardware manufacturers and devices proliferated, operating systems became more complex. To facilitate systems programming and improve extensibility, most operating systems are written to be independent of a system's particular hardware configuration. Operating systems use device drivers, often provided by hardware manufacturers, to perform device-specific I/O operations. This enables the operating system to support a new device simply by using the appropriate device driver. In fact, device drivers are such an integral part of today's systems that they comprise approximately 60 percent of the source code for the Linux kernel.[1]

Many hardware components have been designed to interact with the operating system in a way that facilitates operating system extensibility. For example, **plug-and-play** devices identify themselves to the operating system when they are

Biographical Note

Gordon Moore and Moore's Law

Dr. Gordon E. Moore earned his B.S. in Chemistry from the University of California at Berkeley and Ph.D. in Chemistry and Physics from the California Institute of Technology.[2] He co-founded the Intel Corporation, the largest processor manufacturer in the computing industry. Moore is currently a Chairman Emeritus of Intel Corporation.[3] He is also known for his prediction regarding the progress of computing power that has been named **Moore's law**. Contrary to its name, Moore's law is not a provable fact. In Moore's 1965 paper, "Cramming More Components onto Integrated Circuits," he observed that the number of transistors in processors had doubled roughly every year.[4] **Transistors** are miniature switches that con-

trol electric current (just as a light switch is turned on or off). The faster the switch can be flipped, the faster the processor can execute; the more transistors, the more tasks a processor can do at once. Moore predicted that the increase in transistor count would continue for about a decade. By 1975, Moore adjusted his "law" to predict that transistor counts would double every 24 months.

Currently, processor performance is doubling roughly every 18 months and transistor count is doubling every 24 months (Fig. 2.1). A key factor that enables this is that the cost per transistor in processors is decreasing exponentially. There are other trends related to Moore's law. For one, the size of transistors is becoming exponentially smaller.

The reduction in transistor size has outpaced the growth of the number of transistors on the die (i.e., the chip containing the processor), providing increased computational power from smaller processors. Smaller transistors also operate faster than large ones.

Recent advances in nanotechnology (technology at the scale of molecules) have enabled semiconductor manufacturers to create transistors consisting of a handful of atoms. Soon, however, researchers will be limited by the size of an atom when designing a transistor. To continue to extend Moore's law, companies such as Intel are investigating new techniques to modify transistor construction and create high-performance alternatives to transistor technology.[5]

connected to the computer (see Section 2.4.4, Plug and Play). This enables the operating system to select and use an appropriate device driver with little or no user interaction, simplifying the installation of a new device. From the user perspective, devices that are added to the system are ready to use almost immediately.

The hardware discussions in the next several sections focus on general-purpose computers (e.g., personal computers and servers)—special-purpose computers, such as those in cell phones or cars, are beyond the scope of this book. We discuss the common hardware components found in typical computer systems, then focus on hardware components specifically designed to support operating system functionality.

Self Review

1. Why are operating systems more difficult to design today than 50 years ago?
2. How do drivers and interfaces such as plug-and-play facilitate operating system extensibility?

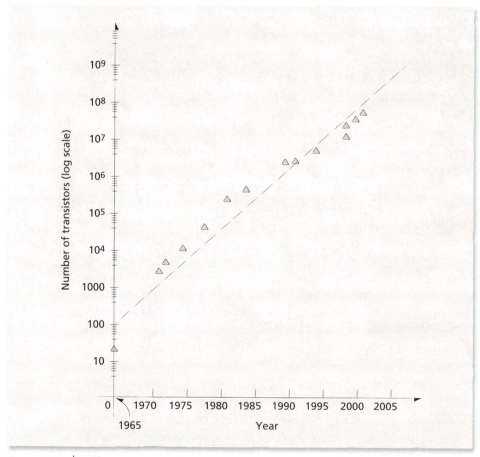

Figure 2.1 | *Transistor count plotted against time for Intel processors.*[6]

Ans. **1)** The operating systems of 50 years ago managed a small number of programs and hardware devices. Today's operating systems typically manage a large number of programs and a set of hardware devices that vary from one computer to another. **2)** Drivers free the operating system designer from the details of interacting with hardware devices. Operating systems can support new hardware simply by using the appropriate device driver. Plug-and-play devices enable the operating system to easily identify a computer's hardware resources, which facilitates installation of devices and their corresponding drivers. From the user perspective, a device is ready to use almost immediately after it is installed.

2.3 Hardware Components

A computer's hardware consists of its physical devices—processor(s), main memory and input/output devices. The following subsections describe hardware components that an operating system manages to meet its users' computing needs.

2.3.1 Mainboards

Computers rely on interactions between many hardware devices to satisfy the requirements of the system. To enable communication among independent devices, computers are equipped with one or more **printed circuit boards (PCBs)**. A PCB is a hardware component that provides electrical connections between devices at various locations on the board.

The **mainboard** (also called the **motherboard**), the central PCB in a system, can be thought of as the backbone of a computer. The mainboard provides slots into which other components—such as the processor, main memory and other hardware devices—are inserted. These slots provide access to the electrical connections between the various hardware components and enable users to customize their computers' hardware configuration by adding devices to, and removing them from, the slots. The mainboard is one of four hardware components required to execute instructions in a general-purpose computer. The other three are the processor (Section 2.3.2, Processors), main memory (Section 2.3.5, Main Memory) and secondary storage (Section 2.3.6, Secondary Storage).

Traditional metal wires are too wide for establishing the large number of electrical connections between components in today's systems. Thus, mainboards typically consist of several extremely thin layers of silicon containing microscopic electrical connections called **traces** that serve as communication channels and provide connectivity on the board. A large set of traces forms a high-speed communication channel known as a **bus**.

Most mainboards include several computer chips to perform low-level operations. For example, mainboards typically contain a **basic input/output system (BIOS)** chip that stores instructions for basic hardware initialization and management. The BIOS is also responsible for loading the initial portion of the operating system into memory, a process called **bootstrapping** (see Section 2.4.3, Bootstrapping). After the operating system has been loaded, it can use the BIOS to communicate with a system's hardware to perform low-level (i.e., basic) I/O operations. Mainboards also contain chips called **controllers** that manage data transfer on the board's buses. A mainboard's **chipset** is the collection of controllers, coprocessors, buses and other hardware integrated onto the mainboard that determine the system's hardware capabilities (e.g., which types of processors and memory are supported).

A recent trend in mainboard design is to integrate powerful hardware components onto the PCB. Traditionally, many of these were inserted into slots as **add-on cards**. Many of today's mainboards include chips that perform graphics processing, networking and RAID (Redundant Array of Independent Disks) operations. These **on-board devices** reduce the overall system cost and have contributed significantly to the continuing sharp decline in computer prices. A disadvantage is that they are permanently attached to the mainboard and cannot be replaced easily.

Self Review

1. What is the primary function of the mainboard?
2. Why is the BIOS crucial to computer systems?

Ans: **1)** The mainboard serves as the backbone for communication between hardware components, allowing them to communicate via the electrical connections on the board. **2)** The BIOS performs basic hardware initialization and management and loads the initial component of the operating system into memory. The BIOS also provides instructions that enable the operating system to communicate with system hardware.

2.3.2 Processors

A **processor** is a hardware component that executes a stream of machine-language instructions. Processors can take many forms in computers, such as a **central processing unit (CPU)**, a graphics **coprocessor** or a digital signal processor (DSP). A CPU is a processor that executes the instructions of a program; a coprocessor, such as a graphics or digital signal processor, is designed to efficiently execute a limited set of special-purpose instructions (such as 3D transformations). In embedded systems, processors might perform specific tasks, such as converting a digital signal to an analog audio signal in a cell phone—an example of a DSP. As a primary processor in the system, a CPU executes the bulk of the instructions, but might increase efficiency by sending computationally intensive tasks to a coprocessor specifically designed to handle them. Throughout the rest of this book, we use the term "processor" or "general-purpose processor" when referring to a CPU.

The instructions a processor can execute are defined by its instruction set. The size of each instruction, or the **instruction length**, might differ among architectures and within each architecture—some processors support multiple instruction sizes. The processor architecture also determines the amount of data that can be operated on at once. For instance, a 32-bit processor manipulates data in discrete units of 32 bits.

Modern processors perform many resource management operations in hardware to boost performance. Such features include support for virtual memory and hardware interrupts—two important concepts discussed later in this book.

Despite the variety of processor architectures, several components are present in almost all contemporary processors. Such components include the instruction fetch unit, branch predictor, execution unit, registers, caches and a bus interface (Fig. 2.2). The **instruction fetch unit** loads instructions into high-speed memory called instruction registers so that the processor can execute the instruction quickly. The **instruction decode unit** interprets the instruction and passes the corresponding input for the execution unit to perform the instruction. The main portion of the execution unit is the **arithmetic and logic unit (ALU)**, which performs basic arithmetic and logical operations, such as addition, multiplication and logical comparisons (note that the "V" shape of the ALU is common in architecture diagrams).

The bus interface allows the processor to interact with memory and other devices in the system. Because processors typically operate at much higher speeds than main memory, they contain high-speed memory called cache that stores copies of data in main memory. Caches increase processor efficiency by enabling fast access to data and instructions. Because high-speed caches are significantly more expensive than main memory, they tend to be relatively small. The caches are classified in levels—Level 1 (L1) is the fastest and most expensive cache and is located on the processor; the Level 2 (L2) cache, which is larger and slower than the L1 cache,

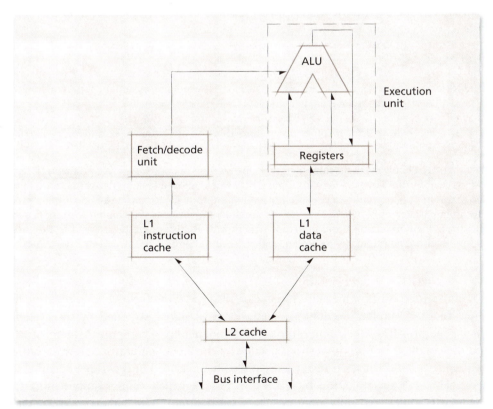

Figure 2.2 | Processor components.

is often located on the mainboard, but is increasingly being integrated onto the processor to improve performance.[7]

Registers are high-speed memories located on a processor that hold data for immediate use by the processor. Before a processor can operate on data, the data must be placed in registers. Storing processor instructions in any other slower type of memory would be inefficient, because the processor would idle while waiting for data access. Registers are hard-wired to the processor circuitry and physically located near the execution units, making access to registers faster than access to the L1 cache. The size of the registers is determined by the number of bits the processor can operate on at once. For example, a 32-bit processor can store 32 bits of data in each register. The majority of processors in personal computers today are 32-bit processors; 64-bit processors are becoming increasingly popular.[8]

Each processor architecture provides a different number of registers, and each register serves a particular purpose. For example, the Intel Pentium 4 processor provides 16 program execution registers. Typically, half of these registers are reserved for use by applications for quick access to data values and pointers during execution. Such registers are called **general-purpose registers**. IBM's PowerPC 970 processor (used in Apple's G5 computers) contains 32 general-purpose registers. The other registers (often called control registers) store system-specific information, such as the program counter, which the processor uses to determine the next instruction to execute.[9]

Self Review

1. Differentiate between a CPU and a coprocessor. How might a system benefit from multiple CPUs? How might a system benefit from multiple coprocessors?
2. What aspects of a system does a processor architecture specify?
3. Why is access to register memory faster than access to any other type of memory, including L1 cache?

Ans: **1)** A CPU executes machine-language instructions; a coprocessor is optimized to perform special-purpose instructions. Multiple CPUs would allow a system to execute more than one program at once; multiple coprocessors could improve performance by performing processing in parallel with a CPU. **2)** A CPU's architecture specifies the computer's instruction set, virtual memory support and interrupt structure. **3)** Registers are hard-wired to the processor circuitry and physically located near the execution units.

2.3.3 Clocks

Computer time is often measured in **cycles**, also called a **clocktick**. The term cycle refers to one complete oscillation of an electrical signal provided by the system clock generator. The clock generator sets the cadence for a computer system, much like the conductor of an orchestra. Specifically, the clock generator determines the frequency at which buses transfer data, typically measured in cycles per second, or hertz (Hz). For example, the **frontside bus (FSB)**, which connects processors to memory modules, typically operates at several hundred megahertz (MHz; one megahertz is one million hertz).

Most modern desktop processors execute at top speeds of hundreds of megahertz (MHz) or even several billion hertz, or gigahertz (GHz), which is often faster than the frontside bus. Processors and other devices generate **derived speeds** by multiplying or dividing the speed of the frontside bus.[10] For example, a 2GHz processor with a 200MHz frontside bus uses a multiplier of 10 to generate its cycles; a 66MHz sound card uses a divider of 2.5 to generate its cycles.

Self Review

1. (T/F) All components of a system operate at the same clock speed.
2. What problems might arise if one component on a bus has an extremely high multiplier and another component on the same bus has an extremely high divider?

Ans: **1)** False. Devices usually use a multiplier or a divider that defines the device's speed relative to the speed of the frontside bus. **2)** Bottlenecks could occur, because a component with a high divider will operate at a much slower speed than a device with a high multiplier. A high-multiplier device that relies on information from a high-divider device will be made to wait.

2.3.4 Memory Hierarchy

The size and the speed of memory are limited by the laws of physics and economics. Almost all electronic devices transfer data using electrons passing through traces on PCBs. There is a limit to the speed at which electrons can travel; the longer the wire between two terminals, the longer the transfer will take. Further, it is prohibitively expensive to equip processors with large amounts of memory that can respond to requests for data at (or near) processor speeds.

The cost/performance trade-off characterizes the **memory hierarchy** (Fig. 2.3). The fastest and most expensive memory is at the top and typically has a small capacity. The slowest and least expensive memory is at the bottom and typically has a large capacity. Note that the size of each block represents how capacity increases for slower memories, but the figure is not drawn to scale.

Registers are the fastest and most expensive memory on a system—they operate at the same speed as processors. Cache memory speeds are measured according to their latency—the time required to transfer data. Latencies are typically measured in nanoseconds or processor cycles. For example, the L1 cache for an Intel Pentium 4 processor operates at a latency of two processor cycles.[11] Its L2 cache operates with a latency of approximately 10 cycles. In many of today's processors, the L1 and L2 cache are integrated onto the processor so that they can exploit the processor's high-speed interconnections. L1 caches typically store tens of kilobytes of data while L2 caches typically store hundreds of kilobytes or several megabytes. High-end processors might contain a third level of processor cache (called the L3 cache) that is slower than the L2 cache but is faster than main memory.

Next in the hierarchy is **main memory**—also called **real memory** or **physical memory**. Main memory introduces additional latency because data must pass through the frontside bus, which typically operates at a fraction of processor speeds. Main memory in today's architectures exhibits latencies of tens or hundreds of pro-

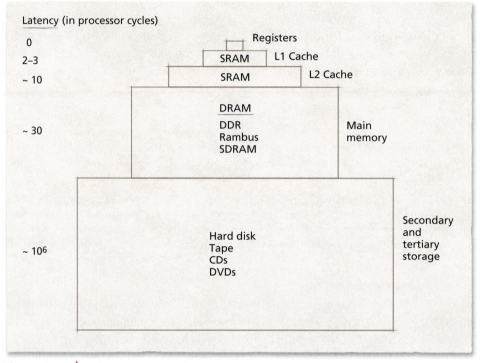

Figure 2.3 | *Memory hierarchy.*

cessor cycles.[12] Current general-purpose main memory sizes range from hundreds of megabytes (PCs) to tens or hundreds of gigabytes (high-end servers). Main memory is discussed in Section 2.3.5, Main Memory, and in Chapter 9, Real Memory Organization and Management. Registers, caches and main memory are typically **volatile** media, so their data vanishes when they lose power.

The hard disk and other storage devices such as CDs, DVDs and tapes are among the least expensive and slowest data storage units in a computer system. Disk storage device latencies are typically measured in milliseconds, typically a million times slower than processor cache latencies. Rather than allow a processor to idle while a process waits for data from secondary storage, the operating system typically executes another process to improve processor utilization. A primary advantage to secondary storage devices such as hard disks is that they have large capacities, often hundreds of gigabytes. Another advantage to secondary storage is that data is stored on a persistent medium, so data is preserved when power is removed from the device. Systems designers must balance the cost and the performance of various storage devices to meet the needs of users (see the Operating Systems Thinking feature, Caching).

Self Review

1. What is the difference between persistent and volatile storage media?
2. Why does the memory hierarchy assume a pyramidal shape?

Ans: **1)** Volatile media lose their data when the computer is turned off, whereas persistent media retain the data. In general, volatile storage is faster and more expensive than persistent storage. **2)** If a storage medium is less expensive, users can afford to buy more of it; thus, storage space increases.

2.3.5 Main Memory

Main memory consists of volatile **random access memory (RAM)**, "random" in the sense that processes can access data locations in any order. In contrast, data locations on a sequential storage medium (e.g., tape) must be read sequentially. Unlike tapes and hard disks, memory latencies for each main memory address are essentially equal.

The most common form of RAM is **dynamic RAM (DRAM)**, which requires that a refresh circuit periodically (a few times every millisecond) read the contents or the data will be lost. This differs from **static RAM (SRAM)**, which does not need to be refreshed to maintain the data it stores. SRAM, which is commonly employed in processor caches, is typically faster and more expensive than DRAM.

An important goal for DRAM manufacturers is to narrow the gap between processor speed and memory-transfer speed. Memory modules are designed to minimize data access latency within the module and maximize the number of times data is transferred per second. These techniques reduce overall latency and increase

Operating Systems Thinking

Caching

We all use caching in our everyday lives. Generally speaking, a cache is a place for storing provisions that can be accessed quickly. Squirrels stashing acorns as they prepare for the winter is a form of caching. We keep pencils, pens, staples, tape and paper clips in our desk drawers so that we can access them quickly when we need them (rather than having to walk down the hall to the supply closet). Operating systems employ many caching techniques, such as caching a process's data and

instructions for rapid access in high-speed cache memories and caching data from disk in main memory for rapid access as a program runs.

Operating systems designers must be cautious when using caching because in computer systems, cached data is a copy of the data whose original is being maintained at a higher level in the memory hierarchy. The cached copy is usually the one to which changes are made first, so it can quickly become out of sync with

the original data, causing inconsistency. If a system were to fail when the cache contains updated data and the original does not, then the modified data could be lost. So operating systems frequently copy the cached data to the original—this process is called flushing the cache. Distributed file systems often place cache on both the server and the client, which makes it even more complex to keep the cache consistent.

bandwidth—the amount of data that can be transferred per unit of time. As manufacturers develop new memory technologies, the memory speed and capacity tend to increase and the cost per unit of storage tends to decrease, in accordance with Moore's law.

Self Review

1. Compare main memory to disk in terms of access time, capacity and volatility.
2. Why is main memory called random access memory?

Ans: **1)** Access times for main memory are much smaller than those for disk. Disks typically have a larger capacity than main memory, because the cost per unit storage for disks is less than for main memory. Main memory is typically volatile, whereas disks store data persistently. **2)** Processes can access main memory locations in any order and at about the same speed, regardless of location.

2.3.6 Secondary Storage

Due to its limited capacity and volatility, main memory is unsuitable for storing data in large amounts or data that must persist after a power loss. To permanently store large quantities of data, such as data files and applications software, computers use **secondary storage** (also called **persistent** or **auxiliary storage**) that maintains its data after the computer's power is turned off. Most computers use hard disks for secondary storage.

Although hard disk drives store more and cost less than RAM, they are not practical as a primary memory store because access to hard disk drives is much slower than access to main memory. Accessing data stored on a hard disk requires mechanical movement of the read/write head, rotational latency as the data spins to the head, and transfer time as the data passes by the head. This mechanical movement is much slower than the speed of electrical signals between main memory and a processor. Also, data must be loaded from the disk into main memory before it can be accessed by a processor.[13] A hard disk is an example of a **block device**, because it transmits data in fixed-size blocks of bytes (normally hundreds of bytes to tends of kilobytes).

Some secondary storage devices record data on lower-capacity media that can be removed from the computer, facilitating data backup and data transfer between computers. However, this type of secondary storage typically exhibits higher latency than other devices such as hard disks. A popular storage device is the **compact disk (CD)**, which can store up to 700MB per side. Data on CDs is encoded in digital form and "burned" onto the CD as a series of pits on an otherwise flat surface that represent ones and zeroes. **Write-once, read-many (WORM)** disks, such as write-once compact disks (CD-R) and write-once digital versatile disks (DVD-R) are removable. Other types of persistent storage include Zip disks, floppy disks, Flash memory cards and tapes.

Data recorded on a CD-RW (rewritable CD) is stored in metallic material inside the plastic disk. Laser light changes the reflective property of the recording medium, creating two states representing one and zero. CD-Rs and CD-ROMs consist of a dye between plastic layers that cannot be altered, once it has been burned by the laser.

Recently, digital versatile disk (DVD; also called digital video disk) technology, which was originally intended to record movies, has become an affordable data storage medium. DVDs are the same size as CDs, but store data in thinner tracks on up to two layers per side and can store up to 5.6 GB of data per layer.

Some systems contain levels of memory beyond secondary storage. For example, large data-processing systems often have tape libraries that are accessed by a robotic arm. Such storage systems, often classified as tertiary storage, are characterized by larger capacity and slower access times than secondary storage.

Self Review

1. Why is accessing data stored on disk slower than accessing data in main memory?
2. Compare and contrast CDs and DVDs.

Ans: **1)** Main memory can be accessed by electrical signals alone, but disks require mechanical movements to move the read/write head, rotational latency as the disk spins to move the requested data to the head and transfer time as the data passes by the head. **2)** CDs and DVDs are the same size and are accessed by laser light, but DVDs store data in multiple layers using thinner tracks and thus have a higher capacity.

2.3.7 Buses

A bus is a collection of traces (or other electrical connections) that transport information between hardware devices. Devices send electrical signals over the bus to communicate with other devices. Most buses consist of a **data bus**, which transports data, and an **address bus**, which determines the recipient or sources of that data.[14] A **port** is a bus that connects exactly two devices. A bus that several devices share to perform I/O operations is also called an **I/O channel**.[15]

Access to main memory is a point of contention for channels and processors. Typically, only one access to a particular memory module may occur at any given time; however, the I/O channels and the processor may attempt to access main memory simultaneously. To prevent the two signals from colliding on the bus, the memory accesses are prioritized by a hardware device called a controller, and channels are typically given priority over processors. This is called **cycle stealing**, because the I/O channel effectively steals cycles from the processor. I/O channels consume a small fraction of total processor cycles, which is typically offset by the enhanced I/O device utilization.

Recall that the frontside bus (FSB) connects a processor to main memory. As the FSB speed increases, the amount of data transferred between main memory and a processor increases, which tends to increase performance. Bus speeds are measured in MHz (e.g., 133MHz and 200MHz). Some chipsets implement an FSB of 200MHz but effectively operate at 400MHz, because they perform two memory transfers per clock cycle. This feature, which must be supported by both the chipset and the RAM, is called **double data rate (DDR)**. Another implementation, called **quad pumping**, allows up to four data transfers per cycle, effectively quadrupling the system's memory bandwidth.

The **Peripheral Component Interconnect (PCI) bus** connects peripheral devices, such as sound cards and network cards, to the rest of the system. The first version of the PCI specification required that the PCI bus operate at 33MHz and be 32 bits wide, which considerably limited the speed with which data was transferred to and from peripheral devices. PCI Express is a recent standard that provides for variable-width buses. With PCI Express, each device is connected to the system by up to 32 lanes, each of which can transfer 250MB per second in each direction—a total of up to 16GB per second of bandwidth per link.[16]

The **Accelerated Graphics Port (AGP)** is primarily used with graphics cards, which typically require tens or hundreds of megabytes of RAM to perform 3D graphics manipulations in real time. The original AGP specification called for a 32-bit 66MHz bus, which provided approximately 260MB per second of bandwidth. Manufacturers have increased the speed of this bus from its original specification—denoting an increase in speed by a factor of 2 as 2x, by a factor of 4 as 4x, and so on. Current specifications allow for 2x, 4x and 8x versions of this protocol, permitting up to 2GB per second of bandwidth.

Self Review

1. How does FSB speed affect system performance?
2. How do controllers simplify access to shared buses?

Ans: **1)** The FSB determines how much data can be transferred between processors and main memory per cycle. If a processor generates requests for more data than can be transferred per cycle, system performance will decrease, because that processor may need to wait until its requested transfers complete. **2)** Controllers prioritize multiple simultaneous requests to access a bus so that devices do not interfere with one another.

2.3.8 Direct Memory Access (DMA)

Most I/O operations transfer data between main memory and an I/O device. In early computers, this was accomplished using **programmed I/O (PIO)**, which specifies a byte or word to be transferred between main memory and an I/O device, then waits idly for the operation to complete. This led to wasting a significant number of processor cycles while waiting for PIO operations to complete. Designers later implemented interrupt-driven I/O, which enabled a processor to issue an I/O request and immediately continue to execute software instructions. The I/O device notified the processor when the operation was complete by generating an interrupt.[17]

Direct memory access (DMA) improves upon these techniques by enabling devices and controllers to transfer blocks of data to and from main memory directly, which frees the processor to execute software instructions (Fig. 2.4). A direct memory access (DMA) channel uses an I/O controller to manage data transfer between I/O devices and main memory. To notify the processor, the I/O control-

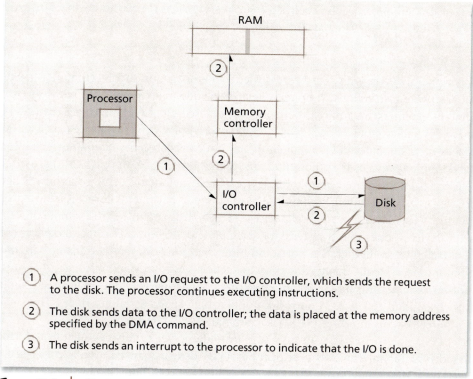

1. A processor sends an I/O request to the I/O controller, which sends the request to the disk. The processor continues executing instructions.

2. The disk sends data to the I/O controller; the data is placed at the memory address specified by the DMA command.

3. The disk sends an interrupt to the processor to indicate that the I/O is done.

Figure 2.4 | *Direct memory access (DMA).*

ler generates an interrupt when the operation is complete. DMA improves performance significantly in systems that perform large numbers of I/O operations (e.g., mainframes and servers).[18]

DMA is compatible with several bus architectures. On legacy architectures (i.e., architectures that are still in use but are no longer actively produced), such as the Industry Standard Architecture (ISA), extended ISA (EISA) or Micro Channel Architecture (MCA) buses, a DMA controller (also called a "third-party device") manages transfers between main memory and I/O devices (see the Operating Systems Thinking feature, Legacy Hardware and Software). PCI buses employ "first-party" DMA using **bus mastering**—a PCI device takes control of the bus to perform the operation. In general, first-party DMA transfer is more efficient than third-party transfer and has been implemented by most modern bus architectures.[19]

Self Review

1. Why is DMA more efficient than PIO?
2. How does first-party DMA differ from third-party DMA?

Ans: 1) In a system that uses PIO, a processor waits idly for each memory transfer to complete. DMA frees processors from performing the work necessary to transfer information between main memory and I/O devices, which enables the processor to execute instructions instead. **2)** Third-party DMA requires a controller to manage access to the bus. First-party DMA enables devices to take control of the bus without additional hardware.

2.3.9 Peripheral Devices

A peripheral device is any hardware device that is not required for a computer to execute software instructions. Peripheral devices include many types of I/O devices (e.g., printers, scanners and mice), network devices (e.g., network interface cards and modems) and storage devices (e.g., CD, DVD and disk drives). Devices such as the processor, mainboard and main memory are not considered peripheral devices. Internal peripheral devices (i.e., those that are located inside the computer case) are often referred to as integrated peripheral devices; these include modems, sound cards and internal CD-ROM drives. Perhaps the most common peripheral device is a hard disk. Figure 2.5 lists several peripheral devices.[20] Keyboards and mice are example of **character devices**—ones that transfer data one character at a time. Peripheral devices can be attached to computers via ports and other buses.[21] **Serial ports** transfer data one bit at a time, typically connecting devices such as keyboards and mice; **parallel ports** transfer data several bits at a time, typically connecting printers.[22] **Universal Serial Bus (USB)** and **IEEE 1394 ports** are popular high-speed serial interfaces. The **small computer systems interface (SCSI)** is a popular parallel interface.

USB ports transfer data from and provide power to devices such as external disk drives, digital cameras and printers. USB devices can be attached to, recognized by and removed from the computer while the computer is on without damaging the system's hardware (a technique called "hot swapping"). USB 1.1 allows data transfer at speeds of 1.5Mbit (megabits, or 1 million bits; 8 bits = 1 byte) per second and 12Mbit per second. Because computers required fast access to large quantities of data on USB devices such as disk drives, USB 2.0 was developed to provide data transfers at speeds up to 480Mbit per second.[23]

Operating Systems Thinking

Legacy Hardware and Software

The latest versions of operating systems are designed to support the latest available hardware and software functionality. However, the vast majority of hardware and software that is "out there" is often older equipment and applications that individuals and organizations have invested in and want to keep using, even when a new operating system is installed. The older items are called legacy hardware and legacy software. An enormous challenge for OS designers is to provide support for such legacy systems, one that real-world operating systems must meet.

Device	Description
CD-RW drive	Reads data from, and writes data to, optical disks.
Zip drive	Transfers data to and from a removable, durable magnetic disk.
Floppy drive	Reads data from, and writes data to, removable magnetic disks.
Mouse	Transmits the change in location of a pointer or cursor in a graphical user interface (GUI).
Keyboard	Transmits characters or commands that a user types.
Multifunction printer	Can print, copy, fax and scan documents.
Sound card	Converts digital signals to audio signals for speakers. Also can receive audio signals via a microphone and produce a digital signal.
Video accelerator	Displays graphics on the screen; accelerates two- and three-dimensional graphics.
Network card	Sends data to and receives data from other computers.
Digital camera	Records, and often displays, digital images.
Biometric device	Scans human characteristics, such as fingerprints and retinas, typically for identification and authentication purposes.
Infrared device	Communicates data between devices via a line-of-sight wireless connection.
Wireless device	Communicates data between devices via an omnidirectional wireless connection.

Figure 2.5 | Peripheral devices.

The IEEE 1394 standard, branded as "iLink" by Sony and "FireWire" by Apple, is commonly found in digital video cameras and mass storage devices (e.g., disk drives). FireWire can transfer data at speeds up to 800Mbit per second; future revisions are expected to scale to up to 2Gbit (gigabits, or 1 billion bits) per second. Similar to USB, FireWire allows devices to be "hot swappable" and can provide power to devices. Further, the FireWire specification allows multiple devices to communicate without being attached to a computer.[24] For example, a user can directly connect two FireWire hard disks to copy the contents of one to the other.

Other interfaces used for connecting peripheral devices to the system include the small computer systems interface (SCSI) and the Advanced Technology Attachment (ATA), which implements the Integrated Drive Electronics (IDE) interface. These interfaces transfer data from a device such as a hard drive or a DVD drive to a mainboard controller, where it can be routed to the appropriate bus.[25] More recent interfaces include Serial ATA (SATA), which permits higher transfer rates than ATA, and several wireless interfaces including Bluetooth (for short-range wireless connections) and IEEE 802.11g (for medium-range, high-speed wireless connections).

SCSI (pronounced "scuh-zee") was developed in the early 1980s as a high-speed connection for mass storage devices. It is primarily used in high-performance environments with many large-bandwidth devices.[26] The original SCSI specification allowed a maximum data transfer rate of 5MB per second and supported eight devices on an 8-bit bus. Current specifications, such as Ultra320 SCSI, permit data transfer at up to 320MB per second for 16 devices on a 16-bit bus.[27]

Self Review

1. What is the main difference between a peripheral device, such as a printer, and a device such as a processor?
2. Compare and contrast USB and FireWire.

Ans: **1)** Peripheral devices are not required for a computer to execute software instructions. By contrast, all computers need at least one processor to run. **2)** Both USB and FireWire provide large bandwidths and powered connections to devices. FireWire has a greater capacity than USB and enables devices to communicate without being attached to a computer.

2.4 Hardware Support for Operating Systems

Computer architectures contain features that perform operating system functions quickly in hardware to improve performance. They also provide features that enable the operating system to rigidly enforce protection, which improves the security and integrity of the system.

2.4.1 Processor

Most operating systems rely on processors to implement their protection mechanisms by preventing processes from accessing privileged instructions or accessing memory that has not been allocated to them. If processes attempt to violate a system's protection mechanisms, the processor notifies the operating system so that it can respond. The processor also invokes the operating system to respond to signals from hardware devices.

User Mode, Kernel Mode and Privileged Instructions

Computer systems generally have several different **execution modes**.[28] Varying the mode of a machine makes it possible to build more robust, fault-tolerant and secure systems. Normally, when the machine is operating in a particular mode, applications have access to only a subset of the machine's instructions. For user applications, the subset of instructions the user may execute in **user mode** (also called the **user state** or **problem state**) precludes, for example, the direct execution of input/output instructions; a user application allowed to perform arbitrary input/output could, for example, dump the system's master list of passwords, print the information of any other user or destroy the operating system. The operating system ordinarily executes with **most trusted user status** in **kernel mode** (also called the **supervisor state**); it has access to all the instructions in the machine's instruction set. In kernel mode, a processor may execute privileged instructions and access resources to perform tasks on behalf of processes. Such a user mode/kernel mode dichotomy has been adequate for most modern computing systems. In highly secure systems, however, it is desirable to have more than two states to allow finer-grained protection. Multiple states allow access to be granted by the **principle of least privilege**—any particular user should be granted the least amount of privilege and access required to accomplish its designated tasks (see the Operating Systems Thinking feature, Principle of Least Privilege).

It is interesting that as computer architectures have evolved, the number of **privileged instructions** (i.e., those instructions not accessible in user mode) has tended to increase. This indicates a trend toward incorporating more operating systems functions in hardware.

Memory Protection and Management

Most processors provide mechanisms for memory protection and memory management. **Memory protection**, which prevents processes from accessing memory that has not been assigned to them (such as other users' memory and the operating system's memory), is implemented using processor registers that can be modified only by privileged instructions (see the Operating Systems Thinking feature, Protection). The processor checks the values of these registers to ensure that processes cannot access memory that has not been allocated to them. For example, in systems that do not use virtual memory, processes are allocated only a contiguous block of memory addresses. The system can prevent such processes from accessing memory locations that have not been allocated to them by providing **bounds registers** that specify the addresses of the beginning and end of a process's allocated memory. Protection is enforced by determining whether a given address is within the allocated block. Most hardware protection operations are performed in parallel with the execution of program instructions, so they do not degrade performance.

Most processors also contain hardware that translates virtual addresses referenced by processes to corresponding addresses in main memory. Virtual memory systems allow programs to reference addresses that need not correspond to the lim-

Operating Systems Thinking

Principle of Least Privilege

Generally speaking, the principle of least privilege says that in any system, the various entities should be given only the capabilities that they need to accomplish their jobs but no more. The government employs this principle in awarding security clearances. You employ it when deciding who gets the extra keys to your home. Businesses employ it when giving employees access to critical and confidential information. Operating systems employ it in many areas.

ited set of **real** (or **physical**) **addresses** available in main memory.[29] Using hardware, the operating system dynamically translates a process's virtual addresses into physical addresses at runtime. Virtual memory systems allow processes to reference address spaces much larger than the number of addresses available in main memory, which allows programmers to create applications that are independent (for the most part) of the constraints of physical memory. Virtual memory also facilitates programming for timesharing systems, because processes need not be aware of the actual location of their data in main memory. Memory management and protection are discussed in detail in Chapters 9–11.

Interrupts and Exceptions

Processors inform the operating system of events such as program execution errors and changes in device status (e.g., a network packet has arrived or a disk I/O has completed). A processor can do so by repeatedly requesting the status of each device, a technique called **polling**. However, this can lead to significant execution overhead when polled devices have not changed status.

Instead, most devices send a signal called an **interrupt** to the processor when an event occurs. The operating system can respond to a change in device status by notifying processes that are waiting on such events. **Exceptions** are interrupts generated in response to errors, such as hardware failures, logic errors and protection violations (see the Anecdote, Origins of the Term "Glitch"). Instead of causing the

Operating Systems Thinking

Protection

The earliest computers had primitive operating systems capable of running only one job at a time. That changed rapidly as parallel processing capabilities were added to local systems and as distributed systems were developed in which parallel activities occur across networks of computers like the Internet. Operating systems must be concerned with various kinds of protection, especially when connected to the Internet.

The operating system and its data must be protected from being clobbered by errant user programs, either accidentally or maliciously. User programs must be protected from clobbering one another. Such protection must be enforced on the local machine and it must be enforced among users and operating system components spread across computer networks. We study protection in many chapters of this book, especially in Chapter 9, Real Memory Organization and Management and Chapter 10, Virtual Memory Organization. We consider protection in the form of file access controls in Chapter 13, File and Database Systems. We discuss protection in general throughout the main portion of the book and then discuss it in the context of the Linux and Windows XP case studies in Chapters 20 and 21, respectively.

system to fail, a processor will typically invoke the operating system to determine how to respond. For example, the operating system may determine that the process causing the error should be terminated or that the system must be restarted. If the system must fail, the operating system can do so gracefully, reducing the amount of lost work. Processes can also register exception handlers with the operating system. When the operating system receives an exception of the corresponding type, it calls the process's exception handler to respond. Interrupt mechanisms and exception handling are discussed in Section 3.4, Interrupts.

Self Review

1. What is the rationale for implementing multiple execution states?
2. How do exceptions differ from other types of interrupts?

Ans: **1)** Multiple execution states provide protection by preventing most software from maliciously or accidentally damaging the system and accessing resources without authorization. These operations are restricted to kernel mode, which enables the operating system to execute privileged instructions. **2)** Exceptions indicate that an error has occurred (e.g., division by zero or a protection violation) and invoke the operating system to determine how to respond. The operating system may then decide to do nothing or to terminate a process. If the operating system encounters a serious error that prevents it from executing properly, it may restart the computer.

Anecdote

Origins of the Term "Glitch"

There are a number of theories on the etymology of the computer term "glitch" which is typically used as a synonym for "bug." Many suggest that it is derived from the Yiddish word "glitshen," meaning "to slip." Here is another take on this. In the mid 1960s during the height of the space program, one of the top computer vendors built the first on-board computer system. The morning of the launch, the computer vendor took out full-page ads in major publications around the world, proclaiming that its computer was safely guiding the astronauts on their mission. That day, the computer failed, causing the space capsule to spin wildly out of control, putting the astronauts' lives at risk. The next morning, one of the major newspapers referred to this as the "Greatest Lemon in the Company's History!"

Lesson to operating systems designers: Always keep Murphy's Law in mind, "If something can go wrong, it will." And don't forget the common addendum, "and at the most inopportune time."

2.4.2 Timers and Clocks

An **interval timer** periodically generates an interrupt that causes a processor to invoke the operating system. Operating systems often use interval timers to prevent processes from monopolizing the processor. For example, the operating system may respond to the timer interrupt by removing the current process from the processor so that another can run. A **time-of-day clock** enables the computer to keep track of "wall clock time," typically accurate to thousandths or millionths of a second. Some time-of-day clocks are battery powered, allowing them to tick even when there is no external power supplied to the computer. Such clocks provide a measure of continuity in a system; for example, when the operating system loads, it may read the time-of-day clock to determine the current time and date.

Self Review

1. How does an interval timer prevent one process from monopolizing a processor?
2. Processors often contain a counter that is incremented after each processor cycle, providing a measure of time accurate to nanoseconds. Compare and contrast this measure of time to that provided by the time-of-day clock.

Ans: **1)** The interval timer generates interrupts periodically. The processor responds to each interrupt by invoking the operating system, which can then assign a different process to a processor. 2) A processor counter enables the system to determine with high precision how much time has passed between events, but does not maintain its information when the system is powered down. Because a time-of-day clock is battery powered, it is more appropriate for determining wall clock time. However, it measures time with coarser granularity than a processor counter.

2.4.3 Bootstrapping

Before an operating system can begin to manage resources, it must be loaded into memory. When a computer system is powered up, the BIOS initializes the system hardware, then attempts to load instructions into main memory from a region of secondary storage (e.g., a floppy disk, hard disk or CD) called the **boot sector**, a technique called bootstrapping (Fig. 2.6). The processor is made to execute these instructions, which typically load operating system components into memory, initialize processor registers and prepare the system to run user applications.

In many systems, the BIOS can load an operating system from a predefined location on a limited number of devices (e.g., the boot sector of a hard disk or a compact disk). If the boot sector is not found on a supported device, the system will not load and the user will be unable to access any of the computer's hardware. To enable greater functionality at boot time, the Intel Corporation has developed the **Extensible Firmware Interface (EFI)** as a replacement for the BIOS. EFI supports a shell through which users can directly access computer devices, and it incorporates device drivers to support access to hard drives and networks immediately after powering up the system.[30]

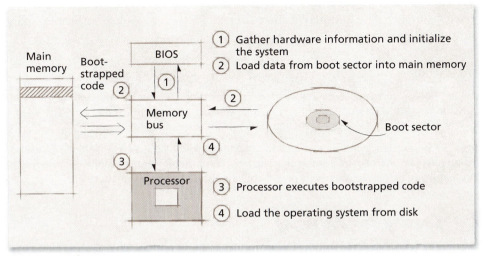

Main memory / **Boot-strapped code**

BIOS

Memory bus

Processor

1. Gather hardware information and initialize the system
2. Load data from boot sector into main memory

Boot sector

3. Processor executes bootstrapped code
4. Load the operating system from disk

Figure 2.6 | *Bootstrapping.*

Self Review

1. How does EFI address the limitations of BIOS?
2. Why should the operating system prevent users from accessing the boot sector?

Ans: **1)** A typical BIOS contains low-level instructions that provide limited functionality and restrict how software is initially loaded. EFI supports drivers and provides a shell, enabling a user to interact with a system and customize the way that the operating system is loaded. **2)** If users could access the boot sector, they could accidentally or maliciously modify operating system code, making the system unusable or enabling an attacker to gain control of the system.

2.4.4 Plug and Play

Plug-and-play technology allows operating systems to configure and use newly installed hardware without user interaction. A plug-and-play hardware device

1. uniquely identifies itself to the operating system,

2. communicates with the operating system to indicate the resources and services it requires to function properly, and

3. identifies its corresponding driver and allows the operating system to use it to configure the device (e.g., assign the device to a DMA channel and allocate to the device a region of main memory).[31]

These features enable users to add hardware to a system and use the hardware immediately with proper operating system support.

As mobile computing devices become more popular, an increasing number of systems rely on batteries for power. Consequently, plug-and-play has evolved to include power management features that enable a system to dynamically adjust its power consumption to increase battery life. The **Advanced Configuration and Power Interface (ACPI)** defines a standard interface for operating systems to configure devices and manage their power consumption. All recent Windows operating systems support plug-and-play; Linux version 2.6 is compatible with many plug-and-play devices.[32]

Self Review

1. Why, do you suppose, is it necessary for a plug-and-play device to uniquely identify itself to the operating system?
2. Why is power management particularly important for mobile devices?

Ans: **1)** Before an operating system can configure and make a device available to users, it must determine the resource needs that are unique to the device. **2)** Mobile devices rely on battery power; managing a device's power consumption can improve battery life.

2.5 Caching and Buffering

In Section 2.3.4, we discussed how computers contain a hierarchy of storage devices that operate at different speeds. To improve performance, most systems perform caching by placing copies of information that processes reference in faster storage. Due to the high cost of fast storage, caches can contain only a small portion of the information contained in slower storage. As a result, cache entries (also called **cache lines**) must be managed appropriately to minimize the number of times referenced information is not present in cache, an event called a **cache miss**. When a cache miss occurs, the system must retrieve the referenced information from slower storage. When a referenced item is present in the cache, a **cache hit** occurs, enabling the system to access data at relatively high speed.[33]

To realize increased performance from caching, systems must ensure that a significant number of memory references result in cache hits. As we discuss in Section 11.3, Demand Paging, it is difficult to predict with high accuracy the information that processes will soon reference. Therefore, most caches are managed using **heuristics**—rules of thumb and other approximations—that yield good results with relatively low execution overhead (see the Operating Systems Thinking Feature, Heuristics).

Examples of caches include the L1 and L2 processor caches, which store recently used data to minimize the number of cycles during which the processor is idle. Many operating systems allocate a portion of main memory to cache data from secondary storage such as disks, which typically exhibit latencies several orders of magnitude larger than main memory.

A **buffer** is storage area that temporarily holds data during transfers between devices or processes that operate at different speeds.[34] Buffers improve system performance by allowing software and hardware devices to transmit data and requests **asynchronously** (i.e., independently of one another). Examples of buffers include hard disk buffers, the keyboard buffer and the printer buffer.[35, 36] Because hard disks operate at much slower speeds than main memory, operating systems typically buffer data corresponding to write requests. The buffer holds the data until the hard disk has completed the write operation, enabling the operating system to execute other processes while waiting for the I/O to complete. A keyboard buffer is often used to hold characters typed by users until a process can acknowledge and respond to the corresponding keyboard interrupts.

Spooling (simultaneous peripheral operations online) is a technique in which an intermediate device, such as a disk, is interposed between a process and a low-speed or buffer-limited I/O device. For example, if a process attempts to print a document but the printer is busy printing another document, the process, instead of waiting for the printer to become available, writes its output to disk. When the printer becomes available, the data on disk is printed. Spooling allows processes to request operations from a peripheral device without requiring that the device be ready to service the request.[37] The term "spooling" comes from the notion of winding thread onto a spool from which it can be unwound as needed.

Self Review

1. How does caching improve system performance?
2. Why do buffers generally not improve performance if one device or process produces data significantly faster than it is consumed?

Ans: **1)** Caches improve performance by placing in fast storage information that a process is likely to reference soon; processes can reference data and instructions from a cache much faster than from main memory. **2)** If the producing entity is much faster than the consuming entity, the buffer would quickly fill, then the relationship would be limited by the relatively

Operating Systems Thinking

Heuristics

A heuristic is a "rule of thumb"— a strategy that sounds reasonable and when employed, typically yields good results. It often does not have a basis in mathematics because the system to which it applies is sufficiently complex to defy easy mathematical analysis. As you leave your home each morning, you may use the heuristic, "If it looks like rain, take my umbrella." You do this because from your experience, "looks like rain" is a reasonable (although

not perfect) indicator that it will rain. By applying this heuristic in the past, you avoided a few soakings, so you tend to rely on it. As you look at the pile of paperwork on your desk and schedule your work for the day, you may use another heuristic, "Do the shortest tasks first." This one has the satisfying result that you get a bunch of tasks done quickly; on the downside, it has the unfortunate side effect of postponing (possibly important) lengthier

tasks. Worse yet, if a steady stream of new short tasks arrives for you to do, you could indefinitely postpone important longer tasks. We will see operating systems heuristics in many chapters of the book, especially in the chapters that discuss resource management strategies, such as Chapter 8, Processor Scheduling and Chapter 12, Disk Performance Optimization.

slow speed of the consuming entity—the producing entity would have to slow down because it would repeatedly find the buffer full and would have to wait (rather than execute at its normally faster speed) until the consumer eventually freed space in the buffer. Similarly, if the consuming entity were faster, it would repeatedly find the buffer empty and would have to slow down to about the speed of the producing entity.

2.6 Software Overview

In this section we review basic concepts of computer programming and software. Programmers write instructions in various programming languages; some are directly understandable by computers, while others require translation. Programming languages can be classified generally as either machine, assembly or high-level languages.

2.6.1 Machine Language and Assembly Language

A computer can understand only its own **machine language**. As the "natural language" of a particular computer, machine language is defined by the computer's hardware design. Machine languages generally consist of streams of numbers (ultimately reduced to 1s and 0s) that instruct computers how to perform their most elementary operations. Machine languages are machine dependent—a particular machine language can be used on only one type of computer. The following section of an early machine-language program, which adds *overtime pay* to *base pay* and stores the result in *gross pay*, demonstrates the incomprehensibility of machine language to humans:

```
1300042774
1400593419
1200274027
```

As the popularity of computers increased, machine-language programming proved to be slow and error prone. Instead of using the strings of numbers that computers could directly understand, programmers began using English-like abbreviations to represent the computer's basic operations. These abbreviations formed the basis of **assembly languages**. Translator programs called **assemblers** convert assembly-language programs to machine-language. The following section of a simplified assembly-language program also adds *overtime pay* to *base pay* and stores the result in *gross pay*, but it presents the steps somewhat more clearly to human readers:

```
LOAD    BASEPAY
ADD     OVERPAY
STORE   GROSSPAY
```

This assembly-language code is clearer to humans, but computers cannot understand it until it is translated into machine language by an assembler program.

Self Review

1. (T/F) Computers typically execute assembly code directly.
2. Is software written in machine language portable?

Ans: 1) False. Assemblers translate assembly code into machine-language code before the code can execute. 2) No; machine languages are machine dependent, so software written in machine language executes only on machines of the same type.

2.6.2 Interpreters and Compilers

Although programming is faster in assembly languages than in machine language, assembly languages still require many instructions to accomplish even the simplest tasks. To increase programmer efficiency, **high-level languages** were developed. High-level languages accomplish more substantial tasks with fewer statements, but require translator programs called **compilers** to convert high-level language programs into machine language. High-level languages enable programmers to write instructions that look similar to everyday English and that contain common mathematical notations. For example, a payroll application written in a high-level language might contain a statement such as

```
grossPay = basePay + overTimePay
```

This statement produces the same result as the machine-language and assembly-language instructions in the prior sections.

Whereas compilers convert high-level language programs to machine language programs, **interpreters** are programs which directly execute source code or code has been reduced to a low-level language that is not machine code. Programming languages such as Java compile to a format called **bytecode** (although Java also can be compiled to machine language), which acts as machine code for a so-called virtual machine. Thus, bytecode is not dependent on the physical machine on which it executes, which promotes application portability. A Java interpreter analyzes each statement and executes the bytecode on the physical machine. Due to the execution-time overhead incurred by translation, programs executed via interpreters tend to execute slower than those that have been compiled to machine code.[38, 39]

Self Review

1. Discuss the benefits of high-level languages over assembly languages.
2. Why are programs compiled to bytecode more portable than those compiled to machine code?

Ans: 1) High-level language programs require many fewer instructions than assembly-language programs; also, programming in high-level languages is easier than in assembly language because high-level languages more closely mirror everyday English and common mathematical notations. 2) Bytecode is compiled to execute on a virtual machine that can be installed on many different platforms. By contrast, programs compiled to machine language can execute only on the type of machine for which the program was compiled.

2.6.3 High-Level Languages

Although hundreds of high-level languages have been developed, relatively few have achieved broad acceptance. Today, programming languages tend to be either structured or object oriented. In this section we enumerate some of the more popular languages, then discuss how they relate to each programming model.

IBM developed **Fortran** in the mid-1950s to create scientific and engineering applications that require complex mathematical computations. Fortran is still widely used, mainly in high-performance environments such as mainframes and supercomputers.

COmmon Business Oriented Language (COBOL) was developed in the late 1950s by a group of computer manufacturers, government agencies and industrial computer users. COBOL is designed for business applications that manipulate large volumes of data. A considerable portion of today's business software is still programmed in COBOL.

The **C** language, which Dennis Ritchie developed at Bell Laboratories in the early 1970s, gained widespread recognition as the development language of the UNIX operating system. In the early 1980s at Bell Laboratories, Bjarne Stroustrup developed **C++**, an extension of C. C++ provides capabilities for **object-oriented programming (OOP)**. **Objects** are reusable software components that model items in the real world. Object-oriented programs are often easier to understand, debug and modify than programs developed with previous techniques. Many of today's popular operating systems are written in C or C++.

When the World Wide Web exploded in popularity in 1993, Sun Microsystems saw immediate potential for using its new object-oriented **Java** programming language to create applications that could be downloaded over the Web and executed in Web browsers. Sun announced Java to the public in 1995, gaining the attention of the business community because of the widespread interest in the Web. Java has become a widely used software development language; it is used to generate Web pages dynamically, build large-scale enterprise applications, enhance the functionality of Web servers, provide applications for consumer devices (for example, cell phones, pagers and PDAs) and for many other purposes.

In 2000, Microsoft announced **C#** (pronounced "C-Sharp") and its .NET strategy. The C# programming language was designed specifically to be the key development language for the .NET platform; it has roots in C, C++ and Java. C# is object-oriented and has access to .NET's powerful library of prebuilt components, enabling programmers to develop applications quickly.

Self Review

1. Classify each of the following programming languages as structured or object oriented:
   a) C#; **b)** C; **c)** Java; **d)** C++.
2. What are some benefits of OOP?

Ans: **1) a)** object oriented; **b)** structured; **c)** object oriented; **d)** object-oriented. **2)** Object-oriented programs are often easier to understand, debug and modify than programs developed with previous techniques. Also OOP focuses on creating reusable software components.

2.6.4 Structured Programming

During the 1960s, software development efforts often ran behind schedule, costs greatly exceeded budgets and finished products were unreliable. People began to realize that software development was a far more complex activity than they had imagined. Research activity addressing these issues resulted in the evolution of **structured programming**—a disciplined approach to creating programs that are clear, correct and easy to modify.

This research led to the development of the **Pascal** programming language by Professor Nicklaus Wirth in 1971. Pascal was named after the 17th-century mathematician and philosopher Blaise Pascal. Designed for teaching structured programming, it rapidly became the preferred introductory programming language at most colleges. The language lacked many features needed to make it useful in commercial, industrial and government applications.

The **Ada** programming language was developed under the sponsorship of the U.S. Department of Defense (DoD) during the 1970s and early 1980s. It was named after Lady Ada Lovelace, daughter of the poet Lord Byron. Lady Lovelace is generally credited as being the world's first computer programmer, having written an application in the middle 1800s for the Analytical Engine mechanical computing device designed by Charles Babbage. Ada was one of the first languages designed to facilitate concurrent programming, which is discussed with examples in pseudocode and Java in Chapter 5, Asynchronous Concurrent Execution, and Chapter 6, Concurrent Programming.

Self Review

1. What problems in early software development did structured programming languages address?
2. How did the Ada programming language differ from other structured programming languages such as Pascal and C?

Ans: **1)** In the early days of programming, developers did not have a systematic approach to constructing complex programs, resulting in unnecessarily high costs, missed deadlines and unreliable products. Structured programming filled the need for a disciplined approach to software development. **2)** Ada was designed to facilitate concurrent programming.

2.6.5 Object-Oriented Programming

As the benefits of structured programming were realized in the 1970s, improved software technology began to appear. However, not until object-oriented programming became widely established in the 1980s and 1990s did software developers finally feel they had the necessary tools to improve the software development process dramatically.

Object technology is a packaging scheme for creating meaningful software units. Almost any noun can be represented as a software object. Objects have **properties** (also called **attributes**), such as color, size and weight; and they perform **actions** (also called **behaviors** or **methods**), such as moving, sleeping or drawing. **Classes** are types of related objects. For example, all cars belong to the "car" class, even though individual cars vary in make, model, color and options packages. A class specifies the general format of its objects, and the properties and actions available to an object depend on its class. An object is related to its class in much the same way as a building is related to its blueprint.

Before object-oriented languages appeared, **procedural programming languages** (such as Fortran, Pascal, BASIC and C) focused on actions (verbs) rather than objects (nouns). This made programming a bit awkward. However, using today's popular object-oriented languages, such as C++, Java and C#, programmers can program in an object-oriented manner that more naturally reflects the way in which people perceive the world, resulting in significant gains in programmer productivity.

Object technology permits properly designed classes to be reused in multiple projects. Using libraries of classes can greatly reduce the effort required to implement new systems. However, some organizations report that the key benefit from object-oriented programming is not software reusability, but rather the production of software that is more understandable because it is better organized and easier to maintain.

Object-oriented programming allows programmers to focus on the "big picture." Instead of worrying about the minute details of how reusable objects are implemented, they can focus on the behaviors and interactions of objects. Programmers can also focus on modifying one object without worrying about the effect on another object. A road map that shows every tree, house and driveway would be difficult, if not impossible, to read. When such details are removed and only the essential information (roads) remains, the map becomes easier to understand. In the same way, an application that is divided into objects is easier to understand, modify and update because it hides much of the detail.

Self Review

1. How is the central focus of object-oriented programming different from that of structured programming?
2. How do objects facilitate modifications to existing software?

Ans: **1)** Object-oriented programming focuses on manipulating objects (nouns), whereas procedural programming focuses on actions (verbs). **2)** Objects hide much of the detail of an overall application, allowing programmers to focus on the big picture. Programmers can focusing on modifying one object without worrying about the effect on another object.

2.7 Application Programming Interfaces (APIs)

Today's applications require access to many resources that are managed by the operating system, such as files on disk and data from remote computers. Because the operating system must act as a resource manager, it typically will not allow processes to acquire these resources without first explicitly requesting them.

Application programming interfaces (APIs) provide a set of routines that programmers can use to request services from the operating system (Fig. 2.7). In most of today's operating systems, communication between software and the operating system is performed exclusively through APIs. Examples of APIs include the Portable Operating System Interface (POSIX) standards and the **Windows API** for developing Microsoft Windows applications. POSIX recommends standard APIs that are based on early UNIX systems and are widely used in UNIX-based operating systems. The Win32 API is Microsoft's interface for applications that execute in a Windows environment.

Processes execute function calls defined by the API to access services provided by a lower layer of the system. These function calls may issue **system calls** to request services from the operating system. System calls are analogous to interrupts for hardware devices—when a system call occurs, the system switches to kernel mode and the operating system executes to service the system call.

Self Review

1. Why must processes issue system calls to request operating system services?
2. How does the POSIX attempt to improve application portability?

Ans: **1)** To protect the system, the operating system cannot allow processes to access operating system services or privileged instructions directly. Instead, the services that an operating system can provide to processes are packaged into APIs. Processes can access these

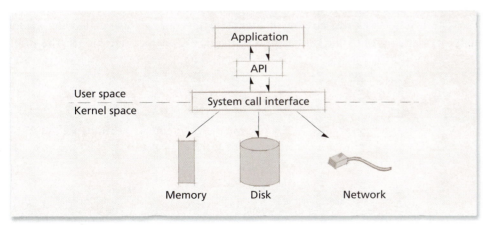

Figure 2.7 | *Application programming interface (API).*

services only through the system call interface, which essentially puts the operating system in control. **2)** Software written using a particular API can be run only on systems that implement the same API. POSIX attempts to address this problem by specifying a standard API for UNIX-based systems. Even many non-UNIX systems now support POSIX.

2.8 Compiling, Linking and Loading

Before a program written in a high-level language can execute, it must be translated into machine language, linked with various other machine-language programs on which it depends and loaded into memory. In this section we consider how programs written in high-level languages are **compiled** into machine-language code and we describe how linkers and loaders prepare compiled code for execution.[40]

2.8.1 Compiling

Although each type of computer can understand only its own machine language, nearly all programs are written in high-level languages. The first stage in the process of creating executable programs is compiling the high-level programming language code to machine language. A compiler accepts **source code**, which is written in a high-level language, as input and returns **object code**, containing the machine-language instructions to execute, as output. Nearly all commercially available programs are delivered as object code, and some distributions (i.e., open-source software) also include the source code.[41]

The compiling process can be divided into several phases; one view of compiling is presented in Fig. 2.8. Each phase modifies the program so that it can be interpreted by the next phase, until the program has been translated into machine code. First, the source code is passed to the **lexer** (also called **lexical analyzer** or **scanner**), which separates the characters of a program's source into **tokens**. Examples of tokens include keywords (e.g., `if`, `else` and `int`), identifiers (e.g., named variables and constants), operators (e.g., `-`, `+`, `*` and `/`) and punctuation (e.g., semicolons).

The lexer passes this stream of tokens to the **parser** (also called the **syntax analyzer**), which groups the tokens into syntactically correct statements. The **inter-**

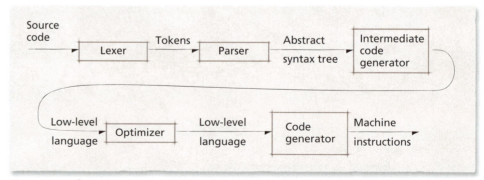

Figure 2.8 | *Compiler phases.*

mediate code generator converts this syntactic structure into a stream of simple instructions that resemble assembly language (although it does not specify the registers used for each operation). The **optimizer** attempts to improve the code's execution efficiency and reduce the program's memory requirements. In the final phase, the **code generator** produces the object file containing the machine-language instructions.[42, 43]

Self Review

1. What is the difference between compiling and assembling?
2. Could a Java program run directly on a physical machine instead of on a virtual machine?

Ans: **1)** The assembly process simply translates assembly-language instructions into machine language. A compiler translates high-level language code into machine-language code and may also optimize the code. **2)** A Java program could run on a physical machine by using a compiler that translates Java source code or bytecode into the corresponding machine language.

2.8.2 Linking

Often, programs consist of several independently developed subprograms, called **modules**. Functions to perform common computer routines such as I/O manipulations or random number generation are packaged into precompiled modules called **libraries**. **Linking** is the process of integrating the various modules referenced by a program into a single executable unit.

When a program is compiled, its corresponding object module contains program data and instructions retrieved from the program's source file. If the program referenced functions or data from another module, the compiler translates these into **external references**. Also, if the program makes functions or data available to other programs, each of these is represented as an **external name**. Object modules store these external references and names in a data structure called a **symbol table** (Fig. 2.9). The integrated module produced by the linker is called a **load module**.

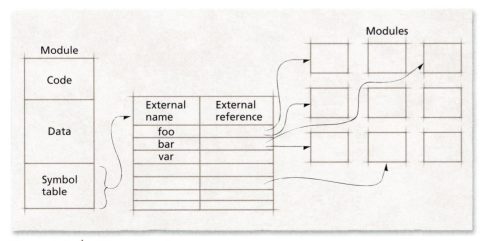

Figure 2.9 | *Object module.*

Input to the linker can include object modules, load modules and control statements, such as the location of referenced library files.[44]

The linker often is provided with several object files that form a single program. These object files typically specify the locations of data and instructions using addresses that are relative to the beginning of each file, called **relative addresses**.

In Fig. 2.10, symbol X in object module A and symbol Y in object module B have the same relative address in their respective modules. The linker must modify these addresses so that they do not reference invalid data or instructions when the modules are combined to form a linked program. **Relocating** addresses ensures that each statement is uniquely identified by an address within a file. When an address is modified, all references to it must be updated with the new location. In the resulting load module, X and Y have been relocated to new relative addresses that are unique within the load module. Often, linkers also provide relative addressing in the load module; however, the addresses are assigned such that they are all relative to the beginning of the entire load module.

Linkers also perform **symbol resolution**, which converts external references in one module to their corresponding external names in another module.[45, 46] In

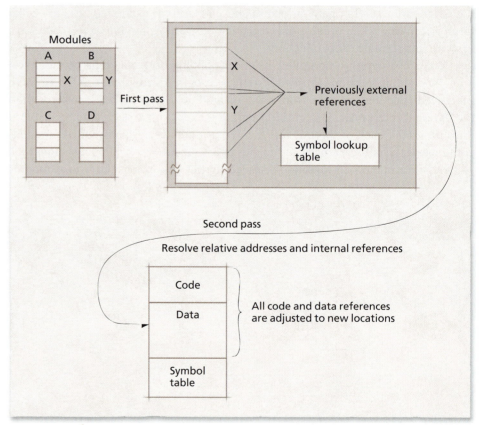

Figure 2.10 | *Linking process.*

Fig. 2.11, the external reference to symbol C in object module 2 is resolved with the external name C from object module 1. Once an external reference is paired with the corresponding name in a separate module, the address of the external reference must be modified to reflect this integration.

Often, linkage occurs in two passes. The first pass determines the size of each module and constructs a symbol table. The symbol table associates each symbol (such as a variable name) with an address, so that the linker can locate the reference. On the second pass, the linker assigns addresses to different instruction and data units

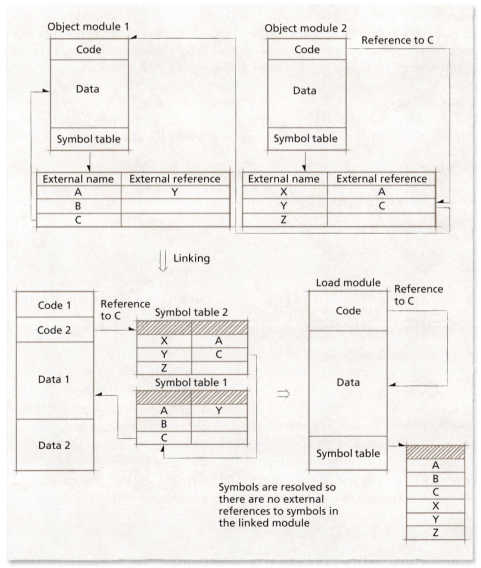

Figure 2.11 | Symbol resolution.

and resolves external symbol references.[47] Because a load module can become the input of another linking pass, the load module contains a symbol table, in which all symbols are external names. Notice that, in Fig. 2.11, the external reference to symbol Y is not listed in the load module's symbol table because it has been resolved.

The time at which a program is linked depends on the environment. A program can be linked at compile time if the programmer includes all necessary code in the source file so that there are no references to external names. This is accomplished by searching for the source code for any externally referenced symbols and placing those symbols in the resulting object file. This method typically is not feasible because many programs rely on **shared libraries**, which are collections of functions that can be shared between different processes. Many programs can reference the same functions (such as library functions that manipulate input and output streams) without including them in their object code. This type of linking is typically performed after compilation but before loading. As discussed in the Mini Case Study, Mach, shared libraries enable the Mach microkernel to emulate multiple operating systems.

This same process can be performed at load time (see Section 2.8.3, Loading). Linking and loading are sometimes both performed by one application called a

Mini Case Study

Mach

The **Mach** system was developed at Carnegie-Mellon University from 1985–1994 and was based on CMU's earlier Accent research OS.[48] The project was directed by Richard Rashid, now the senior vice president of Microsoft Research.[49] Mach was one of the first and best-known microkernel operating systems (see Section 1.13.3, Microkernel Architecture). It has been incorporated into later systems, including Mac OS X, NeXT and OSF/1, and had a strong influence on Windows NT (and ultimately on Windows XP,

which we discuss in Chapter 21).[50, 51, 52] An open-source implementation, GNU Mach, is used as the kernel for the GNU Hurd operating system, which is currently under development.[53]

A powerful capability of the Mach microkernel system is that it can emulate other operating systems. Mach achieves this using "transparent shared libraries."[54] A transparent shared library implements the actions for the system calls of the OS it is emulating, then intercepts system calls made

by programs that are written to run on the emulated OS.[55, 56] The intercepted system calls can then be translated into Mach system calls, and any results are translated back into the emulated form.[57, 58] Thus the user's program does not have to be ported to run on a system running Mach. In addition, any number of these transparent libraries can be in memory, so Mach can emulate multiple operating systems simultaneously.[59]

linking loader. Linking can also occur at runtime, a process called **dynamic linking**. In this case, references to external functions are not resolved until the process is loaded into memory or issues a call to the function. This is useful for large programs that use programs controlled by another party, because a dynamically linked program does not have to be relinked when a library that it uses is modified.[60] Further, because dynamically linked programs are not linked until they are in main memory, shared library code can be stored separately from other program code. Thus, dynamic linking also saves space in secondary storage because only one copy of a shared library is stored for any number of programs that use it.

Self Review

1. How does linking facilitate the development of large programs built by many developers?
2. What is one possible drawback of using a dynamic linker? What is a benefit?

Ans: **1)** Linking permits programs to be written as many separate modules. The linker combines these modules into a final load module when all pieces of the program have been compiled. **2)** If a library cannot be found during execution, an executing program will be forced to terminate, possibly losing all of the work performed up to that point. A benefit is that programs that are dynamically linked do not have to be relinked when a library changes.

2.8.3 Loading

Once the linker has created the load module, it passes it to a **loader** program. The loader is responsible for placing each instruction and data unit at a particular memory address, a process called **address binding**. There are several techniques for loading programs into main memory, most of which are important only for systems that do not support virtual memory. If the load module already specifies physical addresses in memory, the loader simply places the instruction and data units at the addresses specified by the programmer or compiler (assuming the memory addresses are available), a technique called **absolute loading**. **Relocatable loading** is performed when the load module contains relative addresses that need to be converted to actual memory addresses. The loader is responsible for requesting a block of memory space in which to place the program, then relocating the program's addresses to correspond to its location in memory.

In Fig. 2.12, the operating system has allocated the block of memory beginning with memory address 10,000. As the program is loaded, the loader must add 10,000 to each address in the load module. The loader updates the memory address of the variable `Example` in the Fig. 2.12 to 10,450 from its original relative address of 450.

Dynamic loading is a technique that loads program modules upon first use.[61] In many virtual memory systems, each process is assigned its own set of virtual addresses starting at zero, so the loader is responsible for loading the program into a valid memory region.

We review the entire compiling, linking and loading process (using load-time address binding) from source code to execution in Fig. 2.13. The programmer begins by writing the source code in some high-level language—in this case, C.

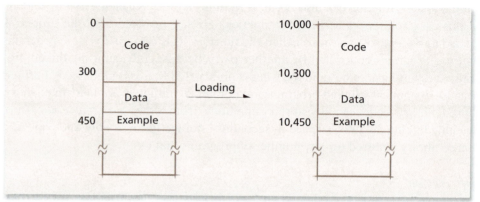

Figure 2.12 | *Loading.*

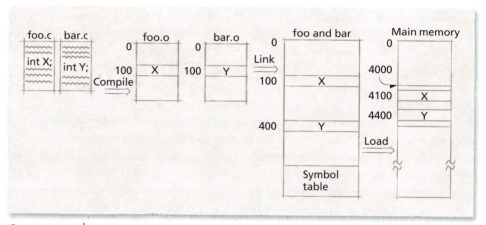

Figure 2.13 | *Compiling, linking and loading.*

Next, the compiler transforms the foo.c and bar.c source-code files into machine language, creating the object modules foo.o and bar.o. In the code, the programmer has defined variable X in foo.c and variable Y in bar.c; both are located at relative address 100 in their respective object modules. The object modules are placed in secondary storage until requested by the user or another process, at which point the modules must be linked.

In the next step, the linker integrates the two modules into a single load module. The linker accomplishes this task by collecting information about module sizes and external symbols in the first pass and linking the files together in the second pass. Notice that the linker relocates variable Y to relative address 400.

In the third step, the loader requests a block of memory for the program. The operating system provides the address range of 4000 to 5050, so the loader relocates variable X to the absolute address 4100 and variable Y to the absolute address 4400.

Self Review

1. How might absolute loading limit a system's degree of multiprogramming?
2. How does dynamic loading improve a system's degree of multiprogramming?

Ans: **1)** Two programs that specify overlapping addresses cannot execute at the same time, because only one can be resident at the same location in memory at once. **2)** Modules are loaded as needed, so memory contains only the modules that are used.

2.9 Firmware

In addition to hardware and software, most computers contain **firmware**, executable instructions stored in persistent, often read-only, memory attached to a device. Firmware is programmed with **microprogramming**, which is a layer of programming below a computer's machine language.

Microcode (i.e., microprogram instructions) typically includes simple, fundamental instructions necessary to implement all machine-language operations.[62] For example, a typical machine instruction might specify that the hardware perform an addition operation. The microcode for this instruction specifies the actual primitive operations that hardware must perform, such as incrementing the pointer that references to the current machine instruction, adding each bit of the numbers, storing the result in a new register and fetching the next instruction.[63, 64]

Professor Maurice Wilkes, the creator of the early EDSAC computer, first introduced the concepts of microprogramming in 1951.[65] However, not until the IBM System/360 appeared in 1964 was microcode used on a wide scale. Machine instruction sets implemented in microcode reached a peak with the VAX operating system, but have declined in recent years, because the execution of microcode instructions limits a processor's maximum speed. Thus, operations formerly performed by microcode instructions are now performed by processor hardware.[66] Today, many hardware devices, including hard drives and peripheral devices, contain miniature processors. The instructions for these processors are often implemented using microcode.[67]

Self Review

1. (T/F) There are no instructions smaller than machine-language instructions.
2. Describe the role of firmware in a computer system.

Ans: **1)** False. Microcode specifies a layer of programming below a processor's machine language. **2)** Firmware specifies simple, fundamental instructions necessary to implement machine-language instructions.

2.10 Middleware

Software plays an important role in distributed systems in which computers are connected across a network. Often, the computers that compose a distributed system are heterogeneous—they use different hardware, run different operating systems and communicate across different network architectures using various network protocols. The nature of distributed systems requires middleware to enable interactions among multiple processes running on one or more computers across a network.

Middleware allows an application running on one computer to communicate with an application running on a remote computer, enabling communications between computers in distributed systems. Middleware also permits applications to run on heterogeneous computer platforms, as long as each computer has the middleware installed. Middleware simplifies application development, because developers do not need to know the details of how the middleware performs its tasks. Developers can concentrate on developing programs rather than developing communication protocols. **Open DataBase Connectivity (ODBC)** is an example of an API for database access that permits applications to access databases through middleware called an ODBC driver. When developing such applications, developers need to provide only the database to which the application should connect. The ODBC driver handles connecting to the database and retrieving the information required by the application. Section 17.3.1, Middleware, through Section 17.3.4, CORBA (Common Object Request Broker Architecture), discuss common middleware implementations and protocols that form the backbone of many distributed systems.

Self Review

1. What are the costs and benefits of using middleware?
2. How does middleware facilitate the construction of heterogeneous systems?

Ans: 1) Middleware promotes program modularity and facilitates application programming, because the developer does not need to write code to manage interactions between processes. However, communication between middleware and processes incurs overhead compared to direct communication. 2) Middleware facilitates communication between computers using different protocols by translating messages into different formats as they are passed between sender and receiver.

Web Resources

www.pcguide.com
Provides articles discussing various aspects of computer hardware and the motivation for creating various interfaces; covers a broad range of topics relating to computer architecture.

www.tomshardware.com
Tom's Hardware Guide is one of the most thorough hardware review sites on the Web.

www.anandtech.com
Reviews new and emerging hardware.

developer.intel.com
Provides technical documentation about Intel products, articles on current technologies and topics investigated by their research and development teams.

www.ieee.org
IEEE defines many standards in computer hardware design. Members may access its journals online.

sourceforge.net
World's most popular site for open-source software development; provides resources and utilities for software developers.

Summary

An operating system is primarily a resource manager, so the design of an operating system is intimately tied to the hardware and software resources the operating system must manage.

A PCB is a hardware component that provides electrical connections between devices at various locations on the PCB. The mainboard is the PCB to which devices such as processors and main memory are attached.

A processor is a hardware component that executes a stream of machine-language instructions. A CPU is a processor that executes the instructions of a program; a coprocessor executes special-purpose instructions (such as graphics or audio) efficiently. In this book, we use the term "processor" to refer to a CPU. Registers are high-speed memory located on a processor that hold data for immediate use by the processor. Before a processor can operate on data, the data must be placed in registers. The instruction length is the size of a machine-language instruction; some processors support multiple instruction lengths.

Computer time is measured in cycles; each cycle is one complete oscillation of an electrical signal provided by the system clock generator. Processor speeds are often measured in GHz (billions of cycles per second).

The memory hierarchy is a scheme for categorizing memory, which places the fastest and most expensive memory at the top and the slowest and least expensive memory at the bottom. It has a steep, pyramidal shape in which register memory occupies the hierarchy's top level, followed by L1 cache memory, L2 cache memory, main memory, secondary storage and tertiary storage. A system's main memory is the lowest data store in the memory hierarchy that the processor can reference directly. Main memory is volatile, meaning it loses its contents when the system loses power. Secondary storage, such as hard disks, CDs, DVDs and floppy disks, persistently store large quantities of data at a low cost per unit storage.

A bus is a collection of thin electrical connections called traces that transport information between hardware devices. A port is a bus connecting two devices. I/O channels are special-purpose components devoted to handling I/O independently of the computer system's main processors.

A peripheral device is hardware that is not required for a computer to execute instructions. Printers, scanners and mice are peripheral devices; processors and main memory are not.

Some hardware exists specifically to improve performance and simplify the design of operating systems. Computer systems generally have several different execution states. For user applications, the subset of instructions the user may execute in user mode precludes, for example, the direct execution of input/output instructions. The operating system ordinarily executes with most trusted user status in kernel mode; in kernel mode, a processor may execute privileged instructions and access resources to perform tasks on behalf of processes. Memory protection, which prevents processes from accessing memory that has not been assigned to them (such as other users' memory and the operating system's memory), is implemented using processor registers that can be modified only by privileged instructions. Most devices send a signal called an interrupt to the processor when an event occurs. The operating system can respond to a change in device status by notifying processes that are waiting on such events.

Programmed I/O (PIO) is a technique whereby a processor idles while data is transferred between a device and main memory. By contrast, direct memory access (DMA) enables devices and controllers to transfer blocks of data to and from main memory directly, which frees the processor to execute software instructions.

Interrupts allow hardware to send signals to the processor, which notifies the operating system of the interrupt. The operating system decides what action to take in response to the interrupt.

A computer contains several types of clocks and timers. An interval timer is useful for preventing a process from monopolizing a processor. After a designated interval, the timer generates an interrupt to gain the attention of the processor; as a result of this interrupt, the processor might then be assigned to another application. The time-of-day clock keeps track of "wall clock time."

Bootstrapping is the process of loading initial operating system components into memory. This process is performed by a computer's BIOS.

Plug-and-play technology allows operating systems to configure newly installed hardware without user interaction. To support plug-and-play, a hardware device must uniquely identify itself to the operating system, communicate with the operating system to indicate the resources and services the device requires to function properly, and identify the driver that supports the device and allows software to configure the device (e.g., assign the device to a DMA channel).

Caches are relatively fast memory designed to increase program execution speed by maintaining copies of data that will be accessed soon. Examples of caches are the L1 and L2 processor caches and the main memory cache for hard disks.

A buffer is a temporary storage area that holds data during I/O transfers. Buffer memory is used primarily to coordinate communication between devices operating at different speeds. Buffers can store data for asynchronous processing, coordinate input/output between devices operating at different speeds or allow signals to be delivered asynchronously.

Spooling is a buffering technique in which an intermediate device, such as a disk, is interposed between a process and a low-speed or buffer-limited I/O device. Spooling allows processes to request operations from a peripheral device without requiring that the device be ready to service the request.

Three types of programming languages are machine, assembly and high-level languages. Machine languages consist of streams of numbers (ultimately reduced to 1s and 0s) that instruct computers how to perform their most elementary operations. A computer can understand only its own machine language. Assembly languages represent machine-language instructions using English-like abbreviations. High-level languages enable programmers to write instructions that look similar to everyday English and that contain common mathematical notations. High-level languages accomplish more substantial tasks with fewer statements, but require translator programs called compilers to convert high-level language programs into machine language. C, C++, Java and C# are examples of high-level languages.

Today, high-level languages tend to fall into two types, structured programming languages and object-oriented programming languages. Structured programming is a disciplined approach to creating programs that are clear, correct and easy to modify. Pascal and Fortran are structured programming languages. Object-oriented programs focus on manipulating objects (nouns) to create reusable software that is easy to modify and understand. C++, C# and Java are object-oriented programming languages.

APIs allow a program to request services from the operating system. Programs call API functions, which may access the operating system by making system calls.

Before a high-level-language program can execute, it must be translated into machine code and loaded into memory. Compilers transform high-level-language code into machine code. Linkers assign relative addresses to different program or data units and resolve external references between subprograms. Loaders convert these addresses into physical addresses and place the program or data units into main memory.

Most computers contain firmware, which specifies software instructions but is physically part of a hardware device. Most firmware is programmed with microprogramming, which is a layer of programming below a computer's machine language.

Middleware enables communication among multiple processes running on one or more computers across a network. Middleware facilitates heterogeneous distributed systems and simplifies application programming.

Key Terms

absolute loading—Loading technique in which the loader places the program in memory at the address specified by the programmer or compiler.

Accelerated Graphics Port (AGP)—Popular bus architecture used for connecting graphics devices; AGPs typically provide 260MB/s of bandwidth.

Ada—Concurrent, procedural programming language developed by the DoD during the 1970s and 1980s.

address binding—Assignment of memory addresses to program data and instructions.

address bus—Part of a bus that specifies the memory location from or to which data is to be transferred.

add-on card—Device that extends the functionality of a computer (e.g., sound and video cards).

Advanced Configuration and Power Interface (ACPI)—Interface to which a plug-and-play device must conform so that Microsoft Windows operating systems can manage the device's power consumption.

application programming—Software development that entails writing code that requests services and resources from the operating system to perform tasks (e.g., text editing, loading Web pages or payroll processing).

application programming interface (API)—Set of functions that allows an application to request services from a lower level of the system (e.g., the operating system or a library module).

Arithmetic and Logic Unit (ALU)—Component of a processor that performs basic arithmetic and logic operations.

assembler—Translator program that converts assembly-language programs to machine language.

assembly language—Low-level language that represents basic computer operations as English-like abbreviations.

attribute (of an object)—See property.

asynchronous transmission—Transferring data from one device to another that operates independently via a buffer to eliminate the need for blocking; the sender can perform other work once the data arrives in the buffer, even if the receiver has not yet read the data.

auxiliary storage—See secondary storage.

bandwidth—Measure of the amount of data transferred over a unit of time.

behavior (of an object)—See method.

basic input/output system (BIOS)—Low-level software instructions that control basic hardware initialization and management.

block device—Device such as a disk that transfers data in fixed-size groups of bytes, as opposed to a character device, which transfers data one byte at a time.

boot sector—Specified location on a disk in which the initial operating system instructions are stored; the BIOS instructs the hardware to load these initial instructions when the computer is turned on.

bootstrapping—Process of loading initial operating system components into system memory so that they can load the rest of the operating system.

bounds register—Register that stores information regarding the range of memory addresses accessible to a process.

buffer—Temporary storage area that holds data during I/O between devices operating at different speeds. Buffers enable a faster device to produce data at its full speed (until the buffer fills) while waiting for the slower device to consume the data.

bus—Collection of traces that form a high-speed communication channel for transporting information between different devices on a mainboard.

bus mastering—DMA transfer in which a device assumes control of the bus (preventing others from accessing the bus simultaneously) to access memory.

bytecode—Intermediate code that is intended for virtual machines (e.g., Java bytecode runs on the Java Virtual Machine).

C—Procedural programming language developed by Dennis Ritchie that was used to create UNIX.

C++—Object-oriented extension of C developed by Bjarne Stroustup.

C#—Object-oriented programming language developed by Microsoft that provides access to .NET libraries.

cache hit—Request for data that is present in the cache.

cache line—Entry in a cache.

cache miss—Request for data that is not present in the cache.

central processing unit (CPU)—Processor responsible for the general computations in a computer.

character device—Device such as a keyboard or mouse that transfers data one byte at a time, as opposed to a block device, which transfers data in fixed-size groups of bytes.

chipset—Collection of controllers, coprocessors, buses and other hardware specific to the mainboard that determine the hardware capabilities of a system.

class—Type of an object. Determines an object's methods and attributes.

clocktick—See cycle.

COmmon Business Oriented Language (COBOL)—Procedural programming language developed in the late 1950s that was designed for writing business software that manipulates large volumes of data.

code generator—Part of a compiler responsible for producing object code from a higher-level language.

compact disk (CD)—Digital storage medium in which data is stored as a series of microscopic pits on a flat surface.

compile—Translate high-level-language source code into machine code.

compiler—Application that translates high-level-language source code into machine code.

controller—Hardware component that manages access to a bus by devices.

coprocessor—Processor, such as a graphics or digital signal processor, designed to efficiently execute a limited set of special-purpose instructions (e.g., 3D transformations).

cycle (clock)—One complete oscillation of an electrical signal. The number of cycles that occur per second determines a device's frequency (e.g., processors, memory and buses) and can be used by the system to measure time.

cycle stealing—Method that gives channels priority over a processor when accessing the bus to prevent signals from channels and processors from colliding.

data bus—Bus that transfers data to or from locations in memory that are specified by the address bus.

derived speed—Actual speed of a device as determined by the frontside bus speed and clock multipliers or dividers.

direct memory access (DMA)—Method of transferring data from a device to main memory via a controller that requires only interrupting the processor when the transfer completes. I/O transfer via DMA is more efficient than programmed I/O or interrupt-driven I/O because the processor does not need to supervise the transfer of each byte or word of data.

double data rate (DDR)—Chipset feature that enables a frontside bus to effectively operate at twice its clock speed by performing two memory transfers per clock cycle. This feature must be supported by the system's chipset and RAM.

dynamic linking—Linking mechanism that resolves references to external functions when the process first makes a call to the function. This can reduce linking overhead because external functions that are never called while the process executes are not linked.

dynamic loading—Method for loading that specifies memory addresses at runtime.

dynamic RAM (DRAM)—RAM that must be continuously read by a refresh circuit to keep the contents in memory.

execution mode—Operating system execution mode (e.g., user mode or kernel mode) that determines which instructions can be executed by a process.

exception—Error caused by a process. Processor exceptions invoke the operating system, which determines how to respond. Processes can register exception handlers that are executed when the operating system receives the corresponding exception.

Extensible Firmware Interface (EFI)—Interface designed by Intel that improves upon a traditional BIOS by supporting device drivers and providing a shell interface at boot time.

external name—Symbol defined in a module that can be referenced by other modules.

external reference—Reference from one module to an external name in a different module.

firmware—Microcode that specifies simple, fundamental instructions necessary to implement machine-language instructions.

Fortran—Procedural programming language developed by IBM in the mid-1950s for scientific applications that require complex mathematical computations.

frontside bus (FSB)—Bus that connects a processor to main memory.

general-purpose register—Register that can be used by processes to store data and pointer values. Special-purpose registers cannot be accessed by user processes.

heuristics—Technique that solves complex problems using rules of thumb or other approximations that incur low execution overhead and generally provide good results.

high-level language—Programming language that uses English-like identifiers and common mathematical notation to represent programs using fewer statements than assembly-language programming.

IEEE 1394 port—Commonly used serial port that provides transfer speeds of up to 800MB per second, sometimes supplies power to devices and allows devices to be hot swappable; these ports are commonly referred to as FireWire (from Apple) or iLink (from Sony).

instruction decode unit—Component of a processor that interprets instructions and generates appropriate control signals that cause the processor to perform each instruction.

instruction fetch unit—Component of a processor that loads instructions from the instruction cache so they can be decoded and executed.

instruction length—Number of bits that comprise an instruction in a given architecture. Some architectures support variable-length instructions; instruction lengths also vary among different architectures.

intermediate code generator—Stage of the compilation process that receives input from the parser and outputs a stream of instructions to the optimizer.

interpreter—Application that can execute code other than machine code (e.g., high-level-language instructions).

interrupt—Message that informs the system that another process or device has completed an operation or produced an error. An interrupt causes the processor to pause program execution and invoke the operating system so it can respond to the interrupt.

interval timer—Hardware that generates periodic interrupts that cause operating system code to execute, which can ensure that a processor will not be monopolized by a malicious or malfunctioning process.

I/O channel—Component responsible for handling device I/O independently of a main processor.

Java—Object-oriented programming language developed by Sun Microsystems that promotes portability by running on a virtual machine.

kernel mode—Execution mode of a processor that allows processes to execute privileged instructions.

lane—Route between two points in a PCI Express bus. PCI Express devices are connected by a link that may contain up to 32 lanes.

lexer—See lexical analyzer.

lexical analyzer—Part of a compiler that separates the source code into tokens.

library module—Precompiled module that performs common computer routines, such as I/O routines or mathematical functions.

linking—Process of integrating a program's object modules into a single executable file.

linking loader—Application that performs both linking and loading.

loader—Application that loads linked executable modules into memory.

load module—Integrated module produced by a linker that consists of object code and relative addresses.

Mach—Early microkernel operating system, designed at Carnegie-Mellon University by a team led by Richard Rashid. Mach has influenced the design of Windows NT and has been used to implement Mac OS X.

machine language—Language that is defined by a computer's hardware design and can be natively understood by the computer.

mainboard—Printed circuit board that provides electrical connections between computer components such as processor, memory and peripheral devices.

main memory—Volatile memory that stores instructions and data; it is the lowest level of the memory hierarchy that can be directly referenced by a processor.

memory hierarchy—Classification of memory from fastest, lowest-capacity, most expensive memory to slowest, highest-capacity, least expensive memory.

memory protection—Mechanism that prevents processes from accessing memory used by other processes or the operating system.

method (of an object)—Part of an object that manipulates object attributes or performs a service.

microcode—Microprogramming instructions.

microprogramming—Layer of programming below a computer's machine language that includes instructions necessary to implement machine-language operations. This enables processors to divide large, complex instructions into simpler ones that are performed by its execution unit.

module—Independently developed subprogram that can be combined with other subprograms to create a larger, more complex program; programmers often use precompiled library modules to perform common computer functions such as I/O manipulations or random number generation.

Moore's law—Prediction regarding the evolution of processor design that asserts the number of transistors in a processor will double approximately every 18 months.

motherboard—See mainboard.

most trusted user status—See kernel mode.

object—Reusable software component that can model real-world items through properties and actions.

object code—Code generated by a compiler that contains machine-language instructions that must be linked and loaded before execution.

object-oriented programming (OOP)—Style of programming that allows programmers to quickly build complex software systems by reusing components called objects, built from "blueprints" called classes.

on-board device—Device that is physically connected to a computer's mainboard.

Open DataBase Connectivity (ODBC)—Protocol for middleware that permits applications to access a variety of databases that use different interfaces. The ODBC driver handles connections to the database and retrieves information requested by applications. This frees the application programmer from writing code to specify database-specific commands.

optimizer—Part of the compiler that attempts to improve the execution efficiency and reduce the space requirement of a program.

parallel port—Interface to a parallel I/O device such as a printer.

parser—Part of the compiler that receives a stream of tokens from the lexical analyzer and groups the tokens so they can be processed by the intermediate code generator.

Pascal—Structured programming language developed in 1971 by Wirth that became popular for teaching introductory programming courses.

Peripheral Components Interconnect (PCI) bus—Popular bus used to connect peripheral devices, such as network and sound cards, to the rest of the system. PCI provides a 32-bit or 64-bit bus interface and supports transfer rates of up to 533MB per second.

persistent storage—See secondary storage.

physical address—See real address.

physical memory—See main memory.

plug-and-play—Technology that facilitates driver installation and hardware configuration performed by the operating system.

polling—Technique to discover hardware status by repeatedly testing each device. Polling can be implemented in lieu of interrupts but typically reduces performance due to increased overhead.

port—Bus that connects two devices.

principle of least privilege—Resource access policy that states that a user should only be granted the amount of privilege and access that the user needs to accomplish its designated task.

printed circuit board (PCB)—Piece of hardware that provides electrical connections to devices that can be placed at various locations throughout the board.

privileged instruction—Instruction that can be executed only from kernel mode. Privileged instructions perform operations that access protected hardware and software resources (e.g., switching the processor between processes or issuing a command to a hard disk).

problem state—See user mode.

procedural programming language—Programming language that is based on functions rather than objects.

processor—Hardware component that executes machine-language instructions and enforces protection for system resources such as main memory.

programmed I/O (PIO)—Implementation of I/O for devices that do not support interrupts in which the transfer of every word from memory must be supervised by the processor.

property (of an object)—Part of an object that stores data about the object.

quad pumping—Technique for increasing processor performance by performing four memory transfers per clock cycle.

random access memory (RAM)—Memory whose contents can be accessed in any order.

real address—Address in main memory.

real memory—See main memory.

register—High-speed memory located on a processor that holds data for immediate use by the processor.

relative address—Address that is specified based on its location in relation to the beginning of a module.

relocatable loading—Method of loading that translates relative addresses in a load module to absolute addresses based on the location of a requested block of memory.

relocating—Process of adjusting the addresses of program code and data.

scanner—See lexical analyzer.

secondary storage—Memory that typically stores large quantities of data persistently. Secondary storage is one level lower than main memory in the memory hierarchy. After a computer is powered on, information is shuttled between secondary storage and main memory so that program instructions and data can be accessed by a processor. Hard disks are the most common form of secondary storage.

serial port—Interface to a device that transfers one bit at a time (e.g, keyboards and mice).

small computer systems interface (SCSI)—Interface designed to support multiple devices and high-speed connections. The SCSI interface supports a large number of devices than the less inexpensive IDE interface and is popular in Apple systems and computers containing large numbers of peripheral devices.

shared library—Collection of functions shared between several programs.

source code—Program code typically written in a high-level language or assembly language that must be compiled or interpreted before it can be understood by a computer.

spool (simultaneous peripheral operations online)—Method of I/O in which processes write data to secondary storage where it is buffered before being transferred to a low-speed device.

static RAM (SRAM)—RAM that does not need to be refreshed and will hold data as long as it receives power.

structured programming—Disciplined approach to creating programs that are clear, correct and easy to modify.

supervisor state—See kernel mode.

symbol resolution—Procedure performed by a linker that matches external references in one module to external names in another.

symbol table—Part of an object module that lists an entry for each external name and each external reference found in the module.

syntax analyzer—See parser.

system call—Procedure call that requests a service from an operating system. When a process issues a system call, the processor execution mode changes from user mode to kernel mode to execute operating system instructions that respond to the call.

systems programming—Development of software to manage a system's devices and applications.

trace—Tiny electrically conducting line that forms part of a bus.

transistor—Miniature switch that either allows or prevents current from passing to enable processors to perform operations on bits.

time-of-day clock—Clock that measures time as perceived outside of a computer system, typically accurate to thousandths or millionths of a second.

token—Characters in a program, separated by the lexical analyzer, that generally represent keywords, identifiers, operators or punctuation.

universal serial bus (USB)—Serial bus interface that transfers data up to 480Mbits per second, can supply power to its devices and supports hot swappable devices.

user mode—Mode of operation that does not allow processes to directly access system resources.

user state—See user mode.

volatile storage—Storage medium that loses data in the absence of power.

Windows API—Microsoft's interface for applications that execute in a Windows environment. The API enables programmers to request operating system services, which free the application programmer from writing the code to perform these operations and enables the operating system to protect its resources.

Write-Once, Read-Many (WORM) medium—Storage medium that can be modified only once, but whose contents can be accessed repeatedly.

Exercises

2.1 Distinguish among hardware, software and firmware.

2.2 Some hardware devices follow.

    i. mainboard

    ii. processor

    iii. bus

    iv. memory

    v. hard disk

    vi. peripheral device

    vii. tertiary storage device

    viii. register

    ix. cache

Indicate which of these devices is best defined by each of the following. (Some items can have more than one answer.)

    a. executes program instructions

    b. not required for a computer to execute program instructions.

    c. volatile storage medium.

    d. the PCB that connects a system's processors to memory, secondary storage and peripheral devices.

    e. fastest memory in a computer system

    f. set of traces that transmit data between hardware devices

    g. fast memory that improves application performance.

    h. lowest level of memory in the memory hierarchy that a processor can reference directly.

2.3 Processor speeds have doubled roughly every 18 months. Has overall computer performance doubled at the same rate? Why or why not?

2.4 Sort the following list from fastest and most expensive memory to cheapest and least expensive memory: secondary storage, registers, main memory, tertiary storage, L2 cache, L1 cache. Why do systems contain several data stores of different size and speed? What is the motivation behind caching?

2.5 What are some costs and benefits of using nonvolatile RAM in all caches and main memory?

2.6 Why is it important to support legacy architectures?

2.7 Relate the principle of least privilege to the concepts of user mode, kernel mode and privileged instructions.

2.8 Describe several techniques for implementing memory protection.

2.9 Double buffering is a technique that allows an I/O channel and a processor to operate in parallel. On double-buffered input, for example, while a processor consumes one set of data in one buffer, the channel reads the next set of data into the other buffer so that the data will (hopefully) be ready for the processor. Explain in detail how a triple-buffering scheme might operate. In what circumstances would triple buffering be effective?

2.10 Describe two different techniques for handling the communications between a processor and devices.

2.11 Explain how DMA improves system performance. and cycle stealing.

2.12 Why is it appropriate for channel controllers to steal cycles from processors when accessing memory?

2.13 Explain the notion of spooling and why it is useful. How, do you suppose, does an input spooling system designed to read punched cards from a card reader operate?

2.14 Consider the following types of programming languages:

    i. machine language

    ii. assembly language

    iii. high-level language

    iv. object-oriented programming language

    v. structured programming language

Indicate which of these categories is best defined by each of the following. (Some items can have more than one answer.)

    a. focuses on manipulating things (nouns)

    b. requires a translator programmer to convert the code into something a specific processor can understand

  c. written using 1's and 0's

  d. defines a disciplined approach to software development and focuses on actions (verbs).

  e. specifies basic computer operations using English-like abbreviations for instructions

  f. Java and C++

  g. Fortran and Pascal

  h. enables programmers to write code using everyday English words and mathematical notation

2.15 Briefly describe how a program written in a high-level language is prepared for execution.

2.16 Compare and contrast absolute loaders with relocating loaders. Give several motivations for the concept of relocatable loading.

2.17 What is microprogramming? Why is the term "firmware" appropriate for describing microcode that is part of a hardware device?

Suggested Projects

2.18 Prepare a research paper on MRAM, a form of nonvolatile RAM (see `www.research.ibm.com/resources/news/20030610_mram.shtml`).

2.19 Prepare a research paper on MEMS (MicroElectroMechanical System) storage, a secondary storage device intended to improve access times over hard disks (see `www.pdl.cmu.edu/MEMS/`).

2.20 Research the difference between the SCSI interface and the IDE interface for secondary storage devices. Why has IDE become the more popular choice?

2.21 Prepare a research paper on the design and implementation of Microsoft's .NET framework.

Recommended Reading

Several textbooks describe computer organization and architecture. Hennessy and Patterson's text is an excellent summary of computer architecture.[68] Blaauw and Brooks, Jr. also discuss computer architecture, providing detailed coverage of low-level mechanisms in computers.[69] For discussion of the most recent hardware technologies, however, only online journals can truly keep pace—see the Web Resources section.

    An excellent essay regarding software engineering in the development of the OS/360 is *The Mythical Man-Month*, by Frederick P. Brooks.[70] Steve Maguire's *Debugging the Development Process* is a discussion of how to manage project teams, drawing from his managerial experience at Microsoft.[71] *Code Complete* by Steve McConnell is a valuable resource on good programming practices and software design.[72]

    A review of compiler design and techniques can be found in a text by Aho et. al.[73] For those interested in modern compiler techniques, see the text by Grune et al.[74] Levine's text is an excellent resource for students interested in concerns and techniques regarding linking and loading an application.[75] The bibliography for this chapter is located on our Web site at `www.deitel.com/books/os3e/Bibliography.pdf`.

Works Cited

1. Wheeler, D. A., "More Than a Gigabuck: Estimating GNU/Linux's Size," June 30, 2001, updated July 29, 2002, Ver. 1.07, <`www.dwheeler.com/sloc/`>.

2. "Intel Executive Bio—Gordon E. Moore," *Intel Corporation*, October 30, 2003, <`www.intel.com/pressroom/kits/bios/moore.htm`>.

3. "Intel Executive Bio—Gordon E. Moore," *Intel Corporation*, October 30, 2003, <`www.intel.com/pressroom/kits/bios/moore.htm`>.

4. Moore, G., "Cramming More Components onto Integrated Circuits," *Electronics*, Vol. 38, No. 8, April 19, 1965.

5. "Expanding Moore's Law: The Exponential Opportunity," *Intel Corporation*, updated Fall 2002, 2002.

6. Gilheany, S., "Evolution of Intel Microprocessors: 1971 to 2007," Berghell Associates, March 28, 2002, <`www.berghell.com/whitepapers/Evolution%20of%20Intel%20Microprocessors%201971%20to%202007.pdf`>.

7. "Processors," *PCTechGuide*, <www.pctechguide.com/02procs.htm>.

8. "Registers," *PCGuide*, <www.pcguide.com/ref/cpu/arch/int/compRegisters-c.html>.

9. *PowerPC Microprocessor Family: Programming Environments Manual for 64- and 32-Bit Microprocessors*, Ver. 2.0, *IBM*, June 10, 2003.

10. "Clock Signals, Cycle Time and Frequency," *PCGuide.com*, April 17, 2001, <www.pcguide.com/intro/fun/clock.htm>.

11. "IA-32 Intel Architecture Software Developer's Manual," *System Programmer's Guide*, Vol. 1, 2002, p. 41.

12. De Gelas, J., "Ace's Guide to Memory Technology," *Ace's Hardware*, July 13, 2000, <www.aceshardware.com/Spades/read.php?article_id=5000172>.

13. "Hard Disk Drives," *PCGuide*, April 17, 2001, <www.pcguide.com/ref/hdd/>.

14. "System Bus Functions and Features," *PCGuide*, <www.pcguide.com/ref/mbsys/buses/func.htm>.

15. Gifford, D., and A. Spector, "Case Study: IBM's System/360-370 Architecture," *Communications of the ACM*, Vol. 30, No. 4, April 1987, pp. 291–307.

16. "PCI Express," *PCI-SIG*, <www.pcisig.com/specifications/pciexpress/>.

17. Scott, T. A., "Illustrating Programmed and Interrupt Driven I/O," *Proceedings of the Seventh Annual CCSC Midwestern Conference on Small Colleges*, October 2000, pp. 230–238.

18. Hennessy, J., and D. Patterson, *Computer Organization and Design*, San Francisco: Morgan Kaufmann Publishers, 1998, pp. 680–681.

19. "DMA Channel Function and Operation," *PCGuide.com*, <www.pcguide.com/ref/mbsys/res/dma/func.htm>.

20. "Peripheral Device," *Webopedia*, December 14, 2001, <www.webopedia.com/TERM/P/peripheral_device.html>.

21. "Serial Port," *CNET Glossary*, <www.cnet.com/Resources/Info/Glossary/Terms/serialport.html>.

22. "Serial Port," *CNET Glossary*, <www.cnet.com/Resources/Info/Glossary/Terms/serialport.html>.

23. "USB," *Computer Peripherals*, <peripherals.about.com/library/glossary/bldefusb.htm>.

24. Liu, P., and D. Thompson, "IEEE 1394: Changing the Way We Do Multimedia Communications," *IEEE Multimedia*, April 2000, <www.computer.org/multimedia/articles/firewire.htm>.

25. "IDE/ATA vs. SCSI: Interface Drive Comparison," *PCGuide.com*, <www.pcguide.com/ref/hdd/if/comp.htm>.

26. "SCSI FAQ," <www.faqs.org/faqs/scsi-faq/part1/>.

27. <www.scsita.org/aboutscsi/termsTermin.html>.

28. Gifford, D., and A. Spector, "Case Study: IBM's System/360-370 Architecture," *Communications of the ACM*, Vol. 30, No. 4, April 1987, pp. 291-307.

29. Denning, P., "Virtual Memory," *ACM Computing Surveys*, Vol. 2, No. 3, September 1970, pp. 153–189.

30. "Intel Developer Forum Day 3—More from the Tech Showcase," *Anandtech.com*, February 20, 2003, <www.anandtech.com/showdoc.html?i=1791&p=2>.

31. "Plug and Play Technology", *Microsoft Windows Platform Development*, March 21, 2003, <www.microsoft.com/hwdev/tech/pnp/default.asp>.

32. "Plug and Play for Windows 2000 and Windows XP," *Microsoft Windows Platform Development*, March 21, 2003, <www.microsoft.com/hwdev/tech/PnP/PnPNT5_2.asp>.

33. Smith, A., "Cache Memories," *ACM Computing Surveys*, Vol. 14, No. 3, September 1982, pp. 473–530.

34. "Buffer," *Data Recovery Glossary*, <www.datarecovery-group.com/glossary/buffer.html>.

35. "Buffer," *Webopedia*, September 1, 1997, <www.webopedia.com/TERM/B/buffer.html>.

36. "Definition: Buffer," *FS-1037*, August 23, 1996, <www.its.bldrdoc.gov/fs-1037/dir-005/_0739.htm>.

37. "Spooling," S*un Product Documentation: Glossary, Solaris 2.4 System Administrator AnswerBook*, <docs.sun.com/db/doc/801-6628/6i108opae?a=view>.

38. Glass, R. L., "An Elementary Discussion of Compiler/Interpreter Writing," *ACM Computing Surveys (CSUR)*, Vol. 1, No. 1, January 1969.

39. "Interpreter (Computer Software)," *Wikipedia, The Free Encyclopedia*, modified February 19, 2003, <www.wikipedia.org/wiki/Interpreter_(computer_software)>.

40. Presser, L., and J. White, "Linkers and Loaders," *ACM Computer Surveys*, Vol. 4, No. 3, September 1972, pp. 149–151.

41. "Object Code," April 7, 2001, <whatis.techtarget.com/definition/0,,sid9_gci539287,00.html>.

42. Aho, A., and J. Ullman, *Principles of Compiler Design*, Reading, MA: Addison-Wesley, 1977, pp. 6–7.

43. "Compiler," *IBM Reference/Glossary*, <www-1.ibm.com/ibm/history/reference/glossary_c.html>.

44. Presser, L., and J. White, "Linkers and Loaders," *ACM Computer Surveys*, Vol. 4, No. 3, September 1972, p. 153.

45. Levine, J., *Linkers and Loaders*, San Francisco: Morgan Kaufman Publishers, 2000, p. 5.

46. Presser, L., and J. White, "Linkers and Loaders," *ACM Computer Surveys*, Vol. 4, No. 3, September 1972, p. 164.

47. Levine, J., *Linkers and Loaders*, San Francisco: Morgan Kaufman Publishers, 2000, p. 6.

48. Carnegie-Mellon University, "The Mach Project Home Page," February 21, 1997, <www-2.cs.cmu.edu/afs/cs/project/mach/public/www/mach.html>.

49. Microsoft Corporation, "Microsoft–PressPass Rick Rashid Biography," 2003, <www.microsoft.com/presspass/exec/rick/default.asp>.

50. Westmacott, I., "The UNIX vs. NT Myth," July 1997, <webserver.cpg.com/wa/2.6>.

51. Carnegie-Mellon University, "The Mach Project Home Page," February 21, 1997, <www-2.cs.cmu.edu/afs/cs/project/mach/public/www/mach.html>.

52. Apple Computer, Inc., "Mac OS X Technologies—Darwin," 2003, <www.apple.com/macosx/technologies/darwin.html>.

53. Free Software Foundation, "GNU Mach," May 26, 2003, <www.gnu.org/software/hurd/gnumach.html>.

54. Rashid, R., et al., "Mach: A System Software Kernel," *Proceedings of the 1989 IEEE International Conference, COMPCON 89*, February 1989, <ftp://ftp.cs.cmu.edu/project/mach/doc/published/syskernel.ps>.

55. Coulouris, G.; J. Dollimore; and T Kindberg, "UNIX Emulation in Mach and Chorus," *Distributed Systems: Concepts and Design*, Addison-Wesley, 1994, pp. 597-584, <www.cdk3.net/oss/Ed2/UNIXEmulation.pdf>.

56. Rashid, R., et al., "Mach: A System Software Kernel," *Proceedings of the 1989 IEEE International Conference, COMPCON 89*, February 1989, <ftp://ftp.cs.cmu.edu/project/mach/doc/published/syskernel.ps>.

57. Coulouris, G.; J. Dollimore; and T Kindberg, "UNIX Emulation in Mach and Chorus," *Distributed Systems: Concepts and Design*, Addison-Wesley, 1994, pp. 597-584, <www.cdk3.net/oss/Ed2/UNIXEmulation.pdf>.

58. Rashid, R., et al., "Mach: A System Software Kernel," *Proceedings of the 1989 IEEE International Conference, COMPCON 89*, February 1989, <ftp://ftp.cs.cmu.edu/project/mach/doc/published/syskernel.ps>.

59. Rashid, R., et al., "Mach: A System Software Kernel," *Proceedings of the 1989 IEEE International Conference, COMPCON 89*, February 1989, <ftp://ftp.cs.cmu.edu/project/mach/doc/published/syskernel.ps>.

60. Presser, L., and J. White, "Linkers and Loaders," *ACM Computer Surveys*, Vol. 4, No. 3, September 1972, p. 151.

61. Presser, L., and J. White, "Linkers and Loaders," *ACM Computer Surveys*, Vol. 4, No. 3, September 1972, p. 150.

62. Hennessy, J., and D. Patterson, *Computer Organization and Design*, San Francisco: Morgan Kaufmann Publishers, 1998, pp. 399–400.

63. Rauscher, T., and P. Adams, "Microprogramming: A Tutorial and Survey of Recent Developments," *IEEE Transactions on Computers*, Vol. C-29, No. 1, January 1980, pp. 2–20.

64. Hennessy, J., and D. Patterson, *Computer Organization and Design*, San Francisco: Morgan Kaufmann Publishers, 1998, pp. 424–425.

65. Wilkes, M., "The Best Way to Design an Automatic Calculating Machine," *Report of the Machine University Computer Inaugural Conference*, Electrical Engineering Department of Manchester University, Manchester, England, July 1951, pp. 16–18.

66. Hennessy, J., and D. Patterson, *Computer Organization and Design*, San Francisco: Morgan Kaufmann Publishers, 1998, pp. 424–425.

67. "Firmware," *PCGuide*, April 17, 2001, <www.pcguide.com/ref/hdd/op/logicFirmware-c.html>.

68. Hennessy, J., and D. Patterson, *Computer Organization and Design*, San Francisco: Morgan Kaufmann Publishers, 1998.

69. Blaauw, G., and F. Brooks, Jr., *Computer Architecture*, Reading, MA: Addison-Wesley, 1997.

70. Brooks, F. P., *The Mythical Man-Month*, Reading, MA: Addison-Wesley, 1995.

71. Maguire, S., *Debugging the Development Process: Practical Strategies for Staying Focused, Hitting Ship Dates, and Building Solid Teams*, Microsoft Press, 1994.

72. McConnell, S., *Code Complete*, Microsoft Press, 1993.

73. Aho, A.; R. Sethi; and J. Ullman, *Compilers: Principles, Techniques, and Tools*, Reading, MA: Addison-Wesley, 1986.

74. Grune, D.; H. Bal; C. Jacobs; and K. Langendoen, *Modern Compiler Design*, New York: John Wiley, 2000.

75. Levine, J., *Linkers and Loaders*, San Francisco: Morgan Kaufman Publishers, 2000.

Processes and Threads

It was surprising that Nature had gone tranquilly on with her golden process in the midst of so much devilment.
—Stephen Crane—

Part 2

To realize maximum performance and meet user needs, operating systems perform many activities simultaneously, using the abstractions of process and thread to keep track of the parallel activities. In the next six chapters, you will study how operating systems manage processes and threads to ensure that they coexist peacefully, cooperate smoothly and do not collide with one another as they go about their business. You will learn how to write your own multithreaded Java applications. Sometimes processes and threads need to wait when there is contention over resources—you will study indefinite postponement and deadlock—problems that can ensue if waiting entities are not managed properly. To keep processes and threads progressing efficiently, you will learn how operating systems schedule their most valuable hardware resource: processors.

There is nothing more requisite in business than dispatch.
—Joseph Addison—

Learn to labor and to wait.

—Henry Wadsworth Longfellow—

Many shall run to and fro, and knowledge shall be increased.

—Daniel 12:2—

You will wake, and remember, and understand.

—Robert Browning—

It was surprising that Nature had gone tranquilly on with her golden process in the midst of so much devilment.

—Stephen Crane—

Chapter 3

Process Concepts

Objectives

After reading this chapter, you should understand:

- *the concept of a process.*
- *the process life cycle.*
- *process states and state transitions.*
- *process control blocks (PCBs)/process descriptors.*
- *how processors transition between processes via context switching.*
- *how interrupts enable hardware to communicate with software.*
- *how processes converse with one another via interprocess communication (IPC).*
- *UNIX processes.*

Chapter Outline

3.1 Introduction

Many systems in nature have the ability to perform multiple actions at the same time. For example, the human body performs a great variety of operations in parallel—or, as we will say, **concurrently**. Respiration, blood circulation, thinking, walking and digestion, for example, can occur concurrently, as can the senses—sight, touch, smell, taste and hearing. Computers, too, perform operations concurrently. It is common for desktop computers to be compiling a program, sending a file to a printer, rendering a Web page, playing a digital video clip and receiving e-mail concurrently (see the Operating Systems Thinking feature, Customers Ultimately Want Applications).

In this chapter we formally introduce the notion of a **process**, which is central to understanding how today's computer systems perform and keep track of many simultaneous activities. We introduce some of the more popular definitions of process. We present the concept of discrete **process states** and discuss how and why processes make transitions between these states. We also discuss various operations that operating systems perform to service processes, such as creating, destroying, suspending, resuming and waking up processes.

3.1.1 Definition of Process

The term "process" in the context of operating systems was first used by and the designers of the Multics system in the 1960s (see the Mini Case Study, CTSS and Multics and the Biographical Note, Fernando J. Corbató).[1] Since that time, process, used somewhat interchangeably with **task**, has been given many definitions, such as: a program in execution, an asynchronous activity, the "animated spirit" of a procedure, the "locus of control" of a procedure in execution, that which is manifested by

Operating Systems Thinking

Customers Ultimately Want Applications

Ultimately, computers exist to run useful applications. Operating systems designers can lose sight of this because they tend to be concerned with complex technical issues of operating systems architecture and engineering. But they cannot operate in a void; they must know their user community; the kinds of applications those users will be running and what results the users really want from those applications. Hardware stores sell many tools to help you perform household chores. The tool designer needs to be aware that few people are interested in simply purchasing tools; rather they ultimately buy the tools for the tasks they perform. Customers do not really want saws, hammers and drills—they want cuts, nails in wood and holes.

the existence of a data structure called a "process descriptor" or a "process control block" in the operating system, that entity to which processors are assigned and the "dispatchable" unit. A program is to a process as sheet music is to a symphony orchestra playing the music.

Two key concepts are presented by these definitions. First, a process is an entity. Each process has its own address space, which typically consists of a **text region**, **data region** and **stack region**. The text region stores the code that the processor executes. The data region stores variables and dynamically allocated memory that the process

Mini Case Study

CTSS and Multics

In the early 1960s, a team of programmers at MIT's Project MAC, led by Professor Fernando Corbató, developed the Compatible Time-Sharing System (CTSS) which allowed users to command the computing power of an IBM 7090 (which eventually became an IBM 7094) with typewriterlike terminals.[2, 3] CTSS ran a conventional batch stream to keep the computer working while giving fast responses to interactive users editing and debugging programs. The computing capabilities provided by CTSS resembled those provided to personal computer users today—namely, a highly interactive environment in which the computer gave rapid responses to large numbers of relatively trivial requests.

In 1965 the same MIT group, in cooperation with Bell Labs and GE, began working on the Multics

(Multiplexed Information and Computing Service) operating system, the successor to CTSS. Multics was a large and complex system; the designers envisioned a general-purpose computer utility that could be "all things to all people." Although it did not achieve commercial success, it was used by various research centers until the last system was shut down in 2000.[4]

A variety of Multics features influenced the development of future operating systems, including UNIX, TSS/360, TENEX and TOPS-20.[5] Multics used a combination of segmentation and paging for its virtual memory system, with paging controlled only by the operating system, while segments were manipulated by user programs as well.[6] It was one of the first operating systems to be written in a high-level systems-pro-

gramming language, IBM's PL/I.[7, 8] Its designers coined the term "process" as it is currently used in operating systems. Multics was built for security. It included a discretionary access mechanism called **ACL** (Access Control List), which was a list of permissions on a memory segment which would look familiar to UNIX users. Later versions included a mandatory access control, **AIM** (Access Isolation Mechanism), an enhancement to ACL where every user and object was assigned a security classification, which helped Multics become the first operating system to get a B2 security rating from the U.S. government.[9, 10, 11] In 1976 the first commercial relational database system was written, the **Multics Relational Data Store**.[12]

uses during execution. The stack region stores instructions and local variables for active procedure calls. The contents of the stack grow as a process issues nested procedure calls and shrink as called procedures return.[13] Second, a process is a "program in execution." A program is an inanimate entity; only when a processor "breathes life" into a program does it become the active entity we call a process.

Self Review

1. Why is a process's address space divided into multiple regions?
2. (T/F) The terms "process" and "program" are synonymous.

Ans: **1)** Each region of an address space typically contains information that is accessed in a similar way. For example, most processes read and execute instructions, but do not modify their instructions. Processes read from and write to the stack, but in last-in-first-out order. Processes read and write data in any order. Separating a process's address space into different regions enables the operating system to enforce such access rules. **2)** False. A process is a program in execution; a program is an inanimate entity.

3.2 Process States: Life Cycle of a Process

The operating system must ensure that each process receives a sufficient amount of processor time. For any system, there can be only as many truly concurrently executing processes as there are processors. Normally, there are many more processes

Biographical Note

Fernando J. Corbató

Fernando Jose Corbató received his Ph.D. in Physics from MIT in 1956. Corbató was a professor at MIT from 1965 to 1996, retiring as a Professor Emeritus in the Department of Electrical Engineering and Computer Science.[14] He was a founding member of MIT's Project MAC and led the development of the CTSS and Multics project.[15, 16] He coauthored technical papers on Multics and on the project management issues of that large cooperation among MIT Project MAC, General Electric, and Bell Labs.

Corbató received the 1990 Turing Award for his work on CTSS and Multics.[17] His award lecture was "On Building Systems That Will Fail," in which he describes how the intrinsic complexity of large and innovative projects will always lead to mistakes, drawing largely from his Multics experiences. In his lecture he advised developers to assume that any given error will occur and that they should therefore plan how to handle it.[18]

than processors in a system. Thus, at any given time, some processes can execute and some cannot.

During its lifetime, a process moves through a series of discrete **process states**. Various events can cause a process to change state. A process is said to be *running* (i.e., in the *running* **state**) if it is executing on a processor. A process is said to be *ready* (i.e., in the *ready* **state**) if it could execute on a processor if one were available. A process is said to be *blocked* (i.e., in the *blocked* **state**) if it is waiting for some event to happen (such as an **I/O completion event,** for example) before it can proceed. There are other process states, but for now we will concentrate on these three.

For simplicity, let us consider a uniprocessor system, although the extension to multiprocessing (see Chapter 15, Multiprocessor Management) is not difficult. In a uniprocessor system only one process may be *running* at a time, but several may be *ready* and several *blocked*. The operating system maintains a **ready list** of *ready* processes and a **blocked list** of *blocked* processes. The ready list is maintained in priority order, so that the next process to receive a processor is the first one in the list (i.e., the process with the highest priority). The blocked list is typically unordered—processes do not become **unblocked** (i.e., *ready*) in priority order; rather, they unblock in the order in which the events they are waiting for occur. As we will see later, there are situations in which several processes may block awaiting the same event; in these cases it is common to prioritize the waiting processes.

Self Review

1. (T/F) At any given time, only one process can be executing instructions on a computer.
2. A process enters the *blocked* state when it is waiting for an event to occur. Name several events that might cause a process to enter the *blocked* state.

Ans: **1)** False. On a multiprocessor computer, there can be as many processes executing instructions as there are processors. **2)** A process may enter the blocked state if it issues a request for data located on a high-latency device such as a hard disk or requests a resource that is allocated to another process and is currently unavailable (e.g., a printer). A process may also block until an event occurs, such as a user pressing a key or moving a mouse.

3.3 Process Management

As the operating system interleaves the execution of its processes, it must carefully manage them to ensure that no errors occur as the processes are interrupted and resumed. Processes should be able to communicate with the operating system to perform simple tasks such as starting a new process or signaling the end of process execution. In this section, we discuss how operating systems provide certain fundamental services to processes—these include creating processes, destroying processes, suspending processes, resuming processes, changing a process's priority, blocking processes, waking up processes, dispatching processes, enabling processes to interact via interprocess communication (IPC) and more. We also discuss how operating systems manage process resources to allow multiple processes to actively contend for processor time at once.

3.3.1 *Process States and State Transitions*

When a user runs a program, processes are created and inserted into the ready list. A process moves toward the head of the list as other processes complete their turns using a processor. When a process reaches the head of the list, and when a processor becomes available, that process is given a processor and is said to make a **state transition** from the *ready* state to the *running* state (Fig. 3.1). The act of assigning a processor to the first process on the ready list is called **dispatching** and is performed by a system entity called the **dispatcher**. Processes that are in the *ready* or *running* states are said to be awake, because they are actively contending for processor time. The operating system manages state transitions to best serve processes in the system. To prevent any one process from monopolizing the system, either accidentally or maliciously, the operating system sets a hardware **interrupting clock** (also called an **interval timer**) to allow a process to run for a specific time interval or **quantum**. If the process does not voluntarily yield the processor before the time interval expires, the interrupting clock generates an interrupt, causing the operating system to gain control of the processor (see Section 3.4, Interrupts). The operating system then changes the state of the previously *running* process to *ready* and dispatches the first process on the ready list, changing its state from *ready* to *running*. If a *running* process initiates an input/output operation before its quantum expires, and therefore must wait for the I/O operation to complete before it can use a processor again, the *running* process voluntarily relinquishes the processor. In this case, the process

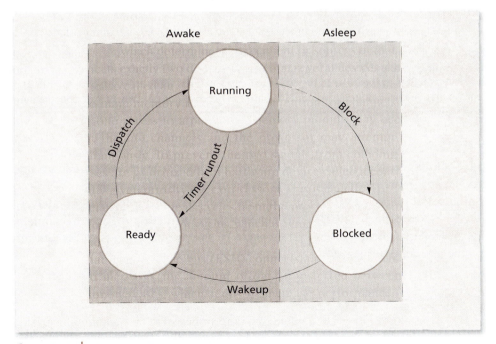

Figure 3.1 | *Process state transitions.*

is said to **block** itself, pending the completion of the I/O operation. Processes in the *blocked* state are said to be asleep, because they cannot execute even if a processor becomes available. The only other allowable state transition in our three-state model occurs when an I/O operation (or some other event the process is waiting for) completes. In this case, the operating system transitions the process from the *blocked* to the *ready* state.

We have defined four possible state transitions. When a process is dispatched, it transitions from *ready* to *running*. When a process's quantum expires, it transitions from *running* to *ready*. When a process blocks, it transitions from *running* to *blocked*. Finally, when a process wakes up because of the completion of some event it is awaiting, it transitions from *blocked* to *ready*. Note that the only state transition initiated by the user process itself is block—the other three transitions are initiated by the operating system.

In this section, we have assumed that the operating system assigns each process a quantum. Some early operating systems that ran on processors without interrupting clocks employed **cooperative multitasking**, meaning that each process must voluntarily yield the processor on which it is running before another process can execute. Cooperative multitasking is rarely used in today's systems, however, because it allows processes to accidentally or maliciously monopolize a processor (e.g., by entering an infinite loop or simply refusing to yield the processor in a timely fashion).

Self Review

1. How does the operating system prevent a process from monopolizing a processor?
2. What is the difference between processes that are awake and those that are asleep?

Ans: **1)** An interrupting clock generates an interrupt after a specified time quantum, and the operating system dispatches another process to execute. The interrupted process will run again when it gets to the head of the ready list and a processor again becomes available. **2)** A process that is awake is in active contention for a processor; a process that is asleep cannot use a processor even if one becomes available.

3.3.2 Process Control Blocks (PCBs)/Process Descriptors

The operating system typically performs several operations when it creates a process. First, it must be able to identify each process; therefore, it assigns a **process identification number (PID)** to the process. Next, the operating system creates a **process control block (PCB)**, also called a **process descriptor**, which maintains information that the operating system needs to manage the process. PCBs typically include information such as:

- PID
- process state (e.g., *running*, *ready* or *blocked*)
- **program counter** (i.e., a value that determines which instruction the processor should execute next)
- scheduling priority

- credentials (i.e., data that determines the resources this process can access)
- a pointer to the process's **parent process** (i.e., the process that created this process)
- pointers to the process's **child processes** (i.e., processes created by this process) if any
- pointers to locate the process's data and instructions in memory
- pointers to allocated resources (such as files).

The PCB also stores the register contents, called the **execution context**, of the processor on which the process was last running when it transitioned out of the *running* state. The execution context of a process is architecture specific but typically includes the contents of general-purpose registers (which contain process data that the processor can directly access) in addition to process management registers, such as registers that store pointers to a process's address space. This enables the operating system to restore a process's execution context when the process returns to the *running* state.

When a process transitions from one state to another, the operating system must update information in the process's PCB. The operating system typically maintains pointers to each process's PCB in a systemwide or per-user **process table** so that it can access the PCB quickly (Fig. 3.2). The process table is one of many operating system data structures we discuss in this text (see the Operating Systems Thinking feature, Data Structures in Operating Systems). When a process is termi-

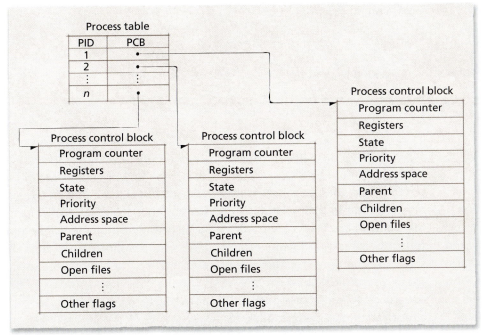

Figure 3.2 | *Process table and process control blocks.*

nated (either voluntarily or by the operating system), the operating system frees the process's memory and other resources, removes the process from the process table and makes its memory and other resources available to other processes. We discuss other process manipulation functions momentarily.[19]

Self Review

1. What is the purpose of the process table?
2. (T/F) The structure of a PCB is dependent on the operating system implementation.

Ans: **1)** The process table enables the operating system to locate each process's PCB. **2)** True.

3.3.3 Process Operations

Operating systems must be able to perform certain process operations, including:

- create a process
- destroy a process
- suspend a process
- resume a process
- change a process's priority
- block a process
- wake up a process
- dispatch a process
- enable a process to communicate with another process (this is called inter-process communication).

Operating Systems Thinking

Data Structures in Operating Systems

Computer science students generally study data structures, both those on the main topic of a full course and as portions of many upper-level courses, such as compilers, databases, networking and operating systems. Data structures are used abundantly in operating systems. Queues are used wherever entities need to wait—processes waiting for a processor, I/O requests waiting for devices to become available, processes waiting for access to their critical sections and so on. Stacks are used for supporting the function call return mechanism. Trees are used to represent file system directory structures, to keep track of the allocation of disk space to files, to build hierarchical page directory structures in support of virtual address translation, and so on. Graphs are used when studying networking arrangements, deadlock resource allocation graphs, and the like. Hash tables are used to access PCBs quickly (using a PID as the key).

A process may **spawn** a new process. If it does, the creating process is called the **parent process** and the created process is called the **child process**. Each child process is created by exactly one parent process. Such creation yields a **hierarchical process structure** similar to Fig. 3.3, in which each child has only one parent (e.g., A is the one parent of C; H is the one parent of I), but each parent may have many children (e.g., B, C, and D are the children of A; F and G are the children of C).In UNIX-based systems, such as Linux, many processes are spawned from the *init* process, which is created when the kernel loads (Fig. 3.4). In Linux, such processes include *kswapd*, *xfs* and *khubd*—these processes perform memory, file system and device management operations, respectively. Many of these processes are discussed further in Chapter 20, Case Study: Linux. The *login* process authenticates users to the operating system. This is typically accomplished by requiring a user to enter a valid username and corresponding password. We discuss other means of authentication in Chapter 19, Security. Once the *login* process authenticates the user, it spawns a shell, such as *bash* (Bourne-*again sh*ell), that allows the user to interact with the operating system (Fig. 3.4). The user may then issue commands to the shell to execute programs such as *vi* (a text editor) and *finger* (a utility that displays user information). Destroying a process involves obliterating it from the system. Its memory and other resources are returned to the system, it is purged from any system lists or tables and its process control block is erased, i.e., the PCB's memory space is made available to other processes in the system. Destruction of a process is more complicated when the process has spawned other processes. In some operating systems, each spawned process is destroyed automatically when its parent is destroyed; in others, spawned processes proceed independently of their parents, and the destruction of a parent has no effect on its children.

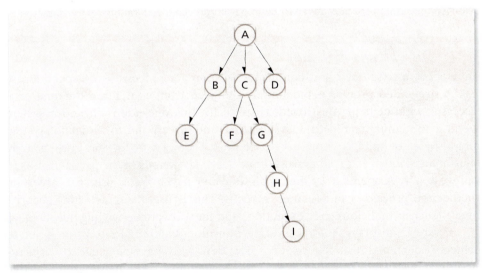

Figure 3.3 | *Process creation hierarchy.*

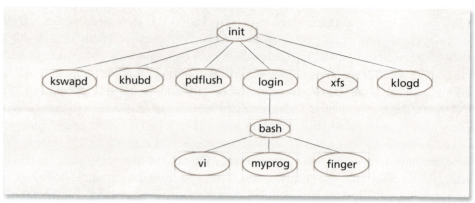

Figure 3.4 | *Process hierarchy in Linux.*

Changing the priority of a process normally involves modifying the priority value in the process's control block. Depending on how the operating system implements process scheduling, it may need to place a pointer to the PCB in a different priority queue (see Chapter 8, Processor Scheduling). The other operations listed in this section are explained in subsequent sections.

Self Review

1. (T/F) A process may have zero parent processes.
2. Why is it advantageous to create a hierarchy of processes as opposed to a linked list?

Ans: **1)** True. The first process that is created, often called *init* in UNIX systems, does not have a parent. Also, in some systems, when a parent process is destroyed, its children proceed independently without their parent. **2)** A hierarchy of processes allows the operating system to track parent/child relationships between processes. This simplifies operations such as locating all the child processes of a particular parent process when that parent terminates.

3.3.4 Suspend and Resume

Many operating systems allow administrators, users or processes to suspend a process. A **suspended** process is indefinitely removed from contention for time on a processor without being destroyed. Historically, this operation allowed a system operator to manually adjust the system load and/or respond to threats of system failure. Most of today's computers execute too quickly to permit such manual adjustments. However, an administrator or a user suspicious of the partial results of a process may suspend it (rather than **aborting** it) until the user can ascertain whether the process is functioning correctly. This is useful for detecting security threats (such as malicious code execution) and for software debugging purposes.

Figure 3.5 displays the process state-transition diagram of Fig. 3.1 modified to include suspend and resume transitions. Two new states have been added, *suspendedready* and *suspendedblocked*. Above the dashed line in the figure are the **active states**; below it are the **suspended states**.

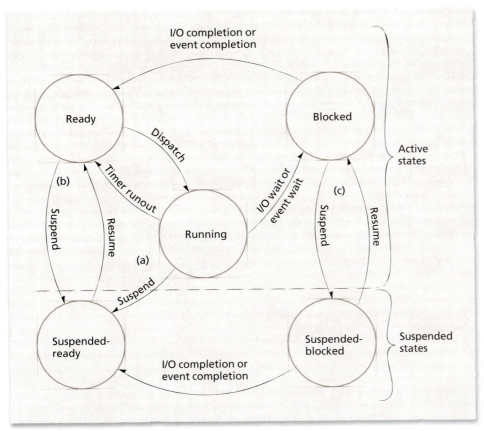

Figure 3.5 | Process state transitions with suspend and resume.

A suspension may be initiated by the process being suspended or by another process. On a uniprocessor system a *running* process may suspend itself, indicated by Fig. 3.5(a); no other process could be running at the same moment to issue the suspend. A *running* process may also suspend a *ready* process or a *blocked* process, depicted in Fig. 3.5(b) and (c). On a multiprocessor system, a *running* process may be suspended by another process running at that moment on a different processor.

Clearly, a process suspends itself only when it is in the *running* state. In such a situation, the process makes the transition from *running* to *suspendedready*. When a process suspends a *ready* process, the *ready* process transitions from *ready* to *suspendedready*. A *suspendedready* process may be made ready, or **resumed**, by another process, causing the first process to transition from *suspendedready* to *ready*. A *blocked* process will make the transition from *blocked* to *suspendedblocked* when it is suspended by another process. A *suspendedblocked* process may be resumed by another process and make the transition from *suspendedblocked* to *blocked*.

One could argue that instead of suspending a *blocked* process, it is better to wait until the I/O completion or event completion occurs and the process becomes *ready*; then the process could be suspended to the *suspendedready* state. Unfortunately, the completion may never come, or it may be delayed indefinitely. The designer must choose between performing the suspension of the *blocked* process or creating a mechanism by which the suspension will be made from the *ready* state when the I/O or event completes. Because suspension is typically a high-priority activity, it is performed immediately. When the I/O or event completion finally occurs (if indeed it does), the *suspendedblocked* process makes the transition from *suspendedblocked* to *suspendedready*.

Self Review

1. In what three ways can a process get to the *suspendedready* state?
2. In what scenario is it best to suspend a process rather than abort it?

Ans: **1)** A process can get to the *suspendedready* state if it is suspended from the *running* state, if it is suspended from the *ready* state by a *running* process or if it is in the *suspendedblocked* state and the I/O completion or event completion it is waiting for occurs. **2)** When a user or system administrator is suspicious of a process's behavior but does not want to lose the work performed by the process, it is better to suspend the process so that it can be inspected.

3.3.5 Context Switching

The operating system performs a **context switch** to stop executing a *running* process and begin executing a previously *ready* process.[20] To perform a context switch, the kernel must first save the execution context of the *running* process to its PCB, then load the *ready* process's previous execution context from its PCB (Fig. 3.6).

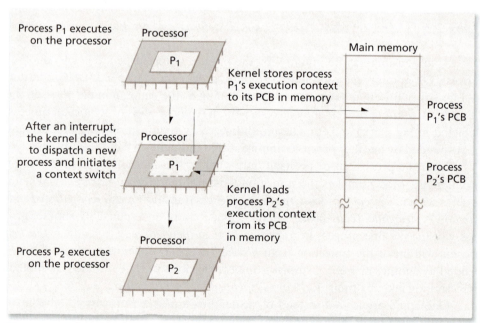

Figure 3.6 | *Context switch.*

Context switches, which are essential in a multiprogrammed environment, introduce several operating system design challenges. For one, context switches must be essentially transparent to processes, meaning that the processes are unaware they have been removed from the processor. During a context switch a processor cannot perform any "useful" computation—i.e., it performs tasks that are essential to operating systems but does not execute instructions on behalf of any given process. Context switching is pure overhead and occurs so frequently that operating systems must minimize context-switching time.

The operating system accesses PCBs often. As a result, many processors contain a hardware register that points to the PCB of the currently executing process to facilitate context switching. When the operating system initiates a context switch, the processor safely stores the currently executing process's execution context in the PCB. This prevents the operating system (or other processes) from overwriting the process's register values. Processors further simplify and speed context switching by providing instructions that save and restore a process's execution context to and from its PCB, respectively.

In the IA-32 architecture, the operating system dispatches a new process by specifying the location of its PCB in memory. The processor then performs a context switch by saving the execution context of the previously running process. The IA-32 architecture does not provide instructions to save and restore a process's execution context, because the processor performs these operations without software intervention.[21]

Self Review

1. From where does an operating system load the execution context for the process to be dispatched during a context switch?
2. Why should an operating system minimize the time required to perform a context switch?

Ans: **1)** The process to be dispatched has its context information stored in its PCB. **2)** During a context switch, a processor cannot perform instructions on behalf of processes, which can reduce throughput.

3.4 Interrupts

As discussed in Chapter 2, Hardware and Software Concepts, interrupts enable software to respond to signals from hardware. The operating system may specify a set of instructions, called an **interrupt handler**, to be executed in response to each type of interrupt. This allows the operating system to gain control of the processor to manage system resources.

A processor may generate an interrupt as a result of executing a process's instructions (in which case it is often called a **trap** and is said to be **synchronous** with the operation of the process). For example, synchronous interrupts occur when a process attempts to perform an illegal action, such as dividing by zero or referencing a protected memory location.

Interrupts may also be caused by some event that is unrelated to a process's current instruction (in which case they are said to be **asynchronous** with process execution; see the Operating Systems Thinking feature, Asynchronism vs. Synchronism). Hardware devices issue asynchronous interrupts to communicate a status change to the processor. For example, the keyboard generates an interrupt when a user presses a key; the mouse generates an interrupt when it moves or when one of its buttons is pressed.

Interrupts provide a low-overhead means of gaining the attention of a processor. An alternative to interrupts is for a processor to repeatedly request the status of each device. This approach, called **polling**, increases overhead as the complexity of the computer system increases. Interrupts eliminate the need for a processor to repeatedly poll devices.

A simple example of the difference between polling and interrupts can be seen in microwave ovens. A chef may either set a timer to expire after an appropriate number of minutes (the timer sounding after this interval interrupts the chef), or the chef may regularly peek through the oven's glass door and watch as the roast cooks (this kind of regular monitoring is an example of polling).

Interrupt-oriented systems can become overloaded—if interrupts arrive too quickly, the system may not be able to keep up with them. A human air traffic controller, for example, could easily be overwhelmed by a situation in which too many planes converged in a narrow area.

In networked systems, the network interface contains a small amount of memory in which it stores each packet of data that it receives from other computers.

Operating Systems Thinking

Asynchronism vs. Synchronism

When we say events occur asynchronously with the operation of a process, we mean that they happen independently of what is going on in the process. I/O operations can proceed concurrently and asynchronously with an executing process. Once the process initiates an asynchronous I/O operation, the process can continue executing while the I/O operation proceeds. When the I/O completes, the process is notified. That notification can come at any time. The process can deal with it at that moment or can proceed with other tasks and deal with the I/O-completion interrupt at an appropriate time. So interrupts are often characterized as an asynchronous mechanism. Polling is a synchronous mechanism. The processor repeatedly tests a device until the I/O is complete. Synchronous mechanisms can spend a lot of time waiting or retesting a device until an event occurs. Asynchronous mechanisms can proceed with other work and waste no time testing for events that have not happened, which generally improves performance.

Each time the network interface receives a packet, it generates an interrupt to inform a processor that data is ready for processing. If a processor cannot process data from the network interface before the interface's memory fills, packets might be lost. Systems typically implement queues to hold interrupts to be processed when a processor becomes available. These queues, of course, consume memory that is limited in size. Under heavy load, the system might not be able to enqueue all arriving interrupts, meaning that some could be lost.

Self Review

1. What does it mean for an interrupt to be synchronous?
2. What is an alternative to interrupts and why is it rarely used?

Ans: **1)** A synchronous interrupt occurs due to software execution. **2)** A system can perform polling, in which the processor periodically checks the status of devices. This technique is rarely used, because it creates significant overhead when the processor polls devices whose status has not changed. Interrupts eliminate this overhead by notifying a processor only when a device's status changes.

3.4.1 Interrupt Processing

We now consider how computer systems typically process hardware interrupts. (Note that there are other interrupt schemes.)

1. The interrupt line, an electrical connection between the mainboard and a processor, becomes active—devices such as timers, peripheral cards and controllers send signals that activate the interrupt line to inform a processor that an event has occurred (e.g., a period of time has passed or an I/O request has completed). Most processors contain an interrupt controller that orders interrupts according to their priority so that important interrupts are serviced first. Other interrupts are queued until all higher-priority interrupts have been serviced.

2. After the interrupt line becomes active, the processor completes execution of the current instruction, then pauses the execution of the current process. To pause process execution, the processor must save enough information so that the process can be resumed at the correct place and with the correct register information. In early IBM systems, this data was contained in a data structure called the program status word (PSW). In the Intel IA-32 architecture, such process state is referred to as the task state segment (TSS). The TSS is typically stored in a process's PCB.[22]

3. The processor then passes control to the appropriate interrupt handler. Each type of interrupt is assigned a unique value that the processor uses as an index into the **interrupt vector**, which is an array of pointers to interrupt handlers. The interrupt vector is located in memory that processes cannot access, so that errant processes cannot modify its contents.

4. The interrupt handler performs appropriate actions based on the type of interrupt.

5. After the interrupt handler completes, the state of the interrupted process (or some other "next process" if the kernel initiates a context switch) is restored.

6. The interrupted process (or some other "next process") executes. It is the responsibility of the operating system to determine whether the interrupted process or some other "next process" executes. This important decision, which can significantly impact the level of service each application receives, is discussed in Chapter 8, Processor Scheduling. For example, if the interrupt signaled an I/O completion event that caused a high-priority process to transition from *blocked* to *ready*, the operating system might preempt the interrupted process and dispatch the high-priority process.

Let us consider how the operating system and hardware interact in response to clock interrupts (Fig. 3.7). At each timer interval, the interrupting clock generates an interrupt that allows the operating system to execute to perform system management operations such as process scheduling. In this case, the processor is executing process P_1 (1) when the clock issues an interrupt (2). Upon receiving the interrupt, the processor accesses the interrupt vector entry that corresponds to the timer interrupt (3).

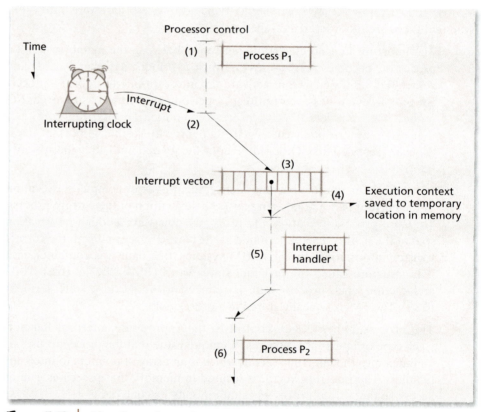

Figure 3.7 | *Handling interrupts.*

The processor then saves the process's execution context to memory (4) so that the P_1's execution context is not lost when the interrupt handler executes.[23] The processor then executes the interrupt handler, which determines how to respond to the interrupt (5). The interrupt handler may then restore the state of the previously executing process (P_1) or call the operating system processor scheduler to determine the "next" process to run. In this case, the handler calls the process scheduler, which decides that process P_2, the highest-priority waiting process, should obtain the processor (6). The context for process P_2 is then loaded from its PCB in main memory, and process P_1's execution context is saved to its PCB in main memory.

Self Review

1. Why are the locations of interrupt handlers generally not stored in a linked list?
2. Why is the process's execution context saved to memory while the interrupt handler executes?

Ans: **1)** To avoid becoming overwhelmed by interrupts, the system must be able to process each interrupt quickly. Traversing a linked list could significantly increase a system's response time if the number of interrupt types were large. Therefore, most systems use an interrupt vector (i.e., an array) to quickly access the location of an interrupt handler. **2)** If the process's execution context is not saved in memory, the interrupt handler could overwrite the process's registers.

3.4.2 Interrupt Classes

The set of interrupts a computer supports is dependent on the system's architecture. Several types of interrupts are common to many architectures; in this section we discuss the interrupt structure supported by the Intel IA-32 specification,[24] which is implemented in Intel® Pentium® processors. (Intel produced over 80 percent of the personal computer processors shipped in 2002.[25])

The IA-32 specification distinguishes between two types of signals a processor may receive: interrupts and exceptions. **Interrupts** notify the processor that an event has occurred (e.g., a timer interval has passed) or that an external device's status has changed (e.g., an I/O completion). The IA-32 architecture also provides **software-generated interrupts**—processes can use these to perform system calls. **Exceptions** indicate that an error has occurred, either in hardware or as a result of a software instruction. The IA-32 architecture also uses exceptions to pause a process when it reaches a breakpoint in code.[26]

Devices that generate interrupts, typically in the form of I/O signals and timer interrupts, are external to a processor. These interrupts are asynchronous with the running process, because they occur independently of instructions being executed by the processor. Software-generated interrupts, such as system calls, are synchronous with the running process, because they are generated in response to an instruction. Figure 3.8 lists several types of interrupts recognized by the IA-32 architecture.

Interrupt Type	*Description of Interrupts in Each Type*
I/O	These are initiated by the input/output hardware. They notify a processor that the status of a channel or device has changed. I/O interrupts are caused when an I/O operation completes, for example.
Timer	A system may contain devices that generate interrupts periodically. These interrupts can be used for tasks such as timekeeping and performance monitoring. Timers also enable the operating system to determine if a process's quantum has expired.
Interprocessor interrupts	These interrupts allow one processor to send a message to another in a multiprocessor system.

Figure 3.8 | *Common interrupt types recognized in the Intel IA-32 architecture.*

The IA-32 specification classifies exceptions as **faults**, **traps** or **aborts** (Fig. 3.9). Faults and traps are exceptions to which an exception handler can respond to allow processes to continue execution. A fault indicates an error that an exception handler can correct. For example, a page fault occurs when a process attempts to access data that is not in memory (we discuss page faults in Chapter 10, Virtual Memory Organization, and in Chapter 11, Virtual Memory Management). The operating system can correct this error by placing the requested data in main memory. After the problem is corrected, the processor restarts the process that caused the error at the instruction that caused the exception.

Traps do not typically correspond to correctable errors, but rather to conditions such as overflows or breakpoints. For example, as a process instructs a processor to increment the value in an accumulator, the value might exceed the capacity

Exception Class	*Description of Exceptions in Each Class*
Fault	These are caused by a wide range of problems that may occur as a program's machine-language instructions are executed. These problems include division by zero, data (being operated upon) in the wrong format, attempt to execute an invalid operation code, attempt to reference a memory location beyond the limits of real memory, attempt by a user process to execute a privileged instruction and attempt to reference a protected resource.
Trap	These are generated by exceptions such as overflow (when the value stored by a register exceeds the capacity of the register) and when program control reaches a breakpoint in code.
Abort	This occurs when the processor detects an error from which a process cannot recover. For example, when an exception-handling routine itself causes an exception, the processor may not be able to handle both errors sequentially. This is called a double-fault exception, which terminates the process that initiated it.

Figure 3.9 | *Intel IA-32 exception classes.*

of the accumulator. In this case, the operating system can simply notify the process that an overflow occurred. After executing the trap's exception handler, the processor restarts the process at the next instruction following the one that caused the exception.

Aborts indicate errors from which the process (or perhaps even the system) cannot recover, such as hardware failure. In this case, the processor cannot reliably save the process's execution context. Typically, as a result, the operating system terminates prematurely the process that caused the abort.

Most architectures and operating systems prioritize interrupts, because some require more immediate action than others. For example, responding to a hardware failure is more important than responding to an I/O-completion event. Interrupt priorities can be implemented in both hardware and software simultaneously. For example, a processor might block or queue interrupts of a lower priority than that of the interrupt the processor is currently handling. At times, the kernel can become so overloaded with interrupts that it can no longer respond to them. Rapid response to interrupts and quick return of control to interrupted processes is essential to maximizing resource utilization and achieving a high degree of interactivity. Most processors therefore allow the kernel to **disable** (or **mask**) an interrupt type. The processor may then ignore interrupts of that type or store them in a queue of pending interrupts that are delivered when that type of interrupt is reenabled. In the IA-32 architecture, the processor provides a register that indicates whether interrupts are disabled.[27]

Self Review

1. In the IA-32 architecture, what two types of signals can a processor receive?
2. In the IA-32 architecture, what is the difference between a fault and a trap?

Ans: **1)** A processor can receive interrupts or exceptions. Interrupts indicate that an event has occurred; exceptions indicate that an error has occurred. **2)** A fault restarts a process from the instruction that caused the exception. Faults are generally errors that can be corrected. A trap restarts a process at the next instruction following the one that caused the exception. Traps are usually generated by system calls and by the arrival of program control at breakpoints.

3.5 Interprocess Communication

In multiprogrammed and networked environments, it is common for processes to communicate with one another. Many operating systems provide mechanisms for interprocess communication (IPC) that, for example, enable a text editor to send a document to a print spooler or a Web browser to retrieve data from a distant server. Interprocess communication is also essential for processes that must coordinate (i.e., synchronize) activities to achieve a common goal. The case studies on Linux (see Section 20.10, Interprocess Communication) and Windows XP (see Section 21.10, Interprocess Communication) discuss how IPC is implemented in popular operating systems.

3.5.1 Signals

Signals are software interrupts that notify a process that an event has occurred. Unlike other IPC mechanisms we discuss, signals do not allow processes to specify data to exchange with other processes.[28] A system's signals depend on the operating system and the software-generated interrupts supported by a particular processor. When a signal occurs, the operating system first determines which process should receive the signal and how that process will respond to the signal.

Processes may catch, ignore or mask a signal. A process **catches** a signal by specifying a routine that the operating system calls when it delivers the signal.[29] A process may also **ignore** the signal. In this case, the process relies on the operating system's **default action** to handle the signal. A common default action is to **abort**, which causes the process to exit immediately. Another common default action is called a **memory dump**, which is similar to aborting. A memory dump causes a process to exit, but before doing so, the process generates a **core file** that contains the process's execution context and data from its address space, which is useful for debugging. A third default action is to simply ignore the signal. Two other default actions are to suspend and, subsequently, resume a process.[30]

A process can also block a signal by **masking** it. When a process masks a signal of a specific type (e.g., the suspend signal), the operating system does not deliver signals of that type until the process clears the signal mask. Processes typically block a signal type while handling another signal of the same type. Similar to masked interrupts, masked signals may be lost, depending on the operating system implementation.

Self Review

1. What is the major drawback of using signals for IPC?
2. What are the three ways in which a process can respond to a signal?

Ans: **1)** Signals do not support data exchange between processes. **2)** A process can catch, ignore or mask a signal.

3.5.2 Message Passing

With the increasing prominence of distributed systems, there has been a surge of interest in message-based interprocess communication.[31, 32, 33, 34, 35, 36] We discuss message-based communication in this section; particular implementations are discussed in the Linux and Windows XP case studies.[37, 38]

Messages can be passed in one direction at a time—for any given message, one process is the sender and the other is the receiver. Message passing may be bidirectional, meaning that each process can act as either a sender or a receiver while participating in interprocess communication. One model of message passing specifies that processes send and receive messages by making calls such as

```
send( receiverProcess, message );
receive( senderProcess, message );
```

The send and receive calls are normally implemented as system calls accessible from many programming language environments. A **blocking send** must wait for the receiver to receive the message, requiring that the receiver notify the sender when the message is received (this notification is called an acknowledgment). A **nonblocking send** enables the sender to continue with other processing even if the receiver has not yet received (and acknowledged) the message; this requires a message buffering mechanism to hold the message until the receiver receives it. A blocking send is an example of **synchronous communication**; a nonblocking send is an example of **asynchronous communication**. The send call may explicitly name a receiving process, or it may omit the name, indicating that the message is to be **broadcast** to all processes (or to some "working group" with which the sender generally communicates).

Asynchronous communication with nonblocking sends increases throughput by reducing the time that processes spend waiting. For example, a sender may send information to a busy print server; the system will buffer this information until the print server is ready to receive it, and the sender will continue execution without having to wait on the print server.

If no message has been sent, then a blocking receive call forces the receiver to wait; a nonblocking receive call enables the receiver to continue with other processing before it next attempts a receive. A receive call may specify that a message is to be received from a particular sender, or the receive may receive a message from any sender (or from any member of a group of senders).

A popular implementation of message passing is a **pipe**—a region of memory protected by the operating system that serves as a buffer, allowing two or more processes to exchange data. The operating system synchronizes access to the buffer—after a writer completes writing to the buffer (possibly filling it), the operating system pauses the writer's execution and allows a reader to read data from the buffer. As a process reads data, that data is removed from the pipe. When the reader completes reading data from the buffer (possibly emptying it), the operating system pauses the reader's execution and allows the writer to write data to the buffer.[39] Detailed treatments of pipes are provided in the Linux and Windows XP case studies at the end of the book. See Section 20.10.2, Pipes, and Section 21.10.1, Pipes, respectively.

In our discussions of interprocess communication between processes on the same computer, we always assumed flawless transmission. In distributed systems, on the other hand, transmissions can be flawed and even lost. So senders and receivers often cooperate using an **acknowledgment protocol** for confirming that each transmission has been properly received. A timeout mechanism can be used by the sender waiting for an acknowledgment message from the receiver; on timeout, if the acknowledgment has not been received, the sender can retransmit the message. Message passing systems with retransmission capabilities can identify each new message with a sequence number. The receiver can examine these numbers to be sure that it has received every message and to resequence out-of-sequence messages. If an acknowledgment message is lost and the sender decides to retransmit, it assigns the same sequence number to the retransmitted message as to the originally transmitted one. The receiver detecting several messages with the same sequence number knows to keep only one of them.

One complication in distributed systems with send/receive message passing is in naming processes unambiguously so that explicit send and receive calls reference the proper processes. Process creation and destruction can be coordinated through some centralized naming mechanism, but this can introduce considerable transmission overhead as individual machines request permission to use new names. An alternate approach is to have each computer ensure unique process names for its own processes; then processes may be addressed by combining the computer name with the process name. This, of course, requires centralized control in determining a unique name for each computer in a distributed system, which could potentially incur significant overhead if computers are frequently added and removed from the network. In practice, distributed systems pass messages between computers using numbered ports on which processes listen, avoiding the naming problem (see Chapter 16, Introduction to Networking).

As we will see in Chapter 17, Introduction to Distributed Systems, message-based communication in distributed systems presents serious security problems. One of these is the **authentication problem**: How do the senders and receivers know that they are not communicating with imposters who may be trying to steal or corrupt their data? Chapter 19, Security, discusses several authentication approaches.

There are several IPC techniques that we discuss later in the book. In addition to signals and pipes, processes may communicate via shared memory (discussed in Chapter 10, Virtual Memory Organization), sockets (discussed in Chapter 16, Introduction to Networking) and remote procedure calls (discussed in Chapter 17). They also may communicate to synchronize activities using semaphores and monitors., which are discussed in Chapter 5, Asynchronous Concurrent Execution, and Chapter 6, Concurrent Programming, respectively.

Self Review

1. Why do distributed systems rely on message passing instead of signals?
2. When a process performs a blocking send, it must receive an acknowledgment message to unblock. What problem might result from this scheme, and how can it be avoided?

Ans: **1)** Signals are typically architecture specific, meaning that signals supported by one computer may not be compatible with signals supported by another. Also, signals do not allow processes to transmit data, a capability required by most distributed systems. **2)** The sender may never receive an acknowledgment message, meaning that the process could be blocked indefinitely. This can be remedied by a timeout mechanism—if the sender does not receive an acknowledgment after a period of time, the send operation is assumed to have failed and it can be retried.

3.6 Case Study: UNIX Processes

UNIX and UNIX-based operating systems provide an implementation of processes that has been borrowed by many other operating systems (see the Mini Case Study,

UNIX Systems). In this section, we describe the structure of UNIX processes, discuss several UNIX features that motivate the discussion in the following chapters and introduce how UNIX allows users to perform process management operations.

Each process must store its code, data and stack in memory during execution. In a real memory system, processes would locate such information by referencing a range of physical addresses. The range of valid main memory addresses for each process is determined by the size of main memory and the memory consumed by other processes. Because UNIX implements virtual memory, all UNIX processes are provided with a set of memory addresses, called a **virtual address space**, in which the process may store information. The virtual address space contains a text region, data region and stack region.[40]

The kernel maintains a process's PCB in a protected region of memory that user processes cannot access. In UNIX systems, a PCB stores information including the contents of processor registers, the process identifier (PID), the program counter and the system stack.[41, 42] The PCBs for all processes are listed in the process table, which allows the operating system to access information (e.g., priority) regarding every process.[43]

UNIX processes interact with the operating system via system calls. Figure 3.10 lists several of these. A process can spawn a child process by using the fork system call, which creates a copy of the parent process.[44, 45] The child process receives a copy of the parent process's data and stack segments and any other resources.[46, 47] The text segment, which contains the parent's read-only instructions, is shared with its child. Immediately following the fork, the parent and child process contain identical data and instructions. This means that the two processes must perform exactly the same actions unless either the parent or child can determine its identity. The fork system call therefore returns different values; the parent process

Mini Case Study

UNIX Systems

In the days before Windows, Macintosh, Linux or even DOS, operating systems typically worked on only one model of computer, managing system resources, running batch streams and little more.[48] From 1965 to 1969, a group of research teams from Bell Laboratories, General Electric and Project MAC at MIT developed the **Multics** operating system—a general-purpose computer utility, designed to be "all things to all people."[49] It was large, expensive and complex. In 1969, Bell Labs withdrew from the project and their own small team, led by Ken Thompson, began designing a more practical operating system to run machines at Bell Labs. *(Continued on the next page.)*

Mini Case Study

UNIX Systems (Cont.)

Thompson implemented the basic components of the operating system, which Brian Kernighan named UNICS, a joke on the "multi" aspect of Multics; the spelling eventually changed to UNIX. Over the next few years, UNIX was rewritten in an interpreted implementation of Thompson's language B (based on Martin Richard's BCPL programming language), and soon after in Dennis Ritchie's faster, compiled C language.[50]

Due to a federal anti-trust lawsuit, AT&T (which owned Bell Labs) was not allowed to sell computer products, so they distributed UNIX source code to universities for a small fee to cover just the expense of producing the magnetic tapes. A group of students at the University of California at Berkeley, led by Bill Joy (later a cofounder of Sun Microsystems), modified the UNIX source code, evolving the operating system into what became known as **Berkeley Software Distribution UNIX (BSD UNIX)**.[51]

Industry software developers were drawn to UNIX because it was free, small and customize-able. To work with UNIX, developers had to learn C, and they liked it. Many of these developers also taught in colleges, and C gradually replaced Pascal as the preferred teaching language in college programming courses. Sun Microsystems based its SunOS on BSD UNIX, then later teamed up with AT&T to design the **Solaris** operating system based on AT&T's System V Release 4 UNIX.[52] A group of other UNIX developers, concerned that Sun's association with AT&T would give Sun an unfair business lead over other UNIX developers, formed the **Open Software Foundation (OSF)** to produce their own non-proprietary version of UNIX called **OSF/1**; the fierce competition between OSF and AT&T-backed Sun was dubbed the UNIX Wars.[53]

Several important operating systems are based on UNIX technology. Professor Andrew Tanenbaum of the Vrije Universiteit in Amsterdam built Minix in 1987, a stripped-down version of UNIX that was designed for teaching OS basics and is still used for this purpose in some college courses. Linus Torvalds, a Finnish graduate student, used Minix to begin writing the well-known open-source Linux operating system—now a whole family of systems in its own right (see Chapter 20, Case Study: Linux).[54] Linux is the most popular open-source operating system, and companies including IBM, Hewlett-Packard, Sun Microsystems and Intel all offer Linux versions as an operating system option for their servers. OpenBSD is another open-source project, led by Theo de Raadt, and is recognized as the most secure operating system available (see Chapter 19, Security).[55, 56, 57, 58] FreeBSD is also open-source and is known for its ease of use.[59] Yet another BSD descendant, NetBSD, has focused on portability to a variety of systems.[60, 61] IBM's AIX, based on both System V and BSD,[62] runs on some of IBM's servers. IBM claims AIX has a high degree of source-code compatibility with Linux.[63] Hewlett-Packard's HP-UX is becoming a strong competitor to AIX and Solaris, achieving the highest ratings in all the categories in a 2002 D.H. Brown Associates report, placing ahead of both Solaris and AIX.[64, 65, 66]

receives the PID of the child and the child process receives a value of zero. This convention allows the child process to recognize that it is newly created. Application programmers can use this convention to specify new instructions for the child process to execute.

A process can call exec to load a new program from a file; exec is often performed by a child process immediately after it is spawned.[67] When the parent creates a child process, the parent can issue a wait system call, which blocks the parent until the specified child process terminates.[68] After a process has completed its work, it issues the exit system call. This tells the kernel that the process has finished; the kernel responds by freeing all of the process's memory and other resources, such as open files. When a parent process exits, its child processes are typically relocated in the process hierarchy to be children of the *init* process.[69, 70] If a parent process is terminated by a kill signal from another process, that signal is also sent to its child processes.

UNIX process priorities are integers between –20 and 19 (inclusive) that the system uses to determine which process will run next. A lower numerical priority value indicates a higher scheduling priority.[71] Processes that belong to the operating system, called kernel processes, often have negative integer values and typically have higher scheduling priority than user processes.[72] Operating system processes that perform maintenance operations periodically, called daemons, typically execute with the lowest possible priority.

Many applications require several independent components to communicate during execution, requiring interprocess communication (IPC). UNIX provides several mechanisms to enable processes to exchange data, such as signals and pipes (see Section 3.5, Interprocess Communication, and Section 20.10.2, Pipes).[73]

System Call	Description
fork	Spawns a child process and allocates to that process a copy of its parent's resources.
exec	Loads a process's instructions and data into its address space from a file.
wait	Causes the calling process to block until its child process has terminated.
signal	Allows a process to specify a signal handler for a particular signal type.
exit	Terminates the calling process.
nice	Modifies a process's scheduling priority.

Figure 3.10 | *UNIX system calls.*

Self Review

1. Why can a parent and its child share the parent's text segment after a fork system call?
2. Why must a process use IPC to share data with other processes?

Ans: **1)** The text segment contains instructions that cannot be modified by either process, meaning that both the parent and child process will execute the same instructions regardless of whether the operating system maintains one, or multiple, copies of the segment in memory. Therefore, the operating system can reduce memory consumption by sharing access to the text region between a parent and its child. **2)** The operating system does not allow unrelated processes to share the data segment of their address spaces, meaning that data stored by one process is inaccessible to an unrelated process. Therefore, the operating system must provide some mechanism to make data from one process available to another.

Web Resources

msdn.microsoft.com/library/en-us/dllproc/base/about_processes_and_threads.asp
Provides a description of processes in Windows XP.

www.freebsd.org/handbook/basics-processes.html
Includes a description of how the FreeBSD operating system handles processes. Mac OS X is based (in part) on FreeBSD.

www.linux-tutorial.info/cgi-bin/display.pl?83&99980&0&3
Discusses how Linux handles processes.

docs.sun.com/db/doc/806-4125/6jd7pe6bg?a=view
Provides a process state-transition diagram for Sun Microsystem's Solaris operating system.

www.beyondlogic.org/interrupts/interupt.htm
Overviews interrupts and provides a detailed description of interrupt handling in the Intel architecture.

developer.apple.com/documentation/Hardware/Device-Managers/pci_srvcs/pci_cards_drivers/PCI_BOOK.16d.html
Documents the interrupt model in Apple Macintosh computers.

Summary

A process, which is a program in execution, is central to understanding how today's computer systems perform and keep track of many simultaneous activities. Each process has its own address space, which may consist of a text region, data region and stack region. A process moves through a series of discrete process states. For example, a process can be in the *running* state, *ready* state or *blocked* state. The ready list and blocked list store references to processes that are not *running*.

When a process reaches the head of the ready list, and when a processor becomes available, that process is given the processor and is said to make a transition from the *ready* state to the *running* state. The act of assigning a processor to the first process on the ready list is called dispatching. To prevent any one process from monopolizing the system, either accidentally or maliciously, the operating system sets a hardware interrupting clock (or interval timer) to allow a process to run for a specific time interval or quantum. If a *running* process initiates an input/output operation before its quantum expires, the process is said to block itself pending the completion of the I/O operation. Alternatively, the operating system can employ cooperative multitasking in which each process runs until completion or until it voluntarily relinquishes its processor. This can be dangerous, because cooperative multitasking does not prevent processes from monopolizing a processor.

The operating system typically performs several operations when it creates a process, including assigning a process identification number (PID) to the process and creating a process control block (PCB), or process descriptor, which stores the program counter (i.e., the pointer to the next instruction the process will execute), PID, scheduling priority and the process's execution context. The operating system maintains pointers to each process's PCB in the process table so that it can access PCBs quickly. When a process terminates (or is terminated by the operating system), the operating system removes the process from the process table and frees all of the process's resources, including its memory.

A process may spawn a new process—the creating process is called the parent process and the created process is called the child process. Exactly one parent process creates a child. Such creation yields a hierarchical process structure. In some systems, a spawned process is destroyed automatically when its parent is destroyed; in other systems, spawned processes proceed independently of their parents, and the destruction of a parent has no effect on the destroyed parent's children.

A suspended process is indefinitely removed from contention for time on the processor without being destroyed. The suspended states are *suspendedready* and *suspendedblocked*. A suspension may be initiated by the process being suspended or by another process; a suspended process must be resumed by another process.

When the operating system dispatches a ready process to a processor, it initiates a context switch. Context switches must be transparent to processes. During a context switch a processor cannot perform any "useful" computation, so operating systems must minimize context-switching time. Some architectures reduce overhead by performing context-switching operations in hardware.

Interrupts enable software to respond to signals from hardware. An interrupt may be specifically initiated by a running process (in which case it is often called a trap and said to be synchronous with the operation of the process), or it may be caused by some event that may or may not be related to the running process (in which case it is said to be asynchronous with the operation of the process). An alternative to interrupts is for the processor to repeatedly request the status of each device, an approach called polling.

Interrupts are essential to maintaining a productive and protected computing environment. When an interrupt occurs, the processor will execute one of the kernel's interrupt-handling functions. The interrupt handler determines how the system should respond to interrupts. The locations of the interrupt handlers are stored in an array of pointers called the interrupt vector. The set of interrupts a computer supports depends on the system's architecture. The IA-32 specification distinguishes between two types of signals a processor may receive: interrupts and exceptions.

Many operating systems provide mechanisms for interprocess communication (IPC) that, for example, enable a Web browser to retrieve data from a distant server. Signals are software interrupts that notify a process that an event has occurred. Signals do not allow processes to specify data to exchange with other processes. Processes may catch, ignore or mask a signal.

Message-based interprocess communication can occur in one direction at a time or it may be bidirectional. One model of message passing specifies that processes send and receive messages by making calls. A popular implementation of message passing is a pipe—a region of memory protected by the operating system that allows two or more processes to exchange data. One complication in distributed systems with send/receive message passing is in naming processes unambiguously so that explicit send and receive calls reference the proper processes.

UNIX processes are provided with a set of memory addresses, called a virtual address space, which contains a text region, data region and stack region. In UNIX systems, a PCB stores information including the contents of processor registers, the process identifier (PID), the program counter and the system stack. All processes are listed in the process table, which allows the operating system to access information regarding every process. UNIX processes interact with the operating system via system calls. A process can spawn a child process by using the fork system call, which creates a copy of the parent process. UNIX process priorities are integers between –20 and 19 (inclusive) that the system uses to determine which process will run next; a lower numerical priority value indicates a higher scheduling priority. The kernel also provides IPC mechanisms, such as pipes, to allow unrelated processes to transfer data.

Key Terms

abort—Action that terminates a process prematurely. Also, in the IA-32 specification, an error from which a process cannot recover.

Access Control List (ACL) (Multics)—Multics' discretionary access control implementation.

Access Isolation Mechanism (AIM) (Multics)—Multics' mandatory access control implementation.

address space—Set of memory locations a process can reference.

Berkeley Software Distribution (BSD) UNIX—UNIX version modified and released by a team led by Bill Joy at the University of California at Berkeley. BSD UNIX is the parent of several UNIX variations.

blocked state—Process state in which the process is waiting for the completion of some event, such as an I/O completion, and cannot use a processor even if one is available.

blocked list—Kernel data structure that contains pointers to all *blocked* processes. This list is not maintained in any particular priority order.

child process—Process that has been spawned from a parent process. A child process is one level lower in the process hierarchy than its parent process. In UNIX systems, child processes are created using the fork system call.

concurrent program execution—Technique whereby processor time is shared among multiple active processes. On a uniprocessor system, concurrent processes cannot execute simultaneously; on a multiprocessor system, they can.

context switching—Action performed by the operating system to remove a process from a processor and replace it with another. The operating system must save the state of the process that it replaces. Similarly, it must restore the state of the process being dispatched to the processor.

cooperative multitasking—Process scheduling technique in which processes execute on a processor until they voluntarily relinquish control of it.

data region—Section of a process's address space that contains data (as opposed to instructions). This region is modifiable.

disable (mask) interrupts—When a type of interrupt is disabled (masked), interrupts of that type are not delivered to the process that has disabled (masked) the interrupts. The interrupts are either queued to be delivered later or dropped by the processor.

dispatcher—Operating system component that assigns the first process on the ready list to a processor.

exception—Hardware signal generated by an error. In the Intel IA-32 specification, exceptions are classified as traps, faults and aborts.

fault—In the Intel IA-32 specification, an exception as the result of an error such as division by zero or illegal access to memory. Some faults can be corrected by appropriate operating system exception handlers.

I/O completion interrupt—Message issued by a device when it finishes servicing an I/O request.

hierarchical process structure—Organization of processes when parent processes spawn child processes and, in particular, only one parent creates a child.

interrupt—Hardware signal indicating that an event has occurred. Interrupts cause the processor to invoke a set of software instructions called an interrupt handler.

interrupt handler—Kernel code that is executed in response to an interrupt.

interrupt vector—Array in protected memory containing pointers to the locations of interrupt handlers.

interrupting clock (interval timer)—Hardware device that issues an interrupt after a certain amount of time (called a quantum), e.g., to prevent a process from monopolizing a processor.

message passing—Mechanism to allow unrelated processes to communicate by exchanging data.

Multics Relational Data Store (MRDS)—First commercial relational database system, included in Multics.

Open Software Foundation (OSF)—Coalition of UNIX developers that built the OSF/1 UNIX clone to compete with AT&T's and Sun's Solaris. The OSF and the AT&T/Sun partnership were the participants in the UNIX Wars.

OSF/1—UNIX clone built by the Open Software Foundation to compete with Solaris.

parent process—Process that has spawned one or more child processes. In UNIX, this is accomplished by issuing a fork system call.

pipe—Message passing mechanism that creates a direct data stream between two processes.

polling—Technique to discover hardware status by repeatedly testing each device. Polling can be implemented in lieu of interrupts but typically reduces performance due to increased overhead.

process—Entity that represents a program in execution.

process control block (PCB)—Data structure containing information that characterizes a process (e.g., PID, address space and state); also called a process descriptor.

process descriptor—See process control block (PCB).

process identification number (PID)—Value that uniquely identifies a process.

process priority—Value that determines the importance of a process relative to other processes. It is often used to determine how a process should be scheduled for execution on a processor relative to other processes.

process state—Status of a process (e.g., *running*, *ready*, *blocked*, etc.).

process table—Data structure that contains pointers to all processes in the system.

program counter—Pointer to the instruction a processor is executing for a running process. After the processor completes the instruction, the program counter is adjusted to point to the next instruction the processor should execute.

quantum—Unit of time during which a process can execute before it is removed from the processor. Helps prevent processes from monopolizing processors.

ready **state**—Process state from which a process may be dispatched to the processor.

ready list—Kernel data structure that organizes all *ready* processes in the system. The ready list is typically ordered by process scheduling priority.

resume—Remove a process from a suspended state.

running **state**—Process state in which a process is executing on a processor.

signal—Message sent by software to indicate that an event or error has occurred. Signals cannot pass data to their recipients.

Solaris—UNIX version based on both System V Release 4 and SunOS, designed by AT&T and Sun collaboratively.

spawning a process—A parent process creating a child process.

stack region—Section of process's address space that contains instructions and values for open procedure calls. The contents of the stack grow as a process issues nested procedure calls and shrink as called procedures return.

state transition—Change of a process from one state to another.

suspended state—Process state (either *suspendedblocked* or *suspendedready*) in which a process is indefinitely removed from contention for time on a processor without being destroyed. Historically, this operation allowed a system operator to manually adjust the system load and/or respond to threats of system failure.

suspendedblocked **state**—Process state resulting from the process being suspended while in the *blocked* state. Resuming such a process places it into the *blocked* state.

suspendedready **state**—Process state resulting from the process being suspended while in the *ready* state. Resuming such a process places it into the *ready* state.

text region—Section of a process's address space that contains instructions that are executed by a processor.

trap—In the IA-32 specification, an exception generated by an error such as overflow (when the value stored by a register exceeds the capacity of the register). Also generated when program control reaches a breakpoint in code.

unblock—Remove a process from the *blocked* state after the event on which it was waiting has completed.

virtual address space—Set of memory addresses that a process can reference. A virtual address space may allow a process to reference more memory than is physically available in the system.

Exercises

3.1 Give several definitions of process. Why, do you suppose, is there no universally accepted definition?

3.2 Sometimes the terms user and process are used interchangeably. Define each of these terms. In what circumstances do they have similar meanings?

3.3 Why does it not make sense to maintain the blocked list in priority order?

3.4 The ability of one process to spawn a new process is an important capability, but it is not without its dangers. Consider the consequences of allowing a user to run the process in Fig. 3.11. Assume that fork() is a system call that spawns a child process.

```
1   int main() {
2
3       while( true ) {
4           fork();
5       }
6
7   }
```

Figure 3.11 | *Code for Exercise 3.4.*

a. Assuming that a system allowed such a process to run, what would the consequences be?

b. Suppose that you as an operating systems designer have been asked to build in safeguards against such processes. We know (from the "Halting Problem" of computability theory) that it is impossible, in the general case, to predict the path of execution a program will take. What are the consequences of this fundamental result from computer science on your ability to prevent processes like the above from running?

c. Suppose you decide that it is inappropriate to reject certain processes, and that the best approach is to place certain runtime controls on them. What controls might the operating system use to detect processes like the above at runtime?

d. Would the controls you propose hinder a process's ability to spawn new processes?

e. How would the implementation of the controls you propose affect the design of the system's process handling mechanisms?

3.5 In single-user dedicated systems, it is generally obvious when a program goes into an infinite loop. But in multiuser systems running large numbers of processes, it cannot easily be determined that an individual process is not progressing.

a. Can the operating system determine that a process is in an infinite loop?

b. What reasonable safeguards might be built into an operating system to prevent processes in infinite loops from running indefinitely?

3.6 Choosing the correct quantum size is important to the effective operation of an operating system. Later in the text we will consider the issue of quantum determination in depth. For now, let us anticipate some of the problems.

Consider a single-processor timesharing system that supports a large number of interactive users. Each time a process gets the processor, the interrupting clock is set to interrupt after the quantum expires. This allows the operating system to prevent any single process from monopolizing the processor and to provide rapid responses to interactive processes. Assume a single quantum for all processes on the system.

a. What would be the effect of setting the quantum to an extremely large value, say 10 minutes?

b. What if the quantum were set to an extremely small value, say a few processor cycles?

c. Obviously, an appropriate quantum must be between the values in (a) and (b). Suppose you could turn a dial and vary the quantum, starting with a small value and gradually increasing. How would you know when you had chosen the "right" value?

d. What factors make this value right from the user's standpoint?

e. What factors make it right from the system's standpoint?

3.7 In a block/wakeup mechanism, a process blocks itself to wait for an event to occur. Another process must detect that the event has occurred, and wake up the blocked process. It is possible for a process to block itself to wait for an event that will never occur.

a. Can the operating system detect that a blocked process is waiting for an event that will never occur?

b. What reasonable safeguards might be built into an operating system to prevent processes from waiting indefinitely for an event?

3.8 One reason for using a quantum to interrupt a running process after a "reasonable" period is to allow the operating system to regain the processor and dispatch the next process. Suppose that a system does not have an interrupting clock, and the only way a process can lose the processor is to relinquish it voluntarily. Suppose also that no dispatching mechanism is provided in the operating system.

a. Describe how a group of user processes could cooperate among themselves to effect a user-controlled dispatching mechanism.

b. What potential dangers are inherent in this scheme?

c. What are the advantages to the users over a system-controlled dispatching mechanism?

3.9 In some systems, a spawned process is destroyed automatically when its parent is destroyed; in other systems, spawned processes proceed independently of their parents, and the destruction of a parent has no effect on its children.

a. Discuss the advantages and disadvantages of each approach.

b. Give an example of a situation in which destroying a parent should specifically not result in the destruction of its children.

3.10 When interrupts are disabled on most devices, they remain pending until they can be processed when interrupts are again enabled. No further interrupts are allowed. The functioning of the devices themselves is temporarily halted. But in real-time systems, the environment that generates the interrupts is often disassociated from the computer system. When interrupts are disabled on the computer system, the environment keeps on generating interrupts anyway. These interrupts can be lost.

a. Discuss the consequences of lost interrupts.

b. In a real-time system, is it better to lose occasional interrupts or to halt the system temporarily until interrupts are again enabled?

3.11 As we will see repeatedly throughout this text, management of waiting is an essential part of every operating system. In this chapter we have seen several waiting states, namely *ready, blocked, suspendedready* and *suspendedblocked*. For each of these states discuss how a process might get into the state, what the process is waiting for, and the likelihood that the process could get "lost" waiting in the state indefinitely.

What features should operating systems incorporate to deal with the possibility that processes could start to wait for an event that might never happen?

3.12 Waiting processes do consume various system resources. Could someone sabotage a system by repeatedly creating processes and making them wait for events that will never happen? What safeguards could be imposed?

3.13 Can a single-processor system have no processes ready and no process running? Is this a "dead" system? Explain your answer.

3.14 Why might it be useful to add a *dead* state to the state-transition diagram?

3.15 System A runs exactly one process per user. System B can support many processes per user. Discuss the organizational differences between operating systems A and B with regard to support of processes.

3.16 Compare and contrast IPC using signals and message passing.

3.17 As discussed in Section 3.6, Case Study: UNIX Processes, UNIX processes may change their priority using the `nice` system call. What restrictions might UNIX impose on using this system call, and why?

Suggested Projects

3.18 Compare and contrast what information is stored in PCBs in Linux, Microsoft's Windows XP, and Apple's OS X. What process states are defined by each of these operating systems?

3.19 Research the improvements made to context switching over the years. How has the amount of time processors spend on context switches improved? How has hardware helped to make context switching faster?

3.20 The Intel Itanium line of processors, which are designed for high-performance computing, are implemented according to the IA-64 (64-bit) specification. Compare and contrast the IA-32 architecture's method of interrupt processing discussed in this chapter with that of the IA-64 architecture (see `developer.intel.com/design/itanium/manuals/245318.pdf`).

3.21 Discuss an interrupt scheme other than that described in this chapter. Compare the two schemes.

Recommended Reading

Randell and Horning describe basic process concepts as well as management of multiple processes.[74] Lampson considers some basic process concepts, including context switching.[75] Quarterman, Silberschatz and Peterson discuss how BSD UNIX 4.3 manages processes.[76] The case studies in Part 8 describe how Linux and Windows XP implement and manage processes. Information on how processors handle interrupts is available in computer architecture books such as *Computer Organization and Design* by Patterson and Hennessey.[77]

Interprocess communication is a focal point of microkernel (see Section 1.13.3, Microkernel Architecture) and exokernel operating system architectures. Because the performance of such systems relies heavily on the efficient operation of IPC mechanisms, considerable research has been devoted to the topic of improving IPC performance. Early message-based architectures[78] such as Chorus were distributed operating systems, but as early as 1986, microkernels such as Mach[79] were developed. IPC performance improvement to support effective microkernels is reflected in the literature.[80, 81]

IPC mechanisms differ from one operating system to another. Most UNIX systems share the mechanisms presented in this chapter. Descriptions of such implementations can be found in the Linux manual pages, but the reader is encouraged to read Chapter 20, Case Study: Linux, first. *Understanding the Linux Kernel*[82] discusses IPC in Linux and *Inside Windows 2000*[83] discusses IPC in Windows 2000 (almost all of which applies to Windows XP as well). The bibliography for this chapter is located on our Web site at `www.deitel.com/books/os3e/Bibliography.pdf`.

Works Cited

1. Daley, Robert C., and Jack B. Dennis, "Virtual Memory, Processes, and Sharing in Multics," *Proceedings of the ACM Symposium on Operating System Principles*, January 1967.

2. Corbató, F.; M. Merwin-Daggett, and R.C. Daley, "An Experimental Time-Sharing System," *Proceedings of the Spring Joint Computer Conference (AFIPS)*, Vol. 21, 1962, pp. 335–344.

3. Van Vleck, T., "The IBM 7094 and CTSS," March 3, 2003, <www.multicians.org/thvv/7094.html>.

4. Van Vleck, T., "Multics General Information and FAQ," September 14, 2003, <www.multicians.org/general.html>.

5. Van Vleck, T., "Multics General Information and FAQ," September 14, 2003, <www.multicians.org/general.html>.

6. Green, P., "Multics Virtual Memory: Tutorial and Reflections," 1993, <ftp://ftp.stratus.com/pub/vos/multics/pg/mvm.html>.

7. Van Vleck, T., "Multics General Information and FAQ," September 14, 2003, <www.multicians.org/general.html>.

8. Green, P., "Multics Virtual Memory: Tutorial and Reflections," 1993, <ftp://ftp.stratus.com/pub/vos/multics/pg/mvm.html>.

9. Van Vleck, T., "Multics General Information and FAQ," September 14, 2003, <www.multicians.org/general.html>.

10. Van Vleck, T., "Multics Glossary—A," <www.multicians.org/mga.html>.

11. Van Vleck, T., "Multics Glossary—B," <www.multicians.org/mgb.html>.

12. McJones, P., "Multics Relational Data Store (MRDS)," <www.mcjones.org/System_R/mrds.html>.

13. Peterson, J. L.; J. S. Quarterman; and A. Silbershatz, "4.2BSD and 4.3BSD as Examples of the UNIX System," *ACM Computing Surveys*, Vol. 17, No. 4, December 1985, p. 388.

14. MIT Laboratory for Computer Science, "Prof. F. J. Corbató," April 7, 2003, <www.lcs.mit.edu/people/bioprint.php3?PeopleID=86>.

15. F. Corbató, M. Merwin-Daggett, and R.C. Daley, "An Experimental Time-Sharing System," *Proc. Spring Joint Computer Conference (AFIPS)*, 335–344.

16. MIT Laboratory for Computer Science, "Prof. F. J. Corbató," April 7, 2003, <www.lcs.mit.edu/people/bioprint.php3?PeopleID=86>.

17. MIT Laboratory for Computer Science, "Prof. F. J. Corbató," April 7, 2003, <www.lcs.mit.edu/people/bioprint.php3?PeopleID=86>.

18. F. Corbató, "On Building Systems That Will Fail," *Communications of the ACM*, Vol. 34, No. 9, September 1991, pp. 72–81.

19. "UNIX System Calls Links," <www.softpanorama.org/Internals/unix_system_calls_links.shtml>.

20. Lampson, B. W., "A Scheduling Philosophy for Multiprocessing System," *Communications of the ACM,* Vol. 11, No. 5, 1968, pp. 347–360.

21. *IA-32 Intel Architecture Software Developer's Manual*, Vol. 3, *System Programmer's Guide*, 2002, pp. 6-1–6-15.

22. *IA-32 Intel Architecture Software Developer's Manual*, Vol. 3, *System Programmer's Guide*, 2002.

23. *IA-32 Intel Architecture Software Developer's Manual*, Vol. 3, *System Programmer's Guide*, 2002, pp. 5-16.

24. *IA-32 Intel Architecture Software Developer's Manual*, Vol. 3, *System Programmer's Guide*, 2002.

25. Krazit, T., "Study: Intel's Q2 Market Share Up, AMD's Down," *InfoWorld*, July 31, 2002, <archive.infoworld.com/articles/hn/xml/02/07/31/020731hnstudy.xml>.

26. *IA-32 Intel Architecture Software Developer's Manual*, Vol. 3, *System Programmer's Guide*, 2002, pp. 5–2, 5–5.

27. *IA-32 Intel Architecture Software Developer's Manual*, Vol. 3, *System Programmer's Guide*, 2002, pp. 2-8.

28. Bar, M., "Kernel Korner: The Linux Signals Handling Model," *Linux Journal*, May 2000, <www.linuxjournal.com/article.php?sid=3985>.

29. Bovet, D., and M. Cesati, *Understanding the Linux Kernel*, O'Reilly, 2001, p. 253.

30. Bar, M., "Kernel Korner: The Linux Signals Handling Model," *Linux Journal,* May 2000, <www.linuxjournal.com/article.php?sid=3985>.

31. Gentleman, W. M., "Message Passing Between Sequential Processes: The Reply Primitive and the Administrator Concept," *Software—Practice and Experience*, Vol. 11, 1981, pp. 435–466.

32. Schlichting, R. D., and F. B. Schneider, "Understanding and Using Asynchronous Message Passing Primitives," in *Proceedings of the Symposium on Principles of Distributed Computing*, August 18–20, 1982, Ottawa, Canada, ACM, New York, pp. 141–147.

33. Stankovic, J. A., "Software Communication Mechanisms: Procedure Calls versus Messages," *Computer*, Vol. 15, No. 4, April 1982.

34. Staustrup, J., "Message Passing Communication versus Procedure Call Communication," *Software—Practice and Experience*, Vol. 12, No. 3, March 1982, pp. 223–234.

35. Cheriton, D. R., "An Experiment Using Registers for Fast Message-Based Interprocess Communications," *Operating Systems Review*, Vol. 18, No. 4, October 1984, pp. 12–20.

36. Olson, R., "Parallel Processing in a Message-Based Operating System," *IEEE Software*, Vol. 2, No. 4, July 1985, pp. 39–49.

37. Andrews, G. R., "Synchronizing Resources," *ACM Transactions on Programming Languages and Systems*, Vol. 3, No. 4, October 1981, pp. 405–430.

38. Andrews, G., and F. Schneider, "Concepts and Notations for Concurrent Programming," *ACM Computing Surveys*, Vol. 15, No. 1, March 1983, pp. 3–44.

39. Bovet, D., and M. Cesati, *Understanding the Linux Kernel*, O'Reilly, 2001, pp. 524-532.

40. Thompson, K., "UNIX Implementation," *UNIX Programer's Manual: 7th ed., Vol. 2b,* January 1979, <cm.bell-labs.com/7thEdMan/bswv7.html>.

41. Thompson, K., "UNIX Implementation," *UNIX Programer's Manual: 7th ed., Vol. 2b,* January 1979, <cm.bell-labs.com/7thEdMan/bswv7.html>.

42. *FreeBSD Handbook: Processes,* 2002, <www.freebsd.org/handbook/basics-processes.html>.

43. Thompson, K., "UNIX Implementation," *UNIX Programer's Manual: 7th ed., Vol. 2b,* January 1979, <cm.bell-labs.com/7thEdMan/bswv7.html>.

44. Thompson, K., "UNIX Implementation," *UNIX Programer's Manual: 7th ed., Vol. 2b,* January 1979, <cm.bell-labs.com/7thEdMan/bswv7.html>.

45. Ritchie, D., and K. Thompson, "The UNIX Time-Sharing System," *Communications of the ACM,* July 1974, pp. 370-372.

46. *FreeBSD Handbook: Processes,* 2002, <www.freebsd.org/handbook/basics-processes.html>.

47. Thompson, K., "UNIX Implementation," *UNIX Programer's Manual: 7th ed., Vol. 2b,* January 1979, <cm.bell-labs.com/7thEdMan/bswv7.html>.

48. Lucent Technologies, "The Creation of the UNIX Operating System," 2002, <www.bell-labs.com/history/unix/>.

49. Organick, E., *The Multics System: An Examination of Its Structure,* Cambridge, MA: MIT Press, 1972.

50. Lucent Technologies, "The Creation of the UNIX Operating System," 2002, <www.bell-labs.com/history/unix/>.

51. Sun Microsystems, "Executive Bios: Bill Joy," <www.sun.com/aboutsun/media/ceo/mgt_joy.html>.

52. Calkins, B., "The History of Solaris," December 15, 2001, <unixed.com/Resources/history_of_solaris.pdf>.

53. Lucent Technologies, "The Creation of the UNIX Operating System," 2002, <www.bell-labs.com/history/unix/>.

54. Torvalds, L., "Linux History," July 31, 1992, <www.li.org/linuxhistory.php>.

55. Holland, N., "1—Introduction to OpenBSD," July 23, 2003, <www.openbsd.org/faq/faq1.html>.

56. Howard, J., "Daemon News: The BSD Family Tree," April 2001, <www.daemonnews.org/200104/bsd_family.html>.

57. Jorm, D., "An Overview of OpenBSD Security," August 8, 2000, <www.onlamp.com/pub/a/bsd/2000/08/08/OpenBSD.html>.

58. Security Electronics Magazine, "OpenBSD: Secure by Default," January 2002, <www.semweb.com/jan02/itsecurityjan.htm>.

59. Howard, J., "Daemon News: The BSD Family Tree," April 2001, <www.daemonnews.org/200104/bsd_family.html>.

60. The NetBSD Foundation, Inc., "About the NetBSD Project," July 17, 2003, <www.netbsd.org/Misc/about.html>.

61. Howard, J., "Daemon News: The BSD Family Tree," April 2001, <www.daemonnews.org/200104/bsd_family.html>.

62. Coelho, J., "comp.aix.unix Frequently Asked Questions (Part 1 of 5)," October 10, 2000, <www.faqs.org/faqs/aix-faq/part1/>.

63. IBM, "AIX Affinity with Linux: Technology Paper," <www-1.ibm.com/servers/aix/products/aixos/linux/affinity_linux.pdf>.

64. Springer, I., "comp.sys.hp.hpux FAQ," September 20, 2003, <www.faqs.org/faqs/hp/hpux-faq/>.

65. Hewlett-Packard Company, "HP-UX 11i Operating System," <www.hp.com/products1/unix/operating/>.

66. Hewlett-Packard Company, "Hewlett Packard Receives Top UNIX Ranking from D.H. Brown," May 30, 2002, <www.hp.com/hpinfo/newsroom/press/30may02b.htm>.

67. *FreeBSD Hypertext Man Pages,* 2002 <www.freebsd.org/cgi/man.cgi?query=execve&sektion=2>.

68. Ritchie, D., and K. Thompson, "The UNIX Time-Sharing System," *Communications of the ACM,* July 1974, pp. 370-372.

69. Ritchie, D., and K. Thompson, "The UNIX Time-Sharing System," *Communications of the ACM,* July 1974, pp. 370-372.

70. "Exit," *The Open Group Base Specifications, Issue 6, IEEE Std 1003.1,* 2003 Edition, <www.opengroup.org/onlinepubs/007904975/functions/_Exit.html>.

71. *UNIXhelp for Users, Version 1.3.2: Nice,* <unixhelp.ed.ac.uk/CGI/man-cgi?nice>.

72. Thompson, K., "UNIX Implementation," *UNIX Programer's Manual: 7th ed., Vol. 2b,* January 1979, <cm.bell-labs.com/7thEdMan/bswv7.html>.

73. *The Design and Implementation of 4.4BSD Operating System: Interprocess Communication,* 2002, <www.freebsd.org/doc/en_US.ISO8859-1/books/design-44bsd/x659.html>.

74. Horning, J. J., and B. Randell, "Process Structuring," *ACM Computing Surveys,* Vol. 5, No. 1, March 1973, pp. 5–29.

75. Lampson, B. W., "A Scheduling Philosophy for Multiprocessing System," *Communications of the ACM,* Vol. 11, No. 5, 1968, pp. 347–360.

76. Peterson, J. L.; J. S. Quarterman; and A. Silbershatz, "4.2BSD and 4.3BSD as Examples of the UNIX System," *ACM Computing Surveys,* Vol. 17, No. 4, December 1985, p. 388.

77. Hennessy, J., and D. Patterson, *Computer Organization and Design,* San Francisco: Morgan Kaufmann Publishers, Inc., 1998.

78. Guillemont, M., "The Chorus Distributed Operating System: Design and Implementation," *Proceedings of the ACM International Symposium on Local Computer Networks,* Firenze, April 1982, pp. 207–223.

79. Accetta, M. J.; R. V. Baron; W. Bolosky; D. B. Golub; R. F. Rashid; A. Tevanian; and M. W. Young, "Mach: A New Kernel Foundation for UNIX Development," *Proceedings of the Usenix Summer'86 Conference,* Atlanta, Georgia, June 1986, pp. 93–113.

80. Liedtke, Jochen, "Improving IPC by Kernel Design," *Proceedings of the Fourteenth ACM Symposium on Operating Systems Principles,* December 5–8, 1993, pp.175–188.

81. Liedtke, Jochen, "Toward Real Microkernels," *Communications of the ACM,* Vol. 39, No. 9, September 1996, pp. 70–77.

82. Bovet, D., and M. Cesati, *Understanding the Linux Kernel,* O'Reilly, 2001, p. 253.

83. Solomon, D., and M. Russinovich, *Inside Windows 2000,* 3d ed., Redmond: Microsoft Press, 2000.

The spider's touch, how exquisitely fine!
Feels at each thread, and lives along the line.
 —Alexander Pope—

You cannot conceive the many without the one.
 —Plato—

There is a time for many words, and there is also a time for sleep.
 —Homer—

To be awake is to be alive.
 —Henry David Thoreau—

Only a signal shown and a distant voice in the darkness.
 —Henry Wadsworth Longfellow—

Chapter 4

Thread Concepts

Objectives

After reading this chapter, you should understand:

- *the motivation for creating threads.*
- *the similarities and differences between processes and threads.*
- *the various levels of support for threads.*
- *the life cycle of a thread.*
- *thread signaling and cancellation.*
- *the basics of POSIX, Linux, Windows XP and Java threads.*

Chapter Outline

4.1 Introduction

Early operating systems enabled computers to execute several programs concurrently, but the programming languages of the time did not enable programmers to specify concurrent activities (see the Operating Systems Thinking feature, Concurrency). Rather, these languages generally provided only a simple set of control structures that enabled programmers to specify a single thread of control. The types of concurrent operations that computers performed were generally implemented by operating system primitives available only to highly experienced systems programmers.

The Ada programming language, developed by the United States Department of Defense in the late 1970s and early 1980s, was one of the first languages to provide explicit concurrency primitives. Ada was made widely available to defense contractors building military command-and-control systems. However, Ada has not been widely adopted by universities and commercial industry.

Operating Systems Thinking

Concurrency

We will see numerous examples in the text of things that can happen concurrently. I/O operations can proceed concurrently with program execution, several processors can be executing concurrently, several users can be using a system concurrently. Several processes can be trying to access shared data concurrently. Several computers can be operating on the same network concurrently.

We study concurrency issues throughout the book. This and the preceding chapter discuss processes and threads—abstractions used by the operating system to manage concurrent activities. Chapters 5 and 6 are concerned with concurrent programming and the subtle issues of enabling concurrent processes and threads to work together to solve common problems of coordination and data sharing. Chapter 7 deals with deadlock and indefinite postponement of concurrent processes and threads. Chapter 8 deals with scheduling a processor among concurrent processes and threads. Chapters 9 and 11 deal with memory organization and management issues among concurrent threads and processes. Chapter 15 deals with concurrent processes and threads on multiprocessor systems. Chapter 16 deals with computer networking and the fascinating protocols used to ensure that computers functioning concurrently on the same network do not "collide" with one another. Chapters 17 and 18 deal with the problems of building concurrent applications, pieces of which are distributed across a computer network. Chapter 19 deals with issues of security and protection among concurrent users operating on individual and networked computers. The case study chapters on Linux and Windows XP show real-world implementations of concurrency control.

In recent years, many general-purpose programming languages, including Java, C#, Visual C++ .NET, Visual Basic .NET and Python, have made concurrency primitives available to the applications programmer. The programmer specifies that applications contain "threads of execution," each thread designating a portion of a program that may execute concurrently with the other threads. This technology, called **multithreading**, gives the programmer powerful capabilities not directly available in languages such as C and C++, the languages on which Java and C# are based. C and C++ are called single-threaded languages. [*Note:* On many computer platforms, C and C++ programs can perform multithreading by using specific code libraries, but these are not part of the ANSI/ISO standard versions of these languages.] Operating system support for threads is essential to supporting languages that provide multithreading semantics.

Writing multithreaded programs can be tricky. Although the human mind can perform functions concurrently, people find it difficult to jump between parallel "trains of thought." To see why multithreaded applications can be difficult to program and understand, try the following experiment: Open three books to page 1 and try reading the books concurrently. Read a few words from the first book, then read a few words from the second book, then read a few words from the third book, then loop back and read the next few words from the first book, and so on. After this experiment, you will appreciate some of the key challenges of multithreading—switching between books, reading briefly, remembering your place in each book, moving the book you are reading closer so you can see it, pushing books you are not reading aside—and amid all this chaos, trying to comprehend the content of the books!

Self Review

1. The text mentions that multithreading capabilities are not directly available in languages such as C and C++. How do programmers still manage to write multithreaded code in these languages?
2. What key advantage would you get by running a multithreaded application on a multiprocessor system over running it on a uniprocessor system?

Ans: **1)** There are specific code libraries that help with multithreading. However, these libraries are not part of the ANSI/ISO C and C++ standards, so programs written using them are not as portable as "standard C and C++" programs. **2)** The multiple threads of the application that perform parallel tasks could run truly simultaneously on separate processors, speeding application execution.

4.2 Definition of Thread

Due to the broad support for multithreading in programming languages, virtually all recent operating systems provide at least some support for threads. A thread, sometimes called a **lightweight process (LWP)**, shares many attributes of a process. Threads are scheduled on a processor, and each thread can execute a set of instructions independent of other processes and threads. However, threads are not meant to exist alone—they normally belong to traditional processes, sometimes referred to as **heavyweight processes (HWP)**. Threads within a process share many of the process's resources—most notably its address space and open files—to improve the efficiency with which they perform their tasks. The name "thread" refers to a single thread of instructions or thread of control; threads within a process can execute concurrently and cooperate to attain a common goal. On a multiprocessor system, multiple threads may be able to execute simultaneously.

Threads possess a subset of the resources contained in a process. Resources such as processor registers, the stack and other thread-specific data (TSD), such as signal masks (data that describes which signals a thread will not receive, discussed in Section 4.7.1, Thread Signal Delivery) are local to each thread, while the address space belongs to the process that contains the threads and is global to the threads (Fig. 4.1). Depending on the thread implementation for the particular platform, threads may be managed by the operating system or by the user application that creates them.

Although many operating systems support threads, the implementations vary considerably. Win32 threads,[1] C-threads[2] and POSIX threads[3] are examples of threading libraries with disparate APIs. **Win32 threads** are used in the Microsoft 32-bit Windows operating systems; **C-threads** are created from a thread library in the Mach microkernel (on which Macintosh OS X is built) and are also supported by Solaris and Windows NT operating systems. The POSIX specification provides the **Pthreads** standard. The primary goal of Pthreads is to allow multithreaded programs to be portable across multiple operating system platforms. POSIX has been implemented in a variety of operating systems, including Solaris, Linux and Windows XP.

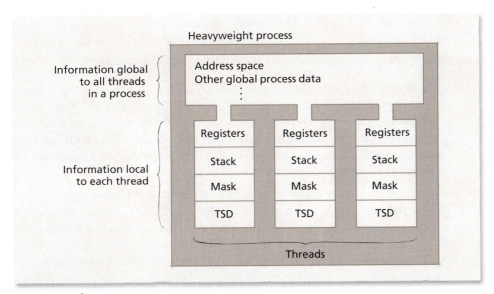

Figure 4.1 | *Thread relationship to processes.*

Self Review

1. Why are traditional processes called heavyweight processes?
2. Why is it difficult to write portable multithreaded applications?

Ans: **1)** The primary distinction between relative "weights" of traditional processes and threads is how address spaces are allocated. When a process is created, it is allocated its own address space. When a thread is created, it shares the process's address space, so threads are 'lighter weight" than processes. **2)** There is no standard threading library that is implemented on all platforms.

4.3 Motivation for Threads

In the previous chapter, we introduced the notion of a process and described how computer systems benefit from improved efficiency and performance when multiple processes execute concurrently. When the process concept was introduced by the Multics project in the 1960s, computers typically contained a single processor and applications were relatively small.[4] Processes of that era were designed to execute a single thread of control on one processor at a time. Subsequent trends in software and hardware design indicated that systems could benefit from multiple threads of execution per process. Some motivating factors for multithreading are:

- *Software design*—Due to modularity and compiler design, many of today's applications contain segments of code that can be executed independent of the rest of the application. Separating independent code segments into individual threads can improve application performance and can make inherently parallel tasks simpler to express in code (see the Operating Systems Thinking feature, Parallelism).

- *Performance*—A problem with single-threaded applications is independent activities cannot be scheduled to execute on multiple processors. In a multithreaded application, threads can share a processor (or set of processors), so that multiple tasks are performed in parallel. Concurrent parallel execution can significantly reduce the time required for a multithreaded application to complete its task, especially in multiprocessor systems, when compared to a single-threaded application that can execute on only one processor at a time and must perform its operations sequentially. Also, in multithreaded processes, ready threads can execute while others are blocked (i.e., while awaiting I/O completion).

- *Cooperation*—Many applications rely on independent components to communicate and synchronize activities. Before threads, these components executed as multiple "heavyweight" processes that established interprocess communication channels via the kernel.[5, 6] Performance with a multiple-lightweight-thread approach is often much better than that with a multiple-heavyweight-process approach because a process's threads can communicate using their shared address space.

Multithreaded applications are ubiquitous in today's computer systems. A Web server is one environment in which threads can dramatically improve performance and interactivity. Web servers typically receive requests from remote applications for Web pages, images and other files. It is common for Web servers to service each request with a separate thread. The process that receives requests may contain one thread that listens for requests from the Internet. For each request received, a new thread is spawned that interprets the request, retrieves the specified Web page and transmits the Web page to the client (typically a Web browser). After the new thread is spawned, its parent can continue to listen for new requests. Because many Web servers are multiprocessor systems, several requests can be received and fulfilled concurrently by different threads, improving both throughput and response time. The overhead incurred by creating and destroying a thread to service each request is substantial. As a result, most of today's Web servers maintain a pool of threads that are assigned to service new requests as they arrive. These threads are not destroyed after servicing the request; rather, they are reassigned to the pool to be reassigned to incoming requests. We discuss thread pooling in greater detail in Section 4.6.3, Combining User- and Kernel-Level Threads.

Word processors use threads to enhance user productivity and improve interactivity. Each time the user types a character at the keyboard, the operating system receives a keyboard interrupt and issues a signal to the word processor. The word processor responds by storing the character in memory and displaying it on the

Operating Systems Thinking

Parallelism

One way to implement parallelism is to do so on the local machine with techniques like multiprogramming, multithreading, multiprocessing and massive parallelism. Computer hardware is built to be able to perform processing in parallel with input/output. Multiprocessors are built to have several processors working in parallel—massive parallelism carries that to the extreme with hundreds, thousands or even more processors working in parallel.

Today, another kind of parallelism is becoming prominent, namely distributed computing over computer networks. We study distributed computing in Chapters 16 through 18 where we examine computer networking and the issues of building distributed operating systems. An operating system is primarily a resource manager. For years, those resources were the hardware, software and data of the local computer system. Today, a distributed operating system must manage resources no matter where they reside, whether on the local computer system or on computer systems distributed across computer networks like the Internet.

screen. Because today's computers can execute hundreds of millions of processor instructions between successive keystrokes, word processors can execute several other threads between keyboard interrupts. For example, many of today's word processors detect misspelled words as they are typed and periodically save a copy of the document to disk to prevent loss of data. Each feature is implemented with a separate thread—as a result, the word processor can respond to keyboard interrupts even if one or more of its threads are blocked due to an I/O operation (e.g., saving a copy of the file to disk).

Self Review

1. How does improved software design help to make multithreaded applications execute faster?
2. Why is it typically more efficient for threads of the same process to communicate than it is for separate processes to communicate?

Ans: **1)** Many applications contain segments of code that can execute independently of one another. When these segments of code are assigned to separate threads, they can, for example, execute on multiple processors simultaneously. **2)** Threads of the same process can communicate via their shared address space and do not have to rely on IPC mechanisms that invoke the kernel.

4.4 Thread States: Life Cycle of a Thread

As discussed in Section 3.2, Process States: Life Cycle of a Process, each process can be viewed as transitioning between a series of discrete process states. In this model, each process contains a single thread of control; therefore, we could have also stated that each thread of control moves through a series of discrete states. When processes contain multiple threads of control, we can view each thread as transitioning between a series of discrete **thread states**. Thus, much of the discussion of process states and state transitions in Section 3.2, applies to thread states and state transitions.

For example, consider the following set of states, based largely on the Java thread implementation (Fig. 4.2).[7] In Java, a new thread begins its life cycle in the ***born*** state. It remains in the *born* state until the program starts the thread, which places the thread in the ***ready*** state (sometimes called the ***runnable*** state). In other operating systems, a thread is started upon creation, eliminating the *born* state. The highest-priority *ready* thread enters the ***running*** state (i.e., begins executing) when it obtains a processor.

A *running* thread enters the ***dead*** state when it completes its task or otherwise terminates. Some threading libraries allow a thread to terminate another thread, which forces the latter into the *dead* state. Once a thread enters the *dead* state, its resources are released and it is removed from the system.

A thread enters the ***blocked*** state when it must wait for the completion of an I/O request (e.g., reading data from disk). A *blocked* thread is not dispatched to a processor until its I/O request has been completed. At that point, the thread returns to the *ready* state, so that it can resume execution when a processor becomes available.

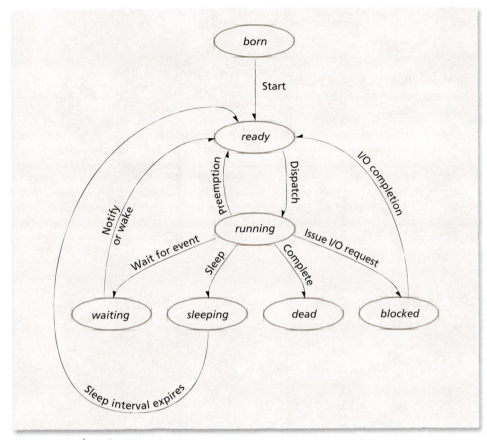

Figure 4.2 | *Thread life cycle.*

When a thread must wait for an event (e.g., mouse movement or a signal from another thread), it can enter the ***waiting*** state. Once in this state, it returns to the *ready* state when another thread **notifies** it (the term **awakens** it is also used). When a *waiting* thread receives a notify event, the thread transitions from *waiting* to *ready*.

A *running* thread can enter the ***sleeping*** state for a specified period of time (called a **sleep interval**). A *sleeping* thread returns to the *ready* state when its designated sleep interval expires. *Sleeping* threads cannot use a processor, even if one is available. Threads sleep when they momentarily do not have work to perform. For example, a word processor may contain a thread that periodically writes a copy of the current document to disk for recovery purposes. If the thread did not sleep between successive backups, it would require a loop in which it continually tests if it should write a copy of the document to disk. This loop would consume processor time without performing productive work, reducing system performance. In this case, it is more efficient for the thread to specify a sleep interval (equal to the period between successive backups) and enter the *sleeping* state. The *sleeping* thread is returned to the *ready* state when its sleep interval expires, at which point it writes a copy of the document to disk and reenters the *sleeping* state.

Self Review

1. How can a thread enter the *dead* state?
2. How are the waiting, blocked and sleeping states similar? How are they different?

Ans: **1)** A thread enters the dead state when it completes its task or when another thread terminates it. **2)** These states are similar in that the threads in them could not use a processor, even if one were available. A *blocked* thread cannot be dispatched because it is waiting on an I/O operation that it requested. In this case, the operating system is responsible for ensuring that it eventually unblocks the thread. A *waiting* thread cannot be dispatched until it receives an event from hardware or software that the operating system does not initiate (e.g., a key press or a signal from another thread). In this case, the operating system cannot control whether or when a *waiting* thread will eventually be awakened. A *sleeping* thread cannot execute because it has explicitly notified the system that it should not execute until its sleep interval expires.

4.5 Thread Operations

Threads and processes have many operations in common such as

- create
- exit (i.e., terminate)
- suspend
- resume
- sleep
- wake.

In many ways, thread creation is similar to process creation. When a process spawns a thread, the threading library initializes thread-specific data structures that store information such as register contents, the program counter and a thread ID. Unlike process creation, thread creation does not require the operating system to initialize resources that are shared between the parent process and its threads (e.g., the address space). Many operating systems require fewer instructions to share resources than they do to initialize them, so in these systems, thread creation is faster than process creation.[8] Likewise, thread termination is often faster than process termination. The reduced overhead due to thread creation and termination encourages software developers to implement parallel tasks using multiple threads instead of multiple processes, when feasible.

Some thread operations do not correspond precisely to process operations. They include:

- **cancel**—A thread or process can cause a thread to terminate prematurely by cancelling it. Unlike process termination, thread cancellation is not guaranteed to terminate the thread. This is because threads may disable, or mask, signals; if a thread masks the cancellation signal, it will not receive the signal until the thread reenables the cancellation signal.[9] However, a thread cannot mask an abort signal.

- **join**—In some thread implementations (e.g., Windows XP), when a process is initialized, it creates a **primary thread**. The primary thread acts as any other thread, except that if it returns, the process terminates. To prevent a process from terminating before all its threads complete execution, the primary thread typically sleeps until each thread it creates has completed execution. In this case, the primary thread is said to join each of the threads it creates. When a thread joins another thread, the former does not execute until the latter terminates.[10]

Although most thread implementations support the operations discussed in this section, other thread operations are specific to particular thread libraries. In the sections that follow, we introduce several popular thread implementations and discuss issues the designer must address when creating a threading library.

Self Review

1. How does the cancellation signal differ from the abort signal, discussed in Section 3.5.1, Signals?
2. Why does thread creation typically require fewer processor cycles than process creation?

Ans: **1)** When a thread receives an abort, it is terminated immediately (i.e., threads cannot mask abort signals). When a thread is cancelled, it may continue to exist until it unmasks the cancellation signal. **2)** Unlike process creation, thread creation requires that the operating system initialize only resources that are local to the thread of control. Global resources (e.g., the process's address space) can be shared using pointers, which requires significantly fewer processor cycles than initialization.

4.6 Threading Models

Thread implementations vary among operating systems, but almost all operating systems support one of three primary threading models. This section examines the three most popular threading models: user-level threads, kernel-level threads, and a combination of the two.

4.6.1 User-Level Threads

Early operating systems supported processes that contained only a single execution context.[11] As a result, each multithreaded process was responsible for maintaining thread state information, scheduling threads and providing thread-synchronization primitives. These **user-level threads** perform threading operations in user space, meaning that threads are created by runtime libraries that cannot execute privileged instructions or access kernel primitives directly.[12] User-level threads are transparent to the operating system—it treats each multithreaded process as a single execution context. This means that the operating system dispatches the multithreaded process as a unit, as opposed to dispatching each individual thread. For this reason, user-level thread implementations are also called **many-to-one** thread mappings, because the operating system maps all threads in a multithreaded process to a single execution context (Fig. 4.3).

When a process employs user-level threads, user-level libraries perform scheduling and dispatching operations on the process's threads because the operating system is unaware that the process contains multiple threads. The multithreaded process continues to execute until its quantum expires or until it is otherwise preempted by the kernel.[13]

There are several benefits to implementing threads in user space instead of in kernel space. User-level threads do not require that the operating system support threads. Therefore, user-level threads are more portable because they do not rely on a particular operating system's threading API. Another advantage is that, because the threading library, not the operating system, controls how threads are scheduled, application developers can tune the threading library's scheduling algorithm to meet the needs of specific applications.[14]

Also, user-level threads do not invoke the kernel for scheduling decisions or synchronization procedures. Recall from Section 3.4.1, Interrupt Processing, that a system loses a number of processor cycles to overhead when an interrupt, such as a system call, occurs. Therefore, user-level multithreaded processes that frequently perform threading operations (e.g., scheduling and synchronization) benefit from low overhead relative to threads that rely on the kernel for such operations.[15]

User-level thread performance varies depending on the system and on process behavior. Many of the deficiencies of user-level threads relate to the fact that the kernel views a multithreaded process as a single thread of control. For instance, user-level threads do not scale well to multiprocessor systems, because the kernel cannot simultaneously dispatch a process's threads to multiple processors, so user-level

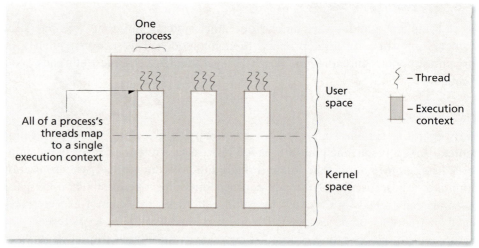

Figure 4.3 | *User-level threads.*

threads can result in suboptimal performance in multiprocessor systems.[16] In a many-to-one thread mapping, the entire process blocks when any of its threads requests a blocking I/O operation, because the entire multithreaded process is the only thread of control that the operating system recognizes. Even if the multithreaded process contains threads in the *ready* state, none of its threads can execute until the *blocked* thread becomes *ready*. This can slow progress to a crawl for multithreaded processes that block frequently. After a user-level thread blocks, the kernel will dispatch another process, which may contain threads of a lower priority than the *ready* threads contained in the *blocked* process. Therefore, user-level threads also do not support systemwide scheduling priority, which could be particularly detrimental to real-time multithreaded processes.[17] Note that some threading libraries translate blocking system calls into nonblocking system calls to address this problem.[18]

Self Review

1. Explain why user-level thread implementations promote portability.
2. In many-to-one thread mappings, why does the operating system block the entire multithreaded process when a single thread blocks?

Ans: **1)** User-level threads present an API to applications that is independent of the operating system's API. **2)** To the operating system, the entire multithreaded process is a single thread of control. Therefore, when the operating system receives a blocking I/O request, it blocks the entire process.

4.6.2 Kernel-Level Threads

Kernel-level threads attempt to address the limitations of user-level threads by mapping each thread to its own execution context. As a result, kernel-level threads are often described as a **one-to-one thread mapping** (Fig. 4.4). Such mappings require the operating system to provide each user thread with a kernel thread that

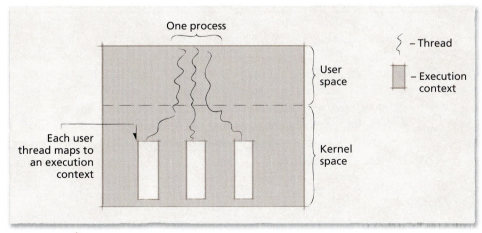

Figure 4.4 | *Kernel-level threads.*

the operating system can dispatch. Kernel threads differ from heavyweight processes because they share their process's address space. Each kernel thread also stores thread-specific data, such as register contents and a thread identifier, for each thread in the system. When a user process requests a kernel-level thread using system calls defined by the operating system's API, the operating system creates a kernel thread that executes the user thread's instructions.

There are several benefits to a one-to-one mapping. The kernel can dispatch a process's threads to several processors at once, which can improve performance for applications designed for concurrent execution.[19] Also, the kernel can manage each thread individually, meaning that the operating system can dispatch a process's *ready* threads even if one of its threads is *blocked*. Therefore, applications that perform blocking I/O can execute other threads while waiting for the I/O operation to complete. This can improve interactivity for applications that must respond to user input and can improve performance, in general, as long as the application can benefit from concurrent execution.

Kernel-level threads enable the operating system's dispatcher to recognize each user thread individually. If the operating system implements a priority-based scheduling algorithm, a process that uses kernel-level threads can adjust the level of service each thread receives from the operating system by assigning scheduling priorities to each of its threads.[20] For example, a process can improve its interactivity by assigning a high priority to a thread that responds to user requests and lower priorities to its other threads.

Kernel-level threads are not always the optimal solution for multithreaded applications. Kernel-level thread implementations tend to be less efficient than user-level thread implementations because scheduling and synchronization operations invoke the kernel, which increases overhead. Also, software that employs kernel-level threads is often less portable than software that employs user-level threads—the application programmer that uses kernel-level threads must modify the program to use the thread API for each operating system on which it runs.[21] Operating systems that conform to standard interfaces such as POSIX reduce this problem (see the Operating Systems Thinking feature, Standards Conformance). Another disadvantage is that kernel-level thread tend to consume more resources than user-level threads.[22] Finally, kernel-level threads require that the operating system manage all threads in the system. Whereas a user-level library might be required to manage tens or hundreds of threads, the operating system may be required to manage thousands. Consequently, the application developer must be sure that the operating system's memory management and scheduling subsystems scale well to large numbers of threads.

Self Review

1. In what scenarios are kernel-level threads more efficient than user-level threads?
2. Why is application software written for kernel-level threads less portable than software written for user-level threads?

Ans: **1)** If an application contains threads that block or that can perform their instructions in parallel, kernel-level threads are more efficient than user-level threads. **2)** Application software written using kernel-level threads depends on a particular operating system's thread API.

4.6.3 Combining User- and Kernel-Level Threads

Some operating systems, such as Solaris and Windows XP, have attempted to bridge the gap between many-to-one and one-to-one mappings by creating a hybrid implementation of threads. The combination of the user- and kernel-level thread implementation is known as the **many-to-many** thread mapping (Fig. 4.5).[23] As its name suggests, this implementation maps many user-level threads to a set of kernel threads. Some refer to this technique as **m-to-n thread mapping**, because the number of user threads and the number of kernel threads need not be equal.[24]

One-to-one thread mappings require that the operating system allocate data structures that represent kernel threads. As a result, the amount of memory consumed by kernel thread data structures can become significant as the number of threads in the system increases. Many-to-many thread mappings reduce this overhead by implementing **thread pooling**. This technique allows an application to specify the number of kernel-level threads it requires. For example, in Fig. 4.5, process P_1 has requested three kernel-level threads. Note that the threads T_1 and T_2 are mapped to a single kernel-level thread—a many-to-one mapping. This requires that

Operating Systems Thinking

Standards Conformance

Imagine trying to access the Internet without the standardized network protocols. Or imagine trying to buy a lamp if wall plugs were not standardized. Even more fundamentally, imagine what driving would be like if cities were to assign different meanings to red and green lights than the current standards of "stop" and "go." There are several major national and international organizations that promote computer-industry standards, such as POSIX, ANSI (the American National Stan-

dards Institute) in the United States, ISO (the International Organization for Standardization), OMG (the Object Management Group), W3C (the World Wide Web consortium) and many more.

An operating systems designer must be aware of the many standards to which a system must conform. These standards often are not static; rather, they evolve with the changing needs of the world community of computer and communications users.

There are drawbacks to standards as well—they can slow or even stifle innovation. They force operating systems development organizations (and others) to spend significant time and money conforming to a vast array of standards, many of which are obscure or even outdated. We refer to standards and standards organizations throughout the book and carefully consider the meaning and impact of standards conformance.

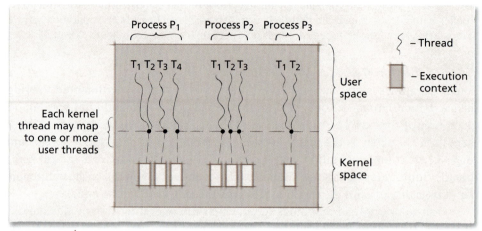

Figure 4.5 | *Hybrid threading model.*

the application maintain state information for each of its threads. Application developers are encouraged to use many-to-one mappings for threads that exhibit a low degree of parallelism (i.e., cannot benefit from simultaneous execution). Process P_1's other threads (T_3 and T_4) are each mapped to a kernel-level thread. These threads are managed by the operating system, as discussed in the previous section.

Thread pooling can significantly reduce the number of costly thread creation and destruction operations. For example, Web and database systems often create a new thread to respond to each incoming request for service. Thread pooling allows kernel threads to remain in the system after a user thread dies. The kernel thread can then be allocated to a new user thread that is created at a later time. This improves system response times in environments such as Web servers because requests can be assigned to threads that already exist in the pool. These persistent kernel threads are called **worker threads** because they typically perform several different functions, depending on the threads that are assigned to them.[25]

An advantage of a many-to-one thread mapping is that applications can improve performance by customizing the threading library's scheduling algorithm. However, as discussed in Section 4.6.1, User-Level Threads, if a single user-level thread blocks, the operating system blocks the entire multithreaded process. Another limitation to a many-to-one thread mapping is that a process's threads cannot simultaneously execute on multiple processors. Scheduler activations attempt to address these limitations to user-level threads. A **scheduler activation** is a kernel thread that can notify a user-level threading library of events (e.g., a thread has blocked or a processor is available). This type of kernel thread is called a "scheduler activation," because the user-level threading library can perform thread-scheduling operations when "activated" by an event notification, sometimes called an upcall.

When a multithreaded process is created, the operating system creates a scheduler activation that executes the process's user-level threading-library initialization code, which creates threads and requests additional processors for its threads, if necessary. The operating system creates an additional scheduler activation for each processor allocated to a process, enabling the user-level library to assign different threads to execute simultaneously on multiple processors.

When a user-level thread blocks, the operating system saves the state of the thread to its scheduler activation and creates a new scheduler activation to notify the user-level library that one of its threads has blocked. The user-level threading library can then save the state of the *blocked* thread from its scheduler activation and assign a different thread to that scheduler activation. This mechanism prevents the entire multithreaded process from being blocked when one of its threads blocks.[26]

The primary limitation of the many-to-many threading model is that it complicates operating system design, and there is no standard way in which to implement it.[27] For example, Solaris 2.2's many-to-many threading model allowed user applications to specify the number of kernel threads assigned to each process; Solaris 2.6 introduced scheduler activations. Interestingly, Solaris 8 abandoned its predecessors' many-to-many thread mapping in favor of a simpler and scalable one-to-one thread mapping scheme.[28] Windows XP, which does not support scheduler activations, dynamically adjusts the number of worker threads in its thread pools in response to system load.[29, 30]

Self Review

1. Why is it inefficient for an application to specify a thread pool size that is larger than the maximum number of *ready* user threads at any point during the application's execution?
2. How do scheduler activations improve performance in a many-to-many thread mapping?

Ans: **1)** Each worker thread in the thread pool consumes system resources such as memory. If worker threads outnumber *ready* user threads, the system incurs overhead due to unnecessary thread creation and inefficient memory allocation. **2)** Scheduler activations allow the application to indicate how threads should be scheduled to maximize throughput.

4.7 Thread Implementation Considerations

In this section, we discuss differences among thread implementations relating to thread signal delivery and thread cancellation. These differences highlight fundamental issues related to thread operations and thread management.

4.7.1 Thread Signal Delivery

Signals interrupt process execution, as do hardware interrupts, but signals are generated by software—either by the operating system or by user processes. Signals became a standard interprocess communication mechanism after appearing in the UNIX operating system. The original UNIX operating system did not support threads, so signals were designed for use with processes.[31]

As discussed in Section 3.5.1, Signals, when the operating system delivers a signal to a process, the process pauses execution and invokes a **signal handler** to respond to the signal. When the signal handler completes, the process resumes execution (assuming the process has not exited).[32]

There are two types of signals: synchronous and asynchronous. A **synchronous signal** occurs as the direct result of an instruction executed by the process or thread. For example, if a process or thread performs an illegal memory operation, the operating system sends the process a synchronous signal indicating the exception. An **asynchronous signal** occurs due to an event unrelated to the current instruction; such signals must specify a process ID to indicate the signal recipient. Asynchronous signals are commonly used to notify a process of I/O completion, suspend a process, continue a process or indicate that a process should terminate (see Section 20.10.1, Signals, for a list of POSIX signals).

When every process in the system contains a single thread of control, signal delivery is straightforward. If the signal is synchronous (e.g., an illegal memory operation), it is delivered to the process currently executing on the processor that initiated the signal (by generating an interrupt). If the signal is asynchronous, the operating system can deliver it to the target process if it is currently *running*, or the operating system can add the signal to a queue of **pending signals** to be delivered when the recipient process enters the *running* state.

Now consider the case of a multithreaded process. If the signal is synchronous, it is reasonable to deliver it to the thread currently executing on the processor that initiated the signal (by generating an interrupt). However, if the signal is asynchronous, the operating system must be able to identify the signal's recipient. One solution is to require that the sender specify a thread ID. However, if the process employs a user-level thread library, the operating system cannot determine which thread should receive the signal.

Alternatively, the operating system can implement signals such that the sender specifies a process ID. In this case, the operating system must decide whether to deliver the signal to all threads, several threads or one thread in the process. This may seem strange, but in fact this is the signal model that UNIX systems and the POSIX specification employ, and the aim is to provide compatibility with applications originally written for the UNIX operating system (see the Anecdote, Engineering).

According to the POSIX specification, processes send signals by specifying a process identifier, not a thread identifier. To solve the thread signal delivery problem, POSIX uses signal masking. A **signal mask** allows a thread to disable signals of a particular type, so that it does not receive signals of that type. A thread can thereby mask all signals except those that it wishes to receive (Fig. 4.6). In this approach, when the operating system receives a signal for a process, it delivers that signal to all threads in the process that are not masking signals of that type. Depending on the signal type and the default action (see Section 3.5.1, Signals), signals may be queued for delivery after the thread unmasks the signal, or the signal may simply be dropped. For example, in Fig. 4.6, each shape represents a signal of a different type (e.g., suspend, resume, terminate). In this case, the operating system attempts to deliver the triangle signal to a multithreaded process. Note that both threads 1 and 3 are masking the triangle signal. Thread 2 is not masking it; therefore, the operating system delivers the triangle signal to thread 2, which then invokes the process's corresponding signal handler.

Signal masking allows a process to divide signal handling among different threads. For example, a word processor may contain a thread that masks all signals except keyboard events. The sole purpose of this thread would be to record user keystrokes. Signal masking also enables the operating system to control which thread receives a signal.

When implementing a POSIX signal delivery mechanism, the operating system must be able to locate a signal mask for each user thread. A one-to-one thread mapping simplifies this problem because the operating system can attach a signal mask to each kernel thread, which corresponds to exactly one user thread. However, if the system employs a many-to-many model, signal masking can become complex. Consider the case where an asynchronous signal is generated for a process and the only thread that does not mask that signal is not currently *running*. In this case, the operating system can choose to add the signal to a list of pending signals or to drop the signal. As a general rule, because signals are often used to notify processes and threads of important events, the operating system should not drop signals. [*Note:* The POSIX specification dictates that the operating system may drop a signal if all threads in the process have masked it and the corresponding signal-handler action is to ignore the signal.[33]]

One way to implement pending signals for a many-to-many threading model is to create a kernel thread for each multithreaded process that monitors and delivers its asynchronous signals. The Solaris 7 operating system employed a thread called the Asynchronous Signal Lightweight Process (ASLWP) that monitored sig-

Engineering

The field of operating systems often seems more like engineering than science. A friend once told me his definition of engineering: "If it's scratched paint it; if it won't fit, smash it and it will fit." This explanation is certainly crude, but it points to the resourcefulness of operating systems designers.

Lesson to operating systems designers: Occasionally, when you dig deep into an operating system, you'll see examples of this kind of painting and smashing.

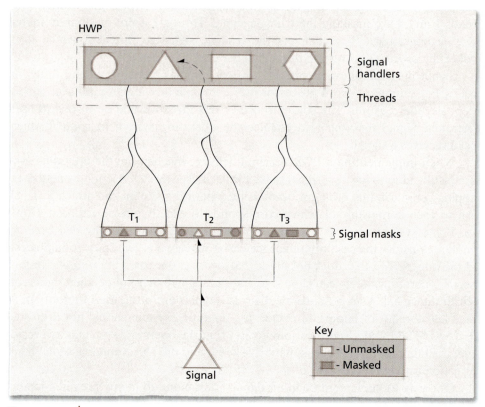

Figure 4.6 | *Signal masking.*

nals and managed pending signals so that they would be delivered to the appropriate thread, even if that thread was not *running* at the time of the signal.[34]

If a multithreaded process employs a user-level library, the operating system simply delivers all signals to the process because it cannot distinguish individual threads. The user-level library registers signal handlers with the operating system, which are then executed upon receipt of a signal. The process's user-level thread library can then deliver the signal to any of its threads that do not mask it.[35, 36]

Self Review

1. Why is synchronous signal delivery simpler than asynchronous signal delivery?
2. Explain how the ASLWP solves to the signal-handling problem in a many-to-many threading model.

Ans: **1)** Unlike an asynchronous signal, a synchronous signal is generated due to a process or thread that is currently executing on a processor. The operating system can easily identify the recipient of the signal by determining which process or thread is currently running on the processor that generated the interrupt corresponding to the signal. **2)** An operating system can create a thread that stores each asynchronous signal until its recipient enters the *running* state (at which point the signal is delivered).

4.7.2 Thread Termination

When a thread terminates by completing execution normally (e.g., by an exit call to a threading library or by exiting the method that contains the thread's code), the operating system can immediately remove the thread from the system. Threads can also terminate prematurely, due to either an exception (such an illegal memory reference) or a cancellation signal from a process or thread. Because threads cooperate by means such as modifying shared data, an application may produce subtle erroneous results when one of its threads unexpectedly terminates. Consequently, threading libraries must carefully determine how and when to remove the thread from the system. A thread can choose to disable cancellation by masking the cancellation signal. Typically it will do so only while performing a task that should not be interrupted before termination, such as completing a modification to a shared variable.[37]

Self Review

1. Name three ways a thread can terminate.
2. Why should a thread be allowed to disable its cancellation signal?

Ans: **1)** A thread can terminate by completing execution, raising a fatal exception or receiving a cancellation signal. **2)** A thread that modifies a value in its process's shared address space may leave data in an inconsistent state if terminated prematurely.

4.8 POSIX and Pthreads

POSIX (Portable Operating Systems Interface for Computing Environments) is a set of standards for operating system interfaces, published by the IEEE's Portable Application Standards Committee (PASC), that are largely based on UNIX System V.[38] The POSIX specification defines a standard interface between threads and their threading library (see the Anecdote, Standards and Conformance: Plug-to-Plug Compatibility). Threads that use the POSIX threading API are called **Pthreads** (sometimes referred to as POSIX threads or POSIX 1003.1c threads).[39]   The POSIX specification is not concerned with the details of the implementation of the threading interface—Pthreads can be implemented in the kernel or by user-level libraries.

POSIX states that the processor registers, the stack and the signal mask are maintained individually for each thread, and any other resource information must be globally accessible to all threads in the process.[40] POSIX also defines a signal model to address many of the concerns discussed in Section 4.7, Thread Implementation Considerations. According to POSIX, when a thread generates a synchronous signal due to an exception such as an illegal memory operation, the signal is delivered only to that thread. If the signal is not specific to a thread, such as a signal to kill a process, then the threading library delivers that signal to a thread that does not mask it. If multiple threads leave the kill signal unmasked, that signal is delivered to one of those threads. More importantly, one may not use the kill signal to terminate a particular thread—if a thread acts upon a kill signal, the entire process, including all of its threads, will terminate. This example demonstrates another important property of the POSIX signal model: although signal masks are stored individually in each thread, signal handlers are global to all of a process's threads.[41, 42]

To terminate a particular thread, POSIX provides a cancellation operation that specifies a target thread, the result of which depends on the target thread's cancellation mode. If the target thread chooses **asynchronous cancellation**, the thread can be terminated at any point during its execution. If the thread **defers cancellation**, it will not be cancelled until it explicitly checks for a cancellation request. Deferred cancellation allows a thread to complete a series of operations before being abruptly terminated. A thread may also **disable cancellation**, meaning that it is not notified that a cancellation operation has been requested.[43]

In addition to the common operations discussed in Section 4.5, Thread Operations, the POSIX specification provides functions that support more advanced operations. It allows programs to specify various levels of parallelism and implement a variety of scheduling policies, including user-defined algorithms and real-time scheduling. The specification also addresses synchronization using locks, semaphores and condition variables (see Chapter 5, Asynchronous Concurrent Execution).[44, 45, 46]

Few of today's most popular operating systems provide complete native Pthreads implementations, i.e., in the kernel. However, POSIX threading libraries exist to provide a wide range of support for various operating systems. For example, although Linux does not conform to POSIX by default, the Native POSIX Thread

Anecdote

Standards and Conformance: Plug-to-Plug Compatibility

The story goes that a manufacturer of tape drives in the 1960s wanted to produce tape drives that were equivalent in capabilities to those produced by a major computer vendor. Their business strategy was to advertise that their drives were "plug-to-plug compatible" with those of the major vendor and to sell the drives at a lower price. The drives were built to conform to the major vendor's specifications. The problem was that when they tried to attach these tape drives to the computer systems of the major vendor, the drives would not work. They retested their drives and were puzzled by the fact that their drives were in perfect conformance with the specifications. Why didn't the drives work? Upon careful research, they discovered that the specification had bugs. They corrected these bugs and joked that maybe they should advertise their drives as being "bug-to-bug compatible" with those of the major vendor.

Lesson to operating systems designers: We live in a world of abundant and evolving standards. Achieving standards conformance is crucial to the success of modern operating systems. But standards are subject to human error just as operating systems are.

Library (NPTL) project aims to provide a conforming POSIX threading library that employs kernel-level threads in Linux.[47] Similarly, the interface to the Microsoft Windows line of operating systems (namely the Win32 API) does not conform to POSIX, but users can install a POSIX subsystem. [Note: Sun Microsystem's Solaris 9 operating system provides two threading libraries: a Pthreads library that conforms to POSIX and a legacy Solaris threads library (called UI threads). There is little difference between Pthreads and Solaris threads—Solaris has been designed so that calls to Pthread and Solaris thread functions from within the same application are valid.[48]

Self Review

1. What is the primary reason to create standard thread interfaces such as Pthreads?
2. Which threading model does the POSIX standard require?

Ans: **1)** Standard threading interfaces allow applications to be portable, which reduces software development time for applications that must operate on multiple platforms. **2)** The POSIX standard does not require a specific implementation. Therefore, the threads can be implemented as user-level, kernel-level or hybrid threads.

4.9 Linux Threads

Support for threads in the Linux operating system was introduced as user-level threads in version 1.0.9 and as kernel-level threads in version 1.3.56.[49] Although Linux supports threads, it is important to note that many Linux kernel subsystems do not distinguish between threads and processes. In fact, Linux allocates the same type of process descriptor to processes and threads, both of which are called **tasks**. Linux uses the UNIX-based system call fork to spawn child tasks. Linux responds to the fork system call by creating a new task that contains a copy of all of its parent's resources (e.g., address space, register contents, stack).

To enable threading, Linux provides a modified version of the fork system call named clone. Similar to fork, clone creates a copy of the calling task—in the process hierarchy, the copy becomes the child of the task that issued the clone system call. Unlike fork, clone accepts arguments that specify which resources to share with the child process. At the highest level of resource sharing, tasks created by clone correspond to threads discussed in Section 4.2, Definition of Thread.

As of version 2.6 of the kernel, Linux provides a one-to-one thread mapping that supports an arbitrary number of threads in the system. All tasks are managed by the same scheduler, meaning that processes and threads with equal priority receive the same level of service. The scheduler has been designed to scale well to a large number of processes and threads. The combination of a one-to-one mapping and an efficient scheduling algorithm provides Linux with a highly scalable thread implementation (see the Operating Systems Thinking feature, Scalability). Although Linux does not support POSIX threads by default, it is distributed with a POSIX threading library. In the 2.4 kernel, a threading library called LinuxThreads provided POSIX functionality but did not entirely conform to the POSIX specification. A more recent project, Native POSIX Thread Library (NPTL), has achieved nearly complete POSIX conformance and is likely to become the default threading library for the 2.6 kernel.[50]

Each task in the process table stores information about the current task state (e.g., *running, stopped, dead*). A task in the *running* state may be dispatched to a processor (Fig. 4.7). A task enters the *sleeping* state when it sleeps, blocks or otherwise cannot execute on a processor. It enters the *stopped* stated when it receives a stop (i.e., suspend) signal. The *zombie* state indicates that a task has been terminated but has not yet been removed from the system. For example, if a task contains several threads, it will enter the *zombie* state while notifying its threads that it received a termination signal. A task in the *dead* state may be removed from the system. These states are further discussed in Section 20.5.1, Process and Thread Organization.

Self Review

1. Explain the difference between the `fork` and `clone` system calls in Linux.
2. What is the difference between the *zombie* state and the *dead* state?

Ans: **1)** When a task issues a `fork` system call, it spawns a child task and allocates it to a copy of its parent's resources. When a task issues a `clone` system call, the task specifies which resources it shares with the task it spawns. Tasks created using the clone system call are analogous to threads. **2)** A task in the *zombie* state is not removed from the system so other threads can be notified of its termination. A task in the *dead* state may be immediately removed from the system.

Operating Systems Thinking

Scalability

Users' computing needs tend to increase with time. Operating systems need to be scalable, i.e., they need to be able to adjust dynamically as more hardware and software capabilities are added to a system. A multiprocessor operating system, for example, should scale smoothly from managing a two-processor configuration to managing a four-processor configuration. We will see that most systems today employ a device-driver architecture that makes it easy to add new types of devices, even ones that did not exist when the operating system was implemented. Throughout the book, we discuss techniques for making operating systems scalable. We conclude with discussions of scalability in Linux and Windows XP.

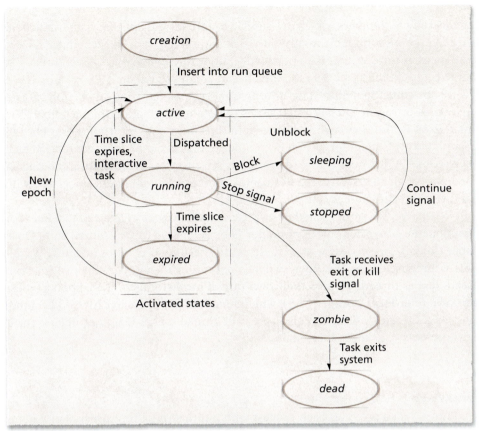

Figure 4.7 | Linux task state-transition diagram.

4.10 Windows XP Threads

In Windows XP, a process consists of program code, an execution context, resources (e.g., open files) and one or more associated threads. The execution context includes such items as the process's virtual address space and various attributes (e.g., security attributes). Threads are the actual unit of execution; threads execute a piece of a process's code in the process's context, using the process's resources. In addition to its process's context, a thread contains its own execution context which includes its runtime stack, the state of the machine's registers and several attributes (e.g, scheduling priority).[51]

   When the system initializes a process, the process creates a **primary thread**. It acts as any other thread, except that if the primary thread returns, the process terminates, unless the primary thread explicitly directs the process not to terminate. A thread can create other threads belonging to its process.[52] All threads belonging to the same process share that process's virtual address space. Threads can maintain their own private data in **thread local storage (TLS)**.

Fibers

Threads can create **fibers**, which are similar to threads, except that a fiber is scheduled for execution by the thread that creates it, rather than the scheduler. Fibers make it easier for developers to port applications that employ user-level threads. A fiber executes in the context of the thread that creates the fiber.[53]

It fiber must maintain state information, such as the next instruction to execute processor registers. The thread stores this state information for each fiber. The thread itself is also a unit of execution, and thus must convert itself into a fiber to separate its own state information from other fibers executing in its context. In fact, the Windows API forces a thread to convert itself into a fiber before creating or scheduling other fibers. The thread's context remains, and all fibers associated with that thread execute in that context.[54]

Whenever the kernel schedules a thread that has been converted to a fiber for execution, the converted fiber or another fiber belonging to that thread runs. Once a fiber obtains the processor, it executes until the thread in whose context it executes is preempted, or the fiber switches execution to another fiber within that thread. Just as threads possess their own thread local storage (TLS), fibers possess their own **fiber local storage (FLS)**, which functions for fibers exactly as TLS functions for a thread. A fiber can also access its thread's TLS. If a fiber deletes itself (i.e., terminates), its thread terminates.[55]

Thread Pools

Windows XP also provides each process with a thread pool that consists of a number of worker threads, which are kernel-mode threads that execute functions specified by user threads. Because the functions specified by user threads may outnumber worker threads, Windows XP maintains requests to execute functions in a queue. The thread pool consists of worker threads that sleep until a request is queued to the pool.[56] The thread that queues the request must specify the function to execute and must provide context information.[57] The thread pool is created the first time a thread submits a function to the pool.

Thread pools have many purposes. Web servers and databases can use them to handle client requests (e.g., from Web browsers). Instead of incurring the costly overhead of creating and destroying a thread for each request, the process simply queues the request to its pool of worker threads. Also, several threads that spend most of their time sleeping (e.g., waiting for events to occur) can be replaced by a single worker thread that awakens each time one of these events occurs. Furthermore, applications can use the thread pool to accomplish asynchronous I/O by queuing a request to its pool of worker threads to execute the I/O completion routines. Using thread pools can make an application more efficient and simpler, because developers do not have to create and delete as many threads. However, thread pools transfer some control from the programmer to the system, which can introduce inefficiency. For example, the system grows and shrinks the size of a process's thread pool in response to request volume; in some cases, the programmer can better estimate how many threads are needed.[58]

Thread States

In Windows XP, threads can be in any one of eight states (Fig. 4.8). A thread begins in the **initialized** **state** during thread creation. Once initialization concludes, the thread enters the **ready** **state**. Threads in the ready state are waiting to use a processor. A thread that the dispatcher has decided will execute next enters the **standby** **state** as it awaits its turn for a processor. A thread is in the standby state, for example, during the context switch from the previously executing thread to that thread. Once the thread obtains a processor, it enters the **running** **state**. A thread transitions out of the *running* state if it terminates execution, exhausts its quantum, is preempted, is suspended or waits on an object. When a thread completes its instructions, it enters the **terminated** **state**. The system does not necessarily delete a *terminated* thread immediately, which can reduce thread creation overhead if the process reinitializes that thread. The system deletes a thread after its resources have been freed. If a *running* thread is preempted or exhausts its quantum, it returns to the *ready* state.

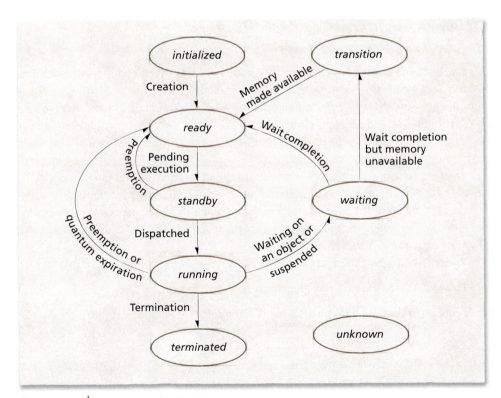

Figure 4.8 | Windows XP thread state-transition diagram.

A *running* thread enters the ***waiting state*** while waiting for an event (e.g., an I/O completion event). Also, another thread (with sufficient access rights) or the system can suspend a thread, forcing it into the *waiting* state until the thread is resumed. When the thread completes its wait, it either returns to the *ready* state or enters the ***transition state***. The system places a thread in the *transition* state if the thread's data is not currently available (e.g., because the thread has not executed recently and the system needed its memory for other purposes), but the thread is otherwise ready to execute. The thread enters the *ready* state once the system pages the thread's kernel stack back into memory. The system places a thread in the ***unknown state*** when the thread's state is unclear (usually because of an error).[59, 60]

Self Review

1. What purpose do fibers serve in Windows XP?
2. How does a primary thread differ from other threads?

Ans: **1)** Fibers exist to improve compatibility with applications that schedule their own threads (e.g., user-level threads). **2)** Unlike other threads, when a primary thread returns, the process to which it belongs terminates.

4.11 Java Multithreading Case Study, Part I: Introduction to Java Threads

As we will see in subsequent chapters, the concurrency introduced by processes and threads has significantly impacted software design. In this and the following optional case studies, we provide examples of real programs that demonstrate and solve problems introduced by concurrency. We have chosen to implement these programs in Java due to its portability across most popular platforms. This case study assumes a basic knowledge of Java.

In this section, we overview various thread-related methods in the Java API. We use many of these methods in live-code examples. The reader should refer to the Java API directly for more details on using each method, especially the exceptions thrown by each method (see `java.sun.com/j2se/1.4/docs/api/java/lang/Thread.html`).

Class `Thread` (package `java.lang`) has several constructors. The constructor

```
public Thread( String threadName )
```

constructs a `Thread` object whose name is `threadName`. The constructor

```
public Thread()
```

constructs a `Thread` whose name is `"Thread-"` concatenated with a number, like `Thread-1`, `Thread-2`, and so on.

The code that "does the real work" of a thread is placed in its **run** method. The run method can be overridden in a subclass of `Thread` or it may be implemented in a **Runnable** object; Runnable is a Java interface that allows the programmer to control a thread's life cycle with the run method in an object of a class that does not extend Thread.

A program launches a thread's execution by calling the thread's **start** method, which, in turn, calls method run. After start launches the thread, start returns to its caller immediately. The caller then executes concurrently with the launched thread.

The static method **sleep** is called with an argument specifying how long (in milliseconds) the currently executing thread should sleep; while a thread sleeps, it does not contend for the processor, so other threads can execute. This can give lower-priority threads a chance to run.

Method **setName** sets a thread's name, which facilitates debugging by allowing the programmer to identify which thread is executing. Method **getName** returns the name of the Thread. Method **toString** returns a String consisting of the name of the thread, the priority of the thread and the thread's **ThreadGroup** (analogous to the parent process of a group of threads). The static method **currentThread** returns a reference to the currently executing Thread.

Method **join** waits for the Thread to which the message is sent to terminate before the calling Thread can proceed; no argument or an argument of 0 milliseconds to method join indicates that the current Thread will wait forever for the target Thread to die before the Thread proceeds. Such waiting can be dangerous; it can lead to two particularly serious problems called deadlock and indefinite postponement—we discuss these concepts in Chapter 7, Deadlock and Indefinite Postponement.

Java implements thread signaling using the **interrupt** method. Calling the **interrupt** method on a thread that is blocked (because that thread's wait, join or sleep method was called) raises (throws) its InterruptedException exception handler. The static method **interrupted** returns true if the current thread has been interrupted and false otherwise. A program can invoke a specific thread's **isInterrupted** method to determine whether that thread has been interrupted.

Creating and Executing Threads

Figure 4.9 demonstrates basic threading techniques, such as constructing Thread objects and using Thread method sleep. The program creates three threads of execution. Each thread displays a message indicating that it is going to sleep for a random interval from 0 to 5000 milliseconds, then goes to sleep. When each thread awakens, it displays its name, indicates that it is done sleeping, terminates and enters the *dead* state. You will see that method main (i.e., the main thread of execution) terminates before the application terminates. The program consists of two classes—ThreadTester (lines 4–23), which creates the three threads, and PrintThread (lines 25–59), which contains in its run method the actions each PrintThread will perform.

Class PrintThread (lines 25–59) extends Thread, so that each PrintThread object can execute concurrently. The class consists of instance variable sleepTime

```
1   // Fig. 4.9: ThreadTester.java
2   // Multiple threads printing at different intervals.
3
4   public class ThreadTester {
5
6      public static void main( String [] args )
7      {
8         // create and name each thread
9         PrintThread thread1 = new PrintThread( "thread1" );
10        PrintThread thread2 = new PrintThread( "thread2" );
11        PrintThread thread3 = new PrintThread( "thread3" );
12
13        System.err.println( "Starting threads" );
14
15        thread1.start(); // start thread1; place it in ready state
16        thread2.start(); // start thread2; place it in ready state
17        thread3.start(); // start thread3; place it in ready state
18
19        System.err.println( "Threads started, main ends\n" );
20
21     } // end main
22
23  } // end class ThreadTester
24
25  // class PrintThread controls thread execution
26  class PrintThread extends Thread {
27     private int sleepTime;
28
29     // assign name to thread by calling superclass constructor
30     public PrintThread( String name )
31     {
32        super( name );
33
34        // pick random sleep time between 0 and 5 seconds
35        sleepTime = ( int ) ( Math.random() * 5001 );
36     } // end PrintThread constructor
37
38     // method run is the code to be executed by new thread
39     public void run()
40     {
41        // put thread to sleep for sleepTime amount of time
42        try {
43           System.err.println( getName() + " going to sleep for " +
44              sleepTime + " milliseconds" );
45
```

Figure 4.9 | Java threads being created, starting, sleeping and printing. (Part 1 of 2.)

```
46             Thread.sleep( sleepTime );
47          } // end try
48
49          // if thread interrupted during sleep, print stack trace
50          catch ( InterruptedException exception ) {
51             exception.printStackTrace();
52          } // end catch
53
54          // print thread name
55          System.err.println( getName() + " done sleeping" );
56
57       } // end method run
58
59    } // end class PrintThread
```

Sample Output 1:

```
Starting threads
Threads started, main ends

thread1 going to sleep for 1217 milliseconds
thread2 going to sleep for 3989 milliseconds
thread3 going to sleep for 662 milliseconds
thread3 done sleeping
thread1 done sleeping
thread2 done sleeping
```

Sample Output 2:

```
Starting threads
thread1 going to sleep for 314 milliseconds
thread2 going to sleep for 1990 milliseconds
Threads started, main ends

thread3 going to sleep for 3016 milliseconds
thread1 done sleeping
thread2 done sleeping
thread3 done sleeping
```

Figure 4.9 | Java threads being created, starting, sleeping and printing. (Part 2 of 2.)

(line 27), a constructor (lines 29–36) and a run method (lines 38–57). Variable sleepTime stores a random integer value chosen when a new PrintThread object's constructor is called. Each thread controlled by a PrintThread object sleeps for the amount of time specified by the corresponding PrintThread object's sleepTime, then outputs its name.

The `PrintThread` constructor (lines 29–36) initializes `sleepTime` to a random integer from 0 to 5000. When a `PrintThread` is assigned a processor for the first time, its `run` method begins executing. Lines 43–44 display a message indicating the name of the currently executing thread and stating that the thread is going to sleep for a certain number of milliseconds. Line 43 uses the currently executing thread's `getName` method to obtain the thread's name, which was specified as a string argument to the `PrintThread` constructor and passed to the superclass `Thread` constructor in line 32. Note that line 43 uses `System.err` to print the message because `System.err` is unbuffered, meaning that it prints its argument immediately after being called. Line 46 invokes static `Thread` method `sleep` to place the thread into the *sleeping* state. At this point, the thread loses the processor, and the system allows another thread to execute. When the thread awakens, it reenters the *ready* state, where it waits until the system assigns it a processor. When the `Print-Thread` object enters the *running* state again, line 55 outputs the thread's name in a message that indicates the thread is done sleeping; then method `run` terminates. This places the thread in the *dead* state, at which point its resources can be freed.

`ThreadTester` method `main` (lines 6–21) creates and names three `Print-Thread` objects (lines 9–11). When debugging a multithreaded program, these names identify which threads are executing. Lines 15–17 invoke each thread's `start` method to transition all three `PrintThread` objects from the *born* state to the *ready* state. Method `start` returns immediately from each invocation; then line 19 outputs a message indicating that the threads were started. Note that all code in this program, except for the code in method `run`, executes in the `main` thread. The `PrintThread` constructor also executes in the `main` thread, since each `Print-Thread` object is created in method `main`. When method `main` terminates (line 21), the program itself continues running, because there are still threads that are alive (i.e., the threads were started and have not yet reached the *dead* state) and are not daemon threads. The program terminates when its last thread dies. When the system assigns a processor to a `PrintThread` for the first time, the thread enters the *running* state, and the thread's `run` method begins executing.

The sample outputs for this program show each thread's name and sleep time as the thread goes to sleep. The thread with the shortest sleep time normally awakens first, indicates that it is done sleeping and terminates. Note in the second sample output that `thread1` and `thread2` each output their name and sleep time before method `main` completes its execution. This situation demonstrates that, once multiple threads are in the *ready* state, any thread can be assigned the processor.

Self Review

1. Why should programmers name Java threads?
2. How does Java allow programmers to create threads from objects that do not extend `Thread`?

Ans:　1) Naming Java threads allows the programmer to identify each thread when debugging. 2) A class can implement the `Runnable` interface so that objects of the class can control the life cycles of threads with their `run` methods.

Web Resources

www.serpentine.com/~bos/threads-faq/
Contains a frequently-asked-questions (FAQ) page about threads. Aside from answering basic thread questions, it provides links to books on threads, discusses some common pitfalls programmers encounter when implementing operating system support for threads and directs readers to thread packages available on the Internet.

www.linux-mag.com/2001-05/compile_01.html
This *Linux Magazine* article by Benjamin Chelf gives an overview of thread implementations. Chelf describes in detail how Linux handles Pthreads, providing sample Linux code.

publib.boulder.ibm.com/iseries/v5r1/ic2924/
index.htm?info/apis/rzah4mst.htm
Provides a complete API for programming Pthreads and defines basic thread concepts.

sources.redhat.com/pthreads-win32/
Contains an implementation of Pthreads for 32-bit Windows environments.

java.sun.com/docs/books/tutorial/essential/threads/
Sun's tutorial on Java threads.

java.sun.com/j2se/1.4.1/docs/api/
Java API containing a specification of the Thread class.

archive.devx.com/dotnet/articles/pa061702/
pa061702-1.asp
Article that overviews multithreading using the .NET platform, including a concise presentation of multithreading concepts.

www.microsoft.com/msj/0499/pooling/pooling.aspx
Article that describes thread pooling in Windows XP.

java.sun.com/docs/hotspot/threads/threads.html
White paper that documents the relationship between Java threads and Solaris threads.

developer.apple.com/documentation/MacOSX/Conceptual/SystemOverview/InverEnvironissues/
chapter_14_section_3.html
Describes the thread manager in Macintosh OS X.

Summary

In recent years, several general-purpose programming languages, such as Java, C#, Visual C++ .NET, Visual Basic .NET and Python, have made concurrency primitives available to the applications programmer. The programmer specifies that applications contain threads of execution, each thread designating a portion of a program that may execute concurrently with other threads. This technology, called multithreading, gives the programmer powerful capabilities. Operating system support for threads is essential to supporting languages that provide multithreading semantics.

Threads, sometimes called lightweight processes (LWPs), share many resources—most notably the address space of their process—to improve the efficiency with which they perform their tasks. The name "thread" refers to a single thread of instructions or thread of control; threads within a process execute concurrently to attain a common goal. Resources such as processor registers, the stack and other thread-specific data (TSD) are local to each thread, while all threads share the address space of their process. Depending on the thread implementation, threads may be managed by the operating system or by a user application. Although many operating systems support threads, the implementations vary considerably.

Threads have become prominent due to trends in software design, scalability and cooperation. Each thread transitions among a series of discrete thread states. Threads and processes have many operations in common, such as create, exit, resume and suspend. Unlike process creation, thread creation does not requires the operating system to initialize resources that are shared between the parent process and its threads (e.g., the address space). This reduces the overhead of thread creation and termination when compared to process creation and termination. Some thread operations do not correspond precisely to process operations, such as *cancel* and *join*.

Thread implementations vary among operating systems, but almost all operating systems support user-level threads, kernel-level threads or a combination of the two. User-level threads perform threading operations in user space, meaning that threads are created by runtime libraries that cannot execute privileged instructions or access kernel primitives directly. User-level thread implementations are also called many-to-one thread mappings, because the operating system maps all threads in a multithreaded process to a single execution context. Although user-level threads vary in performance among applications, many of their deficiencies relate to the fact that the kernel views a multithreaded process as a single thread of control.

Kernel-level threads attempt to address the limitations of user-level threads by mapping each thread to its own execution context. As a result, kernel-level threads provide a one-to-one thread mapping. Their benefits include increased scalability, interactivity and throughput. Due to overhead and reduced portability, however, kernel-level threads are not always the optimal solution for multi-threaded applications.

The combination of the user- and kernel-level thread implementation is known as the many-to-many thread mapping. Some refer to this technique as *m*-to-*n* thread mapping because the number of user and kernel threads need not be equal. Many-to-many thread mappings reduce overhead due to one-to-one thread mappings by implementing thread pooling, which allows an application to specify the number of kernel-level threads it requires. Persistent kernel threads that occupy the thread pool are called worker threads. A technique that enables a user-level library to schedule its threads is called a scheduler activation. It occurs when the operating system calls a user-level threading library that determines if any of its threads need rescheduling. Scheduler activations can reduce context-switching overhead due to inappropriate scheduling decisions in the kernel by allowing the threading library to determine the scheduling policy that best addresses the application's needs.

When the operating system delivers a signal to a process, the process pauses execution and invokes a signal handler to respond. There are two types of signals: synchronous (which occur as the direct result of an instruction being executed) or asynchronous (which occur as the result of an event unrelated to the instructions being executed). Signal delivery introduces several design challenges in threading implementations. The threading library must determine each signal's recipient so that asynchronous signals are delivered properly. Each thread is usually associated with a set of pending signals that are delivered when it executes. One way to control which threads receive signals of a particular type is to require that each thread specify a signal mask that disables signals of particular types. A thread can thereby mask all signals except those that it wishes to receive.

Thread termination, or cancellation, also differs between thread implementations. Because multiple threads share the same address space, prematurely terminating a thread can cause subtle errors in processes. Some thread implementations allow a thread to determine when it can be terminated to prevent the process from entering an inconsistent state.

Threads that use the POSIX threading API are called Pthreads (sometimes referred to as POSIX threads or POSIX 1003.1c threads). POSIX states that the processor registers, the stack and the signal mask are maintained individually for each thread, and any other resource information must be globally accessible to all threads in the process. POSIX specifies how operating systems should deliver signals to Pthreads in addition to specifying several thread-cancellation modes.

Linux allocates the same type of process descriptor to processes and threads, both of which are called tasks. Linux uses the UNIX-based system call fork to spawn child tasks. To enable threading, Linux provides a modified version named clone, which accepts arguments that specify which resources to share with the child task. At the highest level of resource sharing, tasks created by clone correspond to threads discussed in Section 4.2, Definition of Thread.

In Windows XP, threads—not processes—are dispatched to a processor; threads execute a piece of the process's code in the process's context, using the process's resources. In addition to its process's context, a thread contains its own execution context, which includes its runtime stack, the state of the machine's registers and several attributes (e.g, scheduling priority). When the system initializes a process, the process creates a primary thread, which typically terminates the process upon completion. Windows XP threads can create fibers, which are similar to threads, except that a fiber is scheduled for execution by the thread that creates it, rather than the scheduler. Windows XP provides each process with a thread pool that consists of a number of worker threads, which are kernel-mode threads that execute functions specified by user threads.

The Java programming language allows the application programmer to create threads that are portable to many computing platforms. Java uses class Thread to create threads, which execute code specified in a Runnable object's run method. Java supports operations such as naming, starting and joining threads.

Key Terms

asynchronous cancellation (POSIX)—Cancellation mode in which a thread is terminated immediately upon receiving the cancellation signal.

asynchronous signal—Signal generated for reasons unrelated to the current instruction of the running thread.

blocked state—Thread state in which the thread is awaiting notification of some event, such as completion of an I/O operation, before it can again become *ready*.

born state—Thread state in which a new thread begins its life cycle.

C-threads—Threads supported natively in the Mach micro-kernel (on which Macintosh OS X is built).

cancellation of a thread—Thread operation that terminates the target thread. Three modes of cancellation are disabled, deferred and asynchronous cancellation.

dead **state**—Thread state entered after a thread completes its task or otherwise terminates.

deferred cancellation (POSIX)—Cancellation mode in which a thread is terminated only after explicitly checking that it has received a cancellation signal.

disabled cancellation (POSIX)—Cancellation mode in which a thread does not receive pending cancellation signals.

fiber (Windows XP)—Unit of execution in Windows XP created by a thread and scheduled by the thread. Fibers facilitate portability for applications that schedule their own threads.

fiber local storage (FLS) (Windows XP)—Area of a process's address space where a fiber can store data that only the fiber can access.

heavyweight process (HWP)—A traditional process, which may contain one or more threads. The process is "heavyweight" because it is allocated its own address space upon creation.

initialized **state** (Windows XP)—Thread state in which the thread is created by the operating system.

join—Thread operation that causes the calling thread to block until the thread it joins terminates. A primary thread often joins each of threads it creates so that its corresponding process does not exit until all of its threads have terminated.

kernel-level thread—Thread created by an operating system (also called kernel thread).

lightweight process (LWP)—A single thread of program instructions (also called a thread of execution or thread of control). Threads are "lightweight" because they share their address space with other threads in the same process.

main thread of execution—Thread created upon process creation (also called primary thread).

many-to-many (*m*-to-*n*) thread mapping—Threading model in which a set of user threads is assigned to a set of kernel threads so that applications can benefit both from kernel-level threads and user-level features such as scheduler activations. In practice the number of user threads is greater than or equal to the number of kernel threads in the system to minimize memory consumption.

many-to-one thread mapping—Threading model in which all user-level threads in a process are assigned to one kernel thread.

mask a signal—Prevent a signal from being delivered. Signal masking enables a multithreaded process to specify which of its threads will handle signals of a particular type.

multithreading—Technique that incorporates multiple threads of execution within a process to perform parallel activities, possibly simultaneously.

notify—Thread operation that transitions its target thread from the *waiting* to the *ready* state.

one-to-one mapping—Threading model in which each user-level thread is assigned to a kernel-level thread.

pending signal—Signal that has not been delivered to a thread because the thread is not *running* and/or because the thread has masked signals of that type.

primary thread—Thread created upon process creation (also called main thread of execution). When the primary thread returns, its process terminates.

Pthread (POSIX 1003.1c thread)—Thread that conforms to the POSIX 1003.1c standard.

ready **(or** *runnable***) state**—Thread state from which a thread can transition to the *running* state and execute on a processor. In Windows XP, a *ready* thread transitions to the *standby* state, from which it transitions to the *running* state.

running **state**—Thread state in which a thread executes on a processor.

scheduler activation—Mechanism that allows a user-level library to schedule kernel threads.

signal handler—Code that is executed in response to a particular signal type.

signal mask—Data structure that specifies which signals are not delivered to a thread. Depending on the signal type and default action, masked signals are either queued or dropped.

sleep interval—Period of time (specified by the thread that is about to enter the *sleeping* state) during which a thread remains in the *sleeping* state.

sleeping **state**—Thread state in which a thread cannot execute until being returned to the *ready* state after the sleep interval expires.

standby **state** (Windows XP)—Thread state denoting a thread that has been selected for execution.

synchronous signal—Signal generated due to execution of the currently *running* thread's instructions.

task—Linux representation of an execution context (i.e., process or thread).

terminated **state** (Windows XP)—Thread state that denotes a thread has finished executing.

thread —Entity that describes an independently executable stream of program instructions (also called a thread of execution or thread of control). Threads facilitate parallel execution of concurrent activities within a process.

thread local storage (TLS) —Windows XP implementation of thread-specific data. A thread can share its address space with other threads of that process, but hide its private data in its TLS.

thread pooling —Threading technique that employs a number of kernel threads that exist for the duration of the process that creates them. This technique can improve performance by reducing the number of costly thread creation and termination operations.

thread state —Status of a thread (e.g., *running*, *ready*, *blocked*, and so on).

transition state (Windows XP)—Thread state denoting a thread that has completed a wait but is not yet ready to run because its kernel stack has been paged out of memory.

unknown state (Windows XP)—Thread state denoting that the some error has occurred and the system does not know the state of the thread.

user-level threads —Threading model in which all threads in a process are assigned to one execution context.

wake —Thread operation that transitions its target from the *waiting* state to the *ready* state.

waiting state —Thread state from which a thread cannot execute until transitioning to the *ready* state via a wake or notify operation.

Win32 thread —Threads natively supported in the Microsoft 32-bit Windows line of operating systems.

worker thread —Kernel thread that is a member of a thread pool. Worker threads may be mapped to any user thread in the process that created its thread pool.

Exercises

4.1 Compare and contrast thread dispatching in kernel-level threads and in user-level threads.

4.2 Would an algorithm that performs several independent calculations concurrently (e.g., matrix multiplication) be more efficient if it used threads, or if it did not use threads? Why is this a hard question to answer?

4.3 Name two situations other than a Web or database server for which thread pooling may be useful. Another possibility is an online interactive multi-player game. Several such games can have hundreds of active players simultaneously, each of whom can be represented by a thread. In these environments, users frequently enter and exit the game, meaning that thread pools can provide an efficient way to allocate threads. In general, any environment in which threads are rapidly created and destroyed, but variance in the total number of threads in the system at any given time is small, can benefit from thread pools.

4.4 Why are scheduler activations less portable than either user-level or kernel-level threads?

4.5 In Section 4.7.1, Thread Signal Delivery, we explained how signals may specify their targets using thread identifiers or process identifiers. Suggest an alternative way to implement signals to solve the asynchronous signal delivery problem.

4.6 Section 4.7.1, Thread Signal Delivery, discusses how Solaris 7 employed a thread called the Asynchronous Lightweight Process (ASLWP) to monitor and deliver pending asynchronous signals. How can this solution be simplified if the operating system represents threads using one-to-one thread mappings?

4.7 Compare and contrast asynchronous, deferred and disabled cancellation in Pthreads.

4.8 How do the Linux `fork` and `clone` system calls differ? How are they alike?

4.9 According to the discussion in Section 4.10, Windows XP Threads, which thread mappings does Windows XP support?

Suggested Projects

4.10 Research how threads are implemented in Windows XP, OS X, and Linux. Compare and contrast the implementations. How do these implementations differ from POSIX Pthreads?

4.11 Prepare a research paper on Java's implementation of threads. What information does the Java Virtual Machine keep track of for each thread? Does the implementation depend on the platform on which the JVM is running?

4.12 Research the Solaris compatible Thread Library. Prepare a research paper on how this library works. How does it handle the thread signal delivery and termination problems that were mentioned in the text? Does it conform to the POSIX standard?

4.13 Research three types of systems that use thread pooling. What average number of threads does each of these systems use?

4.14 Research how threads are managed in multiprocessor systems and distributed systems.

Recommended Reading

The concept of a lightweight process originated in Sun Microsystem's implementation of lightweight processes.[61] Lightweight processes soon became synonymous with threads, due to the development of the POSIX Pthreads specification and the introduction of the Java programming language. As programmers increasingly used threads in applications, operating system designers developed several levels of support for threads. One of the more successful models is Anderson et al.'s scheduler activations.[62] The paper also discusses many issues relevant to user- and kernel-level threads. Likewise, Benjamin provides a clear discussion of threading models.[63] The reader will also find the evolution of multithreading support in Sun Microsystem's Solaris operating system to be particularly sensitive to operating system design concerns regarding thread implementations.[64]

In recent years, the level of support for Pthreads across different operating systems has increased significantly. Blelloch describes Pthread implementation concerns and presents a case study on Solaris threads.[65] Butenhof's *Programming with POSIX Threads* discusses the POSIX specification and demonstrates how to program with Pthreads.[66] For more information regarding threads and thread programming, see Kleiman et al.'s *Programming with Threads*[67] and Birrell's *An Introduction to Programming with Threads*.[68] Ousterhout discusses how improper use of threads can reduce performance.[69]

Works Cited

1. "Process and Thread Functions," *MSDN Library*. Microsoft Corporation. February 2003, <msdn.microsoft.com/library/default.asp?url=/library/en-us/dllproc/base/process_and_thread_functions.asp>.

2. Manuel Pavón Valderrama, "The Unofficial GNU Mach IPC Beginner's Guide," August 19, 2002, <www.nongnu.org/hurdextras/ipc_guide/mach_ipc_cthreads.html>.

3. IEEE Standards Press, 1996, *9945-1:1996 (ISO/IEC) [IEEE/ANSI Std 1003.1 1996 Edition] Information Technology–Portable Operating System Interface (POSIX)–Part 1: System Application: Program Interface (API) [C Language] (ANSI)*.

4. Daley, Robert C., and Jack B. Dennis, "Virtual Memory, Processes, and Sharing in Multics," *Proceedings of the ACM Symposium on Operating System Principles*, January 1967.

5. "Multithreading in the Solaris Operating Environment, A Technical White Paper," Sun Microsystems, 2002.

6. O'Sullivan, B., "Answers to Frequently Asked Questions for comp.programming.threads: Part 1 of 1," Rev, 1.10, Last modified September 3, 1997, <www.serpentine.com/~bos/threads-faq/>.

7. "Lesson: Threads: Doing Two or More Tasks at Once," The Java Tutorial, Sun Microsystems, Inc., <java.sun.com/docs/books/tutorial/essential/threads/index.html>.

8. Appleton, R., "Understanding a Context Switching Benchmark," Modified October 23, 2001, <cs.nmu.edu/~randy/Research/Papers/Scheduler/understanding.html>.

9. "pthread_cancel," Documentation Overview, Glossary, and Master Index, © Digital Equipment Corporation 1996, All Rights Reserved; Product Version: Digital UNIX Version 4.0 or higher, March 1996, <www.cs.arizona.edu/computer.help/policy/DIGITAL_unix/AA-Q2DPC-TKT1_html/thrd0115.html#pt_cancel_13>.

10. "2.1.4 Waiting for a Thread to Terminate," Documentation Overview, Glossary, and Master Index, Product Version: Digital UNIX Version 4.0 or higher, March 1996, <www.cs.arizona.edu/computer.help/policy/DIGITAL_unix/AA-Q2DPC-TKT1_html/thrd0021.html#join_thread_sec>.

11. "Comp.os.research: Frequently Answered Questions, The History of Threads," Modified August 13, 1996, <www.faqs.org/faqs/os-research/part1/section-10.html>.

12. Anderson, T. E.; B. N. Bershad; E. D. Lazowska; and H. M. Levy, "Scheduler Activations: Effective Kernel Support for User-Level Management of Parallelism," *ACM Transactions on Computer Systems,* Vol. 10, No. 1, February 1992, p. 54.

13. Benjamin, C., "The Fibers of Threads," *Compile Time (Linux Magazine)*, May 2001, <www.linux-mag.com/2001-05/compile_06.html>.

14. Anderson, T. E.; B. N. Bershad; E. D. Lazowska; and H. M. Levy, "Scheduler Activations: Effective Kernel Support for User-Level Management of Parallelism," *ACM Transactions on Computer Systems,* Vol. 10, No. 1, February 1992, p. 54.

15. D.G. Feitelson, "Job Scheduling in Multiprogrammed Parallel Systems," *IBM Research Report RC 19790*, October 1994, 2d rev., August 1997, p. 121.

16. C. Benjamin, "The Fibers of Threads," *Compile Time (Linux Magazine)*, May 2001, <www.linux-mag.com/2001-05/compile_06.html>.

17. Feitelson, D. G., "Job Scheduling in Multiprogrammed Parallel Systems," IBM Research Report RC 19790, October 1994, 2d rev., August 1997, p. 121.

18. "Package java.nio.channels," Java 2 Platform SE v1.4.2, 2003 <java.sun.com/j2se/1.4.2/docs/api/java/nio/channels/package-summary.html#multiplex>.

19. Benjamin, C., "The Fibers of Threads," *Compile Time (Linux Magazine)*, May 2001, <www.linux-mag.com/2001-05/compile_06.html>.

20. Feitelson, D. G., "Job Scheduling in Multiprogrammed Parallel Systems," IBM Research Report RC 19790, October 1994, 2d rev., August 1997, p. 121.

21. Feitelson, D. G., "Job Scheduling in Multiprogrammed Parallel Systems," IBM Research Report RC 19790, October 1994, 2d rev., August 1997, p. 121.

22. Anderson, T. E.; B. N. Bershad; E. D. Lazowska; and H. M. Levy, "Scheduler Activations: Effective Kernel Support for User-Level Management of Parallelism," *ACM Transactions on Computer Systems*, Vol. 10, No. 1, February 1992, p. 54.

23. Benjamin, C., "The Fibers of Threads," *Compile Time (Linux Magazine)*, May 2001, <www.linux-mag.com/2001-05/compile_06.html>.

24. Benjamin, C., "The Fibers of Threads," *Compile Time (Linux Magazine)*, May 2001, <www.linux-mag.com/2001-05/compile_06.html>.

25. Richter, J., "New Windows 2000 Pooling Functions Greatly Simplify Thread Management," *Microsoft Systems Journal*, April 1999, <www.microsoft.com/msj/0499/pooling/pooling.aspx>.

26. Benjamin, C., "The Fibers of Threads," *Compile Time (Linux Magazine)*, May 2001, <www.linux-mag.com/2001-05/compile_06.html>.

27. Benjamin, C., "The Fibers of Threads," *Compile Time (Linux Magazine)*, May 2001, <www.linux-mag.com/2001-05/compile_06.html>.

28. "Multithreading in the Solaris Operating Environment, A Technical White Paper," Sun Microsystems, 2002.

29. "I've Got Work To Do—Worker Threads and Work Queues," *NT Insider*, Vol. 5, No. 5, October 1998 (updated August 20, 2002), <www.osronline.com/article.cfm?id=65>.

30. "System Worker Threads," *MSDN Library*, June 6, 2003, <msdn.microsoft.com/en-us/kmarch/hh/kmarch/synchro_9y1z.asp>.

31. McCracken, D., "POSIX Threads and the Linux Kernel," *Proceedings of the Ottawa Linux Symposium 2002*, p. 335.

32. Troan, E., "A Look at the Signal API," *Linux Magazine*, January 2000, <www.linux-mag.com/2000-01/compile_01.html>.

33. Drepper, Ulrich, "Requirements of the POSIX Signal Model," modified May 17, 2003, <people.redhat.com/drepper/posix-signal-model.xml>.

34. "Multithreading in the Solaris Operating Environment, A Technical White Paper," Sun Microsystems, 2002.

35. "Multithreading in the Solaris Operating Environment, A Technical White Paper," Sun Microsystems, 2002.

36. Drepper, Ulrich, "Requirements of the POSIX Signal Model," modified May 17, 2003, <people.redhat.com/drepper/posix-signal-model.xml>.

37. Butenhof, David R., *Programming with POSIX Threads*, Boston, MA: Addison-Wesley, 1997, p. 144.

38. "POSIX Thread API Concepts," *IBM iSeries information Center*, <publib.boulder.ibm.com/iseries/v5r1/ic2924/index.htm?info/apis/whatare.htm>, modified October 16, 2002.

39. O'Sullivan, B., "Answers to Frequently Asked Questions for comp.programming.threads: Part 1 of 1," rev. 1.1, <www.serpentine.com/~bos/threads-faq/>, last modified September 3, 1997.

40. McCracken, D., "POSIX Threads and the Linux Kernel," *Proceedings of the Ottawa Linux Symposium 2002*, p. 332.

41. Butenhof, David R., *Programming with POSIX Threads*, Boston, MA: Addison-Wesley, 1997, pp. 214–215.

42. Drepper, Ulrich, "Requirements of the POSIX Signal Model," modified May 17, 2003, <people.redhat.com/drepper/posix-signal-model.xml>.

43. Butenhof, David R., *Programming with POSIX Threads*, Boston, MA: Addison-Wesley, 1997, pp. 143–144.

44. Blelloch, G. E., and G. J. Narlikar, "Pthreads for Dynamic and Irregular Parallelism," *Conference on High Performance Networking and Computing, Proceedings of the 1998 ACM/IEEE Conference on Supercomputing*, 1998, San Jose, CA.

45. Rangaraju, K., "Unravel the Complexity of Thread Programming," <www.fawcette.com/javapro/2002_02/magazine/features/krangaraju/>.

46. "Threads Index," *The Open Group Base Specifications, Issue 6*, 2003, <www.opengroup.org/onlinepubs/007904975/idx/threads.html>.

47. Drepper, U., and I. Molnar, "The Native POSIX Thread Library for Linux," January 30, 2003, <people.redhat.com/drepper/nptl-design.pdf>.

48. "Multithreaded Programming Guide," Sun Microsystems, May 2002, pp. 11, 175.

49. Walton, S., "Linux Threads Frequently Asked Questions," January 21, 1997, <www.tldp.org/FAQ/Threads-FAQ/>.

50. Drepper, U., and I. Molnar, "The Native POSIX Thread Library for Linux," January 30, 2003, <people.redhat.com/drepper/nptl-design.pdf>.

51. "Processes and Threads," *MSDN Library*, <msdn.microsoft.com/library/en-us/dllproc/base/about_processes_and_threads.asp>.

52. "About Processes and Threads," *MSDN Library*, February 2003, <msdn.microsoft.com/library/en-us/dllproc/base/about_processes_and_threads.asp>.

53. "Fibers," *MSDN Library*, February 2003, <msdn.microsoft.com/library/en-us/dllproc/base/fibers.asp>.

54. "Convert Thread To Fiber," *MSDN Library*, February 2003, <msdn.microsoft.com/library/en-us/dllproc/base/convertthreadtofiber.asp>.

55. "Fibers," *MSDN Library*, February 2003, `<msdn.microsoft.com/library/en-us/dllproc/base/fibers.asp>`.

56. "Thread Pooling," *MSDN Library* February 2003 `<msdn.microsoft.com/library/en-us/dllproc/base/thread_pooling.asp>`.

57. "Queue User Worker Item," *MSDN Library,* February 2003, `<msdn.microsoft.com/library/en-us/dllproc/base/queueuserworkitem.asp>`.

58. Richter, J., "New Windows 2000 Pooling Functions Greatly Simplify Thread Management," *Microsoft Systems Journal*, April 1999, `<www.microsoft.com/msj/0499/pooling/pooling.aspx>`.

59. "Win_32 Thread," *MSDN Library,* July 2003, `<msdn.microsoft.com/library/en-us/wmisdk/wmi/win32_thread.asp>`.

60. Solomon, D., and M. Russinovich, *Inside Windows 2000,* 3d ed., Redmond: Microsoft Press, 2000, pp. 348–349.

61. Sun Microsystems, "Lightweight Processes," *SunOS System Service Overview*, Mountain View, CA: Sun Microsystems, December 1987, pp. 143–174.

62. Anderson, T. E.; B. N. Bershad; E. D. Lazowska; and H. M. Levy, "Scheduler Activations: Effective Kernel Support for User-Level Management of Parallelism," *ACM Transactions on Computer Systems*, Vol. 10, No. 1, February 1992, p. 54.

63. Benjamin, C., "The Fibers of Threads," *Compile Time (Linux Magazine)*, May 2001, `<www.linux-mag.com/2001-05/compile_06.html>`.

64. "Multithreading in the Solaris Operating Environment, A Technical White Paper," Sun Microsystems, 2002.

65. Blelloch, G. E., and G. J. Narlikar, "Pthreads for Dynamic and Irregular Parallelism," *Conference on High Performance Networking and Computing, Proceedings of the 1998 ACM/IEEE Conference on Supercomputing*, 1998, San Jose, CA.

66. Butenhof, David R., *Programming with POSIX Threads*, Boston, MA: Addison-Wesley, 1997: pp. 143–144.

67. Kleiman, S.; D. Shah; and B. Smaalders, *Programming with Threads*, Prentice Hall PTR, 1997.

68. Birrell, A. D., *An Introduction to Programming with Threads*. Technical Report 35, Digital Equipment Corporation, Systems Research Center, Palo Alto, CA, 1989.

69. Ousterhout, J., "Why threads are a bad idea (for most purposes)." In *USENIX Technical Conference* (Invited Talk), Austin, TX, January 1996.

Do not put me to't, For I am nothing if not critical.

—William Shakespeare—

A person with one watch knows what time it is; a person with two watches is never sure.

—Proverb—

Busy leisure.

—Johann Elias Schlegel—

A really busy person never knows how much he weighs.

—Edgar Watson Howe—

Delays breed dangers.

—John Lyly—

By delaying he preserved the state.

—Quintus Ennius—

Chapter 5

Asynchronous Concurrent Execution

Objectives

After reading this chapter, you should understand:

- *the challenges of synchronizing concurrent processes and threads.*

- *critical sections and the need for mutual exclusion.*

- *how to implement mutual exclusion primitives in software.*

- *hardware mutual exclusion primitives.*

- *semaphore usage and implementation.*

Chapter 5

Chapter Outline

Web Resources | Summary | Key Terms | Exercises | Recommended Reading | Works Cited

5.1 Introduction

In the previous two chapters, we introduced the concept of units of execution—processes and threads. Once again, we will focus our discussion on threads in this chapter, but most of what we say can apply to processes as well. If more than one thread exists in a system at the same time, then the threads are said to be **concurrent**.[1, 2, 3] Two concurrent threads can execute completely independently of one another, or they can execute in cooperation. Threads that operate independently of one another but must occasionally communicate and synchronize to perform cooperative tasks are said to execute **asynchronously**.[4, 5] Asynchronism is a complex topic—this chapter and Chapter 6, Concurrent Programming, discuss the organization and management of systems that support **asynchronous concurrent threads**.

We begin with a Java example that demonstrates the difficulty of writing correct programs even with as few as two asynchronous concurrent threads. If coded improperly, such programs can produce undesired and unpredictable results. In the remainder of the chapter, we discuss various mechanisms that programmers can use to create correct programs with asynchronous concurrent threads. In the next chapter, we present two classic asynchronism problems and implement their solutions in Java.

Self Review

1. (T/F) Communication and synchronization are necessary only for asynchronously executing threads.
2. (T/F) Threads that occasionally communicate, even though they normally operate independently of one another are said to execute synchronously.

Ans: **1)** False. Communication and synchronization are necessary for asynchronously executing threads and processes. **2)** False. Such threads are said to execute asynchronously.

5.2 Mutual Exclusion

Consider a mail server that processes e-mail for an organization. Suppose we want the system to continuously monitor the total number of e-mails that have been sent since the day began. Assume that the receipt of an e-mail is handled by one of several concurrent threads. Each time one of these threads receives an e-mail from a user, the thread increments a processwide shared variable, `mailCount`, by 1. Consider what happens if two threads attempt to increment `mailCount` simultaneously. First, assume that each thread runs the assembly-language code

```
LOAD mailCount
ADD 1
STORE mailCount
```

Assume that the `LOAD` instruction copies `mailCount` from memory to a register, the `ADD` instruction adds the immediate constant 1 from memory to the value in the register, and the `STORE` instruction copies the value in the register to memory. Suppose `mailCount` is currently 21687. Now suppose the first thread executes the `LOAD` and `ADD` instructions, thus leaving 21688 in the register (but not yet updating the value in `mailCount` in memory, which is still 21687). Then, due to a quantum expiration, the first thread loses the processor and the system context switches to the second thread. The second thread now executes all three instructions, thus setting `mailCount` to 21688. This thread loses the processor, and the system context switches back to the first thread, which then continues by executing the STORE instruction—also placing 21688 into `mailCount`. Due to the uncontrolled access to the shared variable `mailCount`, the system has essentially lost track of one of the e-mails—`mailCount` should be 21689. In the case of an e-mail management application, such an error may seem minor. A similar error occurring in a mission-critical application such as air traffic control could cost lives.

The cause of this incorrect result is the writing of the shared variable `mail-Count`. Clearly, many concurrent threads may read data simultaneously without this difficulty. But when one thread reads data that another thread is writing, or when one thread writes data that another thread is also writing, indeterminate results can occur.[6, 7, 8]

We can solve this problem by granting each thread **exclusive access** to `mail-Count`. While one thread increments the shared variable, all other threads desiring to do so will be made to wait. When the executing thread finishes accessing the shared variable, the system will allow one of the waiting processes to proceed. This is called **serializing** access to the shared variable. In this manner, threads will not be able to access shared data simultaneously. As each thread proceeds to update the shared variable, all others are excluded from doing so simultaneously. This is called **mutual exclusion**.[9, 10, 11] As we will see in this and subsequent chapters, waiting threads must be carefully managed to ensure that they will be able to proceed within a "reasonable" amount of time.

Self Review

1. In the `mailCount` example above, would it be acceptable if several threads simultaneously read the value without updating it?
2. (T/F) Suppose each of two threads that share a variable needs to update that shared variable at some point during the thread's execution. If the threads are not made to mutually exclude each other from updating the shared variable simultaneously, then on any execution of two threads, the system will fail.

Ans: **1)** Yes, mutual exclusion is necessary only when threads update the shared variable. **2)** False. It is possible that the threads will attempt to update the shared variable at different times, and the program could thus function correctly.

5.2.1 Java Multithreading Case Study, Part II: A Producer/Consumer Relationship in Java

In a **producer/consumer relationship**, the **producer** portion of the application generates data and stores it in a shared object, and the **consumer** portion reads data from the shared object. One example of a common producer/consumer relationship is print spooling. A word processor spools data to a buffer (typically a file) and that data is subsequently consumed by the printer as it prints the document. Similarly, an application that copies data onto compact discs places data in a fixed-size buffer that is emptied as the CD-RW drive burns the data onto the compact disk.

Consider a multithreaded producer/consumer relationship implemented in Java in which a **producer thread** generates data and places it into a buffer capable of holding a single value and a **consumer thread** reads data from the buffer. If the producer waiting to put the next data into the buffer determines that the consumer has not yet read the previous data from the buffer, the producer should call `wait` so the consumer gets a chance to read unconsumed data before it is overwritten. When the consumer reads the data, it should call `notify` to allow the (possibly waiting) producer to store the next value. `Object` method `notify` transitions a thread from the *waiting* state to the *ready* state. If the consumer finds the buffer empty (because the producer has not yet produced its first data) or finds that the previous data has already been read, the consumer should call `wait` to place itself in the *waiting* state; otherwise, the consumer might read "garbage" from an empty buffer or might erroneously process the same data again. When the producer places the next data into the buffer, the producer should call `notify` to allow the (possibly waiting) consumer thread to proceed, so the consumer can read the new data. Note that `notify` has no effect when none of an application's threads are waiting.

Let us implement this example in Java to see how logic errors can arise if we do not synchronize access among multiple threads manipulating shared data. The example that follows (Fig. 5.1–Fig. 5.5) implements a producer/consumer relationship in which a producer thread sequentially writes numbers (1 to 4) into a shared buffer—a memory location shared between two threads (a single `int` variable called `buffer` in Fig. 5.4). The consumer thread reads this data from the shared buffer and displays the data. The program's output (three samples are shown in Fig. 5.5) shows the values that the producer writes (produces) into the shared buffer and the values that the consumer reads (consumes) from the shared buffer.

Each value the producer writes to the shared buffer must be consumed exactly once (and in order) by the consumer thread. However, the threads in this example are not **synchronized**, meaning that they do not cooperate when performing their tasks (which, as we have seen, is especially important when one of the threads is writing to the buffer). Therefore, data (possibly multiple values) can be lost if the producer places new data into the shared buffer before the consumer consumes the previous data, and data can be incorrectly duplicated (possibly many times) if the consumer consumes data again before the producer produces the next value. The consequence of not synchronizing access to shared data is somewhat like the consequence of not having a traffic light at a busy intersection.

To show these possibilities, the consumer in the following example keeps a total of all the values it reads. The producer produces values from 1 to 4 in order. In the traditional producer/consumer relationship, the consumer reads each produced value once and only once. In addition, the consumer cannot read each value until after the producer has produced it. Therefore, the producer must always produce a value before the consumer reads that value, and the total of the values consumed in our example must be 10. However, if you execute this program several times (see the sample outputs of Fig. 5.5), you will see that the total is rarely, if ever, 10. The producer and consumer threads in the example each sleep for random intervals of up to three seconds between performing their tasks, simulating some lengthy delay such as waiting for user input or for some event to occur. Thus, we do not know exactly when the producer will attempt to write a new value, nor do we know when the consumer will attempt to read a value.

The Java program consists of interface Buffer (Fig. 5.1) and four classes— Producer (Fig. 5.2), Consumer (Fig. 5.3), UnsynchronizedBuffer (Fig. 5.4) and SharedBufferTest (Fig. 5.5). Interface Buffer declares methods set and get that a Buffer must implement to enable a Producer thread to place a value in the Buffer and enable a Consumer thread to retrieve a value from the Buffer, respectively. This interface is implemented in Fig. 5.4 (line 4).

Class Producer (Fig. 5.2)—a subclass of Thread (line 5)—contains field sharedLocation (line 7), a constructor (lines 9–14) and a run method (lines 18–40). The constructor initializes Buffer reference sharedLocation (line 13) with a reference to an object that implements the Buffer interface. That object is created in main (Fig. 5.5; lines 6–18) and passed to the constructor as the parameter shared (Fig. 5.2; line 10); the constructor initializes the Buffer reference sharedLocation (line 13) to be a reference to the parameter shared. The producer thread in this program executes the tasks specified in method run (lines 18–40). The for statement in lines 20–35 loops four times. Each iteration of the loop invokes Thread method sleep (line 25) to place the producer thread into the sleeping state for a random time interval between 0 and 3 seconds (to simulate a lengthy operation).

[*Note:* Normally, a thread awakens when its sleep time expires. A sleeping thread can be awakened early if another thread calls the sleeping thread's interrupt method. If this occurs, sleep "throws" an exception (of type Interrupt-edException) to indicate that the thread was interrupted before its sleep time expired. In Java, this exception must be "handled," which requires the sleep method call to appear in a try block that is followed by a catch handler. The try block contains the code that might throw an exception. The catch handler specifies the type of exception it handles. In this example, the catch handler prints a stack trace, then the program continues with the next statement after the try…catch sequence.]

```java
1   // Fig. 5.1: Buffer.java
2   // Buffer interface specifies methods to access buffer data.
3
4   public interface Buffer
5   {
6      public void set( int value );   // place value into Buffer
7      public int get();               // return value from Buffer
8   }
```

Figure 5.1 | Buffer interface used in producer/consumer examples.

When the thread awakens, line 26 passes the value of control variable `count` to the `Buffer` object's `set` method to change the shared buffer's value. When the loop completes, lines 37–38 display a message in the console window indicating that the thread finished producing data and that the thread is terminating. Next, method `run` terminates (line 40) and the producer thread enters the *dead* state. It is important to note that any method called from a thread's `run` method (such as `Buffer` method `set` in line 26) executes as part of that thread of execution. In fact, each thread has its own method-call stack.

```java
1   // Fig. 5.2: Producer.java
2   // Producer's run method controls a producer thread that
3   // stores values from 1 to 4 in Buffer sharedLocation.
4
5   public class Producer extends Thread
6   {
7       private Buffer sharedLocation; // reference to shared object
8
9       // Producer constructor
10      public Producer( Buffer shared )
11      {
12          super( "Producer" ); // create thread named "Producer"
13          sharedLocation = shared; // initialize sharedLocation
14      } // end Producer constructor
15
16      // Producer method run stores values from
17      // 1 to 4 in Buffer sharedLocation
18      public void run()
19      {
20          for ( int count = 1; count <= 4; count++ )
21          {
22              // sleep 0 to 3 seconds, then place value in Buffer
23              try
24              {
25                  Thread.sleep( ( int ) ( Math.random() * 3001 ) );
26                  sharedLocation.set( count ); // write to the buffer
27              } // end try
28
29              // if sleeping thread interrupted, print stack trace
30              catch ( InterruptedException exception )
31              {
32                  exception.printStackTrace();
33              } // end catch
34
35          } // end for
```

Figure 5.2 | Producer class represents the producer thread in a producer/consumer relationship. (Part 1 of 2.)

```
36
37              System.err.println( getName() + " done producing." +
38                  "\nTerminating " + getName() + "." );
39
40        } // end method run
41
42  } // end class Producer
```

Figure 5.2 | Producer *class represents the producer thread in a producer/consumer relationship. (Part 2 of 2.)*

Class `Consumer` (Fig. 5.3) contains instance variable `sharedLocation` (line 7), a constructor (lines 9–14) and a `run` method (lines 16–41). The constructor initializes `Buffer` reference `sharedLocation` (line 13) with a reference to an object that implements the `Buffer` interface. That object is created in `main` (Fig. 5.5) and passed to the constructor as the parameter `shared` (Fig. 5.3; line 10). As we will see (Fig. 5.5; lines 12–13), this is the same `UnsynchronizedBuffer` object that is used to initialize the `Producer` object; thus, the producer and consumer threads share the object. The consumer thread in this program performs the tasks specified in method `run` (Fig. 5.3; lines 16–41). The loop in lines 22–36 loops four times. Each iteration of the loop invokes `Thread` method `sleep` (line 27) to put the consumer thread into the sleeping state for a random time interval between 0 and 3 seconds. Next, line 28 uses the `Buffer`'s `get` method to retrieve the value in the shared buffer, then adds the value to variable `sum`. When the loop completes, lines 38–39 display a line in the console window indicating the sum of the consumed values and the fact that the consumer thread is terminating. Then, method `run` terminates (line 41), and the consumer thread enters the *dead* state.

```
1   // Fig. 5.3: Consumer.java
2   // Consumer's run method controls a thread that loops four
3   // times and reads a value from sharedLocation each time.
4
5   public class Consumer extends Thread
6   {
7       private Buffer sharedLocation; // reference to shared object
8
9       // Consumer constructor
10      public Consumer( Buffer shared )
11      {
12          super( "Consumer" ); // create thread named "Consumer"
13          sharedLocation = shared; // initialize sharedLocation
14      } // end Consumer constructor
```

Figure 5.3 | Consumer *class represents the consumer thread in a producer/consumer relationship. (Part 1 of 2.)*

```
15
16       // read sharedLocation's value four times and sum the values
17       public void run()
18       {
19          int sum = 0;
20
21          // alternate between sleeping and getting Buffer value
22          for ( int count = 1; count <= 4; ++count )
23          {
24             // sleep 0-3 seconds, read Buffer value and add to sum
25             try
26             {
27                Thread.sleep( ( int ) ( Math.random() * 3001 ) );
28                sum += sharedLocation.get();
29             }
30
31             // if sleeping thread interrupted, print stack trace
32             catch ( InterruptedException exception )
33             {
34                exception.printStackTrace();
35             }
36          } // end for
37
38          System.err.println( getName() + " read values totaling: "
39             + sum + ".\nTerminating " + getName() + "." );
40
41       } // end method run
42
43    } // end class Consumer
```

Figure 5.3 | *Consumer class represents the consumer thread in a producer/consumer relationship. (Part 2 of 2.)*

[*Note*: We use a randomly generated interval with method `sleep` in method run of both the `Producer` and `Consumer` classes to emphasize the fact that, in multithreaded applications, it is unclear when and for how long each thread will perform its task. Normally, these thread-scheduling issues are the job of the operating system. In this program, our thread's tasks are quite simple—for the producer, loop four times, each time setting a value in the shared buffer; for the consumer, loop four times, each time retrieving a value from the shared buffer and adding the value to variable `sum`. Without the `sleep` method call, and if the producer were to execute first, it most likely would complete its task before the consumer got a chance to execute; if the consumer were to execute first, most likely it would consume the "null" value (-1, specified in `UnsynchronizedBuffer`, line 6 of Fig. 5.4) four times, then terminate (displaying the invalid sum, -4) before the producer produced even its first value.]

Class UnsynchronizedBuffer (Fig. 5.4) implements interface Buffer (line 4) defined in Fig. 5.1 and declares the variable buffer (line 6), shared between the Producer and Consumer. Variable buffer is initialized with the value −1. This value is used to demonstrate the case in which the Consumer attempts to consume a value before the Producer places a value in buffer. Methods set (lines 8–15) and get (lines 17–24) do not synchronize access to field buffer (we will see how to do this shortly). Method set simply assigns its parameter to buffer (line 14) and method get simply returns the value of buffer (line 23). Note that each method uses class Thread's static method currentThread to obtain a reference to the currently executing thread, then uses that thread's method getName to obtain the thread's name for output purposes (lines 11 and 20).

Class SharedBufferTest (Fig. 5.5) contains method main (lines 6–18), which launches the application. Line 9 instantiates a shared UnsynchronizedBuffer object and assigns it to Buffer reference sharedLocation. This object stores the data that will be shared between the producer and consumer threads. Lines 12–13 create the Producer object producer and the Consumer object consumer. Each of

```java
1   // Fig. 5.4: UnsynchronizedBuffer.java
2   // UnsynchronizedBuffer represents a single shared integer.
3
4   public class UnsynchronizedBuffer implements Buffer
5   {
6      private int buffer = -1; // shared by Producer and Consumer
7
8      // place value into buffer
9      public void set( int value )
10     {
11        System.err.println( Thread.currentThread().getName() +
12           " writes " + value );
13
14        buffer = value;
15     } // end method set
16
17     // return value from buffer
18     public int get()
19     {
20        System.err.println( Thread.currentThread().getName() +
21           " reads " + buffer );
22
23        return buffer;
24     } // end method get
25
26  } // end class UnsynchronizedBuffer
```

Figure 5.4 | *UnsynchronizedBuffer class maintains the shared integer that is accessed by a producer thread and a consumer thread via methods* set *and* get

the constructor calls in these lines passes sharedLocation as the argument to the constructor (lines 9–14 of Fig. 5.2 for Producer and lines 9–14 of Fig. 5.3 for Consumer), so that each thread accesses the same Buffer. Next, lines 15–16 of Fig. 5.5 invoke method start on the producer and consumer threads, respectively, to place them in the *ready* state. This launches the execution of these threads by making an implicit call to each thread's run method. A thread's run method will be called when the thread is dispatched to a processor for the first time. After the producer and consumer threads are started, method main (i.e., the main thread of execution) terminates and the main thread enters the *dead* state. Once both the producer and consumer threads enter the *dead* state (which occurs when their run methods terminate), the program terminates.

Recall from the overview of this example that the Producer thread must produce a value before the Consumer thread consumes a value, and every value produced by the producer must be consumed exactly once by the consumer. However, when we study the first output of Fig. 5.5, we see that the consumer retrieved the value –1 before the producer ever placed a value in the buffer. The first value produced (1) was consumed three times. Furthermore, the consumer finished executing before the producer had an opportunity to produce the values 2, 3 and 4, so those three values were lost. An incorrect total of 2 was produced.

In the second output, we see that the value 1 was lost, because the values 1 and 2 were produced before the consumer thread could read the value 1 (so the

```
1   // Fig. 5.5: SharedBufferTest.java
2   // SharedBufferTest creates producer and consumer threads.
3
4   public class SharedBufferTest
5   {
6       public static void main( String [] args )
7       {
8           // create shared object used by threads
9           Buffer sharedLocation = new UnsynchronizedBuffer();
10
11          // create producer and consumer objects
12          Producer producer = new Producer( sharedLocation );
13          Consumer consumer = new Consumer( sharedLocation );
14
15          producer.start();  // start producer thread
16          consumer.start();  // start consumer thread
17
18      } // end main
19
20  } // end class SharedCell
```

Figure 5.5 | SharedBuffer *class enables threads to modify a shared object without synchronization. (Part 1 of 2.)*

Sample Output 1:

```
Consumer reads -1
Producer writes 1
Consumer reads 1
Consumer reads 1
Consumer reads 1
Consumer read values totaling: 2.
Terminating Consumer.
Producer writes 2
Producer writes 3
Producer writes 4
Producer done producing.
Terminating Producer.
```

Sample Output 2:

```
Producer writes 1
Producer writes 2
Consumer reads 2
Producer writes 3
Consumer reads 3
Producer writes 4
Producer done producing.
Terminating Producer.
Consumer reads 4
Consumer reads 4
Consumer read values totaling: 13.
Terminating Consumer.
```

Sample Output 3:

```
Producer writes 1
Consumer reads 1
Producer writes 2
Consumer reads 2
Producer writes 3
Consumer reads 3
Producer writes 4
Producer done producing.
Terminating Producer.
Consumer reads 4
Consumer read values totaling: 10.
Terminating Consumer.
```

Figure 5.5 | SharedBuffer *class enables threads to modify a shared object without synchronization. (Part 2 of 2.)*

value 2 overwrote the value 1 in the buffer). Also, the value 4 was consumed twice. Once again, an incorrect total was produced. The last sample output demonstrates that it is possible, with some luck, to get a proper output; clearly, this behavior cannot be guaranteed.

This example demonstrates that access to a shared object by concurrent threads must be controlled carefully; otherwise, a program may produce incorrect results. We provide a solution to this problem in the next chapter. The remainder of this chapter discusses how threads control concurrent access to shared data by enforcing mutually exclusive access to that data.

Self Review

1. (T/F) In the producer/consumer example shown in Fig. 5.1–Fig. 5.5, the output would be correct and consistent if the calls to `sleep` were removed.
2. What are the smallest and largest possible values of `sum` at the end of the execution of the example shown in Fig. 5.1–Fig. 5.5, and how would those values be achieved?

Ans: **1)** False. The `sleep` calls were put there simply to emphasize the fact that there is uncertainty within a system regarding the order and timing in which instructions are executed. Still, we cannot predict the speeds at which these threads will advance, so the outputs could still be incorrect. **2)** The smallest value would occur if the consumer tried consuming four values before the producer produced any. In this case, `sum` would be –4. The largest value would occur if the producer produced four values before the consumer consumed any. In this case, the consumer would consume the value four times, and `sum` would be 16.

5.2.2 Critical Sections

Mutual exclusion needs to be enforced only when threads access shared modifiable data. When threads are performing operations that do not conflict with one another (e.g., reading variables), the system should allow the threads to proceed concurrently. When a thread is accessing shared modifiable data, it is said to be in a **critical section** (or **critical region**).[12] To prevent the kinds of errors we encountered earlier, the system should ensure that only one thread at a time can execute the instructions in its critical section for a particular resource. If one thread attempts to enter its critical section while another is in its own critical section, the first thread should wait until the executing thread exits the critical section. Once a thread has exited its critical section, a waiting thread (or one of the waiting threads, if there are several), may enter and execute its critical section. Any thread that does not need to enter its critical section may execute regardless of whether a critical section is occupied.

A system that enforces mutual exclusion must carefully control access to, and execution in, critical sections. A thread in a critical section has exclusive access to shared, modifiable data, and all other threads currently requiring access to that data are kept waiting. Therefore, a thread should execute a critical section as quickly as possible. A thread must not block inside its critical section, and critical sections must be carefully coded to avoid—for example—the possibility of infinite loops. If a thread in a critical section terminates, either voluntarily or involuntarily, then the operating system, in performing its **termination housekeeping**, must release mutual exclusion so that other threads may enter their critical sections.

Enforcing mutually exclusive access to critical sections is one of the key problems in concurrent programming. Many solutions have been devised: some software solutions and some hardware solutions; some rather low-level and some high-level; some requiring voluntary cooperation among threads and some demanding rigid adherence to strict protocols. We will examine a variety of these solutions in the upcoming sections.

Self Review

1. Why is it important for a thread to execute a critical section as quickly as possible?
2. What might happen if the operating system did not perform termination housekeeping?

Ans: **1)** If other threads are waiting to execute their critical sections, they will be delayed from doing so while any thread is in its critical section. If critical sections do not execute quickly, overall system performance could suffer. **2)** A thread could terminate while in its critical section, and never release mutual exclusion. The threads waiting to enter their critical sections would never be able to enter. As we will see in Chapter 7, Deadlock and Indefinite Postponement, these threads will deadlock.

5.2.3 Mutual Exclusion Primitives

The following pseudocode properly describes the e-mail counting mechanism of Section 5.2, Mutual Exclusion. Notice that we use the words `enterMutualExclusion()` and `exitMutualExclusion()`. These words are constructs that encapsulate the thread's critical section—when a thread wants to enter its critical section, the thread must first execute `enterMutualExclusion()`; when a thread exits the critical section, it executes `exitMutualExclusion()`. Because these constructs invoke the most fundamental operations inherent to mutual exclusion, they are sometimes called **mutual exclusion primitives**.

```
while (true) {
    Receive e-mail              // executing outside critical section
    enterMutualExclusion()      // want to enter critical section
        Increment mailCount     // executing inside critical section
    exitMutualExclusion()       // leaving critical section
}
```

Let us consider how these primitives can provide mutual exclusion. For simplicity in the example presented in this and the next several sections, we shall assume only two concurrent threads and one processor. Handling *n* concurrent processes or threads is a considerably more complex topic, which we discuss in Section 5.4.3, N-Thread Mutual Exclusion: Lamport's Bakery Algorithm. We will also discuss how mutual exclusion is enforced on multiprocessor systems.

Assume that threads T_1 and T_2 of the same process are both executing in the system. Each thread manages e-mail messages, and each thread contains instructions that correspond to the preceding pseudocode. When T_1 reaches the `enterMutualEx-`

`clusion()` line, the system must determine whether T_2 is already in its critical section. If T_2 is not in its critical section, then T_1 enters its critical section, increments shared variable `mailCount` and executes `exitMutualExclusion()` to indicate that T_1 has left its critical section. If, on the other hand, when T_1 executes `enterMutual-Exclusion()`, T_2 is in its critical section, then T_1 must wait until T_2 executes `exitMutualExclusion()`, at which point T_1 enters its critical section. If T_1 and T_2 simultaneously execute `enterMutualExclusion()`, then only one of the threads will be allowed to proceed, and one will be kept waiting. For the moment, we shall assume that the system randomly selects the thread that will proceed. [As we will see, such a policy could lead to indefinite postponement of one of the threads if the other is always selected when the threads repeatedly try to enter their critical sections.] In the next several sections, we discuss various mechanisms for implementing the `enterMutualExclusion()` and `exitMutualExclusion()` mutual exclusion primitives.

Self Review

1. What will happen if a thread does not call `enterMutualExclusion()` before accessing shared variables in a critical section?
2. What will happen if a thread that is in its critical section does not call `exitMutualExclusion()`?

Ans: **1)** If other threads also enter their critical section, there could be indeterminate results that could have serious consequences. **2)** All other threads that are waiting to enter their critical sections would never be allowed to do so. As we will see in Chapter 7, Deadlock and Indefinite Postponement, all of these other threads would eventually deadlock.

5.3 Implementing Mutual Exclusion Primitives

Each initial mutual exclusion solutions that we discuss provides an implementation of `enterMutualExclusion()` and `exitMutualExclusion()` that exhibits the following properties:

1. The solution is implemented purely in software on a machine without specially designed mutual exclusion machine-language instructions. Each machine-language instruction is executed **indivisibly**—i.e., once started, it completes without interruption. If a system contains multiple processors, several threads could try to access the same data item simultaneously. As we will see, many mutual exclusion solutions for uniprocessor systems rely on access to shared data, meaning that they might not work on multiprocessor systems (see Section 15.9, Multiprocessor Mutual Exclusion). For simplicity, we will assume that the system contains one processor. Again, we will deal with multiprocessor systems later.

2. No assumption can be made about the relative speeds of asynchronous concurrent threads. This means that any solution must assume that a thread can be preempted or resumed at any time during its execution and that the rate of execution of each thread may not be constant or predictable.

3. A thread that is executing instructions outside its critical section cannot prevent any other threads from entering their critical sections.

4. A thread must not be indefinitely postponed from entering its critical section. [*Note*: Once inside an improperly coded critical section, a thread could certainly "misbehave" in ways that could lead to indefinite postponement or even deadlock. We discuss these issues in depth in Chapter 7, Deadlock and Indefinite Postponement.]

Self Review

1. Why do you suppose that we cannot predict the relative speeds of asynchronous concurrent threads?
2. How can an improperly coded thread cause indefinite postponement or deadlock?

Ans: **1)** One reason is that hardware interrupts, which may be randomly distributed, can disrupt thread execution at any time. Over any given period, these interrupts may allow some threads to execute longer than others. In addition, biases in resource-scheduling algorithms may favor certain threads. **2)** A thread that never left its critical section (e.g., by entering an infinite loop) would eventually indefinitely postpone or deadlock all other threads as they tried to enter their critical sections.

5.4   Software Solutions to the Mutual Exclusion Problem

An elegant software implementation of mutual exclusion was first presented by the Dutch mathematician Dekker. In the next section we follow Dijkstra's development of **Dekker's Algorithm**, an implementation of mutual exclusion for two threads.[13] The arguments presented introduce many of the subtleties in concurrent programming that make this such an interesting field of study. Then, we discuss simpler and more efficient algorithms developed by G. L. Peterson[14] and L. Lamport.[15]

5.4.1   Dekker's Algorithm

In this section we examine several attempts to implement mutual exclusion. Each implementation contains a problem that the subsequent one overcomes. The section culminates in the presentation of a correct software implementation to mutual exclusion that is free of deadlock and indefinite postponement.

First Version (Introducing Lockstep Synchronization and Busy Waiting)

Figure 5.6 shows a first effort at specifying the code for enforcing mutual exclusion between two threads. The pseudocode is presented using a C-like syntax. Each thread's instructions can be broken into three parts: noncritical instructions (i.e., instructions that do not modify shared data), critical instructions (i.e., instructions that do modify shared data) and the instructions that ensure mutual exclusion (i.e., instructions that implement `enterMutualExclusion()` and `exitMutualExclusion()`). Each thread repeatedly enters and exits its critical section until it is done.

Under this version of mutual exclusion, the system uses a variable called `threadNumber`, to which both threads have access. Before the system starts execut-

```
1    System:
2
3    int threadNumber = 1;
4
5    startThreads(); // initialize and launch both threads
6
7    Thread T₁:
8
9    void main() {
10
11      while ( !done )
12      {
13         while ( threadNumber == 2 ); // enterMutualExclusion
14
15         // critical section code
16
17         threadNumber = 2; // exitMutualExclusion
18
19         // code outside critical section
20
21      } // end outer while
22
23   } // end Thread T1
24
25   Thread T₂:
26
27   void main() {
28
29      while ( !done )
30       {
31         while ( threadNumber == 1 );   // enterMutualExclusion
32
33         // critical section code
34
35         threadNumber = 1; // exitMutualExclusion
36
37         // code outside critical section
38
39      } // end outer while
40
41   } // end Thread T2
```

Figure 5.6 | *Mutual exclusion implementation—version 1.*

ing the threads, `threadNumber` is set to 1 (line 3). Then the system starts both threads. The `enterMutualExclusion()` primitive is implemented as a single `while` loop that loops indefinitely until variable `threadNumber` becomes equal to the number of the thread (see lines 13 and 31 in threads T_1 and T_2, respectively). The `exitMutualExclusion()` primitive is implemented as a single instruction that sets `threadNumber` to the number of the other thread (see lines 17 and 35 in threads T_1 and T_2, respectively).

Consider one way in which execution might proceed under this implementation. Assume T_1 begins executing first. The thread executes the `while` loop (line 13) that acts as `enterMutualExclusion()`. Because `threadNumber` is initially 1, T_1 enters its critical section (the code indicated by the comment in line 15). Now assume that the system suspends T_1 and begins executing T_2. The second thread finds `threadNumber` equal to 1 and remains "locked" in the `while` loop (line 31). This guarantees mutual exclusion, because T_2 cannot enter its critical section until T_1 exits its critical section and sets `threadNumber` to 2 (line 17).

Eventually, T_1 finishes executing in its critical section (recall that we are assuming that the critical sections contain no infinite loops and that threads do not die or block inside critical sections). At this point, T_1 sets `threadNumber` to 2 (line 17) and continues to its "noncritical" instructions. Now T_2 is free to enter its critical section.

Although this implementation guarantees mutual exclusion, the solution has significant drawbacks. In the `enterMutualExclusion()` primitive, the thread uses the processor to perform essentially no work (i.e., the thread repeatedly tests the value of `threadNumber`. Such a thread is said to be **busy waiting.** Busy waiting can be an ineffective technique for implementing mutual exclusion on uniprocessor systems. Recall that one goal of multiprogramming is to increase processor utilization. If our mutual exclusion primitive uses processor cycles to perform work that is not essential to the thread, then processor time is wasted. This overhead, however, is limited to short periods of time (i.e., when there is contention between the threads to enter their critical sections).

A more damaging drawback of this implementation is that it violates one of the key constraints we identified in Section 5.3, Implementing Mutual Exclusion Primitives, namely that a thread that is not in its critical section should not affect a thread that desires to enter its own critical section. For example, T_1 must enter the critical section first, because the system initially sets `threadNumber` to 1. If T_2 tries to go first, it begins execution and unsuccessfully attempts to enter its critical section. Eventually, T_1 executes, entering its critical section and setting `threadNumber` to 2. Thus, T_2 may be delayed considerably before it may enter its critical section. In fact, the threads must enter and leave their critical sections in strict alternation. If one thread needs to enter its critical section more frequently than the other, the faster thread will be constrained to operate at the speed of the slower thread. This is called the **lockstep synchronization** problem.* The next mutual exclusion implementation eliminates this problem but introduces another.

---

* Of course, the problem in Section 5.2.1 required lockstep synchronization because the buffer was of unit size. However, almost all buffers contain several entries, meaning that lockstep synchronization causes inefficient behavior if the producer and consumer operate at different speeds.

Second Version (Violating Mutual Exclusion)

Figure 5.7 contains a solution that attempts to eliminate the lockstep synchronization of the previous implementation. In the first solution, the system maintained
only a single global variable—this forced the lockstep synchronization. Version 2
maintains two variables—t1Inside that is true if T_1 is inside its critical section, and
t2Inside that is true if T_2 is inside its critical section.

```
 1   System:
 2
 3   boolean t1Inside = false;
 4   boolean t2Inside = false;
 5
 6   startThreads(); // initialize and launch both threads
 7
 8   Thread T₁:
 9
10   void main() {
11
12      while ( !done )
13       {
14          while ( t2Inside ); // enterMutualExclusion
15
16          t1Inside = true; // enterMutualExclusion
17
18          // critical section code
19
20          t1Inside = false; // exitMutualExclusion
21
22          // code outside critical section
23
24       } // end outer while
25
26   } // end Thread T1
27
28   Thread T₂:
29
30   void main() {
31
32      while ( !done )
33       {
34          while ( t1Inside ); // enterMutualExclusion
35
36          t2Inside = true; // enterMutualExclusion
37
38          // critical section code
```

Figure 5.7 | *Mutual exclusion implementation—version 2. (Part 1 of 2.)*

```
39
40          t2Inside = false; // exitMutualExclusion
41
42          // code outside critical section
43
44      } // end outer while
45
46  } // end Thread T2
```

Figure 5.7 | *Mutual exclusion implementation—version 2. (Part 2 of 2.)*

By using two variables to govern access to the critical sections (one for each thread), we are able to eliminate lockstep synchronization in our second mutual exclusion implementation. T_1 will be able to continuously enter its critical section as many times as necessary while t2Inside is false. Also, if T_1 enters the critical section and sets t1Inside to true, then T_2 will busy wait. Eventually, T_1 will finish its critical section and perform its mutual exclusion exit code, setting t1Inside to false.

Although this solution eliminates the lockstep synchronization issue, it unfortunately does not guarantee mutual exclusion. Consider the following situation. Variables t1Inside and t2Inside are both false, and both threads attempt to enter their critical sections at the same time. T_1 tests the value of t2Inside (line 14), determines that the value is false and proceeds to the next statement. Now suppose that the system preempts T_1 before it can execute line 16 (which it needs to do to keep T_2 out of its own critical section). T_2 now executes, determines that t1Inside is false and so T_2 enters its critical section. While T_2 is in its critical section, T_2 is preempted and T_1 resumes execution in line 16, setting t1inside to true and entering its critical section. Both threads are concurrently executing their critical sections, violating mutual exclusion.

Third Version (Introducing Deadlock)

Version 2 failed because between the time a thread determines in its while test that it can go ahead (lines 14 and 34) and the time the thread sets a flag to say that it is in its critical section (lines 16 and 36), there is the possibility that the other thread could gain control, pass its while test and enter its critical section. To correct this problem, once a thread attempts the while test, it must be assured that the other process cannot proceed past its own while test. Version 3 (Fig. 5.8) attempts to resolve this problem by having each thread set its own flag prior to entering the while loop. Thus, T_1 indicates its desire to enter its critical section by setting t1WantsToEnter to true. If t2WantsToEnter is false, then T_1 enters its critical section and prevents T_2 from entering its own critical section. Thus mutual exclusion is guaranteed, and it seems that we have a correct solution. We ensure that, once a thread signals its intent to enter the critical section, another thread cannot enter the critical section.

```
 1    System:
 2
 3    boolean t1WantsToEnter = false;
 4    boolean t2WantsToEnter = false;
 5
 6    startThreads(); // initialize and launch both threads
 7
 8    Thread T1:
 9
10    void main()
11    {
12       while ( !done )
13       {
14          t1WantsToEnter = true; // enterMutualExclusion
15
16          while ( t2WantsToEnter ); // enterMutualExclusion
17
18          // critical section code
19
20          t1WantsToEnter = false; // exitMutualExclusion
21
22          // code outside critical section
23
24       } // end outer while
25
26    } // end Thread T1
27
28    Thread T2:
29
30    void main()
31    {
32       while ( !done )
33       {
34          t2WantsToEnter = true; // enterMutualExclusion
35
36          while ( t1WantsToEnter ); // enterMutualExclusion
37
38          // critical section code
39
40          t2WantsToEnter = false; // exitMutualExclusion
41
42          // code outside critical section
43
44       } // end outer while
45
46    } // end Thread T2
```

Figure 5.8 | *Mutual exclusion implementation—version 3.*

One problem has been solved, but another has been introduced. If each thread sets its flag before proceeding to the `while` test, then each thread will find the other's flag set and will loop forever in the `while`. This is an example of a two-process **deadlock**, which is discussed in depth in Chapter 7, Deadlock and Indefinite Postponement.

Version Fourth (Introducing Indefinite Postponement)

To create an effective mutual exclusion implementation, we need a way to "break out" of the infinite loops we encountered in the previous version. Version 4 (Fig. 5.9) accomplishes this by forcing each looping thread to repeatedly set its flag to false for brief periods. This allows the other thread to proceed through its `while` loop with its own flag set to true.

```
1   System:
2
3   boolean t1WantsToEnter = false;
4   boolean t2WantsToEnter = false;
5
6   startThreads(); // initialize and launch both threads
7
8   Thread T1:
9
10  void main()
11  {
12     while ( !done )
13     {
14        t1WantsToEnter = true;   // enterMutualExclusion
15
16        while ( t2WantsToEnter )  // enterMutualExclusion
17        {
18           t1WantsToEnter = false;  // enterMutualExclusion
19
20           // wait for small, random amount of time
21
22           t1WantsToEnter = true;
23        } // end while
24
25        // critical section code
26
27        t1WantsToEnter = false; // exitMutualExclusion
28
29        // code outside critical section
30
31     } // end outer while
32
```

Figure 5.9 | *Mutual exclusion implementation—version 4. (Part 1 of 2.)*

```
33   } // end Thread T1
34
35   Thread T2:
36
37   void main()
38   {
39      while ( !done )
40      {
41         t2WantsToEnter = true;  // enterMutualExclusion
42
43         while ( t1WantsToEnter )  // enterMutualExclusion
44         {
45            t2WantsToEnter = false;  // enterMutualExclusion
46
47            // wait for small, random amount of time
48
49            t2WantsToEnter = true;
50         } // end while
51
52         // critical section code
53
54         t2WantsToEnter = false; // exitMutualExclusion
55
56         // code outside critical section
57
58      } // end outer while
59
60   } // end Thread T2
```

Figure 5.9 | *Mutual exclusion implementation—version 4. (Part 2 of 2.)*

The fourth version guarantees mutual exclusion and prevents deadlock, but allows for another potentially devastating problem to develop, namely, **indefinite postponement.** Because we cannot make any assumptions about the relative speeds of asynchronous concurrent threads, we must consider all possible execution sequences. The threads could, for example, proceed in tandem. Each thread can set its flag to true (line 14), then make the while test (line 16), then enter the body of the while loop, then set its flag to false (line 18), then wait for a random amount of time (line 20), then set its flag to true (line 22), then repeat the sequence beginning with the while test. As the threads do this, the tested conditions (lines 18 and 45) will remain true. Of course, such an execution sequence would occur with low probability—but nevertheless it could occur. If a system using this type of mutual exclusion were controlling a space flight, a heart pacemaker, or an air traffic control system, the possibility of indefinite postponement and subsequent system failure could put people's lives at risk. Therefore, version four, also, is an unacceptable solution to the mutual exclusion problem.

Dekker's Algorithm (A Proper Solution)

Figure 5.10 illustrates **Dekker's Algorithm**—a correct, two-thread mutual exclusion solution implemented purely in software with no special-purpose hardware instructions. Dekker's Algorithm still uses a flag to indicate a thread's desire to enter its critical section, but it also incorporates the concept of a "favored thread" that will enter the critical selection in the case of a tie (i.e., when each thread simultaneously wishes to enter its critical section).

```
1   System:
2
3   int favoredThread = 1;
4   boolean t1WantsToEnter = false;
5   boolean t2WantsToEnter = false;
6
7   startThreads(); // initialize and launch both threads
8
9   Thread T1:
10
11  void main()
12  {
13     while ( !done )
14     {
15        t1WantsToEnter = true;
16
17        while ( t2WantsToEnter )
18        {
19           if ( favoredThread == 2 )
20           {
21              t1WantsToEnter = false;
22              while ( favoredThread == 2 ); // busy wait
23              t1WantsToEnter = true;
24           } // end if
25
26        } // end while
27
28        // critical section code
29
30        favoredThread = 2;
31        t1WantsToEnter = false;
32
33        // code outside critical section
34
35     } // end outer while
36
37  } // end Thread T1
```

Figure 5.10 | *Dekker's Algorithm for mutual exclusion. (Part 1 of 2.)*

```
38
39   Thread T2:
40
41   void main()
42   {
43      while ( !done )
44      {
45         t2WantsToEnter = true;
46
47         while ( t1WantsToEnter )
48         {
49            if ( favoredThread == 1 )
50            {
51               t2WantsToEnter = false;
52               while ( favoredThread == 1 ); // busy wait
53               t2WantsToEnter = true;
54            } // end if
55
56         } // end while
57
58         // critical section code
59
60         favoredThread = 1;
61         t2WantsToEnter = false;
62
63         // code outside critical section
64
65      } // end outer while
66
67   } // end Thread T2
```

Figure 5.10 | *Dekker's Algorithm for mutual exclusion. (Part 2 of 2.)*

Let us examine how Dekker's Algorithm eliminates the possibility of the indefinite postponement experienced in version 4. First note that in this algorithm, the enterMutualExclusion primitive is implemented by lines 15–26 and 45–56; the exitMutualExclusion primitive is implemented by lines 30–31 and 60–61. T_1 indicates its desire to enter its critical section by setting its flag to true (line 15). The thread then proceeds to the while test (line 17) and determines whether T_2 also wants to enter its critical section. If T_2's flag is set to false, there is no contention between threads attempting to enter their critical sections, so T_1 skips the body of the while loop and enters its critical section (line 28).

Suppose, however, that when T_1 performs the while test (line 17), it discovers that T_2's flag is set to true. In this case, there is contention between threads attempting to enter their respective critical sections. Thread T_1 enters the body of its while loop, where the thread examines the value of variable favoredThread, which is used to resolve such conflicts (line 19). If thread T_1 is the favored thread, then T_1 skips the body of the `if` and repeatedly executes the `while` test, waiting for T_2 to set `t2WantsToEnter` to `false`, which, as we will see, it must eventually do. If T_1 determines that T_2 is the favored thread (line 19), T_1 is forced into the body of the `if` statement, where T_1 sets `t1WantsToEnter` to `false` (line 21), then loops inside the ensuing `while` as long as T_2 remains the favored thread (line 22). By setting `t1WantsToEnter` to `false`, T_1 allows T_2 to enter its own critical section.

Eventually, T_2 exits its critical section and executes its mutual exclusion exit code (lines 60–61). These statements set `favoredThread` back to T_1 and set `t2WantsToEnter` to `false`. T_1 may now pass the inner `while` test (line 22) and set `t1WantsToEnter` to `true` (line 23). T_1 then executes the outer `while` test (line 17). If `t2WantsToEnter` (which was recently set to `false`) is still `false`, then T_1 enters its critical section (line 28) and is guaranteed exclusive access. If, however, T_2 has quickly tried to reenter its own critical section, then `t2WantsToEnter` will be set to `true`, and T_1 is once again forced into the body of the outer `while` (line 19).

This time, however, T_1 is the favored thread. T_1 therefore skips the body of the `if` and repeatedly executes the outer `while` test (line 17) until T_2 sets `t2WantsToEnter` to `false`, allowing T_1 to enter its critical section.

Dekker's Algorithm guarantees mutual exclusion while preventing deadlock and indefinite postponement. However, the proof of this statement is not immediately apparent, due to the complex nature of mutual exclusion. For example, consider the following interesting possibility. As T_1 exits the inner busy wait loop (line 22), the system might preempt T_1 before it sets `t1WantsToEnter` to `true`. This would allow T_2 to loop around and attempt to reenter its own critical section. T_2 would then set `t2WantsToEnter` to `true` and reenter its critical section. When T_1 eventually resumes execution, it sets `t1WantsToEnter` to `true`. Because it is T_1's turn (and because `t1WantsToEnter` is now set to `true`), if T_2 tries to reenter (line 47), it must set `t2WantsToEnter` to `false` and enter its inner busy wait (line 52). T_1 now will be able to enter its critical section. Thus, this circumstance, which may seem complicated at first, does not result in indefinite postponement. A rigorous proof that the algorithm never results in indefinite postponement is a more complicated task (see the Anecdote, Why Should You Believe That Your Software Is Functioning Correctly?), and one which the reader will find in the literature.[16]

Self Review

1. Identify the key problem in each of our first four attempts at implementing mutual exclusion.
2. (T/F) If the algorithm presented in Fig. 5.9 were modified such that the threads waited for different amounts of time (e.g., T_1 waits from 0 to 0.2 seconds while T_2 waits from 0.5 to 0.7 seconds), this algorithm would not suffer from indefinite postponement.

Ans: 1) Version 1: Required T_1 to go first and demanded strict alternation. Version 2: Violated mutual exclusion; both threads could enter their critical sections at once. Version 3: Enabled the two threads to deadlock so that neither would ever enter its critical section. Version 4: Allowed the (albeit remote) possibility of the two threads indefinitely postponing one another (if they operated in tandem). **2)** False. The point is that no assumptions can be made about the relative speeds of asynchronous concurrent threads. Even though the random time intervals might indeed be different, we cannot assume how fast the rest of the algorithm will run.

5.4.2 Peterson's Algorithm

The development of Dekker's Algorithm in the previous section introduces some subtle problems that arise due to concurrency and asynchronism in multiprogrammed systems. For many years, this algorithm represented the state of the practice in busy-wait solutions for enforcing mutual exclusion. In 1981, G. L. Peterson published a simpler algorithm for enforcing two-process mutual exclusion with busy waiting (Fig. 5.11).[17]

To illustrate the correctness of Peterson's Algorithm, let us examine the algorithm as executed by thread T_1. Before entering its critical section, T_1 indicates that it wishes to do so by setting `t1WantsToEnter` to `true` (line 15). To avoid indefinite postponement, T_1 sets `favoredThread` to 2 (line 16), allowing T_2 to enter its critical section. T_1 then busy waits while `t2WantsToEnter` is `true` and `favoredThread` is 2. If either condition becomes false, it is safe for T_1 to enter its critical section (line 20).

Anecdote

Why Should You Believe That Your Software Is Functioning Correctly?

Dijkstra was always thought-provoking. Here is one of his best: Suppose you have software that determines whether a very large number is prime or not. If the software determines that the number is not prime, it prints out the factors of the number, which you can multiply together to see if the product is indeed the original number. But what if the software says a number is prime? Why should you believe it?

Lesson to operating systems designers: This is one of the most profound points about computing that you may ever ponder. We put remarkable trust in computers in our personal lives and in our careers. But how can we be sure that complex software really does what it is supposed to do? How can we certify that software is indeed correct, especially when we know that we cannot possibly exhaustively test complex software? The answer may lie in the research field called "proving program correctness." This field still has many important unsolved problems—only small, relatively trivial programs have been proven correct to date. It is a wonderful topic for Ph.D. candidates in computer science.

After executing the instructions in its critical section, T_1 sets `t1WantsToEnter` to `false` (line 22) to indicate that it has completed its critical section.

Now let us consider how preemption affects the behavior of thread T_1. If there is no contention for the critical section when thread T_1 performs its mutual exclusion entry code, `t2WantsToEnter` is `false` when thread T_1 executes line 18; thread T_1 enters its critical section (line 20). Consider the case in which thread T_1 is preempted immediately following entry into its critical section. Because thread T_2 must set `favoredThread` to 1 (line 37), the test that T_2 performs in line 39 will cause T_2 to busy wait until thread T_1 has exited its critical section and set `t1WantsToEnter` to `false`.

However, if `t2WantsToEnter` is `true` when thread T_1 attempts to enter its critical section (line 18), then T_2 must have been preempted while attempting to enter its critical section. One possibility is that T_2 was preempted while executing code in its critical section, meaning `favoredThread = 2` and `t2WantsToEnter = true`. In this case, T_1 must simply busy wait at line 18 until T_2 completes its critical section and sets `t2WantsToEnter` to `false`, thereby causing the `while` condition to fail in line 18 and allowing T_1 to proceed.

If thread T_1 discovers that both `t2WantsToEnter` is `true` and `favoredThread` to 2 in line 18, T_1 will busy wait in its `while` loop (line 18), because it had set `favoredThread` to 2 immediately before executing line 18. Thread T_1 will wait until T_2 regains the processor and sets `favoredThread` to 1 (line 37). At this point, T_2 must busy wait because `t1WantsToEnter` is `true` and `favoredThread` is 1. When thread T_1 regains control of a processor, it performs the test in its `while` loop and enters its critical section (line 20).

If thread T_1 discovers that `t2WantsToEnter` is `true` and `favoredThread` to 1 in line 18, T_1 may safely enter its critical section, because `t1WantsToEnter` is `true` and `favoredThread` is 1; thread T_2 must busy wait until T_1 completes executing its critical section and sets `t1WantsToEnter` to `false`.

We will now provide a formal proof that Peterson's Algorithm guarantees mutual exclusion. We do so by proving that T_2 cannot execute while T_1 is inside its critical section. Note that the algorithm is unchanged if every instance of the characters 1 and 2 is swapped. Consequently, if we prove that T_2 cannot execute while T_1 is inside its critical section, we have also proven that T_1 cannot execute while T_2 is inside its critical section.

```
1   System:
2
3   int favoredThread = 1;
4   boolean t1WantsToEnter = false;
5   boolean t2WantsToEnter = false;
6
7   startThreads(); // initialize and launch both threads
```

Figure 5.11 | *Peterson's Algorithm for mutual exclusion. (Part 1 of 2.)*

```
 8
 9   Thread T1:
10
11   void main()
12   {
13      while ( !done )
14      {
15         t1WantsToEnter = true;
16         favoredThread = 2;
17
18         while ( t2WantsToEnter && favoredThread == 2 );
19
20         // critical section code
21
22         t1WantsToEnter = false;
23
24         // code outside critical section
25
26      } // end while
27
28   } // end Thread T1
29
30   Thread T2:
31
32   void main()
33   {
34      while ( !done )
35      {
36         t2WantsToEnter = true;
37         favoredThread = 1;
38
39         while ( t1WantsToEnter && favoredThread == 1 );
40
41         // critical section code
42
43         t2WantsToEnter = false;
44
45         // code outside critical section
46
47      } // end while
48
49   } // end Thread T2
```

Figure 5.11 | *Peterson's Algorithm for mutual exclusion. (Part 2 of 2.)*

To begin the proof, we observe that the value of favoredThread is set immediately before a thread executes its while loop. Furthermore, each thread sets the value in favoredThread such that the other thread is favored if both threads wish to enter their critical sections. Also, `t1WantsToEnter` is controlled exclusively by thread T_1; similarly, `t2WantsToEnter` is modified exclusively by thread T_2. Now assume that T_1 is the only thread executing inside its critical section—this implies that `t1WantsToEnter = true` and either `favoredThread = 1` or `t2WantsToEnter = false`.

For T_2 to enter its critical section (line 39), either

- `t1WantsToEnter` must be `false`,
- `favoredThread` must be 2, or
- both `t1WantsToEnter` is `false` and `favoredThread` is 2.

This proof will assume that T_2 has successfully entered its critical section while T_1 executes inside its critical section and show that Peterson's Algorithm guarantees mutual exclusion because this cannot occur (i.e., proof by contradiction). In the first case (`t1WantsToEnter` is `false`), T_2 has entered its critical section because `t1WantsToEnter` is `false` and `favoredThread` is either 1 or 2. However, as described earlier in this section, `t1WantsToEnter` must be `true` if thread T_1 is also executing inside its critical section—the only time `t1WantsToEnter` is `false` is after T_1 has exited its critical section (line 22) and before it attempts to reenter it (line 15). Thus thread T_2 could not have entered its critical section because `t1WantsToEnter` was `false`. This also implies that thread T_2 could not have entered its critical section given the third condition (both `t1WantsToEnter` is `false` and `favoredThread` is 2).

We now must show by contradiction that T_2 cannot enter its critical section because `favoredThread` cannot be set to 2 while T_1 executes inside its critical section. To enter its critical section, T_2 must have set `t2WantsToEnter` to `true` (line 36), then `favoredThread` to 1 (line 37) before exiting the `while` loop in line 39. Therefore, if thread T_2 executes in its critical section while thread T_1 executes in its critical section, the value of `favoredThread` must have changed after thread T_2 executed line 37. Note that the only time `favoredThread` is set to 2 is when T_1 executes line 16 of its mutual exclusion entry code, requiring that T_1 exit its critical section. Note that thread T_2 has already set `t2WantsToEnter` to `true` in line 36. Consequently, when thread T_1 attempts to enter its critical section in line 18, it will busy wait, because both `t2WantsToEnter` is `true` and `favoredThread` is 2. Although T_2 may enter its critical section, now T_1 must wait until T_2 exits its critical section. This contradicts the statement that T_2 and T_1 are both executing inside their critical sections. Because we have shown by contradiction that T_2 and T_1 cannot concurrently execute inside their critical sections, we have proven that Peterson's Algorithm ensures mutual exclusion.

Deadlock and indefinite postponement are impossible in Peterson's Algorithm as long as no thread terminates unexpectedly. [*Note:* As always, we mean that deadlock and indefinite postponement could not be caused by the mutual exclusion entry and exit code. They nevertheless could occur if the threads misbehaved in their critical sections.] For deadlock to occur, both T_1 and T_2 must concurrently busy wait in their `while` loops. This will not occur, because `favoredThread` is either 1 or 2 and is not modified during the `while` loop, meaning that the `while` test will always fail for one thread, allowing it to enter its critical section. For indefinite postponement to occur, one thread would have to be able to continually complete and reenter its critical section while the other thread busy waited. Because each thread sets the value of `favoredThread` to the number corresponding to the other thread before entering the `while` loop, Peterson's Algorithm ensures that the two threads will alternate execution of their critical sections, meaning that indefinite postponement cannot occur.

Self Review

1. What major similarity is there between Dekker's Algorithm and Peterson's Algorithm?
2. What variable is necessary to prevent indefinite postponement?

Ans: **1)** They both have the same three global variables. **2)** Removing the `favoredThread` variable would allow for the possibility of indefinite postponement.

5.4.3 N-Thread Mutual Exclusion: Lamport's Bakery Algorithm

Dijkstra was the first to present a software implementation of *n*-thread mutual exclusion primitives.[18] Knuth responded with a solution that eliminated the possibility of indefinite postponement in Dijkstra's algorithm, but still allowed a process to experience a (potentially) lengthy delay.[19] This generated a series of efforts to find algorithms with shorter delays. Eisenberg and McGuire presented a solution guaranteeing that a process will enter its critical section within $n - 1$ tries.[20] Lamport developed a solution that is particularly applicable to networks of computers (see the Biographical Note, Leslie Lamport).[21] The algorithm, which we discuss in depth in this section, uses a "take-a-ticket" system like those employed in busy bakeries, and has been dubbed **Lamport's Bakery Algorithm**. Burns et al. offer a solution to *n*-thread mutual exclusion that uses a single shared variable.[22] Carvalho and Roucairol discuss enforcing mutual exclusion in computer networks.[23]

Lamport was the first to introduce an algorithm that allows threads to enter critical sections quickly when access to the critical section is not contested (which is often the case).[24] Such **fast mutual exclusion algorithms** tend to suffer from inefficiency when the critical section is indeed a point of contention. Anderson and Kim present an algorithm that allows for fast entry into a critical section in the absence of contention and for good performance under contention.[25]

Many of the early solutions to the *n*-thread mutual exclusion problem are difficult to understand because they require a large number of shared variables and complicated loops that determine if a thread can enter its critical section. Lamport's algorithm provides a simpler solution that borrows from a common real-world scenario—waiting for service at a bakery. Moreover, Lamport's algorithm does not require that any operation occur atomically.

Lamport's algorithm is modeled on a bakery in which one employee services customer requests for baked goods; this employee can service exactly one customer at a time. If only one customer is present, the transaction is simple: the customer requests baked goods, the employee retrieves the items, the customer pays for the food and exits the bakery. However, when multiple customers concurrently request service, the employee must determine in what order to serve the customers. Many bakeries serve customers in first-come-first-served order by requiring that they take a numbered ticket from a ticket dispenser as they enter the bakery. The tickets are dispensed in ascending order (i.e., if the current ticket contains a value n, the next

Biographical Note

Leslie Lamport

Leslie Lamport received his Ph.D. in Mathematics from Brandeis University in 1972.[26] He has worked for the Massachusetts Computer Associates, SRI International, Digital Equipment Corporation/Compaq and is currently at Microsoft Research.[27] He believes that his development of a method to structure logical proofs in a hierarchical fashion that is easier to read will be his most memorable work,[28] but he is also well known for several computer science contributions in the area of mutual exclusion of processes that share data.

One of Lamport's major contributions was the bakery algorithm for synchronizing processes using first-come-first-served priority (see Section 5.4.3, N-Thread Mutual Exclusion: Lamport's Bakery Algorithm). Important features of the bakery algorithm are that it eliminates indefinite postponement and is resilient to processes

that terminate prematurely. This simple algorithm mimics the synchronization used for customers at a bakery.[29] Each process that hits the entry gate to its critical section gets a number which is one higher than the previous process's number, just as each new customer to a bakery takes a new ticket with an ordering number on it. As a process exits its critical section, the next number is "called," and the process holding that number is allowed to proceed.[30]

Lamport produced numerous papers on methods for writing formal specifications for concurrent programs, and on proving program correctness. As part of his work on proofs, he also designed a logic system called the Temporal Logic of Actions (TLA), which can be used to verify both circuit and software logic.[31, 32]

Some of Lamport's mutual exclusion work demonstrated that mutual exclusion can be attained

without any atomic statements, which require specific hardware support.[33] He designed at least four algorithms of varying complexity and degrees of fault tolerance.[34] He also invented the first mutual exclusion algorithm that runs in short, constant time if no process is currently executing in its critical section.[35]

Lamport's most famous paper, "Time, Clocks, and the Ordering of Events in a Distributed System," describes a logical clock mechanism that is used to determine the order of events' occurrences, and a method using these clocks to synchronize distributed processes.[36, 37, 38]

Aside from his work in mutual exclusion, Lamport also developed the LaTeX typesetting system in 1985, based on Donald Knuth's TeX typesetting language.[39]

ticket contains the value $n + 1$). After each transaction, the employee serves the customer possessing the ticket with the lowest numerical value, which ensures that customers are served in first-come-first-served order.

Figure 5.12 presents an implementation of Lamport's algorithm for n threads. In Lamport's algorithm, each thread represents a customer that must "take a ticket" to determine when the thread can enter its critical section. When a thread possesses a ticket with the lowest numerical value, it can enter its critical section. Mutual exclusion is enforced by resetting the thread's ticket value when it exits its critical section. Unlike a real-world ticket dispenser, Lamport's algorithm allows multiple threads to obtain the same ticket number. As we will see, Lamport's algorithm includes a tie-breaking mechanism to ensure that only one thread can execute in its critical section at a time.

```
1   System:
2
3   // array that records which threads are taking a ticket
4   boolean choosing[n];
5
6   // value of the ticket for each thread initialized to 0
7   int ticket[n];
8
9   startThreads(); // initialize and launch all threads
10
11  Thread Tx:
12
13  void main()
14  {
15      x = threadNumber(); // store current thread number
16
17      while ( !done )
18      {
19          // take a ticket
20          choosing[x] = true; // begin ticket selection process
21          ticket[x] = maxValue( ticket ) + 1;
22          choosing[x] = false; // end ticket selection process
23
24          // wait for number to be called by comparing current
25          // ticket  value to other thread's ticket value
26          for ( int i = 0; i < n; i++)
27          {
28              if ( i == x )
29              {
30                  continue; // no need to check own ticket
31              } // end if
32
```

Figure 5.12 | *Lamport's Bakery Algorithm. (Part 1 of 2.)*

```
33              // busy wait while thread[i] is choosing
34              while ( choosing[i] != false );
35
36              // busy wait until current ticket value is lowest
37              while ( ticket[i] != 0 && ticket[i] < ticket[x] );
38
39              // tie-breaker code favors smaller thread number
40              if ( ticket[i] == ticket[x] && i < x )
41
42                  // loop until thread[i] leaves its critical section
43                  while ( ticket[i] != 0 ); // busy wait
44          } // end for
45
46          // critical section code
47
48          ticket[x] = 0; // exitMutualExclusion
49
50          // code outside critical section
51
52      } // end while
53
54  } // end Thread TX
```

Figure 5.12 | *Lamport's Bakery Algorithm. (Part 2 of 2.)*

Lines 3–7 declare two arrays that are shared among all *n* threads participating in mutual exclusion. The boolean array choosing (line 4) is of size *n*; if thread T*x* is currently selecting a ticket value, then choosing[x] is true. Otherwise, choosing[x] is false. The integer array ticket (line 7) contains values corresponding to each thread's ticket. Similar to choosing, thread T*x*'s ticket value is contained in ticket[x]. In this example, the initial value for each thread's ticket is zero.

Lines 13–54 represent the code executed by thread T$_x$, one of the *n* threads attempting to execute their critical sections. Each thread participating in the bakery algorithm executes the same enterMutualExclusion (lines 19–44) and exitMutualExclusion (line 48) constructs. When a thread is started, it executes line 15, which stores an integer value in variable x to uniquely identify the thread. The thread uses this value to determine its corresponding entries in the choosing and ticket arrays.

Each thread "takes a ticket" by executing the code in lines 19–22. Line 20 indicates that the current thread is attempting to take a ticket by setting choosing[x] to true. As we will soon see, this step is necessary to ensure that mutual exclusion is enforced if multiple threads concurrently determine their ticket values. The thread calls method maxValue (line 21), which returns the largest value in the integer array ticket. The thread then adds one to that value and stores it as its ticket value, ticket[x] (line 21). Note that if there are numerous threads in the system, method maxValue can take substantial time to execute, increasing the likelihood that the thread that calls `maxValue` will be preempted before the method completes. After the thread has assigned its ticket value to `ticket[x]` (line 21), the thread sets `choosing[x]` to `false` (line 22), indicating that it is no longer selecting a ticket value. Note that when a thread exits its critical section (line 48), the ticket value is set to zero, meaning that a thread's ticket value is nonzero only if it wishes to enter its critical section.

Unlike a real-world bakery, in which an employee calls each customer's number in turn for service, the bakery algorithm requires that each thread determine when it can enter its critical section (lines 24–44). Before entering its critical section, a thread must execute the `for` loop (lines 26–44) that determines the state of all threads in the system. If thread T_i, the thread to examine, and thread T_x, the thread executing the `for` statement, are identical (line 28), T_x executes the `continue` statement (line 30), which skips the remaining statements in the body of the `for` loop and proceeds directly to increment `i` in line 26.

Otherwise, T_x determines if T_i is choosing a ticket value (line 34). If T_x does not wait until T_i has chosen its ticket before entering its critical section, mutual exclusion can be violated. To understand why, let us first examine the other two conditions that are tested in each iteration of the `for` loop.

Line 37 tests if the current thread possesses a ticket value that is less than or equal to the ticket value for the thread it is examining. This condition is analogous to a real-world bakery—each thread must wait until it possesses the lowest nonzero ticket value.

Unlike a real-world bakery, however, two or more threads in the system may obtain the same ticket value. For example, consider a thread T_a that is preempted after method `maxValue` returns and before the thread assigns a new value to `ticket[a]` in line 21. If the next thread that executes calls `maxValue`, the method will return the same value as it did to T_a. As a result, any of the threads could obtain the same ticket value. Therefore, in the case of a tie, line 40 indicates that the thread with the lowest unique identifier proceeds first.

Let us return to line 34 to examine how mutual exclusion is violated if thread T_x does not wait if T_i is selecting a ticket value. For example, consider what happens if thread T_a is preempted after returning from method `maxValue` but before adding one to the ticket value (line 21). Assume for this example that `maxValue` returns the value 215. After T_a is preempted, several other threads execute their mutual exclusion entry code. Consider two threads, T_b and T_c, that execute after T_a is preempted and complete the ticket selection code (lines 19–22), leaving thread T_b with ticket value 216 (note that T_a's ticket value is currently 0) and T_c with ticket value 217. It is possible for T_b to complete its mutual exclusion entry code (lines 19–44), execute its critical section (line 46) and exit its critical section (line 48) before T_a regains control of a processor. It is likewise possible for T_c to enter its critical section before T_a regains control of a processor.

If T_c is preempted while executing code in its critical section and T_a regains control of a processor, T_a completes the instruction in line 21 by setting its ticket value to 216, which is lower than that of T_c. Thus, T_a could execute its mutual exclusion entry code and enter its critical section before T_c exits its critical section, thereby violating mutual exclusion. For this reason, T_x must wait until T_i has completed its ticket selection (line 34) before comparing ticket values in lines 36–43.

When T_x has passed all of the tests for each thread (lines 28–43), T_x is guaranteed exclusive access to its critical section. When T_x exits its critical section, it sets its ticket value to 0 (line 48) to indicate that it is no longer executing in its critical section nor is it attempting to enter its critical section.

In addition to being one of the simplest n-thread mutual exclusion algorithms, Lamport's bakery algorithm exhibits several interesting properties. For example, it does not require its instructions to be executed atomically. Recall from Section 5.3, Implementing Mutual Exclusion Primitives, that we required instructions to execute atomically. This was necessary because both Dekker's and Peterson's algorithms require multiple threads to modify a shared variable to control access to their critical sections. If each thread could read and modify this variable simultaneously on different processors, the threads might read inconsistent values of their shared variables. This might allow both threads to enter their critical sections simultaneously, violating mutual exclusion. Although many architectures provide a small set of atomic instructions (see Section 5.5, Hardware Solutions to the Mutual Exclusion Problem), it is rare to find a multiprocessor system that provides hardware to prevent threads from reading and writing data simultaneously.

Lamport's Bakery Algorithm provides an elegant solution to mutual exclusion on multiprocessor systems, because each thread is assigned its own set of variables that control access to its critical section. Although all threads in the system share the arrays `choosing` and `ticket`, thread T_x is the only thread that can modify values in `choosing[x]` and `ticket[x]`. This prevents threads from reading inconsistent data, because the variables a thread examines while performing its mutual exclusion entry code cannot be simultaneously modified by another thread.

Another interesting property of the bakery algorithm is that threads that are waiting to enter their critical sections are admitted in first-come-first-served (FCFS) order unless multiple threads possess the same ticket value. Finally, Lamport's algorithm can continue to enforce mutual exclusion even if one or more threads fail, provided that the system sets each failed thread's value in the `choosing` array to `false` and each thread's value in the `ticket` array to 0. Given this final provision, Lamport's Bakery Algorithm cannot suffer from deadlock or indefinite postponement, a property that is particularly important in multiprocessor and distributed systems, where the failure of a hardware device such as a processor does not necessarily result in system failure.

Self Review

1. Describe why n-thread mutual exclusion might be difficult in a distributed or networked system.
2. What would happen if the system did not perform housekeeping tasks such as setting the ticket values to zero and `choosing` values to `false` for terminated threads?

3. Suppose multiple threads obtain the same ticket value. In the sample code provided, the thread with the lowest unique identifier enters its critical section first. Does it matter in what order these threads enter their critical sections?

Ans: **1)** There is latency between a computer's sending a message and the receiving computer's actually receiving it, meaning that mutual exclusion algorithms must account for delays between when a thread modifies a shared variable and when another thread attempts to enter its critical section. **2)** The whole system could suffer from indefinite postponement. Suppose a thread terminated while choosing a ticket number, and therefore choosing for that thread would be set to true forever. Other threads wishing to enter mutual exclusion would wait forever for the terminated thread to set the choosing array entry to false. **3)** Unless the programmer wishes to assign priorities to threads that possess the same ticket value, the order in which threads with identical ticket values enter their critical section does not matter. Lines 34 and 37 of Fig. 5.12 ensure that no thread with a higher or lower ticket value can enter its critical section before the threads with identical ticket values. The system need only ensure that each of the threads with the same ticket value eventually enters its critical section.

5.5 Hardware Solutions to the Mutual Exclusion Problem

In the preceding examples the software solutions to the mutual exclusion problem that make few assumptions about the system's instruction set and hardware capabilities. As discussed in Chapter 2, Hardware and Software Concepts, hardware designers tend to implement mechanisms previously handled by software to improve performance and reduce development time. This section presents several mechanisms provided in hardware to help solve the problem of mutual exclusion.

5.5.1 Disabling Interrupts

The reason mutual exclusion primitives are needed in a uniprocessor system is largely that preemption allows multiple threads to access shared data asynchronously, which can result in program errors. Threads are typically preempted by interrupts such as the interrupting clock (to signal quantum expiration). Therefore, a simple way to enforce mutual exclusion is to disable (or mask) interrupts. Unfortunately, the disabling of interrupts places limitations on what software can do inside a critical section. For example, a thread that enters an infinite loop in its critical section after disabling interrupts will never yield its processor. On a uniprocessor system, the operating system could no longer use timer interrupts to gain control of the processor, meaning that the system will hang. In real-time systems, such as an air traffic control system, such a result could put people's lives at risk.

Disabling interrupts is not a viable solution for mutual exclusion in a multiprocessor system. After all, its purpose is to ensure that preemption will not occur. However, in a multiprocessor system, two threads can execute at the same time, each on a different processor. If these threads are unsynchronized, disabling interrupts alone does not prevent them from simultaneously executing inside their critical sections. Therefore, simply disabling interrupts on either processor (or both) is insufficient to enforce mutual exclusion. In general, operating system designers avoid disabling interrupts to provide mutual exclusion. However, there are a limited set of solutions in which it is optimal for the kernel to disable interrupts for trusted code whose execution requires a short period of time. See the Linux and Windows XP case studies in Chapters 20 and 21, respectively, for examples of how current operating systems enforce mutual exclusion by disabling interrupts.

Self Review

1. (T/F) If a thread enters an infinite loop after disabling interrupts on a multiprocessor system, the operating system can no longer execute.
2. Why should a thread avoid requesting blocking I/O in a critical section in a uniprocessor system while interrupts are disabled?

Ans: **1)** False. The operating system can execute on any processor on which interrupts are not disabled. The thread in the infinite loop can be aborted or restarted, but any data it shares with other threads may be left in an inconsistent state, which may cause program errors. **2)** When a thread requests blocking I/O, the operating system places that thread in the *blocked* state until it receives an I/O completion event. Since such events are generated by hardware interrupts, but the operating system would never receive this signal while interrupts remained disabled. As a result, the thread will remain waiting in the *blocked* state for an event it will never receive. This is an example of deadlock, which is further discussed in Chapter 7, Deadlock and Indefinite Postponement.

5.5.2 Test-and-Set Instruction

Disabling interrupts is rarely a practical solution to the synchronization problem, so other techniques include the use of special hardware instructions. Recall from our previous examples that shared data can become corrupted because the system may preempt a thread after it has read the value at a memory location, but before the thread can write a new value to the location. The **test-and-set** instruction enables a thread to perform this operation **atomically** (i.e., indivisibly).[40, 41] Such operations are also described as atomic **read-modify-write (RMW) memory operations**, because the processor reads a value from memory, modifies its value in its registers and writes the modified value to memory without interruption.[42]

The previous examples of software mutual exclusion required that a thread read a variable to determine that no other thread is executing a critical section, then set a variable, known as a **lock**, to indicate that the thread is executing its critical section. The difficulty in guaranteeing mutually exclusive access to critical sections in software was that a thread could be preempted between testing the availability of a critical section and setting a lock to keep other threads from entering their critical sections. The `testAndSet` instruction eliminates the possibility of preemption occurring during this interval.

The instruction

```
testAndSet( a, b )
```

works as follows. First the instruction reads the value of b, which may be either `true` or `false`. Then, the value is copied into a, and the instruction sets the value of b to `true`.

Figure 5.13 shows how a thread can employ `testAndSet` to enforce mutual exclusion. The global boolean variable, `occupied`, is true if either thread is in its critical section. Thread T_1 decides to enter its critical section based on its local boolean variable, `p1MustWait`. If `p1MustWait` is true, T_1 must wait; otherwise, the thread may enter its critical section. Thread T_1 initially sets variable `p1MustWait` to `true`. Then the thread repeatedly calls `testAndSet` on `p1MustWait` and the global variable `occupied`. If T_2 is not in its critical section, the value of `occupied` is `false`. In this case, the `testAndSet` assigns `false` to variable `p1MustWait` and sets `occupied` to `true`. The `while` fails at this point and T_1 enters its critical section. Because the indivisible hardware instruction set `occupied` to `true`, T_2 will be unable to enter its critical section until T_1 has reset `occupied` to `false`.

```
1   System:
2
3   boolean occupied = false;
4
5   startThreads(); // initialize and launch both threads
6
7   Thread T1:
8
9   void main()
10  {
11     boolean p1MustWait = true;
12
13     while ( !done )
14     {
15        while ( p1MustWait )
16        {
17           testAndSet( p1MustWait, occupied );
18        }
19
20        // critical section code
21
22        p1MustWait = true;
23        occupied = false;
24
25        // code outside critical section
26
27     } // end while
28
29  } // end Thread T1
30
31  Thread T2:
32
```

Figure 5.13 | `testAndSet` *instruction for mutual exclusion. (Part 1 of 2.)*

```
33   void main()
34   {
35      boolean p2MustWait = true;
36
37      while ( !done )
38      {
39         while ( p2MustWait )
40         {
41            testAndSet( p2MustWait, occupied );
42         }
43
44         // critical section code
45
46         p2MustWait = true;
47         occupied = false;
48
49         // code outside critical section
50
51      } // end while
52
53   } // end Thread T2
```

Figure 5.13 | testAndSet *instruction for mutual exclusion.* *(Part 2 of 2.)*

Now suppose that T₂ already is in its critical section when T₁ wants to enter. In this case, `occupied` remains `true` during T₁'s repeated `while` tests. Therefore, T₁ continues its busy waiting until T₂ eventually leaves its critical section and sets `occupied` to `false`. At this point, the `testAndSet` assigns `occupied`'s value to `p1MustWait`, thus allowing T₁ to enter its critical section.

Although `testAndSet` as used here does guarantee mutual exclusion, the solution may suffer from indefinite postponement. It is possible for a thread to exit the critical section and loop around to call `testAndSet` before the competing thread has a chance to execute again.

Self Review

1. Does the algorithm in Fig. 5.13 prevent indefinite postponement?
2. (T/F) The `testAndSet` instruction enforces mutual exclusion.

Ans: **1)** No, the algorithm in Fig. 5.13 requires a `favoredProcess` variable as discussed in Section 5.4.1, Dekker's Algorithm, to prevent indefinite postponement. **2)** False. The `testAndSet` instruction is a tool that programmers use to simplify software solutions to mutual exclusion but the instruction itself does not enforce mutual exclusion.

5.5.3 Swap Instruction

To simplify synchronization code and improve program efficiency, most architectures provide several atomic instructions. However, each architecture supports a different set of atomic operations, meaning the `testAndSet` instruction might not be available to the application or system programmer. In this section, we demonstrate how another instruction that performs an atomic read-modify-write memory operation can provide functionality identical to the `testAndSet` instruction.

It is common for programs to exchange (or swap) values stored in two different variables (consider, for example, the Quicksort algorithm). Although the concept is simple, a successful exchange of values between two variables in most high-level programming languages requires three instructions and the creation of a temporary variable:

```
temp = a;
a = b;
b = temp;
```

Because such swapping operations are performed regularly, many architectures support a **swap** instruction that enables a thread to exchange the values of the two variables atomically.

The instruction

```
swap( a, b )
```

proceeds as follows. First the instruction loads the value of b, which may be either `true` or `false`, into a temporary register. Then, the value of a is copied to b and the value of the temporary register is copied to a.

Figure 5.14 shows how a thread can employ `swap` to enforce mutual exclusion. Similar to Fig. 5.13, the global boolean variable, `occupied`, is `true` if either thread is in its critical section. Thread T_1 decides to enter its critical section based on its local boolean variable, `p1MustWait`. Similarly, thread T_2 decides to enter its critical section based on its local variable `p2MustWait`. Note that the `swap` instruction can be used interchangeably with the `testAndSet` instruction in this algorithm. The only difference between Fig. 5.13 and Fig. 5.14 is that we have created a "fast track" to the critical section, in which control of the critical section can be obtained by the execution of one fewer instruction (i.e., by testing the loop condition after the `swap` instruction).

```
1   System:
2
3   boolean occupied = false;
4
5   startThreads(); // initialize and launch both threads
6
7   Thread T₁:
8
9   void main()
10  {
11      boolean p1MustWait = true;
12
```

Figure 5.14 | swap *instruction for mutual exclusion.* (Part 1 of 2.)

```
13        while ( !done )
14        {
15           do
16           {
17              swap( p1MustWait, occupied );
18           } while ( p1MustWait );
19
20           // critical section code
21
22           p1MustWait = true;
23           occupied = false;
24
25           // code outside critical section
26
27        } // end while
28
29     } // end Thread T1
30
31     Thread T2:
32
33     void main()
34     {
35        boolean p2MustWait = true;
36
37        while ( !done )
38        {
39           do
40           {
41              swap( p2MustWait, occupied );
42           } while ( p2MustWait );
43
44           // critical section code
45
46           p2MustWait = true;
47           occupied = false;
48
49           // code outside critical section
50
51        } // end while
52
53     } // end Thread T2
```

Figure 5.14 | swap *instruction for mutual exclusion.* (Part 2 of 2.)

Self Review

1. Why might it be more likely for a swap instruction to be on a system than a testAndSet?

Ans: Many algorithms require some sort of swapping, so a hardware instruction, swap, is very useful for algorithms other than just those providing mutual exclusion.

5.6 Semaphores

Another mechanism that a system can provide to implement mutual exclusion is the **semaphore**, as described by Dijkstra in his seminal paper on cooperating sequential processes (see the Biographical Note, Edsger W. Dijkstra).[43] A sema-

Biographical Note

Edsger W. Dijkstra

One of computer science's most famous and prolific researchers was Edsger Wybe Dijkstra. Born in 1930 in the Netherlands, he received his Ph.D. in Computing Science from the University of Amsterdam and worked as a programmer at the Mathematisch Centrum in Amsterdam. He later served as a Professor of Mathematics at the Eindhoven Institute of Technology, then as a professor of Computer Science at the University of Texas at Austin. Dijkstra died in 2002.[44]

Perhaps his best-known contribution to computer science was his article that started the structured programming revolution, "GOTO Considered Harmful,"[45] a letter to the editor published in *Communications of the ACM* in March of 1968. Dijkstra claimed that the GOTO statement, unless used carefully, quickly results in "spaghetti code"—meaning the path of execution is nearly impossible to follow.[46]

Dijkstra's main contributions to operating system design were the semaphore construct (the first object invented for use in mutual exclusion algorithms) and the layered design (an improvement over the older monolithic approach, where components that provide similar functions are grouped together in layers). He implemented both concepts in his **THE multiprogramming system**—an operating system built for the Dutch EL X8 computer.[47] He later expanded the concept of a layered system to enable the construction of a more general operating system, where the enhanced layered design could be used to build operating systems for any computer.[48] In his description of the THE system, he described how semaphores could be used for synchronization. He is also known for posing the Dining Philosophers synchronization problem, which illustrates subtle difficulties in parallel programming (see Section 7.2.4, Example: Dining Philosophers).

In 1972, Dijkstra received the Turing Award—computer science's top honor—for his work on the ALGOL programming language which introduced block structure (to define variable scopes and mark control structure bodies) and other concepts used by most modern languages.[49, 50, 51] Yet another achievement for Dijkstra was **Dijkstra's Algorithm**. This efficient algorithm takes a weighted graph and finds the shortest paths from a given node to each of the other nodes.

Dijkstra wrote over 1300 documents, mostly in the form of his EWDs—short essays (named after his initials) that were numbered in sequence and distributed informally to the computer science community.[52] Some were technical and serious, while others, such as "How Do We Tell Truths That Might Hurt?" were mainly humorous.[53] In another EWD—"The End of Computer Science?" written in 2000—he attacked the quality of today's software and argued that more computer science research is needed to improve basic design concepts.[54]

phore contains a **protected variable** whose integer value, once initialized, can be accessed and altered by only one of two operations, **P** and **V**. [*Note*: P and V are short for the Dutch words, *proberen*, which means "to test," and *verhogen*, which means "to increment."] A thread calls the *P* operation (also called the **wait** operation) when it wants to enter its critical section and calls the *V* operation (also called the **signal** operation) when it wants to exit its critical section. Before a semaphore can be used for synchronization, it must be initialized. Initialization sets the value of the protected variable to indicate that no thread is executing in its critical section. It also creates a queue that stores references to threads waiting to enter their critical sections protected by that semaphore. Note that *P* and *V* are simply abstractions that encapsulate and hide the details of mutual exclusion implementations. These operations can be applied to a system with any number of cooperating threads.

5.6.1 Mutual Exclusion with Semaphores

Figure 5.15 demonstrates how mutual exclusion is enforced using a semaphore. The system initializes the semaphore occupied to 1; such semaphores are called **binary semaphores**. This value indicates that the critical section is available.

The program in Fig. 5.15 uses the *P* and *V* operations as the enterMutualExclusion() and exitMutualExclusion() primitives from Section 5.2.3, Mutual Exclusion Primitives. When a thread wants to enter a critical section that is protected by semaphore *S*, the thread calls *P(S)*, which operates as follows

```
1   System:
2
3   // create semaphore and initialize value to 1
4   Semaphore occupied = new Semaphore(1);
5
6   startThreads(); // initialize and launch both threads
7
8   Thread Tₓ:
9
10  void main()
11  {
12     while ( !done )
13     {
14        P( occupied );   // wait
15
16        // critical section code
17
18        V( occupied ); // signal
19
20        // code outside critical section
21     } // end while
22  } // Thread TX
```

Figure 5.15 | *Mutual exclusion with semaphores.*

> *If S > 0*
>   *S = S - 1*
> *Else*
>   *The calling thread is placed in the semaphore's queue of waiting threads*

Because Fig. 5.15 initializes the semaphore value to 1, only one thread will be allowed into the critical section at a time. When this thread calls P, the semaphore's value is reduced to 0. When another thread calls P, that thread will be blocked.

After a thread finishes executing in its critical section, the thread calls $V(S)$. This operation proceeds as follows

> *If any threads are waiting on S*
>   *Resume the "next" waiting thread in the semaphore's queue*
> *Else*
>   *S = S + 1*

Thus, if any threads are waiting on the semaphore, the "next" thread, which depends on the semaphore implementation, executes. Otherwise, the value of S is incremented, allowing one more thread to enter its critical section.

A proper semaphore implementation requires that P and V be indivisible operations. Also, if several threads attempt a $P(S)$ simultaneously, the implementation should guarantee that only one thread will be allowed to proceed. The others will be kept waiting, but the implementation of P and V can guarantee that threads will not suffer indefinite postponement. For example, when a thread blocks on a semaphore, the system might place that thread in a queue associated with the semaphore. When another thread calls P, the system can select one of the threads in the queue to release. We shall assume a first-in-first-out queuing discipline for threads blocked on a semaphore (to avoid indefinite postponement).

Self Review

1. What could potentially happen if a thread called the V without having called the P operation?
2. What could potentially happen if threads that blocked on a semaphore were not dequeued in a first-in-first-out order?

Ans: **1)** One scenario is that the semaphore is initially 1 and no threads are waiting. The V increments the semaphore's value to 2. Now two threads using P could both enter their critical sections. **2)** A thread could suffer from indefinite postponement.

5.6.2 *Thread Synchronization with Semaphores*

In the previous section, we saw how a program can use a semaphore to protect access to a critical section. Semaphores also can be used to synchronize two or more concurrent threads. For example, suppose one thread, T_1, wants to be notified about the occurrence of a particular event. Suppose some other thread, T_2, is capable of detecting that this event has occurred. To synchronize these two threads, T_1 executes some preliminary instructions, then calls P on a semaphore that has been initialized to 0, causing T_1 to block. Eventually, T_2 executes V to signal that the event has occurred. This allows T_1 to proceed (with the semaphore still zero).

This mechanism succeeds even if T_2 detects the event and signals it with V before T_1 waits for the event by calling P. The semaphore will have been incremented from 0 to 1, so when T_1 calls P, the operation will simply decrement the semaphore from 1 to 0, and T_1 will proceed without waiting for the event.

One example of thread synchronization is the producer/consumer relationship, introduced in Section 5.2.1, Java Multithreading Case Study, Part II. Figure 5.16 shows how to implement this relationship with semaphores. Both threads share a variable called `sharedValue`. The producer generates values and assigns them to this variable, and the consumer retrieves and processes the values the producer places in this variable. Each thread may need to wait for an event to occur before it can accomplish its task. The consumer may need to wait for a value to be produced (indicated by the producer signaling semaphore `valueProduced`); the producer must wait for a previously produced value to be consumed (indicated by the consumer signaling semaphore `valueConsumed`).

```
1   System:
2   // semaphores that synchronize access to sharedValue
3   Semaphore valueProduced = new Semaphore(0);
4   Semaphore valueConsumed = new Semaphore(1);
5   int sharedValue; // variable shared by producer and consumer
6
7   startThreads(); // initialize and launch both threads
8
9   Producer Thread:
10
11  void main()
12  {
13     int nextValueProduced; // variable to store value produced
14
15     while ( !done )
16     {
17        nextValueProduced = generateTheValue(); // produce value
18        P( valueConsumed ); // wait until value is consumed
19        sharedValue = nextValueProduced; // critical section
20        V( valueProduced );  // signal that value has been produced
21
22     } // end while
23
24  } // end producer thread
```

Figure 5.16 | *Producer/consumer relationship implemented with semaphores. (Part 1 of 2.)*

```
25
26    Consumer Thread:
27
28    void main()
29    {
30       int nextValue; // variable to store value consumed
31
32       while ( !done )
33       {
34          P( valueProduced ); // wait until value is produced
35          nextValueConsumed = sharedValue; // critical section
36          V( valueConsumed ); // signal that value has been consumed
37          processTheValue( nextValueConsumed ); // process the value
38
39       } // end while
40
41    } // end consumer thread
```

Figure 5.16 | Producer/consumer relationship implemented with semaphores. (Part 2 of 2.)

The implementation of each thread is straightforward. The producer generates a new value (line 17), then waits on semaphore valueConsumed (line 18). The semaphore's value is initially 1 (line 4), so the producer assigns the newly created value nextValueProduced to shared variable sharedValue (line 19). Then the producer signals semaphore valueProduced (line 20). The consumer waits on this semaphore (line 34) and, when the producer signals valueProduced (line 20), the consumer assigns the shared variable sharedValue to a local variable nextValue-Consumed (line 35). The consumer then signals semaphore valueConsumed (line 36), which allows the producer to create a new value, and so on. The semaphores ensure mutually exclusive access to shared variable sharedValue and ensure that the threads alternate so that the consumer always reads the value that the producer has just created.

Self Review

1. (T/F) A thread can be in only one semaphore's waiting queue at a time.
2. What happens if semaphore valueProduced is initialized to a value of 1 instead of a value of 0?

Ans: 1) True. A thread is blocked when placed in a semaphore's queue of waiting threads, meaning that thread is unable to execute code that waits on any other semaphore. 2) The consumer could potentially consume a value before the produced produces it.

5.6.3 Counting Semaphores

A **counting semaphore** (also called a **general semaphore**) is a semaphore that is initialized to an integral value greater than zero and commonly greater than one. A counting semaphore is particularly useful when a resource is to be allocated from a pool of identical resources. The semaphore is initialized to the number of resources in the pool. Each *P* operation decrements the semaphore by 1, indicating that another resource has been removed from the pool and is in use by a thread. Each *V* operation increments the semaphore by 1, indicating that a thread has returned a resource to the pool and the resource may be reallocated to another thread. If a thread attempts a *P* operation when the semaphore has been decremented to zero, then the thread must wait until a resource is returned to the pool by a *V* operation.

Self Review

1. Describe how to implement a binary semaphore with a counting semaphore.
2. (T/F) The *V* operation on a counting semaphore always adds 1 to the count.

Ans: **1)** Just initialize the counting semaphore to a value of one. **2)** False. If one or more threads are waiting, *V* lets one of the threads proceed and does not increment the count.

5.6.4 Implementing Semaphores

Semaphores can be implemented in user applications and in the kernel. Given Dekker's algorithm or the availability of a `testAndSet` or `swap` machine instruction, it is straightforward to implement *P* and *V* with busy waiting. However, busy waiting wastes processor cycles that could be put to better use in a multiprogrammed system. In Chapter 3, Process Concepts, we studied the thread-state switching mechanisms implemented in the kernel. We noted that a thread requesting an I/O operation voluntarily blocks itself pending completion of the I/O. The blocked thread does not busy wait—it remains asleep until the system awakens it and moves it to the ready list.

Semaphore operations can be implemented in the kernel by blocking waiting threads to avoid busy waiting.[55] A semaphore is implemented as a protected variable and a queue in which threads can wait for *V* operations. When a thread attempts a *P* operation on a semaphore whose value is zero, the thread relinquishes the processor and blocks itself to await a *V* operation on the semaphore. The system places the thread in the queue of threads waiting on that semaphore. (We assume a first-in-first-out queue discipline. Other disciplines have been investigated.)[56] The system then reassigns the processor to the next ready thread. The thread in the semaphore queue eventually moves to the head of the queue. A subsequent *V* operation removes the thread from the semaphore queue and places it on the ready list.[57]

Of course, threads attempting simultaneous *P* and *V* operations on a semaphore must be guaranteed exclusive access to the semaphore by the kernel. In the case of uniprocessor systems, because *P* and *V* are so short, their indivisibility can be ensured by simply disabling interrupts while *P* and *V* operations are executing. This prevents the processor from being usurped until the operation is complete (at which point interrupts are again enabled). This should be done with care, or it could lead to poor performance or even deadlock (see the Anecdote, Unclear Requirements).

In the kernel of a multiprocessor system, one of the processors can be given the job of controlling the ready list and determining which processors run which threads.[58] Another approach to implementing a kernel for a multiprocessor system is to control access (via busy waiting) to a shared ready list.[59] A distributed operating system kernel could have one processor control the ready list, but normally each processor manages its own ready list and essentially has its own kernel.[60, 61, 62, 63] As a thread migrates between various processors of a distributed system, control of that thread is passed from one kernel to another.

Self Review

1. What is a major benefit of implementing semaphores in the kernel?
2. Consider a semaphore allows the thread with the highest priority to proceed when V is called. What potential problem can this cause?

Ans: 1) Semaphores can avoid busy waiting. The kernel can suspend a thread that attempts a P operation when the semaphore's current value is 0, and move it back to the *ready* queue when a V operation is called. This could increase performance. 2) Threads in the semaphore's wait queue may be indefinitely postponed by higher-priority threads.

Unclear Requirements

In his early years in industry, HMD worked for a company that developed custom software solutions for a wide range of clients. One client-an actuarial firm-sent him the following requirements: Develop a program that will print a list of the "Connecticut pension-ers who died this year in alpha-betical order." This crossed his eyes, because pensioners, of course, rarely die in alphabetical order! His client was inaccessible for a few days, so HMD created a report program that worked as he thought it should-one that printed a alphabetized list of all the Connecticut pensioners who died that year-which turns out to be what the client really wanted. That client was much more careful when specifying the requirements for future projects.

Lesson to operating systems designers: Before you build a complex piece of software like a substantial component of an operating system, be sure that the requirements are absolutely clear. You not only need to "solve the problem right;" you need to "solve the right problem" in the first place.

Web Resources

www.ddj.com/documents/s=924/ddj9801g/9801g.htm
Describes a method for implementing mutual exclusion in Java. It describes, both generally and specifically for Java, how a programmer might implement mutual exclusion between a number of threads.

www.cs.utexas.edu/users/EWD/
Contains electronic copies of manuscripts authored by E. W. Dijkstra, including his seminal paper that introduced semaphores.

www.osdata.com/topic/language/asm/coproc.htm
Describes several machine-language instructions for concurrency, such as test-and-set and swap.

developer.java.sun.com/developer/Books/performance2/chap3.pdf
Chapter from Sun's multithreaded and network programming book. It describes how to handle mutual exclusion in Java. The discussion is motivated by describing some circumstances that mutual exclusion helps avoid; then the article provides a thorough treatment of implementing mutual exclusion to avoid these unwanted circumstances.

www.teamten.com/lawrence/242.paper/242.paper.html
Provides a survey of mutual exclusion algorithms implemented by operating systems running in a multiprocessor environment.

Summary

When more than one thread exists in a system at the same time, the threads are said to be concurrent. Two concurrent threads can execute completely independently of one another, or they can execute in cooperation. Processes that operate independently of one another but must occasionally communicate and synchronize to perform cooperative tasks are said to execute asynchronously.

When one thread reads data that another thread is writing, or when one thread writes data that another thread is also writing, indeterminate results can occur. We can solve this problem by granting each thread exclusive access to the shared variable. While one thread increments the shared variable, all other threads desiring to do so will be made to wait. This is called mutual exclusion. When the executing thread finishes accessing the shared variable, the system will allow one of the waiting processes to proceed. This is called serializing access to the shared variable. In this manner, threads will not be able to access shared data simultaneously.

In a producer/consumer relationship, the producer thread generates data and stores it in a shared object, and the consumer thread reads data from the shared object. We demonstrated how logic errors can arise with unsynchronized access among multiple threads to shared data—data could be lost if the producer places new data into the shared buffer before the consumer consumes the previous data, and data could be incorrectly duplicated if the consumer consumes data again before the producer produces the next value. If this logic were part of an air traffic control application, people's lives could be at risk.

Mutual exclusion needs to be enforced only when threads access shared modifiable data—when threads are performing operations that do not conflict with one another (i.e., reading data), the system should allow the threads to proceed concurrently. When a thread is accessing shared modifiable data, the thread is said to be in its critical section (or critical region). To prevent the kinds of errors we encountered earlier, the system should ensure that only one thread can execute the instructions in its critical section at a time. If one thread attempts to enter its critical section while another thread executes its critical section, the first thread should wait until the executing thread exits its critical section. Once a thread has exited its critical section, a waiting thread (or one of the waiting threads, if there are several), may enter and execute its critical section. If a thread in its critical section terminates, either voluntarily or involuntarily, then the operating system, in performing its termination housekeeping, must release mutual exclusion so that other threads may enter their critical sections.

We discussed the enterMutualExclusion() and exitMutualExclusion() primitives, which invoke the most fundamental operations inherent to mutual exclusion. These primitives exhibit the following properties: each machine-language instruction is executed indivisibly; no assumption is made about the relative speeds of asynchronous concurrent threads; a thread that is executing instructions outside its critical section cannot prevent other threads from entering their critical sections; and a thread cannot be indefinitely postponed from entering its critical section.

An elegant software implementation of mutual exclusion primitives was first presented by Dekker. We followed Dijkstra's development of Dekker's Algorithm, which provides mutual exclusion while addressing the problems of busy waiting, lockstep synchronization, deadlock and indefinite postponement. We then discussed simpler and more efficient algorithms developed by G. L. Peterson and L. Lamport. Lamport's Bakery Algorithm, which is designed for distributed systems, demonstrates a software mutual exclusion algorithm for n threads that is valid in multiprocessor systems and that does not require its operations to be performed atomically.

Several hardware mechanisms have been developed to help implement mutual exclusion. A simple way to enforce mutual exclusion using hardware is to disable (or mask) interrupts. This solution benefits from simplicity; however, the disabling of interrupts can be disastrous if a thread misbehaves inside a critical section. Moreover, disabling interrupts is not a viable solution for mutual exclusion in a multiprocessor system. Other hardware techniques have been developed, including the use of special hardware instructions. The test-and-set and swap instructions enable a thread to perform atomic read-modify-write (RMW) memory operations. These instructions eliminate the possibility of preemption between the instruction that determines if a thread can enter its critical section and the instruction that sets a variable to indicate that no other thread may enter the critical section.

Another mutual exclusion mechanism is semaphores, as described by Dijkstra. A semaphore contains a protected variable whose integer value, once initialized, can be accessed and altered only by calling one of two operations, P and V. A thread calls the P operation (also called the wait operation) when it wants to enter a critical section; the thread calls the V operation (also called the signal operation) when it wants to exit the critical section. Before a semaphore can be used for synchronization, it must be initialized. Initialization sets the value of the protected variable to indicate that no thread is executing in a critical section. A counting semaphore (also called a general semaphore) may be initialized to a value greater than one. Counting semaphores are particularly useful when resources are to be allocated from a pool of identical resources. Semaphores can be implemented in user applications and in the kernel. Given Dekker's Algorithm or the availability of a `testAndSet` or `swap` machine instruction, it is straightforward to implement P and V with busy waiting. However, busy waiting wastes processor cycles that could be put to better use in a multiprogrammed system. Semaphore operations can also be implemented in the kernel to avoid busy waiting by blocking waiting threads.

Key Terms

atomic operation—Operation performed without interruption.

asynchronous concurrent threads—Threads that exist simultaneously but operate independently of one another and that occasionally communicate and synchronize to perform cooperative tasks.

binary semaphore—Semaphore whose value can be no greater than one, typically used to allocate a single resource.

busy waiting—Form of waiting where a thread continuously tests a condition that will let the thread proceed eventually; while busy waiting, a thread uses processor time.

concurrent—The description of a process or thread that exists in a system simultaneously with other processes and/or threads.

consumer—Application that reads and processes data from a shared object.

consumer thread—Thread whose purpose is to read and process data from a shared object.

counting semaphore—Semaphore whose value may be greater than one, typically used to allocate resources from a pool of identical resources.

critical region—See critical section.

critical section—Section of code that performs operations on a shared resource (e.g., writing data to a shared variable). To ensure program correctness, at most one thread can simultaneously execute in its critical section.

deadlock—State of a thread when it cannot continue execution because it is waiting for an event that will never occur.

Dekker's Algorithm—Algorithm that ensures mutual exclusion between two threads and prevents both indefinite postponement and deadlock.

Dijkstra's Algorithm—Efficient algorithm to find the shortest paths in a weighted graph.

disable interrupts—To temporarily ignore interrupts to allow a thread on a uniprocessor system to execute its critical section atomically.

fast mutual exclusion algorithm—Implementation of mutual exclusion that avoids the overhead of a thread performing multiple tests when no other thread is contending for its critical section. This first fast mutual exclusion algorithm was proposed by Lamport.

general semaphore—See counting semaphore.

indefinite postponement—Situation in which a thread waits for an event that might never occur.

indivisible operation—See atomic operation.

Lamport's Bakery Algorithm—*N*-thread mutual exclusion algorithm based on a "take a ticket" system.

lockstep synchronization—Situation where asynchronous threads execute code in strict alternation.

mutual exclusion—Restriction whereby execution by a thread of its critical section precludes execution by other threads of their critical sections. Mutual exclusion is crucial to correct execution when multiple threads access shared writable data.

mutual exclusion lock—Variable that indicates if a thread is executing its critical section; if the lock indicates that a thread is in its critical section, other threads are locked out of their own critical sections.

mutual exclusion primitives—Fundamental operations that are needed to implement mutual exclusion: `enterMutualExclusion()` and `exitMutualExclusion()`.

P operation—Operation on a semaphore. If the variable in the semaphore is 0, then the *P* operation blocks the calling thread. If the variable is greater than 0, the operation will decrement the variable by one and allow the calling thread to proceed.

producer—Thread or process that creates and places data into a shared object.

producer thread—Thread that creates and places data into a shared object.

producer/consumer relationship—Interaction between threads that produce data (called producers) and threads that consume produced data (called consumers) that illustrates many of the intricacies of asynchronous concurrent execution.

protected variable (semaphores)—Integer variable storing the state of a semaphore that can be accessed and altered only by calling *P* or *V* on that semaphore.

read-modify-write (RMW) memory operation—Operation that atomically reads the contents of a variable, changes the contents (possibly based on what it has read) and writes the new value to memory. These operations simplify mutual exclusion algorithms by providing atomic operations.

semaphore—Mutual exclusion abstraction that uses two atomic operations (*P* and *V*) to access a protected integer variable that determines if threads may enter their critical sections.

serialize—To control access to a shared variable such that only one thread can access the variable at a time; another thread can access the variable only after the first has finished.

signal (semaphores)—Operation on a semaphore that increments the value of the semaphore's variable. If threads are sleeping on the semaphore, the signal wakes one and decrements the semaphore's value by 1.

swap instruction—Operation that exchanges the values of two variables atomically. This instruction simplifies mutual exclusion implementations by eliminating the possibility that a thread will be preempted while performing a read-modify-write memory operation.

termination housekeeping—In the case of mutual exclusion algorithms, task performed by the operating system to ensure that mutual exclusion is not violated and that threads can continue to execute if a thread terminates while executing its critical section.

test-and-set—Instruction implemented in hardware that atomically tests the value of a variable and sets the value of the variable to true. This instruction simplifies mutual exclusion implementations by eliminating the possibility that a thread will be preempted while performing a read-modify-write memory operation.

THE Multiprogramming System—First layered operating system architecture, created by Edsger Dijkstra.

V operation—Operation on a semaphore that increments the value of the semaphore's variable if there are no threads waiting on the semaphore. If threads are waiting, the *V* operation wakes one of these.

wait (semaphores)—If the variable in the semaphore is 0, then the operation blocks the calling thread. If the variable is greater than 0, the operation will decrement the variable by one and allow the calling thread to proceed. Wait is also called the *P* operation.

Exercises

5.1 Give several reasons why the study of concurrency is appropriate and important for students of operating systems.

5.2 Explain why the following statement is false: When several threads access shared information in main memory,

mutual exclusion must be enforced to prevent the production of indeterminate results.

5.3 Dekker's Algorithm, `testAndSet`, `swap`, and the semaphore operations *P* and *V* may all be used to enforce mutual exclusion. Compare and contrast these various schemes. Consider their respective advantages and disadvantages.

5.4 When two threads simultaneously attempt `enterMutualExclusion()`, we have assumed that the "winner" is selected at random. Discuss the ramifications of this assumption. Give a better method. Discuss how such a method might be implemented on a multiprocessor system where several threads could in fact attempt `enterMutualExclusion()` at precisely the same moment.

5.5 Comment on the use of mutual exclusion primitives in Fig. 5.17.

5.6 What is the real significance of Dekker's Algorithm?

5.7 In Dekker's Algorithm (Fig. 5.10), it is possible for T_2 to leave its critical section, execute its mutual exclusion exit code, execute its mutual exclusion entry code, and ultimately reenter its critical section before T_1 gets the chance it has been waiting for to enter its own critical section. Could T_2 actually reenter its own critical section many times before T_1 got a chance? If it could, then explain precisely how this could happen and indicate if this situation is an example of indefinite postponement. If it could not happen, then explain precisely how it is prevented.

5.8 Explain how the example concurrent program that enforces mutual exclusion with `testAndSet` (Fig. 5.13) could lead to indefinite postponement. Indicate why this possibility would nevertheless be highly unlikely. Under what circumstances would it be acceptable to use this mutual exclusion technique? Under what circumstances would it be completely unacceptable?

5.9 Perform an exhaustive analysis of Dekker's Algorithm. Does it have any weaknesses? If not, explain why.

5.10 The solution for n-thread mutual exclusion presented by Eisenberg and McGuire[64] guarantees that any single process will enter its critical section within $n - 1$ tries in the worst case. Should one hope for better performance with n processes?

5.11 Mutual exclusion primitives can be implemented with busy waiting or with blocking. Discuss the applicability and relative merits of each approach.

5.12 Explain in detail how binary semaphores and binary semaphore operations can be implemented in the kernel of an operating system.

5.13 Explain how the disabling and enabling of interrupts is useful in implementing mutual exclusion primitives on uniprocessor systems.

5.14 Show how to implement semaphore operations with `testAndSet`.

5.15 Some computers have a `swap` instruction that, like `testAndSet`, simplifies the implementation of mutual exclusion primitives. The `swap` instruction simply exchanges the values of two booleans and thus requires a temporary holding area; the `swap` instruction is executed indivisibly.

    a. Express `swap` as a procedure header in a high-level language.

    b. Show how your `swap` procedure (assuming it is executed indivisibly) may be used to implement the `enterMutualExclusion()` and `exitMutualExclusion()` primitives.

```
1   // perform instructions outside of a critical section
2
3   enterMutualExclusion();
4
5      // perform instructions inside a critical section
6
7      enterMutualExclusion();
8
9         // perform instructions inside a nested critical section
10
11      exitMutualExclusion();
12
13      // perform instructions inside a critical section
14
15   exitMutualExclusion();
16
17   // perform instructions outside of a critical section
```

Figure 5.17 | Code for Exercise 5.5.

5.16 As mentioned in the text, critical sections that reference nonintersecting sets of shared variables may indeed be executed simultaneously. Suppose the mutual exclusion primitives are each modified to include a parameter list of the particular shared variables to be referenced in a critical section.

> **a.** Comment on the use of these new mutual exclusion primitives in Fig. 5.18.
>
> **b.** Suppose the two threads in Fig. 5.19 operate concurrently. What are the possible outcomes?

5.17 In Dekker's Algorithm, what (if anything) would happen if the two assignment statements in the mutual exclusion exit code were reversed?

5.18 Show that Peterson's Algorithm (Fig. 5.11) is *bounded fair*[65]; i.e., a thread cannot be delayed indefinitely on any delay condition that occurs with indefinite repetition. In particular,

show that any thread waiting to enter its critical section will be delayed no longer than the time it takes for the other thread to enter and leave its own critical section once.

5.19 Present a detailed analysis of Peterson's Algorithm to demonstrate that it works properly. In particular, show that deadlock cannot occur, that indefinite postponement cannot occur, and that mutual exclusion is enforced.

5.20 Show that if a system implementing Lamport's Bakery Algorithm does not perform termination housekeeping, the system could suffer from indefinite postponement.

5.21 Based on your understanding of the kernel and interrupt handling, describe how semaphore operations may be implemented on a uniprocessor system.

```
1    // perform instructions outside of a critical section
2
3    enterMutualExclusion(a);
4
5       // perform instructions inside a critical section
6
7       enterMutualExclusion(b);
8
9          // perform instructions inside a nested critical section
10
11      exitMutualExclusion(b);
12
13      // perform instructions inside a critical section
14
15   exitMutualExclusion(a);
16
17   // perform instructions outside of a critical section
```

Figure 5.18 | New mutual exclusion primitives for Exercise 5.16(a).

Thread T₁

```
1    enterMutualExclusion(a);
2
3    enterMutualExclusion(b);
4
5    exitMutualExclusion(b);
6
7    exitMutualExclusion(a);
```

Thread T₂

```
1    enterMutualExclusion(b);
2
3    enterMutualExclusion(a);
4
5    exitMutualExclusion(a);
6
7    exitMutualExclusion(b);
```

Figure 5.19 | Code for Exercise 5.16(b).

5.22 In the text we implied that busy waiting can be wasteful. Is it always wasteful? What alternatives exist? Discuss the pros and cons of busy waiting.

5.23 If many threads attempt a *P* operation, which one should be allowed to proceed? What are the key issues here? What criteria might you use to decide which thread should proceed on a uniprocessor system? What criteria might you use on a multiprocessor system?

5.24 A system supports only binary semaphores. Show that counting semaphores may be simulated on this system by using binary semaphores.

5.25 One requirement in the implementation of a *P* and *V* is that each of these operations must be executed indivisibly; i.e., once started, each operation runs to completion without interruption. Give an example of a simple situation in which, if these operations are not executed indivisibly, mutual exclusion may not be properly enforced.

5.26 Suppose the only mutual exclusion primitive provided to user-level threads is a command that disables interrupts for the next 32 instructions, then reenables interrupts. Explain the benefits and drawbacks of this approach.

5.27 How could cooperating threads implement mutual exclusion primitives in the system mentioned in the previous exercise?

5.28 Does the code in Fig. 5.20 provide mutual exclusion? If not, show an interleaving in which mutual exclusion is not preserved?

5.29 Name one other mutual exclusion constraint the algorithm in Fig. 5.20 violates.

```
1    System:
2
3    int turn = 1;
4    boolean t1WantsToEnter = false;
5    boolean t2WantsToEnter = false;
6
7    startThreads(); // initialize and launch both threads
8
9    Thread T₁:
10
11   void main()
12   {
13      while ( !done )
14      {
15         t1WantsToEnter = true;
16
17         while ( turn != 1 )
18         {
19            while ( t2WantsToEnter );
20
21            turn = 1;
22         } // end while
23
24         // critical section code
25
26         t1WantsToEnter = false;
27
```

Figure 5.20 | *Algorithm for Exercise 5.28. (Part 1 of 2.)*

```
28            // code outside critical section
29        } // end outer while
30    } // end Thread T1
31
32    Thread T2:
33
34    void main()
35    {
36        while ( !done )
37        {
38            t2WantsToEnter = true;
39
40            while ( turn != 2 )
41            {
42                while ( t1WantsToEnter );
43
44                turn = 2;
45            } // end while
46
47            // critical section code
48
49            t2WantsToEnter = false;
50
51            // code outside critical section
52        } // end outer while
53    } // end Thread T2
```

Figure 5.20 | *Algorithm for Exercise 5.28. (Part 2 of 2.)*

Suggested Projects

5.30 Prepare a research paper on Lamport's "fast mutual exclusion" algorithm. How does it work? Where is it used?

5.31 Research mutual exclusion in distributed systems. What research is currently being done in that field?

5.32 Research mutual exclusion multiprocessor systems. Why might this be easier than mutual exclusion in distributed systems?

5.33 Many mutual exclusion algorithms are verified using computer programs. Research how these programs manage to verify that a certain algorithm is correct.

5.34 Dijkstra is probably best known for his shortest-path algorithm. However, he also contributed greatly in other fields of computer science. For example, we know from the text that he invented semaphores. Prepare a biography of E. W. Dijkstra and the important contributions he made to the field of computer science. See, for example, www.cs.utexas.edu/users/EWD/.

5.35 Research the Ada concurrency primitives. How is mutual exclusion guaranteed in this language?

Suggested Simulations

5.36 Implement semaphores in Java. Then use them to provide synchronization between two threads in a producer/consumer program.

Recommended Reading

The problem of process synchronization was identified early and often in the literature.[66, 67, 68] The related problem of mutual exclusion has been studied in detail, and many resources are available that present solutions.[69, 70, 71] Dijkstra first described the problem on mutual exclusion, identified critical sections and applied Dekker's Algorithm to solve the problem.[72] Subsequently, Peterson[73] and Lamport[74] presented novel approaches to implementing software mutual exclusion, both of which simplified code by introducing a more structured approach. Though Dijkstra first presented a solution to *n*-thread mutual exclusion, Knuth,[75] Eisenberg and McGuire[76], Lamport,[77] Anderson and Kim[78] and others have continued to improve on the original algorithm. Dijkstra also introduced semaphores in his seminal paper on mutual exclusion.[79] In response, researchers developed techniques to improve upon the concept of semaphores.[80, 81, 82, 83] The bibliography for this chapter is located on our Web site at www.deitel.com/books/os3e/Bibliography.pdf.

Works Cited

1. Atwood, J. W., "Concurrency in Operating Systems," *Computer*, Vol. 9, No. 10, October 1976, pp. 18–26.

2. Thomas, R. H., "A Majority Consensus Approach to Concurrency Control," *ACM Transactions on Database Systems*, Vol. 4, 1979, pp. 180–209.

3. Wegner, P., and S. A. Smolka, "Processes, Tasks and Monitors: A Comparative Study of Concurrent Programming Primitives," *IEEE Transactions on Software Engineering*, Vol. SE-9, No. 4, 1983, pp. 446–462.

4. Chandy, K. M., and J. Misra, "Asynchronous Distributed Simulation via a Sequence of Parallel Computations," *Communications of the ACM*, Vol. 24, No. 4, April 1981.

5. Schlichting, R. D., and F. B. Schneider, "Understanding and Using Asynchronous Message Passing Primitives," *Proceedings of the Symposium on Principles of Distributed Computing*, August 18–20, 1982, Ottawa, Canada, ACM, New York, pp. 141–147.

6. Bernstein, A. J., "Program Analysis for Parallel Processing," *IEEE Transactions on Computers*, Vol. 15, No. 5, October 1966, pp. 757–762.

7. Courtois, P. J.; Heymans, F.; and D. L. Parnas, "Concurrent Control with Readers and Writers," *Communications of the ACM*, Vol. 14, No. 10, October 1971, pp. 667–668.

8. Lamport, L., "Concurrent Reading and Writing," *Communications of the ACM*, Vol. 20, No. 11, November 1977, pp. 806–811.

9. Ricart, G., and A. K. Agrawala, "An Optimal Algorithm for Mutual Exclusion in Computer Networks," *Communications of the ACM*, Vol. 24, No. 1, January 1981, pp. 9–17.

10. Jones, D. W., "An Empirical Comparison of Priority Queue and Event Set Implementations," *Communications of the ACM*, Vol. 29, No. 4, April 1986, pp. 300–311.

11. Raynal, M., *Algorithms for Mutual Exclusion*, Cambridge, MA: MIT Press, 1986.

12. Dijkstra, E. W., "Cooperating Sequential Processes," Technological University, Eindhoven, Netherlands, 1965, reprinted in F. Genuys, ed., *Programming Languages*, New York: Academic Press, 1968, pp. 43–112.

13. Dijkstra, E. W., "Cooperating Sequential Processes," Technological University, Eindhoven, Netherlands, 1965, reprinted in F. Genuys, ed., *Programming Languages*, New York: Academic Press, 1968, pp. 43–112.

14. Peterson, G. L., "Myths About the Mutual Exclusion Problem," *Information Processing Letters*, Vol. 12, No. 3, June 1981, pp. 115–116.

15. Lamport, L., "A New Solution of Dijkstra's Concurrent Programming Problem," *Communications of the ACM*, Vol. 17, No. 8, August 1974, pp. 453–455.

16. Dijkstra, E. W., "Cooperating Sequential Processes," Technological University, Eindhoven, Netherlands, 1965, reprinted in F. Genuys, ed., *Programming Languages*, New York: Academic Press, 1968, pp. 43–112.

17. Peterson, G. L., "Myths About the Mutual Exclusion Problem," *Information Processing Letters*, Vol. 12, No. 3, June 1981, pp. 115–116.

18. Dijkstra, E. W., "Solution of a Problem in Concurrent Programming Control," *Communications of the ACM*, Vol. 8, No. 5, September 1965, p. 569.

19. Knuth, D., "Additional Comments on a Problem in Concurrent Programming Control," *Communications of the ACM*, Vol. 9, No. 5, May 1966, pp. 321–322.

20. Eisenberg, M. A., and M. R. McGuire, "Further Comments on Dijkstra's Concurrent Programming Control Problem," *Communications of the ACM*, Vol. 15, No. 11, November 1972, p. 999.

21. Lamport, L., "A New Solution to Dijkstra's Concurrent Programming Problem," *Communications of the ACM*, Vol. 17, No. 8, August 1974, pp. 453–455.

22. Burns, J. E.; P. Jackson; N. A. Lynch; M. J. Fischer; and G. L. Peterson, "Data Requirements for Implementation of *N*-Process Mutual Exclusion Using a Single Shared Variable," *Journal of the ACM*, Vol. 29, No. 1, January 1982, pp. 183–205.

23. Carvalho, O. S. F., and G. Roucairol, "On Mutual Exclusion in Computer Networks," *Communications of the ACM*, Vol. 26, No. 2, February 1983, pp. 146–147.

24. Leslie Lamport, "A Fast Mutual Exclusion Algorithm," *ACM Transactions on Computer Systems (TOCS)*, Vol. 5, No. 1, pp.1-11, Feb. 1987.

25. Anderson, James H., and Yong-Jik Kim, "An Improved Lower Bound for the Time Complexity of Mutual Exclusion," *Proceedings of the Twentieth Annual ACM Symposium on Principles of Distributed Computing*, pp. 90-99, August 2001, Newport, Rhode Island, United States.

26. Lamport, L., "The Writings of Leslie Lamport," September 8, 2003, <research.microsoft.com/users/lamport/pubs/pubs.html>.

27. Lamport, L., "The Writings of Leslie Lamport," September 8, 2003, <research.microsoft.com/users/lamport/pubs/pubs.html>.

28. Milojicic, D., "A Discussion with Leslie Lamport," September 2002, <dsonline.computer.org/0208/f/lam_print.htm>.

29. Anderson, J., "Lamport on Mutual Exclusion: 27 Years of Planting Seeds," August 2001, <www.cs.unc.edu/~anderson/papers/lamport.pdf>. *Proceedings of the 20th Annual ACM Symposium on Principles of Distributed Computing*, pp. 3–12.

30. Lamport, L., "A New Solution of Dijkstra's Concurrent Programming Problem," *Communications of the ACM*, Vol. 17, No. 8, August 1974, pp. 453–455, <research.microsoft.com/users/lamport/pubs/bakery.pdf>.

31. Lamport, L., "TLA: The Temporal Logic of Actions," August 26, 2003, <research.microsoft.com/users/lamport/tla/tla.html>.

32. Lamport, L., et al., "Specifying and Verifying Systems with TLA+," September 2002, <research.microsoft.com/users/lamport/pubs/spec-and-verifying.pdf>.

33. Anderson, J., "Lamport on Mutual Exclusion: 27 Years of Planting Seeds," August 2001, <www.cs.unc.edu/~anderson/papers/lamport.pdf>. *Proceedings of the 20th Annual ACM Symposium on Principles of Distributed Computing*, pp. 3–12.

34. Anderson, J., "Lamport on Mutual Exclusion: 27 Years of Planting Seeds," August 2001, <www.cs.unc.edu/~anderson/papers/lamport.pdf>. *Proceedings of the 20th Annual ACM Symposium on Principles of Distributed Computing*, pp. 3–12.

35. Lamport, L., "A Fast Mutual Exclusion Algorithm," November 14, 1985, <research.microsoft.com/users/lamport/pubs/fast-mutex.pdf>.

36. Lamport, L., "The Writings of Leslie Lamport," September 8, 2003, <research.microsoft.com/users/lamport/pubs/pubs.html>.

37. Anderson, J., "Lamport on Mutual Exclusion: 27 Years of Planting Seeds," August 2001, <www.cs.unc.edu/~anderson/papers/lamport.pdf>. *Proceedings of the 20th Annual ACM Symposium on Principles of Distributed Computing*, pp. 3–12.

38. Lamport, L., "Time, Clocks, and the Ordering of Events in a Distributed System," *Communications of the ACM*, Vol. 21, No. 7, July 1978, pp. 558–565, <research.microsoft.com/users/lamport/pubs/time-clocks.pdf>.

39. The LaTeX Project, "LaTeX Project home page," January 27, 2003, <www.latex-project.org/>.

40. Gilbert, Philip, and W. J. Chandler, "Interference Between Communicating Parallel Processes," *Communications of the ACM*, Vol. 15, No. 6, June 1972, p. 436.

41. Presser, Leon, "Multiprogramming Coordination," *ACM Computing Surveys (CSUR)*, Vol. 7, No. 1, January 1975, p. 38.

42. Kruskal, Clyde P.; Larry Rudolph; and Marc Snir, "Efficient Synchronization of Multiprocessors with Shared Memory," *ACM Transactions on Programming Languages and Systems (TOPLAS)*, October 1988, p. 580.

43. Dijkstra, E. W., "Cooperating Sequential Processes," Technological University, Eindhoven, Netherlands, 1965, reprinted in F. Genuys, ed., *Programming Languages*, New York: Academic Press, 1968, pp. 43–112.

44. Computer Science Department of the University of Texas at Austin, "E. W. Dijkstra Archive: Obituary," August 2002, <www.cs.utexas.edu/users/EWD/obituary.html>.

45. Dijkstra, E., "GOTO Considered Harmful," March 1968, <www.acm.org/classics/oct95/>. Reprinted from *Communications of the ACM*, Vol. 11, No. 3, March 1968, pp. 147–148.

46. Dijkstra, E., "GOTO Considered Harmful," March 1968, <www.acm.org/classics/oct95/>. Reprinted from *Communications of the ACM*, Vol. 11, No. 3, March 1968, pp. 147–148.

47. Dijkstra, E., "Appendix of The Structure of the "THE" Multiprogramming System," May 1968, <www.acm.org/classics/mar96/>. Reprinted from *Communications of the ACM*, Vol. 11, No. 5, May 1968, pp. 345–346.

48. Dijkstra, E., "Structure of an Extendable Operating System," November 1969, <www.cs.utexas.edu/users/EWD/ewd02xx/EWD275.PDF>.

49. Computer Science Department of the University of Texas at Austin, "E. W. Dijkstra Archive: Obituary," August 2002, <www.cs.utexas.edu/users/EWD/obituary.html>.

50. T Whaley, "CS 313—Edsger Wybe Dijkstra," <cs.wlu.edu/~whaleyt/classes/313/Turing/Grieco-Dijkstra.htm>.

51. Department of Computer and Information Science of the University of Michigan at Dearborn, "The ALGOL Programming Language," November 24, 1996, <www.engin.umd.umich.edu/CIS/course.des/cis400/algol/algol.html>.

52. Computer Science Department of the University of Texas at Austin, "E. W. Dijkstra Archive: Obituary," August 2002, <www.cs.utexas.edu/users/EWD/obituary.html>.

53. Dijkstra, E., "How Do We Tell Truths That Might Hurt?" 1975, <www.cs.utexas.edu/users/EWD/ewd04xx/EWD498.PDF>.

54. Dijkstra, E., "The End of Computing Science?" 2000, <www.cs.utexas.edu/users/EWD/ewd13xx/EWD1304.PDF>.

55. Hansen, P. Brinch, "The Nucleus of a Multiprogramming System," *Communications of the ACM*, Vol. 13, No. 4, April 1970, pp. 238–241, 250.

56. Stark, Eugene, "Semaphore Primitives and Starvation-Free Mutual Exclusion," *Journal of the Association for Computing Machinery*, Vol. 29, No. 4, October 1982, pp. 1049-1072.

57. Denning, P. J.; Dennis, T.D.; and J. A. Brumfield, "Low Contention Semaphores and Ready Lists," *Communications of the ACM*, Vol. 24, No. 10, October 1981, pp. 687–699.

58. Brinch Hansen, P., "Edison: A Multiprocessor Language," *Software Practice and Experience*, Vol. 11, No. 4, April 1981, pp. 325–361.

59. Linux kernel source code, version 2.5.75, <miller.cs.wm.edu/lxr3.linux/http/source/ipc/sem.c?v=2.5.75>.

60. Hansen, P. Brinch, "Distributed Processes—a Concurrent Programming Concept," *Communications of the ACM*, Vol. 21, No. 11, November 1978, pp. 934–941.

61. Lamport, L., "Time, Clocks, and the Ordering of Events in a Distributed System," *Communications of the ACM*, Vol. 21, No. 7, July 1978, pp. 558–565.

62. Lamport, L., "The Implementation of Reliable Distributed Multiprocess Systems," *Computer Networks*, Vol. 2, No. 2, April 1978, pp. 95–114.

63. Ricart, G., and A. K. Agrawala, "An Optimal Algorithm for Mutual Exclusion in Computer Networks," *Communications of the ACM*, Vol. 24, No. 1, January 1981, pp. 9–17.

64. Eisenberg, M. A., and M. R. McGuire, "Further Comments on Dijkstra's Concurrent Programming Control Problem," *Communications of the ACM*, Vol. 15, No. 11, November 1972, p. 999.

65. Andrews, G. R., and F. B. Schneider, "Concepts and Notations for Concurrent Programming," *ACM Computing Surveys*, Vol. 15, No. 1, March 1983, pp. 3–44.

66. Bernstein, A. J., "Program Analysis for Parallel Processing," *IEEE Transactions on Computers*, Vol. 15, No. 5, October 1966, pp. 757–762.

67. Courtois, P. J.; F. Heymans; and D. L. Parnas, "Concurrent Control with Readers and Writers," *Communications of the ACM*, Vol. 14, No. 10, October 1971, pp. 667–668.

68. Lamport, L., "Concurrent Reading and Writing," *Communications of the ACM*, Vol. 20, No. 11, November 1977, pp. 806–811.

69. Ricart, G., and A. K. Agrawala, "An Optimal Algorithm for Mutual Exclusion in Computer Networks," *Communications of the ACM*, Vol. 24, No. 1, January 1981, pp. 9–17.

70. Jones, D. W., "An Empirical Comparison of Priority Queue and Event Set Implementations," *Communications of the ACM*, Vol. 29, No. 4, April 1986, pp. 300–311

71. Raynal, M., *Algorithms for Mutual Exclusion*, Cambridge, MA: MIT Press, 1986.

72. Dijkstra, E. W., "Cooperating Sequential Processes," Technological University, Eindhoven, Netherlands, 1965, reprinted in F. Genuys, ed., *Programming Languages*, New York: Academic Press, 1968, pp. 43–112.

73. Peterson, G. L., "Myths About the Mutual Exclusion Problem," *Information Processing Letters*, Vol. 12, No. 3, June 1981, pp. 115–116.

74. Lamport, L., "A New Solution of Dijkstra's Concurrent Programming Problem," *Communications of the ACM*, Vol. 17, No. 8, August 1974, pp. 453–455.

75. Knuth, D., "Additional Comments on a Problem in Concurrent Programming Control," *Communications of the ACM*, Vol. 9, No. 5, May 1966, pp. 321–322.

76. Eisenberg, M. A., and M. R. McGuire, "Further Comments on Dijkstra's Concurrent Programming Control Problem," *Communications of the ACM*, Vol. 15, No. 11, November 1972, p. 999.

77. Lamport, L., "A New Solution to Dijkstra's Concurrent Programming Problem," *Communications of the ACM*, Vol. 17, No. 8, August 1974, pp. 453–455.

78. Anderson, James H., and Yong-Jik Kim, "An Improved Lower Bound for the Time Complexity of Mutual Exclusion," *Proceedings of the Twentieth Annual ACM Symposium on Principles of Distributed Computing*, pp. 90-99, August 2001, Newport, Rhode Island, United States.

79. Dijkstra, E. W., "Cooperating Sequential Processes," Technological University, Eindhoven, Netherlands, 1965, reprinted in F. Genuys, ed., *Programming Languages*, New York: Academic Press, 1968, pp. 43–112.

80. Denning, P. J.; Dennis, T.D.; and J. A. Brumfield, "Low Contention Semaphores and Ready Lists," *Communications of the ACM*, Vol. 24, No. 10, October 1981, pp. 687–699.

81. Lamport, L., "Time, Clocks, and the Ordering of Events in a Distributed System," *Communications of the ACM*, Vol. 21, No. 7, July 1978, pp. 558–565.

82. Lamport, L., "The Implementation of Reliable Distributed Multiprocess Systems," *Computer Networks*, Vol. 2, No. 2, April 1978, pp. 95–114.

83. Ricart, G., and A. K. Agrawala, "An Optimal Algorithm for Mutual Exclusion in Computer Networks," *Communications of the ACM*, Vol. 24, No. 1, January 1981, pp. 9–17.

High thoughts must have high language.

—Aristophanes—

As writers become more numerous, it is natural for readers to become more indolent.

—Oliver Goldsmith—

When the last reader reads no more.

—Oliver Wendell Holmes—

The first precept was never to accept a thing as true until I knew it as such without a single doubt.

—René Descartes—

This shows how much easier it is to be critical than to be correct.

—Benjamin Disraeli—

Chapter 6

Concurrent Programming

Objectives

After reading this chapter, you should understand:

- *how monitors synchronize access to data.*

- *how condition variables are used with monitors.*

- *solutions for classic problems in concurrent programming such as readers and writers and circular buffer.*

- *Java monitors.*

- *remote procedure calls.*

Chapter Outline

6.1 Introduction

In the last chapter we presented Dekker's Algorithm and Peterson's Algorithm for the implementation of mutual exclusion primitives, and we studied Dijkstra's semaphores. These mechanisms have a number of weaknesses. They are so primitive that it is difficult to use them to express solutions to more complex concurrency problems, and their presence in concurrent programs increases the already difficult problem of proving program correctness. Their malicious or accidental misuse could lead to subtle bugs that might corrupt the operation of a concurrent system.

The semaphore approach, in particular, has many weaknesses.[1] If a *P* operation is omitted, then mutual exclusion is not enforced. If a *V* operation is omitted, then threads waiting because of *P* operations could become deadlocked. Once the *P* operation begins, the thread cannot back out and take an alternate course of action while the semaphore remains in use. A thread may wait on only one semaphore at a time; this could lead to deadlock in resource-allocation situations. For example, two threads may each hold a resource that the other thread is waiting to use. This is the classic case of two-thread deadlock, which we will discuss in Chapter 7, Deadlock and Indefinite Postponement.

To combat this problem, researchers have developed higher-level mutual exclusion constructs that simplify solving complex concurrency problems, facilitate proving program correctness and are difficult for a programmer to misuse or corrupt.

Concurrent programming is much more difficult than sequential programming. Concurrent programs are harder to write, debug, modify, and prove correct (see the Anecdote, Exhaustive Testing Is Impossible). So why is the programming community so intent on concurrent programming?

There has been a surge of interest in concurrent programming languages because they enable us to express more natural solutions to problems that are inherently parallel. Furthermore, the true hardware parallelism possible with multiprocessors (see Chapter 15, Multiprocessor Management) and distributed systems (see Chapter 17, Introduction to Distributed Systems) can only be harnessed through concurrent programming. The potential applications for concurrent programming are numerous. There has been much discussion on concurrency in computer networks,[2] distributed systems[3, 4, 5, 6, 7] and real-time systems.[8, 9, 10] Certainly, operating systems themselves are important examples of concurrent systems. So are air traffic control systems, mission-critical systems, and real-time process control systems (such as those that control gasoline refineries, chemical manufacturing plants and food processing plants). It is widely believed that human vision is an inherently parallel task. Weather forecasting will almost certainly take great strides forward when massive parallelism reaches the scale of billions or even trillions of concurrent processors.

In this chapter, we consider high-level constructs and languages for concurrent programming. In particular, we investigate monitors, condition variables, interprocess communication using remote procedure calls and the Java programming language's concurrent programming facilities. The pseudocode examples in

Section 6.2, Monitors, use a C-like syntax; the rest of the chapter uses complete Java programs. The chapter concludes with a lengthy literature section indicating the richness of concurrent programming as a research area.

What approach should implementors take when building concurrent systems today? Prior to the 1990s, high-level concurrent programming languages included to Ada,[11] Concurrent Pascal,[12,13] Distributed Processes,[14] Concurrent C,[15] Communicating Sequential Processes,[16,17] Modula-2,[18,19,20] VAL[21] and *MOD (for distributed programming).[22] With the exception of Ada, these languages were generally

Exhaustive Testing Is Impossible

Testing is a hard problem. As you may study in courses on automata theory, a computer may be viewed as a finite state machine. How many states can a computer have? One possible view is that if the machine stores n bits, then the number of states is 2 raised to the nth power. A machine that has even a small main memory—perhaps tens of megabytes—could have far more states than there are atoms in the universe! Consider this experiment: A complex piece of software takes a 1 or 0 as input and yields a 1 or 0 as output. Each time the tester inputs a 1 for a large number of test cases, the software outputs a 1; each time the tester inputs a 0, the software outputs a 0. The

tester concludes that the software is simply passing its input through to its output and seems to be working fine. But suppose the software actually contains a counter of the number of times it has been called, and when the counter reaches a certain large value, it performs some other (possibly devastating) action. If in testing that software, it is called fewer than that number of times, then that test case will not occur and the software "problem" will not be detected.

Dijkstra emphasized that "testing reveals the presence of bugs, but not their absence." Since it is simply not possible to exhaustively test every system we build, this means that even after a system

has been "thoroughly" tested, it could still contain "lurking bugs" that may not surface until long after the system has been deployed. This places a huge burden on the shoulders of operating systems developers. When can we truly say that a system is ready for deployment? Obviously, this decision depends on the nature of the system. Is it a mission-critical or business-critical system? Are human lives at stake? Is it a special-purpose system whose use will be carefully confined to a narrow, controlled audience, or is it a general-purpose system that could be employed in a great diversity of applications, many of which cannot be determined when the system is under development.

Lesson to operating systems designers: Since the systems you build cannot possibly be tested exhaustively, you must "design for testability," minimizing the chance of bugs and providing testing capabilities to help system testers certify that your system is ready for deployment.

developed by academics for research purposes and tend to lack many of the features needed to implement real systems. Today, many popular programming languages support concurrency, including Java, C#, Visual C++ .NET, Visual Basic .NET and Python. Concurrent programming presents opportunities for computer science students as they prepare for careers in industry, where few people are experienced in this complex subject.

Self Review

1. Why have researchers sought higher-level mutual exclusion constructs?
2. What notable high-level concurrent programming language developed prior to the 1990s did indeed include the features needed to implement real systems?

Ans: **1)** These constructs facilitate proving program correctness and are difficult to misuse or corrupt. **2)** Ada.

6.2 Monitors

A **monitor** is an object that contains both the data and procedures needed to perform allocation of a particular **serially reusable** shared resource or group of serially reusable shared resources. The notion of a monitor was suggested by Dijkstra,[23] then by Brinch Hansen,[24, 25] then refined by Hoare.[26] There has been much discussion in the literature on this important topic.[27, 28, 29, 30, 31, 32, 33, 34, 35] Monitors have become an important software construct—in fact, the Java programming language makes extensive use of monitors to implement mutual exclusion.

To accomplish resource allocation using monitors, a thread must call a **monitor entry routine**. Many threads may want to enter the monitor at the same time, but mutual exclusion is rigidly enforced at the monitor boundary—only one thread at a time is allowed to enter. A thread that tries to enter the monitor when it is in use is made to wait by the monitor. Because the monitor guarantees mutual exclusion, concurrency problems (such as indeterminate outcomes) are avoided.

Data inside a monitor may be either global to all routines within the monitor or local to a specific routine. Monitor data is accessible only within the monitor; there is no way for threads outside the monitor to access monitor data. This is a form of **information hiding**—a software architectural technique that improves modularity and facilitates the development of more reliable software systems (see the Operating Systems Thinking feature, Information Hiding).

If a thread calls a monitor entry routine while no other threads are executing inside the monitor, the thread acquires a lock on the monitor and enters it. While the thread is in the monitor, other threads may not enter the monitor to acquire the resource. If a thread calls a monitor entry routine while the monitor is locked, the monitor makes the calling thread *wait* outside the monitor until the lock on the monitor is released (i.e., when a thread is no longer executing inside the monitor). Once inside the monitor, a thread might need to wait because the resource has been allocated to another thread. Because mutual exclusion is enforced at the boundary of the monitory, a thread waiting for a resource must do so outside the monitor to allow another thread into the monitor to return the resource.

Eventually, the thread that has the resource will call a monitor entry routine to release the resource. This routine could merely free the resource and wait for another requesting thread to arrive. But there may be threads waiting for the resource, so the monitor entry routine calls *signal* to allow one of the waiting threads to enter the monitor and acquire the resource. If a thread signals the return (also called the release) of the resource, and no threads are waiting, then the signal has no effect (but, of course, the monitor has recaptured the resource, which it can now allocate to arriving threads). To avoid indefinite postponement, a monitor gives a higher priority to waiting threads than to newly arriving ones.

Self Review

1. Why must a thread wait for a resource outside a monitor?
2. How does a monitor prevent multiple threads from concurrently executing inside the monitor?

Ans: **1)** If the thread were to wait inside a monitor for a resource, no other threads could enter the monitor to return the resource. As we will see in Chapter 7, Deadlock and Indefinite Postponement, this could cause all the threads waiting for the resource to deadlock. **2)** The monitor enforces mutual exclusion at its border using the kinds of techniques discussed in Chapter 5, Asynchronous Concurrent Execution.

 Operating Systems Thinking

Information Hiding

Information hiding is one of the most fundamental techniques of software engineering. It is implemented in many ways in operating systems. When one function or method calls another, the caller does not need to know the details of how the callee is implemented; the caller merely has to know the interface to the callee—what arguments must be passed and in what order, and what return values are expected. Information hiding has many advantages. It makes the caller's job easier. It does not need to be familiar with the (possibly enormous) complexity of how the callee is implemented. It also makes it easier to modify systems—a called function can usually be replaced easily without requiring changes in the caller, as long as the interface to the callee remains the same.

Today's operating systems arguably have tens of thousands (or more) components that are constantly being evolved to adapt to new hardware and software trends and tuned to perform better. Information hiding places a crucial role in making these enormous and highly modular systems understandable and maintainable.

6.2.1 Condition Variables

Monitors implement both mutual exclusion and synchronization between threads of execution. A thread currently inside a monitor may need to wait outside the monitor until another thread performs an action inside the monitor. For example, in the producer/consumer relationship, the producer finding that the consumer still has not read the value in a single shared buffer must wait outside the monitor governing the shared buffer so that the consumer can consume the buffer contents. Similarly, a consumer finding that the shared buffer is empty must wait outside the monitor until the producer fills the buffer. A thread inside a monitor uses a **condition variable** to wait on a condition outside the monitor. A monitor associates a separate condition variable with each distinct situation that might cause a thread to have to wait. We define the `wait` and `signal` operations as:

```
wait (conditionVariable)
signal (conditionVariable)
```

Condition variables are different from "conventional" variables. Every condition variable has an associated queue. A thread calling **wait** on a particular condition variable is placed into the queue associated with that condition variable (while in that queue, the thread is outside the monitor, so that another thread can eventually enter the monitor and call `signal`). A thread calling **signal** on a particular condition variable causes a thread waiting on that condition variable to be removed from the queue associated with it and to reenter the monitor. We may assume a first-in-first-out (FIFO) queue discipline, although priority schemes can be useful in certain situations.[36, 37]

Before that thread can reenter the monitor, the thread calling `signal` must first exit the monitor. Brinch Hansen (see the Biographical Note, Per Brinch Hansen), noting that many `signal` statements immediately preceded a `return` statement (i.e., the thread exits the monitor), proposed a **signal-and-exit** monitor, in which a thread immediately exits the monitor upon signaling.[38] The monitors in the following examples are signal-and-exit monitors. Alternatively, a **signal-and-continue** monitor allows a thread inside the monitor to signal that the monitor will soon become available, but still maintain a lock on the monitor until the thread exits the monitor. A thread can exit the monitor by waiting on a condition variable or by completing execution of the code protected by the monitor. The thread released by a signal-and-continue monitor must wait until the signalling thread exits the monitor. As we discuss in Section 6.3, Java Monitors, the Java programming language implements signal-and-continue monitors.

Self Review

1. What problem might occur if a priority queue (instead of a FIFO queue) were used for a condition variable?
2. (T/F) Each monitor contains exactly one condition variable.

Ans: **1)** A lower-priority thread could be indefinitely postponed by a stream of higher-priority threads calling `wait` in the monitor enter the priority queue. **2)** False. A monitor contains a separate condition variable for each distinct situation that might cause a thread to call `wait` in the monitor.

6.2.2 Simple Resource Allocation with Monitors

Suppose several threads are contending for a resource that requires exclusive access. A simple monitor for handling the allocation and deallocation of such a resource is shown in Fig. 6.1.

Line 4 declares state variable `inUse` which keeps track of whether the resource is in use or not. Line 5 declares a condition variable that is waited on by a thread finding the resource unavailable and signaled by a thread returning the resource (and thus making it available). Lines 7–17 and 19–25 declare two monitor entry routines. To indicate that these are monitor entry routines (rather than routines private to the monitor), we prefix each routine with the pseudocode keyword `monitorEntry`.

Biographical Note

Per Brinch Hansen

Per Brinch Hansen has devoted his research to concurrent programming, which is the technique of designing software that has parallel paths of execution. He received his Masters in Electrical Engineering from the Technical University of Denmark in 1962 and has been a professor at the California Institute of Technology, the University of Southern California and the University of Copenhagen, Denmark. He is currently a professor of Electrical Engineering and Computer Science at Syracuse University.[39]

While working at the Regnecentralen, Copenhagen, Brinch Hansen developed the RC 4000 Multiprogramming System for the RC (RegneCentralen) 4000 computer. This operating system was the first to separate system functions into a kernel module.[40]

Brinch Hansen introduced the concept of the monitor construct—an object that encapsulates both shared data and the procedures that operate on that shared data—in his book, *Operating Systems Principles*, published by Prentice Hall in 1973 (see Section 6.2, Monitors).[41] He incorporated monitors into his Concurrent Pascal language (an extension of Pascal, which allowed only sequential programming), for users to define access controls on shared data so that programs written in Concurrent Pascal could be checked at compile time for sharing violations.[42] As a demonstration of Concurrent Pascal, Brinch Hansen used it to write **Solo**, a simple operating system that was secure (meaning that errors would be detected by the system instead of crashing the program—not the more common meaning of safe from attacks) without using hardware support.[43, 44, 45] He later designed the concurrent programming language Joyce.[46]

```
1   // Fig. 6.1: Resource allocator monitor
2
3   // monitor initialization (performed only once)
4   boolean inUse = false; // simple state variable
5   Condition available; // condition variable
6
7   // request resource
8   monitorEntry void getResource()
9   {
10      if ( inUse ) // is resource in use?
11      {
12         wait( available ); // wait until available is signaled
13      } // end if
14
15      inUse = true; // indicate resource is now in use
16
17   } // end getResource
18
19   // return resource
20   monitorEntry void returnResource()
21   {
22      inUse = false; // indicate resource is not in use
23      signal( available ); // signal a waiting thread to proceed
24
25   } // end returnResource
```

Figure 6.1 | Simple resource allocation with a monitor in pseudocode.

Line 8 begins method `getResource`, which a thread calls to request the resource associated with the condition variable `available`. Line 10 tests the state variable `inUse` to see whether the resource is in use. If this value is `true`, meaning that the resource has been allocated to another thread, the calling thread must `wait` on condition variable `available` (line 12). After calling `wait`, the thread exits the monitor and is placed in the queue associated with the condition variable `available`. As we will see, this allows the thread that is using the resource to enter the monitor and release the resource by signaling condition variable `available`. When the resource is not in use, the requesting thread executes line 15, which sets `inUse` to `true`, providing the thread exclusive access to the resource.

Line 20 begins method `returnResource`, which a thread calls to release the resource. Line 22 sets the value of `inUse` to `false` to indicate that the resource is no longer in use and can be allocated to another thread. Line 23 calls `signal` on condition variable `available` to alert any waiting thread that the resource is now free. If there are any threads waiting in the queue associated with `available` (as a result of executing line 12), the next waiting thread reenters the monitor and executes line 15, obtaining exclusive access to the resource. If there are no threads waiting on `available`, `signal` has no effect.

The beauty of the monitor in Fig. 6.1 is that it performs exactly as a binary semaphore; method `getResource` acts as the *P* operation; method `returnResource` acts as the *V* operation. Because the simple one-resource monitor can be used to implement semaphores, monitors are at least as powerful as semaphores. Note that the monitor initialization (lines 3–5) is performed before threads begin using the monitor; in this case `inUse` is set to false to indicate that the resource is initially available.

Self Review

1. What would happen if `returnResource()` did not `signal` the condition variable `available`?
2. What purpose does the keyword `monitorEntry` serve?

Ans: 1) All of the threads waiting on condition variable `available` would deadlock—they will wait forever. 2) Keyword `monitorEntry` distinguishes between monitor entry routines, which are accessible by all threads and can be executed by only one thread at a time, and private monitor methods, which are accessible only within the monitor.

6.2.3 Monitor Example: Circular Buffer

In this section we discuss the **circular buffer** (sometimes called the **bounded buffer**) and how it is useful in situations in which a producer thread passes data to a consumer thread. Because the producer and consumer access the same data and may operate at different rates, synchronization between the two threads is essential.

We can use an array to implement the circular buffer. In the circular buffer implementation of the solution to the producer/consumer problem, the producer deposits data in the successive elements of the array. The consumer removes them in the order in which they were deposited (FIFO). The producer can be several items ahead of the consumer. Eventually, the producer fills the last element of the array. When it produces more data, it must "wrap around" and again begin depositing data in the first element of the array (assuming, of course, that the consumer has removed the data previously put there by the producer). The array effectively closes in a circle, hence the term circular buffer.

Because of the fixed size of the circular buffer, the producer will occasionally find all the array elements full; in this case the producer must wait until the consumer empties an array element. Similarly, there will be times when the consumer wants to consume, but the array will be empty; in this case the consumer must wait until the producer deposits data into an array element. The monitor in Fig. 6.2 (based on the example presented by Hoare)[47] implements a circular buffer and the appropriate synchronization mechanisms to handle the producer/consumer relationship.

```
1  // Fig. 6.2: Circular buffer monitor
2
```

Figure 6.2 | *Monitor pseudocode implementation of a circular buffer. (Part 1 of 2.)*

```
3    char circularBuffer[] = new char[ BUFFER_SIZE ]; // buffer
4    int writerPosition = 0; // next slot to write to
5    int readerPosition = 0; // next slot to read from
6    int occupiedSlots = 0;  // number of slots with data
7    Condition hasData;       // condition variable
8    Condition hasSpace;      // condition variable
9
10   // monitor entry called by producer to write data
11   monitorEntry void putChar( char slotData )
12   {
13      // wait on condition variable hasSpace if buffer is full
14      if ( occupiedSlots == BUFFER_SIZE )
15      {
16         wait( hasSpace ); // wait until hasSpace is signaled
17      } // end if
18
19      // write character to buffer
20      circularBuffer[ writerPosition ] = slotData;
21      ++occupiedSlots; // one more slot has data
22      writerPosition = (writerPosition + 1) % BUFFER_SIZE;
23      signal( hasData ); // signal that data is available
24   } // end putChar
25
26   // monitor entry called by consumer to read data
27   monitorEntry void getChar( outputParameter slotData )
28   {
29      // wait on condition variable hasData if the buffer is empty
30      if ( occupiedSlots == 0 )
31      {
32         wait( hasData ); // wait until hasData is signaled
33      } // end if
34
35      // read character from buffer into output parameter slotData
36      slotData = circularBuffer[ readPosition ];
37      occupiedSlots--; // one fewer slots has data
38      readerPosition = (readerPosition + 1) % BUFFER_SIZE;
39      signal( hasSpace ); // signal that character has been read
40   } // end getChar
```

Figure 6.2 | *Monitor pseudocode implementation of a circular buffer. (Part 2 of 2.)*

We shall assume that the array `circularBuffer` contains BUFFER_SIZE entries consisting of one character (line 3). Variables `writerPosition` and `readerPosition` (lines 4–5) indicate in which slot of the circular buffer the next item is to be placed by a producer and from which slot of the circular buffer the next item is to be removed by a consumer, respectively.

A producer adds data to the buffer by calling method putChar (lines 10–24). Line 14 tests if the buffer is full. If it is, the producer waits on the condition variable hasSpace (line 16). When it does this, the producer leaves the monitor and waits in the queue associated with the condition variable hasSpace. As we will soon see, this allows a consumer to enter the monitor, consume data in the circular buffer and signal condition variable hasSpace. This enables the producer to continue; it writes the data to the buffer (line 20), increments the number of occupied slots (line 21) and updates the writerPosition variable (line 22). Finally, line 23 signals condition variable hasData to enable a waiting consumer, if there is one, to proceed.

A consumer reads data from the buffer by calling method getChar (lines 26–40). Note the use of the output parameter slotData in the pseudocode (indicated by keyword outputParameter in line 27). Many languages support such a capability. Data written to the output parameter is immediately available in the caller's argument. Line 30 tests if the buffer is empty. If it is, the consumer waits on condition variable hasData (line 32). When the consumer can continue, it reads the data from the buffer directly into the output parameter slotData (line 36), immediately making the data available in the caller's argument. The consumer then decrements the number of occupied slots (line 37) and updates readerPosition (line 38). Line 39 signals condition variable hasSpace to enable a waiting producer, if there is one, to proceed.

The beauty of the circular buffer is that it allows the producer to "get ahead" of the consumer. The producer can create a new value without waiting for the consumer to read the previous value (as is necessary in the single buffer producer/consumer relationship). These extra values are placed in the empty slots of the circular buffer. The consumer will still read the values in the correct order. The circular buffer reduces the amount of time the producer must wait before producing another value, thus improving system performance. The larger the circular buffer, the more values the producer can produce before it must wait for the consumer to empty the buffer. If the producer and consumer work at approximately the same speed, using the circular buffer can increase the average speed of the application. If there is a difference in the average speeds of the threads, this advantage is nullified. For example, if the producer works consistently faster than the consumer, the circular buffer will quickly become full and stay full, forcing the producer to wait each time for the consumer to free up space. Similarly, if the consumer works consistently faster than the producer, then the consumer will typically find the circular buffer empty and will almost always have to wait for the producer to create a value. In these last two cases, using the circular buffer will simply waste memory rather than increasing the speed of the application.

Operating systems can use a circular buffer to implement spooling control. One common example of spooling occurs when a thread generates lines to be printed on a relatively slow output device such as a printer. Because the thread can produce the lines much faster than the printer can print them, and because we would like the thread to be able to complete its execution as quickly as possible, the thread's output lines can be directed to a circular buffer. The circular buffer may be in primary storage, or more likely on disk. The thread creating the lines to be printed is often called a **spooler**. Another thread reads the lines from the `circularBuffer` and writes them to the printer. But this second thread, often called a **despooler**, runs at the slower speed of the printer. The `circularBuffer` has sufficient storage to "take up the slack" resulting from the mismatch in the speeds of the spooler and despooler threads. Of course, we assume the system does not indefinitely generate print lines faster than the printer can print them; if it did, the buffer would always be full and would be of little value in "smoothing" the printing operation.

Self Review

1. Name the two situations in which a circular buffer is less efficient than a single-value buffer in the producer/consumer relationship.
2. Would this monitor support one producer and two consumers such that each element that the producer produces is consumed by exactly one consumer? Why or why not?

Ans: **1)** If the difference in the average speeds of the producer and consumer is significant, the advantage of the circular buffer is nullified. If the producer consistently ran faster than the consumer, it would almost always find the buffer full and would have to wait each time for a consumer to consume. If the consumer consistently ran faster than the producer, it would almost always find the buffer empty and would have to wait each time for a producer to produce. In these cases, a single-value buffer can be used without loss of performance. **2)** Yes. Mutual exclusion would still be enforced by the monitor. The producer would still produce values as normal. Only one consumer would read each piece of data from the producer.

6.2.4 Monitor Example: Readers and Writers

In computer systems, it is common to have some consumer threads (called readers) that read data and producer threads (called writers) that write it. For example, in an airline reservation system there may be many more readers than writers—many inquiries will be made against the database of available flight information before the customer actually selects and commits to a particular seat on a particular flight.

Because readers do not change the contents of the database, many readers may access the database at once. But a writer can modify the data, so it must have exclusive access. When a writer is active, no other readers or writers may be active. This exclusion needs to be enforced only at the record level. It is not necessary to grant a writer exclusive access to the entire database—doing so could dramatically hurt performance.

The problem of designing a concurrent program to control access of readers and writers to a database was first posed and solved by Courtois, Heymans, and Parnas.[48] The solution in Fig. 6.3 is based on that developed by Hoare.[49]

The monitor in Figure 6.3 may be used to control access to an entire database, a subset of the database consisting of many or few records, or even a single record. In any of these cases, the following discussion applies. Only one writer may be active at a time; when a writer is active, the boolean variable `writeLock` (line 4) is `true`. No readers may be active when a writer is active. The integer variable, `readers` (line 3), indicates the number of active readers. When the number of readers is

```
1   // Fig. 6.3: Readers/writers problem
2
3   int readers = 0; // number of readers
4   boolean writeLock = false; // true if a writer is writing
5   Condition canWrite; // condition variable
6   Condition canRead; // condition variable
7
8   // monitor entry called before performing read
9   monitorEntry void beginRead()
10  {
11     // wait outside monitor if writer is currently writing or if
12     // writers are currently waiting to write
13     if ( writeLock || queue( canWrite ) )
14     {
15        wait( canRead ); // wait until reading is allowed
16     } // end if
17
18     ++readers; // there is another reader
19
20     signal( canRead ); // allow waiting readers to proceed
21  } // end beginRead
22
23  // monitor entry called after reading
24  monitorEntry void endRead()
25  {
26     --readers; // there are one fewer readers
27
28     // if no more readers are reading, allow a writer to write
29     if ( readers == 0 )
30     {
31        signal ( canWrite ); // allow a writer to proceed
32     } // end if
33
34  } // end endRead
35
36  // monitor entry called before performing write
37  monitorEntry void beginWrite()
38  {
39     // wait if readers are reading or if a writer is writing
40     if ( readers > 0 || writeLock )
41     {
42        wait( canWrite ); // wait until writing is allowed
43     } // end if
44
```

Figure 6.3 | Monitor pseudocode for solving the readers and writers problem. (Part 1 of 2.)

```
45      writeLock = true; // lock out all readers and writers
46   } // end beginWrite
47
48   // monitor entry called after performing write
49   monitorEntry void endWrite()
50   {
51      writeLock = false; // release lock
52
53      // if a reader is waiting to enter, signal a reader
54      if ( queue( canRead ) )
55      {
56         signal( canRead ); // cascade in waiting readers
57      } // end if
58      else // signal a writer if no readers are waiting
59      {
60         signal( canWrite ); // one waiting writer can proceed
61      } // end else
62
63   } // end endWrite
```

Figure 6.3 | *Monitor pseudocode for solving the readers and writers problem.*
(Part 2 of 2.)

reduced to zero (line 29), then one waiting writer (if there is one) becomes active
(line 31). If a new reader cannot proceed (line 13), it waits on the condition variable
canRead (line 15). If a new writer cannot proceed (line 40), it waits on the condition
variable canWrite (line 42).

When a reader wishes to read, it calls monitor entry beginRead (lines 8–21); a
reader that has finished calls endRead (lines 23–34). In beginRead, a new reader can
proceed as long as no thread is writing and no writer thread is waiting to write (line
13). The latter condition is important for preventing indefinite postponement of waiting writers; it is tested by using the boolean function, queue, which determines
whether or not threads are waiting on the condition variable specified in its argument.
Note that procedure beginRead ends by signaling canRead (line 20) to allow another
waiting reader to begin reading. This causes the next reader in the queue of waiting
readers to become active and, in turn, signal the next waiting reader to proceed. This
"chain reaction," also called a cascade, will continue until all waiting readers have
become active. While this chaining is progressing, all arriving threads are forced to
wait because the monitor observes the rule that signaled threads are serviced before
arriving threads. If arriving readers were allowed to proceed, then a continuous
stream of arriving readers would cause indefinite postponement of waiting writers.
Since the readers do not interfere with one another and can be run in parallel on multiprocessor systems, this is an efficient way to service these threads.

When a thread is done reading, it calls monitor entry endRead (lines 23–34),
which decrements the number of readers by 1 (line 26). Eventually, this decrementing causes the number of readers to become zero, at which point the thread signals

canWrite (line 31) to allow a waiting writer, if there is one, to proceed (preventing indefinite postponement of waiting writers).

When a thread wishes to write, it calls monitor entry beginWrite (lines 36–46). Because a writer must have exclusive access, if there are any readers or if there is an active writer (line 40), the new writer must wait on condition variable canWrite (line 42). When the writer is able to proceed (because canWrite is signaled in line 31 or line 60), writeLock is set to true (line 45). This keeps out any other readers and writers.

When a writer finishes, it calls monitor entry endWrite (lines 48–63). This procedure sets writeLock to false (line 51) so that either readers or another writer can become active. The monitor then must signal another waiting thread to proceed (lines 53–61). Should it give preference to a waiting reader or a waiting writer? If it gives preference to a waiting writer, then it will be possible for a steady stream of incoming writers to cause the indefinite postponement of waiting readers. Therefore, as a writer finishes, it first checks if there is a waiting reader (line 54). If so, then canRead is signaled (line 56) and the waiting reader proceeds (and this, of course, cascades in all waiting readers). If there is no waiting reader, then canWrite is signaled (line 60) and a waiting writer is allowed to proceed.

Self Review

1. Figure 6.3 cascades in waiting readers, but never cascades in waiting writers. Why?
2. What safeguard is there against a steady stream of readers indefinitely postponing a writer?

Ans: **1)** Readers don't interfere with one another, so many readers can safely read at once. Each writer, however, must have exclusive access, or indeterminate results could occur. **2)** In monitory entry beginRead, if there are any writers waiting to write (line 13), then a thread that wishes to read must wait on condition variable canRead (line 15).

6.3 Java Monitors

In the following sections, we present complete, working Java multithreaded solutions to common concurrent programming problems. Monitors are associated with every object created in Java. Monitors are also the primary mechanism to provide mutual exclusion and synchronization in multithreaded Java applications. The keyword **synchronized** imposes mutual exclusion on an object in Java. In this section, we explain how Java monitors differ from the pseudocode monitors discussed in the previous section.

When a thread attempts to execute a method protected by a Java monitor (i.e., the method is declared synchronized), it must first enter that monitor's **entry set** (commonly referred to as an **entry queue**), which is a queue of threads awaiting entry into the monitor. If there is no contention for entry into the monitor, a thread will immediately enter the monitor. If a thread is already inside the monitor, other threads must remain in the entry set until the monitor becomes available.

Java monitors are typically referred to as signal-and-continue monitors.[50] Recall that a signal-and-continue monitor allows a thread inside the monitor to signal that the monitor will soon become available, but still maintain a lock on the monitor until it exits. A thread can exit the monitor by waiting on a condition variable or by completing execution of the code protected by the monitor.

A thread, executing in a monitor, that must wait on a condition variable issues the wait call. The wait method causes the thread to release the lock on the monitor and wait on an unnamed condition variable. After calling wait, a thread is placed in the **wait set** (also commonly referred to as the **wait queue**), a queue of threads waiting to reenter the monitor for the object. Threads remain in the wait set until signaled (notified) by another thread. Because the condition variable is implicit in Java, a thread may be signaled, reenter the monitor and find that the condition on which it waited has not been met. Consequently, a thread may be signaled several times before the condition on which it is waiting is met.

Threads issue signals by calling method notify or notifyAll. The **notify** method wakes a single thread in the wait set. The algorithm that determines which thread will enter the monitor next varies, depending on the Java virtual machine (JVM) implementation. As a result, the programmer cannot rely on a particular queuing discipline when notify is called.

Another pitfall of the notify method is that the order in which some JVM implementations remove threads from the entry and wait sets might introduce lengthy service delays for particular threads in these sets—creating the possibility of indefinite postponement. As a result, if more than two threads access a monitor, it is best to use the **notifyAll** method, which wakes all threads in the entry and wait sets. When all threads are awake, the thread scheduler determines which thread acquires the monitor. The thread scheduler employs a queue discipline that prevents indefinite postponement.[51, 52] Because notifyAll wakes all threads waiting to enter the monitor (as opposed to notify, which wakes a single thread), notifyAll incurs more overhead than notify. In the simple case of two-thread synchronization, notify yields higher performance than notifyAll without suffering from indefinite postponement.

Self Review

1. What is the difference between signal-and-continue monitors and signal-and-exit monitors? Which type does Java use?

Ans: **1)** Java uses signal-and-continue monitors. They allow a thread to signal that it will soon be exiting the monitor, yet retain control of the monitor. Signal-and-exit monitors require that a thread release its lock on the monitor immediately after signaling.

6.4 Java Multithreading Case Study, Part III: Producer/Consumer Relationship in Java

In this section, we present a Java implementation of the producer/consumer relationship investigated in Section 5.2.1, Java Multithreading Case Study, Part II. The application in Fig. 6.4 and Fig. 6.5 demonstrates a producer and a consumer accessing a single shared buffer, with synchronization provided by a monitor. In this case, the producer produces a new value only when the buffer is empty, making the buffer full; the consumer consumes a value only when the buffer is full, making the buffer empty. This example reuses interface Buffer (Fig. 5.1) and classes Producer (Fig. 5.2) and Consumer (Fig. 5.3) from the example of Section 5.2.1. Reusing these classes from the example without synchronization enables us to demonstrate that the threads accessing the shared object are unaware that they are being synchronized. The code that performs the synchronization is placed in the set and get methods of class SynchronizedBuffer (Fig. 6.4), which implements interface Buffer (line 4). Thus, the Producer's and Consumer's run methods simply call the shared object's set and get methods as in the example of Section 5.2.1.

Class SynchronizedBuffer (Fig. 6.4) contains two fields—buffer (line 6) and occupiedBuffers (line 7). Method set (lines 9–43) and method get (lines 45–79) are now synchronized methods (lines 10 and 46); thus, only one thread can enter any of these methods at a time on a particular SynchronizedBuffer object. Although occupiedBuffers (line 7) is logically a condition variable, it is of type int; there is no object or type in Java that directly represents a condition variable. The methods in SynchronizedBuffer use occupiedBuffers in conditional expressions (lines 16 and 52) to determine whether it is the producer's or the consumer's turn to perform a task. If occupiedBuffers is zero, buffer is empty and the producer can place a value into buffer (line 34). This condition (line 52) also means that the consumer must wait (line 59) in the get method to read the value of buffer (again, because it is empty). If occupiedBuffers is one, the consumer can read the value from buffer, because it contains new information. This condition (line 16) also means that the producer must wait to place a value into buffer, because it is currently full.

```java
1   // Fig. 6.4: SynchronizedBuffer.java
2   // SynchronizedBuffer synchronizes access to a shared integer.
3
4   public class SynchronizedBuffer implements Buffer
5   {
6      private int buffer = -1; // shared by producer and consumer
7      private int occupiedBuffers = 0; // counts occupied buffers
8
9      // place value into buffer
10     public synchronized void set( int value )
11     {
12        // for display, get name of thread that called this method
13        String name = Thread.currentThread().getName();
14
```

Figure 6.4 | SynchronizedBuffer synchronizes access to a shared integer. (Part 1 of 3.)

```
15         // while no empty buffers, place thread in waiting state
16         while ( occupiedBuffers == 1 )
17         {
18            // output thread and buffer information, then wait
19            try
20            {
21               System.err.println( name + " tries to write." );
22               displayState( "Buffer full. " + name + " waits." );
23               wait(); // wait until buffer is empty
24            } // end try
25
26            // if waiting thread interrupted, print stack trace
27            catch ( InterruptedException exception )
28            {
29               exception.printStackTrace();
30            } // end catch
31
32         } // end while
33
34         buffer = value; // set new buffer value
35
36         // indicate producer cannot store another value
37         // until consumer retrieves current buffer value
38         ++occupiedBuffers;
39
40         displayState( name + " writes " + buffer );
41
42         notify(); // tell waiting thread to enter ready state
43      } // end method set; releases lock on SynchronizedBuffer
44
45      // return value from buffer
46      public synchronized int get()
47      {
48         // for display, get name of thread that called this method
49         String name = Thread.currentThread().getName();
50
51         // while no data to read, place thread in waiting state
52         while ( occupiedBuffers == 0 )
53         {
54            // output thread and buffer information, then wait
55            try
56            {
57               System.err.println( name + " tries to read." );
58               displayState( "Buffer empty. " + name + " waits." );
```

Figure 6.4 | SynchronizedBuffer *synchronizes access to a shared integer.*
(Part 2 of 3.)

```
59              wait();// wait until buffer contains new values
60          } // end try
61
62          // if waiting thread interrupted, print stack trace
63          catch ( InterruptedException exception )
64          {
65              exception.printStackTrace();
66          } // end catch
67
68       } // end while
69
70       // indicate that producer can store another value
71       // because consumer just retrieved buffer value
72       --occupiedBuffers;
73
74       displayState( name + " reads " + buffer );
75
76       notify(); // tell waiting thread to become ready
77
78       return buffer;
79    } // end method get; releases lock on SynchronizedBuffer
80
81    // display current operation and buffer state
82    public void displayState( String operation )
83    {
84       StringBuffer outputLine = new StringBuffer( operation );
85       outputLine.setLength( 40 );
86       outputLine.append( buffer + "\t\t" + occupiedBuffers );
87       System.err.println( outputLine );
88       System.err.println();
89    } // end method displayState
90
91 } // end class SynchronizedBuffer
```

Figure 6.4 | SynchronizedBuffer synchronizes access to a shared integer. (Part 3 of 3.)

When the Producer thread's run method invokes synchronized method set (from line 26 of Fig. 5.2), the thread attempts to acquire a lock on the SynchronizedBuffer monitor object. [*Note:* When we talk about "acquiring a lock" on a Java monitor, we mean "gaining mutually exclusive access to a monitor" in the generic discussion of monitors in Section 6.2, Monitors.] If the lock is available, the Producer thread acquires the lock. Then the loop in method set (lines 16–32 of Fig. 6.4) determines whether occupiedBuffers is equal to one. If so, buffer is full, so line 21 outputs a message indicating that the Producer thread is trying to write a value, and line 22 invokes method displayState (lines 81–89) to output another message indicating that the buffer is full and that the Producer thread is in the *waiting* state. Note that method `displayState` is not declared `Synchronized` because it is called in method `main` (line 18 of Fig. 6.5) before the producer and consumer threads are created and thereafter only from inside `Synchronized` methods `get` and `set` (lines 10 and 46 of Fig. 6.4). Only one thread can execute inside the `SynchronizedBuffer`'s monitor at once and `displayState` is accessed only from inside the monitor, so mutually exclusive access is enforced without needing to declare `displayState` `Synchronized`.

Line 23 invokes method `wait` (inherited from `Object` by `Synchronized-Buffer`; all Java classes inherit from `Object` directly or indirectly) to place the thread that called method `set` (i.e., the Producer thread) in the *waiting* state for the `SynchronizedBuffer` object. The call to `wait` causes the calling thread to release the lock on the `SynchronizedBuffer` object. This is important because the thread cannot currently perform its task—and holding the lock would prevent other threads from accessing the object. This would result in deadlock, because the condition variable on which the first thread was waiting would never change. After the producer thread calls `wait` in line 23, another thread can attempt to acquire the `SynchronizedBuffer` object's lock and invoke the object's `set` or `get` methods— in particular, a consumer thread can now empty the buffer, eventually allowing the waiting producer to proceed.

The producer thread remains in the *waiting* state until it is notified by another thread that it may proceed—at which point the producer thread returns to the *ready* state and waits for a processor. When the producer thread returns to the *running* state, the thread implicitly attempts to reacquire the lock on the `Synchro-nizedBuffer` object. If the lock is available, the producer reacquires the lock and method `set` continues executing with the next statement after `wait`. Because `wait` is called in a loop (lines 15–32), the loop continuation condition is tested to determine whether the thread can proceed with its execution. If not, `wait` is invoked again; otherwise, method `set` continues with the next statement after the loop.

Line 34 in method `set` assigns the argument `value` to `buffer`. Line 38 increments `occupiedBuffers` to indicate that the `buffer` now contains a value (i.e., a consumer can read the value, but a producer cannot put another value there yet). Line 40 invokes method `displayState` to output a line to the console window indicating that the producer is writing a new value into the `buffer`. Line 42 invokes method `notify` (inherited from `Object`). If the consumer thread is waiting, it enters the *ready* state, where it can attempt its task again (as soon as the thread is assigned a processor). Method `notify` returns immediately and method `set` returns to its caller. [*Note:* Invoking method `notify` works correctly in this program because only one thread calls method `get` at any time (the consumer thread). Programs that have multiple threads waiting on a condition should invoke `notifyAll` to ensure that multiple threads receive notifications properly.] When method `set` returns, it implicitly releases the lock on the `SynchronizedBuffer` object.

Methods `get` and `set` are implemented similarly. When the consumer thread's `run` method invokes `synchronized` method `get` (from line 28 of Fig. 5.3), the thread attempts to acquire a lock on the `SynchronizedBuffer` object. When it acquires the lock, the while loop (lines 51–68 of Fig. 6.4) determines whether occupiedBuffers is equal to 0. If so, the buffer is empty, so line 57 outputs a message indicating that the consumer thread is trying to read a value, and line 58 invokes method displayState to output another message indicating that the buffer is empty and that the consumer thread waits. Line 59 invokes method wait to place the consumer thread that called method get in the *waiting* state for the SynchronizedBuffer object. Again, the call to wait causes the calling thread to release the lock on the SynchronizedBuffer object, so another thread can attempt to acquire the lock and invoke the object's set or get method. If the lock on the SynchronizedBuffer is not available (e.g., if the ProducerThread has not yet returned from method set) the consumer thread is blocked until the lock becomes available.

The consumer thread object remains in the *waiting* state until it is notified by the producer thread that it may proceed—at which point the consumer thread returns to the *ready* state and waits a processor. When it returns to the *running* state, the thread implicitly attempts to reacquire the lock on the SynchronizedBuffer object. If the lock is available, the consumer thread reacquires it and method get continues executing with the next statement after the wait. Because wait is called in a loop (lines 51–68), the loop continuation condition is tested to determine whether the thread can proceed. If not, wait is invoked again; otherwise, method get continues with the next statement after the loop. Line 72 decrements occupiedBuffers to indicate that buffer is now empty, line 74 outputs a line to the console window indicating the value the consumer just read and line 76 invokes method notify. If the producer thread is waiting for the lock on this SynchronizedBuffer object, it enters the ready state. As soon as it is assigned a processor, the thread will attempt to reacquire the lock and continue performing its task. Method notify returns immediately, then method get returns the value of buffer to its caller (line 78). [*Note:* Again, invoking method notify works correctly in this program because only one thread calls method set at any time (the producer thread).] When method get returns, the lock on the SynchronizedBuffer object is released.

Class SharedBufferTest2 (Fig. 6.5) is similar to class SharedBufferTest (Fig. 5.5). SharedBufferTest2 contains method main (lines 6–27), which launches the application. Line 9 instantiates a shared SynchronizedBuffer and assigns its reference to SynchronizedBuffer variable sharedLocation. We use a SynchronizedBuffer variable rather than a Buffer variable, so that main can invoke SynchronizedBuffer method displayState, which is not declared in interface Buffer. The SynchronizedBuffer object stores the data that is shared between the producer and consumer threads. Lines 11–18 display the column heads for the output. Lines 21–22 create a Producer object and a Consumer object, respectively, and pass sharedLocation to each constructor, so each object is initialized with a reference to the same SynchronizedBuffer. Next, lines 24–25 invoke method start on the producer and consumer threads to place them in the *ready* state. This launches these threads and sets up the initial call to each thread's run method. Finally, method main terminates and the main thread of execution dies.

Study the three sample outputs in Fig. 6.5. Observe that every integer produced is consumed exactly once. The synchronization and the variable occupiedBuffers ensure that the producer and consumer can execute only when it is their turn. The producer must go first; the consumer must wait if the producer has not produced since the consumer last consumed; the producer must wait if the consumer has not yet consumed the value that the producer most recently produced. In the first and second sample outputs, notice the comments indicating when the producer and consumer must wait to perform their respective tasks. In the third sample output, notice that the producer and consumer were fortuitously able to perform their tasks without waiting.

Self Review

1. Why does the displayState method not need to be declared as synchronized?
2. (T/F) If the notify method is never called in the get method, the producer will never finish producing because it will be indefinitely postponed at line 23 of Fig. 6.4.

Ans: **1)** Although occupiedBuffers is a shared resource, the only time that displayState is called is inside synchronized methods or when the program contains only one thread. **2)** False. It is possible that the buffer will never fill, in which case the producer will never execute line 23. This is the case in the third output of Fig. 6.5.

```
1    // Fig. 6.5: SharedBufferTest2.java
2    // SharedBufferTest2creates producer and consumer threads.
3
4    public class SharedBufferTest2
5    {
6       public static void main( String [] args )
7       {
8          // create shared object used by threads
9          SynchronizedBuffer sharedLocation = new SynchronizedBuffer();
10
11         // Display column heads for output
12         StringBuffer columnHeads =
13            new StringBuffer( "Operation" );
14         columnHeads.setLength( 40 );
15         columnHeads.append( "Buffer\t\tOccupied Count" );
16         System.err.println( columnHeads );
17         System.err.println();
18         sharedLocation.displayState( "Initial State" );
19
20         // create producer and consumer objects
21         Producer producer = new Producer( sharedLocation );
22         Consumer consumer = new Consumer( sharedLocation );
23
24         producer.start(); // start producer thread
```

Figure 6.5 | Threads modifying a shared object with synchronization. (Part 1 of 4.)

```
25          consumer.start(); // start consumer thread
26
27      } // end main
28
29  } // end class SharedBufferTest2
```

Sample Output 1:

Operation	Buffer	Occupied Count
Initial State	-1	0
Consumer tries to read.		
Buffer empty. Consumer waits.	-1	0
Producer writes 1	1	1
Consumer reads 1	1	0
Consumer tries to read.		
Buffer empty. Consumer waits.	1	0
Producer writes 2	2	1
Consumer reads 2	2	0
Producer writes 3	3	1
Consumer reads 3	3	0
Consumer tries to read.		
Buffer empty. Consumer waits.	3	0
Producer writes 4	4	1
Consumer reads 4	4	0
Producer done producing.		
Terminating Producer.		
Consumer read values totaling: 10.		
Terminating Consumer.		

Figure 6.5 | *Threads modifying a shared object with synchronization. (Part 2 of 4.)*

Sample Output 2:

Operation	Buffer	Occupied Count
Initial State	-1	0
Consumer tries to read. Buffer empty. Consumer waits.	-1	0
Producer writes 1	1	1
Consumer reads 1	1	0
Producer writes 2	2	1
Producer tries to write. Buffer full. Producer waits.	2	1
Consumer reads 2	2	0
Producer writes 3	3	1
Consumer reads 3	3	0
Producer writes 4	4	1
Producer done producing. Terminating Producer. Consumer reads 4	4	0
Consumer read values totaling: 10. Terminating Consumer.		

Sample Output 3:

Operation	Buffer	Occupied Count
Initial State	-1	0
Producer writes 1	1	1

Figure 6.5 | Threads modifying a shared object with synchronization. (Part 3 of 4.)

Sample Output 3 (Cont.):

Operation	Buffer	Occupied Count
Initial State	-1	0
Producer writes 1	1	1
Consumer reads 1	1	0
Producer writes 2	2	1
Consumer reads 2	2	0
Producer writes 3	3	1
Consumer reads 3	3	0
Producer writes 4	4	1
Producer done producing. Terminating Producer. Consumer reads 4	4	0
Consumer read values totaling: 10. Terminating Consumer.		

Figure 6.5 | *Threads modifying a shared object with synchronization. (Part 4 of 4.)*

6.5 Java Multithreading Case Study, Part IV: Circular Buffer in Java

The program of Section 6.4 uses thread synchronization to guarantee that two threads manipulate data in a shared buffer correctly. However, the application may not perform optimally. If the two threads operate at different speeds, one of them will spend more (or even most) of its time waiting. If the producer thread produces values faster than the consumer can consume them, the producer will spend most of its time waiting for the consumer. Similarly, if the consumer consumes faster than the producer can produce them, the consumer will spend most of its time waiting for the producer. Even when the threads operate at the same relative speeds, over a period of time, occasionally those threads may become "out of sync," causing one of them to wait for the other. We cannot and should not make assumptions about the relative speeds of asynchronous concurrent threads. Too many interactions occur with the operating system, the network, the user and other system components that can cause the threads to operate at different and unpredictable speeds. When this happens in the producer/consumer example, one thread must wait. When threads spend a significant portion of their time waiting, programs may become less efficient, the system may become less responsive to interactive users and applications may suffer long delays because the processor is not used efficiently.

To minimize the waiting time for threads that share resources and operate at the same average speeds, we know from earlier in this chapter that we can implement a circular buffer that provides extra buffer slots into which the producer can place values at times when it is running faster than the consumer and from which the consumer can retrieve those values when it is running faster than the producer.

The key to using a circular buffer is to provide it with sufficient buffer slots to handle the anticipated "extra" production. If, over a period of time, we determine that the producer often produces as many as three more values than the consumer can consume, we can provide a buffer of three or more slots to handle the extra production. If the number of buffer slots is too small, threads will wait more; if too large, that would waste memory.

The Java program of Fig. 6.6–Fig. 6.7 demonstrates a producer and a consumer accessing a circular buffer (in this case, a shared array of three cells) with synchronization. In this version of the producer/consumer relationship, the consumer consumes a value only when the array is not empty and the producer produces a value only when the array is not full.

Class Producer is slightly modified from the version presented in Fig. 5.2; this version produces values from 11 to 20 (rather than 1–4). Class Consumer is slightly modified from the version in Fig. 5.3; this version consumes ten (rather than four) values from the circular buffer.

The significant changes of Fig. 6.4–Fig. 6.5 occur in CircularBuffer (Fig. 6.6), which replaces SynchronizedBuffer (Fig. 6.4). CircularBuffer contains four fields. Array buffers (line 8) implements the circular buffer as a three-element integer array. Variable occupiedBuffers (line 11) is the condition variable that can be used to determine whether a producer can write into the circular buffer (i.e., when occupiedBuffers is less than the number of elements in buffers) and whether a consumer can read from the circular buffer (i.e., when occupiedBuffers is greater than 0). Variable readLocation (line 14) indicates the position in buffers from which the next value can be read by a consumer. Variable writeLocation (line 15) indicates the next location in buffers in which a value can be placed by a producer.

```
1   // Fig. 6.6: CircularBuffer.java
2   // CircularBuffer synchronizes access to an array of
3   // shared buffers.
```

Figure 6.6 | SynchronizedBuffer controls access to a shared array of integers. (Part 1 of 5.)

```
4
5   public class CircularBuffer implements Buffer
6   {
7      // each array element is a buffer
8      private int buffers[] = { -1, -1, -1 };
9
10     // occupiedBuffers maintains count of occupied buffers
11     private int occupiedBuffers = 0;
12
13     // variables that maintain read and write buffer locations
14     private int readLocation = 0;
15     private int writeLocation = 0;
16
17     // place value into buffer
18     public synchronized void set( int value )
19     {
20        // get name of thread that called this method
21        String name = Thread.currentThread().getName();
22
23        // while buffer full, place thread in waiting state
24        while ( occupiedBuffers == buffers.length )
25        {
26           // output thread and buffer information, then wait
27           try
28           {
29              System.err.println( "\nAll buffers full. " +
30                 name + " waits." );
31              wait(); // wait until space is available
32           } // end try
33
34           // if waiting thread interrupted, print stack trace
35           catch ( InterruptedException exception )
36           {
37              exception.printStackTrace();
38           } // end catch
39
40        } // end while
41
42        // place value in writeLocation of buffers
43        buffers[ writeLocation ] = value;
44
45        // output produced value
46        System.err.println( "\n" + name + " writes " +
47           buffers[ writeLocation ] + " " );
48
```

Figure 6.6 | SynchronizedBuffer *controls access to a shared array of integers.*
(*Part 2 of 5.*)

```
49          // indicate that one more buffer is occupied
50      ++occupiedBuffers;
51
52          // update writeLocation for future write operation
53      writeLocation = ( writeLocation + 1 ) % buffers.length;
54
55          // display contents of shared buffers
56      System.err.println( createStateOutput() );
57
58      notify(); // return a waiting thread to ready state
59   } // end method set
60
61   // return value from buffer
62   public synchronized int get()
63   {
64      // get name of thread that called this method
65      String name = Thread.currentThread().getName();
66
67      // while buffer is empty, place thread in waiting state
68      while ( occupiedBuffers == 0 )
69      {
70         // output thread and buffer information, then wait
71         try
72         {
73            System.err.println( "\nAll buffers empty. " +
74               name + " waits." );
75            wait(); // wait until buffer contains new data
76         } // end try
77
78         // if waiting thread interrupted, print stack trace
79         catch ( InterruptedException exception )
80         {
81            exception.printStackTrace();
82         } // end catch
83
84      } // end while
85
86      // obtain value at current readLocation
87      int readValue = buffers[ readLocation ];
88
89      // output consumed value
90      System.err.println( "\n" + name + " reads " +
91         readValue + " " );
92
93      // decrement occupied buffers value
```

Figure 6.6 | SynchronizedBuffer controls access to a shared array of integers.
(Part 3 of 5.)

```
94          --occupiedBuffers;
95
96          // update readLocation for future read operation
97          readLocation = ( readLocation + 1 ) % buffers.length;
98
99          // display contents of shared buffers
100         System.err.println( createStateOutput() );
101
102         notify(); // return a waiting thread to ready state
103
104         return readValue;
105      } // end method get
106
107      // create state output
108      public String createStateOutput()
109      {
110         // first line of state information
111         String output = "(buffers occupied: " +
112            occupiedBuffers + ")\nbuffers: ";
113
114         for ( int i = 0; i < buffers.length; ++i )
115         {
116            output += " " + buffers[ i ] + "   ";
117         } // end for
118
119         // second line of state information
120         output += "\n            ";
121
122         for ( int i = 0; i < buffers.length; ++i )
123         {
124            output += "---- ";
125         } // end for
126
127         // third line of state information
128         output += "\n            ";
129
130         // append readLocation (R) and writeLocation (W)
131         // indicators below appropriate buffer locations
132         for ( int i = 0; i < buffers.length; ++i )
133         {
134            if ( i == writeLocation &&
135               writeLocation == readLocation )
136            {
137               output += " WR  ";
138            } // end if
```

Figure 6.6 | *SynchronizedBuffer controls access to a shared array of integers.*
(Part 4 of 5.)

```
139              else if ( i == writeLocation )
140              {
141                 output += "  W   ";
142              } // end if
143              else if ( i == readLocation )
144              {
145                 output += "  R   ";
146              } // end if
147              else
148              {
149                 output += "        ";
150              } // end else
151
152          } // end for
153
154          output += "\n";
155
156          return output;
157      } // end method createStateOutput
158
159 } // end class CircularBuffer
```

Figure 6.6 | SynchronizedBuffer *controls access to a shared array of integers.*
(*Part 5 of 5.*)

CircularBuffer method set (lines 17–59) performs the same tasks as did the SynchronizedBuffer in Fig. 6.4, with a few modifications. The while loop in lines 23–40 determines whether the producer must wait (i.e., all buffers are full). If so, lines 29–30 output that the producer is waiting to perform its task. Then line 31 invokes method wait to place the producer thread in the *waiting* state for the CircularBuffer object. When execution eventually continues in line 43 after the while loop, the value written by the producer is placed in the circular buffer at location writeLocation. Next, lines 46–47 output the value produced. Line 50 increments occupiedBuffers—there is now at least one value in the buffer that the consumer can read. Then, line 53 updates writeLocation for the next call to CircularBuffer method set. The output continues at line 56 by invoking method createStateOutput (lines 107–157), which outputs the number of occupied buffers, the contents of the buffers and the current writeLocation and readLocation. Finally, line 58 invokes method notify to indicate that the consumer thread waiting on the CircularBuffer object (if indeed the consumer is waiting) should proceed.

Method get (lines 61–105) of class CircularBuffer also performs the same tasks as it did in Fig. 6.4, with a few minor modifications. The while loop in lines 67–84 determines whether the consumer must wait (i.e., all buffer slots are empty). If the consumer thread must wait, lines 73–74 output that the consumer is waiting to perform its task. Then, line 75 invokes method wait to place the consumer thread in the *waiting* state for the CircularBuffer object. When execution eventually continues at line 87 after the `while` loop, `readValue` is assigned the value at location `readLocation` in the circular buffer. Lines 90–91 output the consumed value. Line 94 decrements the `occupiedBuffers`—there is now at least one open position in the buffer in which the producer thread can place a value. Then, line 97 updates `readLocation` for the next call to `CircularBuffer` method `get`. Line 100 invokes method `createStateOutput` to output the number of occupied buffers, the contents of the buffers and the current `writeLocation` and `readLocation`. Finally, line 102 invokes method `notify` to indicate that the producer thread waiting for the `CircularBuffer` object (if indeed the producer is waiting) should proceed, and line 104 returns the consumed value to the calling method. Note that because Java implements signal-and-continue monitors, this program does not require the output parameter discussed in Section 6.2.3, Monitor Example: Circular Buffer.

Class `CircularBufferTest` (Fig. 6.7) contains the `main` method (lines 8–24) that launches the application. Line 13 creates the CircularBuffer object `sharedLocation`. Lines 19–20 create the `producer` and `consumer` threads, and lines 22–23 start them. The sample outputs include the current `occupiedBuffers`, the contents of the buffers and the current `writeLocation` and `readLocation`. In the output, the letters W and R represent the current `writeLocation` and `readLocation`, respectively. Notice that, after the third value is placed in the third element of the buffer, the fourth value is inserted back at the beginning of the array—this is the circular buffer effect.

```
1   // Fig. 6.7: CircularBufferTest.java
2   // CircularBufferTest shows two threads manipulating a
3   // circular buffer.
4
5   // set up the producer and consumer threads and start them
6   public class CircularBufferTest
7   {
8      public static void main ( String args[] )
9      {
10        // create shared object for threads; use a reference
11        // to a CircularBuffer rather than a Buffer reference
12        // to invoke CircularBuffer method createStateOutput
13        CircularBuffer sharedLocation = new CircularBuffer();
14
15        // display initial state of buffers in CircularBuffer
16        System.err.println( sharedLocation.createStateOutput() );
17
18        // set up threads
19        Producer producer = new Producer( sharedLocation );
20        Consumer consumer = new Consumer( sharedLocation );
21
```

Figure 6.7 | CircularBufferTest *instantiates producer and consumer threads.* (Part 1 of 6.)

```
22          producer.start(); // start producer thread
23          consumer.start(); // start consumer thread
24      } // end main
25
26  } // end class CircularBufferTest
```

Sample Output:

```
(buffers occupied: 0)
buffers:  -1    -1    -1
          ---- ---- ----
           WR


All buffers empty. Consumer waits.

Producer writes 11
(buffers occupied: 1)
buffers:  11    -1    -1
          ---- ---- ----
           R    W

Consumer reads 11
(buffers occupied: 0)
buffers:  11    -1    -1
          ---- ---- ----
               WR

Producer writes 12
(buffers occupied: 1)
buffers:  11    12    -1
          ---- ---- ----
                R    W


Producer writes 13
(buffers occupied: 2)
buffers:  11    12    13
          ---- ---- ----
           W         R
```

Figure 6.7 │ CircularBufferTest *instantiates producer and consumer threads.*
(Part 2 of 6.)

Sample Output (Cont.):

```
Consumer reads 12
(buffers occupied: 1)
buffers:  11    12    13
          ----  ----  ----
          W           R


Producer writes 14
(buffers occupied: 2)
buffers:  14    12    13
          ----  ----  ----
                W     R


Producer writes 15
(buffers occupied: 3)
buffers:  14    15    13
          ----  ----  ----
                      WR


All buffers full. Producer waits.

Consumer reads 13
(buffers occupied: 2)
buffers:  14    15    13
          ----  ----  ----
                R     W


Producer writes 16
(buffers occupied: 3)
buffers:  14    15    16
          ----  ----  ----
                WR


All buffers full. Producer waits.
```

Figure 6.7 | CircularBufferTest *instantiates producer and consumer threads.*
(Part 3 of 6.)

Sample Output (Cont.):

```
Consumer reads 14
(buffers occupied: 2)
buffers:   14    15    16
          ----  ----  ----
            W     R

Producer writes 17
(buffers occupied: 3)
buffers:   17    15    16
          ----  ----  ----
                 WR


Consumer reads 15
(buffers occupied: 2)
buffers:   17    15    16
          ----  ----  ----
                 W     R


Consumer reads 16
(buffers occupied: 1)
buffers:   17    15    16
          ----  ----  ----
            R     W


Consumer reads 17
(buffers occupied: 0)
buffers:   17    15    16
          ----  ----  ----
                 WR


Producer writes 18
(buffers occupied: 1)
buffers:   17    18    16
          ----  ----  ----
                 R     W
```

Figure 6.7 | CircularBufferTest *instantiates producer and consumer threads.* (Part 4 of 6.)

Sample Output (Cont.):

```
Consumer reads 18
(buffers occupied: 0)
buffers:   17    18    16
           ---- ---- ----
                       WR


All buffers empty. Consumer waits.

Producer writes 19
(buffers occupied: 1)
buffers:   17    18    19
           ---- ---- ----
            W          R


Consumer reads 19
(buffers occupied: 0)
buffers:   17    18    19
           ---- ---- ----
            WR


Producer writes 20
(buffers occupied: 1)
buffers:   20    18    19
           ---- ---- ----
            R     W

Producer done producing.
Terminating Producer.

Consumer reads 20
(buffers occupied: 0)
buffers:   20    18    19
           ---- ---- ----
                 WR
```

Figure 6.7 | CircularBufferTest *instantiates producer and consumer threads.*
(Part 5 of 6.)

Sample Output (Cont.):

```
Consumer read values totaling: 155.
Terminating Consumer.
```

Figure 6.7 | `CircularBufferTest` *instantiates producer and consumer threads.*
(Part 6 of 6.)

Self Review

1. What are the potential costs and benefits of making the circular buffer larger?
2. What would happen if line 102 of Fig. 6.6 was omitted?

Ans: **1)** The potential benefit is that the producer can produce more and block less if the consumer is temporarily slower than the producer. However, this could result in wasted memory if both the consumer and producer work at the same speed, if one works much faster than the other or if the producer rarely, if ever, gets far enough ahead of the consumer to take advantage of the extra space. **2)** The consumer thread would complete without issuing the `notify`. If the producer fortuitously never waits for the consumer (indeed a rare occurrence), then the system would function correctly. More commonly, however, if the producer were waiting it would never be able to proceed, i.e., the producer could be deadlocked.

Web Resources

`developer.java.sun.com/developer/Books/`
`performance2/chap4.pdf`
This page from Sun's Web site provides a detailed description of how to use Java monitors.

`hissa.nist.gov/rbac/5277/titlerpc.html`
Compares several popular RPC implementations.

`java.sun.com/docs/books/tutorial/essential/`
`threads/synchronization.html`
This is Sun's example of implementing mutual exclusion in the consumer/producer relationship in Java.

Summary

Concurrent programs are harder to write, debug, modify, and prove correct than non-concurrent programs. Nonetheless, there has been a surge of interest in concurrent programming languages because they enable us to express more naturally solutions to problems that are inherently parallel. The proliferation of multiprocessing systems, distributed systems and massively parallel architectures has also fueled the surge.

A monitor is an object that contains both the data and procedures needed to perform allocation one or more serially reusable shared resources. Monitor data is accessible only within the monitor; there is no way for threads outside the monitor to access monitor data directly. To accomplish a resource allocation function using monitors, a thread must call a monitor entry routine. Many threads might want to enter the monitor at various times, but mutual exclusion is rigidly enforced at the monitor boundary. A thread that tries to enter the monitor when it is in use is made to wait by the monitor.

Eventually, the thread that has the resource will call a monitor entry routine to return the resource. There might be threads waiting for the resource, so the monitor entry routine calls `signal` to allow one of the waiting threads to acquire the resource and enter the monitor. To avoid indefinite postponement, a monitor gives higher priority to waiting threads than to newly arrived threads.

Before a thread can reenter the monitor, the thread calling `signal` must first exit the monitor. A signal-and-exit monitor requires a thread to immediately exit the monitor upon signaling. Alternatively, a signal-and-continue monitor allows a thread inside the monitor to signal that the monitor will soon become available, but still maintain a lock on the monitor until the thread exits the monitor. A thread can exit the monitor by waiting on a condition variable or by completing execution of the code protected by the monitor.

A thread currently inside a monitor may need to wait outside the monitor until another thread performs an action inside the monitor. A monitor associates a separate condition variable with each distinct situation that might cause a thread to have to wait. Every condition variable has an associated queue. A thread calling wait on a particular condition variable is placed into the queue associated with that condition variable; a thread calling signal on a particular condition variable causes a thread waiting on that condition variable (if there is such a thread) to be removed from the queue associated with that condition variable and to enter the monitor.

In the circular buffer implementation of the solution to the producer/consumer problem, the producer deposits data in the successive elements of the shared array. The consumer removes them in the order in which they were deposited (FIFO). The producer can be several items ahead of the consumer. Eventually, the producer fills the last element of the array. When it produces more data, it must "wrap around" and again begin depositing data in the first element of the array.

Because of the fixed size of the circular buffer, the producer will occasionally find all the array elements full; in this case the producer must wait until the consumer empties an array element. Similarly, there will be times when the consumer wants to consume, but the array will be empty; in this case the consumer must wait until the producer deposits data into an array element.

If the two threads operate at different speeds, one of them will spend more (or even most) of its time waiting. If the producer thread produces values faster than the consumer can consume them, the producer thread spends most of its time waiting for the consumer to remove the next value from the array. Similarly, if the consumer thread consumes values faster than the producer can produce them, the consumer thread spends most of its time waiting for the producer to place the next value into the array.

In computer systems, it is common to have some threads (called readers) that read data and others (called writers) that write it. Because readers do not change the contents of the database, many readers can access the database at once. But a writer can modify the data, so it must have exclusive access. A new reader can proceed as long as no thread is writing and no writer thread is waiting to write. Each new reader signals the next waiting reader to proceed. This causes a "chain reaction" that continues until all waiting readers have become active. While this chaining is in progress, all arriving threads are forced to wait. During the chaining, arriving readers cannot enter the monitor, because the monitor observes the rule that signaled threads are serviced before arriving threads. If arriving readers were allowed to proceed, then a continuous stream of arriving readers would indefinitely postpone waiting writers. When the last reader leaves the monitor, the thread signals a waiting writer to proceed. When a writer finishes, it first checks if there is a waiting reader. If there is, the waiting reader proceeds (again cascading in all waiting readers). If there is no waiting reader, a waiting writer is allowed to proceed.

Monitors are the primary mechanism providing mutual exclusion and synchronization in multithreaded Java applications. The keyword synchronized imposes mutual exclusion on an object in Java. Java monitors are signal-and-continue monitors, allowing a thread to signal that the monitor will soon become available, but still maintain a lock on the monitor until the thread exits the monitor.

In Java, the wait method causes the calling thread to release the lock on the monitor and wait on an unnamed condition variable. After calling wait, a thread is placed in the wait set. A thread remains in the wait set until signaled by another thread. Because the condition variable is implicit in Java, a thread may be signaled, reenter the monitor and find that the condition on which it waited has not been met.

Threads issue signals by calling method notify or notifyAll. The notify method wakes a thread in the wait set. If more than two threads may access a monitor, it is best to use the notifyAll method, which wakes all threads in the wait set. Because notifyAll wakes all threads attempting to enter the monitor (instead of a single thread), notify can yield higher performance in some applications.

Key Terms

bounded buffer—See circular buffer.

circular buffer—In the producer/consumer relationship, a fixed-size region of shared memory that stores multiple values produced by a producer. If the producer occasionally produces values faster than the consumer, a circular buffer reduces the time the producer spends waiting for a consumer to consume the values, when compared to a buffer that stores a single value. If the consumer temporarily consumes values faster than the producer, a circular buffer can similarly reduce the time a consumer spends waiting for the producer to produce values.

condition variable—Variable that contains a value and an associated queue. When a thread waits on a condition variable inside a monitor, it exits the monitor and is placed in the condition variable's queue. Threads wait in the queue until signaled by another thread.

entry queue—See entry set.

entry set—In Java, a queue of threads waiting to enter a monitor after calling a `synchronized` method.

information hiding—Software architectural technique that facilitates the development of more reliable software systems by preventing direct access to data within an object by outside objects.

monitor—Concurrency construct that contains both the data and procedures needed to provide mutual exclusion while allocating a serially reusable shared resource or group of serially reusable shared resources.

monitor entry routine—Monitor routine that can be called by any thread, but that can be executed by only one thread at a time. Unlike private monitor routines, which can be called only by threads executing inside the monitor, monitor entry routines enforce mutual exclusion.

notify—Java method that wakes one thread in a monitor's wait set. The thread that is awakened depends on the JVM implementation.

notifyAll—Java method that awakens all threads in a monitor's wait and entry sets. Method `notifyAll` ensures that waiting threads are not indefinitely postponed, but incurs more overhead than `notify`.

serially reusable shared resource—Resource that can be used by only one thread at a time.

signal-and-continue monitor—Monitor that allows a thread to signal that the monitor is available, but does not require the thread to release the lock until it exits the monitor, at which point a signaled thread may enter the monitor.

signal-and-exit monitor—Monitor that requires a thread to release the lock on the monitor as soon as the thread signals another thread.

Solo—Small operating system created by Per Brinch Hansen to demonstrate fail-safe concurrent programming.

synchronization—Coordination between asynchronous concurrent threads to sequentialize their access to shared resources.

synchronized—Java keyword that imposes mutual exclusive access to code inside an object.

wait queue—See wait set.

wait set—In Java, a set of threads waiting to reacquire the lock on a monitor.

Exercises

6.1 Compare and contrast the use of monitors and semaphore operations.

6.2 When a resource is returned by a thread calling a monitor, the monitor gives priority to a waiting thread over a new requesting thread. Why?

6.3 How do condition variables differ from conventional variables? Does it make sense to initialize condition variables?

6.4 The text has stated repeatedly that no assumptions should be made about the relative speeds of asynchronous concurrent threads. Why?

6.5 What factors, do you suppose, would affect a designer's choice of the number of slots a circular buffer should have?

6.6 Why is it considerably more difficult to test, debug, and prove program correctness for concurrent programs than for sequential programs?

6.7 The text states that information hiding is a system structuring technique that contributes to the development of more reliable software systems. Why, do you suppose, is this so?

6.8 Refer to the monitor described in Fig. 6.2 and answer each of the following questions.

    a. Which procedure places data into the circular buffer?

    b. Which procedure removes data from the circular buffer?

    c. Which queuing discipline best describes the operation of the circular buffer?

d. Is this true: `writerPosition >= readerPosition`?

e. Which statements perform monitor initialization?

f. Which statement(s) can "wake up" a thread waiting on a condition variable?

g. Which statement(s) can put a thread "to sleep"?

h. Which statement(s) ensure that the buffer "wraps around"?

i. Which statement(s) modify a shared critical variable to indicate that another slot in the buffer is available?

6.9 In the readers and writers monitor presented in Fig. 6.3 why does it make sense to cascade in all waiting readers? Could this cause indefinite postponement of waiting writers? Under what circumstances might you choose to limit the number of waiting readers you would initiate when reading is allowed?

6.10 *(The Sleeping Barber Problem)*[53] A barbershop has a cutting room with one chair and a waiting room with *n* chairs. Customers enter the waiting room one at a time if space is available, otherwise they go to another shop. Each time the barber finishes a haircut the customer leaves to go to another store, and a waiting customer, if there is one, enters the cutting room and has a haircut. Customers may enter the waiting room one at a time, or waiting customers may enter the (empty) cutting room one at a time, but these events are mutually exclusive. If the barber discovers that the waiting room is empty, the barber falls asleep in the waiting room. An arriving customer, finding the barber asleep, wakes the barber and has a haircut; otherwise the arriving customer waits. Use a monitor to coordinate the operation of the barber and the clients. If you know Java, also implement your monitor in Java.

6.11 *(The Cigarette Smokers Problem)*[54] [*Note:* One of the authors, HMD, worked with S. Patil and Jack Dennis in the Computation Structures Group at M.I.T.'s Project Mac.] This has become one of the classic problems in concurrency control. Three smokers are represented by threads S1, S2, and S3. Three vendors are represented by threads V1, V2, and V3. Each smoker requires tobacco, a wrapper, and a match to smoke; when these resources are available, the smoker smokes the cigarette to completion, then becomes eligible to smoke again. S1 has tobacco, S2 has wrappers, and S3 has matches. V1 supplies tobacco and wrappers, V2 supplies wrappers and matches, and V3 supplies matches and tobacco. V1, V2, and V3 operate in mutual exclusion; only one of these threads can operate at a time and the next vendor cannot operate until resources supplied by the previous vendor have been consumed by a smoker. Use a monitor to coordinate the operation of the smoker and vendor threads.

6.12 Semaphores are at least as powerful as monitors. Show how to implement a monitor by using semaphores.

6.13 Use semaphores to solve the readers and writers problem.

6.14 Implement the readers and writers problem. Model your solution after the readers and writers solution in Fig. 6.2 and the Java-based circular-buffer solution in Fig. 6.6 and Fig. 6.7.

6.15 Should a waiting thread receive priority over a thread first attempting to enter a monitor? What priority scheme, if any, should be imposed on waiting threads?

Suggested Project

6.16 Prepare a research paper on concurrent programming in video game consoles. Does the hardware provide mutual exclusion primitives to the application programmer?

Suggested Simulation

6.17 Extend the producer/consumer solution without a circular buffer presented in Fig. 6.1 to handle multiple producers.

Recommended Reading

Solutions to problems in concurrent programming have been known for quite some time. Dijkstra[55] was the first to truly address such concerns, and he was soon followed by many others.[56, 57, 58, 59] Recent developments in mutual exclusion algorithms pertain to distributed systems and are beyond the scope of this chapter. However, the reader is encouraged to study Lamport's survey of the mutual exclusion problem and some powerful results.[60, 61] Initial development of the concept of a monitor has been attributed to Brinch Hansen[62] and Hoare.[63] An excellent survey of monitors, which describes their history, taxonomy and usage, is presented by Buhr.[64] For more detailed information about the Java programming language and concurrent programming, see *Java How to Program*[65] and *Concurrent Programming in Java: Design Principles and Pattern, 2nd ed.*[66] The bibliography for this chapter is located on our Web site at www.deitel.com/books/os3e/Bibliography.pdf.

Works Cited

1. "Rationale for the Design of the Ada Programming Language," *ACM SIGPLAN Notices*, Vol. 14, No. 6, June 1979, Part B.

2. Carvalho, O. S. F., and G. Roucairol, "On Mutual Exclusion in Computer Networks," *Communications of the ACM*, Vol. 26, No. 2, February 1983, pp. 146–147.

3. Liskov, B., and R. Scheifler, "Guardians and Actions: Linguistic Support for Robust, Distributed Programs," *ACM Transactions on Programming Languages and Systems*, Vol. 5, No. 3, 1983, pp. 381–404.

4. Shatz, S. M., "Communication Mechanisms for Programming Distributed Systems," *Computer*, Vol. 17, No. 6, June 1984, pp. 21–28.

5. Fisher, D. A., and R. M. Weatherly, "Issues in the Design of a Distributed Operating System for Ada," *Computer*, Vol. 19, No. 5, May 1986, pp. 38–47.

6. Liskov, B. H.; M. Herlihy; and L. Gilbert, "Limitations of Synchronous Communication with Static Process Structure in Languages for Distributed Computing," *Proceedings of the 13th ACM Symposium on Principles of Programming Languages,* St. Petersburg, Florida, January 1986.

7. Shatz, S. M., and J. Wang, "Introduction to Distributed-Software Engineering," *Computer*, Vol. 20, No. 10, October 1987, pp. 23–32.

8. Roberts, E. S.; A. Evans, Jr.; C. R. Morgan; and E. M. Clarke, "Task Management in Ada—A Critical Evaluation for Real-Time Multiprocessors," *Software—Practice and Experience*, Vol. 11, No. 10, October 1981, pp. 1019–1051.

9. Nielsen, K. W., and K. Shumate, "Designing Large Real-Time Systems with Ada," *Communications of the ACM*, Vol. 30, No. 8, August 1987, pp. 695–715.

10. Ford, R., "Concurrent Algorithms for Real-Time Memory Management," *IEEE Software*, Vol. 5, No. 5, September 1988, pp. 10–24.

11. "Preliminary Ada Reference Manual," *ACM SIGPLAN Notices*, Vol. 14, No. 6, June 1979, Part A.

12. Brinch Hansen, P., "The Programming Language Concurrent Pascal," *IEEE Transactions on Software Engineering*, Vol. SE-1, No. 2, June 1975, pp. 199–207.

13. Coleman, D.; Gallimore, R. M.; Hughes, J. W.; and M. S. Powell, "An Assessment of Concurrent Pascal," *Software—Practice and Experience*, Vol. 9, 1979, pp. 827–837.

14. Brinch Hansen, P., "Distributed Processes: A Concurrent Programming Concept," *Communications of the ACM*, Vol. 21, No. 11, November 1978, pp. 934–941.

15. Gehani, N. H., and W. D. Roome, "Concurrent C," *Software—Practice and Experience*, Vol. 16, No. 9, 1986, pp. 821–844.

16. Kieburtz, R. B., and A. Silberschatz, "Comments on 'Communicating Sequential Processes,' " *ACM Transactions on Programming Languages and Systems*, Vol. 1, No. 2, 1979, pp. 218–225.

17. Hoare, C. A. R., *Communicating Sequential Processes*, Englewood Cliffs, NJ: Prentice-Hall, 1985.

18. Hoppe, J., "A Simple Nucleus Written in Modula-2: A Case Study," *Software—Practice and Experience*, Vol. 10, No. 9, September 1980, pp. 697–706.

19. Wirth, N., *Programming in Modula-2*, New York: Springer-Verlag, 1982.

20. Ogilvie, J. W. L., *Modula-2 Programming*, New York: McGraw-Hill, 1985.

21. McGraw, J. R., "The VAL Language: Description and Analysis," *ACM Transactions on Programming Languages*, Vol. 4, No. 1, January 1982, pp. 44–82.

22. Cook, R. P., "*MOD—A Language for Distributed Programming," *IEEE Transactions on Software Engineering*, Vol. SE-6, No. 6, 1980, pp. 563–571.

23. Dijkstra, E. W., "Hierarchical Ordering of Sequential Processes," *Acta Informatica*, Vol. 1, 1971, pp. 115–138.

24. Brinch Hansen, P., "Structured Multiprogramming," *Communications of the ACM*, Vol. 15, No. 7, July 1972, pp. 574–578.

25. Brinch Hansen, P., *Operating System Principles*, Englewood Cliffs, N.J.: Prentice Hall, 1973.

26. Hoare, C. A. R., "Monitors: An Operating System Structuring Concept," *Communications of the ACM*, Vol. 17, No. 10, October 1974, pp. 549–557. Corrigendum, *Communications of the ACM*, Vol. 18, No. 2, February 1975, p. 95.

27. Brinch Hansen, P., "The Solo Operating System: Processes, Monitors, and Classes," *Software—Practice and Experience*, Vol. 6, 1976, pp. 165–200.

28. Howard, J. H., "Proving Monitors," *Communications of the ACM*, Vol. 19, No. 5, May 1976, pp. 273–279.

29. Howard, J. H., "Signaling in Monitors," *Second International Conference on Software Engineering*, San Francisco, October 1976, pp. 47–52.

30. Lister, A. M., and K. J. Maynard, "An Implementation of Monitors," *Software—Practice and Experience*, Vol. 6, No. 3, July 1976, pp. 377–386.

31. Kessels, J. L. W., "An Alternative to Event Queues for Synchronization in Monitors," *Communications of the ACM*, Vol. 20, No. 7, July 1977, pp. 500–503.

32. Keedy, J., "On Structuring Operating Systems with Monitors," *Australian Computer Journal*, Vol. 10, No. 1, February 1978, pp. 23–27, reprinted in *Operating Systems Review*, Vol. 13, No. 1, January 1979, pp. 5–9.

33. Lampson, B. W., and D. D. Redell, "Experience with Processes and Monitors in MESA," *Communications of the ACM*, Vol. 23, No. 2, February 1980, pp. 105–117.

34. Wegner, P., and S. A. Smolka, "Processes, Tasks and Monitors: A Comparative Study of Concurrent Programming Primitives," *IEEE Transactions on Software Engineering*, Vol. SE-9, No. 4, July 1983, pp. 446–462.

35. Buhr, P. A.; Fortier, M.; and Coffin, M., "Monitor Classifications," *ACM Computing Surveys*, Vol. 27, No. 1, March 1995, pp. 63–107.

36. Hoare, C. A. R., "Monitors: An Operating System Structuring Concept," *Communications of the ACM*, Vol. 17, No. 10, October 1974, pp. 549–557.

37. Buhr, P. A.; Fortier, M.; and Coffin, M., "Monitor Classification," *ACM Computing Surveys*, Vol. 27, No. 1, March 1995, pp. 63–107.

38. Brinch Hansen, P., "The Programming Language Concurrent Pascal," *IEEE Transactions on Software Engineering*, No. 2, June 1975, 199–206.

39. Syracuse University, "Biography," <web.syr.edu/~pbhansen/html/biography.html>.

40. Syracuse University, "Biography," <web.syr.edu/~pbhansen/html/biography.html>.

41. Brinch Hansen, P., *Operating System Principles*, Englewood Cliffs, N.J.: Prentice Hall, 1973.

42. Brinch Hansen, P., "The Purpose of Concurrent Pascal," *Proceedings of the International Conference on Reliable Software*, pp. 305–309, 1975.

43. Syracuse University, "Biography," <web.syr.edu/~pbhansen/html/biography.html>.

44. Brinch Hansen, P., "Java's Insecure Parallelism," *SIGPLAN Notices*, Vol. 34, No. 4, pp. 38–45, April 1999.

45. Brinch Hansen, P., "The Solo Operating System," *Software—Practice and Experience*, Vol. 6, No. 2, pp. 141–205, April–June 1976.

46. Brinch Hansen, P., "Joyce—A Programming Language for Distributed Systems," *Software—Practice and Experience*, Vol. 17, No. 1, January 1987, pp. 29-50.

47. Hoare, C. A. R., "Monitors: An Operating System Structuring Concept," *Communications of the ACM*, Vol. 17, No. 10, October 1974, pp. 549–557. Corrigendum, *Communications of the ACM*, Vol. 18, No. 2, February 1975, p. 95.

48. Courtois, P. J.; Heymans, F.; and D. L. Parnas, "Concurrent Control with Readers and Writers," *Communications of the ACM*, Vol. 14, No. 10, October 1971, pp. 667–668.

49. Hoare, C. A. R., "Monitors: An Operating System Structuring Concept," *Communications of the ACM*, Vol. 17, No. 10, October 1974, pp. 549–557. Corrigendum, *Communications of the ACM*, Vol. 18, No. 2, February 1975, p. 95.

50. Hartley, S. J., "Concurrent Programming Using the Java Language," Modified: 30 December 1997, <www.mcs.drexel.edu/~shartley/ConcProgJava/monitors.html>.

51. Venners, B. "Thread Synchronization", Chapter 20 of *Inside the Java Virtual Machine*, last updated April 18, 2003, <www.artima.com/insidejvm/ed2/threadsynch.html>.

52. Christopher, T. W., and , G. K. Thiruvathukal, *High-Performance Java Platform Computing, Multithreaded and Networked Programming*, Upper Saddle River, NJ: Prentice Hall PTR, February 2001, pp. 89–93.

53. Dijkstra, E. W., "Solution of a Problem in Concurrent Programming Control," *Communications of the ACM*, Vol. 8, No. 5, September 1965, p. 569.

54. Patil, S. S., "Limitations and Capabilities of Dijkstra's Semaphore Primitives for Coordination among Processes," *M.I.T. Project MAC Computational Structures Group Memo 57*, February 1971.

55. Dijkstra, E. W., "Hierarchical Ordering of Sequential Processes," *Acta Informatica*, Vol. 1, 1971, pp. 115–138.

56. Knuth, D., "Additional Comments on a Problem in Concurrent Programming Control," *Communications of the ACM*, Vol. 9, No. 5, May 1966, pp. 321–322.

57. Bernstein, A. J. "Program Analysis for Parallel Processing," *IEEE Transactions on Computers*, Vol. 15, No. 5, October 1966, pp. 757–762.

58. Courtois, P. J.; Heymans, F.; and D. L. Parnas, "Concurrent Control with Readers and Writers," *Communications of the ACM*, Vol. 14, No. 10, October 1971, pp. 667–668.

59. Lamport, L., "Concurrent Reading and Writing," *Communications of the ACM*, Vol. 20, No. 11, November 1977, pp. 806–811.

60. Lamport, L., "The Mutual Exclusion Problem: Part I—A Theory of Interprocess Communication," *Journal of the ACM (JACM)*, Vol. 33 No. 2, April 1986, pp. 313–326.

61. Lamport, L., "The Mutual Exclusion Problem: Part II—Statement and Solutions," *Journal of the ACM (JACM)*, Vol. 33 No. 2, April 1986, pp. 327–348.

62. Brinch Hansen, P., "Structured Multiprogramming," *Communications of the ACM*, Vol. 15, No. 7, July 1972, pp. 574–578.

63. Hoare, C. A. R., "Monitors: An Operating System Structuring Concept," *Communications of the ACM*, Vol. 17, No. 10, October 1974, pp. 549–557. Corrigendum, *Communications of the ACM*, Vol. 18, No. 2, February 1975, p. 95.

64. Buhr, P. A.; Fortier, M.; and M. Coffin, "Monitor Classification," *ACM Computing Surveys*, Vol. 27, No. 1, March 1995 pp. 63–107.

65. Deitel, H. M. and P. J. Deitel, *Java How to Program*, 5th ed., Upper Saddle River, NJ: Prentice Hall, 2003.

66. Lea, D., *Concurrent Programming in Java: Design Principles and Pattern, 2nd ed.*, Reading, MA: Addison-Wesley, 1999.

We had better wait and see.

— H. H. Asquith —

Every man is the center of a circle, whose fatal circumference he cannot pass.

— John James Ingalls —

Hold me but safe within the bond
Of one immortal look.

— Robert Browning —

Detection is, or ought to be, an exact science, and should be treated in the same cold and unemotional manner.

— Sir Arthur Conan Doyle —

Delays have dangerous ends.

— William Shakespeare —

Chapter 7

Deadlock and Indefinite Postponement

Objectives

After reading this chapter, you should understand:

- *the problem of deadlock.*
- *the four necessary conditions for deadlock to exist.*
- *the problem of indefinite postponement.*
- *the notions of deadlock prevention, avoidance, detection and recovery.*
- *algorithms for deadlock avoidance and detection.*
- *how systems can recover from deadlocks.*

Chapter Outline

7.1 Introduction

In the previous four chapters, we discussed asynchronous, concurrent processes and threads. A multiprogrammed system provides many benefits, but as discussed in Chapter 6, Concurrent Programming, multiprogramming also introduces additional complexity. One problem that arises in multiprogrammed systems is **deadlock**. A process or thread is in a state of deadlock (or is **deadlocked**) if it is waiting for a particular event that will not occur. In a system deadlock, one or more processes are deadlocked.[1, 2] The remainder of this chapter will focus on processes, but most of the discussion applies to threads as well.

In multiprogrammed computing systems, resource sharing is one of the primary goals. When resources are shared among a set of processes, each process maintaining exclusive control over particular resources allocated to it, deadlocks can develop in which some processes will never be able to complete execution. The result can be loss of work and reduced system throughput and system failure.

This chapter discusses the problem of deadlock and summarizes the four major areas of deadlock research, namely **deadlock prevention**, **avoidance**, **detection** and **recovery**. It also considers the closely related problem of indefinite postponement, also called **starvation**, in which a process that is not deadlocked could wait for an event that might never occur or might occur unpredictably far in the future because of biases in the systems resource-scheduling policies. In some cases, the price for making a system free of deadlock is high. For some systems, such as those that are mission critical, the price must be paid no matter how high, because allowing a deadlock to develop could be catastrophic, especially if it puts human life at risk. This chapter also discusses solutions to the problems of deadlock and indefinite postponement in terms of trade-offs between their overhead and their anticipated benefits.

Self Review

1. A system designer decides to try to avoid any possibility of deadlock by creating a multiprogrammed system that does not share resources. What is wrong with this idea?
2. Compare and contrast deadlock with indefinite postponement.

Ans: **1)** It would be highly inefficient, because each process would need its own set of resources. Also, asynchronous concurrent programs often require shared resources such as semaphores. **2)** Deadlock and indefinite postponement are similar in that they occur when processes wait for an event. Deadlock occurs because the event will never occur; indefinite postponement occurs because it is uncertain when or even whether the event will ever occur (due to biases in a system's resource-scheduling policies).

7.2 Examples of Deadlock

Deadlocks can develop in many ways. If a process is given the task of waiting for an event to occur, and if the system includes no provision for signaling that event, then we have a one-process deadlock.[3] Such deadlocks are extremely difficult to detect. Deadlocks in real systems often involve multiple processes competing for multiple resources of multiple types. Let us consider several common examples.

7.2.1 Traffic Deadlock

Figure 7.1 illustrates a kind of deadlock that occasionally develops in cities. A number of automobiles are attempting to drive through a busy neighborhood, and the traffic is completely snarled. The police have to unwind the jam by slowly and carefully backing cars out of the congested area. Eventually the traffic begins to flow normally, but not without much annoyance, effort, and loss of time (see the Anecdote, One-Lane Bridge).

Self Review

1. Assuming that there are no cars beyond the ellipses in Fig. 7.1, what minimum number of cars would have to back up to relieve the deadlock and which car(s) would they be?
2. If cars could be removed by airlifting in Fig. 7.1, what minimum number of cars, and which one(s), would have to be removed to relieve the deadlock?

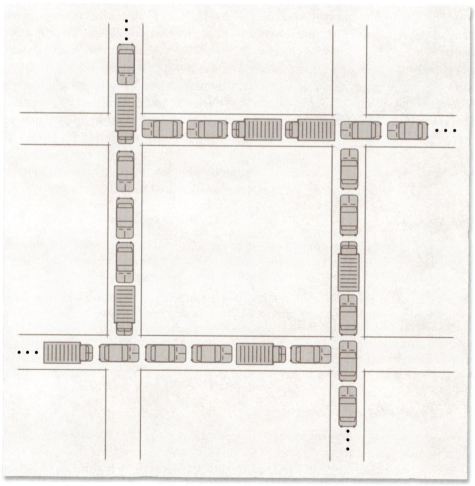

Figure 7.1 | *Traffic deadlock example.*[4]

Ans: **1.)** In Fig. 7.1, only two cars would need to back up to allow every other car to eventually move—any one of the cars abutting an ellipsis, then the car ahead of that one in the intersection. **2.)** Only one car has to be removed—namely, any one of the four cars in the intersections.

7.2.2 Simple Resource Deadlock

Most deadlocks in operating systems develop because of the normal contention for **dedicated resources** (i.e., resources that may be used over time by many processes but by only one process at a time, sometimes called **serially reusable resources**). For example, a printer can print jobs for only one process at a time (otherwise pieces of many print jobs would be interwoven). A simple example of a resource deadlock is illustrated in Fig. 7.2. This **resource allocation graph** shows two processes as rectangles and two resources as circles. An arrow from a resource to a process indicates that the resource belongs to, or has been allocated to, the process. An arrow from a process to a resource indicates that the process is requesting, but has not yet been allocated, the resource. The diagram illustrates a deadlocked system: Process P_1 holds resource R_1 and needs resource R_2 to continue. Process P_2 holds resource R_2 and needs resource R_1 to continue. Each process is waiting for the other to free a resource that the other process will not free. This **circular wait** is characteristic of deadlocked systems (see the Operating Systems Thinking feature, Waiting, Deadlock and Indefinite Postponement). Holding resources tenaciously in this way, a is sometimes referred to as a **deadly embrace**.

One-lane Bridge

A former operating systems student of HMD's was one of the original designers of the IBM personal computer. When we studied deadlock in class, he shared a deadlock anecdote with me. Two drivers were approaching a one-lane bridge. They reached the middle of the bridge at the same time, forcing a confrontation. They got out of their cars and went nose to nose. One driver said, "I don't back up for idiots." The other driver calmly got back in his car and started backing up. He said, "No problem—I do."

Lesson to operating system designers: Processes are neither stubborn nor cooperative, so deadlock is a painful experience at best. Usually, one or more processes will have to be "backed out" of the deadlock, losing some or all of their work.

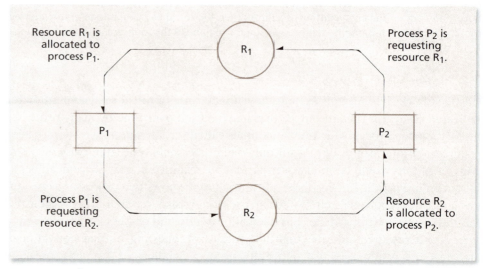

Processes labeled: "Resource R₁ is allocated to process P₁.", "Process P₂ is requesting resource R₁.", "Process P₁ is requesting resource R₂.", "Resource R₂ is allocated to process P₂."

Figure 7.2 | *Resource deadlock example. This system is deadlocked because each process holds a resource being requested by the other process and neither process is willing to release the resource it holds.*

Self Review

1. If the traffic deadlock in Fig. 7.1 were to be represented using a resource-allocation graph, what would the processes be? What would the resources be?
2. Suppose several arrows are pointing from a process to resources in a resource-allocation graph. What does that mean? How does it affect the possibility of deadlock?

Ans: **1)** The cars would be the processes. The resources would be the sections of the street that the cars occupy. Each car currently holds the section of the street directly below it and is requesting the section in front of it. **2)** It means that the process is requesting several resources. The possibility of deadlock depends on whether those resources are allocated to other processes, some of which, in turn, are requesting resources held by the process we are discussing.

7.2.3 Deadlock in Spooling Systems

A spooling system improves system throughput by disassociating a program from slow devices such as printers. For example, if a program sending lines to the printer must wait for each page to be printed before it can transmit the next page, then it will execute slowly. To speed the program's execution, a spooling system routes output pages to a much faster device, such as a hard disk, where they are temporarily stored until they can be printed.

Spooling systems can be prone to deadlock. Some spooling systems require that the complete output from a program be available before printing can begin. Several partially completed jobs generating pages to a spool file can become deadlocked if the disk's available space fills before any job completes. The user or system administrator may kill one or more jobs to make sufficient spooling space available for the remaining jobs to complete.

Typically, the system administrator specifies the amount of space for spooling files. One way to make deadlocks less likely is to provide considerably more space for spooling files than is likely to be needed. This solution may not be feasible if space is at a premium. A more common solution is to restrain the input spoolers so that they do not accept additional print jobs when the spooling files begin to reach some **saturation threshold**, such as 75 percent full. This may reduce system throughput, but it is the price paid to reduce the likelihood of deadlock.

Today's systems are more sophisticated than this. They might allow printing to begin before the job is completed so that a full, or nearly full, spooling file can begin emptying while a job is still executing. This concept has been applied to streaming audio and video clips, where the audio and video begin to play before the clips download fully. In many systems spooling space allocation has been made more dynamic, so that if existing space starts to fill, then more space may be made available.

Operating Systems Thinking

Waiting, Deadlock and Indefinite Postponement

Operating systems must manage many different types of waiting scenarios, which rely on an abundant use of queues to do so. Processes and threads must wait for a processor to become available before they can execute; they often wait for I/O requests to complete and for requested resources to become available. I/O requests themselves must wait for the I/O devices to become available. Processes and threads sharing data may have to wait until a process or thread currently accessing that data finishes and leaves a critical section. In the producer/consumer relationship, the producer passes information to the consumer via a shared region of memory; when that region becomes full, the producer cannot continue to produce more information, so it must wait for the consumer to empty some data; when that region becomes empty the consumer must wait for the producer to generate more data.

You will see extensive examples of waiting scenarios throughout this book. Operating systems must manage waiting carefully to avoid two serious problems, namely deadlock and indefinite postponement, each of which is discussed in detail in this chapter. In a deadlock scenario, processes and threads are waiting for events that will never happen; a simple two-process deadlock has each process waiting on a resource that only one process at a time can use and that the other process is holding. Both processes cease progressing; this can be fatal in mission-critical systems where human lives may be at stake. Indefinite postponement (also called starvation) typically occurs when a process is waiting in line and other processes, perhaps those of a higher priority, are allowed to get in line in front of the waiting process. A steady stream of arriving high-priority processes is said to indefinitely postpone the lower-priority process. This could be as dangerous as deadlock in a mission-critical system. So take waiting seriously—if it is mismanaged, system failures could occur.

Self Review

1. Suppose a spooling system has a saturation threshold of 75 percent and limits the maximum size of each file to 25 percent of the total spooling file size. Could deadlock occur in this system?
2. Suppose a spooling system has a saturation threshold of 75 percent and limits the maximum size of each file to 25 percent of the total spooling file size. Describe a simple way to ensure that deadlock will never occur in the system. Explain how this could lead to inefficient resource allocation.

Ans: **1)** Yes, deadlock can still occur in this system. For instance, several jobs can begin transferring their outputs. When the spooling file reaches the 75 percent threshold, new jobs are not allowed. However, jobs that have begun are allowed to continue spooling, which may result in deadlock if there is insufficient space in the spooling file. **2)** A simple adjustment would be to allow only one job to continue spooling data when the file reaches the threshold. This would be inefficient because it would limit the maximum job size to much less than the available spooling space.

7.2.4 Example: Dining Philosophers

Dijkstra's problem of the **Dining Philosophers**,[5, 6] illustrates many of the subtle problems inherent in concurrent programming. The problem is this:

> *Five philosophers sit around a circular table. Each leads a simple life alternating between thinking and eating spaghetti. In front of each philosopher is a dish of spaghetti that is constantly replenished by a dedicated wait staff. There are exactly five forks on the table, one between each adjacent pair of philosophers. Eating spaghetti (in the most proper manner) requires that a philosopher use both adjacent forks (simultaneously). Develop a concurrent program free of deadlock and indefinite postponement that models the activities of the philosophers.*

If the solution to this problem were not free of deadlock and indefinite postponement, one or more philosophers would starve. The program must, of course, enforce mutual exclusion—two philosophers cannot use the same fork at once. A typical philosopher behaves as shown in Fig. 7.3.

The problems of mutual exclusion, deadlock and indefinite postponement lie in the implementation of method `eat`. Consider the simple, yet dangerous implementation in Fig. 7.4. Because the philosophers operate asynchronously and con-

```
1   void typicalPhilosopher()
2   {
3      while ( true )
4      {
5         think();
6         eat();
7      } // end while
8
9   } // end typicalPhilospher
```

Figure 7.3 | *Dining philosopher behavior.*

```
1   void eat()
2   {
3       pickUpLeftFork();
4       pickUpRightFork();
5       eatForSomeTime();
6       putDownRightFork();
7       putDownLeftFork();
8   } // eat
```

Figure 7.4 | Implementation of method eat

currently, it is possible for each philosopher to execute line 3 before any philosopher executes line 4. In this case, each philosopher will hold exactly one fork, and no forks will remain available on the table. The philosophers will all deadlock and starve.

One way to break the deadlock when each philosopher holds a left fork is to force one or more philosophers to put their left fork down so that another philosopher may grab it as a right fork. To implement this rule, `pickUpRightFork()` can specify that a philosopher puts down the left fork if that philosopher cannot obtain the right fork. However, in this case, it is possible (albeit unlikely) that each philosopher will pick up and put down its left fork repeatedly in tandem without ever obtaining the two forks it needs to eat spaghetti. In this case, the philosophers are not deadlocked, but "livelocked," suffering from indefinite postponement, and they will still starve. The solution must prevent deadlock (by forcing philosophers to put down forks) but also prevent livelock (indefinite postponement) by guaranteeing that each philosopher will obtain both forks from time to time. In the exercises, you will be asked to develop a complete solution to the Dining Philosophers problem.

Self Review

1. Could the implementation of the eat method in Fig. 7.4 allow the philosophers to live in harmony without starving?
2. Consider the eat method in Fig. 7.4. Suppose lines 3 and 4 were replaced with `pickUpBothForksAtOnce()`; would that implementation prevent deadlock? Would it prevent the philosophers from starving?

Ans: **1)** Yes. We cannot predict the relative speeds of asynchronous concurrent processes. It is possible that not all five philosophers will pick up their left fork at once. Various philosophers could acquire the two forks they need, then release them to give the other philosophers a chance to eat. **2)** Yes, it would prevent deadlock, assuming that `pickUpBothForksAtOnce()` can be performed atomically, but it would still allow indefinite postponement. This could occur, for example, if two of the philosophers were to continually pick up two forks, eat, put down the forks and pick them up again before any of the other philosophers could grab them; those other philosophers would starve.

7.3 Related Problem: Indefinite Postponement

In any system that requires processes to wait as a result of resource-allocation and process scheduling decisions, a process may be delayed indefinitely while other processes receive the system's attention. This situation, called indefinite postponement, indefinite blocking, or starvation, can be as devastating as deadlock.

Indefinite postponement may occur because of biases in a system's resource-scheduling policies. When resources are scheduled on a priority basis, it is possible for a given process to wait for a resource indefinitely, as processes with higher priorities continue to arrive. Waiting is a fact of life and is certainly an important aspect of what goes on inside computer systems, so systems should be designed to manage waiting processes fairly and efficiently. Some systems prevent indefinite postponement by increasing a process's priority gradually as it waits for a resource—this technique is called **aging**. Eventually, the waiting process's priority will exceed the priorities of all processes, and the it will be serviced.

Self Review

1. Dekker's Algorithm and Peterson's Algorithm prevented a process from being indefinitely postponed from entering its critical section. Describe how indefinite postponement was prevented. How is this related to aging?
2. Suppose an interactive process appears to be "dead in the water." Does this mean that the process is definitely deadlocked? Could it be indefinitely postponed? Are there other possibilities?

Ans: **1)** Both Dekker's Algorithm and Peterson's Algorithm made the waiting process the favored process when the resource was available again. This is similar to aging, because the waiting process earns a higher priority by waiting. **2)** This is an interesting question. From the user's perspective, an interactive process would appear "dead in the water" if the system simply stopped responding to the interactive user's requests. The process could be deadlocked, but it does not have to be. It could be suffering from indefinite postponement, but it does not have to be. It could also be waiting for an event that may happen shortly, it could be locked in an infinite loop or it could be doing a lengthy calculation that will soon finish. Anyone who has experienced a system that appears to "hang" knows how frustrating this can be. What services should the operating system provide to help the user in such situations? We address these issues throughout the book.

7.4 Resource Concepts

As a resource manager, the operating system is responsible for the allocation of a vast array of resources of various types; this is part of what makes operating system design so interesting. We consider resources that are **preemptible**, such as processors and main memory. Processors are perhaps the most frequently preempted resources on a computer system. Processors must be rapidly switched (i.e., multiplexed) among all active processes competing for system service to ensure that these processes progress at a reasonable rates. Whenever a particular process reaches a point at which it cannot effectively use a processor (such as during a long wait for input/output completion), the operating system dispatches another process to that processor. As we will see in Chapters 9, 10 and 11, a user program currently occupying a particular range of locations in main memory may be removed or preempted by another program. Preemption is thus extremely critical to the success of multiprogrammed computer systems.

Certain resources are **nonpreemptible**; they cannot be removed from the processes to which they are assigned until the processes voluntarily release them. For example, tape drives and optical scanners are normally assigned to a particular process for periods of minutes or hours.

Some resources may be **shared** among several processes, while others are dedicated to a single process at a time. Although a single processor can normally belong to only one process at a time, its multiplexing among many processes creates the illusion of simultaneous sharing. Disk drives are sometimes dedicated to single processes, but typically they contain files that can be accessed by many processes. Disks can be multiplexed among many processes requesting I/O.

Data and programs certainly are resources that the operating system must control and allocate. On multiprogramming systems, many users may simultaneously want to use an editor program. If the operating system maintained in main memory a separate copy of the editor for each program, there would be a significant amount of redundant data, wasting memory. A better technique is for the operating system to load one copy of the code in memory and to make the copy available to each user. If a process were allowed to modify this shared code, other processes might behave unpredictably. As a result, this code must be **reentrant**, meaning the code is not modified as it executes. Code that may be changed but is reinitialized each time it is used is said to be **serially reusable**. Reentrant code may be shared by several processes simultaneously, whereas serially reusable code may be used correctly by only one process at a time.

When we call particular resources shared, we must be careful to state whether they may be used by several processes simultaneously by only one process at a time. The latter kind—serially reusable resources—are the ones that tend to become involved in deadlocks.

Self Review

1. (T/F) Processes do not deadlock as a result of contending for the processor.
2. (T/F) Nonpreemptible resources must be hardware.

Ans: **1)** True. The processor is a preemptible resource that can easily be taken from a process, assigned to other processes and returned to the original process, enabling it to proceed normally. **2)** False. Certain software resources are nonpreemptible, e.g., monitors.

7.5 Four Necessary Conditions for Deadlock

Coffman, Elphick and Shoshani[7] proved that the following four conditions are necessary for deadlock to exist:

1. A resource may be acquired exclusively by only one process at a time (**mutual exclusion condition**).

2. A process that has acquired an exclusive resource may hold that resource while the process waits to obtain other resources (**wait-for condition**, also called the **hold-and-wait condition**).

3. Once a process has obtained a resource, the system cannot remove it from the process's control until the process has finished using the resource (**no-preemption condition**).

4. Two or more processes are locked in a "circular chain" in which each process is waiting for one or more resources that the next process in the chain is holding (**circular-wait condition**).

Because these are *necessary* conditions, the existence of a deadlock implies that each of them must be in effect. As we will see later, this observation helps us develop schemes to prevent deadlocks. Taken together, all four conditions are necessary and **sufficient** for deadlock to exist (i.e., if they are all in place, the system is deadlocked).

Self Review

1. Describe how the four necessary conditions for deadlock apply to spooling systems.
2. Which of the four conditions would be violated if a user could remove jobs from a spooling system?

Ans: **1)** No two jobs can simultaneously write data to the same location in the spooling file. Partially spooled jobs remain in the spooling file until more space is available. Jobs cannot remove other jobs from the spooling file. Finally, when the spooling file is full, each job waits for all of the other jobs to free up space. **2)** This would violate the "no-preemption" condition.

7.6 Deadlock Solutions

Deadlock has been one of the more productive research areas in computer science and operating systems. There are four major areas of interest in deadlock research—deadlock prevention, deadlock avoidance, deadlock detection and deadlock recovery.

In **deadlock prevention** our concern is to condition a system to remove any possibility of deadlocks occurring. Prevention is a clean solution as far as deadlock itself is concerned, but prevention methods can often result in poor resource utilization.

In **deadlock avoidance** the goal is to impose less stringent conditions than in deadlock prevention in an attempt to get better resource utilization. Avoidance methods do not precondition the system to remove all possibility of deadlock. Instead, they allow the possibility to loom, but whenever a deadlock is approached, it is carefully sidestepped.

Deadlock detection methods are used in systems in which deadlocks can occur. The goal is to determine if a deadlock has occurred, and to identify the processes and resources that are involved.

Deadlock recovery methods are used to clear deadlocks from a system so that it may operate free them, and so that the deadlocked processes may complete their execution and free their resources. Recovery is a messy problem at best, typically requiring that one or more of the deadlocked processes be flushed from the system. The flushed processes are normally restarted from the beginning when sufficient resources are available, with much or all of the work done by these processes being lost.

Self Review

1. Compare and contrast deadlock prevention and deadlock avoidance.
2. Some systems ignore the problem of deadlock. Discuss the costs and benefits of this approach.

Ans: **1.)** Deadlock prevention makes deadlock impossible but results in lower resource utilization. With deadlock avoidance, when the threat of deadlock approaches, it is sidestepped and resource utilization is higher. Systems using either deadlock prevention or deadlock avoidance will be free of deadlocks. **2)** Systems that ignore deadlock may fail when deadlock occurs. This is an unacceptable risk in mission-critical systems, but it may be appropriate in other systems where deadlocks rarely occur and the "cost" of dealing with an occasional deadlock is lower than the costs of implementing deadlock prevention or avoidance schemes.

7.7 Deadlock Prevention

This section considers various methods of deadlock prevention and examines the effects on both users and systems, especially from the standpoint of performance.[8, 9, 10, 11, 12, 13] Havender,[14] observing that a deadlock cannot occur if a system denies any of the four necessary conditions, suggested the following deadlock prevention strategies:

- Each process must request all its required resources at once and cannot proceed until all have been granted.

- If a process holding certain resources is denied a further request, it must release its original resources and, if necessary, request them again together with the additional resources.

- A linear ordering of resources must be imposed on all processes; i.e., if a process has been allocated certain resources, it may subsequently request only those resources later in the ordering.

In the sections that follow, we consider each strategy independently and discuss how each denies one of the necessary conditions (see the Anecdote, No Nuts, Bolts or Screws Allowed). Note that Havender presents three strategies, not four. The first necessary condition, namely that processes claim exclusive use of the resources they require, is not one that we want to break, because we specifically want to allow **dedicated** (i.e., serially reusable) resources.

Self Review

1. What is the basic premise of Havender's research on deadlock prevention?

Ans: Deadlock cannot occur in systems in which any of the necessary conditions for deadlock are precluded.

7.7.1 Denying the "Wait-For" Condition

Havender's first strategy requires that all of the resources a process needs to complete its task must be requested at once. The system must grant them on an "all or none" basis. If all the resources needed by a process are available, then the system may grant them all to the process at once, and the process may continue to execute. If they are not all available, then the process must wait until they are. While the process waits, however, it may not hold any resources. Thus the "wait-for" condition is denied, and deadlocks cannot occur.

Although this strategy successfully prevents deadlock, it wastes resources. For example, a program requiring four tape drives at one point in its execution must request, and receive, all four before it begins executing. If all four drives are needed throughout the execution of the program, then there is no serious waste. But, suppose the program needs only one tape drive to begin execution (or worse yet, none

Anecdote

No Nuts, Bolts or Screws Allowed

Some years ago, HMD had the privilege of visiting one of the automated factories of one of the largest computer vendors. At the time, the factory—run almost exclusively by robots—was producing small inexpensive printers for personal computers. The head of the factory made a strong point. He observed that printers have a significant number of moving parts and that the company's engineers had traced failures of previous lines of printers to nuts, bolts and screws that had loosened as a consequence of mechanical motion. So when they designed the printer that was being produced at this factory, the design team made a pact that all the parts of this printer (there were about 80 of them including the casing) would be designed to snap into place—no nuts, bolts or screws would be allowed in the design. The head of the factory then proceeded to assemble one of the printers by hand from the pieces sitting on his table. At the end of the demo, he plugged the printer into a wall socket and printed several pages to show that it was up and running. He mentioned that the "mean-time-to-failure" of this type of printer was proven to be miniscule compared to previous lines.

Lesson to operating systems designers: One way to minimize the chance of system failure is to eliminate as many "points of failure" as possible at the design stage. This works well with another design heuristic—KIS (keep it simple). Both of these heuristics are appealing, but can be difficult to implement. As you read this book, keep this anecdote in mind, searching for points of failure that you may be able to eliminate in future operating systems designs.

at all) and then does not need the remaining tape drives for several hours. The requirement that the program must request, and receive, all four tape drives before execution begins means that substantial resources will sit idle for several hours.

One approach to getting better resource utilization in these circumstances is to divide a program into several threads that run relatively independently of one another. Then resource allocation can be controlled by each thread rather than for the entire process. This can reduce waste, but it involves a greater overhead in application design and execution.

This Havender strategy could cause indefinite postponement if, for example, it favored waiting processes with small resource needs over those attempting to accumulate many resources. A steady stream of processes arriving with small resource needs could indefinitely postpone a process with more substantial needs. One way to avoid this is to handle the needs of the waiting processes in first-come-first-served order. Unfortunately, accumulating the full complement of resources for a process with substantial needs would cause considerable waste, as the gradually accumulating resources would sit idle until all were available.

In large mainframe computer environments with expensive resources, there is some controversy over whom to charge for these unused resources. Because the resources are being accumulated for a specific user, some designers feel this user should pay for them, even while they sit idle. Other designers say this would destroy the **predictability of resource charges**; if the user tried to run the process on a busy day, the charges would be much higher than when the machine was lightly loaded.

Self Review

1. Explain how denying the "wait-for" condition can reduce the degree of multiprogramming in a system.
2. Describe under what conditions a process can be indefinitely postponed when using Havender's scheme to deny the "wait-for" condition.

Ans: **1)** If processes in a system require more resources than are available to concurrently execute, the system must force some of those processes to wait until others finish and return their resources. In the worst case, the system may be limited to executing only one process at a time. **2)** A process could request a substantial number of a system's resources. If the operating system gives higher priority to processes that require fewer of system resources, then the process requesting all of the system's resources will be postponed indefinitely while processes that require fewer resources proceed.

7.7.2 Denying the "No-Preemption" Condition

Havender's second strategy denies the "no preemption" condition. Suppose a system does allow processes to hold resources while requesting additional resources. As long as sufficient resources remain available to satisfy all requests, the system cannot deadlock. But consider what happens when a request for additional resources cannot be satisfied. Now a process holds resources that a second process may need in order to proceed, while the second process may hold resources needed by the first process—a two-process deadlock.

Havender's second strategy requires that when a process holding resources is denied a request for additional resources, it must release the resources it holds and, if necessary, request them again together with the additional resources. This strategy effectively denies the "no-preemption" condition—resources can indeed be removed from the process holding them prior to the completion of that process.

Here, too, the means for preventing deadlock can be costly. When a process releases resources, it may lose all of its work to that point. This may seem to be a high price to pay, but the real question is, "How often does this price have to be paid?" If this occurs infrequently, then this strategy provides a relatively low-cost means of preventing deadlocks. If it occurs frequently, however, then the cost is substantial and the effects are disruptive, particularly when high-priority or deadline processes cannot be completed on time because of repeated preemptions.

Could this strategy lead to indefinite postponement? It depends. If the system favors processes with small resource requests over those requesting substantial resources, that alone could lead to indefinite postponement. Worse yet, as the process requests additional resources, this Havender strategy requires the process to give up all the resources it has and request an even larger number. So indefinite postponement can be a problem in a busy system. Also, this strategy requires all resources to be preemptible, which is not always the case (e.g., printers should not be preempted while processing a print job).

Self Review

1. What is the primary cost of denying the "no-preemption" condition?
2. Which of Havender's first two deadlock strategies do you suppose people find more palatable? Why?

Ans: **1)** A process may lose all of its work up to the point that its resources were preempted. Also, the process could suffer indefinite postponement, depending on the system's resource-allocation strategy. **2)** Most people probably would prefer the first strategy, namely, requiring a process to request all the resources it will need in advance. The second strategy requires the process to give up the resources it already has, possibly causing wasteful loss of work. Interestingly, the first strategy could cause waste as well, as processes gradually acquire resources they cannot yet use.

7.7.3 Denying the "Circular-Wait" Condition

Havender's third strategy denies the possibility of a circular wait. In this strategy, we assign a unique number to each resource (e.g., a disk drive, printer, scanner, file) that the system manages and we create a **linear ordering** of resources. A process must then request its resources in a strictly ascending order. For example, if a process requests resource R_3 (where the subscript, 3, is the resource number), then the process can subsequently request only resources with a number greater than 3.

Because all resources are uniquely numbered, and because processes must request resources in ascending order, a circular wait cannot develop (Fig. 7.5). [*Note:* A proof of this property is straightforward. Consider a system that enforces a linear ordering of resources in which R_i and R_j are resources numbered by integers i and j, respectively ($i \neq j$). If the system has a circular wait characteristic of deadlock, then according to Fig. 7.5, at least one arrow (or set of arrows) leads upward from R_i to R_j and an arrow (or set of arrows) exists leading down from R_j to R_i. However, the linear ordering of resources with the requirement that resources be requested in ascending order implies that no arrow can ever lead from R_j to R_i if $j > i$. Therefore deadlock cannot occur in this system.]

Denying the "circular-wait" condition has been implemented in a number of legacy operating systems, but not without difficulties.[15, 16, 17, 18] One disadvantage of this strategy is that it is not as flexible or dynamic as we might desire. Resources must be requested in ascending order by resource number. Resource numbers are assigned for the computer system and must be "lived with" for long periods (i.e., months or even years). If new resources are added or old ones removed at an installation, existing programs and systems may have to be rewritten.

Another difficulty is determining the ordering of resources in a system. Clearly, the resource numbers should be assigned to reflect the order in which most processes actually use the resources. For processes matching this ordering, more efficient operation may be expected. But for processes that need the resources in a different order than that specified by the linear ordering, resources must be acquired and held, possibly for long periods of time, before they are actually used. This can result in poor performance.

An important goal in today's operating systems is to promote software portability across multiple environments. Programmers should be able to develop their applications without being impeded by awkward hardware and software restrictions. Havender's linear ordering truly eliminates the possibility of a circular wait, yet it diminishes a programmer's ability to freely and easily write application code that will maximize an application's performance.

Self Review

1. How does a linear ordering for resource allocation reduce application portability?
2. (T/F) Imposing a linear ordering for resource requests yields higher performance than denying the "no-preemption" condition.

Ans: **1)** Different systems will normally have different sets of resources and may order resources differently, so an application written for one system may need to be modified to run effectively on another. **2)** False. There are situations where each solution results in higher performance because the solution requires insignificant overhead. If a system's processes each request disjoint sets of resources, denying "no preemption" is quite efficient. If a process uses resources in an order corresponding to the system's linear ordering, then denying the "circular wait" condition can result in higher performance.

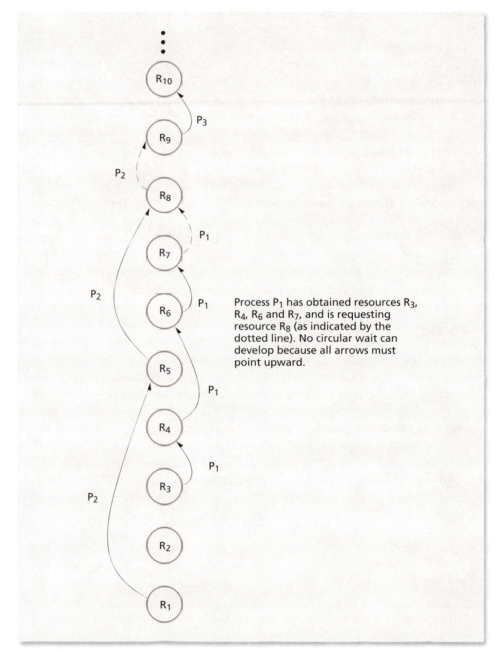

Figure 7.5 | *Havender's linear ordering of resources for preventing deadlock.*

7.8 *Deadlock Avoidance with Dijkstra's Banker's Algorithm*

For some systems, it is impractical to implement the deadlock prevention strategies we discussed in the preceding section. However, if the necessary conditions for a deadlock to occur are in place, it is still possible to avoid deadlock by carefully allocating system resources. Perhaps the most famous deadlock avoidance algorithm is **Dijkstra's Banker's Algorithm**, so named because the strategy is modeled after a banker who makes loans from a pool of capital and receives payments that are returned to that pool.[19, 20, 21, 22, 23] We paraphrase the algorithm here in the context of operating systems resource allocation. Subsequently, much work has been done in deadlock avoidance.[24, 25, 26, 27, 28, 29, 30, 31]

The Banker's Algorithm defines how a particular system can prevent deadlock by carefully controlling how resources are distributed to users (see the Anecdote, Acronyms). A system groups all the resources it manages into **resource types**. Each resource type corresponds to resources that provide identical functionality. To simplify our presentation of the Banker's Algorithm, we limit our discussion to a system that manages only one type of resource. The algorithm is easily extendable to pools of resources of various types; this is left to the exercises.

The Banker's Algorithm prevents deadlock in operating systems that exhibit the following properties:

- The operating system shares a fixed number of resources, t, among a fixed number of processes, n.

- Each process specifies in advance the maximum number of resources that it requires to complete its work.

- The operating system accepts a process's request if that process's **maximum need** does not exceed the total number of resources available in the system, t (i.e., the process cannot request more than the total number of resources available in the system).

- Sometimes, a process may have to wait to obtain an additional resource, but the operating system guarantees a finite wait time.

- If the operating system is able to satisfy a process's maximum need for resources, then the process guarantees that the resource will be used and released to the operating system within a finite time.

Anecdote

Acronyms

Most computer folks are familiar with the acronym WYSIWYG for "what you see is what you get." Few people have seen these two- IWWIWWIWI and YGWIGWIGI, which nicely describe the relationship between the process requesting resources and the operating system attempting to allocate them. The process says, "I want what I want when I want it." The operating system responds, "You'll get what I've got when I get it."

The system is said to be in a **safe state** if the operating system can guarantee that all current processes can complete their work within a finite time. If not, then the system is said to be in an **unsafe state.**

We also define four terms that describe the distribution of resources among processes.

- Let *max(P$_i$)* be the maximum number of resources that process P$_i$ requires during its execution. For example, if process P$_3$ never requires more than two resources, then *max(P$_3$)* = 2.

- Let *loan(P$_i$)* represent process P$_i$'s current **loan** of a resource, where its loan is the number of resources the process has already obtained from the system. For example, if the system has allocated four resources to process P$_5$, then *loan(P$_5$)* = 4.

- Let *claim(P$_i$)* be the current **claim** of a process, where a process's claim is equal to its maximum need minus its current loan. For example, if process P$_7$ has a maximum need of six resources and a current loan of four resources, then we have

$$claim(\,P_7\,) \;=\; max(\,P_7\,) \;-\; loan(\,P_7\,) \;=\; 6 \,-\, 4 \,=\, 2$$

- Let *a* be the number of resources still available for allocation. This is equivalent to the total number of resources (*t*) minus the sum of the loans to all the processes in the system, i.e.,

$$a \;=\; t - \sum_{i\,=\,1}^{n} loan(P_i)$$

So, if the system has a total of three processes and 12 resources, and the system has allocated two resources to process P$_1$, one resource to process P$_2$ and four resources to process P$_3$, then the number of available resources is

$$a \;=\; 12 \,-\, (2 \,+\, 1 \,+\, 4) \;=\; 12 \,-\, 7 \,=\, 5$$

Dijkstra's Banker's Algorithm requires that resources be allocated to processes only when the allocations result in safe states. In that way, all processes remain in safe states at all times, and the system will never deadlock.

Self Review

1. (T/F) An unsafe state is a deadlocked state.
2. Describe the restrictions that the Banker's Algorithm places on processes.

Ans: **1)** False. A process in an unsafe state might eventually deadlock, or it might complete its execution without entering deadlock. What makes the state unsafe is simply that the operating system cannot guarantee that from this state all processes can complete their work. From an unsafe state, it is possible but not guaranteed that all processes could complete their work, so a system in an unsafe state could eventually deadlock. **2)** Each process, before it runs, is required to specify the maximum number of resources it may require at any point during its execution. Each process cannot request more than the total number of resources in the system. Each process must also guarantee that once allocated a resource, the process will eventually return that resource to the system within a finite time.

7.8.1 Example of a Safe State

Suppose a system contains 12 equivalent resources and three processes sharing the resources, as in Fig. 7.6. The second column contains the maximum need for each process, the third column the current loan for each process and the fourth column the current claim for each process. The number of available resources, a, is two; this is computed by subtracting the sum of the current claims from the total number of resources, $t = 12$.

This state is "safe" because it is possible for all three processes to finish. Note that process P_2 currently has a loan of four resources and will eventually need a maximum of six, or two additional resources. The system has 12 resources, of which 10 are currently in use and two are available. If the system allocates these two available resources to P_2, fulfilling P_2's maximum need, then P_2 can run to completion. Note that after P_2 finishes, it will release six resources, enabling the system to immediately fulfill the maximum needs of P_1 (3) and P_3 (3), enabling both of those processes to finish. Indeed, all processes can eventually finish from the safe sate of Fig. 7.6.

Self Review

1. In Fig. 7.6, once P_2 runs to completion, must P_1 and P_3 run sequentially one after the other, or could they run concurrently?
2. Why did we focus initially on allowing P_2 to finish rather than focusing on either P_1 or P_3?

Ans: **1)** P_1 and P_3 each need three more resources to complete. When P_2 finishes, it will release six resources, which is enough to allow P_1 and P_3 to run concurrently. **2)** Because P_2 is the only process whose current claim can be satisfied by the two available resources.

7.8.2 Example of an Unsafe State

Assume a system's 12 resources are allocated as in Fig. 7.7. We sum the values of the third column and subtract from 12 to obtain a value of one for a. At this point, no matter which process requests the available resource, we cannot guarantee that all three processes will finish. In fact, suppose process P_1 requests and is granted the last available resource. A three-way deadlock could occur if indeed each process

Process	max(P_i) (maximum need)	loan(P_i) (current loan)	claim(P_i) (current claim)
P_1	4	1	3
P_2	6	4	2
P_3	8	5	3
Total resources, t, = 12		Available resources, a, = 2	

Figure 7.6 | Safe state.

Process	max(P_i) (maximum need)	loan(P_i) (current loan)	claim(P_i) (current claim)
P_1	10	8	2
P_2	5	2	3
P_3	3	1	2
Total resources, t, = 12		Available resources, a, = 1	

Figure 7.7 | *Unsafe state.*

needs to request at least one more resource before releasing any resources to the pool. It is important to note here that an *unsafe state does not imply the existence of deadlock, nor even that deadlock will eventually occur. What an unsafe state does imply is simply that some unfortunate sequence of events might lead to a deadlock.*

Self Review

1. Why is deadlock possible, but not guaranteed, when a system enters an unsafe state?
2. What minimum number of resources would have to be added to the system of Fig. 7.7 to make the state safe?

Ans: **1)** Processes could give back their resources early, increasing the number of available resources to the point that the state of the system was once again safe and all other processes could finish. **2)** By adding one resource, the number of available resources becomes two, enabling P_1 to finish and return its resources, enabling both P_2 and P_3 to finish. Hence the new state is safe.

7.8.3 Example of Safe-State-to-Unsafe-State Transition

Our resource-allocation policy must carefully consider all resource requests before granting them, or a process in a safe state could enter an unsafe state. For example, suppose the current state of a system is safe, as shown in Fig. 7.6. The current value of *a* is 2. Now suppose that process P_3 requests an additional resource. If the system were to grant this request, then the new state would be as in Fig. 7.8. Now, the current value of *a* is 1, which is not enough to satisfy the current claim of any process, so the state is now unsafe.

Process	max(P_i) (maximum need)	loan(P_i) (current loan)	claim(P_i) (current claim)
P_1	4	1	3
P_2	6	4	2
P_3	8	6	2
Total resources, t, = 12		Available resources, a, = 1	

Figure 7.8 | *Safe-state-to-unsafe-state transition.*

Self Review

1. If process P_2 requested one additional resource in Fig. 7.6, would the system be in a safe or an unsafe state?
2. (T/F) A system cannot transition from an unsafe state to a safe state.

Ans: **1)** The system would still be in a safe state because there is a path of execution that will not result in deadlock. For example, if P_2 requests another resource, then P_2 can complete execution. Then there will be six available resources, which is enough for P_1 and P_3 to finish. **2)** False. As processes release resources, the number of available resources can become sufficiently large for the state of the system to transition from unsafe to safe.

7.8.4 Banker's Algorithm Resource Allocation

Now it should be clear how resource allocation operates under Dijkstra's Banker's Algorithm. The "mutual exclusion," "wait-for," and "no-preemption" conditions are allowed—processes are indeed allowed to hold resources while requesting and waiting for additional resources, and resources may not be preempted from a process holding those resources. As usual, processes claim exclusive use of the resources they require. Processes ease onto the system by requesting one resource at a time; the system may either grant or deny each request. If a request is denied, that process holds any allocated resources and waits for a finite time until that request is eventually granted. The system grants only requests that result in safe states. Resource requests that would result in unsafe states are repeatedly denied until they can eventually be satisfied. Because the system is always maintained in a safe state, sooner or later (i.e., in a finite time) all requests can be satisfied and all users can finish.

Self Review

1. (T/F) The state described by Figure 7.9 is safe.
2. What minimum number of additional resources, when added to the system of Fig. 7.9, would make the state safe?

Ans: **1)** False. There is no guarantee that all of these processes will finish. P_2 will be able to finish by using up the two remaining resources. However, once P_2 is done, there are only three available resources left. This is not enough to satisfy either P_1's claim of 4 or P_3's claim of five. **2)** By adding one more resource, we could allow P_2 to finish and return three resources. These plus the added resource would enable P_1 to finish, returning five resources and enabling P_3 to finish.

Process	max(P_i)	loan(P_i)	claim(P_i)
P_1	5	1	4
P_2	3	1	2
P_3	10	5	5
		$a = 2$	

Figure 7.9 | State description of three processes.

7.8.5 Weaknesses in the Banker's Algorithm

The Banker's Algorithm is compelling because it allows processes to proceed that might have had to wait under a deadlock prevention situation. But the algorithm has a number of weaknesses.

- It requires that there be a fixed number of resources to allocate. Because resources frequently require service, due to breakdowns or preventive maintenance, we cannot count on the number of resources remaining fixed. Similarly, operating systems that support hot swappable devices (e.g., USB devices) allow the number of resources to vary dynamically.

- The algorithm requires that the population of processes remains fixed. This, too, is unreasonable. In today's interactive and multiprogrammed systems, the process population is constantly changing.

- The algorithm requires that the banker (i.e., the system) grant all requests within a "finite time." Clearly, much better guarantees than this are needed in real systems, especially real-time systems.

- Similarly, the algorithm requires that clients (i.e., processes) repay all loans (i.e., return all resources) within a "finite time." Again, much better guarantees than this are needed in real systems.

- The algorithm requires that processes state their maximum needs in advance. With resource allocation becoming increasingly dynamic, it is becoming more difficult to know a process's maximum needs. Indeed, one main benefit of today's high-level programming languages and "friendly" graphical user interfaces is that users are not required to know such low-level details as resource use. The user or programmer expects the system to "print the file" or "send the message" and should not need to worry about what resources the system might need to employ to honor such requests.

For the reasons stated above, Dijkstra's Banker's Algorithm is not implemented in today's operating systems. In fact, few systems can afford the overhead incurred by deadlock avoidance strategies.

Self Review

1. Why does the Banker's Algorithm fail in systems that support hot swappable devices?

Ans: The Banker's Algorithm requires that the number of resources of each type remain fixed. Hot swappable devices can be added and removed from the system at any time, meaning that the number of resources of each type can vary.

7.9 Deadlock Detection

We have discussed deadlock prevention and avoidance—two strategies for ensuring that deadlocks do not occur in a system. Another strategy is to allow deadlocks to occur, locate them and remove them, if possible. **Deadlock detection** is the process of determining that a deadlock exists and identifying the processes and resources involved in the deadlock.[32, 33, 34, 35, 36, 37, 38, 39, 40] Deadlock detection algorithms generally focus on determining if a circular wait exists, given that the other necessary conditions for deadlock are in place.

Deadlock detection algorithms can incur significant runtime overhead. Thus we again face the trade-offs so prevalent in operating systems—is the overhead involved in deadlock detection justified by the potential savings from locating and breaking up deadlocks? For the moment, we shall ignore this issue and concentrate instead on the development of algorithms capable of detecting deadlocks.

7.9.1 Resource-Allocation Graphs

To facilitate the detection of deadlocks, a popular notation (Fig. 7.10) is used in which a directed graph indicates resource allocations and requests.[41] Squares represent processes and large circles represent classes of identical resources. Small circles drawn inside large circles indicate the separate identical resources of each class. For example, a large circle labeled "R_1" containing three small circles indicates that there are three equivalent resources of type R_1 available for allocation in this system.

Figure 7.10 illustrates the relationships that may be indicated in a resource-allocation and request graph. In Fig. 7.10(a), process P_1 is requesting a resource of type R_1. The arrow from P_1 touches only the extremity of the large circle, indicating that the resource request is under consideration.

In Fig. 7.10(b), process P_2 has been allocated a resource of type R_2 (of which there are two). The arrow is drawn from the small circle within the large circle R_2 to the square P_2, to indicate that the system has allocated a specific resource of that type to the process.

Figure 7.10(c) indicates a situation somewhat closer to a potential deadlock. Process P_3 is requesting a resource of type R_3, but the system has allocated the only R_3 resource to process P_4.

Figure 7.10(d) indicates a deadlocked system in which process P_5 is requesting a resource of type R_4, the only one of which the system has allocated to process P_6. Process P_6 is requesting a resource of type R_5, the only one of which the system has allocated to process P_5. This is an example of the "circular wait" necessary for a deadlocked system.

Resource-allocation and request graphs change as processes request resources, acquire them and eventually release them to the operating system.

Self Review

1. Suppose a process has control of a resource of type R_1. Does it matter which small circle points to the process in the resource-allocation graph?
2. What necessary condition for deadlock is easier to identify in a resource-allocation graph than it is to locate by analyzing the resource-allocation data of all the system's processes?

Ans: 1) No; all resources of the same type must provide identical functionality, so it does not matter which small circle within the circle R_1 points to the process. 2) Resource-allocation graphs make it easier to identify circular waits.

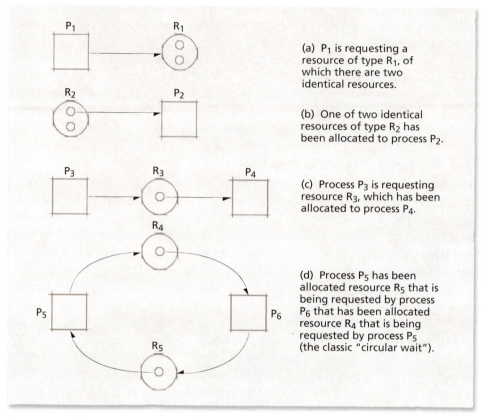

(a) P_1 is requesting a resource of type R_1, of which there are two identical resources.

(b) One of two identical resources of type R_2 has been allocated to process P_2.

(c) Process P_3 is requesting resource R_3, which has been allocated to process P_4.

(d) Process P_5 has been allocated resource R_5 that is being requested by process P_6 that has been allocated resource R_4 that is being requested by process P_5 (the classic "circular wait").

Figure 7.10 | *Resource-allocation and request graphs.*

7.9.2 Reduction of Resource-Allocation Graphs

One technique useful for detecting deadlocks involves graph reductions, in which the processes that may complete their execution, if any, and the processes that will remain deadlocked (and the resources involved in that deadlock), if any, are determined.[42]

If a process's resource requests may be granted, then we say that a graph may be **reduced** by that process. This reduction is equivalent to showing how the graph would look if the process was allowed to complete its execution and return its resources to the system. We reduce a graph by a process by removing the arrows to that process from resources (i.e., resources allocated to that process) and by removing arrows from that process to resources (i.e., current resource requests of that process). If a graph can be reduced by all its processes, then there is no deadlock. If a graph cannot be reduced by all its processes, then the irreducible processes constitute the set of deadlocked processes in the graph.

Figure 7.11 shows a series of graph reductions demonstrating that a particular set of processes is not deadlocked. Figure 7.10(d) shows an irreducible set of processes that constitutes a deadlocked system. It is important to note here that the order in

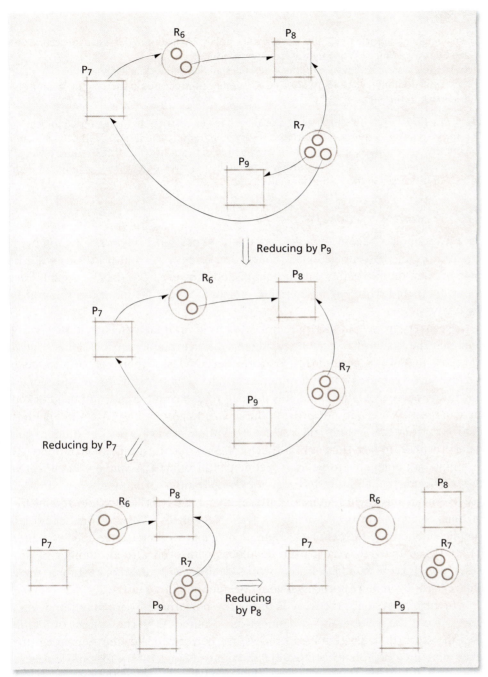

Figure 7.11 | *Graph reductions determining that no deadlock exists.*

which the graph reductions are performed does not matter: The final result will always be the same. We leave the proof of this result to the exercises (see Exercise 7.29).

Self Review

1. Why might deadlock detection be a better policy than either deadlock prevention or deadlock avoidance? Why might it be a worse policy?
2. Suppose a system attempts to reduce deadlock detection overhead by performing deadlock detection only when there are a large number of processes in the system. What is one drawback to this strategy?

Ans: **1.)** In general, deadlock detection places fewer restrictions on resource allocation, thereby increasing resource utilization. However, it requires that the deadlock detection algorithm be performed regularly, which can incur significant overhead. **2)** Because deadlock can occur between two processes, the system might not ever detect some deadlocks if the number of processes in the system is small.

7.10 Deadlock Recovery

Once a system has become deadlocked, the deadlock must be broken by removing one or more of the four necessary conditions. Usually, several processes will lose some or all of the work they have accomplished. However, this may be a small price to pay compared with leaving a system in a state where it cannot use some of its resources.

Recovery from deadlock is complicated by several factors. First, it may not be clear that the system has become deadlocked. For example, most systems contain processes that wake periodically, perform certain tasks, then go back to sleep. Because such processes do not terminate until the system is shut down, and because they rarely enter the active state, it is difficult to determine if they are deadlocked. Second, most systems do not provide the means to suspend a process indefinitely, remove it from the system and resume it (without loss of work) at a later time. Some processes, in fact, such as real-time processes that must function continuously, are simply not amenable to being suspended and resumed. Assuming that effective suspend/resume capabilities did exist, they would most certainly involve considerable overhead and might require the attention of a highly skilled system administrator. Such an administrator is not always available. Finally, recovery from deadlock is complicated because the deadlock could involve many processes (tens, or even hundreds). Given that recovering from deadlocks with even a small number of processes could require considerable work, dealing with deadlock among many hundreds (or even more) processes could be a monumental task.

In current systems, recovery is ordinarily performed by forcibly removing a process from the system and reclaiming its resources.[43, 44] The system ordinarily loses the work that the removed process has performed, but the remaining processes may now be able to complete. Sometimes it is necessary to remove several processes until sufficient resources have been reclaimed to allow the remaining processes to finish. Recovery somehow seems like an inappropriate term here, because some processes are in fact "killed" for the benefit of the others.

Processes may be removed according to some priority order. Here, too, we face several difficulties. For example, the priorities of the deadlocked processes may not exist, so the system may need to make an arbitrary decision. The priorities also may be incorrect or somewhat muddled by special considerations, such as **deadline scheduling**, in which a relatively low-priority process has a high priority temporarily because of an impending deadline. Furthermore, it may require considerable effort to determine the right processes to remove.

The suspend/resume mechanism allows the system to put a temporary hold on a process (temporarily preempting its resources), and, when it is safe to do so, to resume the held process without loss of work. Research in this area is important for reasons other than deadlock recovery. For example, a suspend/resume mechanism can be applied to a system as a whole, allowing a user to shut down the entire system and start it later without loss of work. Such technology has been incorporated into many laptop systems, where limited battery life requires users to minimize power consumption. The **Advanced Configuration and Power Interface** (**ACPI**), a popular specification for power management, defines a sleeping state in which the contents of memory, registers and other system state information are written to a nonvolatile medium (such as the hard disk) and the system is powered off. In Windows XP, this feature is known as "suspend to disk" or "hibernate." When the system starts up again, it resumes from the point at which it entered the sleeping state without loss of work.[45]

Checkpoint/rollback, the precursor to suspend/resume, is widely used in current database systems. Checkpoint/rollback copes with system failures and deadlocks by attempting to preserve as much data as possible from each terminated process. Checkpoint/rollback facilitates suspend/resume capabilities by limiting the loss of work to the time at which the last **checkpoint** (i.e., saved state of the system) was taken. When a process in a system terminates (by accident or intentionally as the result of a deadlock recovery algorithm), the system performs a **rollback** by undoing every operation related to the terminated process that occurred since the last checkpoint.

When databases may have many resources (perhaps millions or more) that must be accessed exclusively, there can be a risk of deadlock. To ensure that data in the database remains in a consistent state when deadlocked processes are terminated, database systems typically perform resource allocations using **transactions**. The changes specified by a transaction are made permanent only if the transaction completes successfully. We discuss transactions in more detail in Chapter 13, File and Database Systems.

Deadlocks could have horrendous consequences in certain real-time systems. A real-time process control system monitoring a gasoline refinery must function without interruption for the refinery's safe and proper operation. A computerized heart pacemaker must literally not "miss a beat." Deadlocks cannot be risked in such environments. What would happen if a deadlock did develop? Clearly, it would have to be detected and removed instantaneously. But is this always possible? These are some of the considerations that keep operating systems designers from restful sleep.

Self Review

1. (T/F) A system can eliminate deadlock by choosing at random an irreducible process in a resource-allocation graph.
2. Why might a system that restarts a process it "kills" to break a deadlock suffer from poor performance?

Ans: **1)** False. There may be multiple circular waits within the system by the time a deadlock is detected. **2)** First, because killing a process causes loss of work. Second, because the restarted process will execute the same code that caused the initial deadlock, and if the system state has not changed, the system can become deadlocked repeatedly.

7.11 Deadlock Strategies in Current and Future Systems

In personal computer systems and workstations, deadlock has generally been viewed as a limited annoyance. Some systems implement the basic deadlock prevention methods suggested by Havender while others ignore the problem—these methods seem to be satisfactory. While ignoring deadlocks may seem dangerous, this approach can actually be rather efficient. Consider that today's systems can contain thousands or millions of serially reusable objects on which processes and threads can deadlock. The time required to execute a deadlock detection algorithm can rise exponentially with the number of serially reusable objects in the system. If deadlock is rare, then the processor time devoted to checking for deadlocks significantly reduces system performance. In systems that are neither mission critical nor business critical, the choice of ignoring deadlock to favor performance often outweighs the need for a solution to the occasional deadlock.

Although some systems ignore deadlock that occurs due to user processes, it is far more important to prevent deadlock in the operating system. Systems such as Microsoft Windows provide debugger support, allowing developers to thoroughly test drivers and applications to ensure that they acquire resources without causing deadlock (e.g., they do not attempt to acquire locks in recursive routines, or they specify lock acquisition in a certain order).[46] Interestingly, once such programs are released, these testing mechanisms are often disabled to improve efficiency.[47]

In real-time, mission-critical or business-critical systems the possibility of deadlock cannot be tolerated. Researchers have developed techniques that handle deadlock while minimizing data loss and maintaining good performance. For example, deadlock is commonly addressed in distributed database systems, which could provide concurrent access to billions of records for millions of users over thousands of sites.[48] Due to the large size of distributed database systems, they often do not employ deadlock prevention or deadlock avoidance algorithms. Instead, they rely on deadlock detection and recovery via checkpoint/rollback (using transactions).[49] These techniques are beyond the scope of this chapter; see Chapter 17, Introduction to Distributed Systems, for an introduction to such methods.

Given current trends, deadlock will continue to be an important area of research for several reasons:

- Many large-scale systems are oriented more toward asynchronous parallel operations than toward the serial operations of the past. Multiprocessing is common, and parallel computation will be prevalent. Networks and distributed systems are ubiquitous. There are, quite simply, more operations going on concurrently, more conflicts over resources and hence more chances of deadlock. Consequently, research on deadlock detection and recovery in distributed systems has become quite active.

- With the increasing tendency of operating systems designers to view data as a resource, the number of resources that operating systems must manage is increasing dramatically. This is particularly evident in Web servers and database systems, which require high resource utilization and performance. This makes most deadlock prevention techniques impractical and deadlock recovery algorithms more important. Researchers have developed advanced transaction-based algorithms that ensure high resource utilization while maintaining a low cost of deadlock recovery.[50]

- Hundreds of millions of computers are incorporated into common devices, particularly small, portable ones such as cell phones, PDAs and navigation systems. These systems, increasingly characterized as Systems-on-a-Chip (SoC), are limited by a small set of resources and the demands of real-time tasks.[51, 52] Deadlock-free resource allocation in such systems is essential, because users cannot rely on an administrator to detect and rid the system of the deadlock.

Self Review

1. Why is deadlock prevention not a primary concern for many operating systems?
2. Why might deadlock in distributed systems be more difficult to detect than in a single computer?

Ans: **1)** Deadlock is rare and is often considered a minor annoyance for most personal computer users, who are often more concerned with operating system performance and features. **2)** Deadlock in distributed systems can be difficult to detect because each computer is managed by a different operating system, requiring each operating system to collect information from other computers in order to construct its resource-allocation graph.

Web Resources

www.diee.unica.it/~giua/PAPERS/CONF/03smc_b.pdf
Discusses an efficient approach to deadlock prevention in a real-time system.

www.db.fmi.uni-passau.de/publications/techreports/dda.html
Describes a solution to deadlock detection in distributed systems.

www.linux-mag.com/2001-03/compile_01.html
This *Compile Time* article describes how to deal with deadlock, using the Dining Philosophers example. The beginning of the article also reviews mutual exclusion primitives (e.g., semaphores) and concurrent programming.

Summary

One problem that arises in multiprogrammed systems is deadlock. A process or thread is in a state of deadlock (or is deadlocked) if the process or thread is waiting for a particular event that will not occur. In a system deadlock, one or more processes are deadlocked. Most deadlocks develop because of the normal contention for dedicated resources (i.e., resources that may be used by only one user at a time). Circular wait is characteristic of deadlocked systems.

One example of a system that is prone to deadlock is a spooling system. A common solution is to restrain the input spoolers so that, when the spooling files begin to reach some saturation threshold, they do not read in more print jobs. Today's systems allow printing to begin before the job is completed so that a full, or nearly full, spooling file can be emptied or partially cleared even while a job is still executing. This concept has been applied to streaming audio and video clips, where the audio and video begin to play before the clips are fully downloaded.

In any system that keeps processes waiting while it makes resource-allocation and process scheduling decisions, it is possible to delay indefinitely the scheduling of a process while other processes receive the system's attention. This situation, variously called indefinite postponement, indefinite blocking, or starvation, can be as devastating as deadlock. Indefinite postponement may occur because of biases in a system's resource scheduling policies. Some systems prevent indefinite postponement by increasing a process's priority as it waits for a resource—this technique is called aging.

Resources can be preemptible (e.g., processors and main memory), meaning that they can be removed from a process without loss of work, or nonpreemptible meaning that they (e.g., tape drives and optical scanners), cannot be removed from the processes to which they are assigned. Data and programs certainly are resources that the operating system must control and allocate. Code that cannot be changed while in use is said to be reentrant. Code that may be changed but is reinitialized each time it is used is said to be serially reusable. Reentrant code may be shared by several processes simultaneously, whereas serially reusable code may be used by only one process at a time. When we call particular resources shared, we must be careful to state whether they may be used by several processes simultaneously or by only one of several processes at a time. The latter kind—serially reusable resources—are the ones that tend to become involved in deadlocks.

The four necessary conditions for deadlock are: a resource may be acquired exclusively by only one process at a time (mutual exclusion condition); a process that has acquired an exclusive resource may hold it while waiting to obtain other resources (wait-for condition, also called the hold-and-wait condition); once a process has obtained a resource, the system cannot remove the resource from the process's control until the process has finished using the resource (no-preemption condition); and two or more processes are locked in a "circular chain" in which each process in the chain is waiting for one or more resources that the next process in the chain is holding (circular-wait condition). Because these are necessary conditions for a deadlock to exist, the existence of a deadlock implies that each of them must be in effect. Taken together, all four conditions are necessary and sufficient for deadlock to exist (i.e., if all these conditions are in place, the system is deadlocked).

The four major areas of interest in deadlock research are deadlock prevention, deadlock avoidance, deadlock detection, and deadlock recovery. In deadlock prevention our concern is to condition a system to remove any possibility of deadlocks occurring. Havender observed that a deadlock cannot occur if a system denies any of the four necessary conditions. The first necessary condition, namely that processes claim exclusive use of the resources they require, is not one that we want to break, because we specifically want to allow dedicated (i.e., serially reusable) resources. Denying the "wait-for" condition requires that all of the resources a process needs to complete its task be requested at once, which can result in substantial resource underutilization and raises concerns over how to charge for resources. Denying the "no-preemption" condition can be costly, because processes lose work when their resources are preempted. Denying the "circular-wait" condition uses a linear ordering of resources to prevent deadlock. This strategy can increase efficiency over the other strategies, but not without difficulties.

In deadlock avoidance the goal is to impose less stringent conditions than in deadlock prevention in an attempt to get better resource utilization. Avoidance methods allow the possibility of deadlock to loom, but whenever a deadlock is approached, it is carefully sidestepped. Dijkstra's Banker's Algorithm is an example of a deadlock avoidance algorithm. In the Banker's Algorithm, the system ensures that a process's maximum resource need does not exceed the number of available resources. The system is said to be in a safe state if the operating system can guarantee that all current processes can complete their work within a finite time. If not, then the system is said to be in an unsafe state.

Dijkstra's Banker's Algorithm requires that resources be allocated to processes only when the allocations result in safe states. It has a number of weaknesses (such as requiring a fixed number of processes and resources) that prevent it from being implemented in real systems.

Deadlock detection methods are used in systems in which deadlocks can occur. The goal is to determine if a deadlock has occurred, and to identify those processes and resources involved in the deadlock. Deadlock detection algorithms can incur significant runtime overhead. To facilitate the detection of deadlocks, a directed graph indicates resource allocations and requests. Deadlock can be detected using graph reductions. If a process's resource requests may be granted, then we say that a graph may be reduced by that process. If a graph can be reduced by all its processes, then there is no deadlock. If a graph cannot be reduced by all its processes, then the irreducible processes constitute the set of deadlocked processes in the graph.

Deadlock recovery methods are used to clear deadlocks from a system so that it may operate free of the deadlocks, and so that the deadlocked processes may complete their execution and free their resources. Recovery typically requires that one or more of the deadlocked processes be flushed from the system. The suspend/resume mechanism allows the system to put a temporary hold on a process (temporarily preempting its resources), and, when it is safe to do so, resume the held process without loss of work.

Checkpoint/rollback facilitates suspend/resume capabilities by limiting the loss of work to the time at which the last checkpoint (i.e., saved state of the system) was taken. When a process in a system terminates (by accident or intentionally as the result of a deadlock recovery algorithm), the system performs a rollback by undoing every operation related to the terminated process that occurred since the last checkpoint. To ensure that data in the database remains in a consistent state when deadlocked processes are terminated, database systems typically perform resource allocations using transactions.

In personal computer systems and workstations, deadlock has generally been viewed as a limited annoyance. Some systems implement the basic deadlock prevention methods suggested by Havender, while others ignore the problem—these methods seem to be satisfactory. While ignoring deadlocks may seem dangerous, this approach can actually be rather efficient. If deadlock is rare, then the processor time devoted to checking for deadlocks significantly reduces system performance. However, given current trends, deadlock will continue to be an important area of research as the number of concurrent operations and number of resources become large, increasing the likelihood of deadlock in multiprocessor and distributed systems. Also, many real-time systems, which are becoming increasingly prevalent, require deadlock-free resource allocation.

Key Terms

Advanced Configuration and Power Interface (ACPI)—Power management specification supported by many operating systems that allows a system to turn off some or all of its devices without loss of work.

aging—Method of preventing indefinite postponement by increasing a process's priority gradually as it waits.

checkpoint—Record of a state of a system so that it can be restored later if a process must be prematurely terminated (e.g., to perform deadlock recovery).

checkpoint/rollback—Method of deadlock and system recovery that undoes every action (or transaction) of a terminated process since the process's last checkpoint.

circular wait—Condition for deadlock that occurs when two or more processes are locked in a "circular chain," in which each process in the chain is waiting for one or more resources that the next process in the chain is holding.

circular-wait necessary condition for deadlock—One of the four necessary conditions for deadlock; states that if a deadlock exists, there will be two or more processes in a circular chain such that each process is waiting for a resource held by the next process in the chain.

deadline scheduling—Scheduling a process or thread to complete by a definite time; the priority of the process or thread may need to be increased as its completion deadline approaches.

deadlock—Situation in which a process or thread is waiting for an event that will never occur.

deadlock avoidance—Strategy that eliminates deadlock by allowing a system to approach deadlock, but ensuring that deadlock never occurs. Avoidance algorithms can achieve higher performance than deadlock prevention algorithms. (See also Dijktra's Banker's Algorithm.)

deadlock detection—Process of determining whether or not a system is deadlocked. Once detected, a deadlock can be removed from a system, typically resulting in loss of work.

deadlock prevention—Process of disallowing deadlock by eliminating one of the four necessary conditions for deadlock.

deadlock recovery—Process of removing a deadlock from a system. This can involve suspending a process temporarily (and preserving its work) or sometimes killing a process (thereby losing its work) and restarting it.

deadly embrace—See deadlock.

dedicated resource—Resource that may be used by only one process at a time. Also known as a serially reusable resource.

Dijkstra's Banker's Algorithm—Deadlock avoidance algorithm that controls resource allocation based on the amount of resources owned by the system, the amount of resources owned by each process and the maximum amount of resources that the process will request during execution. Allows resources to be assigned to processes only when the allocation results in a safe state. (See also safe state and unsafe state.)

Dining Philosophers—Classic problem introduced by Dijkstra that illustrates the problems inherent in concurrent programming, including deadlock and indefinite postponement. The problem requires the programmer to ensure that a set of n philosophers at a table containing n forks, who alternate between eating and thinking, do not starve while attempting to acquire the two adjacent forks necessary to eat.

graph reduction—Altering a resource-allocation graph by removing a process if that process can complete. This also involves removing any arrows leading to the process (from the resources allocated to the process) or away from the process (to resources the process is requesting). A resource-allocation graph can be reduced by a process if all of that process's resource requests can be granted, enabling that process to run to completion and free its resources.

Havender's linear ordering—See linear ordering.

linear ordering (Havender)—Logical arrangement of resources that requires that processes request resources in a linear order. This method denies the circular-wait necessary condition for deadlock.

maximum need (Dijkstra's Banker's Algorithm)—Characteristic of a process in Dijkstra's Banker's Algorithm that describes the largest number of resources (of a particular type) the process will need during execution.

mutual exclusion necessary condition for deadlock—One of the four necessary conditions for deadlock; states that deadlock can occur only if processes cannot claim exclusive use of their resources.

necessary condition for deadlock—Condition that must be true for deadlock to occur. The four necessary conditions are the mutual exclusion condition, no-preemption condition, wait-for condition and circular-wait condition.

no-preemption necessary condition for deadlock—One of the four necessary conditions for deadlock; states that deadlock can occur only if resources cannot be forcibly removed from processes.

nonpreemptible resource—Resource that cannot be forcibly removed from a process, e.g., a tape drive. Such resources are the kind that can become involved in deadlock.

preemptible resource—Resource that may be removed from a process such as a processor or memory. Such resources cannot be involved in deadlock.

reentrant code—Code that cannot be changed while in use and therefore can be shared among processes and threads.

resource allocation graph—Graph that shows processes and resources in a system. An arrow pointing from a process to a resource indicates that the process is requesting the resource. An arrow pointing from a resource to a process indicates that the resource is allocated to the process. Such a graph helps determine if a deadlock exists and, if so, helps identify the processes and resources involved in the deadlock.

resource type—Grouping of resources that perform a common task.

safe state—State of a system in Dijkstra's Banker's Algorithm in which there exists a sequence of actions that will allow every process in the system to finish without the system becoming deadlocked.

saturation threshold—A level of resource utilization above which the resource will refuse access. Designed to reduce deadlock, it also reduces throughput.

serially reusable code—Code that can be modified but is reinitialized each time it is used. Such code can be used by only one process or thread at a time.

serially reusable resource—See dedicated resource.

shared resource—Resource that can be accessed by more than one process.

starvation—Situation in which a thread waits for an event that might never occur, also called indefinite postponement.

sufficient conditions for deadlock—The four conditions–mutual exclusion, no-preemption, wait-for and circular-wait–which are necessary and sufficient for deadlock.

suspend/resume—Method of halting a process, saving its state, releasing its resources to other processes, then restoring its resources after the other processes have released them.

transaction—Atomic, mutually exclusive operation that either completes or is rolled back. Modifications to database entries are often performed as transactions to enable high performance and reduce the cost of deadlock recovery.

unsafe state—State of a system in Dijkstra's Banker's Algorithm that might eventually lead to deadlock because there might not be enough resources to allow any process to finish.

wait-for condition—One of the four necessary conditions for deadlock; states that deadlock can occur only if a process is allowed to wait for a resource while it holds another.

Exercises

7.1 Define deadlock.

7.2 Give an example of a deadlock involving only a single process and a single resource.

7.3 Give an example of a simple resource deadlock involving three processes and three resources. Draw the appropriate resource-allocation graph.

7.4 What is indefinite postponement? How does indefinite postponement differ from deadlock? How is indefinite postponement similar to deadlock?

7.5 Suppose a system allows for indefinite postponement of certain entities. How would you as a systems designer provide a means for preventing indefinite postponement?

7.6 Discuss the consequences of indefinite postponement in each of the following types of systems.
   a. batch processing
   b. timesharing
   c. real-time

7.7 A system requires that arriving processes must wait for service if the needed resource is busy. The system does not use aging to elevate the priorities of waiting processes to prevent

indefinite postponement. What other means might the system use to prevent indefinite postponement?

7.8 In a system of n processes, a subset of m of these processes is currently suffering indefinite postponement. Is it possible for the system to determine which processes are being indefinitely postponed?

7.9 (*The Dining Philosophers*) One of Dijkstra's more delightful contributions is his problem of the Dining Philosophers.[53, 54] It illustrates many of the subtle problems inherent in concurrent programming.

Your goal is to devise a concurrent program (with a monitor) that simulates the behavior of the philosophers. Your program should be free of deadlock and indefinite postponement—otherwise one or more philosophers might starve. Your program must, of course, enforce mutual exclusion—two philosophers cannot use the same fork at once.

Figure 7.12 shows the behavior of a typical philosopher. Comment on each of the following implementations of a typical philosopher.
   a. See Fig. 7.13.
   b. See Fig. 7.14.
   c. See Fig. 7.15.
   d. See Fig. 7.16.

```
1   typicalPhilosopher()
2   {
3      while ( true )
4      {
5         think();
6         eat();
7      } // end while
8   } // end typicalPhilosopher
```

Figure 7.12 | Typical philosopher behavior for Exercise 7.9.

```
1   typicalPhilosopher()
2   {
3      while ( true )
4      {
```

Figure 7.13 | Philosopher behavior for Exercise 7.9(a). (Part 1 of 2.)

```
 5        think();
 6
 7        pickUpLeftFork();
 8        pickUpRightFork();
 9
10        eat();
11
12        putDownLeftFork();
13        putDownRightFork();
14    } // end while
15
16 } // end typicalPhilosopher
```

Figure 7.13 | *Philosopher behavior for Exercise 7.9(a). (Part 2 of 2.)*

```
 1 typicalPhilosopher()
 2 {
 3    while ( true )
 4    {
 5        think();
 6
 7        pickUpBothForksAtOnce();
 8
 9        eat();
10
11        putDownBothForksAtOnce();
12    } // end while
13
14 } // end typicalPhilosopher
```

Figure 7.14 | *Philosopher behavior for Exercise 7.9(b).*

```
 1 typicalPhilosopher()
 2 {
 3    while ( true )
 4    {
 5        think();
 6
 7        while ( notHoldingBothForks )
 8        {
 9            pickUpLeftFork();
10
11            if ( rightForkNotAvailable )
12            {
13                putDownLeftFork();
```

Figure 7.15 | *Philosopher behavior for Exercise 7.9(c). (Part 1 of 2.)*

```
14              } // end if
15              else
16              {
17                  pickUpRightFork();
18              } // end while
19          } // end else
20
21          eat();
22
23          putDownLeftFork();
24          putDownRightFork();
25      } // end while
26
27  } // end typicalPhilosopher
```

Figure 7.15 | *Philosopher behavior for Exercise 7.9(c). (Part 2 of 2.)*

```
1   typicalPhilosopher()
2   {
3       while ( true )
4       {
5           think();
6
7           if ( philosopherID mod 2 == 0 )
8           {
9               pickUpLeftFork();
10              pickUpRightFork();
11
12              eat();
13
14              putDownLeftFork();
15              putDownRightFork();
16          } // end if
17          else
18          {
19              pickUpRightFork();
20              pickUpLeftFork();
21
22              eat();
23
24              putDownRightFork();
25              putDownLeftFork();
26          } // end else
27      } // end while
28
29  } // end typicalPhilosopher
```

Figure 7.16 | *Philosopher behavior for Exercise 7.9(d).*

7.10 Define and discuss each of the following resource concepts.

    a. preemptible resource

    b. nonpreemptible resource

    c. shared resource

    d. dedicated resource

    e. reentrant code

    f. serially reusable code

    g. dynamic resource allocation

7.11 State the four necessary conditions for a deadlock to exist. Give a brief intuitive argument for the necessity of each individual condition.

7.12 In the context of the traffic deadlock, illustrated in Fig. 7.1, discuss each of the necessary conditions for deadlock.

7.13 What are the four areas of deadlock research mentioned in the text? Discuss each briefly.

7.14 Havender's method for denying the "wait-for" condition requires that processes must request all of the resources they will need before the system may let them proceed. The system grants resources on an "all-or-none" basis. Discuss the pros and cons of this method.

7.15 Why is Havender's method for denying the "no-preemption" condition not a popular means for preventing deadlock?

7.16 Discuss the pros and cons of Havender's method for denying the "circular-wait" condition.

7.17 How does Havender's linear ordering for denying the "circular-wait" condition prevent cycles from developing in resource-allocation graphs?

7.18 A process repeatedly requests and releases resources of types R_1 and R_2, one at a time and in that order. There is exactly one resource of each type. A second process also requests and releases these resources one at a time repeatedly. Under what circumstances could these processes deadlock? If so, what could be done to prevent deadlock?

7.19 Explain the intuitive appeal of deadlock avoidance over deadlock prevention.

7.20 In the context of Dijkstra's Banker's Algorithm discuss whether each of the states described in Fig. 7.17 and Fig. 7.18 is safe or unsafe. If a state is safe, show how it is possible for all processes to complete. If a state is unsafe, show how it is possible for deadlock to occur.

7.21 The fact that a state is unsafe does not necessarily imply that the system will deadlock. Explain why this is true. Give an example of an unsafe state and show how all of the processes could complete without a deadlock occurring.

7.22 Dijkstra's Banker's Algorithm has a number of weaknesses that preclude its effective use in real systems. Comment on why each of the following restrictions may be considered a weakness in the Banker's Algorithm.

    a. The number of resources to be allocated remains fixed.

    b. The population of processes remains fixed.

    c. The operating system guarantees that resource requests will be serviced in a finite time.

    d. Users guarantee that they will return held resources within a finite time.

    e. Users must state maximum resource needs in advance.

7.23 (*Banker's Algorithm for Multiple Resource Types*) Consider Dijkstra's Banker's Algorithm as discussed in Section 7.8, Deadlock Avoidance with Dijkstra's Banker's Algorithm. Suppose that a system using this deadlock avoidance scheme has n processes and m different resource types; assume that multiple resources of each type may exist and that the number of resources of each type is known. Develop a version of the Banker's Algorithm that will enable such a system to avoid deadlock. [*Hint:* Under what circumstances could a particular process be guaranteed to complete its execution, and thus return its resources to the pool?]

7.24 Could the Banker's Algorithm still function properly if resources could be requested in groups? Explain your answer carefully.

Process	max(P_i)	loan(P_i)	claim(P_i)
P_1	4	1	3
P_2	6	4	2
P_3	8	5	3
P_4	2	0	2
		$a = 1$	

Figure 7.17 | Resource description for State A.

Process	max(P_i)	loan(P_i)	claim(P_i)
P1	8	4	4
P2	8	3	5
P3	8	5	3
		a = 2	

Figure 7.18 | Resource description for State B.

7.25 A system that uses Banker's-Algorithm deadlock avoidance has five processes (1, 2, 3, 4, and 5) and uses resources of four different types (A, B, C, and D). There are multiple resources of each type. Is the state of the system depicted by Fig. 7.19 and Fig. 7.20 safe? Explain your answer. If the system is safe, show how all the processes could complete their execution successfully. If the system is unsafe, show how deadlock might occur.

7.26 Suppose a system with n processes and m identical resources uses Banker's Algorithm deadlock avoidance. Write a function boolean isSafeState1(int[][] maximumNeed, int[][] loans. int[] available) that determines whether the system is in a safe state.

7.27 Suppose a system uses the Banker's Algorithm with n processes, m resource types, and multiple resources of each type. Write a function boolean isSafeState2(int[][] maximumNeed, int[][] loans, int[] available) that determines whether the system is in a safe state.

7.28 In a system in which it is possible for a deadlock to occur, under what circumstances would you use a deadlock detection algorithm?

7.29 In the deadlock detection algorithm employing the technique of graph reductions, show that the order of the graph reductions does not matter, the same final state will result. [Hint: No matter what the order, after each reduction, the available resource pool increases.]

7.30 Why is deadlock recovery such a difficult problem?

7.31 Why is it difficult to choose which processes to "flush" in deadlock recovery?

7.32 One method of recovering from deadlock is to kill the lowest-priority process (or processes) involved in the deadlock. This (these) process(es) could then be restarted and once again allowed to compete for resources. What potential problem might develop in a system using such an algorithm? How would you solve this problem?

Process	Current Loan				Maximum Need				Current Claim			
	A	B	C	D	A	B	C	D	A	B	C	D
1	1	0	2	0	3	2	4	2	2	2	2	2
2	0	3	1	2	3	5	1	2	3	2	0	0
3	2	4	5	1	2	7	7	5	0	3	2	4
4	3	0	0	6	5	5	0	8	2	5	0	2
5	4	2	1	3	6	2	1	4	2	0	0	1

Figure 7.19 | System state describing current loan, maximum need and current claim.

Total Resources				Resources Available			
A	B	C	D	A	B	C	D
13	13	9	13	3	4	0	1

Figure 7.20 | System state describing total number of resources and available resources.

7.33 Why will deadlock probably be a more critical problem in future operating systems than it is today?

7.34 Do resource malfunctions that render a resource unusable generally increase or decrease the likelihood of deadlocks and indefinite postponement? Explain your answer.

7.35 The vast majority of computer systems in use today do allow at least some kinds of deadlock and indefinite postponement situations to develop, and many of these systems provide no automatic means of detecting and recovering from these problems. In fact, many designers believe that it is virtually impossible to certify a system as absolutely free of the possibilities of deadlock and indefinite postponement. Indicate how these observations should affect the design of "mission-critical" systems.

Suggested Projects

7.38 Prepare a research paper on how current operating systems deal with deadlock.

7.39 Research how real-time systems ensure that deadlock never occurs. How do they manage to eliminate deadlock yet maintain performance?

Suggested Simulations

7.41 (*Deadlock Detection and Recovery Project*) Write a simulation program to determine whether a deadlock has occurred in a system of n identical resources and m processes. Have each process generate a set of resources that it wants (e.g., 3 of resource A, 1 of resource B and 5 of resource C). Then, from each set, request the resources one type at a time in a random order and with random pauses between types. Have each process hold onto all the resources that it has acquired until it can get all of them. Deadlocks should start developing. Now have another thread check for deadlocks every few seconds. It should report when a deadlock has occurred and start killing threads involved in the deadlock. Try different heuristics for choosing processes to kill and see which type of heuristic results in the best average time between deadlocks.

7.42 (*Deadlock Prevention Simulation Project*) Write a simulation program to compare various deadlock prevention schemes

7.36 The table in Fig. 7.21 shows a system in an unsafe state. Explain how all of the processes may manage to finish execution without the system becoming deadlocked.

7.37 A system has three processes and four identical resources. Each process requires at most two of the resources at any given time.

   a. Can deadlock occur in this system? Explain.

   b. If there are m processes, and each could request up to n resources, how many resources must be available in the system to ensure that deadlock will never occur?

   c. If there are m processes and r resources in the system, what maximum number of resources, n, could each process request, if all processes must have the same maximum?

7.40 Determine how Web servers and other business-critical systems address the problem of deadlock.

discussed in Section 7.7, Deadlock Prevention. In particular, compare deadlock prevention by denying the "wait-for" condition (Section 7.7.1, Denying the "Wait-For" Condition) with deadlock prevention by denying the "no-preemption" condition (Section 7.7.2, Denying the "No-Preemption" Condition). Your program should generate a sample user population, user arrival times, user resource needs (assume the system has n identical resources) in terms both of maximum needs and of when the resources are actually required, and so on. Each simulation should accumulate statistics on job turnaround times, resource utilization, number of jobs progressing at once (assume that jobs may progress when they have the portion of the n resources they currently need), and the like. Observe the results of your simulations and draw conclusions about the relative effectiveness of these deadlock prevention schemes.

Process	loan(P_i)	max(P_i)	claim(P_i)
P_1	1	5	4
P_2	1	3	2
P_3	5	10	5
	$a = 1$		

Figure 7.21 | *Example of a system in an unsafe state.*

7.43 (*Deadlock Avoidance Simulation Project*) Write a simulation program to examine the performance of a system of *n* identical resources and *m* processes operating under banker's-algorithm resource allocation. Model your program after the one you developed in Exercise 7.42. Run your simulation and compare the results with those observed in your deadlock prevention simulations. Draw conclusions about the relative effectiveness of deadlock avoidance vs. the deadlock prevention schemes studied.

7.44 (*Deadlock Prevention and Avoidance Comparison*) Create a program that simulates arriving jobs with various resource needs (listing each resource that will be needed and the time at which it will be needed). This can be a random-number-based driver program. Use your simulation to determine how deadlock prevention and deadlock avoidance strategies yield higher resource utilization.

Recommended Reading

Though many operating systems simply ignore the problem of deadlock, there has been considerable research in the field to create effective algorithms to solve the problem. Dijkstra, Isloor and Marsland[55] and Zobel[56] characterize the problem of deadlock. Dijkstra was one of the first to document the problem of deadlock in multiprogrammed systems, presenting both the Dining Philosophers problem and the banker's algorithm for deadlock avoidance.[57, 58] Coffman, Elphick and Shoshani later provided a framework for research in this area by classifying the four necessary conditions for deadlock.[59] Holt[60, 61] developed resource-allocation graphs to aid in deadlock prevention, while Habermann[62] presented a family of deadlock avoidance techniques. In discussing the UNIX System V operating system, Bach indicates how deadlocks may develop in areas such as interrupt handling.[63] Kenah et al. discuss the detection and handling of deadlocks in Digital Equipment Corporation's VAX/VMS operating system.[64]

Today's systems rarely implement deadlock prevention or avoidance mechanisms. In fact, in distributed systems, conventional deadlock prevention and avoidance mechanisms are not feasible, because each computer in a distributed system may be managed by a different operating system. Researchers have developed deadlock detection mechanisms[65] coupled with checkpoint/rollback capabilities[66] to reduce loss of work. Research into deadlock is currently focused on developing efficient deadlock detection algorithms and applying them to distributed systems, networks and other deadlock-prone environments.[67] The bibliography for this chapter is located on our Web site at www.deitel.com/books/os3e/Bibliography.pdf.

Works Cited

1. Isloor, S. S., and T. A. Marsland, "The Deadlock Problem: An Overview," *Computer*, Vol. 13, No. 9, September 1980, pp. 58–78.

2. Zobel, D., "The Deadlock Problem: A Classifying Bibliography," *Operating Systems Review*, Vol. 17, No. 4, October 1983, pp. 6–16.

3. Holt, R. C., "Some Deadlock Properties of Computer Systems," *ACM Computing Surveys*, Vol. 4, No. 3, September 1972, pp. 179–196.

4. Coffman, E. G., Jr.; Elphick, M. J.; and A. Shoshani, "System Deadlocks," *Computing Surveys*, Vol. 3, No. 2, June 1971, p. 69.

5. Dijkstra, E. W., "Cooperating Sequential Processes," Technological University, Eindhoven, Netherlands, 1965, reprinted in F. Genuys, ed., *Programming Languages*, New York: Academic Press, 1968.

6. Dijkstra, E. W., "Hierarchical Ordering of Sequential Processes," *Acta Informatica*, Vol. 1, 1971, pp. 115–138.

7. Coffman, E. G., Jr.; Elphick, M. J.; and A. Shoshani, "System Deadlocks," *Computing Surveys*, Vol. 3, No. 2, June 1971, pp. 67–78.

8. Habermann, A. N., "Prevention of System Deadlocks," *Communications of the ACM*, Vol. 12, No. 7, July 1969, pp. 373–377, 385.

9. Holt, R. C., "Comments on the Prevention of System Deadlocks," *Communications of the ACM*, Vol. 14, No. 1, January 1971, pp. 36–38.

10. Holt, R. C., "On Deadlock Prevention in Computer Systems," Ph.D. Thesis, Ithaca, NY.: Cornell University, 1971.

11. Parnas, D. L., and A. N. Haberman, "Comment on Deadlock Prevention Method," *Communications of the ACM*, Vol. 15, No. 9, September 1972, pp. 840–841.

12. Newton, G., "Deadlock Prevention, Detection, and Resolution: An Annotated Bibliography," *ACM Operating Systems Review*, Vol. 13, No. 2, April 1979, pp. 33–44.

13. Gelernter, D., "A DAG Based Algorithm for Prevention of Store-and-Forward Deadlock in Packet Networks," *IEEE Transactions on Computers*, Vol. C-30, No. 10, October 1981, pp. 709–715.

14. Havender, J. W., "Avoiding Deadlock in Multitasking Systems," *IBM Systems Journal*, Vol. 7, No. 2, 1968, pp. 74–84.

15. Brinch Hansen, P., *Operating System Principles*, Englewood Cliffs, NJ: Prentice Hall, 1973.

16. Scherr, A. L., "Functional Structure of IBM Virtual Storage Operating Systems, Part II: OS/VS2-2 Concepts and Philosophies," *IBM Systems Journal*, Vol. 12, No. 4, 1973, pp. 382–400.

17. Auslander, M. A.; Larkin, D. C.; and A. L. Scherr, "The Evolution of the MVS Operating System," *IBM Journal of Research and Development*, Vol. 25, No. 5, 1981, pp. 471–482.

18. Kenah, L. J.; Goldenberg, R. E.; and S. F. Bate, *VAX/VMS Internals and Data Structures*, Version 4.4, Bedford, MA: Digital Press, 1988.

19. Brinch Hansen, P., *Operating System Principles*, Englewood Cliffs, NJ: Prentice Hall, 1973.

20. Dijkstra, E. W., *Cooperating Sequential Processes*, Technological University, Eindhoven, The Netherlands, 1965.

21. Dijkstra, E. W., *Cooperating Sequential Processes*, Technological University, Eindhover, Netherlands, 1965, Reprinted in F. Genuys, ed., *Programming Languages*, New York: Academic Press, 1968.

22. Habermann, A. N., "Prevention of System Deadlocks," *Communications of the ACM*, Vol. 12, No. 7, July 1969, pp. 373–377, 385.

23. Madduri, H., and R. Finkel, "Extension of the Banker's Algorithm for Resource Allocation in a Distributed Operating System," *Information Processing Letters*, Vol. 19, No. 1, July 1984, pp. 1–8.

24. Havender, J. W., "Avoiding Deadlock in Multitasking Systems," *IBM Systems Journal*, Vol. 7, No. 2, 1968, pp. 74–84.

25. Fontao, R. O., "A Concurrent Algorithm for Avoiding Deadlocks," *Proc. Third ACM Symposium on Operating Systems Principles*, October 1971, pp. 72–79.

26. Frailey, D. J., "A Practical Approach to Managing Resources and Avoiding Deadlock," *Communications of the ACM*, Vol. 16, No. 5, May 1973, pp. 323–329.

27. Devillers, R., "Game Interpretation of the Deadlock Avoidance Problem," *Communications of the ACM*, Vol. 20, No. 10, October 1977, pp. 741–745.

28. Lomet, D. B., "Subsystems of Processes with Deadlock Avoidance," *IEEE Transactions on Software Engineering*, Vol. SE-6, No. 3, May 1980, pp. 297–304.

29. Merlin, P. M., and P. J. Schweitzer, "Deadlock Avoidance in Store-and-Forward Networks—I: Store and Forward Deadlock," *IEEE Transactions on Communications*, Vol. COM-28, No. 3, March 1980, pp. 345–354.

30. Merlin, P. M., and P. J. Schweitzer, "Deadlock Avoidance in Store-and-Forward Networks—II: Other Deadlock Types," *IEEE Transactions on Communications*, Vol. COM-28, No. 3, March 1980, pp. 355–360.

31. Minoura, T., "Deadlock Avoidance Revisited," *Journal of the ACM*, Vol. 29, No. 4, October 1982, pp. 1023–1048.

32. Murphy, J. E., "Resource Allocation with Interlock Detection in a Multitask System," *AFIPS FJCC Proc.*, Vol. 33, No. 2, 1968, pp. 1169–1176.

33. Newton, G., "Deadlock Prevention, Detection, and Resolution: An Annotated Bibliography," *ACM Operating Systems Review*, Vol. 13, No. 2, April 1979, pp. 33–44.

34. Gligor, V., and S. Shattuch, "On Deadlock Detection in Distributed Systems," *IEEE Transactions on Software Engineering*, Vol. SE-6, No. 5, September 1980, pp. 435–440.

35. Ho, G. S., and C. V. Ramamoorthy, "Protocols for Deadlock Detection in Distributed Database Systems," *IEEE Transactions on Software Engineering*, Vol. SE-8, No. 6, November 1982, pp. 554–557.

36. Obermarck, R., "Distributed Deadlock Detection Algorithm," *ACM Transactions on Database Systems*, Vol. 7, No. 2, June 1982, pp. 187–208.

37. Chandy, K. M., and J. Misra, "Distributed Deadlock Detection," *ACM Transactions on Computer Systems*, Vol. 1, No. 2, May 1983, pp. 144–156.

38. Jagannathan, J. R., and R. Vasudevan, "Comments on 'Protocols for Deadlock Detection in Distributed Database Systems'," *IEEE Transactions on Software Engineering*, Vol. SE-9, No. 3, May 1983, p. 371.

39. Kenah, L. J.; Goldenberg, R. E.; and S. F. Bate, *VAX/VMS Internals and Data Structures*, version 4.4, Bedford, MA: Digital Press, 1988.

40. Pun H. Shiu, YuDong Tan, Vincent J. Mooney, "A Novel Parallel Deadlock Detection Algorithm and Architecture" *Proceedings of the Ninth International Symposium on Hardware/Software Codesign*, April 2001.

41. Holt, R. C., "Some Deadlock Properties of Computer Systems," *ACM Computing Surveys*, Vol. 4, No. 3, September 1972, pp. 179–196.

42. Holt, R. C., "Some Deadlock Properties of Computer Systems," *ACM Computing Surveys*, Vol. 4, No. 3, September 1972, pp. 179–196.

43. Kenah, L. J.; R. E. Goldenberg; and S. F. Bate, *VAX/VMS Internals and Data Structures*, version 4.4, Bedford, MA: Digital Press, 1988.

44. Thomas, K., *Programming Locking Applications*, IBM Corporation, 2001, <www-124.ibm.com/developerworks/oss/dlm/currentbook/dlmbook_index.html>.

45. Compaq Computer Corporation, Intel Corporation, Microsoft Corporation, Phoenix Technologies Ltd., Toshiba Corporation, "Advanced Configuration and Power Management," rev. 2.0b, October 11, 2002, p. 238

46. "Driver Development Tools: Windows DDK, Deadlock Detection," *Microsoft MSDN Library*, June 6, 2003, <msdn.microsoft.com/library/en-us/ddtools/hh/ddtools/dv_8pkj.asp>.

47. "Kernel-Mode Driver Architecture: Windows DDK, Preventing Errors and Deadlocks While Using Spin Locks," *Microsoft MSDN Library*, June 6, 2003, <msdn.microsoft.com/library/en-us/kmarch/hh/kmarch/synchro_5ktj.asp>.

48. Krivokapic, N.; Kemper, A.; and E. Gudes, "Deadlock Detection in Distributed Database Systems: A New Algorithm and Com-

parative Performance Analysis," *The VLDB Journal—The International Journal on Very Large Data Bases*, Vol. 8, No. 2, 1999, pp. 79–100.

49. Krivokapic, N.; Kemper, A.; and E. Gudes, "Deadlock Detection in Distributed Database Systems: A New Algorithm and Comparative Performance Analysis," *The VLDB Journal—The International Journal on Very Large Data Bases*, Vol. 8, No. 2, 1999, pp. 79–100.

50. Krivokapic, N.; Kemper, A.; and E. Gudes, "Deadlock Detection in Distributed Database Systems: A New Algorithm and Comparative Performance Analysis," *The VLDB Journal—The International Journal on Very Large Data Bases*, Vol. 8, No. 2, 1999, pp. 79–100.

51. Magarshack, P., and P. Paulin, "System-on-chip Beyond the Nanometer Wall," *Proceedings of the 40th Conference on Design Automation,* Anaheim, CA: ACM Press, 2003, pp. 419–424.

52. Benini, L.; Macci, A.; and M. Poncino, "Energy-Aware Design of Embedded Memories: A Survey of Technologies, Architectures, and Techniques," *ACM Transactions on Embedded Computer Systems (TECS)*, Vol. 2, No. 1, 2003, pp. 5–32.

53. Dijkstra, E. W., "Solution of a Problem in Concurrent Programming Control," *Communications of the ACM*, Vol. 8, No. 5, September 1965, p. 569.

54. Dijkstra, E. W., "Hierarchical Ordering of Sequential Processes," *Acta Informatica*, Vol. 1, 1971, pp. 115–138.

55. Isloor, S. S., and T. A. Marsland, "The Deadlock Problem: An Overview," *Computer*, Vol. 13, No. 9, September 1980, pp. 58–78.

56. Zobel, D., "The Deadlock Problem: A Classifying Bibliography," *Operating Systems Review*, Vol. 17, No. 4, October 1983, pp. 6–16.

57. Dijkstra, E. W., "Cooperating Sequential Processes," Technological University, Eindhoven, Netherlands, 1965, reprinted in F. Genuys, ed., *Programming Languages,* New York: Academic Press, 1968.

58. Dijkstra, E. W., "Hierarchical Ordering of Sequential Processes," *Acta Informatica,* Vol. 1, 1971, pp. 115–138.

59. Coffman, E. G., Jr.; Elphick, M. J.; and A. Shoshani, "System Deadlocks," *Computing Surveys*, Vol. 3, No. 2, June 1971, pp. 67–78.

60. Holt, R. C., "Comments on the Prevention of System Deadlocks," *Communications of the ACM*, Vol. 14, No. 1, January 1971, pp. 36–38.

61. Holt, R. C., "On Deadlock Prevention in Computer Systems," Ph.D. Thesis, Ithaca, NY.: Cornell University, 1971.

62. Habermann, A. N., "Prevention of System Deadlocks," *Communications of the ACM*, Vol. 12, No. 7, July 1969, pp. 373–377, 385.

63. Bach, M. J., *The Design of the UNIX Operating System*, Englewood Cliffs, NJ: Prentice Hall, 1986.

64. Kenah, L. J.; Goldenberg, R. E.; and S. F. Bate, *VAX/VMS Internals and Data Structures,* version 4.4, Bedford, MA: Digital Press, 1988.

65. Obermarck, R., "Distributed Deadlock Detection Algorithm," *ACM Transactions on Database Systems*, Vol. 7, No. 2, June 1982, pp. 187–208.

66. Krivokapic, N.; Kemper, A.; and E. Gudes, "Deadlock Detection in Distributed Database Systems: A New Algorithm and Comparative Performance Analysis," *The VLDB Journal—The International Journal on Very Large Data Bases*, Vol. 8, No. 2, 1999, pp. 79–100.

67. Shiu, P. H.; Tan, Y.; and V. J. Mooney, "A Novel Parallel Deadlock Detection Algorithm and Architecture," *Proceedings of the Ninth International Symposium on Hardware/Software Codesign*, April 2001.

The heavens themselves, the planets and this center observe degree, priority, and place, ...

—William Shakespeare—

Nothing in progression can rest on its original plan. We may as well think of rocking a grown man in the cradle of an infant.

—Edmund Burke—

For every problem there is one solution which is simple, neat, and wrong.

—H. L. Mencken—

There is nothing more requisite in business than dispatch.

—Joseph Addison—

Chapter 8

Processor Scheduling

Objectives

After reading this chapter, you should understand:

- *the goals of processor scheduling.*

- *preemptive vs. nonpreemptive scheduling.*

- *the role of priorities in scheduling.*

- *scheduling criteria.*

- *common scheduling algorithms.*

- *the notions of deadline scheduling and real-time scheduling.*

- *Java thread scheduling.*

Chapter Outline

8.1 Introduction

We have discussed how multiprogramming enables an operating system to use its resources more efficiently. When a system has a choice of processes to execute, it must have a strategy—called a **processor scheduling policy** (or **discipline**)—for deciding which process to run at a given time. A scheduling policy should attempt to satisfy certain performance criteria, such as maximizing the number of processes that complete per unit time (i.e., throughput), minimizing the time each process waits before executing (i.e., latency), preventing indefinite postponement of processes, ensuring that each process completes before its stated deadline, or maximizing processor utilization. Some of these goals, such as maximizing processor utilization and throughput, are complementary; others conflict with one another—a system that ensures that processes will complete before their deadlines may not achieve the highest throughput. In this chapter, we discuss the problems of determining when processors should be assigned, and to which processes. Although we focus on processes, many of the topics we describe apply to jobs and threads as well.

Self Review

1. When might a system that ensures that processes will complete before their deadlines not achieve the highest throughput?
2. Which performance criterion is the most important in an operating system? Why is this a hard question to answer?

Ans: **1)** This occurs, for example, when several short processes are delayed while the system dispatches a long process that must meets its deadline. **2)** No one performance criterion is more important than the others for every operating system. It depends on the goals of the system. For example, in real-time systems, giving processes and threads immediate, predictable service is more important than high processor utilization. In supercomputers that perform lengthy calculations, processor utilization is typically more important than minimizing latency.

8.2 Scheduling Levels

In this section we consider three levels of scheduling (Fig. 8.1). **High-level scheduling**—also called **job scheduling** or **long-term scheduling**—determines which jobs the system allows to compete actively for system resources. This level is sometimes called **admission scheduling**, because it determines which jobs gain admission to the system. Once admitted, jobs are initiated and become processes or groups of processes. The high-level scheduling policy dictates the **degree of multiprogramming**—the total number of processes in a system at a given time.[1] Entry of too many processes into the system can saturate the system's resources, leading to poor performance. In this case, the high-level scheduling policy may decide to temporarily prohibit new jobs from entering until other jobs complete.

After the high-level scheduling policy has admitted a job (which may contain one or more processes) to the system, the **intermediate-level scheduling** policy determines which processes shall be allowed to compete for processors. This policy

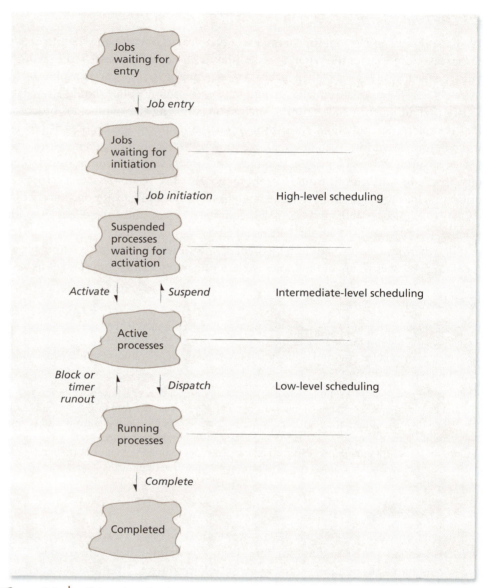

Figure 8.1 | *Scheduling levels.*

responds to short-term fluctuations in system load. It temporarily suspends and resumes processes to achieve smooth system operation and to help realize certain systemwide performance goals. The intermediate-level scheduler acts as a buffer between the admission of jobs to the system and the assignment of processors to the processes representing these jobs.

A system's **low-level scheduling** policy determines which active process the system will assign to a processor when one next becomes available. In many of today's systems, the low- and intermediate-level schedulers are the only schedulers.

(In this case, job initiation is performed by the intermediate-level scheduler.) High-level schedulers are often limited to large mainframe systems that perform batch processing.

Low-level scheduling policies often assign a **priority** to each process, reflecting its importance—the more important a process, the more likely the scheduling policy is to select it to execute next. We discuss priorities in Section 8.4, Priorities, and throughout this chapter. The low-level scheduler (also called the **dispatcher**) also assigns (i.e., **dispatches**) a processor to the selected process. The dispatcher operates many times per second and must therefore reside in main memory at all times.

In this chapter we discuss many low-level scheduling policies. We present each in the context of certain scheduling objectives and criteria (which we discuss in Section 8.5, Scheduling Objectives, and Section 8.6, Scheduling Criteria), and we describe how they relate to one another. Coffman and Kleinrock discuss popular scheduling policies and indicate how users who know which one the system employs can actually achieve better performance by taking appropriate measures.[2] Ruschitzka and Fabry give a classification of scheduling algorithms, and they formalize the notion of priority.[3]

Self Review

1. How should the intermediate scheduler respond to fluctuations in system load?
2. Which level of scheduler should remain resident in main memory? Why?

Ans: **1)** The intermediate scheduler can prohibit processes from proceeding to the low-level scheduler when the system becomes overloaded and can allow these processes to proceed when the system load returns to normal. **2)** The low-level scheduler should remain resident in main memory because it executes frequently, requiring it to respond quickly to reduce scheduling overhead.

8.3 Preemptive vs. Nonpreemtpive Scheduling

Scheduling disciplines are either preemptive or nonpreemptive. A scheduling discipline is **nonpreemptive** if, once the system has assigned a processor to a process, the system cannot remove that processor from that process. A scheduling discipline is **preemptive** if the system can remove the processor from the process it is running. Under a nonpreemptive scheduling discipline, each process, once given a processor, runs to completion or until it voluntarily relinquishes its processor. Under a preemptive scheduling discipline, the processor may execute a portion of a process's code and then perform a context switch.

Preemptive scheduling is useful in systems in which high-priority processes require rapid response. In real-time systems (discussed in Section 8.9, Real-Time Scheduling), for example, the consequences of not responding to an interrupt could be catastrophic.[4, 5, 6, 7] In interactive timesharing systems, preemptive scheduling helps guarantee acceptable user response times. Preemption is not without cost—context switches incur overhead (see the Operating Systems Thinking feature,

Overhead). To make preemption effective, the system must maintain many processes in main memory, so that the next process is ready when a processor becomes available. As we will see in Chapter 10, Virtual Memory Organization, only a portion of each process typically is in main memory at any time; the less active portions typically reside on disk.

In nonpreemptive systems, short processes can experience lengthy service delays while longer processes complete, but turnaround times are more predictable, because incoming high-priority processes cannot displace waiting processes. Because a nonpreemptive system cannot remove a process from a processor until it completes, errant programs that never complete (e.g., by entering an infinite loop) may never relinquish control of the system. Also, in a nonpreemptive system, executing unimportant processes can make important processes wait.

To prevent users from monopolizing the system (either maliciously or accidentally), a preemptive system can take the processor away from a process. As discussed in Chapter 3, Process Concepts, this is typically implemented by setting an interrupting clock or interval timer that periodically generates an interrupt, which allows the operating system to execute. Once a processor is assigned to a process, the process executes until it voluntarily releases its processor, or until the clock interrupt or some other interrupt occurs. The operating system may then decide whether the running process should continue or some other "next" process should execute.

The interrupting clock helps guarantee reasonable response times to interactive users, prevents the system from getting hung up on a user in an infinite loop,

Operating Systems Thinking

Overhead

Ultimately, computer systems exist to run applications for users. Although operating systems certainly perform important tasks, they consume valuable system resources in doing so; that resource consumption is said to be overhead, because the resources are not directly used by user applications to perform useful work. Operating systems designers seek to minimize that overhead while maximizing the portion of the systems resources that can be allocated to user applications. As we will see, overhead can improve performance by improving resource utilization; it can also reduce performance to provide a higher level of protection and security. As computer power continues to increase with costs decreasing, the resource consumption lost to overhead can become less of an issue. However, designers should be aware of a system's workload when considering overhead. For example, a large overhead for a small load may become relatively small under a heavy load; a small overhead for a small load may become relatively large under a heavy load.

and allows processes to respond to time-dependent events. Processes that need to run periodically depend on the interrupting clock.

In designing a preemptive scheduling mechanism, one must carefully consider the arbitrariness of priority schemes. It does not make sense to build a sophisticated mechanism to faithfully implement a priority preemption scheme when the priorities themselves are not meaningfully assigned.

Self Review

1. When is nonpreemptive scheduling more appropriate than preemptive scheduling?
2. Can a program that enters an infinite loop monopolize a preemptive system?

Ans: **1)** Nonpreemptive scheduling provides predictable turnaround times, which is important for batch processing systems that must provide users with accurate job-completion times. **2)** This depends on the priority of the process and the scheduling policy. In general, a preemptive system containing a process executing an infinite loop will experience reduced throughput but will still be able to execute other processes periodically. A high-priority process that enters an infinite loop, however, may execute indefinitely if all other processes in the system have a lower priority. In general, preemptive systems are less affected by such programs than nonpreemptive systems. Operating systems typically deal with such situations by limiting the maximum time a process can use a processor.

8.4 Priorities

Schedulers often use priorities to determine how to schedule and dispatch processes. Priorities may be statically assigned or may change dynamically. Priorities quantify the relative importance of processes.

Static priorities remain fixed, so static-priority-based mechanisms are relatively easy to implement and incur relatively low overhead. Such mechanisms are not, however, responsive to changes in environment, even those that could increase throughput and reduce latency.

Dynamic priority mechanisms are responsive to change. For example, the system may want to increase the priority of a process that holds a key resource needed by a higher-priority process. After the first process relinquishes the resource, the system lowers the priority, so that the higher-priority process may execute. Dynamic priority schemes are more complex to implement and have greater overhead than static schemes. Hopefully, the overhead is justified by the increased responsiveness of the system.

In multiuser systems, an operating system must provide reasonable service to a large community of users but should also provide for situations in which a member of the user community needs special treatment. A user with an important job may be willing to pay a premium, i.e., to **purchase priority**, for a higher level of service. This extra charge is merited because resources may need to be withdrawn from other paying customers. If there were no extra charge, then all users would request the higher level of service.

Self Review

1. Why is it worthwhile to incur the higher cost and increased overhead of a dynamic priority mechanism?
2. Why would a dynamic scheduler choose to favor a low-priority process requesting an underutilized resource?

Ans: **1)** A carefully designed dynamic priority mechanism could yield a more responsive system than would a static priority mechanism. 2) The underutilized resource is likely to be available, allowing the low-priority process to complete and exit the system sooner than a higher-priority process waiting for a saturated resource.

8.5 Scheduling Objectives

A system designer must consider a variety of factors when developing a scheduling discipline, such as the type of system and the users' needs. For example, the scheduling discipline for a real-time system should differ from that for an interactive desktop system; users expect different results from these kinds of systems. Depending on the system, the user and designer might expect the scheduler to:

- *Maximize throughput.* A scheduling discipline should attempt to service the maximum number of processes per unit time.

- *Maximize the number of interactive processes receiving "acceptable" response times.*

- *Maximize resource utilization.* The scheduling mechanisms should keep the resources of the system busy.

- *Avoid indefinite postponement.* A process should not experience an unbounded wait time before or while receiving service.

- *Enforce priorities.* If the system assigns priorities to processes, the scheduling mechanism should favor the higher-priority processes.

- *Minimize overhead.* Interestingly, this is not generally considered to be one of the most important objectives. Overhead often results in wasted resources. But a certain portion of system resources effectively invested as overhead can greatly improve overall system performance.

- *Ensure predictability.* By minimizing the statistical variance in process response times, a system can guarantee that processes will receive predictable service levels (see the Operating Systems Thinking feature, Predictability).

A system can accomplish these goals in several ways. In some cases, the scheduler can prevent indefinite postponement of processes through aging—gradually increasing a process's priority as the process waits for service. Eventually, its priority becomes high enough that the scheduler selects that process to run.

The scheduler can increase throughput by favoring processes whose requests can be satisfied quickly, or whose completion frees other processes to run. One such strategy favors processes holding key resources. For example, a low-priority process may be holding a key resource that is required by a higher-priority process. If the resource is nonpreemptible, then the scheduler should give the low-priority process more execution time than it ordinarily would receive, so that it will release the key resource sooner. This technique is called **priority inversion**, because the relative priorities of the two processes are reversed so that the high-priority one will obtain the resource it requires to continue execution. Similarly, the scheduler may choose to favor a process that requests underutilized resources, because the system will be more likely to satisfy this process's requests in a shorter period of time.

Many of these goals conflict with one another, making scheduling a complex problem. For example, the best way to minimize response times is to have sufficient resources available whenever they are needed. The price for this strategy is that overall resource utilization will be poor. In real-time systems, fast, predictable responses are crucial, and resource utilization is less important. In other types of systems, the economics often makes effective resource utilization imperative.

Despite the differences in goals among systems, many scheduling disciplines exhibit similar properties:

- **Fairness**. A scheduling discipline is fair if all similar processes are treated the same, and no process can suffer indefinite postponement due to scheduling issues (see the Operating Systems Thinking feature, Fairness).

- **Predictability**. A given process always should run in about the same amount of time under similar system loads.

- **Scalability**. System performance should degrade gracefully (i.e., it should not immediately collapse) under heavy loads.

Operating Systems Thinking

Predictability

Predictability is as important in your everyday life as it is in computers. What would you do if you stopped for a red traffic light, and the light stayed red for a long time, much longer than any red light delay you had ever experienced. You would probably become annoyed and fidgety, and after waiting for what you thought was a reasonable amount of time; you might be inclined to go through the light, a potentially dangerous action.

Similarly, you have a sense of how long common tasks should take to perform on your computer. It is challenging for operating systems to ensure predictability, especially given that the load on a system can vary considerably based on the system load and the nature of the tasks being performed. Predictability is especially important for interactive users who demand prompt, consistent response times. Predictability is also important for real-time jobs, where human lives may be at stake (we discuss real-time scheduling in Section 8.9, Real-Time Scheduling). We discuss predictability issues throughout the book.

Self Review

1. How do the goals of reducing the variance in response times and enforcing priorities conflict?
2. Is scheduling overhead always "wasteful"?

Ans: **1)** In preemptive systems, high-priority processes can preempt lower-priority ones at any time, thereby increasing the variance in response times. **2)** No, the overhead incurred by effective scheduling operations can increase resource utilization.

8.6 Scheduling Criteria

To realize a system's scheduling objectives, the scheduler should consider process behavior. A **processor-bound** process tends to use all the processor time that the system allocates for it. An **I/O-bound** process tends to use the processor only briefly before generating an I/O request and relinquishing it. Processor-bound processes spend most of their time using the processor; I/O-bound processes spend most of their time waiting for external resources (e.g., printers, disk drives, network connections, etc.) to service their requests, and only nominal time using processors.

A scheduling discipline might also consider whether a process is batch or interactive. A **batch process** contains work for the system to perform without interacting with the user. An **interactive process** requires frequent inputs from the user. The system should provide good response times to an interactive process, whereas a batch process generally can suffer reasonable delays. Similarly, a scheduling discipline should be sensitive to the urgency of a process. An overnight batch process

Operating Systems Thinking

Fairness

How many times have you expressed annoyance saying, "That's not fair!" You have probably heard the expression, "Life is not fair." We all know what fairness is and most people would agree that it is a "good thing" but not universally achieved. We discuss fairness issues in many chapters throughout this book. We will see priority-based scheduling strategies that yield good performance for most users, processes, threads, I/O requests and the like, but do so at the expense of other users, processes, threads and I/O requests that wind up being mistreated. "That's not fair," you say, yet it is hard to ignore how these strategies achieve the system's objectives, such as improving overall system performance.

Operating systems must keep fairness in mind, but always in the context of other considerations. Fairness issues are particularly important in designing resource scheduling strategies, as we will see when we investigate processor scheduling in this chapter and disk scheduling in Chapter 12, Disk Performance Optimization.

does not require immediate responses. A real-time process control system that monitors a gasoline refinery must be responsive, possibly to prevent an explosion.

When the second edition of this book was published, users interacted with processes by issuing trivial requests using a keyboard. In this environment, a scheduler could favor an interactive process with little effect on other processes, because the time required to service interactive processes (e.g., by displaying text) was nominal. As computers became more powerful, system designers and application programmers included features such as graphics and GUIs to improve user-friendliness. Although some systems still use text-based interfaces, most of today's users interact via GUIs, using a mouse to perform actions such as opening, resizing, dragging and closing windows. Users expect systems to respond quickly so that these actions produce smooth movement. Unlike text display, this can be a computationally intensive task requiring the system to redraw the screen many times per second. Favoring these interactive processes can significantly reduce the level of service provided to other processes in the system. In the case of a batch process, this temporary reduction in service may be acceptable, though perhaps not for processes that execute in real time (e.g., multimedia applications).

In a system that employs priorities, the scheduler should favor processes with higher priorities. Schedulers can base their decisions on how frequently a higher priority process has preempted a lower-priority one. Under some disciplines, frequently preempted processes receive less favored treatment. This is because the process's short runtime before preemption does not justify the overhead incurred by a context switch each time the process is dispatched. One can argue to the contrary that such processes should receive more favored treatment to make up for previous "mistreatment."

Preemptive scheduling policies often maintain information about how much real execution time each process has received. Some designers believe a process that has received little execution time should be favored. Others believe a process that has received much execution time could be near completion and should be favored to help it reach completion, free its resources for other processes to use and exit the system as soon as possible. Similarly, a scheduler may maintain an estimate of how much time remains before a process completes. It is easy to prove that average waiting times can be minimized by running those processes first that require the minimum runtime until completion. Unfortunately, a system rarely knows exactly how much more time each process needs to complete.

Self Review

1. Are interactive processes generally processor bound or I/O bound? How about batch processes?
2. The scheduler rarely knows exactly how much more time each process needs to complete. Consider a system that schedules processes based on this estimation. How can processes abuse this policy?

Ans: **1)** Interactive processes often wait for input from users, so they are generally I/O bound, but an interactive process could certainly enter a phase during which it is primarily processor bound. Batch processes do not interact with users and are often processor bound. Batch processes that require frequent access to disk or other I/O devices are I/O bound. **2)** Processes would tend to underestimate their times to completion to receive favored treatment from the scheduler.

8.7 Scheduling Algorithms

In previous sections we discussed scheduling policies, which specify the goal of the scheduler (e.g., maximizing throughput or enforcing priorities). In the subsections that follow we discuss scheduling algorithms that determine at runtime which process runs next. These algorithms decide when and for how long each process runs; they make choices about preemptibility, priorities, running time, time-to-completion, fairness and other process characteristics. As we will see, some systems require the use of a particular type of scheduler (e.g., real-time systems typically require preemptive, priority-based schedulers). Others rely on process behavior when making scheduler decisions (e.g., favoring I/O-bound processes).

8.7.1 First-In-First-Out (FIFO) Scheduling

Perhaps the simplest scheduling algorithm is **first-in-first-out (FIFO)**, also called first-come-first-served (FCFS) (Fig. 8.2). Processes are dispatched according to their arrival time at the ready queue. FIFO is nonpreemptive—once a process has a processor, the process runs to completion. FIFO is fair in that it schedules processes according to their arrival times, so all processes are treated equally, but somewhat unfair because long processes make short processes wait, and unimportant processes make important processes wait. FIFO is not useful in scheduling interactive processes because it cannot guarantee short response times.

FIFO is rarely used as a master scheme in today's systems, but it is often found within other schemes. For example, many scheduling schemes dispatch processes according to priority, but processes with the same priority are dispatched in FIFO order.

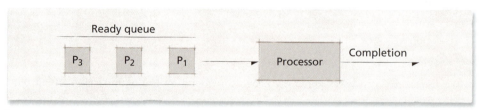

Figure 8.2 | *First-in-first-out scheduling.*

Self Review

1. Can indefinite postponement occur in a system that uses a FIFO scheduler? Assume that all processes eventually run to completion (i.e., no process enters an infinite loop).
2. (T/F) FIFO scheduling is rarely found in today's systems.

Ans: **1)** No, indefinite postponement cannot occur, because arriving processes must enter at the back of the queue, meaning they cannot prevent already waiting processes from executing. **2)** False. FIFO can be found within many of today's scheduling algorithms (e.g., priority-based schedulers that dispatch processes with the same priority in FIFO order).

8.7.2 Round-Robin (RR) Scheduling

In **round-robin (RR)** scheduling (Fig. 8.3), processes are dispatched FIFO but are given a limited amount of processor time called a **time slice** or a **quantum**.[8] If a process does not complete before its quantum expires, the system preempts it and gives the processor to the next waiting process. The system then places the preempted process at the back of the ready queue. In Fig. 8.3, process P_1 is dispatched to a processor, where it executes either until completion, in which case it exits the system, or until its time slice expires, at which point it is preempted and placed at the tail of the ready queue. The scheduler then dispatches process P_2.

Round-robin is effective for interactive environments in which the system needs to guarantee reasonable response times. The system can minimize preemption overhead through efficient context-switching mechanisms and by keeping waiting processes in main memory.

Like FIFO, round-robin is commonly found within more sophisticated processor scheduling algorithms but is rarely the master scheme. As we will see throughout this section, many more sophisticated scheduling algorithms degenerate to either FIFO or round-robin when all processes have the same priority. For this reason, FIFO and round-robin are two of the three scheduling algorithms required by the POSIX specification for real-time systems (we discuss real-time scheduling in Section 8.9, Real-Time Scheduling).[9]

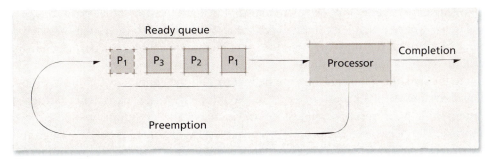

Figure 8.3 | *Round-robin scheduling.*

Selfish Round-Robin

Kleinrock discussed a variant of round-robin called **selfish round-robin (SRR)** that uses aging to gradually increase process priorities over time.[10] In this scheme, as each process enters the system, it first resides in a holding queue, where it ages until the its priority reaches the level of processes in the active queue. At this point, it is placed in the active queue and scheduled round-robin with other processes in the queue. The scheduler dispatches only processes in the active queue, meaning that older processes are favored over those that have just entered the system.

In SRR, a process's priority increases at a rate a while in the holding queue, and at a rate b, where $b \leq a$, in the active queue. When $b < a$, processes in the holding queue age at a higher rate than those in the active queue, so they will eventually enter the active queue and contend for the processor. Tuning the parameters a and b impacts how a process's age affects average latency and throughput. For example, as a becomes much larger than b, then processes that enter the system will spend little, if any, time in the holding queue. If $b << a$, then processes spend an insignificant amount of time in the holding queue, so SRR degenerates to round-robin. If $b = a$, every process in the system ages at the same rate, so SRR degenerates to FIFO. Exercise 8.23 investigates some properties of the SRR scheme.

Quantum Size

Determination of quantum size, q, is critical to the effective operation of a computer system with preemptive scheduling.[11] Should the quantum be large or small? Should it be fixed or variable? Should it be the same for all processes, or should it be determined separately for each process?

First, let us consider the behavior of the system as the quantum gets either extremely large or extremely small. As the quantum gets large, processes tend to receive as much time as they need to complete, so the round-robin scheme degenerates to FIFO. As the quantum gets small, context-switching overhead dominates; performance eventually degrades to the point that the system spends most of its time context switching with little, if any, useful work accomplished.

Just where between zero and infinity should the quantum be set? Consider the following experiment. Suppose a circular dial is marked with values between $q = 0$ and $q = c$, where c is an extremely large value. We begin with the dial positioned at zero. As we turn the dial, the quantum for the system increases. Assume that the system is operational and there are many interactive processes. As we initially rotate the dial, the quantum sizes are near zero, and the context-switching overhead consumes most of the processor's cycles. The interactive users experience a sluggish system with poor response times. As we increase the quantum, response times improve. The percentage of processor consumed by overhead is small enough that the processes receive some processor service, but response times are still not as fast as each user might prefer.

As we turn the dial more, response times continue to improve. Eventually, we reach a quantum size for which most of the interactive processes receive prompt responses from the system, but it is still not clear if the quantum setting is optimal. We turn the dial a bit further, and response times become slightly better. As we continue to turn the dial, response times start to become sluggish again. The quantum, as it gets larger, eventually becomes large enough for each process to run to completion upon receiving the processor. The scheduling is degenerating to FIFO, in which longer processes make shorter ones wait, and the average waiting time increases as the longer processes run to completion before yielding the processor.

Consider the supposedly optimal value of the quantum that yielded good response times. It is a small fraction of a second. Just what does this quantum represent? It is large enough so that the vast majority of interactive requests require less time than the duration of the quantum. When an interactive process begins executing, it normally uses the processor only briefly—just long enough to generate an I/O request, then block—at which point the process then yields the processor to the next process. The quantum is larger than this compute-until-I/O time. Each time a process obtains the processor, there is great likelihood that the process will run until it generates an I/O request. This maximizes I/O utilization and provides relatively rapid response times for interactive processes. It does so with minimal impact to processor-bound processes, which continue to get the lion's share of processor time because I/O-bound processes block soon after executing.

Just what is the optimal quantum in actual seconds? Clearly, the size varies from system to system and under different loads. It also varies from process to process, but our particular experiment is not geared to measuring differences in processes.

In Linux, the default quantum assigned to a process is 100ms, but can vary from 10 to 200ms, depending on process priority and behavior. High-priority and I/O-bound processes receive a larger quantum than low-priority and processor-bound processes.[12] In Windows XP, the default quantum assigned to a process is an architecture-specific value equalling 20ms on most systems. This value can vary depending on whether the process executes in the foreground or background of the GUI.[13]

When all processes are processor bound, the additional overhead detracts from system performance. However, even when only processor-bound processes are active, preemption still is useful. For example, consider that processor-bound processes could be controlling a real-time, mission critical system—it would be devastating if a process entered an infinite loop or even a phase in which it demanded more processor time than expected. More simply, many processor-bound systems support occasional interactive processes, so preemption is needed to ensure that arriving interactive processes receive good response times.

Self Review

1. Imagine turning the quantum dial for a system that contains only I/O-bound processes. After a point $q = c$, increasing the quantum value results in little, if any, change in system performance. What does point c represent, and why is there no change in system performance when $q > c$?
2. The text describes an optimal quantum value that enables each I/O-bound process to execute just long enough to generate an I/O request, then block. Why is this difficult to implement?

Ans: **1)** This point would be the longest period of computation between I/O requests for any processes in the system. Increasing the value of q past c does not affect any processes, because each process blocks before its quantum expires, so the processes cannot take advantage of the additional processor time allocated to them. **2)** In the general case, it is impossible to predict the path of execution a program will take, meaning that the system cannot accurately determine when a process will generate I/O. Therefore, the optimal quantum size is difficult to determine, because it is different for each process and can vary over time.

8.7.3 Shortest-Process-First (SPF) Scheduling

Shortest-process-first (SPF) is a nonpreemptive scheduling discipline in which the scheduler selects the waiting process with the smallest estimated run-time-to-completion. SPF reduces average waiting time over FIFO.[14] The waiting times, however, have a larger variance (i.e., are more unpredictable) than FIFO, especially for large processes.

SPF favors short processes at the expense of longer ones. Many designers advocate that the shorter the process, the better the service it should receive. Other designers disagree, because this strategy does not incorporate priorities (as measured by the importance of a process). Interactive processes, in particular, tend to be "shorter" than processor-bound processes, so this discipline would seem to still provide good interactive response times. The problem is that it is nonpreemptive, so, in general, arriving interactive processes will not receive prompt service.

SPF selects processes for service in a manner ensuring the next one will complete and leave the system as soon as possible. This tends to reduce the number of waiting processes and also the number of processes waiting behind large processes. As a result, SPF can minimize the average waiting time of processes as they pass through the system.

A key problem with SPF is that it requires precise knowledge of how long a process will run, and this information usually is not available. Therefore, SPF must rely on user- or system-supplied run-time estimates. In production environments where the same processes run regularly, the system may be able to maintain reasonable runtime heuristics. In development environments, however, the user rarely knows how long a process will execute.

Another problem with relying on user process duration estimates is that users may supply small (perhaps inaccurate) estimates so that the system will give their programs higher priority. However, the scheduler can be designed to remove this temptation. For example, if a process runs longer than estimated, the system could terminate it and reduce the priority of that user's other processes, even invoking penalties. A second method is to run the process for the estimated time plus a small percentage extra, then "shelve" it (i.e., preserve it in its current form) so that the system may restart it at a later time.[15]

SPF derives from a discipline called short job first (SJF), which might have worked well scheduling jobs in factories but clearly is inappropriate for low-level scheduling in operating systems. SPF, like FIFO, is nonpreemptive and thus not suitable for environments in which reasonable response times must be guaranteed.

Self Review

1. Why is SPF more desirable than FIFO when system throughput is a primary system objective?
2. Why is SPF inappropriate for low-level scheduling in today's operating systems?

Ans: **1)** SPF reduces average wait times, which increases throughput. **2)** SPF does not provide processes with fast response times, which is essential in today's user-friendly, multiprogrammed, interactive systems.

8.7.4 Highest-Response-Ratio-Next (HRRN) Scheduling

Brinch Hansen developed the **highest-response-ratio-next (HRRN)** policy that corrects some of the weaknesses in SPF, particularly the excessive bias against longer processes and the excessive favoritism toward short processes. HRRN is a nonpreemptive scheduling discipline in which each process's priority is a function not only of its service time but also of its time spent waiting for service.[16] Once a process obtains it, the process runs to completion. HRRN calculates dynamic priorities according to the formula

$$\text{priority} = \frac{\text{time waiting} + \text{service time}}{\text{service time}}$$

Because the service time appears in the denominator, shorter processes receive preference. However, because the waiting time appears in the numerator, longer processes that have been waiting will also be given favorable treatment. This technique is similar to aging and prevents the scheduler from indefinitely postponing processes.

Self Review

1. (T/F) With HRRN scheduling, short processes are always scheduled before long ones.
2. Process P_1 has declared a service time of 5 seconds and has been waiting for 20 seconds. Process P_2 has declared a service time of 3 seconds and has been waiting for 9 seconds. If the system uses HRRN, which process will execute first?

Ans: **1)** False. The longer a process waits, the more likely it will be scheduled before shorter processes. **2)** In this case, process P_1 has a priority of 5 and P_2 has a priority of 4, so the system executes P_1 first.

8.7.5 Shortest-Remaining-Time (SRT) Scheduling

Shortest-remaining-time (SRT) scheduling is the preemptive counterpart of SPF that attempts to increase throughput by servicing small arriving processes. SRT was effective for job-processing systems that received a stream of incoming jobs, but it is no longer useful in most of today's operating systems. In SRT, the scheduler selects the process with the smallest estimated run-time-to-completion. In SPF, once a process begins executing, it runs to completion. In SRT, a newly arriving process with a shorter estimated run-time preempts a running process with a longer run-time-to-completion. Again, SRT requires estimates of future process behavior to be effective, and the designer must account for potential user abuse of this system scheduling strategy.

The algorithm must maintain information about the elapsed service time of the running process and perform occasional preemptions. Newly arriving processes with short run-times execute almost immediately. Longer processes, however, have an even longer mean waiting time and variance of waiting times than in SPF. These factors contribute to a larger overhead in SRT than SPF.

The SRT algorithm offers minimum wait times in theory, but in certain situations, due to preemption overhead, SPF might perform better. For example, consider a system in which a running process is almost complete and a new process with a small estimated service time arrives. Should the running process be preempted? The SRT discipline would perform the preemption, but this may not be the optimal choice. One solution is to guarantee that a running process is no longer preemptible when its remaining run time reaches a low-end threshold.

A similar problem arises when a newly arriving process requires slightly less time to complete than the running process. Although the algorithm would correctly preempt the running process, this may not be the optimal policy. For example, if the preemption overhead is greater than the difference in service times between the two processes, preemption results in poorer performance.

As these examples illustrate, the operating systems designer must carefully weigh the overhead of resource-management mechanisms against the anticipated benefits. Also we see that relatively simple scheduling policies can yield poor performance for subtle reasons.

Self Review

1. Is SRT an effective processor scheduling algorithm for interactive systems?
2. Why is SRT an ineffective scheduling algorithm for real-time processes?

Ans: **1)** At first glance, SRT may seem to be an effective algorithm for interactive processes if the tasks performed before issuing I/O are short in duration. However, SRT determines priority based on the run-time-to-completion, not the run-time-to-I/O. Some interactive processes, such as a shell, execute for the lifetime of the session, which would place the shell at the lowest priority level. **2)** SRT can result in a large variance of response times, whereas real-time processes require a small variance in response times to ensure that they will always complete their tasks within a particular period of time.

8.7.6 Multilevel Feedback Queues

When a process obtains a processor, especially when the process has not as yet had a chance to establish a behavior pattern (e.g., how long it typically runs before generating an I/O request, or which portions of memory the process is currently favoring), the scheduler cannot determine the precise amount of processor time the process will require. I/O-bound processes normally use the processor only briefly before generating an I/O request. Processor-bound processes might use the processor for hours at a time if the system makes it available on a nonpreemptible basis. A scheduling algorithm should typically favor short processes, favor I/O-bound processes to get good I/O device utilization and good interactive response times and should determine the nature of a process as quickly as possible and schedule the process accordingly.

Multilevel feedback queues (Fig. 8.4) help accomplish these goals.[17] A new process enters the queuing network at the tail of the highest queue. The process progresses through that queue in FIFO order until the process obtains a processor. If the process completes its execution, or if it relinquishes the processor to wait for I/O completion or the completion of some other event, exits the queuing network. If a process's quantum expires before the process voluntarily relinquishes the processor, the system places the process at the tail of the next lower-level queue. As long as the process uses the full quantum provided at each level, it continues to move to the tail of the next lower queue. Usually there is some bottom-level queue through which the

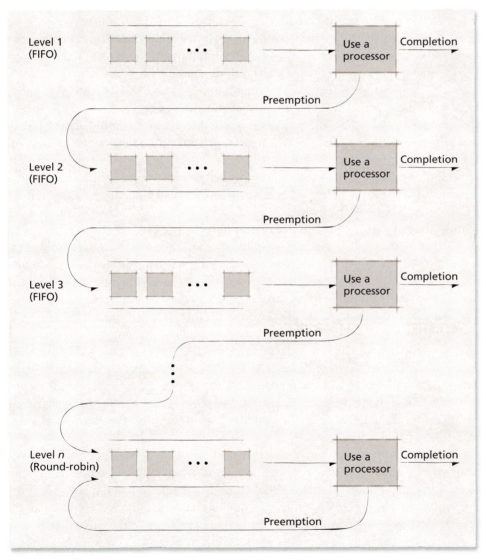

Figure 8.4 | *Multilevel feedback queues.*

process circulates round-robin until it completes. The process that next gets a processor is the one at the head of the highest nonempty queue in the multilevel feedback queue. A running process is preempted by one arriving in a higher queue.

In this system, a process in a lower queue can suffer indefinite postponement, if a higher queue always contains at least one process. This can occur in systems that have a high rate of incoming processes to be serviced, or in which there are several I/O-bound processes consuming their quanta.

In many multilevel feedback schemes, the scheduler increases a process's quantum size as the process moves to each lower-level queue. Thus, the longer a process has been in the queuing network, the larger the quantum it receives each time it obtains the processor. We will soon see why this is appropriate.

Let us examine the treatment that processes receive by considering how this discipline responds to different process types. Multilevel feedback queues favor I/O-bound processes and other processes that need only small bursts of processor time, because they enter the network with high priority and obtain a processor quickly. The discipline chooses for the first queue a quantum large enough so that the vast majority of I/O-bound processes (and interactive processes) issue an I/O request before that quantum expires. When a process requests I/O, it leaves the queuing network, having received the desired favored treatment. The process reenters the network when it next becomes *ready*.

Now consider a processor-bound process. The process enters the network with high priority, and the system places it in the highest-level queue. At this point the queuing network does not "know" whether the process is processor bound or I/O bound—the network's goal is to decide this quickly. The process obtains the processor quickly, uses its full quantum, its quantum expires, and the scheduler moves the process to the next lower queue. Now the process has a lower priority, and incoming processes obtain the processor first. This means that interactive processes will still continue to receive good response times, even as many processor-bound processes sink lower in the queuing network. Eventually, the processor-bound process does obtain the processor, receives a larger quantum than in the highest queue and again uses its full quantum. The scheduler then places the process at the tail of the next-lower queue. The process continues moving to lower queues, waits longer between time slices and uses its full quantum each time it gets the processor (unless preempted by an arriving process). Eventually, the processor-bound process arrives at the lowest-level queue, where it circulates round-robin with other processor-bound processes until it completes.

Multilevel feedback queues are therefore ideal for separating processes into categories based on their need for the processor. When a process exits the queuing network, it can be "stamped" with the identity of the lowest-level queue in which it resided. When the process reenters the queuing network, the system can place it directly in the queue in which it last completed operation—the scheduler here is employing the heuristic that a process's recent-past behavior is a good indicator of its near-future behavior. This technique allows the scheduler to avoid placing a returning processor-bound process into the higher-level queues, where it would interfere with service to high-priority short processes or to I/O-bound processes.

Unfortunately, if the scheduler always places a returning process in the lowest queue it occupied the last time it was in the system, the scheduler is unable to respond to changes in a process's behavior (e.g., the process may be transitioning from being processor bound to being I/O bound). The scheduler can solve this problem by recording not only the identity of the lowest-level queue in which the process resided, but also the amount of its quantum that was unused during its last execution. If the process consumes its entire quantum, then it is placed in a lower-level queue (if one is available). If the process issues an I/O request before its quantum expires, it can be placed in a higher-level queue. If the process is entering a new phase in which it will change from being processor bound to I/O bound, initially it may experience some sluggishness as the system determines that its nature is changing, but the scheduling algorithm will respond to this change.

Another way to make the system responsive to changes in a process's behavior is to allow the process to move up one level in the feedback queuing network each time it voluntarily relinquishes the processor before its quantum expires. Similarly, the scheduler—when assigning a priority—can consider the time a process has spent waiting for service. The scheduler can age the process by promoting it and placing it in the next higher queue after it has spent a certain amount of time waiting for service.

One common variation of the multilevel feedback queuing mechanism is to have a process circulate round-robin several times through each queue before it moves to the next lower queue. Also, the number of cycles through each queue may be increased as the process moves to the next lower queue. This variation attempts to further refine the service that the scheduler provides to I/O-bound versus processor-bound processes.

Multilevel feedback queuing is a good example of an **adaptive mechanism**, i.e., one that responds to the changing behavior of the system it controls.[18, 19] Adaptive mechanisms generally require more overhead than nonadaptive ones, but the resulting sensitivity to changes in the system makes the system more responsive and helps justify the increased overhead. As we discuss in Section 20.5.2, Process Scheduling, the Linux process scheduler employs an adaptive mechanism borrowing from multilevel feedback queues. [*Note:* In the literature, the terms "process scheduling" and "processor scheduling" have been used equivalently.]

Self Review

1. What scheduling objectives should be evaluated when choosing the number of levels to use in a multilevel feedback queue?
2. Why are adaptive mechanisms desirable in today's schedulers?

Ans: **1)** One major objective is the variance in response times. Increasing the number of levels can cause processor-bound processes to wait longer, which increases the variance in response times. Another objective to consider is resource utilization. As the number of levels increases, many processes can execute and issue I/Os before their quanta expire, resulting in effective use of both processor time and I/O devices. **2)** In today's computers, many applications can be both computationally intensive and I/O bound. For example, a streaming video player must perform I/O to retrieve video clip data from a remote server, then must perform computationally intensive operations to decode and display the video images. Similarly, an interactive game such as a flight simulator must respond to user input (e.g., joystick movements) while rendering complicated 3D scenes. Adaptive mechanisms enable the system to provide alternate responses to these processes as they alternate between I/O-bound and processor-bound behavior.

8.7.7 Fair Share Scheduling

Systems generally support various sets of related processes. For example, UNIX (and other multiuser) systems group processes that belong to an individual user. **Fair share scheduling (FSS)** supports scheduling across such sets of processes.[20, 21, 22, 23] Fair share scheduling enables a system to ensure fairness across groups of processes by restricting each group to a certain subset of the system resources. In the UNIX environment, for example, FSS was developed specifically to "give a pre-specified rate of system resources ... to a related set of users."[24]

Let us consider an example in which fair share scheduling would be useful. Imagine a research group whose members all share one multiuser system. They are divided into two groups. The principal investigators—of which there are few—use the system to perform important, computationally intensive work such as running simulations. The research assistants—of which there are many—use the system for less intensive work such as aggregating data and printing results. Now imagine that many research assistants and only one principal investigator are using the system. The research assistants may consume a majority of the processor time, to the detriment of the principal investigator, who must perform the more important work. However, if the system allowed the research assistants group to use only 25 percent of the processor time and allowed the principal investigators group to use 75 percent, the principal investigator would not suffer such service degradation. In this way, fair share scheduling ensures that the performance of a process is affected only by the population of its process group, and not by the user population as a whole.

Let us investigate how fair share scheduling operates in a UNIX system. Normally, UNIX considers resource-consumption rates across all processes (Fig. 8.5). Under FSS, however, the system apportions the resources to various **fair share groups** (Fig. 8.6). It distributes resources not used by one fair share group to other fair share groups in proportion to their relative needs.

UNIX commands establish fair share groups and associate specific users with them.[25] For the purpose of this discussion, assume that UNIX uses a priority round-robin process scheduler.[26] Each process has a priority, and the scheduler associates processes of a given priority with a priority queue for that value. The process scheduler selects the ready process at the head of the highest-priority queue. Processes

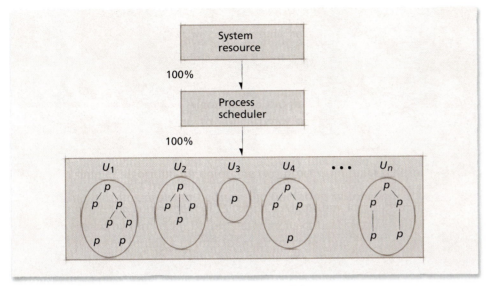

Figure 8.5 | Standard UNIX process scheduler. The scheduler grants the processor to users, each of whom may have many processes. (Property of AT&T Archives. Reprinted with permission of AT&T.)[27]

within a given priority are scheduled round-robin. A process requiring further service after being preempted receives a lower priority. Kernel priorities are high and apply to processes executing in the kernel; user priorities are lower. Disk events receive higher priority than terminal events. The scheduler assigns the user priority as the ratio of recent processor usage to elapsed real time; the lower the elapsed time, the higher the priority.

The fair share groups are prioritized by how close they are to achieving their specified resource-utilization goals. Groups doing poorly receive higher priority; groups doing well, lower priority.

Self Review

1. In FSS, why should groups that are not achieving their resource-utilization goals be given higher priority?
2. How does FSS differ from standard process scheduling disciplines?

Ans: **1)** Processes that are using fewer resources than specified by their resource-utilization goals are probably suffering from low levels of service. By increasing their priority, the system ensures that these processes execute long enough to use their required resources. **2)** FSS apportions resources to groups of processes, whereas standard process schedulers allow all processes to compete for all resources on an equal footing.

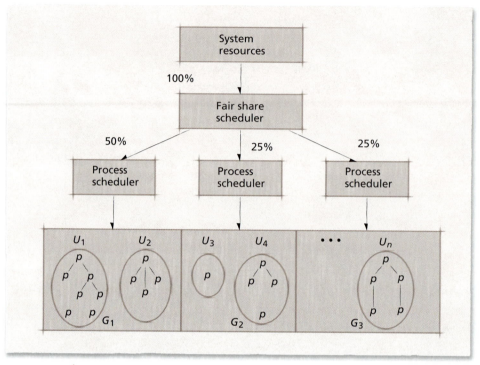

Figure 8.6 | *Fair share scheduler. The fair share scheduler divides system resource capacity into portions, which are then allocated by process schedulers assigned to various fair share groups. (Property of AT&T Archives. Reprinted with permission of AT&T.)*[28]

8.8 Deadline Scheduling

In **deadline scheduling**, certain processes are scheduled to be completed by a specific time or deadline. These processes may have high value if delivered on time and little or no value otherwise.[29, 30, 31]

Deadline scheduling is complex. First, the user must supply the precise resource requirements in advance to ensure that the process is completed by its deadline. Such information is rarely available. Second, the system should execute the deadline process without severely degrading service to other users. Also, the system must carefully plan its resource requirements through to the deadline. This may be difficult, because new processes may arrive, making unpredictable demands. Finally, if many deadline processes are active at once, scheduling could become extremely complex.

The intensive resource management that deadline scheduling requires may generate substantial overhead (see the Operating Systems Thinking feature, Intensity of Resource Management vs. Relative Resource Value). Net consumption of system resources may be high, degrading service to other processes.

As we will see in the next section, deadline scheduling is important to real-time process scheduling. Dertouzos demonstrated that when all processes can meet their deadlines regardless of the order in which they are executed, it is optimal to schedule processes with the earliest deadlines first.[32] However, when the system becomes overloaded, the system must allocate significant processor time to the scheduler to determine the proper order in which to execute processes so that they meet their deadlines. Recent research focuses on the speed[33, 34] or number[35] of processors the system must allocate to the scheduler so that deadlines are met.

Self Review

1. Why is it important for the user to specify in advance the resources a process needs?
2. Why is it difficult to meet a process's stated deadline?

Ans: **1)** This allows the scheduler to ensure that resources will be available for the process so that it can complete its task before its deadline. **2)** New processes may arrive and place unpredictable demands on the system that prevent it from meeting a process's deadline, resources could fail, the process could dramatically change its behavior and so on.

8.9 Real-Time Scheduling

A primary objective of the scheduling algorithms that we presented in Section 8.7, Scheduling Algorithms, is to ensure high resource utilization. Processes that must execute periodically (such as once a minute) require different scheduling algorithms. For example, the unbounded wait times for SPF could be catastrophic for a process that checks the temperature of a nuclear reactor. Similarly, a system using SRT to schedule a process that plays a video clip could produce choppy playback. **Real-time scheduling** meets the needs of processes that must produce correct output by a certain time (i.e., that have a **timing constraint**).[36] A real-time process may divide its instructions into separate tasks, each of which must complete by a dead-

Operating Systems Thinking

Intensity of Resource Management vs. Relative Resource Value

Operating systems manage hardware and software resources. A recurring theme you will see throughout this book is that the intensity with which operating systems need to manage particular resources is proportional to the relative value of those resources, and to their scarcity and intensity of use. For example, the processor and high-speed cache memories are managed much more intensively than secondary storage and other I/O devices. The operating systems designer must be aware of trends that could affect the relative value of system resources and people time and must respond quickly to change.

line. Other real-time processes might perform a certain task periodically, such as updating the locations of planes in an air traffic control system. Real-time schedulers must ensure that timing constraints are met (see the Mini Case Study, Real-Time Operating Systems).

Real-time scheduling disciplines are classified by how well they meet a process's deadlines. **Soft real-time scheduling** ensures that real-time processes are dispatched before other processes in the system, but does not guarantee which, if any, will meet their timing constraints.[37, 38] Soft real-time scheduling is commonly implemented in personal computers, where smooth playback of multimedia is desirable, but occasional choppiness under heavy system loads is tolerated. Soft real-time systems can benefit from high interrupting clock rates to prevent the system from getting "stuck" executing one process while others miss their deadlines. However, the

Mini Case Study

Real-Time Operating Systems

A real-time system differs from a standard system in that every operation must give results that are both correct and returned within a certain amount of time.[39] Real-time systems are used in time-critical applications such as monitoring sensors. They are often small, embedded systems. Real-time operating systems (RTOSs) must be carefully designed to achieve these goals. (Real-time process scheduling is discussed in Section 8.9, Real-Time Scheduling.)

The control program for the SAGE (Semi-Automatic Ground Environment) project may have been the first real-time operating system.[40, 41] SAGE was an Air Force project to defend against possible

bomber attacks in the Cold War.[42] Implemented in the end of the 1950s, this system integrated 56 IBM AN/FSQ-7 digital vacuum-tube computers that monitored data from radar systems across the country to track all planes in the United States airspace.[43, 44] It analyzed this information and directed the interceptor fighter planes, thus requiring real-time response.[45] The operating system to handle this task was the largest computer program of its time.[46]

In contrast, today's RTOSs aim for minimal size. There are many available, but QNX and VxWorks lead the field. QNX implements the POSIX standard APIs with its own microkernel and is tailored to embedded systems.

It also uses message passing for interprocess communication.[47] Similarly, VxWorks is a microkernel system that complies with the POSIX standard and is widely used in embedded systems.[48] QNX performs better than VxWorks on Intel x86 platforms,[49] but QNX was not available on other processors until version 6.1 (the current version is 6.2).[50] VxWorks, however, has concentrated on the PowerPC processor and has a history of cross-platform compatibility.[51] VxWorks is currently the most common RTOS for embedded systems.[52] Additional RTOSs include Windows CE .NET,[53] OS-9,[54] OSE,[55] and Linux distributions such as uCLinux.[56]

system can incur significant overhead if the interrupt rate is too high, resulting in poor performance or missed deadlines.[57]

Hard real-time scheduling guarantees that a process's timing constraints are always met. Each task specified by a hard real-time process must complete before its deadline; failing to do so could produce catastrophic results, including invalid work, system failure or even harm to the system's users.[58, 59] Hard real-time systems may contain **periodic processes** that perform their computations at regular time intervals (e.g., gathering air traffic control data every second) and **asynchronous processes** that execute in response to events (e.g., responding to high temperatures in a power plant's core).[60]

Static Real-Time Scheduling Algorithms

Static real-time scheduling algorithms do not adjust process priority over time. Because priorities are calculated only once, static real-time scheduling algorithms tend to be simple and incur little overhead. Such algorithms are limited because they cannot adjust to variable process behavior and depend on resources staying up and running to ensure that timing constraints are met.

Hard real-time systems tend to use static scheduling algorithms, because they incur low overhead and it is relatively easy to prove that each process's timing constraints will be met. The **rate-monotonic (RM)** algorithm, for example, is a preemptive, priority-based round-robin algorithm that increases a process's priority linearly (i.e., monotonically) with the frequency (i.e., the rate) with which it must execute. This static scheduling algorithm favors periodic processes that execute frequently.[61] The **deadline rate-monotonic** algorithm can be used when a periodic process specifies a deadline that is not equal to its period.[62]

Dynamic Real-Time Scheduling Algorithms

Dynamic real-time scheduling algorithms schedule processes by adjusting their priorities during execution, which can incur significant overhead. Some algorithms attempt to minimize the scheduling overhead by assigning static priorities to some processes and dynamic priorities to others.[63]

Earliest-deadline-first (EDF) is a preemptive scheduling algorithm that dispatches the process with the earliest deadline. If an arriving process has an earlier deadline than the running process, the system preempts the running process and dispatches the arriving process. The objective is to maximize throughput by satisfying the deadlines of the largest number of processes per unit time (analogous to the SRT algorithm) and minimize the average wait time (which prevents short processes from missing their deadlines while long processes execute). Dertouzos proved that, if a system provides hardware preemption (e.g., timer interrupts) and the real-time processes being scheduled are not interdependent, EDF minimizes the amount of time by which the "most tardy" process misses its deadline.[64] However, many real-time systems do not provide hardware preemption, so other algorithms must be employed.[65]

The **minimum-laxity-first** algorithm is similar to EDF but bases priority on a process's **laxity**. Laxity is a measure of a process's importance based on the amount of time until its deadline and the remaining execution time until its task (which may be periodic) has completed. Laxity is computed using the formula

$$L = D - (T + C),$$

where L is the laxity, D the process's deadline, T the current time and C the process's remaining execution time. For example, if the current time is 5, the deadline for a process is 9 and the process requires 3 units of time to complete, the laxity is 1. If a process has 0 laxity, it must be dispatched immediately or it will miss its deadline. Priorities in minimum-laxity-first are more accurate than those in EDF because they are determined by including the remaining processor time each process requires to complete its task. However, such information is often unavailable.[66]

Self Review

1. Why are most hard real-time scheduling algorithms static?

2. When does the minimum-laxity-first algorithm degenerate to EDF? Can this ever occur?

Ans: **1)** Hard real-time systems must guarantee that processes' deadlines are met. Static scheduling algorithms facilitate proving this property for a particular system and reduce the implementation overhead. **2)** The minimum-laxity-first algorithm degenerates to the EDF algorithm when C is identical for all processes at any given time. It is possible, though highly unlikely, that this would occur.

8.10   Java Thread Scheduling

As discussed in Section 4.6, Threading Models, operating systems provide various levels of support for threads. When scheduling a multithreaded process that implements user-level threads, the operating system is unaware that the process is multithreaded and therefore dispatches the process as one unit, requiring a user-level library to schedule its threads. If the system supports kernel-level threads, it may schedule each thread independently from others within the same process. Still other systems support scheduler activations that assign each process to a kernel-level thread that enables the process's user-level library to perform scheduling operations.

System designers must determine how to allocate quanta to threads, and in what order and with what priorities to schedule threads within a process. For example, a "fair-share" approach divides the quantum allocated to a process among its threads. This prevents a multithreaded process from receiving high levels of service simply by creating a large number of threads. Further, the order in which threads are executed can impact their performance if they rely on one another to continue their tasks. In this section, we present Java thread scheduling. Thread scheduling in Windows XP is discussed in Section 21.6.2, Thread Scheduling. The Linux scheduler (which dispatches both processes and threads) is discussed in Section 20.5.2, Process Scheduling.

One feature of the Java programming language and its virtual machine is that every Java applet or application is multithreaded. Each Java thread is assigned a priority in the range between `Thread.MIN_PRIORITY` (a constant of 1) and `Thread.MAX_PRIORITY` (a constant of 10). By default, each thread is given priority `Thread.NORM_PRIORITY` (a constant of 5). Each new thread inherits the priority of the thread that creates it.

Depending on the platform, Java implements threads in either user or kernel space (see Section 4.6, Threading Models).[67, 68] When implementing threads in user space, the Java runtime relies on **timeslicing** to perform preemptive thread scheduling. Without timeslicing, each thread in a set of equal-priority threads runs to completion, unless it leaves the *running* state and enters the *waiting, sleeping* or *blocked* state, or it is preempted by a higher-priority thread. With timeslicing, each thread receives a quantum during which it can execute.

The Java thread scheduler ensures that the highest-priority thread in the Java virtual machine is *running* at all times. If there are multiple threads at the priority level, those threads execute using round-robin. Figure 8.7 illustrates Java's multilevel priority queue for threads. In the figure, assuming a single-processor computer, threads A and B each execute for a quantum at a time in round-robin fashion until both threads complete execution. Next, thread C runs to completion. Threads D, E and F each execute for a quantum in round-robin fashion until they all complete execution. This process continues until all threads run to completion. Note that, depending on the operating system, arriving higher-priority threads could indefinitely postpone the execution of lower-priority ones.

A thread can call the `yield` method of class `Thread` to give other threads a chance to execute. Because the operating system preempts the current thread whenever a higher-priority one becomes *ready*, a thread cannot `yield` to a higher-priority thread. Similarly, `yield` always allows the highest-priority *ready* thread to run, so if all of the *ready* threads are of lower priority than the thread calling `yield`, the current thread will have the highest priority and will continue executing. Therefore, a thread `yields` to give threads of an equal priority a chance to run. On a timesliced system this is unnecessary, because threads of equal priority will each execute for their quantum (or until they lose the processor for some other reason), and other threads of equal priority will execute round-robin. Thus `yield` is appropriate for nontimesliced systems (e.g., early versions of Solaris[69]), in which a thread would ordinarily run to completion before another thread of equal priority would have an opportunity to run.

Self Review

1. Why does Java provide the `yield` method? Why would a programmer ever use `yield`?
2. (T/F) A Java thread of lower priority will never run while a thread of higher priority is *ready*.

Ans: **1)** Method `yield` allows the current thread to voluntarily release the processor and let a thread of equal priority execute. Because Java applications are designed to be portable and because the programmer cannot be certain that a particular platform supports timeslicing,

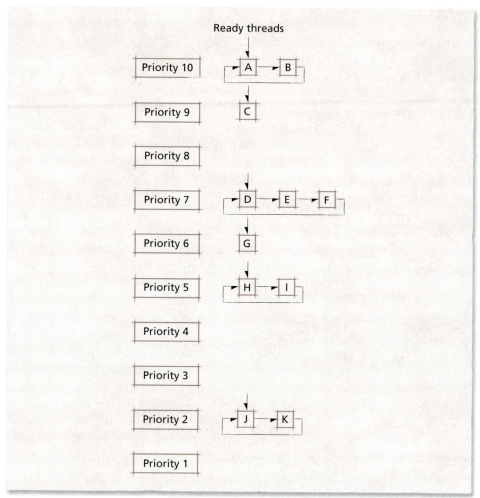

Figure 8.7 | Java thread priority scheduling.

programmers use `yield` to ensure that their applications execute properly on all platforms. **2)** True. Java schedulers will execute the highest-priority *ready* thread.

Web Resources

www.linux-tutorial.info/cgi-bin/dis-play.pl?85&0&0&0&3
This portion of the Linux tutorial describes process scheduling in Linux.

developer.apple.com/techpubs/mac/Processes/Pro-cesses-16.html
Describes process scheduling for the Apple Macintosh.

www.oreilly.com/catalog/linuxkernel/chapter/ch10.html
Contains the online version of O'Reilly's Linux kernel book. This page details process scheduling in Linux version 2.4.

www.javaworld.com/javaworld/jw-07-2002/jw-0703-java101.html
Describes thread scheduling in Java.

csl.cse.ucsc.edu/rt.shtml
Details the results of the real-time operating system scheduler research unit at the University of California, Santa Cruz.

www.ittc.ku.edu/kurt/
Describes the Kansas University real-time scheduler that uses a modified Linux kernel.

Summary

When a system has a choice of processes to execute, it must have a strategy—called a processor scheduling policy (or discipline)—for deciding which process to run at a given time. High-level scheduling—sometimes called job scheduling or long-term scheduling—determines which jobs the system allows to compete actively for system resources. The high-level scheduling policy dictates the degree of multiprogramming—the total number of processes in a system at a given time. After the high-level scheduling policy has admitted a job (which may contain one or more processes) to the system, the intermediate-level scheduling policy determines which processes shall be allowed to compete for a processor. This policy responds to short-term fluctuations in system load. A system's low-level scheduling policy determines which *ready* process the system will assign to a processor when one next becomes available. Low-level scheduling policies often assign a priority to each process, reflecting its importance—the more important a process, the more likely the scheduling policy is to select it to execute next.

A scheduling discipline can be preemptive or nonpreemptive. To prevent users from monopolizing the system (either maliciously or accidentally), preemptive schedulers set an interrupting clock or interval timer that periodically generates an interrupt. Priorities may be statically assigned or be changed dynamically during the course of execution.

When developing a scheduling discipline, a system designer must consider a variety of objectives, such as the type of system and the users' needs. These objectives may include maximizing throughput, maximizing the number of interactive users receiving "acceptable" response times, maximizing resource utilization, avoiding indefinite postponement, enforcing priorities, minimizing overhead and ensuring predictability of response times. To accomplish these goals, a system can use techniques such as aging processes and favoring processes whose requests can be satisfied quickly. Many scheduling disciplines exhibit fairness, predictability and scalability.

Operating system designers can use system objectives to determine the criteria on which scheduling decisions are made. Perhaps the most important concern is how a process uses the processor (i.e., whether it is processor bound or I/O bound). A scheduling discipline might also consider whether a process is batch or interactive. In a system that employs priorities, the scheduler should favor processes with higher priorities.

Schedulers employ algorithms that make choices about preemptibility, priorities, running time and other process characteristics. FIFO (also called FCFS) is a nonpreemptive algorithm that dispatches processes according to their arrival time at the ready queue. In round-robin (RR) scheduling, processes are dispatched FIFO but are given a limited amount of processor time called a time slice or a quantum. A variant of round-robin called selfish round-robin (SRR) initially places a process in a holding queue until its priority reaches the level of processes in the active queue, at which point, the process is placed in the active queue and scheduled round-robin with others in the queue. Determination of quantum size is critical to the effective operation of a computer system. The "optimal" quantum is large enough so that the vast majority of I/O-bound and interactive requests require less time than the duration of the quantum. The optimal quantum size varies from system to system and under different loads.

Shortest-process-first (SPF) is a nonpreemptive scheduling discipline in which the scheduler selects the waiting process with the smallest estimated run-time-to-completion. SPF reduces average waiting time over FIFO but increases the variance in response times. Shortest-remaining-time (SRT) scheduling is the preemptive counterpart of SPF that selects the process with the smallest estimated run-time-to-completion. The SRT algorithm offers minimum wait times in theory, but in certain situations, due to preemption overhead, SPF might actually perform better. Highest-response-ratio-next (HRRN) is a nonpreemptive scheduling discipline in which the priority of each process is a function not only of its service time but also of the amount of time it has been waiting for service.

Multilevel feedback queues allow a scheduler to dynamically adjust to process behavior. The process that gets a processor next is the one that reaches the head of the highest nonempty queue in the multilevel feedback queuing network. Processor-bound processes are placed at the lowest-level queue, and I/O-bound processes tend to be located in the higher-level queues. A running process is preempted by a process arriving in a higher queue. Multilevel feedback queuing is a good example of an adaptive mechanism.

Fair share scheduling (FSS) supports scheduling across related processes and threads. It enables a system to ensure fairness across groups of processes by restricting each group to a certain subset of system resources. In the UNIX environment, for example, FSS was developed specifically to "give a prespecified rate of system resources … to a related set of users."

In deadline scheduling, certain processes are scheduled to be completed by a specific time or deadline. These processes may have high value if delivered on time and be worthless otherwise. Deadline scheduling can be difficult to implement.

Real-time scheduling must repeatedly meet processes' deadlines as they execute. Soft real-time scheduling ensures that real-time processes are dispatched before other processes in the system. Hard real-time scheduling guarantees that a process's deadlines are met. Hard real-time processes must meet their deadlines; failing to do so could be catastrophic, resulting in invalid work, system failure or even harm to the system's users. The rate-monotonic (RM) algorithm is a static scheduling priority-based round-robin algorithm in which priorities are increase (monotonically) with the rate at which a process must be scheduled.

The earliest-deadline-first (EDF) is a preemptive scheduling algorithm that favors the process with the earliest deadline. The minimum-laxity-first algorithm is similar to EDF, but bases priority on a process's laxity, which measures the difference between the time a process requires to complete and the time remaining until that its deadline.

The operating system may dispatch a process's threads individually or it may schedule a multithreaded process as a unit, requiring user-level libraries to schedule their threads. System designers must determine how to allocate quanta to threads, in what order, and what priorities to assign in scheduling threads within a process. In Java, each thread is assigned a priority in the range 1–10. Depending on the platform, Java implements threads in either user or kernel space (see Section 4.6, Threading Models). When implementing threads in user space, the Java runtime relies on timeslicing to perform preemptive thread scheduling. The Java thread scheduler ensures that the highest-priority thread in the Java virtual machine is running at all times. If there are multiple threads at the same priority level, those threads execute using round-robin. A thread can call the `yield` method to give other threads of an equal priority a chance to run.

Key Terms

adaptive mechanism—Control entity that adjusts a system in response to its changing behavior.

admission scheduling—See high-level scheduling.

aging of priorities—Increasing a process's priority gradually, based on how long it has been in the system.

asynchronous real-time process—Real-time process that executes in response to events.

batch process—Process that executes without user interaction.

deadline rate-monotonic scheduling—Scheduling policy in real-time systems that meets a periodic process's deadline that does not equal its period.

deadline scheduling—Scheduling policy that assigns priority based on processes' completion deadlines to ensure that processes complete on time.

degree of multiprogramming—Total number of processes in main memory at a given time.

dispatcher—Entity that assigns a processor to a process.

dispatching—Act of assigning a processor to a process.

dynamic real-time scheduling algorithm—Scheduling algorithm that uses deadlines to assign priorities to processes throughout execution.

earliest-deadline-first (EDF)—Scheduling policy that gives a processor to the process with the closest deadline.

fairness—Property of a scheduling algorithm that treats all processes equally.

fair share group—Group of processes that receives a percentage of the processor time under a fair share scheduling (FSS) policy.

fair share scheduling (FSS)—Scheduling policy developed for AT&T's UNIX system that places processes in groups and assigns these groups a percentage of processor time.

first-in-first-out (FIFO)—Nonpreemptive scheduling policy that dispatches processes according to their arrival time in the ready queue.

job scheduling—See high-level scheduling.

hard real-time scheduling—Scheduling policy that ensures processes meet their deadlines.

highest-response-ratio-next (HRRN)—Scheduling policy that assigns priority based on a process's service time and the amount of time the process has been waiting.

high-level scheduling—Determining which jobs a system allows to compete actively for system resources.

interactive process—Process that requires user input as it executes.

intermediate-level scheduling—Determining which processes may enter the low-level scheduler to compete for a processor.

I/O-bound—Process that tends to use a processor for a short time before generating an I/O request and relinquishing a processor.

latency (process scheduling)—Time a task spends in a system before it is serviced.

laxity—Value determined by subtracting the sum of the current time and a process's remaining execution time from the process's deadline. This value decreases as a process nears its deadline.

long-term scheduling—See high-level scheduling.

low-level scheduling—Determining which process will gain control of a processor.

minimum-laxity-first—Scheduling policy that assigns higher priority to processes that will finish with minimal processor usage.

multilevel feedback queue—Process scheduling structure that groups processes of the same priority in the same round-robin queue. Processor-bound processes are placed in lower-priority queues because they are typically batch processes that do not require fast response times. I/O-bound processes, which exit the system quickly due to I/O, remain in high-priority queues. These processes often correspond to interactive processes that should experience fast response times.

nonpreemptive scheduling—Scheduling policy that does not allow the system to remove a processor from a process until that process voluntarily relinquishes its processor or runs to completion.

periodic real-time process—Real-time process that performs computation at a regular time interval.

predictability—Goal of a scheduling algorithm that ensures that a process takes the same amount of time to execute regardless of the system load.

preemptive scheduling—Scheduling policy that allows the system to remove a processor from a process.

priority—Measure of a process's or thread's importance used to determine the order and duration of execution.

processor-bound—Process that consumes its quantum when executing. These processes tend to be calculation intensive and issue few, if any, I/O requests.

processor scheduling discipline—See processor scheduling policy.

processor scheduling policy—Strategy used by a system to determine when and for how long to assign processors to processes.

purchase priority—to pay to receive higher priority in a system.

quantum—Amount of time that a process is allowed to run on a processor before the process is preempted.

rate-monotonic (RM) scheduling—Real-time scheduling policy that sets priority to a value that is proportional to the rate at which the process must be dispatched.

real-time scheduling—Scheduling policy that bases priority on timing constraints.

round-robin (RR) scheduling—Scheduling policy that permits each *ready* process to execute for at most one quantum per round. After the last process in the queue has executed once, the scheduler begins a new round by scheduling the first process in the queue.

scalability (scheduler)—Characteristic of a scheduler that ensures system performance degrades gracefully under heavy loads.

selfish round-robin (SRR) scheduling—Variant of round-robin scheduling in which processes age at different rates. Processes that enter the system are placed in a holding queue, where they wait until their priority is high enough for them to be placed in the active queue, in which processes compete for processor time.

shortest-process-first (SPF) scheduling—Nonpreemptive scheduling algorithm in which the scheduler selects a process with the smallest estimated run-time-to-completion and runs the process to completion.

shortest-remaining-time (SRT) scheduling—Preemptive version of SPF in which the scheduler selects a process with the smallest estimated remaining run-time-to-completion.

soft real-time scheduling—Scheduling policy that guarantees that real-time processes are scheduled with higher priority than non-real-time processes.

static real-time scheduling algorithm—Scheduling algorithm that uses timing constraints to assign fixed priorities to processes before execution.

throughput—Number of processes that complete per unit time.

time slice—See quantum.

timeslicing—Scheduling each process to execute for at most one quantum before preemption.

timing constraint—Time period during which a process (or subset of a process's instructions) must complete.

Exercises

8.1 Distinguish among the following three levels of schedulers.

    a. high-level scheduler

    b. intermediate-level scheduler

    c. dispatcher

8.2 Which level of scheduler should make a decision on each of the following questions?

    a. Which ready process should be assigned a processor when one becomes available?

    b. Which of a series of waiting batch processes that have been spooled to disk should next be initiated?

    c. Which processes should be temporarily suspended to relieve a short-term burden on the processor?

    d. Which temporarily suspended process that is known to be I/O bound should be activated to balance the multiprogramming mix?

8.3 Distinguish between a scheduling policy and a scheduling mechanism.

8.4 The following are common scheduling objectives.

    a. to be fair

    b. to maximize throughput

    c. to maximize the number of interactive users receiving acceptable response times

    d. to be predictable

    e. to minimize overhead

    f. to balance resource utilization

    g. to achieve a balance between response and utilization

    h. to avoid indefinite postponement

    i. to obey priorities

    j. to give preference to processes that hold key resources

    k. to give a lower grade of service to high overhead processes

    l. to degrade gracefully under heavy loads

Which of the preceding objectives most directly applies to each of the following?

    i. If a user has been waiting for an excessive amount of time, favor that user.

    ii. The user who runs a payroll job for a 1000-employee company expects the job to take about the same amount of time each week.

    iii. The system should admit processes to create a mix that will keep most devices busy.

    iv. The system should favor important processes.

    v. An important process arrives but cannot proceed because an unimportant process is holding the resources the important process needs.

    vi. During peak periods, the system should not collapse from the overhead it takes to manage a large number of processes.

    vii. The system should favor I/O-bound processes.

    viii. Context switches should execute as quickly as possible.

8.5 The following are common scheduling criteria.

    a. I/O boundedness of a process

    b. processor boundedness of a process

    c. whether the process is batch or interactive

    d. urgency of a fast response

    e. process priority

    f. frequency of a process is being preempted by higher-priority processes

    g. priorities of processes waiting for resources held by other processes

    h. accumulated waiting time

    i. accumulated execution time

    j. estimated run-time-to-completion.

For each of the following, indicate which of the preceding scheduling criteria is most appropriate.

    i. In a real-time spacecraft monitoring system, the computer must respond immediately to signals received from the spacecraft.

    ii. Although a process has been receiving occasional service, it is making only nominal progress.

    iii. How often does the process voluntarily give up the processor for I/O before its quantum expires?

    iv. Is the user present and expecting fast interactive response times, or is the user absent?

    v. One goal of processor scheduling is to minimize average waiting times.

    vi. Processes holding resources in demand by other processes should have higher priorities.

    vii. Nearly complete processes should have higher priorities.

8.6 State which of the following are true and which false. Justify your answers.

a. A process scheduling discipline is preemptive if the processor cannot be forcibly removed from a process.

b. Real-time systems generally use preemptive processor scheduling.

c. Timesharing systems generally use nonpreemptive processor scheduling.

d. Turnaround times are more predictable in preemptive than in nonpreemptive systems.

e. One weakness of priority schemes is that the system will faithfully honor the priorities, but the priorities themselves may not be meaningful.

8.7 Why should processes be prohibited from setting the interrupting clock?

8.8 State which of the following refer to "static priorities" and which to "dynamic priorities."

a. are easier to implement

b. require less runtime overhead

c. are more responsive to changes in a process's environment

d. require more careful deliberation over the initial priority value chosen

8.9 Give several reasons why deadline scheduling is complex.

8.10 Give an example showing why FIFO is not an appropriate processor scheduling scheme for interactive users.

8.11 Using the example from the previous problem, show why round-robin is a better scheme for interactive users.

8.12 Determining the quantum is a complex and critical task. Assume that the average context-switching time between processes is s, and the average amount of time an I/O-bound process uses before generating an I/O request is t ($t \gg s$). Discuss the effect of each of the following quantum settings, q.

a. q is slightly greater than zero

b. $q = s$

c. $s < q < t$

d. $q = t$

e. $q > t$

f. q is an extremely large number

8.13 Discuss the effect of each of the following methods of assigning q.

a. q fixed and identical for all users

b. q fixed and unique to each process

c. q variable and identical for all processes

d. q variable and unique to each process

i. Arrange the schemes above in order from lowest to highest runtime overhead.

ii. Arrange the schemes in order from least to most responsive to variations in individual processes and system load.

iii. Relate your answers in (i) and (ii) to one another.

8.14 State why each of the following is incorrect.

a. SPF never has a higher throughput than SRT.

b. SPF is fair.

c. The shorter the process, the better the service it should receive.

d. Because SPF gives preference to short processes, it is useful in timesharing.

8.15 State some weaknesses in SRT. How would you modify the scheme to get better performance?

8.16 Answer each of the following questions about Brinch Hansen's HRRN strategy.

a. How does HRRN prevent indefinite postponement?

b. How does HRRN decrease the favoritism shown by other strategies to short new processes?

c. Suppose two processes have been waiting for about the same time. Are their priorities about the same? Explain your answer.

8.17 Show how multilevel feedback queues accomplish each of the following scheduling goals.

a. favor short processes.

b. favor I/O-bound processes to improve I/O device utilization.

c. determine the nature of a process as quickly as possible and schedule the process accordingly.

8.18 One heuristic often used by processor schedulers is that a process's past behavior is a good indicator of its future behavior. Give several examples of situations in which processor schedulers following this heuristic would make bad decisions.

8.19 An operating systems designer has proposed a multilevel feedback queuing network in which there are five levels. The quantum at the first level is 0.5 seconds. Each lower level has a quantum twice the size of the quantum at the previous level. A process cannot be preempted until its quantum expires. The system runs both batch and interactive processes, and these consist of both processor-bound and I/O-bound processes.

a. Why is this scheme deficient?

b. What minimal changes would you propose to make the scheme more acceptable for its intended process mix?

8.20   The SPF strategy can be proven to be optimal in the sense that it minimizes average response times. In this problem, you will demonstrate this result empirically by examining all possible orderings for a given set of five processes. In the next problem, you will actually prove the result. Suppose five different processes are waiting to be processed, and that they require 1, 2, 3, 4 and 5 time units, respectively. Write a program that produces all possible permutations of the five processes (5! = 120) and calculates the average waiting time for each permutation. Sort these into lowest to highest average waiting time order and display each average time side by side with the permutation of the processes. Comment on the results.

8.21   Prove that the SPF strategy is optimal in the sense that it minimizes average response times. [*Hint:* Consider a list of processes each with an indicated duration. Pick any two processes arbitrarily. Assuming that one is larger than the other, show the effect that placing the smaller process ahead of the longer one has on the waiting time of each process. Draw an appropriate conclusion.]

8.22   Two common goals of scheduling policies are to minimize response times and to maximize resource utilization.

  a.   Indicate how these goals are at odds with one another.

  b.   Analyze each of the scheduling policies presented in this chapter from these two perspectives. Which are biased toward minimizing user response times? Which are biased toward maximizing resource utilization?

  c.   Develop a new scheduling policy that enables a system to be tuned to achieve a good balance between these conflicting objectives.

8.23   In the selfish round-robin scheme, the priority of a process residing in the holding queue increases at a rate a until the priority is as high as that of processes in the active queue, at which point the process enters the active queue and its priority continues to increase, but now at the rate b. Earlier we stated that $b \leq a$. Discuss the behavior of an SRR system if $b > a$.

8.24   How does a fair share scheduler differ in operation from a conventional process scheduler?

8.25   In a uniprocessor system with n processes, how many different ways are there to schedule an execution path?

8.26   Suppose a system has a multilevel feedback queue scheduler implemented. How could one adapt this scheduler to form the following schedulers?

  a.   FCFS

  b.   round-robin

8.27   Compare and contrast EDF and SPF.

8.28   When are static real-time scheduling algorithms more appropriate than dynamic real-time scheduling algorithms?

8.29   Before Sun implemented its current Solaris operating system, Sun's UNIX system,[70] primarily used for workstations, performed process scheduling by assigning base priorities (a high of –20 to a low of +20 with a median of 0), and making priority adjustments. Priority adjustments were computed in response to changing system conditions. These were added to base priorities to compute current priorities; the process with the highest current priority was dispatched first.

The priority adjustment was strongly biased in favor of processes that had recently used relatively little processor time. The scheduling algorithm "forgot" processor usage quickly to give the benefit of the doubt to processes with changing behavior. The algorithm "forgot" 90 percent of recent processor usage in 5 * n seconds; n is the average number of runnable processes in the last minute.[71] Consider this process scheduling algorithm when answering each of the following questions.

  a.   Are processor-bound processes favored more when the system is heavily loaded or when it is lightly loaded?

  b.   How will an I/O-bound process perform immediately after an I/O completion?

  c.   Can processor-bound processes suffer indefinite postponement?

  d.   As the system load increases, what effect will processor-bound processes have on interactive response times?

  e.   How does this algorithm respond to changes in a process's behavior from processor bound to I/O bound or vice versa?

8.30   The VAX/VMS[72] operating system ran a wide variety of computers, from small to large. In VAX/VMS, process priorities range from 0–31, with 31 being the highest priority assigned to critical real-time processes. Normal processes receive priorities in the range 0–15; real-time processes receive priorities in the range 16–31. The priorities of real-time processes normally remain constant; no priority adjustments are applied. Real-time processes continue executing (without suffering quantum expirations) until they are preempted by processes with higher or equal priorities, or until they enter various *wait* states.

Other processes are scheduled as normal processes with priorities 0–15. These include interactive and batch processes, among others. Normal process priorities do vary. Their base priorities normally remain fixed, but they receive dynamic priority adjustments to give preference to I/O-bound over processor-bound processes. A normal process retains the processor until it is preempted by a more important process, until it enters a special state such as an event wait, or until its quantum expires. Processes with the same current priorities are scheduled round-robin.

Normal processes receive priority adjustments of 0 to 6 above their base priorities. Such positive increments occur, for example, when requested resources are made available, or when a condition on which a process is waiting is signaled. I/O-bound processes tend to get positive adjustments in priority, while processor-bound processes tend to have current priorities near their base priorities. Answer each of the following questions with regard to the VAX/VMS process scheduling mechanisms.

a. Why are the priorities of real-time processes normally kept constant?

b. Why are real-time processes not susceptible to quantum expirations?

c. Which normal processes, I/O bound or processor bound, generally receive preference?

d. Under what circumstances can a real-time process lose the processor?

e. Under what circumstances can a normal process lose the processor?

f. How are normal processes with the same priorities scheduled?

g. Under what circumstances do normal processes receive priority adjustments?

Suggested Projects

8.31 Prepare a research paper that compares and contrasts how Windows XP, Linux, and Mac OS X schedule processes.

8.32 Although the operating system is typically responsible for scheduling processes and threads, some systems allow user processes to make scheduling decisions. Research how this is done for process scheduling in exokernel operating systems (see www.pdos.lcs.mit.edu/pubs.html#Exokernels) and for thread scheduling in user-level threads and scheduler activations.

8.33 Research how real-time scheduling is implemented in embedded systems.

8.34 Research the scheduling policies and mechanisms that are commonly used in database systems.

Suggested Simulations

8.35 One solution to the problem of avoiding indefinite postponement of processes is aging, in which the priorities of waiting processes increase the longer they wait. Develop several aging algorithms and write simulation programs to examine their relative performance. For example, a process's priority may be made to increase linearly with time. For each of the aging algorithms you choose, determine how well waiting processes are treated relative to high-priority arriving processes.

8.36 One problem with preemptive scheduling is that the context-switching overhead may tend to dominate if the system is not carefully tuned. Write a simulation program that determines the effects on system performance of the ratio of context-switching overhead to typical quantum time. Discuss the factors that determine context-switching overhead and the factors that determine the typical quantum time. Indicate how achieving a proper balance between these (i.e., tuning the system) can dramatically affect system performance.

Recommended Reading

Coffman and Kleinrock discuss popular scheduling policies and indicate how users who know which scheduling policy the system employs can actually achieve better performance by taking appropriate measures.[73] Ruschitzka and Fabry give a classification of scheduling algorithms, and they formalize the notion of priority.[74] Today's schedulers typically combine several techniques described in this chapter to meet particular system objectives. Recent research in the field of processor scheduling focuses on optimizing performance in settings such as Web servers, real-time systems and embedded devices. Stankovic et al. present a discussion of real-time scheduling concerns,[75] Pop et. al present scheduling concerns in embedded systems[76] and Bender et al. discuss scheduling techniques for Web server transactions.[77] SMART (Scheduler for Multimedia And Real-Time applications), which combines real-time and traditional scheduling techniques to improve multimedia performance, was developed in response to increasing popularity of multimedia applications on workstations and personal computers.[78]

Dertouzos demonstrated that when all processes can meet their deadlines regardless of the order in which they are executed, it is optimal to schedule processes with the earliest deadlines first.[79] However, when the system becomes overloaded, the optimal scheduling policy cannot be implemented without allocating significant processor time to the scheduler.

Recent research focuses on the speed[80, 81] or number[82] of processors the system must allocate to the scheduler so that it meets its deadlines. The bibliography for this chapter is located on our Web site at www.deitel.com/books/os3e/Bibliography.pdf.

Works Cited

1. Ibaraki, T.; Abdel-Wahab, H. M.; and T. Kameda, "Design of Minimum-Cost Deadlock-Free Systems," *Journal of the ACM*, Vol. 30, No. 4 October 1983, p. 750.

2. Coffman, E. G., Jr., and L. Kleinrock, "Computer Scheduling Methods and Their Countermeasures," *Proceedings of AFIPS, SJCC*, Vol. 32, 1968, pp. 11–21.

3. Ruschitzka, M., and R. S. Fabry, "A Unifying Approach to Scheduling," *Communications of the ACM*, Vol. 20, No. 7, July 1977, pp. 469–477.

4. Abbot, C., "Intervention Schedules for Real-Time Programming," *IEEE Transactions on Software Engineering*, Vol. SE-10, No. 3, May 1984, pp. 268–274.

5. Ramamritham, K., and J. A. Stanovic, "Dynamic Task Scheduling in Hard Real-Time Distributed Systems," *IEEE Software*, Vol. 1, No. 3, July 1984, pp. 65–75.

6. Volz, R. A., and T. N. Mudge, "Instruction Level Timing Mechanisms for Accurate Real-Time Task Scheduling," *IEEE Transactions on Computers*, Vol. C-36, No. 8, August 1987, pp. 988–993.

7. Potkonjak, M., and W. Wolf, "A Methodology and Algorithms for the Design of Hard Real-Time Multitasking ASICs," *ACM Transactions on Design Automation of Electronic Systems (TODAES)* Vol, 4, No. 4, October 1999.

8. Kleinrock, L., "A Continuum of Time-Sharing Scheduling Algorithms," *Proceedings of AFIPS, SJCC*, 1970, pp. 453–458.

9. "sched.h—Execution Scheduling (REALTIME)," The Open Group Base Specifications Issue 6, IEEE Std. 1003.1, 2003 edition, <www.opengroup.org/onlinepubs/007904975/basedefs/sched.h.html>.

10. Kleinrock, L., "A Continuum of Time-Sharing Scheduling Algorithms," *Proceedings of AFIPS, SJCC*, 1970, pp. 453–458.

11. Potier, D.; Gelenbe, E.; and J. Lenfant, "Adaptive Allocation of Central Processing Unit Quanta," *Journal of the ACM*, Vol. 23, No. 1, January 1976, pp. 97–102.

12. Linux source code, version 2.6.0-test3, sched.c, lines 62–135 <miller.cs.wm.edu/lxr3.linux/http/source/kernel/sched.c?v=2.6.0-test3>.

13. Solomon, D., and M. Russinovich, *Inside Windows 2000,* 3rd ed., Redmond: Microsoft Press, 2000, pp. 338, 347.

14. Bruno, J.; Coffman, E. G., Jr.; and R. Sethi, "Scheduling Independent Tasks to Reduce Mean Finishing Time," *Communications of the ACM*, Vol. 17, No. 7, July 1974, pp. 382–387.

15. Deitel, H. M., "Absentee Computations in a Multiple Access Computer System," M.I.T. Project MAC, MAC-TR-52, Advanced Research Projects Agency, Department of Defense, 1968.

16. Brinch Hansen, P., "Short-Term Scheduling in Multiprogramming Systems," *Third ACM Symposium on Operating Systems Principles*, Stanford University, October 1971, pp. 103–105.

17. Kleinrock, L., "A Continuum of Time-Sharing Scheduling Algorithms," *Proceedings of AFIPS, SJCC*, 1970, pp. 453–458.

18. Blevins, P. R., and C. V. Ramamoorthy, "Aspects of a Dynamically Adaptive Operating System," *IEEE Transactions on Computers*, Vol. 25, No. 7, July 1976, pp. 713–725.

19. Potier, D.; Gelenbe, E.; and J. Lenfant, "Adaptive Allocation of Central Processing Unit Quanta," *Journal of the ACM*, Vol. 23, No. 1, January 1976, pp. 97–102.

20. Newbury, J. P., "Immediate Turnaround—An Elusive Goal," *Software Practice and Experience*, Vol. 12, No. 10, October 1982, pp. 897–906.

21. Henry, G. J., "The Fair Share Scheduler," *Bell Systems Technical Journal*, Vol. 63, No. 8, Part 2, October 1984, pp. 1845–1857.

22. Woodside, C. M., "Controllability of Computer Performance Tradeoffs Obtained Using Controlled-Share Queue Schedulers," *IEEE Transactions on Software Engineering*, Vol. SE-12, No. 10, October 1986, pp. 1041–1048.

23. Kay, J., and P. Lauder, "A Fair Share Scheduler," *Communications of the ACM*, Vol. 31, No. 1, January 1988, pp. 44–55.

24. Henry, G. J., "The Fair Share Scheduler," *Bell Systems Technical Journal*, Vol. 63, No. 8, Part 2, October 1984, p. 1846.

25. "Chapter 9, Fair Share Scheduler," *Solaris 9 System Administrator Collection*, November 11, 2003, <docs.sun.com/db/doc/806-4076/6jd6amqqo?a=view>.

26. Henry, G. J., "The Fair Share Scheduler," *Bell Systems Technical Journal*, Vol. 63, No. 8, Part 2, October 1984, p. 1848.

27. Henry, G. J., "The Fair Share Scheduler," *Bell Systems Technical Journal*, Vol. 63, No. 8, Part 2, October 1984, p. 1847.

28. Henry, G. J., "The Fair Share Scheduler," *Bell Systems Technical Journal*, Vol. 63, No. 8, Part 2, October 1984, p. 1846.

29. Nielsen, N. R., "The Allocation of Computing Resources—Is Pricing the Answer?" *Communications of the ACM*, Vol. 13, No. 8, August 1970, pp. 467–474.

30. McKell, L. J.; Hansen, J. V.; and L. E. Heitger, "Charging for Computer Resources," *ACM Computing Surveys*, Vol. 11, No. 2, June 1979, pp. 105–120.

31. Kleijnen, A. J. V., "Principles of Computer Charging in a University-Type Organization," *Communications of the ACM*, Vol. 26, No. 11, November 1983, pp. 926–932.

32. Dertouzos, M. L., "Control Robotics: The Procedural Control of Physical Processes," *Proc. IFIP Congress*, 1974, pp. 807–813.

33. Kalyanasundaram, B., and K., Pruhs, "Speed Is As Powerful As Clairvoyance," *Journal of the ACM (JACM)*, Vol. 47, No. 4, July, 2002, pp. 617–643.

34. Lam, T., and K. To, "Performance Guarantee for Online Deadline Scheduling in the Presence of Overload," *Proceedings of the TWELFTH ANNUal ACM-SIAM Symposium on Discrete Algorithms*, January 7–9, 2001, pp. 755–764.

35. Koo, C.; Lam, T.; Ngan, T.; and K. To, "Extra Processors Versus Future Information in Optimal Deadline Scheduling," *Proceedings of the Fourteenth Annual ACM Symposium on Parallel Algorithms and Architectures*, 2002, pp. 133–142.

36. Stankovic, J., "Real-Time and Embedded Systems," *ACM Computing Surveys*, Vol. 28, No. 1, March 1996, pp. 205-208.

37. Xu, J., and D. L. Parnas, "On Satisfying Timing Constraints in Hard-Real-Time Systems," *Proceedings of the Conference on Software for Critical Systems*, New Orleans, Louisiana, 1991, pp. 132–146.

38. Stewart, D., and P. Khosla, "Real-Time Scheduling of Dynamically Reconfigurable Systems," *Proceedings of the IEEE International Conference on Systems Engineering*, Dayton, Ohio, August 1991, pp. 139–142.

39. van Beneden, B., "Comp.realtime: Frequently Asked Questions (FAQs) (Version 3.6)," May 16, 2002 <www.faqs.org/faqs/realtime-computing/faq/>.

40. MITRE Corporation, "MITRE—About Us—MITRE History—Semi-Automatic Ground Environment (SAGE)," January 7, 2003 <www.mitre.org/about/sage.html>.

41. Edwards, P., "SAGE," *The Closed World*, Cambridge, MA: MIT Press, 1996, <www.si.umich.edu/~pne/PDF/cw.ch3.pdf>.

42. Edwards, P., "SAGE," *The Closed World*, Cambridge, MA: MIT Press, 1996, <www.si.umich.edu/~pne/PDF/cw.ch3.pdf>.

43. MITRE Corporation, "MITRE—About Us—MITRE History—Semi-Automatic Ground Environment (SAGE)," January 7, 2003 <www.mitre.org/about/sage.html>.

44. Edwards, P., "SAGE," *The Closed World*, Cambridge, MA: MIT Press, 1996, <www.si.umich.edu/~pne/PDF/cw.ch3.pdf>.

45. MITRE Corporation, "MITRE—About Us—MITRE History—Semi-Automatic Ground Environment (SAGE)," January 7, 2003 <www.mitre.org/about/sage.html>.

46. Edwards, P., "SAGE," *The Closed World*, Cambridge, MA: MIT Press, 1996, <www.si.umich.edu/~pne/PDF/cw.ch3.pdf>.

47. QNX Software Systems Ltd., "The Philosophy of QNX Neutrino," <www.qnx.com/developer/docs/momentics621_docs/neutrino/sys_arch/intro.html>.

48. Wind River Systems, Inc., "VxWorks 5.x." <www.windriver.com/products/vxworks5/vxworks5x_ds.pdf>.

49. Dedicated Systems Experts, "Comparison between QNX RTOS V6.1, VxWorks AE 1.1, and Windows CE .NET," June 21, 2001 <www.eon-trade.com/data/QNX/QNX61_VXAE_CE.pdf>.

50. QNX Software Systems Ltd., "QNX Supported Hardware," <www.qnx.com/support/sd_hardware/platform/processors.html>.

51. Timmerman, M., "RTOS Evaluation Project Latest News," *Dedicated Systems Magazine*, 1999, <www.omimo.be/magazine/99q1/1999q1_p009.pdf>.

52. Wind River Systems, Inc., "VxWorks 5.x.," <www.windriver.com/products/vxworks5/vxworks5x_ds.pdf>.

53. Microsoft Corporation, "Windows CE .NET Home Page," <www.microsoft.com/windows/embedded/ce.net/default.asp>.

54. Radisys Corporation, "RadiSys: Microware OS-9," <www.radisys.com/oem_products/op-os9.cfm?MS=Microware%20Enhanced%20OS-9%20Solution>.

55. Enea Embedded Technology, "Welcome to Enea Embedded Technology," <www.ose.com>.

56. Real Time Linux Foundation, Inc., "Welcome to the Real Time Linux Foundation Web Site," <www.realtimelinuxfoundation.org>.

57. Etsion, Y.; Tsafrir, D.; and D. Feiteelson, "Effects of Clock Resolution on the Scheduling of Interactive and Soft Real-Time Processes," *SIGMETRICS'03*, June 10–14, 2003, pp. 172–183.

58. Xu, J., Parnas, D. L., "On Satisfying Timing Constraints in Hard-Real-Time Systems," *Proceedings of the Conference on Software for Critical Systems*, New Orleans, Louisiana, 1991, pp. 132–146.

59. Stewart, D., and P. Khosla, "Real-Time Scheduling of Dynamically Reconfigurable Systems," *Proceedings of the IEEE International Conference on Systems Engineering*, Dayton, Ohio, August 1991, pp. 139–142.

60. Xu, J., and D. L. Parnas, "On Satisfying Timing Constraints in Hard-Real-Time Systems," *Proceedings of the Conference on Software for Critical Systems*, New Orleans, Louisiana, 1991, pp. 132–146.

61. Stewart, D., and P. Khosla, "Real-Time Scheduling of Dynamically Reconfigurable Systems," *Proceedings of the IEEE International Conference on Systems Engineering*, Dayton, Ohio, August 1991, pp. 139–142.

62. Potkonjak, M., W. Wolf, "A Methodology and Algorithms for the Design of Hard Real-Time Multitasking ASICs," *ACM Transactions on Design Automation of Electronic Systems (TODAES)*, Vol. 4, No. 4, October 1999.

63. Xu, J., and D. L. Parnas, "On Satisfying Timing Constraints in Hard-Real-Time Systems," *Proceedings of the Conference on Software for Critical Systems*, New Orleans, Louisiana, 1991, pp. 132–146.

64. Dertouzos, M. L., "Control Robotics: The Procedural Control of Physical Processes," *Information Processing*, Vol. 74, 1974.

65. Stewart, D., and P. Khosla, "Real-Time Scheduling of Dynamically Reconfigurable Systems," *Proceedings of the IEEE International Conference on Systems Engineering*, Dayton, Ohio, August 1991, pp. 139–142.

66. Stewart, D., and P. Khosla, "Real-Time Scheduling of Dynamically Reconfigurable Systems," *Proceedings of the IEEE International Conference on Systems Engineering*, Dayton, Ohio, August 1991, pp. 139–142.

67. "A Look at the JVM and Thread Behavior," June 28, 1999, <www.javaworld.com/javaworld/javaqa/1999-07/04-qa-jvmthreads.html>.

68. Austin, C., "Java Technology on the Linux Platform: A Guide to Getting Started," October 2000, <developer.java.sun.com/developer/technicalArticles/Programming/linux/>.

69. Holub, A., "Programming Java Threads in the Real World, Part 1," *JavaWorld*, September 1998, <www.javaworld.com/javaworld/jw-09-1998/jw-09-threads.html>.

70. Courington, W., *The UNIX System: A Sun Technical Report*, Mountain View, CA: Sun Microsystems, Inc., 1985.

71. Courington, W., *The UNIX System: A Sun Technical Report*, Mountain View, CA: Sun Microsystems, Inc., 1985.

72. Kenah, L. J.; Goldenberg, R. E.; and S. F. Bate, *VAX/VMS Internals and Data Structures: Version 4.4*, Bedford, MA: Digital Equipment Corporation, 1988.

73. Coffman, E. G., Jr., and L. Kleinrock, "Computer Scheduling Methods and Their Countermeasures," *Proceedings of AFIPS, SJCC*, Vol. 32, 1968, pp. 11–21.

74. Ruschitzka, M., and R. S. Fabry, "A Unifying Approach to Scheduling," *Communications of the ACM*, Vol. 20, No. 7, July 1977, pp. 469–477.

75. Stankovic, J. A.; Spuri, M.; Natale, M. D.; and G. C. Buttazzo, "Implications of Classical Scheduling Results for Real-Time Systems," *IEEE Computer*, Vol. 28, No. 6, 1995, pp. 16–25.

76. Pop, P.; Eles, P.; and Z. Peng, "Scheduling with Optimized Communication for Time-Triggered Embedded Systems," *Proceedings of the Seventh International Workshop on Hardware/Software Codesign*, March 1999.

77. Bender, M. A.; Muthukrishnan, S.; and R. Rajarama, "Improved Algorithms for Stretch Scheduling," *Proceedings of the Thirteenth Annual ACM-SIAM Symposium on Discrete Algorithms*, January 2002.

78. Nieh, J., and M. S. Lam, "The Design, Implementation and Evaluation of SMART: a Scheduler for Multimedia Applications," *ACM SIGOPS Operating Systems Review, Proceedings of the Sixteenth ACM Symposium on Operating Systems Principles*, October 1997.

79. Dertouzos, M. L., "Control Robotics: The Procedural Control of Physical Processes," *Proc. IFIP Congress*, 1974, pp. 807–813.

80. Kalyanasundaram, B., and K., Pruhs, "Speed Is As Powerful As Clairvoyance," *Journal of the ACM (JACM)*, Vol. 47, No. 4, July, 2002, pp. 617–643.

81. Lam, T., and K. To, "Performance Guarantee for Online Deadline Scheduling in the Presence of Overload," *Proceedings of the TWELFTH ANNUal ACM-SIAM Symposium on Discrete Algorithms*, January 7–9, 2001, pp. 755–764.

82. Koo, C.; Lam, T.; Ngan, T.; and K. To, "Extra Processors Versus Future Information in Optimal Deadline Scheduling," *Proceedings of the Fourteenth Annual ACM Symposium on Parallel Algorithms and Architectures*, 2002, pp. 133–142.

Real and Virtual Memory

Lead me from the unreal to the real!
—The Upanishads—

Part 3

Memory is second only to processors in importance and in the intensity with which it is managed by the operating system. The next three chapters follow the elegant evolution in memory organizations from the earliest simple single-user, real memory systems to today's popular virtual memory multiprogramming systems. You will learn the motivation for virtual memory and you will focus on schemes for implementing it—paging, segmentation and a combination of the two. You will study the three key types of memory management strategies: fetch (both demand and anticipatory), placement and replacement. You will see that a crucial factor for performance in virtual memory systems is an effective page replacement strategy when available memory becomes scarce, and you will learn a variety of these strategies and Denning's working set model.

The fancy is indeed no other than a mode of memory emancipated from the order of time and space.
—Samuel Taylor Coleridge—

Nothing ever becomes real till it is experienced—even a proverb is no proverb to you till your life has illustrated it.

—John Keats—

Let him in whose ears the low-voiced
Best is killed by the clash of the First,
Who holds that if way to the
Better there be, it exacts a full look at the worst, ...

—Thomas Hardy—

Remove not the landmark on the boundary of the fields.

—Amenemope—

Protection is not a principle, but an expedient.

—Benjamin Disraeli—

A great memory does not make a philosopher, any more than a dictionary can be called a grammar.

—John Henry Cardinal Newman—

Chapter 9

Real Memory Organization and Management

Objectives

After reading this chapter, you should understand:

- *the need for real (also called physical) memory management.*

- *the memory hierarchy.*

- *contiguous and noncontiguous memory allocation.*

- *fixed- and variable-partition multiprogramming.*

- *memory swapping.*

- *memory placement strategies.*

Chapter Outline

9.1 Introduction

The organization and management of the **real memory** (also called **main memory**, **physical memory** or **primary memory**) of a computer system has been a major influence on operating systems design.[1] Secondary storage—most commonly disk and tape—provides massive, inexpensive capacity for the abundance of programs and data that must be kept readily available for processing. It is, however, slow and not directly accessible to processors. To be run or referenced directly, programs and data must be in main memory.

In this and the next two chapters, we discuss many popular schemes for organizing and managing a computer's memory. This chapter deals with real memory; Chapters 10 and 11 discuss virtual memory. We present the schemes approximately as they evolved historically. Most of today's systems are virtual memory systems, so this chapter is primarily of historical value. However, even in virtual memory systems, the operating system must manage real memory. Further, some systems, such as certain types of real-time and embedded systems, cannot afford the overhead of virtual memory—so to them, real memory management remains crucial. Many of the concepts presented in this chapter lay the groundwork for the discussion of virtual memory in the next two chapters.

9.2 Memory Organization

Historically, main memory has been viewed as a relatively expensive resource. As such, systems designers have attempted to optimize its use. Although its cost has declined phenomenally over the decades (roughly according to Moore's Law, as discussed in Chapter 2; see the Operating Systems Thinking feature, There Are No Upper Limits to Processing Power, Memory, Storage and Bandwidth), main memory is still relatively expensive compared to secondary storage. Also, today's operating systems and applications require ever more substantial quantities (Fig. 9.1). For example, Microsoft recommends 256MB of main memory to efficiently run Windows XP Professional.

We (as operating system designers) view main memory in terms of **memory organization**. Do we place only a single process in main memory, or do we place several processes in memory at once (i.e., do we implement multiprogramming)? If main memory contains several processes simultaneously, do we give each the same amount of space, or do we divide main memory into portions (called **partitions**) of different sizes? Do define partitions rigidly for extended periods, or dynamically, allowing the system to adapt quickly to changes in the needs of processes? Do we require that processes run in a specific partition, or anywhere they will fit? Do we require the system to place each process in one contiguous block of memory locations, or allow it to divide processes into separate blocks and place them in any available slots in main memory? Systems have been based on each of these schemes. This chapter discusses how each scheme is implemented.

Self Review

1. Why is it generally inefficient to allow only one process to be in memory at a time?
2. What would happen if a system allowed many processes to be placed in main memory, but did not divide memory into partitions?

Ans: **1)** If the single process blocks for I/O, no other processes can use the processor. **2)** The processes would share all their memory. Any malfunctioning or malicious process could damage any or all of the other processes.

9.3 Memory Management

Regardless of which memory organization scheme we adopt for a particular system, we must decide which strategies to use to obtain optimal memory performance.[2] **Memory management strategies** determine how a particular memory organization performs under various loads. Memory management is typically performed by both software and special-purpose hardware.

Operating Systems Thinking

There Are No Upper Limits to Processing Power, Memory, Storage and Bandwidth

Computing is indeed a dynamic field. Processors keep getting faster (and cheaper per executed instruction), main memories keep getting larger (and cheaper per byte), secondary storage media keep getting larger (and cheaper per bit), and communications bandwidths keep getting wider (and cheaper per bit transferred)—all kinds of new devices are being created to interface with, or be integrated into, computers.

Operating systems designers must stay apprised of these trends and the relative rates at which they progress; these trends have an enormous impact on what capabilities operating systems need to have. Early operating systems did not provide capabilities to support computer graphics, graphical user interfaces, networking, distributed computing, Web services, multiprocessing, multithreading, massive parallelism, massive virtual memories, database systems, multimedia, accessibility for people with disabilities, sophisticated security capabilities and so on. All of these innovations over the last few decades have had a profound impact on the requirements for building contemporary operating systems, as you will see when you read the detailed case studies on the Linux and Windows XP operating systems in Chapters 20 and 21. All of these capabilities have been made possible by improving processing power, storage and bandwidth. These improvements will continue, eventually enabling even more sophisticated applications and the operating systems capabilities to support them.

Operating System	Release Date	Minimum Memory Requirement	Recommended Memory
Windows 1.0	November 1985	256KB	
Windows 2.03	November 1987	320KB	
Windows 3.0	March 1990	896KB	1MB
Windows 3.1	April 1992	2.6MB	4MB
Windows 95	August 1995	8MB	16MB
Windows NT 4.0	August 1996	32MB	96MB
Windows 98	June 1998	24MB	64MB
Windows ME	September 2000	32MB	128MB
Windows 2000 Professional	February 2000	64MB	128MB
Windows XP Home	October 2001	64MB	128MB
Windows XP Professional	October 2001	128MB	256MB

Figure 9.1 | Microsoft Windows operating system memory requirements.[3, 4, 5]

The **memory manager** is an operating system component concerned with the system's memory organization scheme and memory management strategies. The memory manager determines how available memory space is allocated to processes and how to respond to changes in a process's memory usage. It also interacts with special-purpose memory management hardware (if any is available) to improve performance. In this and the next two chapters, we describe several different memory management and organization strategies.

Each memory management strategy differs in how it answers certain questions. When does the strategy retrieve a new program and its data to place in memory? Does the strategy retrieve the program and its data when the system specifically asks for it, or does the strategy attempt to anticipate the system's requests? Where in main memory does the strategy place the next program to be run and that program's data? Does it minimize wasted space by packing programs and data as tightly as possible into available memory areas, or does it minimize execution time, placing programs and data as quickly as possible?

If a new program or new data must be placed in main memory and if main memory is currently full, which programs or data already in memory does the strategy replace? Should it replace those that are oldest, those that are used least frequently, or those that were used least recently? Systems have been implemented using these and other memory management strategies.

Self Review

1. When is it appropriate for a memory manager to minimize wasted memory space?
2. Why should memory management organizations and strategies be as transparent as possible to processes?

Ans: **1)** When memory is more expensive than the processor-time overhead incurred by placing programs as tightly as possible into main memory. Also, when the system needs to keep the largest possible contiguous memory region available for large incoming programs and data. **2)** Memory management transparency improves application portability and facilitates development, because the programmer is not concerned with memory management strategies. It also allows memory management strategies to be changed without rewriting applications.

9.4 Memory Hierarchy

In the 1950s and 1960s, main memory was extremely expensive—as much as one dollar per bit! To put that in perspective, Windows XP Professional's recommended 256MB of memory would have cost over 2 billion dollars! Designers made careful decisions about how much main memory to place in a computer system. An installation could buy no more than it could afford but had to buy enough to support the operating system and a given number of processes. The goal was to buy the minimum amount that could adequately support the anticipated workloads within the economic constraints of the installation.

Programs and data must be in main memory before the system can execute or reference them. Those that the system does not need immediately may be kept in secondary storage until needed, then brought into main memory for execution or reference. Secondary storage media, such as tape or disk, are generally far less costly per bit than main memory and have much greater capacity. However, main memory may generally be accessed much faster than secondary storage—in today's systems, disk data transfer may be six orders of magnitude slower than that of main memory.[6, 7]

The **memory hierarchy** contains levels characterized by the speed and cost of memory in each level. Systems move programs and data back and forth between the various levels.[8, 9] This shuttling can consume system resources, such as processor time, that could otherwise be put to productive use. To increase efficiency, current systems include hardware units called memory controllers that perform memory transfer operations with virtually no computational overhead. As a result, systems that exploit the memory hierarchy benefit from lower costs and enlarged capacity.

In the 1960s, it became clear that the memory hierarchy could achieve dramatic improvements in performance and utilization by adding one higher level.[10, 11] This additional level, called **cache**, is much faster than main memory and is typically located on each processor in today's systems.[12, 13] A processor may reference programs and data directly from its cache. Cache memory is extremely expensive compared to main memory, and therefore only relatively small caches are used. Figure 9.2 shows the relationship between cache, primary memory and secondary storage.

Cache memory imposes one more level of data transfer on the system. Programs in main memory are transferred to the cache before being executed—executing programs from cache is much faster than from main memory. Because many processes that access data and instructions once are likely to access them again in the future (a phenomenon known as **temporal locality**), even a relatively small

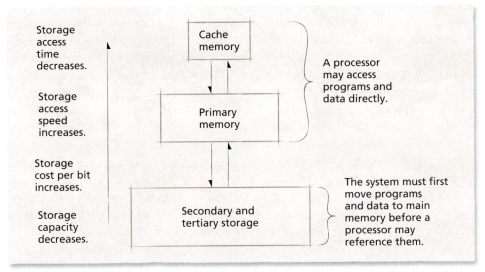

Figure 9.2 | *Hierarchical memory organization*

cache can significantly increase performance (when compared to running programs in a system without cache). Some systems use several levels of cache.

Self Review

1. (T/F) The low cost of main memory coupled with the increase in memory capacity in most systems has obviated the need for memory management strategies.
2. How does a program executing a loop benefit from cache memory?

Ans: **1)** False. Despite the low cost and high capacity of main memory, there continue to be environments that consume all available memory. Also, memory management strategies should be applied to cache, which consists of more expensive, low-capacity memory. In either case, when memory becomes full, a system must implement memory management strategies to obtain the best possible use of memory. **2)** A program executing a loop repeatedly executes the same set of instructions and may also reference the same data. If these instructions and data fit in the cache, the processor can access those instructions and data more quickly from cache than from main memory, leading to increased performance.

9.5 Memory Management Strategies

Memory management strategies are designed to obtain the best possible use of main memory. They are divided into:

1. Fetch strategies
2. Placement strategies
3. Replacement strategies

Fetch strategies determine when to move the next piece of a program or data to main memory from secondary storage. We divide them into two types—**demand**

fetch strategies and **anticipatory fetch strategies**. For many years, the conventional wisdom has been to employ a demand fetch strategy, in which the system places the next piece of program or data in main memory when a running program references it. Designers believed that because we cannot in general predict the paths of execution that programs will take, the overhead involved in making guesses would far exceed expected benefits. Today, however, many systems have increased performance by employing anticipatory fetch strategies, which attempt to load a piece of program or data into memory before it is referenced.

Placement strategies determine where in main memory the system should place incoming program or data pieces.[14, 15] In this chapter we consider the **first-fit**, **best-fit**, and **worst-fit** memory placement strategies. When we discuss paged virtual memory systems in Chapters 10 and 11, we will see that program and data can be divided into fixed-size pieces called pages that can be placed in any available "page frame." In these types of systems, placement strategies are trivial.

When memory is too full to accommodate a new program, the system must remove some (or all) of a program or data that currently resides in memory. The system's **replacement strategy** determines which piece to remove.

Self Review

1. Is high resource utilization or low overhead more important to a placement strategy?
2. Name the two types of fetch strategies and describe when each one might be more appropriate than the other.

Ans: **1)** The answer depends on system objectives and the relative costs of resources and overhead. In general, the operating system designer must balance overhead with high memory utilization to meet the system's goals. **2)** The two types are demand fetch and anticipatory fetch. If the system cannot predict future memory usage with accuracy, then the lower overhead of demand fetching results in higher performance and utilization (because the system does not load from disk information that will not be referenced). However, if programs exhibit predictable behavior, anticipatory fetch strategies can improve performance by ensuring that pieces of programs or data are located in memory before processes reference them.

9.6 Contiguous vs. Noncontiguous Memory Allocation

To execute a program in early computer systems, the system operator or the operating system had to find enough contiguous main memory to accommodate the entire program. If the program was larger than the available memory, the system could not execute it. In this chapter, we discuss the early use of this method, known as **contiguous memory allocation**, and some problems it entailed. When researchers attempted to solve these problems, it became clear that systems might benefit from noncontiguous memory allocation.[16]

In **noncontiguous memory allocation**, a program is divided into blocks or **segments** that the system may place in nonadjacent slots in main memory. This allows making use of holes (unused gaps) in memory that would be too small to hold whole programs. Although the operating system thereby incurs more overhead, this can be justified by the increase in the level of multiprogramming (i.e., the number of processes that can occupy main memory at once). In this chapter we present the techniques that led to noncontiguous physical memory allocation. In the next two chapters we discuss the virtual memory organization techniques of paging and segmentation, each of which requires noncontiguous memory allocation.

Self Review

1. When is noncontiguous preferable to contiguous memory allocation?
2. What sort of overhead might be involved in a noncontiguous memory allocation scheme?

Ans: **1)** When available memory contains no area large enough to hold the incoming program in one contiguous piece, but sufficient smaller pieces of memory are available that, in total, are large enough. **2)** There would be overhead in keeping track of available blocks and blocks that belong to separate processes, and where those blocks reside in memory.

9.7 Single-User Contiguous Memory Allocation

Early computer systems allowed only one person at a time to use a machine. All the machine's resources were dedicated to that user. Billing was straightforward—the user was charged for all the resources whether or not the user's job required them. In fact, the normal billing mechanisms were based on **wall clock time**. The system operator gave the user the machine for some time interval and charged a flat hourly rate.

Figure 9.3 illustrates the memory organization for a typical **single-user contiguous memory allocation system**. Originally, there were no operating systems—the programmer wrote all the code necessary to implement a particular application, including the highly detailed machine-level input/output instructions. Soon, system

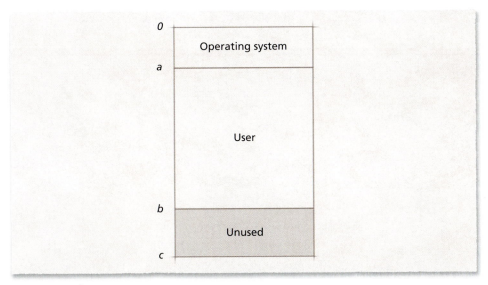

Figure 9.3 | Single-user contiguous memory allocation.

designers consolidated input/output coding that implemented basic functions into an **input/output control system (IOCS)**.[17] The programmer called IOCS routines to do the work instead of having to "reinvent the wheel" for each program. The IOCS greatly simplified and expedited the coding process. The implementation of input/output control systems may have been the beginning of today's concept of operating systems.

9.7.1 Overlays

We have discussed how contiguous memory allocation limited the size of programs that could execute on a system. One way in which a software designer could overcome the memory limitation was to create **overlays**, which allowed the system to execute programs larger than main memory. Figure 9.4 illustrates a typical overlay. The programmer divides the program into logical sections. When the program does not need the memory for one section, the system can replace some or all of it with the memory for a needed section.[18]

Overlays enable programmers to "extend" main memory. However, manual overlay requires careful and time-consuming planning, and the programmer often

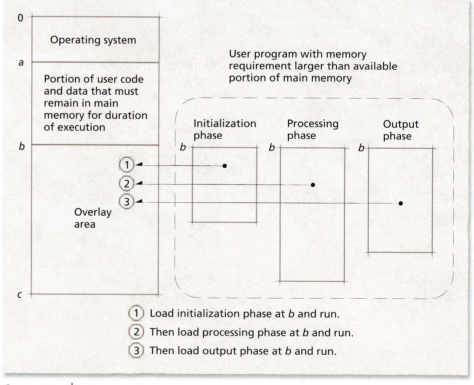

Figure 9.4 | *Overlay structure.*

must have detailed knowledge of the system's memory organization. A program with a sophisticated overlay structure can be difficult to modify. Indeed, as programs grew in complexity, by some estimates as much as 40 percent of programming expenses were for organizing overlays.[19] It became clear that the operating system needed to insulate the programmer from complex memory management tasks such as overlays. As we will see in subsequent chapters, virtual memory systems obviate the need for programmer-controlled overlays, in the same way that the IOCS freed the programmer from repetitive, low-level I/O manipulation.

Self Review

1. How did the IOCS facilitate program development?
2. Describe the costs and benefits of overlays.

Ans: **1)** Programmers were able to perform I/O without themselves having to write the low-level commands that were now incorporated into the IOCS, which all programmers could use instead of having to "reinvent the wheel." **2)** Overlays enabled programmers to write programs larger than real memory, but managing these overlays increased program complexity, which increased the size of programs and the cost of software development.

9.7.2 Protection in a Single-User System

In single-user contiguous memory allocation systems, the question of protection is simple. How should the operating system be protected from destruction by the user's program?

A process can interfere with the operating system's memory—either intentionally or inadvertently—by replacing some or all of its memory contents with other data. If it destroys the operating system, then the process cannot proceed. If the process attempts to access memory occupied by the operating system, the user can detect the problem, terminate execution, possibly fix the problem and relaunch the program.

Without protection, the process may alter the operating system in a more subtle, nonfatal manner. For example, suppose the process accidentally changes certain input/output routines, causing the system to truncate all output records. The process could still run, but the results would be corrupted. If the user does not examine the results until the process completes, then the machine resource has been wasted. Worse yet, the damage to the operating system might cause outputs to be produced that the user cannot easily determine to be inaccurate. Clearly, the operating system must be protected from processes.

Protection in single-user contiguous memory allocation systems can be implemented with a single **boundary register** built into the processor, as in Fig. 9.5, and which can be modified only by a privileged instruction. The boundary register contains the memory address at which the user's program begins. Each time a process references a memory address, the system determines if the request is for an address greater than or equal to that stored in the boundary register. If so, the system services the memory request. If not, then the program is trying to access the operating

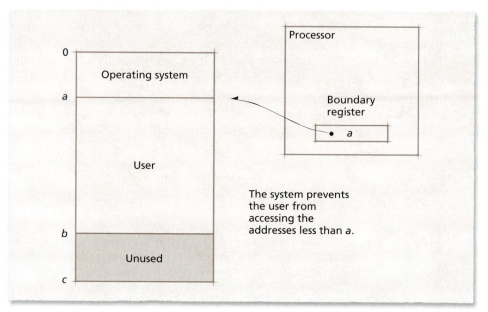

system. The system intercepts the request and terminates the process with an appropriate error message. The hardware that checks boundary addresses operates quickly to avoid slowing instruction execution.

Of course, the process must access the operating system from time to time to obtain services such as input/output. Several system calls (also called **supervisor calls**) are provided that may be used to request services from the operating system. When a process issues a system call (e.g., to write data to a disk), the system detects the call and switches from the user mode to the kernel mode (or **executive mode**) of execution. In kernel mode, the processor may execute operating system instructions and access data to perform tasks on behalf of the process. After the system has performed the requested task, it switches back to user mode and returns control to the process.[20]

The single boundary register represents a simple protection mechanism. As operating systems have become more complex, designers have implemented more sophisticated mechanisms to protect the operating system from processes and to protect processes from one another. We discuss these mechanisms in detail later.

Self Review

1. Why is a single boundary register insufficient for protection in a multiuser system?
2. Why are system calls necessary for an operating system?

Ans: 1) The single boundary would protect the operating system from being corrupted by user processes, but not protect processes from corrupting each other. 2) System calls enable processes to request services from the operating system while ensuring that the operating system is protected from its processes.

9.7.3 Single-Stream Batch Processing

Early single-user real memory systems were dedicated to one job for more than the job's execution time. Jobs generally required considerable **setup time** during which the operating system was loaded, tapes and disk packs were mounted, appropriate forms placed in the printer, time cards "punched in," and so on. When jobs completed, they required considerable **teardown time** as tapes and disk packs were removed, forms removed, time cards "punched out." During job setup and teardown the computer sat idle.

Designers realized that if they could automate various aspects of **job-to-job transition**, they could reduce considerably the amount of time wasted between jobs. This led to the development of **batch-processing** systems (see the Operating Systems Thinking feature, Change Is the Rule Rather Than the Exception). In **single-stream batch processing**, jobs are grouped in batches by loading them consecutively onto tape or disk. A **job stream processor** reads the **job control language** statements (that define each job) and facilitates the setup of the next job. It issues directives to the system operator and performs many functions that the operator previously performed manually. When the current job terminates, the job stream reader reads in the control-language statements for the next job and performs appropriate housekeeping chores to facilitate the transition to the next job. Batch-processing systems greatly improved resource utilization and helped demonstrate the real value of operating systems and **intensive resource management**. Single-stream batch-processing systems were the state of the art in the early 1960s.

Self Review

1. (T/F) Batch-processing systems removed the need for a system operator.
2. What was the key contribution of early batch-processing systems?

Operating Systems Thinking

Change Is the Rule Rather Than the Exception

Historically, change is the rule rather than the exception and that those changes happen faster than anticipated and often are far more wrenching than imagined. You see this in the computer field all the time. Just look at who the leading companies were in the 1960s and 1970s; today many of those companies are gone or have far less prominent positions in the industry. Look at the way computers and operating systems were designed in those decades; today those designs, in many cases, are profoundly different. Throughout the book we discuss many architectural issues and many software engineering issues that designers must consider as they create operating systems that adapt well to change.

Ans: **1)** False. A system operator was needed to set up and "tear down" the jobs and control them as they executed. **2)** They automated various aspects of job-to-job transition, considerably reducing the amount of wasted time between jobs and improved resource utilization.

9.8 Fixed-Partition Multiprogramming

Even with batch-processing operating systems, single-user systems still wasted a considerable amount of the computing resource (Fig. 9.6). A typical process would consume the processor time it needed to generate an input/output request; the process could not continue until the I/O finished. Because I/O speeds were extremely slow compared with processor speeds (and still are), the processor was severely underutilized.

Designers saw that they could further increase processor utilization by implementing multiprogramming systems, in which several users simultaneously compete for system resources. The process currently waiting for I/O yields the processor if another process is ready to do calculations. Thus, I/O operations and processor calculations can occur simultaneously. This greatly increases processor utilization and system throughput.

To take maximum advantage of multiprogramming, several processes must reside in the computer's main memory at the same time. Thus, when one process requests input/output, the processor may switch to another process and continue to perform calculations without the delay associated with loading programs from secondary storage. When this new process yields the processor, another may be ready

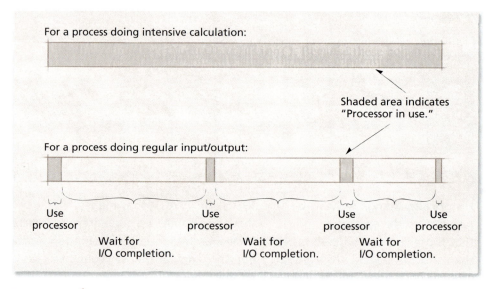

Figure 9.6 | *Processor utilization on a single-user system. [Note: In many single-user jobs, I/O waits are much longer relative to processor utilization periods indicated in this diagram.]*

to use it. Many multiprogramming schemes have been implemented, as discussed in this and the next several sections.

The earliest multiprogramming systems used **fixed-partition multiprogram-ming**.[21] Under this scheme, the system divides main memory into a number of fixed-size **partitions**. Each partition holds a single job, and the system switches the processor rapidly between jobs to create the illusion of simultaneity.[22] This technique enables the system to provide simple multiprogramming capabilities. Clearly, multi-programming normally requires more memory than does a single-user system. However, the improved resource use for the processor and the peripheral devices justifies the expense of the additional memory.

In the earliest multiprogramming systems, the programmer translated a job using an absolute assembler or compiler (see Section 2.8, Compiling, Linking and Loading). While this made the memory management system relatively straightfor-ward to implement, it meant that a job had its precise location in memory determined before it was launched and could run only in a specific partition (Fig. 9.7). This restric-tion led to wasted memory. If a job was ready to run and the program's partition was occupied, then that job had to wait, even if other partitions were available. Figure 9.8 shows an extreme example. All the jobs in the system must run in partition 3 (i.e., the programs' instructions all begin at address c). Because this partition currently is in use, all other jobs are forced to wait, even though the system has two other partitions in which the jobs could run (if they had been compiled for these partitions).

To overcome the problem of memory waste, developers created relocating compilers, assemblers and loaders. These tools produce a relocatable program that can run in any available partition that is large enough to hold that program (Fig. 9.9). This scheme eliminates some of the memory waste inherent in multipro-

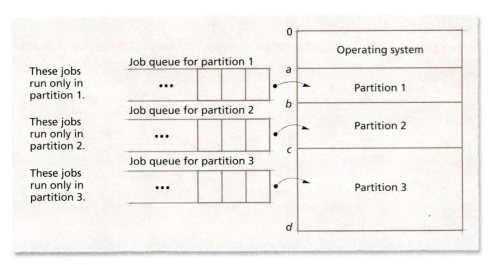

Figure 9.7 | Fixed-partition multiprogramming with absolute translation and loading.

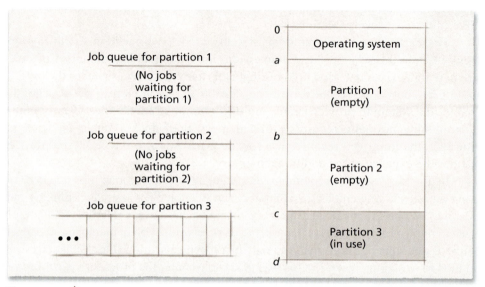

Figure 9.8 | *Memory waste under fixed-partition multiprogramming with absolute translation and loading.*

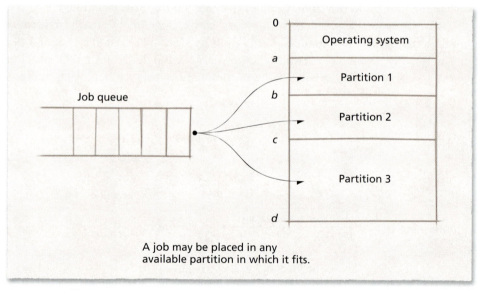

Figure 9.9 | *Fixed-partition multiprogramming with relocatable translation and loading.*

gramming with absolute translation and loading; however, relocating translators and loaders are more complex than their absolute counterparts.

As memory organization increased in complexity, designers had to augment the protection schemes. In a single-user system, the system must protect only the operating system from the user process. In a multiprogramming system, the system must protect the operating system from all user processes and protect each process from all the others. In contiguous-allocation multiprogramming systems, such as those discussed in this section, protection often is implemented with multiple boundary registers. The system can delimit each partition with two boundary registers—low and high, also called the **base** and **limit** registers (Fig. 9.10). When a pro-

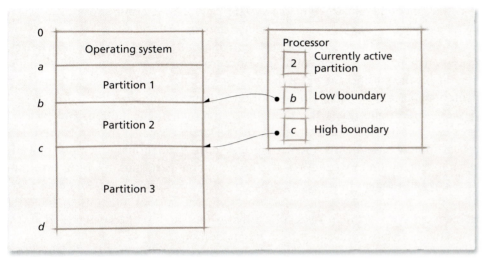

Figure 9.10 | *Memory protection in contiguous-allocation multiprogramming systems.*

Anecdote

Compartmentalization

When HMD was interviewing for a job in computer security at the Pentagon, his last interview of the day was with the person ultimately responsible for all Pentagon computer systems. When offered the job, HMD was enthusiastic: "Yes sir, if I come to the Pentagon you can count on me to work day and night to ensure that the enemy can't compromise our computer systems." The employer smiled and said, "Harvey, I'm not that concerned about the enemy. I just want to make sure that the Navy doesn't know what the Air Force is doing."

Lesson to operating systems designers: A key goal of operating systems is compartmentalization. Operating systems must provide a working environment in which a great diversity of users can operate concurrently, knowing that their work is private and protected from other users.

cess issues a memory request, the system checks whether the requested address is greater than or equal to the process's low boundary register value and less than the process's high boundary register value (see the Anecdote, Compartmentalization). If so, the system honors the request; otherwise, the system terminates the program with an error message. As with single-user systems, multiprogramming systems provide system calls that enable user programs to access operating system services.

One problem prevalent in all memory organizations is that of **fragmentation**—the phenomenon wherein the system cannot use certain areas of available main memory (see the Operating Systems Thinking feature, Spatial Resources and Fragmentation).[23] Fixed-partition multiprogramming suffers from **internal fragmentation**, which occurs when the size of a process's memory and data is smaller than that of the partition in which the process executes.[24] (We discuss external fragmentation in Section 9.9, Variable-Partition Multiprogramming.)

Figure 9.11 illustrates the problem of internal fragmentation. The system's three user partitions are occupied, but each program is smaller than its corresponding partition. Consequently, the system may have enough main memory space in which to run another program but has no remaining partitions in which to run the program. Thus, some of the system's memory resources are wasted. In the next section we discuss another memory organization scheme that attempts to solve the problem of fixed partitions. We shall see that, although this scheme makes improvements, the system can still suffer from fragmentation.

Operating Systems Thinking

Spatial Resources and Fragmentation

Consider a common scenario: A restaurant in a shopping mall wants to expand, but no larger unoccupied stores are available in the mall, so the mall owners must wait for adjacent stores to become available, and then knock down some walls to create a larger space. An office building may initially start off as en empty "shell;" as customers rent spaces,

the walls are built to delineate the separate office spaces. When a customer wants to expand its space, it may be difficult to do so because no larger space may be available and the adjacent spaces may not be available. In both of these cases the units desiring to expand may not be able to find a sufficiently large contiguous space and may have to settle for

using several noncontiguous, smaller spaces. This is called fragmentation and it is a recurring theme in operating systems. In this book, you will see how main memory and secondary storage can each suffer various forms of fragmentation and how operating systems designers deal with these problems.

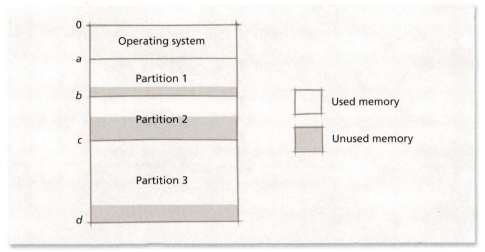

Figure 9.11 | Internal fragmentation in a fixed-partition multiprogramming system.

Self Review

1. Explain the need for relocating compilers, assemblers and loaders.
2. Describe the benefits and drawbacks of large and small partition sizes.

Ans: 1) Before such tools, programmers manually specified the partition into which their program had to be loaded, which potentially wasted memory and processor utilization, and reduced application portability. 2) Larger partitions allow large programs to run, but result in internal fragmentation for small programs. Small partitions reduce the amount of internal fragmentation and increase the level of multiprogramming by allowing more programs to reside in memory at once, but limit program size.

9.9 Variable-Partition Multiprogramming

Fixed-partition multiprogramming imposes restrictions on a system that result in inefficient resource use. For example, a partition may be too small to accommodate a waiting process, or so large that the system loses considerable resources to internal fragmentation. An obvious improvement, operating system designers decided, would be to allow a process to occupy only as much space as needed (up to the amount of available main memory). This scheme is called **variable-partition multiprogramming**.[25, 26, 27]

9.9.1 Variable-Partition Characteristics

Figure 9.12 shows how a system allocates memory under variable-partition multiprogramming. We continue to discuss only contiguous-allocation schemes, where a process must occupy adjacent memory locations. The queue at the top of the figure contains available jobs and information about their memory requirements. The operating system makes no assumption about the size of a job (except that it does

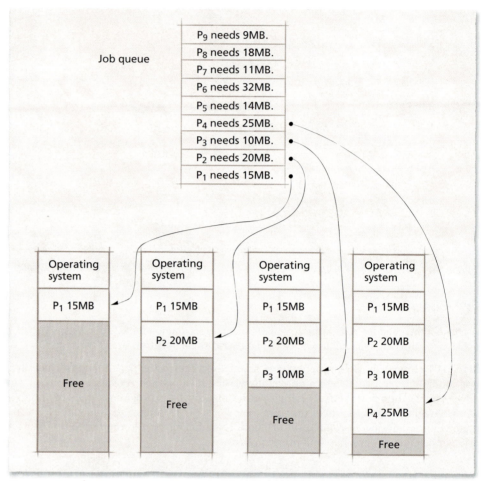

Figure 9.12 | *Initial partition assignments in variable-partition programming.*

not exceed the size of available main memory). The system progresses through the queue and places each job in memory, where there is available space, at which point it becomes a process. In Fig. 9.12, main memory can accommodate the first four jobs; we assume the free space that remains after the system has placed the job corresponding to process P_4 is less than 14KB (the size of the next available job).

Variable-partition multiprogramming organizations do not suffer from internal fragmentation, because a process's partition is exactly the size of the process. But every memory organization scheme involves some degree of waste. In variable-partition multiprogramming, the waste does not become obvious until processes finish and leave **holes** in main memory, as shown in Fig. 9.13. The system can continue to place new processes in these holes. However, as processes continue to complete, the holes get smaller, until every hole eventually becomes too small to hold a new process. This is called **external fragmentation**, where the sum of the holes is

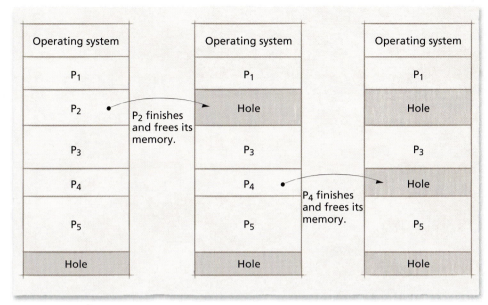

Figure 9.13 | Memory "holes" in variable-partition multiprogramming.

enough to accommodate another process, but the size of each hole is too small to accommodate any available process.[28]

The system can take measures to reduce some of its external fragmentation. When a process in a variable-partition multiprogramming system terminates, the system can determine whether the newly freed memory area is adjacent to other free memory areas. The system then records in a **free memory list** either (1) that the system now has an additional hole or (2) that an existing hole has been enlarged (reflecting the merging of the existing hole and the new adjacent hole).[29, 30] The process of merging adjacent holes to form a single, larger hole is called **coalescing** and is illustrated in Fig. 9.14. By coalescing holes, the system reclaims the largest possible contiguous blocks of memory.

Even as the operating system coalesces holes, the separate holes distributed throughout main memory may still constitute a significant amount of memory—enough in total to satisfy a process's memory requirements, although no individual hole is large enough to hold the process.

Another technique for reducing external fragmentation is called **memory compaction** (Fig. 9.15), which relocates all occupied areas of memory to one end or the other of main memory.[31] This leaves a single large free memory hole instead of the numerous small holes common in variable-partition multiprogramming. Now all of the available free memory is contiguous, so that an available process can run if its memory requirement is met by the single hole that results from compaction. Sometimes memory compaction is colorfully referred to as **burping the memory**. More conventionally, it is called **garbage collection**.[32]

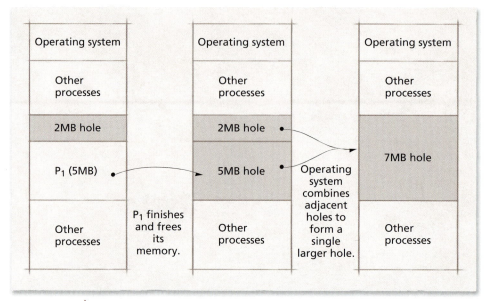

Figure 9.14 | *Coalescing memory "holes" in variable-partition multiprogramming.*

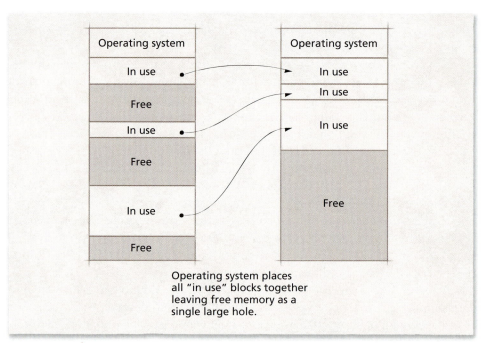

Figure 9.15 | *Memory compaction in variable-partition multiprogramming.*

Compaction is not without drawbacks. Compaction overhead consumes system resources that could otherwise be used productively. The system also must cease all other computation during compaction. This can result in erratic response times for interactive users and could be devastating in real-time systems. Furthermore, compaction must relocate the processes that currently occupy the main memory. This means that the system must now maintain relocation information, which ordinarily is lost when the system loads a program. With a normal, rapidly changing job mix, the system may compact frequently. The consumed system resources might not justify the benefits of compaction.

Self Review

1. Explain the difference between internal fragmentation and external fragmentation.
2. Describe two techniques to reduce external fragmentation in variable-partition multiprogramming systems.

Ans: **1)** Internal fragmentation occurs in fixed-partition environments when a process is allocated more space than it needs, leading to wasted memory space inside each partition. External fragmentation occurs in variable-partition environments when memory is wasted due to holes developing in memory between partitions. **2)** Coalescing merges adjacent free memory blocks into one larger block. Memory compaction relocates partitions to be adjacent to one another to consolidate free memory into a single block.

9.9.2 Memory Placement Strategies

In a variable-partition multiprogramming system, the system often has a choice as to which memory hole to allocate for an incoming process. The system's **memory placement strategy** determines where in main memory to place incoming programs and data.[33, 34, 35] Three strategies frequently discussed in the literature are illustrated in Fig. 9.16.[36]

- **First-fit strategy**—The system places an incoming job in main memory in the first available hole that is large enough to hold it. First-fit has intuitive appeal in that it allows the system to make a placement decision quickly.

- **Best-fit strategy**—The system places an incoming job in the hole in main memory in which it fits most tightly and which leaves the smallest amount of unused space. To many people, best fit is the most intuitive strategy, but it requires the overhead of searching all of the holes in memory for the best fit and tends to leave many small, unusable holes. Note in Fig. 9.16 that we maintain the entries of the free memory list in ascending order; such sorting is relatively expensive.

- **Worst-fit strategy**—At first this appears to be a whimsical choice. Upon closer examination, though, worst-fit also has strong intuitive appeal. Worst fit says to place a job in main memory in the hole in which it fits worst (i.e., in the largest possible hole). The intuitive appeal is simple: After the job is placed in this large hole, the remaining hole often is also large and thus able to hold a relatively large new program. The worst-fit strategy also requires the overhead of finding the largest hole and tends to leave many small, unusable holes.

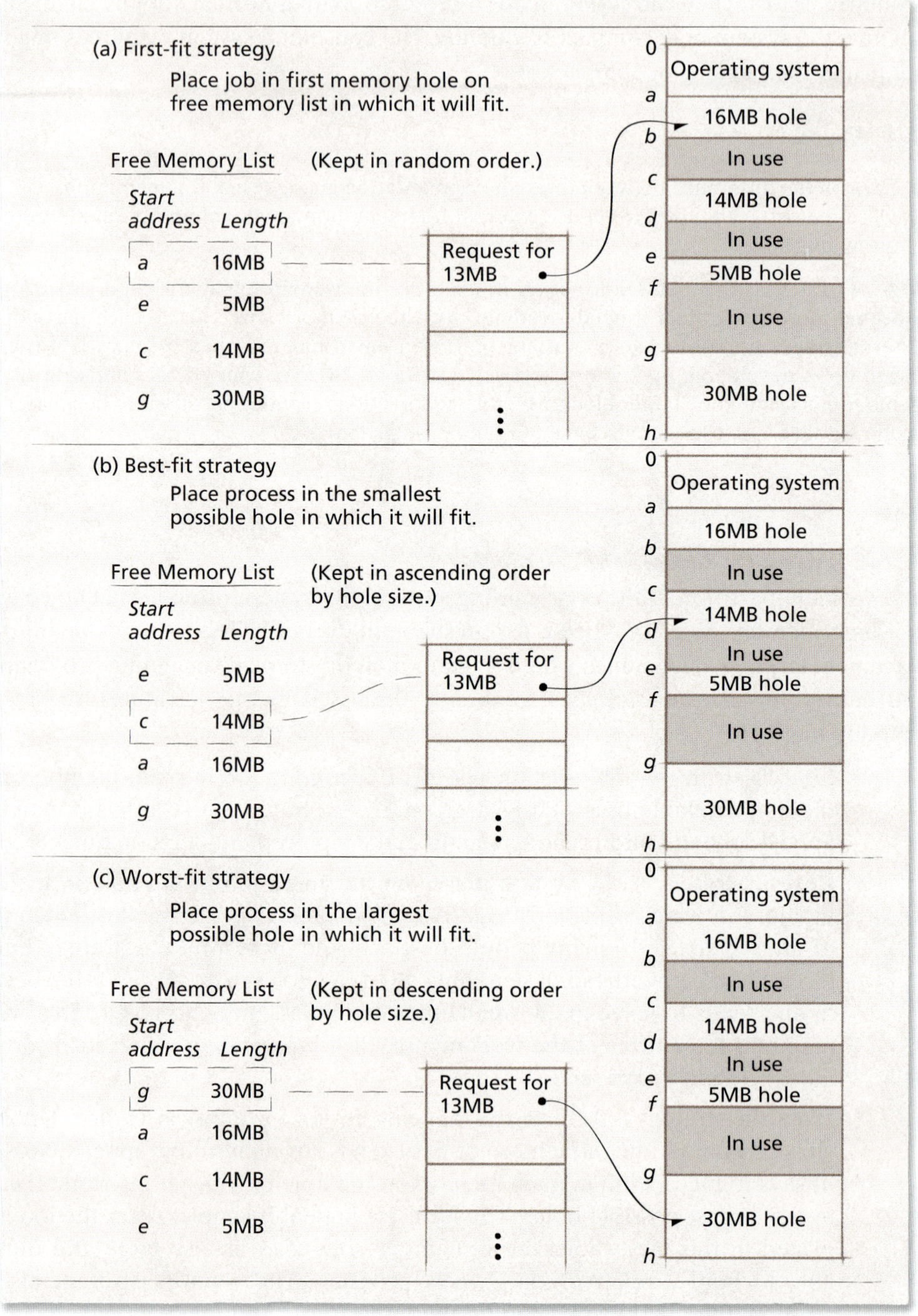

(a) First-fit strategy

Place job in first memory hole on free memory list in which it will fit.

Free Memory List   (Kept in random order.)

Start address	Length
a	16MB
e	5MB
c	14MB
g	30MB

Request for 13MB

0
Operating system
a
16MB hole
b
In use
c
14MB hole
d
In use
e
5MB hole
f
In use
g
30MB hole
h

(b) Best-fit strategy

Place process in the smallest possible hole in which it will fit.

Free Memory List   (Kept in ascending order by hole size.)

Start address	Length
e	5MB
c	14MB
a	16MB
g	30MB

Request for 13MB

0
Operating system
a
16MB hole
b
In use
c
14MB hole
d
In use
e
5MB hole
f
In use
g
30MB hole
h

(c) Worst-fit strategy

Place process in the largest possible hole in which it will fit.

Free Memory List   (Kept in descending order by hole size.)

Start address	Length
g	30MB
a	16MB
c	14MB
e	5MB

Request for 13MB

0
Operating system
a
16MB hole
b
In use
c
14MB hole
d
In use
e
5MB hole
f
In use
g
30MB hole
h

Figure 9.16 | *First-fit, best-fit and worst-fit memory placement strategies.*

A variation of first-fit, called the **next-fit strategy**, begins each search for an available hole at the point where the previous search ended.[37] Exercise 9.20 at the end of this chapter examines the next-fit strategy in detail.

Self Review

1. Why is first-fit an appealing strategy?
2. (T/F) None of the memory placement strategies in this section result in internal fragmentation.

Ans: **1)** First-fit is intuitively appealing because it does not require that the free memory list be sorted, so it incurs little overhead. However, it may operate slowly if the holes that are too small to hold the incoming job are at the front of the free memory list. **2)** True.

9.10 Multiprogramming with Memory Swapping

In all the multiprogramming schemes we have discussed in this chapter, the system maintains a process in main memory until it completes. An alternative to this scheme is **swapping**, in which a process does not necessarily remain in main memory throughout its execution.

In some swapping systems (Fig. 9.17), only one process occupies main memory at a given time. That process runs until it can no longer continue (e.g., because it must wait for I/O completion), at which time it relinquishes both the memory and the processor to the next process. Thus, the system dedicates the entire memory to one process for a brief period. When the process relinquishes the resource, the system **swaps** (or **rolls**) out the old process and swaps (or rolls) in the next process. To swap a process out, the system stores the process's memory contents (as well as its PCB) in secondary storage. When the system swaps the process back in, the process's memory contents and other values are retrieved from secondary storage. The system normally swaps a process in and out many times before the process completes.

Many early timesharing systems were implemented with this swapping technique. Response times could be guaranteed for a few users, but designers knew that they needed better techniques to handle large numbers of users. The swapping systems of the early 1960s led to today's paged virtual memory systems. Paging is considered in detail in the next two chapters on virtual memory systems.

More sophisticated swapping systems have been developed that allow several processes to remain in main memory at once.[38, 39] In these systems, the system swaps a process out only when an incoming process needs that memory space. With a sufficient amount of main memory, these systems greatly reduce the time spent swapping.

Self Review

1. Explain the overhead of swapping in terms of processor utilization. Assume that memory can hold only one process at a time.
2. Why were swapping systems in which only a single process at a time was in main memory insufficient for multiuser interactive systems?

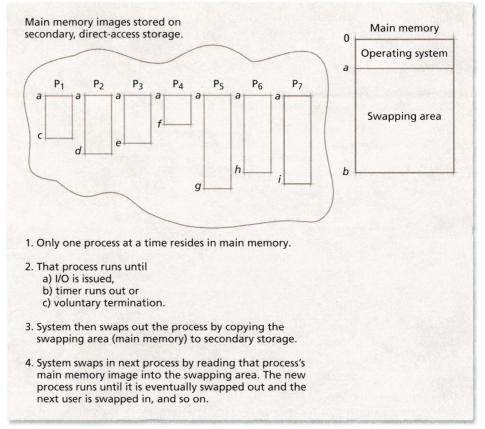

Main memory images stored on secondary, direct-access storage.

1. Only one process at a time resides in main memory.

2. That process runs until
   a) I/O is issued,
   b) timer runs out or
   c) voluntary termination.

3. System then swaps out the process by copying the swapping area (main memory) to secondary storage.

4. System swaps in next process by reading that process's main memory image into the swapping area. The new process runs until it is eventually swapped out and the next user is swapped in, and so on.

Figure 9.17 | *Multiprogramming in a swapping system in which only a single process at a time is in main memory.*

Ans: **1)** Enormous numbers of processor cycles are wasted when swapping a program between disk and memory. **2)** This type of swapping system could not provide reasonable response times to a large number of users, which is required for interactive systems.

Web Resources

www.kingston.com/tools/umg/default.asp
Describes the role of memory in a computer. Although the discussion is geared toward today's computers (which use virtual memory, a topic introduced in the next chapter), it describes many fundamental memory concepts.

www.linux-mag.com/2001-06/compile_01.html
Describes the working of the `malloc()` function in C, which allocates memory to newly created variables. The article also considers some basic allocation strategies that were discussed above (including first-fit, next-fit and worst-fit).

www.memorymanagement.org
Presents memory management techniques and garbage collection. The site also contains a glossary of over 400 memory management terms and a beginner's guide to memory management.

Summary

The organization and management of the real memory (also called main memory, physical memory or primary memory) of a computer system has been one of the most important influences upon operating systems design. Although most of today's systems implement virtual memory, certain types of real-time and embedded systems cannot afford the overhead of virtual memory—real memory management remains crucial to such systems.

Regardless of which memory organization scheme we adopt for a particular system, we must decide which strategies to use to obtain optimal memory performance. Memory management strategies determine how a particular memory organization performs under various policies. Memory management is typically performed by both software and special-purpose hardware. The memory manager is a component of the operating system that determines how available memory space is allocated to processes and how to respond to changes in a process's memory usage. The memory manager also interacts with special-purpose memory management hardware (if any is available) to improve performance.

Programs and data must be in main memory before the system can execute or reference them. The memory hierarchy contains levels characterized by the speed and cost of memory in each level. Systems with several levels of memory perform transfers that move programs and data back and forth between the various levels. Above the main memory level in the hierarchy is cache, which is much faster than main memory and is typically located on each processor in today's systems. Programs in main memory are transferred to the cache, where they are executed much faster than they would be from main memory. Because many processes that access data and instructions once are likely to access them again in the future (a phenomenon known as temporal locality), even a relatively small cache can significantly increase performance (when compared to running programs in a system without cache).

Memory management strategies are divided into fetch strategies, which determine when to move the next piece of a program or data to main memory from secondary storage, placement strategies, which determine where in main memory the system should place incoming program or data pieces, and replacement strategies, which determine which piece of a program or data to replace to accommodate incoming program and data pieces.

Contiguous memory allocation systems store a program in contiguous memory locations. In noncontiguous memory allocation, a program is divided into blocks or segments that the system may place in nonadjacent slots in main memory. This allows the memory management system to make use of holes (unused gaps in memory) that would otherwise be too small to hold programs. Although the operating system incurs more overhead in managing noncontiguous memory allocation, this can be justified by the increase in the level of multiprogramming (i.e., the number of processes that can occupy main memory at once).

Early computer systems allowed only one person at a time to use a machine. These computer systems typically did not contain an operating system. Later, system designers consolidated input/output coding that implemented basic functions into an input/output control system (IOCS), so the programmer no longer had to code input/output instructions directly. With overlays, the system could execute programs larger than main memory. However, manual overlay requires careful and time-consuming planning, and the programmer often must have detailed knowledge of the system's memory organization.

Without protection in a single-user system, a process can interfere with the operating system's memory—either intentionally or inadvertently—by replacing some or all of its memory contents with other data. Protection in single-user contiguous memory allocation systems can be implemented with a single boundary register built into the processor. Processes must access the operating system from time to time to obtain services such as input/output. The operating system provides several system calls (also called supervisor calls) that may be used to request such services from the operating system.

Early single-user real memory systems were dedicated to one job for more than the job's execution time. Jobs generally required considerable setup and teardown time, during which the computer sat idle. The development of batch-processing systems improved utilization. In single-stream batch-processing, jobs are grouped in batches by loading them consecutively onto tape or disk. Even with batch-processing operating systems, single-user systems still wasted a considerable amount of the computing resource. Therefore, designers chose to implement multiprogramming systems, in which several users simultaneously compete for system resources.

The earliest multiprogramming systems used fixed-partition multiprogramming, in which the system divides main memory into a number of fixed-size partitions., each holding a single job. The system switches the processor rapidly between jobs to create the illusion of simultaneity. To overcome the problem of memory waste, developers created relocating compilers, assemblers and loaders.

In contiguous-allocation multiprogramming systems, protection often is implemented with multiple boundary registers, called the base and limit registers, for each process. One problem prevalent in all memory organizations is that of fragmentation—the phenomenon wherein the system is unable to make use of certain areas of available main memory. Fixed-partition multiprogramming suffers from internal fragmentation, which occurs when the size of a process's memory and data is smaller than the partition in which the process executes.

Variable-partition multiprogramming allows a process to occupy only as much space as needed (up to the amount of available main memory). Waste does not become obvious until processes finish and leave holes in main memory, resulting in external fragmentation. The system can take measures to reduce some of its external fragmentation by implementing a free memory list to coalesce holes, or perform memory compaction.

The system's memory placement strategy determines where in main memory to place incoming programs and data.

The first-fit strategy places an incoming job in main memory in the first available hole that is large enough to hold it. The best-fit strategy places the job in the hole in main memory in which it fits most tightly and which leaves the smallest amount of unused space. The worst-fit strategy places the job in main memory in the hole in which it fits worst (i.e., in the largest possible hole). A variation of the first-fit, called the next-fit strategy, begins each search for an available hole at the point where the previous search ended.

Memory swapping is a technique in which a process does not necessarily remain in main memory throughout its execution. When a process in memory cannot execute, the system swaps (or rolls) out the old process and swaps (or rolls) in the next process. More sophisticated swapping systems have been developed that allow several processes to remain in main memory at once. In these systems, the system swaps a process out only when an incoming process needs that memory space. With a sufficient amount of main memory, these systems greatly reduce the time spent swapping.

Key Terms

anticipatory fetch strategy—Method of bringing pages into main memory before they are requested so they will be immediately available when they are requested. This is accomplished by predicting which operations a program will perform next.

base register—Register containing the lowest memory address a process may reference.

best-fit memory placement strategy—Memory placement strategy that places an incoming job in the smallest hole in memory that can hold the job.

boundary register—Register for single-user operating systems that was used for memory protection by separating user memory space from kernel memory space.

burping the memory—See memory compaction.

cache memory—Small, expensive, high-speed memory that holds copies of programs and data to decrease memory access times.

coalescing memory holes—Process of merging adjacent holes in memory in variable partition multiprogramming systems. This helps create the largest possible holes available for incoming programs and data.

contiguous memory allocation—Method of assigning memory such that all of the addresses in the process's entire address space are adjacent to one another.

demand fetch strategy—Method of bringing program parts or data into main memory as they are requested by a process.

executive mode—Protected mode in which a processor can execute operating system instructions on behalf of a user (also called kernel mode).

external fragmentation—Phenomenon in variable-partition memory systems in which there are holes distributed throughout memory that are too small to hold a process.

fetch strategy—Method of determining when to obtain the next piece of program or data for transfer from secondary storage to main memory.

first-fit memory placement strategy—Memory placement strategy that places an incoming process in the first hole that is large enough to hold it.

fixed-partition multiprogramming—Memory organization that divides main memory into a number of fixed-size partitions, each holding a single job.

fragmentation (of main memory)—Phenomenon wherein a system is unable to make use of certain areas of available main memory.

free memory list—Operating system data structure that points to available holes in memory.

garbage collection—See memory compaction.

hole — An unused area of memory in a variable-partition multiprogramming system.

input/output control system (IOCS) — Precursor to modern operating systems that provided programmers with a basic set of functions to perform I/O.

intensive resource management — Notion of devoting substantial resources to managing other resources to improve overall utilization.

internal fragmentation — Phenomenon in fixed-partition multiprogramming systems in which there holes occur when the size of a process's memory and data is smaller than the partition in which the process executes.

job control language — Commands interpreted by a job stream processor that define and facilitate the setup of the next job in a single-stream batch-processing system.

job stream processor — Entity in single-stream batch-processing systems that controls the transition between jobs.

job-to-job transition — Time during which jobs cannot execute in single-stream batch-processing systems while one job is purged from the system and the next job is loaded and prepared for execution.

limit register — Register used in fixed-partition multiprogramming systems to mark where a process's memory partition ends.

memory compaction — Relocating all partitions in a variable-partition multiprogramming system to one end of main memory to create the largest possible memory hole.

memory hierarchy — Model that classifies memory into levels corresponding to speed, size and cost.

memory management strategy — Specification of how a particular memory organization performs operations such as fetching, placing and replacing memory.

memory manager — Component of an operating system that implements the system's memory organization and memory management strategies.

memory organization — Manner in which the system views main memory, addressing concerns such as how many processes exist in memory, where to place programs and data in memory and when to replace those pieces with other pieces.

next-fit memory placement strategy — Variation of the first-fit memory placement strategy that begins each search for an available hole at the point where the previous search ended.

noncontiguous memory allocation — Method of memory allocation that divides a program into several, possibly nonadjacent, pieces that the system places throughout main memory.

overlay — Concept created to enable programs larger than main memory to run. Programs are broken into pieces that do not need to exist simultaneously in memory. An overlay contains one such piece of a program.

partition — Portion of main memory allocated to a process in fixed- and variable-partition multiprogramming. Programs are placed into partitions so that the operating system can protect itself from user processes and so that processes are protected from each other.

physical memory — See main memory.

placement strategy (main memory) — Strategy that determines where in the main memory to place incoming programs and data.

replacement strategy (main memory) — Method that a system uses to determine which piece of program or data to displace to accommodate incoming programs or data.

roll — See swap.

setup time — Time required by a system operator and the operating system to prepare the next job to be executed.

single-stream batch-processing system — Batch-processing system that places ready jobs in available partitions from one queue of pending jobs.

single-user contiguous memory allocation system — System in which programs are placed in adjacent memory addresses and the system services only one program at a time.

supervisor call — Request by a user process to the operating system to perform an operation on its behalf (also called a system call).

swap — Method of copying a process's memory contents to secondary storage, removing the process from memory and allocating the freed memory to a new process.

teardown time — Time required by a system operator and the operating system to remove a job from a system after the job has completed.

temporal locality — Property of events that are closely related over time. In memory references, temporal locality occurs when processes reference the same memory locations repeatedly within a short period.

variable-partition multiprogramming — Method of assigning partitions that are the exact size of the job entering the system.

wall clock time — Measure of time as perceived by a user.

worst-fit strategy — Memory placement strategy that places an incoming job in the largest hole in memory.

Exercises

9.1 In hierarchical memory systems, a certain amount of overhead is involved in moving programs and data between the various levels of the hierarchy. Discuss why the benefits derived from such systems justify the overhead involved.

9.2 Why did demand fetching endure as the conventional wisdom for so long? Why are anticipatory fetch strategies receiving so much more attention today than they did decades ago?

9.3 Discuss how memory fragmentation occurs in each of the memory organization schemes presented in this chapter.

9.4 In what circumstances are overlays useful? When may a section of main memory be overlayed? How does overlaying affect program development time? How does overlaying affect program modifiability?

9.5 Discuss the motivations for multiprogramming. What characteristics of programs and machines make multiprogramming desirable? In what circumstances is multiprogramming undesirable?

9.6 You are given a hierarchical memory system consisting of four levels—cache, primary memory, secondary memory and tertiary memory. Assume that programs may be executed in any of the memory levels. Each level consists of an identical amount of memory, and the range of memory addresses in each level is identical. Cache runs programs the fastest, primary memory is ten times slower than the cache, secondary memory is ten times slower than primary memory and tertiary memory is ten times slower than secondary memory. There is only one processor and it may execute only one program at a time.

   a. Assume that programs and data may be shuttled from any level to any other level under the operating system's control. The time it takes to transfer items between two particular levels is dependent upon the speed of the lowest (and slowest) level involved in the transfer. Why might the operating system choose to shuttle a program from cache directly to secondary memory, thus bypassing primary memory? Why would items be shuttled to slower levels of the hierarchy? Why would items be shuttled to faster levels of the hierarchy?

   b. The scheme above is somewhat unconventional. It is more common for programs and data to be moved only between adjacent levels of the hierarchy. Give several arguments against allowing transfers directly from the cache to any level other than primary memory.

9.7 As a systems programmer in a large computer installation using a fixed-partition multiprogramming system, you have the task of determining if the current partitioning of the system should be altered.

   a. What information would you need to help you make your decision?

   b. If you had this information readily available, how would you determine the ideal partitioning?

   c. What are the consequences of repartitioning such a system?

9.8 A simple scheme for relocating programs in multiprogramming environments involves the use of a single relocation register. All programs are translated to locations beginning at zero, but every address developed as the program executes is modified by adding to it the contents of the processor's relocation register. Discuss the use and control of the relocation register in variable-partition multiprogramming. How might the relocation register be used in a protection scheme?

9.9 Placement strategies determine where in the main memory incoming programs and data should be loaded. Suppose a job waiting to begin execution has a memory requirement that can be fulfilled immediately. Should the job be loaded and begin execution immediately?

9.10 Charging for resources in multiprogramming systems can be complex.

   a. In a dedicated system, the user is normally charged for the entire system. Suppose that in a multiprogramming system only one user is currently on the system. Should the user be charged for the entire system?

   b. Multiprogramming operating systems generally consume substantial system resources, as they manage multiple-user environments. Should users pay for this overhead, or should it be "absorbed" by the operating system?

   c. Most people agree that charges for computer system usage should be fair, but few can define precisely what "fairness" is. Another attribute of charging schemes, but one which is easier to define, is predictability. We want to know that if a job costs a certain amount to run once, running it again in similar circumstances will cost approximately the same amount. Suppose that in a multiprogramming environment we charge by wall clock time, i.e., the total real time involved in running the job from start to completion. Would such a scheme yield predictable charges? Why?

9.11 Discuss the advantages and disadvantages of noncontiguous memory allocation.

9.12 Many designers believe that the operating system should always be given a "most trusted" status. Some designers feel that even the operating system should be curtailed, particularly in its ability to reference certain areas of memory. Discuss the pros and cons of allowing the operating system to access the full range of real addresses in a computer system at all times.

9.13 Developments in operating systems have generally occurred in an evolutionary rather than revolutionary fashion. For each of the following transitions, describe the primary motivations that led operating systems designers to produce the new type of system from the old.

    a. Single-user dedicated systems to multiprogramming

    b. Fixed-partition multiprogramming systems with absolute translation and loading to fixed-partition multiprogramming systems with relocatable translation and loading

    c. Fixed-partition multiprogramming to variable-partition multiprogramming

    d. Contiguous memory allocation systems to noncontiguous memory allocation systems

    e. Single-user dedicated systems with manual job-to-job transition to single-user dedicated systems with single-stream batch-processing systems

9.14 Consider the problem of jobs waiting in a queue until sufficient memory becomes available for them to be loaded and executed. If the queue is a simple first-in-first-out structure, then only the job at the head of the queue may be considered for placement in memory. With a more complex queuing mechanism, it might be possible to examine the entire queue to choose the next job to be loaded and executed. Show how the latter discipline, even though more complex, might yield better throughput than the simple first-in-first-out strategy. What problem could the latter approach suffer from?

9.15 One pessimistic operating systems designer says it really does not matter what memory placement strategy is used. Sooner or later a system achieves steady state and all of the strategies perform similarly. Do you agree? Explain.

9.16 Another pessimistic designer asks why we go to the trouble of defining a strategy with an official-sounding name like first-fit. This designer claims that a first-fit strategy is equivalent to nothing more than random memory placement. Do you agree? Explain.

9.17 Consider a swapping system with several partitions. The absolute version of such a system would require that programs be repeatedly swapped in and out of the same partition. The relocatable version would allow programs to be swapped in and out of any available partitions large enough to hold them, possibly different partitions on successive swaps. Assuming that main memory is many times the size of the average job, discuss the advantages of this multiple-user swapping scheme over the single-user swapping scheme described in the text.

9.18 Sharing procedures and data can reduce the main memory demands of jobs, thus enabling a higher level of multiprogramming. Indicate how a sharing mechanism might be implemented for each of the following schemes. If you feel that sharing is inappropriate for certain schemes, say so and explain why.

    a. fixed-partition multiprogramming with absolute translation and loading

    b. fixed-partition multiprogramming with relocatable translation and loading

    c. variable-partition multiprogramming

    d. multiprogramming in a swapping system that enables two jobs to reside in main memory at once, but that multiprograms more than two jobs.

9.19 Much of the discussion in this chapter assumes that main memory is a relatively expensive resource that should be managed intensively. Imagine that main memory eventually becomes so abundant and so inexpensive, that users could essentially have all they want. Discuss the ramifications of such a development on

    a. operating system design and memory management strategies

    b. user application design.

9.20 In this exercise, you will examine the next-fit strategy and compare it to first-fit.

    a. How would the data structure used for implementing next-fit differ from that used for first-fit?

    b. What happens in first-fit if the search reaches the highest-addressed block of memory and discovers it is not large enough?

    c. What happens in next-fit when the highest-addressed memory block is not large enough?

    d. Which strategy uses free memory more uniformly?

    e. Which strategy tends to cause small blocks to collect at low memory addresses?

    f. Which strategy does a better job keeping large blocks available?

9.21 *(Fifty-Percent Rule)* The more mathematically inclined student may want to attempt to prove the "fifty-percent rule" developed by Knuth.[40, 41] The rule states that at steady state a variable-partition multiprogramming system will tend to have approximately half as many holes as there are occupied memory blocks. It assumes that the vast majority of "fits" are not exact (so that fits tend *not* to reduce the number of holes).

9.22 A variable-partition multiprogramming system uses a free memory list to track available memory. The current list contains entries of 150KB, 360KB, 400KB, 625KB, and 200KB. The system receives requests for 215KB, 171KB, 86KB, and 481KB, in that order. Describe the final contents of the free memory list if the system used each of the following memory placement strategies.

- **a.** best-fit
- **b.** first-fit
- **c.** worst-fit
- **d.** next-fit

9.23 This exercise analyzes the worst-fit and best-fit strategies discussed in Section 9.9, Variable-Partition Multiprogramming, with various data structures.

- **a.** Discuss the efficiency of worst-fit when locating the appropriate memory hole in a free memory list stored in the following data structures.
  - **i.** unsorted array
  - **ii.** array sorted by size of hole
  - **iii.** unsorted linked list
  - **iv.** linked list sorted by size of hole
  - **v.** binary tree
  - **vi.** balanced binary tree
- **b.** Discuss the efficiency of best-fit when locating the appropriate memory hole in a free memory list stored in the following data structures.
  - **i.** unsorted array
  - **ii.** array sorted by size of hole
  - **iii.** unsorted linked list
  - **iv.** linked list sorted by size of hole
  - **v.** binary tree
  - **vi.** balanced binary tree
- **c.** Comparing your results from parts a and b, it might appear that one algorithm is more efficient than the other. Why is this an invalid conclusion?

Suggested Projects

9.24 Prepare a research paper on the use of real memory management in real-time systems.

9.25 Prepare a research paper describing variations on the traditional memory hierarchy.

Suggested Simulations

9.26 Develop a simulation program to investigate the relative effectiveness of the first-fit, best-fit, and worst-fit memory placement strategies. Your program should measure memory utilization and average turnaround time for the various memory placement strategies. Assume a real memory system with 1GB capacity, of which 300MB is reserved for the operating system. New processes arrive at random intervals between 1 and 10 minutes (in multiples of 1 minute), the sizes of the processes are random between 50MB and 300MB in multiples of 10MB, and the durations range from 5 to 60 minutes in multiples of 5 minutes in units of 1 minute. Your program should simulate each strategy over a long enough interval to achieve steady-state operation.

- **a.** Discuss the relative difficulties of implementing each strategy.
- **b.** Indicate any significant performance differences you observed.
- **c.** Vary the job arrival rates and job size distributions and observe the results for each strategy.
- **d.** Based on your observations, state which strategy you would choose if you were actually implementing a physical memory management system.
- **e.** Based on your observations, suggest some other memory placement strategy that you think would be more effective than the ones you have investigated here. Simulate its behavior. What results do you observe?

For each of your simulations, assume that the time it takes to make the memory placement decision is negligible.

9.27 Simulate a system that initially contains 100MB of free memory, in which processes frequently enter and exit the system. The arriving processes are between 2MB and 35MB in size, and their execution times vary between 2 and 5 seconds. Vary the rate of arrival between two processes per second and one process every 5 seconds. Evaluate memory utilization and throughput when using the first-fit, best-fit and worst-fit strategies. Keeping each placement strategy constant, vary the process scheduling algorithm to evaluate its effect on throughput and average wait times. Incorporate scheduling algorithms from Chapter 8, such as FIFO and SPF, and evaluate other algorithms, such as smallest-process-first and largest-process-first. Be sure to determine which, if any, of these algorithms can suffer from indefinite postponement.

Recommended Reading

As a result of the widespread usage of virtual memory, many of the techniques in this chapter are no longer discussed in the literature. Belady et al.[42] provided a thorough treatment of the history of memory management in IBM systems. Mitra[43] and Pohm and Smay[44] give a description of the memory hierarchy that has become the standard in architectures for decades. Bayes[45] and Stephenson[46] presented the primary strategies for memory allocation and placement. Denning[47] presented the pitfalls of single-user contiguous memory allocation, while Knight[48] and Coffman and Ryan[49] investigated the implementation of partitioned memory. Memory placement algorithms were presented by Knuth,[50] Stephenson[51] and Oldehoeft and Allan;[52] memory swapping concepts, which are vital to virtual memory, are presented in further detail in the next chapter.

Recent research has focused on optimizing the use of the memory hierarchy. Several memory management strategies have focused on a faster and more expensive resource, cache.[53] The literature also reports application-specific tuning of the memory architecture to improve performance.[54, 55]

Embedded systems are designed differently than general-purpose systems. Whereas general-purpose systems will provide enough resources to perform a wide variety of tasks concurrently, embedded systems provide the bare minimum necessary to meet their design goals. Due to size and cost considerations, resources in embedded systems are much more scarce than in general-purpose systems. The *ACM Transactions on Embedded Computing Systems*, in their November 2002 and February 2003 issues, explored a great deal of research on the topic of memory management in embedded systems.[56] The bibliography for this chapter is located on our Web site at `www.deitel.com/books/os3e/Bibliography.pdf`.

Works Cited

1. Belady, L. A.; Parmelee, R. P.; and C. A. Scalzi, "The IBM History of Memory Management Technology," *IBM Journal of Research and Development*, Vol. 25, No. 5, September 1981, pp. 491–503.

2. Belady, L. A.; Parmelee, R. P.; and C. A. Scalzi, "The IBM History of Memory Management Technology," *IBM Journal of Research and Development*, Vol. 25, No. 5, September 1981, pp. 491–503. "How Much Memory Does My Software Need?" <`www.crucial.com/library/softwareguide.asp`>, viewed July 15, 2003.

3. Belady, L. A.; Parmelee, R. P.; and C. A. Scalzi, "The IBM History of Memory Management Technology," *IBM Journal of Research and Development*, Vol. 25, No. 5, September 1981, pp. 491–503. "How Much Memory Does My Software Need?" <`www.crucial.com/library/softwareguide.asp`>, viewed July 15, 2003.

4. "Microsoft/Windows Timeline," <`www.technicalminded.com/windows_timeline.htm`>, last modified February 16, 2003.

5. "Windows Version History," <`support.microsoft.com/default.aspx?scid=http://support.microsoft.com:80/support/kb/articles/Q32/9/05.asp&NoWebContent=1`>, last reviewed September 20, 1999.

6. Anand Lal Shimpi, "Western Digital Raptor Preview: 10,000 RPM and Serial ATA," *AnandTech.com*, March 7, 2003, <`www.anandtech.com/storage/showdoc.html?i=1795&p=9`>.

7. Todd Tokubo, "Technology Guide: DDR RAM," *GamePC.com*, September 14, 2000, <`www.gamepc.com/labs/view_content.asp?id=ddrguide&page=3`>.

8. Baskett, F.; Broune, J. C.; and W. M. Raike, "The Management of a Multi-level Non-paged Memory System," *Proceedings Spring Joint Computer Conference*, 1970, pp. 459–465.

9. Lin, Y. S., and R. L. Mattson, "Cost-Performance Evaluation of Memory Hierarchies," *IEEE Transactions Magazine*, MAG-8, No. 3, September 1972, p. 390.

10. Mitra, D., "Some Aspects of Hierarchical Memory Systems," *JACM*, Vol. 21, No. 1, January 1974, p. 54.

11. Pohm, A. V., and T. A. Smay, "Computer Memory Systems," *IEEE Computer*, October 1981, pp. 93–110.

12. Pohm, A. V., and T. A. Smay, "Computer Memory Systems," *IEEE Computer*, October 1981, pp. 93–110.

13. Smith, A. J., "Cache Memories," *ACM Computing Surveys*, Vol. 14, No. 3, September 1982, pp. 473–530.

14. Bays, C., "A Comparison of Next-fit, First-fit, and Best-fit," *Communications of the ACM*, Vol. 20, No. 3, March 1977, pp. 191–192.

15. Stephenson, C. J., "Fast Fits: New Methods for Dynamic Storage Allocation," *Proceedings of the 9th Symposium on Operating Systems Principles*, ACM, Vol. 17, No. 5, October 1983, pp. 30–32.

16. Belady, L. A.; R. P. Parmelee; and C. A. Scalzi, "The IBM History of Memory Management Technology," *IBM Journal of Research and Development*, Vol. 25, No. 5, September 1981, pp. 491–503.

17. Feiertag, R. J. and Organick, E. I., "The Multics Input/Output System," *ACM Symposium on Operating Systems Principles*, 1971, pp. 35–41.

18. Denning, P. J., "Third Generation Computer Systems," *ACM Computing Surveys*, Vol. 3, No. 4, December 1971, pp. 175–216.

19. Denning, P. J., "Third Generation Computer Systems," *ACM Computing Surveys*, Vol. 3, No. 4, December 1971, pp. 175–216.

20. Dennis, J. B., "A Multiuser Computation Facility for Education and Research," *Communications of the ACM*, Vol. 7, No. 9, September 1964, pp. 521–529.

21. Belady, L. A.; Parmelee, R. P.; and C. A. Scalzi, "The IBM History of Memory Management Technology," *IBM Journal of Research and Development*, Vol. 25, No. 5, September 1981, pp. 491–503.

22. Knight, D. C., "An Algorithm for Scheduling Storage on a Non-Paged Computer," *Computer Journal*, Vol. 11, No. 1, February 1968, pp. 17–21.

23. Denning, P., "Virtual Memory", *ACM Computing Surveys*, Vol. 2, No. 3, September 1970, pp. 153–189.

24. Randell, B., "A Note on Storage Fragmentation and Program Segmentation," *Communications of the ACM*, Vol. 12, No. 7, July 1969, pp. 365–372.

25. Knight, D. C., "An Algorithm for Scheduling Storage on a Non-Paged Computer," *Computer Journal*, Vol. 11, No. 1, February 1968, pp. 17–21.

26. Coffman, E. G., and T. A. Ryan, "A Study of Storage Partitioning Using a Mathematical Model of Locality," *Communications of the ACM*, Vol. 15, No. 3, March 1972, pp. 185–190.

27. Belady, L. A.; Parmelee, R. P.; and C. A. Scalzi, "The IBM History of Memory Management Technology," *IBM Journal of Research and Development*, Vol. 25, No. 5, September 1981, pp. 491–503.

28. Randell, B., "A Note on Storage Fragmentation and Program Segmentation," *Communications of the ACM*, Vol. 12, No. 7, July 1969, pp. 365–372.

29. Margolin, B. H.; Parmelee, R. P.; and M. Schatzoff, "Analysis of Free-Storage Algorithms," *IBM Systems Journal*, Vol. 10, No. 4, 1971, pp. 283–304.

30. Bozman, G.; Buco, W.; Daly, T. P.; and W. H. Tetzlaff, "Analysis of Free-Storage Algorithms—Revisited," *IBM Systems Journal*, Vol. 23, No. 1, 1984, pp. 44–66.

31. Baskett, F.; Broune, J. C.; and W. M. Raike, "The Management of a Multi-level Non-paged Memory System," *Proceedings Spring Joint Computer Conference*, 1970, pp. 459–465.

32. Davies, D. J. M., "Memory Occupancy Patterns in Garbage Collection Systems," *Communications of the ACM*, Vol. 27, No. 8, August 1984, pp. 819–825.

33. Knuth, D. E., *The Art of Computer Programming: Fundamental Algorithms*, Vol. 1, 2nd ed., Reading, MA: Addison-Wesley, 1973.

34. Stephenson, C. J., "Fast Fits: New Methods for Dynamic Storage Allocation," *Proceedings of the 9th Symposium on Operating Systems Principles, ACM*, Vol. 17, No. 5, October 1983, pp. 30–32.

35. Oldehoeft, R. R., and S. J. Allan, "Adaptive Exact-fit Storage Management," *Communications of the ACM*, Vol. 28, No. 5, May 1985, pp. 506–511.

36. Shore, J., "On the External Storage Fragmentation Produced by First-fit and Best-fit Allocation Strategies," *Communications of the ACM*, Vol. 18, No. 8, August 1975, pp. 433–440.

37. Bays, C., "A Comparison of Next-fit, First-fit, and Best-fit," *Communications of the ACM*, Vol. 20, No. 3, March 1977, pp. 191–192.

38. Ritchie, D. M., and K. T. Thompson, "The UNIX Time-sharing System," *Communications of the ACM*, Vol. 17, No. 7, July 1974, pp. 365–375.

39. Belady, L. A.; Parmelee, R. P.; and C. A. Scalzi, "The IBM History of Memory Management Technology," *IBM Journal of Research and Development*, Vol. 25, No. 5, September 1981, pp. 491–503.

40. Knuth, D. E., *The Art of Computer Programming: Fundamental Algorithms*, Vol. 1, 2nd ed., Reading, MA: Addison-Wesley, 1973.

41. Shore, J. E., "Anomalous Behavior of the Fifty-Percent Rule," *Communications of the ACM*, Vol. 20, No. 11, November 1977, pp. 812–820.

42. Belady, L. A.; Parmelee, R. P.; and C. A. Scalzi, "The IBM History of Memory Management Technology," *IBM Journal of Research and Development*, Vol. 25, No. 5, September 1981, pp. 491–503.

43. Mitra, D., "Some Aspects of Hierarchical Memory Systems," *JACM*, Vol. 21, No. 1, January 1974, p. 54.

44. Pohm, A. V., and T. A. Smay, "Computer Memory Systems," *IEEE Computer*, October 1981, pp. 93–110.

45. Bays, C., "A Comparison of Next-fit, First-fit, and Best-fit," *Communications of the ACM*, Vol. 20, No. 3, March 1977, pp. 191–192.

46. Stephenson, C. J., "Fast Fits: New Methods for Dynamic Storage Allocation," *Proceedings of the 9th Symposium on Operating Systems Principles*, ACM, Vol. 17, No. 5, October 1983, pp. 30–32.

47. Denning, P. J., "Third Generation Computer Systems," *ACM Computing Surveys*, Vol. 3, No. 4, December 1971, pp. 175–216.

48. Knight, D. C., "An Algorithm for Scheduling Storage on a Non-Paged Computer," *Computer Journal*, Vol. 11, No. 1, February 1968, pp. 17–21.

49. Coffman, E. G., and T. A. Ryan, "A Study of Storage Partitioning Using a Mathematical Model of Locality," *Communications of the ACM*, Vol. 15, No. 3, March 1972, pp. 185–190.

50. Knuth, D. E., *The Art of Computer Programming: Fundamental Algorithms*, Vol. 1, 2nd ed., Reading, MA: Addison-Wesley, 1973.

51. Stephenson, C. J., "Fast Fits: New Methods for Dynamic Storage Allocation," *Proceedings of the 9th Symposium on Operating Systems Principles*, ACM, Vol. 17, No. 5, October 1983, pp. 30–32.

52. Oldehoeft, R. R., and S. J. Allan, "Adaptive Exact-fit Storage Management," *Communications of the ACM*, Vol. 28, No. 5, May 1985, pp. 506–511.

53. Luk, C. and Mowry, T. C., "Architectural and Compiler Support for Effective Instruction Prefetching: A Cooperative Approach," *ACM Transactions on Computer Systems (TOCS)*, Vol. 19 No. 1, February 2001.

54. Mellor-Crummey, J.; Whalley, D; and K. Kennedy, "Improving Memory Hierarchy Performance for Irregular Applications," *Proceedings of the 13th International Conference on Supercomputing*, May 1999.

55. Mellor-Crummey, J.; Fowler, R.; and D. Whalley, "Tools for Application-oriented Performance Tuning," *Proceedings of the 15th International Conference on Supercomputing*, June 2001.

56. Jacob, B. and S. Bhattacharyya, "Introduction to the Two Special Issues on Memory," *ACM Transactions on Embedded Computing Systems (TECS)*, February 2003, Vol. 2, No. 1.

The fancy is indeed no other than a mode of memory emancipated from the order of time and space.

—Samuel Taylor Coleridge—

Lead me from the unreal to the real!

—*The Upanishads*—

O happy fault, which has deserved to have such and so mighty a Redeemer.

—The Missal—*The Book of Common Prayer*—

But every page having an ample marge,
And every marge enclosing in the midst
A square of text that looks a little blot.

—Alfred, Lord Tennyson—

Addresses are given to us to conceal our whereabouts.

—Saki (H.H. Munro)—

Chapter 10

Virtual Memory Organization

Objectives

After reading this chapter, you should understand:

- *the concept of virtual memory.*
- *paged virtual memory systems.*
- *segmented virtual memory systems.*
- *combined segmentation/paging virtual memory systems.*
- *sharing and protection in virtual memory systems.*
- *the hardware that makes virtual memory systems feasible.*
- *the IA-32 Intel architecture virtual memory implementation.*

Chapter Outline

10.1 Introduction

In the preceding chapter, we discussed basic memory management techniques, each of which ultimately must contend with limited memory space. One solution is larger main memories; however, it is often prohibitively expensive to build systems with sufficiently large fast-access memory. Another solution would be to create the illusion that more memory exists. This is a fundamental idea behind **virtual memory**,[1,2,3] which first appeared in the Atlas computer system constructed at the University of Manchester in England in 1960 (see the Mini Case Study, Atlas).[4,5,6,7] Figure 10.1 shows how memory organizations have evolved from single-user real memory systems to multiuser, segmentation/paging virtual memory systems.

This chapter describes how a system implements virtual memory (see the Operating Systems Thinking feature, Virtualization). Specifically, we present the techniques the operating system and the hardware use to convert virtual addresses to physical addresses; and we discuss the two most common noncontiguous alloca-

Mini Case Study

Atlas

The Atlas project began in 1956 at the University of Manchester, England. The project, originally called the MUSE (short for micro-SEcond; "micro" is represented by the Greek letter "mu"), was launched to compete with the high-performance computers being produced by the United States.[8] In 1959, Ferranti Ltd. joined the project as a corporate sponsor, and the first Atlas computer was completed at the end of 1962.[9] Though the Atlas computer was produced for only about 10 years, it made significant contributions computing technology. Many of these appeared in the computer's operating system, the Atlas Supervisor.

The Atlas Supervisor operating system was the first to implement virtual memory.[10] Setting a new standard for job throughput, the Atlas Supervisor was able to execute 16 jobs at once.[11] It also provided its operators with detailed runtime statistics, whereas most other systems required operators to determine them manually. The Atlas Supervisor was also one of the earliest computers to design detailed hardware guidelines in early stages of development to simply systems programming.[12]

Although Atlas was the most powerful computer when it was completed in 1962, it was mostly ignored by the industry.[13] Only three Atlas computers were ever sold, the last in 1965, only three years after its completion.[14] A contributing factor to Atlas's short lifetime was that its programs had to be written in Atlas Autocode, a language much like Algol 60, but not accepted by most programmers.[15] Atlas's designers were eventually forced to implement more popular languages such as Fortran.[16] Another reason for Atlas's quick demise was that limited resources were devoted to developing it. A year after Atlas's release, ICT bought Ferranti's computer projects. ICT discontinued Atlas in favor of its own series of computers known as the 1900s.[17]

Real	Real		Virtual		
Single-user dedicated systems	Real memory multiprogramming systems		Virtual memory multiprogramming systems		
	Fixed-partition multi-programming	Variable-partition multi-programming	Pure paging	Pure segmentation	Combined paging and segmentation
	Absolute	Re-locatable			

Figure 10.1 | *Evolution of memory organizations.*

tion techniques—paging and segmentation. Address translation and noncontiguous allocation enable virtual memory systems to create the illusion of a larger memory and to increase the degree of multiprogramming. In the next chapter we focus on how a system manages the processes in virtual memory to optimize performance. Much of the information is based on Denning's survey on virtual memory (see the Biographical Note, Peter Denning).[18]

Operating Systems Thinking

Virtualization

We will see many examples in this book of how software can be used to make resources appear different than they really are. This is called virtualization. We will study virtual memories that appear to be far larger than the physical memory that is installed on the underlying computer. We will study virtual machines, which create the illusion that the computer being used to execute applications is really quite different from the underlying hardware. The Java virtual machine enables programmers to develop portable applications that will run on different computers running different operating systems (and hardware). Virtualization is yet another way of using abundant processor power to provide intriguing benefits to computer users. As computers become more complex, virtualization techniques can help hide that complexity from users, who instead see a simpler, easier-to-use virtual machine defined by the operating system. Virtualization is common in distributed systems, which we cover in detail in Chapters 17 and 18. Distributed operating systems create the illusion of there being a single large machine when in fact massive numbers of computers and other resources are interconnected in complex ways across networks like the Internet.

At the end of this chapter (just before the Web Resources section), you will find two operating systems Mini Case Studies—IBM Mainframe Operating Systems and Early History of the VM Operating System. As you finish reading this chapter, you will have studied the evolution of both real memory and virtual memory organizations. The history of IBM mainframe operating systems closely follows this evolution.

Self Review

1. Give an example of when it might be inefficient to load an entire program into memory before running it.
2. Why is increasing the size of main memory an insufficient solution to the problem of limited memory space?

Ans: **1)** Many programs have error-processing functions that are rarely, if ever, used. Loading these functions into memory reduces space available to processes. **2)** Purchasing additional main memory is not always economically feasible. As we will see, a better solution is to create the illusion that the system contains more memory than the process will ever need.

Biographical Note

Peter Denning

Peter J. Denning is best known for his work on virtual memory in the 1960s. One of his most important papers, "The Working Set Model for Program Behavior," was published in 1968, the same year he received his Ph.D. in Computer Science from MIT.[19] This paper introduced the concept of working sets (discussed in Section 11.7, Working Set Model) for use in virtual memory management and explained why the use of working sets leads to a page-replacement could improve performance over other replacement schemes.[20] Denning's theory is based on observations that programs spend most of their time using only a small subset of their virtual memory pages, which he called the working set. A program's working set changes from time to time as program execution moves along its phases. He proposed that a program will run efficiently if its current working set is kept in main memory at all times.

Denning has since taught at Princeton University, founded the Research Institute for Advanced Computer Science at the NASA Ames Research Center and led the computer science departments of Purdue, George Mason University and now the Naval Postgraduate School. He has published hundreds of articles and several books on computer science topics and was president of the ACM from 1980–1982.[21]

Denning has made significant contributions to computer science education. He won several teaching awards, managed the creation of the ACM Digital Library (an online collection of articles from ACM journals) and chaired the ACM Education Board which publishes the ACM curriculum.[22] He has also been recognized for his efforts to educate the nontechnical community about computer science topics.[23]

10.2 Virtual Memory: Basic Concepts

As we discussed in the previous section, virtual memory systems provide processes with the illusion that they have more memory than is built into the computer (see the Anecdote, Virtual Memory Unnecessary). Thus, there are two types of addresses in virtual memory systems: those referenced by processes and those available in main memory. The addresses that processes reference are called **virtual addresses**. Those available in main memory are called **physical** (or **real**) **addresses**. [*Note:* In this chapter we use the terms "physical address," "real address" and "main memory address" interchangeably.]

Whenever a process accesses a virtual address, the system must translate it to a real address. This happens so often that using a general-purpose processor to perform such translations would severely degrade system performance. Thus, virtual memory systems contain special-purpose hardware called the **memory management unit (MMU)** that quickly maps virtual addresses to real addresses.

A process's **virtual address space**, V, is the range of virtual addresses that the process may reference. The range of real addresses available on a particular computer system is called that computer's **real address space**, R. The number of addresses in V is denoted $|V|$, and the number of addresses in R is denoted $|R|$. In virtual memory systems, it is normally the case that $|V| \gg |R|$ (i.e., the virtual address space is much larger than the real address space).

If we are to permit a user's virtual address space to be larger than its real address space, we must provide a means for retaining programs and data in a large auxiliary storage. A system normally accomplishes this goal by employing a two-level storage scheme (Fig. 10.2). One level is the main memory (and caches) in which in which instructions and data must reside to be accessed by a processor running a process. The other level is secondary storage, which consists of large-capacity

Anecdote

Virtual Memory Unnecessary

When the concept of virtual memory was first introduced, designers mused that virtual memory systems would never be needed if computers could be built with a million words of memory. That was thought to be absurd, so work proceeded on building virtual memory systems. Many of today's desktop systems have a thousand times that much main memory and the vast majority of these systems employ virtual memory.

Lesson to operating systems designers: Take Moore's Law seriously. Hardware capabilities will continue to improve at an exponential pace and software requirements will increase as fast.

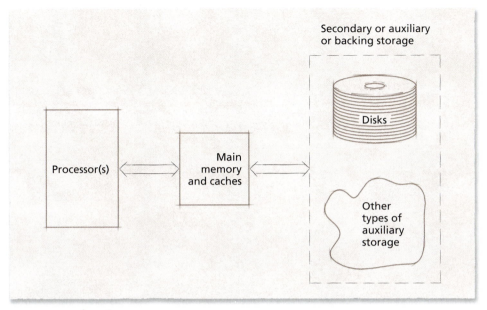

Figure 10.2 | Two-level storage.

storage media (typically disks) capable of holding the programs and data that can-not all fit into the limited main memory.

When the system is ready to run a process, the system loads the process's code and data from secondary storage into main memory. Only a small portion of these needs to be in main memory at once for the process to execute. Figure 10.3 illus-trates a two-level storage system in which items from various processes' virtual memory spaces have been placed in main memory.

A key to implementing virtual memory systems is how to map virtual addresses to physical addresses. Because processes reference only virtual addresses, but must execute in main memory, the system must map (i.e., translate) virtual addresses to physical addresses as processes execute (Fig. 10.4). The system must perform the translation quickly, otherwise the performance of the computer system would degrade, nullifying the gains associated with virtual memory.

Dynamic address translation (DAT) mechanisms convert virtual addresses to physical addresses during execution. Systems that use dynamic address translation exhibit the property that the contiguous addresses in a process's virtual address space need not be contiguous in physical memory—this is called **artificial contiguity** (Fig. 10.5).[24] Dynamic address translation and artificial contiguity free the program-mer from concerns about memory placement (e.g., the programmer need not create overlays to ensure the system can execute the program). The programmer can con-centrate on algorithm efficiency and program structure, rather than on the underly-ing hardware structure. The computer is (or can be) viewed in a logical sense as an implementor of algorithms rather than in a physical sense as a device with unique characteristics, some of which may impede the program development process.

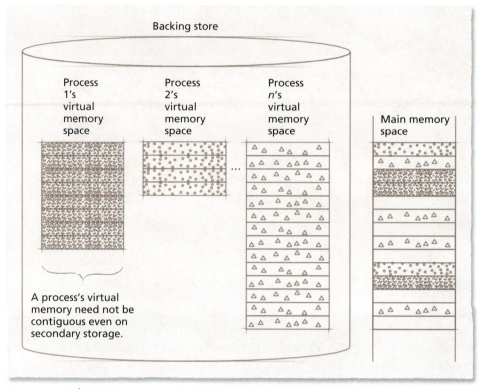

Figure 10.3 | *Pieces of address spaces exist in memory and in secondary storage.*

Self Review

1. Explain the difference between a process's virtual address space and the system's physical address space.
2. Explain the appeal of artificial contiguity.

Ans: **1)** A process's virtual address space refers to the set of addresses a process may reference to access memory when running on a virtual memory system. Processes do not see physical addresses, which locate physical locations in main memory. **2)** Artificial contiguity simplifies programming by enabling a process to reference its memory as if it were contiguous, even though its data and instructions may be scattered throughout main memory.

10.3 Block Mapping

Dynamic address translation mechanisms must maintain **address translation maps** indicating which regions of a process's virtual address space, V, are currently in main memory and where they are located. If this mapping had to contain entries for every address in V, then the mapping information would require more space than is available in main memory, so this is infeasible. In fact, the amount of mapping information must be only a small fraction of main memory, otherwise it would take up too much of the memory needed by the operating system and user processes.

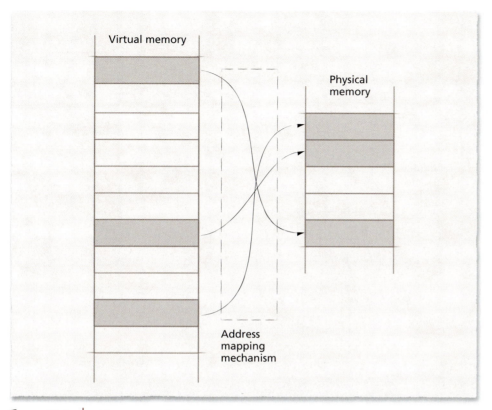

Figure 10.4 | *Mapping virtual addresses to real addresses.*

The most widely implemented solution is to group information in **blocks**; the system then keeps track of where in main memory each virtual memory block has been placed. The larger the average block size, the smaller the amount of mapping information. Larger blocks, however, can lead to internal fragmentation and can take longer to transfer between secondary storage and main memory.

There is some question as to whether the blocks should be all the same size or of different sizes. When blocks are a fixed size (or several fixed sizes), they are called **pages** and the associated virtual memory organization is called **paging**. When blocks may be of different sizes, they are called **segments**, and the associated virtual memory organization is called **segmentation**.[25, 26] Some systems combine the two techniques, implementing segments as variable-size blocks composed of fixed-size pages. We discuss paging and segmentation in detail in the following sections.

In a virtual memory system with **block mapping**, the system represents addresses as ordered pairs. To refer to a particular item in the process's virtual address space, a process specifies the block in which the item resides and the **displacement** (or **offset**) of the item from the start of the block (Fig. 10.6). A virtual address, v, is denoted by an ordered pair (b, d), where b is the block number in which the referenced item resides, and d is the displacement from the start of the block.

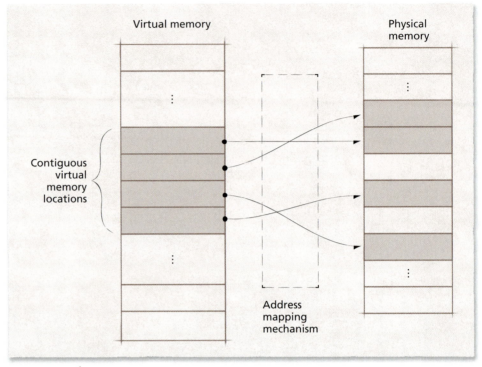

Figure 10.5 | *Artificial contiguity.*

| Block number
b | Displacement
d | Virtual address
v = (b, d) |

Figure 10.6 | *Virtual address format in a block mapping system.*

The translation from a virtual memory address $v = (b, d)$ to a real memory address, r, proceeds as follows (Fig. 10.7). The system maintains in memory a **block map table** for each process. The process's block map table contains one entry for each block of the process, and the entries are kept in sequential order (i.e., the entry for block 0 precedes that for block 1, etc.). At context-switch time, the system determines the real address, a, that corresponds to the address in main memory of the new process's block map table. The system loads this address into a high-speed special-purpose register called the **block map table origin register**. During execution, the process references a virtual address $v = (b, d)$. The system adds the block number, b, to the base address, a, of the process's block map table to form the real address of the entry for block b in the block map table. [*Note:* For simplicity, we assume that the size of each entry in the block map table is fixed and that each address in memory stores an entry of that size.] This entry contains the address, b', for the start of block b in main

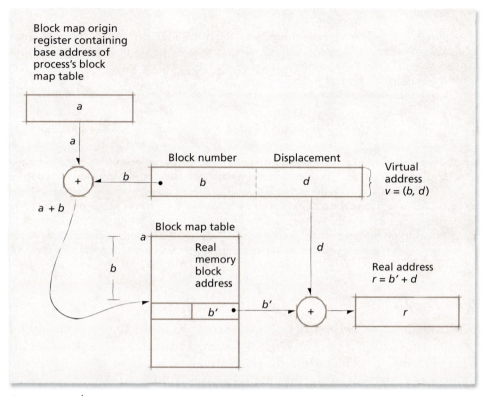

Figure 10.7 | Virtual address translation with block mapping.

memory. The system then adds the displacement, d, to the block start address, b', to form the desired real address, r. Thus, the system computes the real address, r, from the virtual address, $v = (b, d)$, through the equation $r = b' + d$, where b' is stored in the block map table cell located at real memory address $a + b$.

The block mapping techniques employed in segmentation, paging and combined segmentation/paging systems are all similar to the mapping shown in Fig. 10.7. It is important to note that block mapping is performed dynamically by high-speed, special-purpose hardware as a process runs. If not implemented efficiently, this technique's overhead could cause performance degradation that would negate much of the benefit of using virtual memory. For example, the two additions indicated in Fig. 10.7 must execute much faster than conventional machine-language add instructions. They are performed within the execution of each machine-language instruction for each virtual address reference. If the additions took as long as machine-language adds, then the computer might run at only a small fraction of the speed of a purely real-memory-based computer. Similarly, the block address translation mechanism must access entries in the block mapping table much faster than other information in memory. The system normally places entries from the block mapping table in a high-speed cache to dramatically decrease the time needed to retrieve them.

Self Review

1. Suppose a block mapping system represents a virtual address $v = (b, d)$ using 32 bits. If block displacement, d, is specified using n bits, how many blocks does the virtual address space contain? Discuss how setting $n = 6$, $n = 12$ and $n = 24$ affects memory fragmentation and the overhead incurred by mapping information.
2. Why is the start address of a process's block map table, a, placed in a special high-speed register?

Ans: **1)** The system will have 2^{32-n} blocks. If $n = 6$, then the block size would be small and there would be limited internal fragmentation, but the number of blocks would be so large as to make implementation infeasible. If $n = 24$, then the block size would be large and there would be significant internal fragmentation, but the block mapping table would not consume much memory at all. If $n = 12$, the system achieves a balance between moderate internal fragmentation and a reasonably sized block map table. Over the years, $n = 12$ has been quite popular in paging systems, yielding a page size of $2^{12} = 4{,}096$ bytes, as we will see in Chapter 11, Virtual Memory Management. **2)** Placing a in a high-speed register facilitates fast address translation, which is crucial in making the virtual memory implementation feasible.

10.4 Paging

A virtual address in a paging system is an ordered pair (p, d), where p is the number of the page in virtual memory on which the referenced item resides, and d is the displacement within page p at which the referenced item is located (Fig. 10.8). A process may run if the page it is currently referencing is in main memory. When the system transfers a page from secondary storage to main memory, it places the page in a main memory block, called a **page frame**, that is the same size as the incoming page. In discussing paging systems in this chapter, we assume that the system uses a single fixed page size. As we will explain in Chapter 11, Virtual Memory Management, it is common for today's systems to provide more than one page size.[27] Page frames begin at physical memory addresses that are integral multiples of the fixed page size, p_s (Fig. 10.9). The system may place an incoming page in any available page frame.

Dynamic address translation under paging proceeds as follows (Fig. 10.10). A running process references a virtual memory address $v = (p, d)$. A page mapping mechanism, looks up page p in the process's **page map table** (often simply called the **page table**) and determines that page p is in page frame p'. Note that p' is a page frame number, not a physical memory address. Assuming page frames are num-

Figure 10.8 | *Virtual address format in a pure paging system.*

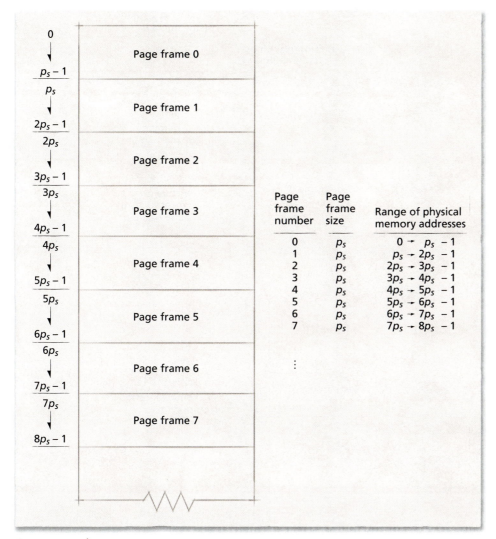

0			

Figure 10.9 | *Main memory divided into page frames.*

bered {0, 1, 2, …, n}, the physical memory address at which page frame p' begins is the product of p' and the fixed page size, $p \times p_s$. The referenced address is formed by adding the displacement, d, to the physical memory address at which page frame p' begins. Thus, the real memory address is $r = (p' \times p_s) + d$.

Consider a system using n bits to represent both real and virtual addresses; the page number is represented by the most-significant $n - m$ bits and the displacement is represented by m bits. Each real address can be represented as the ordered pair, $r = (p', d)$, where p' is the page frame number and d is the displacement within page p' at which the referenced item is located. The system can form a real address by concatenating p' and d, which places p' in the most-significant bits of the real mem-

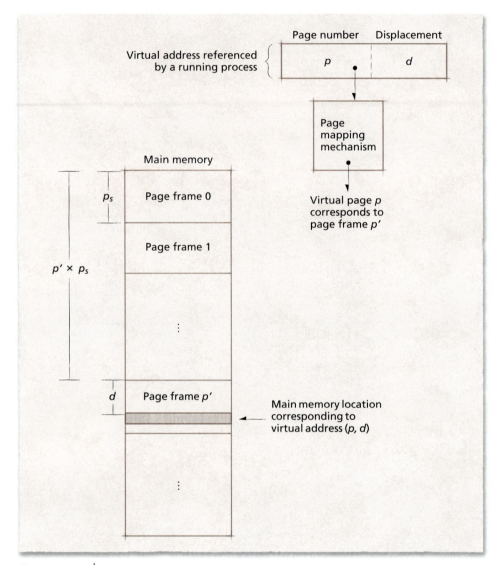

Figure 10.10 | *Correspondence between virtual memory addresses and physical memory addresses in a pure paging system.*

ory address and places d in the least-significant bits of the real memory address. For example, consider a 32-bit system ($n = 32$) using 4KB pages ($m = 12$). Each page frame number is represented using 20 bits, so that page frame number 15 would be represented as the binary string 00000000000000001111. Similarly, a displacement of 200 would be represented as the 12-bit binary string 000011001000. The 32-bit address of this location in main memory is formed simply by concatenating the two strings, yielding 00000000000000001111000011001000. This demonstrates how paging simplifies block mapping by using the concatenation operation to form a real memory address. On the contrary, with variable-size blocks, the system must perform an addition operation to form the real memory address from the ordered pair $r = (b', d)$.

Now let us consider dynamic address translation in more detail. One benefit of a paged virtual memory system is that not all pages belonging to a process must reside in main memory at the same time—main memory must contain only the page (or pages) in which the process is currently referencing an address (or addresses). The advantage is that more processes may reside in main memory at the same time. The disadvantage comes in the form of increased complexity in the address translation mechanism. Because main memory normally does not contain all of a process's pages at once, the page table must indicate whether or not a mapped page currently resides in main memory. If it does, the page table indicates the number of the page frame in which it resides. Otherwise, the page table yields the location in secondary storage at which the referenced page can be found. When a process references a page that is not in main memory, the processor generates a **page fault**, which invokes the operating system to load the missing page into memory from secondary storage.

Figure 10.11 shows a typical **page table entry (PTE)**. A resident bit, r, is set to 0 if the page is not in main memory and 1 if it is. If the page is not in main memory, then s is its secondary storage address. If the page is in main memory, then p' is its frame number. Over the next several subsections we consider several implementations of the page mapping mechanism.

Self Review

1. Does the page mapping mechanism require that s and p' be stored in separate cells of a PTE, as shown in Fig. 10.11?
2. Compare and contrast the notions of a page and a page frame.

Ans: **1)** No. To reduce the amount of memory consumed by PTEs, many systems contain only one cell to store either the page frame number or the secondary storage address. If the

Page resident bit	Secondary storage address (if page is not in main memory)	Page frame number (if page is in main memory)
r	s	p'

$r = 0$ if page is not in main memory
$r = 1$ if page is in main memory

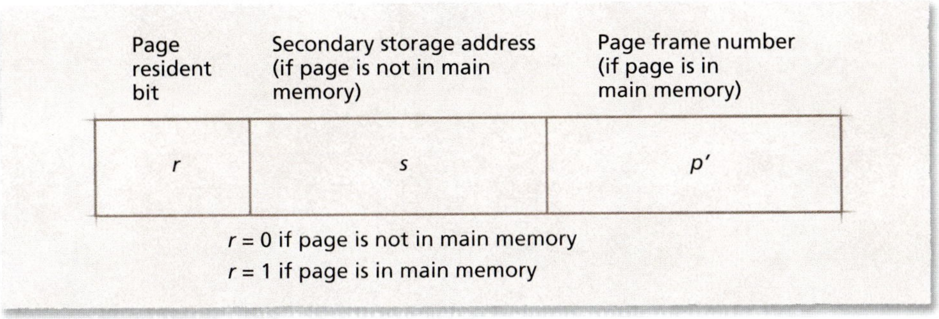

Figure 10.11 | Page table entry.

resident bit is on, the PTE stores a page frame number, but not a secondary storage address. If the resident bit is off, the PTE stores a secondary storage address, but not a page frame number. **2)** Pages and page frames are identical in size; a page refers to a fixed-size block of a process's virtual memory space and a page frame refers to a fixed-size block of main memory. A virtual memory page must be loaded into a page frame in main memory before a processor can access its contents.

10.4.1 Paging Address Translation by Direct Mapping

In this section we consider the **direct-mapping** technique for translating virtual addresses to physical addresses in a pure paging system. Direct mapping proceeds as illustrated in Fig. 10.12.

A process references virtual address $v = (p, d)$. At context-switch time the operating system loads the main memory address of a process's page table into the **page table origin register**. To determine the main memory address that corresponds to the referenced virtual address, the system first adds the process's page table base address, b, to the referenced page number, p (i.e., p is the index into the page table). This result, $b + p$, is the main memory address of the PTE for page p. [*Note:* For simplicity, we assume that the size of each entry in the page table is fixed and that each address in memory stores an entry of that size.] This PTE indicates that virtual page p corresponds to page frame p'. The system then concatenates p' with the displacement, d, to form the real address, r. This is an example of direct mapping,

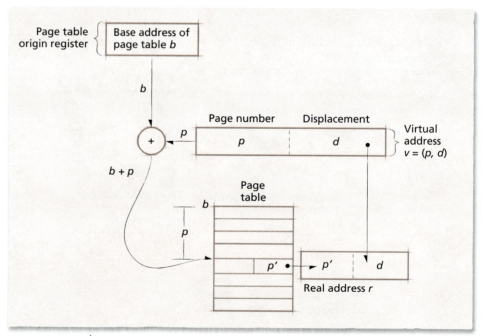

Figure 10.12 | *Paging address translation by direct mapping.*

because the page table contains one entry for every page in this process's virtual memory space, V. If the process contains n pages in V, then the direct-mapped page table for the process contains entries successively for page 0, page 1, page 2, ..., page $n - 1$. Direct mapping is much like accessing an array location via subscripting; the system can locate *directly* any entry in the table with a single access to the table.

The system maintains the virtual address being translated and the base address of the page table in high-speed registers on each processor, which enables operations on these values to be performed quickly (within a single instruction execution cycle). However, a system typically keeps the direct-mapped page table— which can be quite large—in main memory. Consequently, a reference to the page table requires one complete main memory cycle. Because the main memory access time ordinarily represents the largest part of an instruction execution cycle, and because we require an additional main memory access for page mapping, the use of direct-mapping page address translation can cause the computer system to run programs at about half speed (or even worse for machines that support multiple address instructions)! To achieve faster translation, one may implement the complete direct-mapped page table in high-speed cache memory. Due to the cost of high-speed cache memory and the potentially large size of virtual address spaces, maintaining the entire page table in cache memory is typically not viable. We discuss a solution to this problem in Section 10.4.3, Paging Address Translation with Direct/Associative Mapping.

Self Review

1. Why should the size of page table entries be fixed?
2. What type of special-purpose hardware is required for page address translation by direct mapping?

Ans: **1)** The key to virtual memory is that address translation must occur quickly. If the size of page table entries is fixed, the calculation that locates the entries is simple, which facilitates fast page address translation. **2)** A high-speed processor register is needed to store the base address of the page table.

10.4.2 Paging Address Translation by Associative Mapping

One way to increase the performance of dynamic address translation is to place the entire page table into a content-addressed (rather than location-addressed) **associative memory**, which has a cycle time greater than an order of magnitude faster than main memory.[28, 29, 30] [31] Figure 10.13 illustrates how dynamic address translation proceeds with pure **associative mapping**. A process refers to virtual address $v = (p, d)$. Every entry in the associative memory is searched simultaneously for page p. The search returns p' as the page frame corresponding to page p, and p' is concatenated with d, forming the real address, r. Note that the arrows into the associative map enter every cell of the map, indicating that every cell of the associative memory is searched simultaneously for a match on p. This is what makes associative memory prohibitively expensive, even compared to direct-mapped cache. Because

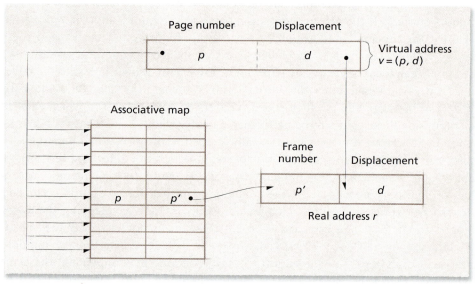

Figure 10.13 | *Paging address translation with pure associative mapping.*

of this expense, pure associative mapping is not used; we show it here in case its economics eventually becomes more favorable.

In the vast majority of systems, using a cache memory to implement pure direct mapping or an associative memory to implement pure associative mapping is too costly. As a result, many designers have chosen a compromise scheme that offers many of the advantages of the cache or associative memory approach at a more modest cost. We consider this scheme in the next section.

Self Review

1. Why is page address translation by pure associative mapping not used?
2. Does page address translation by pure associative mapping require any special-purpose hardware?

Ans: **1)** Associative memory is even more expensive than direct-mapped cache memory. Therefore, it would be prohibitively expensive to build a system that contained enough associative memory to store all of a process's PTEs. **2)** This technique requires an associative memory; however, it does not require a page table origin register to store the location of the start of the page table, because associative memory is content addressed, rather than location addressed.

10.4.3 Paging Address Translation with Direct/Associative Mapping

Much of the discussion to this point has dealt with the computer hardware required to implement virtual memory efficiently. The hardware view presented has been a logical rather a than physical one. We are concerned not with the precise structure of the devices but with their functional organization and relative speeds. This is the view the operating systems designer must have, especially as hardware designs evolve.

Historically, hardware has improved at a much more dramatic pace than improvements in software. Designers have become reluctant to commit themselves to a particular hardware technology because they expect that a better one will soon be available. Operating systems designers, however, must use the capabilities and economics of today's hardware. High-speed cache and associative memories simply are far too expensive to hold the complete address mapping data for full virtual address spaces. This leads to a compromise page-mapping mechanism.

the compromise uses an associative memory, called the **translation lookaside buffer (TLB)**, capable of holding only a small percentage of the complete page table for a process (Fig. 10.14). The TLB's contents may be controlled by the oper-

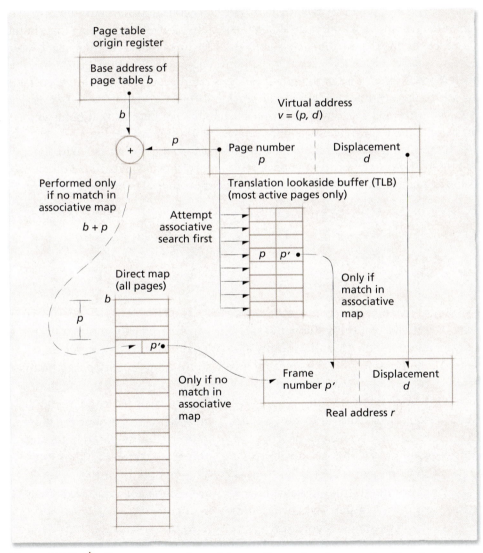

Figure 10.14 | Paging address translation with combined associative/direct mapping.

ating system or by hardware, depending on the architecture.[32] In this chapter, we assume that the TLB is managed by hardware. The page table entries maintained in this map typically correspond to the more-recently referenced pages only, using the heuristic that a page referenced recently is likely to be referenced again in the near future. This is an example of **locality** (more specifically of temporal locality—locality in time), a phenomenon discussed in detail in Chapter 11, Virtual Memory Management (see the Operating Systems Thinking feature, Empirical Results; Locality-Based Heuristics). The TLB is an integral part of today's MMUs.

Dynamic address translation under this scheme proceeds as follows. A process references virtual address $v = (p, d)$. The page mapping mechanism first tries to find page p in the TLB. If the TLB contains p, then the search returns p' as the frame number corresponding to virtual page p, and p' is concatenated with the displacement d to form the real address, r. When the system locates the mapping for p in the TLB, it experiences a **TLB hit**. Because the TLB stores entries in high-speed associative memory, this enables the translation to be performed at the fastest possible speed for the system. The problem, of course, is that because of prohibitive cost, the associative map can hold only a small portion of most virtual address spaces. The challenge is to pick a size within design's economic parameters that holds enough entries so that a large percentage of references will result in TLB hits.

If the TLB does not contain an entry for page p (i.e., the system experiences a **TLB miss**), the system locates the page table entry using a conventional direct map in slower main memory, which increases execution time. The address in the page

Operating Systems Thinking

Empirical Results: Locality-Based Heuristics

Some fields of computer science have significant bodies of theory, built from a mathematical framework. There are indeed aspects of operating systems to which such theoretical treatments apply. But for the most part, operating systems design is based on empirical, (i.e., observed) results and the heuristics that designers and implementers have developed the first operating systems were deployed in the 1950s. For example, we will study the empirical phenomena of spatial locality and temporal locality (i.e., locality in time), which are observed phenomena. If it is sunny in your town, it is likely—but not guaranteed—to be sunny in nearby towns. Also, if it is sunny in your town now, it is likely—but not guaranteed—that is was sunny in your town a short while ago and it will be sunny in your town a short while into the future. We will see many examples of locality in computer systems and we will study many locality-based heuristics in various areas of operating systems such as virtual memory management. Perhaps the most famous locality-based heuristic in operating systems is Peter Denning's working set theory of program behavior, which we discuss in Chapter 11.

table origin register, b, is added to the page number, p, to locate the appropriate entry for page p in the direct-mapped page table in main memory. The entry contains p', the page frame corresponding to virtual page p; p' is concatenated with the displacement, d, to form the real address, r. The system then places the PTE in the TLB so that references to page p in the near future can be translated quickly. If the TLB is full, the system replaces an entry (typically the one least-recently referenced) to make room for the entry for current page.

Empirically, due to the phenomenon of locality, the number of entries in the TLB does not need to be large to achieve good performance. In fact, systems using this technique with only 64 or 128 TLB entries (which, assuming a 4KB page size, covers 256–512KB of virtual memory space) often achieve 90 percent or more of the performance possible with a complete associative map. Note that on a TLB miss, the processor must access main memory to obtain the page frame number. Depending on the hardware and memory management strategy, such misses can cost tens or hundreds of processor cycles, because main memory typically operates at slower speeds than processors do.[33, 34, 35]

Using a combined associative/direct mapping mechanism is an engineering decision based on the relative economics and capabilities of existing hardware technologies. Therefore, it is important for operating systems students and developers to be aware of such technologies as they emerge. The Recommended Reading and Web Resources sections provide several resources documenting these technologies.

Self Review

1. (T/F) The majority of a process's PTEs must be stored in the TLB to achieve high performance.
2. Why does the system need to invalidate a PTE in the TLB if a page is moved to secondary storage?

Ans: 1) False. Processes often achieve 90 percent or more of the performance possible when only a small portion of a process's PTEs are stored in the TLB. 2) If the system does not invalidate the PTE, a reference to the nonresident page will cause the TLB to return a page frame that might contain invalid data or instructions (e.g., a page belonging to a different process).

10.4.4 Multilevel Page Tables

One limitation of address translations using direct mapping is that all of the PTEs of a page table must be in the map and stored contiguously in sequential order by page number. Further, these tables can consume a significant amount of memory. For example, consider a 32-bit virtual address space using 4KB pages. In this system, the page size is 2^{12} bytes, leaving 2^{32-12}, or 2^{20}, page numbers. Thus, each virtual address space would require approximately one million entries, one for each page, for a total addressability of about four billion bytes. A 64-bit virtual address space using 4MB pages would require approximately four trillion entries! Holding such a large page table in memory (assuming that there was enough memory to do so) can severely limit the memory available for actual programs; it also does not makes sense, because processes may need to access only small portions of their address spaces at any given time to run efficiently.

Multilevel (or **hierarchical**) **page tables** enable the system to store in discontiguous locations in main memory those portions of a process's page table that the process is actively using. The remaining portions of can be created the first time they are used and moved to secondary storage when they cease being actively used. Multilevel page tables are implemented by creating a hierarchy—each level containing a table that stores pointers to tables in the level below. The bottom-most level is comprised of tables containing the page-to-page-frame mappings.

For example, consider a system that uses two levels of page tables (Fig. 10.15). The virtual address is the ordered triplet $v = (p, t, d)$, where the ordered pair (p, t) is the page number and d is the displacement into that page. The system first adds the value of p to the address in main memory of the start of the page directory, a, stored in the page directory origin register. The entry at location $a + p$ contains the address of the start of the corresponding page table, b. The system adds t to b to locate the page table entry that stores a page frame number, p'. Finally, the system forms the real address by concatenating p' and the displacement, d.

In most systems, each table in the hierarchy is the size of one page, which enables the operating system to transfer page tables between main memory and

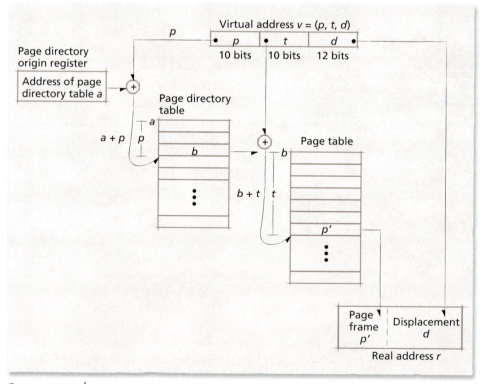

Figure 10.15 | *Multilevel page address translation.*

secondary storage easily. Let us examine how a two-level page table reduces memory consumption compared to direct mapping in a system that provides a 32-bit virtual address space using 4KB pages (which, again, requires 20-bit page numbers). Each page table would contain 2^{20}, or 1,048,576, entries for each process. Considering that typical systems contain tens, if not hundreds, of processes, and that high-end systems can contain thousands of processes, this could lead to considerable memory overhead. If each page table entry were 32 bits, this would consume 4MB of contiguous memory for each process's virtual address space. If the space were sparsely populated (i.e., few page table entries were in use), much of the page table would be unused, resulting in significant memory waste called **table fragmentation**.

Observe how table fragmentation is reduced using a two-level page table as follows. Each 32-bit virtual address is divided into a 10-bit offset into the page directory, p, a 10-bit offset into a page table, t, and a 12-bit displacement into the page, d. In this case, the page directory contains pointers to 2^{10} tables (one entry for each number specified by the 10-bit offset into the page directory, p), each of which holds 2^{10} PTEs (one entry for each number specified by the 10-bit offset into a page table, t). The first 10 bits of the virtual address is used as an index into the first table. The entry at this index is a pointer to the next table, which is a page table containing PTEs. The second 10 bits of the virtual address is used as an index into the page table that locates the PTE. Finally, the PTE provides the page frame number, p', which is concatenated with the last 12 bits of the virtual address to determine the real address.

If a process uses no more than the first 1,024 pages in its virtual address space, the system need only maintain 1,024 (2^{10}) entries for the page directory and 1,024 page table entries, whereas a direct-mapped page table must maintain over one million entries. Multilevel page tables enable the system to reduce table fragmentation by over 99 percent.

The overhead incurred by multilevel page tables is the addition of another memory access to the page mapping mechanism. At first, it may appear that this additional memory cycle would result in worse performance than a direct-mapped page table. Due to locality of reference and the availability of a high-speed TLB, however, once a virtual page has been mapped to a page frame, future references to that page do not incur the memory access overhead. Thus, systems that employ multilevel page tables rely on an extremely low TLB miss rate to achieve high performance.

Multilevel page tables have become common in paged virtual memory systems. For example, the IA-32 architecture supports two levels of page tables (see Section 10.7, Case Study: IA-32 Intel Architecture Virtual Memory).[36]

Self Review

1. Discuss the benefits and drawbacks of using a multilevel paging system instead of a direct-mapped paging system.
2. A designer suggests reducing the memory overhead of direct-mapped page tables by increasing the size of pages. Evaluate the consequences of such a decision.

Ans: **1)** Multilevel paging systems require considerably less main memory space to hold mapping information than direct-mapped paging systems. However, multilevel paging systems require more memory accesses each time a process references a page whose mapping is not in the TLB, and potentially can run more slowly. **2)** Assuming that the size of each virtual address remains fixed, page address translation by direct mapping using large pages reduces the number of entries the system must store for each process. The solution also reduces memory access overhead compared to a multilevel page table. However, as page sizes increase, so do the possibility and magnitude of internal fragmentation. It is possible that the amount of wasted memory due to internal fragmentation could be equal to or greater than the table fragmentation due to storing entries for smaller pages.

10.4.5 Inverted Page Tables

As we discussed in the preceding section, multilevel page tables reduce the number of page table entries that must reside in main memory at once for each process when compared to direct-mapped page tables. In this case, we assumed that processes use only a small, contiguous region of their virtual address spaces, meaning that the system can reduce memory overhead by storing page table entries only for the region of a process's virtual address space that is in use. However, processes in scientific and commercial environments that modify large quantities of data might use a significant portion of their 32-bit virtual address spaces. In this case, multilevel page tables do not necessarily decrease table fragmentation. In 64-bit systems that contain several levels of page tables, the amount of memory consumed by mapping information can become substantial.

An **inverted page table** solves this problem by storing exactly one PTE for each page frame in the system. Consequently, the number of PTEs that must be stored in main memory is proportional to the size of physical memory, not to the size of a virtual address space. The page tables are inverted relative to traditional page tables because the PTEs are indexed by page frame number rather than virtual page number. Note that inverted page tables do not store the secondary storage location of nonresident pages. This information must be maintained by the operating system, and need not be in tables. For example, an operating system might use a binary tree to store the locations of nonresident pages so that they may be found quickly.

Inverted page tables use hash functions to map virtual pages to PTEs.[37, 38] A **hash function** is a mathematical function that takes a number as an input and outputs a number, called a **hash value**, within a finite range. A **hash table** stores each item in the cell corresponding to the item's hash value. Because the domain of a hash function (e.g., a process's virtual page numbers) is generally larger than its range (e.g., the page frame numbers), multiple inputs can result in the same hash value—these are called **collisions**. To prevent multiple items from overwriting each other when mapped to the same cell of the hash table, inverted page tables can implement a variant of a **chaining** mechanism to resolve collisions as follows. When a hash value maps an item to a location that is occupied, a new function is applied to the hash value. The resulting value is used as the position in the table where the input is to be placed. To ensure that the item can be found when referenced, a pointer to this position is appended to the entry in the cell corresponding to the item's original hash value. This process is repeated each time a collision occurs. Inverted page tables typically use linked lists to chain items.

In a paging system implementing inverted page tables, each virtual address is represented by the ordered pair $v = (p, d)$. To quickly locate the hash table entry corresponding to virtual page p, the system applies a hash function to p, which produces a value q (Fig. 10.16). If the qth cell in the inverted page table contains p, then the requested virtual address is in page frame q. If page number in the qth cell of the inverted page table does not match p, the system checks the value of the chaining pointer for that cell. If the pointer is null, then the page is not in memory, so the processor issues a page fault. The operating system can then retrieve the page from secondary storage. Otherwise, there has been a collision at that index in the inverted page table, so the page table entry stores a pointer to the next entry in the chain. The system follows the pointers in the chain until it finds an entry containing p or until the chain ends, at which point the processor issues a page fault to indicate that the page is not resident. The operating system can then retrieve the page from secondary storage. In Fig. 10.16, the system locates an entry corresponding to p after following one chaining pointer to cell p', so p is located in page frame p'.

Although a careful choice of hash functions can reduce the number of collisions in the hash table, each additional chaining pointer requires the system to

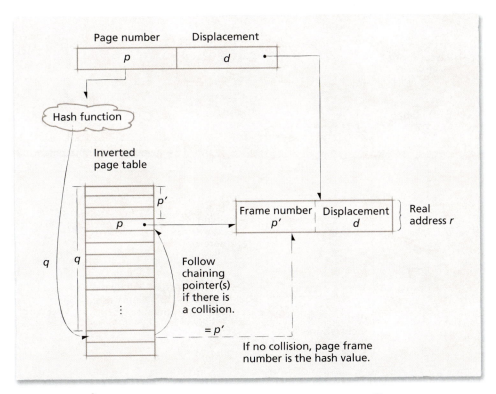

Figure 10.16 | Page address translation using inverted page tables.

access main memory, which can substantially increase address translation time. To improve performance, the system can attempt to reduce the number of collisions by increasing the range of hash values produced by the function. Because the size of the inverted page table must remain fixed to provide direct mappings to page frames, most systems increase the range of the hash function using a **hash anchor table**, which is a hash table containing pointers to entries in the inverted page table (Fig. 10.17). The hash anchor table imposes an additional memory access to virtual-to-physical address translation using inverted page tables and increases table fragmentation. If the hash anchor table is sufficiently large, however, the number of collisions in the inverted page table can be significantly reduced, which can speed address translation. The size of the hash anchor table must be chosen carefully to balance address translation performance with memory overhead.[39, 40]

Inverted page tables are typically found in high-performance architectures, such as the Intel IA-64 and the HP PA-RISC architectures, but are also implemented in the PowerPC architecture, which is found in the consumer line of Apple computers.

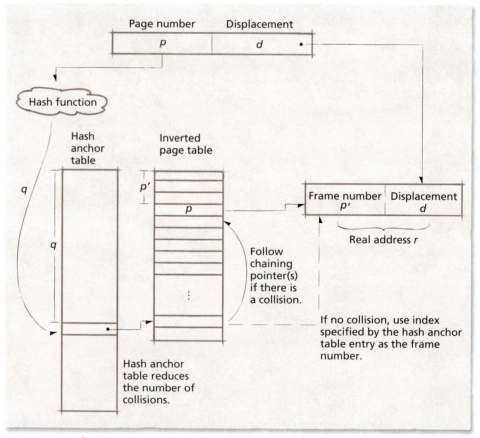

Figure 10.17 | *Inverted page table using a hash anchor table.*

Self Review

1. Compare and contrast inverted page tables (without a hash anchor table) to direct-mapped page tables in terms of memory efficiency and address translation efficiency.
2. Why are PTEs larger in inverted page tables than in direct-mapped page tables?

Ans: **1)** Inverted page tables incur less memory overhead than direct-mapped page tables because an inverted page table contains only one PTE for each physical page frame, whereas a direct-mapped page table contains one PTE for each virtual page. However, address translation may be much slower using an inverted page table than when using a direct-mapped table because the system may have to access memory several times to follow a collision chain. **2)** A PTE in an inverted page table must store a virtual page number and a pointer to the next PTE in the collision chain. A PTE in a direct-mapped page table need only store a page frame number and a resident bit.

10.4.6 Sharing in a Paging System

In multiprogrammed computer systems, especially in timesharing systems, it is common for many users to execute the same programs concurrently. If the system allocated individual copies of these programs to each user, much of main memory would be wasted. The obvious solution is for the system to share those pages common to individual processes.

The system must carefully control sharing to prevent one process from modifying data that another process is accessing. In most of today's systems that implement sharing, programs are divided into separate procedure and data areas. Nonmodifiable procedures are called pure procedures or reentrant procedures. Modifiable data cannot be shared without careful concurrency control. Nonmodifiable data can be shared. Modifiable procedures cannot be shared (although one might envision an esoteric example where doing this with some form of concurrency control would make sense).

All this discussion points to the need to identify each page as either sharable or nonsharable. Once each process's pages have been categorized in this fashion, then sharing in pure paging systems can be implemented as in Fig. 10.18. If the page table entries of different processes point to the same page frame, then this page frame is shared by each of the processes. Sharing reduces the amount of main memory required for a group of processes to run efficiently and can make it possible for a given system to increase its degree of multiprogramming.

One example in which page sharing can substantially reduce memory consumption is with the UNIX fork system call. When a process forks, the data and instructions for both the parent process and its child are initially identical. Instead of allocating an identical copy of data in memory for the child process, the operating system can simply allow the child process to share its parent's virtual address space while providing the illusion that each process has its own, independent virtual address space. This improves performance because it reduces the time required to initialize the child process and reduces memory consumption between the two processes (see the Operating Systems Thinking feature, Lazy Allocation). However, because the

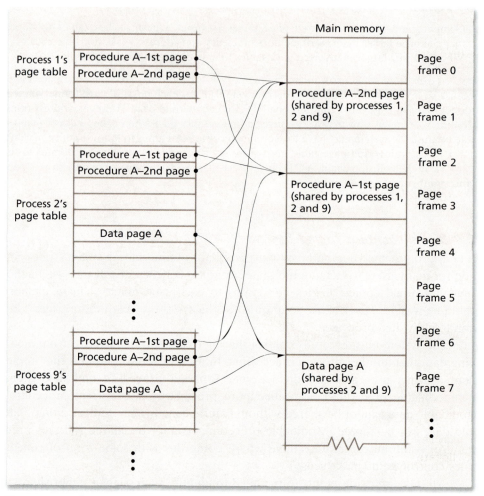

Figure 10.18 | Sharing in a pure paging system.

parent and child are unaware of the sharing, the operating system must ensure that the two processes do not interfere with each other when modifying pages.

Many operating systems use a technique called **copy-on-write** to address this problem. Initially, the system maintains one copy of each shared page in memory, as described previously, for processes P_1 through P_n. If P_1 attempts to modify a page of shared memory, the operating system creates a copy of the page, applies the modification and assigns the new copy to process P_1's virtual address space. The unmodified copy of the page remains mapped to the address space of all other processes sharing the page. This ensures that when one process modifies a shared page, no other processes are affected.

Many architectures provide each PTE with a **read/write bit** that the processor checks each time a process references an address. When the read/write bit is off, the page can be read, but not modified. When the bit is on, the page can be both read and modified. Copy-on-write can thus be implemented by marking each shared page as read-only. When a process attempts to write to a page, the processor on which it executes will cause a page fault, which invokes the kernel. At this point, the kernel can determine that the process is attempting to write to a shared page and perform the copy-on-write.

Copy-on-write speeds process creation and reduces memory consumption for processes that do not modify a significant amount of data during execution. However, copy-on-write can result in poor performance if a significant portion of a process's shared data is modified during program execution. In this case, the process will suffer a page fault each time it modifies a page that is still shared. The overhead associated with invoking the kernel for each exception can quickly outweigh the benefits of copy-on-write. In the next chapter, we consider how sharing affects virtual memory management.

Self Review

1. Why might it be difficult to implement page sharing when using inverted page tables?
2. How does page sharing affect performance when the operating system moves a page from main memory to secondary storage?

Operating Systems Thinking

Lazy Allocation

Lazy resource allocation schemes allocate resources only at the last moment, when they are explicitly requested by processes or threads. For resources that ultimately will not be needed, lazy allocation schemes are more efficient than anticipatory resource allocation schemes, which might attempt to allocate those resources that would not be used, thus wasting the resources. For resources that ultimately will be needed, anticipatory schemes help processes and threads run more efficiently by having the resources they need available when they need them, so those processes and threads do not have to wait for the resources to be allocated. We discuss lazy allocation in various contexts in the book. One classic example of lazy allocation is demand paging, which we study in this chapter and the chapter that follows. With pure demand paging, a process's or thread's pages are brought to memory only as each is explicitly referenced. The advantage of demand paging is that the system never incurs the overhead of transferring a page from secondary storage to main memory unless that page will truly be needed. On the other hand, because such a scheme waits until a page is referenced before bringing it to main memory, the process will experience a significant execution delay as it waits for the disk I/O operation to complete. And while the process or thread is waiting, the portion of that process or thread memory that is in memory is tying up space that could otherwise be used by other running processes. Copy-on-write is another example of lazy allocation.

Ans: **1)** The type of page sharing discussed in this section is accomplished by having PTEs from different process's page tables point to the same page frame number. Because inverted page tables maintain exactly one PTE in memory for each page frame, the operating system must maintain sharing information in a data structure outside the inverted page table. One challenge of this type of page sharing is determining if a shared page is already in memory, because it was recently referenced by a different process, when another process first references it. **2)** When the operating system moves a shared page to secondary storage, it must update the corresponding PTE for every process sharing that page. If numerous processes share the page, this could incur significant overhead compared to that for an unshared page.

10.5 Segmentation

In the preceding chapter, we discussed how a variable-partition multiprogramming system can place a program in memory on a first-fit, best-fit or worst-fit basis. Under variable-partition multiprogramming, each program's memory and data occupy one contiguous section of memory called a partition. An alternative is physical memory **segmentation** (Fig. 10.19). Under this scheme, a program's data and instructions are divided into blocks called **segments**. Each segment consists of contiguous locations; however, the segments need not be the same size nor must they be placed adjacent to one another in main memory.

One advantage of segmentation over paging is that it is a logical rather than a physical concept. In their most general form, segments are not arbitrarily constrained to a certain size. Instead, they are allowed to be (within reasonable limits) as large or as small as they need to be. A segment corresponding to an array is as large as the array. A segment corresponding to a procedural code unit generated by a compiler is as large as it needs to be to hold the code.

In a virtual memory segmentation system, we have the ability to maintain in main memory only those segments that a program requires to execute at a certain time; the remainder of the segments reside on secondary storage.[41] A process may execute while its current instructions and data are located in a segment that resides in main memory. If a process references memory in a segment that does not currently reside in main memory, the virtual memory system must retrieve that segment from secondary storage. Under pure segmentation, the system transfers a segment from secondary storage as a complete unit and places all the locations within that segment in contiguous locations in main memory. An incoming segment may be placed in any available area in main memory that is large enough to hold it. The placement strategies for segmentation are identical to those used in variable-partition multiprogramming.[42]

A virtual memory segmentation address is an ordered pair $v = (s, d)$, where s is the segment number in virtual memory in which the referenced item resides, and d is the displacement within segment s at which the referenced item is located (Fig. 10.20).

Self Review

1. (T/F) Segmented virtual memory systems do not incur fragmentation.
2. How does segmentation differ from variable-partition multiprogramming?

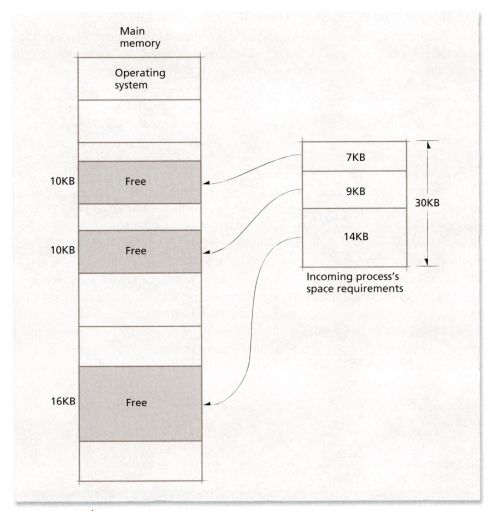

Figure 10.19 | *Noncontiguous memory allocation in a real memory segmentation system.*

Segment number s	Displacement d	Virtual address v = (s, d)

Figure 10.20 | *Virtual address format in a pure segmentation system.*

Ans: **1)** False. Segmented virtual memory systems can incur external fragmentation, exactly as in variable-partition multiprogramming systems. **2)** Unlike programs in a variable-parti-tion multiprogramming system, programs in a segmented virtual memory system can be larger than main memory and need only a portion of their data and instructions in memory to execute. Also, in variable-partition multiprogramming systems, a process occupies one con-tiguous range of main memory, whereas in segmentation systems this need not ne so.

10.5.1 Segmentation Address Translation by Direct Mapping

There are many strategies for implementing segmented address translation. A system can employ direct mapping, associative mapping or combined direct/associative mapping. In this section we consider segmented address translation using direct mapping and maintaining the complete segment map table in a fast-access cache memory.

We consider first the case in which the address translation proceeds normally and consider several problems that may arise. Dynamic address translation under segmentation proceeds as follows. A process references a virtual memory address $v = (s, d)$ to determine where in main memory the referenced segment resides. The system adds the segment number, s, to the segment map table's base address value, b, located in the **segment map table origin register** (Fig. 10.21). The resulting value, $b + s$, is the location of the segment's table map entry. [*Note:* For simplicity, we assume that the size of each entry in the segment map table is fixed and that each address in memory stores an entry of that size.] Each entry contains several pieces of information about the segment, which the mapping mechanism uses to translate the virtual address to a physical address. If the segment currently resides in main memory, the entry contains the segment's main memory starting address, s'. The system adds the displacement, d, to this address to form the referenced location's real memory address, $r = s' + d$. We cannot simply concatenate d to s', as we do in a pure paging system, because segments are of variable size.

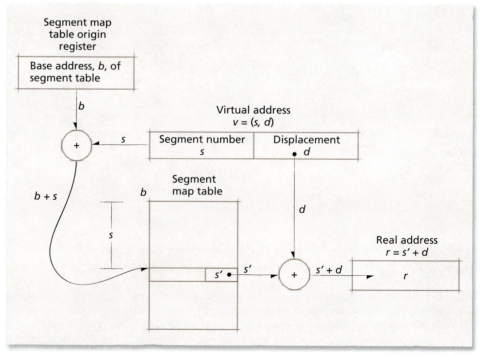

Figure 10.21 | *Virtual address translation in a pure segmentation system.*

Figure 10.22 shows a typical segment map table entry in detail. A resident bit, r, indicates whether or not that segment is currently in main memory. If it is, then s' is the main memory address at which the segment begins. Otherwise a is the secondary storage address from which the segment must be retrieved before the process may proceed. All references to the segment are checked against the segment length, l, to ensure that they fall within the range of the segment. Each reference to the segment is also checked against the **protection bits** to determine if the operation being attempted is allowed. For example, if the protection bits indicate that a segment is read-only, no process is allowed to modify that segment. We discuss protection in segmented systems in detail in Section 10.5.3, Protection and Access Control in Segmentation Systems.

During dynamic address translation, once the segment map table entry for segment s has been located, the resident bit, r, is examined to determine if the segment is in main memory. If it is not, then a **missing-segment fault** is generated, causing the operating system to gain control and load the referenced segment which begins at secondary storage address a. Once the segment is loaded, address translation proceeds with checking that the displacement, d, is less than or equal to the segment length, l. If it is not, then a **segment-overflow exception** is generated, causing the operating system to get control and potentially terminate the process. If it is, the protection bits are checked to ensure that the operation being attempted is allowed. If it is, then the base address, s', of the segment in main memory is added to the displacement, d, to form the real memory address $r = s' + d$ corresponding to virtual memory address $v = (s, d)$. If the operation being attempted is not allowed, then a **segment-protection exception** is generated, causing the operating system to gain control of the system and terminate the process.

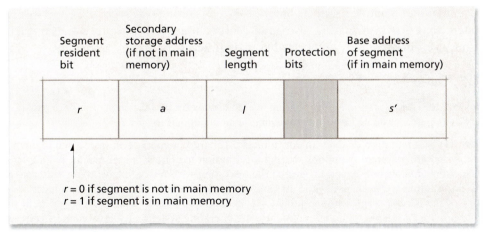

Figure 10.22 | Segment map table entry.

Self Review

1. Why is it incorrect to form the real address, r, by concatenating s' and d?
2. Does the page mapping mechanism require that a and s' be stored in separate cells of a segment map table entry, as shown in Fig. 10.22?

Ans: **1)** Unlike the page frame number p', the segment base address s' is an address in main memory. Concatenating s' and d would result in an address beyond the limit of main memory. Again, concatenation works with paging because the page size is a power of two and the number of bits reserved for the displacement on a page and the number of bits reserved for the page frame number add up to the number of bits in the virtual address. **2)** No. To reduce the amount of memory consumed by segment map table entries, many systems use one cell to store either the segment base address or the secondary storage address. If the resident bit is on, the segment map table entry stores a segment base address, but not a secondary storage address. If the resident bit is off, the segment map table entry stores a secondary storage address, but not a segment base address.

10.5.2 Sharing in a Segmentation System

Sharing segments can incur less overhead than sharing in a direct-mapped pure paging system. For example, to share an array that is stored in three and one-half pages, a pure paging system must maintain separate sharing data for each page on which the array resides. The problem is compounded if the array is dynamic, because the sharing information must be adjusted at execution time to account for the growing or shrinking number of pages that the array occupies. In a segmentation system, on the other hand, data structures may grow and shrink without changing the sharing information associated with the structure's segment.

Figure 10.23 illustrates how a pure segmentation system accomplishes sharing. Two processes share a segment when their segment table entries point to the same segment in main memory.

Although sharing provides obvious benefits, it also introduces certain risks. For example, one process could intentionally or otherwise perform an operation on a segment that negatively affects other processes sharing that segment. Therefore, a system that provides sharing also should provide appropriate protection mechanisms, to ensure that only authorized users may access or modify a segment.

Self Review

1. How does segmentation reduce sharing overhead compared to sharing under pure paging?
2. Can copy-on-write be implemented using segments, and, if so, how?

Ans: **1)** Segmentation enables an entire block of shared memory to fit inside one segment, so the operating system maintains sharing information for one segment. Under paging, this segment might consume several pages, so the operating system would have to maintain sharing information for each page. **2)** Yes. Copy-on-write can be implemented by allocating a copy of the parent's segment map table to its child. If process P_1 (which can be a parent or child process) attempts to modify segment s, the operating system must create a new copy of the segment, located at main memory address s'. The operating system then changes entry s in P_1's segment map table to contain the address s'.

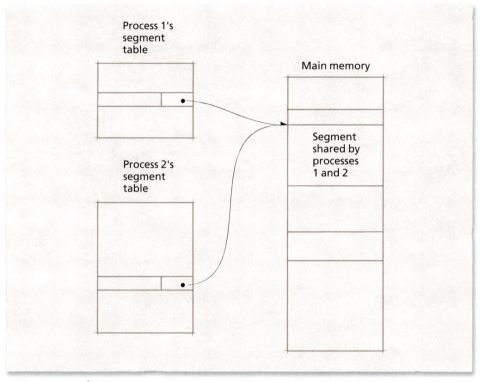

Figure 10.23 | Sharing in a pure segmentation system.

10.5.3 Protection and Access Control in Segmentation Systems

Segmentation promotes program modularity and enables better memory use through noncontiguous allocation and sharing. With these benefits, however, comes increased complexity. For example, a single pair of bounds registers no longer suffices to protect each process from destruction by other processes. Similarly, it becomes more difficult to limit the range of access of any given program. One scheme for implementing memory protection in segmentation systems is the use of **memory protection keys** (Fig. 10.24). In this case, each process is associated with a value, called a protection key. The operating system strictly controls this key, which can be manipulated only by privileged instructions. The operating system employs protection keys as follows. At context-switch time, the operating system loads the process's protection key into a processor register. When the process references a particular segment, the processor checks the protection key of the block containing the referenced item. If the protection key for the process and the requested block are the same, the process can access the segment. For example, in Fig. 10.24, Process 2 can access only those blocks with a protection-key value of 2. If the process attempts to access a block with a different protection key, the hardware prevents the memory access and vectors into the kernel (caused by a segment-protection exception). Although memory protection keys are not the most common protection

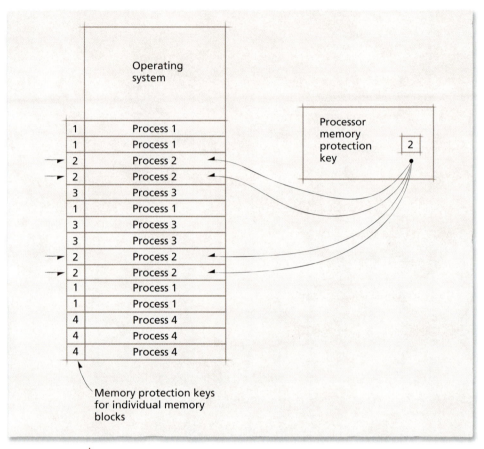

1	Process 1	
1	Process 1	
2	Process 2	◄
2	Process 2	◄
3	Process 3	
1	Process 1	
3	Process 3	
3	Process 3	
2	Process 2	◄
2	Process 2	◄
1	Process 1	
1	Process 1	
4	Process 4	
4	Process 4	
4	Process 4	

Operating system

Processor memory protection key [2]

Memory protection keys for individual memory blocks

Figure 10.24 | *Memory protection with keys in noncontiguous memory allocation multiprogramming systems.*

mechanism in today's systems, they are implemented in the IA-64 Intel architecture (i.e., the Itanium line of processors) and are generally intended for systems containing one virtual address space.[43]

The operating system can exercise further protection control by specifying how a segment may be accessed and by which processes. This is accomplished by assigning each process certain **access rights** to segments. Figure 10.25 lists the most common access control types in use in today's systems. If a process has **read access** to a segment, then it may read data from any address in that segment. If it has **write access** to a segment, then the process may modify any of the segment's contents and may add further information. A process given **execute access** to a segment may pass program control to instructions in that segment for execution on a processor. Execute access to a data segment is normally denied. A process given **append access** to a segment may write additional information to the end of the segment, but may not modify existing information.

By either allowing or denying each of these four access types, it is possible to create 16 different **access control modes**. Some of these are interesting, while others do not make sense. For simplicity, consider the eight different combinations of read, write, and execute access shown in Fig. 10.26.

In mode 0, no access is permitted to the segment. This is useful in security schemes in which the segment is not to be accessed by a particular process. In mode 1, a process is given **execute-only access** to the segment. This mode is useful when a process is allowed to execute instructions in the segment, but may not copy or modify it. Modes 2 and 3 are not useful—it does not make sense to give a process the right to modify a segment without also giving it the right to read the segment. Mode 4 allows a process **read-only access** to a segment. This is useful for accessing nonmodifiable data. Mode 5 allows a process **read/execute access** to a segment. This is useful for

Type of access	Abbreviation	Description
Read	R	This segment may be read.
Write	W	This segment may be modified.
Execute	E	This segment may be executed.
Append	A	This segment may have information added to its end.

Figure 10.25 | Access control types.

Mode	Read	Write	Execute	Description	Application
Mode 0	No	No	No	No access permitted	Security.
Mode 1	No	No	Yes	Execute only	A segment made available to processes that cannot modify it or copy it, but that can run it.
Mode 2	No	Yes	No	Write only	These possibilities are not useful, because granting write access without read access is impractical.
Mode 3	No	Yes	Yes	Write/execute but cannot be read	
Mode 4	Yes	No	No	Read only	Information retrieval.
Mode 5	Yes	No	Yes	Read/execute	A program can be copied or executed but cannot be modified.
Mode 6	Yes	Yes	No	Read/write but no execution	Protects data from an erroneous attempt to execute it.
Mode 7	Yes	Yes	Yes	Unrestricted access	This access is granted to trusted users.

Figure 10.26 | Combining read, write and execute access to yield useful access control modes.

reentrant code. A process may make its own copy of the segment which it may then modify. Mode 6 allows a process **read/write access** to a segment. This is useful when the segment contains data that may be read or written by the process but that must be protected from accidental execution (because the segment does not contain instructions). Mode 7 allows a process **unrestricted access** to a segment. This is useful for allowing a process complete access to its own segments (such as self-modifying code) and for giving it most-trusted status to access other processes' segments.

The simple access control mechanism described in this section is the basis of segment protection implemented in many systems. Figure 10.27 shows one way a system can implement access control, namely by including protection bits in a segment's map table entry. The entry includes four bits—one for each type of access control. The system can now enforce protection during address translation. When a process makes a reference to a segment in virtual memory, the system checks the protection bits to determine if the process has proper authorization. For example, if a process is attempting to execute a segment that has not been granted execution rights, then it does not have authorization to perform its task. In this case, a segment-protection exception is generated, causing the operating system to gain control and terminate the process.

Self Review

1. Which access rights are appropriate for a process's stack segment?
2. What special-purpose hardware is required to implement memory protection keys?

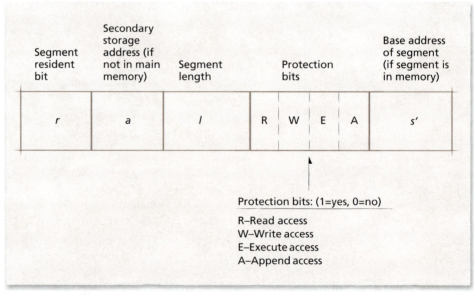

Figure 10.27 | *Segment map table entry with protection bits.*

Ans: **1)** A process should be able to read and write data in its stack segment and append new stack frames to the segment. **2)** A high-speed register is required to store the current process's memory protection key.

10.6 Segmentation/Paging Systems

Both segmentation and paging offer significant advantages as virtual memory organizations. Beginning with systems constructed in the mid-1960s, in particular Multics and IBM's TSS, many computer systems have been built that combine paging and segmentation.[44, 45, 46, 47, 48, 49] These systems offer the advantages of the two virtual memory organization techniques we have presented in this chapter. In a combined segmentation/paging system, segments are usually arranged across multiple pages. All the pages of a segment need not be in main memory at once, and virtual memory pages that are contiguous in virtual memory need not be contiguous in main memory. Under this scheme, a virtual memory address is implemented as an ordered triple $v = (s, p, d)$, where s is the segment number, p the page number within the segment and d the displacement within the page at which the desired item is located (Fig. 10.28).

10.6.1 Dynamic Address Translation in a Segmentation/Paging System

Consider the dynamic address translation of virtual addresses to real addresses in a paged and segmented system using combined associative/direct mapping, as illustrated in Fig. 10.29.

A process references virtual address $v = (s, p, d)$. The most recently referenced pages have entries in the associative memory map (i.e., the TLB). The translation mechanism performs an associative search to attempt to locate (s, p). If the TLB contains (s, p), then the search returns p', the page frame in which page p resides. This value is concatenated with the displacement, d, to form the real memory address r.

If the TLB does not contain an entry for (s, p), the processor must perform a complete direct mapping as follows. The base address, b, of the segment map table (in main memory) is added to the segment number, s, to form the address, $b + s$. This address corresponds to the physical memory location of the segment's entry in the segment map table. The segment map table entry indicates the base address, s', of the page table (in main memory) for segment s. The processor adds the page number, p, to the base address, s', to form the address of the page table entry for page p of segment s. This table entry indicates that p' is the page frame number corresponding to

Segment number	Page number	Displacement	Virtual address
s	p	d	$v = (s, p, d)$

Figure 10.28 | Virtual address format in a segmentation/paging system.

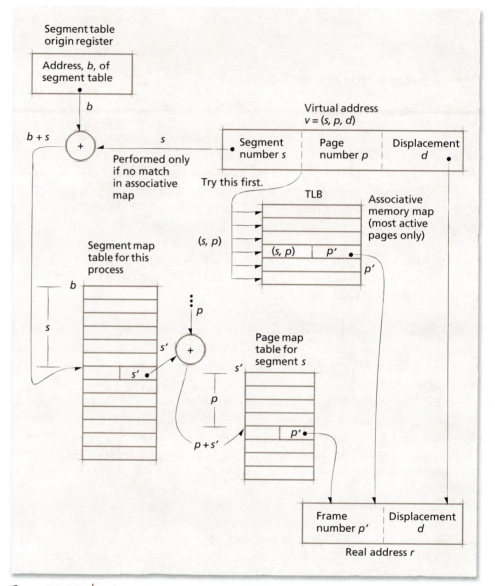

Figure 10.29 | *Virtual address translation with combined associative/direct mapping in a segmentation/paging system.*

virtual page p. This frame number, p', is concatenated with the displacement, d, to form the real address, r. The translation is then loaded into the TLB.

This translation scheme assumes that the process has made a valid memory reference and that every piece of information required for the process is located in main memory. Under many conditions however, the address translation may require extra steps or will fail. The segment map table search may indicate that segment s is not in main memory, thus generating a missing-segment fault and causing the operating system to locate the segment on secondary storage, create a page table for the segment, and load the appropriate page into main memory. If the segment is in main memory, then the reference to the page table may indicate that the desired page is not in main memory, initiating a page fault. This would cause the operating system to gain control, locate the page on secondary storage, and load it into main memory. It is also possible that a process has referenced a virtual memory address that extends beyond the range of the segment, thus generating a segment-overflow exception. Or the protection bits may indicate that the operation to be performed on the referenced virtual address is not allowed, thus generating a segment-protection exception. The operating system must handle all these possibilities.

The associative memory (or, similarly, a high-speed cache memory) is critical to the efficient operation of this dynamic address translation mechanism. If a purely direct mapping mechanism were used, with the complete map being maintained in main memory, the average virtual memory reference would require a memory cycle to access the segment map table, a second one to reference the page table and a third to reference the desired item in main memory. Thus every reference to an item would involve three memory cycles, and the computer system would run only at a small fraction of its normal speed; this would invalidate the benefits of virtual memory.

Figure 10.30 indicates the detailed table structure required by segmentation/paging systems. At the top level is a process table that contains an entry for every process in the system. Each process table entry contains a pointer to its process's segment map table. Each entry of a process's segment map table points to the page table for the associated segment, and each entry in a page table points either to the page frame in which that page resides or to the secondary storage address at which the page may be found. In a system with a large number of processes, segments and pages, this table structure can consume a significant portion of main memory. The benefit of maintaining all the tables in main memory is that address translation proceeds faster at execution time. However, the more tables a system maintains in main memory, the fewer processes it can support, and thus productivity declines. Operating systems designers must evaluate many such trade-offs to achieve the delicate balance needed for a system to run efficiently and to provide responsive service to system users.

Self Review

1. What special-purpose hardware is required for segmentation/paging systems?
2. In what ways do segmentation/paging systems incur fragmentation?

Ans: **1)** Segmentation/paging systems require a high-speed register to store the base address of the segment map table, a high-speed register to store the base address of the corresponding page table and an associative memory map (i.e., a TLB). **2)** Segmentation/paging systems can incur internal fragmentation when a segment is smaller than the page(s) in which it is placed. They also incur table fragmentation by maintaining both segment map tables and page tables in memory. Segmentation/paging systems do not incur external fragmentation (assuming the system uses one page size), because ultimately the memory is divided into fixed-size page frames, which can accommodate any page of any segment.

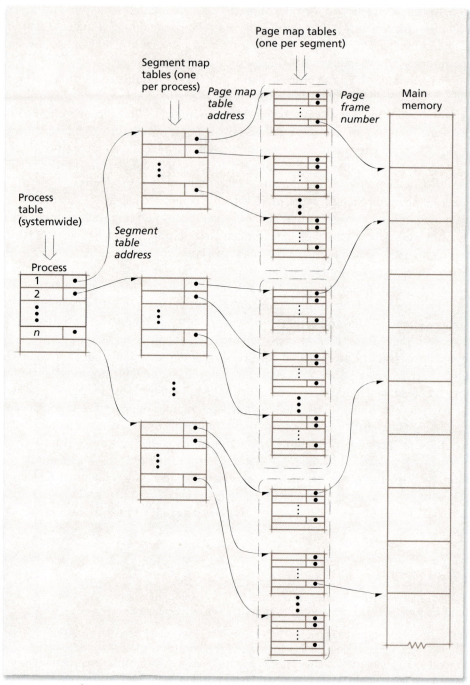

Figure 10.30 | Table structure for a segmentation/paging system.

10.6.2 Sharing and Protection in a Segmentation/Paging System

Segmentation/paging virtual memory systems take advantage of the architectural simplicity of paging and the access control capabilities of segmentation. In such a system the benefits of segment sharing become important. Two processes share memory when each process has a segment map table entry that points to the same page table, as is indicated in Fig. 10.31.

Sharing, whether in paged systems, segmented systems, or segmentation/paging systems, requires careful management by the operating system. In particular, consider what would happen if an incoming page were to replace a page shared by many processes. In this case, the operating system must update the resident bit in the corresponding page table entries for each process sharing the page. The operating system can incur substantial overhead determining which processes are sharing the page and which PTEs in their page tables must be changed. As we discuss in Section 20.6.4, Swapping, Linux reduces this overhead by maintaining a linked list of PTEs that map to a shared page.

Self Review

1. Why are segmentation/paging systems appealing?
2. What are the benefits and drawbacks of maintaining a linked list of PTEs that map to a shared page?

Ans: **1)** Segmentation/paging systems offer the architectural simplicity of paging and the access control capabilities of segmentation. **2)** A linked list of PTEs enables the system to update PTEs quickly when a shared page is replaced. Otherwise, the operating system would need to search each process's page table to determine if any PTEs need to be updated, which can incur substantial overhead. A drawback to the linked list of PTEs is that it incurs memory overhead. In today's systems, however, the cost of accessing main memory to search page tables generally outweighs the memory overhead incurred by maintaining the linked list.

10.7 Case Study: IA-32 Intel Architecture Virtual Memory

In this section, we discuss the virtual memory implementation of the IA-32 Intel architecture (i.e., the Intel Pentium line of processors), which supports either a pure segmentation or a segmentation/paging virtual memory implementation.[50] The set of addresses contained in each segment is called a **logical address space**, and its size depends on the size of the segment. Segments are placed in any available location in the system's **linear address space**, which is a 32-bit (i.e., 4GB) virtual address space. Under pure segmentation, the processor uses linear addresses to access main memory. If paging is enabled, the linear address space is divided into fixed-size page frames that are mapped to main memory.

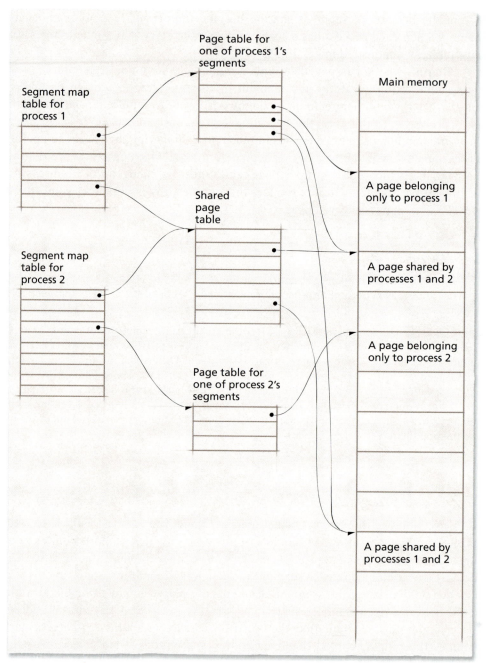

Figure 10.31 | *Two processes sharing a segment in a segmentation/paging system.*

The first stage of dynamic address translation maps segmented virtual addresses to the linear address space. Because there is no way to disable segmentation in the IA-32 specification, this translation occurs for every memory reference. Each segmented virtual address can be represented by the ordered pair $v = (s, d)$, as discussed in Section 10.5.1. In the IA-32 architecture, s is specified by a 16-bit **segment selector** and d by a 32-bit offset (i.e., the displacement within segment s' at which the referenced item is located). The segment index, which is the 13 most-significant bits of the segment selector, specifies an 8-byte entry in the segment map table.

To speed address translation under segmentation, the IA-32 architecture provides six **segment registers**, named CS, DS, SS, ES, FS and GS, to store a process's segment selectors. The operating system normally uses the CS register to store a process's code segment selector (which typically corresponds to the segment containing its executable instructions), the DS register to store a process's data segment selector (which typically corresponds to the segment containing the process's data) and the SS register to store a process's stack segment selector (which typically corresponds to the segment containing its execution stack). The ES, FS and GS registers can be used for any other process segment selectors. Before a process can reference an address, the corresponding segment selector must be loaded into a segment register. This enables the process to reference addresses using the 32-bit offset, so that it does not have to specify the 16-bit segment selector for each memory reference.

To locate a segment map table entry, the processor multiplies the segment index by 8 (the number of bytes per segment map table entry) and adds that value to b, the address stored in the segment map table origin register. The IA-32 architecture provides two segment map table origin registers, the **global descriptor table register (GDTR)** and the **local descriptor table register (LDTR)**. The values of the GDTR and LDTR are loaded at context-switch time.

The system's primary segment map table is the **global descriptor table (GDT)** which contains 8,192 (2^{13}) 8-byte entries. The first entry is not used by the processor—references to a segment corresponding to this entry will generate an exception. Operating systems load the value corresponding to this entry into unused segment registers (e.g., ES, FS and GS) to prevent processes from accessing an invalid segment. If the system uses one segment map table for all of its processes, then the GDT is the only segment map table in the system. For operating systems that must maintain more than 8,192 segments, or that maintain a separate segment map table for each process, the IA-32 architecture provides **local descriptor tables (LDTs)**, each containing 8,192 entries. In this case, the base address of each LDT must be stored in the GDT, because the processor places the LDT in a segment. To perform address translation quickly, the base address of the LDT, b, is placed in the LDTR. The operating system can create up to 8,191 separate segment map tables using LDTs (recall that the first entry in the GDT is not used by the processor).

Each segment map table entry, called a **segment descriptor**, stores a 32-bit **base address**, s', that specifies the location in the linear address space of the start of the segment. The system forms a linear address by adding the displacement, d, to the segment base address, s'. Under pure segmentation, the linear address, $s' + d$, is the real address.

The processor checks each reference against the segment descriptor's resident and protection bits before accessing main memory. The segment descriptor's **present bit** indicates whether the segment is in main memory; if it is, the address translation proceeds normally. If the present bit is off, the processor generates a **segment-not-present exception**, so that the operating system can load the segment from secondary storage. [*Note*: The terms "fault" and "exception" are used differently in the IA-32 specification than in the rest of the text (see Section 3.4.2, Interrupt Classes). The segment-not-present exception corresponds to a missing-segment fault.] The processor also checks each reference against the segment descriptor's 20-bit **segment limit**, l, which specifies the size of the segment. The system uses the segment descriptor's **granularity bit** to determine how to interpret the value specified in the segment's limit. If the granularity bit is off, segments can range in size from 1-byte ($l = 0$) to 1MB ($l = 2^{20} - 1$), in 1 byte increments. In this case, if $d > l$, the system generates a **general protection fault (GPF)** exception, indicating that a process has attempted to access memory outside of its segment. [*Note*: Again, the term "fault" is used differently in the IA-32 specification than in the rest of the text.] If the granularity bit is on, segments can range in size from 4KB ($l = 0$) to 4GB ($l = 2^{20} - 1$), in 4KB increments. In this case, if $d > (l \times 2^{12})$, the processor generates a GPF exception, indicating that a process has attempted to access memory outside of its segment.

The IA-32 architecture maintains a process's access rights to a segment in the **type** field of each segment map table entry. The type field's **code/data bit** determines whether the segment contains executable instructions or program data. Execute access is enabled when this bit is on. The type field also contains a **read/write bit** that determines whether the segment is read-only or read/write.

If paging is enabled, the operating system can divide the linear address space (i.e., the virtual address space in which segments are placed) into fixed-size pages. As we discuss in the next chapter, page size can significantly impact performance; thus, the IA-32 architecture supports 4KB, 2MB and 4MB pages. When 4KB pages are used, the IA-32 architecture maps each linear address to a physical address using a two-level page address translation mechanism. In this case, each 32-bit linear address is represented as $v' = (t, p, d)$, where t is a 10-bit page table number, p is a 10-bit page number, and d is a 12-bit displacement. Page address translation occurs exactly as described in Section 10.4.4. To locate the page directory entry, t is added to the value of the page directory origin register (analogous to the page table origin register). Each 4-byte **page directory entry (PDE)** specifies b, the base address of a page table containing 4-byte page table entries (PTEs). To form the physical address at which the page table entry resides, the processor multiplies p by

4 (because each PTE occupies 4 bytes) and adds b. The most active PTEs and PDEs are stored in a processor's TLB to speed virtual-to-physical address translations.

When 4MB pages are used, each 32-bit linear address is represented as $v' = (p, d)$, where p is a 10-bit page directory number and d is a 22-bit displacement. In this case, page address translation occurs exactly as described in Section 10.4.3.

Each page reference is checked against its PDE's and PTE's read/write bit. When the bit is on, all of the pages in the PDE's page table are read-only; otherwise they are read/write. Similarly, each PTE's read/write bit specifies the read/write access right for its corresponding page.

One limitation of a 32-bit physical addresses space is that the system can access at most 4GB of main memory. Because some systems contain more than that, the IA-32 architecture provides the **Physical Address Extension (PAE)** and **Page Size Extension (PSE)** features, which enable a system to reference 36-bit physical addresses, supporting a maximum memory size of 64GB. The implementation of these features is beyond the scope of the discussion; the reader is encouraged to study these and other features of the IA-32 specification, which can be found online in the *IA-32 Intel Architecture Software Developer's Manual*, Vol. 3, located at `developer.intel.com/design/Pentium4/manuals/`. The Web Resources section contains links to several manuals that describe virtual memory implementations in other architectures, such as the PowerPC and PA-RISC architectures.

Mini Case Study

IBM Mainframe Operating Systems

The first commercial computer with transistor logic for general use was the IBM 7090 which was released in 1959. Its operating system was called **IBSYS**.[51, 52] IBSYS had roughly two dozen components, which included modules for the FORTRAN and COBOL programming languages, in addition to the resource managers.[53]

In 1964 IBM announced its next set of systems, the System/360 line, which consisted of several different models of varying processor power, all running on the same architecture.[54, 55] The smallest models ran under the Disk Operating System or DOS, while the rest came with **OS/360**.[56, 57, 58] Having one operating system run on several different

models of computer was a relatively new concept at the time.[59] OS/360 had three different control options: PCP, MFT, and MVT.[60, 61] OS/360-PCP (for Principal Control Program) was single-tasking and designed for the smallest System/360 models; however, in practice DOS (or TOS for systems with tape drives only) was used *(continued)*

Mini Case Study

IBM Mainframe Operating Systems (Cont.)

on these computers.[62, 63] OS/360-MFT and OS/360-MVT were both multitasking, with a "Fixed number of Tasks" and a "Variable number of Tasks," respectively, which meant that a system running the MFT option had its memory divisions preset by the operator, while under MVT memory could be divided by the system automatically as new jobs arrived.[64, 65] A large project called TSS (Time-Sharing System) to build a multiuser operating system to compete with Multics was eventually cancelled when TSS proved to be too large and to crash too often.[66] Its functionality was implemented as TSO (the Time-Sharing Option) in 1971.[67, 68]

IBM announced the System/370 hardware in 1970, which now included virtual memory support.[69] To utilize this new capability, OS/360-MFT was updated and renamed OS/VS1, while the MVT option was similarly upgraded and named OS/VS2 SVS (Single Virtual Storage), so named because it had only one 16MB virtual address space shared among all users.[70, 71] It was later updated again to allow any number of

such address spaces, and so was renamed OS/VS2 MVS, or simply **MVS** (for Multiple Virtual Storages).[72, 73]

MVS was updated to MVS/370, which soon supported the new cross-memory feature of the System/370 hardware; cross-memory is a mechanism to separate data and code in memory space.[74, 75] Additionally, because 16MB of memory space had quickly been filled by expanding system programs, the processors now used a 26-bit address, allowing for 64MB of real memory; however, while MVS/370 supported this real memory capacity, it still used a 24-bit address and therefore only used 16MB virtual memory spaces.[76, 77]

Two years later, IBM moved on to the 3081 processors running on the 370-XA "Extended Architecture."[78, 79] MVS/370 was updated, new functionality was added, and the resulting package was subsequently released as MVS/XA in 1983.[80, 81] This OS now allowed for 2GB of virtual memory, much more easily satisfying any program's space requirements.[82]

In 1988 IBM upgraded the hardware yet again, moving to the ES/3090 processors on the ESA/370 (Enterprise System Architecture).[83] ESA introduced memory spaces that were used only for data, making it easier to move data around for processing.[84] MVS/XA was moved up to MVS/ESA for these new systems.[85, 86] MVS/ESA was significantly updated in 1991 for the new ESA/390 hardware, which included mechanisms for linking IBM machines into a loose cluster (SYS-PLEX)[87] and changing the settings on I/O devices without the need to take the machine offline (ESCON).[88]

MVS is still the root of IBM's mainframe operating systems, as MVS/ESA was upgraded to OS/390 in 1996 for the System/390 hardware;[89] it is now named **z/OS** and runs on the zSeries mainframes.[90] In addition, IBM's mainframe operating systems have remained backward compatible with earlier versions; OS/390 can run applications written for MVS/ESA, MVS/XA, OS/VS2, or even OS/360.[91]

Mini Case Study

Early History of the VM Operating System

A virtual machine is an illusion of a real machine. It is created by a **virtual machine operating system**, which makes a single real machine appear to be several real machines. From the user's viewpoint, virtual machines can appear to be existing real machines, or they can be dramatically different. The concept has proven valuable, and many virtual machine operating systems have been developed—one of the most widely used is IBM's VM.

VM managed the IBM System/370[92, 93] computer (or compatible hardware), creating the illusion that each of several users had a complete System/370, including many input/output devices. Each user could choose a different operating system. VM can run several operating systems simultaneously, each of them on its own virtual machine. Today's VM users can run versions of the operating systems OS/390, z/OS, TPF, VSE/ESA, CMS and Linux.[94]

Conventional multiprogramming systems share the resources of a single computer among several processes. These processes are each allocated a portion of the real machine's resources. Each process sees a machine smaller in size and capabilities than the real machine executing the process.

Virtual machine multiprogramming systems (Fig. 10.32) share the resources of a single machine in a different manner. They create the illusion that one real machine is actually several machines. They create virtual processors, virtual storage and virtual I/O devices, possibly with much larger capacities than those of the underlying real machine.

The main components of VM are the **Control Program (CP)**, the **Conversational Monitor System (CMS)**, the **Remote Spooling Communications Subsystem (RSCS)**, the **Interactive Problem Control System (IPCS)** and the **CMS Batch Facility**. CP creates the environment in which virtual machines can execute. It provides the support for the various operating systems normally used to control System/370 and compatible computer systems. CP manages the real machine underlying the virtual machine environment. It gives each user access to the facilities of the real machine such as the processor, storage and I/O devices. CP multiprograms complete virtual machines rather than individual tasks or processes. CMS is an applications system with powerful features for interactive development of programs. It contains editors, language translators, various applications packages and debugging tools. Virtual machines running under CP perform much as if they were real machines, except that they operate more slowly, since VM runs many virtual machines simultaneously.

VM's ability to run multiple operating systems simultaneously has many applications.[95, 96] It eases migration between different operating systems or different versions of the same operating system. It enables people to be trained simultaneously with running production systems. System development can occur simultaneously with production runs. Customers can run different operating systems simultaneously to exploit each system's benefits. Running multiple operating systems offers a form of backup in case of failure; this increases availability. Installations may run benchmarks on new operating *(continued)*

Mini Case Study

Early History of the VM Operating System (Cont.)

systems to determine if upgrades are worthwhile; this may be done in parallel with production activity.

Processes running on a virtual machine are not controlled by CP, but rather by the actual operating system running on that virtual machine. The operating systems running on virtual machines perform their full range of functions, including storage management, processor scheduling, input/output control, protecting users from one another, protecting the operating system from the users, spooling, multiprogramming, job and process control, error handling, and so on.

VM simulates an entire machine dedicated to one user. A user at a VM virtual machine sees the equivalent of a complete real machine, rather than many users sharing one set of resources.

CP/CMS began as an experimental system in 1964. It was to be a second-generation timesharing system based on IBM System/ 360 computers.[97] Originally developed for local use at the IBM Cambridge Scientific Center, it soon gained favor as a tool for evaluating the performance of other operating systems.

The first operational version appeared in 1966, consisting of CP-40 and CMS. These components were designed to run on a modified IBM 360/40 with newly incorporated dynamic address translation hardware. At about this time, IBM announced an upgrade to its powerful 360/65. The new system, the 360/67, incorporated dynamic address translation hardware and provided the basis for a general-purpose time-sharing, multiprogramming computer utility called TSS/360.[98] The TSS effort, performed independently of the work on CP/CMS, encountered many difficulties (typical of the large-scale software efforts of the mid-1960s). Meanwhile CP/CMS was successfully moved to the 360/67, and eventually it superseded the TSS effort. CP/CMS evolved into VM/ 370, which became available in 1972 for the virtual storage models of the IBM 370 series.[99]

CTSS, successfully used at MIT through 1974, most strongly influenced the design of CP/CMS. The CP/CMS designers found that the CTSS design was difficult to work with. They felt that a more modular approach would be

appropriate, so they split the resource management portion from the user support portion of the operating system, resulting in CP and CMS, respectively. CP provides separate computing environments that give each user complete access to a full virtual machine; CMS runs on a CP-created virtual machine as a single-user interactive system.

The most significant decision made in the design of CP was that each virtual machine would replicate a real machine. It was clear that the 360 family concept would create a long lifetime for 360 programs; users requiring more power would simply move up in the family to a compatible system with more storage, devices and processor speed. Any decision to produce virtual machines different in structure from a real 360 probably would have resulted in the failure of the CP/CMS system. Instead, the concept has been successful, making VM one of IBM's two leading mainframe operating systems in the 1990s. IBM continues to create new versions of VM for use on its mainframe servers, the latest being z/VM, which supports IBM's 64-bit architecture.[100]

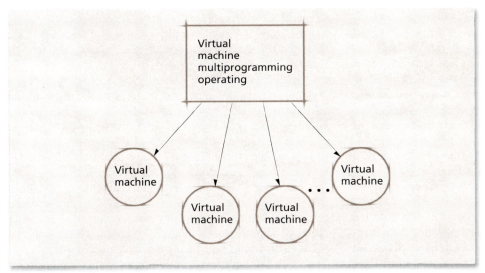

Figure 10.32 | *Virtual machine multiprogramming.*

Web Resources

`www.redhat.com/docs/manuals/linux/RHL-8.0-Manual/admin-primer/s1-memory-concepts.html`
Overview of virtual memory from Red Hat (a Linux vendor).

`www.howstuffworks.com/virtual-memory.htm`
Overview of virtual memory.

`www.memorymanagement.org`
Provides a glossary and guide to physical and virtual memory management.

`developer.intel.com`
Provides technical documentation regarding Intel products, including Pentium and Itanium processors. Their system programmer guides (e.g., for the Pentium 4 processor, `developer.intel.com/design/Pentium4/manuals/`) provide information on how memory is organized and accessed in Intel systems.

`www-3.ibm.com/chips/techlib/techlib.nsf/product-families/PowerPC_Microprocessors_and_Embedded_Processors`
Provides technical documentation regarding PowerPC processors, found in Apple computers. Descriptions of virtual memory management in these processors is located in the software reference manuals (e.g., the PowerPC 970, found in Apple G5 computers, `www-3.ibm.com/chips/techlib/techlib.nsf/products/PowerPC_970_Microprocessor`).

`h21007.www2.hp.com/dspp/tech/tech_TechDocumentDetailPage_IDX/1,1701,958!13!253,00.html`
Describes virtual memory organization for PA-RISC processors. PA-RISC is primarily used in high-performance environments. See also `cpus.hp.com/technical_references/parisc.shtml`.

Summary

Virtual memory solves the problem of limited memory space by creating the illusion that more memory exists than is available in the system. There are two types of addresses in virtual memory systems: those referenced by processes and those available in main memory. The addresses that processes reference are called virtual addresses. The addresses available in main memory are called physical (or real) addresses. Whenever a process accesses a virtual address, it must translate the virtual addresses to a physical address; this is done by the memory management unit (MMU).

A process's virtual address space, V, is the range of virtual addresses that it may reference. The range of physical addresses available on a particular computer system is called that computer's real address space, R. If we are to permit a user's virtual address space to be larger than its real address space, we must provide a means for retaining programs and data in a large auxiliary storage. A system normally accomplishes this by employing a two-level storage scheme consisting of main memory and secondary storage. When the system is ready to run a process, the system loads the process's code and data from secondary storage into main memory. Only a small portion of a process's code and data needs to be in main memory for that process to execute.

Dynamic address translation (DAT) mechanisms convert virtual addresses to physical addresses during execution. Systems that use DAT exhibit the property that the contiguous addresses in a process's virtual address space need not be contiguous in physical memory—this is called artificial contiguity. Dynamic address translation and artificial contiguity free the programmer from concerns about memory placement (e.g., the programmer need not create overlays to ensure the system can execute the program). Dynamic address translation mechanisms must maintain address translation maps indicating which regions of a process's virtual address space, V, are currently in main memory, and where they are located.

Virtual memory systems cannot afford to map addresses individually, so information is grouped into blocks, and the system keeps track of where in main memory the various virtual memory blocks have been placed. When blocks are the same size, they are called pages and the associated virtual memory organization technique is called paging. When blocks may be of different sizes, they are called segments, and the associated virtual memory organization technique is called segmentation. Some systems combine the two techniques, implementing segments as variable-size blocks composed of fixed-size pages.

In a virtual memory system with block mapping, the system represents addresses as ordered pairs. To refer to a particular item in the process's virtual address space, the process specifies the block in which the item resides, and the displacement (or offset) of the item from the start of the block. A virtual address, v, is denoted by an ordered pair (b, d), where b is the block number in which the referenced item resides, and d is the displacement from the start of the block. The system maintains in memory a block map table for each process. The real address, a, that corresponds to the address in main memory of a process's block map table is loaded into a special processor register called the block map table origin register. During execution, the process references a virtual address $v = (b, d)$. The system adds the block number, b, to the base address, a, of the process's

block table to form the real address of the entry for block b in the block map table. This entry contains the address, b', for the start of block b in main memory. The system then adds the displacement, d, to the block start address, b', to form the desired real address, r.

Paging uses a fixed-size block mapping; pure paging systems do not combine segmentation with paging. A virtual address in a paging system is an ordered pair (p, d), where p is the number of the page in virtual memory on which the referenced item resides, and d is the displacement within page p at which the referenced item is located. When the system transfers a page from secondary storage to main memory, the system places the page in a main memory block, called a page frame, that is the same size as the incoming page. Page frames begin at physical memory addresses that are integral multiples of the fixed page size. The system may place an incoming page in any available page frame.

Dynamic address translation under paging is similar to block address translation. A running process references a virtual memory address $v = (p, d)$. A page mapping mechanism uses the value of the page table origin register to locate the entry for page p in the process's page map table (often simply called the page table). The corresponding page table entry (PTE) indicates that page p is in page frame p' (p' is not a physical memory address). The real memory address, r, corresponding to v is formed by concatenating p' and the displacement into the page frame, d, which places p' in the most-significant bits of the real memory address and d in the least-significant bits.

When a process references a page that is not in main memory, the processor generates a page fault, which invokes the operating system to load the missing page into memory from secondary storage. In the PTE for this page, a resident bit, r, is set to 0 if the page is not in main memory and 1 if the page is in main memory.

Page address translation can be performed by direct mapping, associative mapping or combined direct/associative mapping. Due to the cost of high-speed, location-addressed cache memory and the relatively large size of programs, maintaining the entire page table in cache memory is often not viable, which limits the performance of direct-mapping page address translation because the page table must then be stored in much slower main memory. One way to increase the performance of dynamic address translation is to place the entire page table into a content-addressed (rather than location-addressed) associative memory, which has a cycle time perhaps an order of magnitude faster than main memory. In this case, every entry in the associative memory is searched simultaneously for page *p*. In the vast majority of systems, using a cache memory to implement pure direct mapping or an associative memory to implement pure associative mapping is too costly.

As a result, many designers have chosen a compromise scheme that offers many of the advantages of the cache or associative memory approach but at a more modest cost. This approach uses an associative memory, called the translation lookaside buffer (TLB), capable of holding only a small percentage of the complete page table for a process. The page table entries maintained in this map typically correspond to the most-recently referenced pages only, using the heuristic that a page referenced recently in the past is likely to be referenced again in the near future. This is an example of locality (more specifically of temporal locality—locality in time). When the system locates the mapping for *p* in the TLB, it experiences a TLB hit; otherwise a TLB miss occurs, requiring the system to access slower main memory. Empirically, due to the phenomenon of locality, the number of entries in the TLB does not need to be large to achieve good performance.

Multilevel (or hierarchical) page tables enable the system to store in discontiguous locations in main memory those portions of a process's page table that the process is using. These layers form a hierarchy of page tables, each level containing a table that stores pointers to tables in the level below. The bottom-most level is comprised of tables containing address translations. Multilevel page tables can reduce memory overhead compared to a direct-mapping system, at the cost of additional accesses to main memory to perform address translations that are not contained in the TLB.

An inverted page table stores exactly one PTE in memory for each page frame in the system. The page tables are inverted relative to traditional page tables because the PTEs are indexed by page frame number rather than virtual page number. Inverted page tables use hash functions and chaining pointers to map a virtual page to an inverted page table entry, which yields a page frame number. The overhead incurred by accessing main memory to follow each pointer in an inverted page table's hash collision chain can be substantial. Because the size of the inverted page table must remain fixed to provide direct mappings to page frames, most systems employ a hash anchor table that increases the range of the hash function to reduce collisions, at the cost of an additional memory access.

Enabling sharing in multiprogramming systems reduces the memory consumed by programs that use common data and/or instructions, but requires that the system identify each page as either sharable or nonsharable. If the page table entries of different processes point to the same page frame, the page frame is shared by each of the processes. Copy-on-write uses shared memory to reduce process creation time by sharing a parent's address space with its child. Each time a process writes to a shared page, the operating system copies the shared page to a new page that is mapped to that process's address space. The operating system can mark these shared pages as read-only so that the system generates an exception when a process attempts to modify a page. To handle the exception, the operating system allocates an unshared copy of the page to the process that generated the exception. Copy-on-write can result in poor performance if the majority of a process's shared data is modified during program execution.

Under segmentation, a program's data and instructions are divided into blocks called segments. Each segment contains a meaningful portion of the program, such as a procedure or an array. Each segment consists of contiguous locations; however, the segments need not be the same size nor must they be adjacent to one another in main memory. A process may execute while its current instructions and referenced data are in segments in main memory. If a process references memory in a segment not currently resident in main memory, the virtual memory system must retrieve that segment from secondary storage. The placement strategies for segmentation are identical to those used in variable-partition multiprogramming.

A virtual memory segmentation address is an ordered pair $v = (s, d)$, where s is the segment number in which the referenced item resides, and d is the displacement within segment s at which the referenced item is located. The system adds the segment number, s, to the segment map table's base address value, b, located in the segment map table origin register. The resulting value, $b + s$, is the location of the segment map table entry. If the segment currently resides in main memory, the segment map table entry contains the segment's physical memory address, s'. The system then adds the displacement, d, to this address to form the referenced location's real memory address, $r = s' + d$. We cannot simply concatenate s' and d, as we could in a paging system, because segments are of variable size. If the segment is not in main memory, then a missing-segment fault is generated, causing the operating system to gain control and load the referenced segment from secondary storage.

Each reference to a segment is checked against the segment length, l, to ensure that it falls within the segment's range. If it does not, then a segment-overflow exception is generated, causing the operating system to gain control and terminate the process. Each reference to the segment is also checked against the protection bits in the segment map table entry to determine if the operation is allowed. If it is not, then a segment-protection exception is generated, causing the operating system to gain control and terminate the process. Sharing segments can incur less overhead than sharing in a direct-mapped pure paging system, because sharing information for each segment (which may consume several pages of memory) is maintained in one segment map table entry.

One scheme for implementing memory protection in segmentation systems is the use of memory protection keys. In this case, each process is associated with a value, called a protection key. When the process references a particular segment, it checks the protection key of the block containing the referenced item. If the protection key for the processor and the requested block are the same, the process can access the segment. The operating system can exercise further protection control by specifying how a segment may be accessed and by which processes. This is accomplished by assigning each process certain access rights, such as read, write, execute and append. By either allowing or denying each of these access types, it is possible to create different access control modes.

In a combined segmentation/paging system, segments occupy one or more pages. All the pages of a segment need not be in main memory at once, and pages contiguous in virtual memory need not be contiguous in main memory. Under this scheme, a virtual memory address is implemented as an ordered triple $v = (s, p, d)$, where s is the segment number, p the page number within the segment and d is the displacement within the page at which the desired item is located. When a process references a virtual address $v = (s, p, d)$, the system attempts to find the corresponding page frame number p' in the TLB. If it is not present, the system first searches the segment map table, which points to the base of a page table, then uses the page number p as the displacement into the page table to locate the PTE containing the page frame number p'. The displacement, d, is then concatenated to p' to form the real memory address. This translation scheme assumes that the process has made a valid memory reference and that every piece of information required for the process is located in main memory. Under many conditions however, the address translation may require extra steps or may fail.

In segmentation/paging systems, two processes share memory when each process has a segment map table entry that points to the same page table. Sharing, whether in paged systems, segmented systems, or segmentation/paging systems, requires careful management by the operating system.

The IA-32 Intel architecture supports either pure segmentation or segmentation/paging virtual memory. The set of addresses contained in each segment is called a logical address space; segments are placed in any available location in the system's linear address space, which is a 32-bit (i.e., 4GB) virtual address space. Under pure segmentation, a referenced item's linear address is its address in main memory. If paging is enabled, the linear address space is divided into fixed-size page frames that are mapped to main memory. Segment address translation is performed by a direct mapping that uses high-speed processor registers to store segment map table origin registers in the global descriptor table register (GDTR) or in the local descriptor table register (LDTR), depending on the number of segment map tables in the system. The processor also stores segment numbers called segment descriptors in high-speed registers to improve address translation performance. Under segmentation/paging, segments are placed in the 4GB linear address space, which is divided into page frames that map to main memory. The IA-32 architecture uses a two-level page table to perform translations from page numbers to page frame numbers, which are concatenated with the page offset to form a real address.

Key Terms

access control mode—Set of privileges (e.g., read, write, execute and/or append) that determine how a page or segment of memory can be accessed.

access right—Privilege that determines which resources a process may access. In memory, access rights determine which pages or segments a process can access, and in what manner (i.e., read, write, execute and/or append).

address translation map—Table that assists in the mapping of virtual addresses to their corresponding real memory addresses.

append access—Access right that enables a process to write additional information at the end of a segment but not to modify its existing contents; see also execute access, read access and write access.

artificial contiguity—Technique employed by virtual memory systems to provide the illusion that a program's instructions and data are stored contiguously when pieces of them may be spread throughout main memory; this simplifies programming.

associative mapping—Content-addressed associative memory that assists in the mapping of virtual addresses to their corresponding real memory addresses; all entries of the associative memory are searched simultaneously.

associative memory—Memory that is searched by content, not by location; fast associative memories can help implement high-speed dynamic address translation mechanisms.

block—Portion of a memory space (either real or virtual) defined by a range of contiguous addresses.

block map table—Table containing entries that map each of a process's virtual blocks to a corresponding block in main memory (if there is one). Blocks in a virtual memory system are either segments or pages.

block map table origin register—Register that stores the address in main memory of a process's block map table; this high-speed register facilitates rapid virtual address translation.

block mapping—Mechanism that, a virtual memory system, reduces the number of mappings between virtual memory addresses and real memory addresses by mapping blocks in virtual memory to blocks in main memory.

chaining (hash tables)—Technique that resolves collisions in a hash table by placing each unique item in a data structure (typically a linked list). The position in the hash table at which the collision occurred contains a pointer to that data structure.

CMS Batch Facility (VM)—VM Component that allows the user to run longer jobs in a separate virtual machine so that the user can continue interactive work.

virtual machine operating system—Software that creates the virtual machine.

collision (hash tables)—Event that occurs when a hash function maps two different items to the same position in a hash table. Some hash tables use chaining to resolve collisions.

Conversational Monitor System (CMS) (VM)—Component of VM that is an interactive application development environment.

Control Program (CP) (VM)—Component of VM that runs the physical machine and creates the environment for the virtual machine.

copy-on-write—Mechanism that improves process creation efficiency by sharing mapping information between parent and child until a process modifies a page, at which point a new copy of the page is created and allocated to that process. This can incur substantial overhead if the parent or child modifies many of the shared pages.

direct mapping—Address translation mechanism that assists in the mapping of virtual addresses to their corresponding

real addresses, using an index into a table stored in location-addressed memory.

displacement—Distance of an address from the start of a block, page or segment, also called offset.

dynamic address translation (DAT)—Mechanism that converts virtual addresses to physical addresses during execution; this is done at extremely high speed to avoid slowing execution.

execute access—Access right that enables a process to execute instructions from a page or segment; see also read access, write access and append access.

general protection fault (GPF) (IA-32 Intel architecture)—Occurs when a process references a segment to which it does not have appropriate access rights or references an address outside of the segment.

global descriptor table (GDT) (IA-32 Intel architecture)—Segment map table that contains mapping information for process segments or local descriptor table (LDT) segments, which contain mapping information for process segments.

granularity bit (IA-32 Intel architecture)—Bit that determines how the processor interprets the size of each segment, specified by the 20-bit segment limit. When the bit is off, segments range in size from 1 byte to 1MB, in 1-byte increments. When the bit is on, segments range in size from 4KB to 4GB, in 4KB increments.

hash anchor table—Hash table that points to entries in an inverted page table. Increasing the size of the hash anchor table decreases the number of collisions, which improves the speed of address translation, at the cost of the increased memory overhead required to store the table.

hash function—Function that takes a number as input and returns a number, called a hash value, within a specified range. Hash functions facilitate rapidly storing and retrieving information from hash tables.

hash value—Value returned by a hash function that corresponds to a position in a hash table.

hash table—Data structure that indexes items according to their hash values; used with hash functions to rapidly store and retrieve information.

IBSYS—Operating system for the IBM 7090 mainframe.

Interactive Problem Control System (IPCS) (VM)—VM component that provides online analysis and correction of VM software problems.

inverted page table—Page table containing one entry for each page frame in main memory. Inverted page tables incur less table fragmentation than traditional page tables, which typically maintain in memory a greater number of page table entries than page frames. Hash functions map virtual page numbers to an index in the inverted page table.

linear address space (IA-32 Intel architecture)—32-bit (4GB) virtual address space. Under pure segmentation, this address space is mapped directly to main memory. Under segmentation/paging, this address space is divided into page frames that are mapped to main memory.

local descriptor table (LDT) (IA-32 Intel architecture)—Segment map table that contains mapping information for process segments. The system may contain up to 8,191 LDTs, each containing 8,192 entries.

locality—Empirical phenomenon describing events that are closely related in space or time. When applied to memory access patterns, spatial locality states that when a process references a particular address, it is also likely to access nearby addresses; temporal locality states that when a process references a particular address, it is likely to reference it again soon.

logical address space (IA-32 Intel architecture)—Set of addresses contained in a segment.

Memory Management Unit (MMU)—Special-purpose hardware that performs virtual-to-physical address translation.

missing-segment fault—Fault that occurs when a process references a segment that is not currently in main memory. The operating system responds by loading the segment from secondary storage into main memory when space is available.

multilevel paging system—Technique that enables the system to store portions of a process's page table in discontiguous locations in main memory and store only those portions that a process is actively using. Multilevel page tables are implemented by creating a hierarchy of page tables, each level containing a table that stores pointers to tables in the level below. The bottom-most level is comprised of tables containing the page-to-page-frame mappings. This reduces memory waste compared to single-level page tables, but incurs greater overhead due to the increased number of memory accesses required to perform address translation when corresponding mappings are not contained in the TLB.

Multiple Virtual Spaces (MVS)—IBM operating system for System/370 mainframes allowing any number of 16MB virtual address spaces.

offset—See displacement.

OS/360—Operating system for the IBM System/360 mainframes. OS/360 had two major options, MFT and MVT, which stood for "Multiprogramming with a Fixed number of Tasks" and "Multiprogramming with a Variable number of Tasks." OS/360-MVT evolved into MVS, the ancestor of the current IBM mainframe operating system z/OS.

page—Fixed-size set of contiguous addresses in a process's virtual address space that is managed as one unit. A page contains portions of a process's data and/or instructions and can be placed in any available page frame in main memory.

page directory entry (IA-32 Intel architecture)—Entry in a page directory that maps to the base address of a page table, which stores page table entries.

page fault—Fault that occurs as the result of an error when a process attempts to access a nonresident page, in which case the operating system can load it from disk.

page frame—Block of main memory that can store a virtual page. In systems with a single page size, any page can be placed in any available page frame.

page global directory—In a two-tiered multilevel page table, the page global directory is a table of pointers to portions of a process's page table. Page global directories are the top level of a multilevel page table hierarchy.

page map table—See page table.

page table origin register—Register that holds the location of a process's page table in main memory; having this information accessible in a high-speed register facilitates rapid virtual-to-physical address translation.

page table—Table that stores entries that map page numbers to page frames. A page table contains an entry for each of a process's virtual pages.

page table entry (PTE)—Entry in a page table that maps a virtual page number to a page frame number. Page table entries store other information about a page, such as how the page may be accessed and whether the page is resident.

paging—Virtual memory organization technique that divides an address space into fixed-size blocks of contiguous addresses. When applied to a process's virtual address space, the blocks are called pages, which store process data and instructions. When applied to main memory, the blocks are called page frames. A page is stored on secondary storage and loaded into a page frame if one is available. Paging trivializes the memory placement decision and does not incur external fragmentation (for systems that contain a single page size); paging does incur internal fragmentation.

physical address—Location in main memory.

Physical Address Extension (PAE) (IA-32 Intel architecture)—Mechanism that enables IA-32 processors to address up to 64GB of main memory.

physical address space—Range of physical addresses corresponding to the size of main memory in a given computer. The physical address space may be (and is often) smaller than each process's virtual address space.

process table—Table of known processes. In a segmentation/paging system, each entry points to a process's virtual address space, among other items.

pure paging—Memory organization technique that employs paging only, not segmentation.

read access—Access right that enables a process to read data from a page or segment; see also execute access, write access and append access.

real address—See physical address.

Remote Spooling Communications Subsystem (RSCS) (VM)—Component of VM that provides the capability to send and receive files in a distributed system.

segment—Variable-size set of contiguous addresses in a process's virtual address space that is managed as one unit. A segment is typically the size of an entire set of similar items, such as a set of instructions in a procedure or the contents of an array, which enables the system to protect such items with fine granularity using appropriate access rights. For example, a data segment typically is assigned read-only or read/write access, but not execute access. Similarly, a segment containing executable instructions typically is assigned read/execute access, but not write access. Segments tend to create external fragmentation in main memory but do not suffer from internal fragmentation.

segment descriptor (IA-32 Intel architecture)—Segment map table entry that stores a segment's base address, present bit, limit address and protection bits.

segment map table origin register—Register that holds the location of a process's segment map table in main memory; having this information accessible in a high-speed register facilitates rapid virtual-to-physical address translation.

segment-overflow exception—Exception that occurs when a process attempts to access an address that is outside a segment.

segment-protection exception—Exception that occurs when a process attempts to access a segment in ways other than those specified by its access control mode (e.g., attempting to write to a read-only segment).

segment selector (IA-32 Intel architecture)—16-bit value indicating the offset into the segment map table at which the corresponding segment descriptor (i.e., segment map table entry) is located.

table fragmentation—Wasted memory consumed by block mapping tables; small blocks tend to increase the number of blocks in the system, which increases table fragmentation.

translation lookaside buffer (TLB)—High-speed associative memory map that holds a small number of mappings between virtual page numbers and their corresponding page frame numbers. The TLB typically stores recently used page table entries, which improves performance for processes exhibiting locality.

virtual address—Address that a process accesses in a virtual memory system; virtual addresses are translated to real addresses dynamically at execution time.

virtual address space—Range of virtual addresses that a process may reference.

virtual memory—Technique that solves the problem of limited memory by providing each process with a virtual address space (potentially larger than the system's physical address space) that the process uses to access data and instructions.

write access—Access right that enables a process to modify the contents of a page or segment; see also execute access, read access and append access.

z/OS—IBM operating system for zSeries mainframes and the latest version of MVS.

Exercises

10.1 Give several reasons why it is useful to separate a process's virtual memory space from its physical memory space.

10.2 One attraction of virtual memory is that users no longer have to restrict the size of their programs to make them fit into physical memory. Programming style becomes a freer form of expression. Discuss the effects of such a free programming style on performance in a multiprogramming virtual memory environment. List both positive and negative effects.

10.3 Explain the various techniques used for mapping virtual addresses to physical addresses under paging.

10.4 Discuss the relative merits of each of the following virtual memory mapping techniques.

    a. direct mapping

    b. associative mapping

    c. combined direct/associative mapping

10.5 Explain the mapping of virtual addresses to physical addresses under segmentation.

10.6 Consider a pure paging system that uses 32-bit addresses (each of which specifies one byte of memory), contains 128MB of main memory and has a page size of 8KB.

  a. How many page frames does the system contain?

  b. How many bits does the system use to maintain the displacement, d?

  c. How many bits does the system use to maintain the page number, p?

10.7 Consider a pure paging system that uses three levels of page tables and 64-bit addresses. Each virtual address is the ordered set $v = (p, m, t, d)$, where the ordered triple (p, m, t) is the page number and d is the displacement into the page. Each page table entry is 64 bits (8 bytes). The number of bits that store p is n_p, the number of bits that store m is n_m and the number of bits to store t is n_t.

  a. Assume $n_p = n_m = n_t = 18$.

  i. How large is the table at each level of the multi-level page table?

  ii. What is the page size, in bytes?

  b. Assume $n_p = n_m = n_t = 14$.

  i. How large the table at each level of the multi-level page table?

  ii. What is the page size, in bytes?

  c. Discuss the trade-offs of large and small table sizes.

10.8 Explain how memory protection is implemented in virtual memory systems with segmentation.

10.9 Discuss the various hardware features useful for implementing virtual memory systems.

10.10 Discuss how fragmentation manifests itself in each of the following types of virtual memory systems.

  a. segmentation
  b. paging
  c. combined segmentation/paging

10.11 In any computer system, regardless of whether it is a real memory system or a virtual memory system, the computer will rarely reference all the instructions or data brought into main memory. Let us call this *chunk fragmentation,* because it is the result of handling memory items in blocks or chunks rather than individually. Chunk fragmentation might actually account for more waste of main memory than all other types of fragmentation combined.

  a. Why, then, has chunk fragmentation not been given the same coverage in the literature as other forms of fragmentation?

  b. How do virtual memory systems with dynamic memory allocation greatly reduce the amount of chunk fragmentation over that experienced in real memory systems?

  c. What effect would smaller page sizes have on chunk fragmentation?

  d. What considerations, both practical and theoretical, prevent the complete elimination of chunk fragmentation?

  e. What can each of the following do to minimize chunk fragmentation?

  i. the programmer

  ii. the hardware designer

  iii. the operating system designer

10.12 Explain the mapping of virtual addresses to physical addresses under combined segmentation/paging.

10.13 In multiprogramming environments, code and data sharing can greatly reduce the main memory needed by a group of processes to run efficiently. For each of the following types of systems, outline briefly how sharing can be implemented.

  a. fixed-partition multiprogramming

  b. variable-partition multiprogramming

  c. paging

  d. segmentation

  e. combined segmentation/paging

10.14 Why is sharing of code and data so much more natural in virtual memory systems than in real memory systems?

10.15 Discuss the similarities and differences between paging and segmentation.

10.16 Compare and contrast pure segmentation with segmentation/paging combined.

10.17 Suppose you are asked to implement segmentation on a machine that has paging hardware but no segmentation hardware. You may use only software techniques. Is this possible? Explain your answer.

10.18 Suppose you are asked to implement paging on a machine that has segmentation hardware but no paging hardware. You may use only software techniques. Is this possible? Explain your answer.

10.19 As the chief designer of a new virtual memory system you have been given the choice of implementing either paging or segmentation, but not both. Which would you choose? Why?

10.20 Suppose that economical associative memory were to become available. How might such associative memory be incorporated into future computer architectures to improve the performance of the hardware, the operating system, and user programs?

10.21 Give as many ways as you can in which executing a program on a virtual memory system differs from executing the same program on a real memory system. Do these observations lead you to favor real memory approaches or virtual memory approaches?

10.22 Give as many reasons as you can why locality is a reasonable phenomenon. Give as many examples as you can of situations in which locality simply does not apply.

10.23 One popular operating system provides separate virtual address spaces to each of its processes, while another has all processes share a single large address space. Compare and contrast these two different approaches.

10.24 Virtual address translation mechanisms are not without their costs. List as many factors as you can that contribute to the overhead of operating a virtual-address-to-physical-address translation mechanism. How do these factors tend to "shape" the hardware and software of systems that support such address translation mechanisms?

10.25 The Multics system, as originally designed, provided for two page sizes. It was believed that the large number of small data structures could occupy small pages, and that most other procedures and data structures would best occupy one or more large pages. How does a memory organization scheme that supports multiple page sizes differ from one that supports a single page size? Suppose a system were designed to support *n* page sizes. How would it differ from the Multics approach? Is a system that supports a large number of page sizes essentially equivalent to a segmentation system? Explain.

10.26 With multilevel page tables, a process's PTE can be initialized when the process is first loaded, or each PTE can be initialized the first time its corresponding page is referenced. Similarly, the entire multilevel page table structure can be maintained in main memory, or parts of it can be sent to sec-ondary storage. What are the costs and benefits of each approach?

10.27 Why did virtual memory emerge as an important scheme? Why did real memory schemes prove inadequate? What current trends could conceivably negate the usefulness of virtual memory?

10.28 What aspect of paging with a single page size makes page-replacement algorithms so much simpler than segment-replacement algorithms? What hardware or software features might be used in support of segment replacement that could make it almost as straightforward as page replacement in a system with a single page size?

10.29 What aspect of content-addressed associative memory will probably ensure that such memory will remain far more costly than location-addressed cache memory?

10.30 Suppose you are designing a portion of an operating system that requires high-speed information retrieval (such as a virtual address translation mechanism). Suppose that you have been given the option of implementing your search-and-retrieval mechanism with either pure direct mapping, using a high-speed cache, or pure associative mapping. What factors would influence your choice? What interesting kind(s) of question(s) could conceivably be answered by an associative search (in one access) that cannot be answered in a single direct-mapped search?

10.31 Deciding what entries to keep in the TLB is crucial to the efficient operation of a virtual memory system. The percentage of references that get "resolved" via the TLB is called the TLB hit ratio. Compare and contrast the performance of virtual address translation systems that achieve a high (near 100 percent) hit ratio versus those that achieve a low (near 0 percent) hit ratio. List several heuristics not mentioned in the text that you believe would achieve high hit ratios. Indicate examples of how each might fail, i.e., under what circumstances would these heuristics place the "wrong" entries into the TLB?

Suggested Projects

10.32 Describe how the IA-32 architecture enables processes to access up to 64GB of main memory. See developer.intel.com/design/Pentium4/manuals/.

10.33 Compare and contrast the IBM/Motorola PowerPC architecture virtual memory implementation with that of the IA-32 Intel architecture. Discuss how 64-bit processing affects memory organization in the PowerPC. See developer.intel.com/design/Pentium4/manuals/ and www-3.ibm.com/chips/techlib/techlib.nsf/productfamilies/PowerPC_Microprocessors_and_Embedded_Processors.

10.34 Compare and contrast the 64-bit Hewlett-Packard PA-RISC architecture virtual memory implementation with that of the 32-bit Intel IA-32 architecture. See developer.intel.com/design/Pentium4/manuals/ and cpus.hp.com/technical_references/parisc.shtml.

10.35 Survey the differences between the virtual memory implementation in the 32-bit Intel IA-32 architecture and in the 64-bit IA-64 Intel architecture. See developer.intel.com/design/Pentium4/manuals/ and developer.intel.com/design/itanium/manuals/iiasdmanual.htm (select Volume 2: System Architecture).

Recommended Reading

The concept of virtual memory has been around for decades; an early comprehensive survey was produced by Denning.[101] The benefits of virtual memory systems spurred the development of specialized hardware to increase their performance and feasibility.[102] Associative memories for dynamic address translation were presented by Hanlon,[103] and their role in storing TLB entries has been studied thoroughly.[104]

Denning discusses paging in his work on virtual memory; an in-depth treatment of segmentation is provided by Dennis.[105] Further discussions on virtual memory organization, such as combined segmentation and paging, can be found in papers by Daley and Dennis[106] and Denning.[107] Jacob and Mudge[108] provide an excellent survey of virtual memory organization techniques and their implementations in modern systems. Two popular textbooks on computer architecture that describe the implementations of MMUs are Patterson and Hennessy's *Computer Organization and Design*[109] and Blaauw and Brooks's *Computer Architecture*.[110] The bibliography for this chapter is located on our Web site at www.deitel.com/books/os3e/Bibliography.pdf.

Works Cited

1. Shiell, J., "Virtual Memory, Virtual Machines," *Byte*, Vol. 11, No. 11, 1986, pp. 110–121.

2. Leonard, T. E., ed., *VAX Architecture Reference Manual*, Bedford, MA: Digital Press, 1987.

3. Kenah, L. J.; R. E. Goldenberg; and S. F. Bate, *VAX/VMS Internals and Data Structures*, Bedford, MA: Digital Press, 1988.

4. Fotheringham, J., "Dynamic Storage Allocation in the Atlas Computer, Including an Automatic Use of a Backing Store," *Communications of the ACM*, Vol. 4, 1961, pp. 435–436.

5. Kilburn, T.; D. J. Howarth; R. B. Payne; and F. H. Sumner, "The Manchester University Atlas Operating System, Part I: Internal Organization," *Computer Journal*, Vol. 4, No. 3, October 1961, pp. 222–225.

6. Kilburn, T.; R. B. Payne; and D. J. Howarth, "The Atlas Supervisor," *Proceedings of the Eastern Joint Computer Conference, AFIPS*, Vol. 20, 1961.

7. Lavington, S. H., "The Manchester Mark I and Atlas: A Historical Perspective," *Communications of the ACM*, Vol. 21, No. 1, January 1978, pp. 4–12.

8. Manchester University Department of Computer Science, "The Atlas," 1996, <www.computer50.org/kgill/atlas/atlas.html>.

9. Manchester University Department of Computer Science, "History of the Department of Computer Science," December 14, 2001, <www.cs.man.ac.uk/Visitor_subweb/history.php3>.

10. Manchester University Department of Computer Science, "History of the Department of Computer Science," December 14, 2001, <www.cs.man.ac.uk/Visitor_subweb/history.php3>.

11. Lavington, S., "The Manchester Mark I and Atlas: A Historical Perspective," *Communications of the ACM*, January 1978, pp. 4–12.

12. Lavington, S., "The Manchester Mark I and Atlas: A Historical Perspective," *Communications of the ACM*, January 1978, pp. 4–12.

13. Manchester University Department of Computer Science, "The Atlas," 1996, <www.computer50.org/kgill/atlas/atlas.html>.

14. Lavington, S., "The Manchester Mark I and Atlas: A Historical Perspective," *Communications of the ACM*, January 1978, pp. 4–12.

15. Lavington, S., "The Manchester Mark I and Atlas: A Historical Perspective," *Communications of the ACM*, January 1978, pp. 4–12.

16. Manchester University Department of Computer Science "The Atlas," 1996, <www.computer50.org/kgill/atlas/atlas.html>.

17. Lavington, S., "The Manchester Mark I and Atlas: A Historical Perspective," *Communications of the ACM*, January 1978, pp. 4–12.

18. Denning, P., "Virtual Memory," *ACM Computing Surveys*, Vol. 2, No. 3, September 1970, pp. 153–189.

19. George Mason University, "Peter J. Denning—Biosketch," January 1, 2003, <cne.gmu.edu/pjd/pjdbio.html>.

20. Denning, P., "The Working Set Model for Program Behavior," *Communications of the ACM*, Vol. 11, No. 5, May 1968, pp. 323–333.

21. George Mason University, "Peter J. Denning—Biosketch," January 1, 2003, <cne.gmu.edu/pjd/pjdbio.html>.

22. George Mason University, "Peter J. Denning—Biosketch," January 1, 2003, <cne.gmu.edu/pjd/pjdbio.html>.

23. ACM, "Peter J. Denning—ACM Karlstrom Citation 1996," 1996, <cne.gmu.edu/pjd/pjdkka96.html>.

24. Randell, B., and C. J. Kuehner, "Dynamic Storage Allocation Systems," *Proceedings of the ACM Symposium on Operating System Principles*, January 1967, pp. 9.1–9.16.

25. McKeag, R. M., "Burroughs B5500 Master Control Program," in *Studies in Operating Systems*, Academic Press, 1976, pp. 1–66.

26. Oliphint, C., "Operating System for the B5000," *Datamation*, Vol. 10, No. 5, 1964, pp. 42–54.

27. Talluri, M.; S. Kong; M. D. Hill; and D. A. Patterson, "Tradeoffs in Supporting Two Page Sizes," In *Proceedings of the 19th International Symposium on Computer Architecture*, Gold Coast, Australia, May 1992, pp. 415-424.

28. Hanlon, A. G., "Content-Addressable and Associative Memory Systems—A Survey," *IEEE Transactions on Electronic Computers,* August 1966.

29. Lindquist, A. B.; R. R. Seeder; and L. W. Comeau, "A Time-Sharing System Using an Associative Memory," *Proceedings of the IEEE,* Vol. 54, 1966, pp. 1774–1779.

30. Cook, R., et al., "Cache Memories: A Tutorial and Survey of Current Research Directions," *ACM/CSC-ER,* 1982, pp. 99–110.

31. Wang, Z.; D. Burger; K. S. McKinley; S. K. Reinhardt; and C. C. Weems, "Guided Region Prefetching: A Cooperative Hardware/Software Approach," *Proceedings of the 30th Annual International Symposium on Computer Architecture,* 2003, p. 388.

32. Jacob, B. L., and T. N. Mudge, "A Look at Several Memory Management Units, TLB-Refill Mechanisms, and Page Table Organizations," *Proceedings of the Eighth International Conference on Architectural Support for Programming Languages and Operating Systems,* 1998, pp. 295–306.

33. Kandiraju, G. B., and A. Sivasubramaniam, "Characterizing the d-TLB Behavior of SPEC CPU2000 Benchmarks," ACM SIGMETRICS Performance Evaluation Review, *Proceedings of the 2002 ACM SIGMETRICS International Conference on Measurement and Modeling of Computer Systems,* Vol. 30, No. 1, June 2002.

34. Sohoni, S.; R. Min; Z. Xu; and Y. Hu, "A Study of Memory System Performance of Multimedia Applications," ACM SIGMETRICS Performance Evaluation Review, *Proceedings of the 2001 ACM SIGMETRICS International Conference on Measurement and Modeling of Computer Systems,* Vol. 29, No. 1, June 2001.

35. Kandiraju, Gokul B., and Anand Sivasubramaniam, "Going the Distance for TLB Prefetching: An Application-Driven Study," ACM SIGARCH Computer Architecture News, *Proceedings of the 29th Annual International Symposium on Computer Architecture,* Vol. 30, No. 2, May 2002.

36. Jacob, B., and T. Mudge, "Virtual Memory: Issues of Implementation," *IEEE Computer,* Vol. 31, No. 6, June 1998, p. 36.

37. Jacob, B., and T. Mudge, "Virtual Memory: Issues of Implementation," *IEEE Computer,* Vol. 31, No. 6, June 1998, pp. 37–38.

38. Shyu, I., "Virtual Address Translation for Wide-Address Architectures," *ACM SIGOPS Operating Systems Review,* Vol. 29, No. 4, October 1995, pp. 41–42.

39. Holliday, M. A., "Page Table Management in Local/Remote Architectures," *Proceedings of the Second International Conference on Supercomputing,* New York: ACM Press, June 1988, p. 2.

40. Jacob, B., and T. Mudge, "Virtual Memory: Issues of Implementation," *IEEE Computer,* Vol. 31, No. 6, June 1998, pp. 37-38.

41. Dennis, J. B., "Segmentation and the Design of Multiprogrammed Computer Systems," *Journal of the ACM,* Vol. 12, No. 4, October 1965, pp. 589–602.

42. Denning, P., "Virtual Memory," *ACM Computing Surveys,* Vol. 2, No. 3, September 1970, pp. 153–189.

43. *Intel Itanium Software Developer's Manual,* Vol. 2, *System Architecture,* Rev. 2.1, October 2002, pp. 2-431–2-432.

44. Daley, R. C., and J. B. Dennis, "Virtual Memory, Processes and Sharing in Multics," *CACM,* Vol. 11, No. 5, May 1968, pp. 306–312.

45. Denning, P. J., "Third Generation Computing Systems," *ACM Computing Surveys,* Vol. 3, No. 4, December 1971, pp. 175–216.

46. Bensoussan, A.; C. T. Clingen; and R. C. Daley, "The Multics Virtual Memory: Concepts and Design," *Communications of the ACM,* Vol. 15, No. 5, May 1972, pp. 308–318.

47. Organick, E. I., *The Multics System: An Examination of Its Structure,* Cambridge, MA: M.I.T. Press, 1972.

48. Doran, R. W., "Virtual Memory," *Computer,* Vol. 9, No. 10, October 1976, pp. 27–37.

49. Belady, L. A.; R. P. Parmelee; and C. A. Scalzi, "The IBM History of Memory Management Technology," *IBM Journal of Research and Development,* Vol. 25, No. 5, September 1981, pp. 491–503.

50. *IA-32 Intel Architecture Software Developer's Manual,* Vol. 3, *System Programmer's Guide,* 2002, pp. 3-1–3-38.

51. da Cruz, F., "The IBM 7090," July 2003, <www.columbia.edu/acis/history/7090.html>.

52. Harper, J., "7090/94 IBSYS Operating System," August 23, 2001, <www.frobenius.com/ibsys.htm>.

53. Harper, J., "7090/94 IBSYS Operating System," August 23, 2001, <www.frobenius.com/ibsys.htm>.

54. Poulsen, L., "Computer History: IBM 360/370/3090/390," October 26, 2001, <www.beagle-ears.com/lars/engineer/comphist/ibm360.htm>.

55. Suko, R., "MVS ... a Long History," December 15, 2002, <os390-mvs.hypermart.net/mvshist.htm>.

56. Poulsen, L., "Computer History: IBM 360/370/3090/390," October 26, 2001, <www.beagle-ears.com/lars/engineer/comphist/ibm360.htm>.

57. Suko, R., "MVS ... a Long History," December 15, 2002, <os390-mvs.hypermart.net/mvshist.htm>.

58. Mealy, G., "The Functional Structure of OS/360, Part 1: Introductory Survey," *IBM Systems Journal,* Vol. 5, No. 1, 1966, <www.research.ibm.com/journal/sj/051/ibmsj0501B.pdf>.

59. Mealy, G., "The Functional Structure of OS/360, Part 1: Introductory Survey," *IBM Systems Journal,* Vol. 5, No. 1, 1966, <www.research.ibm.com/journal/sj/051/ibmsj0501B.pdf>.

60. Poulsen, L., "Computer History: IBM 360/370/3090/390," October 26, 2001, <www.beagle-ears.com/lars/engineer/comphist/ibm360.htm>.

61. Suko, R., "MVS ... a Long History," December 15, 2002, <os390-mvs.hypermart.net/mvshist.htm>.

62. Poulsen, L., "Computer History: IBM 360/370/3090/390," October 26, 2001, <www.beagle-ears.com/lars/engineer/comphist/ibm360.htm>.

63. Suko, R., "MVS ... a Long History," December 15, 2002 <os390-mvs.hypermart.net/mvshist.htm>.

64. Poulsen, L., "Computer History: IBM 360/370/3090/390," October 26, 2001, <www.beagle-ears.com/lars/engineer/comphist/ibm360.htm>.

65. Suko, R., "MVS ... a Long History," December 15, 2002, <os390-mvs.hypermart.net/mvshist.htm>.

66. Poulsen, L., "Computer History: IBM 360/370/3090/390," October 26, 2001, <www.beagle-ears.com/lars/engineer/comphist/ibm360.htm>.

67. Poulsen, L., "Computer History: IBM 360/370/3090/390," October 26, 2001, <www.beagle-ears.com/lars/engineer/comphist/ibm360.htm>.

68. Suko, R., "MVS ... a Long History," December 15, 2002, <os390-mvs.hypermart.net/mvshist.htm>.

69. Clark, C., "The Facilities and Evolution of MVS/ESA," *IBM Systems Journal*, Vol. 28, No. 1, 1989, <www.research.ibm.com/journal/sj/281/ibmsj2801I.pdf>.

70. Poulsen, L., "Computer History: IBM 360/370/3090/390," October 26, 2001, <www.beagle-ears.com/lars/engineer/comphist/ibm360.htm>.

71. Suko, R., "MVS ... a Long History," December 15, 2002, <os390-mvs.hypermart.net/mvshist.htm>.

72. Poulsen, L., "Computer History: IBM 360/370/3090/390," October 26, 2001, <www.beagle-ears.com/lars/engineer/comphist/ibm360.htm>.

73. Suko, R., "MVS ... a Long History," December 15, 2002, <os390-mvs.hypermart.net/mvshist.htm>.

74. Suko, R., "MVS ... a Long History," December 15, 2002, <os390-mvs.hypermart.net/mvshist.htm>.

75. Clark, C., "The Facilities and Evolution of MVS/ESA," *IBM Systems Journal*, Vol. 28, No. 1, 1989, <www.research.ibm.com/journal/sj/281/ibmsj2801I.pdf>.

76. Suko, R., "MVS ... a Long History," December 15, 2002, <os390-mvs.hypermart.net/mvshist.htm>.

77. D. Elder-Vass, "MVS Systems Programming: Chapter 3a—MVS Internals," July 5, 1998, <www.mvsbook.fsnet.co.uk/chap03a.htm>.

78. Suko, R., "MVS ... a Long History," December 15, 2002, <os390-mvs.hypermart.net/mvshist.htm>.

79. Clark, C., "The Facilities and Evolution of MVS/ESA," *IBM Systems Journal*, Vol. 28, No. 1, 1989, <www.research.ibm.com/journal/sj/281/ibmsj2801I.pdf>.

80. Suko, R., "MVS ... a Long History," December 15, 2002, <os390-mvs.hypermart.net/mvshist.htm>.

81. Clark, C., "The Facilities and Evolution of MVS/ESA," *IBM Systems Journal*, Vol. 28, No. 1, 1989, <www.research.ibm.com/journal/sj/281/ibmsj2801I.pdf>.

82. Elder-Vass, D., "MVS Systems Programming: Chapter 3a—MVS Internals," 5 July 1998, <www.mvsbook.fsnet.co.uk/chap03a.htm>.

83. Suko, R., "MVS ... a Long History," December 15, 2002, <os390-mvs.hypermart.net/mvshist.htm>.

84. Clark, C., "The Facilities and Evolution of MVS/ESA," *IBM Systems Journal*, Vol. 28, No. 1, 1989, <www.research.ibm.com/journal/sj/281/ibmsj2801I.pdf>.

85. Suko, R., "MVS ... a Long History," December 15, 2002, <os390-mvs.hypermart.net/mvshist.htm>.

86. Clark, C., "The Facilities and Evolution of MVS/ESA," *IBM Systems Journal*, Vol. 28, No. 1, 1989, <www.research.ibm.com/journal/sj/281/ibmsj2801I.pdf>.

87. Mainframes.com, "Mainframes.com—SYSPLEX," <www.mainframes.com/sysplex.html>.

88. Suko, R., "MVS ... a Long History," December 15, 2002, <os390-mvs.hypermart.net/mvshist.htm>.

89. IBM, "S/390 Parallel Enterprise Server and OS/390 Reference Guide," May 2000, <www-1.ibm.com/servers/eserver/zseries/library/refguides/pdf/g3263070.pdf>.

90. IBM, "IBM eServer zSeries Mainframe Servers," <www-1.ibm.com/servers/eserver/zseries/>.

91. Spruth, W., "The Evolution of S/390," July 30, 2001, <www-ti.informatik.uni-tuebingen.de/os390/arch/history.pdf>.

92. Case, R. P. and A. Padegs, "Architecture of the IBM System/370," *Communications of the ACM*, January 1978, pp. 73–96.

93. Gifford, D. and A. Spector, "Case Study: IBM's System/360–370 Architecture," *Communications of the ACM*, April 1987, pp. 291–307.

94. IBM, "z/VM General Information, V4.4," 2003, <www.vm.ibm.com/pubs/pdf/HCSF8A60.PDF>.

95. Kutnick, D., "Whither VM?" *Datamation*, December 1, 1985, pp. 73–78.

96. Doran, R. W., "Amdahl Multiple-Domain Architecture," *Computer*, October 1988, pp. 20–28.

97. Adair, A.J.; R. U. Bayles; L. W. Comeau; and R. J. Creasy, "A Virtual Machine System for the 360/40," Cambridge, MA: *IBM Scientific Center Report 320–2007*, May 1966.

98. Lett, A.S. and W. L. Konigsford, "TSS/360: A Time-Shared Operating System," *Proceedings of the Fall Joint Computer Conference*, AFIPS, 1968, Montvale, NJ: AFIPS Press, pp. 15–28.

99. Creasy, R. J., "The Origin of the VM/370 Time-Sharing System," *IBM Journal of R&D*, September 1981, pp. 483–490.

100. IBM, "IBM z/VM and VM/ESA Home Page," <www.vm.ibm.com/>.

101. Denning, P., "Virtual Memory," *ACM Computing Surveys*, Vol. 2, No. 3, September 1970, pp. 153–189.

102. Randell, B., and C. J. Kuehner, "Dynamic Storage Allocation Systems," *Proceedings of the ACM Symposium on Operating System Principles*, January 1967, pp. 9.1–9.16.

103. Hanlon, A. G., "Content-Addressable and Associative Memory Systems—A Survey," *IEEE Transactions on Electronic Computers*, August 1966.

104. Smith, A. J., "Cache Memories," *ACM Computing Surveys*, Vol. 14, No. 3, September 1982, pp. 473–530.

105. Dennis, J. B., "Segmentation and the Design of Multiprogrammed Computer Systems," *Journal of the ACM*, Vol. 12, No. 4, October 1965, pp. 589–602.

106. Daley, R. C., and J. B. Dennis, "Virtual Memory, Processes and Sharing in Multics," *CACM*, Vol. 11, No. 5, May 1968, pp. 306–312.

107. Denning, P. J., "Third Generation Computing Systems," *ACM Computing Surveys*, Vol. 3, No. 4, December 1971, pp. 175–216.

108. Jacob, B., and T. Mudge, "Virtual Memory: Issues of Implementation," *IEEE Computer*, Vol. 31, No. 6, June 1998.

109. Patterson, D., and J. Hennessy, *Computer Organization and Design*, San Francisco: Morgan Kaufmann Publishers, Inc., 1998.

110. Blaauw, G. A., and F. P. Brooks, Jr., *Computer Architecture*, Reading, MA: ACM Press, 1997.

What we anticipate seldom occurs; what we least expect generally happens.

  —Benjamin Disraeli—

Time will run back and fetch the Age of Gold.

  —John Milton—

Faultless to a fault.

  —Robert Browning—

Condemn the fault and not the actor of it?

  —William Shakespeare—

Gather up the fragments that remain, that nothing be lost.

  —John 6:12—

Chapter 11

Virtual Memory Management

Objectives

After reading this chapter, you should understand:

- *the benefits and drawbacks of demand and anticipatory paging.*

- *the challenges of page replacement.*

- *several popular page-replacement strategies and how they compare to optimal page replacement.*

- *the impact of page size on virtual memory performance.*

- *program behavior under paging.*

Chapter Outline

11.1 Introduction

Chapter 9 discussed fetch, placement and replacement memory management strategies for real memory systems. Chapter 10 discussed virtual memory organization, focusing on pure paging systems, pure segmentation systems and hybridized segmentation/paging systems. In this chapter we discuss memory management in virtual memory systems.

Virtual memory fetch strategies determine when a page or segment should be moved from secondary storage to main memory. Demand fetch strategies wait for a process to reference a page or segment before loading it into main memory. Anticipatory fetch strategies use heuristics to predict which pages or segments a process will soon reference—if the likelihood of reference is high and if space is available, then the system brings the page or segment into main memory before the process explicitly references it, thus improving performance when the reference occurs.

Paging systems—either pure paging or segmentation/paging systems—that use only one page size trivialize the placement decision because an incoming page may be placed in any available page frame. Segmentation systems require placement strategies similar to those used in variable-partition multiprogramming (see Section 9.9, Variable-Partition Multiprogramming).

Replacement strategies determine which page or segment to replace to provide space for an incoming page or segment. In this chapter, we concentrate on **page-replacement strategies** that, when properly implemented, help optimize performance in paging systems. The chapter includes a discussion of Denning's Working Set Model of program behavior, which provides a framework for observing, analyzing and improving program execution in paging systems.[1]

Self Review

1. Explain the difference between demand fetch strategies and anticipatory fetch strategies in virtual memory systems. Which one requires more overhead?
2. Why are placement strategies trivial in paging systems that use only one page size?

Ans: **1)** Demand fetch strategies load pages or segments into main memory only when a process explicitly references them. Anticipatory fetch strategies attempt to predict which pages or segments a process will need and load them ahead of time. Anticipatory fetch strategies require more overhead because the system must spend time determining the likelihood that a page or segment will be referenced; as we will see, this overhead can often be small. **2)** Because any incoming page can be placed into any available page frame.

11.2 Locality

Central to most memory management strategies is the concept of locality—that a process tends to reference memory in highly localized patterns.[2, 3] Locality manifests itself in both time and space. Temporal locality is locality over time. For example, if the weather is sunny in a certain town at 3 p.m., then there is a good chance (but certainly no guarantee) that the weather in that town was sunny at 2:30 p.m.

and will be sunny at 3:30 p.m. **Spatial locality** means that nearby items tend to be similar. Again, considering the weather, if it is sunny in one town, then it is likely, but not guaranteed, to be sunny in nearby towns.

Locality is also observed in operating systems environments, particularly in the area of memory management. It is an empirical (i.e., observed) property rather than a theoretical one. It is never guaranteed but is often highly likely. In paging systems, for example, we observe that processes tend to favor certain subsets of their pages, and that these pages tend to be near one another in a process's virtual address space. This behavior does not preclude the possibility that a process may make a reference to a new page in a different area of its virtual memory.

Actually, locality is quite reasonable in computer systems, when one considers the way programs are written and data is organized. Loops, functions, procedures and variables used for counting and totalling all involve temporal locality. In these cases, recently referenced memory locations are likely to be referenced again in the near future. Array traversals, sequential code execution and the tendency of programmers (or compilers) to place related variable definitions near one another all involve spatial locality—they all tend to generate clustered memory references.

Self Review

1. Does locality favor anticipatory paging or demand paging? Explain.
2. Explain how looping through an array exhibits both spatial and temporal locality.

Ans: **1)** Locality favors anticipatory paging because it indicates that the operating system should be able to predict with reasonable probability the pages that a process will use. **2)** Looping through an array exhibits spatial locality because the elements of an array are contiguous in virtual memory. It exhibits temporal locality because the elements are generally much smaller than a page. Therefore, references to two consecutive elements usually result in the same page being referenced twice within a short period of time.

11.3 Demand Paging

The simplest fetch policy implemented in virtual memory systems is **demand paging**.[4] Under this policy, when a process first executes, the system loads into main memory the page that contains its first instruction. Thereafter, the system loads a page from secondary storage to main memory only when the process explicitly references the page. There are several reasons for the appeal of this strategy. Computability results, specifically the Halting Problem, tell us that, in the general case, it is impossible to predict the path of execution a program will take (see the Operating Systems Thinking feature, Computer Theory in Operating Systems).[5,6] Therefore, any attempt to preload pages in anticipation of their use might result in the wrong pages being loaded. The overhead incurred by preloading the wrong pages can impede the performance of the entire system.

Demand paging guarantees that the system brings into main memory only those pages that processes actually need. This potentially allows more processes to occupy main memory—the space is not "wasted" by pages that may not be referenced for some time (or ever).

Demand paging is not without its problems. A process in a demand-paged system must accumulate pages one at a time. As it references each new page, the process must wait while the system transfers that page to main memory. If the process already has many pages in main memory, then this wait time can be particularly costly, because a large portion of main memory is occupied by a process that cannot execute. This factor often affects the value of a process's **space-time product**—a measure of its execution time (i.e., how long it occupies memory) multiplied by the amount of space in main memory the process occupies (see the Operating Systems Thinking feature, Space–Time Trade-offs).[7] The space-time product illustrates not only how much time a process spends waiting, but how much main memory cannot be used while it waits. Figure 11.1 illustrates the concept. The y-axis represents the number of page frames allocated to a process and the x-axis represents "wall clock" time. The space-time product corresponds to the area under the "curve" in the figure; the dotted lines indicate that a process has referenced pages that are not in main memory and must be loaded from the backing store. The shaded region repre-

Operating Systems Thinking

Computer Theory in Operating Systems

Computer science is rich in elegant theoretical fields. Computability theory helps us determine what kinds of things computer software, such as operating systems, can and cannot do. The Halting Problem of computability theory tells us that in the general case, we cannot write a program to determine the execution path of another program. This has many ramifications in operating systems. If we could predict the execution path of a program, then we could for example, implement perfect anticipatory resource allocation, so that the resources are ready (if at all possible) when the process needs them, avoiding lengthy delays. Once we know what computers can and cannot do, complexity theory helps us determine whether those tasks can be performed efficiently and to characterize just how efficiently (or inefficiently) they can be performed. Automata theory helps us understand the power of different classes of computing devices; as we discussed in Chapter 6, this helps us realize that modern computer systems are far too complex to allow exhaustive testing of all possible states of computer hardware and software. This last observation is truly a point to ponder, especially if you must build highly reliable systems.

sents the process's space-time product while it is performing productive work. The unshaded region represents its space-time product while it waits for pages to be loaded from secondary storage. [*Note*: The wait period, *F*, is much larger than indicated by the figure.] Thus, the unshaded region indicates the amount of time during which the process's memory allocation cannot be used. Reducing the space-time product of a process's page waits, in order to improve memory utilization, is an important goal of memory management strategies. As the average page-wait time increases, the benefit of demand paging decreases.[8]

Self Review

1. Why is the space-time product of demand paging higher than that of anticipatory paging?
2. How could demand paging (as compared to anticipatory paging) increase the degree of multiprogramming in a system? How could demand paging decrease the degree of multiprogramming in a system?

Ans: **1)** The reason is that the process has pages in memory that it is not using while it waits for its pages to be painstakingly demand-paged in, one at a time. Anticipatory paging also has a space-time product with associated waste. Pages brought into memory before they are referenced occupy page frames that go unused, thus preventing other processes from using them. As

Operating Systems Thinking

Space-Time Trade-offs

Examples of the space–time trade-off are common in computing and other areas. When moving to a new apartment, if you have a larger truck, you can complete the move in less time, but you will have to pay more to rent the larger truck. When you study searching and sorting algorithms in data structures and algorithms classes, you see how performance can improve when more memory is available (e.g., hash tables). These trade-offs are common in operating systems as well. If the operating system allocates more main memory to an executing program, for example, the program may run significantly faster. With less, more-expensive memory, the operating system must manage the memory more extensively, incurring more processing overhead. With more abundant, cheaper memory, the operating system can manage the memory less intensively, perhaps making cruder decisions while consuming less processor power. We will see in the discussion of RAID systems in Chapter 12, that maintaining redundant copies of data can result in improved system throughput. We will see, however, that increasing the amount of memory available to a process does not always increase the speed at which it runs—we will study Belady's Anomaly which shows that in some circumstances, giving a process more memory could actually degrade performance. Fortunately, this occurs only in rare circumstances.

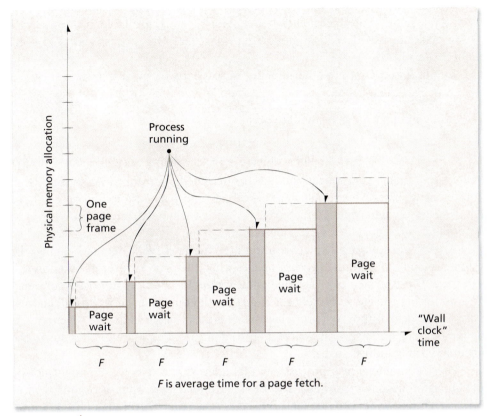

Figure 11.1 | *Space-time product under demand paging.*

we will see, anticipatory paging brings these pages into main memory in groups, which generally reduces the page-wait time compared to loading pages individually using demand paging. **2)** Demand paging could increase the degree of multiprogramming because the system brings into main memory only those pages that processes actually needed. Therefore, more processes can fit into physical memory. However, processes require more execution time because they need to retrieve pages from secondary storage more often (compared with being brought in as a group with anticipatory paging). While the operating system is retrieving pages from secondary storage, the memory that the process takes up is wasted, and thus the degree of multiprogramming might decrease (over what is possible with anticipatory paging).

11.4 Anticipatory Paging

A central theme in resource management is that a resource's relative value influences just how intensively the resource should be managed.[9] As hardware costs continue their dramatic decline, the relative value of machine time to people time is reduced. Operating systems designers are constantly focused on reducing the amount of time people must wait for results from computers.[10]

As we demonstrated in the preceding section, one way to reduce wait times is to avoid the delays in a demand-paged system. In **anticipatory paging** (also called

prefetching and **prepaging**), the operating system tries to predict the pages a process will need and to preload them when memory space is available. If the system is able to make correct decisions about future page use, the process's total runtime can be reduced.[11, 12]

Important criteria that determine the success of a prepaging strategy include:

- prepaged allocation—the amount of main memory allocated to prepaging
- the number of pages that are preloaded at once
- the policy—the heuristic that determines which pages are preloaded (e.g., those predicted by spatial locality or those predicted by temporal locality).[13]

Anticipatory paging strategies should be designed with care. A strategy that requires significant resources (such as processor time, page frames and disk I/O), or that inaccurately determines which pages a process will need, might result in worse performance than in a demand paging system.

Anticipatory paging strategies often are combined with demand paging; the system preloads a few of the process's pages when the process references a nonresident page. These strategies typically exploit spatial locality; i.e., a process referencing a nonresident page will likely reference contiguous pages in its virtual address space in the near future. When a process generates a page fault, the system loads the faulting page and several nearby nonresident pages that are contiguous in the process's virtual address space.

Pages contiguous in a process's virtual address space, however, might not be contiguous on secondary storage. Unlike main memory, secondary storage devices (e.g., hard disks) do not provide uniform access times to data stored at different locations, so the time required to load multiple pages from secondary storage may be significantly greater than that required to load a single page. In this case, processes could suffer greater page-wait times due to anticipatory paging than in demand paging.

One solution is to group pages on secondary storage that are contiguous in a process's virtual address space.[14] As we discuss in Chapter 12, Disk Performance Optimization, the difference between the page-wait times for loading several pages that are contiguous on disk and for loading a single page is relatively small, so anticipatory paging can be performed without significantly increasing the page-wait time compared to demand paging. In Linux, for example, when a process references a nonresident page containing its program instructions or data, the kernel attempts to exploit spatial locality by loading from disk the nonresident page and a small number of pages that are contiguous in the process's address space. By default, the system loads from disk four contiguous pages (16KB on the IA-32 architecture) if main memory is smaller than 16MB, or eight contiguous pages (32KB on the IA-32 architecture) otherwise.[15] This technique can yield good performance for processes that exhibit spatial locality.

Self Review

1. In which scenarios is the Linux anticipatory paging strategy inappropriate?

2. Why is anticipatory paging likely to yield better performance than demand paging? How might it yield poorer performance?

Ans: **1)** If processes exhibit random page-reference behavior, Linux would likely load pages that a process will not reference, leading to memory waste. If main memory is small (on the order of kilobytes), this could significantly reduce the amount of memory available to other processes, tending to increase the number of page faults the system experiences. **2)** It could yield better performance because it is more efficient to bring in several contiguous pages in one I/O transfer than to do several I/O operations (as would be the case in demand paging). Performance could be worse, though, if the process does not actually use the pages that were prepaged in.

11.5 Page Replacement

In a virtual memory system with paging, all of the page frames might be occupied when a process references a nonresident page. In this case, the system must not only bring in a new memory page from auxiliary storage, but must first decide which page in main memory should be replaced (i.e., removed or overwritten) to make room for the incoming page. In this and the next several sections, we investigate page-replacement strategies.

Recall that a page fault occurs if a running process references a nonresident page. In this case, the memory management system must locate the referenced page in secondary storage, load it into main memory and update the appropriate page table entry. Page-replacement strategies typically attempt to reduce the number of page faults a process experiences as it runs from start to finish, hopefully reducing the process's execution time.

If the page chosen for replacement has not been modified since it was last paged in from disk, then the new page can simply overwrite it. If the page has been modified, it must first be written (or evicted) to secondary storage to preserve its contents. A **modified bit**, or **dirty bit**, in the page table entry is set to 1 if the page has been modified and 0 otherwise.

Writing (or **flushing**) a modified page to disk, which requires a disk I/O operation, increases page-wait times if it is performed when a page is replaced. Some operating systems, such as Linux and Windows XP, periodically flush dirty pages to secondary storage to increase the likelihood that the operating system can perform page replacement without first having to write a modified page to disk. Because this periodic flushing can occur asynchronously with process execution, the system incurs little overhead by doing so. If a process references a modified page before the flush is completed, then it is recaptured, thus saving an expensive page-in operation from secondary storage.

When we evaluate a page-replacement strategy, we often compare it to the so-called **optimal page replacement** strategy (also called **OPT** or **MIN**), which states that, to obtain optimum performance, replace the page that will not be referenced again until furthest in the future.[16, 17, 18, 19, 20] Thus, the strategy increases performance by minimizing the number of page faults. This strategy can be demonstrated to be optimal, but it is not realizable, because we cannot, in general, accurately predict the behavior of processes. Instead, the strategy serves as a benchmark to which we compare realizable strategies. A well-designed replacement strategy balances the goals of minimal future page faults with the overhead incurred by attempting to predict future page use.

Self Review

1. What other factor complicates replacement strategies on systems that use pure segmentation (as compared with systems that use pure paging)?
2. Is it possible to perform optimal page replacement for certain types of processes? If so, give an example.

Ans: **1)** Such systems must consider the size of the segment being replaced compared to the size of the incoming segment. **2)** Yes, a trivial example is a process with one data page that is intensively referenced and whose data and instructions are referenced purely sequentially.

11.6 Page-Replacement Strategies

In the subsections that follow, we discuss several strategies that determine which page to replace to accommodate an incoming page. Each strategy is characterized by the heuristic it uses to select a page for replacement and the overhead it incurs. Some replacement strategies are intuitively appealing but lead to poor performance due to poor choice of heuristic. Other strategies predict future page usage well, but their overhead can degrade performance. We also discuss how special-purpose hardware can reduce the overhead incurred by page-replacement strategies.

11.6.1 Random Page Replacement

Random (RAND) page replacement is an easy-to-implement, low-overhead page-replacement strategy. Under this strategy, each page in main memory has an equal likelihood of being selected for replacement. One problem with RAND is that it may accidentally select as the next page to replace the page that will be referenced next (which is, of course, the worst page to replace). A benefit of RAND is that it makes replacement decisions quickly and fairly. Since typically there are many page frames from which to choose, there is only a small probability of replacing a page likely to be referenced again almost immediately. Because of its hit-or-miss approach, RAND is rarely used.

Self Review

1. How is RAND fair? Why is this type of fairness inappropriate for replacement strategies?
2. Could RAND ever operate exactly as OPT?

Ans: **1)** RAND is fair in that all pages in memory are equally likely to be replaced. This is inappropriate for replacement strategies, which, to reduce page faults, must try not to replace pages that will be referenced soon. **2)** Yes, it could accidentally make all the right page-replacement decisions, but it would do this with such miniscule probability that it would be better to answer this question, "No."

11.6.2 First-In-First-Out (FIFO) Page Replacement

In the **first-in-first-out (FIFO) page-replacement** strategy, we replace the page that has been in the system the longest. Figure 11.2 provides a simple example of the FIFO strategy for a process which has been allocated three page frames. The left-most column contains the process's page-reference pattern. Each row in the figure shows the state of the FIFO queue after each new page arrives; pages enter the tail of the queue on the left and exit the head on the right.

Under FIFO page replacement, the system keeps track of the order in which pages enter main memory. When a page must be replaced, the strategy chooses the one that has been in main memory the longest. The intuitive appeal of this strategy seems reasonable—namely, that this page has had its chance and it is time to give another page a chance. Unfortunately, first-in-first-out can replace heavily used pages. For example, on large timesharing systems it is common for many users to share a copy of a text editor as they enter and correct programs. FIFO page replacement on such a system might choose to replace a heavily used editor page. This would be a poor choice, because the page would be recalled to main memory almost immediately, resulting in an increased page-fault rate. Although FIFO can be implemented with relatively low overhead using a queue, it is impractical for most systems. But, as we will see in Section 11.6.7, Modifications to FIFO: Second-Chance and Clock Page Replacement, FIFO forms the basis of various imple-mented page-replacement schemes.

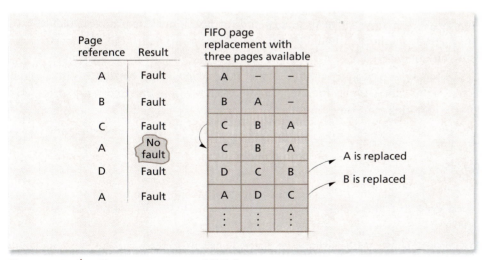

Figure 11.2 | First-in-first-out (FIFO) page replacement.

Self Review

1. Why does FIFO page replacement lead to poor performance for many processes?
2. How does FIFO page replacement compare to OPT for a process executing a loop that references n pages when main memory can hold no more than $n-1$ of that process's pages?

Ans: **1)** FIFO replaces pages according to their age, which, unlike locality, is not a good predictor of how pages will be used in the future. **2)** Assume that the pages are numbered from zero to $n-1$. In this case, when the process references page $n-1$, FIFO replaces the first page the process referenced in the loop. However, the next page the process references after completing one iteration of the loop is the page that was just replaced. To make room for that page, FIFO replaces the second page the process referenced in the previous iteration of the loop. This is, of course, the next page the process will reference in the current iteration. The optimal strategy would be to replace the page that will be referenced the furthest in the future, which is the page that was just referenced. In this case, OPT would result in one page fault per iteration of the loop, whereas FIFO would result in n page faults per iteration of the loop.

11.6.3 FIFO Anomaly

It would seem reasonable that the more page frames allocated to a process, the fewer page faults the process would experience. Belady, Nelson and Shedler discovered that, under FIFO page replacement, certain page reference patterns actually cause more page faults when the number of page frames allocated to a process is increased.[21] This phenomenon is called the **FIFO Anomaly** or **Belady's Anomaly**.

Figure 11.3 illustrates an example of the anomaly. The first table demonstrates how the reference pattern causes the system to load and replace pages (using FIFO) when the system allocates three page frames to the process. The second table shows how the system behaves in response to the same reference pattern, but when four page frames have been allocated. To the left of each table, we indicate whether the new page reference causes a page fault or not. When the process executes with four pages in memory, it actually experiences one more page fault than when it executes with only three pages.

The FIFO Anomaly is more of a curiosity than an important result. Perhaps its real significance to the student is to serve as a warning that operating systems are complex entities that sometimes defy intuition.

Self Review

1. (T/F) When using the FIFO page-replacement strategy, the number of page faults a process generates always increases as the number of page frames allocated to that process increases.

Ans: False. The normal behavior is that page faults will decrease because more of the process's pages can be available in memory, decreasing the chance that a referenced page will not be available. Belady's observation is an anomaly; the behavior he observed occurs infrequently.

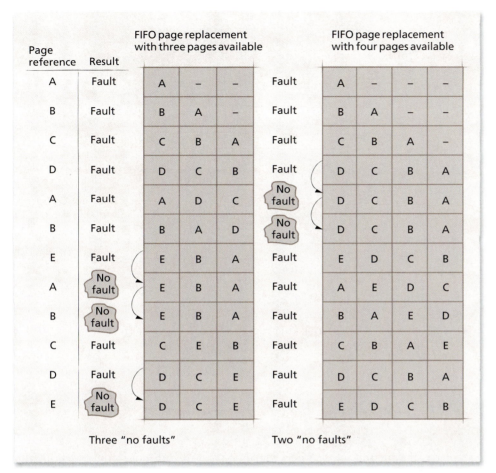

Page reference	Result	FIFO page replacement with three pages available			Result	FIFO page replacement with four pages available			
A	Fault	A	–	–	Fault	A	–	–	–
B	Fault	B	A	–	Fault	B	A	–	–
C	Fault	C	B	A	Fault	C	B	A	–
D	Fault	D	C	B	Fault	D	C	B	A
A	Fault	A	D	C	No fault	D	C	B	A
B	Fault	B	A	D	No fault	D	C	B	A
E	Fault	E	B	A	Fault	E	D	C	B
A	No fault	E	B	A	Fault	A	E	D	C
B	No fault	E	B	A	Fault	B	A	E	D
C	Fault	C	E	B	Fault	C	B	A	E
D	Fault	D	C	E	Fault	D	C	B	A
E	No fault	D	C	E	Fault	E	D	C	B

Three "no faults" — Two "no faults"

Figure 11.3 | FIFO anomaly—page faults can increase with page frame allocation.

11.6.4 Least-Recently-Used (LRU) Page Replacement

The **least-recently-used (LRU)** page-replacement strategy (Fig. 11.4) relies on the locality heuristic that a process's recent past behavior is a good indicator of the process's near future behavior (temporal locality). When the system must replace a page, LRU replaces the page that has spent the longest time in memory without being referenced.

Although LRU can provide better performance than FIFO, the benefit comes at the cost of system overhead.[22] LRU can be implemented with a list structure that contains one entry for each occupied page frame. Every time a page frame is referenced, the system places that page's entry at the head of the list (indicating that the page has been "most-recently referenced"). Older entries migrate toward the tail of the list. When an existing page must be replaced to make room for an incoming one, the system replaces the entry at the tail of the list. The system frees the corresponding page frame (possibly requiring a modified page to be written to secondary stor-

Page reference	Result	LRU page replacement with three pages available		
A	Fault	A	–	–
B	Fault	B	A	–
C	Fault	C	B	A
B	No fault	B	C	A
B	No fault	B	C	A
A	No fault	A	B	C
D	Fault	D	A	B
A	No fault	A	D	B
B	No fault	B	A	D
F	Fault	F	B	A
B	No fault	B	F	A

Figure 11.4 | *Least-recently-used (LRU) page-replacement strategy.*

age), places the incoming page into that page frame and moves the entry for that frame to the head of the list (because that page is now the one that has been most recently referenced). This scheme would faithfully implement LRU; however, it incurs substantial overhead, because the system must update the list every time a page is referenced.

We must always be careful when applying heuristic reasoning in operating system design; the heuristic—such as LRU here—could fail in certain common situations. For example, the page least recently used could be the next page to be referenced by a program that is iterating inside a loop that references several pages. If the page is replaced, the system will be required to reload it almost immediately.

Self Review

1. (T/F) LRU is designed to benefit processes that exhibit spatial locality.
2. Why is "pure" LRU rarely implemented?

Ans: **1)** False. LRU benefits processes that exhibit temporal locality. **2)** LRU incurs the overhead of maintaining an ordered list of pages and reordering that list.

11.6.5 Least-Frequently-Used (LFU) Page Replacement

The **least-frequently-used (LFU)** page-replacement strategy makes replacement decisions based on how intensively each page is being used. Under LFU, the system replaces the page that is least frequently used or least intensively referenced. This strategy is based on the intuitively appealing heuristic that a page that is not being intensively referenced is not as likely to be referenced in the future. LFU can be implemented using a counter that is updated each time its corresponding page is referenced, but this can incur substantial overhead.

The LFU page-replacement strategy, too, could easily select incorrect pages for replacement. For example, the least-frequently used page could be the page brought into main memory most recently. This page has been used once, whereas all other pages in main memory may have been used more than once. In this case, the page-replacement mechanism replaces the new page, when in fact the page would be highly likely to be used immediately. Next, we consider a low-overhead page-replacement strategy that makes reasonable decisions most of the time.

Self Review

1. Why is frequency of page usage a poor heuristic for reducing the number of future page faults?
2. Which page-replacement strategy incurs more execution overhead: LRU or LFU?

Ans: **1)** Frequency measures the number of times a page is referenced, but it does not indicate how many of those references generated page faults. Because page faults require the process to wait for a page to be loaded from secondary storage, they should be treated with greater weight than references to resident pages. If a reference to a page frequently generates a page fault, then that page is being actively used, and keeping it in memory is likely to reduce future page faults. The same is not always true for resident pages that have been referenced frequently, because frequency does not indicate whether a page is still being actively referenced. **2)** The answer depends on the implementation. Both strategies, in their "pure" form, must update page usage on every memory reference, meaning that the two strategies incur similar overhead. LFU updates a counter, while LRU could be rethreading a linked list; the latter would probably involve more overhead.

11.6.6 Not-Used-Recently (NUR) Page Replacement

A popular scheme for approximating LRU with little overhead is the **not-used-recently (NUR)** page-replacement strategy. NUR is based on the idea that a page that has not been used recently is not likely to be used in the near future. The NUR strategy is implemented using the following two hardware bits per page table entry:

- **referenced bit**—set to 0 if the page has not been referenced and set to one if the page has been referenced.
- **modified bit**—set to 0 if the page has not been modified and set to 1 if the page has been modified.

The referenced bit is sometimes called the **accessed bit**. The NUR strategy works as follows. Initially, the system sets the referenced bits of all pages to 0. When a process references a particular page, the system sets the referenced bit of that page to 1. The modified bits on all pages also are initially set to 0. Whenever a page is modified, the system sets the page's modified bit to 1. When the system must replace a page, NUR first attempts to find a page that has not been referenced (because NUR is intended to approximate LRU). If no such page exists, the system must replace a referenced page. In this case, NUR checks the modified bit to determine whether the page has been modified. If the page has not been modified, the system selects it for replacement. Otherwise, the system must replace a page that has been modified. Recall that replacing a modified page incurs the substantial delay of an additional I/O operation as the modified page is written to secondary storage to preserve its contents. Note, however, that periodic flushing of dirty pages can, on average, reduce or eliminate this delay.

Of course, main memory will likely be actively referenced in a multiuser system, so eventually most or all of the pages' referenced bits will be set to 1. When this is the case, NUR loses the ability to identify the most desirable pages to replace. A technique that has been widely implemented to avoid this problem is for the system periodically to set all the referenced bits to 0, then continue as usual. Unfortunately, this makes even active pages vulnerable to replacement, but only for a brief moment after the bits are reset—active pages will have their referenced bits set to 1 again almost immediately.

Pages can be classified into four groups in the NUR scheme (Fig. 11.5). The pages in the lowest-numbered groups should be replaced first, and those in the highest-numbered groups last. Pages within a group are selected randomly for replacement. Note that Group 2 seems to describe an unrealistic situation—namely, pages that have been modified but not referenced. This occurs because of the periodic resetting of the referenced bits (but not of the modified bits).

Schemes like NUR also can be implemented on machines that lack a hardware referenced bit, and even on machines that lack a hardware modified bit.[23] The referenced and modified bits are typically implemented in hardware and set as part of the execution of each machine instruction. Each of these bits can be simulated by intercepting an operating system's fault handlers and exception handlers as follows.

The referenced bit can be simulated by implementing a corresponding software bit and by initializing each entry in the page table to indicate that the page is not present. When a process references a page and causes a page fault, control reverts to the page fault handler, which sets the referenced bit to 1 and resumes

Group	Referenced	Modified	Description
Group 1	0	0	Best choice to replace
Group 2	0	1	[Seems unrealistic]
Group 3	1	0	
Group 4	1	1	Worst choice to replace

Figure 11.5 | *Page types under NUR.*

normal processing. The modified bit is simulated by marking each page as read-only. When a process attempts to modify the page, a memory-access exception occurs; the exception handler gains control, sets the (software-controlled) modified bit on and changes the access control on that page to read/write. Of course, the mechanism that implements the modified bit must still protect genuine read-only pages from being modified, so the operating system must keep track of which pages are truly read-only and which are truly read/write. The operating system must also periodically set each resident page's referenced bit to zero; the size of this interval is crucial to the performance of NUR. The instructions necessary to perform these actions are most likely to be a small set that can execute quickly. Almost all of today's processors include both a referenced and modified bit to boost the performance of memory managers.

Self Review

1. How does the modified bit improve performance in the NUR replacement strategy?
2. How could NUR replace the worst possible page?
3. How can an NUR page be modified but not referenced?

Ans: **1)** The modified bit enables the operating system to determine which pages can be overwritten without first being flushed to disk. Selecting unmodified pages first reduces I/O when performing page replacement. Note that NUR—to implement its heuristic—nevertheless replaces an unreferenced modified page before it replaces a referenced unmodified page. **2)** The next page that is about to be referenced could have its referenced bit reset to zero just before a page-replacement decision is made. **3)** It truly would be referenced, but NUR periodically resets the referenced bits.

11.6.7 Modifications to FIFO: Second-Chance and Clock Page Replacement

A clear weakness of the FIFO strategy is that it may choose to replace a heavily used page that has been in memory for a long time. This possibility can be avoided by implementing FIFO with a referenced bit for each page and replacing a page only if its referenced bit is set to zero.

The **second-chance** variation of FIFO examines the referenced bit of the oldest page; if this bit is off, the strategy immediately selects that page for replacement. If the referenced bit is on, the algorithm turns off the bit and moves the page to the tail of the FIFO queue. Such a page is treated essentially the same as a new arrival. Over time, the page gradually moves to the head of the queue. When it reaches the head, it will be selected for replacement only if the referenced bit is still off.

Active pages will be selected to return to the tail of the list, because their referenced bits will be set, and will thus remain in main memory. A modified page must be flushed to secondary storage before the system can replace it; so when its referenced bit is set off, the page remains "temporarily unreplaceable" until the system completes the transfer. If a process references this page before the flush is completed, then it is recaptured, thus saving an expensive page-in operation from secondary storage.

The **clock page replacement strategy**, which produces essentially the same results as the second-chance algorithm, arranges the pages in a circular list instead of a linear list.[24] Each time a page fault occurs, a list pointer moves around the circular list much as the hand of a clock rotates. When a page's referenced bit is turned off, the pointer is moved to the next element of the list (simulating the movement of this page to the rear of a FIFO queue). The clock algorithm places new arrivals in the first page it encounters with the referenced bit turned off.

Self Review

1. Which strategy incurs more overhead, second chance or clock?
2. Why are second-chance and clock page replacement more efficient than LRU?

Ans: **1)** Second chance requires the system to dequeue and requeue a page each time its resident bit is turned off. Clock generally incurs less overhead, because it modifies the value of a pointer each time a page's resident bit is turned off. **2)** These algorithms reduce the number of times the system updates page usage information.

11.6.8 Far Page Replacement

When programs execute, they tend to reference functions and data in predictable patterns. The **far page-replacement strategy** uses graphs to make replacement decisions based on these predictable patterns. The far strategy has been shown mathematically to perform at near-optimal levels, but it is complex to implement and incurs significant execution-time overhead.[25, 26, 27]

The far strategy creates an access graph (Fig. 11.6) that characterizes a process's reference patterns. Each vertex in the access graph represents one of the process's pages. An edge from vertex v to vertex w means that the process can reference page w after it has referenced page v. For example, if an instruction on page v references data on page w, there will be a directed edge from vertex v to vertex w. Similarly, if a function call to page x returns to page y, there will be an edge from vertex x to vertex y. The graph, which can become quite complex, describes how a process can reference pages as it executes. Access graphs can be created by analyzing a compiled program to determine which pages can be accessed by each instruction on each page, which can require significant execution time. [*Note*: Most studies of the far strategy assume the access graph is constructed before a process is run, although graph construction at runtime has been investigated.][28] The access graph in Fig. 11.6 indicates that, after the process references page B, it will next reference either page A, C, D or E, but it will not reference page G before it has referenced page E.

The replacement algorithm operates in phases much like the clock algorithm. Far initially marks all vertices in the access graph as unreferenced. When the process accesses a page, the algorithm marks as referenced the vertex that corresponds to that page. When the algorithm must select a page for replacement, it chooses the unreferenced page that is furthest away (hence the name "far") from any referenced page in

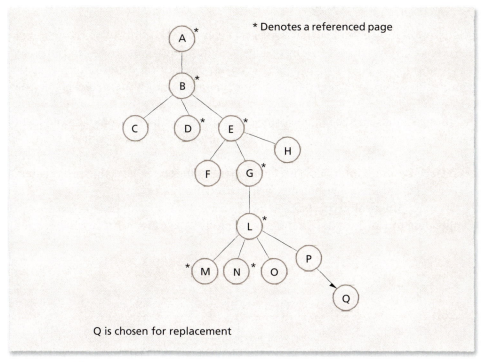

* Denotes a referenced page

Q is chosen for replacement

Figure 11.6 | *Far page-replacement-strategy access graph.*

the access graph (in Fig. 11.6, this corresponds to page Q). The intuitive appeal of this strategy is that the unreferenced page that is furthest from any referenced page is likely to be referenced furthest in the future. If the graph does not contain an unreferenced vertex, the current phase is complete, and the strategy marks all the vertices as unreferenced to begin a new phase.[29] At this point, the algorithm replaces the page furthest in the graph from the most-recently referenced page.

The field of graph theory provides algorithms for building and searching the the kinds of graphs in the far strategy. However, largely due to its complexity and execution-time overhead, far has not been implemented in real systems.

Self Review

1. Despite providing near-optimal performance, what hinders the far page-replacement strategy from being widely implemented?
2. When might the far strategy replace a page that will be referenced soon?

Ans: **1)** Far is complex to implement and it incurs substantial execution-time overhead. **2)** The process may subsequently "walk" the access graph directly to the page that was replaced, at which point it would experience a page fault. This could occur, for example, when a process referenced error-processing routines or issued a series of nested procedure calls.

11.7 Working Set Model

Locality of reference implies that a program can run efficiently even though only a relatively small subset of its pages resides in main memory at any given time. Denning's **working set theory of program behavior** focuses on determining what that favored subset is and maintaining it in main memory to achieve the best performance.[30, 31]

Many studies have been performed that illustrate the phenomenon of locality. Figure 11.7 shows a graph of a process's memory reference pattern across its pages.[32] The darkened areas show which memory areas the process referenced during consecutive time intervals. The figure vividly illustrates how this process tends to favor a subset of its pages during certain execution intervals.

The hypothetical process behaviors in Fig. 11.8 also support the existence of the phenomenon of locality. This figure demonstrates how a process's page fault

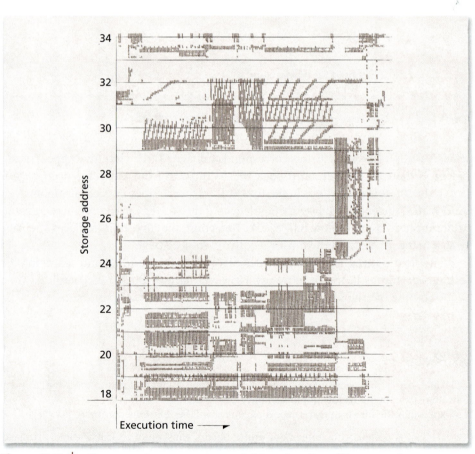

Figure 11.7 | *Storage reference pattern exhibiting locality. (Reprinted by permission from IBM Systems Journal. © 1971 by International Business Machines Corporation.)*

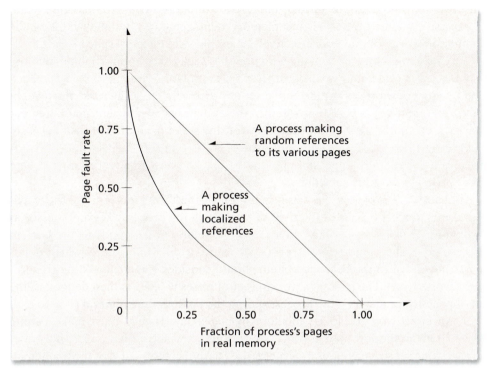

Figure 11.8 │ *Dependency of page fault rate on amount of memory for a process's pages.*

rate depends on the amount of main memory available for its pages. The straight line shows how this relationship would appear if the process exhibited a random reference pattern uniformly distributed over all its pages. The curved line shows how processes typically behave. As the number of page frames available to a process decreases, there is an interval over which it does not dramatically affect the page fault rate. But at a certain point, when the number of page frames decreases further, the number of page faults experienced by the running process rises dramatically. The graph shows that the process's page fault rate remains stable as long as its favored subset remains in main memory. However, when the system cannot allocate enough page frames to the process for its favored subset to remain in memory, the process's page fault rate increases dramatically (because the process is constantly referencing the pages that have been replaced).

The principle of locality and the behavior of processes exhibited in the previous figures all support Denning's working set theory of program behavior.[33, 34] This theory asserts that for a program to run efficiently, the system must maintain the program's favored subset (i.e., its working set) of pages in main memory. Otherwise, the system might experience excessive paging activity causing low processor utilization, called **thrashing**, as the process repeatedly requests the same pages from secondary storage.[35] One way to avoid thrashing might be to give each process enough page frames to hold half its virtual space. Unfortunately, rules like this often result in excessively conservative virtual memory management, ultimately limiting the number of processes that may effectively share physical memory space.

A working set memory management policy seeks to maintain in main memory only the pages that comprise each process's current working set.[36, 37, 38, 39] The decision to add a new process to the active set of processes (i.e., to increase the level of multiprogramming) is based on whether the system has a sufficient main memory space to accommodate the new process's working set of pages. This decision—especially in the case of freshly initiated processes—is typically made with heuristics, because it is generally impossible for the system to know in advance how large a given process's working set will be.

Figure 11.9 provides a precise definition of the term **working set**. The x-axis represents process time (i.e., the time during which the process uses a processor as distinguished from "wall clock" time) and the value t corresponds to the current process time. The value w is the process's **working set window size**, which determines how far into the past the system should consider when calculating the process's working set. The process's working set of pages $W(t, w)$, is then defined as the set of pages referenced by the process during the process-time interval $t - w$ to t.

An effective working set memory management strategy must make careful decisions about the size, w, of its process's working set window. Figure 11.10 illustrates how working set size increases as w increases. This is a consequence of the mathematical definition of working set and is not necessarily an indication of empirically observable working set sizes. The "true" working set of a process is simply the set of pages that must reside in main memory for the process to execute efficiently.

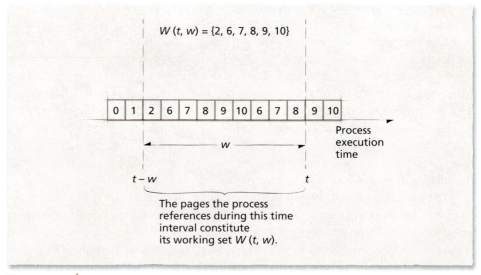

Figure 11.9 | *Definition of a process's working set of pages.*

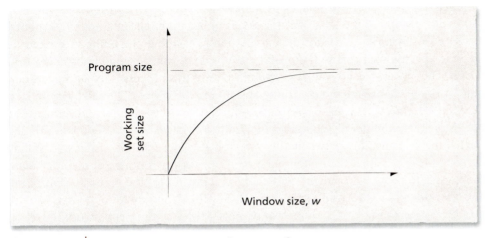

Figure 11.10 | *Working set size as a function of window size.*

Working sets change as a process executes.[40] Sometimes pages are added or deleted. Sometimes dramatic changes occur when the process enters a new phase (i.e., execution requiring a different working set). Thus, any assumptions about the size and content of a process's initial working set do not necessarily apply to subsequent working sets that the process will accumulate. This complicates precise memory management under a working set strategy.

Figure 11.11 shows how a process running under a working set memory management strategy might use main memory. First, as the process demand pages in its initial working set one page at a time, the system gradually allocates it enough memory to hold the working set. At this point, the process's memory use stabilizes

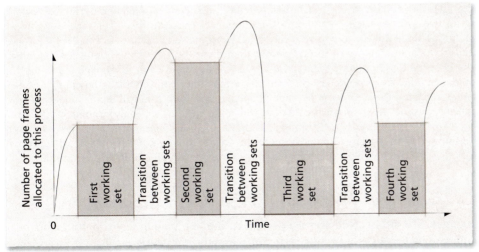

Figure 11.11 | *Main memory allocation under working set memory management.*

as it actively references the pages in its first working set. The process eventually makes a transition to the next working set, as indicated by the curved line from first to second working set. Initially, the curved line rises above the number of pages in the first working set because the process is rapidly demand-paging in its new working set. The system has no way of knowing whether this process is expanding its current working set or changing working sets. Once the process stabilizes in its next working set, the system sees fewer page references in the window and reduces the process's main memory allocation to the number of pages in its second working set. Each time a transition between the working sets occurs, this rising and falling curved line shows how the system adapts. One goal of working set memory management is to reduce the height of each curved portion of the graph to that of the next working set in the graph as quickly as possible. This would, of course, require that the system rapidly determine which pages from the previous working set (if any) are not part of the process's new working set.

The figure illustrates one of the difficulties with a working set memory management strategy, namely that working sets are transient, and a process's next working set may differ substantially from its current one. A memory management strategy must carefully consider this to avoid overcommitting main memory, which can lead to thrashing. Implementing a true working set memory management policy can incur substantial overhead, especially because the composition of working sets can and does change quickly. Morris discusses the use of custom hardware to make working set storage management more efficient.[41]

Self Review

1. Why is it difficult to determine the size of a process's working set?
2. What trade-offs are inherent in choosing a window size, w?

Ans: **1)** If we adhere strictly to Denning's definition, then it is trivial to determine the working set size—it is exactly the number of unique pages that have been referenced within the window, w. If we are concerned with the "true" working set, i.e., the set of pages the process needs to have in memory to run efficiently, then things become more complex. One indication that a process has its working set in memory is a low (or even zero) page fault rate. This could mean that the process has too many pages in memory. If we reduce the number of page frames allocated to the process, at some point the page fault rate will increase, possibly dramatically. Just before it does is the point at which the working set (only) is in memory. **2)** If w is too small, a process's true working set might not be in memory at all times, leading to thrashing. If w is too large, memory might be wasted because pages outside of a process' working set might still be in memory, possibly limiting the degree of multiprogramming.

11.8 Page-Fault-Frequency (PFF) Page Replacement

One measure of how well a process is executing in a paging environment is its page fault rate. A process that faults constantly may be thrashing because it has too few page frames and cannot maintain its working sets in memory. A process that almost never faults may have too many page frames and thus may be impeding the progress of other processes in the system (or preventing the operating system from increasing the degree of multiprogramming). Ideally, processes should operate at some point between these extremes. The **page-fault-frequency (PFF)** algorithm adjusts a process's **resident page set** (i.e., those pages which are currently in memory), based on the frequency at which the process is faulting.[42, 43, 44, 45, 46] Alternatively, PFF may adjust a process's resident page set based on the time between page faults, called the process's **interfault time**.

PFF has a lower overhead than working set page replacement because it adjusts the resident page set only after each page fault; a working set mechanism must operate after each memory reference. Under PFF, when a process makes a request that results in a page fault, the strategy calculates the time since the last page fault. If that time is larger than an upper threshold value, then the system releases all pages unreferenced in that interval. If the time is less than a lower threshold value, the incoming page becomes a member of the process's resident page set.

A benefit of PFF is that it adjusts a process's resident page set dynamically, in response to the process's changing behavior. If a process is switching to a larger working set, then it will fault frequently, and PFF will allocate more page frames. Once the process has accumulated its new working set, the page fault rate will stabilize and PFF will either maintain the resident page set or reduce it. A key to the proper and efficient operation of PFF is maintaining the thresholds at appropriate values.

Some systems might increase performance by adjusting their process scheduling algorithms to the frequency with which a process generates page faults. Presumably, processes generating few page faults have accumulated their working sets in main storage. Processes experiencing large numbers of page faults have not yet established their working sets. The conventional wisdom is to favor processes that have established their working sets. Another viewpoint is that processes with high page fault rates should receive priority because they use a processor only briefly before generating an I/O request. A process that is faulting in its next working set appears to be an I/O-bound process. Once the working set is accumulated, the process will "settle down" to "regular" behavior—some processes will be processor bound and others will be I/O bound.

Self Review

1. How does PFF approximate the working set model?

2. What problems could arise if the PFF upper threshold is too small? What if the lower threshold is too large?

Ans: **1)** Both PFF and the working set model change the size of a process's allocation space dynamically to prevent thrashing. However, the working set model readjusts after every memory access, whereas PFF readjusts only after each page fault. **2)** If the lower threshold were too large, the system would allocate more pages to a process than it needs, which would result in wasted memory. If the upper threshold were too small, the system would release a process's working set pages, leading to thrashing.

11.9 Page Release

Under working set memory management, a process indicates which pages it wants to use by explicitly referencing the pages. Pages that a process no longer requires should be removed from its working set. Under existing memory management strategies, however, needless pages often remain in memory until the management strategy can detect that the process no longer needs them. An alternative strategy would be for the process to issue a **voluntary page release** command to free a page it no longer needs. This would eliminate the delay period caused by letting the process gradually pass the page from its working set.

Voluntary page release could speed program execution for the entire system. One hope in this area is for compilers and operating systems to detect page-release situations, and to do so much sooner than is possible under working set strategies. Realistically, users cannot make such decisions, but applications programmers and systems programmers can.

Self Review

1. Why could voluntary page release yield better performance than a pure working set page-replacement strategy?
2. Why, then, is voluntary page release not widely implemented in today's systems?

Ans: **1)** There is a latency in the working set strategy (i.e., the window size, w) that causes pages no longer needed to "hang around" before being replaced. Voluntary page release could release those pages sooner, leading to more efficient use of memory. **2)** The real issue is whether it is indeed possible to choose the right pages to release. This is hard to do, because we know that we cannot, in the general case, predict the path of execution a program will take.

11.10 Page Size

An important characteristic of a paged virtual memory system is the size of the pages and page frames that the system supports. In today's systems, there is no one "industry standard" page size, and many architectures support multiple page sizes, with demonstrable improvements in performance.[47] When choosing a page size (or page sizes), the system designer should evaluate several concerns, based on the goals and limitations of the system to be designed.

Many early results in the literature, both theoretical and empirical, point to the need for small pages.[48, 49, 50] As both memory and program sizes increase rapidly, larger page sizes have become more desirable. What considerations determine whether a page should be large or small? Several are summarized here:

- A large page size increases the range of memory that the TLB can reference with each entry. This increases the likelihood of TLB hits, which improves dynamic address translation performance.[51]

- In general, a large page size can reduce the number of time-consuming I/O operations that transfer information between main memory and secondary storage. A system transferring such information using a small page size may require several separate I/O operations, which would increase a process's space-time product (see Section 11.3). However, anticipatory paging and (as we discuss in the next chapter) disk scheduling algorithms can reduce this overhead.

- Processes tend to exhibit locality of reference over a small portion of their address spaces, so a smaller page size would help a process establish a smaller, tighter working set, leaving more memory available to other processes.[52]

- A small page size leads to a large number of pages and page frames and correspondingly larger page tables. As discussed in Section 10.4.4, Multilevel Page Tables, these tables can consume a significant portion of main memory (i.e., table fragmentation). Large page sizes reduce table fragmentation by decreasing the number of page table entries (at the cost of increased internal fragmentation).

- In a combined segmentation/paging organization the system may experience internal fragmentation, because procedure and data units rarely comprise an integral number of pages, so a segment is just as likely to have its last page nearly full as nearly empty (Fig. 11.12). Thus, each segment contains, on average, one-half page of internal fragmentation. More fragmentation results in a larger average working set size for programs.[53] The system can reduce the amount of internal fragmentation by employing smaller page sizes.[54]

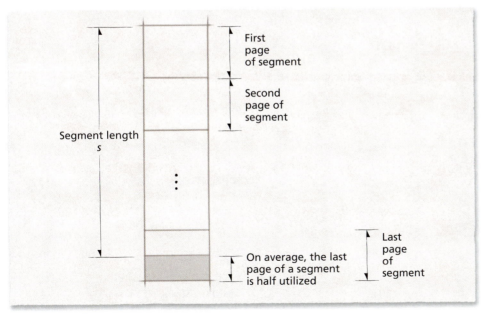

Figure 11.12 | *Internal fragmentation in a paged and segmented system.*

Although supporting multiple page sizes can address many of the limitations of both large and small page sizes, it has several disadvantages. First, operating systems require hardware support for multiple page sizes to provide efficient dynamic address translation. This means that the page address translation hardware must be able to accommodate large and small pages. In the Intel Pentium 4 processor, this is accomplished using multiple TLBs, each of which is dedicated to storing PTEs for one page size. This added hardware complexity increases cost. Also, multiple page sizes introduces the possibility of external fragmentation similar to that in segmentation systems, because blocks are of variable size.[55]

Figure 11.13 lists the page sizes used by several systems. Note the relatively small single page sizes chosen for earlier computers, whereas more recent computers support larger page sizes and multiple page sizes.

Self Review

1. Why are large page sizes more favorable in today's systems than they were decades ago?
2. What are the negatives of having multiple page sizes?

Ans: 1) The cost of memory has become cheaper, leading to systems that contain large memories and applications that require increasingly large amounts of memory. In today's systems, the cost of internal fragmentation due to larger page sizes is of less concern than it was

Manufacturer	Model	Page Size	Real address size
Honeywell	Multics	1KB	36 bits
IBM	370/168	4KB	32 bits
DEC	PDP-10 and PDP-20	512 bytes	36 bits
DEC	VAX 8800	512 bytes	32 bits
Intel	80386	4KB	32 bits
Intel / AMD	Pentium 4 / Athlon XP	4KB or 4MB	32- or 36 bits
Sun	UltraSparc II	8KB, 64KB, 512KB, 4MB	44 bits
AMD	Opteron / Athlon 64	4KB, 2MB and 4MB	32, 40, or 52 bits
Intel-HP	Itanium, Itanium 2	4KB, 8KB, 16KB, 64KB, 256KB, 1MB, 4MB, 16MB, 64MB, 256MB	Between 32 and 63 bits
IBM	PowerPC 970	4KB, 128KB, 256KB, 512KB, 1MB, 2MB, 4MB, 8MB, 16MB, 32MB, 64MB, 128MB, 256MB	32 or 64 bits

Figure 11.13 | *Page sizes in various processor architectures.*[56, 57, 58]

decades ago, when memory was far more expensive. Large pages also require the system to perform fewer costly I/O operations to load a large portion of a process's virtual address space into memory. However, there are many cases in which the operating system must store data which is only a fraction of the page size. In this case, multiple page sizes might improve memory utilization, at the cost of additional memory management overhead. **2)** Both the operating system and hardware must support multiple page sizes to provide efficient memory management. Operating systems must be rewritten so that they efficiently manage multiple page sizes, which requires costly software development. Processors must increase in complexity to support multiple page sizes, which tends to increase their cost.

11.11   Program Behavior under Paging

Many studies have been performed examining the behavior of processes in paging environments.[59, 60, 61, 62, 63, 64, 65, 66, 67, 68, 69, 70, 71, 72, 73, 74, 75, 76, 77, 78, 79, 80] In this section we present some qualitative results of these studies.

Figure 11.14 shows the percentage of a hypothetical process's pages that have been referenced, starting from the time the process begins execution. The initial sharp upward slope indicates that a process tends to reference a significant portion of its pages immediately after execution begins. With time, the slope diminishes, and the graph asymptotically approaches 100 percent. Certainly some processes reference 100 percent of their pages, but the graph is drawn to reflect that many processes may execute for a long time without doing so. This is the case, for example, when certain error-processing routines are rarely invoked.

The number of faults a process experiences depends on the size and behavior of the system's processes. If they have small working sets, the number of page faults experienced by a running process tends to increase as the page size increases. This phenomenon occurs because, as page size increases, more procedures and data that will not be referenced are brought into a fixed-size main memory. Further, as page

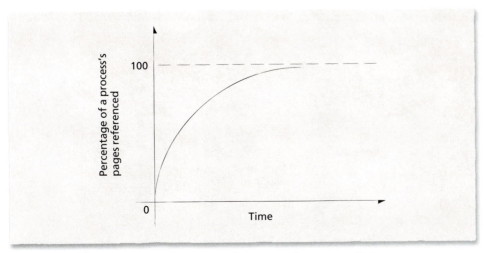

Figure 11.14 | Percentage of a process's pages referenced with time.

size continues to increase, the system incurs more internal fragmentation. Thus, a smaller percentage of a process's limited main memory is occupied by procedures and data that will be referenced. A process with a large working set requires a greater number of small page frames, which can lead to a large number of page faults each time the process runs. If a process's working set contains pages that are contiguous in the process's virtual address space, the number of page faults tends to decrease as the page size increases. This occurs because each page fault loads into memory a significant portion of the process's working set.

Figure 11.15 shows how the average interfault time (i.e., the time between page faults) varies as the number of page frames allocated to a process increases. The graph is nondecreasing—the more page frames a process has, the longer the time between page faults (subject, of course, to occasional strange behavior such as the FIFO anomaly).[81] At one point, the graph bends, and its slope declines sharply. At this point the process has its entire working set in main memory. Initially, the interfault time grows quickly, as more of the working set resides in main memory. Once the physical memory allotment is sufficient to hold the process's working set, the curve bends sharply, indicating that the effect of allocating additional page frames on increasing the interfault time is not as great. Again, the goal of a memory management strategy should be to maintain the working set in main memory.

The qualitative discussions of this section generally point to the validity of the working set concept. As computer architecture and software design evolves, these results will need to be reevaluated.

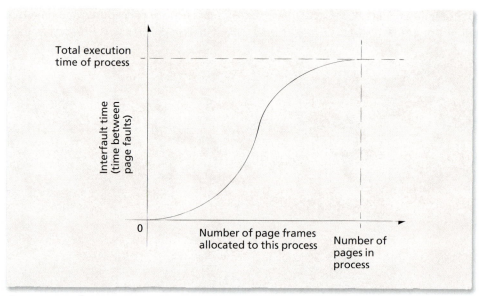

Figure 11.15 | Dependency of interfault time on the number of page frames allocated to a process.

Self Review

1. How does program behavior under paging support the notion of lazy allocation, whereby the operating system does not allocate page frames to a process until the process explicitly references its pages?
2. (T/F) The interfault time for a particular process always increases as the number of page frames allocated to a process increases.

Ans: **1)** Figure 11.14 demonstrates that the operating system would waste considerable memory if it reserved memory that a process would not use until later in its execution. However, if a process references its pages with predictable patterns, anticipatory paging could improve performance by reducing page-wait times. **2)** False. This is indeed the normal behavior, but if the algorithm is subject to Belady's Anomaly, the interfault time might decrease.

11.12 Global vs. Local Page Replacement

When evaluating the page-replacement strategies presented in the previous sections, we provided reference patterns for a single, arbitrary process. In most real systems, the operating system must provide a page-replacement strategy that yields good performance for a number of diverse processes.

When implementing a paged virtual memory system, the operating system designer must decide whether page-replacement strategies should be applied to all processes as a unit (i.e., global strategies) or consider each process individually (i.e., local strategies). Global page-replacement strategies tend to ignore the characteristics of individual process behavior; local page-replacement strategies enable the system to adjust memory allocation according to the relative importance of each process to improve performance.

As we will see, a heuristic that yields good results when applied to individual process behavior can lead to poor performance when applied to the system as a whole. There is no conventional wisdom on this—Linux, for example, implements a global page-replacement strategy and Windows XP implements a local page-replacement strategy (see Section 20.6.3, Page Replacement, and Section 21.7.3, Page Replacement, respectively).[82]

The **global LRU (gLRU)** page-replacement strategy replaces the least-recently-used page in the entire system. This simple strategy does not attempt to analyze individual process behavior or the relative importance of processes when selecting a page to replace. Consider, for example, a system that schedules processes using round robin—the next process to run is the process that has waited the longest. In this case, pages belonging to the next process to run are often the least-recently-used pages, so gLRU is likely to replace the next page to be used. Note that gLRU can result in poor performance regardless of individual process behavior if the system implements a variant of the round-robin scheduling algorithm.

Glass and Cao suggest the SEQ (sequence) global replacement strategy, which is a modified version of LRU that adjusts its strategy based on process behavior.[83] In general, the SEQ strategy uses the LRU strategy to replace pages. As discussed in Section 11.6.4, LRU performs poorly when processes enter loops that reference a sequence of pages that cannot all fit in memory at once. In this case, the optimal page to replace is the page that was most-recently used because it will be referenced furthest in the future (i.e., during the next iteration of the loop). Accordingly, the SEQ strategy uses the heuristic that a process experiencing a sequence of page faults when referencing a series of contiguous pages is exhibiting looping behavior. When such behavior is detected, it applies the most-recently used (MRU) strategy, which is optimal for that reference pattern. If a process experiences page fault when referencing a noncontiguous page, SEQ uses the LRU strategy until another sequence of page faults to contiguous pages is detected.

11.13 Case Study: Linux Page Replacement

In this section we discuss the page-replacement strategy implemented in Linux. More information about memory management in Linux can be found in Section 20.6, Memory Management. When physical memory is full and nonresident data is requested by processes or the kernel, page frames must be freed to fill the request. Pages are divided into active pages and inactive pages. To be considered active, a page must have been referenced recently. One goal of the memory manager is to maintain the current working set inside the collection of active pages.[84]

Linux uses a variation of the clock algorithm to approximate an LRU page-replacement strategy (Fig. 11.16). The memory manager uses two linked lists: the active list contains active pages, the inactive list contains inactive pages. The lists are organized such that the most-recently used pages are near the head of the active list, and the least-recently used pages are near the tail of the inactive list.[85]

When a page is first brought into memory, it is placed in the inactive list and is marked as having been referenced by setting its referenced bit. The memory manager periodically determines whether the page has been subsequently referenced, such as during a page fault. If the page is active or inactive and its referenced bit is off, the bit is turned on. Similar to the clock algorithm, this technique ensures that recently referenced pages are not selected for replacement.

Otherwise, if the page is inactive and is being referenced for the second time (its referenced bit is already on), the memory manager moves the page to the head of the active list, then clears its referenced bit.[86] This allows the kernel to determine whether a page has been referenced more than once recently. If so, the page is placed in the active list so that it is not selected for replacement. To ensure that the active list contains only pages that are being heavily referenced, the memory manager periodically moves any unreferenced pages in the active list to the head of the inactive list.

This algorithm is repeated until the specified number of pages have been moved from the tail of the active list to the head of the inactive list. A page in the inactive list will remain in memory until it is selected for replacement. While a page is in the active list, however, it cannot be selected for replacement.[87]

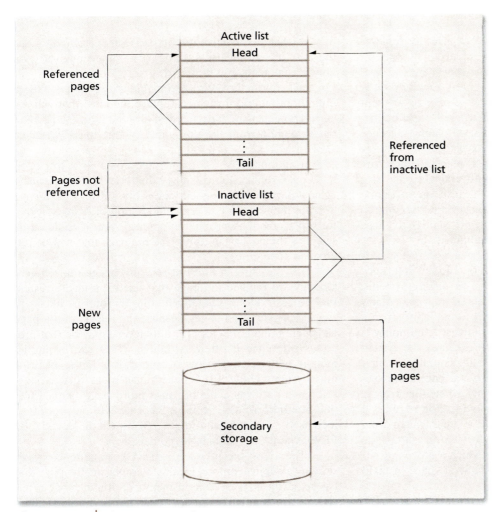

Figure 11.16 | *Linux page replacement overview.*

Web Resources

publib16.boulder.ibm.com/pseries/en_US/aixbman/
admnconc/vmm_overview.htm
Describes virtual memory management in AIX, which is IBM's UNIX-based system.

www.csn.ul.ie/~mel/projects/vm/
Describes virtual memory management for the Linux 2.4 kernel.

www.informit.com/isapi/product_id~%7B6D5ACA10-
5AB0-4627-81E5-65B9F6E080AC%7D/content/index.asp
Describes virtual memory management in Windows 2000 running on an Intel x86 processor.

developer.apple.com/documentation/mac/Memory/Memory-2.html
Describes virtual memory management in the Apple Macintosh operating system.

msdn.microsoft.com/library/default.asp?url=/
library/en-us/appendix/hh/appendix/
enhancements5_3oc3.asp
Discusses memory management enhancements in Windows XP.

www.nondot.org/~sabre/os/articles/MemoryManagement/
Lists links to several articles related to memory management.

Summary

The technique a system employs to select pages for replacement when memory is full is called a replacement strategy. A system's fetch strategy determines when pages or segments should be loaded into main memory. Demand fetch strategies wait for a process to reference a page or segment before loading it. Anticipatory fetch strategies use heuristics to predict which pages a process will soon reference and load those pages or segments. A placement strategy determines where in main memory to place an incoming page or segment. Paging systems with a single page size trivialize the placement decision, because an incoming page may be placed in any available page frame. Segmentation systems require placement strategies similar to those used in variable-partition multiprogramming.

Central to most memory management strategies is the concept of locality—that a process tends to reference memory in highly localized patterns. In paging systems, processes tend to favor certain subsets of their pages, and these pages often tend to be adjacent to one another in a process's virtual address space. The simplest fetch policy is demand paging—when a process first executes, the system loads into main memory the page that contains its first instruction. After that, the system loads a page from secondary storage to main memory only when the process explicitly references that page. Demand paging requires a process to accumulate pages one at a time, which often increases a process's space-time product—a measure of its execution time (i.e., the duration for which a process occupies memory) multiplied by the amount of space in main memory it occupies.

In anticipatory paging, the operating system attempts to predict the pages a process will need and preloads these pages when memory space is available. Anticipatory paging strategies must be carefully designed so that overhead incurred by the strategy does not reduce system performance. A demand prepaging strategy preloads a group of pages into memory when a process references a nonresident page, which can be effective when processes exhibit spatial locality.

When a process generates a page fault, the memory management system must locate the referenced page in secondary storage, load it into a page frame in main memory and update the corresponding page table entry. Most modern architectures support a modified (or dirty) bit in their page table entries; this bit is set to 1 if the page has been modified and 0 otherwise. The operating system uses this bit to quickly determine which pages have been modified, so that it can improve the performance by avoiding the cost of writing (or flushing) a modified page to disk after a page fault.

The optimal page replacement strategy states that, to obtain optimal performance, replace the page that will not be referenced again until furthest into the future. It is possible to demonstrate the optimality of this strategy (called OPT or MIN).

Random (RAND) page replacement is a low-overhead page-replacement strategy that does not discriminate against particular processes. Under this strategy, each page in main memory has an equal likelihood of being selected for replacement. A problem it entails is that it could easily select as the next page to replace the page that will be referenced next.

In the first-in-first-out (FIFO) page-replacement strategy, we replace the page that has been in the system the longest. Unfortunately, first-in-first-out is likely to replace heavily used pages, because the reason that a page has been in main memory for a long time may be that processes reference it often. Although FIFO can be implemented with relatively low overhead, it is impractical for most systems. Under FIFO page replacement, certain page-reference patterns actually cause more page faults when the number of page frames allocated to a process is increased—a counterintuitive phenomenon called the FIFO Anomaly or Belady's Anomaly.

The least-recently-used (LRU) page-replacement strategy exploits temporal locality by replacing the page that has spent the longest time in memory without being referenced. Although LRU can provide better performance than FIFO, the benefit comes at the cost of increased system overhead. Unfortunately, the page least-recently used could be the next page to be referenced by a program that is iterating inside a loop that references several pages.

The least-frequently-used (LFU) page-replacement strategy replaces the page that is least intensively referenced. This strategy is based on the heuristic that a page not referenced often is not likely to be referenced in the future. LFU could select the wrong page for replacement; for example, the least-frequently-used page could easily be the page brought into main memory most recently—a page that any reasonable page-replacement strategy would like to keep in main memory.

The not-used-recently (NUR) replacement strategy approximates LRU with little overhead by using a referenced bit and a modified bit to determine which page has not been used recently and can be replaced quickly. Schemes like NUR also can be implemented on machines that lack a hardware referenced bit and/or modified bit.

The second-chance variation of FIFO examines the referenced bit of the oldest page; if this bit is off, the strategy selects that page for replacement. If the referenced bit is on, the strategy turns off the bit and moves the page to the tail of the FIFO queue. This ensures that active pages are the least likely to be replaced. The clock variation of the second-chance algorithm arranges the pages in a circular list instead of a linear list. When a page's referenced bit is turned off, the pointer is moved to the next element of the list (simulating the movement of this page to the rear of a FIFO list). Second chance and clock produce essentially the same results.

The far strategy creates an access graph that characterizes a process's reference patterns. The algorithm chooses to replace the unreferenced page that is furthest away from any referenced page in the access graph. Although the strategy performs at near-optimal levels, it has not been implemented in real systems, because the access graph is complex to search and manage without hardware support.

Denning's working set theory of program behavior asserts that for a program to run efficiently, the system must maintain that program's favored subset of pages—its working set—in main memory. Otherwise, the system might experience excessive paging activity causing low processor distillation called thrashing as the program repeatedly requests pages from secondary storage. A working set memory management policy seeks to maintain in main memory only the pages that comprise each process's current working set. The decision to add a new process to the active set of processes is based in part on whether the system has sufficient main memory space to accommodate the new process's working set of pages. A process's working set window size specifies how far into the past the system should consider when calculating the process's working set. One challenge of working set memory management is that working sets are transient, and a process's next working set may differ substantially from its current one.

The page-fault-frequency (PFF) algorithm adjusts a process's resident page set (i.e., those pages which are currently in memory), based on the frequency at which the process is faulting. Alternatively, PFF may adjust a process's resident page set based on the time between page faults, called the process's interfault time. An advantage of PFF over working set page replacement is lower overhead—PFF adjusts the resident page set only after each page fault, whereas a working set mechanism must operate after each memory reference. If a process is switching to a larger working set, then it will fault frequently and PFF will allocate more page frames. Once the process has accumulated its new working set, the page fault rate will stabilize and PFF will either maintain the resident page set or reduce it. The key to the proper and efficient operation of PFF is maintaining the thresholds at appropriate values.

Under all memory management strategies, needless pages can remain in main memory until the management strategy detects that the process no longer needs them, which can be well after the page is no longer needed. One way to solve this problem would be for the process to issue a voluntary page release to free a page frame that it knows it no longer needs, eliminating the delay period caused by letting the process gradually pass the page from its working set. The real hope in this area is for compilers and operating systems to detect page-release situations, and to do so much sooner than is possible under working set strategies.

An important characteristic of a paged virtual memory system is the size of the pages and page frames that the system supports. Some systems improve performance and utilization by providing multiple page sizes. Small page sizes reduce internal fragmentation and can reduce the amount of memory required to contain a process's working set, leaving more memory available to other processes. Large page sizes reduce wasted memory from table fragmentation, enable each TLB entry to map a larger region of memory, and reduce the number of I/O operations the system performs to load a process's working set into memory. The use of multiple page sizes requires both hardware and software support, which can be costly to implement, and introduces the possibility of external fragmentation due to variable page sizes.

Processes tend to reference a significant portion of their pages within a short time after execution begins, then access most (or all) of their remaining pages at a slower rate. The average interfault time (i.e., the time between page faults) monotonically increases in general—the more page frames a process has, the longer the time between page faults (subject, of course, to strange behavior such as that observed in the FIFO Anomaly).

When implementing a paged virtual memory system, the operating system designer must decide whether page-replacement strategies should be applied to all processes as a unit (i.e., global strategies) or consider each process individually (i.e., local strategies). Global page-replacement strategies tend to ignore the characteristics of individual process behavior; local page-replacement strategies enable the system to adjust memory allocation according to the relative importance of each process to improve performance. The global LRU (gLRU) page-replacement strategy replaces the least-recently-used page in the entire system. The SEQ

(sequence) global replacement strategy, uses the LRU strategy to replace pages until sequence of page faults to contiguous pages is detected, at which point it uses the most-recently-used (MRU) page-replacement strategy.

Key Terms

accessed bit—See referenced bit.

anticipatory paging—Technique that preloads a process's nonresident pages that are likely to be referenced in the near future. Such strategies attempt to reduce the number of page faults a process experiences.

Belady's Anomaly—See FIFO Anomaly.

clock page-replacement strategy—Variation of the second-chance page-replacement strategy that arranges the pages in a circular list instead of a linear list. A list pointer moves around the circular list, much as the hand of a clock rotates, and replaces the page nearest the pointer (in circular order) that has its referenced bit turned off.

demand paging—Technique that loads a process's nonresident pages into memory only when the process explicitly references the page.

dirty bit—Page table entry bit that specifies whether the page has been modified (also known as the modified bit).

far page-replacement strategy—Graph-based page-replacement strategy that analyzes a program's reference patterns to determine which page to replace. This strategy replaces the page that is furthest from any referenced page in the graph and that has not been referenced recently.

FIFO Anomaly—Phenomenon in FIFO page-replacement strategy whereby increasing a process's page frame allocation increases the number of page faults it experiences; normally, page faults should decrease as more page frames become available.

first-in-first-out (FIFO) page replacement—Page-replacement strategy that replaces the page that has been in memory longest. FIFO incurs low overhead but generally does not predict future page usage accurately.

flushing a page—Copying the contents of a modified page in main memory to secondary storage so another page can be placed in its frame. When this occurs, the page's dirty bit is cleared, which enables the operating system to quickly determine that the page can be overwritten by an incoming page, which can reduce page-wait times.

global least-recently-used (gLRU) page replacement—Global page-replacement strategy that replaces the page that has

not been referenced for the longest time in the entire system. LRU can perform poorly because variants of round-robin scheduling cause the system to exhibit a large-scale looping reference pattern. The SEQ variant of gLRU page replacement attempts to improve performance by replacing the most-recently-used page when it detects a looping reference pattern.

interfault time—Time between a process's page faults. This is used in the page-fault-frequency page-replacement strategy to determine when to increase or decrease a program's page frame allocation.

least-frequently-used (LFU) page replacement—Page-replacement strategy that replaces the page that is least frequently used or least intensively referenced. LFU is easy to implement, but generally does not predict future page usage well.

least-recently-used (LRU) page replacement—Page-replacement strategy that replaces the page that has not been referenced for the longest time. LRU generally predicts future page usage well but incurs significant overhead.

modified bit—Page table entry bit that indicates whether a page has been modified and hence must be copied to secondary storage before being replaced (also known as the dirty bit).

not-used-recently (NUR) page replacement—Low-overhead approximation to the LRU page-replacement strategy; uses referenced bits and dirty bits to replace a page. NUR first attempts to replace a page that has not been referenced recently and that has not been modified. If no such page is available, the strategy replaces a dirty page that has not been referenced recently, a clean page that has been referenced recently or a referenced page that has been referenced recently, in that order.

optimal (OPT) page replacement—Unrealizable page-replacement strategy that replaces the page that will not be used until furthest in the future. This strategy has been shown to be optimal.

page-fault-frequency (PFF) page replacement—Algorithm that adjusts a process's resident page set based on the frequency with which the process is faulting. If a process is switching to a larger working set, then it will fault frequently, and PFF will allocate more page frames. Once the process has accumulated its new working set, the page fault rate will stabilize, and PFF will either maintain the resident page set or reduce it. The key to the proper and efficient operation of PFF is maintaining the thresholds at appropriate values.

page-replacement strategy—Strategy that determines which page to replace to provide space for an incoming page. Page replacement strategies attempt to optimize performance by predicting future page usage.

prefetching—See anticipatory paging.

prepaging—See anticipatory paging.

random (RAND) page replacement—Page-replacement strategy in which each page in main memory has an equal likelihood of being selected for replacement. Although this strategy is fair and incurs little overhead, it does not attempt to predict future page usage.

referenced bit—Page table entry bit indicating whether a page has been referenced recently. Several strategies reset this bit to more accurately determine how recently a page has been referenced.

resident page set—Set of a process's pages that are currently in memory; these pages may be referenced without generating a page fault. The resident page set might differ in size from a process's working set, which is the set of pages that must be in memory for a process to execute efficiently.

second-chance page-replacement strategy—Variation of FIFO page replacement that uses the referenced bit and a FIFO queue to determine which page to replace. If the oldest page's referenced bit is off, second chance replaces the page; otherwise it turns off the referenced bit on the oldest page and moves it the tail of the FIFO queue. If its referenced bit is on, the strategy turns off the bit and examines the next page or pages until it locates a page with its referenced bit turned off.

space-time product—Value that measures the product of a process's execution time (i.e., the duration for which a process occupies memory) and the amount of real-memory space the process occupies. Ideally, memory management strategies should reduce this quantity to increase a system's degree of multiprogramming.

spatial locality—Empirical property that, in paging systems, states that processes tend to favor certain subsets of their pages, and that these pages tend to be near one another in a process's virtual address space. A process accessing sequential indices of an array exhibits spatial locality.

thrashing—Excessive paging activity causing low processor utilization that occurs when a process's memory allocation is smaller than its working set. This results in poor performance, as the process spends most of its time waiting as pages are transferred between secondary storage and main memory.

voluntary page release—Occurrence when a process explicitly releases a page frame that it no longer needs. This can improve performance by reducing the number of unused page frames allocated to a process, leaving more memory available.

working set—A program's favored subset of pages in main memory. Given a working set window, w, the process's working set of pages $W(t, w)$, is defined as the set of pages it references during the process-time interval $t - w$ to t.

working set theory of program behavior—Theory presented by Denning; which asserts that for a program to run efficiently, the system must maintain that program's favored subset (i.e., its working set) of pages in main memory. Given a working set window, w, the process's working set of pages $W(t, w)$, is defined as the set of pages referenced by the process during the process-time interval $t - w$ to t. Choosing the window size, w, is a crucial aspect of implementing working set memory management.

working set window size—Value that determines how far into the past the system should consider to determine what pages are in the process's working set.

Exercises

11.1 Discuss the goals of each of the following memory management strategies in the context of virtual memory systems with paging.

   a. fetch strategy

   b. placement strategy

   c. replacement strategy

11.2 Explain why memory management in pure segmentation systems is quite similar to memory management in variable-partition multiprogramming systems.

11.3 One particular virtual memory computer system with combined segmentation and paging supports a degree of multiprogramming of 10. Instruction pages (reentrant code) are maintained separately from data pages (which are modifiable).

You have studied the system in operation and have made the following observations: (1) Most procedure segments are many pages long and (2) most data segments use only a small fraction of a page.

Your associate has proposed that one way to get better utilization out of memory is to pack several of each user's data segments onto an individual page. Comment on this proposal considering issues of:

    a. memory use

    b. execution efficiency

    c. protection

    d. sharing

11.4 Today there is much interest in anticipatory paging and in anticipatory resource allocation in general. What useful information might each of the following supply to an anticipatory paging mechanism?

    a. the programmer

    b. the compiler

    c. the operating system

    d. a log of past executions of the program

11.5 It is known that in the general case we cannot predict the path of execution of an arbitrary program. If we could, then we would be able to solve the Halting Problem—which is known to be unsolvable. Explain the ramifications for the effectiveness of anticipatory resource-allocation mechanisms.

11.6 Suppose a memory manager has narrowed its page-replacement decision to one of two pages. Suppose that one of the pages is shared by several processes, and the other is in use by only a single process. Should the memory manager always replace the nonshared page? Explain.

11.7 Discuss each of the following unconventional (if not whimsical) page-replacement schemes in the context of a virtual memory multiprogramming system servicing both batch and interactive processes.

    a. "Global LIFO"—The page brought into main memory most recently is replaced.

    b. "Local LIFO"—The page brought in most recently by the process which requested the incoming page is replaced.

    c. "Tired Page"—The most heavily referenced page in the system is replaced.

    d. "Battered Page"—The most heavily modified page in the system is replaced. One variant would count the number of writes to the page. Another would consider the percentage of the page that has been modified.

11.8 Suppose a memory manager decides which page to replace solely on the basis of examining the referenced and modified bits for each page frame. List several incorrect decisions the memory manager might make.

11.9 List several reasons why it is necessary to prevent certain pages from being paged out of main memory.

11.10 Why is it generally more desirable to replace an unmodified page rather than a modified one? In what circumstances might it be more desirable to replace a modified page?

11.11 For each of the following pairs of replacement strategies, explain how a page-reference sequence could result in both strategies choosing (1) the same page for replacement and (2) a different page for replacement.

    a. LRU, NUR

    b. LRU, LFU

    c. LRU, FIFO

    d. NUR, LFU

    e. LFU, FIFO

    f. NUR, FIFO.

11.12 The optimal (MIN) page-replacement strategy is unrealizable because the future cannot be predicted. There are circumstances, however, in which MIN can be implemented. What are they?

11.13 Suppose a memory manager has chosen a modified page for replacement. This page must be sent to secondary storage before the new page may be placed in its page frame. Therefore, the memory manager requests an I/O operation to write this page to secondary storage. An entry is made in a list of I/O requests waiting to be serviced. Thus the page will remain in main memory for some time before the requested I/O operation is performed. Now suppose that, while the other I/O requests are serviced, a running process requests the page to be replaced. How should the memory manager react?

11.14 Design an experiment for a paged system to demonstrate the phenomena of temporal and spatial locality.

11.15 A programmer who writes programs specifically to exhibit good locality can expect marked improvement in their execution efficiency. List several strategies a programmer can use to improve locality. In particular, what high-level language features should be emphasized?

11.16 Suppose the bus between memory and secondary storage is experiencing heavy page traffic. Does this imply thrashing? Explain.

11.17 Why might a global page-replacement policy (in which an incoming page may replace a page of any process) be more susceptible to thrashing than a local page-replacement policy (in which an incoming page may replace only a page belonging to the same process)?

11.18 Discuss the trade-offs between giving each process more page frames than it needs (to prevent thrashing) and the resulting fragmentation of main memory.

11.19 Suggest a heuristic that a memory manager might use to determine if main memory has become overcommitted.

11.20 The working set of a process may be defined in several ways. Discuss the merits of each of the following schemes for deciding which pages constitute a process's working set.

    a. those pages that the process has referenced in the last w seconds of wall-clock time

    b. those pages that the process has referenced in the last w seconds of virtual time (i.e., time during which the process was running on a processor)

    c. the last k different pages referenced by the process

    d. those pages on which a process made its last r instruction or data references

    e. those pages that the process has referenced in the last w seconds of virtual time with a frequency greater than f times per virtual second.

11.21 Give an example in which a working set page-replacement strategy would replace:

    a. the best possible page

    b. the worst possible page

11.22 One difficulty in implementing a working set memory management strategy is that when a process requests a new page, it is difficult to determine whether that process is transitioning to a new working set or is expanding its current working set. In the first case it is better for the memory manager to replace one of the process's pages; in the latter it is better for the memory manager to increase the process's page frame allocation. How might a memory manager decide which case is appropriate?

11.23 Suppose all active processes have established their working sets in main memory. As localities change, working sets could grow and main memory could become overcommitted, causing thrashing. Discuss the relative merits of each of the following preventive strategies for preventing this.

    a. Never initiate a new process if main memory is already 80 percent or more committed.

    b. Never initiate a new process if main memory is already 97 percent or more committed.

    c. When a new process is initiated, assign it a maximum working set size beyond which it will not be allowed to grow.

11.24 The interaction between the various components of an operating system is critical to achieving good performance. Discuss the interaction between the memory manager and the job initiator (i.e., admission scheduler) in a virtual-memory multiprogramming system. In particular, suppose the memory manager uses a working set memory-management approach.

11.25 Consider the following experiment and explain the observations.

    A process is run by itself on a paged machine. It begins execution with its first procedure page. As it runs, the pages it needs are demand-paged into available page frames. The number of available page frames far exceeds the number of pages in the process. But there is a dial external to the computer that allows a person to set the maximum number of page frames the process may use.

    Initially, the dial is set at two frames, and the program is run to completion. The dial is then set at three frames, and again the program is run to completion. This continues until the dial is eventually set to the number of available page frames in main memory, and the process is run for the last time. For each run, the run time of the process is recorded.

    Observations:

    As the dial is changed from two to three to four, the run times improve dramatically. From four to five to six, the run times still improve each time, but less dramatically. With the dial settings of seven and higher, the run time remains essentially constant.

11.26 An operating systems designer has proposed the "PD memory management strategy" that operates as follows. Exactly two page frames are allocated to each active process. These frames hold the most recently referenced procedure page, called the P-page, and the most recently referenced data page, called the D-page. When a page fault occurs, if the referenced page is a procedure page, the strategy replaces the P-page, and if the referenced page is a data page, the strategy replaces the D-page.

    The designer says that the chief virtue of the scheme is that it trivializes all aspects of memory management and thus has low overhead.

    a. How are each of the following memory management strategies handled under the PD scheme?

        i. fetch

        ii. placement

        iii. replacement

    b. In what circumstances would PD actually yield better results than working set memory management?

    c. In what circumstances would PD yield poor results?

11.27 Summarize the arguments for and against (1) small page sizes and (2) large page sizes.

11.28 The Multics system was originally designed to manage 64-word pages and 1024-word pages (the dual-page-size scheme was eventually abandoned).

    a. What factors do you suppose motivated this design decision?

    b. What effect does this dual-page-size approach have on memory management strategies?

11.29 Discuss the use of each of the following hardware features in virtual memory systems.

    a. dynamic address mapping mechanisms

    b. associative memory

    c. direct-mapped cache memory

    d. "page-referenced" bit

    e. "page-modified" bit

    f. "page-in-transit" bit (signifying that a page is currently being input to a particular page frame)

11.30 If programs are carefully organized in a paged system so that references are highly localized to small groups of pages, the resulting performance improvements can be impressive. Most programs today are being written in high-level languages, however, so the programmer does not generally have access to information rich enough to aid in producing programs with good organization. Because the path of execution a program will take cannot be predicted, it is difficult to know precisely which sections of code will be used intensively.

One hope for improving program organization is called dynamic program restructuring. Here, the operating system monitors the execution characteristics of a program, rearranging the code and data so that the more active items are placed together on pages.

    a. What execution characteristics of a large program should be monitored to facilitate dynamic program restructuring?

    b. How would a dynamic program restructuring mechanism use this information to make effective restructuring decisions?

11.31 The key to the proper and efficient operation of the page-fault-frequency (PFF) page-replacement strategy is the selection of the threshold interfault time values. Answer each of the following questions.

    a. What are the consequences of selecting too large an upper value?

    b. What are the consequences of selecting too small a lower value?

    c. Should the values remain fixed, or should they be adjusted dynamically?

    d. What criteria would you use to adjust the values dynamically?

11.32 Compare and contrast the page-fault-frequency (PFF) page-replacement strategy with the working set (WS) page-replacement strategy. Be sure to consider each of the following:

    a. execution-time overhead

    b. memory overhead for holding the information necessary to support the strategy

11.33 A possible weakness of the second-chance page-replacement strategy is that if the list of pages is short, then an active page that has just moved to the back of the list after having had its referenced bit set off could quickly move to the front of the list and be selected for replacement before its referenced bit is set on. Comment on this phenomenon. Is it an anomaly in second-chance page replacement? Defend your answer carefully.

11.34 Suppose a system is not currently thrashing. List as many factors as you can that might cause it to begin thrashing. What measures should the operating system take, once thrashing is detected? Can thrashing be absolutely prevented? If so, at what cost? If not, explain why not.

11.35 A system receives a series of page references in the following order: 1, 1, 3, 5, 2, 2, 6, 8, 7, 6, 2, 1, 5, 5, 5, 1, 4, 9, 7, 7. The system has five page frames. If all of the frames are initially empty, calculate the number of page faults using each of these algorithms:

    a. FIFO

    b. LRU

    c. second chance

    d. OPT

11.36 Should a process be penalized for generating excessive page faults?

11.37 Consider a process experiencing a large number of page faults. Describe the effect, if any, of increasing this process's scheduling priority.

Suggested Projects

11.38 Some types of processes perform well under certain page-replacement strategies and poorly under others. Discuss the possibility of implementing a memory manager that would dynamically determine a process's type and then select and use the appropriate page-replacement strategy for that process.

11.39 Suppose you are aware of the page-replacement strategy used by the multiuser timesharing system on which you are running. For each of the page-replacement strategies discussed in this chapter, what countermeasures might you take to force the operating system to give your process(es) favored treatment, when in fact the operating system might normally do otherwise? What measures might an operating system take to detect such processes and prevent them from obtaining such preferred treatment? Prepare a paper describing your solution.

Suggested Simulations

11.42 Develop a simulator program that will enable you to compare and contrast the operation of each of the page-replacement strategies discussed in this chapter. Your simulator needs to be concerned with transitions between pages in virtual space, but not with the instruction-by-instruction execution of programs. Assign a random but high probability to the event of remaining on the same page on which the previous instruction was executed. When page transitions occur, the probability of transferring to the next page (or the previous page) in virtual space should be higher than that of transferring to some remote page. Assume a moderately loaded system so that page-replacement decisions are common. Assume that the same replacement strategy applies to all processes on the system for a given run of the simulation. Your simulator should maintain statistics on the performance of each replacement strategy. Include features to enable you to fine-tune the simulator; i.e., you should be able to adjust the working set window size, the page-fault-frequency threshold values, and so on. When the simulator is completed, develop a new page-replacement strategy and compare the results to those of the other strategies in the text.

11.43 Develop a simulation program to investigate how changing the number of pages allocated to a process affects the number of page faults it experiences. Use reference strings that simulate spatial locality over both large and small regions of memory and temporal locality over both large and small periods. Also test the simulation using reference strings that are

essentially random. Describe the optimal page-replacement algorithm for each reference string. You might also wish to simulate the effect of multiprogramming by interleaving different reference patterns.

11.44 Develop a program that simulates page-fault-frequency (PFF) page replacement for a particular reference string. Determine the effect of changing the threshold values each time the program runs. Use reference strings that simulate spatial locality over both large and small regions of memory and temporal locality over both large and small periods. Also test the simulation using reference strings that are essentially random. Describe the optimal page-replacement algorithm for each reference string. Enhance your simulation so that it dynamically adjusts these values in response to the reference string it encounters.

11.45 Develop a program that compares page-fault-frequency (PFF) page replacement and working set (WS) page replacement for a particular reference string. Determine the effect of changing the threshold values for PFF and window size for WS each time the program runs. Use reference strings that simulate spatial locality over both large and small regions of memory and temporal locality over both large and small periods. Also test the simulation using reference strings that are essentially random. Describe the optimal page-replacement algorithm for each reference string.

11.40 Prepare a research paper that describes how Intel's Pentium 4 supports three different page sizes. How does the processor choose which size to use? Also, is there any communication between the TLBs?

11.41 Prepare a research paper on hardware support for the working set model.

Recommended Reading

Owing to its wide application in operating system design, virtual memory management is a rich field. Seminal papers, such as Denning's discussion of the working set model[88] and his summary of virtual memory concepts,[89] offer a clear presentation of the concerns in virtual memory management, most of which are still valid today. Fetch policies were discussed by Aho et al.[90] and further analyzed by Kaplan et al.[91]

Optimal page replacement was discussed by Belady,[92] who also discovered the FIFO anomaly.[93] Though common

algorithms such as FIFO and approximations to LRU can be found as pieces of some memory management algorithms, typically they are not used alone. More sophisticated algorithms involving graphs and coloring have been developed in the literature.[94, 95] Morris discusses the use of custom hardware to make working set storage management more efficient.[96]

The question of the most appropriate page size has been studied in the literature.[97, 98, 99] To meet different application needs, modern general-purpose processors have begun to support multiple page sizes.[100] Program behavior under paging continues to be the subject of many studies that seek to increase system throughput and performance by reducing the number of page faults.[101, 102, 103, 104, 105, 106, 107, 108] The bibliography for this chapter is located on our Web site at www.deitel.com/books/os3e/Bibliography.pdf.

Works Cited

1. Denning, P. J., "The Working Set Model for Program Behavior," *Communications of the ACM*, Vol. 11, No. 5, May 1968, pp. 323–333.

2. Belady, L. A., "A Study of Replacement Algorithms for Virtual Storage Computers," *IBM Systems Journal*, Vol. 5, No. 2, 1966, pp. 78–101.

3. Baer, J., and G. R. Sager, "Dynamic Improvement of Locality in Virtual Memory Systems," *IEEE Transactions on Software Engineering*, Vol. SE-1, March 1976, pp. 54–62.

4. Aho, A. V.; P. J. Denning; and J. D. Ullman, "Principles of Optimal Page Replacement," *Journal of the ACM*, Vol. 18, No. 1, January 1971, pp. 80–93.

5. Minsky, M. L., *Computation: Finite and Infinite Machines*, Englewood Cliffs, N.J.: Prentice-Hall, 1967.

6. Hennie, F., *Introduction to Computability*, Reading, MA: Addison-Wesley, 1977.

7. Buzen, J. P., "Fundamental Laws of Computer System Performance," *Proceedings of the 1976 ACM SIGMETRICS Conference on Computer Performance Modeling Measurement and Evaluation*, 1976, pp. 200–210.

8. Randell, B., and C. J. Kuehner, "Dynamic Storage Allocation Systems," *CACM*, Vol. 11, No. 5, May 1968, pp. 297–306.

9. Lorin, H., and H. Deitel, *Operating Systems*, Reading, MA: Addison-Wesley, 1981.

10. Trivedi, K. S., "Prepaging and Applications to Array Algorithms," *IEEE Transactions on Computers*, Vol. C-25, September 1976, pp. 915–921.

11. Smith, A. J., "Sequential Program Prefetching in Memory Hierarchies," *Computer*, Vol. 11, No. 12, December 1978, pp. 7–21.

12. Trivedi, K. S., "Prepaging and Applications to Array Algorithms," *IEEE Transactions on Computers*, Vol. C-25, September 1976, pp. 915–921.

13. Kaplan, S., et al., "Adaptive Caching for Demand Prepaging," *Proceedings of the Third International Symposium on Memory Management*, 2002, pp. 114–116.

14. Linux Source, <lxr.linux.no/source/mm/memory.c?v=2.5.56>, line 1010 (swapin_readahead).

15. Linux Source, <lxr.linux.no/source/mm/swap.c?v=2.6.0-test2>, line 100 (swap_setup).

16. Belady, L. A., "A Study of Replacement Algorithms for Virtual Storage Computers," *IBM Systems Journal*, Vol. 5, No. 2, 1966, pp. 78–101.

17. Denning, P. J., "Virtual Memory," *ACM Computing Surveys*, Vol. 2, No. 3, September 1970, pp. 153–189.

18. Mattson, R. L.; J. Gecsie; D. R. Slutz; and I. L. Traiger, "Evaluation Techniques for Storage Hierarchies," *IBM Systems Journal*, Vol. 9, No. 2, 1970, pp. 78–117.

19. Prieve, B. G., and R. S. Fabry, "VMIN—An Optimal Variable Space Page Replacement Algorithm," *Communications of the ACM*, Vol. 19, No. 5, May 1976, pp. 295–297.

20. Budzinski, R.; E. Davidson; W. Mayeda; and H. Stone, "DMIN: An Algorithm for Computing the Optimal Dynamic Allocation in a Virtual Memory Computer," *IEEE Transactions on Software Engineering*, Vol. SE-7, No. 1, January 1981, pp. 113–121.

21. Belady, L. A., and C. J. Kuehner, "Dynamic Space Sharing in Computer Systems," *Communications of the ACM*, Vol. 12, No. 5, May 1969, pp. 282–288.

22. Turner, R., and H. Levy, "Segmented FIFO Page Replacement," *Proceedings of the 1981 ACM SIGMETRICS Conference on Measurement and Modeling of Computer Systems*, 1981, pp. 48–51.

23. Babaoglu, O., and W. Joy, "Converting a Swap-Based System to Do Paging in an Architecture Lacking Page-Referenced Bits," *Proceedings of the Eighth Symposium on Operating Systems Principles, ACM*, Vol. 15, No. 5, December 1981, pp. 78–86.

24. Carr, R. W., *Virtual Memory Management*. UMI Research Press, 1984.

25. Borodin, A.; S. Irani; P. Raghavan; and B. Schieber, "Competitive Paging with Locality of Reference," in *Proceedings of the 23rd Annual ACM Symposium on Theory of Computing*, New Orleans, Louisiana, May 1991, pp. 249–259.

26. Irani, S.; A. Karlin; and S. Phillips, "Strongly Competitive Algorithms for Paging with Locality of Reference," *Proceedings of the Third Annual ACM-SIAM Symposium on Discrete Algorithms*, 1992, pp. 228–236.

27. Albers, S.; L. Favrholdt; and O. Giel, "On Paging with Locality of Reference," *Proceedings of the Thirty-Fourth Annual ACM Symposium on Theory of Computation*, 2002, pp. 258–267.

28. Fiat, A., and Z. Rosen, "Experimental Studies of Access Graph Based Heuristics: Beating the LRU Standard?" in *Proceedings of the Eighth Annual ACM-SIAM Symposium on Discrete Algorithms*, New Orleans, Louisiana, January 1997, pp. 63–72.

29. Fiat, A., and Z. Rosen, "Experimental Studies of Access Graph Based Heuristics: Beating the LRU Standard?" In *Proceedings of the Eighth Annual ACM-SIAM Symposium on Discrete Algorithms*, New Orleans, Louisiana, January 1997, pp. 63–72.

30. Denning, P. J., "The Working Set Model for Program Behavior," *Communications of the ACM*, Vol. 11, No. 5, May 1968, pp. 323–333.

31. Denning, P. J., "Resource Allocation in Multiprocess Computer Systems," Ph.D. Thesis, Report MAC-TR-50 M.I.T. Project MAC, May 1968.

32. Hatfield, D., "Experiments on Page Size, Program Access Patterns, and Virtual Memory Performance," *IBM Journal of Research and Development*, Vol. 15, No. 1, January 1972, pp. 58–62.

33. Denning, P. J., "The Working Set Model for Program Behavior," *Communications of the ACM*, Vol. 11, No. 5, May 1968, pp. 323–333.

34. Denning, P. J., "Working Sets Past and Present," *IEEE Transactions on Software Engineering*, Vol. SE-6, No. 1, January 1980, pp. 64–84.

35. Denning, P. J., "Thrashing: Its Causes and Preventions," *AFIPS Conference Proceedings*, Vol. 33, 1968 FJCC, pp. 915–922.

36. Rodriguez-Rosell, J., "Empirical Working Set Behavior," *Communications of the ACM*, Vol. 16, No. 9, 1973, pp. 556–560.

37. Fogel, M., "The VMOS Paging Algorithm: A Practical Implementation of the Working Set Model," *Operating Systems Review*, Vol. 8, No. 1, January 1974, pp. 8–16.

38. Levy, H. M., and P. H. Lipman, "Virtual Memory Management in the VAX/VMS Operating System," *Computer*, Vol. 15, No. 3, March 1982, pp. 35–41.

39. Kenah, L. J.; R. E. Goldenberg; and S. F. Bate, *VAX/VMS Internals and Data Structures*, Bedford, MA: Digital Press, 1988.

40. Bryant, P., "Predicting Working Set Sizes," *IBM Journal of Research and Development*, Vol. 19, No. 3, May 1975, pp. 221–229.

41. Morris, J. B., "Demand Paging through the Use of Working Sets on the Maniac II," *Communications of the ACM*, Vol. 15, No. 10, October 1972, pp. 867–872.

42. Chu, W. W., and H. Opderbeck, "The Page Fault Frequency Replacement Algorithm," *Proceedings AFIPS Fall Joint Computer Conference*, Vol. 41, No. 1, 1972, pp. 597–609.

43. Opderdeck, H., and W. W. Chu, "Performance of the Page Fault Frequency Algorithm in a Multiprogramming Environment," *Proceedings of IFIP Congress*, 1974, pp. 235–241.

44. Sadeh, E., "An Analysis of the Performance of the Page Fault Frequency (PFF) Replacement Algorithm," *Proceedings of the Fifth ACM Symposium on Operating Systems Principles*, November 1975, pp. 6–13.

45. Chu, W. W., and H. Opderbeck, "Program Behavior and the Page-Fault-Frequency Replacement Algorithm," *Computer*, Vol. 9, No. 11, November 1976, pp. 29–38.

46. Gupta, R. K., and M. A. Franklin, "Working Set and Page Fault Frequency Replacement Algorithms: A Performance Comparison," *IEEE Transactions on Computers*, Vol. C-27, August 1978, pp. 706–712.

47. Ganapathy, N., and C. Schimmel, "General Purpose Operating System Support for Multiple Page Sizes," *Proceedings of the USENIX Conference*, 1998.

48. Batson, A. P.; S. Ju; and D. Wood, "Measurements of Segment Size," *Communications of the ACM*, Vol. 13, No. 3, March 1970, pp. 155–159.

49. Chu, W. W., and H. Opderbeck, "Performance of Replacement Algorithms with Different Page Sizes," *Computer*, Vol. 7, No. 11, November 1974, pp. 14–21.

50. Denning, P. J., "Working Sets Past and Present," *IEEE Transactions on Software Engineering*, Vol. SE-6, No. 1, January 1980, pp. 64–84.

51. Ganapathy, N., and C. Schimmel, "General Purpose Operating System Support for Multiple Page Sizes," *Proceedings of the USENIX Conference*, 1998.

52. Talluri, M.; S. Kong; M. D. Hill; and D. A. Patterson, "Tradeoffs in Supporting Two Page Sizes," in *Proceedings of the 19th International Symposium on Computer Architecture*, Gold Coast, Australia, May 1992, pp. 415-424.

53. Talluri, M.; S. Kong; M. D. Hill; and D. A. Patterson, "Tradeoffs in Supporting Two Page Sizes," in *Proceedings of the 19th International Symposium on Computer Architecture*, Gold Coast, Australia, May 1992, pp. 415-424.

54. McNamee, D., "Flexible Physical Memory Management," Department of Computer Science and Engineering, University of Washington, September 1995.

55. Talluri, M.; S. Kong; M. D. Hill; and D. A. Patterson, "Tradeoffs in Supporting Two Page Sizes," in *Proceedings of the 19th International Symposium on Computer Architecture*, Gold Coast, Australia, May 1992, pp. 415–424.

56. *IA-32 Intel Architecture Software Developer's Manual*, Vol. 3, *System Programmer's Guide*, Intel, 2002, p. 3–19.

57. "UltraSPARC II Detailed View," Modified July 29, 2003, <www.sun.com/processors/UltraSPARC-II/details.html>.

58. *PowerPC Microprocessor Family: Programming Environments Manual for 64 and 32-Bit Microprocessors*, Version 2.0, IBM, June 10, 2003, pp. 258, 282.

59. Belady, L. A., "A Study of Replacement Algorithms for Virtual Storage Computers," *IBM Systems Journal*, Vol. 5, No. 2, 1966, pp. 78–101.

60. Fine, E. G.; C. W. Jackson; and P. V. McIsaac, "Dynamic Program Behavior under Paging," *ACM 21st National Conference Proceedings*, 1966, pp. 223–228.

61. Coffman, E. G., Jr., and L. C. Varian, "Further Experimental Data on the Behavior of Programs in a Paging Environment," *Communications of the ACM*, Vol. 11, No. 7, July 1968, pp. 471–474.

62. Freibergs, I. F., "The Dynamic Behavior of Programs," *Proceedings AFIPS Fall Joint Computer Conference*, Vol. 33, Part 2, 1968, pp. 1163–1167.

63. Hatfield, D., "Experiments on Page Size, Program Access Patterns, and Virtual Memory Performance," *IBM Journal of Research and Development*, Vol. 15, No. 1, January 1972, pp. 58–62.

64. Freibergs, I. F., "The Dynamic Behavior of Programs," *Proceedings AFIPS Fall Joint Computer Conference*, Vol. 33, Part 2, 1968, pp. 1163–1167.

65. Spirn, J. R., and P. J. Denning, "Experiments with Program Locality," *AFIPS Conference Proceedings*, Vol. 41, 1972 FJCC, pp. 611–621.

66. Morrison, J. E., "User Program Performance in Virtual Storage Systems," *IBM Systems Journal*, Vol. 12, No. 3, 1973, pp. 216–237.

67. Rodriguez-Rosell, J. "Empirical Working Set Behavior," *Communications of the ACM*, Vol. 16, No. 9, 1973, pp. 556–560.

68. Chu, W. W., and H. Opderbeck, "Performance of Replacement Algorithms with Different Page Sizes," *Computer*, Vol. 7, No. 11, November 1974, pp. 14–21.

69. Oliver, N. A., "Experimental Data on Page Replacement Algorithms," *Proceedings of AFIPS*, 1974 NCC 43, Montvale, N.J.: AFIPS Press, 1974, pp. 179–184.

70. Opderdeck, H., and W. W. Chu, "Performance of the Page Fault Frequency Algorithm in a Multiprogramming Environment," *Proceedings of IFIP Congress*, 1974, pp. 235–241.

71. Sadeh, E., "An Analysis of the Performance of the Page Fault Frequency (PFF) Replacement Algorithm," *Proceedings of the Fifth ACM Symposium on Operating Systems Principles*, November 1975, pp. 6–13.

72. Baer, J., and G. R. Sager, "Dynamic Improvement of Locality in Virtual Memory Systems," *IEEE Transactions on Software Engineering*, Vol. SE-1, March 1976, pp. 54–62.

73. Potier, D., "Analysis of Demand Paging Policies with Swapped Working Sets," *Proceedings of the Sixth ACM Symposium on Operating Systems Principles*, November 1977, pp. 125–131.

74. Franklin, M. A.; G. S. Graham; and R. K. Gupta, "Anomalies with Variable Partition Paging Algorithms," *Communications of the ACM*, Vol. 21, No. 3, March 1978, pp. 232–236.

75. Gupta, R. K., and M. A. Franklin, "Working Set and Page Fault Frequency Replacement Algorithms: A Performance Comparison," *IEEE Transactions on Computers*, Vol. C-27, August 1978, pp. 706–712.

76. Denning, P. J., "Working Sets Past and Present," *IEEE Transactions on Software Engineering*, Vol. SE-6, No. 1, January 1980, pp. 64–84.

77. Irani, S.; A. Karlin; and S. Phillips, "Strongly Competitive Algorithms for Paging with Locality of Reference," *Proceedings of the Third Annual ACM-SIAM Symposium on Discrete Algorithms*, 1992, pp. 228–236.

78. Glass, G., and Pei Cao, "Adaptive Page Replacement Based on Memory Reference Behavior," *Proceedings of the 1997 ACM SIGMETRICS International Conference on Measurement and Modeling of Computer Systems*, pp. 115–126, June 15–18, 1997, Seattle, Washington.

79. Ganapathy, N., and C. Schimmel, "General Purpose Operating System Support for Multiple Page Sizes," *Proceedings of the USENIX Conference*, 1998.

80. Albers, S.; L. Favrholdt; and O. Giel, "On Paging with Locality of Reference," *Proceedings of the 34th Annual ACM Symposium on Theory of Computation*, 2002, pp. 258–267.

81. Franklin, M. A.; G. S. Graham; and R. K. Gupta, "Anomalies with Variable Partition Paging Algorithms," *Communications of the ACM*, Vol. 21, No. 3, March 1978, pp. 232–236.

82. Glass, G., and Pei Cao, "Adaptive Page Replacement Based on Memory Reference Behavior," *Proceedings of the 1997 ACM SIGMETRICS International Conference on Measurement and Modeling of Computer Systems*, p.115-126, June 15-18, 1997, Seattle, Washington, United States.

83. Glass, G., and Pei Cao, "Adaptive Page Replacement Based on Memory Reference Behavior," *Proceedings of the 1997 ACM SIGMETRICS International Conference on Measurement and Modeling of Computer Systems*, p.115-126, June 15-18, 1997, Seattle, Washington, United States.

84. A. Arcangeli, "Le novita' nel Kernel Linux," December 7, 2001, <old.lwn.net/2001/1213/aa-vm-talk/mgp00001.html>.

85. A. Arcangeli, "Le novita' nel Kernel Linux," December 7, 2001, <old.lwn.net/2001/1213/aa-vm-talk/mgp00001.html>.

86. Linux kernel source code version 2.5.75, <www.kernel.org>.

87. Linux kernel source code version 2.5.75, <www.kernel.org>.

88. Denning, P. J., "The Working Set Model for Program Behavior," *Communications of the ACM*, Vol. 11, No. 5, May 1968, pp. 323–333.

89. Denning, P. J., "Virtual Memory," *ACM Computing Surveys*, Vol. 2, No. 3, September 1970, pp. 153–189.

90. Aho, A. V.; P. J. Denning; and J. D. Ullman, "Principles of Optimal Page Replacement," *Journal of the ACM*, Vol. 18, No. 1, January 1971, pp. 80–93.

91. Kaplan, S., et al., "Adaptive Caching for Demand Prepaging," *Proceedings of the Third International Symposium on Memory Management*, 2002, pp. 114–116.

92. Belady, L. A., "A Study of Replacement Algorithms for Virtual Storage Computers," *IBM Systems Journal*, Vol. 5, No. 2, 1966, pp. 78–101.

93. Belady, L. A., and C. J. Kuehner, "Dynamic Space Sharing in Computer Systems," *Communications of the ACM*, Vol. 12, No. 5, May 1969, pp. 282–288.

94. Irani, S.; A. Karlin; and S. Phillips, "Strongly Competitive Algorithms for Paging with Locality of Reference," *Proceedings of the Third Annual ACM-SIAM Symposium on Discrete Algorithms*, 1992, pp. 228–236.

95. Albers, S.; L. Favrholdt; and O. Giel, "On Paging with Locality of Reference," *Proceedings of the 34th Annual ACM Symposium on Theory of Computation*, 2002, pp. 258–267.

96. Morris, J. B., "Demand Paging through the Use of Working Sets on the Maniac II," *Communications of the ACM*, Vol. 15, No. 10, October 1972, pp. 867–872.

97. Batson, A. P.; S. Ju; and D. Wood, "Measurements of Segment Size," *Communications of the ACM*, Vol. 13, No. 3, March 1970, pp. 155–159.

98. Chu, W. W., and H. Opderbeck, "Performance of Replacement Algorithms with Different Page Sizes," *Computer*, Vol. 7, No. 11, November 1974, pp. 14–21.

99. Denning, P. J., "Working Sets Past and Present," *IEEE Transactions on Software Engineering*, Vol. SE-6, No. 1, January 1980, pp. 64–84.

100. Ganapathy, N., and C. Schimmel, "General Purpose Operating System Support for Multiple Page Sizes," *Proceedings of the USENIX Conference*, 1998.

101. Freibergs, I. F., "The Dynamic Behavior of Programs," *Proceedings AFIPS Fall Joint Computer Conference*, Vol. 33, Part 2, 1968, pp. 1163–1167.

102. Hatfield, D., "Experiments on Page Size, Program Access Patterns, and Virtual Memory Performance," *IBM Journal of Research and Development*, Vol. 15, No. 1, January 1972, pp. 58–62.

103. Morrison, J. E., "User Program Performance in Virtual Storage Systems," *IBM Systems Journal*, Vol. 12, No. 3, 1973, pp. 216–237.

104. Sadeh, E., "An Analysis of the Performance of the Page Fault Frequency (PFF) Replacement Algorithm," *Proceedings of the Fifth ACM Symposium on Operating Systems Principles*, November 1975, pp. 6–13.

105. Gupta, R. K., and M. A. Franklin, "Working Set and Page Fault Frequency Replacement Algorithms: A Performance Comparison," *IEEE Transactions on Computers*, Vol. C-27, August 1978, pp. 706–712.

106. Denning, P. J., "Working Sets Past and Present," *IEEE Transactions on Software Engineering*, Vol. SE-6, No. 1, January 1980, pp. 64–84.

107. Irani, S.; A. Karlin; and S. Phillips, "Strongly Competitive Algorithms for Paging with Locality of Reference," *Proceedings of the Third Annual ACM-SIAM Symposium on Discrete Algorithms*, 1992, pp. 228–236.

108. Albers, S.; L. Favrholdts; and O. Giel, "On Paging with Locality of Reference," *Proceedings of the 34th Annual ACM Symposium on Theory of Computation*, 2002, pp. 258–267.

Secondary Storage, Files and Databases

A fair request should be followed by the deed in silence.
—Dante—

Part 4

Computers store programs and vast amounts of data as files and databases on secondary storage devices. The following two chapters explain how operating systems organize and manage data on these devices. We explain the operation of the enormously popular moving-head disk storage device and show how to achieve maximum performance with seek and rotational optimization strategies. RAID (Redundant Arrays of Independent Disks) systems, which achieve high levels of performance and fault tolerance, are presented. We discuss file systems and examine how files are allocated on disk, how free space is managed and how file data is accessed and protected. File servers, and how they are used in distributed systems, are explained. We introduce database systems, and discuss relational databases and the kinds of operating systems services that support database systems.

'Tis in my memory lock'd, And you yourself shall keep the key of it.
—William Shakespeare—

The path of duty lies in what is near, and man seeks for it in what is remote.
    —Mencius—

A fair request should be followed by the deed in silence.
    —Dante—

... the latter, in search of the hard latent value with which it alone is concerned, sniffs round the mass as instinctively and unerringly as a dog suspicious of some buried bone.
    —William James—

Go where we will on the surface of things, men have been there before us.
    —Henry David Thoreau—

The wheel that squeaks the loudest is the one that gets the grease.
    —Josh Billings (Henry Wheeler Shaw)—

Chapter 12

Disk Performance Optimization

Objectives

After reading this chapter, you should understand:

- *how disk input/output is accomplished.*

- *the importance of optimizing disk performance.*

- *seek optimization and rotational optimization.*

- *various disk scheduling strategies.*

- *caching and buffering.*

- *other disk performance improvement techniques.*

- *key schemes for implementing redundant arrays of independent disks (RAID).*

Chapter Outline

Web Resources | Summary | Key Terms | Exercises | Recommended Reading | Works Cited

12.1 Introduction

In recent years, processor and main memory speeds have increased more rapidly than those of secondary storage devices, such as hard disks. As a result, processes requesting data on secondary storage tend to experience relatively long service delays. In this chapter, we discuss the characteristics of moving-head disk storage and consider how operating system designers can manage such devices to provide better service to processes. We explain how to optimize disk performance by reordering disk requests to increase throughput, decrease response times and reduce the variance of response times. We also discuss how operating systems reorganize data on disk and exploit buffers and caches to boost performance. Finally, we discuss Redundant Arrays of Independent Disks (RAIDs), which improve disk access times and fault tolerance by servicing requests using multiple disks at once.

12.2 Evolution of Secondary Storage

In early computers, persistent data was stored on punched cards and punched paper tape, which used the absence or presence of holes to represent bits of data.[1] Writing software and loading it into the computer using such media was both labor intensive and slow. The need for an inexpensive, rewritable persistent storage device led researchers to develop magnetic storage, which records bits of data by changing the direction of magnetization of regions on the medium's surface. To access data, a current-carrying device called a **read-write head** hovers above the medium as it moves. The head reads data by measuring how the magnetized medium changes the current; it "writes" data by using the current to change the magnetization on the medium. A challenge in building these devices is that the head must float extremely close to the medium's surface without touching it.

In 1951, the designers of **UNIVAC 1 (UNIVersal Automatic Computer)** introduced **magnetic tape storage**, which was both persistent and rewritable.[2] Magnetic tape is a form of sequential access storage, like audio or video cassettes. Such a medium is inappropriate for transaction-processing applications, where, for example, the system must be able to locate and update any record in a fraction of a second. To address this problem, IBM introduced the first commercial **hard disk drive**, the **RAMAC (Random Access Method of Accounting and Control)**, in 1957. Hard disk drives are random access (also called direct access) devices because they are not limited to accessing data sequentially. RAMAC's capacity totalled five megabytes, and its cost was $50,000; it was generally rented to installations for hundreds of dollars per month.[3, 4] Although hard disks provided better performance than magnetic tape storage, their high cost limited their use to large installations.

As the decades passed, hard drive capacity and performance increased, while costs declined. Typical personal computer hard disk capacity increased from hundreds of megabytes to several gigabytes during the 1990s while prices fell to a few pennies per megabyte. By 2003, hard drive capacity had exceeded 200GB and cost less than a dollar per gigabyte.[5] Due to mechanical constraints that we discuss in the next section, hard disk speeds have improved more slowly than their capacity. As processor speeds increased and applications consumed larger amounts of data, systems became increasingly I/O bound.[6]

Research in persistent storage technology continues to focus on increasing capacity and performance. Some solutions attempt to improve the performance of existing magnetic disk devices; others employ novel techniques and media.

Self Review

1. Why have many of today's systems become I/O bound?
2. Why are disks more appropriate than tapes for secondary storage?

Ans: **1)** Processor speeds have increased faster than hard disk speeds. **2)** Magnetic tape performs well only in an application in which data is accessed sequentially. In transaction-processing applications and in multiprogrammed systems, requests to access secondary storage from multiple processes can lead to essentially random access patterns. In this case, direct access storage devices are essential.

12.3 Characteristics of Moving-Head Disk Storage

Unlike main memory, which provides (nearly) uniform access speed to all of its contents, moving-head disk storage exhibits variable access speed that depends on the relative positions of the read-write head and the requested data. Figure 12.1 shows a simplified view of a moving-head disk.[7,8,9] Data is recorded on a series of

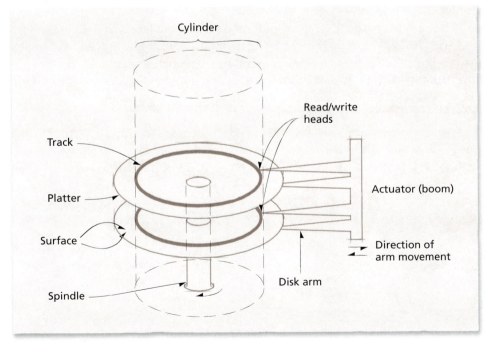

Figure 12.1 | *Schematic side view of a moving-head disk.*

magnetic disks, or **platters**, connected to a **spindle** that rotates at high speed (typically thousands of revolutions per minute[10]).

The data on each disk surface is accessed by a read-write head that is separated by a small amount of space from the surface (much smaller than a particle of smoke). For example, the disk in Fig. 12.1 contains two platters, each having two surfaces (top and bottom) and four read-write heads, one for each surface. A read-write head can access data immediately below (or above) it. Therefore, before data can be accessed, the portion of the disk surface at which the data is to be read (or written) must rotate until it is immediately below (or above) the read-write head. The time it takes for data to rotate from its current position to the beginning of the read-write head is called **rotational latency time**. A disk's average rotational latency is simply half the time it takes to complete one revolution. Most hard disks exhibit average rotational latency on the order of several milliseconds (Fig. 12.2).

As the platters spin, each read-write head sketches out a circular **track** of data on a disk surface. Each read-write head is positioned at the end of a **disk arm**, which is attached to an **actuator** (also called a **boom** or **moving-arm assembly**). The disk arm moves parallel to the surface of the disk. When the disk arm moves the read-write heads to a new position, a different vertical set of circular tracks, or **cylinder**, becomes accessible. The process of moving the disk arm to a new cylinder is called a **seek** operation.[11, 12] To locate small units of data, disks divide tracks into several **sectors**, often 512 bytes (Fig. 12.3).[13] Therefore, an operating system can locate a particular data item by specifying the head (which indicates which disk surface to read from), the cylinder (which indicates which track to read from), and the sector in which the data is located.

To access a particular record of data on a moving-head disk, several operations are usually necessary (Fig. 12.4). First, the disk arm must move to the appropriate cylinder (i.e., perform a **seek operation**). The time it takes for the head to move from its current cylinder to the one containing the data record is called the **seek time**. Then the portion of the disk on which the data record is stored must rotate until it is immediately under (or over) the read-write head. Then the record, which is of arbitrary size, must be made to spin by the read-write head. This is called **transmission time**. Because each of these operations involves mechanical movement, the total time a disk access takes is often an appreciable fraction of a second

Model (Environment)	Average Seek Time (ms)	Average Rotational Latency (ms)
Maxtor DiamondMax Plus 9 (High-end desktop)	9.3	4.2
WD Caviar (High-end desktop)	8.9	4.2
Toshiba MK8025GAS (Laptop)	12.0	7.14
WD Raptor (Enterprise)	5.2	2.99
Cheetah 15K.3 (Enterprise)	3.6	2.0

Figure 12.2 | *Hard disk track-to-track seek times and latency times.*[14, 15, 16, 17, 18]

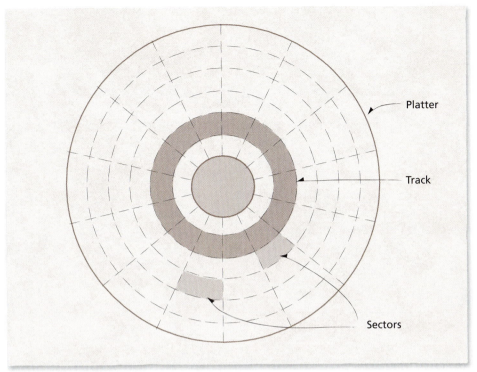

Figure 12.3 | *Schematic top view of a disk surface.*

(several milliseconds at least). During this same period of time, a processor can execute tens or even hundreds of millions of instructions.

Self Review

1. One focus of research in the field of storage technology is on increasing a hard disk's areal density (i.e., amount of data per unit area). How does increasing the areal density alone affect disk access times?
2. (T/F) Rotational latency is identical for every disk access.

Ans: **1)** As the amount of data per unit area increases, then the amount of data contained in each track increases. If a particular data record is located on a single track, the transmission time decreases compared to that for a lower areal density because more data can be read per unit time. **2)** False. The rotational latency depends on the location of the beginning of the requested sector relative to the position of the arm.

12.4 Why Disk Scheduling Is Necessary

Many processes can generate requests for reading and writing data on a disk simultaneously. Because these processes sometimes make requests faster than they can be serviced by the disk, waiting lines or queues build up to hold disk requests. Some early computing systems simply serviced these requests on a **first-come-first-served**

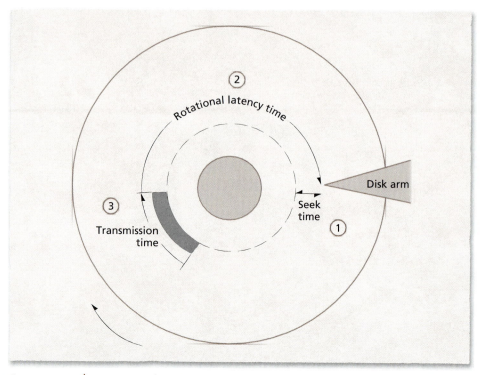

Figure 12.4 | Components of a disk access.

(FCFS) basis, in which the earliest arriving request is serviced first.[19] FCFS is a fair method of allocating service, but when the **request rate** (i.e., the **load**) becomes heavy, can be long waiting times.

FCFS exhibits a **random seek pattern** in which successive requests can cause time-consuming seeks from the innermost to the outermost cylinders. To reduce the time spent seeking records, it seems reasonable to order the request queue in some manner other than FCFS.[20] This process, called **disk scheduling**, can significantly improve throughput.[21]

Disk scheduling involves a careful examination of pending requests to determine the most efficient way to service them. A disk scheduler examines the positional relationships among waiting requests, then reorders the queue so that the requests will be serviced with minimum mechanical motion.

Because FCFS does not reorder requests, it is considered by many to be the simplest disk scheduling algorithm. The two most common types of scheduling are **seek optimization** and **rotational optimization.** Because seek times tend to be greater than latency times, most scheduling algorithms concentrate on minimizing total seek time for a set of requests. As the gap between rotational latency and seek times narrows, minimizing the rotational latency of a set of requests can also improve overall system performance, especially under heavy loads.

Self Review

1. Indicate which type of disk scheduling algorithm is most appropriate in the following scenarios: seek time is significantly greater than latency time, seek time and latency time are nearly equal, seek time is significantly shorter than latency time.
2. Which characteristics of disk geometry are most important to seek optimization and rotational optimization?

Ans: **1)** When seek time is significantly greater than latency time, access times are most affected by seek operations, so the system should implement seek optimization. When seek times and latency times are nearly equal, the system can benefit from combining both seek and rotational optimization techniques. If seek time is much shorter than latency time, then access times are most affected by latency time, so the system should concentrate on rotational optimization. Because today's processors are so fast, both forms of optimization should be employed to improve overall performance. **2)** Cylinder locations are most important when optimizing seek times, and sector locations are most important when optimizing latency times.

12.5 *Disk Scheduling Strategies*

A system's disk scheduling strategy depends on the system objectives, but most strategies are evaluated by the following criteria

- *throughput*—the number of requests serviced per unit time
- ***mean response time***—the average time spent waiting for a request to be serviced
- *variance of response times*—a measure of the predictability of response times. Each disk request should be serviced within an acceptable time period (i.e., the strategy should prevent indefinite postponement).

Clearly, a scheduling policy should attempt to maximize throughput and minimize the mean response time. Many scheduling policies attempt to accomplish these goals by minimizing the time spent performing lengthy seeks. When throughput and mean response time are optimized, average system performance improves, but individual requests may be delayed.

Variance measures how individual requests are serviced relative to average system performance. The smaller the variance, the more likely it is that most disk requests are serviced after waiting for a similar amount of time. Therefore, variance can be seen as a measure of fairness and of predictability. We desire a scheduling policy that minimizes variance (or at least keeps it at reasonable levels) to avoid erratic service times. In a business-critical system, such as a Web server, a high variance of response times could result in loss of sales if, for example, users' requests to purchase products were indefinitely postponed or suffer lengthy waits. In mission-critical systems, the result of such a delay could be catastrophic.

The following sections describe several common scheduling policies. We use the set of disk requests in Fig. 12.5 to demonstrate the result of each policy on an arbitrary series of requests. The arbitrary series of requests is intended to demonstrate how each policy orders disk requests, it does not necessarily indicate the relative performance of each policy in a real system. In the examples that follow, we

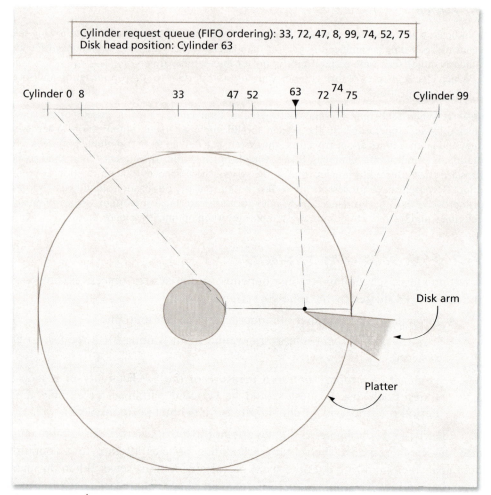

Figure 12.5 | Disk request pattern.

assume that the disk contains 100 cylinders, numbered 0–99, and that the read/write head is initially located at cylinder 63, unless stated otherwise. For simplicity, we also assume that the disk scheduler has already determined the cylinder number corresponding to each request.

Self Review

1. Why is minimizing the variance of response times an important goal in disk scheduling?
2. We mentioned that FCFS is a fair scheduling algorithm. Which of the criteria mentioned in this section most directly relates to fairness?

Ans: **1)** Otherwise the system could experience erratic response times. In a business-critical system, this could cause a company to lose customers; in a mission-critical system, it could put people's lives at risk. **2)** FCFS is fair in the sense that arriving requests cannot get in line ahead of waiting requests. This helps reduce the variance of response times.

12.5.1 First-Come-First-Served (FCFS) Disk Scheduling

FCFS scheduling uses a FIFO queue so that requests are serviced in the order in which they arrive.[22, 23, 24] FCFS is fair in the sense that a request's position in the queue is unaffected by arriving requests. This ensures that no request can be indefinitely postponed, but it also means that FCFS might perform a lengthy seek operation to service the next waiting request, even if another request in the queue is closer and can be serviced faster. Although this technique incurs low execution-time overhead, it can result in low throughput due to lengthy seeks.

When requests are uniformly distributed over the disk surfaces, FCFS scheduling leads to a random seek pattern because it ignores positional relationships among the pending requests (Fig. 12.6). This is acceptable when the load on a disk is light. However, as the load grows, FCFS tends to saturate (i.e., overwhelm) the device, and response times become large. The random seek pattern of FCFS results in low variance (because arriving requests cannot get ahead of waiting requests), but this is of little solace to the request sitting at the back of the disk queue while the disk arm rambles around in a torrid "disk dance."

Self Review

1. One measure of fairness is a low variance in response times. In this sense, is FCFS disk scheduling fair?
2. Can indefinite postponement occur with FCFS disk scheduling? Explain.

Ans: **1)** Yes, in this sense it is fair, but because no attempt is made to minimize response times, average response times tend to be longer than necessary. **2)** No. Indefinite postponement cannot occur because arriving requests can never be placed ahead of requests in the queue.

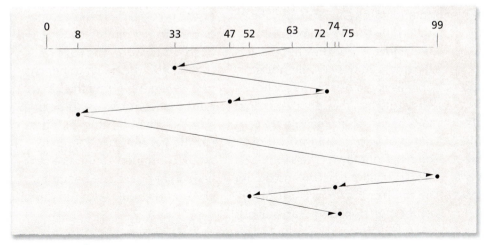

Figure 12.6 | Seek pattern under the FCFS strategy.

12.5.2 Shortest-Seek-Time-First (SSTF) Disk Scheduling

Shortest-seek-time-first (SSTF) scheduling next services the request that is closest to the read-write head's current cylinder (and thus incurs the shortest seek time), even if that is not the first one in the queue.[25, 26, 27, 28] SSTF does not ensure fairness and can lead to indefinite postponement because its seek pattern tends to be highly localized, which can lead to poor response times for requests to the innermost and outermost tracks (Fig. 12.7).

By reducing average seek times, SSTF achieves higher throughput rates than FCFS, and mean response times tend to be lower for moderate loads. One significant drawback is that it leads to higher variances of response times because of the discrimination against the outermost and innermost tracks; in the extreme, starvation (see Chapter 7) of requests far from the read/write heads could occur if new arrivals tend to be clustered near the middle cylinders. The high variance is acceptable in batch-processing systems, where throughput and mean response times are more important goals. However, SSTF is inappropriate for interactive systems, where the system must ensure that each user experiences prompt, predictable response times (see the Anecdote, Every Problem Has a Solution and Every Solution Has a Problem).

Every Problem Has a Solution and Every Solution Has a Problem

This true story happened to a neighbor who is in no way involved with the computer industry. Her husband left for work shortly before she did and he forgot to close the garage door that day. When she was leaving her home to go to work, she walked into her garage and found a skunk had pushed over a garbage pail and was sitting next to the door to her car merrily chomping on the garbage. She called the town's animal control department, but they had a backlog and said they would not be able to come out for a few hours. They told her, though, that skunks love bacon, so she should fry up a batch of bacon and throw it out on her front lawn. The skunk would smell the bacon and go out on the front lawn to eat it. She could then hop in her car, pull out of the garage, close the garage door with her remote control and head off to work. She followed that advice. But much to her chagrin, when she threw the bacon onto the front lawn, another skunk came out of the woods to eat the bacon, while the first skunk continued eating the garbage in her garage. She got to work a few hours late that day.

Lesson to operating systems designers: Always try to anticipate the consequences of your design choices.

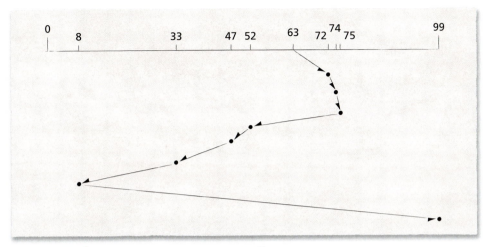

Figure 12.7 | Seek pattern under the SSTF strategy.

Self Review

1. To which scheduling algorithm from Chapter 8 is SSTF most similar? How do they differ?

2. Compare the overhead incurred by SSTF and FCFS.

Ans: **1)** SSTF is most similar to the shortest-process-first (SPF) strategy. Unlike SPF, SSTF does not require future knowledge (such as runtime-to-completion)—the request's location is sufficient information to determine which request to service next. **2)** Both FCFS and SSTF must maintain a queue of waiting requests in memory. Because FCFS maintains a simple FIFO queue, the execution time required to determine which request to service next is small and is unaffected by the number of requests in the queue. SSTF incurs overhead by either maintaining a sorted list (or lists) of requests or by searching the entire request queue for the appropriate request to service. In this case, the overhead incurred by SSTF is proportional to the number of requests in the queue (whereas the overhead of FCFS is constant—simply the amount of time it takes to insert entries at the back of the queue and remove them from the front).

12.5.3 SCAN Disk Scheduling

Denning developed the **SCAN** disk scheduling strategy to reduce the unfairness and variance of response times exhibited by SSTF.[29] SCAN chooses the request that requires the shortest seek distance in a **preferred direction** (Fig. 12.8). Thus, if the preferred direction is currently outward, the SCAN strategy chooses the shortest seek distance in the outward direction. SCAN does not change its preferred direction until it reaches the outermost cylinder or the innermost cylinder. In this sense, it is called the **elevator algorithm**, because an elevator continues in one direction servicing requests before reversing direction.

   SCAN behaves much like SSTF in terms of high throughput and good mean response times. However, because SCAN ensures that all requests in a given direction will be serviced before the requests in the opposite direction, it offers a lower variance of response times than SSTF. SCAN, like SSTF, is a cylinder-oriented strategy.

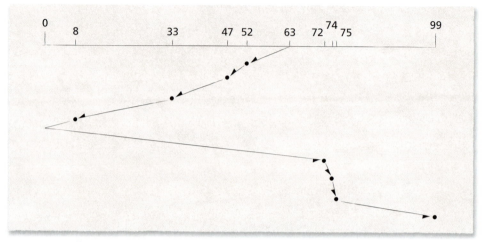

Figure 12.8 | *Seek pattern under the SCAN strategy.*

Because the read-write heads oscillate between opposite ends of each platter in SCAN, the outer tracks are visited less often than the midrange tracks, but generally more often than they would be using SSTF. Because arriving requests can be serviced before waiting requests, both SSTF and SCAN can suffer indefinite postponement.

Self Review

1. One limitation of the SCAN algorithm is that it might perform unnecessary seek operations. Indicate where this occurs in Fig. 12.8.
2. Can requests be indefinitely postponed under SCAN?

Ans: **1)** The unnecessary seek operation occurs after servicing the request to cylinder 8. Because there are no further requests in the preferred direction, it would be more efficient to change direction after servicing that request. We examine a modification to the SCAN strategy that addresses this limitation in Section 12.5.6, LOOK and C-LOOK Disk Scheduling. **2)** One could imagine a scenario in which processes issue continuous requests to the same cylinder, so that the read/write head becomes "stuck" on that cylinder.

12.5.4 C-SCAN Disk Scheduling

In the **Circular SCAN (C-SCAN)** modification to the SCAN disk scheduling strategy, the arm moves from the outer cylinder to the inner cylinder, servicing requests on a shortest-seek basis (Fig. 12.9). When the arm has completed its inward sweep, it jumps (without servicing requests) to the outermost cylinder, then resumes its inward sweep, processing requests. C-SCAN maintains high levels of throughput while further limiting variance of response times by avoiding discrimination against the innermost and outermost cylinders.[30, 31] As in SCAN, requests in C-SCAN can be indefinitely postponed if requests to the same cylinder continuously arrive (although this is less likely than with SCAN or SSTF). In the sections that follow, we discuss modifications to SCAN that address this problem.

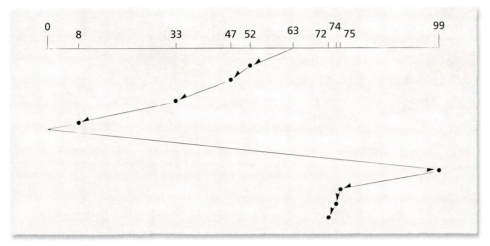

Figure 12.9 | *Seek pattern under the C-SCAN strategy.*

Simulation results in the literature indicate that the best disk scheduling policy might operate in two stages.[32] Under a light load, the SCAN policy is best. Under medium to heavy loads, C-SCAN and other adaptations to the SCAN policy yield better results. C-SCAN with rotational optimization handles heavy loading conditions effectively.[33]

Self Review

1. Which criteria of disk scheduling strategies does C-SCAN improve upon?
2. (T/F) C-SCAN incurs essentially the same execution-time overhead as SCAN.

Ans: **1)** C-SCAN reduces variance of response times compared to SCAN because it is less biased against the outermost and innermost cylinders. **2)** False. C-SCAN incurs overhead over SCAN when it finishes its inward sweep and skips requests while moving the head to the outermost cylinder.

12.5.5 FSCAN and N-Step SCAN Disk Scheduling

The **FSCAN** and **N-Step SCAN** modifications to the SCAN strategy eliminate the possibility of indefinitely postponing requests.[34, 35] FSCAN uses the SCAN strategy to service only those requests waiting when a particular sweep begins (the "F" stands for "freezing" the request queue at a certain time). Requests arriving during a sweep are grouped together and ordered for optimum service during the return sweep (Fig. 12.10).

N-Step SCAN services the first n requests in the queue using the SCAN strategy. When the sweep is complete, the next n requests are serviced. Arriving requests are placed at the end of the request queue (Fig. 12.11). N-Step SCAN can be tuned by varying the value for n. When $n = 1$, N-Step SCAN degenerates to FCFS. As n approaches infinity, N-Step SCAN degenerates to SCAN.

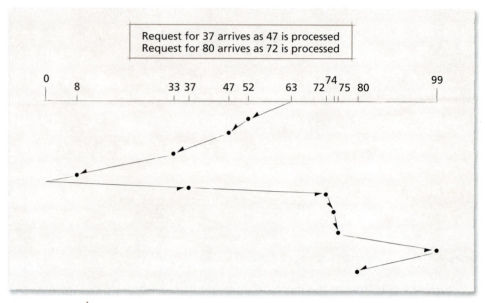

Figure 12.10 | *Seek pattern under the FSCAN strategy.*

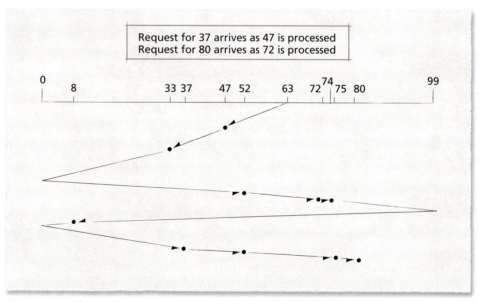

Figure 12.11 | *Seek pattern under the N-Step SCAN strategy (n = 3).*

FSCAN and *N*-Step SCAN offer good performance due to high throughput and low mean response times. Because they prevent indefinite postponement, their distinguishing characteristic is a lower variance of response times than with SSTF and SCAN, especially when requests would be indefinitely postponed under the latter two strategies.

Self Review

1. Explain how FSCAN can lead to lower throughput than SCAN.
2. Compare and contrast FSCAN and *N*-Step SCAN.

Ans: 1) If a request to a cylinder in the preferred direction arrives after FSCAN freezes the queue, the disk head will pass by the cylinder without servicing the request until the next pass. 2) Both strategies use SCAN to service a portion of the request queue to prevent indefinite postponement. FSCAN services all the requests in the queue before beginning a sweep in a new preferred direction; *N*-Step SCAN services only the next *n* requests in the queue.

12.5.6 LOOK and C-LOOK Disk Scheduling

The **LOOK** variation of the SCAN strategy "looks" ahead to the end of the current sweep to determine the next request to service. If there are no more requests in the current direction, LOOK changes the preferred direction and begins the next sweep (Fig. 12.12). In this sense, it is appropriate to call this the elevator algorithm, because an elevator continues in one direction until it reaches the last request in that direction, then reverses direction. This strategy eliminates unnecessary seek operations exhibited by other variations of the SCAN strategy (compare the left side of Fig. 12.12 to the corresponding location in Fig. 12.8).

    Circular LOOK (C-LOOK) variation of the LOOK strategy uses the same technique as C-SCAN to reduce the bias against requests located at the extreme ends of the platters. When there are no more requests on a current inward sweep, the read/write head moves to the request closest to the outer cylinder (without servicing requests in between) and begins the next sweep. The C-LOOK policy is characterized by a potentially lower variance of response times compared to LOOK and high throughput (although generally lower than LOOK).[36] Figure 12.13 summarizes each of the disk scheduling strategies we have discussed.

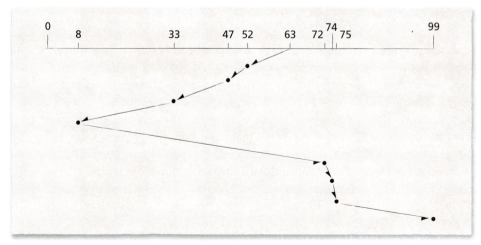

Figure 12.12 | *Seek pattern under the LOOK strategy.*

Strategy	Description
FCFS	Services requests in the order in which they arrive.
SSTF	Services the request that results in the shortest seek distance first.
SCAN	Head sweeps back and forth across the disk, servicing requests according to SSTF in a preferred direction.
C-SCAN	Head sweeps inward across the disk, servicing requests according to SSTF in the preferred (inward) direction. Upon reaching the innermost track, the head jumps to the outermost track and resumes servicing requests on the next inward pass.
FSCAN	Requests are serviced the same as SCAN, except newly arriving requests are postponed until the next sweep. Avoids indefinite postponement.
N-Step SCAN	Services requests as in FSCAN, but services only *n* requests per sweep. Avoids indefinite postponement.
LOOK	Same as SCAN except the head changes direction upon reaching the last request in the preferred direction.
C-LOOK	Same as C-SCAN except the head stops after servicing the last request in the preferred direction, then services the request to the cylinder nearest the opposite side of the disk.

Figure 12.13 | *Seek optimization strategies summary.*

Self Review

1. Why does C-LOOK typically exhibit throughput lower than that of LOOK?

2. Under C-LOOK, in what order would the requests presented in Fig. 12.5 be serviced?

Ans: **1)** The time spent seeking from one end of the platter to the furthest request from the position of the read/write head at the end of the sweep increases the mean response time, which decreases throughput. **2)** 52, 47, 33, 8, 99, 75, 74, 72

12.6 Rotational Optimization

Because the dominant component of access time in early hard drives was seek time, research focused on seek optimization. However, today's hard disks exhibit seek times and average latencies that are of the same order of magnitude, meaning that rotational optimization can often improve performance.[37] Processes that access data sequentially tend to access entire tracks of data and thus do not benefit much from rotational optimization. However, when there are numerous requests to small pieces of data randomly distributed throughout the disk's cylinders, rotational optimization can improve performance significantly. In this section, we discuss how to combine seek and rotational optimization strategies to achieve maximum performance.

12.6.1 SLTF Scheduling

Once the disk arm arrives at a particular cylinder, there might be many requests pending on the various tracks of that cylinder. The **shortest-latency-time-first**

(SLTF) strategy examines all of these requests and services the one with the shortest rotational delay first (Fig. 12.14). This strategy has been shown to be close to the theoretical optimum and is relatively easy to implement.[38] Rotational optimization is sometimes referred to as **sector queuing**; requests are queued by sector position around the disk, and the nearest sectors are serviced first.

Self Review

1. Why is sector queuing easy to implement?
2. Is rotational optimization appropriate for today's hard disks? Why?

Ans: **1)** Sector queuing determines the best access pattern for sectors on a track. Assuming that sectors are at fixed locations and that the disk can spin only in one direction, sector queuing simply is a sorting problem. **2)** Yes, rotational optimization is appropriate. Today's hard disks exhibit seek times and average latencies that are of the same order of magnitude.

12.6.2 SPTF and SATF Scheduling

The **shortest-positioning-time-first (SPTF)** strategy next services the request that requires the shortest **positioning time**, which is the sum of the seek time and rotational latency time. Like SSTF, SPTF results in high throughput and a low mean

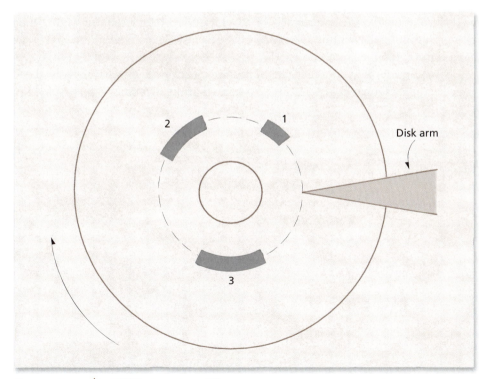

Figure 12.14 | *SLTF scheduling. The requests will be serviced in the indicated order regardless of the order in which they arrived.*

response time, and it can also indefinitely postpone requests to the innermost and outermost cylinders.[39]

A variation of SPTF is the **shortest-access-time-first (SATF)** strategy, which next services the request that requires the shortest access time (i.e., positioning time plus transmission time). SATF exhibits higher throughput than SPTF, but large requests can be indefinitely postponed by a series of smaller requests, and requests to the innermost or outermost cylinders can be indefinitely postponed by requests to midrange cylinders. Both SPTF and SATF can improve performance by implementing the "look-ahead" mechanisms described in Section 12.5.6.[40]

Figure 12.15 demonstrates the difference between SPTF and SATF. In Fig. 12.15(a), the disk receives two requests for data records of the same size, A and B, that are located on adjacent cylinders. Data record A is located in the same cylinder as the read/write head, but approximately one-half rotation away from the read/write head. Data record B is near the read/write head but is located on an adjacent cylinder. In this case, the transmission time is identical for A and B because A and B are the same size, so SATF reduces to SPTF. Thus, for this particular disk, both SATF and SPTF would service the request for data record B first, because the disk takes less time to perform a single-cylinder seek operation than to rotate the platter 180 degrees. If the seek time is adequately small, the disk can service the request for B, then reposition the head to service the request for A within one disk rotation. On the contrary, SSTF would service A first, requiring more than one revolution of the platter to service both requests. Thus, SATF and SPTF can increase throughput compared to SSTF.

Now consider that data record B consumes an entire track whereas A is stored in one sector, as shown in Fig. 12.15(b). Assume that the location of the first byte of

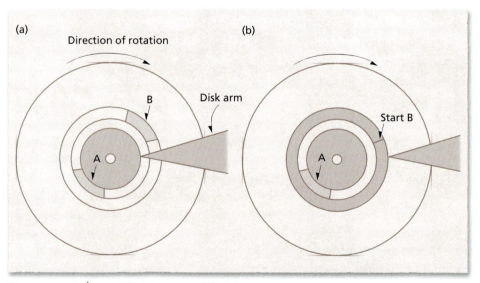

Figure 12.15 | SPTF (a) and SATF (b) disk scheduling examples.

each record is the same as in the previous example. In this case, SPTF would service requests in exactly the same order as in the previous example, because the positioning times are the same. However, SATF would service request A first, because request A requires one half of a rotation plus nominal transmission time, whereas request B requires a nominal rotational latency time plus a transmission time equal to the time required for the platter to complete one revolution.

SPTF and SATF require knowledge of disk characteristics including latency time, track-to-track seek times and relative locations of sectors. Unfortunately, many of today's hard drives expose misleading geometry. For example, many disks hide error-checking and correcting data from the operating system (so that it cannot be unintentionally or maliciously modified), so consecutively numbered sectors may not precisely correspond to contiguous physical locations on disk. On some systems, when bad sectors are detected, alternate ones are assigned. For example, if sector 15 becomes unusable, the disk might send its requests to a reserved sector other than 14 or 16. These alternate sectors can be widely dispersed over the disk surfaces, causing seeks where none might actually be expected.

These features, such as using alternate sectors, which improve data integrity, tend to counteract efforts to improve disk performance using scheduling strategies, because the disk provides the operating system with incomplete or misleading positional information.[41] Although some architectures and hard disks provide commands to retrieve the real geometry of the disk, this feature is not supported by all disks. Other hard disk architectural features complicate disk scheduling strategies; for more information, see the links provided in the Web Resources section at the end of the chapter.

A straightforward performance enhancement technique is to decrease rotational latency by increasing the rotational speed of the disk. However, designers have encountered significant problems when increasing the rotations per minute (RPM) of a hard disk. Faster-rotating disks consume greater amounts of energy (a key concern on laptop computers with limited battery power), radiate more heat, make more noise and require more costly mechanical and electrical mechanisms to control them.[42] Given these and other problems, RPM speed has increased only modestly (only a few percent a year over the past decade) to approximately 5,400 to 7,200 RPM for PCs and 10,000–15,000 RPM for servers and high-end machines.[43]

Self Review

1. What is the difference between the SPTF and SATF algorithms? Why would a designer choose one over the other?
2. What factors prevent operating systems from obtaining accurate knowledge of hard disk geometries?

Ans: **1)** SPTF services the request that it can begin accessing within the shortest period of time. SATF services the request that it can complete accessing within the shortest time. Although SATF has higher throughput, it favors requests to small amounts of data over requests to large amounts of data. Thus, SATF is more appropriate for systems that issue many requests for small data records. SPTF is more appropriate for systems that generate requests for both large and small data records, because it does not consider the size of a request. **2)** Some types of hard disk hide information, such as the location of error-protection data and bad sectors.

12.7 System Considerations

When is disk scheduling useful? When might it degrade performance? These questions must be answered in the context of the overall system. The sections that follow discuss several considerations that might influence a designer's decisions.

Storage as Limiting Resource

When disk storage proves to be a **bottleneck**, some designers recommend adding more disks to the system (see the Operating Systems Thinking feature, Saturation and Bottlenecks). This does not always solve the problem, because the bottleneck could be caused by a large request load on a relatively small number of disks. When this situation is detected, disk scheduling may be used as a means of improving performance and eliminating the bottleneck.

System Load

Disk scheduling might not be useful in a batch-processing system with a relatively low degree of multiprogramming. Scheduling becomes more effective as the randomness of multiprogramming increases, which increases the system load and leads to erratic disk request patterns. For example, file servers in local area networks can receive requests from hundreds of users, which normally results in the kind of ran-

Operating Systems Thinking

Saturation and Bottlenecks

Operating systems often manage hardware and software configurations. When a system is performing poorly, you might be inclined to speak of the problem "in the whole"—the "whole system" is performing poorly. In fact, its often the case that only one or a few resources have become saturated, i.e., they have reached their capacity and cannot service requests any faster. Such resources are called bottlenecks. Locating bottlenecks and dealing with them by adding resources in only one or a few areas of the system, could result in overall system improvement at a relatively modest cost. Systems should be built in ways that make it easy to locate bottlenecks. Chapter 14 presents a thorough treatment of performance issues, including saturation and bottlenecks.

dom request patterns that are best serviced using disk scheduling. Similarly, **online transaction processing (OLTP)** systems, such as Web and database servers, typically receive many disk requests to randomly distributed locations containing small amounts of data (e.g., HTML files and database records). Research has shown that disk scheduling algorithms such as C-LOOK and SATF (with look-ahead) can improve performance in this type of environment.[44, 45]

Nonuniform Request Distributions

Much of the analytical work in the literature assumes that request distributions are uniform. Conclusions based on the assumption of uniformity may be invalid on systems whose request distributions are not uniformly distributed over the disk surfaces. **Nonuniform request distributions** are common in certain situations, and their consequences have been investigated.[46] In one study, Lynch determined that the vast majority of disk references are to the same cylinder as the immediately preceding reference.[47]

One common cause of highly localized nonuniform request distributions is the use of large sequential files on dedicated disks. When an operating system allocates space for the adjacent records of a user's sequential file, it usually places adjacent records on the same track. When a track is full, additional records are placed on adjacent tracks within the same cylinder; when a cylinder is full, additional records are placed on adjacent cylinders. Thus requests for successive records in a sequential file often cause no seeking at all. When needed, seeks are short, because they are usually to immediately adjacent cylinders. Obviously, an FCFS disk scheduling policy would be adequate in this situation. In fact, overhead incurred in more complex scheduling strategies might actually result in degraded performance.

File Organization Techniques

As we discuss in Chapter 13, File and Database Systems, sophisticated file organization techniques can cause a proliferation of requests with large seek times. In some cases, file data retrieval may involve reference to a master index, reference to a cylinder index, and then location of the actual record, a process that could incur several seek delays. Because the master index and cylinder index are normally stored on disk (but separate from the main data area), these seeks can be costly. Such file organization techniques are convenient for the applications designer but can degrade performance.

Self Review

1. Why do many systems exhibit nonuniform request distributions?
2. Why does disk scheduling become more effective as system load increases?

Ans: **1)** File data is often stored and accessed sequentially, so a request to a particular cylinder is likely to be followed by a request to the same cylinder, or to an adjacent cylinder. **2)** As system load increases, request patterns tend to become more random, which could lead to substantial seek activity. Disk scheduling improves performance by reducing the number of wasteful seek operations.

12.8 Caching and Buffering

Many systems maintain a **disk cache buffer**, which is a region of main memory that the operating system reserves for disk data. In one context, the reserved memory acts as a cache, allowing processes quick access to data that would otherwise need to be fetched from disk. The reserved memory also acts as a buffer, allowing the operating system to delay writing modified data until the disk experiences a light load or until the disk head is in a favorable position to improve I/O performance. For example, an operating system may delay writing modified data to disk to allow time for multiple requests to contiguous locations to enqueue, so that they can be serviced with one I/O request.

The disk cache buffer presents several challenges to operating system designers. Because the size of the disk cache must be limited to allow enough memory for active processes, the designer must implement some replacement strategy. The cache-replacement question is similar to the page-replacement question, and designers use many of the same heuristics. Most commonly, designers choose a strategy that replaces the least-recently used item in the disk cache buffer.

A second concern arises because disk caching can lead to inconsistencies. Disk cache buffers are maintained in volatile memory, so if the system fails or loses power while modified data is in the cache buffer, those changes are lost. To safeguard data against such problems, the contents of the disk cache buffer are periodically flushed to the hard disk; this reduces the probability of data loss if the system crashes.

A system that employs **write-back caching** does not write modified data to disk immediately. Instead, the cache is written to disk periodically, enabling the operating system to batch multiple I/Os that are serviced using a single request, which can improve system performance. A system that employs **write-through caching** writes data both to the disk cache buffer and to disk each time cached data is modified. This technique prevents the system from batching requests, but reduces the possibility of inconsistent data in the event of a system crash.[48]

Many of today's hard disk drives maintain an independent high-speed buffer cache (often called an on-board cache) of several megabytes.[49] If requested data is stored in the on-board cache, the hard drive can deliver the data at or near the speed of main memory. Additionally, some hard disk interface controllers (e.g., SCSI and RAID controllers) maintain their own buffer caches separate from main memory. When requested data is not located in the main memory buffer cache, on-board buffer caches improve I/O performance by servicing requests without performing relatively slow mechanical operations.[50] However, one study showed that disks that include on-board caches typically use replacement strategies that adapt poorly to random request patterns, leading to suboptimal performance.[51] It is also likely that on-board buffer caches and main memory buffer caches will contain the same data, which leads to inefficient resource utilization.

Self Review

1. What are the trade-offs when selecting the size of the system's disk cache buffer?
2. State when write-back caching and write-through caching are appropriate, and why.

Ans: **1)** A small disk cache buffer allows enough memory for active processes, but is likely to contain only a small portion of requested data, so many requests must be serviced using the disk. A small cache buffer also limits the number of write requests that can be buffered simultaneously, which means that data will need to be flushed frequently. A large cache buffer reduces the number of I/O operations the system performs, but can reduce the memory available to store process instructions and data, which could lead to thrashing. **2)** Write-back caching enables the system to batch modified data to reduce the number of disk requests, but does not prevent loss of buffered data in the event of a power or system failure. Thus, write-back caching is appropriate for systems where performance is more important than reliability (e.g., some supercomputers). Because write-through caching immediately sends modified data to disk, it is appropriate for systems that cannot tolerate loss of data (e.g., database systems).

12.9 Other Disk Performance Techniques

We have considered optimizing the performance of rotational storage devices using scheduling policies and optimizing system architecture. In this section we analyze several other disk performance optimization techniques.

As files and records are added and deleted, a disk's data tends to become dispersed throughout the disk, or **fragmented**. Even sequential files, which one would expect to exhibit low access latency, become severely fragmented, which increases access time. Many operating systems provide **defragmentation** (or **disk reorganization**) programs that can be used periodically to reorganize files. This allows the consecutive records of sequential files to be placed contiguously on the disk. Systems that use noncircular variations of the SCAN strategy tend to visit the midrange cylinders more frequently than the outermost ones. For these systems, frequently referenced items can be placed on the midrange tracks to reduce average access times.

Also, operating systems can place files that are likely to be modified near free space to reduce future fragmentation—as the files grow, new data can be placed in the adjacent free space instead of elsewhere on disk. Some operating systems allow users to **partition** a disk into separate areas. Files are then restricted to these partitions, so fragmentation is reduced.[52] However, partitions can lead to wasted memory similar to internal fragmentation in paged virtual memory systems.

Some systems use **data compression** techniques to reduce the amount of space required by information on disk (see the Operating Systems Thinking feature, Compression and Decompression). Data compression decreases the size of a record by replacing common bit patterns with shorter ones. Therefore, compressed data consumes less space without losing information. This can ultimately reduce the number of seeks, latency times and transmission times. However, it can require substantial processor time to compress the data and later to decompress it to make it available to applications.

Systems that need to access certain information quickly benefit from placing multiple copies of that data at different positions on the disk (see the Operating

Systems Thinking feature, Redundancy). This can substantially reduce seek and rotation times, but the redundant copies can consume a significant portion of the disk. This technique is more useful for read-only data, or for data that changes nominally. Frequent changes degrade the performance of the scheme, because each of the copies must be updated regularly; another danger is that a system crash could leave the multiple copies in an inconsistent state.

In a multiple-disk system in which only one disk request may be serviced at a time, performance can be improved by replicating frequently referenced data on separate drives, which enables higher throughput. Some RAID techniques, discussed in Section 12.10, implement this concept.

Additionally, record **blocking** can yield significant performance improvements. When contiguous records are read or written as a single block, only a single seek is required; if these records are read or written individually, then one seek per record could be required.

Systems that monitor disk access attempts can try to keep frequently accessed data in a favorable position in the memory hierarchy (i.e., in main or cache memory) while transferring infrequently referenced data to slower storage (such as a hard disk or compact disk). This yields an overall performance improvement, but it might provide poor response to users of infrequently accessed data. This is unacceptable if the infrequently accessed data belongs to high-priority applications. It might also be helpful to dedicate a disk to a single high-performance application.

In many environments, there are often short periods when there are no waiting requests for the disk to service and the disk arm sits idle, waiting for the next

Operating Systems Thinking

Compression and Decompression

An excellent use of abundant, cheap processor power is compression and decompression of data. On hard disks, this helps reduce the space required to store files. It is also important in network transmissions. The world's networking infrastructure bandwidths tend to increase much slower than processor power does. The capital investment in networking infrastructure, especially transmission lines, is enormous. It simply is not feasible to keep upgrading the entire world's networking infrastructure every time a faster transmission technology becomes available. This means that the ratio of processor speeds to transmission speeds will tend to increase over time, with processor power remaining relatively cheap compared to transmission bandwidth. Compression enables messages to be shrunk for transmission over relatively slow networks, essentially increasing network throughput. Compressed messages must be decompressed at the receiving end to be usable. Operating systems will increasingly include compression and decompression mechanisms.

request.[53] If the disk arm is currently at one edge of the disk, it is likely that a long seek will be required to process the next request. By contrast, if the disk arm is in the center of the disk, or at some **hot spot** of disk activity, the average seek time will be less. Moving the disk arm to a location that will minimize the next seek is known as **disk arm anticipation**.[54]

Disk arm anticipation can be useful in environments where the disk request patterns of processes exhibit locality. For best results, the arm should move to the hot spot of disk activity (rather than simply the center of the disk). When processes issue requests to sequential locations on disk, however, moving the head to the center of the disk after servicing each request can lead to excessive seek activity. In this case, disk arm anticipation might degrade performance.[55]

Self Review

1. How do defragmentation and disk reorganization improve performance?
2. Why might data compression techniques become more practical in the future?
3. Under what conditions is it inappropriate to move the read/write head to the center of the disk during idle periods?
4. Why does multiprogramming complicate efforts to anticipate the next request?

Ans: **1)** Defragmentation places file data in contiguous blocks on disk, which improves access times by reducing seek activity when accessing sequential data. Disk reorganization places frequently or heavily used data in favorable locations on disk (e.g., midrange tracks for noncircular scheduling strategies) to reduce average seek times. **2)** There is a growing gap between processor speed and disk speed. The reduced access time due to data compression

Operating Systems Thinking

Redundancy

We will see many examples of redundancy being employed in operating systems for a variety of reasons. A common use of redundancy is creating backups to ensure that if one copy of information is lost, it can be restored. A multiprocessing system can have a pool of identical processors available to assign to processes and threads as needed. Such redundancy has several advantages. Although the system could still function with only a single processor, having the extra processors yields better performance because the processors can all work in parallel. It is also effective for fault tolerance—if one processor fails, the system can continue operating. RAID reduces access times to data on disks by placing redundant copies of that data on separate disks that may function in parallel. We can also place redundant copies of the data on different regions of the same disk, so that we can minimize the movement of the read/write head and the amount of rotational movement of the disk before the data becomes accessible, thus increasing performance. Redundancy, of course, has its price. The resources costs money and the hardware and the software to support them can become more complex. This is yet another example of trade-offs in operating systems.

might outweigh the overhead incurred by compressing and decompressing data. **3)** If programs generally exhibit spatial locality, and the area of locality is not at the center of the disk, then moving the head to the center of the disk during each idle period requires a wasteful seek to return to the disk's hot spot when requests resume. **4)** A multiprogrammed system can service requests from multiple concurrent processes, which may lead to several hot spots on the disk. In this case, it is difficult to determine which, if any, hot spot the read/write head should move to when it is idle.

12.10 Redundant Arrays of Independent Disks (RAID)

RAID (Redundant Arrays of Independent Disks) is a family of techniques that use multiple disks (called an array of disks) that are organized to provide high performance and/or reliability. RAID was originally proposed by Patterson, Gibson and Katz; in their paper, the "I" in RAID denotes "Inexpensive," but this has been changed to "Independent" because many RAID systems employ expensive, high-performance disks.[56]

Patterson et al. recognized that processor speed, main memory size and secondary storage size were increasing rapidly while I/O transfer rates (particularly in hard disks) were growing at a much slower pace. Computer systems were becoming increasingly I/O bound—they could not service I/O requests as quickly as they were generated, and could not transfer data as quickly as it was capable of being consumed. To improve throughput and transfer rates, the authors recommended creating arrays of disks that could be accessed simultaneously.[57]

12.10.1 RAID Overview

In their original paper, Patterson et al. proposed five different organizations, or **levels**, of disk arrays.[58] Each RAID level is characterized by **data striping** and **redundancy**. Data striping entails dividing storage into fixed-size blocks called **strips**. Contiguous strips of a file are typically placed on separate disks so that requests for file data can be serviced using multiple disks at once, which improves access times. A **stripe** consists of the set of strips at the same location on each disk in the array. In Fig. 12.16, a portion of a file is divided into four strips of identical length, each on a different disk in the array. Because each strip is placed at the same location on each disk, the four strips form one stripe. Striping distributes a system's data across multiple disks, which enables higher throughput than a single-disk system because data can be accessed from multiple disks simultaneously.

When selecting a strip size, the system designer should consider the average size of disk requests. Smaller strip sizes, also called **fine-grained strips**, tend to spread file data across several disks. Fine-grained strips can reduce each request's access time and increase transfer rates, because multiple disks simultaneously retrieve portions of the requested data. While these disks service a request, they cannot be used to service other requests in the system's request queue.

Large strip sizes, also called **coarse-grained strips**, enable some files to fit entirely within one strip. In this case, some requests can be serviced by only a por-

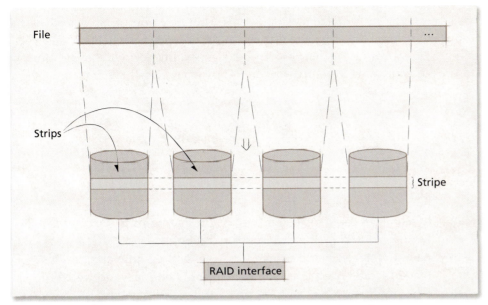

Figure 12.16 | Strips and stripe created from a single file in RAID systems.

tion of the disks in the array, so it is more likely that multiple requests can be serviced simultaneously. However, smaller requests are serviced by one disk at a time, which reduces transfer rates for individual requests compared to fine-grained strips.

Systems such as Web servers and databases, which typically access multiple small records simultaneously, benefit from coarse-grained strips, because several I/O operations can occur concurrently. Systems such as supercomputers that require fast access to a small number of records benefit from fine-grained strips, which provide high transfer rates for individual requests.[59]

The increased transfer rate provided by RAID systems have a price. As the number of disks in the array increases, so does the likelihood of disk failure. For example, if the **mean-time-to-failure (MTTF)** of a single disk is 200,000 hours (roughly 23 years), the MTTF for a 100-disk array would be 2,000 hours (about three months).[60] If one disk in an array fails, any files containing strips on that disk are lost. In business-critical and mission-critical systems, this loss of data could be catastrophic (see the Operating Systems Thinking feature, Mission-Critical Systems). As a result, most RAID systems store information that enables the system to recover from errors, a technique called redundancy. RAID systems use redundancy to provide fault tolerance (i.e., to sustain failures without loss of data; see the Operating Systems Thinking feature, Fault Tolerance).

A straightforward way to provide redundancy is **disk mirroring**, a technique that places each unique data item on two disks. A drawback to mirroring is that only half of the storage capacity of the array can be used to store unique data. As we discuss in the sections that follow, some RAID levels employ a more sophisticated approach that reduces this overhead.[61]

To realize the improved performance of striped disks with redundancy, the system must efficiently divide files into strips, form files from strips, determine the locations of strips in the array and implement the redundancy scheme. Using a general-purpose processor for this purpose can significantly degrade the performance of processes competing for processor time. Thus, many RAID systems contain spe-

Operating Systems Thinking

Mission-Critical Systems

There are systems where the cost of failure is so high that enormous investment must be made in resources to ensure that the systems do not fail and perform well enough to meet their requirements. Such systems are often called mission-critical or business-critical systems. If an air traffic control system were to fail, human lives could be lost. If the New York Stock Exchange systems were to fail, the world's stock markets could crash. Thus, operating systems must be designed to meet the unique reliability and performance requirements of particular applications systems. In some cases, the operating system must make extraordinary resource commitments to particular applications, far greater than what general-purpose applications would normally receive. In the Linux and Windows XP case studies, we will see, for example, that real-time applications can be given special treatment.

Operating Systems Thinking

Fault Tolerance

Computer systems are employed in many key aspects of our personal and professional lives. We depend on computers not to fail. Fault tolerant systems are designed to keep operating, even in the presence of problems that might typically cause system failure. Redundancy is a popular means of achieving fault tolerance—if a component fails, another "equal" component takes over. It is costly to design fault tolerance into a system, but the costs can be small compared to the costs of system failure, especially in business-critical or mission-critical systems. We discuss issues of fault tolerance in many parts of the book, with particular emphasis on these techniques in our treatments of RAID, multiprocessing in Chapter 15, computer networking in Chapter 16, distributed systems in Chapter 17, distributed file systems in Chapter 18 and computer security in Chapter 19.

cial-purpose hardware called a **RAID controller** to perform such operations quickly. RAID controllers also simplify RAID implementation by enabling the operating system simply to pass read and write requests to the RAID controller, which then performs striping and maintains redundant information as necessary. However, RAID controllers can significantly increase the cost of a RAID system.

A systems designer choosing to adopt a RAID system must balance cost, performance and reliability. Typically, improving one characteristic worsens the other two. For example, to reduce the cost of the RAID system, one might reduce the number of disks in the array. A smaller number of disks often reduces performance by limiting transfer rates and can reduce reliability by limiting the array's capacity to store redundant information.

Self Review

1. Explain when fine-grained and coarse-grained strips are appropriate in RAID systems.
2. Why should RAID systems provide some degree of fault tolerance?

Ans: **1)** Fine-grained strips are appropriate for systems requiring individual I/O operations to be performed quickly. Coarse-grained strips are appropriate for systems that must fulfill many I/O requests simultaneously. **2)** The greater the number of disks in an array, the more likely it is that one of them will fail. Thus, RAID systems should provide additional fault tolerance.

12.10.2 Level 0 (Striping)

RAID level 0 uses a striped disk array with no redundancy. Figure 12.17 illustrates a RAID 0 configuration containing four striped disks. If an application requests to read data stored in strips A and B of the array data from both strips can be read simultaneously, because they are on separate disks (D_1 and D_2). Further, the RAID controller can simultaneously service a write request to strip K, located on disk D_3.

RAID level 0 was not one of the five original levels of RAID and is not considered a "true" RAID level because it does not provide fault tolerance. If one of the disks fails, all the data in the array that depend on the failed disk are lost. Depending on the array's strip size, all data stored in the array could become unusable with the loss of a single disk.[62]

RAID level 0 is simple to implement and does not incur storage overhead to provide fault tolerance. Further, a RAID 0 system with n disks performs reads and writes at a rate up to n times greater than that of a single disk. RAID 0 systems are appropriate for systems where high performance and low cost are more important than reliability.[63, 64]

Self Review

1. Why is RAID level 0 not considered a "true" RAID level?
2. What are the benefits of RAID level 0?

Ans: **1)** RAID level 0 does not provide fault tolerance through redundancy. **2)** RAID level 0 provides high transfer rates, is simple to implement and does not incur storage overhead to provide fault tolerance.

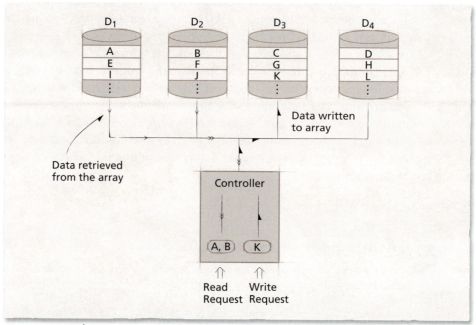

Figure 12.17 | *RAID level 0 (striping).*

12.10.3 Level 1 (Mirroring)

RAID level 1 employs disk **mirroring** (also called **shadowing**) to provide redundancy, so each disk in the array is duplicated. Stripes are not implemented in level 1, reducing both hardware complexity and system performance. Figure 12.18 displays a RAID 1 array. Notice that disks D_1 and D_2 contain the same data, and disks D_3 and D_4 contain the same data. Level 1 arrays permit multiple I/O operations to be serviced simultaneously. For example, in Fig. 12.18, requests to read data stored on blocks A and B can be serviced concurrently by each disk of the mirrored pair, D_1 and D_2. To ensure consistency, modified data must be written to a pair of mirrored disks, so multiple write requests to the same mirrored pair must be serviced one at a time. Note that in Fig. 12.18, read requests for blocks A and B can be serviced by disks D_1 and D_2 while a write request to block I is serviced by disks D_3 and D_4.

   Although RAID level 1 provides the highest degree of fault tolerance of any RAID level, only half of the array's disk capacity can be used to store unique data. Thus, the cost per unit storage in a RAID 1 array is twice that in a RAID 0 array. Because each block of data is stored on a pair of disks, the system can sustain multiple disk failures without loss of data. For example, if disk D_3 fails, the system can continue to operate using the mirrored data on D_4. A new disk can subsequently be installed to replace D_3. Recovering and rebuilding data from a failed disk, called **data regeneration**, entails copying the redundant data from the mirrored disk. However, if both disks in a mirrored pair fail, their data is unrecoverable.[65]

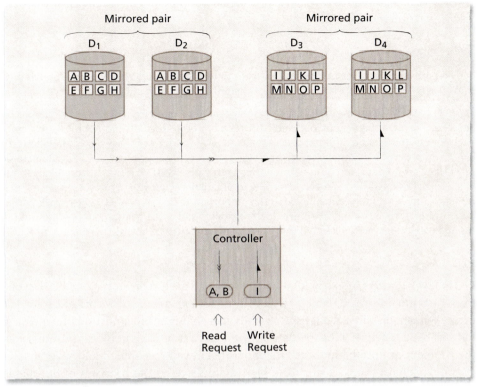

Figure 12.18 | *RAID level 1 (mirroring).*

Some RAID systems contain "spare" disks (also called **hot spare disks** or **online spares**) that can replace failed disks, much like a spare tire for an automobile. Some systems also feature hot swappable disk drives that can be replaced while the system is online, which allows data regeneration to occur as the system runs—necessary in high-availability environments such as online transaction-processing systems.[66]

Level 1 arrays are characterized by the following advantages and disadvantages:

- High storage overhead—only half of the array's storage capacity can be used to store unique data.

- Fast average read transfer rates—two different read requests to data stored in the same mirrored pair can be serviced simultaneously.

- Slower average write transfer rates—multiple write requests to a mirrored pair must be performed one at a time. However, write requests to different mirrored pairs can be performed simultaneously.

- High fault tolerance—RAID level 1 can sustain multiple drive failures without loss of data or availability. It provides the highest degree of fault tolerance among the most popular RAID levels.

- High cost—the storage overhead increases cost per unit capacity.

RAID 1 is best suited for environments in which reliability is a higher priority than cost or performance.[67]

Self Review

1. Compare and contrast RAID 0 and RAID 1 in terms of cost, performance and reliability.
2. Why is RAID 1 appropriate for business- and mission-critical systems?

Ans: **1)** RAID 0 costs less than RAID 1 when capacity is held fixed. Read and write performance is dependent on system load and strip sizes, but both RAID 0 and RAID 1 can service read requests for data on different disks simultaneously. RAID 0 can service write requests for data on different disks simultaneously; RAID 1 can perform write requests simultaneously only if they are to data stored on different mirrored pairs. RAID 0 is much more likely to fail than a single disk; RAID 1 is much less likely to fail than a single disk. **2)** In these systems, performance, reliability and availability are more important than cost. RAID 1 offers high performance for read requests and extremely high reliability, and it can continue to operate without loss of data if one or more disks fail (but at reduced performance levels).

12.10.4 Level 2 (Bit-Level Hamming ECC Parity)

RAID level 2 arrays are striped at the bit level, so each strip stores one bit. Level 2 arrays are not mirrored, which reduces the storage overhead incurred by level 1 arrays. When a disk in a RAID system fails, it is analogous to a portion of a message that has been corrupted during data transfer, such as during network transmission. The problem of unreliable transmission has been well researched and several solutions have been proposed (for examples of solutions to the problem of unreliable transmission, see `www.eccpage.com`). RAID level 2 borrows from a technique that is commonly implemented in memory modules called **Hamming error-correcting codes (Hamming ECCs)**, which uses parity bits to check for errors in data transmitted from disks and to correct them, if possible.[68]

Parity bits can be calculated as follows. Consider an array in which each stripe stores four bits. When the RAID system receives a request to write the data 0110 to a stripe, it determines the **parity** of the sum of the bits, i.e., whether the sum is odd or even. In this case, the parity sum (2) is even, so the system writes the stripe to the corresponding four data disks of the array and a 0, representing even parity, to a parity disk. [*Note*: Although data is striped at the bit level, most requests correspond to data in multiple stripes that can be written at once to improve performance.] RAID systems generally place parity bits on a separate disk, so that reads and writes to each stripe can be performed by all disks simultaneously. When the stripe is next accessed, the system reads the stripe and its corresponding parity bit, calculates the stripe's parity and compares it to the value read from the parity disk. If a disk error causes the third bit of the stripe to change from 1 to 0 (i.e., the stripe stores 0100), the stripe will have odd parity, and the system can detect the error by comparing the parity to the value stored on the parity disk.

A limitation of this particular form of parity is that it cannot detect an even number of errors. For example, if both the second and third bits change from 1 to 0 (i.e., the stripe stores 0000), the stripe will still have even parity. Further, this technique does not enable the system to determine which, if any, bits have errors.

Hamming error-correcting codes (Hamming ECCs) use a more sophisticated approach to enable the system to detect up to two errors, correct up to one error and determine the location of the error in a stripe (the algorithm behind Hamming ECC parity generation is beyond the scope of this book; it is described at www2.rad.com/networks/1994/err_con/hamming.htm). The size of Hamming ECC codes, and thus the number of parity disks, increases according to the logarithm of the number of data disks. For example, an array of 10 data disks requires four parity disks; an array of 25 data disks requires five parity disks.[69] Thus, level 2 arrays containing a large number of disks incur significantly less storage overhead than level 1 arrays.

Figure 12.19 illustrates a level 2 array containing four data disks and three parity disks. Stripe A is composed of the strips A_0–A_3, which occupy the first strips on the data disks D_1–D_4. Stripe A's corresponding Hamming ECC is composed of the bits A_x–A_z, which occupy the first strips on the parity disks P_1–P_3.

Consider a write request to store data in strips A_0, A_1, A_2, A_3, B_0 and B_1. In this case, because the Hamming ECC code is computed for each write, the controller must write stripes A and B, and the Hamming ECC code for each stripe. Even

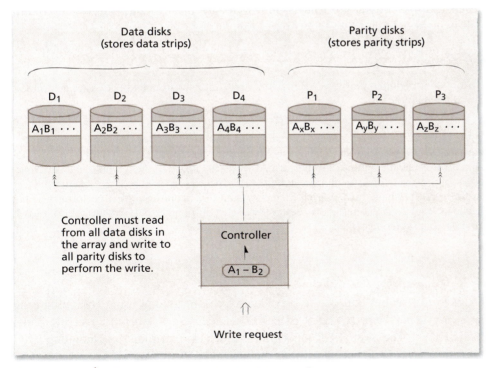

Figure 12.19 | RAID level 2 (bit-level ECC parity).

though only two of the four bits in stripe B are modified, the entire B stripe must be read and its Hamming ECC code calculated and written to disk. This process, which degrades performance because the system must access the array twice for each write, is called a **read–modify–write cycle**.

Although the ECC disks reduce the overhead associated with redundancy when compared to mirroring, they can degrade performance because multiple requests cannot be serviced simultaneously. Each read request requires the array to access all disks, compute the ECC, and compare it with the value retrieved from the parity disks. Some systems reduce this bottleneck by computing parity information only for write requests. However, the system must access all disks to maintain parity information when performing a write, meaning that write requests must be serviced one at a time.

One way to increase the maximum number of concurrent reads and writes using a RAID level 2 array is to divide the system's disks into several small RAID level 2 arrays. Unfortunately, this technique increases storage overhead, because smaller groups require a a larger ratio of parity disks to data disks. For example, a 32-data-disk level 2 array requires six parity disks. If the system were divided into eight groups of four data disks, the resulting arrays would require 24 parity disks.[70]

The primary reason that RAID 2 is not implemented in today's systems is that modern disk drives maintain Hamming ECCs or comparable fault-tolerance mechanisms transparently in hardware. Almost all current SCSI and IDE drives contain built-in error detection and disk monitoring.[71]

Self Review

1. How does dividing a large RAID level 2 array into subgroups affect cost, performance and reliability?
2. Why is RAID level 2 rarely implemented?

Ans: **1)** Dividing a level 2 array into subgroups improves performance because multiple requests can be serviced simultaneously. Subgroups do not affect reliability, because the same error-checking routines are performed for each subgroup. As a whole, the subgroups require more parity disks than a single large array, which increases cost. **2)** Because modern hardware devices have built-in error detection and disk monitoring that perform the same checks as level 2 arrays, designers seek a lower-cost and higher-performance alternative to providing fault tolerance.

12.10.5 Level 3 (Bit-Level XOR ECC Parity)

RAID level 3 stripes data at the bit or byte level. Instead of using Hamming ECC for parity generation, RAID 3 uses **XOR (exclusive or) error-correcting codes (XOR ECCs)**. The XOR ECC algorithm is much simpler than the Hamming ECC. It is called XOR ECC because it uses the logical XOR operation:

$$(a \ \text{XOR} \ b) = 0 \ \text{ when } a \text{ and } b \text{ are both zero or both one;}$$
$$= 1 \ \text{ otherwise.}$$

It follows that $(a \text{ XOR } (b \text{ XOR } c)) = 0$ only when an even number of the arguments are 1 or 0. RAID level 3 exploits this fact to perform nested XOR operations on each byte to generate its XOR ECC. For example, consider stripe A in Fig. 12.20. Let $A_0 = 1$, $A_1 = 0$, $A_2 = 0$ and $A_3 = 1$; or, more succinctly, $A = 1001$. The system uses nested XOR operations to compute A's parity. If the number of 1's or 0's is even, the parity bit, A_p, is 0; otherwise, A_p is 1. In this case there are two 1's, so $A_p = 0$. If the system stripes at the byte level, the XOR ECC is calculated for each bit, so each parity strip stores 8 bits.

XOR ECC uses only one disk to hold parity information, regardless of the size of the array. Note that, unlike Hamming ECCs, XOR ECCs do not enable the system to detect which bit contains erroneous data. This is acceptable, because most parity errors in RAID systems result from the failure of an entire disk, which is easy to detect. For example, assume that disk D_2 has failed (Fig. 12.20). In this case, when the system attempts to read stripe A, it finds $A = 1x01$ (where x is the unknown bit) and $A_p = 0$. Because $A_p = 0$, stripe A must have stored an even number of 1's. Thus, the system can determine that $A_2 = 0$ and regenerate the lost data. This technique can be applied to recover from any single data disk failure; if the parity disk fails, recovery entails recomputing the parity from the data disks.[72]

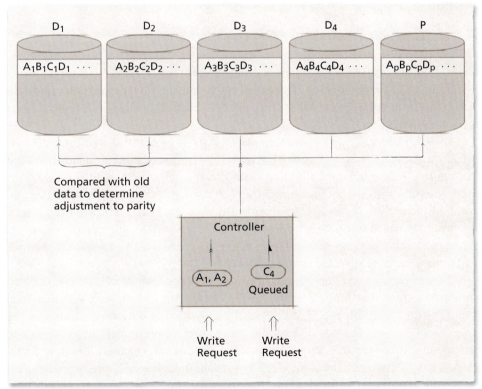

Figure 12.20 | *RAID level 3 (bit-level, single parity disk).*

Due to fine-grained striping, most reads require access to the entire array. Further, due to parity generation, only one write can be performed at a time. Similar to RAID level 2, this yields high transfer rates when reading and writing large files, but, in general, only one request can be serviced at a time.[73] The primary advantage of RAID level 3 is that it is easy to implement, offers reliability similar to RAID level 2, and entails significantly lower storage overhead than RAID level 2.[74]

Self Review

1. Compare and contrast RAID levels 2 and 3.
2. Why is XOR ECC parity, instead of Hamming ECC parity, sufficient for most RAID systems?

Ans: **1)** Both RAID levels 2 and 3 provide fault tolerance using parity to reduce the overhead of mirroring, both use dedicated parity disks and, in general, both cannot service multiple requests simultaneously. RAID level 2 incurs greater storage overhead than level 3. **2)** Although XOR ECCs cannot determine which disk has failed, the system can easily determine this, because failed disks do not respond to requests. Therefore, the system can regenerate one failed disk using a single parity disk.

12.10.6 Level 4 (Block-Level XOR ECC Parity)

RAID level 4 systems are striped using fixed-size blocks (typically much larger than a byte) and use XOR ECC to generate parity data, which requires a single parity disk. Figure 12.21 depicts a RAID 4 array. Note that the only organizational difference between level 3 and level 4 arrays is that each data strip in a level 4 array stores more data.

In RAID levels 2 and 3, each request's data is typically stored on each data disk in the array. However, because RAID level 4 permits coarse-grained strips, it is possible that requested data might be stored on a small fraction of the disks in the array. Thus, if parity is not determined for each read, the system can potentially service multiple read requests simultaneously. Because the ECC codes are used primarily for data regeneration as opposed to error checking and correcting, many systems eliminate the parity calculation when reads are performed so that multiple read requests can be serviced simultaneously.[75]

When servicing a write request, however, the system must update parity information to ensure that no data is lost in the event of a disk failure. When coarse-grained strips are employed, write requests rarely modify data on each disk in the array. Again, accessing each disk in the array to compute parity information can lead to substantial overhead. Fortunately, the system can calculate the new parity bit, A_p', simply by using the data block before modification, A_d, the modified data block, A_d', and the corresponding parity block on disk, A_p:

$$A_p' = (A_d \text{ XOR } A_d') \text{ XOR } A_p.[76]$$

You will be asked to prove this relation in the exercises. This technique eliminates wasteful disk I/O operations, because writes do not require access to the
entire array. However, because each write request must update the parity disk,
write requests must be performed one at a time, creating a write bottleneck. As we
discuss in the next section, RAID level 5 removes the write bottleneck, so RAID
level 4 is rarely implemented.[77, 78, 79, 80]

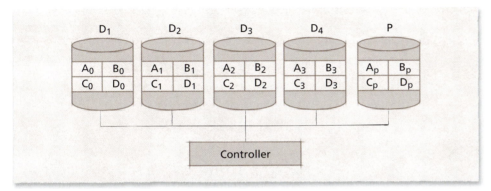

Figure 12.21 | RAID level 4 (block-level parity).

Self Review

1. How does RAID level 4 offer higher performance than RAID level 3?
2. Why can RAID level 4 perform only one write at a time?

Ans: **1)** RAID level 4 permits coarse-grained striping, which enables multiple read requests
to be performed simultaneously and reduces the number of disks accessed for each write
request. **2)** RAID level 4 uses one parity disk that must be accessed to update parity information each time data in the array is modified.

12.10.7 Level 5 (Block-Level Distributed XOR ECC Parity)

RAID level 5 arrays are striped at the block level and use XOR ECC parity, but
parity blocks are distributed throughout the array of disks (Fig. 12.22).[81] Note that
in Fig. 12.22, the parity for the first stripe is placed on disk D_5, while the parity for
the second stripe is placed on disk D_4. Because parity blocks are distributed across
many disks, multiple parity strips can be accessed simultaneously, removing the
write bottleneck for many requests. For example, consider how RAID level 5 services write requests to strips A_1 and C_2. The controller accesses disk D_2 to write
strip A_1 and disk D_5 to update the corresponding parity block, A_p. The controller
can simultaneously access disk D_4 to write strip C_2 and access disk D_3 to update its
corresponding parity block, C_p.
    Although RAID level 5 improves write performance by distributing parity,
level 5 arrays must still perform a read–modify–write cycle for each write request,

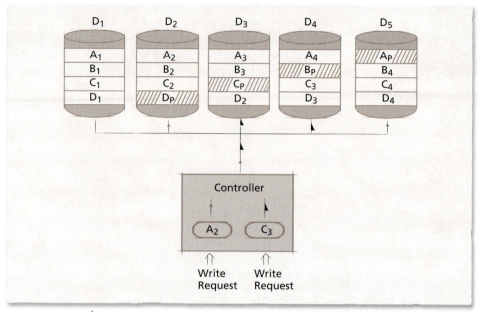

Figure 12.22 | *RAID level 5 (block-level distributed parity).*

requiring at least four I/O operations to service each write request. If a system consistently writes small amounts of data, the number of costly I/O operations can significantly degrade performance.[82]

Several methods have been developed to address this issue. Caching recently accessed data and parity blocks can reduce the number of I/O operations in the read–modify–write cycle. **Parity logging** can improve RAID level 5 performance by storing the difference between the old parity and new parity (called the **update image**) in memory instead of performing a read–modify–write cycle. Because a single update image can store parity information corresponding to multiple write requests, the system can reduce I/O overhead by performing a single update to the parity block in the array after several writes have been performed.[83] A similar performance-enhancing technique is called **AFRAID** (**A Frequently Redundant Array of Independent Disks**). Instead of performing the read–modify–write cycle with every write, parity data generation is deferred to times when system load is light. This can greatly improve performance in environments characterized by intermittent bursts of requests generating small writes.[84]

Although RAID level 5 increases performance relative to RAID levels 2–4, it is complex to implement, which increases its cost. Also, because parity is distributed throughout the array, data regeneration is more complicated than in other RAID levels.[85] Despite its limitations, RAID level 5 is frequently adopted due to its effective balance of performance, cost and reliability. Level 5 arrays are considered general-purpose arrays and are often found in file and application servers, enterprise resource planning and other business systems.[86] Figure 12.23 compares the six levels of RAID presented in this chapter.

RAID Level	Read Concurrency	Write Concurrency	Redundancy	Striping Level
0	Yes	Yes	None	Block
1	Yes	No	Mirroring	None
2	No	No	Hamming ECC parity	Bit
3	No	No	XOR ECC parity	Bit/byte
4	Yes	No	XOR ECC parity	Block
5	Yes	Yes	Distributed XOR ECC parity	Block

Figure 12.23 | *Comparison of RAID levels 0-5.*

Other RAID Levels

Many other RAID levels exist, each borrowing from one or more of the RAID levels we discussed in the preceding sections.[87] Unfortunately, there is no standard naming convention for RAID levels, which often leads to confusing or misleading names. Some of the more notable RAID levels include

- RAID level 6—extends RAID 5 by distributing two parity blocks per stripe for higher reliability upon disk failure.[88]
- RAID level 0+1—a set of striped disks (level 0) whose image is mirrored to a second set of disks (level 1).
- RAID level 10—a set of mirrored data (level 1) that is striped across another set of disks (level 0), requiring a minimum of four disks.

Other RAID arrays that have been developed include levels 0+3, 0+5, 50, 1+5, 51 and 53.[89] RAID level 7, which is a high-performance, high-cost solution, is a proprietary technique whose name is trademarked by the Storage Computer Corporation.[90]

Self Review

1. How does RAID level 5 address the write bottleneck in RAID level 4?
2. What techniques have been implemented to improve performance in RAID systems that receive many requests for small writes?

Ans: **1)** RAID level 5 distributes parity information across all disks in the array so that multiple write operations can be performed simultaneously. **2)** Caching recently accessed data improves write performance by reducing the number of I/O operations generated by read–modify–write cycles. Delaying the update of parity information improves performance by reducing the number of disks accessed to perform each write operation.

Web Resources

www.disk-tape-data-recovery.com/storage-history.htm
Provides a short history of persistent data storage media.

www.almaden.ibm.com/sst/storage/index.shtml
Describes physical limitations of storage technology and promising fields of research IBM has pursued to solve them.

colossalstorage.net/colossal11.htm
Provides links to sites describing evolving storage technologies.

www.cosc.brocku.ca/~cspress/HelloWorld/1999/03-mar/disk_scheduling_algorithms.html
Contains an article from *Hello World*, a magazine for computer science students; the article overviews disk scheduling algorithms.

www.pcguide.com/ref/hdd/index.htm
Discusses hard disk characteristics.

www.microsoft.com/windows2000/techinfo/administration/fileandprint/defrag.asp
Describes how to use the disk defragmenting utilities in Windows 2000.

www.pcguide.com/ref/hdd/perf/raid/
Provides an in-depth introduction to RAID.

www.acnc.com/04_00.html
Provides a summary of most RAID levels.

linas.org/linux/raid.html
Contains articles about RAID and its implementation in Linux systems.

www.pdl.cmu.edu/RAID/
Overviews RAID and provides links to current RAID research.

Summary

As processor and main memory speeds increase more rapidly than those of secondary storage devices, optimizing disk performance has become important to realizing optimal performance. Magnetic storage records data by changing the direction of magnetization of regions, each representing a 1 or a 0. To access data, a current-carrying device called a read/write head hovers above the medium as it moves.

Most modern computers use hard disks as secondary storage. As the platters spin, each read-write head sketches out a circular track of data on a disk surface. All read-write heads are attached to a single disk arm (also called an actuator, boom or moving-arm assembly). When the disk arm moves the read/write heads to a new position, a different set of tracks, or cylinder, becomes accessible. The process of moving the disk arm to a new cylinder is called a seek operation. The time it takes for the head to move from its current cylinder to the one containing the data record being accessed is called the seek time. The time it takes for data to rotate from its current position to a position adjacent to the read/write head is called latency time. Then the record, which is of arbitrary size, must be made to spin by the read/write head so that the data can be read from or written to the disk. This is called transmission time.

Many processes can generate requests for reading and writing data on a disk simultaneously. Because these processes sometimes make requests faster than they can be serviced by the disk, queues build up to hold disk requests. Some early computing systems simply serviced these requests on a first-come-first-served (FCFS) basis, in which the earliest arriving request is serviced first. FCFS is a fair method of allocating service, but when the request rate (i.e., the load) becomes heavy, FCFS results in long waiting times.

FCFS exhibits a random seek pattern in which successive requests can cause time-consuming seeks from the innermost to the outermost cylinders. To reduce the time spent seeking records, it seems reasonable to order the request queue in some other manner than FCFS. This reordering is called disk scheduling. The two most common types of scheduling are seek optimization and rotational optimization. Disk scheduling strategies often are evaluated by comparing their throughput, mean response time and variance of response times.

First-come-first-served scheduling uses a FIFO queue so that requests are serviced in the order they arrive. Although this technique incurs low execution-time overhead, it can result in low throughput due to lengthy seeks.

Shortest-seek-time-first (SSTF) scheduling next services the request that is closest to the read-write head's current cylinder (thus incurring the shortest seek time), even if that is not the first one in the queue. By reducing average seek times, SSTF achieves higher throughput rates than FCFS, and mean response times tend to be lower for moderate loads. One significant drawback is that higher variances occur on response times because of the discrimination against the outermost and innermost tracks; in the extreme, indefinite postponement of requests far from the read-write heads could occur.

The SCAN scheduling strategy reduces unfairness and variance of response times by choosing the request that requires the shortest seek distance in a preferred direction.

Thus, if the preferred direction is currently outward, the SCAN strategy chooses the shortest seek distance in the outward direction. SCAN behaves much like SSTF in terms of high throughput and good mean response time. However, because SCAN ensures that all requests in a given direction will be serviced before the requests in the opposite direction, it offers a lower variance of response times than SSTF.

The circular SCAN (C-SCAN) modification to the SCAN strategy moves the arm from the outer cylinder to the inner cylinder, servicing requests on a shortest-seek basis. When the arm has completed its inward sweep, it jumps (without servicing requests) to the outermost cylinder, then resumes its inward sweep processing requests. C-SCAN maintains high levels of throughput while further limiting variance of response times by avoiding the discrimination against the innermost and outermost cylinders. SCAN is often called the elevator algorithm.

The FSCAN and *N*-Step SCAN modifications to the SCAN strategy eliminate the possibility of indefinitely postponing requests. FSCAN uses the SCAN strategy to service only those requests waiting when a particular sweep begins (the "F" stands for "freezing" the request queue at a certain time). Requests arriving during a sweep are grouped together and ordered for optimum service during the return sweep. *N*-Step SCAN services the first *n* requests in the queue using the SCAN strategy. When the sweep is complete, the next *n* requests are serviced. Arriving requests are placed at the end of the request queue, which prevents requests in the current sweep from being indefinitely postponed. FSCAN and N-Step SCAN offer good performance due to high throughput, low mean response times and a lower variance of response times than SSTF and SCAN.

The LOOK variation of the SCAN strategy (also called the elevator algorithm) "looks" ahead to the end of the current sweep to determine the next request to service. If there are no more requests in the current direction, LOOK changes the preferred direction and begins the next sweep, stopping when passing a cylinder that corresponds to a request in the queue. This strategy eliminates unnecessary seek operations experienced by other variations of the SCAN strategy by preventing the read/write head from moving to the innermost or outermost cylinders unless it is servicing a request to those locations.

The circular LOOK (C-LOOK) variation of the LOOK strategy uses the same technique as C-SCAN to reduce the bias against requests located at extreme ends of the platters. When there are no more requests on a current sweep, the read/write head moves to the request closest to the outer cylinder (without servicing requests in between)

and begins the next sweep. The C-LOOK strategy is characterized by potentially lower variance of response times compared to LOOK, and by high throughput, although lower than that of LOOK.

In many environments, there are often short periods when there are no waiting requests for the disk to service and the disk arm sits idle, waiting for the next request. If the disk arm is in the center of the disk, or at some hot spot of disk activity, the average seek time will be less. Moving the disk arm to a location that will hopefully minimize the next seek is known as disk arm anticipation. It can be useful in environments where processes's disk request patterns exhibit locality and where there is typically enough time to move the disk arm between disk requests. If a request is received during anticipatory movement, moving the head to the originally specified location and then to the requested cylinder increases response time. Allowing the seek to a hot spot to be interrupted to adjust to requests provides the greatest performance boost.

Rotational optimization was used extensively with early fixed-head devices such as drums, and can improve performance in today's hard disks, which exhibit seek times and average latencies of the same order of magnitude. The shortest-latency-time-first (SLTF) strategy examines all pending requests and services the one with the shortest rotational delay first. Rotational optimization is sometimes referred to as sector queuing; requests are queued by sector position around the disk, and the nearest sectors are serviced first.

The STLF strategy works well for fixed-head disks but does not incorporate the positioning time, which is the seek time plus latency, of moving-head disks. The shortest-positioning-time-first (SPTF) strategy next services the request that requires the shortest positioning time. SPTF results in high throughput and a low mean response time, similar to SSTF, and can also indefinitely postpone requests to the innermost and outermost cylinders.

A variation of SPTF is the shortest-access-time-first (SATF) strategy, which next services the request that requires the shortest access time (i.e., positioning time plus transmission time). SATF exhibits higher throughput than SPTF, but large requests can be indefinitely postponed by a series of smaller requests. Requests to the innermost or outermost cylinders can be indefinitely postponed by requests to intermediate cylinders. SPTF and SATF can improve performance by implementing the "look-ahead" mechanisms employed by the LOOK and C-LOOK strategies.

One reason why SPTF and SATF are rarely implemented is that they require knowledge of disk characteristics including latency, track-to-track seek times and relative locations of sectors. Unfortunately, many of today's hard drives hide such geometry or expose misleading geometries due to hidden error-checking data and bad sectors.

When disk storage proves to be a bottleneck, some designers recommend adding more disks to the system. This does not always solve the problem, because the bottleneck could be caused by a large request load on a relatively small number of disks. When this situation is detected, disk scheduling may be used as a means of improving performance and eliminating the bottleneck. Disk scheduling might not be useful in a batch-processing system with a relatively low degree of multiprogramming. Scheduling becomes more effective as the degree of multiprogramming increases, which increases the system load and leads to unpredictable disk request patterns.

Nonuniform request distributions are common in certain situations and their consequences have been investigated. One study determined that the vast majority of disk references are to the same cylinder as the immediately preceding reference. Sophisticated file organization techniques can cause a proliferation of requests with large seek times. Such techniques are convenient for the applications designer but can complicate implementation and degrade performance.

Many systems maintain a disk cache buffer, which is a region of main memory that the operating system reserves for disk data. In one context, the reserved memory acts as a cache, allowing processes quick access to data that would otherwise need to be fetched from disk. The reserved memory also acts as a buffer, allowing the operating system to delay writing the data to improve I/O performance. The disk cache buffer presents several challenges to operating system designers, because memory allocated to the cache buffer reduces the amount allocated to processes. Also, because memory is volatile, power or system failures can lead to inconsistencies.

Write-back caching writes buffered data to disk periodically, enabling the operating system to use a single request to batch multiple I/Os, which can improve system performance. Write-through caching writes data both to the disk cache buffer and to disk each time cached data is modified. This technique prevents the system from batching requests but reduces the possibility of inconsistent data in the event of a system crash.

Many of today's hard disk drives maintain an independent high-speed buffer cache (often called an on-board cache) of several megabytes. If data requested is stored in the on-board cache, the hard drive can deliver the data at or near the speed of main memory. However, one study showed that disks that include on-board caches typically use replacement strategies that adapt poorly to random request patterns, leading to suboptimal performance.

Disks tend to become fragmented as files and records are added and deleted. Many operating systems provide defragmentation (or disk reorganization) programs that can be used periodically to reorganize files. This allows the consecutive records of sequential files to be placed contiguously on the disk. Also, operating systems can place files that are likely to be modified near free space to reduce future fragmentation. Some operating systems allow users to partition a disk into separate areas. Files are then restricted to these areas, so fragmentation is reduced. Some systems use data compression techniques to reduce the amount of space required by information on disk. Data compression decreases the size of a record by replacing common bit patterns with shorter ones. This can reduce seeks, latency times and transmission times, but may require substantial processor time to compress the data for storage on the disk, and to decompress the data to make it available to applications.

Systems that need to access certain information quickly benefit from placing multiple copies of that data at different positions on the disk. This can substantially reduce seek and rotation times, but the redundant copies can consume a significant portion of the disk. Also, if one copy is modified, all other copies must be modified, which can degrade performance. Additionally, record blocking can yield significant performance improvements by reading contiguous records as a single block, requiring only a single seek. Systems that monitor disk access attempts can try to keep frequently accessed data in a favorable position in the memory hierarchy (i.e., in main or cache memory) while transferring infrequently referenced data to slower storage (such as a hard disk or compact disk).

Redundant Arrays of Independent Disks (RAID) is a family of techniques that use arrays of disks to address the problem of relatively slow disk transfer speeds. Each array organization, called a level, is characterized by data striping and redundancy. Storage is divided into fixed-size strips; contiguous strips on each disk generally store noncontiguous data or data from different files. A stripe consists of the set of strips at the same location on each disk in the array.

When selecting a strip size, the system designer should consider the average size of disk requests. Smaller strip sizes, also called fine-grained strips, tend to spread file data across several disks. Fine-grained strips can reduce each request's access time and increase transfer rates because multiple disks simultaneously retrieve portions of the requested data. While these disks service a request, they cannot be used to service other requests in the system's request queue.

Large strip sizes, also called coarse-grained strips, enable more files to fit entirely within one strip. In this case, some requests can be serviced by only a portion of the disks in the array, so it is more likely that multiple requests can be serviced simultaneously. However, smaller requests are serviced by one disk at a time, which reduces transfer rates for individual requests.

Systems such as Web servers and databases, which typically access multiple small records simultaneously, benefit from coarse-grained strips because several I/O operations can occur concurrently; systems such as supercomputers that require fast access to a small number of records benefit from fine-grained strips, which provide high transfer rates for individual requests.

As the number of disks in the array increases, so does the likelihood that one of those disks will fail, measured by the mean-time-to-failure (MTTF). Most RAID systems maintain copies of data to help enable them to recover from errors and failures, a technique called redundancy. Disk mirroring is a redundancy technique that maintains copies of each data item on two disks. A drawback to mirroring is that only half of the storage capacity of the array can be used to store unique data.

To realize the improved performance of striped disks with redundancy, the system must efficiently divide files into strips, form files from strips, determine the locations of strips in the array and implement redundancy. Many RAID systems contain special-purpose hardware called a RAID controller to perform such operations quickly. The designer must balance cost, performance and reliability when selecting a RAID level. Typically, improving one characteristic worsens the other two.

RAID level 0 uses a striped disk array with no redundancy. Level 0 arrays are not fault tolerant; if one disk fails, all the data in the array that depend on the failed disk are lost. Depending on the array's strip size, all data stored in the array could become unusable with the loss of a single disk. Although RAID 0 is not fault tolerant, it is simple to implement, yields high transfer rates and does not incur any storage overhead.

RAID level 1 employs disk mirroring (also called shadowing) to provide redundancy, so each disk in the array is duplicated. Stripes are not implemented in level 1, reducing both hardware complexity and system performance. While this results in the highest degree of fault tol-erance of any RAID level, only half of the array's capacity can be used to store unique data, which increases cost. For each mirrored pair, two read requests can be serviced simultaneously, but only one request can be serviced at a time during a write. Recovering and rebuilding data from a failed disk, called data regeneration, entails copying the redundant data from the mirrored disk. If both disks in a mirrored pair fail, their data is unrecoverable.

Some RAID systems contain "spare" disks (also called hot spare disks or online spares) that can replace failed disks, much like a spare tire for an automobile. Some systems also feature hot swappable disk drives that can to be replaced while the system is online. In these systems, data regeneration can occur while the system continues to run, which is necessary in high-availability environments such as online transaction processing systems. RAID 1 is best suited for business-critical and mission-critical environments in which reliability has higher priority than cost or performance.

RAID level 2 arrays are striped at the bit level, so each strip stores one bit. Level 2 arrays are designed to reduce the storage overhead incurred by implementing fault tolerance using mirroring. Instead of maintaining redundant copies of each data item, RAID level 2 uses a technique of storing parity information called Hamming error-correcting codes (Hamming ECCs), which allow the system to detect up to two errors, correct up to one error and determine the location of the error in a stripe. The size of Hamming ECC codes, and thus the number of parity disks, increases in proportion to the logarithm (base 2) of the number of data disks. Thus, level 2 arrays containing a large number of disks incur significantly less storage overhead than level 1 arrays.

Although the ECC disks reduce the overhead associated with redundancy when compared to mirroring, they can degrade performance, because multiple requests cannot be serviced simultaneously. Each read request requires the array to access all disks, compute the ECC, and compare it with the value retrieved from the parity disks. Similarly, when servicing a write request, the Hamming ECC must be calculated for each stripe that is written. Further, the system must perform a read–modify–write cycle, which degrades performance because the system must access the entire array twice for each write. One way to enable concurrency using a RAID level 2 array is to divide the system's disks into several small RAID level 2 arrays, but this increases storage overhead and cost. The primary reason that RAID 2 is not implemented in today's systems is that modern disk drives perform Hamming ECCs or comparable protection transparently in hardware.

RAID level 3 stripes data at the bit or byte level. RAID 3 uses XOR (exclusive or) error-correcting codes (XOR ECCs), which use the logical XOR operation to generate parity information. XOR ECC uses only one disk to hold parity information, regardless of the size of the array. The system can use the parity bits to recover from any single disk failure; if the parity disk fails, it can be rebuilt from the array's data disks. Due to parity checking RAID level 3 reads and writes require access to the entire array. Similar to RAID level 2, this yields high transfer rates when reading and writing large files, but only one request can be serviced at a time.

RAID level 4 systems are striped using fixed-size blocks (typically larger than a byte) and use XOR ECC to generate parity data that is stored on a single parity disk. Because level 4 arrays enable coarse-grained striping, the system can potentially service multiple read requests simultaneously, if parity is not determined for each read. When servicing a write request, however, the system must update parity information to ensure that no data is lost in the event of a disk failure. This means that write requests must be performed one at a time, creating a write bottleneck.

RAID level 5 arrays are striped at the block level and use XOR ECC for parity, but parity blocks are distributed throughout the array of disks. Because parity blocks are distributed across many disks, multiple parity blocks can be accessed simultaneously, removing the write bottleneck for many requests. Although RAID level 5 improves write per-formance by distributing parity, level 5 arrays must still perform a read–modify–write cycle for each write request, requiring at least four I/O operations to service each write request.

Caching recently accessed data and parity blocks can reduce the number of I/O operations in the read–modify–write cycle. Parity logging can improve RAID level 5 performance by storing the difference between the old parity and new parity (called the update image) in memory instead of performing a read–modify–write cycle. A Frequently Redundant Array of Independent Disks (AFRAID) improves performance by deferring parity data generation to times at which the system load is light.

Although RAID level 5 increases performance relative to RAID levels 2–4, it is complex to implement, which increases its cost. Also, because parity is distributed throughout the array, data regeneration is more complicated than in other RAID levels. Despite its limitations, RAID level 5 is frequently adopted for its effective balance of performance, cost and reliability. Level 5 arrays are considered general-purpose arrays and are often found in file and application servers, enterprise resource planning (ERP) and other business systems.

Many other RAID levels exist, each borrowing from one or more of RAID levels 0–5. Unfortunately, there is no standard naming convention for RAID levels, which often leads to confusing or misleading names.

Key Terms

A Frequently Redundant Array of Independent Disks (AFRAID) (RAID)—RAID implementation that defers parity data generation to times when the system's load is light to improve performance when a system performs many small writes.

actuator—See disk arm.

anticipatory movement—Movement of the disk arm during disk arm anticipation.

block—Fixed-size unit of data, typically much larger than a byte. Placing contiguous data records in blocks enables the system to reduce the number of I/O operations required to retrieve them.

blocking—Grouping of contiguous records into larger blocks that can be read using a single I/O operation. This technique reduces access times by retrieving many records with a single I/O operation.

boom—See disk arm.

bottleneck—Condition that occurs when a resource receives requests faster than it can process them, which can slow process execution and reduce resource utilization. Hard disks are a bottleneck in most systems.

circular LOOK (C-LOOK) disk scheduling—Disk scheduling strategy that moves the arm in one direction, servicing requests on a shortest-seek basis. When there are no more requests on a current sweep, the read-write head moves to the request closest to the cylinder opposite its current location (without servicing requests in between) and begins the next sweep. The C-LOOK policy is characterized by potentially lower variance of response times compared to LOOK; it offers high throughput (although lower than that of LOOK).

circular SCAN (C-SCAN) disk scheduling—Disk scheduling strategy that moves the arm in one direction, servicing requests on a shortest-seek basis. When the arm has completed its a sweep, it jumps (without servicing requests) to the cylinder opposite its current location, then resumes its inward sweep processing requests. C-SCAN maintains high levels of throughput while further limiting variance of response times by avoiding the discrimination against the innermost and outermost cylinders.

coarse-grained strip (RAID)—Strip size that enables average files to be stored in a small number of strips. In this case, some requests can be serviced by only a portion of the disks in the array, so it is more likely that multiple requests can be serviced simultaneously. If requests are small, they are serviced by one disk at a time, which reduces their average transfer rates.

cylinder—Set of tracks that can be accessed by the read-write heads for a specific position of the disk arm.

data compression—Technique that decreases the size of a data record by replacing repetitive patterns with shorter bit strings. This can reduce seeks, and transmission times, but may require substantial processor time to compress the data for storage on the disk, and to decompress the data to make it available to applications.

data regeneration (RAID)—Reconstruction of lost data (due to disk errors or failures) in RAID systems.

data striping (RAID)—Technique in RAID systems that divides contiguous data into fixed-size strips that can be placed on different disks. This enables multiple disks to service requests for data.

defragmentation—Moving parts of files so that they are located in contiguous blocks on disk. This can reduce access times when reading from or writing to files sequentially.

disk arm—Moving-head disk component that moves read-write heads linearly, parallel to disk surfaces.

disk arm anticipation—Moving the disk arm to a location that will minimize the next seek. Disk arm anticipation can be useful in environments where process disk request patterns exhibit locality and when the load is light enough that there is sufficient time to move the disk arm between disk requests without degrading performance.

disk cache buffer—A region of main memory that the operating system reserves for disk data. In one context, the reserved memory acts as a cache, allowing processes quick access to data that would otherwise need to be fetched from disk. The reserved memory also acts as a buffer, allowing the operating system to delay writing the data to improve I/O performance by batching multiple writes into a small number of requests.

disk mirroring (RAID)—Data redundancy technique in RAID that maintains a copy of each disk's contents on a separate disk. This technique provides high reliability and

simplifies data regeneration but incurs substantial storage overhead, which increases cost.

disk reorganization—Technique that moves file data on disk to improve its access time. One such technique is defragmentation, which attempts to place sequential file data contiguously on disk. Another technique attempts to place frequently requested data on tracks that result in low average seek times.

disk scheduling—Technique that orders disk requests to maximize throughput and minimize response times and the variance of response times. Disk scheduling strategies improve performance by reducing seek times and rotational latencies.

elevator algorithm—See SCAN disk scheduling.

first-come-first-served (FCFS) disk scheduling—Disk scheduling strategy in which the earliest arriving request is serviced first. FCFS is a fair method of allocating service, but when the request rate (i.e., the load) becomes heavy, FCFS can result in long waiting times. FCFS exhibits a random seek pattern in which successive requests can cause time-consuming seeks from the innermost to the outermost cylinders.

fine-grained strip (RAID)—Strip size that causes average files to be stored in multiple stripes. Fine-grained strips can reduce each request's access time and increase transfer rates because multiple disks simultaneously retrieve portions of the requested data.

FSCAN disk scheduling—Disk scheduling strategy that uses SCAN to service only those requests waiting when a particular sweep begins (the "F" stands for "freezing" the request queue at a certain time). Requests arriving during a sweep are grouped together and ordered for optimum service during the return sweep.

fragmented disk—Disk that stores files in discontinuous blocks as the result of file creation and deletion. Such disks exhibit high seek times when reading files sequentially. Disk defragmentation can reduce or eliminate the problem.

Hamming error-correcting codes (Hamming ECCs)—Technique of generating parity bits that enables systems to detect and correct errors in data transmission.

hard disk drive—Magnetic, rotational secondary storage device that provides persistent storage for, and random access to, data.

hot spare disk (RAID)—Disk in a RAID system that is not used until a disk fails. Once the system regenerates the failed disk's data, the hot spare disk replaces the failed disk.

hot spot—Disk cylinder that contains frequently requested data. Some disk arm anticipation techniques move the disk head to hot spots to reduce average seek times.

load—See request rate.

level (RAID)—A particular organization of a RAID system, such as level 1 (mirroring) or level 2 (Hamming ECC parity). See also RAID level 0, RAID level 1, RAID level 2, RAID level 3, RAID level 4 and RAID level 5.

LOOK disk scheduling—Variation of the SCAN disk scheduling strategy that "looks" ahead to the end of the current sweep to determine the next request to service. If there are no more requests in the current direction, LOOK changes the preferred direction and begins the next sweep, stopping when passing a cylinder that corresponds to a request in the queue. This strategy eliminates unnecessary seek operations experienced by other variations of SCAN by preventing the read-write head from moving to the innermost or outermost cylinder unless it needs to service a request at those cylinders.

magnetic tape storage—Rewritable magnetic storage medium that accesses data sequentially. Its sequential nature makes it unsuitable for direct access applications.

mean response time (disk scheduling)—Average time a system spends waiting for a disk request to be serviced.

mean-time-to-failure (MTTF) (RAID)—Average time before a single-disk failure.

mirroring (RAID)—See disk mirroring.

moving-arm assembly—See disk arm.

nonuniform request distribution—Set of disk requests that are not uniformly distributed across disk surfaces. This occurs because processes exhibit spatial locality, leading to localized request patterns.

N-Step SCAN disk scheduling—Disk scheduling strategy that services the first *n* requests in the queue using the SCAN strategy. When the sweep is complete, the next *n* requests are serviced. Arriving requests are placed at the end of the request queue. *N*-Step SCAN offer good performance due to high throughput, low mean response times and a lower variance of response times than SSTF and SCAN.

online spare—See hot spare disk.

online transaction processing (OLTP)—Type of system that typically receives many disk requests to randomly distributed locations containing small amounts of data (e.g., databases and Web servers). Such systems significantly improve performance using disk scheduling algorithms.

partition—Area of a disk whose boundaries cannot be crossed by file data. Partitions can reduce disk fragmentation.

parity—Technique that detects an even number of errors in data transmission. Parity information is generated by determining whether the data contains an even (or odd) number of 1's (or 0's). This parity information is generated after transmission and compared to the value generated before transmission. Error-correction codes (ECCs), such as Hamming or XOR, use the parity of a string of bits to detect and correct errors. Parity enables RAID systems to provide fault tolerance with lower storage overhead than mirrored systems.

parity logging (RAID)—Technique that increases write performance in RAID systems using parity by postponing writes to the parity disk while the system is busy. Because parity logging stores information in volatile memory, parity information could be lost if the system loses power.

platter—Magnetic disk medium that stores bits on its surfaces.

positioning time—Access time plus latency. Positioning time is used by the SPTF strategy to order requests.

preferred direction—Direction in which the disk head is moving in SCAN-based scheduling algorithms.

RAID (Redundant Array of Independent Disks)—Family of techniques that use an array of disks to improve disk transfer rates while providing fault tolerance.

RAID controller—Special-purpose hardware that efficiently performs operations such as dividing files into strips, forming files from strips, determining the locations of strips in the array and implementing the array's fault-tolerance mechanism.

RAID level 0—RAID system that uses a striped disk array with no redundancy. Level 0 arrays are not fault tolerant; if one disk fails, all the data in the array that depend on the failed disk are lost. Depending on the array's strip size, all data stored in the array could become unusable with the loss of a single disk. Although RAID 0 is not fault tolerant, it is simple to implement, yields high transfer rates and does not incur any storage overhead. Level 0 arrays are implemented in systems where performance is more important than fault tolerance, such as supercomputers.

RAID level 1—RAID system that employs disk mirroring (also called shadowing) to provide redundancy, so that each disk in the array is duplicated. Stripes are not implemented in level 1, reducing both hardware complexity and system performance. While this results in the highest degree of fault tolerance of any RAID level, only half of the array's capacity can be used to store unique data, which increases cost. Level 1 arrays are implemented in systems where high availability is more important than cost, such as database systems.

RAID level 2—RAID system that is striped at the bit level (i.e., each strip stores one bit). Level 2 arrays are designed to reduce the storage overhead incurred by implementing fault tolerance using mirroring. Instead of maintaining redundant copies of each data item, RAID level 2 uses a version of Hamming error-correcting codes (Hamming ECCs) to store parity information that allows the system to detect up to two errors, correct up to one error and determine the location of the error in a stripe. The size of Hamming ECC codes, and thus the number of parity disks, increases according to the logarithm (base 2) of the number of data disks. Thus, level 2 arrays containing a large number of disks incur significantly less storage overhead than level 1 arrays.

RAID level 3—RAID system that stripes data at the bit or byte level. RAID 3 uses XOR (exclusive or) error-correcting codes (XOR ECCs), which use the logical XOR operation to generate parity information. XOR ECC uses only one disk to hold parity information, regardless of the size of the array. The system can use the parity bits to recover from any single disk failure. Due to parity checking, RAID level 3 reads and writes require access to the entire array. Similar to RAID level 2, this yields high transfer rates when reading and writing large files, but only one request can be serviced at a time.

RAID level 4—RAID system that is striped using fixed-size blocks (typically larger than a byte) and uses XOR ECC to generate parity data that is stored on a single parity disk. Because level 4 arrays enable coarse-grained striping, the system can potentially service multiple read requests simultaneously, if parity is not determined for each read. When servicing a write request, however, the system must update parity information to ensure that no data is lost in the event of a disk failure. This means that write requests must be performed one at a time, creating a write bottleneck.

RAID level 5—RAID system that is striped at the block level and uses XOR ECC for parity, but distributes parity blocks throughout the array of disks. Because parity blocks are distributed across many disks, multiple parity strips can be accessed simultaneously, removing the write bottleneck for many requests. Although RAID level 5 increases performance relative to RAID levels 2–4, it is complex to implement and more costly. Level 5 arrays are considered general-purpose arrays and are often found in file and application servers, enterprise resource planning (ERP) and other business systems.

RAMAC (Random Access Method of Accounting and Control)—First commercial hard drive produced by IBM.

random seek pattern—Series of requests to cylinders randomly distributed across disk surfaces. FCFS causes random seek patterns that result in high response times and low throughput.

read–modify–write cycle (RAID)—Operation that reads a stripe, modifies its contents and parity, then writes the stripe to the array. It is performed for each write request in RAID systems that use parity. Some systems reduce the cost of read–modify–write cycles by caching strips or by updating parity information only periodically.

read-write head—Moving-head disk component that hovers over a disk surface, reading and writing bits as the disk moves.

redundancy—Technique that maintains multiple identical resources to enable recovery upon failure.

Redundant Array of Independent Disks (RAID)—See RAID.

reliability—Measure of fault tolerance. The more reliable a resource, the less likely it is to fail.

request rate—Measure of request frequency. The higher the request rate, the greater the system load. Systems experiencing a high disk request rate tend to benefit from disk scheduling.

rotational latency—Time required for a disk to rotate a requested data item from its current position to a position adjacent to the read-write head.

rotational optimization—Disk scheduling technique that reduces access times by next servicing the request to the nearest sector in the read-write head's current cylinder.

SCAN disk scheduling—Disk scheduling strategy that reduces unfairness and variance of response times as compared to SSTF by servicing the request that requires the shortest seek distance in a preferred direction. SCAN behaves much like SSTF in terms of high throughput and good mean response times. However, because SCAN ensures that all requests in a given direction will be serviced before the requests in the opposite direction, it offers a lower variance of response times than SSTF. Also called the elevator algorithm.

sector—Smallest portion of a track that can be accessed by an I/O request.

sector queuing—See rotational optimization.

seek operation—Operation that moves the disk head to a different cylinder.

seek time—Time it takes for the read/write head to move from its current cylinder to the cylinder containing the requested data record.

seek optimization—Disk scheduling technique that reduces seek times by generally servicing requests to the cylinder near the read-write head.

shadowing (RAID)—See mirroring.

shortest-access-time-first (SATF) disk scheduling—Disk scheduling strategy that next services the request that requires the shortest access time (i.e., positioning time plus transmission time). SATF exhibits higher throughput than SPTF, but large requests can be indefinitely postponed by a series of smaller requests, and requests to the innermost or outermost cylinders can be indefinitely postponed by requests to intermediate cylinders.

shortest-latency-time-first (SLTF) disk scheduling—Disk scheduling strategy that examines all of the waiting requests and services the one with the shortest rotational delay first. This strategy has been shown to be close to the theoretical optimum and is relatively easy to implement.

shortest-positioning-time-first (SPTF) disk scheduling—Disk scheduling strategy that next services the request that requires the shortest positioning time. SPTF results in high throughput and a low mean response time, similar to SSTF, and can also indefinitely postpone requests to the innermost and outermost cylinders.

shortest-seek-time-first (SSTF) disk scheduling—Disk scheduling strategy that next services the request that is closest to the read-write head's current cylinder (and thus incurs the shortest seek time), even if that is not the first one in the queue. By reducing average seek times, SSTF achieves higher throughput rates than FCFS, and mean response times tend to be lower for moderate loads. One significant drawback is that higher variances occur on response times because of the discrimination against the outermost and innermost tracks; in the extreme, starvation of requests far from the read-write heads could occur.

spindle—Moving-head disk component that spins platters at high speeds.

strip (RAID)—Smallest unit of data operated on by a RAID system. The set of strips at the same location on each disk is called a stripe.

stripe (RAID)—Set of strips at the same location on each disk in a RAID system. Striping enables RAID systems to access files using multiple disks at once, which improves transfer times.

track—Circular region of data on a platter. Sequential file data is typically placed contiguously on one track to improve access time by reducing seeking activity.

transmission time—Time required for a data record to pass by the read-write head.

UNIVAC 1 (UNIVersal Automatic Computer)—First computer to introduce a magnetic storage tape.

update image (RAID)—Method to reduce parity computation time by storing the difference between new and old parities in memory instead of performing a read–modify–write cycle.

write-back caching—Technique that writes buffered data to disk periodically, enabling the operating system to batch multiple I/Os that are serviced using a single request, which can improve system performance.

write-through caching—Technique that writes data both to the disk cache buffer and to disk each time cached data is modified. This technique prevents the system from batching requests, but reduces the possibility of inconsistent data in the event of a system crash.

XOR (exclusive-or) operation—Operation on two bits that returns 1 if the two bits are not the same, 0 otherwise. RAID levels 3–5 use the XOR operation to generate parity bits.

Exercises

12.1 What are the essential goals of disk scheduling? Why is each important?

12.2 Suppose that on a particular model of disk drive, average seek times approximately equal average latency times. How might this affect a designer's choice of disk scheduling strategies?

12.3 What makes a given disk scheduling discipline fair? Just how important is fairness compared to other goals of disk scheduling disciplines?

12.4 Disk scheduling disciplines that are not fair generally have a larger variance of response times than FCFS. Why is this true?

12.5 Under light loading conditions, virtually all the disk scheduling disciplines discussed in this chapter degenerate to which scheme? Why?

12.6 One criterion that influences the desirability of implementing disk scheduling is the disk scheduling mechanism's runtime overhead. What factors contribute to this overhead? Suppose t is the average seek time on a system with FCFS disk scheduling. Suppose *s* is the approximate time it would take to schedule an average disk request if another form of disk scheduling were in use. Assume all other factors are favorable to incorporating disk scheduling on this system. For each of the following cases, comment on the potential effectiveness of incorporating disk scheduling on the system.

     a. $s = 0.01t$

     b. $s = 0.1t$

     c. $s = t$

     d. $s = 10t$

12.7 Latency optimization usually has little effect on system performance except under extremely heavy loads. Why?

12.8 On interactive systems it is essential to ensure reasonable response times to users. Reducing the variance of response times is still an important goal, but it is not sufficient to prevent an occasional user from suffering indefinite postponement. What additional mechanism would you incorporate into a disk scheduling discipline on an interactive system to help ensure reasonable response times and to avoid the possibility of indefinite postponement?

12.9 Argue why some people refuse to consider FCFS to be a disk scheduling discipline. Is there a scheme for servicing disk requests that we would be even less inclined to call disk scheduling than FCFS?

12.10 In what sense is LOOK fairer than SSTF? In what sense is C-LOOK fairer than LOOK?

12.11 Give a statistical argument for why FCFS offers a small variance of response times.

12.12 Argue why SSTF tends to favor requests to midrange tracks at the expense of the requests to the innermost and outermost tracks.

12.13 Chapter 7, Deadlock and Indefinite Postponement, suggests a scheme for avoiding indefinite postponement. Suggest an appropriate modification to the SSTF scheme to create a "nonstarving SSTF." Compare this new version with regular SSTF with regard to throughput, mean response times, and variance of response times.

12.14 It is possible that while a disk request for a particular cylinder is being serviced, another request for that cylinder will arrive. Some disk scheduling disciplines would service this new request immediately after processing the current request. Other disciplines preclude the servicing of the new request until the return sweep of the disk arm. What dangerous situation might occur in a disk scheduling discipline that allowed immediate servicing of a new request for the same cylinder as the previous request?

12.15 Why does SCAN have a lower variance of response times than SSTF?

12.16 Compare the throughput of FSCAN with that of SCAN.

12.17 Compare the throughput of C-SCAN with that of SCAN.

12.18 How does a latency optimization scheme operate?

12.19 A disk storage bottleneck may not always be removed by adding more disk drives. Why?

12.20 How does the level of multiprogramming affect the need for disk scheduling?

12.21 Suppose controller saturation is indicated. Might disk scheduling be useful? What other actions should be taken?

12.22 Why is it desirable to assume uniform request distributions when considering disk scheduling disciplines? In what types of systems might you expect to observe relatively uniform request distributions? Give several examples of systems that tend to have nonuniform request distributions.

12.23 Would disk scheduling be useful for a single-user, dedicated disk in a sequential file processing application? Why?

12.24 The VSCAN scheduling strategy combines SSTF and SCAN according to a variable R.[91] VSCAN determines the next request to service using SSTF, but each request to a cylinder that requires the read/write head to change direction is weighted by a factor R. The "distances" to requests in the opposite direction are computed as follows. If C is the number of cylinders on the disk and S is the number of cylinders between the current location of the head and the next request, then VSCAN uses the distance, $D = S + R \times C$. Thus, VSCAN uses R to add an extra cost to the requests in the unpreferred direction.

12.25 If $R = 0$, to which disk scheduling policy does VSCAN degenerate?

12.26 If $R = 1$, to which disk scheduling policy does VSCAN degenerate?

12.27 Discuss the benefit of choosing a value, R, somewhere between 0 and 1.

12.28 In what circumstances might disk scheduling actually result in poorer performance than FCFS?

12.29 Compare the essential goals of disk scheduling with those of processor scheduling. What are the similarities? What are the differences?

12.30 What factors contribute to the need for seeking?

12.31 A sequential file "properly" stored on an empty disk can be retrieved with minimal seeking. But disks tend to become heavily fragmented as files are added and deleted. Thus, successive references to "adjacent" records in a disk file can result in substantial seeking throughout the disk. Discuss the notion of file reorganization as a scheme for minimizing seeks. Under what circumstances should a file be reorganized? Should every file on the disk be reorganized or should this operation be limited to certain files only?

12.32 A designer has proposed the use of multiple disk arms to greatly improve the response times of a disk subsystem. Discuss the advantages and disadvantages of such a scheme.

12.33 We mentioned that the LOOK algorithm is like the algorithm followed by elevators in buildings. In what ways is this an appropriate analogy?

12.34 Suggest other techniques besides disk scheduling and file reorganization for minimizing seeks.

12.35 The SCAN strategy often exhibits significantly higher throughput than the C-SCAN algorithm. However, system designers sometimes choose C-SCAN over SCAN. Why might this decision be justified?

12.36 In Section 12.10.6, we said that a RAID system can reduce the number of I/O operations when calculating parity by using the formula $A_p' = (A_d$ XOR $A_d')$ XOR A_p. Prove that this relation holds for all strips A_d, A_d' and A_p.

12.37 For each of the following applications, indicate whether the system should use RAID level 0, RAID level 1, or RAID level 5 and explain why.

12.38 Storing account transactions for a financial institution

12.39 Storing high-resolution telescope images (that have been transferred from a tape drive) before processing on a supercomputer

12.40 Running a personal Web server

Suggested Projects

12.41 Research disk scheduling in Linux. What scheduling strategies does Linux use? How are these strategies implemented? For an introduction to Linux disk scheduling, see Section 20.8.3, Block Device I/O.

12.42 Prepare a research paper discussing the techniques that hard disk manufacturers employ to improve performance. See the links in the Web Resources section.

12.43 Prepare a report briefly describing five RAID levels other than the 6 covered in detail in this chapter.

Suggested Simulations

12.44 Develop monitors (see Chapter 6, Concurrent Programming) to implement each of the following disk scheduling disciplines.

   a. FCFS

   b. SSTF

   c. SCAN

   d. N-Step SCAN

   e. C-SCAN

12.45 In this chapter, we have investigated several cylinder-oriented disk scheduling strategies including FCFS, SSTF, SCAN, *N*-Step SCAN, and C-SCAN, F-SCAN, LOOK and C-LOOK. Write a simulation program to compare the performance of these scheduling methods under light, medium, and heavy loads. Define a light load as one in which there is usually either 0 or 1 requests waiting for the entire disk. Define a medium load as one in which each cylinder has either 0 or 1 request waiting. Define a heavy load as one in which many cylinders are likely to have many requests pending. Use random

number generation to simulate the arrival time of each request as well as the actual cylinder for each request.

12.46 The availability of moving-head disk storage has contributed greatly to the success of modern computing systems. Disks offer relatively fast and direct access to enormous amounts of information. Industry forecasters see a solid future for disk-based secondary storage systems, and researchers continue developing new and improved disk scheduling disciplines. Propose several new disk scheduling schemes and compare them with those presented in this chapter.

Develop a program that simulates a disk that contains two platters (i.e., four surfaces), four read/write heads, 25 cylinders and 20 sectors per track. This disk should store the current position of the read/write head and provide functions such as read, write and seek. These functions should return the number of milliseconds required to service each request (track-to-track seek times of 2 ms, average seek times of 10 ms and average latencies of 5 ms are reasonable). Then create a simulation program that generates a uniform distribution of requests specifying a location by platter, cylinder and sector and a size by the number of requested sectors. These requests should be sent to your disk scheduler, which then orders them and sends them to the disk for service by calling its read, write and seek functions. Use the values returned by the disk to determine each scheduling algorithm's throughput, response time and variance of response times.

12.47 Extend the simulation in the previous exercise to incorporate rotational latency. For each strategy, did performance increase or decrease as a result?

Recommended Reading

Because disks are a bottleneck in most systems, disk performance optimization continues to be an active area of research and analysis in the literature. Denning discussed how disk scheduling algorithms can improve performance.[92] As hard disks became the dominant form of secondary storage, research into improving their performance continued.[93,94,95,96,97,98,99] Researchers regularly perform comparative analyses of disk scheduling algorithms, often using sophisticated simulations of hard disk activity.[36,39] Patterson et al. introduced the notion of

RAID in their seminal paper;[100] subsequent research has further explored the trade-offs between various RAID levels.[101,102] As the gap between main memory and hard disk speeds grows at an increasing pace, microelectromechanical storage (MEMS) devices, which access a rectangular media using chips containing thousands of read/write heads, show promise as a technology to replace the hard disk as high-capacity, low-cost storage.[103,104] The bibliography for this chapter is located on our Web site at www.deitel.com/books/os3e/Bibliography.pdf.

Works Cited

1. Kozierok, C., "Life Without Hard Disk Drives," *PCGuide*, April 17, 2001, <www.pcguide.com/ref/hdd/histWithout-c.html>.

2. Khurshudov, A., *The Essential Guide to Computer Data Storage*, Upper Saddle River, NJ: Prentice Hall PTR., 2001, p. 6.

3. "RAMAC," *Whatis.com*, April 30, 2001, <searchstorage.techtarget.com/sDefinition/0,,sid5_gci548619,00.html>.

4. Khurshudov, A., *The Essential Guide to Computer Data Storage*, Upper Saddle River, NJ: Prentice Hall PTR, 2001, p. 90.

5. "Cost of Hard Drive Space," September 20, 2002, <www.littletechshop.com/ns1625/winchest.html>.

6. Patterson, D.; G. Gibson; and R. Katz, "A Case for Redundant Arrays of Inexpensive Disks," *Proceedings of the ACM SIGMOD*, June 1998, p. 109.

7. Gotlieb, C., and G. MacEwen, "Performance of Movable-Head Disk Storage Devices," *Journal of the ACM*, Vol. 20, No. 4, October 1973, pp. 604–623.

8. Smith, A., "On the Effectiveness of Buffered and Multiple Arm Disks," *Proceedings of the Fifth Symposium on Computer Architecture*, 1978, pp. 109–112.

9. Pechura, M., and J. Schoeffler, "Estimated File Access Time of Floppy Disks," *Communications of the ACM*, Vol. 26, No. 10, October 1983, pp. 754–763.

10. Kozierok, C., "Spindle Speed," *PCGuide*, April 17, 2001, <www.pcguide.com/ref/hdd/op/spinSpeed-c.html>.

11. Walters, S., "Estimating Magnetic Disc Seeks," *Computer Journal*, Vol. 18, No. 1, 1973, pp. 412–416.

12. Kollias, J., "An Estimate of Seek Time for Batched Searching of Random or Indexed Sequential Structured Files," *Computer Journal*, Vol. 21, No. 2, 1978, pp. 21–26.

13. Kozierok, C., "Hard Disk Tracks, Cylinders and Sectors," modified April 17, 2001, <www.pcguide.com/ref/hdd/geom/tracks.htm>.

14. "DiamondMax Plus 9," Maxtor Corporation, May 14, 2003, <www.maxtor.com/en/documentation/data_sheets/diamondmax_plus_9_data_sheet.pdf>.

15. "WD Caviar Hard Drive 250GB 7200 RPM," October 28, 2003, <www.westerndigital.com/en/products/Products.asp?DriveID=41>.

16. "MK8025GAS," Toshiba America, Inc., October 28, 2003, <sdd.toshiba.com/main.aspx?Path=/81820000000700000010000659800001516/81820000011d000000010000659c000003fd/8182000001c8000000010000659c00000599/8182000001e5000000010000659c000005cb/8182000006db000000010000659c00001559>.

17. "WD Raptor Enterprise Serial ATA Hard Drive 36.7 GB 10,000 RPM," October 28, 2003, <www.westerndigital.com/en/products/WD360GD.asp>.

18. "Cheetah 15K.3," *Seagate Technology*, March 27, 2003, <www.seagate.com/docs/pdf/datasheet/disc/ds_cheetah15k.3.pdf>.

19. Wilhelm, N., "An Anomaly in Disk Scheduling: A Comparison of FCFS and SSTF Seek Scheduling Using an Empirical Model for Disk Accesses," *Communications of the ACM*, Vol. 19, No. 1, January 1976, pp. 13–17.

20. Wong, C., "Minimizing Expected Head Movement in One-Dimensional and Two-Dimensional Mass Storage Systems," *ACM Computing Surveys*, Vol. 12, No. 2, 1980, pp. 167–178.

21. Frank, H., "Analysis and Optimization of Disk Storage Devices for Time-Sharing Systems," *Journal of the ACM*, Vol. 16, No. 4, October 1969, pp. 602–620.

22. Teorey, T., "Properties of Disk Scheduling Policies in Multiprogrammed Computer Systems," *Proceedings of AFIPS FJCC,* Vol. 41, 1972, pp. 1–11.

23. Wilhelm, N., "An Anomaly in Disk Scheduling: A Comparison of FCFS and SSTF Seek Scheduling Using an Empirical Model for Disk Access," *Communications of the ACM*, Vol. 19, No. 1, January 1976, pp. 13–17.

24. Hofri, M., "Disk Scheduling: FCFS vs. SSTF Revisited," *Communications of the ACM*, Vol. 23, No. 11, November 1980, pp. 645–653.

25. Denning, P., "Effects of Scheduling on File Memory Operations," *Proceedings of AFIPS, SJCC*, Vol. 30, 1967, pp. 9–21.

26. Teorey, T., "Properties of Disk Scheduling Policies in Multiprogrammed Computer Systems," *Proceedings of AFIPS FJCC*, Vol. 41, 1972, pp. 1–11.

27. Wilhelm, N., "An Anomaly in Disk Scheduling: A Comparison of FCFS and SSTF Seek Scheduling Using an Empirical Model for Disk Access," *Communications of the ACM*, Vol. 19, No. 1, January 1976, pp. 13–17.

28. Hofri, M., "Disk Scheduling: FCFS vs. SSTF Revisited," *Communications of the ACM*, Vol. 23, No. 11, November 1980, pp. 645–653.

29. Denning, P., "Effects of Scheduling on File Memory Operations," *Proceedings of AFIPS, SJCC*, Vol. 30, 1967, pp. 9–21.

30. Teorey, T., "Properties of Disk Scheduling Policies in Multiprogrammed Computer Systems," *Proceedings of AFIPS FJCC*, Vol. 41, 1972, pp. 1–11.

31. Gotlieb, C., and G. MacEwen, "Performance of Movable-Head Disk Storage Devices," *Journal of the ACM*, Vol. 20, No. 4, October 1973, pp. 604–623.

32. Teorey, T., and T. Pinkerton, "A Comparative Analysis of Disk Scheduling Policies," *Communications of the ACM*, Vol. 15, No. 3, March 1972, pp. 177–184.

33. Thomasian, A., and C. Liu, "Special Issue on the PAPA 2002 Workshop: Disk Scheduling Policies with Lookahead," *ACM SIGMETRICS Performance Evaluation Review*, Vol. 30, No. 2, September 2002, pp. 36.

34. Teorey, T., "Properties of Disk Scheduling Policies in Multiprogrammed Computer Systems," *Proceedings of AFIPS FJCC*, Vol. 41, 1972, pp. 1–11.

35. Teorey, T., and T. Pinkerton, "A Comparative Analysis of Disk Scheduling Policies," *Communications of the ACM*, Vol. 15, No. 3, March 1972, pp. 177–184.

36. Worthington, B.; G. Ganger; and Y. Patt, "Scheduling Algorithms for Modern Disk Drives," *Proceedings of the 1994 ACM SIGMETRICS Conference*, May 1994, p. 243.

37. "Hard Disk Specifications," viewed October 2, 2003, <www.storagereview.com/guide2000/ref/hdd/perf/perf/spec/index.html>.

38. Stone, H., and S. Fuller, "On the Near Optimality of the Shortest-Latency-Time-First Drum Scheduling Discipline," *Communications of the ACM*, Vol. 16, No. 6, June 1973, pp. 352–353.

39. Thomasian, A., and C. Liu, "Special Issue on the PAPA 2002 Workshop: Disk Scheduling Policies with Look-Ahead," *ACM SIGMETRICS Performance Evaluation Review*, Vol. 30, No. 2, September 2002, p. 33.

40. Thomasian, A., and C. Liu, "Special Issue on the PAPA 2002 Workshop: Disk Scheduling Policies with Look-Ahead," *ACM SIGMETRICS Performance Evaluation Review*, Vol. 30, No. 2, September 2002, p. 33.

41. Kozierok, C., "Logical Geometry," *PCGuide*, April 17, 2001, <www.pcguide.com/refhdd/perf/perf/extp/pcCaching-c.html>.

42. Khurshudov, A., *The Essential Guide to Computer Data Storage* (Upper Saddle River, NJ: Prentice Hall PTR. 2001), pp. 106–107.

43. "Dell – Learn More – Hard Drives," 2003, <www.dell.com/us/en/dhs/learnmore/learnmore_hard_drives_desktop_popup_dimen.htm>.

44. Chaney, R., and B. Johnson, "Maximizing Hard-Disk Performance: How Cache Memory Can Dramatically Affect Transfer Rate," *Byte*, May 1984, pp. 307–334.

45. Thomasian, A., and C. Liu, "Special Issue on the PAPA 2002 Workshop: Disk Scheduling Policies with Look-Ahead," *ACM SIGMETRICS Performance Evaluation Review*, Vol. 30, No. 2, September 2002, p. 38.

46. Wilhelm, N., "An Anomaly in Disk Scheduling: A Comparison of FCFS and SSTF Seek Scheduling Using an Empirical Model for Disk Accesses," *Communications of the ACM*, Vol. 19, No. 1, January 1976, pp. 13–17.

47. Lynch, W., "Do Disk Arms Move?" *Performance Evaluation Review, ACM Sigmetrics Newsletter*, Vol. 1, December 1972, pp. 3–16.

48. Kozierok, C., "Cache Write Policies and the Dirty Bit," *PCGuide*, April 17, 2001, <www.pcguide.com/ref/mbsys/cache/funcWrite-c.html>.

49. Thomasian, A., and C. Liu, "Special Issue on the PAPA 2002 Workshop: Disk Scheduling Policies with Look-Ahead," *ACM SIGMETRICS Performance Evaluation Review*, Vol. 30, No. 2, September 2002, p. 32.

50. Kozierok, C., "Operating System and Controller Disk Caching," *PCGuide*, April 17, 2001, <www.pcguide.com/refhdd/perf/perf/extp/pcCaching-c.html>.

51. Thomasian, A., and C. Liu, "Special Issue on the PAPA 2002 Workshop: Disk Scheduling Policies with Look-Ahead," *ACM SIGMETRICS Performance Evaluation Review*, Vol. 30, No. 2, September 2002, p. 31.

52. "Disk Optimization Can Save Time and Resources in a Windows NT/2000 Environment," *Raxco Software*, <www.raxco.dk/raxco/perfectdisk2000/download/Optimization_Can_Save_Time.pdf>.

53. King, R., "Disk Arm Movement in Anticipation of Future Requests," *ACM Transactions in Computer Systems*, Vol. 8, No. 3, August 1990, p. 215.

54. King, R., "Disk Arm Movement in Anticipation of Future Requests," *ACM Transactions in Computer Systems*, Vol. 8, No. 3, August 1990, p. 214.

55. King, R., "Disk Arm Movement in Anticipation of Future Requests," *ACM Transactions in Computer Systems,* Vol. 8, No. 3, August 1990, pp. 220, 226

56. "RAID Overview," <www.amsstorage.com/html/raid_overview.html>.

57. Patterson, D.; G. Gibson; and R. Katz, "A Case for Redundant Arrays of Inexpensive Disks," *Proceedings of the ACM SIGMOD,* June 1988, p. 109.

58. Patterson, D.; G. Gibson; and R. Katz, "A Case for Redundant Arrays of Inexpensive Disks," *Proceedings of the ACM SIGMOD,* June 1988, pp. 109–110.

59. Chen, P.; E. Lee; G. Gibson; R. Katz; and D. Patterson, "RAID: High-Performance, Reliable Secondary Storage," *ACM Computing Surveys,* Vol. 26, No. 2, June 1994, pp. 151–152.

60. Chen, P.; E. Lee; G. Gibson; R. Katz; and D. Patterson, "RAID: High-Performance, Reliable Secondary Storage," *ACM Computing Surveys,* Vol. 26, No. 2, June 1994, p. 147.

61. Chen, P.; E. Lee; G. Gibson; R. Katz; and D. Patterson, "RAID: High-Performance, Reliable Secondary Storage," *ACM Computing Surveys,* Vol. 26, No. 2, June 1994, p. 152.

62. "RAID 0: Striped Disk Array without Fault Tolerance," <www.raid.com/04_01_00.html>.

63. "RAID 0: Striped Disk Array without Fault Tolerance," <www.raid.com/04_01_00.html>.

64. Chen, P.; E. Lee; G. Gibson; R. Katz; and D. Patterson, "RAID: High-Performance, Reliable Secondary Storage," *ACM Computing Surveys,* Vol. 26, No. 2, June 1994, p. 152.

65. Patterson, D.; G. Gibson; and R. Katz, "A Case for Redundant Arrays of Inexpensive Disks," *Proceedings of the ACM SIGMOD,* June 1988, p. 112.

66. "RAID Overview," <www.masstorage.com.com/html/raid_overview.html>.

67. "RAID 1: Mirroring and Duplexing," <www.raid.com/04_01_01.html>.

68. "RAID 2: Hamming Code ECC," <www.raid.com/04_01_02.html>.

69. Patterson, D.; G. Gibson; and R. Katz, "A Case for Redundant Arrays of Inexpensive Disks," *Proceedings of the ACM SIGMOD,* June 1988, p. 112.

70. Patterson, D.; G. Gibson; and R. Katz, "A Case for Redundant Arrays of Inexpensive Disks," *Proceedings of the ACM SIGMOD* June 1988, p. 112.

71. "RAID Overview," <www.amsstorage.com.com/html/raid_overview.html>.

72. Patterson, D.; G. Gibson; and R. Katz, "A Case for Redundant Arrays of Inexpensive Disks," *Proceedings of the ACM SIGMOD,* June 1988, p. 112.

73. Chen, P.; E. Lee; G. Gibson; R. Katz; and D. Patterson, "RAID: High-Performance, Reliable Secondary Storage," *ACM Computing Surveys,* Vol. 26, No. 2, June 1994, p. 156.

74. "RAID 3: Parallel Transfer with Parity," <www.raid.com/04_01_03.html>.

75. Patterson, D.; G. Gibson; and R. Katz, "A Case for Redundant Arrays of Inexpensive Disks," *Proceedings of the ACM SIGMOD,* June 1988, p. 113.

76. Patterson, D.; G. Gibson; and R. Katz, "A Case for Redundant Arrays of Inexpensive Disks," *Proceedings of the ACM SIGMOD,* June 1988, p. 113.

77. "RAID Overview," <www.amsstorage.com/html/raid_overview.html>.

78. "RAID 5: Independent Data Disks with Distributed Parity Blocks," <www.raid.com/04_01_05.html>.

79. "RAID Level 4," *PCGuide.com,* <www.pcguide.com/ref/hdd/perf/raid/levels/singleLevel4-c.html>.

80. Patterson, D.; G. Gibson; and R. Katz, "A Case for Redundant Arrays of Inexpensive Disks," *Proceedings of the ACM SIGMOD,* June 1988, p. 114.

81. Patterson, D.; G. Gibson; and R. Katz, "A Case for Redundant Arrays of Inexpensive Disks," *Proceedings of the ACM SIGMOD,* June 1988, p. 114.

82. Savage, S., and J. Wilkes, "AFRAID—A Frequently Redundant Array of Independent Disks," *Proceedings of the 1996 Usenix Conference,* January 1996, p. 27.

83. Chen, P.; E. Lee; G. Gibson; R. Katz; and D. Patterson, "RAID: High-Performance, Reliable Secondary Storage," *ACM Computing Surveys,* Vol. 26, No. 2, June 1994, pp. 166–168.

84. Savage, S., and J. Wilkes, "AFRAID—A Frequently Redundant Array of Independent Disks," *Proceedings of the 1996 Usenix Conference,* January 1996, pp. 27, 37.

85. "RAID 5: Independent Data Disks with Distributed Parity Blocks," <www.raid.com/04_01_05.html>.

86. "RAID Level 5," *PCGuide.com,* <www.pcguide.com/ref/hdd/perf/raid/levels/singleLevel5-c.html>.

87. "Multiple (Nested) RAID Levels," *PCGuide.com,* <www.pcguide.com/ref/hdd/perf/raid/mult.htm>.

88. "RAID 6: Independent Data Disks with Two Independent Parity Schemes," <www.raid.com/04_01_06.html>.

89. "Multiple (Nested) RAID Levels," *PCGuide.com,* <www.pcguide.com/ref/hdd/perf/raid/mult.htm>.

90. "RAID Level 7," *PCGuide.com,* <www.pcguide.com/ref/hdd/perf/raid/levels/singleLevel7-c.html>.

91. Geist, R., and S. Daniel, "A Continuum of Disk Scheduling Algorithms," *ACM Transactions in Computer Systems,* Vol. 5, February 1, 1987, p. 78.

92. Denning, P., "Effects of Scheduling on File Memory Operations," *Proceedings of AFIPS, SJCC,* Vol. 30, 1967, pp. 9–21.

93. Teorey, T., "Properties of Disk Scheduling Policies in Multiprogrammed Computer Systems," *Proceedings of AFIPS FJCC,* Vol. 41, 1972, pp. 1–11.

94. Wilhelm, N., "An Anomaly in Disk Scheduling: A Comparison of FCFS and SSTF Seek Scheduling Using an Empirical Model for Disk Access," *Communications of the ACM,* Vol. 19, No. 1, January 1976, pp. 13–17.

95. Hofri, M., "Disk Scheduling: FCFS vs. SSTF Revisited," *Communications of the ACM*, Vol. 23, No. 11, November 1980, pp. 645–653.

96. Geist, R., and S. Daniel, "A Continuum of Disk Scheduling Algorithms," *ACM Transactions in Computer Systems*, Vol. 5, February 1, 1987, p. 78.

97. King, R., "Disk Arm Movement in Anticipation of Future Requests," *ACM Transactions in Computer Systems,* Vol. 8, No. 3, August 1990, p. 215.

98. Thomasian, A., and C. Liu, "Special Issue on the PAPA 2002 Workshop: Disk Scheduling Policies with Look-Ahead," *ACM SIGMETRICS Performance Evaluation Review*, Vol. 30, No. 2, September 2002, p. 33.

99. Patterson, D.; G. Gibson; and R. Katz, "A Case for Redundant Arrays of Inexpensive Disks," *Proceedings of the ACM SIGMOD,* June 1988, p. 109.

100. Patterson, D.; G. Gibson; and R. Katz, "A Case for Redundant Arrays of Inexpensive Disks," *Proceedings of the ACM SIGMOD,* June 1988, p. 109.

101. Chen, P.; E. Lee; G. Gibson; R. Katz; and D. Patterson, "RAID: High-Performance, Reliable Secondary Storage," *ACM Computing Surveys,* Vol. 26, No. 2, June 1994, pp. 151–152.

102. Savage, S., and J. Wilkes, "AFRAID—A Frequently Redundant Array of Independent Disks," *Proceedings of the 1996 Usenix Conference,* January 1996, pp. 27, 37.

103. Griffin, J., L.; S. W. Schlosser; G. R. Ganger; and D. F. Nagle, "Operating System Management of MEMS-based Storage Devices," *Proceedings of the Fourth Symposium on Operating Systems Design and Implementation (OSDI)*, 2000, pp. 227–242.

104. Uysal, M.; A. Merchant; and G. A. Alvarez, "Using MEMS-based Storage in Disk Arrays," *Proceedings of the Second USENIX Conference on File and Storage Technologies*, March, 2003.

'Tis in my memory lock'd, And you yourself shall keep the key of it.

—William Shakespeare—

E pluribus unus. (One composed of many.)

—Virgil—

I can only assume that a "Do Not File" document is filed in a "Do Not File" file.

—Senator Frank Church, Senate Intelligence Subcommittee Hearing, 1975—

A form of government that is not the result of a long sequence of shared experiences, efforts, and endeavors can never take root.

—Napoleon Bonaparte—

Chapter 13

File and Database Systems

Objectives

After reading this chapter, you should understand:

- *the need for file systems.*
- *files, directories and the operations that can be performed on them.*
- *organizing and managing a storage device's data and free space.*
- *controlling access to data in a file system.*
- *backup, recovery and file system integrity mechanisms.*
- *database systems and models.*

Chapter Outline

13.1 Introduction

Most computer users are familiar with the concept of **file** as a named collection of data that is manipulated as a unit. Files typically reside on secondary storage devices such as disks, CDs or tapes, though they can exist exclusively in volatile main memory. In this chapter, we discuss how systems organize and access file data so that it can be retrieved quickly from high-latency secondary storage devices. We also discuss how operating systems can create an interface that facilitates navigation of a user's files. Because secondary storage often contains files storing sensitive information for several users, we discuss how systems control access to file data. Many systems use files to store important information such as inventories, payrolls and account balances; we discuss how file systems can protect such data from corruption or total loss from disasters such as power and disk failures. Finally, we discuss how systems that manage large amounts of shared data can benefit from databases as an alternative to files.

13.2 Data Hierarchy

Information is stored in computers according to a **data hierarchy**. The lowest level of the data hierarchy is composed of bits. Bits are grouped together in **bit patterns** to represent all data items of interest in computer systems. There are 2^n possible bit patterns for a string of n bits.

The next level in the data hierarchy is fixed-length patterns of bits such as **bytes**, characters and words. When referring to storage, a byte is typically 8 bits. A **word** is the number of bits a processor can operate on at once. Thus, a word is 4 bytes on a 32-bit processor and 8 bytes on a 64-bit processor.

Characters map bytes (or groups of bytes) to symbols such as letters, numbers, punctuation and new lines. Many systems use 8-bit characters and thus can have 2^8, or 256, possible characters in their **character sets**. The three most popular character sets in use today are **ASCII (American Standard Code for Information Interchange), EBCDIC (Extended Binary-Coded Decimal Interchange Code)** and **Unicode**®.

ASCII stores characters as 8-bit bytes and thus can have 256 possible characters in its character set. Due to ASCII's small character size, it does not support international character sets. EBCDIC is often used for representing data in mainframe computer systems, particularly systems developed by IBM; it also stores characters as 8-bit bytes.[1]

Unicode is an internationally recognized standard that is popular in Internet and multilingual applications. Its goal is to use a unique number to represent every character in all the world's languages.[2] Unicode provides 8-, 16- and 32-bit representations of its character set. To simplify conversion from ASCII to Unicode characters, the 8-bit representation of Unicode, called UTF–8 (Unicode character set Translation Format–8 bit), corresponds directly to the ASCII character set. HTML files are typically encoded using UTF–8. UTF–16 and UTF–32 each provide larger character sets, enabling applications to store information containing characters from multiple alphabets, such as Greek, Cyrillic, Chinese and a great many others. However, they require larger files to store the same number of characters when compared to UTF–8. For example, the 12-character string "Hello, world" requires 12 bytes of storage using 8-bit characters, 24 bytes using 16-bit characters and 48 bytes using 32-bit characters.

A **field** is a group of characters (e.g., a person's name, street address or telephone number). A **record** is a group of fields. A student record may contain, for example, separate fields for identification number, name, address, telephone number, cumulative grade point average, major field of study, expected date of graduation and so on. A file is a group of related records. For example, a student file might contain one record for each student in a university; a payroll file might contain one record for every employee in a company. The highest level of the data hierarchy is a file system or database. File systems are collections of files, and databases are collections of data (database systems are discussed in Section 13.12, Database Systems).

The term **volume** is a unit of data storage that may hold multiple files. A physical volume is limited to one storage device; a logical volume—such as one that might be used in a virtual machine—could be draped across many devices. Examples of volumes include CDs, DVDs, tapes and hard disks.

Self Review

1. What are the trade-offs of large character sets?
2. How many possible character can be stored using a 16-bit, 32-bit and 64-bit character set? Why do you suppose that 64-bit character sets are not implemented?

Ans: **1)** Large character sets such as Unicode enable users to store and transmit data in multiple languages. However, large character sets require a large number of bits to represent each character, which increases the size of data they store. **2)** A 16-bit character set can represent 2^{16}, or 65,536, possible characters; a 32-bit character set can represent 2^{32}, or over 4 billion characters; a 64-bit character set can represent 2^{64}, or over 16 quintillion characters. As yet, 64-bit character sets have not been implemented, because they consume a significant amount of space per character to provide a range of characters far beyond what users are likely to need well into future.

13.3 Files

A file is a named collection of data that may be manipulated as a unit by operations such as

- **open**—Prepare a file to be referenced.
- **close**—Prevent further reference to a file until it is reopened.
- **create**—Create a new file.
- **destroy**—Remove a file.
- **copy**—Copy the contents of one file to another.
- **rename**—Change the name of a file.
- **list**—Print or display the contents of a file.

Individual data items within the file may be manipulated by operations like

- **read**—Copy data from a file to a process's memory.
- **write**—Copy data from a process's memory to a file.
- **update**—Modify an existing data item in a file.
- **insert**—Add a new data item to a file.
- **delete**—Remove a data item from a file.

Files may be characterized by attributes such as

- **size**—the amount of data stored in the file.
- **location**—the location of the file (in a storage device or in the system's logical file organization).
- **accessibility**—restrictions placed on access to file data.
- **type**—how the file data is used. For example, an executable file contains machine instructions for a process. A data file may specify the application that is used to access its data.
- **volatility**—the frequency with which additions and deletions are made to a file.
- **activity**—the percentage of a file's records accessed during a given period of time.

Files can consist of one or more records. A **physical record** (or **physical block**) is the unit of information actually read from or written to a storage device. A **logical record** (or **logical block**) is a collection of data treated as a unit by software. When each physical record contains exactly one logical record, the file is said to consist of **unblocked records**. When each physical record may contain several logical records, the file is said to consist of **blocked records**. In a file with fixed-length records, all records are the same length; the block size is ordinarily an integral multiple of the record size. In a file with variable-length records, records may vary in size up to the block size.

Self Review

1. Compare physical records to logical records.
2. Why do you suppose variable-length records incur more storage overhead than fixed-length records?

Ans: **1)** A physical record corresponds to the unit of information read from or written to a storage device. A logical record corresponds to a collection of data treated as a unit by software. **2)** The system needs to determine the length of each record. Two common ways to do this are to end each record with an end-of-record marker, or to precede each record with a length field—each of these takes space. A system that processes fixed-length records need have the length recorded only once.

13.4 File Systems

A **file system** organizes files and manages access to data.[3] File systems are responsible for:

- **File management**—providing the mechanisms for files to be stored, referenced, shared, and secured.

- **Auxiliary storage management**—allocating space for files on secondary or tertiary storage devices.

- **File integrity mechanisms**—ensuring that the information stored in a file is uncorrupted. When file integrity is assured, files contain only the information that they are intended to have.

- **Access methods**—how the stored data can be accessed.

The file system is concerned primarily with managing secondary storage space, particularly disk storage, but it can access file data stored on other media (e.g., main memory).

File systems enable users to create, modify, and delete files; they should also be able to structure files in a manner most appropriate for each application and initiate data transfer between files. Users should also be able to share each other's files in a carefully controlled manner to build upon each other's work. The mechanism for sharing files should provide various types of controlled access such as **read access**, **write access**, **execute access** or various combinations of these.

File systems should exhibit **device independence**—users should be able to refer to their files by **symbolic names** rather than having to use **physical device names**. Symbolic names are logical, user-friendly names, such as `myDirectory:myFile.txt`. Physical device names specify where a file can be found on a device, e.g., disk 2, blocks 782–791. Symbolic names allow file systems to give users a **logical view** of their data by assigning meaningful names to files and file operations. A **physical view** is concerned with the layout of file data on its storage device and the device-specific operations that manipulate the data. The user should not have to be concerned with the particular devices on which data is stored, the form the data takes on those devices or the physical means of transferring data to and from them.

Designing a file system requires knowledge of the user community, including the number of users, the average number and size of files per user, the average duration of user sessions, the nature of applications to be run on the system, and the like. These factors must be carefully considered to determine the most appropriate file organizations and directory structures.

To prevent either accidental loss or malicious destruction of information, file systems should also provide **backup** capabilities that facilitate the creation of redundant copies of data and **recovery** capabilities that enable users to restore any lost or damaged data. In sensitive environments in which information must be kept secure and private, such as in electronic funds transfer systems, criminal records systems, medical records systems, and so on, the file system may also provide **encryp-**

tion and **decryption** capabilities. This makes information useful only to its intended audience—those who possess the decryption keys (encryption and decryption are discussed in Section 19.2, Cryptography; see the Operating Systems Thinking feature, Encryption and Decryption).

Self Review

1. (T/F) File systems manage data only on secondary storage.
2. In what ways is file system management similar to virtual memory management?

Ans: **1)** False. File systems manage files, which represent named collections of data that can be stored on any medium, including main memory. **2)** File system management entails allocating storage, hiding the physical view of storage from applications and controlling access to storage.

13.4.1 Directories

Consider a large-scale timesharing system supporting a large community of users. Each user may have several accounts; each account may have many files. Some files may be small, such as e-mail messages. Other files may be large, such as a master list of parts in an inventory control application.

It is common for user accounts to contain hundreds and even thousands of files. With a user community of several thousand users, a system's disks might easily contain millions of files. These files need to be accessed quickly to limit response times.

To organize and quickly locate files, file systems use **directories**, which are files containing the names and locations of other files in the file system. Unlike other files, a directory does not store user data. Figure 13.1 lists several common directory fields.

Operating Systems Thinking

Encryption and Decryption

Years ago information processed by a computer was largely confined to one local computer system and access to it could be tightly controlled. Operating systems running on today's high-powered computer systems pass massive amounts of information between computers on networks, especially the Internet. Transmission media are insecure and vulnerable, so to protect that information, operating systems software often provides capabilities for encryption and decryption. Both of these operations can be so processor intensive, that it was impractical to employ them on a wide scale years ago. As processor power continues to dramatically increase, more systems will incorporate encryption and decryption into more applications, especially applications that involve vulnerable network transmission.

Directory Field	Description
Name	Character string representing the file's name.
Location	Physical block or logical location of the file in the file system (i.e., a pathname).
Size	Number of bytes consumed by the file.
Type	Description of the file's purpose (e.g., data file or directory file).
Access time	Time the file was last accessed.
Modified time	Time the file was last modified.
Creation time	Time the file was created.

Figure 13.1 | Directory file contents example.[4, 5, 6]

Single-Level File System

The simplest file system organization is a **single-level** (or **flat**) directory structure. In this implementation, the file system stores all of its files using one directory.[7] In a single-level file system, no two files can have the same name. Because most environments contain a large number of files, many of which use the same name, single-level file systems are rarely implemented.

Hierarchically Structured File System

A more appropriate file system for most environments may be organized as follows (Fig. 13.2). A **root** indicates where on the storage device the **root directory** begins. Directories are files that can point to other directories and files. In Fig. 13.2, the root directory points to the various **user directories**. A user directory contains an entry for each of that user's files; each entry points to the location of the corresponding file on the storage device.

File names need be unique only within a given user directory. In such **hierarchically structured file systems**, each directory may contain several subdirectories but no more than one parent directory. The name of a file is usually formed as the **pathname** from the root directory to the file. For example, in a two-level file system with users SMITH, JONES and DOE, in which JONES has files PAYROLL and INVOICES, the pathname for file PAYROLL might be formed as ROOT:JONES:PAYROLL. In this example, ROOT indicates the root directory, and the use of a colon (:) delimits different pieces of the pathname.

Hierarchical file systems are implemented by most general-purpose file systems, but the name of the root directory and the type of delimiter can vary between file systems. A Windows file system's root directory is specified by a letter followed by a colon (e.g., C:), and a UNIX-based file systems uses a slash (/). Windows systems use a backslash (e.g., C:\Jones\Payroll) as a delimiter and UNIX-based systems use a slash (e.g., /jones/payroll). Various Linux and Windows XP file systems are considered in depth in the case studies (see Section 20.7.3, Second Extended File System (ext2fs), and Section 21.8.2, NTFS).

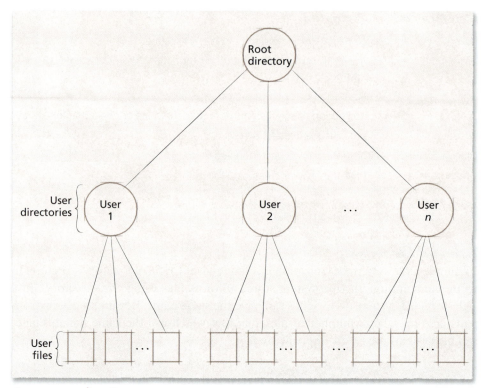

Figure 13.2 | *Two-level hierarchical file system.*

Relative Pathnames

Many file systems support the notion of a **working directory** to simplify navigation using pathnames. The working directory (represented by the directory entry ". " in Windows and UNIX-based file systems) enables users to specify a pathname that does not begin at the root directory. For example, suppose the current working directory has been set to /home/hmd/ in the file system in Fig. 13.3. The **relative path** to /home/hmd/os/chapter13 would be os/chapter13.[8] This feature reduces the size of the pathname when accessing files. When a file system encounters a relative pathname, it forms the **absolute path** (i.e., the path beginning at the root) by concatenating the working directory and the relative path. The file system then traverses the directory structure to locate the requested file.

The file system typically maintains a reference to the working directory's **parent directory**, the directory one level higher in the file system hierarchy. For example, in Fig. 13.3, home is the parent directory for the hmd, pjd and drc directories. In Windows and UNIX-based systems, ". ." is a reference to the parent directory.[9]

Links

A **link** is a directory entry that references a data file or directory that is typically located in a different directory.[10] Users often employ links to simplify file system

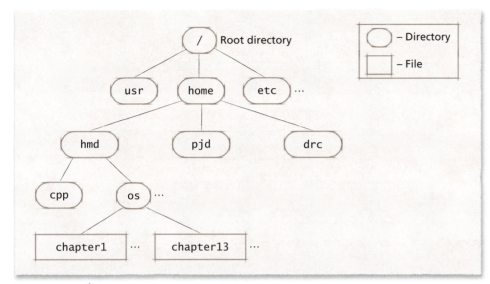

Figure 13.3 | *Example hierarchical file system contents.*

navigation and to share files. For example, suppose that a user's working directory is /home/drc/ and the user shares another user's files located in the /home/hmd/os/ directory. By creating a link to /home/hmd/os/ in the user's working directory, the user can access the shared files simply using the relative pathname os/.

A **soft link** (also called a symbolic link in UNIX-based systems, a "shortcut" on Windows systems and "alias" on MacOS systems) is a directory entry containing the pathname for another file. The file system locates the target of the soft link by traversing the directory structure using the specified pathname.[11]

A **hard link** is a directory entry that specifies the location of the file (typically a block number) on the storage device. The file system locates a hard link's file data by directly accessing the physical block it references.[12]

Figure 13.4 illustrates the difference between soft links and hard links. Files foo and bar are located at block numbers 467 and 843, respectively. The directory entry foo_hard is a hard link because it specifies the same block number (467) as foo's directory entry. The directory entry foo_soft is a soft link because it specifies the pathname for foo (in this case, ./foo).

Recall from Section 12.9 that disk reorganization and defragmentation can be used to improve disk performance. During such operations, the physical location of a file can change, requiring the file system to update the file's location in its directory entry. Because a hard link specifies a physical location of a file, the hard link references invalid data when the physical location of the corresponding file changes. To address this issue, a file system can store in a file a pointer to each of its hard links. When the file's physical location changes, the file system can use these pointers to find hard links that require updating.

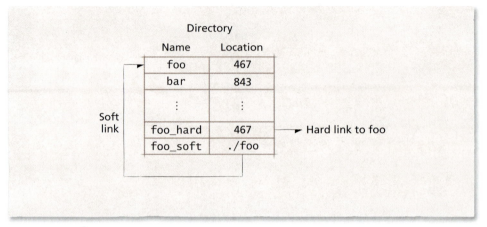

Figure 13.4 | *Links in a file system.*

Because soft links store the logical location of the file in the file system, which does not change during defragmentation or disk reorganization, they do not require updating when file data is moved. However, if a user moves a file to a different directory or renames the file, any soft links to that file are no longer valid. This behavior can be useful in some cases. For example, a user may wish to replace a program file with a new version of the program with the same name. In this case, the file that was originally linked can be moved, renamed or replaced, but the soft link will continue to reference a valid file (the new version of the program). Traditionally, file systems do not update soft links when a file is moved to a different directory.

When a user destroys a link to a file, the file system must determine whether to destroy the corresponding file as well. For this purpose, file systems typically maintain a count of the number of hard links to a file. When the count reaches zero, the file system contains no references to the file data, so the file can be safely removed. Because soft links do not reference the physical location of file data, they are not considered when determining whether a file should be destroyed.

Self Review

1. Why are single-level file systems inappropriate for most systems?
2. Describe the difference between hard links and soft links.

Ans: **1)** The reason is that most systems require that the file system support multiple files of the same name, a feature that single-level file systems do not provide. **2)** Hard links are directory entries that specify the location of a file on its storage device; soft links specify a file's pathname. Hard links reference the same data even if the file name changes. Soft links locate a file according to its logical location in the file system. Thus, the data referenced by a soft link's pathname can change when a new file is assigned that pathname.

13.4.2 Metadata

Most file systems store data other than user data and directories, such as the locations of a storage device's free blocks (to ensure that new file data does not overwrite blocks that are being used) and the time at which a file was last modified (for accounting purposes). This information, called **metadata**, protects the integrity of the file system and cannot be modified directly by users.

Before a file system can access data, its storage device is typically **formatted**. Formatting is a system-dependent operation, but typically entails inspecting the storage device for any unusable sectors, erasing any data on the device and creating the file system's root directory. Many file systems also create a **superblock** to store information that protects the integrity of the file system. A superblock might contain:

- a **file system identifier** that uniquely identifies the type of file system
- the number of blocks in the file system
- the location of the storage device's free blocks
- the location of the root directory
- the date and time at which the file system was last modified
- information indicating whether the file system needs to be checked (e.g., due to a system failure that prevented buffered data from being written to secondary storage).[13, 14, 15]

If the superblock is corrupted or destroyed, the file system might be unable to access file data. Subtle errors in superblock data (such as the location of the storage device's free blocks) could cause the file system to overwrite existing file data. To reduce the risk of lost data, most file systems distribute redundant copies of the superblock throughout the storage device. Thus, the file system can use redundant copies of the superblock to determine whether the primary superblock is damaged and, if so, replace it.

File Descriptors

When a file is opened, the operating system first locates information about the file by traversing the directory structure. To avoid further (possibly lengthy) traversals, the system maintains a table in main memory that keeps track of open files. In many systems, the file open operation returns a **file descriptor**, a non-negative integer that indexes into the open-file table. From this point on, access to the file is directed through the file descriptor.

The open-file table often contains **file control blocks**. These specify the information that the system needs to manage a file, sometimes called **file attributes**. They are highly system-dependent structures. A typical file control block might include a file's

- symbolic name
- location in secondary storage
- organization structure (e.g., sequential, direct access, and so on)
- device type (e.g., hard disk, CD-ROM)
- access control data (such as which users can access the file and the type of access that is permitted)

- type (data file, object program, C source program, and so on)
- disposition (permanent vs. temporary)
- creation date and time
- date and time last modified
- access activity counts (number of reads, for example).

Ordinarily, file control blocks are maintained on secondary storage. They are brought to main memory when a file is opened to improve the efficiency of file operations.

Self Review

1. Why should the file system maintain redundant copies of critical metadata such as super-blocks?
2. Why do file systems prevent users from accessing metadata directly?

Ans: **1)** Because metadata such as superblocks store information that identify the file system and provide the location of its files and free space, file system data could be lost if the superblock is damaged. Maintaining multiple copies of the superblock data enables the system to recover if the superblock is damaged, which reduces the risk of data loss. **2)** If access were not tightly controlled, accidental misuse of file system metadata could lead to inconsistencies and loss of data.

13.4.3 Mounting

Users often require access to information that is not part of the native file system (i.e., the file system that is permanently mounted on a particular system and whose root is referenced by the root directory). For example, many users store data on a second hard disk, DVD or another workstation in a network in computers. For this reason, operating systems provide the ability to **mount** multiple file systems. Mounting combines multiple file systems into one **namespace**—a set of files that can be identified by a single file system. The unified namespace allows users to access data from different locations as if all files were located inside the native file system.[16]

The mount command assigns a directory, called the **mount point**, in the native file system to the root of the mounted file system. Early Windows file systems provided a flat mounting structure; each mounted file system was assigned a letter and was located at the same level of the directory structure. Typically for example, the file system containing the operating system was mounted at C: and the next file system at D:.

UNIX-compatible file systems (such as the UNIX File System, the Fast File System and the Second Extended File System), and versions of Microsoft's NTFS 5.0 and greater, feature mount points that can be located anywhere in the file system. The contents of the native file system's directory at the mount point are temporarily hidden while another file system is mounted at that directory.[17, 18]

In UNIX systems, some file systems are mounted at one of the directories located in /mnt/. Consider in Fig. 13.5. The mount command places the root of file

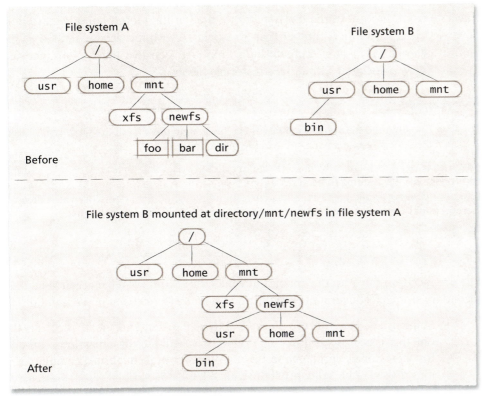

Figure 13.5 | *Mounting a file system.*

system B over the directory `/mnt/newfs/` of file system A. After the mount operation, files from file system B can be accessed from `/mnt/newfs/` in file system A. For example, one can access the file system B's `/usr/bin/` directory from file system A's `/mnt/newfs/usr/bin/` directory. When a file system is mounted, the contents of the directory at the mount point are unavailable to users until the file system is unmounted.

File systems manage mounted directories with **mount tables**. These contain information about mount point pathnames and the device that stores each mounted file system. When the native file system encounters a mount point, it uses the mount table to determine the device and type of file system that is mounted at that directory. Most operating systems support multiple file systems for removable storage, such as Universal Disk Format (UDF) for DVDs and the ISO 9660 file system for CDs. Once the operating system has determined the device's file system type, it uses the appropriate file system to access the file on the specified device. The unmount command allows the user to disconnect mounted file systems. This call updates the mount table and enables users to access any files that were hidden by the mounted system.[19]

Users can create soft links to files in mounted file systems. When the file system encounters the soft link, it uses the specified pathname to traverse the directory structure. When the file system encounters a mount point, it begins the directory traversal from the root of the file system mounted at the mount point. A hard link, however, specifies a block number that is associated with the device that stores the link. In general, users cannot create hard links between two file systems, because they are often associated with different storage devices.

Self Review

1. (T/F) The mounted file system and the native file system must be of the same type.
2. Can a file system create a hard link to a file in a mounted file system?

Ans: **1)** False. A primary advantage to mounting file systems is that they enable multiple heterogeneous file systems to be accessed via a single file system interface. **2)** No, hard links reference device-specific block numbers corresponding to the file system on which they are stored, so they cannot be used to specify physical locations in other file systems.

13.5 File Organization

File organization refers to the manner in which the records of a file are arranged on secondary storage.[20] Several file organization schemes have been implemented:

- **Sequential**—Records are placed in physical order. The "next" record is the one that physically follows the previous record. This organization is natural for files stored on magnetic tape, an inherently sequential medium. Disk files may also be sequentially organized, but for various reasons discussed later in this chapter, records in a sequential disk file are not necessarily stored contiguously.

- **Direct**—Records are directly (randomly) accessed by their physical addresses on a direct access storage device (DASD). The application user places the records on DASD in any order appropriate for a particular application.[21]

- **Indexed sequential**—Records on disk are arranged in logical sequence according to a key contained in each record. The system maintains an index containing the physical addresses of certain principal records. Indexed sequential records may be accessed sequentially in key order, or they may be accessed directly, by a search through the system-created index.

- **Partitioned**—This is essentially a file of sequential subfiles. Each sequential subfile is called a **member**. The starting address of each member is stored in the file's directory. Partitioned files have been used to store program libraries or macro libraries.

Self Review

1. Which file organization technique is most appropriate for tape storage? Why?
2. For which media is direct file organization most appropriate?

Ans: **1)** Sequential file organization is most appropriate for tape storage because it is a sequential access medium. **2)** Direct file organization is most appropriate for random access devices, such as main memory and moving-head disks.

13.6 File Allocation

The problem of allocating and freeing space on secondary storage is somewhat like that experienced in main memory allocation under variable-partition multiprogramming. As files are allocated and freed, it is common for the space on secondary storage to become increasingly fragmented, with files being spread throughout widely dispersed blocks; this can cause performance problems.[22] As discussed in Section 12.9, the system can perform defragmentation, but doing so while the file system is in use can lead to poor response times.

Because processes often access portions of a file sequentially, this leads us to try to store all the data in a file contiguously to improve performance. For example, users searching a file for information often use file scan options to locate the next record or the previous record. These scans should result in minimal seek activity when possible.

Spatial locality tells us that once a process has referred to a data item on a page, it is likely to reference additional data items on that page; it is also likely to reference data items on pages contiguous to that page in the user's virtual address space. Therefore it is desirable to store nonresident, logically contiguous pages of a user's virtual memory space as physically contiguous pages on secondary storage, especially if several pages are stored per physical block.

Because files often grow or shrink over time, and because users rarely know in advance how large their files will be, contiguous storage allocation systems have generally been replaced by more dynamic noncontiguous storage allocation systems. As we will see, these systems attempt to allocate parts of files contiguously to exploit locality, but enable files to change in size with minimal overhead.

Self Review

1. Compare the problem of fragmentation in file systems to that in virtual memory systems.
2. Why is it beneficial to allocate storage in blocks of a system's page size or a multiple of the page size?

Ans: 1) In both systems, fragmentation can lead to wasted storage if no data is small enough to fit in the storage "holes." Unlike main memory, which provides essentially uniform access time for each of its addresses, secondary storage devices such as disks can exhibit high access times if data is fragmented, because the storage device is likely to perform many seek operations to access file data. 2) This enables the system to exploit spatial locality by using a single I/O operation to load into memory several pages that are likely to be referenced in the near future.

13.6.1 Contiguous File Allocation

File systems that employ contiguous allocation place file data at contiguous addresses on the storage device. The user specifies the amount of space needed to store the file in advance. If the desired amount of contiguous space is not available, the file cannot be created.

An advantage of contiguous allocation is that successive logical records typically are physically adjacent to one another. This speeds access compared to systems in which successive logical records are dispersed throughout secondary storage, requiring additional seek operations. Locating file data is straightforward, because the directories need store only the address of the start of the file and the file's length.

A disadvantage to contiguous allocation schemes is that they exhibit the same types of external fragmentation problems inherent in memory allocation for variable-partition multiprogramming systems (see Section 9.9). Also, contiguous allocation can result in poor performance as files grow and shrink over time. If a file grows beyond the size originally specified and there are no adjacent free blocks, the file must be transferred to a new area of adequate size, leading to additional I/O operations. To provide for anticipated expansion, users might overestimate their storage needs, leading to inefficient storage allocation. Contiguous allocation is particularly useful for write-once CDs and DVDs, which do not allow files to grow or shrink over time.

Self Review

1. Explain the benefits of using a contiguous file allocation scheme.
2. Explain the disadvantages of using a contiguous file allocation scheme.

Ans: **1)** Locating file data is straightforward. Also, files can be accessed quickly, because the storage device does not need to perform lengthy seeks after it locates the first block. **2)** Contiguous allocation schemes can lead to significant external fragmentation and poor performance when a file grows too large to be stored contiguously at its current location and must be moved.

13.6.2 Linked-List Noncontiguous File Allocation

Most file systems implemented on rewritable secondary storage media use noncontiguous allocation. One approach to noncontiguous file allocation is to implement a sector-based linked list. In this scheme, each directory entry points to the first sector of a file on a moving-head storage device such as a hard disk. The data portion of a sector stores the contents of the file; the pointer portion stores a pointer to the file's next sector. Because files often occupy multiple sectors, a disk's read/write head must sequentially access each file sector until it finds the requested record.

Noncontiguous allocation solves some of the problems inherent in contiguous allocation schemes, but it has its own drawbacks. Because a file's records may be dispersed throughout the disk, direct and sequential access to logical records can involve many additional seeks besides the first seek to the file. Pointers in the list structure also reduce the amount of space available for file data in each sector.

One scheme used to manage secondary storage more efficiently and reduce file-traversal overhead is called **block allocation**. In this scheme, instead of allocating individual sectors, blocks (often called **extents**) of contiguous sectors are allocated. The system tries to allocate new blocks to a file by choosing free blocks as close as possible to existing file data blocks, preferably on the same cylinder. Each access to the file involves determining the appropriate block and sector within the block.

In block **chaining**, each entry in a directory points to the first block of a file (Fig. 13.6). The blocks comprising a file each contain two portions: a data block and a pointer to the next block. The smallest unit of allocation is a fixed-size block that ordinarily consists of many sectors. Locating a particular record requires searching the block chain until the appropriate block is found, then searching that block until the appropriate record is found. The chain must be searched from the beginning, and if the blocks are dispersed throughout the disk (which is normal), the search process can be slow, as block-to-block seeks occur. Insertion and deletion are performed simply by modifying the pointer in the previous block. Some systems use doubly linked lists to facilitate searching; the blocks are threaded both forward and backward so that a search may proceed in either direction.

Block size can significantly impact file system performance. If blocks are split between files (e.g., a file that requires 2.5 blocks occupies three blocks on disk), large block sizes can result in a considerable amount of internal fragmentation. Large block sizes, however, reduce the number of I/O operations required to access file data. Small block sizes may cause file data to be spread across multiple blocks, which tend to be dispersed throughout the disk. This could lead to poor performance. In practice, block sizes typically range from one to eight kilobytes.[23, 24, 25]

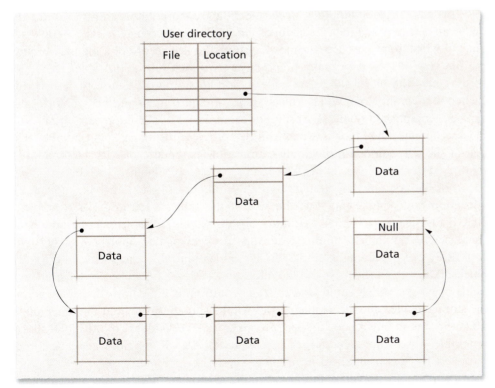

Figure 13.6 | *Noncontiguous file allocation using a linked list.*

Self Review

1. What is the primary disadvantage of linked-list noncontiguous file allocation?

2. What are the trade-offs between choosing a large block size and a small block size?

Ans: **1)** In the worst case, the file system must access each of the file's blocks (when using a singly linked list) or half of the file's blocks (when using a doubly linked list) to locate file data, which could lead to long access times. As we discuss in the next sections, several popular file allocation techniques place a lower limit on access times, which tends to improve performance. **2)** A large block size generally reduces the number of I/O operations required to retrieve a particular record, at the cost of wasted storage due to internal fragmentation. A small block size reduces the amount of internal fragmentation but if file data is scattered throughout a device such as a hard disk, it can lead to poor access times.

13.6.3 Tabular Noncontiguous File Allocation

Tabular noncontiguous file allocation stores pointers to file blocks contiguously in tables to reduce the number of lengthy seeks required to access a particular record (Fig. 13.7). Directory entries indicate the first block of a file. For example, the first block of file C in Fig. 13.7 is 2. The current block number is used as an index into the block allocation table to determine the location of the next block. Therefore, the value of file C's next block number is stored in location 2 in the block allocation table. In this case, file C's next block is 5. The block allocation table's entry for a file's last block stores the value null.

Because the pointers that locate file data are stored in a central location, the table can be cached so that the chain of blocks that compose a file can be traversed quickly, which improves access times. Locating the last record of a file may require the file system to follow many pointers in the block allocation table. To reduce access times, the block allocation table should be stored contiguously on disk and cached in main memory. When a file system contains a small number of blocks, this can be accomplished relatively easily. For example, a 1.44MB floppy disk using 1KB blocks contains 1,440 blocks, which can be addressed using an 11-bit number. The size of the corresponding block allocation table is the size of each block address multiplied by the number of blocks—in this case, approximately 2,000 bytes.

For file systems that contain a greater number of blocks, the size of each file allocation table entry, and thus the size of the table, is greater. For example, a 200GB disk using 4KB blocks contains 50,000,000 blocks, which can be addressed using a 26-bit number. In this case, the block allocation table consumes over 160MB. In the preceding example, the file allocation table was stored in only two blocks; however, in this case the file allocation table is spread across tens of thousands of blocks, which could lead to fragmentation. If file data is dispersed across the storage device, the file's table entries will be spread throughout the block table. Thus, the system might need to load into memory several blocks of the block allocation table, which could lead to poor access times. Also, if the block allocation table is cached, it can consume significant memory.

A popular implementation of tabular noncontiguous file allocation is Microsoft's **FAT file system**. Microsoft first incorporated a **file allocation table**

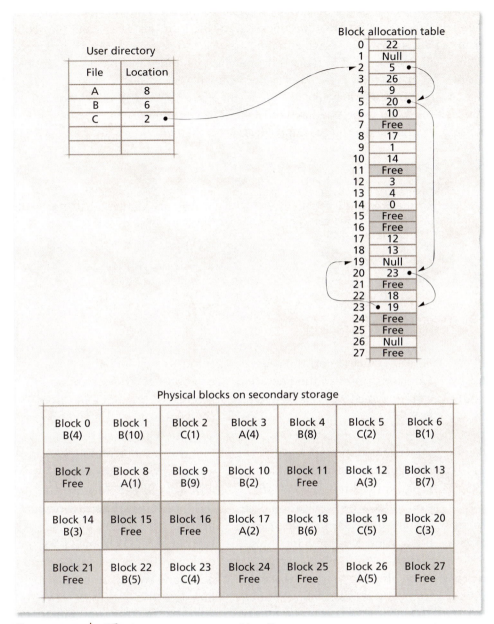

Figure 13.7 | Tabular noncontiguous file allocation.

(FAT) into its release of MS-DOS 1.0 (see the Mini Case Study, MS-DOS).[26] The FAT stores information about each block, including whether the block is currently allocated and the number of the next block in the file. The first version of the FAT file system, called FAT12, allocated 12 bits per entry in the FAT. This meant that a disk managed by FAT12 could contain no more than 2^{12} (4,096) blocks. This was sufficient for small disks containing few files, but FAT12 resulted in significant wasted memory for larger disks. For example, to address an entire 64MB disk, the file system required a minimum block size of 8KB. In this case, small files could incur significant internal fragmentation. As disks grew larger, Microsoft created FAT16 and FAT32, which increased the number of addressable blocks and enabled the file system to access large disks using small block sizes.[27, 28]

When Microsoft introduced FAT in the early 1980s, disk drives were small, allowing the FATs to be small and efficient. FAT continues to be effective for low-capacity storage media such as floppy disks.[29]

Self Review

1. How is tabular file allocation more efficient than linked-list file allocation?
2. What was the primary limitation of FAT12? How did later versions of FAT solve this problem? Why is FAT no longer appropriate to manage today's hard disks?

Mini Case Study

MS-DOS

Microsoft **MS-DOS** was based on a disk operating system written by Tim Paterson for Seattle Computing Products (SCP) in 1980.[30] At the time, SCP needed an operating system for their memory board for the new Intel 16-bit 8086 processor.[31] Digital Research's (CP/M) Control Program for Microcomputers was the major microcomputer operating system at the time, but an updated version for the 8086 processor was not ready when SCP's memory boards went on sale.[32] Paterson was asked to write a new operating system, which was named QDOS (Quick and Dirty Operating System). As the name implies, it was completed in just a few months but had not been thoroughly tested and debugged.

For the remainder of the year, Paterson improved the operating system, which was released as 86-DOS.[33]

Several important goals guided the design of 86-DOS. First, it had to be compatible with programs written for CP/M to exploit its large application base, requiring 86-DOS to have a similar application programming interface (API).[34, 35, 36] To make 86-DOS more efficient than CP/M, Paterson wrote it in assembly language and incorporated the File Allocation Table (FAT) disk management system, based on Microsoft's Stand-Alone Disk BASIC system (see Section 13.6.3, Tabular Noncontiguous File Allocation).[37, 38, 39]

In 1981, IBM solicited vendors for an operating system to

run their first line of personal computers.[40] They attempted to license the popular CP/M from Digital Research, but CP/M creator Gary Kildall refused to sign IBM's highly restrictive nondisclosure agreements.[41] In the meantime, IBM worked with Microsoft to produce software for the new IBM PCs.[42] Microsoft had been licensing 86-DOS from SCP for several months for development purposes and was asked by IBM to purchase all rights to DOS.[43, 44, 45] SCP accepted the offer and 86-DOS, renamed MS-DOS, became the de facto operating system for the IBM Personal Computer and compatible microcomputers.[46]

Ans: **1)** Block allocation tables can store the locations of the file system's data contiguously, reducing the number seeks required to locate a particular record. **2)** FAT12 could not address more than 4,096 blocks, which necessitated large block sizes to address large disks, leading to internal fragmentation. FAT16 and FAT32 addressed this issue by increasing the number of blocks the file allocation table could reference by allowing more bits per entry. This increased the size of the file allocation table, which led to increased file access times and wasted memory in file system caches.

13.6.4 Indexed Noncontiguous File Allocation

Another popular noncontiguous allocation strategy is to use **index blocks** to point to data in a file. Each file has one or more index blocks. An index block contains a list of pointers that point to file data blocks. A file's directory entry points to its index block. To locate a record, the file system traverses the directory structure to determine the location of the file's index block on disk. It then loads the index block into memory and uses the pointers to determine the physical location of a particular block. Often, large files will consume more blocks than the number of pointers that a single index block can store. Most index block implementations reserve the last few entries to store pointers to more index blocks, a technique called **chaining** (Fig. 13.8).

The primary advantage of index block chaining over simple linked-list implementations is that searching may take place in the index blocks themselves. They may be kept close together in secondary storage to minimize seeking. To speed file traversal, index blocks are typically cached in main memory. Once the appropriate record is located via the index blocks, the data block containing that record is read into main memory. Index block chaining is analogous to storing a separate block allocation table for each file, which can be more efficient than systemwide block allocation tables, because references to each file's blocks are stored contiguously in each of its index blocks. File systems typically place index blocks near the data blocks they reference, so the data blocks can be accessed quickly after their index block is loaded.

Index blocks are called **inodes** (i.e., index nodes) in UNIX-based operating systems.[47] A file's inode stores the file's attributes, such as the its owner, size, time of creation and the time of last modification. It also stores the addresses of some of the file's data blocks and pointers to continuation index blocks called **indirect blocks**. Inode structures support up to three levels of indirect blocks (Fig. 13.9). The first indirect block points to data blocks; these data blocks are singly indirect. The second indirect block contains pointers that reference only other indirect blocks. These indirect blocks point to data blocks that are doubly indirect. The third indirect block points only to other indirect blocks that point only to more indirect blocks that point to data blocks; these data blocks are triply indirect. The power of this hierarchical structure is that it places a relatively low limit on the maximum number of pointers that must be followed to locate file data—it enables inodes to locate any data block by following at most four pointers (the inode and up to three levels of indirect blocks).

Inodes are investigated in detail in the Linux case study in Section 20.7.3, Second Extended File System (ext2fs). Another file system that uses index blocks is

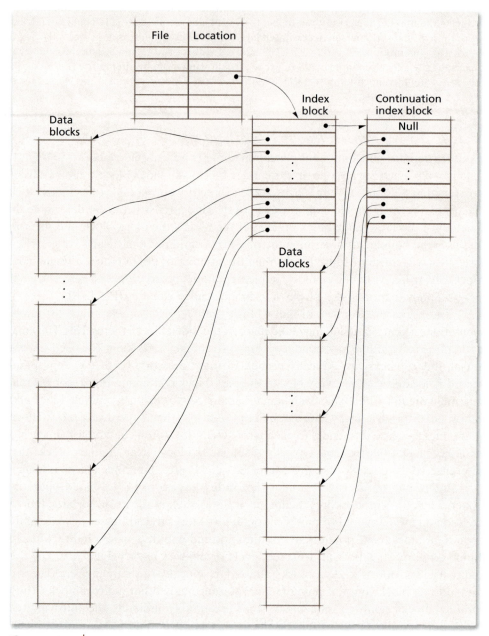

Figure 13.8 | *Index block chaining.*

Microsoft's NTFS, which is discussed in the Windows XP case study in Section 21.8.2, NTFS. Indexed noncontiguous allocation yields good performance with low overhead for many environments and has been implemented in many general-purpose computer systems.

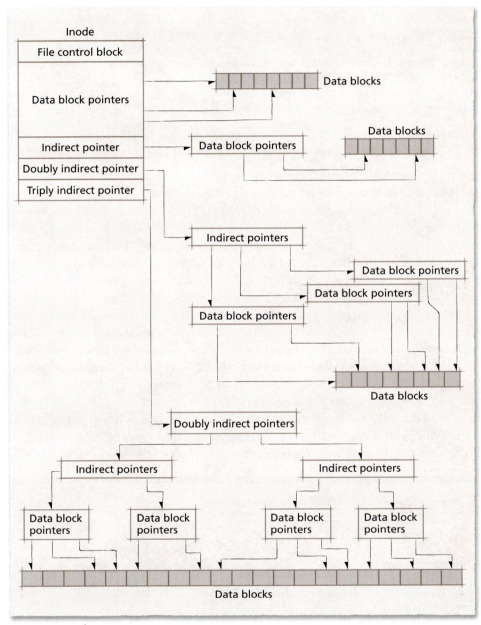

Figure 13.9 | *Inode structure.*

Self Review

1. How does placing index blocks near the data they reference improve access time?
2. Compare indexed noncontiguous file allocation to tabular noncontiguous file allocation when files are, on average, small (e.g., less than or equal to one block).

Ans: **1)** When the file system reads an index block, the disk arm will be near the data it references, reducing or even eliminating seeks. **2)** In tabular noncontiguous file allocation, a small file will consume one data block and one entry in the block allocation table. In indexed noncontiguous file allocation, a small file requires a block for the index block and one data block, which results in substantial storage overhead. Further, several small files can be located by loading a single block of the file allocation table into memory. A file system using indexed file allocation must access a different index block for each file that it references, which can slow access time due to many seeks.

13.7 Free Space Management

As files grow and shrink, file systems maintain a record of the location of blocks that are available to store new data (i.e., free blocks). A file system may use a **free list** to keep track of free space (Fig. 13.10). The free list is a linked list of blocks containing the locations of free blocks. The last entry of a free list block stores a pointer to the next free list block; the last entry of the last free list block stores a null pointer to indicate that there are no further free list blocks. When the system needs to allocate a new block to a file, it finds the address of a free block in the free list, writes the new data to a free block and removes that block's entry from the free list.

The file system typically allocates blocks from the beginning of the free list and appends freed blocks to the end of the list. Pointers to the head and tail of the free list can be stored in the file system's superblock. A free block can be located by following a single pointer; likewise, adding a block to the free list requires the system to follow one pointer. Therefore, this technique requires little overhead to perform free list maintenance operations. As files are created and deleted, however, the storage device's free space can become fragmented, and adjacent entries in the free list will point to noncontiguous blocks. As a result, sequential file data will be allocated noncontiguous blocks, which generally increases file access time. Alterna-

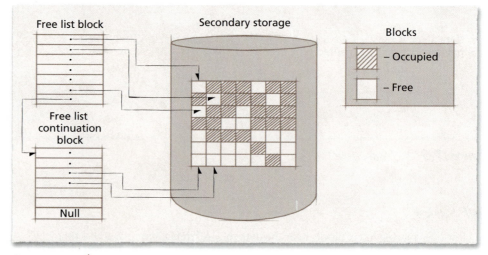

Figure 13.10 | *Free space management using a free list.*

tively, the file system can attempt to allocate contiguous blocks by searching or sorting the free list, both of which incur significant overhead.[48]

Another common method of free space management is the **bitmap** (Fig. 13.11). A bitmap contains one bit for each block in the file system, where the ith bit corresponds to the ith block in the file system. In one implementation, a bit in the bitmap is 1 when the corresponding block is in use and 0 when it is not.[49] The bitmap generally spans multiple blocks. Thus, if each block stores 32 bits, the 15th bit of the third bitmap corresponds to block 79. One of the primary advantages to bitmaps over free lists is that the file system can quickly determine if contiguous blocks are available at certain locations on secondary storage. For example, if a user appends data to a file that ends at block 60, the file system can directly access the 61st entry of the bitmap to determine if the block is free. A disadvantage to bitmaps is that the file system may need to search the entire bitmap to find a free block, resulting in execution overhead. In many cases this overhead is trivial, because processor speeds are so much faster than I/O speeds in today's systems.

Self Review

1. Compare free lists to free space bitmaps in terms of time required to find the next free block, reclaim a free block and allocate a contiguous group of blocks.
2. Which free space management technique mentioned in this section results in lowest storage overhead?

Ans: **1)** Free lists are more efficient for allocating one free block, because the file system need only follow the pointer to the head of the free list. Bitmaps require an exhaustive search until a free block is found. Given a particular block, file systems can use bitmaps to determine if there are contiguous free blocks by directly inspecting their entries. To find contiguous blocks in a free list, the file system must search or sort the free list, requiring significant execution time on average. **2)** Often a bitmap is smaller than a free list, because a bitmaprep-

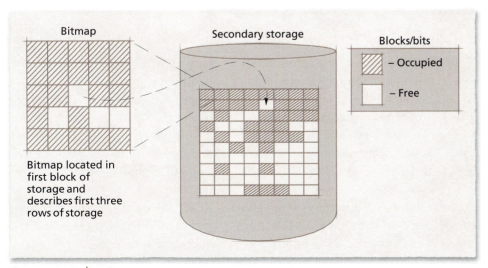

Figure 13.11 | *Free space management using a bitmap.*

resents each block using a single bit, but a free list uses a block number, which can be as large as 32 or 64 bits. A file system's bitmap size is constant, while the free list's size depends on the number of free blocks in the system. Thus, when a file system contains few free blocks, a free list consumes less space than a bitmap.

13.8 File Access Control

Files are often used to store sensitive data such as credit card numbers, passwords, social security numbers and more, so file systems should include mechanisms to control user access to data (see the Operating Systems Thinking feature, Security). In the sections that follow, we discuss common techniques for implementing file access control.

13.8.1 Access Control Matrix

One way to control access to files is to create a two-dimensional **access control matrix** (Fig. 13.12) listing all the users and all the files in the system. The entry a_{ij} is 1 if user i is allowed access to file j; otherwise $a_{ij} = 0$. For example, in Fig. 13.12, user 5 can access all ten files and user 4 can access only file 1. In an installation with a large number of users and a large number of files, this matrix would be quite large. Further, allowing one user access to another user's files is the exception rather than the rule, so the matrix would be extremely sparse. To make such a matrix concept useful, it would be necessary to use codes to indicate various kinds of access such as read-only, write-only, execute-only, read/write, and so on. This could substantially increase the size of the matrix.

Operating Systems Thinking

Security

Computer security has always been an important concern, especially for people responsible for business-critical and mission-critical systems. But the nature of the security problems changes with advances in technology, so operating systems designers must always be evaluating new technology trends and their susceptibility to attack. Early computer systems often weighed many tons and were kept in secure rooms; there was no networking. Today's systems, especially hand-held computers, laptops and even desktop machines can easily be stolen. Now, virtually all systems are capable of being networked, which creates numerous challenges as proprietary information is transmitted over insecure transmission media. Early encryption/decryption schemes have become easy to "crack" with today's high-powered computers, so much more sophisticated schemes have been developed. We discuss security issues throughout the book and devote all of Chapter 19 to this crucial topic. The case study chapters on Linux and Windows XP discuss security considerations and capabilities in those popular operating systems.

File\User	1	2	3	4	5	6	7	8	9	10
1	1	1	0	0	0	0	0	0	0	0
2	0	0	1	0	1	0	0	0	0	0
3	0	1	0	1	0	1	0	0	0	0
4	1	0	0	0	0	0	0	0	0	0
5	1	1	1	1	1	1	1	1	1	1
6	0	0	0	0	0	1	1	0	0	0
7	1	0	0	0	0	0	0	0	0	1
8	1	0	0	0	0	0	0	0	0	0
9	1	1	1	1	0	0	0	0	1	1
10	1	1	0	0	1	1	0	0	0	1

Figure 13.12 | Access control matrix.

Self Review

1. Why is file access control necessary?
2. Why are access control matrices inappropriate for most systems?

Ans: **1)** Any user can reference any pathname in a file system. File systems control access to files to protect personal and sensitive information from users that do not have proper authorization. **2)** Access control matrices are generally large and sparsely populated, leading to wasted storage and inefficient access times when enforcing access control policies.

13.8.2 Access Control by User Classes

A technique that requires considerably less space than the uses of an access control matrix is the control of access to various **user classes**. A common file access classification scheme is

- **Owner**—Normally, this is the user who created the file. The owner has unrestricted access to the file and typically can change file permissions.

- **Specified user**—The owner specifies that another individual may use the file.

- **Group** (or project)—Users are often members of a group working on a particular project. In this case the various members of the group may all be granted access to each other's project-related files.

- **Public**—Most systems allow a file to be designated as public so that it may be accessed by any member of the system's user community. By default, public access rights typically allow users to read or execute a file, but not to write it.

This access control data can be stored as part of the file control block and often consumes an insignificant amount of space. Security is an important issue in operating system design and is covered in greater detail in Chapter 19, Security.

Self Review

1. How do user classes reduce the storage overhead incurred by access control information?

2. Describe the advantages and disadvantages of storing access control data as part of the file control block.

Ans: **1)** User classes enable the file owner to grant permissions to a group of users using one entry. **2)** The advantage is that there is essentially no overhead if the user is granted access to a file, because the file system needs to read the file control block before opening the file anyway. However, if access is denied, the file system will have wastefully performed several lengthy seeks to access the file control block for a file that the user cannot open.

13.9 Data Access Techniques

In many systems, several processes may be requesting file data from various files spread across the storage device, leading to many seeks. Instead of instantly responding to immediate user I/O demands, the operating system may use several techniques to improve performance.

Today's operating systems generally provide many access methods. These are sometimes grouped as **queued access methods** and **basic access methods**. The queued methods provide more powerful capabilities than the basic methods.

Queued access methods are used when the sequence in which records are to be processed can be anticipated, such as in sequential and indexed sequential accessing. The queued methods perform **anticipatory buffering** and scheduling of I/O operations. Such methods attempt to have the next record available for processing as soon as the previous record has been processed. More than one record at a time is maintained in main memory; this allows processing and I/O operations to be overlapped, improving performance.

The basic access methods are normally used when the sequence in which records are to be processed cannot be anticipated, particularly with direct accessing. Also there are many situations, such as database applications, in which user applications want to control record accesses without incurring the overhead of anticipatory buffering. In the basic methods, the access method reads and writes physical blocks; blocking and deblocking (if appropriate to the application) is performed by the user application.

Memory-mapped files map file data to a process's virtual address space instead of using a file system cache.[50] Because references to memory-mapped files occur in a process's virtual address space, the virtual memory manager can make page-replacement decisions based on each process's reference pattern. Memory-mapped files also simplify application programming, because developers can access file data using pointers instead of specifying read, write and seek operations.

When a process issues a write request, the data is typically buffered in main memory (to improve I/O performance) and its corresponding page is marked as dirty. When a memory-mapped file's modified page is replaced, the page is written to its corresponding file on secondary storage. When the file is closed, the system flushes all dirty pages to secondary storage. To reduce the risk of data loss due to a system failure, dirty memory-mapped pages are flushed typically to secondary storage periodically.[51]

Self Review

1. Compare and contrast queued access methods and basic access methods.
2. How do memory-mapped files simplify application programming?

Ans: **1)** Queued access methods perform anticipatory buffering, which attempts to load into memory a block that is likely to be used in the near future. Basic access methods do not attempt to schedule or buffer I/O operations, which is more appropriate when the system cannot predict future requests or when the file system must reduce the risk of losing data during a system failure. **2)** Memory-mapped files enable programmers to access file data using pointers instead of file operations such as read, write and seek.

13.10 Data Integrity Protection

Computer systems often store critical information, such as inventories, financial records and/or personal information. System crashes, natural disasters and malicious programs can destroy this information. The results of such events can be catastrophic.[52] Operating systems and data storage systems should be fault tolerant in that they account for the possibility of disasters and provide techniques to recover from them.

13.10.1 Backup and Recovery

Most systems implement backup techniques to store redundant copies of information and recovery techniques that enable the system to restore data after a system failure. Backup and recovery strategies can also protect systems against user-generated events, such as an unintentional deletion of important data (see the Operating Systems Thinking feature, Backup and Recovery).

Physical safeguards are the lowest level of data protection. Physical obstacles such as locks and alarm systems can prevent unauthorized access to computers that store sensitive data. Because main memory typically is volatile (i.e., it loses its contents when the power is shut off), power outages can result in the loss of data not yet transferred to secondary storage. An uninterruptable power supply (UPS) can be used to protect data from being lost due to a power outage.[53]

Natural disasters such as fires and earthquakes can destroy all data at a site. Thus, some organizations maintain a backup site, geographically removed from the primary site to protect data in case of a site failure.[54] Although these precautions are important, they do not protect data from operating system crashes or disk-head malfunctions.

Performing periodic backups is the most common technique used to prevent data loss. **Physical backups** duplicate a storage device's data at the bit level. In some cases, the system copies only allocated blocks of data. Physical backups are simple to implement, but they store no information about the logical structure of the file system. The file system's data may be stored in different formats, depending on the system architecture, so physical backups cannot easily be restored on computers using different architectures. Also, because a physical backup does not read the file system's logical structure, it cannot distinguish among the files it contains. Thus, physical backups must record and restore the entire file system to ensure that all data has been duplicated, even if most of a file system's data has not been modified since the last physical backup.[55]

A **logical backup** stores file system data and its logical structure. Thus, logical backups inspect the directory structure to determine which files need to be backed up, then write these files to a backup device (e.g., a tape, CD or DVD) in a common, often compressed, archival format. For example, the tape archive (tar) format is commonly used to store, transport and back up multiple files on UNIX-based systems (see www.gnu.org/software/tar/tar.html). Because logical backups store data in a common format using a directory structure, they permit operating systems with different native file formats to read and restore the backup data, so file data can be restored on multiple heterogeneous systems. Logical backups also enable the user to restore a single file from the backup (e.g., an accidentally deleted file),

Operating Systems Thinking

Backup and Recovery

Have you ever lost several hours work because of a system failure? HMD was working on a massive project with hundreds of software engineers when lightning struck our building and we lost all of the system updates for the last week. Fortunately, each of us had backups of our own work, but it still took us several days to recover—a painful and costly experience.

Should users be responsible for performing (potentially time-consuming) backups or should these be done automatically by the system? Backups consume significant resources. How often should backups be done? How much data should be backed up each time? Should backups be done as full system bit images or should they be done with incremental logging

of each change to the system? Answering these questions requires the system administrator to balance the overhead of performing frequent backups with the risk of lost work due to infrequent backups. Incorporating backup and recovery features into operating systems is crucial.

which is typically faster than restoring the entire file system. However, because logical backups can read only data exposed by the file system, they may omit information such as hidden files and metadata that are copied by a physical backup when copying each bit on the file system's storage device. Saving files in a common format can be inefficient due to the overhead incurred when translating between the native file format and the archival format.[56]

Incremental backups are logical backups that store only file system data that has changed since the previous backup. The system can record which files have been modified and write them to the backup file periodically. Because incremental backups require less time and fewer resources than backing up an entire file system, they can be performed more often, reducing the risk of lost data due to disasters.

Self Review

1. Compare and contrast logical backups and physical backups.
2. Why are physical safeguards insufficient for preventing loss of data in the event of a disaster?

Ans: **1)** Logical backups are readable by file systems with different file formats, support incremental backups and enable fine-grained recovery, such as restoring a single file. Physical backups are typically easier to create, because the file system structure does not need to be traversed. However, physical backups do not support incremental or partial backups and are typically incompatible with different systems. **2)** Physical safeguards prevent access to data but do not prevent loss of data due to natural disasters, such as fires and earthquakes, or to hardware and power failures. In fact, there is no way to guarantee absolute security of files.

13.10.2 Data Integrity and Log-Structured File Systems

None of the techniques discussed so far address the possibility that significant activity may occur between the time of the last backup and the time at which a failure occurs (see the Operating Systems Thinking feature, Murphy's Law and Robust Systems). Further, backups often require a lengthy restoration process, during which time the system is not operational.

In systems that cannot tolerate data loss or downtime, RAID and transaction-based file systems are appropriate. In Section 12.10, Redundant Arrays of Independent Disks (RAID), we discussed how RAID levels 1–5 improve a system's mean-time-to-failure and can restore data in the event of a single disk failure. We also discussed how mirroring and hot swappable disks enable RAID systems to continue to operate when disks fail, providing high availability.

Logging and Shadow Paging

If a system failure occurs during a write operation, the file system data may be left in an inconsistent state. For example, an electronic transfer of funds might require a banking system to withdraw money from one account and deposit it in another. If the system fails between withdrawing and depositing the funds, it could lose the money. Transaction-based logging reduces the risk of data loss by using **atomic transactions**, which perform a group of operations in their entirety, or not at all. If an error occurs that prevents a transaction from completing, it is **rolled back** by returning the system to the state before the transaction began.[57]

Atomic transactions can be implemented by recording the result of each operation in a log file instead of modifying existing data. Once the transaction has completed, it is **committed** by recording a special value in the log. At some time in the future, the log is transferred to permanent storage. If the system fails before the transaction completes, any operations recorded after the previous committed transaction are ignored. When the system recovers, it reads the log file and compares it to the data in the file system to determine the state of the file system at the last commit point.

To enable the system to undo any number of operations, in many systems the log file is not deleted after its operations are written to permanent storage. Because logs can become large, reprocessing transactions to find the state of the system at the last commit point can be time consuming. To reduce the time spent reprocessing transactions in the log, most transaction-based systems maintain **checkpoints** that point to the last transaction that has been transferred to permanent storage. If the system crashes, it need only examine transactions after the checkpoint.

Shadow paging implements atomic transactions by writing modified data to a free block instead of the original block. Once the transaction commits, the file system updates its metadata to point to the new block and releases the old block, or **shadow page**, as free space. If the transaction fails, the file system rolls back the transaction by releasing the new blocks as free space.[58]

Operating Systems Thinking

Murphy's Law and Robust Systems

Most everyone is familiar with one form or another of Murphy's Law, named for U.S. Air Force Capt. Edward Murphy who cursed one of his error-prone technicians by saying, "If there is any way to do it wrong, he'll find it." Today's most common variant is "If something can go wrong, it will." Often, "and at the most inopportune time" is appended to the law. Operating system designers are well advised to keep Murphy's Law in mind. They need to constantly ask questions like, "What can go wrong?" "What is the likelihood of such problems?" "What are the consequences of such problems?" "How can the operating system be designed to prevent such problems?" "If certain problems cannot be prevented, how should the operating system deal with them?" A robust system deals with a wide range of inputs and unexpected situations in a manner that allows the system to keep operating.

Log-Structured File Systems (LFS)

Transaction logging and shadow paging prevent file system data from entering an inconsistent state but do not necessarily guarantee that the file system itself will be in a consistent state. For example, moving a file from one directory to another requires the file system to delete the file's original directory entry and create an entry in its new directory. A system failure (e.g., due to a power failure) that occurs between deleting the original directory entry and creating the new one can result in loss of file data. To address this limitation, a **log-structured file system (LFS)**, also called a **journaling file system**, performs file system operations as logged transactions.[59] Examples of log-structured file systems include Microsoft's NTFS Journaling File System and the Red Hat's ext3 file system for Linux.[60, 61]

In an LFS, the entire disk serves as a log file to record transactions. New data is written sequentially in the log file's free space. For example, in Fig. 13.13, the LFS receives a request to create files foo and bar in a new directory. The file system performs the requested operation first by writing foo's data to the log, then by writing foo's metadata (e.g., an inode), which enables the file system to locate foo's data. Similarly, the LFS writes bar's data and corresponding file metadata. Finally, the file system writes the new directory entry to the log. Note that if the file system writes a file's metadata before writing file data to the log, the system could fail before the file's data is written. This could leave the file system in an inconsistent state, because metadata will reference invalid data blocks (i.e., those that were not written before the system failed).

Because modified directories and metadata are always written to the end of the log, an LFS might need to read the entire log to locate a particular file, leading to poor read performance. To reduce this problem, an LFS caches locations of file system metadata and occasionally writes **inode maps** or superblocks, which indicate the location of other metadata (Fig. 13.13). This enables the operating system to locate and cache file metadata quickly when the system boots. Subsequently, file data can be accessed quickly by determining its location from the file system's caches. As the size of the file system cache increases, its performance improves at the cost of reducing the amount of memory available to user processes.[62]

To reduce overhead, some file systems store only metadata in the log. In this case, the file system modifies metadata first by writing an entry to the log, then by updating the entry in the file system. The operation commits only after the metadata has been updated both in the log and in the file system. This ensures file system integrity with relatively low overhead but does not ensure file integrity in the event of a system failure.[63]

Because data is written sequentially in an LFS, each write request is performed sequentially, which can substantially reduce write times. By comparison, noncontiguous file allocation implementations might require the file system to traverse the directory structure, which may be distributed throughout the disk, leading to long access times.

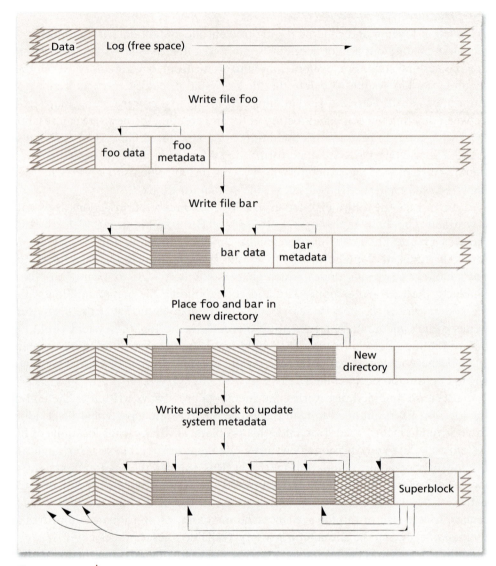

Figure 13.13 | Log-structured file system.

When the log fills, an LFS must determine how to recover free space for incoming data. An LFS can inspect the content of the log periodically to determine which blocks can be freed because the log contains a modified copy of their data. The LFS can thread new data through these blocks, which are likely to be highly fragmented. Unfortunately, threading can reduce read and write performance to levels lower than those in conventional file systems, because the disk might need to perform many seeks to access data. To address this issue, an LFS can create contiguous free space in the log by copying data to a contiguous region at the end of the log. While performing this I/O-intensive operation, however, users will experience poor response times.[64]

Self Review

1. Explain how data stored by a RAID level 1 array, which offers a high level of redundancy, could enter an inconsistent state.
2. Explain the difference between logging and shadow paging.

Ans: 1) If a power failure occurs while data in a mirrored pair is being written, the array may contain incomplete copies of file data or file system metadata on both disks. **2)** Logging keeps track of when a transaction was started, and when it completed. If the transaction fails, it rolls back to the last commit point. Shadow paging involves allocating new data blocks to write the new data, then freeing the old data blocks when the transaction is complete.

13.11   File Servers and Distributed Systems

One approach to handling nonlocal file references in a computer network is to route all such requests to a **file server**, i.e., a computer system dedicated to resolving intercomputer file references.[65, 66, 67, 68, 69] This approach centralizes control of these references, but the file server could become a bottleneck, because all client computers would send all requests to the server. A better approach is to let the separate computers communicate directly with one another; this is the approach taken by Sun Microsystem's **Network File System (NFS)**. In an NFS network, each computer maintains a file system that can act as a server and/or a client.

Through the 1970s, file systems generally stored and managed the files of a single computer system. On multiuser timesharing systems the files of all users were under the control of a centralized file system. Today, the trend is toward **distributed file systems** in computer networks.[70, 71, 72, 73] A real complication is that such networks often connect a wide variety of computer systems with different operating systems and file systems.

A distributed file system enables users to perform operations on remote files in a computer network in much the same manner as on local files.[74, 75, 76, 77, 78] NFS provides distributed file system capabilities for networks of heterogeneous computer systems; it is so widely used that it has become an international standard.[79] File servers and distributed file systems are discussed in Section 18.2, Distributed File Systems.

Self Review

1. Why is a single file server impractical for environments such as large organizations?
2. What is the primary advantage to having each client in a distributed file system also be a server?

Ans: 1) If the file server fails, the whole file system becomes unavailable. A central file server can also become a bottleneck. **2)** This removes the bottleneck of central file servers and can enable the file system to be operational even if one or more clients fail.

13.12   Database Systems

A **database** is a centrally controlled, integrated collection of data; a **database system** involves the data, the hardware on which the data resides and the software that controls access to data (called a **database management system** or **DBMS**). Databases are commonly implemented on Web servers and in online transaction-processing environments, where multiple processes require quick access to a large store of shared data.

13.12.1 Advantages of Database Systems

In conventional file systems, multiple applications often store the same information at different pathnames and in different formats (e.g., a text file stored as a Postscript and as a PDF file). To eliminate this redundancy, database systems organize data according to its content instead of by pathname. For example, a Web site may contain separate applications to charge orders to customer credit cards, send bills to those customers and print labels for packages to be delivered to customers. All of these applications must access customer information such as name, address, phone number, and the like. However, each application must format the information differently to perform its task (e.g., send credit card information or print a label). A database would store only one copy of each customer's information and enable each application to access the information and format it as required. To enable this access to shared data, databases incorporate a querying mechanism that allows applications to specify which information to retrieve.

Database systems use standardized data organization techniques (e.g., hierarchical, relational, object oriented), the structure of which cannot be altered by applications. Database systems are susceptible to attack due to centralized control and location of data, so they are designed with elaborate security mechanisms.[80, 81]

Self Review

1. How do database systems reduce redundant data typically stored by traditional file systems?
2. Why is security extremely important in database systems?

Ans: **1)** Database systems address data according to its content so that no two records contain the same information. For example, a database might store a single copy of customer information and enable multiple applications to access that information using queries. **2)** Databases provide centralized control to large stores of data, which may contain sensitive information. If a malicious user gains unauthorized access to a database, that user may be able to access all data stored by the system. This is more serious than in traditional file systems, because access rights are typically stored for each file, so a user that obtains unauthorized access to a file system may not be able to access all of its files.

13.12.2 Data Access

Database systems exhibit **data independence**, because a database's organizational structure and access techniques are hidden from applications. Unlike a hierarchically structured file system, which requires all applications to access data using pathnames, a data-independent system enables multiple applications to access the same data using different logical views. Consider the customer information stored by the Web site in the preceding section. In this case, a credit card transaction processing application may view customer information as a list of credit card number and expiration dates; the application that performs billing may view customer information as names, addresses and dollar amounts. Data independence makes it possible for the system to modify its storage structure and data access strategy in response to the installation's changing requirements without needing to modify functioning applications.

Database languages facilitate data independence by providing a standard way to access information. A database language consists of a **data definition language (DDL)**, a **data manipulation language (DML)** and a **query language**. A DDL specifies how data items are organized and related and a DML is used to modify data. A query language allows users to create queries, which search the database for data that meets certain criteria. Database languages can be executed directly from a command line or through programs written using higher-level host languages, such as C++ or Java. The **Structured Query Language (SQL)**, which consists of a DDL, DML and a query language, is a popular query language that enables users to find data items that have certain properties, create tables, specify integrity constraints, manage consistency and enforce security.[82, 83, 84]

A **distributed database** is a database that is spread throughout the computer systems of a network. Distributed databases facilitate efficient data access across many sets of data that reside on different computers.[85] In such systems each data item is typically stored at the location at which it is most frequently used, while remaining accessible to other network users. Distributed systems provide the control and efficiency of local processing with the advantages of information accessibility over a geographically dispersed organization. They can be costly to implement and operate, however, and they can suffer from increased vulnerability to security attacks and breaches.

Self Review

1. How do databases facilitate access to data for application developers?
2. Explain the difference between a DDL and a DML.

Ans: **1)** Database languages facilitate data independence, so programmers can access data according to a logical view that is most appropriate for their applications. **2)** A DDL defines the organization of and relationships between data elements. A DML is used to modify data.

13.12.3 Relational Database Model

Databases are based on models that describe how data and their relationships are viewed. The relational model developed by Codd is a logical structure rather than a physical one; the principles of relational database management can be considered without concerning oneself with the physical implementation of the underlying data structures.[86, 87, 88, 89, 90]

A relational database is composed of **relations** (tables). Figure 13.14 illustrates a relation that might be used in a personnel system. The name of the relation is EMPLOYEE and its primary purpose is to organize the various attributes of each

Relation: EMPLOYEE

	Number	Name	Department	Salary	Location
	23603	Jones, A.	413	1100	New Jersey
	24568	Kerwin, R.	413	2000	New Jersey
A tuple	34589	Larson, P.	642	1800	Los Angeles
	35761	Myers, B.	611	1400	Orlando
	47132	Neumann, C.	413	9000	New Jersey
	78321	Stevens, T.	611	8500	Orlando

Primary key   An attribute

Figure 13.14 | *Relation in a relational database.*

employee. Any particular element (row) of the relation is called a **tuple**. This rela-tion is a set of six tuples. In this example, the first attribute (column) in each tuple, the employee number, is used as the **primary key** for referencing data in the rela-tion. The tuples of the relation are uniquely identifiable by primary key.

Each attribute of the relation belongs to a single **domain.** Tuples must be unique within a relation, but particular attribute values may be duplicated between tuples. For example, three different tuples in the example contain department num-ber 413. The number of attributes in a relation is the **degree** of the relation. Rela-tions of degree 2 are **binary relations**, relations of degree 3 are **ternary relations**, and relations of degree *n* are *n*-**ary relations**.

Users of a database are often interested in different data items and different relationships among them. Most users will want only certain subsets of the table rows and columns. Many users will wish to combine smaller tables into larger ones to produce more complex relations. Codd called the subset operation **projection** and the combination operation **join**.

Using the relation of Fig. 13.14 we might, for example, use the projection operation to create a new relation called DEPARTMENT-LOCATOR whose pur-pose is to show where departments are located (Fig. 13.15).

The Structured Query Language (SQL) operates on relational databases. The SQL query in Fig. 13.16 generates the table in Fig. 13.15. Line 1 begins with "--", the SQL delimiter for a comment. The SELECT clause (line 2) specifies the columns, Department and Location, of the new table. The keyword DISTINCT indicates that the table should contain only unique entries. The FROM clause (line 3) indicates that

Relation: DEPARTMENT-LOCATOR

Department	Location
413	NEW JERSEY
611	ORLANDO
642	LOS ANGELES

Figure 13.15 | *Relation formed by projection.*

```
1   -- SQL query to generate the table in Fig. 13.15
2   SELECT DISTINCT Department, Location
3   FROM EMPLOYEE
4   ORDER BY Department ASC
5
```

Figure 13.16 | *SQL query.*

the columns will be projected from the EMPLOYEE table (Fig. 13.14). On line 4, an ORDER BY clause indicates the column (in this case, Department) that is used to sort the query result and ASC indicates that the sort will be in ascending order.

The relational model has several advantages.

1. The tabular representation used in implementations the relational model is easy to implement in a physical database system.

2. It is relatively easy to convert virtually any other type of database structure into the relational model. Thus the model may be viewed as a universal form of representation.

3. The projection and join operations are easy to implement and make the creation of new relations required for particular applications easy to perform.

4. Access control to sensitive data is straightforward to implement. The sensitive data is merely placed in separate relations, and access to these relations is controlled by some sort of authority or access scheme.

Self Review

1. What is the difference between the join and projection operations in relational databases?
2. (T/F) In a relation, each attribute value must be unique among tuples.

Ans: **1)** The join operation forms a relation from more than one relation; the projection operation forms a relation from a subset of a relation's attributes. **2)** False. Multiple tuples may have the same attribute value.

13.12.4 Operating Systems and Database Systems

Stonebraker discusses various operating system services that support database management systems, namely buffer pool management, the file system, scheduling, process management, interprocess communication, consistency control and paged virtual memory.[91] He observes that because most of these features are not specifically optimized to DBMS environments, DBMS designers have tended to bypass operating system services in favor of supplying their own. He concludes that efficient, minimal operating systems are the most desirable for supporting the kinds of database management systems that supply their own optimized services. Database support is becoming more common in today's systems. For example, Microsoft intends to use a database to store all user data in the next version of the Windows operating system.[92]

Self Review

1. Why should operating systems generally avoid direct support for database systems?
2. Why might more operating systems directly support database systems in the future?

Ans: **1)** Each database system may have different needs, which are difficult for the operating system to predict. These database systems generally exhibit higher performance when supplying their own optimized services. **2)** If an operating system uses a single database as the primary way to store user information, it should certainly provide optimized services for that database.

Web Resources

www.linux-tutorial.info/cgi-bin/display.pl?95&0&0&0&3
Contains a tutorial describing file systems in Linux.

www.redhat.com/docs/manuals/linux/RHL-8.0-Manual/admin-primer/s1-storage-basics.html
Overviews file system concepts.

www.itworld.com/nl/db_mgr/
Contains articles about data management strategies.

www.winnetmag.com/articles/index.cfm?articleid=3455
Includes information about the Windows NT file system.

www.osta.org/specs/pdf/udf201.pdf
Contains the 2.01 revision of the Universal Disk Format (UDF) file system, which is commonly used to organize data on DVDs.

storageconference.org/
Contains articles and presentations from the annual cooperative IEEE-NASA Storage Conference, highlighting techniques and technologies that manage mass storage devices.

www.sqlcourse.com/
Provides an interactive tutorial, teaching the basics of SQL.

Summary

Information is stored in computers according to a data hierarchy. The lowest level of the data hierarchy is composed of bits. Bits are grouped together in bit patterns to represent all data items of interest in computer systems. The next level in the data hierarchy is fixed-length patterns of bits such as bytes, characters and words. A byte is typically 8 bits. A word is the number of bits a processor can operate on at once. Characters map bytes (or groups of bytes) to symbols such as letters, numbers, punctuation and new lines. The three most popular character sets in use today are ASCII (American Standard Code for Information Interchange), EBCDIC (Extended Binary-Coded Decimal Interchange Code) and Unicode.

A field is a group of characters. A record is a group of fields. A file is a group of related records. The highest level of the data hierarchy is a file system or database. A volume is a unit of data storage that may hold multiple files.

A file is a named collection of data that may be manipulated as a unit by operations such as open, close, create, destroy, copy, rename and list. Individual data items within a file may be manipulated by operations like read, write, update, insert and delete. File characteristics include location, accessibility, type, volatility and activity. Files can consist of one or more records.

A file system organizes files and manages access to data. File systems are responsible for file management, auxiliary storage management, file integrity mechanisms and access methods. A file system primarily is concerned with managing secondary storage space, particularly disk storage.

File systems should exhibit device independence—users should be able to refer to their files by symbolic names rather than having to use physical device names. File systems should also provide backup and recovery capabilities to prevent either accidental loss or malicious destruction of information. The file system may also provide encryption and decryption capabilities to make information useful only to its intended audience.

File systems use directories, which are files containing the names and locations of other files in the file system, to organize and quickly locate files. A directory entry stores information such as a file name, location, size, type and accessed, modified and creation times. The simplest file system organization is the single-level (or flat) system, which stores all of its files using one directory. In single-level file systems, no two files can have the same name and the file system must perform a linear search of the directory contents to locate each file, which can lead to poor performance.

In a hierarchical file system, a root is used to indicate where on the storage device the root directory begins. The root directory points to the various directories, each of which contains an entry for each of its files. File names need be unique only within a given user directory. The name of a file is usually formed as the pathname from the root directory to the file.

Many file systems support the notion of a working directory to simplify navigation using pathnames. The working directory enables users to specify a pathname that does not begin at the root directory (i.e., a relative path). When a file system encounters a relative pathname, it forms the absolute path (i.e., the path beginning at the root) by concatenating the working directory and the relative path.

A link, which is a directory entry that references a data file or directory located in a different directory, facilitates data sharing and can make it easier for users to access files located throughout a file system's directory structure. A soft link is a directory entry containing the pathname for another file. A hard link is a directory entry that specifies the location of the file (typically a block number) on the storage device. Because a hard link specifies a physical location of a file, it references invalid data when the physical location of its corresponding file changes. Because soft links store the logical location of the file in the file system, they do not require updating when file data is moved. However, if a user moves a file to different directory or renames the file, any soft links to that file are no longer valid.

Metadata is information that protects the integrity of the file system and cannot be modified directly by users. Many file systems store in a superblock critical information that protects the integrity of the file system, such as the file system identifier and the location of the storage device's free blocks. To reduce the risk of date loss, most file systems distribute redundant copies of the superblock throughout the storage device.

The file open operation returns a file descriptor which is a non-negative integer index into the open-file table. From this point on, access to the file is directed through the file descriptor. To enable fast access to file-specific information such as permissions, the open-file table often contains file control blocks, also called file attributes, which are highly system-dependent structures that might include the file's symbolic name, location in secondary storage, access control data and so on.

The mount operation combines multiple file systems into one namespace so that they can be referenced from a single root directory. The mount command assigns a directory, called the mount point, in the native file system to the root of the mounted file system. File systems manage mounted directories with mount tables, which contain information about the location of mount points and the devices to which they point. When the native file system encounters a mount point, it uses the mount table to determine the device and type of the mounted file system. Users can create soft links to files in mounted file systems but cannot create hard links between file systems.

File organization refers to the manner in which the records of a file are arranged on secondary storage. File organization schemes include sequential, direct, indexed nonsequential and partitioned.

The problem of allocating and freeing space on secondary storage is somewhat like that experienced in primary storage allocation under variable-partition multiprogramming. Because files tend to grow or shrink over time, and because users rarely know in advance how large their files will be, contiguous storage allocation systems have generally been replaced by more dynamic noncontiguous storage allocation systems.

File systems that employ contiguous allocation place file data at contiguous addresses on the storage device. One advantage of contiguous allocation is that successive logical records typically are physically adjacent to one another. Contiguous allocation schemes exhibit the same types of external fragmentation problems inherent in memory allocation for variable-partition multiprogramming systems. Contiguous allocation may result in poor performance if files grow and shrink over time. If a file grows beyond the size originally specified and no contiguous free blocks are available, it must be transferred to a new area of adequate size, leading to additional I/O operations.

Using a sector-based linked-list noncontiguous file allocation scheme, a directory entry points to the first sector of a file. The data portion of a sector stores the contents of the file; the pointer portion points to the file's next sector. Sectors belonging to a common file form a linked list.

When performing block allocation, the system allocates blocks of contiguous sectors (sometimes called extents). In block chaining, entries in the user directory point to the first block of each file. The blocks comprising a file each contain two portions: a data block and a pointer to the next block. When locating a record, the chain must be searched from the beginning, and if the blocks are dispersed throughout the storage device (which is normal), the search process can be slow as block-to-block seeks occur. Insertion and deletion are done by modifying the pointer in the previous block.

Large block sizes can result in a considerable amount of internal fragmentation. Small block sizes may cause file data to be spread across multiple blocks dispersed throughout the storage device, leading to poor performance as the storage device performs many seeks to access all the records of a file.

Tabular noncontiguous file allocation uses tables storing pointers to file blocks to reduce the number of lengthy seeks required to access a particular record. Directory entries indicate the first block of a file. The current block number is used as an index into the block allocation table to determine the location of the next block. If the current block is the file's last block, then its block allocation table entry is null. Because the pointers that locate file data are stored in a central location, the table can be cached so that the chain of blocks that compose a file can be traversed quickly, which improves access times. However, to locate the last record of a file, the file system might need to follow many pointers in the block allocation table, which could take significant time. When a storage device contains many blocks, the block allocation table can become large and fragmented, reducing file system performance. A popular implementation of tabular noncontiguous file allocation is Microsoft's FAT file system.

In indexed noncontiguous file allocation, each file has an index block or several index blocks. The index blocks contain a list of pointers that point to file data blocks. A file's directory entry points to its index block, which may reserve the last few entries to store pointers to more index blocks, a technique called chaining.

The primary advantage of index block chaining over simple linked-list implementations is that searching may take place in the index blocks themselves. File systems typically place index blocks near the data blocks they reference, so the data blocks can be accessed quickly after their index block is loaded. Index blocks are called inodes (i.e., index nodes) in UNIX-based operating systems.

Some systems use a free list—a linked list of blocks containing the locations of free blocks—to manage the storage device's free space. The file system typically allocates blocks from the beginning of the free list and appends freed blocks to the end of the list. This technique requires little overhead to perform free list maintenance operations, but files are allocated in noncontiguous blocks, which increases file access time.

A bitmap contains one bit for each block in memory, where the ith bit corresponds to the ith block on the storage device. A primary advantage of bitmaps over free lists is that the file system can quickly determine if contiguous blocks are available at certain locations on secondary storage. A disadvantage is that the file system may need to search the entire bitmap to find a free block, resulting in substantial execution overhead.

In a two-dimensional access control matrix, the entry a_{ij} is 1 if user i is allowed access to file j; otherwise $a_{ij} = 0$. In an installation with a large number of users and a large number of files, this matrix generally would be large and sparse. A technique that requires considerably less space is to control access to various user classes. User classes can include the file owner, a specified user, group, project or public. This access control data can be stored as part of the file control block and often consumes an insignificant amount of space.

Today's operating systems generally provide many access methods, such as queued and basic access methods. Queued access methods are used when the sequence in which records are to be processed can be anticipated, such as in sequential and indexed sequential accessing. The queued methods perform anticipatory buffering and scheduling of I/O operations. The basic access methods are normally used when the sequence in which records are to be processed cannot be anticipated, particularly with direct accessing.

Memory-mapped files map file data to a process's virtual address space instead of using a file system cache. Because references to memory-mapped files occur in a process's virtual address space, the virtual memory manager can make page-replacement decisions based on each process's reference pattern.

Most file systems implement backup techniques to store redundant copies of information, and recovery techniques that enable the system to restore data after a system failure. Physical safeguards such as locks and fire alarms are the lowest level of data protection. Performing periodic backups is the most common technique used to ensure the continued availability of data. Physical backups duplicate a storage device's data at the bit level. A logical backup stores file system data and its logical structure. Thus, logical backups inspect the directory structure to determine which files need to be backed up, then write these files to a backup device in a common, often compressed, archival format. Incremental backups are logical backups that store only file system data that has changed since the previous backup.

In systems that cannot tolerate loss of data or downtime, RAID and transaction logging are appropriate. If a system failure occurs during a write operation, file data may be left in an inconsistent state. Transaction-based file systems reduce data loss using atomic transactions, which perform a group of operations in their entirety or not at all. If an error occurs that prevents a transaction from completing, it is rolled back by returning the system to the state before the transaction began.

Atomic transactions can be implemented by recording the result of each operation in a log file instead of modifying existing data. Once the transaction has completed, it is committed by recording a sentinel value in the log. To reduce the time spent reprocessing transactions in the log, most transaction-based systems maintain checkpoints that point to the last transaction that has been transferred to permanent storage. If the system crashes, it need only examine transactions after the checkpoint. Shadow paging implements atomic transactions by writing modified data to a free block instead of the original block.

Log-structured file systems (LFS), also called journaling file systems, perform all file system operations as logged transactions to ensure that they do not leave the system in an inconsistent state. In LFS, the entire disk serves as a log file. New data is written sequentially in the log file's free space. Because modified directories and metadata are always written to the end of the log, an LFS might need to read the entire log to locate a particular file, leading to poor read performance. To reduce this problem, an LFS caches locations of file system metadata and occasionally writes inode maps or superblocks that indicate the location of other metadata, enabling the operating system to locate and cache file metadata quickly when the system boots. Some file systems attempt to reduce the cost of log-structured file systems by using a log only to store metadata. This ensures file system integrity with relatively low overhead but does not ensure file integrity in the event of a system failure.

Because data is written sequentially, each LFS write requires only a single seek while there is still space on disk. When the log fills, the file system's fragmented free space from reclaiming invalid blocks can reduce read and write performance to levels lower than those in conventional file systems. To address this issue, an LFS can create contiguous free space in the log by copying valid data to a contiguous region at the end of the log.

One approach to handling nonlocal file references in a computer network is to route all such requests to a file server, i.e., a computer system dedicated to resolving intercomputer file references. This approach centralizes control of these references, but the file server could easily become a bottleneck, because all client computers send all requests to the server. A better approach is to let the separate computers communicate directly with one another.

A database is a centrally controlled collection of data stored in a standardized format; a database system involves the data, the hardware on which the data resides and the software that controls access to data (called a database management system or DBMS). Databases reduce data redundancy and prevent data from being in an inconsistent state. Redundancy is reduced by combining data from separate files. Databases also facilitate data sharing.

An important aspect of database systems is data independence; i.e., applications need not be concerned with how data is physically stored or accessed. From the system's standpoint, data independence makes it possible for the storage structure and accessing strategy to be modified in response to the installation's changing requirements, but without the need to modify functioning applications.

Database languages allow database independence by providing a standard way to access information. A database language consists of a data definition language (DDL), a data manipulation language (DML) and a query language. A DDL specifies how data are organized and related and the DML enables data to be modified. A query language is a part of the DML that allows users to create queries that search the database for data that meets certain criteria. The Structured Query Language (SQL) is currently one of the most popular database languages.

A distributed database, a database that is spread throughout the computer systems of a network, facilitates efficient data access across many sets of data that reside on different computers.

Databases are based on models that describe how data and their relationships are viewed. The relational model is a logical structure rather than a physical one; the principles of relational database management are independent of the physical implementation of data structures. A relational database is composed of relations that indicate the various attributes of an entity. Any particular element of a relation is called a tuple (row). Each attribute (column) of the relation belongs to a single domain. The number of attributes in a relation is the degree of the relation. A projection operation forms a subset of the attributes; a join operation combines relations to produce more complex relations. The relational database model is relatively easy to implement.

Various operating system services support database management systems, namely buffer pool management, the file system, scheduling, process management, interprocess communication, consistency control and paged virtual memory. Most of these features are not specifically optimized to DBMS environments, so DBMS designers have tended to bypass operating system services in favor of supplying their own.

Key Terms

absolute path—Path beginning at the root directory.

access control matrix—Two-dimensional listing of all the users and their access to privileges to files in the system.

accessibility (file)—File property that places restrictions on which users can access file data.

access method—Technique a file system uses to access file data. See also queued access methods and basic access methods.

activity (file)—Percentage of a file's records accessed during a given period of time.

anticipatory buffering—Technique that allows processing and I/O operations to be overlapped by buffering more than one record at a time in main memory.

ASCII (American Standard Code for Information Interchange)—Character set, popular in personal computers and in data communication systems, that stores characters as 8-bit bytes.

atomic transaction—Group of operations that have no effect on the state of the system unless they complete in their entirety.

auxiliary storage management—Component of file systems concerned with allocating space for files on secondary storage devices.

backup—Creation of redundant copies of information.

basic access method—File access method in which the operating system responds immediately to user I/O demands. It is used when the sequence in which records are to be processed cannot be anticipated, particularly with direct accessing.

binary relation—Relation (in a relational database) of degree 2.

bitmap—Free space management technique that maintains one bit for each block in memory, where the ith bit corresponds to the ith block in memory. Bitmaps enable a file system to more easily allocate contiguous blocks but can require substantial execution time to locate a free block.

bit pattern—Lowest level of the data hierarchy. A bit pattern is a group of bits that represent virtually all data items of interest in computer systems.

block allocation—Technique that enables the file system to manage secondary storage more efficiently and reduce file traversal overhead by allocating extents (blocks of contiguous sectors) to files.

blocked record—Record that may contain several logical records for each physical record.

byte—Second-lowest level in the data hierarchy. A byte is typically 8 bits.

character—In the data hierarchy, a fixed-length pattern of bits, typically 8, 16 or 32 bits.

character set—Collection of characters. Popular character sets include ASCII, EBCDIC and Unicode.

chaining—Indexed noncontiguous allocation technique that reserves the last few entries of an index block to store pointers to more index blocks, which in turn point to data blocks. Chaining enables index blocks to reference large files by storing references to its data across several blocks.

checkpoint—Marker indicating which transactions in a log have been transferred to permanent storage. The system need only reapply the transactions from the latest checkpoint to determine the state of the file system, which is faster than reapplying all transactions starting at the beginning of the log.

close (file)—Operation that prevents further reference to a file until it is reopened.

committed transaction—Transaction that has completed successfully.

copy (file)—Operation that creates another version of a file with a new name.

create (file)—Operation that builds a new file.

data definition language (DDL)—Type of language that specifies the organization of data in a database.

data manipulation language (DML)—Type of language that enables data modification.

data-dependent application—Application that relies on a particular file system's organization and access techniques.

data hierarchy—Classification that groups different numbers of bits to extract meaningful data. Bit patterns, bytes and words contain small numbers of bits that are interpreted by hardware and low-level software. Fields, records and files may contain large numbers of bits that are interpreted by operating systems and user applications.

data independence—Property of applications that do not rely on a particular file organization technique or access technique.

database—Centrally controlled collection of data that is stored in a standardized format and can be searched based on logical relations between data. Databases organize data according to content as opposed to pathname, which tends to reduce or eliminate redundant information.

database language—Language that provides for organizing, modifying and querying of structured data.

database management system (DBMS)—Software that controls database organization and operations.

database system—A particular set of data, the storage devices on which it resides and the software that controls its storage and retrieval (called a database management system or DBMS).

decryption—Technique that reverses data encryption so that data can be read in its original form.

degree—Number of attributes in a relation in a relational database.

delete (file)—Operation that removes a data item from a file.

destroy (file)—Operation that removes a file from the file system.

device independence—Property of files that can be referenced by an application using a symbolic name instead of a name indicating the device on which it resides.

direct file organization—File organization technique in which a record is directly (randomly) accessed by its physical address on a direct access storage device (DASD).

directory—File storing references to other files. Directory entries often include a file's name, type, and size.

distributed database—Database that is spread throughout the computer systems of a network.

distributed file system—File system that is spread throughout the computer systems of a network.

domain—Set of possible values for attributes in a relational database system.

EBCDIC (Extended Binary-Coded Decimal Interchange Code)—Eight-bit character set for representing data in mainframe computer systems, particularly systems developed by IBM.

encryption—Technique that transforms data to prevent it from being interpreted by unauthorized users.

execute access—Permission that enables a user to execute a file.

extent—Block of contiguous sectors.

FAT file system—An implementation of tabular noncontiguous file allocation developed by Microsoft.

field—In the data hierarchy, a group of characters (e.g., a person's name, street address or telephone number).

file—Named collection of data that may be manipulated as a unit by operations such as open, close, create, destroy, copy, rename and list. Individual data items within a file may be manipulated by operations like read, write, update, insert and delete. File characteristics include location, accessibility, type, volatility and activity. Files can consist of one or more records.

file allocation table (FAT)—Table storing pointers to file data blocks in Microsoft's FAT file system.

file attribute—See file control block.

file control block—Metadata containing information the system needs to manage a file, such as access control information.

file descriptor—Non-negative integer that indexes into an opened-file table. A process references a file descriptor instead of a pathname to access file data without incurring the overhead of a directory structure traversal.

file integrity mechanism—Mechanism that ensures that the information in a file is uncorrupted. When file integrity is assured, files contain only the information they are intended to have.

file management—Component of a file system concerned with providing the mechanisms for files to be stored, referenced, shared and secured.

file organization—Manner in which the records of a file are arranged on secondary storage (e.g., sequential, direct, indexed sequential and partitioned).

file server—System dedicated to provide remote processes access to its files.

file system—Component of an operating system that organizes files and manages access to data. File systems are concerned with organizing files logically (using pathnames) and physically (using metadata). They also manage their storage device's free space, enforce security policies, maintain data integrity and so on.

file system identifier—Value that uniquely identifies the file system a storage device is using.

flat directory structure—File system organization containing only one directory.

format a storage device—To prepare a device for a file system by performing operations such as inspecting its contents and writing storage management metadata.

free list—Linked list of blocks that contain the addresses of free blocks.

group (file access control)—Set of users with the same file access rights (e.g., members of a group that is working on a particular project).

hard link—Directory entry specifying the location of a file on its storage device.

hierarchically structured file system—File system organization in which each directory can contain multiple subdirectories but exactly one parent.

incremental backup—Backup technique that copies only data in file system that has changed since the last backup.

index block—Block that contains a list of pointers to file data blocks.

indexed sequential file organization—File organization that arranges records in a logical sequence according to a key contained in each record.

indirect block—Index block containing pointers to data blocks in inode-based file systems.

inode—Index block in a UNIX-based system that contains the file control block and pointers to singly, doubly and triply indirect blocks of pointers to file data.

inode map—Block of metadata written to the log of a log-structured file system that indicates the location of the file system's inodes. Inode maps improve LFS performance by reducing the time required to determine file locations in the LFS.

insert (file)—Operation that adds a new data item to a file.

join (database)—Operation that combines relations.

journaling file system—See log-structured file system (LFS).

link—Directory entry that references an existing file. Hard links reference the location of the file on its storage device; soft links store the file's pathname.

list (file)—Operation that prints or displays a file's contents.

location (file)—Address of a file on a storage device or in the system's logical file organization.

log-structured file system (LFS)—File system that performs all file operations as transactions to ensure that file system data and metadata is always in a consistent state. An LFS generally exhibits good write performance because data is also appended to the end of a systemwide log file. To improve read performance, an LFS typically distributes metadata throughout the log and employs large caches to store that metadata so that the locations of file data can be found quickly.

logical backup—Backup technique that stores file data and the file system's directory structure, often in a common, compressed format.

logical block—See logical record.

logical record—Collection of data treated as a unit by software.

logical view—View of files that hides the devices that store them, their format and the system's physical access techniques.

member—Sequential subfile of a partitioned file.

memory-mapped file—File whose data is mapped to a process's virtual address space, enabling a process to reference file data as it would other data. Memory-mapped files are useful for programs that frequently access file data.

metadata—Data that a file system uses to manage files and that is inaccessible to users directly. Inodes and superblocks are examples of metadata.

mount operation—Operation that combines disparate file systems into a single namespace so they can be accessed by a single root directory.

mount point—User-specified directory within the native file system hierarchy where the mount command places the root of a mounted file system.

mount tables—Tables that store the locations of mount points and their corresponding devices.

MS-DOS—Popular operating system for the first IBM Personal Computer and compatible microcomputers.

n-ary relation—Relation of degree n.

namespace—Set of files that can be identified by a file system.

Network File System (NFS)—File system implemented by Sun Microsystems in which each computer maintains a virtual file system that can act as a server and/or a client.

owner (file access control)—User who created the file.

open (file)—Operation that prepares a file to be referenced.

parent directory—In hierarchically structured file systems, the directory that points to the current directory.

partitioned file—File composed of sequential subfiles.

pathname—String identifying a file or directory by its logical name, separating directories using a delimiter (e.g., "/" or "\"). An absolute pathname specifies the location of a file or directory starting at the root directory; a relative pathname specifies the location of a file or directory beginning at the current working directory.

physical backup—Copy of each bit of the storage device; no attempt is made to interpret the contents of its file system.

physical block—See physical record.

physical device name—Name given to a file that is specific to a particular device.

physical record—Unit of information actually read from or written to disk.

physical view—View of file data concerned with the particular devices on which data is stored, the form the data takes on those devices, and the physical means of transferring data to and from those devices.

primary key—In a relational database, a combination of attributes whose value uniquely identifies a tuple.

projection (database)—Operation that creates a subset of attributes.

public (file access control)—File that may be accessed by any member of the system's user community.

queued access method—File access method that does not immediately service user I/O demands. This can improve performance when the sequence in which records are to be processed can be anticipated and requests can be ordered to minimize access times.

query language—Language that allows users to search a database for data that meets certain criteria.

read access—Permission to access a file for reading.

record—In the data hierarchy, a group of fields (e.g., to store several related fields containing information about a student or a customer).

recovery—Restoration of the system's data after a failure.

read (file)—Operation that inputs a data item from a file to a process.

relation—A set of tuples in the relational model.

relational model—A model of data proposed by Codd that is the basis for most modern database systems.

relative path—Path that specifies the location of a file relative to the current working directory.

rename (file)—Operation that changes a file's name.

roll back a transaction—To return the system to the state that existed before the transaction was processed.

root—Beginning of a file system's organizational structure.

root directory—Directory that points to the various user directories.

sequential file organization—File organization technique in which records are placed in sequential physical order. The "next" record is the one that physically follows the previous record.

shadow page—Block of data whose modified contents are written to a new block. Shadow pages are one way to implement transactions.

shadow paging—Transaction implementation that writes modified blocks to a new block. The copy of the block that is unmodified is released as free space when the transaction has been committed.

single-level directory structure—See flat directory structure.

size (file)—Amount of information stored in a file.

soft link—File that specifies the pathname corresponding to the file to which it is linked.

specified user (file access control)—Identity of an individual user (other than the owner) that may use a file.

Structured Query Language (SQL)—Database language that allows users to find data items that have certain properties, and also to create tables, specify integrity constraints, manage consistency and enforce security.

superblock—Block containing information critical to the integrity of the file system (e.g., the location of the file system's free block list or bitmap, the file system identifier and the location of the file system root).

symbolic name—Device-independent name (e.g., a pathname).

ternary relations—Relation of degree 3.

tuple—Particular element of a relation.

type (file)—Description of a file's purpose (e.g., an executable program, data or directory).

unblocked record—Record containing exactly one logical record for each physical record.

Unicode—Character set that supports international languages and is popular in Internet and multilingual applications.

update (file)—Operation that modifies an existing data item in a file.

user classes—Classification scheme that specifies individual users or groups of users that can access a file.

user directory—Directory that contains an entry for each of a user's files; each entry points to where the corresponding file is stored on its storage device.

volatility (file)—Frequency with which additions and deletions are made to a file.

volume—Unit of storage that may hold multiple files.

word—Number of bits a system's processor(s) can process at once. In the data hierarchy, words are one level above bytes.

working directory—Directory that contains files that a user can access directly.

write (file)—Operation that outputs a data item from a process to a file.

write access—Permission to access a file for writing.

Exercises

13.1   A virtual memory system has page size p and its corresponding file system has block size b and fixed-length record size r. Discuss the various relationships among p, b, and r that make sense. Explain why each of these possible relationships is reasonable.

13.2   Give a comprehensive enumeration of reasons why records may not necessarily be stored contiguously in a sequential disk file.

13.3   Suppose a distributed system has a central file server containing large numbers of sequential files for hundreds of users. Give several reasons why such a system may *not* be organized to perform compaction (dynamically or otherwise) on a regular basis.

13.4   Give several reasons why it may *not* be useful to store logically contiguous pages from a process's virtual memory space in physically contiguous areas on secondary storage.

13.5   A certain file system uses "systemwide" names; i.e., once one member of the user community uses a name, that name may not be assigned to new files. Most large file systems, however, require only that names be unique with respect to a given user—two different users may choose the same file name without conflict. Discuss the relative merits of these two schemes, considering both implementation and application issues.

13.6   Some systems implement file sharing by allowing several users to read a single copy of a file simultaneously. Others provide a copy of the shared file to each user. Discuss the relative merits of each approach.

13.7   Indexed sequential files are popular with application designers. Experience has shown, however, that direct access to indexed sequential files can be slow. Why is this so? In what circumstances is it better to access such files sequentially? In what circumstances should the application designer use direct files rather than indexed sequential files?

13.8   When a computer system failure occurs, it is important to be able to reconstruct the file system quickly and accurately.

Suppose a file system allows complex arrangements of pointers and interdirectory references. What measures might the file system designer take to ensure the reliability and integrity of such a system?

13.9   Some file systems support a large number of access classes while others support only a few. Discuss the relative merits of each approach. Which is better for highly secure environments? Why?

13.10 Compare the allocation space for files on secondary storage to real storage allocation under variable-partition multiprogramming.

13.11 In what circumstances is compaction of secondary storage useful? What dangers are inherent in compaction? How can these be avoided?

13.12 What are the motivations for structuring file systems hierarchically?

13.13 One problem with indexed sequential file organization is that additions to a file may need to be placed in overflow areas. How might this affect performance? What can be done to improve performance in these circumstances?

13.14 Pathnames in a hierarchical file system can become lengthy. Given that the vast majority of file references are made to a user's own files, what convention might the file system support to minimize the need for using lengthy pathnames?

13.15 Some file systems store information in exactly the format created by the user. Others attempt to optimize by compressing the data. Describe how you would implement a compression/decompression mechanism. Such a mechanism necessarily trades execution time overhead against the reduced storage requirements for files. In what circumstances is this trade-off acceptable?

13.16 Suppose that a major development in primary storage technology made it possible to produce a storage so large, so fast and so inexpensive that all the programs and data at an installation could be stored in a single "chip." How would the design of a file system for such a single-level storage differ from that for today's conventional hierarchical storage systems?

13.17 You have been asked to perform a security audit on a computer system. The system administrator suspects that the pointer structure in the file system has been compromised, thus allowing certain unauthorized users to access critical system information. Describe how you would attempt to determine who is responsible for the security breach and how it was possible for them to modify the pointers.

13.18 In most computer installations, only a small portion of file backups are ever used to reconstruct a file. Thus there is a trade-off to be considered in performing backups. Do the consequences of not having a file backup available when needed justify the effort of performing the backups? What factors point to the need for performing backups as opposed to not performing them? What factors affect the frequency with which backups should be performed?

13.19 Sequential access from sequential files is much faster than sequential access from indexed sequential files. Why then do many applications designers implement systems in which indexed sequential files are to be accessed sequentially?

13.20 In a university environment how might the user access classes "owner," "group," "specified user," and "public" be used to control access to files? Consider the use of the computer system for administrative as well as academic computing. Consider also its use in support of grant research as well as in academic courses.

13.21 File systems provide access to native files as well as to files from other mounted file systems. What types of files might best be stored in the native file system? in other mounted file systems? What problems are unique to the management of mounted file systems?

13.22 What type and frequency of backup would be most appropriate in each of the following systems?

    a. a batch-processing payroll system that runs weekly

    b. an automated teller machine (ATM) banking system

    c. a hospital patient billing system

    d. an airline reservation system in which customers make reservations for flights as much as one year in advance

    e. a distributed program development system used by a group of 100 programmers

13.23 Most banks today use online teller transaction systems. Each transaction is immediately applied to customer accounts to keep balances correct and current. Errors are intolerable, but because of computer failures and power failures, these systems do "go down" occasionally. Describe how you would implement a backup/recovery capability to ensure that each completed transaction applies to the appropriate customer's account. Also, any transactions only partially completed at the time of a system failure must not apply.

13.24 Why is it useful to reorganize indexed sequential files periodically?

    What criteria might a file system use to determine when reorganization is needed?

13.25 Distinguish between queued access methods and basic access methods.

13.26 How might redundancy of programs and data be useful in the construction of highly reliable systems? Database systems can greatly reduce the amount of redundancy involved in storing data. Does this imply that database systems may in fact be less reliable than nondatabase systems? Explain your answer.

13.27 Many of the storage schemes we discussed for placing information on disk include the extensive use of pointers. If a pointer is destroyed, either accidentally or maliciously, an entire data structure may be lost. Comment on the use of such data structures in the design of highly reliable systems. Indicate how pointer-based schemes can be made less susceptible to damage by the loss of a pointer.

13.28 Discuss the problems involved in enabling a distributed file system of homogeneous computers to treat remote file accesses the same as local file accesses (at least from the user's perspective).

13.29 Discuss the notion of transparency in distributed file systems of heterogeneous computers. How does a distributed file system resolve differences between various computer architectures and operating systems to enable all systems on a network to perform remote file accesses regardless of system differences?

13.30 Figure 13.9 shows an inode data structure. Suppose a file system that uses this structure has filled up the blocks stemming from the doubly indirect pointers. How many disk accesses will it take to write one more byte to the file? Assume that the inode and free block bitmap are both completely in memory, but there is no buffer cache. Also assume that blocks do not have to be initialized.

13.31 A file system can keep track of free blocks by using either a free block bitmap or a free block list. The system has a total of t blocks of size b, u of which are used, and each block number is stored using s bits.

    a. Express size (in bits) of this device's free block bitmap using the given variables.

    b. Express the size (in bits) of this system's free block list in terms of the given variables. Ignore the space consumed by pointers to free list continuation blocks.

13.32 Suppose a system uses 1KB blocks and 16-bit (2-byte) addresses. What is the largest possible file size for this file system for the following inode organizations?

    a. The inode contains 12 pointers directly to data blocks.

    b. The inode contains 12 pointers directly to data blocks and one indirect block. Assume the indirect data block uses all 1,024 bytes to store pointers to data blocks.

    c. The inode contains 12 direct pointers to data blocks, one indirect data block, and one doubly indirect data block.

13.33 Why is it useful to store fixed-length directory entries? What limitation does this impose on file names?

Suggested Projects

13.34 Prepare a research paper on the upcoming WinFS file system and compare it to the NTFS file system. What problems in the NTFS file system does WinFS address?

13.35 Prepare a research paper on the implementation and application of distributed databases.

13.36 Research how operating systems such as Windows and Linux provide file system encryption and decryption capabilities.

Suggested Simulations

13.37 Design a file system. What would you put in each of the inodes (files and directories should have different information)? What would you need for metadata? After you design it, implement a simulated file system in the language of your choice. Then implement the following functions: *create, open, close, read, write, cd* (change directory), and *ls* (to list the files in a directory). If you have more time, figure out how to save your file system to a file and be able to load it later.

Recommended Reading

File system research continues to produce file system implementations that adapt to changing user demands. Golden et al. provide a summary of many common file system functions.[93] For information regarding the NT File System, see Custer's *Inside the Windows NT File System.*[94] Log-structured file systems are discussed in detail by Rosenblum et al.[95] Wang et al. introduce the notion of user-level custom file systems as a technique to improve the performance of I/O-bound Internet servers.[96] The bibliography for this chapter is located on our Web site at www.deitel.com/books/os3e/Bibliography.pdf.

Works Cited

1. Searle, S., "Brief History of Character Codes in North America, Europe, and East Asia," modified March 13, 2002, <tron-web.super-nova.co.jp/characcodehist.html>.

2. "The Unicode® Standard: A Technical Introduction," March 4, 2003, <www.unicode.org/standard/principles.html>.

3. Golden, D., and M. Pechura, "The Structure of Microcomputer File Systems," *Communications of the ACM,* Vol. 29, No. 3, March 1986, pp. 222–230.

4. Linux kernel source code, version 2.6.0-test2, ext2_fs.h, lines 506–511, <lxr.linux.no/source/include/linux/ext2_fs.h?v=2.6.0-test2>.

5. Linux kernel source code, version 2.6.0-test2, iso_fs.h, lines 144–156, <lxr.linux.no/source/include/linux/iso_fs.h?v=2.6.0-test2>.

6. Linux kernel source code, version 2.6.0-test2, msdos_fs.h, lines 151–162, <lxr.linux.no/source/include/linux/msdos_fs.h?v=2.6.0-test2>.

7. Golden, D., and M. Pechura, "The Structure of Microcomputer File Systems," *Communications of the ACM,* Vol. 29, No. 3, March 1986, p. 224.

8. Peterson, J. L.; J. S. Quarterman; and A. Silberschatz, "4.2BSD and 4.3BSD as Examples of the UNIX System," *ACM Computing Surveys,* Vol. 17, No.4, December 1985, p. 395.

9. Appleton, R., "A Non-Technical Look Inside the EXT2 File System," *Kernel Korner,* August 1997.

10. Peterson, J. L.; J. S. Quarterman; and A. Silberschatz, "4.2BSD and 4.3BSD as Examples of the UNIX System," *ACM Computing Surveys,* Vol. 17, No.4, December 1985, p. 395.

11. Peterson, J. L.; J. S. Quarterman; and A. Silberschatz, "4.2BSD and 4.3BSD as Examples of the UNIX System," *ACM Computing Surveys,* Vol. 17, No.4, December 1985, p. 395.

12. Peterson, J. L.; J. S. Quarterman; and A. Silberschatz, "4.2BSD and 4.3BSD as Examples of the UNIX System," *ACM Computing Surveys,* Vol. 17, No.4, December 1985, p. 395.

13. Linux kernel source code, version 2.6.0-test2, ext2_fs_sb.h, lines 25–55, `<lxr.linux.no/source/include/linux/ext2_fs_sb.h?v=2.6.0-test2>`.

14. Linux kernel source code, version 2.6.0-test2, iso_fs_sb.h, lines 7–32, `<lxr.linux.no/source/include/linux/iso_fs_sb.h?v=2.6.0-test2>`.

15. Linux kernel source code, version 2.6.0-test2, msdos_fs_sb.h, lines 38–63, `<lxr.linux.no/source/include/linux/msdos_fs_sb.h?v=2.6.0-test2>`.

16. Thompson, K., "UNIX Implementation," *UNIX Time-Sharing System: UNIX Programmer's Manual,* 7th ed., Vol. 2b, January 1979, p. 9.

17. Levy, E., and A. Silberschatz, "Distributed File Systems: Concepts and Examples," *ACM Computing Surveys,* Vol. 22, No. 4, December 1990, p. 329.

18. "Volume Mount Points," *MSDN Library,* February 2003, `<msdn.microsoft.com/library/default.asp?url=/library/en-us/fileio/base/volume_mount_points.asp>`.

19. Thompson, K., "UNIX Implementation," *UNIX Time-Sharing System: UNIX Programmer's Manual,* 7th ed., Vol. 2b, January 1979, p. 9.

20. Larson, P., and A. Kajla, "File Organization: Implementation of a Method Guaranteeing Retrieval in One Access," *Communications of the ACM,* Vol. 27, No. 7, July 1984, pp. 670–677.

21. Enbody, R. J., and H. C. Du, "Dynamic Hashing Schemes," *ACM Computing Surveys,* Vol. 20, No. 2, June 1988, pp. 85–113.

22. Koch, P. D. L., "Disk File Allocation Based on the Buddy System," *ACM Transactions on Computer Systems,* Vol. 5, No. 4, November 1987, pp. 352–370.

23. McKusick, M.; W. Joy; S. Leffler; and R. Fabry, "A Fast File System for UNIX," *ACM Transactions on Computer Systems,* Vol. 2, No. 3, August 1984, pp. 183–184.

24. "Description of FAT32 File System," *Microsoft Knowledge Base,* February 21, 2002, `<support.microsoft.com/default.aspx?scid=kb;[LN];Q154997>`.

25. Card, R; T. Ts'o, and S. Tweedie, "Design and Implementation of the Second Extended Filesystem," September 20, 2001, `<e2fsprogs.sourceforge.net/ext2intro.html>`.

26. Kozierok, C., "DOS (MS-DOS, PC-DOS, etc.)," *PCGuide,* April 17, 2001, `<www.pcguide.com/ref/hdd/file/osDOS-c.html>`.

27. Kozierok, C., "Virtual FAT (VFAT)," *PCGuide,* April 17, 2001, `<www.pcguide.com/ref/hdd/file/fileVFAT-c.html>`.

28. Kozierok, C., "DOS (MS-DOS, PC-DOS, etc.)," *PCGuide,* April 17, 2001, `<www.pcguide.com/ref/hdd/file/osDOS-c.html>`.

29. "FAT32," *MSDN Library,* `<msdn.microsoft.com/library/default.asp?url=/library/en-us/fileio/storage_29v6.asp>`.

30. Paterson, T., "A Short History of MS-DOS," June 1983, `<www.patersontech.com/Dos/Byte/History.html>`.

31. Rojas, R., "Encyclopedia of Computers and Computer History—DOS," April 2001, `<www.patersontech.com/Dos/Encyclo.htm>`.

32. Hunter, D., "Tim Patterson: The Roots of DOS," March 1983, `<www.patersontech.com/Dos/Softalk/Softalk.html>`.

33. Hunter, D., "Tim Patterson: The Roots of DOS," March 1983, `<www.patersontech.com/Dos/Softalk/Softalk.html>`.

34. Paterson, T., "An Inside Look at MS-DOS," June 1983, `<www.patersontech.com/Dos/Byte/InsideDos.htm>`.

35. Rojas, R., "Encyclopedia of Computers and Computer History—DOS," April 2001, `<www.patersontech.com/Dos/Encyclo.htm>`.

36. Rojas, R., "Encyclopedia of Computers and Computer History—DOS," April 2001, `<www.patersontech.com/Dos/Encyclo.htm>`.

37. Hunter, D., "Tim Patterson: The Roots of DOS," March 1983, `<www.patersontech.com/Dos/Softalk/Softalk.html>`.

38. Paterson, T., "An Inside Look at MS-DOS," June 1983, `<www.patersontech.com/Dos/Byte/InsideDos.htm>`.

39. Rojas, R., "Encyclopedia of Computers and Computer History—DOS," April 2001, `<www.patersontech.com/Dos/Encyclo.htm>`.

40. The Online Software Museum, "CP/M: History," `<museum.sysun.com/museum/cpmhist.html>`.

41. The Online Software Museum, "CP/M: History," `<museum.sysun.com/museum/cpmhist.html>`.

42. Rojas, R., "Encyclopedia of Computers and Computer History—DOS," April 2001, `<www.patersontech.com/Dos/Encyclo.htm>`.

43. Hunter, D., "Tim Patterson: The Roots of DOS," March 1983, `<www.patersontech.com/Dos/Softalk/Softalk.html>`.

44. Rojas, R., "Encyclopedia of Computers and Computer History—DOS," April 2001, `<www.patersontech.com/Dos/Encyclo.htm>`.

45. The Online Software Museum, "CP/M: History," `<museum.sysun.com/museum/cpmhist.html>`.

46. Rojas, R., "Encyclopedia of Computers and Computer History—DOS," April 2001, `<www.patersontech.com/Dos/Encyclo.htm>`.

47. McKusick, M.; W. Joy; S. Leffler; and R. Fabry, "A Fast File System for UNIX," *ACM Transactions on Computer Systems,* Vol. 2, No. 3, August 1984, p. 183.

48. Hecht, M., and J. Gabbe, "Shadowed Management of Free Disk Pages with a Linked List," *ACM Transactions on Database Systems,* Vol. 8, No. 4, December 1983, p. 505.

49. Hecht, M., and J. Gabbe, "Shadowed Management of Free Disk Pages with a Linked List," *ACM Transactions on Database Systems,* Vol. 8, No. 4, December 1983, p. 503.

50. Betourne, C., et al., "Process Management and Resource Sharing in the Multiaccess System ESOPE," *Communications of the ACM*, Vol. 13, No. 12, December 1970, p. 730.

51. Green, P., "Multics Virtual Memory—Tutorial and Reflections," <ftp://ftp.stratus.com/pub/vos/multics/pg/mvm.html>, 1999.

52. Choy, M.; H. Leong; and M. Wong, "Disaster Recovery Techniques for Database Systems," *Communications of the ACM*, Vol. 43, No. 11, November 2000, p. 273.

53. Chen, P.; W. Ng; S. Chandra; C. Aycock; G. Rajamani; and D. Lowell, "The Rio File Cache: Surviving Operating System Crashes," *Proceedings of the Seventh International Conference on Architectural Support for Programming Languages and Operating Systems*, 1996, p. 74.

54. Choy, M.; H. Leong; and M. Wong, "Disaster Recovery Techniques for Database Systems," *Communications of the ACM*, Vol. 43, No. 11, November 2000, p. 273.

55. Hutchinson, N.; S. Manley; M. Federwisch; G. Harris; D. Hitz; S. Kleiman; and S. O'Malley, "Logical vs. Physical File System Backup," *Proceedings of the Third Symposium on Operating System Design and Implementation*, 1999, pp. 244–245.

56. Hutchinson, N.; S. Manley; M. Federwisch; G. Harris; D. Hitz; S. Kleiman; and S. O'Malley, "Logical vs. Physical File System Backup," *Proceedings of the Third Symposium on Operating System Design and Implementation*, 1999, pp. 240, 242–243.

57. Tanenbaum, A., and R. Renesse, "Distributed Operating Systems," *Computing Surveys*, Vol. 17, No.4, December 1985, p. 441.

58. Brown, M.; K. Kolling; and E. Taft, "The Alpine File System," *ACM Transactions on Computer Systems*, Vol. 3, No. 4, November 1985, pp. 267–270.

59. Ousterhout, J. K., and M. Rosenblum, "The Design and Implementation of a Log-Structured File System," *ACM Transactions on Computer Systems*, Vol. 10, No. 1, February 1992.

60. "What's New in File and Print Services," June 16, 2003, <www.microsoft.com/windowsserver2003/evaluation/overview/technologies/fileandprint.mspx>.

61. Johnson, M. K., "Whitepaper: Red Hat's New Journaling File System: ext3," 2001, <www.redhat.com/support/wpapers/redhat/ext3/>.

62. Ousterhout, J. K., and M. Rosenblum, "The Design and Implementation of a Log-Structured File System," *ACM Transactions on Computer Systems*, Vol. 10, No. 1, February 1992.

63. Piernas J.; T. Cortes; and J. M. García, "DualFS: A New Journaling File System without Meta-Data Duplication," *Proceedings of the 16th International Conference on Supercomputing*, 2002, p. 137.

64. Matthews, J. N.; D. Roselli; A. M. Costello; R. Y. Wang; and T. E. Anderson, "Improving the Performance of Log-Structured File Systems with Adaptive Methods," *Proceedings of the Sixteenth ACM Symposium on Operating Systems Principles*, 1997, pp. 238–251.

65. Birrell, A. D., and R. M. Needham, "A Universal File Server," *IEEE Transactions on Software Engineering*, Vol. SE-6, No. 5, September 1980, pp. 450–453.

66. Mitchell, J. G., and J. Dion, "A Comparison of Two Network-Based File Servers," *Proceedings of the Eighth Symposium on Operating Systems Principles*, Vol. 15, No. 5, December 1981, pp. 45–46.

67. Christodoulakis, S., and C. Faloutsos, "Design and Performance Considerations for an Optical Disk-Based, Multimedia Object Server," *Computer*, Vol 19, No. 12, December 1986, pp. 45–56.

68. Mehta, S., "Serving a LAN," *LAN Magazine*, October 1988, pp. 93–98.

69. Fridrich, M., and W. Older, "The Felix File Server," *Proceedings of the Eighth Symposium on Operating System Principles*, Vol. 15, No. 5, December 1981, pp. 37–44.

70. Wah, B. W., "File Placement on Distributed Computer Systems," *Computer*, Vol. 17, No. 1, January 1984, pp. 23–32.

71. Mullender, S., and A. Tanenbaum, "A Distributed File Service Based on Optimistic Concurrency Control," *Proceedings of the 10th Symposium on Operating Systems Principles*, ACM, Vol. 19, No. 5, December 1985, pp. 51–62.

72. Morris, J. H.; M. Satyanarayanan; M. H. Conner; J. H. Howard; D. S. H. Rosenthal; and F. D. Smith, "Andrew: A Distributed Personal Computing Environment," *Communications of the ACM*, Vol. 29, No. 3, March 1986, pp. 184–201.

73. Nelson, M. N.; B. B. Welch; and J. K. Ousterhout, "Caching in the Sprite Network File System," *ACM Transactions on Computer Systems*, Vol. 6, No. 1, February 1988, pp. 134–154.

74. Walsh, D.; R. Lyon; and G. Sager, "Overview of the Sun Network File System," *USENIX Winter Conference*, Dallas, 1985, pp. 117–124.

75. Sandberg, R., et al. "Design and Implementation of the Sun Network File System," *Proceedings of the USENIX 1985 Summer Conference*, June 1985, pp. 119–130.

76. Sandberg, R., *The Sun Network File System: Design, Implementation and Experience*, Mountain View, CA: Sun Microsystems, Inc., 1987.

77. Lazarus, J., *Sun 386i Overview*, Mountain View; CA, Sun Microsystems, Inc., 1988.

78. Schnaidt, P., "NFS Now," *LAN Magazine*, October 1988, pp. 62–69.

79. Shepler, S.; B. Callaghan; D. Robinson; R. Thurlow; C. Beame; M. Eisler; and D. Noveck, "Network File System (NFS) version 4 Protocol," RFC 3530, April 2003, <www.ietf.org/rfc/rfc3530.txt>.

80. Date, C. J., *An Introduction Database Systems*, Reading, MA: Addison-Wesley, 1981.

81. Silberschatz, A.; H. Korth; and S. Sudarshan, *Database System Concepts*, 4th ed., New York: McGraw-Hill, 2002, pp. 3–5.

82. Silberschatz, A.; H. Korth; and S. Sudarshan, *Database System Concepts*, 4th ed., New York: McGraw-Hill, 2002, pp. 135–182.

83. Chen, P., "The Entity-Relationship Model—Toward a Unified View of Data," *ACM Transactions on Database Systems*, Vol. 1, No. 1, 1976, pp. 9–36.

84. Markowitz, V. M., and A. Shoshani, "Representing Extended Entity-Relationship Structures in Relational Databases: A Modular Approach," *ACM Transactions on Database Systems*, Vol. 17, No. 3, 1992. pp. 423–464.

85. Winston, A., "A Distributed Database Primer," *UNIX World*, April 1988, pp. 54–63.

86. Codd, E. F., "A Relational Model for Large Shared Data Banks," *Communications of the ACM*, June 1970.

87. Codd, E. F., "Further Normalization of the Data Base Relational Model," *Courant Computer Science Symposia*, Vol. 6, *Data Base Systems*, Englewood Cliffs, NJ.: Prentice Hall, 1972.

88. Blaha, M. R.; W. J. Premerlani; and J. E. Rumbaugh, "Relational Database Design Using an Object-Oriented Methodology," *Communications of the ACM,* Vol. 13, No. 4, April 1988, pp. 414–427.

89. Codd, E. F., "Fatal Flaws in SQL," *Datamation*, Vol. 34, No. 16, August 15, 1988, pp. 45–48.

90. Relational Technology, *INGRES Overview*, Alameda, CA: Relational Technology, 1988.

91. Stonebraker, M., "Operating System Support for Database Management," *Communications of the ACM*, Vol. 24, No. 7, July 1981, pp. 412–418.

92. Ibelshäuser, O., "The WinFS File System for Windows Longhorn: Faster and Smarter," *Tom's Hardware Guide*, June 17, 2003, <www.tomshardware.com/storage/20030617/>.

93. Golden, D., and M. Pechura, "The Structure of Microcomputer File Systems," *Communications of the ACM,* Vol. 29, No. 3, March 1986, pp. 222–230.

94. Custer, Helen, *Inside the Windows NT File System*, Redmond, WA: Microsoft Press, 1994.

95. Rosenblum, M., and J. K. Ousterhout, "The Design and Implementation of a Log-Structured File System," *ACM Transactions on Computer Systems (TOCS),* Vol. 10, No. 1, February 1992.

96. Wang, Jun; Rui Min; Zhuying Wu; and Yiming Hu, "Boosting I/O Performance of Internet Servers with User-Level Custom File Systems," *ACM SIGMETRICS Performance Evaluation Review*, Vol. 29, No. 2, September 2001, pp. 26–31.

Performance, Processors and Multiprocessor Management

Don't tell me how hard you work. Tell me how much you get done.
—Lewis Carroll—

Part 5

The next two chapters continue our emphasis on performance. Chapter 14 discusses performance measures, monitoring, evaluation, bottlenecks, saturation and feedback loops. The chapter also examines the crucial importance of processor instruction set architectures for maximizing system performance. Chapter 15 discusses the profound performance improvement that is possible in systems that employ multiple processors, especially massive numbers of processors. In the next decade, we expect parallel computing to literally explode, with individual systems tending to become multiprocessors, and with the proliferation of distributed systems. The chapter focuses on multiprocessor systems and discusses architecture, operating system organizations, memory access architectures, memory sharing, scheduling, process migration, load balancing and mutual exclusion.

The most general definition of beauty ... Multeity in Unity.
—Samuel Taylor Coleridge—

Observe due measure, for right timing is in all things the most important factor.

—Hesiod—

Don't tell me how hard you work. Tell me how much you get done.

—James Ling—

It is not permitted to the most equitable of men to be a judge in his own cause.

—Blaise Pascal—

All words,
And no performance!

—Philip Massinger—

Chapter 14

Performance and Processor Design

Objectives

After reading this chapter, you should understand:

- *the need for performance measures.*

- *common performance metrics.*

- *several techniques for measuring relative system performance.*

- *the notions of bottlenecks, saturation and feedback.*

- *popular architectural design philosophies for processors.*

- *processor design techniques that increase performance.*

Chapter Outline

14.1 Introduction

Because an operating system is primarily a resource manager, it is important for operating systems designers, managers and users to be able to determine how effectively a particular system manages its resources. System performance measurements enable consumers to make more informed decisions and help developers build more efficient systems. In this chapter, we describe many performance issues and investigate techniques for measuring, monitoring and evaluating performance; the use of these methods can help designers, managers and users realize maximum performance from computing systems.

The performance of a system depends heavily on its hardware, operating system and the interaction between the two. Therefore, this chapter considers several evaluation techniques that measure the performance of entire systems, rather than just the operating system. We also present an introduction to popular processor-design philosophies and how each seeks to achieve high performance.

Self Review

1. How do you suppose performance evaluation benefits consumers, developers and users?
2. What resource of a computer system probably has the greatest impact on performance?

Ans: **1)** Performance evaluation provides consumers with a basis of comparison to decide between different systems, developers with useful information on how to write software to efficiently use system components and users with information that can facilitate tuning the system to meet the requirements of a specific setting. **2)** The processor(s).

14.2 Important Trends Affecting Performance Issues

In the early years of computer systems development, hardware was the dominant cost, so performance studies concentrated primarily on hardware issues. Now, hardware is relatively inexpensive and prices continue to decline. Software complexity is increasing with the widespread use of multithreading, multiprocessing, distributed systems, database management systems, graphical user interfaces and various application support systems. The software typically hides the hardware from the user, creating a virtual machine defined by the operating characteristics of the software. Cumbersome software causes poor performance, even on systems with powerful hardware, so it is important to consider a system's software performance as well as its hardware performance.

The nature of performance evaluation itself is evolving. Raw and potentially misleading measures, such as clock speed and bandwidth, have become influential in the consumer market, because vendors engineer their products with an eye to these metrics. However, other aspects of performance evaluation are improving. For example, designers have developed more sophisticated benchmarks, acquired better trace data and engineered more comprehensive computer simulation models—we investigate all these techniques later in the chapter. New industry-standard benchmarks and "synthetic programs" are emerging. Unfortunately, there is still no consensus on these standards. Critics charge that performance results can be incorrect or misleading, because the performance evaluation techniques do not necessarily measure relevant features of a program.[1]

Self Review

1. How has the focus of performance studies shifted over the years?
2. Give several examples of how operating systems can improve performance, as discussed in the preceding chapters.

Ans: **1)** In the early years, hardware was the dominant cost, so performance studies focused on hardware issues. Today, it is recognized that sophisticated software can have a substantial effect on performance. **2)** Operating systems can improve disk and processor scheduling policies, implement more efficient thread-synchronization protocols, more effectively manage file systems, perform context switches more efficiently, improve memory management algorithms, etc.

14.3 Why Performance Monitoring and Evaluation Are Needed

In his classic paper, Lucas mentions three common purposes for performance evaluation.[2]

- **Selection evaluation** — The performance evaluator decides whether obtaining a computer system or application from a particular vendor is appropriate.

- **Performance projection** — The performance evaluator estimates the performance of a system that does not exist. It might be a completely new computer system, or an old system with a new hardware or software component.

- **Performance monitoring** — The evaluator accumulates performance data on an existing system or component to ensure that it is meeting its performance goals. Performance monitoring can also help estimate the impact of planned changes and provide system administrators with the data they need in order to make strategic decisions, such as whether to modify an existing process priority system or upgrade a hardware component.

In the early phases of a new system's development, the vendor attempts to predict the nature of applications that will run on the system and the anticipated workloads these applications must handle. Once the vendor begins development and implementation of the new system, performance evaluation and prediction are used to determine the best hardware organization, the resource management strategies that should be implemented in the operating system and whether or not the evolving system meets its performance objectives. Once the product is released to the marketplace, the vendor must be prepared to answer questions from potential users about whether the system can handle certain applications with certain levels of performance. Users are often concerned with choosing an appropriate configuration of a system that services their needs.

When the system is installed at the user's site, both the vendor and the user seek to obtain optimal performance. Administrators fine-tune the system to run at its best in the user's operating environment. This process, called **system tuning,** can often cause dramatic performance improvements, once the system is adjusted to the idiosyncrasies of the user installation.

Self Review

1. When would an evaluator use performance projection in preference to selection evaluation?
2. How does performance monitoring facilitate system tuning?

Ans: **1)** Selection evaluation help an evaluator choose among existing systems. Performance projection helps the evaluator predict the performance of systems that do not exist yet—or how anticipated modifications to existing systems would perform. **2)** An evaluator can monitor performance to determine which modifications would most likely increase system performance.

14.4 Performance Measures

By performance, we mean the efficiency with which a computer system meets its goals. Thus, performance is a relative rather than an absolute quantity, although we often talk of **absolute performance measures** such as the amount of time in which a given computer system can perform a specific computational task. However, whenever a performance measure is taken, it is normally to be used as a basis of comparison.

Performance is often "in the eye of the beholder." For example, a young music student might find a performance of Beethoven's Fifth Symphony thoroughly inspiring, whereas the conductor might be sensitive to the most minor flaws in the way a second violinist plays a certain passage. Similarly, the owner of a large airline reservation system might be pleased with the high utilization reflected by a large volume of reservations processed, whereas an individual user might be experiencing excessive delays on such a busy system.

Quantifying is difficult for some performance measures, such as **ease of use,** and simple for others, such as the speed of a disk-to-memory transfer. The performance evaluator must be careful to consider both types of measures, even though it might be possible to provide neat statistics only for the latter. Some performance measures, such as response time, are user oriented. Others, such as processor utilization, are system oriented.

Some performance results might be deceptive. For example, one operating system might focus on conserving memory by executing complicated page-replacement algorithms, whereas another might avoid these complex routines to save processor cycles for executing user programs. The former would appear more efficient on a system with a high clock speed; the latter, on a processor with a large main memory. In addition, some techniques permit the evaluator to measure the performance of small pieces of a system such as individual components or primitives. Although these tools can be useful for pinpointing specific weaknesses, they do not tell the entire story. The evaluator might discover that an operating system performs all of its primitives efficiently except one. This should not be a major concern, unless that inefficient primitive is used extensively. Without taking into account the frequency with which each primitive is used, measurements can be misleading. Similarly, programs designed to evaluate a system for a particular environment that do not resemble the applications for which the system is intended can yield spurious results.

Some common performance measures are:

- **Turnaround time**—This is the time from submission of a job until the system returns a result to the user.

- **Response time**—This is an interactive system's turnaround time, often defined as the time from a user's pressing an *Enter* key or clicking a mouse until the system displays its response.

- **System reaction time**—In an interactive system, this is often defined as the time from a user's pressing *Enter* or clicking a mouse until the first time slice of service is given to that user's request.

These are probabilistic quantities, and in simulation and modeling studies of systems they are considered to be **random variables**. A random variable is one that can assume a certain range of values, where each value has an associated probability of occurring. We discuss the **distribution of response times**, for example, because users experience a wide range of response times on a particular interactive system over some interval of operation. A probability distribution can meaningfully characterize this range.

When we talk of the **expected value** of a random variable, we are referring to its **mean** or average value. However, means can often be deceiving. A certain mean value can be produced by averaging a series of identical or nearly identical values, or it can be produced by averaging a wide variety of values, some much larger and some much smaller than the calculated mean. Therefore, other performance measures often employed are:

- **Variance in response times** (or of any of the random variables we discuss)—The variance of response times is a measure of **dispersion.** A small variance indicates that the response times experienced by users are generally close to the mean. A large variance indicates that some users are experiencing response times that differ widely from the mean. Some users could be receiving fast service, while others could be experiencing long delays. Thus the variance of response times is a measure of **predictability**; this can be an important performance measure for users of interactive systems.

- **Throughput**—This is the work-per-unit-time performance measurement.

- **Workload**—This is the measure of the amount of work that has been submitted to the system. Often, evaluators define an acceptable level of performance for the typical workload of a computing environment. The system is evaluated compared to the acceptable level.

- **Capacity**—This is a measure of the maximum throughput a system can attain, assuming that whenever the system is ready to accept more jobs, another job is immediately available.

- **Utilization**—This is the fraction of time that a resource is in use. Utilization can be a deceptive measure. Although a high-percent utilization seems desirable, it might be the result of inefficient usage. One way to achieve high processor utilization, for example, is to run a process that is in an infinite loop! Another view of processor utilization also yields interesting insights. We might view a processor at any moment as being idle, in user mode, or in kernel mode. When a processor is in user mode, it is performing operations on behalf of a user. When the processor is in kernel mode, it is performing tasks for the operating system. Some of this time, such as context-switching time, is pure overhead. This overhead component can become large in some systems. Thus, when we measure processor utilization, we must be concerned with how much of this usage is productive work on behalf of the users, and how much is system overhead. Strangely, "poor utilization" is actually a positive measure in certain kinds of systems, such as hard real-time systems, where the system resources must stand ready to respond immediately to incoming tasks, or lives could be at risk. Such systems focus on immediate response rather than resource utilization.

Self Review

1. What is the difference between response time and system reaction time?
2. (T/F) When a processor spends most of its time in user mode, the system achieves efficient processor utilization.

Ans: **1)** Response time is the time required for the system to *finish* responding to a user request (from the time the request is submitted); system reaction time is the time required for the system to *begin* responding to a user request (from the time the request is submitted). **2)** False. If the processor is executing an infinite loop, this system is not using the processor efficiently.

14.5 Performance Evaluation Techniques

Now that we have considered some possible performance measures, we need some way of extracting them. In this section, we describe several important performance evaluation techniques.[3, 4, 5] Some of these isolate different components of a system and report each component's individual performance, allowing developers to identify areas of inefficiency. Others are oriented toward the system as a whole and allow consumers to make comparisons between systems. Still other techniques are application specific and therefore allow only indirect comparisons with other systems,. In the sections that follow, we describe various evaluation techniques and the aspects of system performance they measure.

14.5.1 Tracing and Profiling

Ideally, a system evaluator would measure the performance of several systems, each executing in the same environment. However, this is usually not feasible, especially for corporations whose environments are complex and difficult to duplicate. Such a process can be invasive, compromising the integrity of the environment and nullifying the results. When the performance of a system must be evaluated in a given environment, designers often use **trace** data. A trace is a record of system activity—typically a log of user and application requests to the operating system.

System evaluators can use trace data to characterize a particular system's execution environment by determining the frequency with which user-mode processes request particular kernel services. Before installing a new computing system, evaluators can test the new system using a workload derived from the trace data or using the trace itself. Trace data often can be modified to evaluate "what-if" scenarios. For example, a system administrator might need to determine how a new Web site will affect Web server performance. An existing trace can be modified to estimate how the system will handle its new load.[6]

When operating systems execute in similar environments, standard traces can be developed and executed on those systems to compare performance. Trace data obtained from one installation, however, might not be applicable to another. Such data is, at best, an approximation of system activity at the other installation. In addition, user logs are considered proprietary to the system on which they were recorded; rarely are such logs distributed to the research community or to vendors. Consequently, there is a dearth of trace data available for comparison and evaluation.[7]

Another method for capturing a computing system's execution environment is profiling. **Profiles** record system activity while executing in kernel mode, which can include operations such as process scheduling, memory management and I/O management. For example, a profile might record which kernel operations are performed most often. Alternatively, a profile can simply log all function calls issued by the operating system. Profiles indicate which operating system primitives are most heavily used, enabling system administrators to identify potential targets for optimization and tuning.[8] Evaluators must often employ other performance evaluation techniques in concert with profiles to determine the most effective ways to improve system performance.

Self Review

1. How do evaluators use trace data?
2. Explain the difference between traces and profiles.

Ans:　**1)** Trace data permits evaluators to compare the performance of many different systems that operate in the same computing environment. Trace data describes this environment so that evaluators can obtain performance results relevant to the systems' intended use. **2)** Traces record user requests, whereas profiles log all activity in kernel mode. Therefore, traces describe a computing environment by capturing the user demand for particular kernel services (without regard to the underlying system), and profiles capture operating system activity in a given environment.

14.5.2 Timings and Microbenchmarks

Timings provide a means of performing quick comparisons of computer hardware. Early computer systems were often evaluated by their add times or their memory-cycle times. Timings are useful for indicating the "raw horsepower" of a particular computer system, often in terms of the number of **MIPS (millions of instructions per second)** or **BIPS (billions of instructions per second)** it executes. Some computers perform in the **TIPS (trillion instructions per second)** range.

With the advent of **families of computers**, such as the IBM 360 series, first introduced in 1964, or the Intel Pentium series, a descendant of the Intel x86 series introduced in 1978, it has become common for hardware vendors to offer computers that enable a user to upgrade to faster processors (without replacing other computer components) as the user's needs grow. The computers in a family are compatible in that they can run the same programs but at greater speeds as the user moves up in the family. Timings provide a convenient means for comparing the members of a family of computers.

A **microbenchmark** measures the time required to perform an operating system operation (e.g., process creation). Microbenchmarks are useful for measuring how a design change affects the performance of a specific operation. **Microbenchmark suites** are programs that measure the performance of a number of important operating system primitives, such as memory operations, process creation and context-switch latency.[9] Evaluators also use microbenchmarks to measure system performance for specific operations, such as read/write bandwidth (i.e., how much data the system can transfer per unit time during a read or write) and network connection latency.[10]

Microbenchmarks describe how quickly a system performs a particular operation, not how often that operation is performed. Consequently, they do not measure important evaluation criteria such as throughput and utilization. Microbenchmarks, however, are useful in isolating which operations could be causing a system to perform poorly when coupled with information about how each operation is used.[11]

Until the 1990s, no single microbenchmark suite demonstrated the effect of hardware components on the performance of operating system primitives. In 1995 the **lmbench microbenchmark suite**, which enabled evaluators to measure and compare system performance on a variety of UNIX platforms, was introduced.[12] Although lmbench provided useful performance evaluation data that allowed comparison across multiple platforms, it was inconsistent in the way that it reported statistical data—some tests returned results based on an average of runs while other used just one run of the microbenchmark. lmbench was also limited to performing measurements once per millisecond because it used coarse software timing mechanisms; this is insufficient for measuring fast operations and timing hardware. Researchers at Harvard University addressed these limitations by creating the

hbench microbenchmark suite, which provides a standard and rigorous model for reporting statistics, enabling evaluators to more effectively analyze the relationship between operating system primitives and hardware components.[13] lmbench and hbench represent different microbenchmark philosophies. lmbench focuses on portability, which permits evaluators to compare performance across different architectures; hbench focuses on the relationship between the operating system and its underlying hardware within a particular system.[14, 15]

Self Review

1. How can results from timings and microbenchmarks be misleading? How are they useful?
2. Which performance measure can be combined with microbenchmarks to evaluate operating system performance?

Ans: **1)** Microbenchmarks measure the time required to perform specific primitives (e.g., process creation), and timings perform quick comparisons of hardware operations (e.g., add instructions). Neither of these measurements reflects system performance as a whole. However, microbenchmarks and timings can be useful in pinpointing potential areas of inefficiency and evaluating the effect of small modifications on system performance. **2)** Profiles, which record how often an operating system primitive is used, can be combined with microbenchmarks to evaluate operating system performance.

14.5.3 Application-Specific Evaluation

Although "raw performance" is an important measure, many users are more interested in how well particular applications will perform on a particular system. Seltzer et al. describe a **vector-based methodology** for calculating an application-specific evaluation of a system by combining trace and profile data with timings and microbenchmarks.[16]

In this technique, an evaluator records the results of microbenchmarks for the operating system's primitives. Next, the evaluator constructs a vector by placing the values corresponding to the microbenchmark results in the elements of the vector; this is called the **system vector**. Next, the evaluator profiles the operating system while executing the target application. The evaluator constructs a second vector by inserting the relative demand for each operating system primitive in an element in the vector; this is called the **application vector**. Each element in the system vector describes how long the operating system needs to execute a particular primitive, and the corresponding entry in the application vector describes the application's relative demand for that primitive. For example, if the first entry in the system vector records process creation performance, the first entry in the application vector records how many processes were created while executing a particular application (or group of applications). A characterization of the performance of a given system executing a particular application is calculated by

$$\sum_{i=1}^{th} s_i \times a_i$$

where s_i is the ith entry in the system vector, a_i is the ith entry in the application vector and n is the size of both vectors.[17]

This technique can be useful for comparing how efficiently different operating systems execute a particular application (or group of applications) by considering the demand an application places on each of a system's primitives. The vector-based methodology can be used to select operating system primitives to tune to improve system performance.

Some application behavior depends both on the particular application and on user input. For example, the type of application requests generated in a database system depends on its population of active users. Simply profiling the system without determining the typical stream of user requests can produce misleading results. In such cases, both the application and user requests determine the system's execution environment. Therefore, to provide a more accurate system evaluation, the vector-based methodology can be combined with a trace (Seltzer et al. call this the **hybrid methodology**). In this case, the trace data allows the evaluator to construct the application vector while accounting for how the specific application and typical stream of user requests affect the demand for each operating system primitive.[18]

A **kernel program** is another application-specific performance evaluation tool, although it is not often used. A kernel program can range from an entire program that is typical of one executed at an installation or a simple algorithm such as a matrix inversion. Using the manufacturer's estimated instruction timings, execution of a kernel program is timed for a given machine. Machines are then compared on the basis of differences in the expected execution times. Kernel programs are actually "executed on paper" rather than being run on a particular computer. They are used in selection evaluation before a consumer purchases the system being evaluated. [*Note*: "Kernel" here should not be confused with the kernel of the operating system.][19]

Kernel programs give better results than either timings or microbenchmarks, but they require manual effort to prepare and time. One key advantage of many kernel programs is that they are complete programs, which ultimately is what the user actually runs on the computer system under consideration.

Kernel programs can be helpful in evaluating certain software components of a system. For example, two different compilers might produce dramatically different code, and kernel programs can help an evaluator decide which one generates more efficient code.[20]

Self Review

1. What is a benefit of application-specific evaluation? What is a drawback?
2. Why do you suppose kernel programs are rarely used?

Ans: **1)** Application-specific evaluation is useful in determining whether a system will perform well in executing the particular programs at a given installation. A drawback is that a system must be evaluated by each installation that is considering using it; the system's designers cannot simply publish one set of performance results. **2)** Kernel programs require time and effort to prepare and time. Also, they are "executed on paper" and can introduce human error. Often, it is easier to run the actual program, or one similar to it, on the actual system than calculate the execution time for a kernel program.

14.5.4 Analytic Models

Analytic models are mathematical representations of computer systems or their components.[21, 22, 23, 24, 25] Many types of models are used; those of queuing theory and Markov processes are two of the more popular, because they are relatively manageable and useful.

For evaluators who are mathematically inclined, the analytic model can be relatively easy to create and modify. A large body of mathematical results exists that evaluators can apply in order to estimate the performance of a given computer system or component quickly and fairly accurately. However, several disadvantages of analytic modeling hinder its applicability. One is that evaluators must be highly skilled mathematicians; these people are rare in commercial computing environments. Another is that complex systems are difficult to model precisely; as systems become more complex, analytic modeling becomes less useful.

Today's systems are often so complex that the modeler is forced to make many simplifying assumptions that can diminish the usefulness and applicability of the model. Therefore, an evaluator should use other techniques (e.g., microbenchmarks) in concert with analytic models. Sometimes the results of an evaluation using only analytic models might be invalidated by studies using other techniques. Often the different evaluations tend to reinforce one another, demonstrating the validity of the modeler's conclusions.

Self Review

1. Explain the relative merits of complex and simple analytic models.
2. What are some benefits of using analytic modeling?

Ans: **1)** Complex analytic models are more accurate, but it might not be possible to find a mathematical solution to model a system's behavior. It is easier to represent the behavior of a system with a simpler model, but it might not accurately represent the system. **2)** There is a large body of results that evaluators can draw from when creating models; analytic models can provide accurate and quick performance results; and they can be modified relatively easily when the system changes.

14.5.5 Benchmarks

A **benchmark** is a program that is executed to evaluate a machine. Commonly, a benchmark is a **production program** which is typical of many jobs at the installation. The evaluator is thoroughly familiar with the performance of the benchmark on existing equipment, so when it is run on new equipment, the evaluator can draw meaningful conclusions.[26, 27] Several organizations, such as **Standard Performance Evaluation Corporation (SPEC**; www.specbench.org) and **Business Application Performance Corporation (BAPCo**; www.bapco.com), have developed industry-standard benchmarks targeted for different systems (e.g., Web servers or personal computers). Evaluators can run these benchmarks to compare similar systems from different vendors.

One advantage of benchmarks is that many already exist, so the evaluator merely needs to choose them from known production programs or use industry-standard benchmarks. No timings are taken on individual instructions. Instead, the full program is run on the actual machine using real data, so the computer does most of the work. The chance of human error is minimal because the benchmark time is measured by the computer itself. In environments such as multiprogramming, timesharing, multiprocessing, database, data communications and real-time systems, benchmarks can be particularly valuable, because they run on the actual machine in real circumstances. The effects of such complex systems can be experienced directly instead of being estimated.

Several criteria should be considered when developing a benchmark. First, the results should be repeatable; specifically, every run of the benchmark program on a certain system should produce nearly the same result. Results do not have to be identical, and seldom are, because they can be affected by environment-specific details, such as where an item is stored on disk. Second, benchmarks should accurately reflect the types of applications that will be executed on a system. Finally, the benchmark should be widely used so that more accurate comparisons can be made between systems. A good industry-standard benchmark will have all these properties; however, the latter two often lead to conflicting design decisions. A benchmark that is specific to a certain system might not be widely used; a benchmark that is designed to test multiple systems might not yield as accurate a result for a specific system.[28]

Benchmarks are useful in evaluating hardware as well as software, even under complex operating environments. They also are particularly useful in comparing the operation of a system before and after certain changes are made. Benchmarks are not useful, however, in predicting the effects of proposed changes, unless another system exists with the changes incorporated and on which the benchmarks can be run.

Benchmarks are probably the technique most widely used by organizations and consumers when determining which equipment to purchase from several competing vendors. Their popularity as tools for this purpose led to the need for industry-standard benchmarks. SPEC was founded in 1988 to promote the development of standard, relevant benchmarks. SPEC publishes a variety of benchmarks (often called **SPECmarks**) that can be used to evaluate systems ranging from servers to Java Virtual Machines and publishes performance results obtained using those SPECmarks for thousands of commercial systems. SPEC ratings can be useful for making an informed decision determining which computer components to purchase. However, one must first carefully determine the focus of each SPECmark test to evaluate particular platforms. For example, SPECweb measures systems on which Web servers typically execute and should not be used to compare systems that execute in different environments.[29] If the environment of a particular Web server differs from a "typical" one, the SPEC rating might not be relevant. Furthermore, some of SPEC's benchmarks have been criticized for narrow scope, especially by those who question the assumption that a "typical" workload can accurately approximate a real-world workload for a particular system. To combat such limitations, SPEC continually redesigns its benchmarks to improve their relevance to current systems.[30, 31]

Although SPEC produces some of the best-known benchmarks, there are a number of other popular benchmarks and benchmarking organizations. BAPCo produces several benchmarks, including the popular **SYSmark benchmark** (for desktop systems), **MobileMark** (for systems installed on mobile devices) and **WebMark** (for Internet performance).[32] Other popular benchmarks include the **Transaction Processing Performance Council (TPC) benchmarks**, which target database systems,[33] and the **Standard Application (SAP) benchmarks**, which evaluate a system's scalability.[34]

Self Review

1. How can benchmarks be used to anticipate the effect of proposed changes to a system?
2. Why are there no universally accepted "standard" benchmarks?

Ans: **1)** In general, benchmarks are effective only for determining the results after a change or for performance comparisons between systems, not for anticipating the effect of proposed changes to a system. However, if the proposed changes match the configuration of an existing system, running the benchmark on that system would be useful. **2)** Benchmarks are real programs that are run on real machines, but each machine might contain a different set of hardware that runs a different mix of programs. Therefore, benchmark designers provide "typical" application mixes that are updated regularly to better approximate particular environments.

14.5.6 Synthetic Programs

Synthetic programs (also called **synthetic benchmarks**) are similar to benchmarks, except that they focus on a specific component of the system, such as the I/O subsystem and memory subsystem. Unlike benchmarks, which are typical of real applications, evaluators construct synthetic programs for specific purposes. For example, a synthetic program might target an operating system component (e.g., the file system) or might be constructed to match the instruction frequency distribution of a large set of programs. One advantage of synthetic programs is that they can isolate specific components of a system rather than test the entire system.[35, 36, 37, 38, 39]

Synthetic programs are useful in development environments. As new features become available, synthetic programs can be used to test that they are operational. Evaluators, unfortunately, do not always have sufficient time to code and debug synthetic programs, so they often seek existing benchmark programs that match the desired characteristics of a synthetic program as closely as possible. Evaluators can use synthetic programs with benchmarks and microbenchmarks for a thorough system evaluation. These three techniques provide different levels of abstraction (the system as a whole, a component of the system or a simple primitive) that, combined, give the evaluator an understanding of the performance both of the entire system and of individual parts of the system.

Although no longer used much, the **Whetstone** and the **Dhrystone** are examples of classic synthetic programs. The Whetstone measures how well systems handle floating point calculations, and was thus helpful in evaluating scientific programs. The Dhrystone measures how effectively an architecture runs systems programs. Because the Dhrystone consumes only a small amount of memory, its effectiveness is particularly sensitive to the size of a processor's cache; if the Dhrystone's data and instruction can fit in the cache, it will execute much faster than if the processor must access main memory while it executes. In fact, because the Dhrystone fits in most of today's processor caches, in effect it measures a processor's clock speed and provides no insight into how a system manages memory. One popular synthetic program used extensively today is **WinBench 99**, which tests a system's graphics, disk and video subsytems in a Microsoft Windows environment.[40] Other popular synthetic benchmarks include **IOStone** (which tests file systems),[41] **Hartstone** (for real-time systems)[42] and **STREAM** (for the memory subsystem).[43]

Self Review

1. Explain why synthetic programs are useful for development environments.
2. Should synthetic programs alone be used for a performance evaluation? Why?

Ans: **1)** Synthetic programs can be written fairly quickly and can test specific features for correctness. **2)** No, synthetic programs are "artificial" programs used to test specific components or to characterize a large set of programs (but not one in particular). Therefore, although producing valuable results, they do not necessarily describe how the entire system will perform when executing real programs. It is usually a good idea to use a variety of performance evaluation techniques.

14.5.7 Simulation

Simulation is a technique in which an evaluator develops a computerized model of the system being evaluated.[44, 45, 46, 47, 48] The evaluator tests the model, which presumably reflects the target system, to infer performance data about this system.

With simulation it is possible to prepare a model of a system that does not exist and then run the model to see how the system might behave in certain circumstances. Of course, the simulation must eventually be **validated** against the real system to prove that it is accurate. Simulations can highlight problems early in a system's development cycle. Computerized simulators have become especially popular in the space and transportation industries, because of the severe consequences of building systems that fail.

Simulators are generally of two types:

- **Event-driven simulators**—These are controlled by events that are made to occur in the simulator according to probability distributions.[49]
- **Script-driven simulators**—These are controlled by data carefully manipulated to reflect the anticipated environment of the simulated system; evaluators derive this data from empirical observations.

Simulation requires considerable expertise on the part of the evaluator and can consume substantial computer time. Simulators generally produce huge amounts of data that must be carefully analyzed. However, once simulators are developed, they can be reused effectively and economically.

Just as with analytic models, it is difficult to model a complex system exactly with a simulation. Several common errors cause most inaccuracies. Bugs in simulators will, of course, produce erroneous performance results. Deliberate omissions, resulting from the necessity of simplifying a simulation, can invalidate results as well. This is usually more of a problem for simple simulators. However, complex simulators suffer from the third problem—lack of detail. Complex simulators attempt to model all parts of the system, but inevitably, they do not model all details exactly. The attendant errors also can hinder a simulator's effectiveness. Therefore, to achieve the most accurate performance results, it is important to validate a simulation against the real system.[50]

Self Review

1. Which produces more consistent results, event-driven or script-driven simulators?
2. (T/F) Complex simulators are always more effective than simpler ones.

Ans: **1)** Script-driven simulators produce nearly the same result each run because the system always uses the same inputs. Because event-driven simulators dynamically generate input based on probabilities, the results are less consistent. **2)** False. Although complex simulators attempt to model a system more completely, they still might not model it accurately.

14.5.8 Performance Monitoring

Performance monitoring is the collection and analysis of information regarding system performance for existing systems.[51, 52, 53] It can help determine useful performance measures, such as throughput, response times and predictability. Performance monitoring can locate inefficiencies quickly and help system administrators decide how to improve system performance.

Users can monitor performance using software or hardware techniques. Software monitors might distort performance readings, because the monitors themselves consume system resources. Familiar examples of performance monitoring software are Microsoft Windows's Task Manager[54] and the Linux proc file system[55] (see Section 20.7.4, Proc File System). Hardware monitors are generally more costly, but they have little or no impact on system performance. Many of today's processors maintain several counting registers useful for performance monitoring that record events including clockticks, TLB misses and memory operations (such as a write to main memory).[56]

Monitors generally produce huge volumes of data that must be analyzed, possibly requiring extensive computer resources. However, they indicate precisely how the system is functioning, and this information can be extremely valuable. This is particularly true in development environments in which key design decisions might be based on the observed operation of the system.

Instruction execution traces, or module execution traces, can reveal which areas of a system are most frequently used. A module execution trace might show, for example, that a small subset of modules is being used a large percentage of the time. If designers concentrate their optimization efforts on these modules, they might be able to improve system performance without expending effort and resources on infrequently used portions of the system. Figure 14.1 summarizes performance evaluation techniques.

Self Review

1. Why do software performance monitors influence a system more than hardware performance monitors?
2. Why is performance monitoring important?

Ans: **1)** Software-based performance monitors must compete for system resources that would otherwise be allocated to programs that are being evaluated. This can result in inaccurate performance measurements. Hardware performance monitors operate in parallel with other system hardware, so that measurement does not affect system performance. **2)** Performance monitoring enables administrators to identify inefficiencies, using data describing how the system is functioning.

Technique	Description
Trace	Record of real application requests to the operating system, which identifies a system's workload.
Profile	Record of kernel activity taken during a real session. Profiles indicate the relative usage of operating system primitives.
Timing	Raw measure of hardware performance, which can be used for quick comparisons between related systems.
Microbenchmarks	Raw measure of how quickly an operating system performs an isolated operation.
Application-specific evaluation	Evaluation that determines how efficiently a system executes a particular application.
Analytic modeling	Technique in which an evaluator builds and analyzes a mathematical model of a computer system.
Benchmark	Program typical of one that will be run on the given system, used for comparisons between systems.
Synthetic program	Program that isolates the performance of a particular operating system component.
Simulation	Technique in which a computer model of the system is evaluated. The results of the simulation must be validated against the actual system once the system is built.
Performance monitoring	Ongoing evaluation of a system once it is installed, allowing administrators to assess whether it is meeting its demands and to determine which areas of its performance require improvement.

Figure 14.1 | *Summary of performance evaluation techniques.*

14.6 Bottlenecks and Saturation

Operating systems manage collections of resources that interface and interact in complex ways. Occasionally, resources become **bottlenecks**, limiting the system's overall performance, because they perform their designated tasks slowly relative to other resources. While other system resources might have excess capacity, the bottlenecks cannot pass jobs or processes to these other resources fast enough to keep them busy.[57, 58, 59]

A bottleneck tends to develop at a resource when the traffic there begins to approach its capacity. We say that the resource becomes **saturated**—i.e., processes competing for its attention begin to interfere with one another, because one must wait for others to complete using the resource.[60] A classic example is a virtual memory system that is thrashing (see Chapter 11, Virtual Memory Management). This occurs in paged systems when main memory becomes overcommitted and the working sets of the various active processes cannot be maintained simultaneously in main memory. An active process interferes with another process's use of memory by forcing the system to flush some of the other process's working set to secondary storage to make room for its own working set. Saturation can be dealt with by reducing the load on the system—e.g., thrashing can be eliminated by temporarily suspending less critical, noninteractive processes, if such processes are available.

How can bottlenecks be detected? Quite simply, each resource's request queue should be monitored. When a queue begins to grow quickly, then the **arrival rate** of requests at that resource must be larger than its **service rate**, so the resource has become saturated.

Isolation of bottlenecks is an important part of tuning a system. The bottlenecks can be removed by increasing the capacity of the resources, by adding more resources of that type at that point in the system, or, again, by decreasing the load on those resources. Removing a bottleneck does not always improve throughput, however, because other bottlenecks might also exist in the system. Tuning a system often involves identifying and eliminating bottlenecks until system performance reaches satisfactory levels.

Self Review

1. Why is it important to identify bottlenecks in a system?
2. Thrashing is due to the saturation of what resource? How would an operating system detect thrashing?

Ans: **1)** Identifying bottlenecks allows designers to focus on optimizing sections of a system that are degrading performance. **2)** Main memory. The operating system would notice a high page recapture rate—the pages being paged out to make room for incoming pages would themselves quickly be paged back into main memory.

14.7 Feedback Loops

A **feedback loop** is a technique in which information about the current state of the system can affect arriving requests. These requests can be rerouted if the feedback indicates that the system might have difficulty servicing them. Feedback can be negative, in which case arrival rates might decrease, or positive, in which case arrival rates might increase. Although we divide this section to examine positive and negative feedback situations separately, they do not represent two different techniques. Rather, a request rate at a particular resource might cause either negative or positive feedback (or neither).

14.7.1 Negative Feedback

In **negative feedback** situations, the arrival rate of new requests might decrease as a result of information being fed back. For example, a motorist pulling into a gas station and observing that several cars are waiting at each pump might decide to drive down the street to less crowded station.

In distributed systems, spooled outputs can often be printed by any of several equivalent print servers. If the queue behind one server is too long, the job may be placed in a less crowded queue.

Negative feedback contributes to **stability** in queuing systems. If the scheduler assigns arriving jobs indiscriminately to a busy device, for example, then the queue behind that device might grow indefinitely (even though other devices might be underutilized).

Self Review

1. Explain how negative feedback could improve read performance in Level 1 (mirrored) RAID.
2. How does negative feedback contribute to system stability?

Ans: **1)** If one of the disks in a mirrored pair contains a large queue of read requests, some of these requests could be sent to the other disk in the pair if it contains a smaller queue.
2) Negative feedback prevents one resource from being overwhelmed while other identical resources lie idle.

14.7.2 Positive Feedback

In **positive feedback** situations, the arrival rate of new requests might increase as a result of information being fed back. A classic example occurs in paged virtual memory multiprocessor systems. Suppose the operating system detects that a processor is underutilized. The system might inform the process scheduler to admit more processes to that processor's queue, anticipating that this would place a greater load on the processor. As more processes are admitted, the amount of memory that can be allocated to each process decreases and page faults might increase (because the working sets of all active processes might not fit in memory). Processor utilization will actually decrease as the system thrashes. A poorly designed operating system might then decide to admit even more processes. Of course, this would cause further deterioration in processor utilization.

Operating systems designers must be cautious when designing mechanisms to respond to positive feedback to prevent such unstable situations from developing. The effects of each incremental change should be monitored to see whether it results in the anticipated improvement. If a change causes performance to deteriorate, this signals to the operating system that it might be entering an unstable range and that resource-allocation strategies should be adjusted in order to resume stable operation.

Self Review

1. In some large server systems, users communicate requests to a "front-end" server. This server accepts the user's request and sends it to a "back-end" server for processing. How could a front-end server balance request loads among a set of equivalent back-end servers using feedback loops?
2. This section describes how positive feedback can intensify thrashing. Suggest one possible solution to this problem.

Ans: **1)** Back-end servers with a long queue of requests might send negative feedback to the front-end sever, and back-end servers that are idle might send positive feedback. The front-end server can use these feedback loops to send incoming requests to underloaded instead of overloaded servers. **2)** The system can monitor the number of page recaptures and refuse to admit further processes beyond a certain threshold.

14.8 Performance Techniques in Processor Design

A system's performance depends heavily on the performance of its processors. Conceptually, a processor can be divided into its **instruction set**, which is the set of machine instructions it can perform, and its implementation, which is the physical hardware. An instruction set might be composed of a few basic instructions that perform only simple functions, such as loading a value from memory into a register or adding two numbers. Alternatively, instruction sets can contain an abundance of more complex instructions such as those that solve a specified polynomial equation. The penalty for providing such a large number of complex instructions is more complex hardware, which increases processor cost and might reduce performance for simpler instructions; the benefit is that these complex routines can be performed quickly.

The **instruction set architecture (ISA)** of a processor is an interface that describes the processor, including its instruction set, number of registers and memory size. The ISA is the hardware equivalent to an operating system API.[61] Although a particular ISA does not specify the hardware implementation, the elements of an ISA directly affect how the hardware is constructed and therefore significantly impact performance. Approaches to ISAs have evolved over the years. This section investigates these approaches and evaluates how ISA design decisions affect performance.

1. What trade-offs must be weighed when including single instructions that perform complex routines in an instruction set?
2. Why is the choice of an ISA important?

Ans: **1)** The penalty for adding these instructions is more complex hardware, which might slow the execution of other more frequently used instructions; the benefit is faster execution of these complex routines. **2)** The ISA specifies a programming interface between hardware and low-level software; therefore, it affects how easily code can be generated for the processor and how much memory that code occupies. Also, the ISA directly affects processor hardware, which influences cost and performance.

14.8.1 Complex Instruction Set Computing (CISC)

Until the mid-1980s, the clear trend was to incorporate frequently used sections of code into single machine-language instructions, with the hope of making these functions faster to execute and easier to code in assembly language. The logic was appealing, judging by the number of ISAs that reflected these greatly expanded instruction sets—an approach that has been named **complex instruction set computing (CISC)**, partly echoing the popular term reduced instruction set computing (RISC), which we discuss in the next section.[62]

CISC processors originated when most systems programs were written in assembly language. An instruction set including single instructions that each performed several operations enabled assembly-language programmers to write their programs with fewer lines of code, thus improving programmer productivity. CISC continued to be attractive when high-level languages became widely used for writing operating systems (such as the use of C and C++ in UNIX source code), because special-purpose instructions were added to fit well with the needs of optimizing compilers. Optimizing compilers alter the structure of compiled code (but not the semantics) to achieve higher performance for a particular architecture. CISC instructions mirrored the complex operations of high-level languages rather than the simple operations a processor could execute in one or two clock cycles. These complex instruction sets tended to be implemented via microprogramming. Microprogramming introduces a layer of programming below a computer's machine language; this layer specifies the actual primitive operations that a processor must perform, such as fetching an instruction from memory (see Section 2.9 for a further description). In these CISC architectures, the machine-language instructions were interpreted, so that complex instructions were performed as a series of simpler microprogrammed instructions.[63]

CISC processors became popular largely in response to the decreasing cost of hardware coupled with the increasing cost of developing software with assembly language. CISC processors attempt to move most of the complexity from the software to the hardware. As a side effect, CISC processors also reduce the size of programs, saving memory and easing debugging. Another characteristic of some CISC processors is a trend toward reducing the number of general-purpose registers, to decrease cost and increase space available to other CISC structures, such as the instruction decoder.[64, 65]

One powerful technique to increase performance that developed during the CISC era was pipelining. A pipeline divides a processor's datapath (i.e., the portion of the processor that performs operations on data) into discrete stages. For every clock cycle, a maximum of one instruction can occupy each stage, allowing a processor to perform operations on several instructions simultaneously. In the early 1960s, IBM developed the first pipelined processor, the IBM 7030 (nicknamed "Stretch"). The 7030's pipeline consisted of four stages: instruction fetch, instruction decode, operand fetch and execution. While the processor was executing one instruction, it fetched the operands for the next instruction, decoded another instruction and fetched a fourth instruction. After each clock cycle began, each instruction in the pipeline would move forward one stage; this permitted the 7030 to process up to four instructions at once, which improved performance significantly.[66, 67, 68]

As processor manufacturing technology has improved, chip size and memory bandwidth have become less of a concern. Moreover, advanced compilers can easily perform many optimization techniques previously delegated to the implementation of the CISC instruction set.[69] However, CISC processors still are popular in many personal computers; they also can be found in several high-performance computers. Intel Pentium (`www.intel.com/products/desktop/processors/pentium4/`) and Advanced Micro Devices (AMD) Athlon (`www.amd.com/us-en/Processors/ProductInformation/0,,30_118_756,00.html`) processors are CISC processors.

Self Review

1. (T/F) The widespread use of high-level programming languages eliminated the usefulness of complex instructions.
2. What was the motivation behind the CISC processor-design philosophy?

Ans: **1)** False. Additional complex instructions were created to fit well with the needs of optimizing compilers. **2)** Early operating systems were written primarily in assembly code, so complex instructions simplified programming, because each instruction performed several operations.

14.8.2 Reduced Instruction Set Computing (RISC)

Many of the advantages of CISC processors were rendered unimportant by advances in hardware technology and compiler design. In addition, designers realized that the microcode required to interpret complex instructions slowed the execution of the simpler instructions. Various studies indicated that a large majority of programs generated by popular compilers used only a small portion of their target processors' instruction sets. For example, an IBM study observed that the 10 most frequently executed instructions of the hundreds in the System/370 architecture (Fig. 14.2) accounted for two-thirds of the instruction executions on that machine.[70] The additional instructions incorporated into CISC instruction sets to improve software development time were being used only infrequently. The simplest instructions to implement, such as register-memory transfers (loads and stores), were the most commonly used.

Another IBM study, a static analysis of assembly-language programs written for the IBM Series/1 computer, provided more evidence that large CISC instruction sets might be inefficient. The study observed that programmers tended to generate "semantically equivalent instruction sequences" when working with the rich machine language of the IBM Series/1. The authors concluded that since it is difficult to detect such sequences automatically, either instruction sets should be made sparser, or programmers should restrict their use of instructions.[71] These observations provided compelling motivation for the notion of **reduced instruction set computing (RISC)**. This processor-design philosophy emphasizes that computer architects can optimize performance by concentrating their efforts on making common instructions, such as branches, loads and stores, execute efficiently.[72, 73]

RISC processors execute common instructions efficiently by including relatively few instructions, most of which are simple and can be performed quickly (i.e., in one clock cycle). This means that much of the programming complexity is moved from the hardware to the compiler, which permits RISC processor design to be simple and to optimize for a small set of instructions. Furthermore, RISC control units are implemented in hardware, which reduces execution overhead compared to microcode. RISC instructions, which occupy fixed-length words in memory, are faster and easier to decode than variable-length CISC instructions. Additionally, RISC processors attempt to reduce the number of accesses to main memory by providing many high-speed general-purpose registers in which programs can perform data manipulation.[74]

Providing only simple, uniform-length instructions permits RISC processors to make better use of pipelines than CISC processors do. Pipelined execution in CISC architectures can be slowed by the longer processing times of complex

Opcode	Instruction	% of Executions
BC	Branch Condition	20.2
L	Load	15.5
TM	Test Under Mask	6.1
ST	Store	5.9
LR	Load Register	4.7
LA	Load Address	4.0
LTR	Test Register	3.8
BCR	Branch Register	2.9
MVC	Move Characters	2.1
LH	Load Half Word	1.8

Figure 14.2 | *The 10 most frequently executed instructions on IBM's System/370 architecture.*[75] *(Courtesy of International Business Machines Corporation.)*

instructions; these have the effect of idling sections of the pipeline handling simpler instructions. Additionally, pipelines on CISC machines often contain many stages and require complex hardware to support instructions of various lengths. Pipelines in RISC architectures contain few stages and are relatively straightforward to implement because most instructions require one cycle.[76]

A simple and clever optimizing technique used in many RISC architectures is called **delayed branching**.[77, 78] When a conditional branch is executed, the next sequential instruction might or might not be executed next, depending on the evaluation of the condition. Delayed branching enables this next sequential instruction to enter execution anyway; then, if the branch is not taken, this next instruction can be well along, if not completely finished. RISC optimizing compilers often rearrange machine instructions so that a useful calculation (one that must be executed regardless of whether the branch is taken) is placed immediately after the branch. Because branching occurs more frequently than most people realize (as often as every fifth instruction on some popular architectures), this can yield considerable performance gains.[79] Lilja provides a thorough analysis of delayed branching and several other techniques that can greatly reduce the so-called **branch penalty** in pipelined architectures.[80]

The most significant trade-off in the RISC design philosophy is that its simple, reduced instruction set and register-rich architecture increase context-switching complexity.[81] RISC architectures must save a large number of registers to main memory during a context switch; this reduces context-switching performance compared to CISC architectures due to an increased number of accesses to main memory. Because context switching is pure overhead and occurs frequently, this can significantly impact system performance.

In addition to increased context-switch time, there are other drawbacks to the RISC design. One interesting study tested the effect of instruction complexity on performance; the study selected three increasingly complex instruction subsets of the VAX. The researchers reached several conclusions:[82]

1. Programs written in the simplest of the instruction subsets required as much as 2.5 times the memory of equivalent complex instruction set programs.

2. The cache miss ratio was considerably larger for programs written in the simplest subset.

3. The bus traffic for programs written in the simplest subset was about double that of programs written in the most complex subset.

These results and others like them indicate that RISC architectures can have negative consequences.

Floating point operations execute faster in CISC architectures. Additionally, CISC processors perform better for graphics or scientific programs, which repeatedly execute complex instructions; these programs tend to perform better on CISC machines with optimized complex instructions than on comparable RISC machines.[83]

Figure 14.3 provides a summary comparison between the RISC and CISC design philosophies. Examples of RISC processors include the UltraSPARC

Category	Characteristics of CISC Processors	Characteristics of RISC Processors
Instruction length	Variable, typically 1 to 10 bytes.	Fixed, typically 4 bytes.
Instruction decode	Via microcode.	In hardware.
Number of instructions in ISA	Many (typically several hundred), including many complex instructions.	Few (typically less than one hundred).
Number of instructions per program	Few.	Many (often about 20 percent more than for CISC).
Number of general-purpose registers	Often, few (e.g., eight in the Intel Pentium 4 processor).[84]	Many (typically, 32).
Complexity	In hardware.	In the compiler.
Ability to exploit parallelism through pipelining	Limited.	Broad.
Underlying philosophy	Implement as many operations as possible.	Make the common case fast.
Examples	Pentium, Athlon.	MIPS, SPARC, G5.

Figure 14.3 | *RISC and CISC comparison.*

(www.sun.com/processors), MIPS (www.mips.com) and G5 (www.apple.com/powermac/specs.html) processors.

Self Review

1. Why do RISC processors exploit pipelines better than CISC processors?
2. Why does context switching require more overhead on RISC than on CISC processors?

Ans: **1)** RISC instructions are of fixed length and generally require one cycle to execute, so it is easy to overlap instructions such that most stages in the pipeline are performing meaningful work. The variable-length instructions of CISC processors have the effect of idling sections of the pipeline not needed for simple instructions. **2)** RISC processors contain many more registers than CISC processors, requiring a greater number of memory transfers during a context switch.

14.8.3 Post-RISC Processors

As RISC and CISC processors have evolved, many techniques that were developed to independently increase the performance of one or the other have been integrated into both architectures.[85, 86, 87] Many of these features add complexity to the instruction set or place more responsibility on the hardware to optimize performance. This convergence of architectures has blurred the line between RISC and CISC. The philosophy behind these processors is to increase performance in any way possible, leading Severance et al. to coin the term **fast instruction set computing (FISC)**. Other commonly used names for this modern processor design philosophy are "post-RISC" and "second-generation RISC."[88]

However, some designers adhere to the traditional terminology, "RISC" and "CISC." This school of thought—that the two types of processors have not converged—argues that RISC and CISC refer specifically to the ISA and not to how the ISA is implemented (i.e., additional hardware complexity is irrelevant). Further, they argue that the primary difference is that RISC instructions are of a uniform length and generally execute in one cycle, unlike CISC instructions. As we see in this section, most of the convergence results from the growing similarity of complex hardware in RISC and CISC machines and the expansion of the number of instructions in RISC ISAs, two aspects which these designers argue are not central to ISA design philosophies.[89]

The sections that follow describe many techniques that post-RISC processors employ to improve processor performance. As we will see, these techniques cause processor hardware to be more complex, which increases cost and strays from the RISC tenet of keeping hardware simple.

Superscalar Architecture

Superscalar execution enables more than one instruction to be executed in parallel during each clock cycle. **Superscalar architectures** include multiple execution units on a single chip and, until recently, were primarily used in CISC processors to reduce the time required to decode complex instructions. Today, superscalar execution is found in almost all general-purpose processors, because the parallelism that it allows increases performance. For example, both the Pentium 4 and G5 processors are superscalar. These architectures contain complicated hardware that ensures no two instructions executing simultaneously depend on each other. For example, when a processor executes the machine-code equivalent of an `if…then…else` control structure, the instructions inside the `then` and `else` clauses cannot be executed until the processor has determined the value of the branch condition.[90, 91, 92]

Out-of-Order Execution (OOO)

Out-of-order execution (OOO) is a technique that dynamically reorders instructions at runtime to optimize performance by isolating groups of instructions that can execute simultaneously. OOO facilitates deep pipelines and superscalar design, which require the processor or compiler to detect groups of independent instructions that can be executed in parallel.[93, 94]

Such a mechanism, now common to both RISC and CISC processors, breaks with the RISC philosophy of leaving optimization to the compiler. OOO requires significant additional hardware to detect dependencies and handle exceptions. When an instruction raises an exception, the processor must ensure that the program is in the state in which it would have been after the exception if the instructions had been executed in order.[95, 96]

Branch Prediction

Branch prediction is a mechanism whereby a processor uses heuristics to determine the most probable result of a branch condition. The processor places instructions that are predicted to execute into the pipeline for immediate processing after the branch. If the processor guesses incorrectly, it must remove the predicted code from the pipeline, losing all work performed on that code. This case is slightly worse than the alternative, which is to wait until the result of a branch to fill the pipeline. However, if the processor guesses correctly, performance increases, because the processor can continue to execute instructions immediately after the branch. To achieve high performance using branch prediction, the processor must contain accurate branch prediction units, which also contribute to hardware complexity.[97, 98]

On-Chip Floating-Point and Vector Processing Support

Many modern processors contain on-chip execution units called coprocessors. Designers optimize coprocessors to perform specific operations that the general-purpose arithmetic and logic units (ALUs) execute slowly. These include floating point coprocessors and vector coprocessors. Vector coprocessors execute vector instructions, which operate on a set of data, applying the same instruction to each item in the set (e.g., adding one to each element in an array). Placing these coprocessors on the processor's chip decreases the communication latency between the processor and its coprocessors, dramatically increasing the speed with which these operations are performed, but also increases hardware complexity.[99]

Additional Infrequently-Used Instructions

Perhaps the most significant divergence from the RISC philosophy is the expansion of the instruction sets in today's so-called RISC processors. These ISAs tend to include any instruction that enhances overall performance, regardless of the hardware complexity required to execute that instruction.[100] For example, the Apple PowerMac G5 processor, referred to by many as a RISC processor, contains over a hundred more instructions than its ancestor, the G3. These instructions typically manipulate large (i.e., 128-bit) integers or perform the same instruction on multiple data units, a technique called vector processing.[101]

CISC convergence to RISC

As RISC hardware has become more complex, CISC processors have adopted components of the RISC philosophy. For example, today's CISC processors often contain an optimized core subset of commonly used instructions that are decoded and executed quickly to enable performance comparable to that of RISC when complex instructions are not employed. In fact, the Intel Pentium 4 decodes all instructions into simple, fixed-size **micro-ops** before sending them to the execution unit. Often, the only reason that some complex instructions remain in a CISC ISA is to provide backward compatibility with code written for older versions of a CISC processor.[102] In this way, CISC processors incorporate the benefits of simpler instructions advocated by the RISC philosophy.

Self Review

1. Despite increased additional hardware complexity, what is the primary characteristic that distinguishes today's RISC processors from CISC processors?
2. (T/F) RISC processors are becoming more complex while CISC processors are becoming simpler.

Ans: **1)** Most of today's RISC processors continue to provide instructions of uniform length that require a single clock cycle to execute. **2)** False. RISC processors are indeed becoming more complex. Although CISC processors incorporate RISC design philosophies, their hardware complexity continues to increase.

14.8.4 Explicitly Parallel Instruction Computing (EPIC)

Techniques such as superscalar design, deep pipelines and OOO enable post-RISC processors to exploit parallelism. The hardware required to implement these features while accounting for dependencies across multiple execution units can become prohibitively expensive. In response, designers at Intel and Hewlett Packard proposed a new design philosophy called **Explicitly Parallel Instruction Computing (EPIC)**. EPIC attempts to simplify processor hardware to enable a high degree of parallelism. The EPIC philosophy requires that the compiler, not hardware, determines which instructions can be performed in parallel. This technique exploits **instruction-level parallelism (ILP)**, which refers to sets of machine instructions that can be executed in parallel (i.e., the instructions in the set do not rely on one another to execute).

To support ILP, EPIC employs a variation of the **very long instruction word (VLIW)** method.[103] In the VLIW method, the compiler determines which instructions should be executed in parallel. This simplifies hardware, allowing more room for execution units; the Multiflow computer, the first VLIW machine, had 28 execution, which is substantially more than modern superscalar processors.[104] However, some dependencies are known only at execution time (e.g., because of branch instructions), but VLIWs form the execution path before the program executes. This limits the level of parallelism VLIW designs can exploit.[105]

EPIC borrows from both VLIW processor designs and superscalar processor designs. EPIC processors assist the compiler by providing predictability—no out-of-order execution is used, allowing EPIC compilers to optimize the most likely execution path or paths. However, it is often difficult for a compiler to optimize every path of execution in a program. If the path of execution is incorrectly predicted, the processor ensures program correctness (e.g., by checking data dependencies).[106]

Typical RISC and CISC processors employ branch prediction to probabilistically determine the result of a branch. Instead, EPIC processors execute all possible instructions that could follow a branch in parallel and use only the result of the correct branch once the **predicate** (i.e., the branch comparison) is resolved.[107] This technique is called **branch predication**.

Figure 14.4 illustrates the difference between program execution in an EPIC processor versus a post-RISC processor. In Fig. 14.4(a), the EPIC compiler has pro-

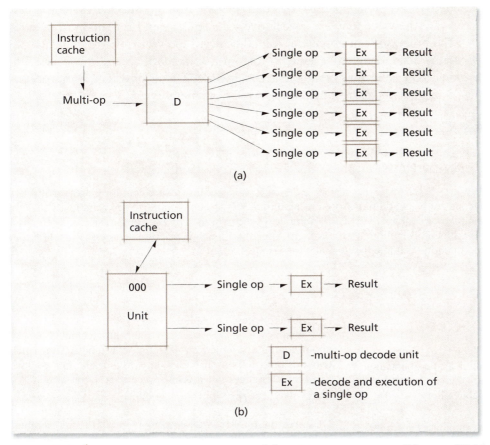

Figure 14.4 | Instruction execution in an (a) EPIC processor and (b) post-RISC processor.

duced a **multi-op instruction**, which is a package of a number of instructions that can be executed in parallel; the number depends on the processor. The processor decodes this multi-op into a number of single operations, then executes each simultaneously on several execution units. Because EPIC processors assist the compiler by providing predictability guarantees, they do not reorder multi-op instructions, and no OOO unit is needed. In Fig. 14.4(b), the post-RISC processor analyzes the instruction stream that it is executing and reorders instructions to find two instructions that can execute simultaneously. The processor places these two instructions into its two execution units (using a superscalar architecture) for simultaneous execution.

Aside from improving performance through parallelism, EPIC processors employ **speculative loading**, a technique that attempts to reduce memory latency. When optimizing program code, the compiler converts each load instruction to a speculative load operation and a verifying load operation. A speculative load retrieves from memory data specified by an instruction that has yet to be executed. Therefore, the processor can execute a speculative load well before the actual data is needed. The verifying load ensures that the data from the speculative load is consistent (i.e., the value that was speculatively loaded has not been modified in memory). The processor can execute at full efficiency if the verifying load validates the speculative load, eliminating much of the cost of memory access. However, if the verifying load determines that the speculative load is inconsistent, the processor must wait while the correct data is retrieved from memory.[108]

Self Review

1. What is a motivation behind the EPIC design philosophy?
2. How do EPIC ISAs reduce the performance cost of branching?

Ans: **1)** Superscalar designs do not scale well, because exponentially more hardware is needed for each additional processing unit. EPIC attempts to move the complexity into the compiler to exploit ILP. **2)** EPIC compilers specify branch predication to execute both possible paths of execution after a branch. After the branch is performed, one path is discarded and the other is immediately ready to execute.

Web Resources

www.opersys.com/LTT/
Provides a trace toolkit for Linux.

www.eecs.harvard.edu/~vino/perf/hbench/
Provides information on hbench, which is a microbenchmark suite. The site includes a link to download a copy of the suite, documentation and related technical publications.

www.specbench.org
SPEC is an organization that develops standard benchmarks. Its Web site describes a number of benchmarks (called SPECmarks) used to evaluate a variety of systems and publishes the results of tests with these benchmarks on real systems.

www.veritest.com/benchmarks/default.asp?visitor=
VeriTest provides computer system evaluation services. This page from its Web site provides excellent information on several commercially available benchmarks and synthetic programs.

arstechnica.com/cpu/4q99/risc-cisc/rvc-1.html
Ars Technica is a Web site that publishes technical articles about computers, aimed at educating consumers. This article contains information on RISC and CISC design philosophies and characteristics of post-RISC processors.

www.intel.com/products/server/processors/server/itanium/
Describes the Intel Itanium processor, one of the first commercially available EPIC processors.

www.bapco.com
BAPCo is an organization that develops standard benchmarks, such as the popular SYSMark for processors. Its Web site describes its benchmarks in detail.

www.linuxjournal.com/article.php?sid=2396
Describes performance monitoring in Linux.

Summary

The performance of a system depends heavily on its hardware, operating system and the interaction between the two. Cumbersome software causes poor performance, even on systems with powerful hardware, so it is important to consider a system's software performance as well as its hardware performance.

Three common purposes for performance evaluation are selection evaluation, performance projection and performance monitoring. Some common performance measures are turnaround time, response time, system reaction time, variance in response time, throughput and capacity.

Some performance results may be deceptive if the evaluation does not use a representative workload or focuses on a small part of the system.

A trace is a record of system activity—typically a log of user and application requests to the operating system. A profile records the activity of a system when executing in kernel mode. These techniques are useful in evaluating systems whose workload depends heavily on the system's execution environment.

Timings are useful for performing quick comparisons in hardware. Timings measure how many instructions a system can execute per second. Similarly, microbenchmarks permit evaluators to make quick comparisons between operating systems (or systems as a whole). A microbenchmark measures how long an operating system operation (e.g., process creation) takes.

An application-specific evaluation enables organizations and consumers to determine whether a particular system is appropriate for a particular installation. The vector-based methodology uses a weighted average of various microbenchmark results suited to a particular application. The hybrid methodology uses a trace to determine the relative weights for each primitive in the average. A kernel program is a typical program that might be run at an installation; it is executed "on paper" using manufacturers' instruction timing estimates.

Analytic models are mathematical representations of computer systems or their components. A large body of mathematical results exists that evaluators can apply in order estimate the performance of a given computer system or component quickly and fairly accurately.

A benchmark is a real program that an evaluator executes on the machine being evaluated. Several organizations have developed industry-standard benchmarks targeted to different kinds of systems. Evaluators use the results from running these benchmarks to compare systems. Benchmarks should be repeatable, accurately reflect the types of applications that will be executed and be widely used.

Synthetic programs are artificial programs that evaluate a specific component of an operating system; they might be constructed to match the instruction frequency distribution of a large set of programs. Synthetic programs are useful in development environments; as new features become available, synthetic programs can be used to test that these features are operational.

Simulation is a technique in which an evaluator develops a computerized model of the target system. The simulation is run to determine how a system might perform when it has been built.

Performance monitoring is the collection and analysis of system performance information for existing systems. A resource becomes a bottleneck when it hinders the progress of the system because it cannot do its job efficiently. A resource becomes saturated when it has no excess capacity to fulfill new requests. In a feedback loop, information is reported to the system about how saturated (or underutilized) a resource is. With negative feedback, the arrival rate of requests at that resource might decrease; with positive feedback, the arrival rate might increase.

A processor's instruction set architecture (ISA) is an interface that describes the processor, including its instruction set, number of registers and memory size. The ISA is like an API that low-level software uses to construct executable programs.

CISC ISAs tend to include a large number of instructions, many of which require multiple cycles to execute; instruction length is variable. Many CISC implementations have few general-purpose registers and complex hardware. CISC processors became popular because they reduced memory cost and facilitated assembly-language programming.

RISC ISAs tend to include a small number of instructions, most of which execute in one cycle; instruction length is fixed. Many RISC implementations have a large number of general-purpose registers and simple hardware. They optimize the most-common instructions. RISC processors became popular because they use pipelines efficiently and eliminate cumbersome hardware, both of which improve performance.

Today, RISC and CISC designs are converging, prompting many to call these modern processors post-RISC, FISC or second-generation RISC. Still, some maintain that this is not the case and that the terms RISC and CISC are still important. This convergence stems from increased hardware complexity and extra infrequently used instructions in RISC processors and from the fact that CISC processors often include an optimized core of RISC-like instructions.

EPIC, a newer processor-design philosophy, attempts to address the limited scalability of superscalar designs. EPIC processors place the responsibility on the compiler to determine the path of execution and use their many execution units to support a high degree of parallelism. EPIC processors also reduce the penalty for main memory accesses by performing speculative loads before execution of a load instruction; the processor performs a verifying load when the instruction is executed, ensuring data integrity. If the data that was speculatively loaded has not changed, then no action is taken as a result of the verifying load; otherwise, the processor reexecutes the instruction using data from the verifying load.

Key Terms

absolute performance measure—Measure of the efficiency with which a computer system meets its goals, described by an absolute quantity such as the amount of time in which a system executes a certain benchmark. This contrasts with relative performance measures such as ease of use, which only can be used to make comparisons between systems.

analytic model—Mathematical representation of a computer system or component of a computer system for the purpose of estimating its performances quickly and relatively accurately.

application vector—Vector that contains the relative demand on operating system primitives by a particular application, used in an application-specific performance evaluation.

arrival rate—Rate at which new requests are made for a resource.

benchmark—Real program that an evaluator executes on the system being evaluated to determine how efficiently the system executes that program; benchmarks are used to compare systems.

BIPS (billion instructions per second)—Unit commonly used to categorize the performance of a particular computer; a rating of one BIPS means a processor can execute one billion instructions per second.

bottleneck—Resource that hinders the progress of the system because it cannot do its job efficiently.

branch penalty—Performance loss in pipelined architectures associated with a branch instruction; this occurs when a processor cannot begin processing the instruction after the branch until the processor knows the outcome of the branch. The branch penalty can be reduced by using delayed branching, branch prediction or branch predication.

branch predication—Technique used in EPIC processors whereby a processor executes all possible instructions that could follow a branch in parallel and uses only the result of the correct branch once the predicate (i.e., the branch comparison) is resolved.

branch prediction—Technique whereby a processor uses heuristics to determine the most probable result of a branch in code; when the processor predicts correctly, performance increases, because the processor can continue to execute instructions immediately after the branch.

Business Application Performance Corporation (BAPCo)—Organization that develops standard benchmarks, such as the popular SYSMark for processors.

capacity—Measure of the maximum throughput a system can attain, assuming that whenever the system is ready to accept more jobs, another job is immediately available.

complex instruction set computing (CISC)—Processor-design philosophy, emphasizing expanded instruction sets that incorporate single instructions that perform several operations.

delayed branching—Optimization technique for pipelined processors in which a compiler places directly after a branch an instruction that must be executed whether or not the branch is taken; the processor begins executing this instruction while determining the outcome of the branch.

Dhrystone—Classic synthetic program that measures how effectively an architecture runs systems programs.

dispersion—Measure of the variance of a random variable.

distribution of response times—Set of values describing the response times for jobs in a system and the relative frequencies with which those values occur.

ease of use—Measure of the comfort and convenience associated with system use.

event-driven simulator—Simulator controlled by events that are made to occur according to probability distributions.

expected value—Sum of a series of values each multiplied by its respective probability of occurrence.

Explicitly Parallel Instruction Computing (EPIC)—Processor-design philosophy whose goals are to provide a high degree of instruction-level parallelism, reduce processor hardware complexity and improve performance.

family of computers—Series of computers that are compatible in that they can run the same programs.

fast instruction set computing (FISC)—Term describing the processor-design philosophy resulting from the convergence of RISC and CISC design philosophies. The FISC design philosophy stresses inclusion of any construct that improves performance.

feedback loop—Technique in which information about the current state of the system can influence the number of requests arriving at a resource (e.g., positive and negative feedback loops).

Hartstone—Popular synthetic benchmark used to evaluate real-time systems.

hbench microbenchmark suite—Popular microbenchmark suite, which enables evaluators to effectively analyze the relationship between operating system primitives and hardware components.

hybrid methodology—Performance evaluation technique that combines the vector-based methodology with trace data to measure performance for applications whose behavior depends strongly on user input.

lmbench microbenchmark—Microbenchmark suite that enables evaluators to measure and compare system performance on a variety of UNIX platforms.

instruction-level parallelism (ILP)—Parallelism that permits two machine instructions to be executed at once. Two instructions exhibit ILP if the execution of one does not affect the outcome of the other (i.e., the two instructions do not depend on each other).

instruction set—Set of machine instructions a processor can perform.

instruction set architecture (ISA)—Interface exposed by a processor that describes the processor, including its instruction set, number of registers and memory size.

IOStone—Popular synthetic benchmark that evaluates file systems.

kernel program—Typical program that might be run at an installation; it is executed "on paper" using manufacturers' instruction timings and used for application-specific performance evaluation.

mean—Average of a set of values.

micro-op—Simple, RISC-like instruction that is the only type of instruction processed by a Pentium processor; the Pentium's instruction decoder converts complex instructions into a series of micro-ops.

microbenchmark—Performance evaluation tool that measures the speed of a single operating system operation (e.g., process creation).

microbenchmark suite—Program that consists of a number of microbenchmarks, typically used to evaluate many important operating system operations.

MIPS (million instructions per second)—Unit commonly used to categorize the performance of a particular computer; a rating of one MIPS means a processor can execute one million instructions per second.

MobileMark—Popular benchmark for evaluating systems installed on mobile devices developed by Business Application Performance Corporation (BAPCo).

multi-op instruction—Instruction word used by an EPIC system in which the compiler packages a number of smaller instructions for the processor to execute in parallel.

negative feedback—Data informing the system that a resource is having difficulty servicing all requests and the processor should decrease the arrival rate for requests at that resource.

out-of-order execution (OOO)—Technique in which a processor analyzes a stream of instructions and dynamically reorders instructions to isolate groups of independent instructions for parallel execution.

performance monitoring—Collection and analysis of system performance information for existing systems; the information includes a system's throughput, response times, predictability, bottlenecks, etc.

performance projection—Estimate of the performance of a system that does not exist, useful for deciding whether to build that system or to modify an existing system's design.

positive feedback—Data informing the system that a resource has excess capacity, so the processor can increase the arrival rate for requests at that resource.

predicate—Logical decision made on a subject (e.g., a branch comparison).

predictability—Measure of the variance of an entity, such as response time. Predictability is particularly important for interactive systems, where users expect predictable (and short) response times.

production program—Program that is run regularly at an installation.

profile—Record of kernel activity taken during a real session, which indicates the operating system functions that are used most often and should therefore be optimized.

random variable—Variable that can assume a certain range of values, where each value has an associated probability.

reduced instruction set computing (RISC)—Processor-design philosophy that emphasizes small, simple instructions sets and optimization of the most-frequently used instructions.

response time—In an interactive system, the time from when a user presses an *Enter* key or clicks a mouse until the system delivers a final response.

saturation—Condition of a resource that has no excess capacity to fulfill new requests.

script-driven simulator—Simulator controlled by data carefully designed to reflect the anticipated environment of the simulated system; evaluators derive this data from empirical observations.

selection evaluation—Analysis regarding whether obtaining a computer system or application from a particular vendor is appropriate.

service rate—Rate at which requests are completed by a resource.

simulation—Performance evaluation technique in which an evaluator develops a computerized model of a system being evaluated. The model is then run to reflect the behavior of the system being evaluated.

SPECmark—Standard benchmark for testing systems; SPEC-marks are published by the Standard Performance Evaluation Corporation (SPEC).

speculative loading—Technique whereby a processor retrieves from memory data specified by an instruction that has yet to be executed; when the instruction is executed, the processor performs a verifying load to ensure the data's consistency.

stability—Condition of a system that functions without error or significant performance degradation.

Standard Application (SAP) benchmarks—Popular benchmarks used to evaluate a system's scalability.

Standard Performance Evaluation Corporation (SPEC)—Organization that develops standard, relevant benchmarks (called SPECmarks), which are used to evaluate a variety of systems; SPEC publishes the results of tests with these benchmarks on real systems.

STREAM—Popular synthetic benchmark which tests the memory subsystem.

superscalar architecture—Technique in which a processor contains multiple execution units so that it can execute more than one instruction in parallel per clock cycle.

synthetic benchmark—Another name for a synthetic program.

synthetic program—Artificial program used to evaluate a specific component of a system or constructed to mirror the characteristics of a large set of programs.

SYSmark benchmark—Popular benchmark for desktop systems developed by Business Application Performance Corporation (BAPCo).

system reaction time—Time from when a job is submitted to a system until the first time slice of service is given to that job.

system tuning—Process of making fine adjustments to a system based on performance monitoring to optimize the system's execution for a specific operating environment.

system vector—Vector containing the results of microbenchmarks for a number of operating system primitives for a specific system, used in an application-specific evaluation.

throughput—Work-per-unit-time performance measurement.

timing—Raw measure of an isolated hardware performance metric, such as a BIPS rating, used for quick comparisons between systems.

TIPS (trillion instructions per second)—Unit used to categorize the performance of a particular computer; a rating of one TIPS means a processor can execute one trillion instructions per second.

trace (performance evaluation)—Record of real system activity, which is executed on systems to test how the system handles a sample workload.

Transaction Processing Performance Council (TPC) benchmarks—Popular benchmarks which target database systems.

turnaround time—Time from when a job is submitted until the system completes executing it.

utilization—Fraction of time that a resource is in use.

validate a model—To demonstrate that a computer model is an accurate representation of the real system the model is simulating.

variance in response times—Measure of how much individual response times deviate from the mean response time.

vector-based methodology—Method of calculating an application-specific evaluation of a system based on the weighted average of the microbenchmark results for the target system's primitives; the weights are determined by the the target application's relative demand for each primitive.

very long instruction word (VLIW)—Technique in which a compiler chooses which instructions a processor should execute in parallel and packages them into a single (very long) instruction word; the compiler guarantees that there are no dependencies between instructions that the processor executes at the same time.

WinBench 99—Popular synthetic program used extensively today in testing a system's graphics, disk and video subsystems in a Microsoft Windows environment.

WebMark—Popular benchmark for Internet performance developed by Business Application Performance Corporation (BAPCo).

Whetstone—Classic synthetic program which measures how well systems handle floating point calculations, and has thus been helpful in evaluating scientific programs.

workload—Measure of the amount of work that has been submitted to a system; evaluators determine typical workloads for a system and evaluate the system using these workloads.

Exercises

14.1 Explain why it is important to monitor and evaluate the performance of a system's software as well as its hardware.

14.2 When a user logged in, some early timesharing systems printed the total number of logged-in users.

a. Why was this information useful to the user?

b. In what circumstances might this not have been a useful indication of load?

c. What factors tended to make this a highly reliable indication of system load on a timesharing system that supported many users?

14.3 Briefly discuss each of the following purposes for performance evaluation.

a. selection evaluation

b. performance projection

c. performance monitoring

14.4 What is system tuning? Why is it important?

14.5 Distinguish between user-oriented and system-oriented performance measures.

14.6 What is system reaction time?
Is it more critical to processor-bound or I/O-bound jobs? Explain your answer.

14.7 In discussing random variables, why can mean values sometimes be deceiving?
What other performance measure is useful in describing how closely the values of a random variable cluster about its mean?

14.8 Why is predictability such an important attribute of computer systems?
In what types of systems is predictability especially critical?

14.9 Some commonly used performance measures follow.

i. turnaround time

ii. throughput

iii. response time

iv. workload

v. system reaction time

vi. capacity

vii. variance of response times

viii. utilization

For each of the following, indicate which performance measure(s) is (are) described.

a. the predictability of a system

b. the current demands on a system

c. a system's maximum capabilities

d. the percentage of a resource in use

e. the work processed per unit time

f. turnaround time in interactive systems

14.10 What performance measure(s) is (are) of greatest interest to each of the following? Explain your answers.

a. an interactive user

b. a batch-processing user

c. a designer of a real-time process control system

d. installation managers concerned with billing users for resource usage

e. installation managers concerned with projecting system loads for the next yearly budget cycle

f. installation managers concerned with predicting the performance improvements to be gained by adding

i. memory

ii. faster processors

iii. disk drives

14.11 There is a limit to how many measurements should be taken on any system. What considerations might cause you to avoid taking certain measurements?

14.12 Simulation is viewed by many as the most widely applicable performance evaluation technique.

a. Give several reasons for this.

b. Even though simulation is widely applicable, it is not as widely used as one might expect. Give several reasons why.

14.13 Some of the popular performance evaluation and monitoring techniques are

i. timings

ii. microbenchmarks

iii. synthetic programs

iv. vector-based methodology

v. simulations

vi. kernel programs

vii. hardware monitors

viii. analytic models

ix. software monitors

x. benchmarks

Indicate which of these techniques is best defined by each of the following. (Some items can have more than one answer.)

a. their validity might be jeopardized by making simplfying assumptions

b. weighted average of instruction timings

c. produced by skilled mathematicians

d. models that are run on a computer

    e. useful for quick comparisons of "raw horsepower" for hardware

    f. particularly valuable in complex software environments

    g. a real program executed on a real machine

    h. useful for determining the performance of operating system primitives

    i. custom-designed programs to exercise specific features of a machine

    j. a real program "executed on paper"

    k. a production program

    l. most commonly developed by using the techniques of queuing theory and Markov processes

    m. often used when it is too costly or time consuming to develop a synthetic program

14.14 What performance evaluation techniques are most applicable in each of the following situations? Explain your answers.

    a. An insurance company has a stable workload consisting of a large number of lengthy batch-processing production runs. Because of a merger, the company must increase its capacity by 50 percent. The company wishes to replace its equipment with a new computer system.

    b. The insurance company described in (a) wishes to increase capacity by purchasing some additional memory and channels.

    c. A computer company is designing a new, ultrahigh-speed computer system and wishes to evaluate several alternative designs.

    d. A consulting firm that specializes in commercial data processing gets a large military contract requiring extensive mathematical calculations. The company wishes to determine if its existing computer equipment will process the anticipated load of mathematical calculations.

    e. Management in charge of a multicomputer network needs to locate bottlenecks as soon as they develop and to reroute traffic accordingly.

    f. A systems programmer suspects that one of the software modules is being called upon more frequently than originally anticipated. The programmer wants to confirm this before devoting substantial effort to recoding the module to make it execute more efficiently.

    g. An operating systems vendor needs to test all aspects of the system before selling its product commercially.

14.15 On one computer system, the processor contains a BIPS meter that records how many billion instructions per second the processor is performing at any instant in time. The meter is calibrated from 0 to 4 BIPS in increments of 0.1 BIPS. All of the workstations to this computer are currently in use. Explain how each of the following situations might occur.

    a. The meter reads 3.8 BIPS and the terminal users are experiencing good response times.

    b. The meter reads 0.5 BIPS and the terminal users are experiencing good response times.

    c. The meter reads 3.8 BIPS and the terminal users are experiencing poor response times.

    d. The meter reads 0.5 BIPS and the terminal users are experiencing poor response times.

14.16 You are a member of a performance evaluation team working for a computer manufacturer. You have been given the task of developing a generalized synthetic program to facilitate the evaluation of a completely new computer system with an innovative instruction set.

    a. Why might such a program be useful?

    b. What features might you provide to make your program a truly general evaluation tool?

14.17 Distinguish between event-driven and script-driven simulators.

14.18 What does it mean to validate a simulation model?

    How might you validate a simulation model of a small timesharing system (which already exists) with disk storage, several CRT terminals, and a shared laser printer?

14.19 What information might a performance evaluator get from an instruction execution trace?

    a module execution trace?

    Which of these is more useful for analyzing the operation of individual programs?

    for analyzing the operation of systems?

14.20 How can bottlenecks be detected?

    How can they be removed?

    If a bottleneck is removed, should we expect a system's performance to improve? Explain.

14.21 What is a feedback loop?

    Distinguish between negative and positive feedback.

    Which of these contributes to system stability?

    Which could cause instability? Why?

14.22 Workload characterization is an important part of any performance study. We must know what a computer is supposed to be doing before we can say much about how well it is doing it. What measurements might you take to help characterize the workload in each of the following systems?

a. a timesharing system designed to support program development

b. a batch-processing system used for preparing monthly bills for an electric utility with half a million customers

c. an advanced workstation used solely by one engineer

d. a microprocessor implanted in a person's chest to regulate heartbeat

e. a local area computer network that supports a heavily used electronic mail system within a large office complex

f. an air traffic control system for collision avoidance

g. a weather forecasting computer network that receives temperature, humidity, barometric pressure and other readings from 10,000 grid points throughout the country over communications lines.

h. a medical database management system that provides doctors around the world with answers to medical questions.

i. a traffic control computer network for monitoring and controlling the flow of traffic in a large city

14.23 A computer system manufacturer has a new multiprocessor under development. The system is modularly designed so that users may add new processors as needed, but the connections are expensive. The manufacturer must provide the connections with the original machine because they are too costly to install in the field. The manufacturer wants to determine the optimal number of processor connections to provide. The chief designer says that three is optimal. The designer believes that placing more than three processors on the system would not be worthwhile and that the contention for memory would be too great. What performance evaluation techniques would you recommend to help determine the optimal number of connections during the design stage of the project? Explain your answer.

14.24 Why are RISC programs generally longer than their CISC equivalents?

Given this, why might RISC programs execute faster than their CISC equivalents?

14.25 Compare branch prediction to branch predication. Which is likely to yield higher performance? Why?

14.26 For each of the following features of modern processors, describe how this feature improves performance and indicate why its inclusion in a processor strays from either a pure RISC or pure CISC design.

a. superscalar architecture

b. out-of-order execution (OOO)

c. branch prediction

d. on-chip vector and floating point support

e. large instruction sets

f. decoding complex, multicycle instructions into simpler, single-cycle instructions.

14.27 How do EPIC processors differ from post-RISC processors?

Given these differences, what could be a hindrance to the adoption of EPIC processors?

Suggested Projects

14.28 It is often difficult to measure performance in a system without influencing the results. Prepare a research paper on the various ways benchmarks minimize the effect they have on a system's performance.

14.29 In recent years, graphics-rendering technology has improved at a phenomenal rate. Prepare a research paper on the architectural features that boost graphics card performance. Also discuss graphics card performance evaluation techniques.

14.30 Prepare a research paper on the IBM PowerPC 970 processor, which powers Apple's PowerMac G5 series. What type of instruction set does it have? What other technology improves the performance of this processor?

14.31 Prepare a research paper on tools such as *gprof* to allow application developers to profile their software.

14.32 Prepare a research paper surveying contemporary studies that compare RISC performance to CISC performance. Describe the strengths and weaknesses of each design philosophy in today's systems.

14.33 In the text, it was indicated that one weakness of the RISC approach is a dramatic increase in context-switching overhead. Give a detailed explanation of why this is so. Write a paper on context switching. Discuss the various approaches that have been used. Suggest how context switching might be handled efficiently in RISC-based systems.

Suggested Simulations

14.34 Obtain versions of popular benchmarks or synthetic programs discussed in the text, such as SYSMark or a SPEC-mark. Run these on several computers and prepare a comparison of the results. Are your results similar to those published by the vendors? What factors might cause differences between the results? Describe your experience using these benchmarks and synthetic programs.

14.35 In this problem, you will undertake a reasonably detailed simulation study. You will write an event-driven simulation program using random-number generation to produce events probabilistically.

At one large batch-processing computer installation the management wants to decide what memory placement strategy will yield the best possible performance. The installation runs a computer with a large main memory that uses variable-partition multiprogramming. Each user program runs in a single group of contiguous storage locations. Users state their memory requirement in advance, and the operating system allocates each user the requested memory when the user's job is initiated. A total of 1024MB of main memory is available for user programs.

The storage requirements of jobs at this installation are distributed as follows.

10MB—30 percent of the jobs
20MB—20 percent of the jobs
30MB—25 percent of the jobs
40MB—15 percent of the jobs
50MB—10 percent of the jobs

Execution times of jobs at this installation are independent of the jobs' storage requirements and are distributed as follows.

1 minute—30 percent of the jobs
2 minutes—20 percent of the jobs
5 minutes—20 percent of the jobs

10 minutes—10 percent of the jobs
30 minutes—10 percent of the jobs
60 minutes—10 percent of the jobs

The load on the system is such that there is always at least one job waiting to be initiated. Jobs are processed strictly first-come-first-served.

Write a simulation program to help you decide which memory placement strategy should be used at this installation. Your program should use random-number generation to produce the memory requirement and execution time for each job according to the distributions above. Investigate the performance of the installation over an eight-hour period by measuring throughput, storage utilization, and other items of interest to you for each of the following memory placement strategies.

a. first fit

b. best fit

c. worst fit

14.36 At the installation described in the previous problem, management suspects that the first-come-first-served job scheduling might not be optimal. In particular, they are concerned that longer jobs tend to keep shorter jobs waiting. A study of waiting jobs indicates that there are always at least 10 jobs waiting to be initiated (i.e., when 10 jobs are waiting and one is initiated, another arrives immediately). Modify your simulation program from the previous exercise so that job scheduling is now performed on a shortest-job-first basis. How does this affect performance for each of the memory placement strategies? What problems of shortest-job-first scheduling become apparent?

Recommended Reading

Lucas's 1971 paper, "Performance Evaluation and Monitoring," provides a survey of performance evaluation.[109] A discussion of recent trends in performance evaluation, particularly benchmarking, is found in *The Seventh Workshop on Hot Topics in Operating Systems* in the section entitled "Lies, Damn Lies, and Benchmarks."[110, 111] The SPEC Web site (www.specbench.org) and the *PC Magazine* benchmarks from VeriTest Web site (www.veritest.com/benchmarks/default.asp)[112] provide information on commercial benchmarks. Patterson and Hennesey's *Computer Organization and Design* describes processor architecture.[113] Stokes[114] and Aletan[115] survey the histories and philosophies of RISC and CISC processors. Flynn, Mitchell and Mulder discuss some benefits of the CISC approach.[116] Schlansker and Rau explain the EPIC design philosophy.[117] The bibliography for this chapter is located on our Web site at www.deitel.com/books/os3e/Bibliography.pdf.

Works Cited

1. Mogul, J., "Brittle Metrics in Operating System Research," *Proceedings of the Seventh Workshop on Hot Operating System Topics*, March 1999, pp. 90–95.

2. Lucas, H., "Performance Evaluation and Monitoring," *ACM Computing Surveys*, Vol. 3, No. 3, September 1971, pp. 79–91.

3. Lucas, H., "Performance Evaluation and Monitoring," *ACM Computing Surveys*, Vol. 3, No. 3, September 1971, pp. 79–91.

4. Ferrari, D.; G. Serazzi; and A. Zeigner, *Measurement and Tuning of Computer Systems*, Englewood Cliffs, NJ: Prentice Hall, 1983.

5. Anderson, G., "The Coordinated Use of Five Performance Evaluation Methodologies," *Communications of the ACM*, Vol. 27, No. 2, February 1984, pp. 119–125.

6. Seltzer, M., et al., "The Case for Application-Specific Benchmarking," *Proceedings of the Seventh Workshop on Hot Topics in Operating Systems,* March 1999, pp. 105–106.

7. Seltzer, M., et al., "The Case for Application-Specific Benchmarking," *Proceedings of the Seventh Workshop on Hot Topics in Operating Systems,* March 1999, pp. 105–106.

8. Spinellis, D., "Trace: A Tool for Logging Operating System Call Transactions," *ACM SIGOPS Operating System Review,* October 1994, pp. 56–63.

9. Bull, J. M., and D. O'Neill, "A Microbenchmark Suite for OpenMP 2.0," *ACM SIGARCH Computer Architecture Notes,* Vol. 29, No. 5, December 2001, pp. 41–48.

10. Keckler, S., et al., "Exploiting Fine-Grain Thread Level Parallelism on the MIT Multi-ALU Processor," *Proceedings of the 25th Annual International Symposium on Computer Architecture,* October 1998, pp. 306–317.

11. Brown, A., and M. Seltzer, "Operating System Benchmarking in the Wake of Lmbench: A Case Study on the Performance of NetBSD on the Intel x86 Architecture," *ACM SIGMETRICS Conference on Measurement and Modeling of Computer Systems* June 1997, pp. 214–224.

12. McVoy, L., and C. Staelin, "lmbench: Portable Tools for Performance Analysis," in *Proceedings of the 1996 USENIX Annual Technical Conference,* January 1996, pp. 279–294.

13. Brown, A., and M. Seltzer, "Operating System Benchmarking in the Wake of lmbench: A Case Study on the Performance of NetBSD on the Intel x86 Architecture," *ACM SIGMETRICS Conference on Measurement and Modeling of Computer Systems,* June 1997, pp. 214–224.

14. McVoy, L., and Staelin, C., "lmbench: Portable tools for Performance Analysis," *In Proceedings of the 1996 USENIX Annual Technical Conference,* January 1996, pp. 279–294.

15. Brown, A., and M. Seltzer, "Operating System Benchmarking in the Wake of Lmbench: A Case Study on the Performance of NetBSD on the Intel x86 Architecture," *ACM SIGMETRICS Conference on Measurement and Modeling of Computer Systems,* June 1997, pp. 214–224.

16. Seltzer, M., et al., "The Case for Application-Specific Benchmarking," *Proceedings of the Seventh Workshop on Hot Topics in Operating Systems,* March 1999, pp. 105–106.

17. Seltzer, M., et al., "The Case for Application-Specific Benchmarking," *Proceedings of the Seventh Workshop on Hot Topics in Operating Systems,* March 1999, pp. 105–106.

18. Seltzer, M., et al., "The Case for Application-Specific Benchmarking," *Proceedings of the Seventh Workshop on Hot Topics in Operating Systems,* March 1999, pp. 102–107.

19. Lucas, H., "Performance Evaluation and Monitoring," *ACM Computing Surveys,* Vol. 3, No. 3, September 1971, pp. 79–91.

20. Lucas, H., "Performance Evaluation and Monitoring," *ACM Computing Surveys,* Vol. 3, No. 3, September 1971, pp. 79–91.

21. Lucas, H., "Performance Evaluation and Monitoring," *ACM Computing Surveys,* Vol. 3, No. 3, September 1971, pp. 79–91.

22. Svobodova, L., *Computer Performance Measurement and Evaluation Methods: Analysis and Applications,* New York: Elsevier, 1977.

23. Kobayashi, H., *Modeling and Analysis: An Introduction to System Performance Evaluation Methodology,* Reading, MA: Addison-Wesley, 1978.

24. Lazowska, E., "The Benchmarking, Tuning, and Analytic Modeling of VAX/VMS," *Conference on Simulation, Measurement and Modeling of Computer Systems,* August 1979, pp. 57–64.

25. Sauer, C., and K. Chandy, *Computer Systems Performance Modeling,* Englewood Cliffs, NJ: Prentice Hall, 1981.

26. Lucas, H., "Performance Evaluation and Monitoring," *ACM Computing Surveys,* Vol. 3, No. 3, September 1971, pp. 79–91.

27. Hindin, H., and M. Bloom, "Balancing Benchmarks Against Manufacturers' Claims," *UNIX World,* January 1988, pp. 42–50.

28. Mogul, J., "Brittle Metrics in Operating System Research," *Proceedings of the Seventh Workshop on Hot Topics in Operating Systems,* March 1999, pp. 90–95.

29. "SpecWeb99," *SPEC (Standard Performance Evaluation Corporation),* September 26, 2003, <www.specbench.org/web99/>.

30. Mogul, J., "Brittle Metrics in Operating System Research," *Proceedings of the Seventh Workshop on Hot Operating System Topics,* March 1999, pp. 90–95.

31. Seltzer, M., et al., "The Case for Application-Specific Benchmarking," *Proceedings of the Seventh Workshop on Hot Topics in Operating Systems,* March 1999, pp. 102–107.

32. "BAPCo Benchmark Products," *BAPCo,* August 5, 2002, <www.bapco.com/products.htm>.

33. "Overview of the TPC Benchmark C," *Transaction Processing Performance Council,* August 12, 2003, <www.tpc.org/tpcc/detail.asp>.

34. "SAP Standard Application Benchmarks," August 12, 2003, <www.sap.com/benchmark>.

35. Bucholz, W., "A Synthetic Job for Measuring System Performance," *IBM Journal of Research and Development,* Vol. 8, No. 4, 1969, pp. 309–308.

36. Lucas, H., "Performance Evaluation and Monitoring," *ACM Computing Surveys,* Vol. 3, No. 3, September 1971, pp. 79–91.

37. Weicker, R., "Dhrystone: A Synthetic Systems Programming Benchmark," *Communications of the ACM,* Vol. 21, No. 10, October 1984, pp. 1013–1030.

38. Dronek, G., "The Standards of System Efficiency," *Unix Review,* March 1985, pp. 26–30.

39. Wilson, P., "Floating-Point Survival Kit," *Byte,* Vol. 21, No. 3, March 1988, pp. 217–226.

40. "WinBench," *PC Magazine,* September 2, 2003, <www.etestinglabs.com/benchmarks/winbench/winbench.asp>.

41. "IOStone: A Synthetic File System Benchmark," *ACM SIGARCH Computer Architecture News,* Vol. 18, No. 2, June 1990, pp. 45–52.

42. "Hartstone: Synthetic Benchmark Requirements for Hard Real-Time Applications," *Proceedings of the Working Group on ADA Performance Issues,* 1990, pp. 126–136.

43. "Unix Technical Response Benchmark Info Page," May 17, 2002, <www.unix.ualberta.ca/Benchmarks/benchmarks.html>.

44. Lucas, H., "Performance Evaluation and Monitoring," *ACM Computing Surveys*, Vol. 3, No. 3, September 1971, pp. 79–91.

45. Nance, R., "The Time and State Relationships in Simulation Modeling," *Communications of the ACM*, Vol. 24, No. 4, April 1981, pp. 173–179.

46. Keller, R., and F. Lin, "Simulated Performance of a Reduction-Based Multiprocessor," *Computer*, Vol. 17, No. 7, July 1984, pp. 70–82.

47. Overstreet, C., and R, Nance, "A Specification Language to Assist in Analysis of Discrete Event Simulation Models," *Communications of the ACM*, Vol. 28, No. 2, February 1985, pp. 190–201.

48. Jefferson, D., et al., "Distributed Simulation and the Time Warp Operating System," *Proceeding of the 11th Symposium on Operating System Principles*, Vol. 21, No. 5, November 1987, pp. 77–93.

49. Overstreet, C., and R. Nance, "A Specification Language to Assist in Analysis of Discrete Event Simulation Models," *Communications of the ACM*, Vol. 28, No. 2, February 1985, pp. 190–201.

50. Gibson, J. et al., "FLASH vs. (Simulated) FLASH: Closing the Simulation Loop," *ACM SIGPLAN Notices*, Vol. 35, No. 11, November 2000, pp. 52–58.

51. Lucas, H., "Performance Evaluation and Monitoring," *ACM Computing Surveys*, Vol. 3, No. 3, September 1971, pp. 79–91.

52. Plattner, B., and J. Nivergelt, "Monitoring Program Execution: A Survey," *Computer*, Vol. 14, No. 11, November 1981, pp. 76–92.

53. Irving, R.; C. Higgins; and F. Safayeni, "Computerized Performance Monitoring Systems: Use and Abuse," *Computer Technology Form No. SA23–1057*, 1986.

54. "Windows 2000 Performance Tools: Leverage Native Tools for Performance Monitoring and Tuning," *InformIT*, January 15, 2001, <www.informit.com/content/index.asp?product_id=%7BA085E192-E708-4AAB-999E-5C339560EAA6%7D>.

55. Gavin, D., "Performance Monitoring Tools for Linux," *Linux Journal*, No. 56, December 1, 1998, <www.linuxjournal.com/article.php?sid=2396>.

56. "IA-32 Intel Architecture Software Developer's Manual," Vol. 3, *System Programmer's Guide*, 2002.

57. Lucas, H., "Performance Evaluation and Monitoring," *ACM Computing Surveys*, Vol. 3, No. 3, September 1971, pp. 79–91.

58. Ferrari, D.; G. Serazzi; and A. Zeigner, *Measurement and Tuning of Computer Systems*, Englewood Cliffs, NJ: Prentice Hall, 1983.

59. Bonomi, M., "Avoiding Coprocessor Bottlenecks," *Byte*, Vol. 13, No. 3, March 1988, pp. 197–204.

60. Coutois, P., "Decomposability, Instability, and Saturation in Multiprogramming Systems," *Communications of the ACM*, Vol. 18, No. 7, 1975, pp. 371–376.

61. Hennessy, J., and D. Patterson, *Computer Organization and Design*, San Francisco, CA: Morgan Kaufmann Publishers, Inc., 1998, p. G-7.

62. Stokes, J., "Ars Technica: RISC vs. CISC in the Post RISC Era," October 1999, <arstechnica.com/cpu/4q99/risc-cisc/rvc-1.html>.

63. Stokes, J., "Ars Technica: RISC vs. CISC in the Post RISC Era," October 1999, <arstechnica.com/cpu/4q99/risc-cisc/rvc-1.html>.

64. Daily, S., "Killer Hardware for Windows NT," *Windows IT Library*, January 1998 <www.windowsitlibrary.com/Content/435/02/toc.html>.

65. DeMone, P., "RISC vs. CISC Still Matters," February 13, 2000, <ctas.east.asu.edu/bgannod/CET520/Spring02/Projects/demone.htm>.

66. Hennessy, J. and D. Patterson, *Computer Organization and Design*, San Francisco, CA: Morgan Kaufmann Publishers, Inc., 1998, p. 525.

67. Rosen, S., "Electronic Computers—A Historical Survey," *ACM Computing Surveys*, Vol. 1, No. 1, January 1969, pp. 26–28.

68. Ramamoorthy, C. V., and H. F. Li, "Pipeline Architecture," *ACM Computing Surveys*, Vol. 9, No. 1, January 1977, pp. 62–64.

69. Aletan, S., "An Overview of RISC Architecture," *Proceedings of the 1992 ACM/SIGAPP Symposium on Applied Computing: Technological Challenges of the 1990's*, 1992, pp. 11–12.

70. Hopkins, M., "Compiling for the RT PC ROMP," *IBM RT Personal Computer Technology*, 1986, pp. 81.

71. Coulter, N. S., and N. H. Kelly, "Computer Instruction Set Usage by Programmers: An Empirical Investigation," *Communications of the ACM*, Vol. 29, No. 7, July 1986, pp. 643–647.

72. Serlin, O., "MIPS, Dhrystones, and Other Tales," *Datamation*, Vol. 32, No. 11, June 1, 1986, pp. 112–118.

73. Aletan, S., "An Overview of RISC Architecture," *Proceedings of the 1992 ACM/SIGAPP Symposium on Applied Computing: Technological Challenges of the 1990's*, 1992, p. 13.

74. Patterson, D. A., "Reduced Instruction Set Computers," *Communications of the ACM*, Vol. 28, No. 1, January 1985, pp. 8–21.

75. Hopkins, M., "Compiling for the RT PC ROMP," *IBM RT Personal Computer Technology*, 1986, pp. 81.

76. Patterson, D. A., "Reduced Instruction Set Computers," *Communications of the ACM*, Vol. 28, No. 1, January 1985, pp. 8–21.

77. Patterson, D., "Reduced Instruction Set Computers," *Communications of the ACM*, Vol. 28, No. 1, January 1985, pp. 8–21.

78. Lilja, D., "Reducing the Branch Penalty in Pipelined Processors," *Computer*, Vol. 21, No. 7, July 1988, pp. 47–55.

79. Huang, I., "Co-synthesis of Pipelined Structures and Structured Reordering Constraints for Instruction Set Processors," *ACM Transactions on Design Automation of Electronic Systems*, Vol. 6, No. 1, January 2001, pp. 93–121.

80. Lilja, D., "Reducing the Branch Penalty in Pipelined Processors," *Computer*, Vol. 21, No. 7, July 1988, pp. 47–55.

81. Wilson, R., "RISC Chips Explore Parallelism for Boost in Speed," *Computer Design*, January 1, 1989, pp. 58–73.

82. Davidson, J. W., and R. A. Vaughan, "The Effect of Instruction Set Complexity on Program Size and Memory Performance," *Proceedings of the Second International Conference on Architectural Support for Programming Languages and Operating Systems*, 1987, pp. 60–64.

83. Wilson, R., "RISC Chips Explore Parallelism for Boost in Speed," *Computer Design,* January 1, 1989, pp. 58–73.

84. "IA-32 Intel Architecture Software Developer's Manual," Vol. 1: Basic Architecture, 2002.

85. Brehob, M., et al., "Beyond RISC—The Post-RISC Architecture," *Michigan State University Department of Computer Science, Technical Report CPS-96-11*, March 1996.

86. Stokes, J., "Ars Technica: RISC vs. CISC in the Post RISC Era," October 1999, <arstechnica.com/cpu/4q99/risc-cisc/rvc-1.html>.

87. Stokes, J., "Ars Technica: RISC vs. CISC in the Post RISC Era," October 1999, <arstechnica.com/cpu/4q99/risc-cisc/rvc-1.html>.

88. Brehob, M., et al., "Beyond RISC—The Post-RISC Architecture," *Michigan State University Department of Computer Science, Technical Report CPS-96-11*, March 1996.

89. DeMone, P., "RISC vs. CISC Still Matters," February 13, 2000, <ctas.east.asu.edu/bgannod/CET520/Spring02/Projects/demone.htm>.

90. Hennessy, J., and D. Patterson, *Computer Organization and Design,* San Francisco, CA: Morgan Kaufmann Publishers, Inc., 1998, p. 510.

91. Jouppi, N., "Superscalar vs. Superpipelined Machines," *ACM SIGARCH Computer Architecture News*, Vol. 16, No. 3, June 1988, pp. 71–80.

92. Ray, J.; J. Hoe; and B. Falsafi, "Dual Use of Superscalar Datapath for Transient-Fault Detection and Recovery," *Proceedings of the 34th Annual ACM/IEEE International Symposium on Microarchitecture,* December 2001, pp. 214–224.

93. Stokes, J., "Ars Technica: RISC vs. CISC in the Post RISC Era," October 1999, <arstechnica.com/cpu/4q99/risc-cisc/rvc-1.html>.

94. Hwu, W. W., and Y. Patt, "Checkpoint Repair for Out-of-Order Execution Machines," *Proceedings of the 14th International Symposium on Computer Architecture,* June 1987, pp. 18–26.

95. Chuang, W., and B. Calder, "Predicate Prediction for Efficient Out-of-Order Execution," *Proceedings of 17th Annual International Conference on Supercomputing,* June 2003, pp. 183–192.

96. Stokes, J., "Ars Technica: RISC vs. CISC in the Post RISC Era," October 1999, <arstechnica.com/cpu/4q99/risc-cisc/rvc-1.html>.

97. Stokes, J., "Ars Technica: RISC vs. CISC in the Post RISC Era," October 1999, <arstechnica.com/cpu/4q99/risc-cisc/rvc-1.html>.

98. Young, C., and M. Smith, "Static Correlation Branch Prediction," *ACM Transactions on Programming Languages and Systems,* Vol. 21, No. 5, September 1999, pp. 1028–1075.

99. Stokes, J., "Ars Technica: RISC vs. CISC in the Post RISC Era," October 1999, <arstechnica.com/cpu/4q99/risc-cisc/rvc-1.html>.

100. Stokes, J., "Ars Technica: RISC vs. CISC in the Post RISC Era," October 1999, <arstechnica.com/cpu/4q99/risc-cisc/rvc-1.html>.

101. "Altivec Fact Sheet," *Motorola Corporation,* 2002, <e-www.motorola.com/files/32bit/doc/fact_sheet/ALTIVECGLANCE.pdf>.

102. Stokes, J., "Ars Technica: RISC vs. CISC in the Post RISC Era," October 1999, <arstechnica.com/cpu/4q99/risc-cisc/rvc-1.html>.

103. Schlansker, M., and B. Rau, "EPIC: Explicitly Parallel Instruction Computing," *Computer*, Vol. 33, No. 2, February 2000, pp. 37–38.

104. Lowney, P., et al., "The Multiflow Trace Scheduling Compiler," *Journal of Supercomputing,* Vol. 7, May 1993: 51–142.

105. Hennessy, J., and D. Patterson, *Computer Organization and Design,* San Francisco, CA: Morgan Kaufmann Publishers, Inc., 1998, p. 528.

106. Schlansker, M., and B. Rau, "EPIC: Explicitly Parallel Instruction Computing," *Computer*, Vol. 33, No. 2, February 2000, pp. 38–39.

107. Schlansker, M., and B. Rau, "EPIC: Explicitly Parallel Instruction Computing," *Computer*, Vol. 33, No. 2, February 2000, pp. 41–44.

108. Schlansker, M., and B. Rau, "EPIC: Explicitly Parallel Instruction Computing," *Computer*, Vol. 33, No. 2, February 2000, pp. 41–44.

109. Lucas, H., "Performance Evaluation and Monitoring," *ACM Computing Surveys,* Vol. 3, No. 3, September 1971, pp. 79–91.

110. Mogul, J., "Brittle Metrics in Operating System Research," *Proceedings of the Seventh Workshop on Hot Topics in Operating Systems,* March 1999, pp. 90–95.

111. Seltzer, M., et al., "The Case for Application-Specific Benchmarking," *Proceedings of the Seventh Workshop on Hot Topics in Operating Systems,* March 1999, pp. 105–106.

112. "PC Magazine Benchmarks from VeriTest," *PC Magazine* <www.veritest.com/benchmarks/default.asp?visitor=>.

113. Hennessy, J., and D. Patterson, *Computer Organization and Design,* San Francisco, CA: Morgan Kaufmann Publishers, Inc., 1998, p. 528.

114. Stokes, J., "Ars Technica: RISC vs. CISC in the Post RISC Era," October 1999, <arstechnica.com/cpu/4q99/risc-cisc/rvc-1.html>.

115. Aletan, S., "An Overview of RISC Architecture," *Proceedings of the 1992 ACM/SIGAPP Symposium on Applied Computing: Technological Challenges of the 1990's,* 1992, pp. 11–12.

116. Flynn, M. J.; C. L. Mitchell; and J. M. Mulder, "And Now a Case for More Complex Instruction Sets," *Computer*, Vol. 20, No. 9, September 1987, pp. 71–83.

117. Schlansker, M., and Rau, B., "EPIC: Explicitly Parallel Instruction Computing," *Computer*, Vol. 33, No. 2, February 2000, pp. 41–44.

What's going to happen in the next decade is that
we'll figure out how to make parallelism work.

—David Kuck quoted in *TIME*, March 28, 1988—

"The question is," said Humpty Dumpty, "which is to be master—that's all."

—Lewis Carroll—

I hope to see my Pilot face to face When I have crossed the bar.

—Alfred, Lord Tennyson—

"If seven maids with seven mops
Swept it for half a year,
Do you suppose," the Walrus said,
"That they could get it clear?"

—Lewis Carroll—

The most general definition of beauty ... Multeity in Unity.

—Samuel Taylor Coleridge—

Chapter 15

Multiprocessor Management

Objectives

After reading this chapter, you should understand:

- *multiprocessor architectures and operating system organizations.*

- *multiprocessor memory architectures.*

- *design issues specific to multiprocessor environments.*

- *algorithms for multiprocessor scheduling.*

- *process migration in multiprocessor systems.*

- *load balancing in multiprocessor systems.*

- *mutual exclusion techniques for multiprocessor systems.*

Chapter Outline

15.9
Multiprocessor Mutual Exclusion

Web Resources | Summary | Key Terms | Exercises | Recommended Reading | Works Cited

15.1 Introduction

For decades, Moore's Law has successfully predicted an exponential rise in processor transistor count and performance, yielding ever more powerful processors. Despite these performance gains, researchers, developers, businesses and consumers continue to demand substantially more computing power than one processor can provide. As a result, **multiprocessing systems**—computers that contain more than one processor—are employed in many computing environments.

Large engineering and scientific applications that execute on supercomputers increase throughput by processing data in parallel on multiple processors. Businesses and scientific institutions use multiprocessing systems to increase system performance, scale resource usage to application requirements and provide a high degree of data reliability.[1] For example, the Earth Simulator in Yokohama, Japan—the most powerful supercomputer as of June, 2003—contains 5,120 processors, each operating at 500MHz (see the Mini Case Study, Supercomputers). The system can

Mini Case Study

Supercomputers

Supercomputer is simply a term for the most powerful contemporary computers. The early supercomputers would be no match for today's inexpensive PCs. The speed of a supercomputer is measured in Flops (Floating-point operations per second).

The first supercomputer was the CDC 6600, manufactured by Control Data Corporation and designed by Seymour Cray, who became known as the father of supercomputing (see the Biographical Note, Seymour Cray).[2, 3] This machine, released in the early 1960's, processed 3 million instructions per second.[4, 5] It was also the first computer to use the RISC (reduced instruction set comput-

ing) architecture.[6, 7] Roughly 10 years and several machines later, Cray designed the Cray-1, one of the earliest vector-processor models.[8] (Vector processors are discussed in Section 15.2.1, Classifying Sequential and Parallel Architectures.) The supercomputers that Cray designed dominated the high-performance field for many years.

According to the supercomputer tracking organization Top500 (www.top500.org), the fastest computer in the world (at the time this book was published) is NEC's Earth Simulator, located in Japan. It operates at a peak speed of roughly 35 teraflops, more than twice the speed of the sec-

ond-fastest computer and tens of thousands of times faster than a typical desktop machine.[9, 10] The Earth Simulator consists of 5,120 vector processors grouped into 640 units of eight processors each, where each unit has 16GB of shared main memory, totalling 10TB of memory.[11, 12] These units are connected by 1500 miles of network cable and are linked to a 640TB disk system and a tape library that can hold over 1.5 petabytes (1,500,000,000,000,000 bytes).[13, 14] This enormous computing capacity is used for research in predicting environmental conditions and events.[15]

execute 35.86 Tflops (trillion floating point operations per second), enabling researchers to model weather patterns, which can be used to predict natural disasters and evaluate how human activities affect nature.[16, 17]

Multiprocessing systems must adapt to different workloads. In particular, the operating system should ensure that

- all processors remain busy
- processes are evenly distributed throughout the system
- execution of related processes is synchronized
- processors operate on consistent copies of data stored in shared memory
- mutual exclusion is enforced.

Techniques used to solve deadlock in multiprocessing and distributed systems are similar and are discussed in Chapter 17, Introduction to Distributed Systems.

This chapter describes multiprocessor architectures and techniques for optimizing multiprocessing systems. These techniques focus on improving performance,

Biographical Note

Seymour Cray

Seymour Cray is known as the father of supercomputing. Shortly after getting his Masters in Applied Mathematics from the University of Minnesota in 1951, he joined Engineering Research Associates (ERA), one of the first companies to build digital computers.[18, 19, 21] At ERA Cray designed the 1103, the first computer designed for scientific research that also sold well to the general market.[20, 22]

In 1957, Cray left the company with William Norris (the founder of ERA) to start Control Data Corporation.[23, 24, 25] By 1960 Cray had designed the CDC 1604, the first computer that com-

pletely replaced vacuum tubes with transistors.[26, 27, 28] In 1962 Cray designed the CDC 6600, the first true "supercomputer," followed by the CDC 7600.[29, 30, 31] He always strove for simplicity, so the CDC 6600 featured a simplified architecture based on a smaller set of instructions—a design philosophy later called RISC (reduced instruction set computing).[32, 33, 34]

Seymour Cray founded Cray Research in 1972 to continue building large scientific computers.[35] The Cray-1, one of the earliest vector-processor computers, was released in 1976 (see Section 15.2.1, Classifying Sequential and Parallel Architectures).[36]

The Cray-1 was much smaller yet more powerful than the CDC 7600.[37] It was also visually interesting, curving around to form a cylinder with a gap, and equipped with a bench running around the outside.[38] It ran at 133 megaflops, which was extraordinarily fast at that time, but slower than today's typical desktop PCs.[39] The Cray-1 was followed by three more Cray models, each progressively faster and more compact than the last. The computational unit (not including the memory banks and cooling equipment) of the Cray-4 was smaller than the human brain.[40]

fairness, cost and fault tolerance. Often, improvement in one of these parameters occurs at the expense of the others. We also consider how design decisions can affect multiprocessor performance.

Self Review

1. Why are multiprocessors useful?
2. How do the responsibilities of a multiprocessor operating system differ from those of a uniprocessor system?

Ans: 1) Many computer users demand more processing power than one processor can provide. For example, businesses can use multiprocessors to increase performance and scale resource usage to application needs. 2) The operating system must balance the workload of various processors, enforce mutual exclusion in a system where multiple processes can execute truly simultaneously and ensure that all processors are made aware of modifications to shared memory.

15.2 Multiprocessor Architecture

The term "multiprocessing system" encompasses any system containing more than one processor. Examples of multiprocessors include dual-processor personal computers, powerful servers that contain many processors and distributed groups of workstations that work together to perform tasks.

Throughout this chapter we present several ways to classify multiprocessors. In this section, we categorize multiprocessing systems by their physical properties, such as the nature of the system's datapath (i.e., the portion of the processor that performs operations on data), the processor interconnection scheme and how processors share resources.

15.2.1 Classifying Sequential and Parallel Architectures

Flynn developed an early scheme for classifying computers into increasingly parallel configurations. The scheme consists of four categories based on the different types of **streams** used by processors.[41] A stream is simply a sequence of bytes that is fed to a processor. A processor accepts two streams—an instruction stream and a data stream.

Single-instruction-stream, single-data-stream (SISD) computers are the simplest type. These are traditional uniprocessors in which a single processor fetches one instruction at a time and executes it on a single data item. Techniques such as pipelining, very long instruction word (VLIW) and superscalar design can introduce parallelism into SISD computers. Pipelining divides an instruction's execution path into discrete stages. This allows the processor to process multiple instructions simultaneously, as long as at most one instruction occupies each stage during a clock cycle. VLIW and superscalar techniques simultaneously issue multiple independent instructions (from one instruction stream) that execute in different execution units. VLIW relies on the compiler to determine which instructions to issue at any given clock cycle, whereas superscalar design requires that the processor make this decision.[42] Additionally, Intel's Hyper-Threading technology introduces parallelism by creating two virtual processors from one physical processor. This gives a multiprocessor-enabled operating system the impression that it is running on two processors that each execute at a little less than half the speed of the physical processor.[43]

Multiple-instruction-stream, single-data-stream (MISD) computers are not commonly used. A MISD architecture would have several processing units that act on a single stream of data. Each unit would execute a different instruction on the data and pass the result to the next unit.[44]

Single-instruction-stream, multiple-data-stream (SIMD) computers issue instructions that act on multiple data items. A SIMD computer consists of one or more processing units. A processor executes a SIMD instruction by performing the same instruction on a block of data (e.g., adding one to every element in an array). If there are more data elements than processing units, the processing units fetch additional data elements for the next cycle. This can increase performance relative to SISD architectures, which would require a loop to perform the same operation one data element at a time. A loop contains many conditional tests, requires the SISD processor to decode the same instruction multiple times and requires the SISD processor to read data one word at a time. By contrast, SIMD architectures read in a block of data at once, reducing costly memory-to-register transfers. SIMD architectures are most effective in environments in which a system applies the same instruction to large data sets.[45, 46]

Vector processors and **array processors** use a SIMD architecture. A vector processor contains one processing unit that executes each vector instruction on a set of data, performing the same operation on each data element. Vector processors rely on extremely deep pipelines (i.e., ones containing many stages) and high clock speeds. Deep pipelines permit the processor to perform work on several instructions at a time so that many data elements can be manipulated at once. An array processor contains several processing units that perform the same instruction in parallel on many data elements. Array processors (often referred to as **massively parallel processors**) might contain tens of thousands of processing elements. Therefore, array processors are most efficient when manipulating large data sets. Vector and array processing are useful in scientific computing and graphics manipulation where the same operation must be applied to a large data set (e.g., matrix transformations).[47, 48] The Connection Machine (CM) systems built by Thinking Machines, Inc., are examples of array processors.[49]

Multiple-instruction-stream, multiple-data-stream (MIMD) computers are multiprocessors in which the processing units are completely independent and operate on separate instruction streams.[50] However, these systems typically contain hardware that allows processors to synchronize with each other when necessary, such as when accessing a shared peripheral device.

Self Review

1. Thread-level parallelism (TLP) refers to the execution of multiple independent threads in parallel. Which multiprocessor architecture exploits TLP?
2. (T/F) Only SIMD processor architectures exploit parallelism.

Ans: **1)** Only MIMD and MISD architectures can execute multiple threads at once. However, the threads executed by a MISD computer manipulate the same data and are not independent. Therefore, only MIMD systems can truly exploit TLP. **2)** False. SISD systems use techniques such as pipelines, VLIW and superscalar design to exploit parallelism; MISD processors execute multiple threads at once; and MIMD processors exploit TLP as described in the previous answer.

15.2.2 Processor Interconnection Schemes

The **interconnection scheme** of a multiprocessor system describes how the system's components, such as processors and memory modules, are physically connected. The interconnection scheme is a key issue for multiprocessor designers because it affects the system's performance, reliability and cost. An interconnection scheme consists of **nodes** and **links**. Nodes are composed of system components and/or **switches** that route messages between components. A link is a connection between two nodes. In many systems, a single node might contain one or more processors, their associated caches, a memory module and a switch. In large-scale multiprocessors, we sometimes abstract the concept of a node and denote a group of nodes as a single supernode.

Designers use several parameters to evaluate interconnection schemes. A node's **degree** is the number of nodes to which it is connected. Designers try to minimize a node's degree to reduce the complexity and cost of its communication interface. Nodes with larger degrees require more complex communication hardware to support communication between the node and its neighbor nodes (i.e., nodes connected to it).[51]

One technique for measuring an interconnection scheme's fault tolerance is to count the number of communication links that must fail before the network is unable to function properly. This can be quantified using the **bisection width**—the minimum number of links that need to be severed to divide the network into two unconnected halves. Systems with larger bisection widths are more fault tolerant than those with smaller bisection widths because more components must fail before the entire system fails.

An interconnection scheme's performance largely depends on communication latency between nodes. This can be measured in several ways, one of which is the average latency. Another performance measure is the **network diameter**—the shortest distance between the two most remote nodes in the interconnection scheme. To determine the network diameter, consider all pairs of nodes in the network and find the shortest path length for each pair—computed by totaling the number of links traversed—then find the largest of these paths. A small network diameter indicates low communication latency and higher performance. Finally, system architects attempt to minimize the **cost of an interconnection scheme**, which is equal to the total number of links in a network.[52]

In the following subsections, we enumerate several successful interconnection models and evaluate them based on the preceding criteria. Many real systems implement variations of these models. For example, they might add extra communication links to increase fault tolerance (by increasing the bisection width) and performance (by decreasing the network diameter).

Shared Bus

The **shared bus** network organization uses a single communication path (i.e., route through which messages travel) between all processors and memory modules (Fig. 15.1).[53] The components' bus interfaces handle transfer operations. The bus is passive, and the components arbitrate among themselves to use the bus. Only one transfer can take place at a time on the bus, because the bus cannot convey two electrical signals at once. Therefore, before a component initiates a transfer, it must first check that both the bus and the destination component are available. One problem with shared buses—**contention**—arises when several components wish to use the bus at once. To reduce contention and bus traffic, each processor maintains its own local cache as shown in Fig. 15.1. When the system can fulfill a memory request from a processor's cache, the processor does not need to communicate over the bus with a memory module. Another option is to construct a **multiple shared bus architecture**, which reduces contention by providing multiple buses that service communication requests. However, these require complex bus arbitration logic and additional links, which increases the system's cost.[54, 55]

The shared bus is a simple and inexpensive scheme to connect a small number of processors. New components can be added to the system by attaching them to the bus, and software handles the detection and identification of the bus components. However, due to contention for the single communication path, shared bus organizations do not scale beyond a small number of processors (in practice 16 or 32 is the maximum).[56] Contention is exacerbated by the fact that processor speed has increased faster than bus bandwidth. As processors get faster, it takes fewer processors to saturate a bus.

Shared buses are dynamic networks, because communication links are formed and discarded (through the shared bus) during execution. Therefore, the criteria used to evaluate interconnection schemes that we discussed earlier do not apply; these criteria are based on static links, which do not change during execution. How-

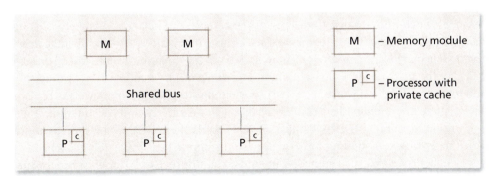

Figure 15.1 | *Shared bus multiprocessor organization.*

ever, compared to other interconnection schemes, a shared bus with several processors is fast and inexpensive, but not particularly fault tolerant—if the shared bus fails, the components cannot communicate.[57]

Designers can leverage the benefits of shared buses in multiprocessors with larger numbers of processors. In these systems, maintaining a single shared bus (or several buses) that connects all processors is impractical, because the bus becomes saturated easily. However, designers can divide the system's resources (e.g., processors and memory) into several small supernodes. The resources within a supernode communicate via a shared bus, and the supernodes are connected using one of the more scalable interconnection schemes described in the sections that follow. Such systems attempt to keep most communication traffic within a supernode to exploit the fast bus architecture, while enabling communication between supernodes.[58] Most multiprocessors with a small number of processors, such as dual-processor Intel Pentium systems, use a shared bus architecture.[59]

Crossbar-Switch Matrix

A **crossbar-switch matrix** provides a separate path from every processor to every memory module (Fig. 15.2).[60] For example, if there are n processors and m memory modules, there will be $n \times m$ total switches that connect each processor to each memory module. We can imagine the processors as the rows of a matrix and the memory modules as the columns. In larger networks, nodes often consist of processor and memory components. This improves memory-access performance (for those accesses between a processor and its associated memory module). In the case of a crossbar-switch matrix, this reduces the interconnection scheme's cost. In this design, each node connects to a switch of degree of $p - 1$, where p is the number of processor-memory nodes in the system (i.e., in this case, $m = n$ because each node contains the same number of processors and memory modules).[61, 62]

A crossbar-switch matrix can support data transmissions to all nodes at once, but each node can accept at most one message at a time. Contrast this with the shared bus, which supports only one transmission at a time. A switch uses an arbitration algorithm such as "service the requesting processor that has been serviced least recently at this switch" to resolve multiple requests. The crossbar-switch design provides high performance. Because all nodes are linked to all other nodes and transmission through switch nodes has a trivial performance cost, the network diameter is essentially one. Each processor is connected to each memory module, so to divide a crossbar-switch matrix into two equal halves, half of the links between processors and memory modules must be cut. The number of links in the matrix is the product of n and m, so the bisection width is $(n \times m) / 2$, yielding strong fault tolerance. As Fig. 15.2 shows, there are many paths a communication can take to reach its destination.

A disadvantage of crossbar-switch matrices is their cost, which increases proportionally to $n \times m$, making large-scale systems impractical.[63] For this reason, crossbar-switches are typically employed in smaller multiprocessors (e.g., 16 processors). However, as hardware costs decline, they are being used more frequently in larger systems. The Sun UltraSPARC-III uses crossbar switches to share memory.[64]

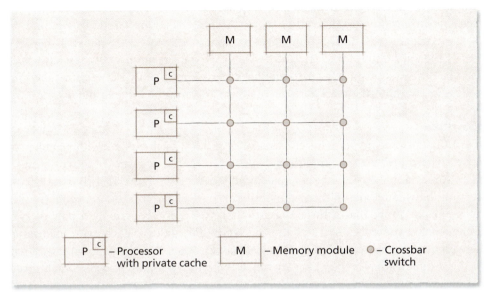

Figure 15.2 | Crossbar-switch matrix multiprocessor organization.

2-D Mesh Network

In a **2-D mesh network** interconnection scheme, each node consists of one or more processors and a memory module. In the simplest case (Fig. 15.3), the nodes in a mesh network are arranged in a rectangle of n rows and m columns, and each node is connected with the nodes directly north, south, east and west of it. This is called a **4-connected 2-D mesh network**. This design keeps each node's degree small, regardless of the number of processors in a system—the corner nodes have a degree of two, the edge nodes have a degree of three and the interior nodes have a degree of four. In Fig. 15.3, where $n = 4$ and $m = 5$, the 2-D mesh network can be divided into two equal halves by cutting the five links between the second and third rows of nodes. In fact, if n is even and m is odd the bisection width is $m + 1$ if $m > n$ and is n otherwise. If the 2-D mesh contains an even number of rows and columns, the bisection width is the

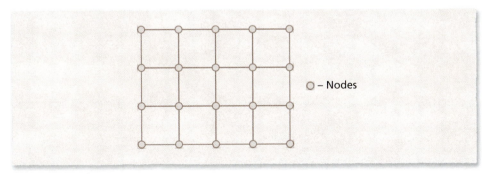

Figure 15.3 | 4-connected 2-D mesh network.

smaller of *m* and *n*. Although not as fault tolerant as a crossbar-switch matrix, a 2-D mesh network is more so than other simple designs, such as a shared bus. Because the maximum degree of a node is four, a 2-D mesh network will have a network diameter that is too substantial for large-scale systems. However, mesh networks have been used in large systems in which communication is kept mainly between neighboring nodes. For example, the Intel Paragon multiprocessor uses a 2-D mesh network.[65]

Hypercube

An *n*-dimensional **hypercube** consists of 2^n nodes, each linked with *n* neighbor nodes. Therefore, a two-dimensional hypercube is a 2×2 mesh network, and a three-dimensional hypercube is conceptually a cube.[66] Figure 15.4 illustrates connections between nodes in three-dimensional (part a) and four-dimensional (part b) hypercubes.[67] Note that a three-dimensional hypercube is actually a pair of two-dimensional hypercubes in which the corresponding nodes in each two-dimensional hypercube are connected. Similarly, a four-dimensional hypercube is actually a pair of three-dimensional hypercubes in which the corresponding nodes in each three-dimensional hypercube are connected.

A hypercube's performance scales better than that of a 2-D mesh network, because each node is connected by *n* links to other nodes. This reduces the network diameter relative to a 2-D mesh network. For example, consider a 16-node multiprocessor implemented as either a 4×4 mesh network or a 4-dimensional hypercube. A 4×4 mesh network has a network diameter of 6, whereas a 4-dimensional hypercube has a network diameter of 4. In some hypercubes, designers add communication links between nonneighbor nodes to further reduce the network diameter.[68] A hypercube's fault tolerance also compares favorably with that of other designs. However, the increased number of links per node increases a hypercube's cost relative to that of a mesh network.[69]

The hypercube interconnection scheme is efficient for connecting a modest number of processors and is more economical than a crossbar-switch matrix. The nCUBE system used in streaming media and digital-advertising systems employs hypercubes of up to 13 dimensions (8,192 nodes).[70]

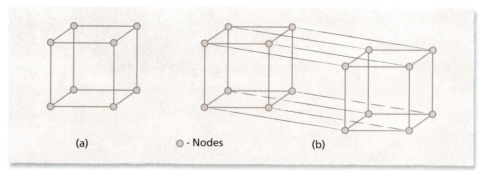

(a)   ⊙ - Nodes   (b)

Figure 15.4 | *3- and 4-dimensional hypercubes.*

Multistage Networks

An alternative processor interconnection scheme is a **multistage network**.[71] As in the crossbar-switch matrix design, some nodes are switches rather than processor nodes with local memory. Switch nodes are smaller, simpler and can be packed more tightly, increasing performance. To understand the benefits of a multistage network over a crossbar-switch matrix, consider the problem of flying between small cities. Instead of offering direct flights between every pair of cities, airlines use large cities as "hubs." A flight between two small cities normally consists of several "legs" in which the traveller first flies to a hub, possibly travels between hubs and finally travels to the destination airport. In this way, airlines can schedule fewer total flights and still connect any small city with an airport to any other. The switching nodes in a multistage network act as hubs for communication between processors, just as airports in large cities do for airlines.

There are many schemes for constructing a multistage network. Figure 15.5 shows a popular multistage network called a **baseline network**.[72] Each nodes on the left is the same as the node on the right. When one processor wants to communicate with another, the message travels through a series of switches. The leftmost switch corresponds to the least significant (rightmost) bit of the destination processor's ID; the middle switch corresponds to the middle bit; and the rightmost switch corresponds to the most significant (leftmost) bit.

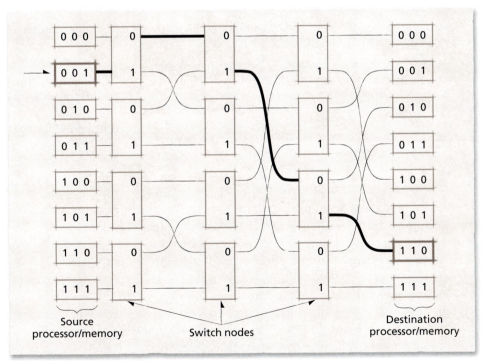

Figure 15.5 | *Multistage baseline network.*

For example, consider the bold path in Fig. 15.5 from the processor with ID 001 to the processor with ID 110. Begin by following the path from processor 001 to the switch. Next, determine the least significant bit (i.e., 0) in the destination processor's ID (110) and follow that path from the current switch to the next switch. From the second switch, follow the path that corresponds to the middle bit (i.e., 1) in the destination processor's ID. Finally, from the third switch, follow the path that corresponds to the most significant bit (i.e., 1) in the destination processor's ID.

Multistage networks represent a cost-performance compromise. This design employs simple hardware to connect large numbers of processors. Any processor can communicate with any other without routing the message through intermediate processors. However, a multistage network has a larger network diameter, so communication is slower than with a crossbar-switch matrix—each message must pass through multiple switches. Also, contention can develop at switching elements, which might degrade performance. IBM's SP series multiprocessor, which evolved to the POWER4, uses a multistage network to connect its processors. The IBM ASCI-White, which can perform over 100 trillion operations per second, is based on the POWER3-II multiprocessor.[73, 74]

Self Review

1. An 8-connected 2-D mesh network includes links to diagonal nodes as well as the links in Fig. 15.3. Compare 4-connected and 8-connected 2-D mesh networks using the criteria discussed in this section.
2. Compare a multistage network to a crossbar-switch matrix. What are the benefits and drawbacks or each interconnection scheme?

Ans: **1)** An 8-connected 2-D mesh network has approximately double the degree for each node and, therefore, approximately double the cost compared to a 4-connected 2-D mesh network. However, the network diameter decreases and the bisection width correspondingly increases, because there are more links in the network. Thus, an 8-connected 2-D mesh network exhibits lower network latency and higher fault tolerance at a higher cost than a 4-connected 2-D mesh network. **2)** A multistage network is cheaper to build than a crossbar-switch matrix. However, multistage networks exhibit reduced performance and fault tolerance.

15.2.3 Loosely Coupled vs. Tightly Coupled Systems

Another defining characteristic of multiprocessors is how the processors share system resources. In a **tightly coupled system** (Fig. 15.6), the processors share most system resources. Tightly coupled systems often employ shared buses, and processors usually communicate via shared memory. A centralized operating system typically manages the system's components. **Loosely coupled systems** (Fig. 15.7) normally connect components indirectly through communication links.[75] Processors sometimes share memory, but often each processor maintains its own local memory, to which it has much faster access than to the rest of memory. In other cases, message passing is the only form of communication between processors, and memory is not shared.

In general, loosely coupled systems are more flexible and scalable than tightly coupled systems. When components are loosely connected, designers can easily add components to or remove components from the system. Loose coupling also increases fault tolerance because components can operate independently of one another. However, loosely coupled systems typically are less efficient, because they communicate by passing messages over a communications link, which is slower than communicating through shared memory. This also places a burden on operating systems programmers, who typically hide most of the complexity of message passing from application programmers. Japan's Earth Simulator is an example of a loosely coupled system.[76]

By contrast, tightly coupled systems perform better but are less flexible. Such systems do not scale well, because contention for shared resources builds up quickly as processors are added. For this reason, most systems with a large number of processors are loosely coupled. In a tightly coupled system, designers can optimize interactions between components to increase system performance. However, this decreases the system's flexibility and fault tolerance, because one component relies on other components. A dual-processor Intel Pentium system is an example of a tightly coupled system.[77]

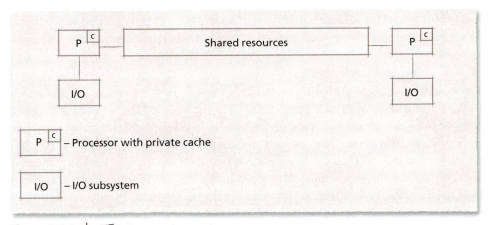

Figure 15.6 | Tightly coupled system.

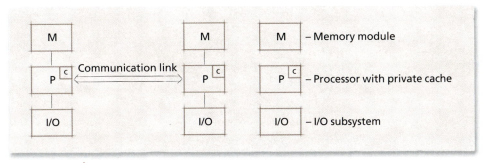

Figure 15.7 | Loosely coupled system.

Self Review

1. Why are many small multiprocessors constructed as tightly coupled systems? Why are many large-scale systems loosely coupled?
2. Some systems consist of several tightly coupled groups of components connected together in a loosely coupled fashion. Discuss some motivations for this scheme.

Ans: **1)** A small system would typically be tightly coupled because there is little contention for shared resources. Therefore, designers can optimize the interactions between system components, thus providing high performance. Typically, large-scale systems are loosely coupled to eliminate contention for shared resources and reduce the likelihood that one failed component will cause systemwide failure. **2)** This scheme leverages the benefits of both interconnection organizations. Each group is small, so tightly coupled systems provide the best performance within a group. Making the overall system loosely coupled reduces contention and increases the system's flexibility and fault tolerance.

15.3 Multiprocessor Operating System Organizations

In organization and structure, multiprocessor operating systems differ significantly from uniprocessor operating systems. In this section, we categorize multiprocessors based on how they share operating system responsibilities. The basic operating system organizations for multiprocessors are master/slave, separate kernels for each processor and symmetric (or anonymous) treatment of all processors.

15.3.1 Master/Slave

The **master/slave multiprocessor organization** designates one processor as the master and the others as slaves (Fig. 15.8).[78] The master executes operating system code; the slaves execute only user programs. The master performs input/output and computation. The slaves can execute processor-bound jobs effectively, but I/O-bound jobs running on the slaves cause frequent calls for services that only the master can perform. From a fault-tolerance standpoint, some computing capability is lost when a slave fails, but the system continues to function. Failure of the master processor is catastrophic and halts the system. Master/slave systems are tightly coupled because all slave processors depend on the master.

The primary problem with master/slave multiprocessing is the hardware asymmetry, because only the master processor execute the operating system. When

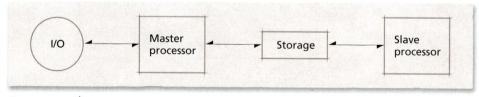

Figure 15.8 | *Master/slave multiprocessing.*

a process executing on a slave processor requires the operating system's attention, the slave processor generates an interrupt and waits for the master to handle the interrupt.

The nCUBE hypercube system is an example of a master/slave system. Its many slave processors handle computationally intensive tasks associated with manipulating graphics and sound.[79]

Self Review

1. (T/F) Master/slave multiprocessors scale well to large-scale systems.
2. For what type of environments are master/slave multiprocessors best suited?

Ans: **1)** False. Only one processor can execute the operating system. Contention will build between processes that are awaiting services (such as I/O) that only the master processor can provide. **2)** Master/slave processors are best suited for environments that mostly execute processor-bound processes. The slave processors can execute these processes without intervention from the master processor.

15.3.2 Separate Kernels

In the **separate-kernels multiprocessor organization**, each processor executes its own operating system and responds to interrupts from user-mode processes running on that processor.[80] A process assigned to a particular processor runs to completion on that processor. Several operating system data structures contain global system information, such as the list of processes known to the system. Access to these data structures must be controlled with mutual exclusion techniques, which we discuss in Section 15.9, Multiprocessor Mutual Exclusion. Systems that use the separate-kernels organization are loosely coupled. This organization is more fault tolerant than the master/slave organization—if a single processor fails, system failure is unlikely. However, the processes that were executing on the failed processor cannot execute until they are restarted on another processor.

In the separate-kernels organization, each processor controls its own dedicated resources, such as files and I/O devices. I/O interrupts return directly to the processors that initiate those interrupts.

This organization benefits from minimal contention over operating system resources, because the resources are distributed among the individual operating systems for their own use. However, the processors do not cooperate to execute an individual process, so some processors might remain idle while one processor executes a multithreaded process. The Tandem system, which is popular in business-critical environments, is an example of a separate-kernels multiprocessor; because the operating system is distributed throughout the loosely coupled processing nodes, it is able to achieve nearly 100 percent availability.[81]

Self Review

1. Why is the separate-kernels organization more fault tolerant than the master/slave organization?
2. For what type of environment would separate-kernels multiprocessor be useful?

Ans: **1)** The separate-kernels organization is loosely coupled. Each processor has its own resources and does not interact with other processors to complete its tasks. If one processor fails, the remainder continue to function. In master/slave organizations, if the master fails, none of the slave processors can perform operating system tasks that must be handled by the master. **2)** A separate-kernels multiprocessor is useful in environments where processes do not interact, such as a cluster of workstations in which users execute independent programs.

15.3.3 Symmetrical Organization

Symmetrical multiprocessor organization is the most complex organization to implement, but is also the most powerful.[82, 83] [*Note:* This organization should not be confused with symmetric multiprocessor (SMP) systems, which we discuss in Section 15.4.1.] The operating system manages a pool of identical processors, any one of which can control any I/O device or reference any storage unit. The symmetry makes it possible to balance the workload more precisely than with the other organizations.

Because many processors might be executing the operating system at once, mutual exclusion must be enforced whenever the operating system modifies shared data structures. Hardware and software conflict-resolution techniques are important.

Symmetrical multiprocessor organizations are generally the most fault tolerant. When a processor fails, the operating system removes that processor from its pool of available processors. The system degrades gracefully while repairs are made (see the Operating Systems Thinking feature, Graceful Degradation). Also, a process running on a symmetrical system organization can be dispatched to any processor. Therefore, a process does not rely on a specific processor as in the separate-kernels organization. The operating system "floats" from one processor to the next.

One drawback of the symmetrical multiprocessor organization is contention for operating system resources, such as shared data structures. Careful design of system data structures is essential to prevent excessive locking that prevents the operating system from executing on multiple processors at once. A technique that minimizes contention is to divide the system data structures into separate and independent entities that can be locked individually.

Even in completely symmetrical multiprocessing systems, adding new processors does not cause system throughput to increase by the new processors' rated capacities. There are many reasons for this, including additional operating system overhead, increased contention for system resources and hardware delays in switching and routing transmissions between an increased number of components. Several performance studies have been performed; one early BBN Butterfly system with 256 processors operated 180 to 230 times faster than a single-processor system.[84]

Self Review

1. Why would doubling the number of processors in a symmetrical organization not double the total processing power?
2. What are some benefits of the symmetrical organization over the master/slave and separate-kernels organizations?

Ans: **1)** Adding processors increases contention for resources and increases operating system overhead, offsetting some of the performance gains attained from adding processors. **2)** The symmetrical organization is more scalable than master/slave because all processors can execute the operating system; this also makes the system more fault tolerant. Symmetrical organization provides better cooperation between processors than separate kernels. This facilitates IPC and enables systems to exploit parallelism better.

15.4 Memory Access Architectures

So far, we have classified multiprocessor systems by hardware characteristics and by how processors share operating system responsibilities. We can also classify multiprocessor systems by how they share memory. For example, consider a system with few processors and a small amount of memory. If the system contains a group of memory modules that is easily accessible by all processors (e.g., via a shared bus), the system can maintain fast memory access. However, systems with many processors and memory modules will saturate the bus that provides access to these memory modules. In this case, a portion of memory can be closely tied to a processor so

Operating Systems Thinking

Graceful Degradation

Things do go wrong. Individual components of systems do fail. Entire systems fail. The question is, "What should a system do after experiencing some degree of failure?" Many systems are designed to degrade gracefully (i.e., continue operating after a failure, but at reduced levels of service). A classic example of graceful degradation occurs in a symmetric multiprocessing system in which any processor can run any process. If one of the processors fails, the system can still function with the remaining processors, but with reduced performance. Graceful degradation occurs in many disk systems that, upon detecting a failed portion of the disk, simply "map around" the failed areas, enabling the user to continue storing and retrieving information on that disk. When a router fails on the Internet, the Internet continues to handle new transmissions by sending them to the remaining functioning routers. Providing for graceful degradation is an important task for operating systems designers, especially as people grow increasingly reliant on hardware devices that eventually fail.

that the processor can access its memory more efficiently. Designers, therefore, must weigh concerns about a system's performance, cost and scalability when determining the system's memory-access architecture. The following sections describe several common memory architectures for multiprocessor systems.

15.4.1 Uniform Memory Access

Uniform-memory-access (UMA) multiprocessor architectures require all processors to share the system's main memory (Fig. 15.9). This is a straightforward extension of a uniprocessor memory architecture, but with multiple processors and memory modules. Typically, each processor maintains its own cache to reduce bus contention and increase performance. Memory-access time is uniform for any processor accessing any data item, except when the data item is stored in a processor's cache or there is contention on the bus. UMA systems are also called **symmetric multiprocessor (SMP)** systems because any processor can be assigned any task and all processors share all resources (including memory, I/O devices and processes). UMA multiprocessors with a small number of processors typically use a shared bus or a crossbar-switch matrix interconnection network. I/O devices are attached directly to the interconnection network and are equally accessible to all processors.[85]

UMA architectures are normally found in small multiprocessor systems (typically two to eight processors). UMA multiprocessors do not scale well—a bus quickly becomes saturated when more than a few processors access main memory simultaneously, and crossbar-switch matrices become expensive even for modest-sized systems.[86, 87]

Self Review

1. Why are mesh networks and hypercubes inappropriate interconnection schemes for UMA systems?
2. How is a UMA system "symmetric?"

Ans: **1)** Mesh networks and hypercubes place processors and memory at each node, so local memory can be accessed faster than remote memory; thus memory-access times are not uni-

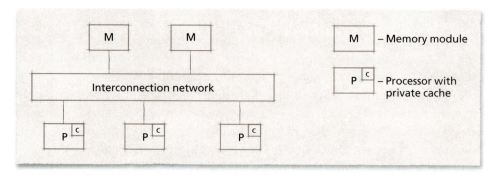

Figure 15.9 | UMA multiprocessor.

form. **2)** It is symmetric because any processor can be assigned any task and all processors share all resources (including memory, I/O devices and processes).

15.4.2 Nonuniform Memory Access

Nonuniform-memory-access (NUMA) multiprocessor architectures address UMA's scalability problems. The primary bottleneck in a large-scale UMA system is access to shared memory—performance degrades due to contention from numerous processors attempting to access shared memory. If a crossbar-switch matrix is used, the interconnection scheme's cost might increase substantially to facilitate multiple paths to shared memory. NUMA multiprocessors handle these problems by relaxing the constraint that memory-access time should be uniform for all processors accessing any data item.

NUMA multiprocessors maintain a global shared memory that is accessible by all processors. The global memory is partitioned into modules, and each node uses one of these memory modules as the processor's local memory. In Fig. 15.10, each node contains one processor, but this is not a requirement. Although the interconnection scheme's implementation might vary, processors are connected directly to their local memory modules and connected indirectly (i.e., through one of the interconnection schemes discussed in Section 15.2.2) to the rest of global memory. This arrangement provides faster access to local memory than to the rest of global memory, because access to global memory requires traversing the interconnection network.

The NUMA architecture is highly scalable because it reduces bus collisions when a processor's local memory services most of the processor's memory requests. A NUMA system can implement a strategy that moves pages to the processor on which those pages are accessed most frequently—a technique called page migration, which is discussed in detail in Section 15.5.2, Page Replication and Migration. Typically, NUMA systems can support a large number of processors, but they are more complex to design than UMAs, and systems with many processors can be expensive to implement.[88, 89]

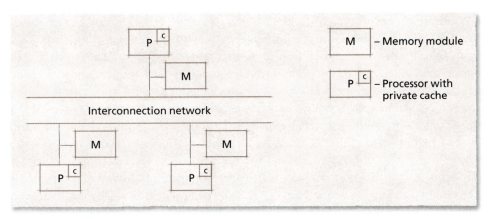

Figure 15.10 | *NUMA multiprocessor.*

Self Review

1. List some advantages of NUMA multiprocessors over UMA. List some disadvantages.
2. What issues does the NUMA design raise for programmers and for operating systems designers?

Ans: **1)** NUMA multiprocessors are more scalable than UMA multiprocessors because NUMA multiprocessors remove the memory-access bottleneck of UMA systems by using large numbers of processors. UMA multiprocessors are more efficient for small systems because there is little memory contention and access to all memory in a UMA system is fast. **2)** If two processes executing on processors at separate nodes use shared memory for IPC, then at least one of the two will not have the memory item in its local memory, which degrades performance. Operating system designers place processes and their associated memory together on the same node. This might require scheduling a process on the same processor each time the process executes. Also, the operating system should be able to move pages to different memory modules based on demand.

15.4.3 Cache-Only Memory Architecture

As described in the previous section, each node in a NUMA system maintains its own local memory, which processors from other nodes can access. Often, local memory access is dramatically faster than global memory access (i.e., access to another node's local memory). **Cache-miss latency**—the time required to retrieve data that is not in the cache—can be significant when the requested data is not present in local memory. One way to reduce cache-miss latency is to reduce the number of memory requests serviced by remote nodes. Recall that NUMA systems place data in the local memory of the processor that accesses the data most frequently. This is impractical for a compiler or programmer to implement, because data access patterns change dynamically. Operating systems can perform this task, but can move only page-size chunks of data, which can slow data migration. Also, different data items on a single page often are accessed by processors at different nodes.[90]

    Cache-Only Memory Architecture (COMA) multiprocessors (also called Cache-Only Memory Access multiprocessors) use a slight variation of NUMA to address this memory placement issue (Fig. 15.11). COMA multiprocessors include one or more processors, each with its associated cache, and a portion of the global shared memory. However, the memory associated with each node is organized as a large cache known as an **attraction memory (AM)**. This allows the hardware to migrate data efficiently at the granularity of a **memory line**—equivalent to a cache line, but in main memory, and typically four or eight bytes.[91] Also, because each processor's local memory is viewed as a cache, different AMs can have copies of the same memory line. With these design modifications, data often resides in the local memory of the processor that uses the data most frequently, which reduces the average cache-miss latency. The trade-offs are memory overhead from duplicating data items in multiple memory modules, and complicated hardware and protocols to ensure that memory updates are reflected in each processor's AM. This overhead results in higher latency for those cache misses that are serviced remotely.[92]

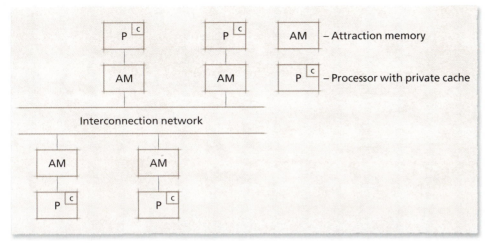

Figure 15.11 | *COMA multiprocessor.*

Self Review

1. What problems inherent in NUMA multiprocessors does the COMA design address?
2. (T/F) The COMA design always increases performance over a NUMA design.

Ans: **1)** Cache misses serviced at remote nodes in both NUMA and COMA systems typically require much more time than cache misses serviced by local memory. Unlike NUMA systems, COMA multiprocessors use hardware to move copies of data items to a processor's local memory (the AM) when referenced. **2)** False. COMA multiprocessors reduce the *number* of cache misses serviced remotely, but they also add overhead. In particular, cache-miss latency increases for cache misses that are serviced remotely, and synchronization is required for data that is copied into several processors' attraction memory.

15.4.4 No Remote Memory Access

UMA, NUMA and COMA multiprocessors are tightly coupled. Although NUMA (and COMA to a lesser extent) multiprocessors scale well, they require complex software and hardware. The software controls access to shared resources such as memory; the hardware implements the interconnection scheme. **NO-Remote-Memory-Access (NORMA) multiprocessors** are loosely coupled multiprocessors that do not provide any shared global memory (Fig. 15.12). Each node maintains its own local memory, and often, NORMA multiprocessors implement a common **shared virtual memory (SVM)**. On an SVM system, when a process requests a page that is not in its processor's local memory, the operating system loads the page into local memory from another memory module (i.e., from a remote computer over a network) or from secondary storage (e.g., a disk).[93, 94] Nodes in NORMA systems that do not support SVM must share data through explicit message passing. Google, which powers its service using 15,000 low-end servers located across the world, is an example of a distributed NORMA multiprocessor system.[95]

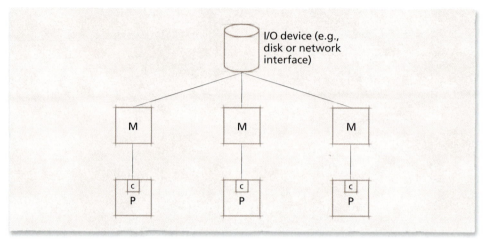

Figure 15.12 | *NORMA multiprocessor.*

NORMA systems are the simplest to build, because they do not require a complex interconnection scheme. However, the absence of shared global memory requires application programmers to implement IPC via message passing and remote procedure calls. On many systems, using shared virtual memory is inefficient, because the system would have to send entire data pages from one processor to the next, and these processors often are not in the same physical machine.[96] We discuss SVM in more detail in Section 15.5.3, Shared Virtual Memory.

Because NORMA multiprocessors are loosely coupled, it is relatively easy to remove or add nodes. NORMA multiprocessors are distributed systems governed by a single operating system, rather than networked computers each with its own operating system. If a node in a NORMA system fails, a user can simply switch to another node and continue working. If one percent of the nodes fails in a NORMA multiprocessor, the system merely runs one percent slower.[97]

Self Review

1. Why are NORMA multiprocessors ideal for workstation clusters?
2. In what environments are NORMA multiprocessors not useful?

Ans: **1)** Different users in a workstation cluster usually do not share memory. However, they share resources such as a file system and processing power, which NORMA systems provide. Also, it is relatively easy to add or remove nodes in NORMA multiprocessors, which can be useful for scaling the system's processing capabilities. **2)** NORMA multiprocessors are not useful in shared-memory environments, especially systems with a single user or a few processors. These can be implemented more efficiently with UMA or NUMA designs.

15.5 Multiprocessor Memory Sharing

When multiple processors with private caches or local memories access shared memory, designers must address the problem of **memory coherence**. Memory is coherent if the value obtained from reading a memory address is always the value that was most recently written to that address.[98] For example, consider two processors that maintain a separate copy of the same page in their local memories. If one processor modifies its local copy, the system should ensure that the other copy of the page is updated to reflect the latest changes. Multiprocessors that allow only one copy of a page to be resident in the system at a time (such as UMA and small NUMA systems) must still ensure **cache coherence**—reading a cache entry reflects the most recent update to that data. Large-scale systems (such as NORMA or large-scale NUMA systems) often permit the same memory page to be resident in the local memory of several processors. These systems must integrate memory coherence into their implementation of shared virtual memory.

Other important design considerations are page placement and replication. Local memory access is much faster than global memory access, so ensuring that data accessed by a processor resides in that processor's local memory can improve performance. There are two common strategies for addressing this issue. **Page replication** maintains multiple copies of a memory page, so that the page can be accessed quickly at multiple nodes (see the Operating Systems Thinking feature, Data Replication and Coherency). **Page migration** transfers pages to the node (or nodes, when used with page replication) where processors access a page most. In Section 15.5.2, Page Replication and Migration, we consider implementations of these two strategies.

Self Review

1. Why is memory coherence important?
2. What are the advantages of allowing multiple copies of the same page to exist in one system?

Operating Systems Thinking

Data Replication and Coherency

We will see several examples of data being duplicated for various reasons in operating systems. Sometimes this is done for backup to ensure recoverability if one copy of the data is lost. It is also done for performance where some copies of the data may be accessed faster than others. Often, it is crucial to ensure coherency, (i.e., that all copies of the data either are identical or will be made so before any differences could cause a problem).

Ans: **1)** Without memory coherence, there is no guarantee that a particular copy of data is the most up-to-date version. Data must be coherent to ensure that applications produce correct results. **2)** If two processes executing on different processors repeatedly read the same memory page, replicating the page allows both processors to keep the page in local memory so that it can be accessed quickly.

15.5.1 Cache Coherence

Memory coherence became a design consideration when caches appeared, because computer architectures allowed different access paths to data (i.e., through the cache copy or the main memory copy). In multiprocessor systems, coherence is complicated by the fact that each processor maintains a private cache.

UMA Cache Coherence

Implementing cache coherence protocols for UMA multiprocessors is simple because caches are relatively small and the bus connecting shared memory is relatively fast. When a processor updates a data item, the system must also update or discard all instances of that data in other processors' caches and in main memory.[99] This can be accomplished by **bus snooping** (also called **cache snooping**). In this protocol, a processor "snoops" the bus by determining whether a requested write from another processor is for a data item in the processor's cache. If the data resides in the processor's cache, the processor removes the data item from its cache. Bus snooping is simple to implement, but generates additional traffic on the shared bus. Alternatively, the system can maintain a centralized directory that records the items that reside in each cache and indicates when to remove stale data (i.e., data that does not reflect the most recent update) from a cache. Another option is for the system to allow only one processor to cache a particular memory item.[100]

Cache-Coherent NUMA (CC-NUMA)

Cache-coherent NUMAs (CC-NUMAs) are NUMA multiprocessors that impose cache coherence. In a typical CC-NUMA architecture, each physical memory address is associated with a **home node**, which is responsible for storing the data item with that main-memory address. (Often, the home node is simply determined by the higher-order bits in the address.) When a cache miss occurs at a node, that node contacts the home node associated with the requested memory address. If the data item is clean (i.e., no other node has a modified version of the data item in its cache), the home node forwards it to the requesting processor's cache. If the data item is dirty (i.e., another node has written to the data item since the last time the main memory entry was updated), the home node forwards the request to the node with the dirty copy; this node sends the data item to both the requestor and the home node. Similarly, requests to modify data are performed via the home node. The node that wishes to modify data at a particular memory address requests exclusive ownership of the data. The most recent version of the data (if not already in the modifying node's cache) is obtained in the same manner as a read request. After the modification, the home node notifies other nodes with copies of the data that the data was modified.[101]

This protocol is relatively simple to implement, because all reads and writes first contact the home node. Although this might seem inefficient, this coherence protocol requires a maximum of only three network communications. (Consider how much traffic would be generated if a writing node had to contact all other nodes.) This protocol also makes it easy to distribute the load throughout the system—by assigning each node as the home node for approximately the same number of addresses—which increases fault tolerance and reduces contention. However, this protocol can perform poorly if most data accesses come from remote nodes.

Self Review

1. What are the advantages and disadvantages of bus snooping?
2. Why is it difficult for the system to establish a home node for memory that is referenced by several different nodes over time? How can the CC-NUMA home-based protocol be modified to support such behavior?

Ans: **1)** Bus snooping is easy to implement and it enables cache coherence. However, it generates additional bus traffic. **2)** If memory-access patterns for a memory region change frequently, then it is difficult to decide which node should be the home node for that region. Although one node might make the majority of the references to that item now, this will soon change and most of the references will come from a remote node. A remedy would be to dynamically change the home node of a data item (this, of course, would imply changing the item's physical memory address).

15.5.2 Page Replication and Migration

NUMA systems have higher memory-access latency than UMA multiprocessors, which limits NUMA's performance. Therefore, maximizing the number of cache misses serviced by local memory is an important NUMA design consideration.[102] The COMA design, described in Section 15.4.3, is one attempt to address the NUMA latency issue. CC-NUMA systems address the latency issue by implementing page-migration or page-replication strategies.[103]

Replicating a page is straightforward. The system copies all data from a remote page to a page in the requesting processor's local memory. To maintain memory coherence, the system uses a data structure that records where all duplicate pages exist. We discuss different strategies for memory coherence in the next section. Page migration occurs in a similar fashion, except that after a page has been replicated, the original node deletes the page from its memory and flushes any associated TLB or cache entries.[104]

Although migrating and replicating pages has obvious benefits, these strategies can degrade performance if they are not implemented correctly. For example, remotely referencing a page is faster than migrating or replicating that page. Therefore, if a process references a remote page only once, it would be more efficient not to migrate or replicate the page.[105] In addition, some pages are better candidates for replication than for migration, and vice versa. For example, pages that are read frequently by processes at different processors would benefit from replication, by enabling all processes to access that page from local memory. Also, the drawback of replication—maintaining coherency on writes—would not be a problem for a read-only page. A page frequently modified by one process is a good candidate for migration; if other processes are reading from that page, replicating the page would not be viable because these processes would have to fetch updates continually from the writing node. Pages that are frequently written by processes at more than one processor are not good candidates for either replication or migration, because they would be migrated or replicated after each write operation.[106]

To help determine the best strategy, many systems maintain each page's access history information. A system might use this information to determine which pages are frequently accessed—these should be considered for replication or migration. The overhead of replicating or migrating a page is not justified for pages that are not frequently accessed. A system also might maintain information on which remote processors are accessing the page and whether these processors are reading from, or writing to, the page. The more page-access information the system gathers, the better decision the system can make. However, gathering this history and transferring it during migration incurs overhead. Thus, the system must collect enough information to make good replication or migration decisions without incurring excessive overhead from maintaining this information.[107]

Self Review

1. How could an ineffective migration/replication strategy degrade performance?
2. For what types of pages is replication appropriate? When is migration appropriate?

Ans: **1)** Migration and replication are more costly than remotely referencing a page. They are beneficial only if the page will be referenced remotely multiple times from the same node. An ineffective strategy might migrate or replicate pages that are, for example, modified by many nodes, requiring frequent updates and thus reducing performance. Also, manipulating pages' access history information imposes additional overhead that can degrade performance.
2) Pages that are read frequently by multiple processors (but not modified) should be replicated. Pages that are written by only one remote node should be migrated to that node.

15.5.3 Shared Virtual Memory

Sharing memory on small, tightly coupled multiprocessors, such as UMA multiprocessors, is a straightforward extension of uniprocessor shared memory because all processors access the same physical addresses with equal access latency. This strategy is impractical for large-scale NUMA multiprocessors due to remote-memory-access latency, and it is impossible for NORMA multiprocessors, which do not share physical memory. Because IPC through shared memory is easier to program than IPC via message passing, many systems enable processes to share memory located on different nodes (and perhaps in different physical address spaces) through shared virtual memory (SVM). SVM extends uniprocessor virtual memory concepts by ensuring memory coherence for pages accessed by various processors.[108]

Two issues facing SVM designers are selecting which coherence protocol to use and when to apply it. The two primary coherence protocols are invalidation and write broadcast. First we describe these protocols, then we consider how to implement them.

Invalidation

In the **invalidation** memory-coherence approach, only one processor may access a page while it is being modified—this is called page ownership. To obtain page ownership, a processor must first invalidate (deny access to) all other copies of the page. After the processor obtains ownership, the page's access mode is changed to read/write, and the processor copies the page into its local memory before accessing it. To obtain read access to a page, a processor must request that the processor with read/write access change its access mode to read-only access. If the request is granted, other processors can copy the page into local memory and read it. Typically, systems employ the policy of always granting requests unless a processor is waiting to acquire page ownership; in the case that a request is denied, the requestor must wait until the page is available. Note that multiple processes modifying a single page concurrently leads to poor performance, because competing processors repeatedly invalidate the other processors' copies of the page.[109]

Write Broadcast

In the **write broadcast** memory-coherence approach, the writing processor broadcasts each modification to the entire system. In one version of this technique, only one processor may obtain write ownership of a page. Rather than invalidating all other existing copies of the page, the processor updates all copies.[110] In a second version, several processors are granted write access to increase efficiency. Because this scheme does not require writers to obtain write ownership, processors must ensure that various updates to a page are applied in the correct order, which can incur significant overhead.[111]

Implementing Coherence Protocols

There are several ways to implement a memory-coherence protocol, though designers must attempt to limit memory-access bus traffic. Ensuring that every write is reflected at all nodes as soon as possible can decrease performance; however, weakening coherence constraints can produce erroneous results if programs use stale data. In general, an implementation must balance performance and data integrity.

Systems that use **sequential consistency** ensure that all writes are immediately reflected in all copies of a page. This scheme does not scale well to large systems due to communication cost and page size. Internode communication is slow compared to accessing local memory; if a process repeatedly updates the same page, many wasteful communications will result. Also, because the operating system manipulates pages, which often contain many data items, this strategy might result in **false sharing**, where processes executing at separate nodes might need access to unrelated data on the same page. In this case, sequential consistency effectively requires the two processes to share the page, even though their modifications do not affect one another.[112]

Systems that use **relaxed consistency** perform coherence operations periodically. The premise behind this strategy is that delaying coherence for remote data by a few seconds is not noticeable to the user and can increase performance and reduce the false sharing effect.[113]

In **release consistency**, a series of accesses begin with an **acquire operation** and end with a **release operation**. All updates between the acquire and the release are batched as one update message after the release.[114] In **lazy release consistency**, the update is delayed until the next acquire attempt for the modified memory. This reduces network traffic, because it eliminates coherence operations for pages that are not accessed again.[115]

One interesting consequence of lazy release consistency is that only a node that attempts to access a modified page receives the modification. If this node also modifies the page, a third node would need to apply two updates before it can access the page. This can lead to substantial page-update overhead. One way to reduce this problem is to provide periodic global synchronization points at which all data must be consistent.[116] An alternative way to reduce this problem is to use a **home-based consistency** approach similar to that used for cache coherence in a CC-NUMA. The home node for each page is responsible for keeping an updated version of the page. Nodes that issue an acquire to a page that has been updated since that its last release must obtain the update from the home node.[117]

The **delayed consistency** approach sends update information when a release occurs, but nodes receiving updates do not apply them until the next acquisition. These updates can be collected until a new acquire attempt, at which point the node applies all update information. This does not reduce network traffic, but it improves performance because nodes do not have to perform coherence operations as frequently.[118]

Lazy data propagation notifies other nodes that a page has been modified at release time. This notification does not supply the modified data, which can reduce bus traffic. Before a node acquires data for modification, it determines if that data has been modified by another node, If so, the former node retrieves update information from the latter. Lazy data propagation has the same benefits and drawbacks as lazy release consistency. This strategy significantly reduces communication traffic, but requires a mechanism to control the size of update histories, such as a global synchronization point.[119]

Self Review

1. What is a benefit of relaxed consistency? A drawback?
2. In many relaxed consistency implementations, data may not be coherent for several seconds. Is this is a problem in all environments? Give an example where it might be a problem.

Ans: **1)** Relaxed consistency reduces network traffic and increases performance. However, the system's memory can be incoherent for a significant period of time, which increases the likelihood that processors will operate on stale data. **2)** This is not a problem in all environments, considering that even sequential consistency schemes may use networks exhibiting latencies of a second or two. However, latency of this magnitude is not desirable for a supercomputer in which many processes interact and communicate through shared memory. The extra latency degrades performance due to frequent invalidations.

15.6 *Multiprocessor Scheduling*

Multiprocessor scheduling has goals similar to those of uniprocessor scheduling—the system attempts to maximize throughput and minimize response time for all processes. Further, the system must enforce scheduling priority.

Unlike uniprocessor scheduling algorithms which only determine in what order processes are dispatched, multiprocessor scheduling algorithms also must determine to which processor they are dispatched, which increases scheduling complexity. For example, multiprocessor scheduling algorithms should ensure that processors are not idle while processes are waiting to execute.

When determining the processor on which a process is executed, the scheduler considers several factors. For example, some strategies focus on maximizing parallelism in a system to exploit application concurrency. Systems often group collaborating processes into a job. Executing a job's processes in parallel improves performance by enabling these processes to execute truly simultaneously. This section introduces several **timesharing scheduling** algorithms that attempt to exploit such parallelism by scheduling collaborative processes on different processors.[120] This enables the processes to synchronize their concurrent execution more effectively.

Other strategies focus on **processor affinity**—the relationship of a process to a particular processor and its local memory and cache. A process that exhibits high processor affinity executes on the same processor through most or all of its life cycle. The advantage is that the process will experience more cache hits and, in the case of a NUMA or NORMA design, possibly fewer remote page accesses than if it were to execute on several processors throughout its life cycle. Scheduling algorithms that attempt to schedule a process on the same processor throughout its life cycle maintain **soft affinity**, whereas algorithms that schedule a process on only one processor maintain **hard affinity**.[121]

Space-partitioning scheduling algorithms attempt to maximize processor affinity by scheduling collaborative processes on a single processor (or single set of processors) under the assumption that collaborative processes will access the same shared data, which is likely stored in the processor's caches and local memory.[122] Therefore, space-partitioning scheduling increases cache and local memory hits. However, it can limit throughput, because these processes typically do not execute simultaneously.[123]

Multiprocessor scheduling algorithms are generally classified as job blind or job aware. **Job-blind scheduling** policies incur minimal scheduling overhead, because they do not attempt to enhance a job's parallelism or processor affinity. **Job-aware scheduling** evaluates each job's properties and attempts to maximize each job's parallelism or processor affinity, which increases performance at the cost of increased overhead.

Many multiprocessor scheduling algorithms organize processes in **global run queues**.[124] Each global run queue contains all the processes in the system that are ready to execute. Global run queues might be used to organize processes by priority, by job or by which process executed most recently.[125]

Alternatively, systems might use a **per-processor run queue**. This is typical of large, loosely coupled systems (such as NORMA systems) in which cache hits and references to local memory should be maximized. In this case, processes are associated with a specific processor and the system implements a scheduling policy for that processor. Some systems use **per-node run queues**; each node might contain more than one processor. This is appropriate for a system in which a process is tied to a particular group of processors. We describe the related issue of process migration, which entails moving processes from one per-processor or per-node run queue to another, in Section 15.7, Process Migration.

Self Review

1. What types of processes benefit from timesharing scheduling? From space-partitioning scheduling?
2. When are per-node run queues more appropriate than global run queues?

Ans: **1)** Timesharing scheduling executes related processes simultaneously, improving performance for processes that interact frequently because processes can react to messages or modifications to shared memory immediately. Space-partitioning scheduling is more appropriate for processes that must sequentialize access to shared memory (and other resources) because their processors are likely to have cached shared data, which improves performance. **2)** Per-node run queues are more appropriate than global run queues in loosely coupled systems, where processes execute much less efficiently when accessing remote memory.

15.6.1 Job-Blind Multiprocessor Scheduling

Job-blind multiprocessor scheduling algorithms schedule jobs or processes on any available processor. The three algorithms described in this section are examples of job-blind multiprocessor scheduling algorithms. In general, any uniprocessor scheduling algorithm, such as those described in Chapter 8, can be implemented as a job-blind scheduling multiprocessor algorithm.

First-Come-First-Served (FCFS) Process Scheduling

First-come-first-served (FCFS) process scheduling places arriving processes in a global run queue. When a processor becomes available, the scheduler dispatches the process at the head of the queue and runs it until the process relinquishes the processor.

FCFS treats all processes fairly by scheduling them according to their arrival times. However, FCFS might be considered unfair because long processes make short processes wait, and low-priority processes can make high-priority processes wait—although a preemptive version of FCFS can prevent the latter from occurring. Typically, FCFS scheduling is not useful for interactive processes, because FCFS cannot guarantee short response times. However, FCFS is easy to implement and eliminates the possibility of indefinite postponement—once a process enters the queue, no other process will enter the queue ahead of it.[126, 127]

Round-Robin Process (RRprocess) Multiprocessor Scheduling

Round-robin process (RRprocess) scheduling places each *ready* process in a global run queue. RRprocess scheduling is similar to uniprocessor round-robin scheduling—a process executes for at most one quantum before the scheduler dispatches a new process for execution. The previously executing process is placed at the end of the global run queue. This algorithm prevents indefinite postponement, but does not facilitate a high degree of parallelism or processor affinity because it ignores relationships among processes.[128, 129]

Shortest-Process-First (SPF) Multiprocessor Scheduling

A system can also implement the **shortest-process-first (SPF)** scheduling algorithm, which dispatches the process that requires the least amount of time to run to completion.[130] Both preemptive and nonpreemptive versions of SPF exhibit lower average waiting times for interactive processes than FCFS does, because interactive processes typically are "short" processes. However, a longer process can be indefinitely postponed if shorter processes continually arrive before it can obtain a processor. As with all job-blind algorithms, SPF does not consider parallelism or processor affinity.

Self Review

1. Is a UMA or a NUMA system more suitable for job-blind multiprocessor scheduling?
2. Which job-blind scheduling strategy discussed in this section is most appropriate for batch processing systems and why?

Ans: **1)** A UMA system is more appropriate for a job-blind algorithm. NUMA systems often benefit from scheduling algorithms that consider processor affinity, because memory access time depends on the node at which a process executes, and nodes in a NUMA system have their own local memory. **2)** SPF is most appropriate because it exhibits high throughput, an important goal for batch-processing systems.

15.6.2 Job-Aware Multiprocessor Scheduling

Although job-blind algorithms are easy to implement and incur minimal overhead, they do not consider performance issues specific to multiprocessor scheduling. For example, if two processes that communicate frequently do not execute simultaneously, they might spend a significant amount of their time busy waiting, which degrades overall system performance. Furthermore, in most multiprocessor systems, each processor maintains its own private cache. Processes in the same job often access the same memory items, so scheduling one job's processes on the same processor tends to increase cache hits and improves memory-access performance. In general, job-aware process-scheduling algorithms attempt to maximize parallelism or processor affinity, at the cost of greater scheduling algorithm complexity.

Smallest-Number-of-Processes-First (SNPF) Scheduling

The **smallest-number-of-processes-first (SNPF)** scheduling algorithm, which can be either preemptive or nonpreemptive, uses a global job priority queue. A job's priority is inversely proportional to the number of processes in the job. If jobs containing the same number of processes compete for a processor, the job that has waited the longest receives priority. In nonpreemptive SNPF scheduling, when a processor becomes available, the scheduler selects a process from the job at the head of the queue and allows it to execute to completion. In preemptive SNPF scheduling, if a new job arrives with fewer processes, it receives priority and its processes are dispatched immediately.[131, 132] SNPF algorithms improve parallelism, because processes that are associated with the same job can often execute concurrently. However, the SNPF algorithms do not attempt to improve processor affinity. Further, it is possible for jobs with many processes to be postponed indefinitely.

Round-Robin Job (RRJob) Scheduling

Round-robin job (RRJob) scheduling employs a global job queue from which each job is assigned to a group of processors (although not necessarily the same group each time the job is scheduled). Every job maintains its own process queue. If the system contains p processors and uses a quantum of length q, then a job receives a total of $p \times q$ of processor time when dispatched. Typically, a job does not contain exactly p processes that each exhaust one quantum (e.g., a process may block before its quantum expires). Therefore, RRJob uses round-robin scheduling to dispatch the job's processes until the job consumes the entire $p \times q$ quanta, the job completes or all of the job's processes block. The algorithm also can divide the $p \times q$ quanta equally among the processes in the job, allowing each to execute until it exhausts its quantum, completes or blocks. Alternatively, if a job has more than p processes, it can select p processes to execute for a quantum length of q.[133]

Similar to RRprocess scheduling, this algorithm prevents indefinite postponement. Further, because processes from the same job execute concurrently, this algorithm promotes parallelism. However, the additional context-switching overhead of round-robin scheduling can reduce job throughput.[134, 135]

Coscheduling

Coscheduling (or **gang scheduling**) algorithms employ a global run queue that is accessed in round-robin fashion. The goal of coscheduling algorithms is to execute processes from the same job concurrently rather than maximize processor affinity.[136] There are several coscheduling implementations—matrix, continuous and undivided. We present only the undivided algorithm, because it corrects some of the deficiencies of the matrix and continuous algorithms.

The **undivided coscheduling algorithm** places processes from the same job in adjacent entries in the global run queue (Fig. 15.13). The scheduler maintains a "window" equal to the number of processors in the system. All processes within a window execute in parallel for at most one quantum. After scheduling a group of processes, the window moves to the next group of processes, which also execute in parallel for one quantum. To maximize processor utilization, if a process in the window is suspended, the algorithm extends the sliding window one process to the right to allow another runnable process to run for the given quantum, even if it is not part of a job that is currently executing.

Because coscheduling algorithms use a round-robin strategy, they prevent indefinite postponement. Furthermore, because processes from the same job often run at the same time, coscheduling algorithms allow programs that are designed to run in parallel to take advantage of a multiprocessing environment. Unfortunately, the processor on which a process might be dispatched to a different processor each time, which can reduce processor affinity.[137]

Dynamic Partitioning

Dynamic partitioning minimizes the performance penalty associated with cache misses by maintaining high processor affinity.[138] The scheduler evenly distributes processors in the system among jobs. The number of processors allocated to a job is always less than or equal to the job's number of runnable processes.

For example, consider a system that contains 32 processors and executes three jobs—the first with eight runnable processes, the second with 16 and the third with 20. If the scheduler were to divide the processors evenly between jobs, one job would receive 10 processors and the other two jobs 11. In this case, the first job has only eight processes, so the scheduler assigns eight processors to that job and evenly distributes the remaining 24 processors (12 each) to the second and third jobs (Example 1 in Fig. 15.14). Therefore, a particular job always executes on a certain

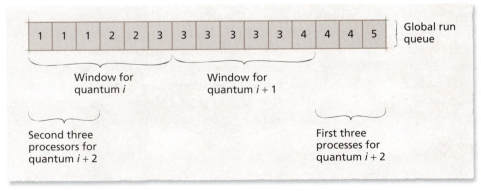

Figure 15.13 | *Coscheduling (undivided version).*

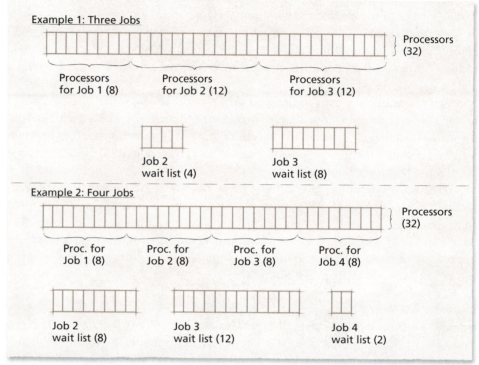

Figure 15.14 | *Dynamic partitioning.*

subset of processors as long as no new jobs enter the system. The algorithm can be extended so that a particular process always executes on the same processor. If every job contains only one process, dynamic partitioning reduces to a round-robin scheduling algorithm.[139]

As new jobs enter the system, the system dynamically updates the processor allocation. Suppose a fourth job containing 10 runnable processes (Example 2 in Fig. 15.14) enters the system. The first job retains its allocation of eight processors, but the second and third jobs each relinquish four processors to the fourth job. Thus, the processors are evenly distributed among the jobs—eight processors per job.[140] The algorithm updates the number of processors each job receives whenever jobs enter or exit the system, or a process within a job changes state from *running* to *waiting* or vice versa. Although the number of processors allocated to jobs changes, a job still executes on either a subset or superset of its previous allocation, which helps maintain processor affinity.[141] For dynamic partitioning to be effective, the performance increase from cache affinity must outweigh the cost of repartitioning.[142]

Self Review

1. How are RRJob and undivided coscheduling similar? How are they different?
2. Describe some of the trade-offs between implementing a global scheduling policy that maximizes processor affinity, such as dynamic partitioning, and per-processor run queues.

Ans: **1)** RRJob and undivided coscheduling are similar in that both schedule processes of a job to execute concurrently in round-robin fashion. Undivided coscheduling simply places processes of the same job next to each other in the global run queue where they wait for the next available processor. RRJob schedules only entire jobs. **2)** Global scheduling is more flexible because it reassigns processes to different processors depending on system load. However, per-processor run queues are simpler to implement and can be more efficient than maintaining global run queue information.

15.7 Process Migration

Process migration entails transferring a process between two processors.[143, 144] This might occur if, for example, a processor fails or is overloaded.

The ability to execute a process on any processor has many advantages. The most obvious is that processes can move to processors that are underutilized to reduce process response times and increase performance and throughput.[145, 146] (We describe this technique, called load balancing, in more detail in Section 15.8, Load Balancing.) Process migration also promotes fault tolerance.[147] For example, consider a program that must perform intensive, uninterrupted computation. If the machine running the program needs to be shut down or becomes unstable, the program's progress might be lost. Process migration allows the program to move to another machine to continue computation perhaps in a more stable environment.

In addition, process migration promotes resource sharing. In large-scale systems, some resources might not be replicated at every node. For example, in a NORMA system, processes might execute on machines with different hardware device support. A process might require access to a RAID array that is available through only one computer. In this case, the process should migrate to the computer with access to the RAID array for better performance.

Finally, process migration improves communication performance. Two processes that communicate frequently should execute on or near the same node to reduce communication latency. Because communication links are often dynamic, process migration can be used to make process placement dynamic.[148]

Self Review

1. What are some benefits provided by process migration?
2. On which types of systems (UMA, NUMA or NORMA) is process migration most appropriate?

Ans: **1)** Process migration promotes fault tolerance by moving processes away from malfunctioning nodes, supports load balancing, can reduce communication latency and promotes resource sharing. **2)** Process migration is appropriate for large-scale NUMA or NORMA systems that use per-processor (or per-node) run queues. Process migration enables these systems to perform load balancing and share resources local to each node.

15.7.1 Flow of Process Migration

Although process migration implementations vary across architectures, many implementations follow the same general steps (Fig. 15.15). First, a node issues a

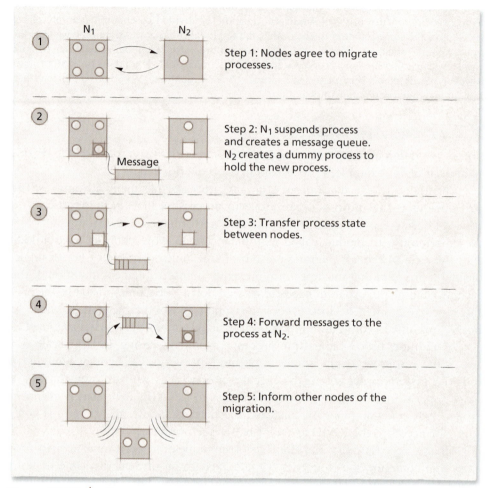

Figure 15.15 | Process migration.

migration request to a remote node. In most schemes, the sender initiates the migration because its node is overloaded or a specific process needs to access a resource located at a remote node. In some schemes, an underutilized node might request processes from other nodes. If the sender and receiver agree to migrate a process, the sender suspends the migrating process. The sender creates a message queue to hold all messages destined for the migrating process. Then, the sender extracts the process's state; this includes copying the process's memory contents (i.e., pages marked as valid in the process's virtual memory), register contents, state of open files and other process-specific information. The sender transmits the extracted state to a "dummy" process that the receiver creates. The two nodes notify all other processes of the migrated process's new location. Finally, the receiver dispatches the new instance of the process, the sender forwards the messages in the migrated process's message queue and the sender destroys the local instance of the process.[149, 150]

Self Review

1. List some items that compose a process's state and that must be migrated with a process.
2. What overhead is incurred in process migration?

Ans: **1)** The sending process must transfer such items as the process's memory contents, register contents and state of open files. **2)** The overhead includes migrating the process and its state, rerouting messages to the receiving node, maintaining two instances of the process for a short time (the old instance and the "dummy process"), suspending the process for a short time and sending messages to other nodes to inform them about the migrated process's new location.

15.7.2 Process Migration Concepts

Memory transfer is the most time-consuming element of migration.[151] To minimize the process migration's performance cost, **residual dependency**—a process's dependency on its former node—must be minimized. For example, the process's former node might contain part of the process's working set or might be executing other processes with which the migrated one was communicating. If migration results in many residual dependencies, a receiving node must communicate with the sending node while executing the migrated process. This increases IPC, which generates more traffic on the interconnection network and degrades performance due to high latencies. Also, residual dependencies decrease fault tolerance, because the migrated process's execution depends on both nodes functioning correctly.[152]

Often, the strategies that result in the highest degree of residual dependency transfer pages from the sender only when the process at the receiving node references them. These **lazy** (or **on-demand**) **migration** strategies reduce the initial process migration time—the duration for which the migrating process is suspended. In lazy migration, the process's state (and other required) information is transferred to the receiver, but the original node retains the process's pages. As the process executes on the remote node, it must initiate a memory transfer for each access to a page that remains at the sending node. Although this technique yields fast initial process migration, memory access can severely decrease an application's performance. Lazy migration is most useful when the process does not require frequent access to the remote address space.[153, 154]

For successful migration, processes should exhibit several characteristics. A migrated process should exhibit transparency—i.e., it should not be adversely affected (except, perhaps, for a slight delay in response time) by migration. In other words, the process should lose no interprocess messages or open file handles.[155] A system also must be scalable—if process's residual dependencies grow with each migration, then a system could quickly be overwhelmed by network traffic as processes request remote pages. Finally, advances in communication technology across multiple architectures have created the need for heterogeneous process migrations—processes should be able to migrate between two different processor architectures in distributed systems. This implies that process state should be stored in a platform-independent format.[156] Section 17.3.6, Process Migration in Distributed Systems, discusses heterogeneous process migration architectures in more detail.

Self Review

1. Why is residual dependency undesirable? Why might some residual dependency be beneficial?
2. How might a migration strategy that results in significant residual dependency not be scalable?

Ans: **1)** Residual dependency is undesirable because it decreases fault tolerance and degrades performance after the transfer. One reason for allowing residual dependency is that it reduces initial transfer time. **2)** If a process that already has a residual dependency migrates again, it will now rely on three nodes. With each migration, the process's state grows (so it can find its memory pages) and its fault tolerance decreases.

15.7.3 Process Migration Strategies

Process migration strategies must balance the performance penalty of transferring large amounts of process data with the benefit of minimizing a process's residual dependency. In some systems, designers assume that most of a migrated process's address space will be accessed at its new node. These systems often implement **eager migration**, which transfers all of a process's pages during initial process migration. This enables the process to execute as efficiently at its new node as it did at its previous one. However, if the process does not access most of its address space, the initial latency and the bandwidth required by eager migration are largely overhead.[157, 158]

To mitigate eager migration's initial cost, **dirty eager migration** transfers only a process's dirty pages. This strategy assumes that there is common secondary storage (e.g., a disk to which both nodes have access). All clean pages are brought in from the common secondary storage as the process references them from the remote node. This reduces initial transfer time and eliminates residual dependency. However, each access to a nonresident page takes longer than it would have using eager migration.[159]

One disadvantage of dirty eager migration is that the migrated process must use secondary storage to retrieve the process's clean pages. **Copy-on-reference migration** is similar to dirty eager migration, except that the migrated process can request clean pages from either its previous node or the common secondary storage. This strategy has the same benefits as dirty eager migration but gives the memory manager more control over the location from which to request pages—access to remote memory may be faster than disk access. However, copy-on-reference migration can add memory overhead at the sender.[160, 161]

The **lazy copying** implementation of copy-on-reference transfers only the minimum state information at initial migration time; often, no pages are transferred. This creates a large residual dependency, forces the previous node to keep pages in memory for the migrated process and increases memory-access latency over strategies that migrate dirty pages. However, the lazy copying strategy eliminates most initial migration latency.[162, 163] Such latency might be unacceptable for real-time processes and is inappropriate for most processes.[164]

All the strategies discussed so far either create residual dependency or incur a large initial migration latency. A method that eliminates most of the initial migration latency and residual dependency is the **flushing** strategy. In this strategy, the sender writes all pages of memory to shared secondary storage when migration begins; the migrating process must be suspended while the data is being written to secondary storage. The process then accesses the pages from secondary storage as needed. Therefore, no actual page migration occurs to slow initial migration, and the process has no residual dependency on the previous node. However, the flushing strategy reduces process performance at its new node, because the process has no pages in main memory, leading to page faults.[165, 166]

Another strategy for eliminating most of the initial migration latency and residual dependency is the **precopy** method, in which the sender node begins transferring dirty pages before the original process is suspended. Any transferred page that the process modifies before it migrates is marked for retransmission. To ensure that a process eventually migrates, the system defines a lower threshold for the number of dirty pages that should remain before the process migrates. When that threshold is reached, the process is suspended and migrated to another processor. With this technique, the process does not need to be suspended for long (compared to other techniques such as eager and copy-on-reference), and memory access at the new node is fast because most data has already been copied. Also, residual dependency is minimal. The process's working set is duplicated for a short time (it exists at both nodes involved in migration), but this a minor drawback.[167, 168]

Self Review

1. Which migration strategies should be used with real-time processes?
2. Although initial migration time is minimal and there is little residual dependency for the precopy strategy, can you think of any "hidden" performance costs this strategy incurs?

Ans: **1)** Real-time processes cannot be suspended for long because this would slow response time. Therefore, strategies such as lazy copying, flushing, copy-on-reference and precopy are best for soft real-time processes. However, hard real-time processes should not be migrated because migration always introduces some indeterministic delay. **2)** The process must continue executing on the sender node while its state is being copied to the receiving node. Because a migration decision was made, it is reasonable to assume that executing on the sending node is no longer desirable and therefore, precopy includes this additional cost.

15.8 Load Balancing

One measure of efficiency in a multiprocessor system is overall processor utilization. In most cases, if processor utilization is high, the system is performing more efficiently. Most multiprocessor systems (especially NUMA and NORMA systems) attempt to maximize processor affinity. This increases efficiency, because the processes do not need to access remote resources as often, but it might reduce processor utilization if all the processes assigned to a particular processor complete. This processor will idle while processes are dispatched to other processors to exploit affinity. **Load balancing** is a technique in which the system attempts to distribute processing loads evenly among processors. This increases processor utilization and shortens run queues for overloaded processors, reducing average process response times.[169]

A load balancing algorithm might assign a fixed number of processors to a job when the job is first scheduled. This is called **static load balancing**. This method yields low runtime overhead, because processors spend little time determining the processors on which a job should execute. However, static load balancing does not account for varying process populations within a job. For example, a job might include many processes initially, but maintain only a few processes throughout the rest of its execution. This can lead to unbalanced run queues, which may lead to processor idling.[170]

Dynamic load balancing attempts to address this issue by adjusting the number of processors assigned to a job throughout its life. Studies have shown that dynamic load balancing performs better than static load balancing when context-switch time is low and system load is high.[171]

Self Review

1. What are some of the benefits of implementing load balancing?
2. What scheduling algorithms benefit from load balancing?

Ans: **1)** Some of the benefits of load balancing include higher processor utilization, which leads to higher throughput, and reduced process response time. **2)** Load balancing is appropriate for scheduling algorithms that maximize processor affinity, such as dynamic partitioning. Also, it can benefit systems that maintain per-processor or per-node run queues.

15.8.1 Static Load Balancing

Static load balancing is useful in environments in which jobs repeat certain tests or instructions and therefore exhibit predictable patterns (e.g., scientific computing).[172] These patterns can be represented as graphs that can be used to model scheduling. Consider the processes in a system as vertices in a graph, and communications between processes as edges. For example, if there is an application in which one process continually analyzes similar data, then feeds that data to another process, this can be modeled as two nodes connected by one edge. Because this relationship will be consistent throughout the application's life, there is no need to adjust the graph.

Due to shared cache and physical memory, communication between processes at the same processor is much faster than communication between processes at different processors. Therefore, static load balancing algorithms attempt to divide the graph into subgraphs of similar size (i.e., each processor has a similar number of processes) while minimizing edges between subgraphs to reduce communication between processors.[173] However, this technique can incur significant overhead for a large number of jobs.[174] Consider the graph in Fig. 15.16. Two dashed lines represent

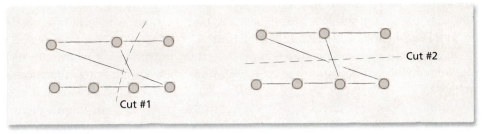

Figure 15.16 | *Static load balancing using graphs.*

possible cuts to divide the processes somewhat evenly. Cut #1 yields four interprocessor communication channels, whereas cut #2 yields only two, thus representing a better grouping of processes.

Static load balancing can be inadequate when communication patterns change dynamically and when processes complete with no new processes to take their places. The first case might perform less efficiently due to high communication latency. In the second case, processor utilization could decrease even when there are processes waiting to obtain a processor. In these cases, dynamic load balancing can improve performance.[175]

Self Review

1. When is static load balancing useful? When is it not useful?
2. In Fig. 15.16, there is a substantial difference between cut #1 and cut #2. Considering that it is difficult to find the most effective cut when there are large numbers of jobs, what does this say about the limitations of static load balancing?

Ans: **1)** Static load balancing is useful in environments where processes might exhibit predictable communication patterns. It is not useful in environments where communication patterns change dynamically and processes are created or terminated unpredictably. **2)** The difference between Cut #1 (four IPC channels) and Cut #2 (two IPC channels) illustrates the performance implications of making bad decisions. Most large systems will have to estimate to find a solution; a wrong estimate could severely degrade performance.

15.8.2 Dynamic Load Balancing

Dynamic load balancing algorithms migrate processes after they have been created in response to system load. The operating system maintains statistical processor load information such as the number of active and blocked processes at a processor, average processor utilization, turnaround time and latency.[176, 177] If many of a processor's processes are blocked or have a large turnaround times, the processor most likely is overloaded. If a processor does not have a high processor utilization rate, it probably is underloaded.

Several policies may be used to determine when to migrate processes in dynamic load balancing. The **sender-initiated policy** activates when the system determines that a processor contains a heavy load. Only then will the system search for underutilized processors and migrate some of the overloaded processor's jobs to them. This is best for systems with light loads, because process migration is costly and, in this case, the policy will rarely be activated.[178, 179]

Conversely, a **receiver-initiated policy** is better for overloaded systems. In this environment, the system initiates process migration when a processor's utilization is low.[180, 181]

Most systems experience heavy and light loads over time. For these systems, the **symmetric policy**, which combines the previous two methods, provides maximum versatility to adapt to environmental conditions.[182, 183] Finally, the **random policy**, in which the system arbitrarily chooses a processor to receive a migrated process, has shown decent results due to its simple implementation and (on average) even distribution of processes. The motivation behind the random policy is that the migrating process's destination will likely have a smaller load than its origin, considering that the original processor is severely overloaded.[184, 185]

The subsections that follow describe common algorithms that determine how processes are migrated. For the purposes of this discussion, consider that the multiprocessor system can be represented by a graph in which each processor and its memory are a vertex and each link is an edge.

Bidding Algorithm

The **bidding algorithm** is a simple sender-initiated migration policy. Processors with smaller loads "bid" for processes on overloaded processors, much as in an auction. The value of a bid is based on the current load of the bidding processor and the distance between the underloaded and overloaded processors in the graph. To reduce the process migration cost, more direct communication paths to the overloaded processor receive higher bid values. The overloaded processor accepts bids from processors that are within a certain distance on the graph. If the overloaded processor receives too many bids, it decreases the distance; if it receives too few, it increases the distance and checks again. The process is sent to the processor with the highest bid.[186]

Drafting Algorithm

The **drafting algorithm** is a receiver-initiated policy that classifies the load at each processor as low, normal or high. Each processor maintains a table describing the other processors' loads using these classifications. Often in large-scale or distributed systems, processors maintain only information about their neighbors. Every time a processor's load changes classification, the processor broadcasts its updated information to the processors in its load table. When a processor receives one of these messages, it appends its own information and forwards the message to its neighbors. In this way, information about load levels eventually reaches all nodes in the network. Underutilized processors use this information to request processes from overloaded processors.[187]

Communications Issues

Inefficient or incorrect communication strategies can overwhelm a system. For example, some process migration implementations employ systemwide broadcasts. The flood of broadcast messages can overwhelm communication channels. Due to communication delays, many overloaded processors could receive a request for a process at the same time and all send their processes to one underloaded processor.[188]

Several strategies have been devised to avoid these problems. For example, the algorithm could restrict processors to communicate only with their immediate neighbors, which reduces the number of messages that are transmitted, but increases the time required for information to reach every node in the system.[189] Alternatively, processors could periodically select a random processor with which to exchange information. In this case, processes are migrated from the processor with the higher load to the one with a lower load.[190] In cases where one processor is severely overloaded and the rest are underloaded, this results in rapid process diffusion.

Figure 15.17 illustrates process diffusion in a system in which nodes communicate only with their neighbors. The overloaded processor, represented by the middle vertex, has 17 processes while all others have one process. After one iteration, the overloaded processor communicates with its neighbors and sends three processes to each. Now those processors have four processes, which is three more than some of their neighbors have. In the second iteration, the processors with four processes send some to their neighbors. Finally, in the third iteration, the overloaded processor once again sends some processes to its neighbors so that now the processor with the heaviest load has only three processes. This example illustrates that even when communications are kept among neighboring processors, load balancing can effectively distribute processing responsibilities throughout the system.

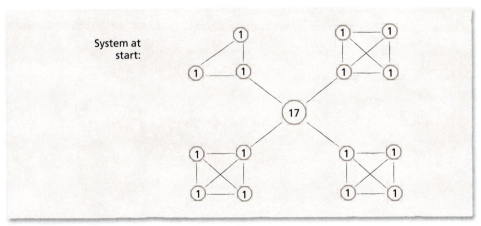

Figure 15.17 | Processor load diffusion. (Part 1 of 2.)

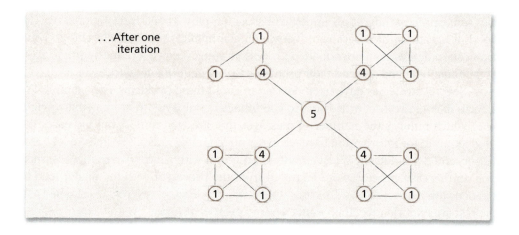

...After one iteration

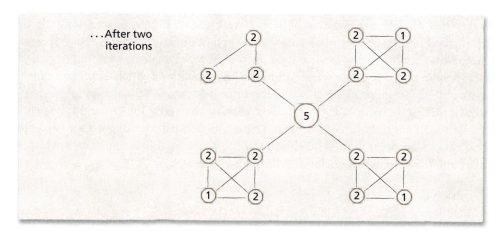

...After two iterations

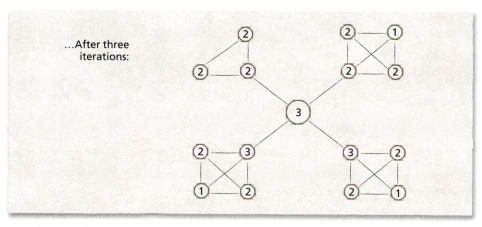

...After three iterations:

Figure 15.17 | Processor load diffusion. (Part 2 of 2.)

Self Review

1. In what type of environment should a sender-oriented policy be used? A receiver-oriented policy? Justify your answers.
2. How does high communication latency hinder the effectiveness of load balancing?

Ans: **1)** A system with a light load should use a sender-oriented policy, whereas a system with a heavy load should use a receiver-oriented policy. In both cases this will reduce unnecessary migrations, because there will be few senders in a system with a light load and few receivers in one with a heavy load. **2)** A node sending a message that it is underloaded might have become overloaded by the time another node receives the message. Thus, the receiving node could further unbalance the system's load by migrating additional processes to the sender.

15.9 Multiprocessor Mutual Exclusion

Many of the mutual exclusion mechanisms we described in Chapter 5 are not adequate for multiprocessor systems. For example, disabling interrupts, which prevents other processes from executing by disabling preemption on uniprocessor systems, does not guarantee mutual exclusion on multiprocessors because several processes can execute simultaneously on different processors. Instructions such as test-and-set can be inefficient when the data these instructions reference is located in remote memory. Test-and-set has another weakness, namely that each of the pending operations requires a separate memory access; these are performed sequentially, because only one access to a memory location may normally occur at a time. Such collisions can quickly saturate various kinds of interconnection networks, causing serious performance problems. Because of nontrivial communication costs and the fact that multiple processes execute at the same time, designers have developed a number of mutual exclusion techniques for multiprocessors. This section introduces mutual exclusion techniques for nondistributed multiprocessing systems. We present distributed mutual exclusion in Section 17.5, Mutual Exclusion in Distributed Systems.

15.9.1 Spin Locks

Multiprocessor operating systems, such as Windows XP and Linux, frequently use **spin locks** for multiprocessor mutual exclusion. A spin lock is called a "lock" because a process that holds a spin lock claims exclusive access to the resource the spin lock protects (e.g., a shared data structure in memory or a critical section of code). In effect, other processes are "locked out" of the resource. Other processes that wish to use the resource "spin" (i.e., busy wait) by continually testing a condition to determine whether the resource is available. In uniprocessing systems, spin locks are wasteful because they consume processor cycles that could be used by other processes, including the one that holds the lock, to do useful work. In multiprocessing systems, the process holding the lock could release it while another process is busy waiting. In this case, it is more efficient for a process to busy wait if the time required for the system to perform a context switch to schedule another process is longer than the average busy-wait time.[191] Also, if a processor contains no other runnable processes in its run queue, it makes sense to keep the process spinning to minimize the response time when the spin lock is released.[192, 193]

When a process holds a spin lock for a long duration (relative to context-switch time), blocking is more efficient. **Delayed blocking** is a technique in which a process spins for a short period of time; if it does not acquire the lock in that time, the process blocks.[194] An **advisable process lock (APL)** presents an alternative solution. When a process acquires an APL, it specifies the amount of time it will hold the lock. Based on the time specified, other processes waiting to acquire the APL can determine if it is more efficient to busy wait for the lock or to block.[195]

Adaptive locks (also called **configurable locks**) add flexibility to a mutual exclusion implementation. At certain times, such as when there are few active processes, spin locks are preferable because a process can acquire a resource soon after it becomes available. At times when system load is high, spinning wastes valuable processor cycles and blocking is preferable. Adaptive locks permit a process to dynamically change the type of lock being used. These locks can be set to blocking, spinning or delayed blocking and can incorporate APL features to customize the lock according to system load and application needs.[196]

When multiple processes simultaneously wait for a spin lock to be released, indefinite postponement can occur. Operating systems can prevent indefinite postponement by granting the spin lock to processes in first-come-first-served order, or by aging processes waiting on the spin lock, as discussed in Section 7.3.

Self Review

1. In what way can spinning be useful in a multiprocessor? Under what conditions is it not desirable in a multiprocessor? Why is spinning not useful in a uniprocessor system?
2. Why might an APL not be useful in all situations?

Ans: **1)** Spinning can be useful because it minimizes the time between when a resource becomes available and when a new process acquires the resource. Spinning is not desirable when system load is high and the expected time before the resource is available is greater than context-switch time; in these cases, spinning uses valuable processor cycles. Spinning is not useful in uniprocessor systems because it blocks the execution of the process holding the resource. **2)** An APL is not useful when a process cannot determine how long it will hold the lock.

15.9.2 Sleep/Wakeup Locks

A **sleep/wakeup lock** provides synchronization similar to a spin lock, but reduces wasted processor cycles and bus traffic. Consider processes P_1 and P_2, both of which request use of a resource protected by a sleep/wakeup lock. P_1 requests the resource first and obtains the lock. When P_2 requests the resource owned by P_1 and does not receive the resource, P_2 responds by sleeping (i.e., blocking). Once P_1 releases the lock, P_1 wakes the highest-priority process waiting for the resource (in this case, P_2). Unlike spin locks (which give the lock to the next waiting process), sleep/wakeup locks can use the processor scheduler to enforce process priorities.

Sleep/wakeup locks can cause waiting processes to be indefinitely postponed, depending on the system's scheduling policy.

Note that unlike a uniprocessor implementation, only the process with the highest priority is awakened. When all threads are awakened, a **race condition** can result because two or more threads may access a resource associated with a lock in a nondeterministic order. Race conditions should be avoided because they can cause subtle errors in applications and are difficult to debug. In uniprocessors, even if all processes are alerted, there can be no race condition because only one process (the one with highest priority in most scheduling algorithms) obtains control of the processor and acquires the lock. In a multiprocessing environment, a broadcast could wake many processes that are competing for the lock, creating a race condition. This would also result in one process obtaining the lock and many processes testing, reblocking and consequently going back to sleep, thus squandering processor time due to context switching. This phenomenon is known as the **thundering herd**.[197]

Self Review

1. What are an advantage and a disadvantage of a sleep/wakeup lock compared to a spin lock?
2. How is the implementation of a sleep/wakeup lock different in a multiprocessor environment than in a uniprocessor environment?

Ans: **1)** A sleep/wakeup lock eliminates wasted processor cycles incurred by spinning. Also, a sleep/wakeup lock ensures that the highest-priority waiting process obtains the lock next. A disadvantage is that reaction to the lock's availability is slower because the new acquirer must awaken and obtain a processor. **2)** In a multiprocessor environment, a releasing process awakens only one waiting process, which prevents a thundering herd that would waste processor cycles and flood communication channels. This is not a problem on uniprocessor systems.

15.9.3 Read/Write Locks

Enforcing mutually exclusive access to shared memory in a multiprocessor system can degrade performance. Only writers need exclusive access to the resource, whereas, in general, multiple readers can access the same memory location at once. Therefore, many systems protect shared memory with a more versatile **read/write lock** rather than a generic mutual exclusion lock.[198] A read/write lock provides mutual exclusion similar to that presented in the readers/writers problem of Section 6.2.4. A read/write lock permits multiple reader processes (i.e., processes that will not alter shared data) to enter their critical sections. Unlike the example in Section 6.2.4, however, read/write locks require that a writer (i.e., a process that will alter shared data) wait until there are no reader or writer processes in their critical sections before entering its critical section.[199]

To implement this locking approach efficiently, the mutual exclusion mechanism must use shared memory. However, in environments in which memory is not shared, such as NORMA systems, message passing must be used. We discuss such techniques in Section 17.5, Mutual Exclusion in Distributed Systems.

Self Review

1. In what situations are read/write locks more efficient than spin locks?
2. A naive implementation of a read/write lock allows any reader to enter its critical section when no writer is in its critical section. How can this lead to indefinite postponement for writers? What is a fairer implementation?

Ans: **1)** Read/write locks are more efficient than spin locks when multiple processes read a memory location, but do not write to it. In this case, multiple processes can be in critical sections at once. **2)** This implementation leads to indefinite postponement if readers continually enter their critical sections before a writer can enter its critical section. A fairer implementation would allow a reader to enter its critical section only if no writer is in or is waiting to enter its critical section as discussed in Section 6.2.4.

Web Resources

www.winntmag.com/Articles/Index.cfm?ArticleID=303&pg=1&show=495
This article describes multiprocessor scheduling in Windows NT.

www.aceshardware.com/Spades/read.php?article_id=30000187
This article describes how the AMD Athlon (with two processors) implements cache coherence. It also discusses bus snooping.

www.mosix.org
This site provides information about MOSIX, a software bundle used on UNIX systems, which implements automatic process migration and load balancing.

www.teamten.com/lawrence/242.paper/242.paper.html
This paper discusses mutual exclusion algorithms for multiprocessors.

users.win.be/W0005997/UNIX/LINUX/IL/atomicity-eng.html
This site explains how to use spin locks to implement mutual exclusion in Linux.

Summary

Many applications demand substantially more computing power than one processor can provide. As a result, multiprocessing systems—computers that use more than one processor to meet a system's processing needs—are often employed. The term "multiprocessing system" encompasses any system with more than one processor. This includes dual-processor personal computers, powerful servers that contain many processors and distributed groups of workstations that work together to perform tasks.

There are several ways to classify multiprocessors. Flynn developed an early scheme for classifying computers into increasingly parallel configurations based on the types of streams used by processors. SISD (single instruction stream, single data stream) computers are traditional uniprocessors that fetch one instruction at a time and execute it on a single data item. MISD (multiple instruction stream, single data stream) computers (which are not commonly used) have multiple processing units, each operating on a piece of data and then passing the result to the next processing unit. SIMD (single instruction stream, multiple data stream) computers, which include array and vector processors, execute instructions on multiple data items in parallel. MIMD (multiple instruction stream, multiple data stream) computers have multiple processing units that operate independently on separate instruction streams.

The interconnection scheme of a multiprocessor system describes how the system physically connects its components, such as processors and memory modules. The interconnection scheme affects the system's performance, reliability and cost, so it is a key issue for multiprocessor designers. A shared bus provides low cost and high performance for a small number of processors but does not scale well, owing to contention on the bus as the number of processors increases. A crossbar-switch matrix provides high fault tolerance and performance but is inappropriate for small systems in which UMA (uniform memory access) is more cost effective. A 2-D mesh network is a simple design that provides adequate performance and fault tolerance at a low cost but that also does not scale well. A hypercube is more scalable than a 2-D mesh network and provides better performance, but at a higher cost. Multistage networks compromise between cost and performance and can be used to build extremely large-scale multiprocessors.

In a tightly coupled system, the processors share most system resources. Loosely coupled systems connect components indirectly through communication links and do not share most resources. Loosely coupled systems are more scalable, flexible and fault tolerant but do not perform as well as tightly coupled systems. Loosely coupled systems also place more burden on programmers, who must implement applications that communicate via IPC rather than shared memory.

Multiprocessors can also be categorized based on how the processors share operating system responsibilities. In the master/slave organization, only the master processor can execute the operating system; the slaves execute only user programs. In the separate-kernels organization, each processor executes its own operating system, and operating system data structures maintain the system's global information. In the symmetrical organization, all processors can control any device and reference any storage unit. This organization enables systems to balance their workloads more precisely.

Multiprocessor systems use several architectures to share memory. UMA multiprocessors require all processors to share all the system's main memory equally owing to shared-memory contention; these systems are not scalable beyond a few processors. NUMA (nonuniform memory access) multiprocessors partition memory into modules, assigning one to each processor as its local memory. COMA (cache-only memory architecture) multiprocessors are similar to NUMA multiprocessors, but treat all memory as a large cache to increase the likelihood that requested data resides in the requesting processor's local memory. NORMA (no remote memory access) multiprocessors are loosely coupled and do not provide any globally shared main memory. NORMA multiprocessors are used to build large-scale distributed systems.

Memory is coherent if the value obtained from reading a memory address is always the same as the value most recently written to that address. UMA cache-coherence protocols include bus snooping and directory-based coherence. CC-NUMAs (cache-coherent NUMAs) often use a home-based approach in which a home node for each memory address is responsible for keeping that data item coherent throughout the system.

Systems that use page replication maintain multiple copies of a memory page so it can be accessed quickly by multiple processors. Systems that use page migration transfer pages to the processor that accesses the pages most. These techniques can be combined to optimize performance.

Shared virtual memory (SVM) provides the illusion of shared physical memory in large-scale multiprocessor systems. Invalidation (in which a writer voids other copies of a page) and write broadcast (in which a writer notifies other processors of updates to a page) are two approaches for implementing memory coherence in SVM systems. These protocols can be strictly applied, but this can be inefficient. Relaxed consistency, in which the system might not be coherent for a few seconds, improves efficiency but sacrifices some data integrity.

Multiprocessor scheduling algorithms must determine both when and where to dispatch a process. Some algorithms maximize processor affinity (the relationship of a process to a particular processor and its local memory) by executing related processes on the same processors. Others maximize parallelism by executing related processes on separate processors simultaneously. Some systems use global run queues, whereas others (typically large-scale systems) maintain per-processor or per-node run queues.

Process migration is the act of transferring a process between two processors or computers. Process migration can increase performance, resource sharing and fault tolerance. To migrate a process, nodes must transfer the process's state, which includes the process's memory pages, register contents, state of open files and kernel context. Migration policies that allow residual dependency (a process's dependency on its former node) decrease fault tolerance and the process's performance after migration. However, eliminating residual dependency makes initial migration slow. Various migration policies balance the goals of minimal residual dependency and fast initial migration.

Load balancing is a technique in which the system attempts to distribute processing responsibility equally among processors to increase processor utilization and decrease process response times. Static load balancing algorithms assign a fixed number of processors to a job when the job is first scheduled. These algorithms are useful in environments, such as scientific computing, where process interactions and execution times are predictable. Dynamic load balancing algorithms change the number of processors assigned to a job throughout the job's life. These algorithms are useful when process interactions are unpredictable, and when processes can be created and terminate at any time.

Many uniprocessor mutual exclusion mechanisms are either inefficient or ineffective for multiprocessors. Designers have developed mutual exclusion techniques specific to multiprocessors. A spin lock is a mutual exclusion lock in which waiting processes spin (i.e., busy wait) for the lock. This is appropriate when system load is low and spinning time is short relative to context-switch time. Spin locks reduce reaction time when resources become available.

With a sleep/wakeup lock, a process releasing the lock wakes up the highest-priority waiting process, which acquires the lock. This reduces the use of processor cycles typical in spin locks. Read/write locks allow one writer or many readers to be in their critical sections at once.

Key Terms

2-D mesh network—Multiprocessor interconnection scheme that arranges nodes in an $m \times n$ rectangle.

4-connected 2-D mesh network—2-D mesh network in which nodes are connected with the nodes directly to the north, south, east and west.

acquire operation—In several coherence strategies, an operation indicating that a process is about to access shared memory.

adaptive lock—Mutual exclusion lock that allows processes to switch between using a spin lock or a blocking lock, depending on the current condition of the system.

advisable process lock (APL)—Locking mechanism in which an acquirer estimates how long it will hold the lock; other processes can use this estimate to determine whether to block or spin when waiting for the lock.

array processor—SIMD (single instruction stream, multiple data stream) system consisting of many (possibly tens of thousands) simple processing units, each executing the same instruction in parallel on many data elements.

attraction memory (AM)—Main memory in a COMA (cache-only memory architecture) multiprocessor, which is organized as a cache.

baseline network—Type of multistage network.

bidding algorithm—Dynamic load balancing algorithm in which processors with smaller loads "bid" for jobs on overloaded processors; the bid value depends on the load of the bidding processor and the distance between the underloaded and overloaded processors.

bisection width—Minimum number of links that need to be severed to divide a network into two unconnected halves.

bus snooping—Coherence protocol in which processors "snoop" the shared bus to determine whether a requested write is to a data item in that processor's cache or, if applicable, local memory.

cache coherence—Property of a system in which any data item read from a cache has the value equal to the last write to that data item.

cache-coherent NUMA (CC-NUMA)—NUMA multiprocessor that maintains cache coherence, usually through a home-based approach.

cache miss latency—Extra time required to access data that does not reside in the cache.

cache-only memory architecture (COMA) multiprocessor—Multiprocessor architecture in which nodes consist of a processor, cache and memory module; main memory is organized as a large cache.

cache snooping—Bus snooping used to ensure cache coherency.

configurable lock—See adaptive lock

contention—In multiprocessing a situation in which several processors compete for the use of a shared resource.

copy-on-reference migration—Process migration technique in which only a process's dirty pages are migrated with the process, and the process can request clean pages either from the sending node or from secondary storage.

cost of an interconnection scheme—Total number of links in a network.

coscheduling—Job-aware process scheduling algorithm that attempts to execute processes from the same job concurrently by placing them in adjacent global-run-queue locations.

crossbar-switch matrix—Processor interconnection scheme that maintains a separate path from every sender node to every receiver node.

degree of a node—Number of other nodes with which a node is directly connected.

delayed blocking—Technique whereby a process spins on a lock for a fixed amount of time before it blocks; the rationale is that if the process does not obtain the lock quickly, it will probably have to wait a long time, so it should block.

delayed consistency—Memory coherence strategy in which processors send update information after a release, but a receiving node does not apply this information until it performs an acquire operation on the memory.

dirty eager migration—Process migration method in which only a process's dirty pages are migrated with the process; clean pages must be accessed from secondary storage.

drafting algorithm—Dynamic load balancing algorithm that classifies each processor's load as low, normal or high; each processor maintains a table of the other processors' loads, and the system uses a receiver-initiated policy to exchange processes.

dynamic load balancing—Technique that attempts to distribute processing responsibility equally by changing the number of processors assigned to a job throughout the job's life.

dynamic partitioning—Job-aware process scheduling algorithm that divides processors in the system evenly among jobs, except that no single job can be allocated more processors than runnable processes; this algorithm maximizes processor affinity.

eager migration—Process migration strategy that transfers the entire address space of a process during the initial phases of migration to eliminate a migrated process's residual dependencies on its original node.

false sharing—Situation that occurs when processes on separate processors are forced to share a page because they are each accessing a data item on that page, although not the same data item.

first-come-first-served (FCFS) process scheduling—Job-blind multiprocessor scheduling algorithm that places arriving processes in a queue; the process at the head of the queue executes until it freely relinquishes the processor.

flushing—Process migration strategy in which the sending node writes all of the process's memory pages to a shared disk at the start of migration; the process then accesses the pages from the shared disk as needed on the receiving node.

gang scheduling—Another name for coscheduling.

global run queue—Process scheduling queue used in some multiprocessor scheduling algorithms, which is independent of the processors in a system and into which every process or job in the system is placed.

hard affinity—Type of processor affinity in which the scheduling algorithm guarantees that a process only executes on a single node throughout its life cycle.

home-based consistency—Memory-coherence strategy in which processors send coherence information to a home node associated with the page being written; the home node forwards update information to other nodes that subsequently access the page.

home node—Node that is the "home" for a physical memory address or page and is responsible for maintaining the data's coherence.

hypercube—Multiprocessor interconnection scheme that consists of 2^n nodes (where n is an integer); each node is linked with n neighbor nodes.

interconnection scheme—Design that describes how a multiprocessor system physically connects its components, such as processors and memory modules.

invalidation—Memory-coherence protocol in which a process first invalidates—i.e., voids—all other copies of a page before writing to the page.

job-aware scheduling—Multiprocessor scheduling algorithms that account for job properties when making scheduling decisions; these algorithms typically attempt to maximize parallelism or processor affinity.

job-blind scheduling—Multiprocessor scheduling algorithms that ignore job properties when making scheduling decisions; these algorithms are typically simple to implement.

lazy copying—Process migration strategy that transfers pages from the sender only when the process at the receiving node references these pages.

lazy data propagation—Technique in which writing processors send coherence information after a release, but not the data; a processor retrieves the data when it accesses a page that it knows is not coherent.

lazy migration—Process migration strategy in multiprocessor systems that does not transfer all pages during initial migration. This increases residual dependency but reduces initial migration time.

lazy release consistency—Memory-coherence strategy in which a processor does not send coherence information after writing to a page until a new processor attempts an acquire operation on that memory page.

load balancing—Technique which attempts to distribute the system's processing responsibility equally among processors.

loosely coupled system—System in which processors do not share most resources; these systems are flexible and fault tolerant but perform worse than tightly coupled systems.

massively parallel processor—Processor that performs a large number of instructions on large data sets at once; array processors are often called massively parallel processors.

master/slave multiprocessor organization—Scheme for delegating operating system responsibilities in which only one processor (the "master") can execute the operating system, and the other processors (the "slaves") can execute only user processes.

memory coherence—State of a system in which the value obtained from reading a memory address is always the same as the most-recently written value at that address.

memory line—Entry in memory that stores one machine word of data, which is typically four or eight bytes.

multiple-instruction-stream, multiple-data-stream (MIMD) computer—Computer architecture consisting of multiple processing units, which execute independent instructions and manipulate independent data streams; this design describes multiprocessors.

multiple-instruction-stream, single-data-stream (MISD) computer—Computer architecture consisting of several processing units, which execute independent instruction streams on a single stream of data; these architectures have no commercial application.

multiple shared bus architecture—Interconnection scheme that employs several shared buses connecting processors and memory. This reduces contention, but increases cost compared to a single shared bus.

multiprocessing system—Computing system that employs more than one processor.

multistage network—Multiprocessor interconnection scheme that uses switch nodes as hubs for communication between processor nodes that each have their own local memory.

network diameter—Shortest path between the two most remote nodes in a system.

network link—Connection between two nodes.

node—System component, such as a processor, memory module or switch, attached to a network; sometimes a group of components might be viewed as a single node.

nonuniform-memory-access (NUMA) multiprocessor—Multiprocessor architecture in which each node consists of a processor, cache and memory module. Access to a processor's associated memory module (called local memory) is faster than access to other memory modules in the system.

no-remote-memory-access (NORMA) multiprocessor—Multiprocessor architecture that does not provide global shared memory. Each processor maintains its own local memory. NORMA multiprocessors implement a common shared virtual memory.

on-demand migration—Another name for lazy process migration.

page migration—Technique in which the system transfers pages to the processor (or processors when used with page replication) that accesses the pages most.

page replication—Technique in which the system maintains multiple copies of a page at different nodes so that it can be accessed quickly by multiple processors.

per-processor run queue—Process scheduling queue associated with a specific processor; processes entering the queue are scheduled on the associated processor independently of the scheduling decisions made in rest of the system.

per-node run queue—Process scheduling queue associated with a group of processors; processes entering the queue are scheduled on the associated node's processors independently of the scheduling decisions made in rest of the system.

precopy—Process migration strategy in which the sender begins transferring dirty pages before the original process is suspended; once the number of untransferred dirty pages at the sender reaches some threshold, the process migrates.

process migration—Transferring a process and its associated state between two processors.

processor affinity—Relationship of a process to a particular processor and a corresponding memory bank.

race condition—Occurs when multiple threads simultaneously compete for the same serially reusable resource, and that resource is allocated to these threads in an indeterminate order. This can cause subtle program errors when the order in which threads access a resource is important.

random policy—Dynamic load balancing policy in which the system arbitrarily chooses a processor to receive a migrated process.

read/write lock—Lock that allows a single writer process or multiple reading processes (i.e., processes that will not alter shared variables) to enter a critical section.

receiver-initiated policy—Dynamic load balancing policy in which processors with low utilization attempt to find overloaded processors from which to receive a migrated process.

relaxed consistency—Category of memory-coherence strategies that permit the system to be in an incoherent state for a few seconds after a write, but improve performance over strict consistency.

release consistency—Memory-coherence strategy in which multiple accesses to shared memory are considered a single access; these accesses begin with an acquire and end with a release, after which coherence is enforced throughout the system.

release operation—In several coherence strategies, this operation indicates that a process is done accessing shared memory.

residual dependency—Dependency of a migrated process on its original node after process migration because some of the process's state remains on the original node.

round-robin job (RRJob) scheduling—Job-aware process scheduling algorithm employing a global run queue in which jobs are dispatched to processors in a round-robin fashion.

round-robin process (RRprocess) scheduling—Job-blind multiprocessor scheduling algorithm that places each process in a global run queue and schedules these process in a round-robin manner.

sender-initiated policy—Dynamic load balancing policy in which overloaded processors attempt to find underloaded processors to which to migrate a process.

separate kernels multiprocessor organization—Scheme for delegating operating system responsibilities in which each processor executes its own operating system, but the processors share some global system information.

sequential consistency—Category of memory-coherence strategies in which coherence protocols are enforced immediately after a write to a shared memory location.

shared bus—Multiprocessor interconnection scheme that uses a single communication path to connect all processors and memory modules.

shared virtual memory (SVM)—An extension of virtual memory concepts to multiprocessor systems; SVM presents the illusion of shared physical memory between processors and ensures coherence for pages accessed by separate processors.

shortest-process-first (SPF) scheduling (multiprocessor)—Job-blind multiprocessor scheduling algorithm, employing a global run queue, that selects the process with the smallest processor time requirement to execute on an available processor.

single-instruction-stream, multiple-data-stream (SIMD) computer—Computer architecture consisting of one or more processing elements that execute instructions from a single instruction stream that act on multiple data items.

single-instruction-stream, single-data-stream (SISD) computer—Computer architecture in which one processor fetches instructions from a single instruction stream and manipulates a single data stream; this architecture describes traditional uniprocessors.

sleep/wakeup lock—Mutual exclusion lock in which waiting processes block, and a releasing process wakes the highest-priority waiting process and gives it the lock.

smallest-number-of-processes-first (SNPF) scheduling—Job-aware process scheduling algorithm, employing a global job-priority queue, where job priority is inversely proportional to the number of processes in a job.

soft affinity—Type of processor affinity in which the scheduling algorithm tries, but does not guarantee, to schedule a process only on a single node throughout its life cycle.

space-partitioning scheduling—Multiprocessor scheduling strategy that attempts to maximize processor affinity by scheduling collaborative processes on a single processor (or single set of processors); the underlying assumption is that these processes will access the same shared data.

spin lock—Mutual exclusion lock in which a waiting process busy waits for the lock; this reduces the process's reaction time when the protected resource's becomes available.

static load balancing—Category of load balancing algorithms that assign a fixed number of processors to a job when it is first scheduled.

stream—Sequence of objects fed to the processor.

switch—Node that routes messages between component nodes.

symmetric multiprocessor (SMP)—Multiprocessor system in which processors share all resources equally, including memory, I/O devices and processes.

symmetrical multiprocessor organization—Scheme for delegating operating system responsibilities in which each processor can execute the single operating system.

symmetric policy—Dynamic load balancing policy that combines the sender-initiated policy and the receiver-initiated policy to provide maximum versatility to adapt to environmental conditions.

thundering herd—Phenomenon that occurs when many processes awaken when a resource becomes available; only one process acquires the resource, and the others test the lock's availability and reblock, wasting processor cycles.

tightly coupled system—System in which processors share most resources; these systems provide higher performance but are less fault tolerant and flexible than loosely coupled systems.

timesharing scheduling—Multiprocessor scheduling technique that attempts to maximize parallelism by scheduling collaborative processes concurrently on different processors.

undivided coscheduling algorithm—Job-aware process scheduling algorithm in which processes of the same job are placed in adjacent locations in the global run queue, and processes are scheduled round-robin.

uniform-memory-access (UMA) multiprocessor—Multiprocessor architecture that requires all processors to share all of main memory; in general, memory-access time is constant, regardless of which processor requests data, except when the data is stored in a processor's cache.

vector processor—Type of SIMD computer containing one processing unit that executes instructions that operate on multiple data items.

write broadcast—Technique for maintaining memory coherence in which the processor that performs a write broadcasts the write throughout the system.

Exercises

15.1 A multiprocessor's interconnection scheme affects the system's performance, cost and reliability.

   a. Of the schemes presented in this chapter, which are best suited for small systems and which for large-scale systems?

   b. Why are some interconnection schemes good for small networks and others for large networks, but none are optimal for all networks?

15.2 For each of the following multiprocessor organizations, describe an environment in which the organization is useful; also, list a drawback for each.

   a. Master/slave multiprocessor organization

   b. Separate-kernels multiprocessor organization

   c. Symmetrical organization

15.3 For each of the following environments, suggest whether the UMA, NUMA or NORMA memory-access architecture would be best and explain why.

   a. An environment consisting of a few interactive processes that communicate using shared memory

   b. Thousands of workstations performing a common task

   c. Large-scale multiprocessor containing 64 processors in a single machine

   d. Dual-processor personal computer

15.4 As we described in the chapter, one important, but difficult, goal of a NUMA multiprocessor designer is maximizing the number of page accesses that can be serviced by local memory. Describe the three strategies, COMA, page migration and page replication, and discuss the advantages and disadvantages of each.

   a. COMA multiprocessor.

   b. Page migration.

   c. Page replication.

15.5 For each of the following multiprocessor scheduling algorithms, use the classifications discussed early in this chapter to describe the type of multiprocessor system that would likely employ it. Justify your answers.

   a. Job-blind multiprocessor scheduling

   b. Job-aware multiprocessor scheduling

   c. Scheduling using per-processor or per-node run queues

15.6 For each of the following system attributes, describe how process migration can increase it in a system and an inefficient implementation reduce it.

   a. Performance

   b. Fault tolerance

   c. Scalability

15.7 In our load balancing discussion, we described how processors decide when and with whom to migrate a process. However, we did not describe how processors decide which process to migrate. Suggest some factors that could help determine which process to migrate. [*Hint:* Consider the benefits of process migration other than load balancing.]

15.8 Can a process waiting for a spin lock be indefinitely postponed even if all processes guarantee to leave their critical sections after a finite amount of time? A process waiting for a sleep/wakeup lock? If you answered yes, suggest a way to prevent indefinite postponement.

Suggested Projects

15.9 Prepare a research paper describing how the Linux operating system supports CC-NUMA multiprocessors. Describe Linux's scheduling algorithm, how Linux maintains cache and memory coherency and the various mutual exclusion mechanisms provided by the operating system. Make sure your research entails reading some source code.

15.10 The cost and performance of different hardware devices are changing at different rates. For example, hardware continues to get cheaper, and processor speed is increasing faster than bus speed. Write a research paper describing the trends in interconnection schemes. Which schemes are becoming more popular? Which less popular? Why?

15.11 Prepare a research paper surveying the load balancing algorithms in use today. What are the motivations behind each

algorithm? For what type of environment is each intended? Are most algorithms static or dynamic?

15.12 Prepare a research paper describing how operating systems implement memory coherence. Include a precise description of the coherence protocol and when it is applied for at least one real operating system.

Suggested Simulations

15.13 Use Java threads to simulate a multiprocessor, with each thread representing one processor. Be sure to synchronize access to global (i.e., shared) variables. Implement shared memory as an array with memory addresses as subscripts. Define an object class called `Process`. Randomly create `Process` objects and implement a scheduling algorithm for them. A `Process` object should describe how long it runs before blocking each time, and when it terminates. It should also spec-

ify when it requires access to a shared memory location and to which location.

15.14 Expand your simulation. Implement per-processor run queues and a load balancing algorithm. Maintain a data structure for a processor's local memory, and implement a function in the `Process` object to randomly add memory locations to the local memory. Be sure to migrate this local memory when migrating a `Process`.

Recommended Reading

Flynn and Rudd provide a synopsis of parallel and sequential architecture classifications in their 1996 paper "Parallel Architectures."[200] Crawley, in his paper "An Analysis of MIMD Processor Interconnection Networks for Nanoelectronic Systems," surveys processor interconnection schemes.[201]

As multiprocessing systems have become more mainstream, much research has been devoted to optimizing their performance. Mukherjee et al. present a survey of multiprocessor operating system concepts and systems in "A Survey of Multiprocessor Operating Systems."[202] More recently Tripathi and Karnik, in their paper "Trends in Multiprocessor and Distributed Operating System Designs," summarize many important topics such as scheduling, memory access and locks.[203]

For more information regarding scheduling algorithms in multiprogrammed environments, see Leutenegger and Ver-

non's "The Performance of Multiprogrammed Multiprocessor Scheduling Policies,"[204] and more recently, Bunt et al's "Scheduling in Multiprogrammed Parallel Systems."[205] Lai and Hudak discuss "Memory Coherence in Shared Virtual Memory Systems."[206] Iftode and Singh survey different implementation strategies for maintaining memory coherence in "Shared Virtual Memory: Progress and Challenges."[207] A comprehensive survey, "Process Migration," has been published by Milojicic et al.,[208] and the corresponding problem of load balancing has been treated thoroughly by Langendorfer and Petri in "Load Balancing and Fault Tolerance in Workstation Clusters: Migrating Groups of Processes."[209] The bibliography for this chapter is located on our Web site at `www.deitel.com/books/os3e/Bibliography.pdf`.

Works Cited

1. Mukherjee, B.; K. Schwan; and P. Gopinath, "A Survey of Multiprocessor Operating Systems," *GIT-CC-92/05*, November 5, 1993, p. 1.

2. Mitchell, R., "The Genius: Meet Seymour Cray, Father of the Supercomputer," *BusinessWeek*, April 30, 1990, <`www.business-week.com/1989-94/pre88/b31571.htm`>.

3. Breckenridge, C., "Tribute to Seymour Cray," November 19, 1996, <`www.cgl.ucsf.edu/home/tef/cray/tribute.html`>.

4. Mitchell, R., "The Genius: Meet Seymour Cray, Father of the Supercomputer," *BusinessWeek*, April 30, 1990, <`www.business-week.com/1989-94/pre88/b31571.htm`>.

5. Breckenridge, C., "Tribute to Seymour Cray," November 19, 1996, <`www.cgl.ucsf.edu/home/tef/cray/tribute.html`>.

6. Mitchell, R., "The Genius: Meet Seymour Cray, Father of the Supercomputer," *BusinessWeek*, April 30, 1990, <`www.business-week.com/1989-94/pre88/b31571.htm`>.

7. Breckenridge, C., "Tribute to Seymour Cray," November 19, 1996, <www.cgl.ucsf.edu/home/tef/cray/tribute.html>.

8. Mitchell, R., "The Genius: Meet Seymour Cray, Father of the Supercomputer," *BusinessWeek*, April 30, 1990, <www.business-week.com/1989-94/pre88/b31571.htm>.

9. Top500, "TOP500 Supercomputer Sites: TOP500 List 06-2003," June 2003, <www.top500.org/list/2003/06/?page>.

10. van der Steen, A., "TOP500 Supercomputer Sites: Intel Itanium 2," <www.top500.org/ORSC/2002/itanium.html>.

11. Habata, S.; M. Yokokawa; and S. Kitawaki, "The Earth Simulator System," *NEC Research and Development*, January 2003, <www.nec.co.jp/techrep/en/r_and_d/r03/r03-no1/rd06.pdf>.

12. JAMSTEC, "Earth Simulator Hardware," <www.es.jamstec.go.jp/esc/eng/ES/hardware.html>.

13. Habata, S.; M. Yokokawa; and S. Kitawaki, "The Earth Simulator System," *NEC Research and Development*, January 2003, <www.nec.co.jp/techrep/en/r_and_d/r03/r03-no1/rd06.pdf>.

14. JAMSTEC, "Earth Simulator Hardware," <www.es.jamstec.go.jp/esc/eng/ES/hardware.html>.

15. JAMSTEC, "Earth Simulator Mission," <www.es.jamstec.go.jp/esc/eng/ESC/mission.html>.

16. "TOP500 Supercomputer Sites," June 1, 2003, <top500.org/lists/2003/06/1/>.

17. "Our Mission and Basic Principles," *The Earth Simulator Center*, October 17, 2003, <www.es.jamstec.go.jp/esc/eng/ESC/mission.html>.

18. Allison, D., "Interview with Seymour Cray," May 9, 1995, <americanhistory.si.edu/csr/comphist/cray.htm>.

19. Breckenridge, C., "Tribute to Seymour Cray," November 19, 1996, <www.cgl.ucsf.edu/home/tef/cray/tribute.html>.

20. Allison, D., "Interview with Seymour Cray," May 9, 1995, <americanhistory.si.edu/csr/comphist/cray.htm>.

21. Mitchell, R., "The Genius: Meet Seymour Cray, Father of the Supercomputer," *BusinessWeek*, April 30, 1990, <www.business-week.com/1989-94/pre88/b31571.htm>.

22. Breckenridge, C., "Tribute to Seymour Cray," November 19, 1996, <www.cgl.ucsf.edu/home/tef/cray/tribute.html>.

23. Allison, D., "Interview with Seymour Cray," May 9, 1995, <americanhistory.si.edu/csr/comphist/cray.htm>.

24. Breckenridge, C., "Tribute to Seymour Cray," November 19, 1996, <www.cgl.ucsf.edu/home/tef/cray/tribute.html>.

25. Mitchell, R., "The Genius: Meet Seymour Cray, Father of the Supercomputer," *BusinessWeek*, April 30, 1990, <www.business-week.com/1989-94/pre88/b31571.htm>.

26. Allison, D., "Interview with Seymour Cray," May 9, 1995, <americanhistory.si.edu/csr/comphist/cray.htm>.

27. Breckenridge, C., "Tribute to Seymour Cray," November 19, 1996, <www.cgl.ucsf.edu/home/tef/cray/tribute.html>.

28. Mitchell, R., "The Genius: Meet Seymour Cray, Father of the Supercomputer," *BusinessWeek*, April 30, 1990, <www.business-week.com/1989-94/pre88/b31571.htm>.

29. Allison, D., "Interview with Seymour Cray," May 9, 1995, <americanhistory.si.edu/csr/comphist/cray.htm>.

30. Breckenridge, C., "Tribute to Seymour Cray," November 19, 1996, <www.cgl.ucsf.edu/home/tef/cray/tribute.html>.

31. Mitchell, R., "The Genius: Meet Seymour Cray, Father of the Supercomputer," *BusinessWeek*, April 30, 1990, <www.business-week.com/1989-94/pre88/b31571.htm>.

32. Allison, D., "Interview with Seymour Cray," May 9, 1995, <americanhistory.si.edu/csr/comphist/cray.htm>.

33. Breckenridge, C., "Tribute to Seymour Cray," November 19, 1996, <www.cgl.ucsf.edu/home/tef/cray/tribute.html>.

34. Mitchell, R., "The Genius: Meet Seymour Cray, Father of the Supercomputer," *BusinessWeek*, April 30, 1990, <www.business-week.com/1989-94/pre88/b31571.htm>.

35. Allison, D., "Interview with Seymour Cray," May 9, 1995, <americanhistory.si.edu/csr/comphist/cray.htm>.

36. Mitchell, R., "The Genius: Meet Seymour Cray, Father of the Supercomputer," *BusinessWeek*, April 30, 1990, <www.business-week.com/1989-94/pre88/b31571.htm>.

37. Mitchell, R., "The Genius: Meet Seymour Cray, Father of the Supercomputer," *BusinessWeek*, April 30, 1990, <www.business-week.com/1989-94/pre88/b31571.htm>.

38. Cray Incorporated, "Historic Cray Systems," <www.cray.com/company/h_systems.html>.

39. Cray Incorporated, "Historic Cray Systems," <www.cray.com/company/h_systems.html>.

40. Allison, D., "Interview with Seymour Cray," May 9, 1995, <americanhistory.si.edu/csr/comphist/cray.htm>.

41. Flynn, M., "Very High-Speed Computing Systems," *Proceedings of the IEEE*, Vol. 54, December 1966, pp. 1901–1909.

42. Flynn, M., and K. Rudd, "Parallel Architectures," *ACM Computing Surveys*, Vol. 28, No. 1, March 1996, p. 67.

43. "Accelerating Digital Multimedia Production with Hyper-Threading Technology," January 15, 2003. <http://cedar.intel.com/cgi-bin/ids.dll/content/content.jsp?cntKey=Generic+Editorial%3a%3ahyperthreading_digital_multimedia&cntType=IDS_EDITORIAL&catCode=CDN&path=5>.

44. Flynn, M., and K. Rudd, "Parallel Architectures," *ACM Computing Surveys*, Vol. 28, No. 1, March 1996, p. 69.

45. Zhou, J., and K. Ross, "Research Sessions: Implementation Techniques: Implementing Database Operations Using SIMD Instructions," *Proceedings of the 2002 ACM SIGMOD International Conference on Management of Data*, June 2002, p. 145.

46. Flynn, M., and K. Rudd, "Parallel Architectures," *ACM Computing Surveys*, Vol. 28, No. 1, March 1996, pp. 68–69.

47. Hennessy, J., and D. Patterson, *Computer Organization and Design*, San Francisco, CA: Morgan Kaufmann, 1998, pp. 751–752.

48. Flynn, M., and K. Rudd, "Parallel Architectures," *ACM Computing Surveys*, Vol. 28, No. 1, March 1996, p. 68.

49. Gelenbe E., "Performance Analysis of the Connection Machine," *Proceedings of the 1990 ACM SIGMETRICS Conference on Measurement and Modeling of Computer Systems*, Vol. 18, No. 1, April 1990, pp. 183–191.

50. Flynn, M., and K. Rudd, "Parallel Architectures," *ACM Computing Surveys*, Vol. 28, No. 1, March 1996, p. 69.

51. Crawley, D., "An Analysis of MIMD Processor Interconnection Networks for Nanoelectronic Systems," *UCL Image Processing Group Report 98/3*, 1998, p. 3.

52. Crawley, D., "An Analysis of MIMD Processor Interconnection Networks for Nanoelectronic Systems," *UCL Image Processing Group Report 98/3*, 1998, p. 3.

53. Bhuyan, L.; Q. Yang; and D. Agrawal, "Performance of Multiprocessor Interconnection Networks," *Computer*, Vol. 20, No. 4, April 1987, pp. 50–60.

54. Rettberg, R., and R. Thomas, "Contention is No Obstacle to Shared-Memory Multiprocessors," *Communications of the ACM*, Vol. 29, No. 12, December 1986, pp. 1202–1212.

55. Crawley, D., "An Analysis of MIMD Processor Interconnection Networks for Nanoelectronic Systems," *UCL Image Processing Group Report 98/3*, 1998, p. 12.

56. Hennessy, J., and D. Patterson, *Computer Organization and Design*, San Francisco, CA: Morgan Kaufmann, 1998, p. 718.

57. Crawley, D., "An Analysis of MIMD Processor Interconnection Networks for Nanoelectronic Systems," *UCL Image Processing Group Report 98/3*, 1998, p. 12.

58. Qin, X., and J. Baer, "A Performance Evaluation of Cluster Architectures," *Proceedings of the 1997 ACM SIGMETRICS International Conference on Measuring and Modeling of Computer Systems*, 1997, p. 237.

59. Friedman, M., "Multiprocessor Scalability in Microsoft Windows NT/2000," *Proceedings of the 26th Annual International Measurement Group Conference*, December 2000, pp. 645–656.

60. Enslow, P., "Multiprocessor Organization—A Survey," *ACM Computing Surveys*, Vol. 9, No. 1, March 1977, pp. 103–129.

61. Bhuyan, L.; Q. Yang; and D. Agrawal, "Performance of Multiprocessor Interconnection Networks," *Computer*, Vol. 20, No. 4, April 1987, pp. 50–60.

62. Stenstrom, P., "Reducing Contention in Shared-Memory Multiprocessors," *Computer*, Vol. 21, No. 11 November 1988, pp. 26–37.

63. Crawley, D., "An Analysis of MIMD Processor Interconnection Networks for Nanoelectronic Systems," *UCL Image Processing Group Report 98/3*, 1998, p. 19.

64. "UltraSPARC-III," `<www.sun.com/processors/UltraSPARC-III/USIIITech.html>`.

65. Crawley, D., "An Analysis of MIMD Processor Interconnection Networks for Nanoelectronic Systems," *UCL Image Processing Group Report 98/3*, 1998, p. 8.

66. Seitz, C., "The Cosmic Cube," *Communications of the ACM*, Vol. 28, No. 1, January 1985, pp. 22–33.

67. Padmanabhan, K., "Cube Structures for Multiprocessors," *Communications of the ACM*, Vol. 33, No. 1, January 1990, pp. 43–52.

68. Hennessy, J., and D. Patterson, *Computer Organization and Design*, San Francisco, CA: Morgan Kaufmann, 1998, p. 738.

69. Crawley, D., "An Analysis of MIMD Processor Interconnection Networks for Nanoelectronic Systems," *UCL Image Processing Group Report 98/3*, 1998, p. 10.

70. "The nCUBE 2s," *Top 500 Supercomputer Sites*, February 16, 1998 `<www.top500.org/ORSC/1998/ncube.html>`.

71. Bhuyan, L.; Q. Yang; and D. Agrawal, "Performance of Multiprocessor Interconnection Networks," *Computer*, Vol. 20, No. 4, April 1987, pp. 50–60.

72. Crawley, D., "An Analysis of MIMD Processor Interconnection Networks for Nanoelectronic Systems," *UCL Image Processing Group Report 98/3*, 1998, p. 15.

73. "Using ASCI White," October 7, 2002, `<www.llnl.gov/asci/platforms/white/>`.

74. "IBM SP Hardware/Software Overview," February 26, 2003, `<www.llnl.gov/computing/tutorials/ibmhwsw/#evolution>`.

75. Skillicorn, D., "A Taxonomy for Computer Architectures," *Computer*, Vol. 21, No. 11, November 1988, pp. 46–57.

76. McKinley, D., "Loosely-Coupled Multiprocessing: Scalable, Available, Flexible, and Economical Computing Power," *RTC Europe*, May 2001, pp. 22–24, `<www.rtceuropeonline.com/may2001/specialreport.pdf>`.

77. McKinley, D., "Loosely-Coupled Multiprocessing: Scalable, Available, Flexible, and Economical Computing Power," *RTC Europe*, May 2001, pp. 22–24, `<www.rtceuropeonline.com/may2001/specialreport.pdf>`.

78. Enslow, P., "Multiprocessor Organization—A Survey," *Computing Surveys*, Vol. 9, No. 1, March 1977, pp. 103–129.

79. Van Lang, T., "Strictly On-Line: Parallel Algorithms for Calculating Underground Water Quality," *Linux Journal*, No. 63, July 1, 1999, `<www.linuxjournal.com/article.php?sid=3021>`.

80. Enslow, P., "Multiprocessor Organization—A Survey," *Computing Surveys*, Vol. 9, No. 1, March 1977, pp. 103–129.

81. Bartlett, J., "A NonStop Kernel," *Proceedings of the Eighth Symposium on Operating System Principles*, December 1981, pp. 22–29.

82. Enslow, P., "Multiprocessor Organization—A Survey," *Computing Surveys*, Vol. 9, No. 1, March 1977, pp. 103–129.

83. Wilson, A., "More Power to You: Symmetrical Multiprocessing Gives Large-Scale Computer Power at a Lower Cost with Higher Availability," *Datamation*, June 1980, pp. 216–223.

84. Rettberg, R., and R. Thomas, "Contention is No Obstacle to Shared-Memory Multiprocessors," *Communications of the ACM*, Vol. 29, No. 12, December 1986, pp. 1202–1212.

85. Mukherjee, B.; K. Schwan; and P. Gopinath, "A Survey of Multiprocessor Operating Systems," *GIT-CC-92/05*, November 5, 1993, p. 2.

86. Tripathi, A., and N. Karnik, "Trends in Multiprocessor and Distributed Operating System Design," *Journal of Supercomputing*, Vol. 9, No. 1/2, 1995, p. 4.

87. Mukherjee, B.; K. Schwan; and P. Gopinath, "A Survey of Multiprocessor Operating Systems," *GIT-CC-92/05*, November 5, 1993, p. 2.

88. Mukherjee, B.; K. Schwan; and P. Gopinath, "A Survey of Multiprocessor Operating Systems," *GIT-CC-92/05*, November 5, 1993, pp. 2–3.

89. Tripathi, A., and N. Karnik, "Trends in Multiprocessor and Distributed Operating System Design," *Journal of Supercomputing*, Vol. 9, No. 1/2, 1995, p. 3.

90. Joe, T., and J. Hennessy, "Evaluating the Memory Overhead Required for COMA Architectures," *Proceedings of the 21st Annual Symposium on Computer Architecture*, April 1994, p. 82.

91. Stenstrom, P.; T. and Joe; A. Gupta, "Comparative Performance Evaluation of Cache-Coherent NUMA and COMA Architectures," *Proceedings of the 19th Annual Symposium on Computer Architecture*, May 1992, p. 81.

92. Stenstrom, P.; T. Joe; and A. Gupta, "Comparative Performance Evaluation of Cache-Coherent NUMA and COMA Architectures," *Proceedings of the 19th Annual Symposium on Computer Architecture*, May 1992, p. 80.

93. Tripathi, A., and N. Karnik, "Trends in Multiprocessor and Distributed Operating System Design," *Journal of Supercomputing*, Vol. 9, No. 1/2, 1995, p. 20.

94. Mukherjee, B.; K. Schwan; and P. Gopinath, "A Survey of Multiprocessor Operating Systems," *GIT-CC-92/05*, November 5, 1993, pp. 2–3.

95. Barroso, L.A.; J. Dean; and U. Hoelzle, "Web Search for a Planet: The Google Cluster Architecture," *IEEE MICRO*, March–April 2003, pp. 22–28.

96. Tripathi, A., and N. Karnik, "Trends in Multiprocessor and Distributed Operating System Design," *Journal of Supercomputing*, Vol. 9, No. 1/2, 1995, p. 3.

97. Tanenbaum, A., and R. Renesse, "Distributed Operating Systems," *Computing Surveys*, Vol. 17, No. 4, December 1985, p. 420.

98. Lai, K., and P. Hudak, "Memory Coherence in Shared Virtual Memory Systems," *ACM Transactions on Computer Systems*, Vol. 7, No. 4, November 1989, p. 325.

99. Lai, K., and P. Hudak, "Memory Coherence in Shared Virtual Memory Systems," *ACM Transactions on Computer Systems*, Vol. 7, No. 4, November 1989, p. 325.

100. "Cache Coherence," *Webopedia.com*, <www.webopedia.com/TERM/C/cache_coherence.html>.

101. Stenstrom, P.; T. Joe; and A. Gupta, "Comparative Performance Evaluation of Cache-Coherent NUMA and COMA Architectures," *Proceedings of the 19th Annual Symposium on Computer Architecture*, May 1992, p. 81.

102. Soundararajan, V., et al., "Flexible Use of Memory for Replication/Migration in Cache-Coherent DSM Multiprocessors," *Proceedings of the 25th Annual Symposium on Computer Architecture*, June 1998, p. 342.

103. Lai, A. and B. Falsafi, "Comparing the Effectiveness of Fine-Grain Memory Caching against Page Migration/Replication in Reducing Traffic in DSM Clusters," *ACM Symposium on Parallel Algorithms and Architecture*, 2000, p. 79.

104. Soundararajan, V., et al., "Flexible Use of Memory for Replication/Migration in Cache-Coherent DSM Multiprocessors," *Proceedings of the 25th Annual Symposium on Computer Architecture*, June 1998, p. 342.

105. Baral, Y.; M. Carikar; and P. Indyk, "On Page Migration and Other Relaxed Task Systems," *ACM Symposium on Discrete Algorithms*, 1997, p. 44.

106. Vergese, B., et al., "Operating System Support for Improving Data Locality on CC-NUMA Computer Servers," *Proceedings of the 7th International Conference on Architectural Support for Programming Languages and Operating Systems*, October 1996, p. 281.

107. Vergese, B., et al., "Operating System Support for Improving Data Locality on CC-NUMA Compute Servers," *Proceedings of the 7th International Conference on Architectural Support for Programming Languages and Operating Systems*, October 1996, p. 281.

108. LaRowe, R.; C. Ellis; and L. Kaplan, "The Robustness of NUMA Memory Management," *Proceedings of the 13th ACM Symposium on Operating System Principles*, October 1991, pp. 137–138.

109. Lai, K., and P. Hudak, "Memory Coherence in Shared Virtual Memory Systems," *ACM Transactions on Computer Systems*, Vol. 7, No. 4, November 1989, pp. 326–327.

110. Lai, K., and P. Hudak, "Memory Coherence in Shared Virtual Memory Systems," *ACM Transactions on Computer Systems*, Vol. 7, No. 4, November 1989, pp. 327–328.

111. Tripathi, A., and N. Karnik, "Trends in Multiprocessor and Distributed Operating System Design," *Journal of Supercomputing*, Vol. 9, No. 1/2, 1995, p. 21.

112. Iftode, L., and J. Singh, "Shared Virtual Memory: Progress and Challenges," *Proceedings of the IEEE Special Issue on Distributed Shared Memory*, Vol. 87, No. 3, March 1999, p. 498.

113. Iftode, L., and J. Singh, "Shared Virtual Memory: Progress and Challenges," *Proceedings of the IEEE Special Issue on Distributed Shared Memory*, Vol. 87, No. 3, March 1999, p. 499.

114. Gharacharloo, K., et al., "Memory Consistency and Event Ordering in Scalable Shared-Memory Multiprocessors," *Proceedings of the 17th Annual Symposium on Computer Architecture*, May 1990, pp. 17–19.

115. Carter, J.; J. Bennett; and J. Zwaenepoel, "Implementation and Performance of Munin," *Proceedings of the 13th ACM Symposium on Operating System Principles*, 1991, pp. 153–154.

116. Iftode, L., and J. Singh, "Shared Virtual Memory: Progress and Challenges," *Proceedings of the IEEE Special Issue on Distributed Shared Memory,* Vol. 87, No. 3, March 1999, pp. 499–500.

117. Dudnicki, C., et al., "Improving Release-Consistent Shared Virtual Memory Using Automatic Update," *Proceedings of the Second IEEE Symposium on High-Performance Computer Architecture,* February 1996, p. 18.

118. "Delayed Consistency and Its Effects on the Miss Rate of Parallel Programs," *Proceedings of Supercomputing '91,* 1991, pp. 197–206.

119. Iftode, L,. and J. Singh, "Shared Virtual Memory: Progress and Challenges," *Proceedings of the IEEE Special Issue on Distributed Shared Memory,* Vol. 87, No. 3, March 1999, p. 500.

120. Tripath, A., and N. M. Karnik, "Trends in Multiprocessor and Distributed Operating System Designs," *Journal of Supercomputing,* Vol. 9, No. 1/2, 1995, p. 14.

121. Tripath, A., and N. M. Karnik, "Trends in Multiprocessor and Distributed Operating System Designs," *Journal of Supercomputing,* Vol. 9, No. 1/2, 1995, p. 14.

122. Tripath, A., and N. M. Karnik, "Trends in Multiprocessor and Distributed Operating System Designs," *Journal of Supercomputing,* Vol. 9, No. 1/2, 1995, p. 14.

123. Tannenbaum, A. S., and R. V. Renesse, "Distributed Operating Systems," *ACM Computing Surveys,* Vol. 17, No. 4, December 1985, p. 436.

124. Bunt, R. B.; D. L. Eager; and S. Majumdar, "Scheduling in Multiprogrammed Parallel Systems," *ACM SIGMETRICS,* 1988, p. 106.

125. Bunt, R. B.; D. L. Eager; and S. Majumdar, "Scheduling in Multiprogrammed Parallel Systems," *ACM SIGMETRICS,* 1988, p. 105.

126. Bunt, R. B.; D. L. Eager; and S. Majumdar, "Scheduling in Multiprogrammed Parallel Systems," *ACM SIGMETRICS,* 1998, p. 106.

127. Gopinath, P., et al., "A Survey of Multiprocessing Operating Systems (Draft)," *Georgia Institute of Technology,* November 5, 1993, p. 15.

128. Mukherjee, B.; K. Schwan; and P. Gopinath, "A Survey of Multiprocessor Operating Systems," *GIT-CC-92/05,* November 5, 1993, 1993, p. 15.

129. Bunt, R. B.; D. L. Eager; and S. Majumdar, "Scheduling in Multiprogrammed Parallel Systems," *ACM SIGMETRICS,* 1998, p. 106.

130. Mukherjee, B.; K. Schwan; and P. Gopinath, "A Survey of Multiprocessor Operating Systems," *GIT-CC-92/05,* November 5, 1993, p. 15.

131. Tripathi, A., and N. M. Karnik, "Trends in Multiprocessor and Distributed Operating System Design," *Journal of Supercomputing,* Vol. 9, No. 1/2, 1995, p. 16.

132. Leutenegger, S. T., and M. K. Vernon, "The Performance of Multiprogrammed Multiprocessor Scheduling Policies," *Proceedings of the ACM Conference on Measurement and Modeling of Computer Systems,* 1990, p. 227.

133. Leutenegger, S. T., and M. K. Vernon, "The Performance of Multiprogrammed Multiprocessor Scheduling Policies," *Proceedings of the ACM Conference on Measurement and Modeling of Computer Systems,* 1990, p. 227.

134. Mukherjee, B.; K. Schwan; and P. Gopinath, "A Survey of Multiprocessor Operating Systems," *GIT-CC-92/05,* November 5, 1993, p. 17.

135. Tripathi, A., and N. M. Karnik, "Trends in Multiprocessor and Distributed Operating System Design," *Journal of Supercomputing,* Vol. 9, No. 1/2, 1995, p. 16.

136. Mukherjee, B.; K. Schwan; and P. Gopinath, "A Survey of Multiprocessor Operating Systems," *GIT-CC-92/05,* November 5, 1993, p. 15.

137. Mukherjee, B.; K. Schwan; and P. Gopinath, "A Survey of Multiprocessor Operating Systems," *GIT-CC-92/05,* November 5, 1993, p. 16.

138. Gupta, A., and A. Tucker, "Process Control and Scheduling Issues for Multiprogrammed Shared-Memory Multiprocessors," *Proceedings of the 12th ACM Symposium on Operating System Principles,* 1989, p. 165.

139. Leutenegger, S. T., and M. K. Vernon, "The Performance of Multiprogrammed Multiprocessor Scheduling Policies," *Proceedings of the ACM Conference on Measurement and Modeling of Computer Systems,* 1990, pp. 227–228.

140. Carlson, B.; L. Dowdy; K. Dussa; and K-H. Park, "Dynamic Partitioning in a Transputer Environment," *Proceedings of the ACM,* 1990, p. 204.

141. Carlson, B.; L. Dowdy; K. Dussa; and K-H. Park, "Dynamic Partitioning in a Transputer Environment," *Proceedings of the ACM,* 1990, p. 204.

142. Carlson, B.; L. Dowdy; K. Dussa; and K-H. Park, "Dynamic Partitioning in a Transputer Environment," *Proceedings of the ACM,* 1990, p. 204.

143. Tripathi, A., and N. M. Karnik, "Trends in Multiprocessor and Distributed Operating System Designs," *Journal of Supercomputing,* Vol. 9, No. 1/2, 1995, p. 17

144. Milojicic, D., et al., "Process Migration," *ACM Computing Surveys,* Vol. 32, No. 3, September 2000, p. 241

145. Milojicic, D., et al., "Process Migration," *ACM Computing Surveys,* Vol. 32, No. 3, September 2000, p. 246

146. Langendorfer, H., and S. Petri, "Load Balancing and Fault Tolerance in Workstation Clusters: Migrating Groups of Processes," *Operating Systems Review,* Vol. 29, No. 4, October 1995, p. 25

147. Milojicic, D., et al., "Process Migration," *ACM Computing Surveys,* Vol. 32, No. 3, September 2000, p. 246

148. Eskicioglu, M., "Design Issues of Process Migration Facilities in Distributed Systems," *IEEE Computer Society Technical Committee on Operating Systems Newsletter,* Vol. 4, No. 2, 1990, pp. 5–6.

149. Steketee, C.; P. Socko; and B. Kiepuszewski, "Experiences with the Implementation of a Process Migration Mechanism for

Amoeba," *Proceedings of the 19th ACSC Conference,* January–February 1996.

150. Eskicioglu, M., "Design Issues of Process Migration Facilities in Distributed Systems," *IEEE Computer Society Technical Committee on Operating Systems Newsletter,* Vol. 4, No. 2, 1990, pp. 5–6.

151. Milojicic, D., et. al., "Process Migration," *ACM Computing Surveys,* Vol. 32, No. 3, September 2000, p. 255

152. Eskicioglu, M., "Design Issues of Process Migration Facilities in Distributed Systems," *IEEE Computer Society Technical Committee on Operating Systems Newsletter,* Vol. 4, No. 2, 1990, p. 10.

153. Milojicic, D., et al., "Process Migration," *ACM Computing Surveys,* Vol. 32, No. 3, September 2000, p. 256

154. Mukherjee, B.; K. Schwan; and P. Gopinath, "A Survey of Multiprocessor Operating Systems," *GIT-CC-92/05,* November 5, 1993, p. 21.

155. Steketee, C.; P. Socko; and B. Kiepuszewski, "Experiences with the Implementation of a Process Migration Mechanism for Amoeba," *Proceedings of the 19th ACSC Conference,* January–February 1996.

156. Milojicic, D., et al., "Process Migration," *ACM Computing Surveys,* Vol. 32, No. 3, September 2000, p. 259

157. Milojicic, D., et al., "Process Migration," *ACM Computing Surveys,* Vol. 32, No. 3, September 2000, p. 256

158. Eskicioglu, M., "Design Issues of Process Migration Facilities in Distributed Systems," *IEEE Computer Society Technical Committee on Operating Systems Newsletter,* Vol. 4, No. 2, 1990, p. 6.

159. Milojicic, D., et al., "Process Migration," *ACM Computing Surveys,* Vol. 32, No. 3, September 2000, p. 256.

160. Milojicic, D., et al., "Process Migration," *ACM Computing Surveys,* Vol. 32, No. 3, September 2000, p. 256

161. Eskicioglu, M., "Design Issues of Process Migration Facilities in Distributed Systems," *IEEE Computer Society Technical Committee on Operating Systems Newsletter,* Vol. 4, No. 2, 1990, p. 7.

162. Douglis, F., and J. Ousterhout, "Transparent Process Migration: Design Alternatives and the Sprite Implementation," *Software Practice and Experience,* Vol. 21, No. 8, p. 764.

163. Zayas, E., "Attacking the Process Migration Bottleneck," *Proceedings of the Eleventh Annual ACM Symposium on Operating System Principles,* 1987, pp. 13–24.

164. Douglis, F., and J. Ousterhout, "Transparent Process Migration: Design Alternatives and the Sprite Implementation," *Software Practice and Experience,* Vol. 21, No. 8, p. 764.

165. Milojicic, D., et al., "Process Migration," *ACM Computing Surveys,* Vol. 32, No. 3, September 2000, p. 256

166. Eskicioglu, M., "Design Issues of Process Migration Facilities in Distributed Systems," *IEEE Computer Society Technical Committee on Operating Systems Newsletter,* Vol. 4, No. 2, 1990, p. 7.

167. Dougli, F., and J. Ousterhout, "Transparent Process Migration: Design Alternatives and the Sprite Implementation," *Software Practice and Experience,* Vol. 21, No. 8, p. 764.

168. Eskicioglu, M., "Design Issues of Process Migration Facilities in Distributed Systems," *IEEE Computer Society Technical Committee on Operating Systems Newsletter,* Vol. 4, No. 2, 1990, pp. 6–7.

169. Mukherjee, B.; K. Schwan; and P. Gopinath, "A Survey of Multiprocessor Operating Systems," *GIT-CC-92/05,* November 5, 1993, p. 14.

170. Mukherjee, B.; K. Schwan; and P. Gopinath, "A Survey of Multiprocessor Operating Systems," *GIT-CC-92/05,* November 5, 1993, p. 14.

171. Mukherjee, B.; K. Schwan; and P. Gopinath, "A Survey of Multiprocessor Operating Systems," *GIT-CC-92/05,* November 5, 1993, pp. 14–15.

172. Diekmann, R.; B. Monien; and R. Preis, "Load Balancing Strategies for Distributed Memory Machines," *World Scientific,* 1997, p. 3.

173. Tannenbaum, A. S., and R. V. Renesse, "Distributed Operating Systems," *ACM Computing Surveys,* Vol. 17, No. 4, December 1985, p. 436.

174. Diekmann, R.; B. Monien; and R. Preis, "Load Balancing Strategies for Distributed Memory Machines," *World Scientific,* 1997, p. 5.

175. Diekmann, R.; B. Monien; and R. Preis, "Load Balancing Strategies for Distributed Memory Machines," *World Scientific,* 1997, p. 7.

176. Tannenbaum, A. S., and R. V. Renesse, "Distributed Operating Systems," *ACM Computing Surveys,* Vol. 17, No. 4, December 1985, p. 438.

177. Milojicic, D., et al., "Process Migration," *ACM Computing Surveys,* Vol. 32, No. 3, September 2000, p. 250.

178. Milojicic, D., et al., "Process Migration," *ACM Computing Surveys,* Vol. 32, No. 3, September 2000, p. 251.

179. Shivarati, N.; P. Kreuger; and M. Singhal, "Load Distributing for Locally Distributed Systems," *IEEE Computer,* 1992, pp. 37–39.

180. Milojicic, D., e. al., "Process Migration," *ACM Computing Surveys,* Vol. 32, No. 3, September 2000, p. 251.

181. Shivarati, N.; P. Kreuger; and M. Singhal, "Load Distributing for Locally Distributed Systems," *IEEE Computer,* 1992, pp. 37–39.

182. Milojicic, D., et al., "Process Migration," *ACM Computing Surveys,* Vol. 32, No. 3, September 2000, p. 251.

183. Shivarati, N.; P. Kreuger; and M. Singhal, "Load Distributing for Locally Distributed Systems," *IEEE Computer,* 1992, pp. 37–39.

184. Milojicic, D., et al., "Process Migration," *ACM Computing Surveys,* Vol. 32, No. 3, September 2000, p. 251.

185. Ahmad, I., and Y-K. Kwok, "Static Scheduling Algorithms for Allocating Directed Task Graphs to Multiprocessors," *Communications of the ACM,* 2000, p. 462.

186. Luling, R., et al., "A Study on Dynamic Load Balancing Algorithms," *Proceedings of the IEEE SPDP,* 1991, p. 686–689.

187. Luling, R., et al., "A Study on Dynamic Load Balancing Algorithms," *Proceedings of the IEEE SPDP,* 1991, p. 686–689.

188. Tannenbaum, A. S., and R. V. Renesse, "Distributed Operating Systems," *ACM Computing Surveys*, Vol. 17, No. 4, December 1985, p. 438.

189. Tannenbaum, A. S., and R. V. Renesse, "Distributed Operating Systems," *ACM Computing Surveys*, Vol. 17, No. 4, December 1985, p. 438.

190. Barak, A., and A. Shiloh, "A Distributed Load Balancing Policy for a Multicomputer," *Software Practice and Experience*, December 15, 1985, pp. 901–913.

191. Tripathi, A., and N. M. Karnik, "Trends in Multiprocessor and Distributed Operating System Designs," *Journal of Supercomputing*, Vol. 9, No 1/2, 1995, p. 11.

192. Mellor-Crummy, J. and M. Scott, "Algorithms for Scalable Synchronization on Shared-Memory Multiprocessors," *ACM Transactions on Computer Systems*, Vol. 9, No. 1, February 1991, p. 22.

193. Mukherjee, B.; K. Schwan; and P. Gopinath, "A Survey of Multiprocessor Operating Systems," *GIT-CC-92/05*, November 5, 1993, p. 24.

194. Tripathi, A., and N. M. Karnik, "Trends in Multiprocessor and Distributed Operating System Designs," *Journal of Supercomputing*, Vol. 9, No 1/2, 1995, pp. 11-12.

195. Tripathi, A., and N. M. Karnik, "Trends in Multiprocessor and Distributed Operating System Designs," *Journal of Supercomputing*, Vol. 9, No 1/2, 1995, p. 12.

196. Mukherjee, B., and K. Schwan, "Experiments with Configurable Locks for Multiprocessors," *GIT-CC-93/05*, January 10, 1993.

197. Tripathi, A., and N. M. Karnik, "Trends in Multiprocessor and Distributed Operating System Designs," *Journal of Supercomputing*, Vol. 9, No 1/2, 1995, p. 13.

198. Mellor-Crummy, J. and M. Scott, "Scalable Reader-Writer Synchronization for Shared-Memory Multiprocessors," *Proceedings of the Third ACM SIGPLAN Symposium on Principles and Practices of Parallel Programming*, 1991, pp. 106–113.

199. Mukherjee, B.; K. Schwan; and P. Gopinath, "A Survey of Multiprocessor Operating Systems," *GIT-CC-92/05*, November 5, 1993, p. 25.

200. Flynn, M., "Very High-Speed Computing Systems," *Proceedings of the IEEE*, Vol. 54, December 1966, pp. 1901–1909.

201. Crawley, D., "An Analysis of MIMD Processor Interconnection Networks for Nanoelectronic Systems," *UCL Image Processing Group Report 98/3*, 1998, p. 3.

202. Mukherjee, B.; K. Schwan; and P. Gopinath, "A Survey of Multiprocessor Operating Systems," *GIT-CC-92/05*, November 5, 1993, p. 1.

203. Tripathi, A., and N. Karnik, "Trends in Multiprocessor and Distributed Operating System Design," *Journal of Supercomputing*, Vol. 9, No. 1/2, 1995, p. 3.

204. Leutenegger, S. T., and M. K. Vernon, "The Performance of Multiprogrammed Multiprocessor Scheduling Policies," *Proceedings of the ACM Conference on Measurement and Modeling of Computer Systems*, 1990, p. 227.

205. Bunt, R. B.; D. L. Eager; and S. Majumdar, "Scheduling in Multiprogrammed Parallel Systems," *ACM SIGMETRICS*, 1988, p. 106.

206. Lai, K., and P. Hudak, "Memory Coherence in Shared Virtual Memory Systems," *ACM Transactions on Computer Systems*, Vol. 7, No. 4, November 1989, p. 325.

207. Iftode, L., and J. Singh, "Shared Virtual Memory: Progress and Challenges," *Proceedings of the IEEE Special Issue on Distributed Shared Memory*, Vol. 87, No. 3, March 1999, p. 498.

208. Milojicic, D., et al., "Process Migration," *ACM Computing Surveys*, Vol. 32, No. 3, September 2000, p. 241

209. Langendorfer, H., and S. Petri, "Load Balancing and Fault Tolerance in Workstation Clusters: Migrating Groups of Processes," *Operating Systems Review*, Vol. 29, No. 4, October 1995, p. 25

Networking and Distributed Computing

Whatever shall we do in that remote spot?
—Napoleon Bonaparte—

Part 6

With the popularization of the Web in 1993, Internet usage literally exploded. Now there is a huge focus on building distributed, Internet-based applications; this is profoundly affecting operating systems design. Chapter 16 introduces computer networking and discusses network topologies and types, and the client/server networking model. We carefully explain the four layers of the Internet's TCP/IP protocol stack. Chapter 17 introduces distributed systems and discusses attributes, communication, synchronization, mutual exclusion and deadlock. The chapter also presents case studies of the Sprite and Amoeba distributed operating systems. Chapter 18 discusses distributed file systems, clustering, peer-to-peer distributed computing, grid computing, Java distributed computing technologies and the emerging technology of Web services.

The humblest is the peer of the most powerful.
—John Marshall Harlan—

Live in fragments no longer. Only connect.
— Edward Morgan Forster —

What networks of railroads, highways and canals were in another age, the networks of telecommunications, information and computerization...are today.
— Bruno Kreisky —

It took five months to get word back to Queen Isabella about the voyage of Columbus, two weeks for Europe to hear about Lincoln's assassination, and only 1.3 seconds to get the word from Neil Armstrong that man can walk on the moon.
— Isaac Asimov —

Chapter 16

Introduction to Networking

Objectives

After reading this chapter, you should understand:

- *the central role of networking in today's computer systems.*

- *various network types and topologies.*

- *the TCP/IP protocol stack.*

- *the capabilities of TCP/IP's application, transport, network and link layers.*

- *protocols such as HTTP, FTP, TCP, UDP, XCP, IP and IPv6.*

- *network hardware and hardware protocols such as Ethernet and Wireless 802.11.*

- *the client/server networking model.*

Chapter Outline

16.1 Introduction

Networks have become almost as important as the computers they connect, enabling users to access resources that are available on remote computers and communicate with other users around the world. Talking on the telephone, watching cable television, using a cellular phone, making a credit card purchase, withdrawing money from an ATM, browsing the Web and sending e-mail are all activities that rely on networked computers. As users, we have come to expect that network communication will occur quickly and without error.

This chapter discusses common network layouts, focusing on how **hosts**—entities that receive and provide services over a network—are connected by **links**—media over which network services are transmitted. If a link breaks, a host fails or a message is lost, network communication can be interrupted. We introduce the **TCP/ IP protocol stack**, which provides well-defined interfaces to enable communication between computers across a network and to allow problems to be fixed as they arise. The TCP/IP protocol stack splits networked communication into four logical levels called **layers**. Each layer provides functionality for the layers above it to ease the development, management and debugging of networks and simplify the programming of applications that rely on those networks. A layer is implemented by following certain **protocols**—sets of rules that govern how two entities should interact. In our discussion of each layer, we consider popular Internet protocols that allow users worldwide to communicate. We conclude by discussing the popular client/server model of network communication.

The concepts presented in this chapter will help you understand the chapters on distributed systems (Chapter 17 and Chapter 18), security (Chapter 19) and the case studies on Linux (Chapter 20) and Windows XP (Chapter 21).

Self Review

1. Why does the TCP/IP protocol stack separate network communication into four layers?
2. What problems can arise during network communication?

Ans: **1)** Separating network communication into four layers modularizes the communication. Developers can focus on one layer at a time. This eases development, management and debugging of networks and networked applications. **2)** Hosts can fail, links can break and messages can be lost.

16.2 Network Topology

Network topology describes the relationship among the hosts, also called **nodes**, on a network. A **logical topology** displays which nodes in a network are directly connected (i.e., which nodes can communicate with each other without relying on any intermediate nodes).[1] Common network topologies (Fig. 16.1) include bus, ring, star, tree, mesh and fully-connected mesh networks.

Nodes on a **bus** (or **linear**) **network** (Fig. 16.1, part a) are all connected to a single, common communication link (called a bus). Bus networks are simple

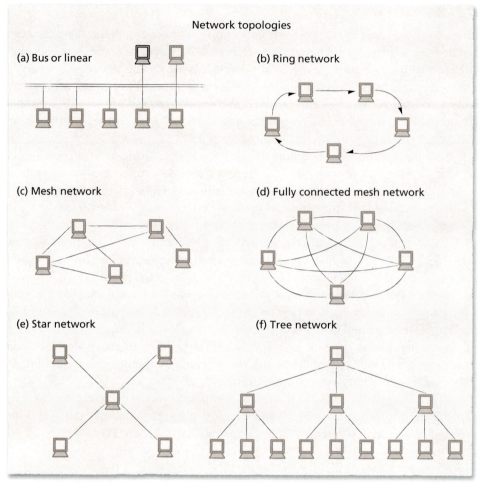

Network topologies

(a) Bus or linear

(b) Ring network

(c) Mesh network

(d) Fully connected mesh network

(e) Star network

(f) Tree network

Figure 16.1 | *Network topologies.*

because they do not require intermediate nodes to forward messages to other nodes. As messages travel along a link, resistance in the medium causes the signal to lose strength—this is known as **attenuation.** Since bus networks do not have intermediate nodes that retransmit messages, the length of the bus communication medium must be limited to minimize attenuation. If any individual node in a bus network fails, the entire network will continue functioning. If the bus itself fails, the entire network will fail. Bus networks are appropriate for homes and small offices.[2, 3]

Ring networks (Fig. 16.1, part b) consist of a set of nodes, each of which maintains exactly two connections to other nodes such that a message sent through one connection can eventually return via the other. Ring networks can grow to be larger than bus networks, because each node in the ring forwards each message; this limits message attenuation but introduces a retransmission delay (i.e., the time required for a node to process a message before retransmitting it). One of the most significant limitations of a ring network is that if one node in a ring fails, then communication in the entire ring will fail. This means that a ring network has limited fault tolerance, since the network cannot recover from a single node failure.

Star networks (Fig. 16.1, part e) contain a single central node, or **hub**, that is connected to all of the other nodes in the network and is responsible for relaying messages between nodes. All transmissions in a star network pass through the hub. Since communications over star networks go through a single intermediate node, attenuation will limit the geographical size of the network, but transmission delay is smaller than in ring networks. The network can survive the failure of one of the outer nodes, but the entire network will fail if the central hub fails. Since the central hub controls all communication, a bottleneck will occur if the network demand exceeds the processing capabilities of the hub. [4, 5]

Tree networks (Fig. 16.1, part f) are hierarchical networks that consist of a root node and several subnodes, called children, that can have subnodes of their own. A tree network can be viewed as multiple star networks. The hub of the first star network is the root of the tree. Each child node in this star serves as a hub for another star network. Hubs are responsible for relaying information to the nodes in their immediate networks. A tree topology is often used to join nodes that communicate with each other frequently, thereby increasing network efficiency. [6, 7]

In **mesh networks** (Fig. 16.1, part c), at least two nodes have more than one path connecting them. A mesh network in which each node is directly connected to every other node is a **fully-connected mesh network** (Fig. 16.1, part d). Mesh networks and fully connected networks are the most fault-tolerant topologies, because typically there are multiple paths between each pair of nodes. The primary disadvantage of mesh networks is the complexity associated with directing messages between nodes that have no direct connection. With fully-connected networks, this is simple since each pair of nodes has a direct link between them. The problem with fully-connected networks is that as the number of nodes increase, the number of links to connect those nodes increases exponentially. [8, 9]

The proliferation of wireless network technology has introduced **ad hoc networks** (see the Mini Case Study, Symbian OS). An ad hoc network is spontaneous—any number of devices may be connected to it at any time. These devices become part of, and leave, the network at random. Ad hoc networks consist of any combination of wireless and wired devices. The network topology can change rapidly, which makes it difficult for the network to be governed by a central node. The variable nature of ad hoc networks makes determining their topology a challenging problem in current research. [10]

Self Review

1. Why would a network for a mission-critical system (e.g., a nuclear power plant or an air traffic control system) not be built with a ring topology?
2. Why do wireless devices require a spontaneous network?

Ans: **1)** A mission-critical system would not use a ring topology because of the lack of fault tolerance. If a single node failed, the entire network would fail. Mission-critical systems require networks with multiple levels of redundancy to ensure continuous operation. **2)** The nature of wireless devices is that as they move from place to place; they join and exit multiple networks. Ad hoc networks do not require a fixed network topology.

16.3 Network Types

The two most prevalent types of networks are **local area networks (LANs)** and **wide area networks (WANs)**. A LAN is a network with limited geographic range designed to optimize data transfer rates between its nodes. Local area networks interconnect resources using high-speed communication paths with network protocols optimized for local area environments such as office buildings or college campuses. LANs benefit by independence from the larger networks. Those that are company or university owned can be upgraded or reorganized at the company or university's discretion. LANs are also free from the congestion that can arise in

Mini Case Study

Symbian OS

Symbian (www.symbian.com), maker of the Symbian operating system, was founded in 1998 by mobile phone manufacturers Ericsson, Nokia, Motorola and Psion to develop a cross-platform mobile phone operating system to replace their individual, incompatible OSs.[11, 12] The result is **Symbian OS**, a small operating system that runs on "smart phones"[13]—mobile phones with the functionality of a PDA (Personal Digital Assistant). Symbian OS is unique in that it was built for mobile phones,[14, 15] while its major competitors such as Windows CE, Linux and PalmOS were all originally designed for different systems, then adapted to mobile phones.

Symbian focuses on size and time efficiency.[16, 17] The Symbian OS complies with open standards such as the POSIX API[18]—the IEEE's Portable Operating System Interface standard—as well as APIs for high-performance graphics and multimedia, mobile browsing and messaging, communications and mobile telephony, security and data management, to make it easier for application developers to write compatible software.[19, 20] Also, since Java is becoming standard on mobile phones and has a large application developer base, an implementation of the Java mobile run-time environment (MIDP) is included.[21, 22]

Symbian's latest release, v7.0s, is intended for third-generation (3G) mobile phones and comes equipped with new functionality to meet the needs of these high-performance wireless devices. Some of the new features of OS v7.0s include a multithreaded framework for multimedia, Java Wireless Messaging 1.0 and Bluetooth 1.1 capability.[23] OS v7.0s also supports W-CDMA (wideband code-division multiple access), which enables 3G mobile phones to transfer data at much higher rates, up to 2Mbps.[24] These new features are built upon the extensive collection of APIs common in all recent Symbian OS releases.

larger networks that must serve millions of users. Since LANs are autonomous, they can be customized to meet the needs of a particular group and can employ any of the network topologies discussed in Section 16.2.[25]

WANs are broader, consisting of many LANs and connecting many computers over great distances; the largest WAN by far is the Internet. WANs generally employ a mesh topology, operate at lower speeds than LANs and have higher error rates because they must interact with multiple, often heterogeneous LANs and WANs.[26]

Self Review

1. What is the purpose of creating smaller subnetworks within a larger network, such as a LAN that comprises a piece of a WAN?
2. What are the disadvantages of WANs compared to LANs?

Ans: **1)** A subnetwork, such as a LAN on a college campus, allows for a group of related computers to be directly connected for faster transmission, higher capacity, greater management flexibility and customization. **2)** WANs often operate at lower speeds and have higher error rates than LANs because they must interact with multiple, often heterogeneous LANs and WANs.

16.4   TCP/IP Protocol Stack

The four layers of networked communication as defined by the TCP/IP protocol stack are the application, transport, network and link layers. The **application layer** is the highest level and provides protocols (e.g., HTTP, FTP) for applications, such as Web browsers and Web servers, to communicate with each other. The **transport layer** is responsible for end-to-end communication of information from the sending process to the receiving process. The **network layer** is responsible for moving the data from one computer to the next (also known as routing). The transport layer relies on the network layer to determine the proper path from one end of the communication to the other. The **link layer** translates information between bits and a physical signal that travels through the physical link (e.g., a network cable).[27]

As a message travels down the stack, each layer receives the message and adds **control information** to the beginning of the message (called a **header**) or to the end of the message (called a **trailer**) to enable communication with the corresponding layer on other hosts. The control information might include, for example, the addresses of the source and destination hosts, or the type or size of data that is being sent. This new message then is passed to the layer below it (or to the physical medium if the message is coming from the link layer). When receiving information over a network, each layer receives data from the layer below it (or from the physical medium in the case of the link layer). The layer strips off the control information from the corresponding layer on the remote host. This data is often used to ensure that the message is valid and directed to the current host. The message then is passed to the layer above it (or to the process if the message is being passed upward by the application layer). We discuss these layers in detail in the sections that follow.

In 1984, the International Organization for Standardization (ISO) introduced the Open Systems Interconnection (OSI) Reference Model to establish an international standard for communication between applications over a network. Although not followed strictly on the Internet, it remains an important model to understand. The OSI protocol stack consists of the four layers we discussed previously plus three additional ones. The seven layers of the OSI model are application, presentation, session, transport, network, data link and physical.

The application, presentation and session layers in OSI correspond to the application layer in the TCP/IP protocol stack. In the OSI model, the **application layer** interacts with the applications and provides network services, such as file transfer and e-mail. The **presentation layer** solves certain compatibility problems, such as when the two end users use different data formats, by translating the application data into a standard format that can be understood by other layers. The **session layer** establishes, manages and terminates the communication between two end users. The transport and network layers correspond with the transport and network layers of the TCP/IP protocol stack, respectively. The data link layer and physical layer in OSI correspond to the link layer in the TCP/IP protocol stack. At the sender, the **data link layer** converts the data representation it receives from the network layer into bits and at the destination, it converts bits received into the data representation for the network layer. The **physical layer** transmits bits over the physical medium, such as cables.[28, 29, 30, 31]

Self Review

1. What type of information is placed in the header or trailer of a message?
2. Briefly list the capabilities of each of the four layers of the TCP/IP protocol stack.

Ans: **1)** Control information is placed in the header or trailer of a message to govern the communication between the two hosts; this information can include the addresses of the two hosts, or the type or size of the data. **2)** The application layer allows applications on remote hosts to communicate with one another. The transport layer is responsible for end-to-end communication between two hosts. The network layer is responsible for sending a packet to the next host toward the destination. The link layer serves as an interface between the network layer and the physical medium through which the information travels.

16.5 Application Layer

The application layer provides a well-defined interface for applications on different computers to communicate with one another; for example opening a remote file, requesting a Web page, transferring an e-mail or calling a remote procedure. Application layer protocols simplify communication between processes on a network and determine how processes should interact.[32] Common protocols of the application layer include Hypertext Transfer Protocol (HTTP), File Transfer Protocol (FTP), Simple Mail Transfer Protocol (SMTP), Domain Name System (DNS) and Secure Socket Shell (SSH).

Many application layer protocols interact with resources on remote hosts. These resources are specified by a **Uniform Resource Identifier (URI)**, which is a name that references a specific resource on a remote host. The more common term **Uniform Resource Locator (URL)** describes URIs that access resources in common protocols such as HTTP or FTP.[33] Most URLs contain the protocol, host, port and path of the resource. The protocol is the application layer protocol that is being used to communicate (e.g., HTTP or FTP). The host is the fully qualified name of the host computer. We discuss computer naming conventions in Section 16.7.1, Internet Protocol (IP). The **port** determines the socket to which a message should be passed—a **socket** is a software construct that represents one endpoint of a connection. Processes use sockets to send and receive messages over a network. The path is the location of the resource on that host.

Consider the URL `http://www.deitel.com/index.html`. The first part, `http://`, denotes that this URL is for HTTP. The second part, `www.deitel.com`, is the host name. Specifically, it accesses the company Web site for Deitel & Associates. The third part of the URL, the port, is omitted. Certain ports have been assigned by the Internet Assigned Numbers Authority as "well-known" ports; these ports are used by common application layer protocols. For example, HTTP commonly uses port 80, whereas FTP commonly uses ports 20 and 21.[34] By omitting the port, this URL connects to port 80, the default port for HTTP. The final part of the URL, `index.html`, specifies the path and name of the resource.

Self Review

1. Name some common protocols of the application layer.
2. Why is the port an important part of a URL?

Ans: **1)** FTP, SMTP, DNS, SSH and HTTP. **2)** The port identifies the socket on the computer to which the message should be passed.

16.5.1 Hypertext Transfer Protocol (HTTP)

The **Hypertext Transfer Protocol (HTTP)** is a versatile application layer protocol. While HTTP is commonly used to transmit HTML documents over the Internet, it allows the transfer of data in several formats using **Multipurpose Internet Mail Extensions** (**MIME**). MIME defines five content types: *text*, *image*, *audio*, *video* and *application*. The first four types are often used in multimedia Web pages; *application* is generally reserved for transferring binary files.

HTTP consists of requests for resources and responses from remote hosts. An **HTTP request** involves an action and a resource's URI. The action specifies the operation to be performed on the resource. The remote host processes the request and replies with an **HTTP response**, which contains in its header a code that tells the client whether the request was processed correctly or an error occurred. If the request was processed correctly, the requested resource is returned along with the header. The header also specifies the MIME type of the resource to notify the requesting application about the type of content it is receiving.[35, 36, 37]

Self Review

1. What would happen if a client sent an HTTP request for a resource that did not exist?
2. What is the purpose of MIME types?

Ans: **1)** The server would reply with an HTTP response that included an error code in the header. **2)** The MIME type provides the client with knowledge about the type of data being transmitted. This aids the client in determining how to process the data.

16.5.2 File Transfer Protocol (FTP)

File Transfer Protocol (FTP) is an application layer protocol that allows the transfer of files between remote hosts. FTP specifies connections between two ports: one port (typically port 21) sends control information that governs the session; the other port (typically port 20) sends the actual data. After a connection is established, the client specifies actions for the FTP server to perform by issuing various commands to the server (Fig. 16.2). The server attempts to satisfy each command, then issues a response with the result.[38]

Self Review

1. What ports do FTP hosts usually use to communicate?
2. What is the purpose of FTP?

Ans: **1)** FTP uses two ports to communicate, typically ports 20 and 21. **2)** FTP allows the transfer of files between hosts.

16.6 Transport Layer

The transport layer is responsible for the end-to-end communication of data between hosts. It receives data from the application layer, breaks it into smaller

Name	Function
CDUP	Change from the current directory to the parent of the current directory.
CWD	Change the working directory.
PWD	Print the path of the working directory.
LIST	List the contents of the working directory.
DELE	Delete the specified file.
RETR	Retrieve the specified file.
STOR	Upload the specified file.
QUIT	Terminate the FTP session.

Figure 16.2 | *FTP commands.*

pieces suitable for transport, appends control information to these pieces and sends them to the network layer.

There are two primary approaches to implementing the transport layer: **connection oriented** and **connectionless**. Connection-oriented services are modeled after the telephone system, in which a connection is established and held for the length of the session. Connectionless services are modeled after the postal service, in which two letters mailed from one place to the same destination may actually take two dramatically different paths through the system and even arrive at different times or not at all.

In a connection-oriented approach, hosts send each other control information—through a technique called **handshaking**—to initiate an end-to-end connection. Many networks are **unreliable**, which means that data sent across them may be damaged or lost (see the Anecdote, Unreliable Communication Lines Can Lead to Embarrassment). These networks do not guarantee anything about the data sent; it could arrive corrupted or out of order, as duplicates or not at all. These networks

Unreliable Communication Lines Can Lead to Embarrassment

This one happened to one of the authors, HMD. In the early 1980s, he was offered a consulting opportunity. To formalize the relationship, he had to send the client a detailed resume along with some other materials by overnight package courier. The package pickup deadline was approaching. HMD quickly updated his resume using a terminal at his home connected by an old-style acoustic coupler to phone lines and in turn to a time-sharing computer at the university where he was a professor at the time. He typed, "Since 1978, Harvey M. Deitel has been an assistant professor at Boston University" and started the printout (which was done on an old-style, 30-character-per-second dot matrix printing terminal). He walked into another room. The package courier came. He asked his wife to please tear off the printout, throw it in the package, seal it and give it to the courier. She said, "Harvey, I don't think you want to send this; you'd better take a look at it." HMD came back into the room. Data transmission over phone lines was a bit unreliable at the time. The printer failed and stopped typing at a most unfortunate point in the middle of the sentence (figure it out)! If HMD had sent the package, he surely would not have been given the consulting job! This was a humbling experience!

Lesson to operating systems designers: You can't design in a vacuum and simply assume that parts of a system "you're not responsible for" will indeed work perfectly. Every part of a system can fail—the software for which operating systems designers and implementors are most directly responsible, the hardware, the communications lines and even the people who work with the system as users or administrators.

make only a "best effort" to deliver data. A connection-oriented approach ensures reliability on unreliable networks. These protocols make communication **reliable**, guaranteeing that sent data will arrive at the intended receiver undamaged and in the correct sequence. Hosts might also exchange information to regulate the termination of the session so that no processes are left running on either host.

In a connectionless approach, the two hosts do not handshake before transmission and reliability is not guaranteed—data sent may never reach the intended recipient. A connectionless approach, however, avoids the overhead associated with handshaking and enforcing reliability; less information often needs to be passed between the hosts.[39, 40, 41, 42, 43]

Self Review

1. Why would a bank not implement a connectionless transport layer?
2. Most streaming media applications require a connectionless transport layer. What are some possible reasons for this?

Ans: **1)** A bank performs business-critical transactions that must be carried out correctly. A connectionless transport layer could lose transactions. **2)** Streaming media applications do not require the reliability of a connection-oriented approach, but benefit by the smaller amount of control information that comes with a connectionless approach.

16.6.1 Transmission Control Protocol (TCP)

The **Transmission Control Protocol (TCP)** is a connection-oriented transmission protocol that guarantees that data (called **segments** in TCP) sent from a sender will arrive at the intended receiver undamaged and in the correct sequence. Both HTTP and FTP rely on TCP to guarantee reliable communication. TCP handles error control, congestion control and retransmission, allowing protocols like HTTP and FTP to send information across a network as simply and reliably as writing to a file on a local computer.

To set up a connection, TCP uses a three-way handshake. One of the purposes of this handshaking is to synchronize sequence numbers between the two hosts. The sequence number of each host increases by one with each segment sent and is placed in each segment's header. The destination host uses these sequence numbers to rearrange the segments if they are received out-of-order. First, the source host sends a **synchronization segment (SYN)** to the destination host. This segment requests that a connection be made and contains the sequence number of the source host. The destination host responds with a **synchronization/acknowledgement segment (SYN/ACK)** which is an acknowledgement of the connection being established and contains the sequence number for the destination host. Finally, the source host responds with an **acknowledgement segment (ACK)** which finalizes the connection.[44]

When the destination host receives a segment, it responds with an acknowledgement (ACK) containing the sequence number of the received segment. If the source host does not receive an ACK for a particular sequence number, it will resend the segment with that sequence number after a certain wait time. This process guarantees that all segments will eventually be received by the destination host, duplicates will be discarded and the segments will be reassembled, if necessary, into the original order.[45, 46, 47, 48, 49]

In addition to reliability, TCP offers flow control and congestion control. **Flow control** regulates the number of segments sent by each host in an attempt not to overwhelm the receiver of those segments. **Congestion control** restricts the number of segments sent from a single host in response to overall network congestion. TCP implements both flow control and congestion control by maintaining a **TCP window** for the sender and receiver. The sender cannot send more segments than specified by the window before receiving an ACK from the receiver. The receiver calculates and sends its window along with each ACK that it sends. There are trade-offs associated with the size of the window advertised. A large window leads to the transmission of many segments. If the network or the receiver cannot handle this volume of segments, some will be discarded leading to retransmission of segments and inefficiency. Smaller windows can reduce throughput and result in the network being underutilized.

Self Review

1. TCP guarantees that segments will be delivered to the application in order, but the segments may not arrive at the host in order. What additional resource must TCP use?
2. What is the difference between flow control and congestion control?

Ans: **1)** TCP must possess a buffer to hold any segments received out of order until the missing segments are received. **2)** Flow control deals with restricting the number of segments sent by the source host so as to not overwhelm the destination host. Congestion control restricts the number of segments sent from a single host to help restrict network congestion.

16.6.2 User Datagram Protocol (UDP)

Applications that do not require the reliable end-to-end transmission guaranteed by TCP may be better served by the connectionless **User Datagram Protocol (UDP)**. UDP incurs the minimum overhead necessary to implement the transport layer. There is no guarantee that UDP segments, called **datagrams**, will reach their destination or arrive in their original order.

There are benefits to using UDP over TCP. UDP has little overhead because UDP headers are small; they do not need to carry the information TCP carries to ensure reliability. UDP also reduces network traffic relative to TCP due to the absence of ACKs, handshaking, retransmissions, etc.

Unreliable communication is acceptable in many situations. First, reliability is not necessary for some applications, so the overhead imposed by a protocol that guarantees reliability can be avoided. Second, some applications, such as streaming audio and video, can tolerate occasional datagram loss. This usually results in a small pause (or "hiccup") in the audio or video being played. If the same application were run over TCP, a lost segment could cause a significant pause, since the protocol would wait until the lost segment was retransmitted and delivered correctly before continuing. Finally, applications that need to implement their own reliability mechanisms different from that provided by TCP can build such mechanisms over UDP.[50, 51, 52]

Self Review

1. If a UDP datagram is lost due to network traffic, how does the host that sent the datagram respond?
2. Why would an application choose to use UDP as its transport layer protocol?

Ans: **1)** The host does nothing. UDP includes no means by which the sending host could learn that a datagram was lost. The host does not retransmit. **2)** An application would use UDP if reliability were not necessary (e.g., as in streaming audio and video applications) or if the application needed to implement its own reliability mechanisms.

16.7 Network Layer

The network layer receives data from the transport layer and is responsible for sending the data (called **datagrams**) to the next stop toward the destination through a process known as routing. **Routing** is the two-step process of determining the next host for a datagram toward the destination and sending the datagram along this path. **Routers** are computers that connect networks. Note that a router determines the next host for a given source and destination given its particular picture of the network at the time. Networks can change quickly and routers cannot determine these changes instantaneously, so a router's knowledge of the network is not always complete and up-to-date.

Routers determine the next host for a given datagram based on information such as network topologies and link quality, which includes strength of signal, error rate and interference. This information is propagated throughout networks using various routing protocols, one of the better known being the **Routing Information Protocol (RIP)**—an application layer protocol operating over UDP. RIP requires each router in a network to transmit its entire **routing table** (a hierarchical matrix listing the current network topology) to its closest neighboring routers. The process is continued until all routers are aware of the current topology. As networks grow in size, each router needs to keep track of the entire network topology. This generates excessive network traffic in large networks, which is why RIP is used almost exclusively on smaller networks.

Routers keep queues to manage datagrams, because it takes time for the router to determine the best route and send the datagram. When a datagram arrives from a network, it is placed into a queue until it can be serviced. Once the queue is full, additional datagrams are simply dropped from the network. It is therefore important to make sure senders do not overwhelm routers. Transport layer protocols must try not to overrun the queues.

Unlike the transport layer, which is concerned with sending data from the originating host to the destination host, the network layer at a particular host sends datagrams only to the next host toward the destination host. This process continues until the datagram reaches its destination host.

Self Review

1. What is the major drawback to the Routing Information Protocol that causes it to be reserved for smaller networks?
2. What happens when network congestion causes a router's queue to fill up with unserviced datagrams?

Ans: **1)** Each router in a network is required to transmit its entire routing table to its closest neighbor, regardless of whether or not changes have occurred. In large networks, these routing tables are larger, which causes increased network traffic. **2)** When a router's queue is full, datagrams that arrive subsequently are discarded. Hosts using TCP will consider this an example of network congestion and slow down transmission.

16.7.1 Internet Protocol (IP)

The **Internet Protocol (IP)** is the dominant network layer protocol for transmitting information over a network. IP allows smaller networks (LANs and small WANs) to be combined into larger networks (WANs, such as the Internet). IP version 4 (IPv4) is the version currently used by most networks. Destinations on the Internet are specified by **IP addresses**, which are 32-bit numbers in IPv4. Thus, there are 2^{32}, or approximately 4 billion, unique IP addresses. IP addresses are generally divided into four octets (8-bit bytes). An 8-bit byte can represent a decimal number from 0 to 256.

One or more host names are mapped to an IP address through the **Domain Name System (DNS)**. When a person enters a host name into a browser, it uses DNS to find the correct IP address for that host name. In this way, an easily remembered name is established as an alias for the IP address. This IP address is then used by the transport and network layers to deliver the data.[53, 54, 55]

Self Review

1. How many possible IPv4 addresses are there?
2. How does a Web browser convert a host name into an IP address?

Ans: **1)** There are 2^{32}, or approximately 4 billion, unique IP addresses. **2)** The Web server uses the Domain Name System (DNS) to convert a host name into an IP address.

16.7.2 Internet Protocol version 6 (IPv6)

Every device that accesses the Internet must be assigned an IP address. As the number of devices (e.g., PDAs and cellular phones) with network access increases, the pool of available IP addresses shrinks. In the near future, the number of remaining 32-bit IP addresses will run out. To combat this problem, the Internet Engineering Task Force has introduced **Internet Protocol version 6 (IPv6)**. IPv5 was proposed in 1990, nine years after IPv4, but it was never implemented.[56] IPv6 eliminates many limitations of IPv4. IPv6 addresses are 128 bits long, yielding 2^{128} (approximately 3.4×10^{38}) possible addressable nodes.

IPv6 specifies three types of addresses: unicast, anycast and multicast. A **unicast address** allows users to send a datagram to a single host. **Anycast addresses** allow users to send a datagram to any one of a group of hosts. For example, a series of routers that provide access to a LAN could be assigned anycast addresses. Incoming datagrams would be delivered to the nearest router with that address. **Multicast addresses** allow users to send datagrams to all hosts in a group.[57]

IPv6's headers are simpler than those of IPv4, because several of the header fields have been eliminated or offered as options in IPv6. This increases the speed with which datagrams are processed. Fewer restrictions are imposed on the header format to increase extensibility; IPv6 provides mechanisms for including additional headers between the required header and the message.

The transition to IPv6 is proving to be gradual. To aid with this transition, some routers have been modified to interpret both IPv6 and IPv4 datagrams. For routers that cannot handle IPv6 addresses, IPv6-enabled routers can implement a technique called **tunneling**, which places IPv6 datagrams inside IPv4 datagrams. When other IPv6-enabled routers eventually receive the datagram, they can strip the IPv4 control information and continue as usual. This method is attractive because it allows routing to continue without interruption. However, it adds processing overhead at routers.[58, 59]

Self Review

1. How many possible IPv6 addresses are there?
2. What is the difference between anycast and multicast addresses?

Ans: 1) There are 2^{128}, or approximately 3.4×10^{38}, unique IPv6 addresses. 2) An anycast address allows a user to send a datagram to any one of a group of hosts. A multicast address allows a user to send a datagram to all hosts within a group.

16.8 Link Layer

The link layer interfaces with the **transmission medium** (often copper wiring or optical fiber). It is responsible for transforming a datagram (called a **frame** in the link layer) into a representation (such as electrical or optical) that is suitable for the specific transmission medium and for sending this representation into the medium. The link layer is also responsible for transforming that representation at the receiving computer back into bit streams that can be interpreted by the upper three layers of the TCP/IP stack. Because transmission media are physical entities, they are susceptible to interference which can cause errors. The link layer attempts to detect and, if possible, correct such errors.[60]

Many implementations of the link layer use a **checksum** to determine if a frame was corrupted. A checksum is the result of a calculation on the bits in the frame. If the checksum calculated by the sender and inserted into the frame matches the checksum calculated by the receiver, it is likely that the frame was not corrupted during transmission. Some systems employ error-correcting codes that enable a receiver to both detect and correct corrupted frames. An example is a Hamming Code, which uses redundant bits to determine which bits in the transmission were corrupted and to correct the frames. If errors cannot be corrected, the sender must resend the original frame.[61]

Self Review

1. What is the benefit of using an error-correcting code such as the Hamming Code?
2. What factors contribute to the overhead of using an error-correcting code such as the Hamming Code?

Ans: **1)** Error-correcting codes can be used to correct errors that occurred during transmission. This removes the need to retransmit corrupted frames. **2)** The complication with error-correcting codes is that they require additional bits to be sent with each frame. This can slow network transmission. These bits must be calculated at the sender and recalculated and checked at the receiver.

16.8.1 Ethernet

Ethernet is a type of LAN first developed at the Xerox Palo Alto Research Center in 1976 and later defined by the **IEEE 802.3** standard. Ethernet uses the **Carrier Sense Multiple Access with Collision Detection (CSMA/CD)** protocol. In 802.3-style CSMA/CD (i.e., CSMA/CD that conforms to the IEEE 802.3 standard), "intelligent" nodes are attached to the medium by hardware devices called **transceivers**. The nodes are deemed "intelligent" because a transceiver tests a shared medium to determine if it is available before transmitting data. When the station connected to the transceiver wishes to transmit, the transceiver sends data into the shared medium, while monitoring that medium to detect a simultaneous transmission called a **collision**. Due to delays in the medium, it is possible that multiple transceivers may decide that the medium is clear and begin transmitting simultaneously. When two frames collide, the data is corrupted.

If transceivers detect a collision, they continue to transmit bytes for a specific period of time to ensure that all transceivers become aware of the collision. Each transceiver, after learning of a collision, waits a random interval before attempting to transmit again. This interval is calculated to maximize throughput while minimizing new collisions—one of the most challenging issues in designing CSMA/CD technology. Ethernet employs a method called **exponential backoff**. The transceiver tracks how many times there has been a collision in trying to transmit a certain frame and uses it to calculate the delay before attempting to retransmit. This is called the **random delay**. Each time there is a collision, the length of the delay doubles—rapidly reducing the probability that the offending transceivers will retransmit at the same time. Eventually the frame is sent without collision.

While this method may seem inefficient, it actually works quite well in practice. If the delay were not random, then more collisions would be likely, resulting in greater loss of time. Due to the high transmission speeds and relatively small frames, multiple successive collisions after random retransmissions are usually rare and indicate a network configuration error or a hardware error.[62, 63]

Self Review

1. What are the possible consequences if a transceiver does not continue to transmit bytes upon detection of a collision?

2. Why are collisions possible in Ethernet transmissions?

Ans: **1)** Other transceivers may not recognize that a collision has occurred. This can cause a transceiver to think a frame has been transferred correctly when it has in fact been corrupted. **2)** Transmission is not instantaneous, so two hosts can decide that the medium is free at the same time and start transmitting.

16.8.2 Token Ring

The **Token Ring** protocol operates on ring networks and employs **tokens** to gain access to the transmission medium. In a Token Ring, the token is actually an empty frame that circulates continuously between machines over a network having a logical ring topology (Fig. 16.3). When a node wishes to send a message, it must first wait for the empty frame to arrive. When the node receives the empty frame, it changes one bit in the header to indicate that the frame is no longer empty and writes its message and the address of the intended recipient to the frame. The node then sends the frame to its neighbor. Each node compares its own address to the address in the frame; if the addresses do not match, the node sends the frame on to the next node.

If the address does match, the machine copies the content of the message, changes the bit in the frame's header and passes the frame to the next node on the ring. When the original sender receives the frame (i.e., the frame has completed one cycle of the ring), it can determine if the message was received. At this point, the sender removes the message from the frame and passes the now-empty frame to its neighbor. The Token Ring protocol also contains complex mechanisms to protect the network from losing the token—if a station failed while holding the token, the token might never be released, thus deadlocking the network.

When the token is being passed without incident, the time to transmit a message is quite predictable, as is the time to recover from various errors. Token Rings are the most common network architecture after Ethernet.[64]

Self Review

1. What would happen if a station failed while it owned the token and there was no mechanism to recover?
2. Describe what happens when a host wants to send information using a Token Ring.

Ans: **1)** The token would never be released and all of the hosts would become deadlocked. **2)** The host must first wait until it receives the empty frame (the token). When the host receives the empty frame, it places its message in it. The frame is sent around the Token Ring until it reaches the destination host, which reads the message and indicates that the message has been read. The frame continues around the Token Ring until it reaches the first host, which then releases the token.

16.8.3 Fiber Distributed Data Interface (FDDI)

Fiber Distributed Data Interface (FDDI) shares many properties of the Token Ring protocol, but operates over fiber-optic cable, allowing it to support more transfers at greater speeds over larger distances. FDDI is built on two Token Rings,

Sending message via a token ring protocol.

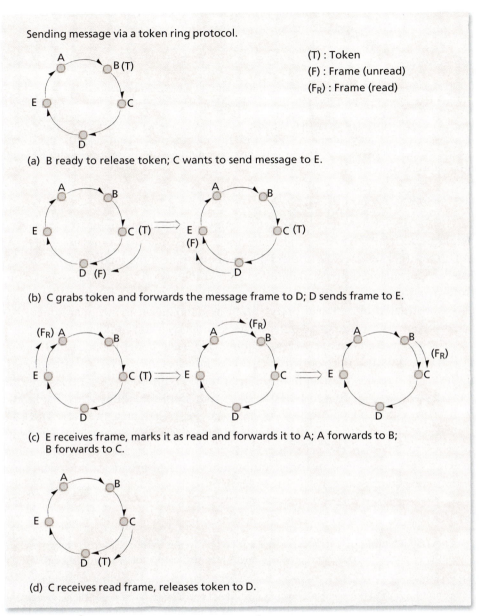

(T) : Token
(F) : Frame (unread)
(F$_R$) : Frame (read)

(a) B ready to release token; C wants to send message to E.

(b) C grabs token and forwards the message frame to D; D sends frame to E.

(c) E receives frame, marks it as read and forwards it to A; A forwards to B;
   B forwards to C.

(d) C receives read frame, releases token to D.

Figure 16.3 | *Sending a message via the Token Ring protocol.*

the second usually being reserved for backup. In FDDI, a token circulates around the optical fiber ring; stations cannot transmit until they obtain the token by receiving it from a preceding station. While the station is transmitting, no token is circulating, thus forcing all other stations to wait before they are allowed to transmit. When it has completed transmission, the transmitting station generates a new token, and other stations may attempt to capture it so they may transmit in turn. If the secondary ring is not needed for backup purposes, FDDI will generally use it to transmit information and tokens in the opposite direction.[65, 66, 67]

Self Review

1. What is the major difference between FDDI and the Token Ring protocol?
2. What is the purpose of the second ring in FDDI?

Ans: **1)** FDDI operates over fiber-optic cable, allowing it to support more transfers at greater speeds over larger distances. FDDI is also built on two Token Rings. **2)** The second ring is provided as backup for the first. If the first ring fails, the second is used to keep the entire network from failing.

16.8.4 IEEE 802.11 (Wireless)

IEEE 802.11 is a wireless protocol which employs a method similar to Ethernet to communicate: **Carrier Sense Multiple Access with Collision Avoidance (CSMA/CA)**. Like Ethernet devices, wireless devices determine if the medium (air) is available before transmission. Availability is a good indication that no message is currently being transferred. However, since wireless networks are spontaneous and can be obstructed by physical objects such as buildings, it is not guaranteed that each device will be aware of all other devices, and a collision could still occur.

To circumvent this issue, 802.11 requires that each sender broadcast a **Request to Send (RTS)** to the entire network. The RTS indicates the sender's desire to transmit data and specifies the length of the transmission, the sender's address and the receiver's address. Upon receiving an RTS and if the medium is available, the receiver broadcasts a **Clear to Send (CTS)** message to the entire network. The CTS message also includes the specified length of transmission. The two stations with the addresses specified in the RTS and CTS can then begin communication. After receiving a CTS message, any other station that wishes to broadcast must wait until the time specified by the CTS (i.e., the length of transmission) has passed.[68]

Self Review

1. What complications arise in wireless networks that do not exist in Ethernet networks?
2. What two messages are required before a wireless host can begin transmitting data?

Ans: **1)** Wireless networks are spontaneous and can often be obstructed by physical objects such as buildings. It is not guaranteed that each device will be aware of all other devices, and collisions could still occur. **2)** The source host must send out an RTS and the destination host must respond with a CTS, before transmission is allowed to begin.

16.9 Client/Server Model

Many distributed applications operate according to a popular networking paradigm known as the **client/server model**. **Clients** are hosts that need various services performed, and **servers** are hosts that provide these services. Typically, clients transmit requests to servers over a network and servers process requests and return the result to the client. For example, an Internet user might request from a server a list of airplane flights departing from a particular location at a particular time. Upon receiving this request, the server might query a local database for the requested flight information, then send the client a message containing the requested list.[69]

We have presented the client/server model essentially as a **two-tier system**. Typically, in such a system, the user interface resides on the client, the data resides on the server and the application logic (i.e., rules for processing and handling data) lies on one or both of these components.

Some developers find it convenient to use a larger number of tiers in their client/server systems for various reasons, including increased flexibility and extensibility in configuring a single system for many clients. In general, architectures consisting of three or more tiers are referred to as *n*-**tier systems**. For example, a **three-tier system** offers a clearer separation of the application logic from the user interface and the data (Fig. 16.4).[70] Ideally, the logic resides in its own layer, possibly on a separate machine, independent of the client and data. This organization affords client/server systems increased flexibility. The trade-off in a multitier system is increased network latency and more areas where the network could fail. Since the three tiers are separate from one another, we can alter or relocate one without affecting the others.

Web applications commonly use a three-tier architecture, consisting of a client browser, a Web server and a relational database.[71] The Web browser on the client machine usually offers the client a graphical user interface (GUI) which facilitates

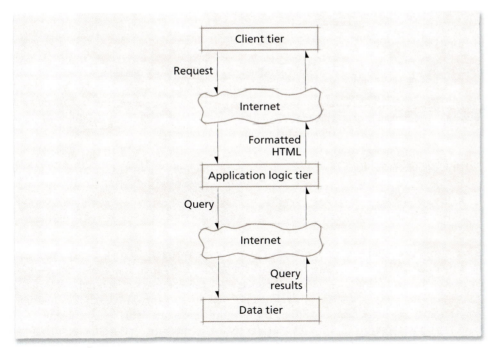

Figure 16.4 | *Three-tier client/server model.*

access to remote documents. The browser interprets pages written in HyperText Markup Language (HTML) and produces their representation on the client monitor. To retrieve a remote document, the browser communicates via HTTP with a Web server, which transmits HTML to the browser also via HTTP. A particular Web server might dynamically produce Web pages by querying a relational database (see Section 13.12.3). For example, imagine that a user visits an online auction site and wishes to view all the computers of a certain type that are currently being auctioned. A request would be sent from the client browser to the auction site's Web server. The server might then query a relational database residing on a remote machine and use the resulting information to dynamically create an HTML page. This page is sent to the browser, which interprets the HTML and displays the information on the client monitor. In this example, the client, server and data tiers are on physically separate machines.

Self Review

1. What are the names of the tiers in a typical three-tier system?
2. What are the benefits and complications associated with increasing the number of tiers of a Web-based system?

Ans: **1)** The client tier, the application logic tier and the data tier. **2)** The benefit is that it further modularizes the system. Each tier can be modified without altering the others. Adding tiers can introduce network latencies as requests are being fulfilled, diminishing application performance.

Web Resources

www.ietf.org/rfc
Provides an index of all of the Requests For Comments (RFCs) that have been published.

www.ietf.org
Internet Engineering Task Force provides links to its working groups and a discussion of the Internet standards process.

www.w3.org
World Wide Web Consortium (W3C) provides guidelines for many Web-based technologies.

www.its.bldrdoc.gov/fs-1037/
Federal Standards 1037 Web site provides a glossary of telecommunications terms.

www.iana.org/
Internet Assigned Numbers Authority sets default port numbers for many common protocols.

Summary

Network topology describes the relationship between different hosts, also called nodes, on a network. A logical topology displays which nodes in a network are directly connected.

Nodes on a bus network are connected to a single, common communication link. Since there are no intermediary nodes to retransmit the message, the length of bus communications medium must be limited to reduce attenuation.

Ring networks consist of a set of nodes, each maintaining exactly two connections to other nodes such that a message sent through one connection can eventually return via the other. Each node in the ring forwards each message, limiting attenuation but introducing a delay for retransmission.

In mesh networks at least two nodes have more than one path connecting them. A fully-connected mesh network directly connects every node to every other node. The presence of multiple paths between any two nodes increases the capacity available for network traffic, enabling higher network throughput.

Star networks contain a hub that is connected to all other nodes in the network. Star networks suffer from lower transmission delay than ring networks, because connections require only one intermediary node. If the central hub fails, however, messages cannot reach their recipients, so fault tolerance can be a problem.

Tree networks are hierarchical networks that consist of a root node and several subnodes, called children, that can have subnodes of their own. A tree topology can be used to join nodes that communicate with each other frequently into a subtree, thereby increasing network efficiency.

The proliferation of wireless network technology has introduced ad hoc networks. An ad hoc network is characterized as being spontaneous—any combination of wireless and wired devices may be connected to it at any time. The network topology is not fixed, which makes it difficult to have a network governed by a central node.

Networks can also be classified by the geographic dispersion of their hosts. A local area network (LAN) has limited geographic dispersion and is designed to optimize data transfer rates between its hosts. LANs interconnect resources using high-speed communication paths with optimized network protocols for local area environments. Advantages of local networks include error rates lower than those of larger networks, greater management flexibility, and independence from the constraints of the public networking system. Wide area networks (WANs) are broader, connecting two or more LANs; the largest WAN is the Internet. WANs generally employ a mesh topology, operate at lower speeds than LANs and have higher error rates, because they handle larger amounts of data being transmitted over far greater distances.

The TCP/IP protocol stack is composed of four logical levels called layers. The application layer is the highest level and provides protocols for applications to communicate. The transport layer is responsible for end-to-end communication. The network layer is responsible for moving the data on to the next step. The transport layer relies on the network layer to determine the proper path from one end of the communication to the other. The link layer provides an interface between the network layer and the underlying physical medium of the connection.

Application layer protocols specify the rules that govern remote interprocess communication and determine how processes should interact. Many of these protocols interact with resources on remote hosts. These resources are specified by a Uniform Resource Identifier (URI), which is a name that references a specific resource on the remote host.

The Hypertext Transfer Protocol (HTTP) is an application layer protocol that allows the transfer of a variety of data formats. HTTP defines a request for a resource and a response. The remote host processes the request and replies with a response, which contains in its header a code that tells the client whether the request was processed correctly or there was an error.

The File Transfer Protocol (FTP) is an application layer protocol that allows file-sharing between remote hosts. FTP specifies connections between two pairs of ports: one pair sends control information that governs the session, the other sends the actual data. After a connection is established, the client specifies actions for the FTP server to perform by issuing various requests to the server. The server attempts to satisfy each request, then issues a response specifying the result.

The transport layer is responsible for the end-to-end communication of messages. In a connection-oriented approach, hosts send each other control information—through a technique called handshaking—to set up a logical end-to-end connection. A connection-oriented approach imposes reliability on unreliable networks. By making communication reliable, these protocols guarantee that data sent from the sender will arrive at the intended receiver undamaged and in the correct sequence. In a connectionless approach, the two hosts do not handshake before transmission, and there is no guarantee that sent messages will be received in their original order, or at all.

The Transmission Control Protocol (TCP) is a connection-oriented transmission protocol. TCP guarantees that segments sent from a sender will arrive at the intended receiver undamaged and in the correct sequence. TCP handles error control, congestion control and retransmission, allowing protocols like HTTP and FTP to send information into the network as simply and reliably as writing to a file on the local computer.

When TCP is given a message to send over a network, TCP must first make a connection with the receiving host using a three-way handshake. The receiving host in TCP accounts for reordering of the segments by using the sequence numbers found in the message headers to reconstruct the original message. When the destination host gets one of these segments, it responds with an ACK segment containing the sequence number of the message. This guarantees that segments will eventually be received by the destination host and that they will be reassembled in the original order.

TCP also implements flow control and congestion control to regulate the amount of data sent by each host.

The connectionless User Datagram Protocol (UDP) provides the minimum overhead necessary for the transport layer. There is no guarantee that UDP datagrams will reach their destination in their original order, or at all.

The network layer receives segments from the transport layer and is responsible for sending these packets to the next stop toward the destination through a process known as routing. Routing is the two-step procedure of first determining the best route between two points and then sending packets along this route. Routers determine the next host for a given datagram based on information, such as network topologies and link quality, which includes strength of signal, error rate and interference which is broadcast throughout networks using various router protocols, such as the Routing Information Protocol (RIP).

Internet Protocol version 4 (IPv4) is the dominant protocol for directing information over a network. Destinations on the Internet are specified by IP addresses, which are 32-bit numbers in IPv4. To make networking simpler for the user, one or more names can be mapped to an IP address through the Domain Name System (DNS).

In the near future, there will be more addressable nodes on the Internet than available addresses using the current system. To combat this problem, the Internet Engineering Task Force introduced Internet Protocol version 6 (IPv6). IPv6 specifies three types of addresses: unicast, anycast and multicast. A unicast address describes a particular host on the Internet. Anycast addresses are designed to be sent to the nearest host with a particular address. Multicast addresses are designed to send packets to a group of hosts.

The link layer interfaces the software-oriented layer with the physical medium over which frames are sent. The link layer is responsible for detecting and, if possible, correcting transmission errors. Some systems employ error-correcting codes to correct the corrupted frames.

Ethernet uses the Carrier Sense Multiple Access with Collision Detection (CSMA/CD) protocol. In 802.3-style CSMA/CD, a transceiver tests a shared medium to determine if it is available before transmitting data. Due to delays in the medium, it is possible that multiple transceivers may decide that the medium is clear and begin transmitting simultaneously. If transceivers detect a collision caused by simultaneous transmissions, they continue to transmit bytes for a specific period of time to ensure that all transceivers become aware of the collision. Each transceiver, after learning of a collision, waits a random interval before attempting to transmit again.

The Token Ring protocol operates on ring networks and employs tokens to gain access to the transmission medium. In a Token Ring, a token that controls access to the transmission medium is actually an empty frame that is continuously circulated between machines over a network having a logical ring topology. When a machine owns the token, it generates data, places it in the frame and sends the frame to its neighbor. Each machine forwards the token until it reaches its destination. At the destination, the machine copies the content of the message, marks the frame as having been delivered and passes the frame to its neighbor. When the original sender receives the frame, it removes the message from the frame and passes the token to its neighbor.

Fiber Distributed Data Interface (FDDI) operates over fiber-optic cable, allowing it to support more transfers at greater speeds over larger distances. FDDI is built on two Token Rings, the second usually being reserved for backup.

802.11 wireless communications employ a method similar to Ethernet to communicate: Carrier Sense Multiple Access with Collision Avoidance (CSMA/CA). This requires that each sender broadcast a Request to Send (RTS) to the entire network. Upon receiving an RTS, the receiver broadcasts a Clear to Send (CTS) message to the entire network if the medium is available.

Typically, in a two-tier client/server system, the user interface resides on the client, the data resides on the server and the application logic lies on one or both of these components. In place of this two-tier model, client/server systems often employ a three-tier system, which offers a clearer separation of the application logic from the user interface and the data. Ideally, the logic resides in its own layer, possibly on a separate machine, independent of the client and data. This organization affords the client/server system increased flexibility and extensibility. The trade-off in a multitier system is increased network latency and more areas where the network could fail.

Key Terms

acknowledgement segment (ACK)—In TCP, a segment that is sent to the source host to indicate that the destination host has received a segment. If a source host does not receive and ACK for a segment, it will retransmit that segment. This guarantees that each transmitted segment is received.

ad hoc network—Network characterized as being spontaneous—any number of wireless or wired devices may be connected to it at any time.

anycast—Type of IPv6 address that enables a datagram to be sent to any host within a group of hosts.

application layer (in OSI)—Interacts with the applications and provides various network services, such as file transfer and e-mail.

application layer (in TCP/IP)—Protocols in this layer allow applications on remote hosts to communicate with each other. The application layer in TCP/IP performs the functionality of the top three layers of OSI—the application, presentation and session layers.

attenuation—Deterioration of a signal due to physical characteristics of the medium.

bus network—Network in which the nodes are connected by a single bus link (also known as a linear network).

Carrier Sense Multiple Access with Collision Avoidance (CSMA/CA)—Protocol used in 802.11 wireless communication. Devices must send a Request To Send (RTS) and receive a Clear To Send (CTS) from the destination host before transmitting.

Carrier Sense Multiple Access with Collision Detection (CSMA/CD)—Protocol used in Ethernet that enables transceivers to test a shared medium to see if it is available before transmitting data. If a collision is detected, transceivers continue transmitting data for a period of time to ensure that all transceivers recognize the collision.

checksum—Result of a calculation on the bits of a message. The checksum calculated at the receiver is compared to the checksum calculated by the sender (which is embedded in the control information). If the checksums do not match, the message has been corrupted.

Clear to Send (CTS)—Message that a receiver broadcasts in the CSMA/CA protocol to indicate that the medium is free. A CTS message is sent in response to a Request to Send (RTS).

client/server model—Popular networking paradigm in which processes that need various services performed (clients) transmit their requests to processes that provide these services (servers). The server processes the request and returns the result to the client. The client and the server are typically on different machines on the network.

client—Process in the client/server model that needs various services performed.

collision—Simultaneous transmission in CSMA/CD protocol.

congestion control—Means by which TCP restricts the number of segments sent by a single host in response to network congestion.

connectionless transport—Method of implementing the transport layer in which there is no guarantee that data will arrive in order or at all.

connection-oriented transport—Method of implementing the transport layer in which hosts send control information to govern the session. Handshaking is used to set up the connection. The connection guarantees that all data will arrive and in the correct order.

control information—Data in the form of headers and/or trailers that allows protocols of the same layer on different machines to communicate. Control information might include the addresses of the source and destination hosts and the type of data or size of the data that is being sent.

data link layer (in OSI)—At the sender, converts the data representation from the network layer into bits to be transmitted over the physical layer. At the receiver, converts the bits into the data representation for the network layer.

datagram—Piece of data transferred using UDP or IP.

Domain Name System (DNS)—System on the Internet used to translate a machine's name to an IP address.

Ethernet (IEEE 802.3)—Network that supports many speeds over a variety of cables. Ethernet uses the Carrier Sense Multiple Access with Collision Detection (CSMA/CD) protocol. Ethernet is the most popular type of LAN.

exponential backoff—Method employed by Ethernet to calculate the interval before retransmission after a collision; this reduces the chance of subsequent collisions on the same transmission, thus increasing throughput.

Fiber Distributed Data Interface (FDDI)—Protocol that shares many properties of a Token Ring, but operates over fiber-optic cable, allowing the transfer of more information at greater speeds. In FDDI, a token circulates around the optical fiber ring; stations cannot transmit until they obtain the token by receiving it from a preceding station. FDDI uses a second Token Ring as backup or to circulate tokens in the reverse direction of the primary Token Ring.

File Transfer Protocol (FTP)—Application layer protocol that moves files between different hosts on a network. FTP specifies connections between two pairs of ports: one pair sends control information that governs the session, the other sends the actual data.

flow control—Means by which TCP regulates the number of segments sent by a host to avoid overwhelming the receiver.

frame—Piece of data in the link layer. Contains both the message and the control information.

fully-connected mesh network—Mesh network in which each node is directly connected to every other node. These networks are faster and more fault tolerant than other networks, but also unrealizable on all but the smallest of networks because of the cost of the potentially enormous number of connections.

handshaking—Mechanism in a connection-oriented transport layer in which hosts send control information to create a logical connection between the hosts.

header—Control information placed in front of a data message.

host—Entity, such as a computer or Internet-enabled cellular phone, that receives and/or provides services over a network. Also called a node.

hub—Central node (such as in a star network) responsible for relaying messages between nodes.

HTTP request—Resource request from an HTTP client to an HTTP server.

HTTP response—Reply message from an HTTP server to an HTTP client, consisting of a status, header and data.

Hypertext Transfer Protocol (HTTP)—Application layer protocol used for transferring HTML documents and other data formats between a client and a server.

IEEE 802.11—One of the standards that governs wireless communication. It dictates that hosts follow the CSMA/CA protocol.

Internet Protocol version 6 (IPv6)—New version of the Internet Protocol that uses 128-bit addresses and specifies three types of addresses: unicast, anycast and multicast.

Internet Protocol (IP)—Primary protocol for directing information over a network. Destinations on the Internet are specified by 32-bit numbers called IP addresses.

IP address—Address of a particular host on the Internet.

layer—Level of abstraction in the TCP/IP protocol stack associated with certain conceptual functions. These layers are the application layer, transport layer, network layer and link layer.

link—Medium over which services are physically transmitted in a network.

link layer (in TCP/IP)—Responsible for interfacing with and controlling the physical medium over which data is sent.

local area network (LAN)—Type of network used to interconnect resources using high-speed communication paths optimized for local area environments, such as office buildings or college campuses.

logical topology—Map of a network that depicts which nodes are directly connected.

mesh network—Network in which at least two nodes have more than one path connecting them. Faster and more fault tolerant than all but fully-connected mesh networks.

multicast—Type of IPv6 address used to send packets to all hosts in a group of related hosts.

Multipurpose Internet Mail Extensions (MIME)—Electronic mail standard defining five content types: text, image, audio, video and application.

network layer—Protocols responsible for sending data to the next host toward the destination. This layer exists in both the TCP/IP model and the OSI model of network communication.

network topology—Representation of the relationships of nodes in a network. Some examples are bus networks, ring networks, star networks, tree networks and mesh networks.

***n*-tier system**—Architecture for network-based applications. The three-tier system, for example, has a client tier, an application logic tier and a data tier.

physical layer (in OSI)—Transmits bits over physical media, such as cables. The data link layer and physical layer in OSI correspond to the link layer in TCP/IP.

port—Identifies the specific socket on a machine to which to send data. For example, HTTP communicates by default on port 80.

presentation layer (in OSI)—Solves compatibility problems by translating the application data into a standard format that can be understood by other layers.

protocol—Set of rules that govern how two entities should interact. Common examples include Transmission Control Protocol (TCP), Internet Protocol (IP) and Hypertext Transfer Protocol (HTTP).

random delay—Interval of time calculated by the exponential backoff method of CSMA/CD before a transceiver can retransmit a frame after a collision.

reliable network—Network which does not damage or lose packets.

Request to Send (RTS)—Message sent from a wireless device in the CSMA/CA protocol that indicates a desire to transmit data, the length of the transmission, the sender address and the receiver address. If the medium is available, the receiver will send a Clear To Send (CTS) message.

ring network—Network consisting of a set of nodes, each maintaining exactly two connections to other nodes in that network. These networks have a low fault tolerance since the failure of any single node can cause the whole network to fail.

router—Computer that is an intermediate destination between the sending host and the receiving host. The router is responsible for determining where to send a datagram next in order for it to eventually reach its destination.

Routing Information Protocol (RIP)—Protocol that defines how routing information is propagated throughout networks. RIP requires routers to share their entire routing table with other routers; this limits its use to small networks.

routing table—Representation of a network used to determine where routers should send datagrams next on their path to their destination.

routing—Determining the best route between two points and sending packets along this route.

segment—Piece of data sent by TCP. It includes the message and the TCP header.

server—Process in the client/server model that performs various services for clients.

session layer (in OSI)—Establishes, manages and terminates the communication between two end users.

socket—Software construct that represents one endpoint of a connection.

star network—Network containing a hub that is directly connected to all other nodes in the network. The hub is responsible for relaying messages between nodes.

Symbian OS—Small operating system for smart phones (mobile phones with the functionality of a PDA).

synchronization segment (SYN)—In TCP, the first handshaking segment sent; contains the sequence number of the source host.

synchronization/acknowledgement segment (SYN/ACK)—In TCP, the second handshaking segment sent; acknowledges that the SYN segment was received and contains the sequence number of the destination host.

TCP/IP Protocol Stack—Hierarchical decomposition of computer communications functions into four levels of abstraction called layers. These layers are the application layer, transport layer, network layer and link layer.

TCP window—Flow-control and congestion-control mechanism in which only a certain amount of data can be sent by the network layer without the receiver explicitly authorizing the sender to send more.

three-tier system—System which offers a separation of the application logic, the user interface and the data. The user interface tier (also called the client tier) communicates with the user. The application logic tier is responsible for the logic associated with the system's function. The data tier stores the information that the user wishes to access.

token—Empty frame used to ensure that only one host is transmitting data at a time in the Token Ring and FDDI protocols.

Token Ring—Protocol in which a token is circulated around a ring network. Only one host can own the token at a time, and only its owner can transmit data.

trailer—Control information appended to the end of a data message.

transceiver—Hardware device that attaches an Ethernet node to the network transmission medium. Transceivers test a shared medium to see if it is available before transmitting data, and monitor the medium to detect a simultaneous transmission called a collision.

Transmission Control Protocol (TCP)—Connection-oriented transmission protocol designed to provide reliable communication over unreliable networks.

transmission medium—Material used to propagate a signal (e.g., optical fiber or copper wire).

transport layer—Set of protocols responsible for end-to-end communication of data in a network. This layer exists in both the TCP/IP model and the OSI model of network communication.

tree network—Hierarchical network that consists of multiple star networks. The hub of the first star network is the root of the tree. Each node that this hub connects serves as a hub for another star network and is a root of a subtree.

tunneling—Process of placing IPv6 datagrams in the body of IPv4 datagrams when communicating with routers that do not support IPv6.

two-tier system—A system in which the user interface resides on the client, the data resides on the server and the application logic lies on one or both of these components.

unicast address—IP address used to deliver data to a single host.

Uniform Resource Identifier (URI)—Name that references a specific resource on the Internet.

Uniform Resource Locator (URL)—A URI used to access a resource in a common protocol such as HTTP and FTP. Consists of the protocol, host name, port and path of the resource.

unreliable network—Network that may damage or lose packets.

User Datagram Protocol (UDP)—Connectionless transmission protocol which allows datagrams to arrive out of order, duplicated or not at all.

wide area network (WAN)—Type of network connecting two or more local area networks, usually operating over great geographical distances. WANs are generally implemented with a mesh topology and high-capacity connections. The largest WAN is the Internet.

Exercises

16.1 What are the pros and cons of using a layered network architecture?

16.2 Why does TCP/IP not specify a single protocol at each layer?

16.3 Compare and contrast connection-oriented services and connectionless services.

16.4 Distinguish between addressing, routing, and flow control. What is a windowing mechanism?

16.5 Explain the operation of CSMA/CD. Compare the predictability of CSMA/CD with token-based approaches. Which of these schemes has the greatest potential for indefinite postponement?

16.6 One interesting problem that occurs in distributed control, token-passing systems, is that the token may get lost. Indeed, if a token is not properly circulating around the net-

work, no station can transmit. Comment on this problem. What safeguards can be built into a token-passing network to determine if a token has been lost, and then to restore proper operation of the network?

16.7 The text said that the Internet is implemented as a mesh network. What would be the consequences if the internet were implemented as a tree network? If it was implemented as a ring network? If it was implemented as a fully-connected mesh network?

16.8 HTTP and FTP are both implemented on top of TCP. What would be the effect if they were implemented on top of UDP?

16.9 Why was CSMA/CD not used for wireless systems?

16.10 Why would an implementation of the link layer utilize error-correcting codes? How would that affect the system?

Suggested Projects

16.11 A number of protocols have been proposed to replace TCP. Researchers at MIT and Berkeley have recently developed the eXplicit Control Protocol (XCP) which is designed to speed up transmissions.[72] Research this protocol and examine what changes it makes to TCP.

16.12 In the text, we mentioned that Routing Information Protocol (RIP) is a means to determine the next host for a datagram. Research RIP and explore how it determines the next host for a datagram.

Suggested Simulations

16.13 Write a simulation program to experiment with routing procedures. Create a mesh network containing some number of nodes and links. Create your own routing protocol to send information about the links throughout the network. Check to

see that each node can efficiently determine the next node along a path between two nodes in the graph. Experiment with "crashing" a node or changing the network topology. How quickly will all of your nodes figure out the new topology?

Recommended Reading

Many books go into greater depth on networking than space permits in an operating systems text. Those include Tanenbaum's classic *Computer Networks*, 4th ed. and *Computer Networking: A Top-Down Approach Including the Internet* by Kurose and Ross.[73, 74]

Requests for Comments (RFCs) describe networking protocols, including TCP, IP, UDP, FTP and SMTP. The Internet Engineering Task Force (IETF) provides free access to every RFC via their Web site (www.ietf.org).

Networking remains a rich research area. Papers such as "Congestion Control for High Bandwidth-Delay Product Networks" and "Why Wi-Fi Wants to be Free" give a technical and

more general idea of how this exciting research area is progressing.[75, 76] Professional groups such as the Institute of Electrical and Electronics Engineers (IEEE; www.ieee.org) and the Association for Computing Machinery (ACM; www.acm.org) are an ideal source of new literature on the topic. Interesting papers available through the ACM include "Frameworks for Component-Based Client/Server Computing," "The Transport Layer: Tutorial and Survey" and "Fundamental Challenges in Mobile Computing."[77, 78, 79] The bibliography for this chapter is located on our Web site at www.deitel.com/books/os3e/Bibliography.pdf.

Works Cited

1. *Federal Standards On-Line,* "Network Topology," <www.its.bldrdoc.gov/fs-1037/>.

2. Abeysundara, B. W., and A. E. Kamal, "High-Speed Local Area Networks and Their Performance: A Survey," *ACM Computing Surveys,* Vol. 23, No. 2, June 1991, p. 231.

3. *Federal Standards On-Line,* "Network Topology," <www.its.bldrdoc.gov/fs-1037/>.

4. Abeysundara, B. W., and A. E. Kamal, "High-Speed Local Area Networks and Their Performance: A Survey," *ACM Computing Surveys,* Vol. 23, No. 2, June 1991, pp. 248–249.

5. *Federal Standards On-Line,* "Network Topology," <www.its.bldrdoc.gov/fs-1037/>.

6. Abeysundara, B. W., and A. E. Kamal, "High-Speed Local Area Networks and Their Performance: A Survey," *ACM Computing Surveys,* Vol. 23, No. 2, June 1991, pp. 248–250.

7. *Federal Standards On-Line,* "Network Topology," <www.its.bldrdoc.gov/fs-1037/>.

8. Abeysundara, B. W., and A. E. Kamal, "High-Speed Local Area Networks and Their Performance: A Survey," *ACM Computing Surveys,* Vol. 23, No. 2, June 1991, pp. 248–250.

9. *Federal Standards On-Line,* "Network Topology," <www.its.bldrdoc.gov/fs-1037/>.

10. Rajaraman, R., "Topology Control and Routing in Ad Hoc Networks: A Survey," *ACM SIGACT News,* Vol. 33, No. 2, June 2002, pp. 60–74.

11. Symbian, "Symbian: About Us," <www.symbian.com/about/about.html>.

12. Blackwood, J., "Why You Can't Ignore Symbian," May 22, 2002, <techupdate.zdnet.com/techupdate/stories/main/0,14179,2866892,00.html>.

13. Mery, D., "Symbian Technology: Why Is a Different Operating System Needed?" March 2002, <www.symbian.com/technology/why-diff-os.html>.

14. Blackwood, J., "Why You Can't Ignore Symbian," May 22, 2002, <techupdate.zdnet.com/techupdate/stories/main/0,14179,2866892,00.html>.

15. Mery, D., "Symbian Technology: Why Is a Different Operating System Needed?" March 2002, <www.symbian.com/technology/why-diff-os.html>.

16. Mery, D., "Symbian Technology: Symbian OS v7.0 Functional Description," March 2003, <www.symbian.com/technology/symbos-v7x-det.html>.

17. Mery, D., "Symbian Technology: Why Is a Different Operating System Needed?" March 2002, <www.symbian.com/technology/why-diff-os.html>.

18. PASC, "The Portable Application Standards Committee," <www.pasc.org>.

19. Mery, D., "Symbian Technology: Why Is a Different Operating System Needed?" March 2002, <www.symbian.com/technology/why-diff-os.html>.

20. Mery, D., "Symbian Technology: Symbian OS v7.0 Functional Description," March 2003, <www.symbian.com/technology/symbos-v7x-det.html>.

21. de Jode, M., "Symbian: Technology: Standards: Symbian on Java," June 2003, <www.symbian.com/technology/standard-java.html>.

22. Dixon, K., "Symbian OS Version 7.0s: Functional Description," Rev. 2.1, June 2003, <www.symbian.com/technology/symbos-v7s-det.html>.

23. Dixon, K., "Symbian OS Version 7.0s: Functional Description," Rev. 2.1, June 2003, <www.symbian.com/technology/symbos-v7s-det.html>.

24. "WCDMA," *SearchNetworking.com,* July 2003, <searchnetworking.techtarget.com/sDefinition/0,,sid7_gci505610,00.html>.

25. Abeysundra, B. W., and A. E. Kamal, "High-Speed Local Area Networks and Their Performance: A Survey," *ACM Computing Surveys,* Vol. 23, No. 2, June 1991, pp. 223–250.

26. *Federal Standards On-Line,* "Network Topology," <www.its.bldrdoc.gov/fs-1037/>.

27. Yanowitz, Jason, "Under the Hood of the Internet: An Overview of the TCP/IP Protocol Suite," <www.acm.org/crossroads/xrds1-1/tcpjmy.html>.

28. TCP/IP and OSI, <searchnetworking.techtarget.com/originalContent/0,289142,sid7_gci851291,00.html>.

29. Tyson, J., "How OSI Works—The Layers," <computer.howstuffworks.com/osi1.htm>.

30. Tyson, J., "How OSI Works—Protocol Stacks," <computer.howstuffworks.com/osi2.htm>.

31. "The 7 Layers of the OSI Model," <webopedia.internet.com/quick_ref/OSI_Layers.asp>.

32. Module 4: Standards and the ISO OSI Model, "ISO OSI—Application Layer (7)," <vvv.it.kth.se/edu/gru/Telesys/96P3_Telesystem/HTML/Module4/ISO-15.html>, modified 11/1/95, © 1995 G. Q. Maguire Jr., KTH/Teleinformatics.

33. "Naming and Addressing: URIs, URLs.," *W3C,* July 2002, <http://www.w3.org/Addressing/>.

34. "Port," *searchNetworking.com,* last modified July 2003, <searchnetworking.techtarget.com/sDefinition/0,,sid7_gci212807,00.html>.

35. "Hypertext Transfer Protocol—HTTP/1.1," RFC 2616, June 1999, <www.ietf.org/rfc/rfc2616.txt>.

36. "Multipurpose Internet Mail Extensions (MIME), Part One: Format of Internet Message Bodies," RFC 2045, November 1996, <www.ietf.org/rfc/rfc2045.txt>.

37. "Uniform Resource Identifiers (URI): General Syntax," RFC 2396, August 1998, <www.ietf.org/rfc/rfc2396.txt>.

38. "File Transfer Protocol (FTP)," RFC 959, October 1985, <www.ietf.org/rfc/rfc0959.txt>.

39. Pouzin, L., "Methods, Tools, and Observations on Flow Control in Packet-Switched Data Networks," *IEEE Transactions on Communications*, April 1981.

40. George, F. D., and G. E. Young, "SNA Flow Control: Architecture and Implementation," *IBM Systems Journal*, Vol. 21, No. 2, 1982, pp. 179–210.

41. Grover, G. A., and K. Bharath-Kumar, "Windows in the Sky—Flow Control in SNA Networks with Satellite Links," *IBM Systems Journal*, Vol. 22, No. 4, 1983, pp. 451–463.

42. Henshall, J., and S. Shaw, *OSI Explained: End-to-End Computer Communication Standards*, Chichester, England: Ellis Horwood Limited, 1988.

43. Iren, S.; P. Amer; and P. Conrad, "The Transport Layer: Tutorial and Survey," *ACM Computing Surveys*, Vol. 31, No. 4, December 1999.

44. "Explanation of the Three-Way Handshake via TCP/IP," <support.microsoft.com:80/support/kb/articles/Q172/9/83.ASP>.

45. "Transmission Control Protocol, DARPA Internet Program, Protocol Specification," RFC 793, September 1981, <www.ietf.org/rfc/rfc0793.txt>.

46. Iren, S.; P. Amer; and P. Conrad, "The Transport Layer: Tutorial and Survey," *ACM Computing Surveys*, Vol. 31, No. 4, December 1999, pp. 360–405.

47. *Federal Standards On-Line*, "Network Topology," <www.its.bldrdoc.gov/fs-1037/> .

48. "The TCP Maximum Segment Size and Related Topics," RFC 789, November 1983, <www.faqs.org/rfcs/rfc879.html>.

49. Deitel, H.; P. Deitel; and S. Santry, *Advanced Java 2 Platform: How to Program*, Prentice Hall, Upper Saddle River, NJ, 2002, pp. 530–592.

50. "User Datagram Protocol," RFC 768, August 1980, <www.ietf.org/rfc/rfc0768.txt>.

51. Iren, S.; P. Amer; and P. Conrad, "The Transport Layer: Tutorial and Survey," *ACM Computing Surveys*, Vol. 31, No. 4, December 1999, pp. 360–405.

52. "Overview of the TCP/IP Protocols," *IT Standards Handbook—The Internet Protocol Suite (Including TCP/IP)*, <www.nhsia.nhs.uk/napps/step/pages/ithandbook/h322-4.htm>.

53. "How Domain Name Servers Work," <computer.howstuffworks.com/dns.htm> .

54. "DNS Demystified," <www.lantimes.com/handson/97/706a107a.html> .

55. "Exploring the Domain Name Space," <hotwired.lycos.com/webmonkey/webmonkey/geektalk/97/03/index4a.html>.

56. "Experimental Internet Stream Protocol, Version 2 (ST-II)," RFC 1190, October 1990, <www.ietf.org/rfc/rfc1190.txt>.

57. "Internet Protocol Version 6 (IPv6) Addressing Architecture," RFC 3513, April 2003, <www.ietf.org/rfc/rfc3513.txt>.

58. "Internet Protocol, Version 6 (IPv6) Specification," RFC 1883, December 1993, <www.ietf.org/rfc/rfc1883.txt>.

59. "IP Version 6 Addressing Architecture," RFC 1884, December 1995, <www.ietf.org/rfc/rfc1884.txt>.

60. "Cyclic Redundancy Check," *Free On-Line Dictionary of Computing*, last modified August 2003, <http://wombat.doc.ic.ac.uk/foldoc/foldoc.cgi?CRC>.

61. Duerincks, G., "Cyclic Redundancy Checks in Ada95," *ACM SIGAda Ada Letters*, Vol. 17, No. 1, January/February 1997, pp. 41–53.

62. Chae, L., "Fast Ethernet: 100BaseT," *Network Magazine*, December 1995, <www.networkmagazine.com/article/NMG20000727S0014>.

63. Intel, "Gigabit Ethernet Solutions (White Paper)," 2001, <www.intel.com/network/connectivity/resources/doc_library/white_papers/gigabit_ethernet/gigabit_ethernet.pdf>.

64. "Token Ring," *searchNetworking.com*, last modified July 2003, <searchnetworking.techtarget.com/sDefinition/0,,sid7_gci213154,00.html>.

65. Mokhoff, N., "Communications: Fiber Optics," *IEEE Spectrum*, January 1981.

66. Schwartz, M., "Optical Fiber Transmission—from Conception to Prominence in 20 Years," *IEEE Communications Magazine*, May 1984.

67. "FDDI," *searchNetworking.com*, last modified April 2003, <searchnetworking.techtarget.com/gDefinition/0,294236,sid7_gci213957,00.html>.

68. Karve, A., "802.11 and Spread Spectrum," *Network Magazine*, December 1997, <www.networkmagazine.com/article/NMG20000726S0001>.

69. Sinha, A., "Client-Server Computing," *Communications of the ACM*, Vol. 35, Issue 7, July 1992, pp. 77–98.

70. Lewandowski, S., "Frameworks for Component-Based Client/Server Computing," *ACM Computing Surveys*, Vol. 30, No. 1, March 1998, pp. 3–27.

71. Lewandowski, S., "Frameworks for Component-Based Client/Server Computing," *ACM Computing Surveys*, Vol. 30, No. 1, March 1998, pp. 3–27.

72. Katabi, D.; M. Handley; and C. Rohrs, "Congestion Control for High Bandwidth-Delay Product Networks," *Proceedings of the 2002 Conference on Applications, Technologies, Architectures, and Protocols for Computer Communications*, August 2002, pp. 89–102.

73. Tanenbaum, A., *Computer Networks*, 4th ed., Upper Saddle River, NJ, Prentice Hall PTR, 2002.

74. Kurose, J., and K. Ross, *Computer Networking: A Top-Down Approach Featuring the Internet*, Reading, MA, Addison-Wesley, 1st ed., 2000.

75. Katabi, D.; M. Handley; and C. Rohrs, "Congestion Control for High Bandwidth-Delay Product Networks," *Proceedings of the 2002 Conference on Applications, Technologies, Architectures, and Protocols for Computer Communications*, August 2002, pp. 89–102.

76. Schmidt T., and A. Townsend, "Why Wi-Fi Wants to Be Free," *Communications of the ACM*, Vol. 46, No. 5, May 2003, pp. 47–52.

77. Lewandowski, S., "Frameworks for Component-Based Client/ Server Computing," *ACM Computing Surveys*, Vol. 30, No. 1, March 1998, pp. 3–27.

78. Iren, S.; P. Amer; and P. Conrad, "The Transport Layer: Tutorial and Survey," *ACM Computing Surveys*, Vol. 31, No. 4, December 1999, pp. 360–405.

79. Satyanarayanan, M., "Fundamental Challenges in Mobile Computing," *Symposium on Principles of Distributed Computing '96*, ACM, 1996, Philadelphia PA.

I wish to have no connection with any ship that does not sail fast; for I intend to go in harm's way.
  —John Paul Jones—

Whatever shall we do in that remote spot?
  —Napoleon Bonaparte—

The art of progress is to preserve order amid change and to preserve change amid order.
  —Alfred North Whitehead—

Order and simplification are the first steps toward the mastery of a subject—the actual enemy is the unknown.
  —Thomas Mann—

The clock, not the steam-engine, is the key machine of the modern industrial age.
  —Lewis Mumford—

It's so awkward to tell one client that you're working on someone else's business …
  —Andrew Forthingham—

You may delay, but Time will not.
  —Benjamin Franklin—

Chapter 17

Introduction to Distributed Systems

Objectives

After reading this chapter, you should understand:

- *the need for distributed computing.*

- *fundamental properties and desirable characteristics of distributed systems.*

- *remote communication in distributed systems.*

- *synchronization, mutual exclusion and deadlock in distributed systems.*

- *examples of distributed operating systems.*

Chapter Outline

17.1 Introduction

As the speed and reliability of networking have improved, computers worldwide have become increasingly interconnected. Remote communication via networks, originally reserved for large computer installations and academic environments, has become pervasive. In **distributed systems**, remote computers cooperate via a network to appear as a local machine. Both distributed systems and network systems spread computation and storage throughout a network of computers. However, users of a **distributed operating system** are given the impression that they are interacting with just one machine, whereas users of a network operating system must be aware of the distributed implementation. Applications of distributed systems are able to execute code on local machines and remote machines and to share data, files and other resources among these machines.

Distributed systems often arise from the need to improve the capacity (e.g., processing power and storage size) and reliability of a single machine. Economic factors can limit the capabilities of a system. By implementing an operating system across several inexpensive machines, it is possible to design a powerful system without expensive machines. For example, it is difficult to connect hundreds of processors on a single mainboard; moreover, most hard disk interfaces do not support the hundreds of disks required for terabytes of storage. Having a single machine with an exorbitant amount of resources is wasteful; a single user would rarely, if ever, take advantage of such capacity. Dividing the resources among a group of machines lets multiple users share the resources, while guaranteeing that there will be enough for the occasional large job. Another reason to adopt a distributed system is to serve a large user base. A **distributed file system** places files on separate machines, while providing the view of a single file system. Distributed file systems can allow vast numbers of users to access the same set of files reliably and efficiently.

Although distributed systems offer many advantages over single-machine operating systems, they can be complex and difficult to implement and manage. For example, they must handle communication delays and reliability problems introduced by the underlying networks. It is harder to manage machine failure in distributed systems; an operating system distributed across n machines is far more likely to experience a system crash than a single-machine operating system. Another challenge is ensuring that each computer in the system has the same view of the entire system.

The discussion of distributed systems in this and the next chapter builds on Chapter 16. In this chapter we discuss distributed communication, distributed file systems and distributed processing. Distributed communication describes how processes on different machines communicate, while distributed processing describes the interaction among distributed processes. Distributed file systems provide a means of managing files within a distributed system.

Self Review

1. What are some benefits of a distributed system?
2. What makes distributed systems complex and difficult to implement and manage?

Ans: **1)** Distributed systems can achieve a high level of performance for a lesser cost than with a single system. Distributed systems can also allow vast numbers of users access to the same files reliably and efficiently. **2)** Handling communication delays and reliability problems introduced by the underlying networks, responding to machine failure and ensuring that each computer in the system has the same view of the entire system.

17.2 Attributes of Distributed Systems

For decades, researchers and professionals have stressed the importance of distributed systems. The explosion of the Internet that occurred with the popularization of the World Wide Web in 1993 has made distributed systems common. This section discusses performance, scalability, connectivity, security, reliability and fault tolerance in distributed systems.

17.2.1 Performance and Scalability

In a centralized system, a single server handles all user requests. With a distributed system, user requests can be sent to different servers working in parallel to increase performance. **Scalability** allows a distributed system to grow (i.e., add more machines to the system) without affecting the existing applications and users.

Self Review

1. How can a distributed systems increase performance?
2. How does scalability make distributed systems better than centralized systems?

Ans: **1)** Multiple servers can handle user requests simultaneously. **2)** Scalability allows the distributed system to grow (i.e., add more machines) without affecting the existing applications and users.

17.2.2 Connectivity and Security

A distributed system can provide seamless access to resources distributed across the network. If the resource is a processor, the distributed system should allow tasks to be executed on any machine. If the resource is a globally shared file system, then remote users should be able to access the file system as they would access a local, private file system. For example, a user should be able to navigate the file system and open a file using a graphical browser or shell instead of connecting to an FTP program.

Connectivity in distributed systems requires communication protocols. The protocols must provide common interfaces to all computers in the system. Many distributed systems require communication of state information to maintain efficient operation. **State information** consists of data that describes the status of one or more resources. Improper state information could lead to inconsistency; transmitting state information too often can flood the network and reduce scalability. Distributed system designers must determine what state information to maintain and how often to make such information known to the system.[1]

Distributed systems can be susceptible to attacks by malicious users if they rely on insecure communications media (i.e., a public network). To improve security, a distributed system should allow only authorized users to access resources and ensure that information transmitted over the network is readable only by the intended recipients. Also, because many users or objects may request resources, the system must provide mechanisms to protect resources from attack. Security and protection are discussed in Chapter 19.

Self Review

1. What facts should distributed system designers consider when designing state information?
2. Give examples of poor state-information design.

Ans: **1)** Distributed system designers need to decide whether the system should keep state information, what state information to maintain and how often to make such information known to the system. **2)** Poor state-information design may keep multiple entries for the status of the same resource, leading to inconsistency; it may cause state information to be transmitted too often, which could flood the network and restrict scalability.

17.2.3 Reliability and Fault Tolerance

The failure of one or more resources on a single machine may cause the whole system to fail or may affect the performance of processes running on the system. A distributed system is more likely to suffer failures than a single-machine system because it has more components that might malfunction.[2]

Distributed systems implement fault tolerance by providing replication of resources across the system. The failure of any one computer will not affect the availability of the system's resources. For example, a distributed file system might keep copies of the same file at different servers. If a user is using a file on a server that crashes, then the distributed file system can direct future requests to a server with a copy of the original file. Replication offers users increased reliability and availability over single-machine implementations.

This comes at a cost. Distributed system designers must develop software that detects and reacts to system failures. Furthermore, designers must provide mechanisms to ensure consistency among the state information at different machines. Such systems must also be equipped to reintegrate failed resources, once they have been repaired.

Self Review

1. Why is a distributed system more likely to suffer faults than a single machine?
2. What is the side effect of increasing reliability and fault tolerance?

Ans: **1)** Distributed systems simply have more components that might malfunction. **2)** Increasing reliability and fault tolerance makes designing distributed systems more complex. The designer must provide mechanisms to switch from a failed machine to a working machine and keep the copies of the duplicated resources consistent across the system.

17.2.4 Transparency

One goal of a distributed system is to provide **transparency** by hiding the distribution aspects from users of the system. Access to a file system that is distributed across several remote computers should be no different than access to a local file system. The user of a distributed file system should be able to access its resources without knowing about the communication between the processes, which process runs the user request and the physical location of the resources.

The ISO Open Distributed Processing Reference Model defines eight types of transparency a distributed system can provide:[3]

- access transparency
- location transparency
- failure transparency
- replication transparency
- persistence transparency
- migration transparency
- relocation transparency
- transaction transparency

Access transparency hides the details of networking protocols that enable communication between distributed computers. It also provides a universal means to access data stored in disparate data formats throughout a system.

Location transparency builds on access transparency to hide the location of resources in the distributed system from those attempting to access them. A distributed file system that provides location transparency allows access to remote files as if they were local files.

Failure transparency is the method by which a distributed system provides fault tolerance. If one or more resources or computers in the network fail, users of the system will be aware only of the reduced performance. Failure transparency is typically implemented by **replication** or checkpoint/recovery. Under replication, a system provides multiple resources that perform the same function. Even if all but one of a set of replicated resources fails, a distributed system can continue to function. A system that employs checkpointing periodically stores the state of an object (such as a process) such that it can be restored (i.e., recovered) if a failure in the distributed system results in the loss of the object.

Replication transparency hides the fact that multiple copies of a resource are available in the system; all access to a group of replicated resources occurs as if there were one such resource available. **Persistence transparency** hides the information about where the resource is stored—memory or disk.

Migration and **relocation transparency** both hide the movement of components of a distributed system. Migration transparency masks the movement of an object from one location to another in the system, such as the movement of a file from one server to another. Relocation transparency masks the relocation of an object from other objects that communicate with it. Finally, **transaction transparency** allows a system to achieve consistency by masking the coordination among a set of resources. Transactions (see Section 13.10.2, Data Integrity and Log-Structured File Systems) include service requests (such as file access and function calls) that change the state of the system. Consequently, transactions often require checkpointing or replication to meet other goals of the distributed system. Transaction transparency hides the implementation of these services.

Self Review

1. Give an example of location transparency.
2. When failure transparency is implemented by replication, what issue(s) should the designers consider?

Ans: **1)** When you access a file in a distributed system, you do not know which server owns the file. **2)** The designers should consider consistency among replicated resources.

17.2.5 Network Operating Systems

A **network operating system** accesses resources on remote computers that run independent operating systems, but is not responsible for resource management at remote locations. Consequently, distributed functions are explicit rather than transparent—a user or process must explicitly specify the resources's location to retrieve a networked file or remotely execute an application. The lack of transparency in network operating systems keeps them from providing some of the benefits of distributed operating systems. However, because network operating systems do not need to ensure transparency, they are easier to implement than distributed operating systems.[4]

Self Review

1. State how network operating systems differ from distributed operating systems.
2. Why are network operating systems easier to implement than distributed operating systems?

Ans: **1)** The network operating system lacks transparency, which means the client must explicitly specify the resource location to access the resource. **2)** Network operating systems do not provide transparency and are not responsible for resource management at remote locations, so network operating systems do not need to implement these capabilities.

17.2.6 Distributed Operating Systems

A **distributed operating system** manages resources located in multiple networked computers. Distributed operating systems employ many of the same communication methods, file system structures and other protocols found in network operating systems, but make the communication transparent so that objects in the system are unaware of the separate computers that provide the service. This level of transparency is difficult to achieve, so it is rare to find a "truly" distributed system.[5]

17.3 Communication in Distributed Systems

One of the primary challenges in designing distributed systems is managing communication between computers. Designers must establish interoperability between heterogeneous computers and applications. In the early years of distributed computing, processes communicated by calling functions from processes located on remote computers. Many of today's applications, however, require interaction between remote objects via method calls. In this section we discuss remote function calls and interactions among remote objects via remote method calls.[6]

Interoperability permits software components to interact among different hardware and software platforms, programming languages and communication protocols. An interface allows heterogeneous systems to communicate in a way that is meaningful to both sides—promoting interoperability. In the client/server model, the client issues a request across the network to the server, and the server processes the request and sends the reply back to the client computer, often using an interface to aid the communication. A **standardized interface** allows each client/server pair to communicate using a single, common interface that is understood by both sides. Standardized interfaces are discussed in Section 17.3.4, CORBA (Common Object Request Broker Architecture).

Self Review

1. Why is interoperability a challenge in distributed systems?
2. Explain how the client/server communication model works.

Ans: **1)** Distributed systems typically consist of heterogeneous computing systems that must somehow be made to interoperate smoothly despite their differences. **2)** In the client/server communication model, the client issues requests across the network to the server, then the server processes the requests and sends the replies back to the client.

17.3.1 Middleware

The machines that compose distributed systems are often heterogeneous—different hardware running different operating systems communicating across different network architectures. In such environments, it is time-consuming and error-prone for the application programmer to provide the routines to convert messages between computers (see the Anecdote, Consequences of Errors). Software known as **middleware** helps provide portability, transparency and interoperability in distributed systems. Portability enables the movement of a system or component from one environment (including both hardware and software) to another without changing the system or component being moved.

Consider a customer purchasing goods from a merchant by writing a check. A bank has issued the customer a book of checks to use for transactions. Upon receipt of a check, the merchant can process it at any bank (even one which did not issue the check), which transparently performs operations to validate the transaction and process the transfer of funds. In this example, the bank (or banks) represents middleware and the merchant and customer represent two computers in a distributed system. Similar to the banks, middleware transparently performs operations to validate transactions and initiate network communication. Middleware provides mechanisms to simplify transactions. Instead of visiting the bank to withdraw funds, paying the merchant and having the merchant visit another bank to deposit the funds, the customer can simply write a check which the merchant deposits directly. In a similar manner, middleware facilitates communication and cooperation among the various components of a distributed system by hiding low-level implementation details from users and applications developers.[7]

Middleware provides standard programming interfaces to enable interprocess communication between remote computers. These interfaces provide portability and transparency.[8] The following sections describe several common implementations and protocols that form the backbone of many distributed systems.

Self Review

1. Why do distributed systems need middleware?
2. How does middleware provide transparency?

Ans: **1)** Distributed systems consist of heterogeneous machines. Middleware enables these heterogeneous machines to work together as a single computer. Middleware provides portability, transparency and interoperability. **2)** Middleware provides standard interfaces so that heterogeneous computers can communicate with each other. It makes calls to procedures on another computer look like local procedure calls.

Consequences of Errors

For $125 million, can you answer how many feet are in a meter? On September 23, 1999, engineers lost contact with NASA's Mars Climate Orbiter, a $125 million satellite orbiting Mars to study its atmosphere. It was later discovered that the Orbiter had entered the Martian atmosphere, which destroyed the spacecraft. The cause for the error? The project team in Colorado was measuring the trajectory of the spacecraft in standard units (e.g., feet and pounds) but the California team was measuring it in metric units (e.g., meters and kilograms). The difference between the two measurements caused the teams to interpret the satellite's bearing incorrectly, which eventually led to the orbiter's loss.

Lesson to operating systems designers: Think twice. Question everything. Dig deeper. The consequences of malfunctions in the systems you design could be serious.

17.3.2 Remote Procedure Call (RPC)

In the mid-1970s, the concept of a **remote procedure call (RPC)** was introduced to provide a structured, high-level approach to interprocess communication in distributed systems. A remote procedure call allows a process executing on one computer to invoke a procedure (or function) in a process executing on another computer. This mechanism assumes a client/server model: The client computer issuing the remote procedure call sends its parameters across the network to the server, where the called procedure resides. Execution occurs at the server, and the result (i.e., the return value of the function) is then transmitted across the network to the client.

A goal of RPC was to simplify the process of writing distributed applications by preserving the syntax of a local procedure (or function) call while transparently initiating network communication. In addition to the primary goal of simplicity, RPC also aimed to be efficient and secure.[9]

To provide transparency to programmers of distributed systems, RPC introduces the concept of a stub. A **stub** prepares outbound data for transmission and translates incoming data so that it may be correctly interpreted. To issue an RPC, a client process makes a call (passing the appropriate parameters) to the procedure in the **client stub**. The client stub performs **marshaling of data**, which packages procedure arguments along with the procedure name into a message for transmission over a network.[10]

To make the remote procedure call, the client stub passes the message (with marshaled parameters) to the server (Fig. 17.1). Upon receipt of the message from the client stub, the server's operating system transmits the message to the **server stub**. The message is then unmarshaled, and the stub sends the parameters to the appropriate local procedure. When the procedure has completed, the server stub marshals the result and sends it back to the client. Finally, the client stub unmarshals the result, notifies the process and passes it the result. From the standpoint of

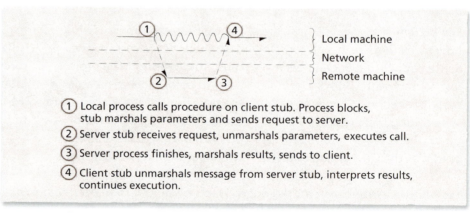

1. Local process calls procedure on client stub. Process blocks, stub marshals parameters and sends request to server.
2. Server stub receives request, unmarshals parameters, executes call.
3. Server process finishes, marshals results, sends to client.
4. Client stub unmarshals message from server stub, interprets results, continues execution.

Figure 17.1 | *RPC communication model.*

the client, this looks no different than making a local procedure call and receiving the return result—the elaborate mechanisms of the RPC are hidden.[11]

There are several complications associated with RPC. RPC can run over either TCP or UDP, which means that different implementations may offer varying levels of reliability. If RPC is operating over UDP, then the RPC implementation must provide communication reliability. Furthermore, each RPC implementation may offer a different level of security (we discuss this topic in Chapter 19, Security and Protection). In fact, we will see that the security capabilities provided by NFS—Section 18.2.2, Network File System (NFS)—are directly related to its underlying RPC implementation.

Another complication is that the process issuing an RPC and its corresponding client stub reside in different memory address spaces. This complicates passing pointers as parameters, which can limit the transparency and capability of RPC. Similarly, RPC does not support global variables, so every variable that a procedure uses must be passed to it as an argument.

Although remote procedure calls promote interoperation in distributed systems, they are not a sufficient solution to the general problem of distributed communication. Performance and security issues have led to the development of additional communication protocols, described in the following sections.

Self Review

1. What is the main benefit of RPC?
2. List several problems with RPC.

Ans: **1)** RPC enables processes to call procedures on remote hosts as easily as making calls to procedures on the local machine. **2)** Problems with RPCs include: **a)** Lack of reliability and security; **b)** limited transparency and capability; **c)** Does not support global variables; **d)** Complex to implement.

17.3.3 Remote Method Invocation (RMI)

Java's RPC protocol, known as **remote method invocation (RMI)**, enables a Java process executing on one computer to invoke a method of an object on a remote computer using the same syntax as a local method call. Similar to RPC, the details of parameter marshaling and message transport in RMI are transparent to the calling program. A key benefit of RMI is that it allows transmission of objects between remote processes. RMI allows Java programmers to implement distributed systems without having to explicitly program sockets.[12]

Three distinct software layers comprise the RMI architecture: the **stub/skeleton layer**, the **remote reference layer (RRL)** and the **transport layer**.[13] The stub/skeleton layer contains parameter-marshaling structures analogous to the client and server stubs of RPC. An RMI stub is a Java object residing on the client machine that provides an interface between the client process and the remote object. When a client process invokes a method on a remote object, the stub method is called first. The stub employs **object serialization** to create its marshaled message, a feature that allows objects to be encoded into byte streams and transmitted from one address space to another. Object serialization enables programs to pass Java objects as parameters and receive objects as return values.[14]

Once the parameters have been serialized by the stub, they are sent to the client-side component of the RMI system's RRL. The RRL uses the transport layer to send the marshaled message between the client and the server. When the server-side component of the RRL receives the marshaled parameters, it directs them to the **skeleton**, which unmarshals the parameters, identifies the object on which the method is to be invoked and calls that method. Upon completion of the method, the skeleton marshals the result and returns it to the client via the RRL and stub.[15]

Self Review

1. What is the function of the stub/skeleton layer in RMI?
2. What benefit does RMI provide over RPC?

Ans: **1)** The stub/skeleton layer marshals and unmarshals parameters. This allows the communication between remote hosts to be hidden from the user. **2)** RMI uses object serialization to enable clients to send objects as arguments in remote method calls and to receive objects as return values from servers.

17.3.4 CORBA (Common Object Request Broker Architecture)

CORBA (Common Object Request Broker Architecture) is a standard specification of distributed systems architecture that has gained wide acceptance.[16] Conceived in the early 1990s by the Object Management Group (OMG), CORBA is an open standard designed to enable interoperation among programs in heterogeneous as well as homogeneous systems. Similar to RMI, CORBA supports objects as parameters or return values in remote procedures during interprocess communication. However, unlike RMI (which is Java based), CORBA is language and system independent, meaning that applications written in different programming languages and on different operating systems interoperate through access to a common CORBA core.[17]

CORBA-based distributed systems have a relatively simple structure. The process on the client passes the procedure call along with the required arguments to the client stub. The client stub marshals the parameters and sends the procedure call through its **Object Request Broker (ORB)**, which communicates with the ORB on the server. The ORB on the server then passes off the procedure call to the server's skeleton, which unmarshals the parameters and passes the call to the remote procedure.[18]

CORBA provides its users language independence with the **interface definition language (IDL)**. IDL allows programmers to strictly define the procedures that can be called on the object; this is known as that object's interface. Applications written in any language can communicate through CORBA by following each object's IDL specification.[19]

Self Review

1. What advantage does CORBA have over RMI?
2. Why might a user chose RMI over CORBA?

Ans: **1)** Unlike RMI, CORBA is language independent, so that applications written in different programming languages can interoperate through access to a common CORBA core. **2)** If the user is working strictly in Java, then CORBA's language independence is unnecesary. Using CORBA also requires the user to learn IDL so that the client and server can communicate properly.

17.3.5 DCOM (Distributed Component Object Model)

In the 1990s, Microsoft independently developed its own distributed object architecture called **DCOM (Distributed Component Object Model)**.[20, 21] DCOM has been included in Windows operating systems since Windows 95 and is CORBA's key competitor in distributed object computing. DCOM is a distributed extension of Microsoft's **Component Object Model (COM)**, which was introduced in 1993 to facilitate component-based development in the Windows environment. The COM specification was designed to allow software components residing in a single address space or in separate address spaces within a single computer to interact with one another.

As in CORBA, objects in DCOM are accessed via interfaces. This allows DCOM objects to be written in a number of different programming languages and on a number of different platforms. Unlike CORBA, however, DCOM objects may have multiple interfaces. When a client requests a DCOM object from a server, the client must also request a specific interface of the object.[22] The client request is first sent to the client stub (called a **proxy**). The client stub communicates over a network with the server stub, which forwards the request to the specific DCOM object. When the DCOM object is finished with the request, it sends the return value back to the server stub. The server stub sends this value back over the network to the proxy, which finally returns the value to the calling process.[23]

Self Review

1. How is DCOM similar to CORBA?
2. What is a benefit of having multiple interfaces for a DCOM object?

Ans: **1)** Both DCOM and CORBA provide support for remote objects written in different programming languages on different platforms. **2)** This allows a single DCOM object to interact differently with different processes.

17.3.6 Process Migration in Distributed Systems

An alternative to remote communication is process migration, which transfers a process between two computers in the distributed system. Recall from Section 15.7 that process migration implements load balancing in multiprocessor systems. Process migration can enable more efficient access to remote resources. For example, consider that computers A and B are networked and that a process residing on computer

A frequently accesses files residing on computer B. The combination of disk and network latency could severely degrade the performance of the process. To reduce this latency, the process from computer A can be transferred to computer B.[24]

Process cloning creates a copy of a process on a remote machine. Because process cloning does not destroy the original process, the two processes may need to synchronize access to shared memory.[25]

Self Review

1. Why is process migration employed in distributed systems?
2. Explain the difference between process migration and process cloning.

Ans: **1)** Process migration allows a process executing on one computer to be transferred to another to utilize the resources efficiently and to distribute the workload among different processors; it can improve performance by enabling processes to execute without incurring network latencies. **2)** In process migration, the process is transferred to, and executed on, a remote computer. In process cloning, a new process is created and executed on the remote computer.

17.4 Synchronization in Distributed Systems

Distributed systems typically contain many processes that cooperate to achieve a common goal. Events at one node in a distributed system often depend on events at other nodes. Determining the order in which events occur is difficult, because communication delays in a distributed network are unpredictable. If two nodes each send a message to a third node, the order of arrival of the two messages might not be the same as the order in which they were sent. This uncertainty can have important consequences if the two messages are related. For example, suppose a distributed system ensures mutual exclusion by having processes broadcast a message whenever they enter or leave a critical section. Suppose one process leaves its critical section and broadcasts a message. Upon receiving this message, another process enters its critical section and broadcasts a second message. If a third process receives the second message before the first, it will appear to that process that mutual exclusion has been violated.

This mutual exclusion example describes a **causally dependent** relationship. The second message (that a process is executing inside its critical section) may occur only if the first message (indicating that a process has exited its critical section) has been broadcast. **Causal ordering** ensures that all processes recognize that a causally dependent event must occur only after the event on which it is dependent.

Causal ordering is implemented by the **happens-before relation**, which is denoted as $a \rightarrow b$. This relation states that if events a and b belong to the same process, then $a \rightarrow b$ if a occurred before b. This relation also states that if event a is the sending of a message and event b is the receiving of that message, then $a \rightarrow b$. Finally, this relation is transitive, so if $a \rightarrow b$ and $b \rightarrow c$ then $a \rightarrow c$. Causal ordering is only a **partial ordering**, because there will be events for which it cannot be determined which occurred earlier. In this case, these events are said to be **concurrent**.

Sometimes, a causal ordering is not strong enough. A **total ordering** ensures that all events are ordered and that causality is preserved.[26]

One way to implement total ordering is through a **logical clock** which assigns a number (or **time stamp**) to each event (such as sending and receiving a message, accessing a variable, etc.) that occurs in the system. Logical clocks do not measure time as such, but rather the order in which events occur; they are often implemented as a simple counter of events. Logical clocks enforce a causal ordering in that if $a \rightarrow b$, then the time associated with event a will be less than that associated with event b.[27]

Scalar logical clocks synchronize the logical clocks on remote hosts and keep a single time value at each host. They ensure causality by following two simple rules. The first rule is that if two events happen within the same process, then the event that happened earlier in actual time will have the earlier time stamp. The second rule is that the event corresponding to receiving a message will have a later time stamp than the event corresponding to sending that message. These two rules also ensure that scalar logical clocks ensure causality.[28]

To follow the first rule, a process will increment its internal clock each time an event occurs. To follow the second rule, when a process receives a message, it will compare the value of its logical clock to the time stamp from the message, set its logical clock to the latter of the two and then increment it.[29]

Self Review

1. How is a logical clock implemented?
2. What would happen if the clocks used by different processes were not synchronized?

Ans: **1)** To implement the logical clock, a process must increment its clock before it executes an event, and a process must append a time stamp (the local time at which the message was sent) to the end of a message. **2)** If the clocks used by different processes were not synchronized, then the time stamp from one process would be interpreted incorrectly by the other process.

17.5 Mutual Exclusion in Distributed Systems

This section discusses how to implement mutual exclusion in distributed systems. The synchronization methods presented in the previous section are used to enforce mutual exclusion.

17.5.1 Mutual Exclusion without Shared Memory

Efficient mutual exclusion algorithms for uniprocessor and shared memory multiprocessors use shared memory. However, in environments with no shared memory, such as NORMA multiprocessors, mutual exclusion must be implemented using some form of message passing, which often requires clock synchronization. **FIFO broadcast** guarantees that when two messages are sent from one process to another, the message that was sent first will arrive first. **Causal broadcast** ensures that when message M_1 is causally dependent on message M_2, then no process receives M_1 before receiving M_2. **Atomic broadcast** guarantees that all messages in a system are received in the same order at each process. Atomic broadcast is also known as **totally ordered broadcast** or **agreed broadcast**.[30, 31]

Self Review

1. What is FIFO broadcast?
2. State the différence between atomic broadcast and causal broadcast.

Ans: **1)** FIFO broadcast guarantees that when two messages are sent from one process to another, the message that was sent first will arrive first. **2)** Causal broadcast does not guarantee the delivery order of unrelated messages. Atomic broadcast guarantees that unrelated messages are delivered in the same order to each process.

17.5.2 Agrawala and Ricart's Distributed Mutual Exclusion Algorithm

G. Ricart and A. K. Agrawala present an algorithm for ensuring mutual exclusion in NORMA systems in their 1981 paper, "An Optimal Algorithm for Mutual Exclusion in Computer Networks"[32] which derives from the work by Lamport.[33] This algorithm requires that a process first send a request message to all other processes in the system and receive a response from each of them before that process can enter its critical section. This algorithm assumes that communication between processes is reliable (i.e., no messages are lost) and that processes do not fail. Algorithms have been developed to address these issues, but they are beyond the scope of this book.

When a process receives a request to enter a critical section and has not sent a request of its own, it sends a reply. If the process has sent its own request, it compares the time stamps of the two requests, and if its own request has a later time stamp than the other request, it sends a reply. If the process's own request has an earlier time stamp than the other request, it delays its reply. Finally, if the time stamps of the requests are equal, the process compares its process number to that of the requesting process. If its own number is higher, it sends a reply, otherwise it delays its reply.

Consider processes P_1, P_2, P_3, each residing on different nodes. Process P_2 wishes to enter its critical section and sends request messages to P_1 and P_3. Processes P_1 and P_3 do not wish to enter their critical sections and immediately respond. Once P_2 has received both of these replies, it enters its critical section. While P_2 executes inside its critical section, both P_1 and P_3 attempt to enter their critical sections. Each process sends its request message, and both happen to have identical time stamps. Process P_2 receives both requests but delays its reply because it is currently inside its critical section. Process P_3 receives the request from P_1 and compares the time stamps. Because both are equal, P_3 then compares process numbers. P_3's number is higher than P_1's, so P_3 sends its reply.

Process P_1 receives the request from P_3 and compares the time stamps. Again, both are equal, but P_1's number is less P_3's, so the reply is delayed. When P_2 exits its critical section, it sends replies to both P_1 and P_3. Process P_2 does not check either time stamp, since it is concerned only about whether it is currently using its critical section, not whether another process is doing so. Process P_1 receives the reply from P_2 and enters its critical section (as it has already received a reply from P_3). Process P_3 receives the reply from P_2 but must still wait on the reply from P_1. Finally, when P_1 is done with its critical section, it sends its reply to P_3, which will then enter its critical section.

Mutual exclusion is ensured by this algorithm. If two processes entered their critical sections at the same time, it would mean that each process sent a request, received the other process's request, compared the time stamps, and found that the other process's request had a lower time stamp than its own. This is not possible; therefore, mutual exclusion is ensured.[34]

This algorithm also prevents indefinite postponement. If a process is indefinitely postponed, requests are being sent with earlier time stamps than its own. But because time stamps increase monotonically, all requests sent after the postponed process's request will have a later time stamp. Eventually, all requests with an earlier time stamp will be fulfilled and the postponed process's request will have the lowest timestamp, allowing the postponed process to proceed. In Exercise 17.12 you will be asked to prove that this algorithm prevents deadlock. [35]

Self Review

1. What are the consequences if a process does fail in this algorithm?
2. If there are n processes within the system, how many messages must be sent before a process can enter its critical section?

Ans: **1)** If a process fails, then other processes will not receive replies from it when they send out a request. If there is no mechanism to determine that a process has failed, the entire system could become deadlocked. **2)** $2(n - 1)$ messages must be sent.

17.6   Deadlock in Distributed Systems

Distributed deadlock occurs when processes spread over different computers in a network wait for events that will not occur. This section addresses how distributed systems complicate the problem of deadlock and provides algorithms to solve them.

17.6.1   Distributed Deadlock

Distributed deadlock can be classified into three types. Resource deadlock is the type discussed in Chapter 7.[36]

As in a centralized system, processes in a distributed system also often block, waiting for signals from other processes. This introduces a new type of deadlock called **communication deadlock**, circular waiting for communication signals. For instance, if P_1 is waiting for a response from P_2, P_2 is waiting for a response from P_3 and P_3 is waiting for a response from P_1, then the system is deadlocked.[37]

Due to the communications delay associated with distributed computing, it is possible that a deadlock detection algorithm, introduced in Chapter 7, might detect a deadlock that does not exist. For example, consider processes P_1 and P_2 executing on different nodes and a third node, N_3, that is testing for deadlock. Process P_1 holds resource R_1 and process P_2 holds resource R_2. Process P_1 releases resource R_1 and sends message M_1 to node N_3. Process P_1 then requests resource R_2 and sends message M_2 to node N_3. Process P_2 releases resource R_2 and sends message M_3 to node N_3. Finally, P_2 requests R_1 and sends message M_4 to node N_3. Suppose that, because of network latency, messages M_2 and M_4 arrive at node N_3 before M_1 and M_3. Node N_3 would then detect a deadlock which did not exist. This is known as **phantom deadlock**.[38]

Self Review

1. When would phantom deadlock occur?
2. Why is it difficult to manage distributed deadlock?

Ans: **1)** Phantom deadlock occurs when communications between two processes are delayed, which leads to a false global state. **2)** In distributed systems, the deadlocked processes are spread over different computers in a network. Managing distributed deadlock requires each process to know the global state of the shared resources and critical sections.

17.6.2 Deadlock Prevention

To prevent deadlocks in uniprocessor machines, it is sufficient to deny one of the four necessary conditions for deadlock (i.e., mutual exclusion, wait for, no preemption and circular wait). These techniques can also be employed to prevent distributed deadlock. Rosenkrantz et al. developed two algorithms designed specifically for distributed systems in their 1978 paper, "System Level Concurrency Control for Distributed Database Systems." Both of these algorithms rely on ordering processes based on when each process was started.[39]

Wound-Wait Strategy

The **wound-wait deadlock prevention strategy** (Fig. 17.2) breaks deadlock by denying the no-preemption condition. Consider the following situation: there are two processes, P_1 and P_2, and P_1 was created before P_2. If process P_1 requests a resource held by P_2, P_1 **wounds** P_2. Process P_2 will then be restarted, freeing all of its resources, including the resource requested by P_1. If P_2 requests a resource held by P_1, P_2 will wait for P_1 to finish using the resource and release it.[40]

Wait-Die Strategy

The **wait-die deadlock prevention strategy** (Fig. 17.3) prevents deadlock by denying the wait-for condition. Consider the following situation: there are two processes, P_1 and P_2, and P_1 was created before P_2. Process P_1 can request a resource held by P_2 and wait for P_2 to release that resource. But if P_2 requests a resource held by P_1, P_2 **dies**. When P_2 dies, it releases all of its resources and restarts.[41]

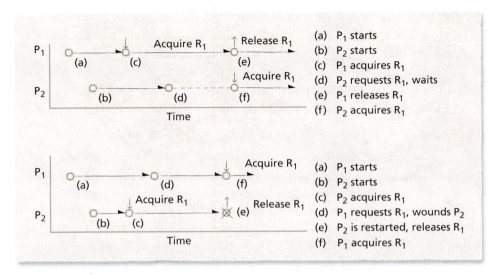

Figure 17.2 | *Wound-wait strategy.*

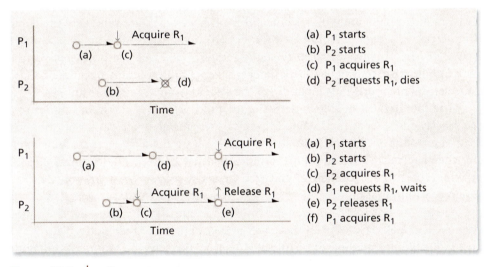

Figure 17.3 | *Wait-die strategy.*

Both of these strategies prevent deadlock, but processes interact differently in each. In the wound-wait strategy, recently created processes will be restarted if they hold a resource requested by an earlier created process. Recently created processes are also forced to wait for earlier created processes. As a process ages, it will wait less often. In the wait-die strategy, recently created processes will die instead of waiting for a resource. As processes age, they may be forced to wait more often.[42]

800 Introduction to Distributed Systems

Self Review

1. How do the wound-wait and wait-die strategies prevent indefinite postponement?
2. What is a problem with the wound-wait and wait-die strategies?

Ans: **1)** In both algorithms, a process that is rolled back many times would eventually get executed, because at some point it would have an earlier time stamp than other processes.
2) In each algorithm, a process may be forced to restart multiple times. This requires the process to repeatedly execute the code preceding the roll back.

17.6.3 Deadlock Detection

In a centralized system, all resources and processes are located on a single machine. In a distributed system, resources and processes are spread over multiple, geographically distant machines. This makes it harder for the system to coordinate interactions between processes. Three distributed deadlock detection strategies are central, hierarchical and distributed. Systems that implement **central deadlock detection** contain a single node that monitors the entire system. Whenever a process requests or releases a resource, it notifies the central node. The node checks the global system for cycles. Upon detection of a cycle, the system may implement a variety of deadlock recovery algorithms. The centralized deadlock detection strategy is simple to implement and is efficient for LANs, which are relatively small and exhibit relatively high communication rates. However, the system may experience decreased performance, because resource requests can create a bottleneck at the central node. Also, central deadlock detection is not fault tolerant, because a failure at the central node prevents all nodes in the system from acquiring resources.[43, 44]

The **hierarchical deadlock detection** method organizes a system's nodes in a tree. Each node, except the leaf nodes, collects the resource allocation information of all dependent nodes. This tree structure provides a higher degree of fault tolerance than centralized systems. Furthermore, because deadlock detection is divided into hierarchies, each branch of the tree needs to have knowledge only of the resources within that branch.[45]

Distributed deadlock detection strategies require each process to determine whether deadlock exists. To do this, each node queries all other nodes. This is the most fault-tolerant method of deadlock detection, because the failure of one node does not prevent other nodes from functioning properly. However, creating efficient algorithms for distributed deadlock detection is difficult, because they must manage synchronized communication among many processes.[46]

Self Review

1. In a distributed system operating over a WAN, why would it be infeasible to use a centralized deadlock detection strategy?
2. What will happen in a hierarchical deadlock detection scheme if a host fails?

Ans: **1)** In a WAN, a deadlock may not be detected for a long time, due to communication delays. This will cause processes involved in the deadlock to wait unnecessarily long for the deadlock to be resolved. **2)** Deadlock detection for all hosts dependent on the failed host will stop. This can cause a reduction in performance.

17.6.4 A Distributed Resource Deadlock Algorithm

Johnston et al. presented a simple algorithm for deadlock detection in distributed systems in their 1991 paper, "A Distributed Algorithm for Resource Deadlock Detection."[47] In this algorithm, each operating system enforces mutual exclusion on its resources and keeps track of which process holds each resource. Processes can be uniquely identified throughout the entire distributed system.

Consider a simple example. Process P_1 begins executing and requests resource R_1. Resource R_1 is available, so its operating system allocates it to P_1. Process P_2 then begins executing and requests resource R_2, which is also available and is allocated to P_2. Process P_2 then requests R_1. Resource R_1 is being used, so P_2 is blocked and R_1's operating system sends P_2 the identifier of process P_1, which holds the resource that P_2 has requested. This value is stored in P_2's *Held_by* variable. Process P_1 also holds all of the resources it needs to execute, so P_2 stores P_1 in its *Wait_for* variable. Finally, P_1 records in its *Request_queue* that process P_2 has requested R_1.

Now process P_3 begins executing. It requests resource R_3, which is available and allocated to P_3. P_3 then requests resource R_2 which is held by process P_2. P_3 blocks, and R_2's operating system sends P_3 the identifier of P_2. P_2 is then stored in P_3's *Held_by* variable. P_2 has an outstanding resource request, so P_3 stores the value that is in P_2's *Wait_for* variable, which is P_1, in its own. Finally, P_2 records in its *Request_queue* that process P_3 has requested R_2.

Process P_4 then begins executing and also requests resource R_2. P_4 blocks, and R_2's operating system sends P_4 the identifier of P_2, which is then stored in P_4's *Held_by* variable. P_2 has an outstanding resource request, so P_4 stores the value of P_2's *Wait_for* variable (which is P_1) in its own. Finally, P_2 records in its *Request_queue* that process P_4 has requested R_2.

Figure 17.4 shows the **transaction wait-for graph (TWFG)** for this system. In a TWFG, each process in the system is a node in the graph. A line between nodes indicates that one process has requested a resource that is being held by another process.

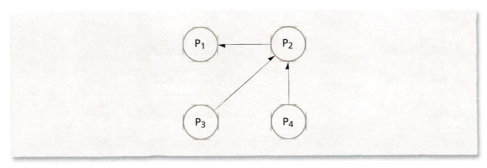

Figure 17.4 | *System without deadlocks.*

Suppose now that process P_1 requests resource R_3, which will complete a circular wait (Fig. 17.5). P_1 now blocks, and R_3's operating system sends P_1 the identifier of the process that holds R_3, which is P_3. This process is stored in P_1's *Held_by* variable. Since P_3 has an outstanding resource request, P_1 stores in its *Wait_for* variable the process in P_3's *Wait_for* variable, which is P_1. Finally, P_3 stores in its *Request_queue* that process P_1 has requested R_3.

When P_1 changes its *Wait_for* variable (from null to P_1), it sends a message to each process in its *Request_queue* to update their own *Wait_for* variables. Process P_2 receives this message, but its *Wait_for* variable is already P_1, so no change is made. P_2 then checks for deadlock. This is done by testing whether the process in the *Wait_for* variable is also in P_2's *Request_queue*. The process in P_2's *Wait_for* variable is P_1, while the only process in its *Request_queue* is P_3, so deadlock is not detected at this step. The message is now forwarded to P_3 and P_4.

Process P_3 receives the message, but its *Wait_for* variable is already P_1 also, so no change is made. P_3 still checks for deadlock, though. The process in P_3's *Wait_for* variable is P_1, which is also in P_3's *Request_queue*, so a deadlock has been detected. In this algorithm, the process that detects the deadlock aborts, so P_3 releases R_3, notifies P_1 that R_3 has been freed, and aborts. P_1's resource request will then be filled, and the deadlock has been removed (Fig. 17.6).

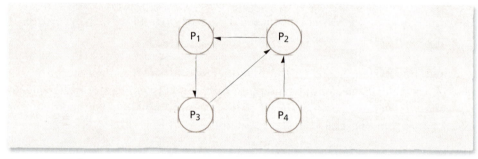

Figure 17.5 | *Deadlock is introduced to the system.*

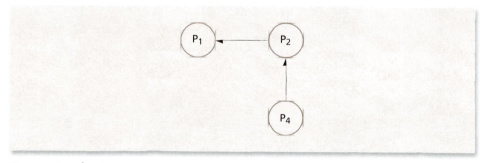

Figure 17.6 | *System after deadlock has been eliminated.*

Self Review

1. How does a process check for deadlock in this algorithm?
2. What information is stored in a process's *Request_queue*?

Ans: 1) A process checks for deadlock by determining whether the process in its *Wait_for* variable is also an entry in its *Request_queue*. If this is the case, deadlock has occurred. 2) The *Request_queue* keeps track of the processes that have requested a resource held by the original process, and of the resource each of those processes requested.

17.7 Case Study: The Sprite Distributed Operating System

Sprite is a distributed operating system developed at the University of California at Berkeley. Sprite connects large numbers of powerful but inexpensive personal workstations in a high-speed LAN. In a Sprite network, large numbers of personal workstations are connected, and many computers could be idle at any given time. These idle workstations allow Sprite to use process migration to balance the workload of the system.[48]

Each workstation in Sprite monitors its own usage to determine if it is idle. When a workstation does not receive any keyboard or mouse input for 30 seconds and when it has fewer running processes than processors, the workstation claims it is idle and reports to a server, called the **central migration server**, that keeps information about idle workstations. The central migration server will then migrate a process to that workstation, called the **target computer**. When the user of the target computer returns (i.e., the workstation receives a keyboard or mouse input), the workstation notifies the central migration server about the return, and the process is migrated back to its original computer, called the **home computer**.[49]

Each workstation in the system runs a Sprite kernel, and these can communicate with each other via RPCs. Sprite uses **implicit acknowledgements** to ensure that messages are delivered reliably. With implicit acknowledgements, the response message is an implied acknowledgement for the request message.

To ensure transparency, the Sprite kernel distinguishes between two kinds of calls. **Location-dependent call**s are system calls that produce different results for different workstations. **Location-independent call**s are system calls that produce the same result for all workstations. The system then provides more location-independent calls by providing the exact same view of the file system for each workstation. When a location-dependent call is required, the system either forwards the call to the home computer for evaluation or transfers the process's state information (such as virtual memory, open files and process identifiers, etc.) from the home computer to the target computer.

The Sprite file system has the same form as a UNIX file system—every client has the exact same view of the hierarchy. The Sprite file system caches files on both the server and client sides. On the server side, when a file is requested, the server checks the server cache first. If the requested file is not cached, the server adds the file to the server cache and sends it to the client. On the client side, when a file is requested, the client checks the client cache first. If the file is in the client cache, then the client gets the file from the client cache. Otherwise, the client gets the file from the server and adds it to the client cache.[50] Section 18.2.5, Sprite File System, discusses the Sprite file system in much more detail.

Self Review

1. Give an example of a location-dependent call.
2. How does Sprite share computer power to balance workload?

Ans: 1) Obtaining the home computer's name is a location-dependent call. 2) Sprite uses a process migration mechanism to enable idle computers to share computer power. When process migration happens, a process on one computer is transferred to an idle computer, distributing the workload among the computers in the system.

17.8 Case Study: The Amoeba Distributed Operating System

Amoeba is a distributed operating system developed at the Vrije Universiteit Amsterdam. Unlike Sprite in which each workstation has its own processors, Amoeba users share processors located in one or more processor pools. A **processor pool** is a collection of processors, each having its own memory and Ethernet connection. The processors in the processor pool are shared equally among users. When a user issues a command to execute a process, the processor pool dynamically allocates the processors for the user. When the user process terminates, the user returns the allocated processors to the processor pool. Like Sprite, Amoeba provides transparency by hiding the number and location of processors from the user.[51]

Each processor in an Amoeba system runs a microkernel, which is a collection of services that supports kernel process management, kernel memory management and the communication between clients and servers. It is also the microkernel's responsibility to manage and schedule the threads in a process.[52]

Amoeba supports two forms of communication—point-to-point and group. In a point-to-point communication, a client stub sends a request message to the server stub and blocks, awaiting the server reply. Amoeba uses **explicit acknowledgement,** which means the client sends an acknowledgement to the server in an additional packet when the client receives the response from the server. In a group communication, messages are sent to all receivers in exactly the same order.

The Amoeba file system has a standard file server called the **bullet server**. The bullet server has a large primary memory. The files stored in it are **immutable**, which means they cannot be modified after being created. If the file is modified, a new file is created to replace the old one, and the old one is deleted from the server.[53]

The bullet server stores files contiguously on the disk, while Sprite stores files in blocks that are not necessarily contiguous. This means that the bullet server can transfer files faster than Sprite. Unlike Sprite, the bullet server supports only server-side caching. Files located in the cache are also stored contiguously. When a client process wants to access a file, it sends the request to the bullet server. The bullet server retrieves the file from disk if it is not in the cache, otherwise the bullet server gets the file from the cache.[54]

Self Review

1. How are processors managed in Amoeba?
2. How is a file stored in the bullet server modified?

Ans: **1)** All processors are located in one or more processor pools. The processors in a pool are not owned by a particular user but are shared among all the users. The processor pool dynamically allocates the processor for each client. When the processors finish their job to execute a client's command, they are returned to the processor pool. **2)** Bullet servers store only immutable files. To modify a file, a bullet server creates a new file to replace the old one, and the old file is deleted from the server.

Web Resources

www.cs.arizona.edu/computer.help/policy/
DIGITAL_unix/AA-QOR5B-TET1_html/TOC.html
Discusses the remote procedure call (RPC) model.

www.omg.org/library/wpjava.html
Demonstrates how Java, RMI and CORBA are used in distributed systems.

java.sun.com/products/jdk/rmi/
Java RMI home page, which contains links for white papers, specifications and RMI tutorials.

java.sun.com/j2se/1.4.2/docs/guide/rmi/spec/rmi-TOC.html
Provides the Java platform's remote method invocation system specification.

www.omg.org/gettingstarted/corbafaq.htm
Introduces CORBA and provides links to detailed specifications.

www.omg.org/docs/formal/02-12-06.pdf
Detailed CORBA architecture and specification.

msdn.microsoft.com/library/default.asp?url=/
library/en-us/dndcom/html/msdn_dcomtec.asp
DCOM technical overview provided by Microsoft.

research.microsoft.com/~ymwang/papers/HTML/
DCOMnCORBA/S.html
Architectural comparison of DCOM and CORBA.

ftp://ftp.cs.vu.nl:/pub/papers/amoeba/
comcom91.ps.Z
Status report on the Amoeba distributed operating system.

www.cs.vu.nl/pub/amoeba/Intro.pdf
Introduction to the Amoeba distributed operating system.

ftp://ftp.cs.vu.nl:/pub/papers/amoeba/cs91.ps.Z
Compares the Amoeba and Sprite distributed operating systems.

Summary

In distributed systems, remote computers cooperate via a network to appear as a local machine. Scalability allows the distributed system to grow without affecting the existing applications and users. Distributed systems can be susceptible to attacks by malicious users if they rely on insecure communications media. To improve security, a distributed system should allow only authorized users to access resources and ensure that information transmitted over the network is readable only by the intended recipients. The system must also provide mechanisms to protect resources from attack. Distributed systems implement fault tolerance by providing replication of resources across the system.

Replication offers users increased reliability and availability over single-machine implementations, but designers must provide mechanisms to ensure consistency among the state information at different machines.

Access transparency hides the details of networking protocols that enable communication between distributed computers. Location transparency builds on access transparency to hide the location of resources in the distributed system.

Failure transparency is the method by which a distributed system provides fault tolerance. Under replication, a system provides multiple resources that perform the same function. A system that employs checkpointing periodically stores the state of an object such that it can be restored if a failure in the distributed system results in the loss of the object.

Replication transparency hides the fact that multiple copies of a resource are available in the system. Persistence transparency hides the information about where the resource is stored—memory or disk.

Migration and relocation transparency both hide the movement of components of a distributed system. The former masks the movement of an object from one location to another in the system; the latter masks the relocation of an object from other objects that communicate with it. Transaction transparency allows a system to achieve consistency by masking the coordination among a set of resources.

A remote procedure call allows a process executing on one computer to invoke a procedure in a process executing on another computer. A goal of RPC was to simplify the process of writing distributed applications by preserving the syntax of a local procedure call while transparently initiating network communication. To issue an RPC, a client process makes a call to the procedure in the client stub, which performs marshaling of data to package procedure arguments along with the procedure name into a message for transmission over a network. The client stub passes the message to the server, which transmits the message to the server stub. The message is then unmarshaled, and the stub sends the parameters to the appropriate local procedure. When the procedure has completed, the server stub marshals the result and sends it back to the client. Finally, the client stub unmarshals the result, notifies the process and passes it the result.

Remote method invocation (RMI) enables a Java process executing on one computer to invoke a method of an object on a remote computer using the same syntax as a local method call. Similar to RPC, the details of parameter marshaling and message transport in RMI are transparent to the calling program.

The stub/skeleton layer of RMI contains parameter-marshaling structures analogous to the client and server stubs of RPC. The stub employs object serialization, which enables programs to pass Java objects as parameters and receive objects as return values. The remote reference layer (RRL) and the transport layer of RMI work together to send the marshaled message between the client and the server. The skeleton unmarshals the parameters, identifies the object on which the method is to be invoked and calls that method. Upon completion of the method, the skeleton marshals the result and returns it to the client via the RRL and stub.

CORBA (Common Object Request Broker Architecture) is an open standard designed to enable interoperation among programs in heterogeneous as well as homogeneous systems. CORBA supports objects as parameters or return values in remote procedures during interprocess communication and is language independent. In CORBA, the process on the client passes the procedure call along with the required arguments to the client stub. The client stub marshals the parameters and sends the procedure call through its Object Request Broker (ORB), which communicates with the ORB on the server. CORBA provides its users language independence with the Interface Definition Language (IDL), which allows programmers to strictly define the procedures that can be called on the object.

Distributed Component Object Model (DCOM) is designed to allow software components residing on remote computers to interact with one another. As in CORBA, objects in DCOM are accessed via interfaces. Unlike CORBA, however, DCOM objects may have multiple interfaces. When a client requests a DCOM object from a server, the client must also request a specific interface of the object.

Process migration transfers a process between two computers in a distributed system. Process migration between remote computers allows processes to exploit a remote resource, but it is a complicated task that often reduces the performance of the process that is being migrated. Process cloning is similar to process migration, except that instead of transferring a process to a remote location, a new process is created on the remote machine.

Determining the order in which events occur is difficult, because communication delays in a distributed network are unpredictable. Causal ordering ensures that all processes recognize that a causally dependent event must occur only after the event on which it is dependent.

Causal ordering is implemented by the happens-before relation, which states that if events a and b belong to the same process, then $a \rightarrow b$ if a occurred before b. This relation also states that if event a is the sending of a message and event b is the receiving of that message, then $a \rightarrow b$. Finally, this relation is transitive. Causal ordering is only a partial ordering. Events for which it cannot be determined which occurred earlier are said to be concurrent. A total ordering ensures that all events are ordered and that causality is preserved.

One way to implement total ordering is through a logical clock which assigns a timestamp to each event that occurs in the system. Scalar logical clocks synchronize the logical clocks on remote hosts and ensure causality.

In environments with no shared memory, mutual exclusion must be implemented over message passing. Message-passing systems use clock synchronization concepts to employ either FIFO broadcast, causal broadcast or atomic broadcast to synchronize the system. FIFO broadcast guarantees that when two messages are sent from one process to another, the message that was sent first will arrive first. Causal broadcast ensures that when message m_1 is causally dependent on message m_2, then no process delivers m_1 before delivering m_2. Atomic broadcast guarantees that all messages in a system are received in the same order at each process.

Ricart and Agrawala's algorithm requires that a process first send a request message to all other processes in the system and receive a response from each of these processes before that process can enter its critical section. When a process receives a request to enter a critical section and has not sent a request of its own, it sends a reply. If the process has sent its own request, it compares the timestamps of the two requests and if the process's own request has a later timestamp than the other request, it sends a reply. If the process's own request has a earlier timestamp than the other request, it delays its reply. Finally, if the timestamps of the requests are equal, the process compares its process number to that of the requesting process. If its own number is higher, it sends a response, otherwise it delays its response.

There are three types of distributed deadlock: resource deadlock, communication deadlock and phantom deadlock. Resource deadlock is the kind of deadlock introduced in Chapter 7. Communication deadlock is circular waiting for communication signals. Due to the communications delay associated with distributed computing, it is possible that a deadlock detection algorithm might detect a deadlock (called phantom deadlock, a perceived deadlock) that does not exist. Although this form of deadlock cannot immediately stop the system, it is a source of inefficiency.

Two algorithms designed to prevent deadlock rely on ordering processes based on when each process was started. The wound-wait strategy breaks deadlock by denying the no-preemption condition. A process will wait for another process if the first process was created before the other. In this strategy, a process will wound (restart) another process if the first process was created after the other. The wait-die strategy breaks deadlock by denying the wait-for condition. In this strategy, a process will wait for another process if the first process was created after the other process. A process will die (restart) itself if it was created before the other process.

Systems that implement central deadlock detection have one site that is dedicated to monitoring the entire system. Whenever a process requests or releases a resource it informs the central site which continuously checks the system for cycles. The central algorithm is simple to implement and is efficient for LANs. However, the system may experience decreased performance and is not fault tolerant.

The hierarchical deadlock detection method arranges each site in the system as a node in a tree. Each node, except the leaf nodes, collects the resource allocation information of all dependent nodes. This tree structure helps to ensure fault tolerance. Furthermore, because deadlock detection is divided into hierarchies and clusters, sites that are irrelevant to deadlock detection on a particular resource do not have to participate in deadlock detection.

Distributed deadlock detection algorithms place the responsibility of deadlock detection with each site. Each site in the system queries all other sites to determine whether any other sites are involved in deadlock. This is the most fault-tolerant method of deadlock detection because the failure of one site will not cause any other site to fail.

Johnston, et al. presented a simple algorithm for deadlock detection in distributed systems. In this algorithm, each process keeps track of the transaction wait-for graph (TWFG) of which they are involved. When a process requests a resource that is being held by another process, the requesting process blocks and the TWFG is updated. As this happens, any deadlocks are detected and removed.

In a Sprite network, large numbers of personal workstations are connected and many computers could be idle at any given time. These idle workstations allow Sprite to use process migration to balance the workload of the system. When the central migration server is notified that a workstation is idle, it will migrate a process to that target computer. When the user of the target computer returns, the workstation notifies the central migration server about the return, and the process is migrated back to the home computer.

The Sprite kernel provides more location-independent calls by providing the exact same view of the file system for each workstation. When a location-dependent call is required, the system either forwards the call to the home computer for evaluation or transfers the process's state information from the home computer to the target computer. The Sprite file system also caches files on both the server and client sides.

Amoeba users share processors located in one or more processor pools. When a user issues a command to execute a process, the processor pool dynamically allocates the processors for the user. When the user process terminates, the user returns the allocated processors to the processor pool. Amoeba provides transparency by hiding the number and location of processors from the user.

Amoeba supports two forms of communication—point-to-point and group. In a point-to-point communication, a client stub sends a request message to the server stub and blocks, awaiting the server reply. In a group communication, messages are sent to all receivers in exactly the same order.

The Amoeba file system has a standard file server called the bullet server which has a large primary memory. The files stored in the bullet server are immutable. If a file is modified, a new file is created to replace the old one, and the old one is deleted from the server. The bullet server also stores files contiguously on the disk so that it can transfer files faster than Sprite.

Key Terms

access transparency—Hides the details of networking protocols that enable communication between computers in a distributed system.

atomic broadcast—Guarantees that all messages in a system are received in the same order at each process. Also known as totally ordered or agreed broadcast.

bullet server—Standard file server used in the Amoeba file system.

causal broadcast—Ensures that when a message is sent from one process to all other processes, any given process will receive the message before it receives a response to the message from a different process.

causal ordering—Ensures that all processes recognize that a causally dependent event must occur only after the event on which it is dependent.

causally dependent—Event B is causally dependent on event A if event B may occur only if event A occurs.

central deadlock detection—A strategy in distributed deadlock detection, in which one site is dedicated to monitoring the TWFG of the entire system. Whenever a process requests or releases a resource, it informs the central site. The site continuously checks the global TWFG for cycles.

central migration server—Workstation in a Sprite distributed operating system that keeps information about idle workstations.

client stub—Stub at the client side that prepares outbound data for transmission and translates incoming data so that it may be correctly interpreted.

Component Object Model (COM)—Introduced in 1993 by Microsoft to facilitate component-based development in the Windows environment.

Common Object Request Broker Architecture (CORBA)—Conceived in the early 1990s by the Object Management Group (OMG), CORBA is a standard specification of distributed systems architecture that has gained wide acceptance.

communication deadlock—One of the two types of distributed deadlock, which is a circular waiting for communication signals.

concurrent—Two events are concurrent if it cannot be determined which occurred earlier by following the happens-before relation.

Distributed Component Object Model (DCOM)—Distributed systems extension of Microsoft's COM.

distributed deadlock—Similar to deadlock in a uniprocessor system, except that the processes concerned are spread over different computers.

distributed deadlock detection strategy—Technique used to find deadlock in a distributed system.

distributed file system—Places files on physically distinct machines, while providing the view of a single file system.

distributed operating system—Provides all of the same services as a traditional operating system, but must provide adequate transparency such that objects in the system are unaware of the computers that provide the service.

distributed system—Remote computers cooperate via a network to provide a unified operating system.

explicit acknowledgement—The client sends an acknowledgement to the server in an additional packet when the client receives the response from the server.

failure transparency—Method by which a distributed system provides fault tolerance so that the client is unaware of the failure of a computer.

FIFO broadcast—Guarantees that when two messages are sent from one process to another, the message that was sent first will arrive first.

happens before relation—A happens before B if A and B belong to the same process and A occurred before B; or A is the sending of a message and B is the receiver of that message.

hierarchical deadlock detection—A strategy in distributed deadlock, which arranges each site in the system as a node in a tree. Each node, except the leaf nodes, collects the resource allocation information of all dependent nodes.

home computer (in process migration)—Computer on which the process originates.

implicit acknowledgement—The response message implies the acknowledgement for the request message.

immutable file—A file that cannot be modified after it is created.

Interface Definition Language (IDL)—A language used to specify the details of the RPCs, which provides a language-independent representation of interfaces and allows distributed applications to transparently call procedures on remote computers.

interoperability—Permits software components to interact among different hardware and software platforms, programming languages and communication protocols.

location-dependent call—System call that depends on the workstation (in Sprite) on which the call is executed. Location-dependent calls produce different results for different workstations.

location-independent call—System call that does not depend on the workstation on which the call is executed. Location-independent calls produce the same result for all workstations.

location transparency—Builds on access transparency to hide the location of resources in a distributed system from those attempting to access them.

logical clock—Assigns a timestamp to each event that happens in a system in order to create a total ordering of events.

marshaling of data—A routine for the client stub to package procedure arguments and return values for transmission over a network.

middleware—A software layer that helps provide portability, transparency, and interoperability in distributed systems.

migration transparency—Masks the movement of an object from one location to another in the system, such as the movement of a file from one server to another.

network operating system—Accesses resources on remote computers that run independent operating systems.

Object Request Broker (ORB)—Component residing on both CORBA client and server, which is responsible for initiating communication between systems.

object serialization—Allows objects to be encoded into byte streams and transmitted from one address space to another.

partial ordering—An ordering of events that follows the happens-before relation. Some events cannot be ordered using this system which is why it is only a partial ordering.

persistence transparency—Hides the information about where the resource is stored—memory or disk.

phantom deadlock—Situation due to communications delay associated with distributed computing, when a deadlock detection algorithm (DDA) might detect a deadlock that does not exist.

process cloning—Creates a copy of a process on a remote machine.

processor pool—Component in Amoeba system, which contains a collection of processors, each having its own memory and Ethernet connection.

proxy—In DCOM, the client-side stub that is responsible for marshaling and unmarshaling messages.

relocation transparency—Masks the relocation of an object from other objects that communicate with it.

remote method invocation (RMI)—Allows Java programmers to implement distributed systems without having to explicitly program sockets.

remote procedure call (RPC)—Allows a process executing on one computer to invoke a procedure (or function) in a process executing on another computer.

remote reference layer (RRL)—Works with the transport layer to send marshaled messages between the client and server in RMI.

replication—Provides multiple resources that perform the same function in a system.

replication transparency—Hides the fact that multiple copies of a resource are available in the system. All access to a group of replicated resources occurs as if there were one such resource available.

scalability—Allows a distributed system to grow (i.e., add more machines to the system) without affecting the existing applications and users.

server stub—A stub at the server side in RPC that prepares outbound data for transmission and translates incoming data so that it may be correctly interpreted.

skeleton—Server-side stub.

standardized interface—Allows each client/server pair to communicate using a single, common interface that is understood by both sides.

state information—Data that describes the status of one or more resources.

stub—prepares outbound data for transmission and translates incoming data so that it may be correctly interpreted

stub/skeleton layer in RMI—Contains parameter-marshaling structures analogous to the client and server stubs of RPC.

target computer (in process migration)—Computer to which the process is migrated.

time stamp—Records the local time at which the message was sent.

total ordering—Ensures that all events are observed in the same order by all processes.

transaction transparency—Allows a system to achieve consistency by masking the coordination among a set of resources.

transaction wait-for graph (**TWFG**)—Graph that represents processes as nodes and dependencies as directed edges, which is used for distributed deadlock detection algorithms.

transparency—Hides the distribution aspects from users of a distributed system.

transport layer (in RMI)—Works with the RRL to send marshaled messages between the client and server in RMI.

wait-die deadlock prevention strategy—Prevents deadlock by denying the wait-for condition. Assigns individual processes unique priorities based on when they were created. A process will wait if it was created after the process it is waiting on. A process will die if it was created before the process it is waiting on.

wound-wait deadlock prevention strategy—Prevents deadlock by denying the no-preemption condition. Assigns individual processes unique priorities based on when they were created. A process requesting a resource held by another process will wound that process if the first one was created before the other. A process will wait if it was created after the process it is waiting on.

wound—When a process is wounded by another process, it will be rolled back.

Exercises

17.1   What are the benefits of distributed systems?

17.2   Define each type of transparency.

17.3   What is the role of middleware? Give examples of middleware.

17.4   Explain how RPC works.

17.5   When the client and the server communicate via RPC, the client blocks until it receives a response from the server. What is the drawback of this design? Give an alternative suggestion to remove this limitation.

17.6   Why is the Interface Definition Language (IDL) important in CORBA?

17.7   Discuss the major differences in DCOM and CORBA.

17.8   Give examples in which process migration is used to exploit resource locality and to balance work load.

17.9   Draw two diagrams, one illustrating that event e_2 is dependent on e_1, the other illustrating that events e_2 and e_1 are concurrent.

17.10   Distinguish FIFO broadcast, causal broadcast and atomic broadcast.

17.11   Suppose processes P_1, P_2 and P_3 share the critical section. P_1 sends a request to enter the critical section at logical time 1. P_2 sends a request to enter the critical section at logical time 2. P_3 sends a request to enter the critical section at logical time 3. Apply Ricart and Agrawala's algorithm to demonstrate how mutual exclusion is achieved.

17.12   Prove that Ricart and Agrawala's algorithm prevents deadlock.

17.13   Suppose processes P_1, P_2 and P_3 have time stamps 1, 2 and 3, respectively. If P_1 requests a resource held by P_2, which process will be rolled back using the wound-wait algorithm?

17.14   Suppose processes P_1, P_2 and P_3 have timestamps 1, 2 and 3, respectively. If P_3 requests a resource held by P_2, which process will be rolled back using the Wait-Die algorithm?

17.15   Compare the Sprite and Amoeba distributed systems.

Recommended Reading

This chapter has only provided a high-level overview of certain middleware technologies. More information on CORBA can

be found through the Object Management Group (OMG).[55] In addition, many of the algorithms introduced in this chapter are discussed in much greater detail in the papers that introduced each algorithm. Agrawala and Ricart's paper provides much greater detail about their mutual exclusion algorithm.[56] Rosenkrantz et. al. discuss in their paper concurrency control in distributed systems.[57] Other resources are the paper by Johnston et al.,[58] which describes their deadlock detection algorithm, and Obermarck's paper,[59] which covers another deadlock detection algorithm not mentioned in this chapter.

Works Cited

1. Tanenbaum, A. S., and M. van Steen, *Distributed Systems, Principles and Paradigms*, Upper Saddle River, NJ: Prentice Hall, 2002, pp. 4–5.

2. Gärtner, F., "Fundamentals of Fault-Tolerant Distributed Computing in Asynchronous Environments," *ACM Computing Surveys*, Vol. 31, No. 1, March 1999.

3. ISO "Open Distributed Processing—Reference Model: Architecture," *Ref. Number: ISO/IEC 10746-3: 1996E*, September 15, 1996, pp. 45–48.

4. Renesse, R. V., and A. S. Tanenbaum, "Distributed Operating Systems," *Computing Surveys*, Vol. 17, No. 4, December 1985, pp. 421–422.

5. Renesse, R. V., and A. S. Tanenbaum, "Distributed Operating Systems," *ACM Computing Surveys*, Vol. 17, No. 4, December 1985, pp. 420 and 425.

6. Wegner, P., "Interoperability," *ACM Computing Surveys*, Vol. 28, No. 1, March 1996, pp. 287.

7. Emmerich, W., "Software Engineering and Middleware: A Roadmap," *Proceedings of the Conference on the Future of Software Engineering 2000*, pp. 117–129.

8. Bernstein, P., "Middleware: A Model for Distributed System Services," *Communications of the ACM*, Vol. 39, No. 2, February 1996, pp. 86–98.

9. Birrell, A., and B. Nelson, "Implementing Remote Procedure Calls," *ACM Transactions on Computer Systems*, Vol. 2, No. 1, February 1984, pp. 41–42.

10. Birrell, A., and B. Nelson, "Implementing Remote Procedure Calls," *ACM Transactions on Computer Systems*, Vol. 2, No. 1, February 1984, pp. 43–44.

11. Birrell, A., and B. Nelson, "Implementing Remote Procedure Calls," *ACM Transactions on Computer Systems*, Vol. 2, No. 1, February 1984, pp. 43–44.

12. "Java™ Remote Method Invocation (RMI)," <java.sun.com/products/jdk/rmi/>.

13. "Java™ Remote Method Invocation," <java.sun.com/marketing/collateral/rmi_ds.html>.

14. "Java™ Remote Method Invocation: Stubs and Skeletons," <java.sun.com/j2se/1.4/docs/guide/rmi/spec/rmi-arch2.html>.

15. "Java™ Remote Method Invocation: 2—Distributed Object Model," 2001, Sun Microsystems, <java.sun.com/j2se/1.4.1/docs/guide/rmi/spec/rmi-objmodel2.html>.

16. "CORBA Basics," <www.omg.org/gettingstarted/corbafaq.htm>.

17. "The Common Object Request Broker: Architecture and Specification," *OMG Document Number 93.12.43*, December 1993.

18. Chung, P., et al., "DCOM and CORBA Side by Side, Step by Step, and Layer by Layer," *C++ Report*, Vol. 10, No. 1, January 1998, pp. 18–29.

19. "The Common Object Request Broker: Architecture and Specification," *OMG Document Number 93.12.43*, December 1993.

20. "DCOM Technical Overview," <msdn.microsoft.com/library/default.asp?url=/library/en-us/dndcom/html/msdn_dcomtec.asp>.

21. Botton, D., "Interfacing ADA 95 to Microsoft COM and DCOM Technologies," *ACM SIGAda Ada Letters, Proceedings of the 1999 Annual ACM SIGAda International Conference on Ada*, September 1999, Vol. 19, No. 3.

22. Chung, P., et. al., "DCOM and CORBA Side by Side, Step by Step, and Layer by Layer," *C++ Report*, Vol. 10, No. 1, January 1998, pp. 18–29. <research.microsoft.com/~ymwang/papers/HTML/DCOMnCORBA/S.html>.

23. DCOM Architecture, <msdn.microsoft.com/library/default.asp?url=/library/en-us/dndcom/html/msdn_dcomarch.asp>.

24. Milojicic, D., et al., "Process Migration," *ACM Computing Surveys*, Vol. 32, No. 3, September 2000, pp. 246.

25. Milojicic, D., et al., "Process Migration," *ACM Computing Surveys*, Vol. 32, No. 3, September 2000, p. 253.

26. Lamport, L., "Time, Clocks, and the Ordering of Events in a Distributed System," *Communications of the ACM*, Vol. 21, No. 7 July 1978, pp. 558–560.

27. Lamport, L., "Time, Clocks, and the Ordering of Events in a Distributed System," *Communications of the ACM*, Vol. 21, No. 7, July 1978, p. 559.

28. Raynal, M., and M. Singhal, "Logical Time: A Way to Capture Causality in Distributed Systems," *Rapport de recherche*, No. 2472, March 1995, pp. 8–9.

29. Raynal, M., and M. Singhal, "Logical Time: A Way to Capture Causality in Distributed Systems," *Rapport de recherche*, No. 2472, March 1995, p. 8.

30. Chockler, G. V.; I. Keidar; and R. Vitenberg, "Group Communication Specifications: A Comprehensive Study," *ACM Computing Surveys*, Vol. 33, No. 4, December 2001, pp. 446–449.

31. Tripathi, A., and N. M. Karnik, "Trends in Multiprocessor and Distributed Operating System Designs," *Journal of Supercomputing*, Vol. 9, No. 1/2, 1995, p. 13.

32. Agrawala, A. K., and G. Ricart, "An Optimal Algorithm for Mutual Exclusion in Computer Networks," *Communications of the ACM*, Vol. 24, No. 1, January 1981.

33. Lamport, L., "A New Solution of Djikstra's Concurrent Programming Problem," *Communications of the ACM*, Vol. 17, No. 8, August 1974.

34. Agrawala, A. K., and G. Ricart, "An Optimal Algorithm for Mutual Exclusion in Computer Networks," *Communications of the ACM*, Vol. 24, No. 1, January 1981, p. 12.

35. Agrawala, A. K., and G. Ricart, "An Optimal Algorithm for Mutual Exclusion in Computer Networks," *Communications of the ACM*, Vol. 24, No. 1, January 1981, p. 13.

36. Knapp, E., "Deadlock Detection in Distributed Databases," *ACM Computing Surveys*, Vol. 19, No. 4, December 1987, p. 309.

37. Chandy, K. M.; J. Misra; and L. M. Haas, "Distributed Deadlock Detection," *ACM Transactions on Computer Systems*, Vol. 1, No. 2, May 1983, p. 148.

38. Obermarck, R., "Distributed Deadlock Detection Algorithm," *ACM Transactions on Database Systems*, Vol. 7, No. 2, June 1982, p. 198.

39. Rosenkrantz, D. J.; R. E. Sterns; and P. M. Lewis, "System Level Concurrency Control for Distributed Database Systems," *ACM Transactions on Database Systems*, Vol. 3, No. 2, June 1978.

40. Rosenkrantz, D. J.; R. E. Sterns; and P. M. Lewis, "System Level Concurrency Control for Distributed Database Systems," *ACM Transactions on Database Systems*, Vol. 3, No. 2, June 1978, pp. 186–187, 192.

41. Rosenkrantz, D. J.; R. E. Sterns; and P. M. Lewis, "System Level Concurrency Control for Distributed Database Systems," *ACM Transactions on Database Systems*, Vol. 3, No. 2, June 1978, pp. 186–197, 191–192.

42. Rosenkrantz, D. J.; R. E. Sterns; and P. M. Lewis, "System Level Concurrency Control for Distributed Database Systems," *ACM Transactions on Database Systems*, Vol. 3, No. 2, June 1978, pp. 192–193.

43. Makki, K., "Detection and Resolution of Deadlocks in Distributed Database Systems," *CIKM '95*, Baltimore, MD, 1995, p. 412.

44. Knapp, E., "Deadlock Detection in Distributed Databases," *ACM Computing Surveys*, Vol. 19, No. 4, December 1987, p. 308.

45. Makki, K., "Detection and Resolution of Deadlocks in Distributed Database Systems," *CIKM '95*, Baltimore, MD, 1995, p. 412.

46. Makki, K., "Detection and Resolution of Deadlocks in Distributed Database Systems," *CIKM '95*, Baltimore, MD, 1995, pp. 412.

47. Johnston, B.; R Javagal; A. Datta; and S. Ghosh, "A Distributed Algorithm for Resource Deadlock Detection," *Proceedings of the Tenth Annual Phoenix Conference on Computers and Communication March*, 1991, pp. 253–255.

48. Ousterhout, J. K.; A. R. Cherenson; F. Douglis; M. N. Nelson; and B. B. Welch, "The Sprite Network Operating System," *IEEE Computer*, Vol. 21, No.2, February 1998, pp. 23–36.

49. Douglis, F., and J. K. Ousterhout "Process Migration in Sprite: A Status Report," *IEEE Computer Society Technical Committee on Operating Systems Newsletter*, Vol. 3, No. 1, Winter 1989, pp. 8–10.

50. Douglis, F., and J. K. Ousterhout, "Transparent Process Migration: Design Alternatives and the Sprite Implementation," *Software–Practice & Experience*, Vol. 21, No. 8, August 1991, pp. 757–785.

51. Tanenbaum, A. S., and G. J. Sharp, "The Amoeba Distributed System," <www.cs.vu.nl/pub/amoeba/Intro.pdf>.

52. Tanenbaum, A. S.; M. F. Kaashoek; R. van Renesse; and H. E. Bal, "The Amoeba Distributed Operating System—A Status Report," *Computer Communications*, Vol. 14, No. 6, July/August 1991, pp. 324–335, <ftp://ftp.cs.vu.nl:/pub/papers/amoeba/comcom91.ps.Z>.

53. Douglis, F.; J. K. Ousterhout; M. F. Kaashoek; and A. S. Tanenbaum, "A Comparison of Two Distributed Systems: Amoeba and Sprite," *Computing Systems*, Vol. 4, No. 3, December 1991, pp. 12–14. <ftp://ftp.cs.vu.nl:/pub/papers/amoeba/cs91.ps.Z>.

54. Douglis, F.; J. K. Ousterhout; M. F. Kaashoek; and A. S. Tanenbaum, "A Comparison of Two Distributed Systems: Amoeba and Sprite," *Computing Systems*, Vol. 4, No. 3, December 1991, pp. 12–14. <ftp://ftp.cs.vu.nl:/pub/papers/amoeba/cs91.ps.Z>.

55. "The Common Object Request Broker: Architecture and Specification," *OMG Document Number 93.12.43*, December 1993.

56. Agrawala, A. K., and G. Ricart, "An Optimal Algorithm for Mutual Exclusion in Computer Networks," *Communications of the ACM*, Vol. 24, No. 1, January 1981.

57. Rosenkrantz, D. J.; R. E. Sterns; and P. M. Lewis, "System Level Concurrency Control for Distributed Database Systems," *ACM Transactions on Database Systems*, Vol. 3, No. 2, June 1978.

58. Johnston, B.; R Javagal; A. Datta; and S. Ghosh, "A Distributed Algorithm for Resource Deadlock Detection," *Proceedings of the Tenth Annual Phoenix Conference on Computers and Communication March*, 1991, pp. 253–255.

59. Obermarck, R., "Distributed Deadlock Detection Algorithm," *ACM Transactions on Database Systems*, Vol. 7, No. 2, June 1982, p. 198.

The humblest is the peer of the most powerful.
    —John Marshall Harlan

O! call back yesterday, bid time return.
    William Shakespeare—

Chapter 18

Distributed Systems and Web Services

Objectives

After reading this chapter, you should understand:

- *characteristics and examples of networked and distributed file systems.*

- *types, benefits and examples of clustering.*

- *the peer-to-peer distributed computing model.*

- *grid computing.*

- *Java distributed computing technologies.*

- *Web services and the Microsoft .NET and Sun ONE platforms.*

Chapter Outline

Web Resources | Summary | Key Terms | Exercises | Recommended Reading | Works Cited

18.1 Introduction

In the preceding chapter, we discussed the basic concepts of distributed systems, including the middleware technologies that help to build transparent and scalable systems. We also discussed how to ensure mutual exclusion in distributed systems and how to prevent and detect distributed deadlocks. In this chapter, we look at another fundamental element of distributed systems—file sharing. Accessing files stored on file servers using a distributed file system is similar to accessing files stored on the user's local computer. We discuss several distributed file systems and give an overview of how data and files are shared among distributed computers. Then, we introduce clustering, which takes advantage of distributed systems and parallel systems to build powerful computers. We discuss the peer-to-peer distributed computing model which is used to remove many central points of failure in applications like instant messengers. Another distributed computing model we discuss is grid computing, which uses unused computer power to solve complex problems. We continue our presentation of Java distributed systems technologies, with discussions of servlets, JSP, Jini, JavaSpaces and JMX, and discuss Web services and how they improve interoperability in distributed systems.

18.2 Distributed File Systems

Networked file systems allow clients to access resources stored on remote computers as the combination of a server name and the path to the resource within that server. **Distributed file systems**, discussed in detail in this chapter, are special examples of networked file systems that allow transparent access to remote files.[1] They take the form of one global file system to which all machines in the system have access. This is achieved by allowing users to mount other file systems (see Chapter 13). Once a remote file system has been mounted, the user can access the files in it as if the files were local. This section addresses the key concepts of distributed file systems and presents case studies on various key distributed file systems.

18.2.1 Distributed File System Concepts

A distributed file server can be either stateful or stateless. A **stateful** server maintains state information about client requests—such as the file name, a pointer to the file and the current position in the file—so that subsequent access to the file is faster and easier. In a **stateless** system, the client must specify this state information in each request. There are benefits to both types of systems: fault tolerance is easier to implement in stateless systems, but stateful systems can reduce the size of request messages and hence offer better performance. Distributed file systems can be characterized by transparency, scalability, security, fault tolerance, and consistency.

Transparency

Distributed file systems provide complete file location transparency; the user sees the distributed file system as a single, global file system. For example, consider a company with offices located in Boston and New York. If a user is in Boston, the system should allow the user to access files located in either Boston or New York. However, the physical location of the files is hidden from the user. To achieve high degrees of transparency, robust naming mechanisms are required.[2]

Scalability

Distributed file systems should also be scalable; allowing new computers to be added to the system easily. Designers of scalable distributed file systems must consider the size of the file system, file management, data duplication and concurrent user access. Other design issues, such as narrow bandwidth, could also limit scalability. Further, if any operations are restricted to a single machine, adding clients could make that machine a bottleneck.[3]

Security

Two key security concerns in distributed file systems are ensuring secure communications and guaranteeing correct file-access permissions. Providing secure communications can be done by encrypting file content. Ensuring correct file access permissions can be complex. In many operating systems, the kernel can determine what files a process has access to based on the identity of the process' user. However, in a distributed system, users may have different user identifications on different machines. This can allow users to access files that they should not and prevent users from accessing files that they are authorized to access.[4]

Fault Tolerance

Fault tolerance is more complex in distributed systems than in conventional systems. When a machine crashes, the system should provide mechanisms to leave the file system in a stable and consistent state. For example, if a client requests a file and blocks while waiting for a server's response and the server then crashes, the client must have some way to guarantee that it will not wait indefinitely. Often, both the client and server will set a timer and abort a call after a timeout, but this introduces complications. What happens if a client sends a request and does not receive a response from the server? It could be that the server has crashed. It could also be that the server is slow or that its response was lost. In the latter case, if the client's request was **idempotent**, i.e., several calls to perform the same operation return the same result (such as when checking a bank balance), then the client can resend its request without introducing inconsistency into the system. However, if the client's request was not idempotent, such as when withdrawing money from a bank account, inconsistencies might arise.[5] A well-designed distributed system makes sure that the same remote procedure calls are executed exactly once regardless of server failures.

High availability is closely related to fault tolerance. In a fault-tolerant system, the failure of a component causes no down time; a backup component immediately takes the place of the failed component and users will not be aware that a failure occurred. In a high-availability system, the failure of a component causes minimal down time. In such systems, often the backup components are used during normal execution for better performance.[6]

Consistency

Consistency is another concern for the designers of distributed systems. Many distributed systems implement **client caching** to avoid the overhead of multiple RPCs. In such cases, clients will keep a local copy of a file and flush it to the server from time to time. Because there are multiple copies of the same file, files can become inconsistent. To avoid inconsistencies, each client must **invalidate** its copy of the file against the copy on the server. The client checks the timestamp of the copy of the file on the server. If it has been updated since the client last copied the file, then the client must download the latest version. If the file has not been updated since the client copied it, then the client can work on its cached copy. Invalidation guarantees that each client will have the same view of the file, but it can lead to inefficiency if it results in the overwriting of work performed by the client. To reduce file access times, sometimes clients will also cache information about files, such as creation or modification dates and location.[7]

Servers can guarantee consistency by issuing locks to clients, giving them exclusive access to a file. When another client needs to access the file, that client must wait for the client that owns the lock to release it. The server still has ultimate control over the file and can revoke the lock if necessary. In fact, most servers **lease** locks and automatically revoke them when the leases expire. If a user still requires a lock, the user must renew the lease before it expires. In some cases, a server may even delegate complete control over the file to the client for a brief period of time. In this situation, other clients must request file access from that client instead of from the server, thereby reducing the load on the server.[8]

Designing a distributed file system involves trade-offs. One means of implementing fault tolerance is replication. But replication requires more components and introduces the problem of consistency. To ensure consistency, systems can employ client invalidation and file locks. But these increase complexity and, in some cases, restrict scalability; and these mechanisms can reduce performance.

Self Review

1. Why is fault tolerance difficult to implement in stateful systems?
2. What problem is raised by client caching?

Ans: **1)** In stateful systems, if the server crashes, it must reconstruct the state information of each client when it restarts. The state information after the server restarts must be consistent with the state information before the crash. **2)** Client caching may cause file inconsistency because multiple copies of a file may be distributed to multiple clients, enabling them to modify the same file at the same time.

18.2.2 Network File System (NFS)

Sun Microsystem's **Network File System (NFS)**, the current de facto standard for network file sharing, is supported natively in most varieties of UNIX and with client and server software available for other common platforms. NFS was originally designed around TCP/IP, so it has been easily adapted to link file systems across the Internet and other wide area networks.[9]

The original version of NFS was released by Sun in 1984 and licensed free to the industry. NFS was revised in 1985 to version 2, which became integrated into various operating systems. In 1989 NFS-2 became the first version of NFS to be standardized by the Internet Engineering Task Force (IETF), becoming an Internet protocol.[10] NFS was revised again with the release of version 3 in 1995.[11]

Figure 18.1 illustrates how NFS works. Before an NFS client can access a remote file, it must use the mount protocol—a mechanism that translates a file path name to a file handle—to mount the directory that holds the remote file. A **file handle** identifies a remote file by its type, location and access permissions. Mounting involves mapping a remote file directory to a client's local directory. To mount the file system, the NFS client makes an RPC (the mount request, which contains the file path of the remote file to be mounted) to the client stub. Upon receiving the mount request, the server skeleton passes the call to the NFS server. The NFS server looks up its local file system and **exports** the local file directory that satisfies the client request, which means the server makes the local directory of files available to the remote client. The server skeleton then returns a file handle of the exported local file directory, which allows the client to access the exported file

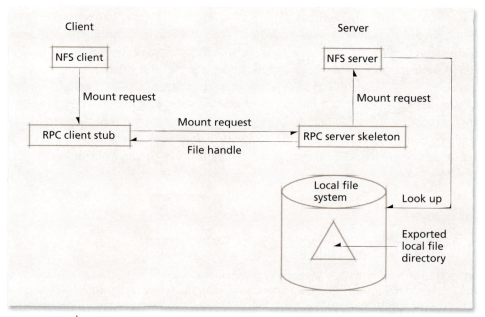

Figure 18.1 | NFS architecture.

directory remotely. The remote client uses this file handle in all subsequent requests to files in the exported file directory.

NFS-2 and NFS-3 assume a stateless server implementation, which makes fault tolerance easier to implement. If a stateless server crashes, the client can simply retry until the server responds. The NFS-2 and NFS-3 permission checks simply rely on the authentication information from RPC, which determines whether the client can access certain information and functions. NFS-2 uses UDP as its transfer protocol, since UDP performs well over local area networks. TCP becomes the protocol of choice on error-prone, high-latency and wide-area networks. Both NFS-2 and NFS-3 support TCP; NFS-3 optimizes its use by allowing transfers of large streams of data. Neither version 2 nor version 3 defines a caching policy to guarantee the consistency of the server and client copies of the file.[12]

Although NFS-2 and NFS-3 are structurally similar, NFS-3 introduces several key differences. First, it supports larger files—file sizes can be stored in 64 bits, while NFS-2 supports only 32-bit file sizes. Second, NFS-3 supports **safe asynchronous writes**, which allow a server to continue executing before a write has been completed. Finally, NFS-3 removes the 8KB limit defined by NFS-2 for any single request or reply.[13] This limit was chosen as a reasonable upper bound for the size of UDP packets being transferred over local area Ethernet.

Following the release of NFS-3, Sun enhanced NFS with a service called **WebNFS**, which allows NFS clients to access WebNFS-enabled servers with a minimum of protocol overhead. WebNFS is specifically designed to take advantage of NFS-3's use of TCP to support efficient file operations over the Internet.

Many features provided by WebNFS have been integrated into version 4 of NFS, which entered development in 1999 as an IETF proposal. NFS version 4 maintains most of the features of prior versions of NFS and provides efficient operation over wide area networks, strong security implementation, stronger interoperability and client caching.[14]

Like its predecessors, NFS-4 uses RPCs to communicate between client and server. NFS-4 offers a new feature, allowing multiple related RPCs to be packaged together into one request. This limits network traffic and increases performance. Also, NFS-4 is stateful, which allows faster access to files. With earlier versions of NFS, the client used the mount protocol to receive the file handle. In NFS-4, the client obtains the file handle without the mount protocol. The client gets a file handle referring to the root of the file system on the server, then traverses the file system to locate the requested file. By removing the mount protocol, the client does not need to mount the different file systems of a server separately.[15]

NFS-4 extends the client-caching scheme through **delegation**, whereby the server temporarily transfers control of a file to a client. When the server grants a read delegation, no other clients can write to that particular file but they can read from it. When the server grants a write delegation, then no other clients can read from or write to that particular file. If another client requests write access to a file with the read or write delegation, or the client requests read access to the file with write delegation, the server will revoke the delegation and request that the original client flush the file to disk.[16]

As discussed earlier, the only security provided by previous versions of NFS was weak authentication from RPC. The developers of NFS-4 were able to take advantage of new RPC security which also supports several cryptographic algorithms which are used when NFS-4 sets up communication sessions and encrypts each RPC.[17]

Self Review

1. Does NFS-2 require stateful server implementation? What is the benefit of such a design?
2. When an NFS-4 client owns the read delegation of a file, can other clients read or write to that file?

Ans: **1)** No, NFS-2 servers must be stateless. With a stateless server, it is easy to implement fault tolerance. **2)** Other clients can read from, but not write to, the file.

18.2.3 Andrew File System (AFS)

Development of the **Andrew File System (AFS)**, a scalable distributed file system, began in 1983 at Carnegie Mellon University. The goal was to provide a distributed file system that would grow to support a large user community while being secure. The designers hoped to exploit advances in workstation processing capabilities to facilitate scalability, efficiency and security. AFS is a global file system that appears as a branch of a traditional UNIX file system at each workstation. It is based on the client-server model and relies on RPCs for communication. Andrew went through three major revisions: AFS-1, AFS-2 and AFS-3.[18, 19]

The entity that governs distributed file access in AFS is called **Vice** (Fig. 18.2). Vice processes run on distributed file servers and interact with a user-level process called **Venus** at each client. Venus interacts with the kernel's **virtual file system**

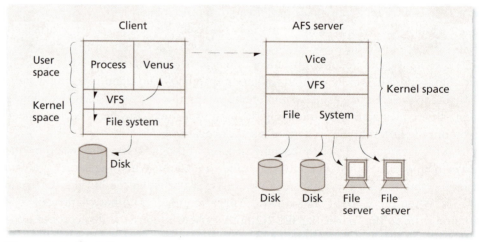

Figure 18.2 | *AFS structure.*

(VFS), which provides the abstraction of a common file system at each client and is responsible for all distributed file operations. AFS obtains scalability from its caching method. The local **nonvolatile storage** (disk) at each workstation serves primarily as a cache to the distributed file system. The data stored in nonvolatile storage is not lost when a machine loses power. When a user process tries to open a file, it makes a request to the VFS which consequently checks to see if the file is in the cache. If it is, the VFS simply accesses the file. If not, the VFS communicates through Venus to Vice, which retrieves the file from the correct server.[20]

In AFS-1 and AFS-2, the cache was updated only at the file level—block updates were not possible. This guaranteed that users working locally on a file would not have to wait long for network access once the file was open. AFS-3 was also upgraded to support block-level caching, which allows large files to be manipulated by clients with small caches.

In AFS-1, each time the VFS tried to open a cached file it would have Venus contact the server to make sure that the file was still valid. This generated many network calls, even when files had not been modified. In AFS-2 and AFS-3, the server becomes responsible for ensuring each client has the most up-to-date copy of its files. Each server keeps track of the files that clients cached. Each time a client closes a file, Venus flushes it to Vice, so the server always keeps the most up-to-date copy of the files. When a file is flushed to Vice, the server performs a **callback** to clients that have that file cached. When a client receives a callback, it knows that its cached version is no longer valid and requests the newest version from the server.

In AFS-1 the server had one process listening on a dedicated port for connection requests. Upon connection, this process would fork another process to handle the Vice functions for the duration of the client's session. Because processes on different machines cannot share main memory, all shared data had to be written to the server's local file system. Furthermore, servers suffered performance problems due to the time associated with the context switches that were required to service different clients. In AFS-2 and AFS-3 there is one dedicated process that services all client requests. This process spawns a separate thread for each client and allows all state information to be loaded into virtual memory. Because the state information tends to be small for each client, it can generally be held in main memory. This eliminates context switches and allows interthread communication through shared memory. The RPC mechanism is incorporated into the thread package to further improve performance.[21]

The overall AFS structure also changed with each revision. In AFS-1 different subtrees were divided among different servers, which were known as the custodians. Each server also had a directory that would allow Vice to direct requests for different subtrees to different servers. Venus located resources based on pathname. This had several drawbacks—resolving an entire path could generate multiple calls to Vice and could span multiple custodians. AFS-2 introduced **volumes** to manage subtrees. Volumes are primarily of administrative value, allowing replication and isolation of certain subtrees, and are transparent to users. Generally each user is assigned a volume. Making the idea of volumes concrete also allowed the implementation of **file identifiers (fids)** in Venus. A fid specifies a volume, an index within a volume and an identifier to guarantee object uniqueness within a volume. The AFS-2 implementation of Venus resolved filenames in this manner, which simplified file lookups and allowed the renaming of directories. Each server had a directory to allow it to find volumes on any other server. AFS-3 was designed to be a large distributed file system. In fact, one continuous AFS-3-based namespace spanned multiple geographically distant universities in the United States. Obviously, there cannot be centralized administration of such a file system as each university typically has its own managerial requirements. Therefore, AFS-3 introduced **cells**, which preserve namespace continuity while allowing different systems administrators to oversee each cell.[22, 23]

The security of AFS is much stronger than that of earlier versions of NFS, partially due to the underlying RPC structure. Because AFS is designed to grow to service many computers, its designers decided that it would not be safe to trust the network or any client. Therefore, every RPC is encrypted and must be authenticated. In AFS-1 and AFS-2 the permissions of a given user are related to the permissions of each group to which the user belongs. In AFS-3 permissions must be specified individually. Upon system login, users must specify a password. Vice sends the encrypted password to an authentication server, which responds with tokens. Secure RPCs use these tokens to provide secure communication. File access is governed by access control lists (ACLs). Section 19.4.3, Access Control Mechanisms, discusses ACL in detail. Each user is allowed to perform certain operations on certain files. Authentication is guaranteed by matching the credentials on each token to the permitted operations in the ACL.[24]

18.2.4 Coda File System

AFS is scalable, indeed able to service thousands of computers, but it has one large drawback—it is not fault tolerant. The crash of one server or disruption of network service can render hundreds of computers inoperable. To deal with this, the designers of AFS began research on Coda in 1987.[25]

Coda is derived from AFS-2. As in AFS-2, Coda uses local nonvolatile storage (e.g., disks) as file caches, and Vice uses callbacks to keep clients up to date. Volumes are the basic division in the file system and Coda performs file lookups in the same way as AFS-2. The goal of fault tolerance led to the addition and modification of several of AFS's features, including the idea of a volume.[26]

In Coda, volumes are logical pieces of the file system and are replicated physically across multiple file servers. Servers that hold the same volume are known as a **volume storage group (VSG)**. Although the multiple servers are transparent to users, the Venus process on each client periodically probes the VSGs of each of its volumes. The members of the VSG with which the client can connect and communicate are known collectively as the client's **available volume storage group (AVSG)** (Fig. 18.3). Coda uses AVSGs to implement fault tolerance.[27]

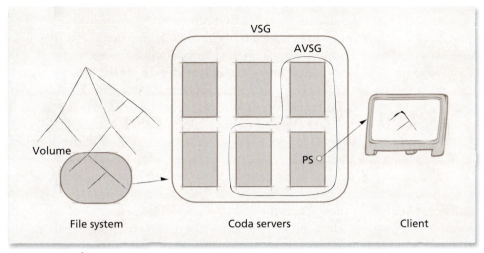

Figure 18.3 | *Coda volume structure.*

When a client process tries to read a file, its request is directed to the local VFS. If the file is in cache, then the read continues as in AFS-2. Otherwise, Venus contacts a member of the AVSG known as the **preferred server (PS)**. Venus downloads a copy of the file from the PS and downloads file version information from each member in the AVSG. If the versions on each server agree, then the client is allowed to use the file. If the versions from different servers do not agree, then the calling process aborts and the outdated copies are updated. After the members of the AVSG have been updated, the requesting client downloads a copy of the file. Note that if the PS or any member of the AVSG crashes, the client can still operate, whereas in AFS-2 the client would be stuck.[28]

Upon closing a file, Coda clients write a copy of the file to each member of the AVSG. The write occurs in two steps using the **Coda Optimistic Protocol**. The first step, COP1, writes the file as we have discussed. The second step, COP2 writes an **update set**, which specifies the members of the AVSG that have successfully performed the COP1, to each of the members of the AVSG. If any of the members are not in the update set, it is assumed that they have not updated (even if they have and their reply was lost) and this is noted to remind the system to update them the next time communication is established. To decrease write delays, COP2 messages are performed asynchronously and are appended on future COP1 messages. If other clients have a copy of the file in cache, then servers will have to perform callbacks.[29]

These operations will provide a consistent view of a file within an AVSG. When a file is opened, it will be the same as the last copy that was written to Coda. However, Coda's replication scheme is optimistic, which means it assumes that files in different AVSGs are consistent and it allows clients to access and modify such files. This guarantees that files will always be available, but it might lead to inconsistencies and the loss of work.

We now discuss Coda's replication scheme and potential consistency issues. Consider a VSG and two clients whose AVSGs are mutually exclusive (Fig. 18.4). It is possible for each client to download, modify and upload the same copy of a file to its AVSG. Now the view of that file within the VSG will not be consistent.

Coda provides some mechanisms to fix inconsistencies. If the file in conflict is a directory, the Coda servers deal with the problem. Each member of the VSG locks the volume that holds the document and one is designated the leader. Logs of the transactions of each server are sent to the leader, which combines the logs and redistributes them. Based on the logs, each server updates its view of the directory. Finally, the volumes are unlocked.

When Coda clients are connected to Coda, they enter a stage called the **hoarding stage**, where they prepare for a possible disconnection from the system by caching any requested files. When the client becomes disconnected, it enters the **emulation stage**, during which all file read requests are serviced from the cache. The files could be stale, but the system is still operable. If the user tries to access a file that is not in cache, the system reports an error. Writes during the emulation stage occur in two steps. First, the file is updated on disk. Second, the **client modification log (CML)** is updated to reflect file changes. Venus modifies the CML so that when a log entry is undone by a later entry, the earlier log entry is removed. The CML also facilitates updates during the **reintegration stage**. Reintegration occurs immediately after the client reconnects to the system when Venus asynchronously updates the server using the CML.[30]

A client may become disconnected for several reasons: All of the servers in a VSG could crash, a network connection could be faulty or the user could intentionally disconnect from the network. Coda handles each of these cases in the same way, and the transition between connected and disconnected states is transparent.

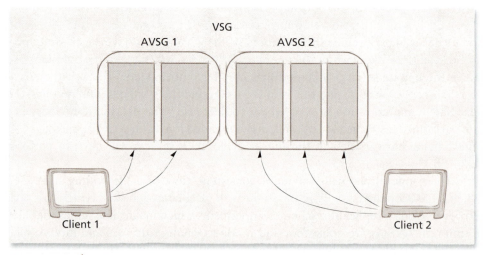

Figure 18.4 | *File consistency issues in mutually exclusive AVSGs.*

This makes Coda particularly attractive for the growing number of mobile computers, and it is one of the primary reasons that Coda is still undergoing improvement.

Self Review

1. In Coda, if client A and client B belong to the same AVSG, does it imply that they belong to the same VSG? If client A and client B belong to the same VSG, does it imply that they belong to the same AVSG?
2. What is the problem with Coda's replication scheme?

Ans: **1)** If client A and client B belong to the same AVSG, then they belong to the same VSG. If client A and client B belong to the same VSG, then they may not belong to the same AVSG. **2)** Coda's replication scheme provides a consistent view of a file within an AVSG but does not guarantee consistency within the VSG. Coda's replication scheme assumes that files in different AVSGs are consistent and allows clients to access and modify such files within different AVSGs, which causes inconsistency within the VSG.

18.2.5 Sprite File System

In Chapter 17, we overviewed the Sprite operating system. This section focus on the Sprite file system. A primary goal for the Sprite file system was transparency. Sprite's developers attained a better level of transparency than that offered by NFS, AFS or Coda. A second goal was to implement complete consistency.[31]

The Sprite file system has the perceived form of a UNIX file system. Unlike NFS or Coda, however, it gives every client the exact same view of the hierarchy. The Sprite file system also goes one step further in UNIX file system emulation by allowing transparent remote access to I/O devices (which are represented as files in UNIX). Although hidden from the user, the Sprite file system is divided into **domains**. Each domain represents a piece of the global file hierarchy and is stored at one server (Fig. 18.5). Except for the domain at the top of the global file hierarchy, the root of one domain is the deepest child of another.[32]

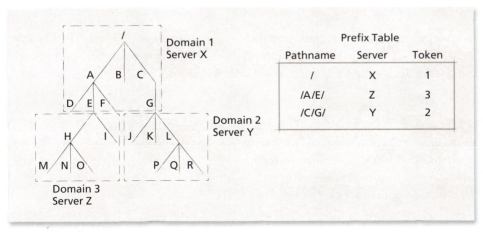

Figure 18.5 | Sprite file system domains.

The kernel of each client keeps a private copy of a **prefix table**, which stores domain information to aid in file lookups (Fig. 18.5). Each entry in the table represents a separate domain and consists of the absolute path to the root directory within the domain, the server that houses the domain and a token that identifies the domain. To look up a file, a client takes an absolute pathname and locates the longest matching prefix within the prefix table. If no such prefix can be found, the client broadcasts a request to every server. The server that houses the domain that matches the path responds with information to populate the client's prefix table, and the client continues. The client then removes the matched prefix from the name and sends what is left to the indicated server along with the domain identification token. The server resolves the name within the specified domain and returns a token pointing to the requested file. If the resolution cannot be completed because the path spans multiple domains, the server returns the pathname of the new domain and the client repeats the process. Sprite processes that access files keep the server address and token identifying the domain of the working directory as part of their state. Processes that access files via relative paths provide this state information in addition to the relative path to allow servers to resolve the entire path.[33]

In Sprite, both the client and the server keep a cache in main memory. To open a file, the client first checks its cache. If the file is not in the client's cache, the client then makes a request to its backing store (which is generally a server). If the server is unable to satisfy the request from its cache, it reads the data in from disk (Fig. 18.6, step a). The server then stores the data in its cache and passes the data to the client. The client retains a copy of the data in its cache as well (Fig. 18.6, step b). When a client writes a block, it writes into its cache. Sprite flushes updated pages to the server every 30 seconds though the cache management algorithm may choose to flush the page sooner. The page will then remain in the server's cache for 30 seconds before it is flushed to disk (Fig. 18.6, step c).

The lazy write-back strategy was chosen to trade an increase in performance for a decrease in fault tolerance. As in UNIX systems, modified pages in a cache will be lost during a crash if they have not been flushed to the server.[34]

Sprite's complete consistency is achieved by its caching protocols. The clients may have inconsistent versions of a file if two or more clients have a copy of the file in cache and at least one client is modifying its copy. This can be divided into two cases: **sequential write-sharing** and **concurrent write-sharing**. Sequential write-sharing occurs when one client modifies a file then another client tries to read or write its own cached copy of the file. To guarantee the highest level of consistency, before a client opens a file it contacts the server and requests the version of that file. If the file on the server is newer than the cached version, the client removes the file from cache and downloads the version from the server. To ensure that delayed write-backs do not hinder this algorithm, the server keeps track of the last client that writes a file. On receiving a read request, the server forces the last client that modifies the file to flush all modified pages to disk immediately, before servicing the request. Concurrent write-sharing occurs when two clients modify cached copies of

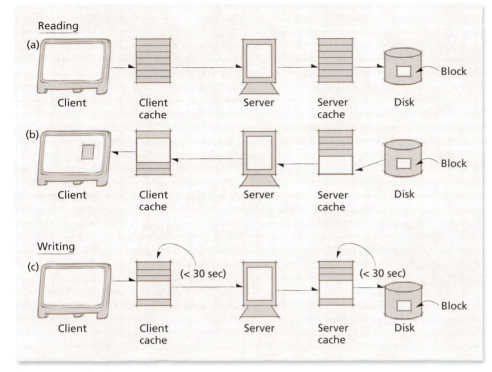

Figure 18.6 | *Reading and writing in the Sprite file system.*

the same file at the same time. To ensure consistency, Sprite disables caching of that file for all clients. Reads and writes are sent directly to the server, and the state of the file therefore appears the same to all clients.

Note that although each client will have a consistent view of the file, there could be synchronization issues associated with this algorithm. Sprite provides locking system calls for applications that cause the inconsistency. This solution also hinders file system performance. The developers of Sprite justified their implementation by observing that concurrent write-sharing is rare.[35]

Cache (in main memory) and virtual memory contend for the same system resources in Sprite—physical memory. Whereas devoting a large portion of physical memory to the virtual memory system increases processing efficiency, devoting a large portion to cache increases network and file system efficiency. Furthermore, some applications rely heavily on virtual memory while others rely on the file system. Sprite allows its cache size to vary dynamically to deal with these issues. Physical memory pages are divided into two sets, a set for cache and a set for virtual memory. The replacement algorithm for each set uses the age of the pages as a guideline for removal when new pages must be swapped in. The set that has the older page loses that page to the set that is swapping in a new page. For example, consider the situation where 16 pages of physical memory are devoted to cache, 16 pages are devoted to virtual memory and one of the virtual memory's pages is the oldest of all 32 pages. If a process tries to bring a page into cache, the oldest virtual memory page is removed and the cache is then allocated 17 total pages.

This introduces a subtle point of inefficiency. What happens if a page is in both virtual memory and cache? Clearly the system is wasting space. To avoid this, virtual memory writes directly to the server when updating files.

We have seen that Sprite is more concerned with performance than with fault tolerance. This point is strengthened when considering how Sprite deals with server crashes. Sprite does not use replication servers. Instead, in the hope that crashes would be infrequent, Sprite's designers implemented a server that would recover quickly from crashes. To do this they placed the burden of state control on the clients, using a log-structured file system with checkpointing on the server (as discussed in Section 13.10.2). The motivation for log-based file system was to improve I/O performance. When clients realize that a server has crashed, they wait until it reboots and then send it information about its files that they have cached. The server uses this information to rebuild its state.[36]

Self Review

1. How is complete consistency achieved in sequential write-sharing?
2. What problem might result from placing the burden of state control on the clients? Propose a solution to this problem.

Ans: **1)** Sequential write-sharing occurs when one client modifies a file and then another client tries to read or write its own cached copy of the file. Before a client opens a file, it contacts the server and requests the version of that file. If the file on the server is newer than the cached version, the client removes the file from cache and downloads the version from the server. To ensure complete consistency, the server keeps track of the last client that writes a file. On receiving a read request, the server forces the last client that modifies the file to flush all modified pages to disk immediately, before servicing the request. **2)** All of the clients will bombard the server with information when it reboots, possibly swamping the network. Sprite's developers built a negative acknowledgement into their implementation. This allows the server to tell the client that it is busy now, but has not crashed and to come back later.

18.3 Multicomputer Systems

As discussed in Chapter 15, multiprocessing is the use of multiple processors to execute separate portions of a computation in parallel. Several classes of machines are generally referred to as multiprocessors, but the most popular are machines that have similar or identical processors and that share a common memory. In contrast, **multicomputer systems** do not share a common memory or bus (although they may share a virtual memory). Each processing unit has access to its own resources. These independent units are connected in a network to operate cooperatively to form a multicomputer system. Multicomputer systems can be either homogenous or heterogeneous. A homogeneous multicomputer system consists of computers that have the same hardware, run the same operating systems and communicate across the same network architectures. A heterogeneous multicomputer system consists of computers that may have different hardware, run different operating systems and communicate across different network architectures.[37]

Modern supercomputers are massively parallel processing (MPP) machines capable of hundreds of gigaflops or even teraflops. A flop is a floating point operation per second.[38] Currently under construction at Los Alamos is the supercomputer Q which will top 100 teraflops. It will be used by scientists to simulate the effects of aging on America's nuclear arsenal, using three-dimensional models of explosions.[39] Los Alamos scientists are also working on a low-end supercomputer called Green Destiny built from off-the-shelf components. Green Destiny provides 160 gigaflops of computing power using 100Base-T Ethernet and 240 667-megahertz Transmeta Corp. processors.[40] Green Destiny is a multicomputer system.

Another method of implementing a multicomputer system is with grid computing which uses middleware that can run like an application on a general-purpose computer. Distributed.net pioneered academic distributed computing over the Internet by having users download an application which performed operations on their own computers.[41] Today there is also SETI@Home, which uses volunteers' computers to process data collected by the Search for Extraterrestrial Intelligence project. Intel, United Devices, and the American Cancer Society have created a screensaver software that performs calculations to aid in pharmaceutical research.[42] Companies such as United Devices are developing software and hardware packages to create enterprise computer grids which will allow organizations to leverage unused processor cycles on their networks to handle computer-intensive tasks. We discuss such grid computing in Section 18.6, Grid Computing.

Distributed processing makes large computations feasible. However, this power comes at the cost of simplicity. Just as in uniprocessing environments, distributed processing must take into account synchronization, mutual exclusion and deadlock. Networking and the lack of shared memory make managing such issues more complex.

Self Review

1. Distinguish multiprocessing and multicomputer systems.
2. What makes distributed processing difficult to implement?

Ans: **1)** With multiprocessing, processors share a common memory. Multicomputer systems do not share a common memory—each processing unit has access to its own resources. **2)** Distributed processing must take into account synchronization, mutual exclusion and deadlock. Networking and the lack of shared memory make managing such issues more complex.

18.4 Clustering

Recall that in a distributed system, several computers handle user requests simultaneously. Each computer processes user requests independently. However, the distributed system must handle communication delays introduced by its underlying networks. Multiprocessing fixes the communication delays by allocating many processors for one computer, making the communications among processes easier and faster. Yet, multiprocessing has its own disadvantages: high cost/performance ratio, limited scalability and not all types of applications running on a system benefit from multiprocessing.[43]

Clustering—interconnecting nodes (single-processor computers or multiprocessor computers) within a high-speed LAN to function as a single parallel computer—is architecturally intermediate between distributed computing and multiprocessing. The set of nodes that forms the single parallel machine is called a **cluster**. Clustering enables multiple computers to work together to solve large and complex problems.[44]

Self Review

1. What is clustering?
2. Why would clustering be employed?

Ans: **1)** Clustering interconnects nodes within a high-speed LAN to function as a single parallel computer. **2)** Clustering takes advantage of multiprocessing and distributed systems while eliminating the communication delays associated with fully distributed systems, providing a powerful computer that is capable of solving large and complex problems.

18.4.1 Clustering Types

There are three major types of clusters. In a **high-performance cluster**, all of the nodes in the cluster are used to perform work. In a **high-availability cluster**, some of the nodes perform work while others serve as backups. If working nodes or their components fail, the backup nodes start running and take over the jobs that were being executed on the failed nodes immediately without interrupting service. In a **load-balancing cluster**, a particular node works as a **load balancer** to distribute the load (such as thousands of requests from the clients) to a set of nodes so that all hardware is efficiently utilized.[45]

High-performance clusters are used for solving large-scale computations that can be divided into smaller problems to be solved in parallel. High-availability clusters are used for mission-critical applications in which failure must be avoided. Load-balancing clusters benefit organizations that handle large volumes of user requests. For example, high-performance clusters are useful for analyzing images from Magnetic Resource Imaging (MRI) scanners, while high-availability clusters are crucial in aircraft control systems and load-balancing clusters are usually used in e-business applications with high user volumes.

Self Review

1. Does a high-availability cluster require that its nodes be working all the time?
2. Argue why a cluster for a particular type of application should have the attributes of all three types of clusters. Consider a search engine being used for an application where lives could be at stake, such as locating organs for transplant.

Ans: **1)** No. High-availability clusters require that only some of their nodes be working while others act as backups. **2)** The cluster should be high performance, because billions of

Web pages would have to be searched in a fraction of a second. It should be high availability to ensure that it is always ready to operate when needed, especially in an emergency. It should be load balancing to spread the load in peak periods, ensuring that individual requests are not delayed.

18.4.2 Clustering Benefits

There are several benefits associated with clustering. It economically interconnects relatively inexpensive components. This reduces the cost for building a clustered system compared to a single parallel computer with the same capability.[46] High performance is another advantage of clustering. Each node in the clustering system shares the workload. Communications among nodes in the cluster are faster than those in unclustered distributed computing systems due to the high-speed LAN between nodes.[47] Clustering can also provide replication of resources across the nodes, so that the failure of any one computer will not affect the availability of the system's resources. If a service on one node is down, other nodes that provide the same service in the cluster can still function and take over the tasks performed by the failed component.[48] Clustering inherits the scalability of distributed systems. A cluster is able to add or remove nodes (or the components of nodes) to adjust its capabilities without affecting the existing nodes in the cluster. Clustering provides better scalability than multiprocessing. For example, the HP 9000 Superdome can have up to 64 processors, while the HP XC clusters can scale up to 512 processors.[49, 50] Clustering achieves reliability and fault tolerance by providing backups for the services and resources. When failure occurs in one running service, the cluster immediately switches the process to the backup service without affecting the performance and capacity of the system, providing uninterrupted service.[51]

Self Review

1. Why is communication among nodes in a cluster faster than among nodes in an unclustered distributed computing system?
2. How does clustering implement fault tolerance?

Ans: **1)** The reason is that a high-speed local area network is generally faster than the wide area networks used in distributed systems. **2)** Clustering provides backups for services and resources.

18.4.3 Clustering Examples

In this section, we consider how clustering is implemented in Linux and Windows. Many Linux clustering solutions are available, the best known being **Beowulf**, a high-performance cluster.[52] In 1994, the NASA Earth and Space Sciences (ESS) project built the first Beowulf cluster to provide parallel computing to address large-scale problems involved in ESS applications. Figure 18.7 shows a typical Beowulf cluster. A Beowulf cluster may contain up to several hundred nodes. Theoretically, all nodes have Linux installed as their operating system and they are interconnected with high-speed Ethernet (often with a bandwidth of 100 Mbps). Each

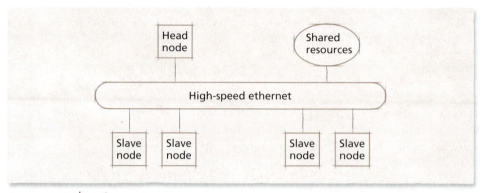

Figure 18.7 | *Typical Beowulf cluster.*

Beowulf cluster has a **head node** (also called a **master node**) that acts as a server to distribute the work load, control access to the cluster and handle the shared resources. All other nodes in the cluster are often called **slave nodes**. The head node usually has a monitor and keyboard, while slave nodes do not. All slave nodes should be configured with the same processor, memory and disk space so that all nodes can complete the same job at approximately the same time. Usually, all the nodes in the cluster are connected within a single room to form a supercomputer.[53]

Windows Server 2003 can be used to build both high-availability clusters and load-balancing clusters. A high-availability cluster built with Windows Server 2003 can have at most eight nodes. All its nodes may share a storage device (Fig. 18.8) or each node may have a local storage, in which case the backup node must keep the exact same data (Fig. 18.9). Unlike the Beowulf cluster, the nodes in the high-availability Windows cluster can be connected either in a LAN or a WAN. In the case of shared storage, only one node is running at a time and that node has the control of the shared storage. When the running node fails, a backup node takes over control of the shared storage. However, if the shared storage breaks down, the entire clus-

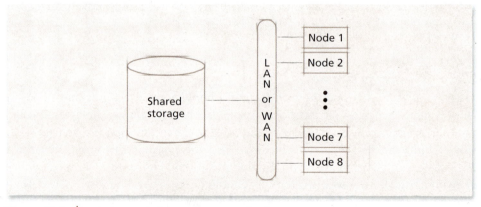

Figure 18.8 | *High-availability cluster with shared storage.*

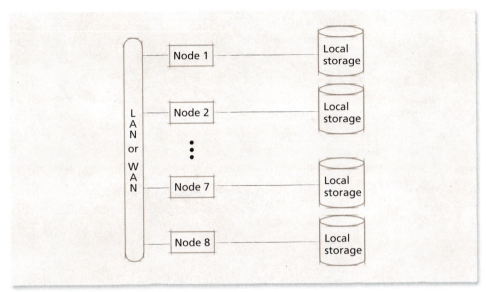

Figure 18.9 | High-availability cluster with local storage.

ter cannot keep running. When each node has its own storage, more than half of the cluster nodes must be active at all times so that when one or more nodes fail, other nodes can continue work effectively. For example, if the cluster has eight nodes, at least five of them must be active and ready to function.[54]

A load-balancing cluster built with Windows Server 2003 can have at most 32 nodes (Fig. 18.10). The cluster does not require sharing storage, because each node can do its job independently. If one node fails, the remaining nodes in the cluster are still capable of handling user requests. Scalability is achieved with the load-balancing cluster, because it is easy to add or remove a node from the cluster. Usually the nodes in the load-balancing cluster are interconnected with high-speed Ethernet.[55]

Self Review

1. List three characteristics that make Beowulf clusters high-performance.
2. What problem does the high-availability cluster with shared storage have?

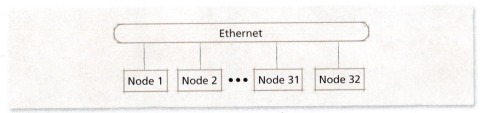

Figure 18.10 | Load-balancing cluster with 32 nodes.

Ans: **1)** All nodes in the Beowulf cluster are interconnected with high-speed Ethernet (often with a bandwidth of 100 Mbps). All nodes can complete the same job approximately at the same time. All nodes work together in parallel to improve performance. **2)** All nodes depend on the shared storage. If the shared storage fails, the entire cluster fails.

18.5 Peer-to-Peer Distributed Computing

In a **peer-to-peer (P2P) application**, each **peer**—a single computer in the P2P system—performs both client and server functions. Such applications distribute processing responsibilities and information to many computers, thus reclaiming otherwise wasted computing power and storage space and eliminating many central points of failure. In the next several subsections we introduce the fundamental concepts of peer-to-peer applications.

18.5.1 Client/Server and Peer-to-Peer Applications

Many network applications operate on the principle that computers should be segregated by function. Some computers, such as servers, offer common stores of programs and data. Other computers, such as clients, access the data provided by the servers. Using a search engine from a Web browser is an example of a client/server application. Clients send queries to servers, which access various databases and respond with the requested information.

P2P applications are different from client/server applications because all computers in the network act as both clients and servers. Each peer has the ability to discover and communicate with other peers and may share resources (such as large multimedia files) with others. P2P applications are similar to the telephone system—a single user can both send and receive information.[56]

Self Review

1. How do client/server applications work?
2. List the advantages of peer-to-peer applications over client/server applications.

Ans: **1)** In a client/server application, the client sends requests to the server, and the server processes the client request, often accessing one or more databases, and sends the response back to the client. **2)** It is easier to set up the network for a peer-to-peer application, and no network administrator is required. In a peer-to-peer application, if one peer fails, others can still function well. In a client/sever application, if the server fails, the entire application fails.

18.5.2 Centralized vs. Decentralized P2P Applications

P2P applications can be implemented in two forms: centralized and decentralized.[57] A **centralized P2P application** uses a central server system that connects to each peer. Centralized P2P applications are similar to the client/server relationship. In a

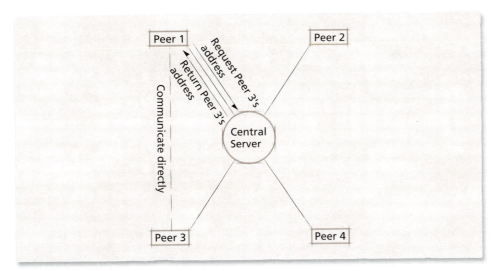

Figure 18.11 | *Centralized P2P instant-messenging application.*

centralized instant messenging application (Fig. 18.11), when peer 1 wants to talk to peer 3, peer 1 must get the address of peer 3 from the server first. Then peer 1 communicates with peer 3 directly. One major weakness of this centralized system is the dependency on the server. If one or more central servers fail, the entire network could fail. The server's capabilities limit the application's overall performance. For instance, Web sites can fail when malicious users overload the Web server(s) with an excessive number of requests. However, centralized architectures also have advantages, such as simplifying management tasks (e.g., monitoring user access by providing single points of network control).

A **pure P2P application**, also called a **decentralized P2P application**, does not have a server and therefore does not suffer from the same deficiencies as applications that depend on servers. In a pure P2P instant messenger application (Fig. 18.12), when peer 1 wants to send a message to peer 3, peer 1 no longer needs to communicate with the server. Instead, peer1 discovers peer3 via distributed search mechanisms and sends messages to peer3 directly. If a peer in a well-designed, pure P2P system fails, all other peers continue to function, so such systems are particularly fault tolerant.

Peer-to-peer applications have disadvantages as well. Anyone with the appropriate software can join the network of peers and often remain anonymous, so determining who is on the network at any moment is difficult. Also, the lack of a server hinders the protection of copyright and intellectual-property rights. Real-time searches can be slow and increase network traffic, as queries propagate throughout the network.[58] Figure 18.13 lists some common peer-to-peer applications.

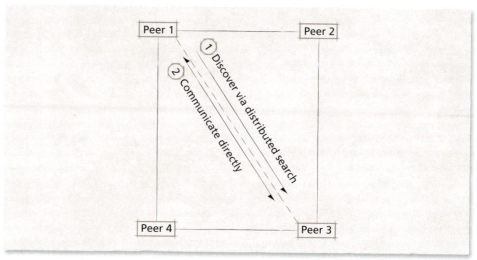

Figure 18.12 | *Pure P2P instant-messaging application.*

Distributed Application	Description
Gnutella	A P2P technology used to share documents on the Internet. Gnutella does not use any servers. There is no authentication, and peers search for files via a distributed search mechanism.[59] (Section 18.5.3, Peer Discovery and Searching, overviews this mechanism.)
KaZaA	A file sharing application that is a hybrid between Gnutella and centralized applications. A server authenticates all users. Certain peers serve as search hubs, which catalog the files of peers connected to them. Searches are distributed to each search hub, which then responds with results that allow direct connections for file transfers.[60]
Groove	A P2P system that allows users to communicate, collaborate and share documents on the Internet and intranet. Groove provides secure communication because users are authenticated and private data is not shared with third parties.[61]
Freenet	Decentralized P2P technology that allows users to share documents on the Internet without fear of censorship. Freenet does not have a central server to govern access. Instead, access to Freenet is anonymous. Documents stored in Freenet are encrypted to improve protection.[62]
Instant messenging	P2P application that enables users to send short text messages and files to one another. Most instant messengers use servers that authenticate all users and route messages between peers.

Figure 18.13 | *Common P2P applications.*

Pure peer-to-peer applications are completely decentralized. Some file sharing applications are not pure peer-to-peer, because they use servers to authenticate users and index each peer's shared files. However, peers connect directly to one another to transfer files. In such a system, centralization improves search performance but makes the network dependent on a server. Performing file transfers between peers decreases the load on the server.

Self Review

1. What are the advantages of centralized P2P applications?
2. What is a benefit of a decentralized P2P application over a centralized one?

Ans: **1)** Centralized P2P applications simplify management tasks, such as monitoring user access by providing single points of network control. **2)** Centralized P2P applications rely on a server for certain operations. If the server fails, those operations will be unavailable.

18.5.3 Peer Discovery and Searching

Peer discovery is the act of finding peers in a P2P application. Pure P2P applications often suffer slow peer discovery and information searching due to the lack of a server. There is no general solution to peer discovery. Gnutella presents one approach for circumventing these problems. Gnutella is a pure peer-to-peer technology that enables distributed information storage and retrieval. Users can search for and download files from any peer on the network. Users first join a Gnutella network by specifying the network address of a known Gnutella peer. Without knowing at least one peer on the network, a user cannot join the network. Each user's Gnutella software functions as a server and uses the HTTP protocol to search for and transfer files.[63]

To perform a search, a peer sends search criteria to the peers connected to it. Those peers then propagate the search throughout the network of peers. If a particular peer can satisfy the search, that peer passes this information back to the originator. The originator then connects directly to the target peer and downloads the information. The peer that made the original query can identify itself only when it connects directly to the peer with the requested file to begin file transfer.

In the Gnutella network, a peer forwards a search request to all of its directly connected peers in parallel. For example, if P_1 receives a request from the user, P_1 forwards the search request to all its directly connected peers first. These peers then work in parallel; each one tries to fulfill the search request and also forwards the request to its directly connected peers.

In the Freenet P2P application, each peer forwards a search request to a single directly-connected peer at a time. For example, if P_1 receives a request from the user, P_1 forwards the search request to P_2 which is one of its directly connected peers. If P_2 cannot answer the request, it forwards the request to one of its directly connected peers. If all the nodes that P_2 can reach cannot answer the request, P_1 then forwards the search request to another one of its directly connected peers.[64]

Searches conducted in both Gnutella and Freenet are called **distributed searches**. Distributed searches make networks more robust by removing single points of failure, such as servers. Not only can peers find information in this way, but peers can search for other peers via distributed searches as well.

Self Review

1. What are some of the problems with distributed searches?
2. Compare Gnutella's distributed search mechanism to Freenets.

Ans: **1)** Distributed searches are costly, possibly generating enormous amounts of network traffic. If poorly implemented P2P systems proliferate, this could have serious ramifications on the performance of the entire Internet. Distributed searches do not guarantee to find the requested files. **2)** Searches in Gnutella will reach close peers before reaching any more distant peers. In Freenet, a search can reach a distant peer before all close peers have been searched.

18.5.4 JXTA

Sun Microsystems, Inc., created Project JXTA (short for Juxtapose) in response to the growing popularity of peer-to-peer applications. Project JXTA strives to create a standard, low-level, platform and language-independent protocol that promotes interoperability among peer-to-peer applications. The current JXTA implementation is written in Java, but developers can implement JXTA in any programming language. JXTA provides a foundation on which developers can build any type of P2P application.

JXTA attempts to solve the following problems of peer-to-peer applications:[65]

1. Security/authentication—Large peer-to-peer network applications, such as AOL Instant Messenger (AIM) and MSN Instant Messenger, use servers to bootstrap users onto the network.[66] This bootstrapping ensures that the same person uses a particular online identity.

2. Peer discovery—Without a server, it is complex to locate other peers on the network.

3. Network incompatibility—Currently, each popular peer-to-peer application has a set of proprietary protocols that are incompatible with other peer-to-peer networks due to the lack of standards. For example, users on the AIM platform cannot communicate with MSN Instant Messenger users.

4. Platform incompatibility—Software developers must rewrite the low-level core aspects of their peer-to-peer applications for each platform they wish to support. Wireless phones and other mobile devices usually have a limited selection of P2P applications, if any.

JXTA attempts to solve these problems by standardizing the low-level protocols that govern peer-to-peer applications. All JXTA-based P2P applications use identical low-level protocols, hence they are compatible with one another.

Networks built with the JXTA protocols consist of three basic types of entities—peers or peer groups, advertisements and pipes. A peer is any entity that uses JXTA protocols (Fig. 18.14) to communicate with other peers. Each peer need support only some of the protocols, so devices with low processing power and memory can still participate in JXTA networks (albeit with limited functionality). **Peer**

Protocol	Function
Peer discovery	Peers use this protocol to find other entities in the JXTA network by searching for advertisements.
Peer resolver	Peers that help a search process (e.g., send and process requests) implement this protocol.
Peer information	Peers obtain information about other peers via this protocol.
Peer membership	Peers use this protocol to learn about the requirements of groups, how to apply for membership, how to modify their membership and how to quit a group. Authentication and security are implemented through this protocol.
Pipe binding	Peers can connect pipes to one another, via advertisements, through this protocol.
Endpoint routing	Peer routers implement this protocol to provide other routing services to other peers (e.g., tunneling through a firewall).

Figure 18.14 | JXTA low-level protocols.[67]

groups are logical constructs that represent sets of peers. JXTA specifies only two rules regarding peer groups:

1. peers can join or leave groups, and
2. the group administrator, if the group has one, controls access to the group.

Advertisements are XML documents formatted according to JXTA specifications that are used by a peer to advertise itself and notify others of its existence. **Pipes** are virtual communication channels that connect two or more peers for sending and receiving messages among peers. At the simplest level, pipes are one-way communication channels. Two peers communicate by configuring two pipes that "flow" in opposite directions. When a source peer needs to send a message to a destination peer, a pipe is dynamically bound to the two peers. Once the pipe is set up, the source peer can send messages to the destination peer via the pipe.

Examples of P2P applications that uses JXTA are: VistaPortal (www.vistaportal.com/), Momentum by InView Software (www.inviewsoftware.com/news/20030305_momentum1.htm) and ifreestyle by Digital Dream (www.digitaldream.jp/en/).[68]

Self Review

1. How do AOL Instant Messenger and MSN Instant Messenger bootstrap users onto the network?
2. How do peers communicate in networks built with the JXTA protocol?

Ans: **1)** Both AOL Instant Messenger and MSN Instant Messenger use central servers to bootstrap users onto the network. **2)** Peers use one-way communication channels called pipes to exchange messages.

18.6 Grid Computing

A few decades ago, the number of computers was relatively small, their computing power was modest and they were expensive and heavily utilized. With the advent of the microprocessor, there are now hundreds of millions of inexpensive, relatively powerful computers in homes and businesses. However, a vast amount of computing power is wasted (e.g., personal computers at home sit idle while people are at work, and work computers sit idle while people are at home). **Grid computing** links potentially vast numbers of computational resources (such as computers, storage devices and scientific instruments) that are distributed over a network to solve complex, massive, computation-intensive problems.

As in other distributed systems, the resources in grid computing are distributed, and users can access them transparently. While clustering typically is localized or centralized, grid computing emphasizes public collaboration. Individuals and research institutes participating in grid computing coordinate resources that are not subject to centralized control. High performance, the goal of grid computing, is achieved by using spare computer power at little or no cost. Grid computing offers better scalability than clusters. For example, the SETI@home project, which is discussed later, runs on half-a-million PCs while an HP XC cluster runs on up to 512 nodes. Grid computing requires sophisticated software to manage distributed computing tasks on such a massive scale.[69, 70, 71]

To enable interoperability of heterogeneous distributed resources, a grid-computing system is often divided into five layers. The **application layer**, which is the highest level, contains applications that use the lower layers to access distributed resources. The **collective layer** is responsible for coordinating distributed resources, such as scheduling a task to analyze data received from a scientific device. The **resources layer** enables applications to request and share a resource. The **connectivity layer** carries out reliable and secure network communications between resources. The **fabric layer** accesses physical resources, such as disks.[72]

The SETI@home (Search for Extraterrestrial Intelligence at home) project (`setiathome.ssl.berkeley.edu/`) is a popular grid-computing implementation. SETI@home enables individuals to participate in a scientific effort seeking intelligent life elsewhere in the universe. Computers belonging to participants, when not in use, download data representing signals from outer space from the SETI@home server, analyze the data and return the results to the SETI@home server.[73, 74]

The Globus Alliance (`www.globus.org/`), based at Argonne National Laboratory, the University of Southern California's Information Sciences Institute, the University of Chicago, the University of Edinburgh and the Swedish Center for Parallel Computers, researches grid-computing resource management and develops software (called the Globus Toolkit) to implement grid computing.[75] United Devices (`www.ud.com`) provides grid-computing solutions for businesses.[76]

Self Review

1. What makes grid computing a promising trend?

2. Why is the grid-computing system divided into several layers?

Ans: **1)** Grid computing helps coordinate distributed resources and allows access to potentially massive amounts of computing resources, enabling complex problems to be solved that usually cannot be approached without enormous computing powers. **2)** Distributed resources are typically heterogeneous, so the layered architecture enables interoperability and modularity.

18.7   Java Distributed Computing

Java is used widely to implement distributed systems. We discussed developing distributed systems using Java's RMI in Section 17.3.3, and CORBA in Section 17.3.4. Sun provides an article about CORBA and Java at `java.sun.com/j2ee/corba/`. The following subsections introduce several additional Java technologies that enable developers to build distributed systems and to share and manage distributed resources.

18.7.1   Java Servlets and JavaServer Pages (JSP)

Java provides a number of built-in networking capabilities that make it easy to develop Internet-based and Web-based applications. This section focuses on both sides of a client-server relationship which is the foundation for the highest-level views of networking in Java, namely **servlets** and **JavaServer Pages (JSP)**. A servlet extends the functionality of a server, most frequently a Web server. Using special syntax, JSP allows Web-page programmers to create pages that use encapsulated Java functionality and even to write **scriptlets** (Java code embedded in a JSP) of actual Java code directly in the page.[77]

A common implementation of the request-response model is between Web browsers and Web servers that interact via the HTTP protocol. When a user accesses a Web site by means of a browser (the client application), a request is sent to the appropriate Web server (the server application). The server normally responds to the client by sending the appropriate HTML Web page. Servlets enhance the functionality of Web servers to provide capabilities such as secure access to Web sites, interacting with databases on behalf of a client, dynamically generating custom documents to be displayed by browsers and maintaining unique session information for each client.

In some ways, JSPs look like standard HTML or XML documents. In fact, JSPs normally include HTML or XML markup. Such markup is known as fixed-template data or fixed-template text. JSPs are generally used when most of the content sent to the client is static text and markup, and only a small portion of the content is generated dynamically with Java code. Servlets are commonly used when a small portion of the content sent to the client is static text or markup. In fact, some servlets do not produce content. Rather, they perform a task on behalf of the client (such as a database query), then invoke other servlets or JSPs to provide a response. Note that in most cases servlet and JSP technologies are interchangeable. The server that executes a servlet is referred to as the **servlet container** or **servlet**

engine. JSPs are translated into servlets by the servlet container, which then compiles and executes them.[78]

Many developers believe that servlets are appropriate for database-intensive applications that communicate with so-called **thin clients**—applications that require minimal client-side support. With these applications, the server is responsible for database access and clients connect to the server using HTTP. Thus, the presentation-logic code for generating dynamic content can be written once and reside on the server for access by clients, to allow programmers to create efficient thin clients.

Sun Microsystems, through the **Java Community Process**, is responsible for the development of the servlet and JavaServer Pages specifications. The reference implementations of these standards are under development by the **Apache Software Foundation** (www.apache.org) as part of the **Jakarta Project** (jakarta.apache.org).[79] As stated on the Jakarta Project's home page, "The goal of the Jakarta Project is to provide commercial-quality server solutions based on the Java platform that are developed in an open and cooperative fashion." The servlet and JSP part of the Jakarta Project is called **Tomcat**—this is the official reference implementation of the JSP and servlet standards. The most recent version can be downloaded from the Apache Software Foundation's Web site.

Servlets and JavaServer Pages have become so popular that they are now supported by most major Web servers and application servers, including the Sun ONE Application Server, Microsoft's Internet Information Services (IIS), the Apache HTTP Server, BEA's WebLogic application server, IBM's WebSphere application server, the World Wide Web Consortium's Jigsaw Web server and many more.

Servlet Life Cycle

Architecturally, all servlets implement a common interface, which enables the servlet container to interact with any servlet, regardless of its functionality. A servlet's life cycle begins when the servlet container loads the servlet into memory—usually in response to the first request that the servlet receives. Before the servlet can handle that request, the servlet container initializes the servlet. Then, the servlet can respond to its first request. Typically, each new request results in a new thread of execution (created by the servlet container). The servlet container can also terminate the servlet to release its resources.[80]

JavaServer Pages (JSP)

JavaServer Pages is an extension of servlet technology. JSPs simplify the delivery of dynamic Web content. Web-application programmers can create dynamic content by reusing predefined components and by interacting with components using server-side Java code. JSP programmers can reuse Java objects and create custom tag libraries that encapsulate complex, dynamic functionality. These libraries enable Web-page designers who are not familiar with Java to enhance Web pages with powerful dynamic content and processing capabilities.

There are four key components to JSPs: directives, actions, scriptlets and tag libraries. Directives are messages to the JSP container that enable the programmer to specify page settings, to include content from other resources and to specify custom tag libraries for use in a JSP. Actions encapsulate functionality in predefined tags that programmers can embed in a JSP. Actions often are performed based on the information sent to the server as part of a particular client request. They also can create Java objects for use in JSP scriptlets. Scriptlets, or scripting elements, enable programmers to insert Java code that interacts with components in a JSP (and possibly other Web-application components) to process requests. The tag-extension mechanism enables programmers to create custom tags. Such tags enable programmers to manipulate JSP content.[81]

When a JSP-enabled server receives the first request for a JSP, the JSP container translates that JSP into a Java servlet that handles the current request and future requests to the JSP. If the new servlet compiles properly, the JSP container invokes the servlet to process the request. The JSP may respond directly to the request or may invoke other Web-application components to assist in processing the request. Overall, a JSP's request/response mechanism and life cycle are identical to that of a servlet.

Self Review

1. Suppose a request for a Web page requires the server to generate its content from a database. Which technology discussed in the previous section is most appropriate to accomplish this?
2. Which JSP component enables programmers to insert Java code into JSP?

Ans: **1)** Servlets should be used, because JSP is used when a small portion of the content is generated dynamically with Java code. **2)** Scriptlets.

18.7.2 Jini

Many network devices, such as printers and Web servers, provide services to network clients. **Jini**—a framework for building reliable and fault-tolerant distributed systems with existing Java technologies—extends this idea of providing services beyond industry computer-based networks and into home-based networks. For example, when you arrive home, your car could use a wireless network to notify your home's lighting service to turn on the lights over the walkway. Each service mentioned here has a well-defined interface. The network-printing service provides an interface that enables applications to print documents. A Web server provides an HTTP interface that enables Web browsers to download documents. Your home's lighting service provides an interface that enables other devices on the network to turn the lights on and off.

To use a Jini service, a Jini client must be able to discover that a service exists and must know the interface for interacting with the service. For example, your car must be able to discover that your home provides a lighting service and must know the service's interface to interact with it. However, the car need not know the implementation of the underlying lighting service.

The Jini **lookup service** is the heart of the Jini architecture (Fig. 18.15). A lookup service maintains information about available Jini services and enables clients to discover and use them. The process of finding the lookup services and obtaining references to them is called **discovery**. A service provider discovers and registers the service interface with one or more lookup services to make itself available to clients. Clients discover the lookup services and request a service they require. The lookup services then send a copy of the service interface to the client. Upon obtaining the service interface, the client communicates with the service provider via RMI, as discussed in Section 17.3.3, using the service interface.[82]

Recall that Jini services register with lookup services to make the Jini service's functionality available to other members in the network. If all goes well, other members use the service, and the service stays up and running perpetually. In reality, however, services fail for many reasons—network outages can make a service unreachable, a physical device associated with a service (e.g., a printer) might need repairs or the service itself could encounter an unrecoverable error. In these and many other situations, a service could become unavailable, and that service might not be able to unregister itself from lookup services to prevent other clients from attempting to use it.

One goal of Jini technology is to make Jini communities "self-healing" and able to recover from these common problems. Therefore, when a Jini service registers with a lookup service, the registration is not permanent. The registration is leased for a specific amount of time, after which the lookup service revokes the registration (a service provider can also renew the lease anytime before it expires).[83] This prevents problematic services from disrupting the entire Jini network. If a Jini

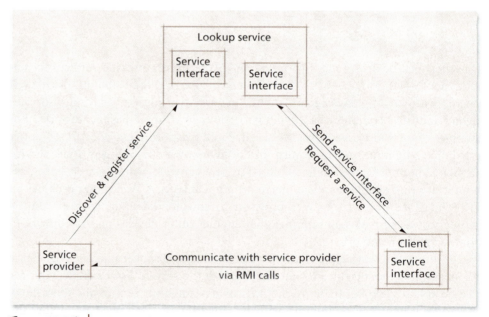

Figure 18.15 | *Jini architecture.*

service fails, the Jini service's lease eventually expires and lookup services will no longer provide the failed Jini service to clients. The leasing strategy that Jini employs is strict—if a Jini service provider does not renew the lease, the lookup service terminates the registration when the lease expires and the service becomes unavailable to clients.

Self Review

1. What information must a Jini client know in order to use a Jini service?
2. What is the function of the Jini lookup service?

Ans: **1)** The Jini client must know the service interface to use a Jini service. **2)** It acts as a registry for Jini services so that a Jini client can find and use the Jini services that are available.

18.7.3 JavaSpaces

JavaSpaces is a Jini service that implements a simple, high-level architecture for building distributed systems. Objects that take part in distributed systems must be able to communicate with one another and share information. The JavaSpaces service provides distributed, shared storage (and shared memory) for Java objects and enables Java objects to communicate, share objects and coordinate tasks using the storage. Any Java-compatible client can put shared objects into the storage.

A JavaSpaces service provides three fundamental operations—write, take and read, which allow the communications between objects stored in JavaSpaces. The **write operation** adds an object into the JavaSpaces service. When clients want to remove an object, they perform a **take operation**. The take operation removes from the JavaSpaces service an object that satisfies the client's search criteria. The **read operation** is similar to the take operation, but it does not remove the matching object from the JavaSpaces service so that other clients can still find it. Clients can perform read operations concurrently, but only one client can perform the take operation to remove the object from JavaSpaces.[84]

JavaSpaces eases the design and development of distributed systems that share Java objects between the service providers and the clients. A JavaSpaces service has six major properties:[85]

1. A JavaSpaces service is a Jini service.

2. Multiple processes can access a JavaSpaces service concurrently, which helps synchronize actions between distributed applications.

3. An object stored in a JavaSpaces service will remain in the service until its lease expires or until a program removes the object from the JavaSpaces service.

4. A JavaSpaces service locates objects by comparing them to a template. The template specifies the search criteria against which the JavaSpaces service compares each object in the JavaSpaces service. When one or more entries match the template, the JavaSpaces service returns a single matching object.

5. JavaSpaces services ensure that operations execute atomically.

6. Objects in a JavaSpaces service are shared. Both service providers and clients can read and take objects from the JavaSpaces service.

Now we demonstrate how to build a distributed image-processing system with the JavaSpaces service (Fig. 18.16). Image processing can be a time-consuming task, especially for large images. However, we can improve performance by using JavaSpaces services to build a distributed image-processing system for applying filters to images (e.g., blur, sharpen, etc.). The client first partitions a large image into smaller pieces and writes them into a JavaSpaces service. Multiple image processors (distributed among the system) run in parallel to take the smaller images from the storage and process them by applying appropriate filters, then write the processed images back into the JavaSpaces service. The client takes the processed subimages from the JavaSpaces service and builds the complete, processed image.

Self Review

1. **(T/F)** After a service provider adds an object to a JavaSpaces service, the object will always be there if no one removes it.
2. How might JavaSpaces be used to implement a chat system?

Ans: 1) False. Even though the client does not execute a take operation, the object will not remain in the JavaSpaces service permanently. Each object stored in a JavaSpaces service has

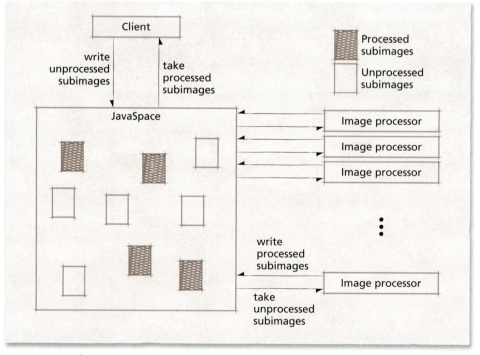

Figure 18.16 | *Distributed image-processing application using JavaSpaces.*

a lease; when its lease expires, the object is removed. **2)** JavaSpaces can be used to build a chat system in which the message sender writes messages to JavaSpaces and the message receiver reads or takes the message from JavaSpaces. The sender can send messages to a particular recipient or to a group of recipients.

18.7.4 Java Management Extensions (JMX)

A crucial function in any distributed system is network management. Businesses increasingly need networks that provide services which are customized to customer demands, consistently available and easily updated. As more organizations add networks and expand existing networks to increase productivity, network management becomes more difficult. The proper functionality of printers, network routers and other devices—many of which play an integral role in the productivity of a firm—is important. As more devices are networked and as networks grow larger, more problems can occur. The demand for managing distributed applications increases when business applications move into distributed environments.[86]

Existing tools for managing networked devices often use both standard and proprietary protocols and management tools. The diversity of such proprietary protocols and tools makes managing a diverse network difficult. Many network management schemes are inflexible and nonautomated. This usually means that significant amounts of time and resources are spent trying to fix and operate large networks. New technologies are required that will help shift the burden of routine tasks to the network management software itself and leave special issues to the network manager.

Recent technological advances have provided network management developers with the tools necessary to develop smart agents that can assume various responsibilities. These tools allow agents to incorporate themselves into frameworks in which numerous agents interact with each other and provide a dynamic and extensible network management solution.

Java Management Extensions (JMX), developed by Sun and other companies in the network management industry, defines a component framework that enables developers to build automated, intelligent and dynamic network management solutions. JMX defines a three-level management architecture—the instrumentation level, the agent level and the manager level (Fig. 18.17). The **instrumentation level** makes any Java-based object manageable so that the management application can access and operate these objects. The **agent level** provides services for exposing the managed resources. The **manager level** gives management applications access to resources created in the instrumentation level and operates these resources via the JMX agents.[87]

Self Review

1. What are the problems with many existing network-management schemes?
2. What are the three levels in JMX architecture? Briefly describe the function of each.

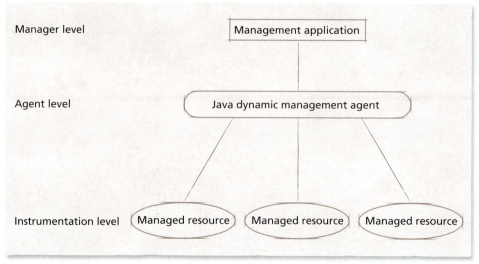

Figure 18.17 | *JMX's three-level management architecture.*

Ans: **1)** Many existing network-management schemes are inflexible and nonautomated, because various networked devices may be managed using diverse protocols and tools and require large amounts of time to fix and operate in a large network. **2)** The three levels are: the instrumentation level, the agent level and the manager level. The instrumentation level makes any Java-based object manageable. The agent level provides services for exposing the managed resources. The manager level gives management applications access to resources and operates these resources via the JMX agents.

18.8 Web Services

Over the past several decades, computing has evolved at an unprecedented pace. This progress impacts organizations in significant ways, forcing information-technology (IT) managers and developers to accept new computing paradigms. Innovations in programming and hardware have led to more powerful and useful technologies, including object-oriented programming, distributed computing, Internet protocols and XML (Extensible Markup Language). At the same time, organizations have learned to leverage the power of their networks and the Internet to gain competitive advantages.

Web services technology, which represents the next stage in distributed computing, will profoundly affect organizations in the future. Web services encompass a set of related standards that can enable any two computer applications to communicate and exchange data via the Internet. Many factors—including software vendors' widespread support for underlying standards—indicate that Web services will radically change IT architectures and partner relationships. Companies are already implementing Web services to facilitate a wide variety of business processes, such as application integration and business-to-business transactions.[88]

For a distributed system to function correctly, application components executing on different computers throughout a network must be able to communicate. In Section 17.3, we discussed technologies such as DCOM and CORBA that enable communication among distributed components. Unfortunately, DCOM and CORBA cannot intercommunicate easily. Their components often communicate via a COM/CORBA bridge. If DCOM's and CORBA's underlying protocols change, programmers must modify the bridge to reflect the changes. Such problems have impeded distributed computing's ability to facilitate business-process integration and automation.

Web services improve distributed computing capabilities by addressing the issue of limited interoperability.[89] Web services operate using open (i.e., nonproprietary) standards, which means that Web services can, theoretically, enable any two software components to communicate—regardless of the technologies used to create the components or the platforms on which the components reside. Also, Web-services-based applications are often easier to debug, because Web services use a text-based communications protocol, rather than the (albeit faster) binary communications protocols employed by DCOM and CORBA. Organizations are implementing Web services to improve communication between DCOM and CORBA components and to create standards-based distributed computing systems. Thus, Web services will help organizations achieve the goals of distributed computing and do so more economically.[90]

The industry's experience with interoperability problems led to the development of open standards for Web services technologies, in an effort to enable cross-platform communication. The primary standard used in Web services is **Extensible Markup Language (XML)**, a language for marking up data so that information can be exchanged between applications and platforms. Microsoft and DevelopMentor developed the **Simple Object Access Protocol (SOAP)** as a messaging protocol for transporting information and instructions between Web services, using XML as a foundation for the protocol. Two other Web services specifications—**Web Services Description Language (WSDL)** and **Universal Description, Discovery and Integration (UDDI)**—are also based on XML. WSDL provides a standard method of describing Web services and their specific capabilities; UDDI defines XML-based rules for building directories in which companies advertise themselves and their Web services.[91]

Open standards enable businesses (running different platforms) to communicate and transfer data without designing costly platform-specific software. Web services improve collaborative software development by allowing developers to create applications by combining code written in any language on any platform. Also, Web services promote modular programming. Each specific function in an application can be exposed as a separate Web service. Individuals or businesses can create their own unique applications by mixing and matching Web services that provide the functionality they need. Modularization is less error prone and promotes software reuse.

A Web service can be as trivial as multiplying two numbers together or as complex as the functions carried out by an entire customer relationship management (CRM) software system. For example, tracking the location and status of a FedEx package is a Web service (`fedex.com/us/tracking`).

Some e-commerce Web sites allow independent developers to harness the power of their sites' technologies by exposing certain functions as Web services. For example, online retailer `Amazon.com` allows developers to build online stores that search its product databases and display detailed product information via Amazon.com Web Services (`www.amazon.com/gp/aws/landing.html`). The Google search engine also can be integrated with other functionality through the Google Web APIs (`www.google.com/apis`), which connect to Google's indices of Web sites using Web services. `Amazon.com` and Google provide access to their sites' features through SOAP and other standard protocols in exchange for increased exposure.

Self Review

1. How are Web services more portable than DCOM?
2. Can a client application written in Java access a Web service written in C#? Why?

Ans: **1)** Web services provide interoperability, platform independence and language independence. **2)** Yes, a client application written in Java can access a Web service written in C#, because Web services technologies use open standards such as XML, SOAP, WSDL and UDDI.

18.8.1 Microsoft's .NET Platform

Microsoft introduced the term Web services during the June 2000 launch of its .NET initiative. Today, Microsoft is one of the dominant companies in the Web services market. The .NET initiative includes the Visual Studio .NET integrated development environment which enables programmers to develop Web services in a variety of languages, including C++, C# and Visual Basic .NET. However, .NET technologies are available only for Windows 2000 and XP. [92]

.NET Web services, which are central to the .NET initiative, extend the concept of software reuse to the Internet by allowing developers to reuse software components that reside on other machines or platforms. Employing Web services as reusable building blocks, programmers can concentrate on their specialties without having to implement every component of an application. For example, a company developing an e-commerce application can subscribe to Web services that process payments and authenticate users. This enables programmers to focus on other, more unique aspects of the e-commerce application.

In .NET, a Web service is an application stored on one machine that can be accessed by another machine over a network. In its simplest form, a Web service created in .NET is a class, or a logical grouping of methods and data that simplifies program organization. Methods are defined within a class to perform tasks and return information when their tasks are complete. .NET Web service classes contain certain methods (called **Web service methods**) that are specified as part of the Web service. These methods can be invoked remotely using RPC.

Self Review

1. Can .NET technologies be used on Linux?
2. How have .NET Web services extended the concept of software reuse to the Internet?

Ans: **1)** No. .NET technologies are available only for Windows 2000 and XP. **2)** .NET Web services allow developers to reuse software components that reside on other machines or platforms.

18.8.2 Sun Microsystems and the Sun ONE Platform

Sun Microsystems' Web services strategy is based on the **Sun Open Net Environment (Sun ONE)**, which consists of three components—a vision, an architecture and a conceptual model for developing standards-based software.[93]

The Sun ONE vision incorporates a model for software development, in which critical business information and applications are available at any time to any type of device, including cell phones and PDAs. Sun ONE's goal is to help developers create networks of distributed applications or Web services that are highly reliable and promote the reuse of components and services.[94]

The Sun ONE architecture is designed to be scalable to ensure reliable access to services. Scalability is crucial; as new technologies and new components are added to systems, more demands are placed on system resources, potentially degrading service.[95]

The Sun ONE platform is comprised of three products: the Solaris™ Operating Environment, the Infrastructure Software and the Sun ONE Studio. The Infrastructure Software includes the Sun ONE Directory Server and the Sun ONE Portal Server, which offer user authentication and personalization. Other Infrastructure Software capabilities include scheduling management, billing and communication. Sun ONE allows programmers to deploy Web services using third-party products. By integrating disparate products, programmers can develop Web services infrastructures that best suit their companies' requirements. Sun ONE incorporates support for open standards, including XML, SOAP, UDDI and WSDL, to help ensure high levels of interoperability and system integration.[96]

Sun ONE promotes the notion that a company's Data, Applications, Reports and Transactions, which compose the conceptual DART model, can be published as services online.[97] Using the DART model, companies can organize business applications and processes that involve data, applications, reports and transactions, so that programmers can map business elements to corresponding services.

Self Review

1. How is Sun ONE more portable than .NET?
2. What does infrastructure software do in Sun ONE?

Ans: **1)** .NET is available only on Windows, while Sun ONE is available for many platforms. **2)** Infrastructure software offers user authentication and personalization. Infrastructure software is also capable of scheduling management, billing and communication.

Web Resources

www.faqs.org/ftp/rfc/pdf/rfc1094.txt.pdf
PDF version of the Network File System version 2 protocol specification.

www.connectathon.org/nfsv3.pdf
PDF version of the Network File System version 3 protocol specification.

www.ietf.org/rfc/rfc2054.txt
Text version of the WebNFS client specification.

www.ietf.org/rfc/rfc3010.txt
Text version of the Network File System version 4 protocol specification.

www.ietf.org/rfc/rfc2203.txt
Text version of the RPCSEC_GSS protocol specification.

www.cs.berkeley.edu/projects/sprite/retrospective.html
Brief retrospective on the Sprite Network Operating System.

www.es.jamstec.go.jp/esc/eng/index.html
Earth simulator home page.

www.distributed.net/pressroom/presskit.php
Provides news and articles for distributed system projects.

library.thinkquest.org/C007645/english/1-parallel.htm
Compares distributed computing and parallel computing and introduces clustering.

www.linux-mag.com/2000-10/clustering_01.html
Discusses Linux clustering in detail.

www.jini.org
The Jini technology site; provides links for downloading the Jini technology implementation.

wwws.sun.com/software/jini/specs/js2_0.pdf
Provides the JavaSpaces service specification.

java.sun.com/products/JavaManagement/wp/
Contains Java Management Extensions (JMX) White Paper.

www.jxta.org
Official Web site for Project JXTA; contains the newest downloads of the source code and opportunities to participate in developing JXTA.

www.openp2p.com
This O'Reilly Network online resource provides articles and links related to peer-to-peer technologies.

java.sun.com/j2ee/corba/
Discusses CORBA technology and the Java platform.

java.sun.com/j2ee
Provides reference material for all Java 2 Enterprise Edition technologies, including servlets and JavaServer Pages.

jakarta.apache.org
The Apache Jakarta Project site provides resources for servlets and JavaServer Pages and the reference implementation of these technologies.

www.webservices.org
The Web Services Community Portal contains the latest news regarding Web services and Web services vendors. There is also a collection of articles and papers relating to Web services technologies.

www.microsoft.com/net
Microsoft's .NET site provides .NET resources, including product information, news, events and downloads.

www.sun.com/sunone
Sun Microsystems' Sun ONE initiative site explains the Open Net Environment and provides news about the products and its users.

www.xmethods.com
Lists free, publicly available Web services and provides links for tutorials and implementations of Web services.

Summary

Networked file systems allow clients to access files stored on remote computers. Distributed file systems, which are the focus of this chapter, are special examples of networked file systems that allow transparent access to remote files.

A distributed file server can be either stateful or stateless. In a stateful system, the server keeps state infor-

mation of the client requests so that subsequent access to the file is easier. In a stateless system, the client must specify which file to access in each request.

Distributed file systems provide the illusion of transparency. Complete file location transparency means that the user is unaware of the physical location of a file within a distributed file system; the user just sees a global file system. Many distributed systems implement client caching to avoid the overhead of multiple RPCs. Clients keep a local copy of a file and flush it to the server from time to time. Because there are multiple copies of the same file, files can become inconsistent. Distributed file systems are designed to share information among large groups of computers. To reach this goal new computers should be able to be added to the system easily. Distributed file systems should be scalable. There are two primary security concerns in distributed file systems: ensuring secure communications and guaranteeing correct file access permissions.

NFS (Network File System) versions 2 and version 3 assume a stateless server implementation, which makes fault tolerance easier to implement than with a stateful server. With stateless servers, if the server crashes, the client can simply retry until the server responds. NFS-4 is stateful. The stateful server allows faster access to files. However, if the server crashes, all the state information of the client is lost, so the client needs to rebuild its state on the server before retrying.

Client-side caching is essential to efficient distributed file system operation. NFS-4 extends the client-caching scheme through delegation, which allows the server to temporarily transfer the control of a file to a client. When the server grants a read delegation of a particular file to the client, then no other client can write to that file. When the server grants a write delegation of a particular file to the client, then no other client can read or write to that file. If another client requests a file that has been delegated, the server will revoke the delegation and request that the original client flush the file to disk.

AFS (Andrew File System) is a global file system that appears as a branch of a traditional UNIX file system at each workstation. AFS is completely location transparent and provides a high degree of availability, which means the files are always available regardless of the user's location. AFS is based on the client-server model and relies on RPCs for communication.

The Sprite file system has the perceived form of a UNIX file system, and every client has the exact same view of the hierarchy. It goes a step further in UNIX file system emulation by allowing transparent remote access to I/O devices (which are represented as files in UNIX). In Sprite, both the client and the server keep a cache. To open a file, the client first checks its cache, then makes a request to its backing store (which is generally a server). If the server is unable to satisfy the request from its cache, it reads the data from disk. Both caches retain a copy of the data when

it is returned to the client. When a client writes a block, it writes into its cache. Sprite flushes updated pages to the server every 30 seconds.

Clustering involves interconnecting nodes (single-processor computers or multiprocessor computers) within a high-speed LAN to function as a single parallel computer. The set of nodes that forms the single parallel machine is called a cluster. Clustering enables multiple computers to work together to solve large and complex problems such as weather prediction.

There are three major types of clusters: high-performance clusters, high-availability clusters and load-balancing clusters. In a high-performance cluster, all the nodes in the cluster work to improve performance. In a high-availability cluster, only some of the nodes in the cluster are working while others act as backups. If working nodes or their components fail, the backup nodes immediately start running and take over the jobs that were being executed on the failed nodes, without interrupting service. In a load-balancing cluster, a particular node works as a load balancer to distribute the load to a set of nodes so that all hardware is efficiently utilized.

P2P (peer-to-peer) applications are different from client/server applications. Instead of segregating computers by function, all computers act as both clients and servers. Each peer has the ability to discover and communicate with other peers. Peers may share resources (such as large multimedia files) with others. P2P applications can be implemented in two forms: centralized and decentralized. A centralized P2P application uses a server that connects to each peer. Centralized P2P applications exemplify the client/server relationship. A pure P2P application, also called a decentralized P2P application, does not have a server and therefore does not suffer from the same deficiencies as applications that depend on servers.

Distributed searches make networks more robust by removing single points of failure, such as servers. Not only can peers find information in this way, but they can search for other peers via distributed searches.

Grid computing links computational resources that are distributed over the wide area network (such as computers, data storages and scientific devices) to solve complex problems. Resources in grid computing are distributed, and users can access these resources transparently without knowing where they are located. Grid computing emphasizes public collaboration—individuals and research institutes coordinate resources that are not subject to a centralized control to deliver qualities of service. Grid computing has the same advantage as clustering—high performance, achieved by cost-effectively using spare computer power and collaborating resources. However, grid computing requires advanced software to manage distributed computing tasks efficiently and reliably.

A Java servlet extends the functionality of a server, most frequently a Web server. Using special syntax, JSP allows Web-page programmers to create pages that use encapsulated Java functionality and even to write scriptlets (Java code embedded in a JSP) of actual Java code directly in the page.

JSPs are generally used when most of the content sent to the client is static text and markup and only a small portion of the content is generated dynamically with Java code. Servlets are commonly used when a small portion of the content sent to the client is static text or markup. In fact, some servlets do not produce content. Rather, they perform a task on behalf of the client (such as a database query), then invoke other servlets or JSPs to provide a response.

Project JXTA strives to create a standard, low-level platform and language-independent protocol that promotes interoperability among peer-to-peer applications. JXTA provides a foundation on which developers can build any type of P2P application.

Jini—a framework for building reliable and fault-tolerant distributed systems with existing Java technologies—extends this idea of providing services beyond computer-based networks and into home-based networks. The JavaSpaces service provides distributed, shared storage (and shared memory) for Java objects and enables Java objects to communicate, share objects and coordinate tasks using the storage. Any Java-compatible client can put shared objects into the storage.

Java Management Extensions (JMX) defines a component framework that enables developers to build automated, intelligent and dynamic network-management solutions.

Web services is an emerging area of distributed computing. Web services encompass a set of related standards that can enable any two computer applications to communicate and exchange data via the Internet. Web services can enable any two software components to communicate—regardless of the technologies used to create the components or the platforms on which the components reside.

Web services improve collaborative software development by allowing developers to create applications by combining code written in any language on any platform. Also, Web services promote modular programming. Each specific function in an application can be exposed as a separate Web service. With separate Web service components, individuals or businesses can create their own unique applications by mixing and matching Web services that provide the functionality they need. Such modularization is less error prone and promotes software reuse

Key Terms

advertisement (in JXTA)—XML document formatted according to JXTA specifications that is used by a peer to advertise itself and notify others of its existence.

agent level (in JMX)—JMX level that provides services for exposing the managed resources.

Andrew File System (AFS)—Scalable distributed file system that would grow to support a large community while being secure. AFS is a global file system that appears as a branch of a traditional UNIX file system at each workstation. AFS is completely location transparent and provides a high degree of availability.

Apache Software Foundation—Provides open-source software, such as Tomcat, the official reference implementation of JSP and servlet specifications.

application layer (in grid computing)—Contains applications that use lower-level layers to access the distributed resources.

available volume storage group (AVSG) (in Coda)—Members of the VSG with which the client can communicate.

Beowulf cluster—Linux clustering solution, which is a high-performance cluster. A Beowulf cluster may contain several nodes or several hundred. Theoretically, all nodes have Linux installed as their operating system and are interconnected with high-speed Ethernet. Usually, all the nodes in the cluster are connected within a single room to form a supercomputer.

callback (in AFS)—Sent by the server to notify the client that the cached file is modified.

cell (in AFS-3)—Unit in AFS-3, which preserves namespace continuity while allowing different systems administrators to oversee each cell.

centralized P2P application—Uses a server that connects to each peer.

client caching—Clients keep local copies of files and flush them to the server after having modified the files.

client modification log (CML) (in Coda)—Log which is updated to reflect file changes on disk.

cluster—Set of nodes that forms what appears to be a single parallel machine.

clustering—Interconnection of nodes within a high-speed LAN so that they function as a single parallel computer.

Coda Optimistic Protocol—Protocol used by Coda clients to write a copy of the file to each of the members of the AVSG, which provides a consistent view of a file within an AVSG.

collective layer (in grid computing)—Layer responsible for coordinating distributed resources, such as scheduling a task to analyze data received from a scientific device.

concurrent write-sharing—Occurs when two clients modify cached copies of the same file.

connectivity layer (in grid computing)—Layer that carries out reliable and secure transactions between distributed resources.

decentralized peer-to-peer application—Also called a pure peer-to-peer application. It does not have a server and therefore does not suffer from the same deficiencies as applications that depend on servers.

delegation (in NFS)—Allows the server to temporarily transfer the control of a file to a client. When the server grants a read delegation of a particular file, then no other clients can write to that file, but they can read it. When the server grants a write delegation of a particular file to the client, then no other clients can read or write that file.

discovery (in Jini)—Process of finding the lookup services and obtaining references to them.

distributed file system—Special examples of networked file systems that allow transparent access to remote files.

distributed search—Searching technology used in peer-to-peer applications to make networks more robust by removing single points of failure, such as servers. In a distributed search, if a peer cannot answer the client's request, the peer forwards the request to its directly connected peers and the search is distributed to the entire peer-to-peer network.

domain (in Sprite file system)—Unit that represents a portion of the global file hierarchy and is stored at one server.

emulation stage—When a Coda client becomes disconnected, it is said to enter the emulation stage. During this stage all file read requests are satisfied from cache. Write requests during the emulation stage occur in two steps. First, the file is updated on disk. Second, a log called the client modification log (CML) is updated to reflect file changes.

export local file—Performed by an NFS server to make the local directory of files available to the remote client via the mount protocol.

Extensible Markup Language (XML)—Language for marking up data so that information can be exchanged between applications and platforms.

fabric layer (in grid computing)—Layer that accesses physical resources, such as disks.

file handle—Identifies a file on the file server with file type, location and access permissions.

file identifiers (fids) (in AFS)—Entity that specifies a volume, an index within a volume and an identifier to guarantee object uniqueness within a volume.

grid computing—Links computational resources that are distributed over the wide area network (such as computers, data storages and scientific devices) to solve complex problems.

head node (in a Beowulf cluster)—Node, also called master node, that acts as a server to distribute the workload, control access to the cluster and handle the shared resources.

high-availability cluster—Cluster in which only some of the nodes are working while other nodes act as backups. The goal of a high-availability cluster is to stay up all the time.

high-performance cluster—Cluster in which all the nodes work to achieve maximum performance.

hoarding stage (in Coda)—Stage that clients enter when they are connected to Coda. In this stage, clients prepare for a possible disconnection from the system by caching any requested file.

idempotent request—A requested operation that if performed several times will return the same result, so it is acceptable to perform the same operation twice.

instrumentation level (in JMX)—Makes any Java-based object manageable so that the management application can access and operate these objects.

invalidate—To invalidate a file, the client checks the time stamp of the copy of the file on the server. If this copy has been updated since the client last copied the file, then the client must download the latest version. If the server copy has not been updated since the client copied it, then the client can work on its cached copy.

Jakarta project—Provides commercial-quality server solutions based on the Java platform that are developed in an open and cooperative fashion.

Java Community Process—Open organization that focus on developing Java technology specifications, including servlet and JavaServer Pages.

Java Management Extensions (JMX)—Developed by Sun and network management industry leaders, which defines a component framework that enables developers to build automated, intelligent and dynamic network management solutions.

JavaServer Pages (JSP)—Allows Web-page programmers to create pages that use encapsulated Java functionality and even to write scriptlets of actual Java code directly in the page.

JavaSpaces—Jini service that implements a simple, high-level architecture for building distributed systems. The Java-Spaces service provides distributed, shared storage (and shared memory) for Java objects and enables Java objects to communicate, share objects and coordinate tasks using the storage.

Jini—Framework for building reliable and fault-tolerant distributed systems with existing Java technologies. Jini extends the idea of providing services beyond industry-based computer networks and into home-based networks.

JXTA—Project created at Sun Microsystems, Inc., which creates a standard, low-level, platform and language-independent protocol that promotes interoperability among peer-to-peer applications.

lease—Agreement between the client and server for controlling file locks.

load-balancing cluster—Cluster in which one particular node works as a load balancer to distribute the load to a set of nodes, so that all hardware is efficiently utilized.

load balancer—Node in a load-balancing cluster that distributes the workload (such as thousands of requests from the clients) to a set of nodes so that all hardware is efficiently utilized.

lookup service—Heart of the Jini architecture, which maintains information about available Jini services and enables clients to discover and use them.

manager level (in JMX)—Level that gives a management application access to managed resources (created in the instrumentation level) and operates these resources via the JMX agents.

master node (in a Beowulf cluster)—Node also known as the head node, that acts as a server to distribute the workload, control the access to the cluster and handle the shared resources.

multicomputer system—System in which processors do not share a common memory or bus. Each processor has access to its own resources. These independent processors are connected in a network to operate cooperatively to form a multicomputer system.

Network File System (NFS)—Current de facto standard for network file sharing, natively supported in most varieties of UNIX (and many other operating systems) with client

and server software available for other common platforms.

network file system—System that allows clients to access files on remote computers. Network file systems do not provide location transparency as distributed file systems do.

nonvolatile storage—The contents of nonvolatile storage are not lost when the machine loses power or is powered off.

peer—Single computer in a peer-to-peer system.

peer discovery—Finding peers in a peer-to-peer application.

peer group—Logical construct that represents a set of peers. A peer group is one of the basic types of entities in a network built with the JXTA protocols.

peer-to-peer (P2P) application—Distributes processing responsibilities and information to many computers, thus reclaiming otherwise wasted computing power and storage space and eliminating central points of failure. In a peer-to-peer system, each peer performs both client and server functions.

pipe (in JXTA)—Virtual communication channel that connects two or more peers for sending and receiving messages among peers.

preferred server (PS) (in Coda)—Member of the AVSG that provides copies of files for Venus.

prefix table (in Sprite)—Table that stores domain information to aid in file lookups. Each entry in the table represents a separate domain and consists of the absolute path to the root directory within the domain, the server which houses the domain and a token that identifies the domain.

pure peer-to-peer application—Also called a decentralized peer-to-peer application. It does not have a server and therefore does not suffer from the same deficiencies as applications that depend on servers.

read operation (in JavaSpaces)—Operation that is similar to the take operation, but does not remove the object from the JavaSpaces service so that other clients can still find it.

reintegration stage (in Coda)—Stage right after the client reconnects to the system during which Venus asynchronously updates the server using the CML.

resources layer (in grid computing)—Layer that enables applications to query and share a resource.

safe asynchronous write (in NFS-3)—Allows a server to return before a write has been completed.

scriptlet—Java code embedded in a JSP.

sequential write-sharing—Occurs when one client modifies a file, then another client tries to read or write its own cached copy of the file. Sequential write-sharing introduces cache inconsistency.

servlet—Enhances the functionality of Web servers to provide capabilities such as secure access to Web sites, interacting with databases on behalf of a client, dynamically generating custom documents to be displayed by browsers and maintaining unique session information for each client.

servlet container—Server that executes a servlet. Also known as servlet engine.

Simple Object Access Protocol (SOAP)—Messaging protocol for transporting information and instructions between Web services, using XML as a foundation for the protocol.

slave node (in a Beowulf cluster)—Beowulf cluster node that is not a head node.

Sprite—Distributed operating system whose goal is transparency and complete consistency.

stateful server—Keeps state information of the client requests—such as the file name, a pointer to the file and the current position in the file—so that the subsequent access to the file is easier and faster.

stateless server—The server does not keep state information of the client requests, so the client must specify which file to access in each request.

Sun Open Net Environment (Sun ONE)—Consists of three components—a vision, an architecture and a conceptual model for developing standards-based software.

take operation (in JavaSpaces)—Removes from the JavaSpaces service an object that matches the given criteria. Take operations, together with write and read operations, allow distributed applications to dynamically exchange objects within JavaSpaces services.

thin client—Application that requires minimal client-side support.

Tomcat—Official reference implementation of the JSP and servlet standards.

Universal Description, Discovery and Integration (UDDI)—Defines XML-based rules for building directories in which companies advertise themselves and their Web services.

update set (in Coda)—Specifies, to each member of the AVSG, the members of the AVSG that have successfully performed the write.

Venus (in AFS)—User-level process that interacts with the Vice processes run on distributed file servers to govern distributed file access.

virtual file system (VFS)—Provides the abstraction of a common file system at each client and is responsible for all distributed file operations.

Vice (in AFS)—Entity that governs distributed file access in AFS.

volume (in AFS-2)—Introduced in AFS-2 to manage subtrees. Volumes are primarily of administrative value, allowing replication and isolation of certain subtrees, and are therefore transparent to users.

volume storage group (VSG) (in Coda)—Volumes are logical pieces of the file system and are replicated physically across multiple file servers. Servers that hold the same volume are known as a volume storage group (VSG).

WebNFS—Allows NFS clients to access WebNFS-enabled servers with a minimum of protocol overhead. Marketed as the file system for the Web, WebNFS is designed to improve NFS functionality and performance over wide area Internet and intranets.

Web service—Technology that encompasses a set of related standards that can enable any two computer applications to communicate and exchange data via the Internet.

Web Services Description Language (WSDL)—Provides a standard method of describing Web services and their specific capabilities.

Web service methods (in .NET)—Methods contained in a .NET Web service class.

write operation (in JavaSpaces)—Operation that adds an object into the JavaSpaces service.

Exercises

18.1 Explain the benefits and drawbacks of client caching in distributed file systems.

18.2 What are the primary concerns of implementing distributed file systems?

18.3 A file server can be either stateful or stateless. What are the advantages and disadvantages of each implementation?

18.4 How can distributed file systems ensure cache consistency?

18.5 Is NFS-4 more secure than NFS-2 and NFS-3? How?

18.6 In AFS-1, each time the VFS tried to open a cached file it would have Venus contact the server to make sure that the file was still valid. What is the problem with this approach? How do AFS-2 and AFS-3 solve this problem?

18.7 Explain how Coda provides fault tolerance.

18.8 Describe the three stages Coda clients go through when reading and writing to a file on the Coda server.

18.9   How does Sprite handle server crashes?

18.10   Describe the differences between high-performance clusters, high-availability clusters and load-balance clusters. Give examples of each of these cluster types in use.

18.11   List the essential elements for building a Beowulf cluster.

18.12   Compare centralized and pure peer-to-peer applications. What are the advantages and disadvantages of each approach?

18.13   Given the peer network of Fig. 18.18, apply the distributed search mechanism used in Gnutella to find the requested resource which is on P_7. Assume the search starts at P_1.

18.14   Given the peer network as shown in Fig. 18.18, apply the distributed search mechanism used in Freenet to find the requested resource, which is on P_7. Assume the search starts at P_1.

18.15   Describe the three basic types of entities of JXTA.

18.16   Explain why the Jini lookup service is the heart of the Jini architecture.

18.17   When a service provider registers a service with a Jini lookup service, is the registration permanent? What is the benefit of this design?

18.18   What problems do DCOM and CORBA have? How can Web services solve this problem?

Suggested Projects

18.19   Research transparency in distributed file systems. What research is currently being done in that field?

18.20   Research client caching in distributed file systems. What research is currently being done in that field?

18.21   Prepare a research paper for Web services. How is it used?

Recommended Reading

Distributed file systems play an important role in distributed systems.[98, 99] Examples of distributed file systems are NFS,[136, 101, 102, 103, 104, 105] AFS,[106, 107] Coda[108] and Sprite.[109, 110, 111, 112] Clustering enables multiple computers to work together to solve large and complex problems.[113, 114] The most popular clustering technologies are Beowulf and Windows Server 2003 clusters.[115, 116] The peer-to-peer distributed computing model is another architecture for building distributed systems.[117, 118, 119] Peer-to-peer applications use a distributed search to find a peer in the network.[120, 121] Sun provides several technologies for developing distributed computing systems with servlets and JavaServer Pages (JSP),[122, 123, 124, 125] including Jini,[126, 127] JavaSpaces[128] and

JMX.[129] Web services is an emerging area of distributed computing. Web services encompass a set of related standards that can enable any two computer applications to communicate and exchange data via the Internet. Web services can enable any two software components to communicate—regardless of the technologies used to create the components or the platforms on which the components reside.[130, 131, 132, 133]

Web services is one of the most recent distributed systems architectures.[134, 135] Distributed systems exist in many forms—distributed object-based systems, distributed file systems, distributed document-based systems and distributed coordination-based systems. Tanenbaum and Steen discuss each of these types

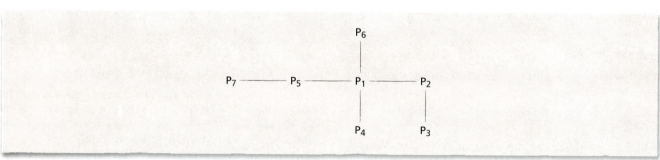

Figure 18.18 | *P2P system with seven peers.*

of distributed systems.[136] Both centralized and decentralized P2P applications have scalability limitations. Grid computing enables the creation of a large-scale infrastructure used to share computing power and data resources.[137, 138]

Works Cited

1. Tanenbaum, A., and R. Renesse, "Distributed Operating Systems," *ACM Computing Surveys*, Vol. 17, No. 4, December 1985, pp. 419–470.

2. Levy, E., and A. Silberschatz, "Distributed File Systems: Concepts and Examples," *ACM Computing Surveys*, Vol. 22, No. 4, December 1990, pp. 321–374.

3. Howard, J. H., et al, "Scale and Performance in a Distributed File System", *ACM Transactions on Computer Systems*, Vol. 6, No. 1, February 1988, pp. 51–81.

4. Andrade, H., "Distributed File Systems", <www.cs.umd.edu/~hcma/818g/>.

5. Tanenbaum, A., and R. Renesse, "Distributed Operating Systems," *ACM Computing Surveys*, Vol. 17, No. 4, December 1985, pp. 429–430.

6. "Difference Between Fault Tolerance and High-Availability," <aix.caspur.it/ibm/web/pssp-3.5/planv2/am0s0mst38.html>.

7. Froese, K. W., and R. B. Bunt, "The Effect of Client Caching on File Server Workloads," *Proceedings of the Twenty-Ninth Hawaii International Conference on System Sciences*, Wailea, HI, January 1996, pp. 15--159.

8. Tanenbaum, A., and R. Renesse, "Distributed Operating Systems," *ACM Computing Surveys*, Vol. 17, No. 4, December 1985, pp. 427–429.

9. Sandberg, R., "The Sun Network Filesystem: Design, Implementation and Experience", *Proceedings of The USENIX Conference*, 1986, pp. 300–314, <www.cs.ucf.edu/~eurip/cop6614/sandbergnfs.pdf>.

10. Nowicki, B., "NFS: Network File System Protocol Specification," March 1989, <www.ietf.org/rfc/rfc1094.txt>.

11. Callaghan, B., "NFS Version 3 Protocol Specification," <www.ietf.org/rfc/rfc1813.txt>, June 1995.

12. Network File Systems: Version 2 Protocol Specification, <docs.freebsd.org/44doc/psd/27.nfsrfc/paper.pdf>.

13. Callaghan, B., "WebNFS Client Specification," October 1996, <www.ietf.org/rfc/rfc2054.txt>.

14. Shepler, S., "RFC 2624—NFS Version 4 Design Considerations," June 1999, <www.faqs.org/rfcs/rfc2624.html>.

15. Pawlowski, B., et al., "The NFS Version 4 Protocol," <www.netapp.com/tech_library/3085.html>.

16. Shepler, S., et al., "NFS Version 4 Protocol," December, 2000, <www.ietf.org/rfc/rfc3010.txt>.

17. Eisler, M., "NFS Version 4 Security," December 1998, <www.ietf.org/proceedings/98dec/slides/nfsv4-eisler-98dec.pdf>.

18. Satyanarayanan, M., "Scalable, Secure and Highly Available Distributed File Access," *IEEE Computer*, May 1990, p. 9.

19. Morris, J. H., et al., "Andrew: A Distributed Personal Computing Environment," *Communications of the ACM*, Vol. 29, No. 3, March 1986, pp. 186–187.

20. Satyanarayanan, M., "Scalable, Secure and Highly Available Distributed File Access," *IEEE Computer*, May 1990, p. 10.

21. Satyanarayanan, M., "Scalable, Secure and Highly Available Distributed File Access," *IEEE Computer*, May 1990, pp. 11–12.

22. Morris, J. H., et al., "Andrew: A Distributed Personal Computing Environment," *Communications of the ACM*, Vol. 29, No. 3, March 1986, p. 193.

23. Satyanarayanan, M., "Scalable, Secure and Highly Available Distributed File Access," *IEEE Computer*, May 1990, p. 12.

24. Satyanarayanan, M., "Scalable, Secure and Highly Available Distributed File Access," *IEEE Computer*, May 1990, pp. 13–15.

25. Coda credits, <www.mit.edu/afs/sipb/project/coda/src/coda/CREDITS>.

26. Satyanarayanan, M., "Scalable, Secure and Highly Available Distributed File Access," *IEEE Computer*, May 1990, p. 15.

27. Satyanarayanan, M., "The Evolution of Coda," *ACM Transactions on Computer Systems*, Vol. 20, No. 2, May 2002, p. 89.

28. Satyanarayanan, M., "The Evolution of Coda," *ACM Transactions on Computer Systems*, Vol. 20, No. 2, May 2002, pp. 89–90.

29. Satyanarayanan, M., "The Evolution of Coda," *ACM Transactions on Computer Systems*, Vol. 20, No. 2, May 2002, pp. 90–91.

30. Satyanarayanan, M., "The Evolution of Coda," *ACM Transactions on Computer Systems*, Vol. 20, No. 2, May 2002, pp. 94–95.

31. Ousterhout, J., "A Brief Retrospective on the Sprite Network Operating System," <www.cs.berkeley.edu/projects/sprite/retrospective.html>.

32. Ousterhout, J., et al., "The Sprite Network Operating System," *IEEE Computer*, February 1988, p. 28.

33. Ousterhout, J., et al., "The Sprite Network Operating System," *IEEE Computer*, February 1988, pp. 28–30.

34. Ousterhout, J., et al., "The Sprite Network Operating System," *IEEE Computer*, February 1988, pp. 30–31.

35. Nelson, M., "Caching in the Sprite Network File System," *ACM Transactions on Computer Surveys*, Vol. 6, No. 1, February 1988, pp. 134–154.

36. Baker, M., and J. Ousterhout, "Availability in the Sprite Distributed File System," *Proceedings of the 4th workshop on ACM SIGOPS European workshop*, September 1990, pp. 1–4.

37. McGregor, J. D., and A. M. Riehl, "The Future of High Performance Super Computers in Science and Engineering," *Communications of the ACM*, Vol. 32, No. 9, September 1989, p. 1092.

38. Earth Simulator Performance, <www.es.jamstec.go.jp/esc/eng/ES/performance.html>.

39. Lyman, J., "The Supercomputing Speed Barrier," *Newsfactor Special Report*, September 13, 2002, <www.techextreme.com/perl/story/19391.html>.

40. Johnson, G., "At Los Alamos, Two Visions of Supercomputing," *New York Times*, June 25, 2002, <www.nytimes.com/2002/06/25/science/physical/25COMP.html?pagewanted=print&position=bottom>.

41. McNett, D., "Press Information," <www.distributed.net/pressroom/presskit.html>.

42. Press Release: "Intel and Scientific Community Announce Cancer Research Program," April 3, 2001, <www.intel.com/pressroom/archive/releases/20010403corp.htm>.

43. Parallel Processing, <library.thinkquest.org/C007645/english/1-parallel.htm?tqskip1=1&tqtime=1020>.

44. Alternatives and forms of DC; <library.thinkquest.org/C007645/english/0-alternatives.htm?tqskip1=1&tqtime=0818>.

45. "Linux Clustering in Depth", *Linux Magazine*, <www.linux-mag.com/2000-10/clustering_01.html>.

46. "Distributed Computing: Power Grid", <www.zdnet.com.au/printfriendly?AT=2000048620-20269390-2>.

47. "Unraveling the Mysteries of Clustering", <www.networkcomputing.com/shared/printArticle.jhtml?article=/1119/1119f2full.html>.

48. The UNIX Operating System: A Robust, Standardized Foundation for Cluster Architectures, <www.unix.org/whitepapers/cluster.html>.

49. HP 9000 Superdome Overview and Features, <www.hp.com/products1/servers/scalableservers/superdome/>.

50. HP High Performance XC Clusters, <www.hp.com/techservers/clusters/5982-0212EN_lo.pdf>.

51. Understanding Clustering, <otn.oracle.com/oramag/oracle/03-jul/o43devejb.html>.

52. Jan Lindheim, C., "Building a Beowulf System", <www.cacr.caltech.edu/research/beowulf/tutorial/beosoft/>.

53. "What's a Beowulf?" <www.phy.duke.edu/brahma/beowulf_book/node9.html>.

54. "Windows Server 2003 Clustering," <www.microsoft.com/windowsserver2003/docs/BDMTDM.doc>.

55. "Windows Server 2003 Clustering," <www.microsoft.com/windowsserver2003/docs/BDMTDM.doc>.

56. Harold, E., *JAVA Network Programming*, Sebastopol, CA: O'Relly & Associates, Inc., 1997, pp. 26–27.

57. "Peer-to-Peer File Sharing," <banners.noticiasdot.com/termometro/boletines/docs/musica-video/varios/2002/musica_P2PWhitePaper.pdf>.

58. "P2P Search Engines," <ntrg.cs.tcd.ie/undergrad/4ba2.02-03/p8.html>.

59. "GNUtella," <ntrg.cs.tcd.ie/undergrad/4ba2.02-03/p5.html>.

60. "Technical: How KaZaA Works," <www.christian-gerner.de/forum/topic-1-279-279.html>.

61. Milojicic, D.; V. Kalogeraki; R. Lukose; K. Nagaraja; J. Pruyne; B. Richard; S. Rollins; and Z. Xu, "Peer-to-Peer Computing", March 2002, <www.hpl.hp.com/techreports/2002/HPL-2002-57.pdf>.

62. "The Free Network Project," <freenet.sourceforge.net/>.

63. Oram, A., "Gnutella and Freenet Represent True Technological Innovation," <www.oreillynet.com/pub/a/network/2000/05/12/magazine/gnutella.html?page=1>.

64. Oram, A., "Gnutella and Freenet Represent True Technological Innovation," <www.oreillynet.com/pub/a/network/2000/05/12/magazine/gnutella.html?page=1>.

65. Gong, L., "Project JXTA: A Technology Overview," <www.jxta.org/project/www/docs/jxtaview_01nov02.pdf>.

66. AOL Instant Messenger™, <www.aim.com/index.adp>.

67. Gong, L., "Project JXTA: A Technology Overview," <www.jxta.org/project/www/docs/jxtaview_01nov02.pdf>.

68. See, S., "Project JXTA Technology Overview," <cosmos.kaist.ac.kr/~hckim/p2p/busan/jxta-overview.pdf>.

69. "Grid Computing," <searchcio.techtarget.com/sDefinition/0,,sid19_gci773157,00.html>.

70. Foster, I., "Internet Computing and the Emerging Grid," <www.nature.com/nature/webmatters/grid/grid.html>.

71. "Grid Computing," <www.nr.no/dart/projects/emerging/grid.html>.

72. Casanova, H., "Distributed Computing Research Issues in Grid Computing," *ACM SIGACT News*, Vol. 33, No. 3, Sept. 2002, p. 54.

73. "Learn about SETI@home," <setiathome.ssl.berkeley.edu/learnmore.html>.

74. Hipschman, R., "How SETI@home Works," <setiathome.ssl.berkeley.edu/about_seti/about_seti_at_home_1.html>.

75. "About the Globus Alliance," <www.globus.org/about/default.asp>.

76. "Overview—The Solution: Grid Computing," <www.ud.com/solutions/>.

77. Deitel, H. M. and P. J. Deitel, *Java How To Program, 5th Edition*, Upper Saddle River, NJ: Prentice Hall, 2003.

78. "Introduction to JavaServer Pages™," Sun Microsystems, 2002, <developer.java.sun.com/developer/onlineTraining/webcasts/pdf/webcamp/dchen/dchen6.pdf>.

79. "The Apache Jakarta Project," <jakarta.apache.org>.

80. "The J2EE™ Tutorial—Servlet Life Cycle," <java.sun.com/j2ee/tutorial/1_3-fcs/doc/Servlets4.html>.

81. McPherson, S., "JavaServer Pages: A Developer's Perspective," April 2000, <developer.java.sun.com/developer/technicalArticles/Programming/jsp/>.

82. "Jini™ Architecture Specification," <wwws.sun.com/software/jini/specs/jini1.2html/jini-spec.html>.

83. "Jini™ Technology Core Platform Specification, LE-Distributed Leasing," <www.jini.org/nonav/standards/davis/doc/specs/html/lease-spec.html>.

84. "JavaSpaces Service Specification," <wwws.sun.com/software/jini/specs/js2_0.pdf>.

85. Freeman, E., and S. Hupfer, "Make room for JavaSpaces, Part 1," <www.javaworld.com/javaworld/jw-11-1999/jw-11-jiniology_p.html>.

86. Kreger, H., "Java Management Extensions for Application Management," <www.research.ibm.com/journal/sj/401/kreger.html>.

87. "Java Management Extensions White Paper," <java.sun.com/products/JavaManagement/wp/>.

88. Deitel, H. M.; P. J. Deitel; B. DuWaldt; and L. K. Trees, *Web Services A Technical Introduction*, Upper Saddle River, NJ: Prentice Hall, 2003, p. 2.

89. Snell, J., "Web Services Interoperability," <www.xml.com/pub/a/2002/01/30/soap.html>.

90. Deitel, H. M.; P. J. Deitel; B. DuWaldt; and L. K. Trees, *Web Services A Technical Introduction*, Upper Saddle River, NJ: Prentice Hall, 2003, pp. 4–5.

91. Deitel, H. M.; P. J. Deitel; J. Gadzik; K. Lomeli; S. Santry; and S. Zhang, *Java Web Services for Experienced Programmers*, Upper Saddle River, NJ: Prentice Hall, 2003, p. 7.

92. Combs, B., "Windows NT/2000," <www.interex.org/pubcontent/enterprise/nov01/nt1101.jsp>.

93. Sun Open Net Environment (Sun ONE), <wwws.sun.com/software/sunone/>.

94. "Sun ONE Overview: Vision," <wwws.sun.com/software/sunone/overview/vision/>.

95. "Sun ONE Overview: Architecture," <wwws.sun.com/software/sunone/overview/architecture/index.html>.

96. Adhikari, R., "Sun Extends Web Services Strategy," *Application Development Trends*, Dec. 2001, p. 12.

97. "Sun ONE Overview: DART Model," <wwws.sun.com/software/sunone/overview/dart/index.html>.

98. Tanenbaum, A., and R. Renesse, "Distributed Operating Systems," *ACM Computing Surveys*, Vol. 17, No. 4, December 1985, pp. 419–470.

99. Levy, E., and A. Silberschatz, "Distributed File Systems: Concepts and Examples," *ACM Computing Surveys*, Vol. 22, No. 4, December 1990, pp. 321–374.

100. Sandberg, R., "The Sun Network Filesystem: Design, Implementation and Experience", *Proceedings of The USENIX Conference*, 1986, pp. 300–314, <www.cs.ucf.edu/~eurip/cop6614/sandbergnfs.pdf>.

101. Nowicki, B., "NFS: Network File System Protocol Specification," March 1989, <www.ietf.org/rfc/rfc1094.txt>.

102. Callaghan, B., "NFS Version 3 Protocol Specification," <www.ietf.org/rfc/rfc1813.txt>, June 1995.

103. Network File Systems: Version 2 Protocol Specification, <docs.freebsd.org/44doc/psd/27.nfsrfc/paper.pdf>.

104. Callaghan, B., "WebNFS Client Specification," October 1996, <www.ietf.org/rfc/rfc2054.txt>.

105. Shepler, S., "RFC 2624—NFS Version 4 Design Considerations," June 1999, <www.faqs.org/rfcs/rfc2624.html>.

106. Satyanarayanan, M., "Scalable, Secure and Highly Available Distributed File Access," *IEEE Computer*, May 1990, p. 9.

107. Morris, J. H., et al., "Andrew: A Distributed Personal Computing Environment," *Communications of the ACM*, Vol. 29, No. 3, March 1986, pp. 186–187.

108. Satyanarayanan, M., "The Evolution of Coda," *ACM Transactions on Computer Systems*, Vol. 20, No. 2, May 2002, p. 89.

109. Ousterhout, J., "A Brief Retrospective on the Sprite Network Operating System," <www.cs.berkeley.edu/projects/sprite/retrospective.html>.

110. Ousterhout, J., et al., "The Sprite Network Operating System," *IEEE Computer*, February 1988, p. 28.

111. Nelson, M., "Caching in the Sprite Network File System," *ACM Transactions on Computer Surveys*, Vol. 6, No. 1, February 1988, pp. 134–154.

112. Baker, M., and J. Ousterhout, "Availability in the Sprite Distributed File System," *Proceedings of the 4th workshop on ACM SIGOPS European workshop*, September 1990, pp. 1–4.

113. Ousterhout, J., et al., "The Sprite Network Operating System," *IEEE Computer*, February 1988, pp. 30–31.

114. Nelson, M., "Caching in the Sprite Network File System," *ACM Transactions on Computer Surveys*, Vol. 6, No. 1, February 1988, pp. 134–154.

115. "What's a Beowulf?" <www.phy.duke.edu/brahma/beowulf_book/node9.html>.

116. "Windows Server 2003 Clustering," <www.microsoft.com/windowsserver2003/docs/BDMTDM.doc>.

117. "Peer-to-Peer File Sharing," <banners.noticiasdot.com/termometro/boletines/docs/musica-video/varios/2002/musica_P2PWhitePaper.pdf>.

118. "P2P Search Engines," <ntrg.cs.tcd.ie/undergrad/4ba2.02-03/p8.html>.

119. "Technical: How KaZaA Works," <www.christian-gerner.de/forum/topic-1-279-279.html>.

120. Oram, A., "Gnutella and Freenet Represent True Technological Innovation," <www.oreillynet.com/pub/a/network/2000/05/12/magazine/gnutella.html?page=1>.

121. Milojicic, D.; V. Kalogeraki; R. Lukose; K. Nagaraja; J. Pruyne; B. Richard; S. Rollins and Z. Xu, "Peer-to-Peer Computing", March 2002, <www.hpl.hp.com/techreports/2002/HPL-2002-57.pdf>.

122. Deitel, H. M. and P. J. Deitel, *Java How To Program, 5th Edition*, Upper Saddle River, NJ: Prentice Hall, 2003.

123. "Introduction to JavaServer Pages™," Sun Microsystems, 2002, <developer.java.sun.com/developer/onlineTraining/webcasts/pdf/webcamp/dchen/dchen6.pdf>.

124. "The J2EE™ Tutorial—Servlet Life Cycle," <java.sun.com/j2ee/tutorial/1_3-fcs/doc/Servlets4.html>.

125. McPherson, S., "JavaServer Pages: A Developer's Perspective," April 2000, <developer.java.sun.com/developer/technicalArticles/Programming/jsp/>.

126. "Jini™ Architecture Specification," <wwws.sun.com/software/jini/specs/jini1.2html/jini-spec.html>.

127. "Jini™ Technology Core Platform Specification, LE-Distributed Leasing," <www.jini.org/nonav/standards/davis/doc/specs/html/lease-spec.html>.

128. "JavaSpaces Service Specification," <wwws.sun.com/software/jini/specs/js2_0.pdf>.

129. "Java Management Extensions White Paper," <java.sun.com/products/JavaManagement/wp/>.

130. Snell, J., "Web Services Interoperability," <www.xml.com/pub/a/2002/01/30/soap.html>.

131. Combs, B., "Windows NT/2000," <www.interex.org/pubcontent/enterprise/nov01/nt1101.jsp>.

132. Sun Open Net Environment (Sun ONE), <wwws.sun.com/software/sunone/>.

133. "Sun ONE Overview: DART Model," <wwws.sun.com/software/sunone/overview/dart/index.html>.

134. Deitel, H. M., P. J. Deitel, B. DuWaldt and L. K. Trees, *Web Services A Technical Introduction*, Upper Saddle River, NJ: Prentice Hall, 2003, pp. 4–5.

135. Deitel, H. M., P. J. Deitel, J. Gadzik, K. Lomeli, S. Santry and S. Zhang, *Java Web Services for Experienced Programmers*, Upper Saddle River, NJ: Prentice Hall, 2003, p. 7.

136. Tanenbaum, A. S., and M. van Steen, *Distributed Systems Principles and Paradigms*, Upper Saddle River, NJ: Prentice Hall, 2002.

137. Foster, I. and C. Kesselman, *The Grid: Blueprint for a New Computing Infrastructure*, San Fransisco, CA: Morgan Kaufmann, 1999.

138. Bester, F.; I. Foster; C. Kesselman; J. Tedesco; and S. Tuecke, "GASS: A Data Movement and Access Service for Wide Area Computing Systems," *In Proceeding of the Sixth Workshop on I/O in Parallel and Distributed Systems*, 1999, pp. 78–88.

Security

'Is it weakness of intellect, birdie?' I cried,
'Or a rather tough worm in your little inside?'
—W. S. Gilbert—

Part 7

Computers are vulnerable to attacks that can compromise data, corrupt files and crash systems—operating system security is at the core of secure computing systems. The next chapter discusses key security topics, including cryptography (secret key and public key), authentication (biometrics, smart cards, Kerberos, single sign-on), access control, security attacks (cryptanalysis, viruses, worms, denial-of-service attacks), attack prevention (firewalls, intrusion detection systems, antivirus software), key agreement protocols, digital signatures, Public Key Infrastructure (PKI), certificates, certificate authorities, secure communication protocols (Secure Sockets Layer, Virtual Private Networks, wireless security), steganography and proprietary vs. open-source security. We include a case study on OpenBSD, arguably the world's most secure operating system.

We have forty million reasons for failure, but not a single excuse.
—Rudyard Kipling—

You can't trust code that you did not totally create yourself. (Especially code from companies that employ people like me.)

— Ken Thompson —
1983 Turing Award Lecture
Association for Computing Machinery, Inc.

We have forty million reasons for failure, but not a single excuse.

— Rudyard Kipling —

There is no such thing as privacy on a computer. The view here is that if you don't want something read, don't put it on the system.

— Thomas Mandel —
quoted in *Time*, April 6, 1987

*'Is it weakness of intellect, birdie?' I cried,
'Or a rather tough worm in your little inside?'*

— W. S. Gilbert —

Chapter 19

Security

Objectives

After reading this chapter, you should understand:

- *public-key/private-key cryptography.*

- *the role of authentication in providing secure systems.*

- *access control models, policies and mechanisms.*

- *security threats, such as viruses, worms, exploits and denial-of-service attacks.*

- *security and authentication protocols, such as SSL and Kerberos.*

- *digital signatures, digital certificates and certificate authorities.*

- *Virtual Private Networks and IPSec.*

Chapter Outline

Web Resources | Summary | Key Terms | Exercises | Recommended Reading | Works Cited

19.1 Introduction

As the personal computing and e-business movements expand, individuals and organizations are storing highly confidential information on their computers and transmitting sensitive information over the Internet. Consumers are submitting credit card numbers to e-commerce sites, and businesses are exposing proprietary data on the Web. At the same time, organizations are experiencing increasing numbers of security breaches. Both individuals and companies are vulnerable to data theft and attacks that can compromise data, corrupt files and crash systems. The computing industry has been responding to these needs, as organizations work to improve Internet and network security. For example, the "trustworthy computing" initiative put forth by Microsoft Chairman Bill Gates is an effort to focus the company's priorities on providing reliable, available and secure applications (see the Operating Systems Thinking feature, Ethical Systems Design).[1]

Computer security addresses the issue of preventing unauthorized access to resources and information maintained by computers. Computer systems must provide mechanisms to manage security threats originating both from outside the computer (via a network connection) and from within the computer (via malicious users and software). Computer security commonly encompasses guaranteeing the privacy

Operating Systems Thinking

Ethical Systems Design

We have entrusted our lives to computers in a manner that demands ethical behavior on the part of operating systems designers.[2] People who work with computers and communication devices are often privy to confidential information they would not ordinarily see. Computer systems control heart pacemakers, monitor air traffic and process confidential financial, medical and criminal records. People who design computer systems must realize that these systems are used and relied upon in critical sit-

uations. Should we build systems that could fail? What is an "acceptable" level of failure? Who is responsible when computer systems fail? Should we build systems so complex that we cannot be certain they will perform properly?[3] Operating systems designers need to be concerned with these and other important ethical issues.

With viruses and worms attacking our computer systems in record numbers, we must think seriously about just how vulnerable our systems are, and about

our professional responsibilities to build dependable systems. Can we continue to build systems that are so easily attacked and compromised, and employ those systems in situations where people's health and lives are at stake? It is software, not computer hardware, which has been most vulnerable to attack. Operating systems designers must conscientiously deal with the same kinds of ethical dilemmas as those faced by other professional people such as doctors, attorneys, scientists and engineers.

and integrity of sensitive data, restricting the use of computer resources and providing protection against malicious attempts to incapacitate the system. **Protection** encompasses mechanisms that shield resources such as hardware and operating system services from attack. Security is quickly becoming one of the richest and most challenging topics in computing; operating system security is at the core of a secure computing system.

This chapter also explores the fundamentals of Internet security, including the implementation of secure electronic transactions and secure networks. We discuss how to achieve network security using current technologies—including cryptography, Public Key Infrastructure (PKI), digital signatures, Secure Sockets Layer (SSL) and Virtual Private Networks (VPNs). We also examine authentication and authorization solutions, firewalls and intrusion detection systems. At the end of the chapter, we discuss UNIX security. Linux operating systems security and Windows XP operating systems security are discussed in Section 20.13 and Section 21.13, respectively.

Self Review

1. Why are security and protection important even for computers that do not contain sensitive data?
2. What is the difference between security and protection?

Ans: **1)** All computers, regardless of the data they manage, are susceptible to security breaches that may crash the system, spread viruses or commit identity theft. **2)** Security addresses the issue of preventing unauthorized access to resources and information maintained by computers. Protection refers to the mechanisms that shield resources such as hardware and operating system services from attack.

19.2 Cryptography

An important goal of computing is to make massive amounts of data easily available. Electronic data transmission, especially over public wires, is inherently insecure. A solution to this problem is to make data unreadable to any unauthorized user, through encryption. Many security mechanisms rely on encryption to protect sensitive data such as passwords.

Cryptography focuses on encoding and decoding data so that it can be interpreted only by the intended recipients. Data is transformed by the use of a **cipher**, or **cryptosystem**—a mathematical algorithm for encrypting messages. A **key**, represented by a string of characters, is input to the cipher. The algorithm transforms the unencrypted data, or **plaintext**, into encrypted data, or **ciphertext**, using the keys as input—different keys result in different ciphertext. The aim is to render the data incomprehensible to any unintended receivers (i.e., those who do not possess the decryption key). Only the intended receivers should have the key to decrypt the ciphertext into plaintext.

First employed by the ancient Egyptians, cryptographic ciphers have been used throughout history to conceal and protect valuable information. Ancient cryptographers encrypted messages by hand, usually with a method based on the alphabetic letters of the message. The ancients' two primary types of ciphers were substitution ciphers and transposition ciphers. In a **substitution cipher**, every occurrence of a given letter is replaced by a different letter. For example, if every "a" were replaced by a "b," every "b" by a "c," and so on, the word "security" would encrypt to "tfdvsjuz." The first prominent substitution cipher was credited to Julius Caesar and is referred to today as the Caesar cipher. Using the Caesar cipher, every instance of a letter is replaced by the letter in the alphabet three places to the right. For example, the word "security" would encrypt to "vhfxulwb."[4]

In a **transposition cipher**, the ordering of the letters is shifted. For example, if every other letter, starting with "s," in the word "security" creates the first word in the ciphertext and the remaining letters create the second word, the word "security" encrypts to "scrt euiy." An encrypted message becomes increasingly robust (i.e., difficult to decipher) when its cipher combines substitution and transposition ciphers. For example, using the substitution cipher in combination with the transposition cipher, the word "security" encrypts to "tdsu fvjz."[5]

The greatest weakness of many early ciphers was their reliance on the sender and receiver remembering the encryption algorithm and maintaining its secrecy. Such algorithms are called **restricted algorithms**. Restricted algorithms are not feasible to implement for a large group of people. Imagine if the security of U.S. government communications relied on every employee keeping a secret—the encryption algorithm could easily be compromised.

Modern cryptosystems rely on algorithms that operate on the individual bits or blocks (a group of bits) of data, rather than letters of the alphabet. Encryption and decryption keys are binary strings with a given key length. For example, 128-bit encryption systems have a key length of 128 bits. Longer keys have stronger encryption; it takes more time and computing power to "break" the encryption. Longer keys also require more processing time to encrypt and decrypt data, reducing system performance. The growth of computer networking has made the security/performance trade-off more challenging.

Until January 2000, the U.S. government placed restrictions on the strength of cryptosystems that could be exported from the United States by limiting the key length of exported encryption algorithms. Today, the regulations are less stringent. Any cryptography product may be exported, as long as the end user is not a foreign government or a member of a country with embargo restrictions.[6]

Self Review

1. Consider a cipher that randomly reorders the letters of each word in a message. Why is such a cipher inappropriate for encryption?
2. What is the primary weakness of restricted algorithms?

Ans: **1)** The receiver would be unable to decipher the ciphertext because it would have no way of knowing how the letters were reordered. **2)** The sender and receiver must remember the encryption algorithm and maintain its secrecy; thus, restricted algorithms are not feasible to implement for a large group of people.

19.2.1 *Secret-Key Cryptography*

Symmetric cryptography, also known as **secret-key cryptography**, uses the same secret key to encrypt and decrypt a message (Fig. 19.1). In this case, the sender encrypts a message using the secret key, then sends the encrypted message to the intended recipient, who decrypts the message using the same secret key. A limitation of secret-key cryptography is that before two parties can communicate securely, they must find a secure way to exchange the secret key.

A solution is to have the key delivered by a courier or other mail service. While this approach may be feasible when two parties communicate, it does not scale well to large networks. Moreover, secret-key encryption cannot be considered completely secure, because message privacy and integrity can be compromised if the key is intercepted as it is passed between the sender and the receiver. Also, because both parties in the transaction use the same key to encrypt and decrypt a message, one cannot determine which party created a message. This enables a third party, posing as one of the two authorized parties, to create a message after capturing the key. Finally, to maintain private communications, a sender needs a different secret key for each receiver. Consequently, secure computing in large organizations would necessitate maintaining large numbers of secret keys for each user, requiring significant data storage.

An alternative approach to the key-exchange problem is to create a central authority, called a **key distribution center (KDC)**, which shares a different secret key with every user in the network. The key distribution center generates a **session key** to be used for a transaction (Fig. 19.2), then delivers the session key to the sender and receiver, encrypted with the secret key they each share with the key distribution center.

For example, suppose a merchant and a customer wish to conduct a secure transaction. They each share unique secret keys with the key distribution center. The KDC generates a session key for the merchant and customer to use in the

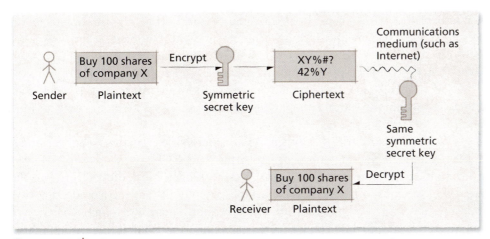

Figure 19.1 | *Encrypting and decrypting a message using a secret key.*

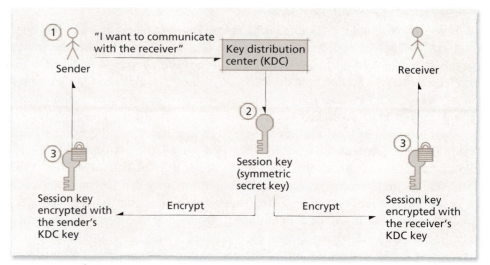

Figure 19.2 | *Distributing a session key with a key distribution center.*

transaction, then sends the session key for the transaction to the merchant, encrypted using the secret key the merchant already shares with the center. The KDC sends the same session key for the transaction to the customer, encrypted using the secret key the customer already shares with the KDC. Once the merchant and the customer obtain the session key for the transaction, they can communicate with each other, encrypting their messages using the shared session key.

A key distribution center reduces the number of courier deliveries of secret keys to each user in the network. In addition, it gives users a new secret key for each communication with other users in the network, which greatly increases the level of security of the network. However, if the security of the key distribution center is compromised, then the security of the entire network is also compromised.

One commonly used symmetric encryption algorithm is the **Data Encryption Standard (DES)**. Horst Feistel of IBM created the **Lucifer algorithm**, which was chosen as the DES by the U.S. government and the National Security Agency (NSA) in the 1970s.[7] DES has a key length of 56 bits and encrypts data in 64-bit blocks. This type of encryption is known as a **block cipher**, because it creates groups of bits from a message, then applies an encryption algorithm to the block as a whole. This technique reduces the amount of computer processing power and time required to encrypt data.

For many years, DES was the encryption standard set by the U.S. government and the American National Standards Institute (ANSI). However, due to advances in technology and computing speed, DES is no longer considered secure—in the late 1990s, specialized DES cracker machines were built that recovered DES keys after a period of several hours.[8] Consequently, the standard for symmetric encryption was replaced by **Triple DES**, or **3DES**, a variant of DES that is essentially three DES systems in series, each with a different secret key that operates on a block.

Though 3DES is more secure, the three passes through the DES algorithm increase encryption overhead, leading to reduced performance.

In October 2000, the U.S. government selected a more secure standard for symmetric encryption to replace DES, called the **Advanced Encryption Standard (AES)**. The **National Institute of Standards and Technology (NIST)**—which sets the cryptographic standards for the U.S. government—chose **Rijndael** as the encryption method for AES. Rijndael is a block cipher developed by Dr. Joan Daemen and Dr. Vincent Rijmen of Belgium. Rijndael can be used with key sizes and block sizes of 128, 192 or 256 bits. Rijndael was chosen as the AES over four other finalists due to its high level of security, performance, efficiency, and flexibility and its low memory requirement for computing systems.[9]

Self Review

1. Discuss the advantages and disadvantages of secret-key cryptography.
2. What limits the strength of most encryption algorithms?

Ans: **1)** An advantage is that encryption and decryption via secret-key cryptography are straightforward because both parties share the same key, making secret-key encryption highly efficient. Disadvantages are that it does not provide authentication and it requires a secure way to transmit the secret key so that a third party does not intercept it. **2)** The primary limitation to most encryption algorithms is the amount of computational power required to implement them.

19.2.2 Public-Key Cryptography

In 1976, Whitfield Diffie and Martin Hellman, researchers at Stanford University, developed **public-key cryptography** to solve the problem of securely exchanging symmetric keys. Public-key cryptography is asymmetric in that it employs two inversely related keys: a **public key** and a **private key**. The private key is kept secret by its owner and the public key is freely distributed. If the public key encrypts a message, only the corresponding private key can decrypt it (Fig. 19.3) and vice

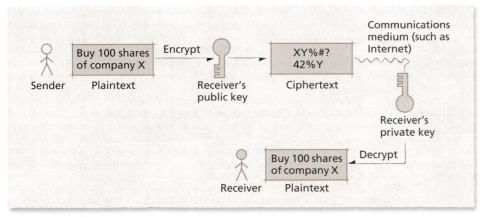

Figure 19.3 | *Encrypting and decrypting a message using public-key cryptography.*

versa. Each party in a transaction possesses both a public key and a private key. To transmit a message securely, the sender uses the receiver's public key to encrypt the message. The receiver then decrypts the message, using his or her unique private key. Assuming that the private key has been kept secret, the message cannot be read by anyone other than the intended receiver. Thus the system ensures the privacy of the message.

Secure public-key algorithms depend on a private key that is computationally infeasible to deduce from the public key within a reasonable amount of time. Such algorithms are called "one-way" or "trap-door" functions, because the message requires little computation to encrypt using the public key, but takes significant computing power and time to decrypt without knowledge of the private key. Moderately secure encryption requires years for a single computer to decrypt. [*Note*: `Distributed.net`'s RC5 competition offers a cash award to decrypt a message encrypted by a one-way function. The competition attracts thousands of users that work in parallel to discover the key. Recently, over 300,000 participants devoted computer power to crack a message encrypted using a 64-bit key. The key was found in August of 2002 after 1,757 days of computation, equivalent to 46,000 2GHz processors working in parallel.[10] The most powerful computer at the time was the Earth Simulator, which contained 5,120 500MHz processors.]

The security of the system relies on the secrecy of the private keys. Therefore, if a third party obtains the private key used in decryption, the security of the entire system is compromised. If system integrity is compromised, the user can simply change the key, rather than change the entire encryption or decryption algorithm.

Both the public key or the private key can be used to encrypt or decrypt a message. For example, if a customer uses a merchant's public key to encrypt a message, only the merchant can decrypt the message, using the merchant's private key. Thus, the merchant's identity can be authenticated, because only the merchant knows the private key. However, the merchant cannot validate the customer's identity, because the encryption key the customer used is publicly available.

If the decryption key is the sender's public key and the encryption key is the sender's private key, the sender of the message can be authenticated. For example, suppose a customer sends a merchant a message encrypted using the customer's private key. The merchant decrypts the message using the customer's public key. Because the customer encrypted the message using his or her private key, the merchant can be confident of the customer's identity. This process authenticates the sender but does not ensure confidentiality, as any third party could decrypt the message with the sender's public key. The problem of proving ownership of a public key is discussed in Section 19.9, Public-Key Infrastructure, Certificates and Certificate Authorities.

These two methods of public-key encryption can be combined to authenticate both participants in a communication (Fig. 19.4). Suppose a merchant wishes to send a message securely to a customer so that only the customer can read it, and also to provide proof to the customer that the merchant sent the message. First, the

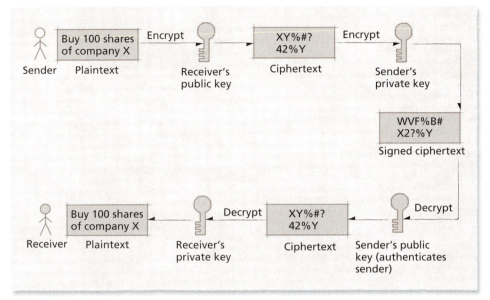

Figure 19.4 | *Authentication with a public-key algorithm.*

merchant encrypts the message using the customer's public key. This step guarantees that only the customer can read the message. Then the merchant encrypts the result using the merchant's private key, which proves the identity of the merchant. The customer decrypts the message in reverse order. First, the customer uses the merchant's public key. Because only the merchant could have encrypted the message with the inversely related private key, this step authenticates the merchant. Then the customer uses the customer's private key to decrypt the next level of encryption. This step ensures that the content of the message remained private in the transmission, because only the customer has the key to decrypt the message.

The most commonly used public-key algorithm is **RSA**, an encryption system developed in 1977 by MIT professors Ron Rivest, Adi Shamir and Leonard Adleman (see the Biographical Note, Rivest, Shamir and Adleman).[11] Their encryption products are built into hundreds of millions of copies of the most popular Internet applications, including Web browsers, commerce servers and e-mail systems. Most secure e-commerce transactions and communications on the Internet use RSA products.

Pretty Good Privacy (PGP), a public-key encryption system that encrypts e-mail messages and files, was designed in 1991 by Phillip Zimmermann.[12] PGP can also provide digital signatures (see Section 19.8.2, Digital Signatures) that confirm the identity of an author of an e-mail or public posting.

PGP is based on a "web of trust"; each client in a network can vouch for another client's identity to prove ownership of a public key. The "web of trust" is used to authenticate each client. If users know the identity of a public key holder, through personal contact or another secure method, they validate the key by signing it with their own key. The web of trust grows as more users validate the keys of others. To learn more about PGP and to download a free copy of the software, visit the MIT Distribution Center for PGP at `web.mit.edu/network/pgp.html`.

Self Review

1. How does secret-key cryptography differ from public-key cryptography?
2. For which types of communication is PGP appropriate?

Ans: **1)** Secret-key cryptography uses the same secret key to encrypt and decrypt a message. Public-key cryptography employs two inversely related keys: a public key and a private key. The private key is kept secret by its owner, while the public key is freely distributed—if the public key encrypts a message, only the corresponding private key can decrypt it. **2)** PGP's security increases as the number of users in the Web of trust increases. Thus, PGP is appropriate for communication among a group of users (e.g., e-mail or public forums).

19.3 Authentication

Identifying users and the actions they are allowed to perform is vital to maintaining a secure computing system. A user can be identified by:

Biographical Note

Rivest, Shamir and Adleman

Ronald Rivest, Adi Shamir and Leonard Adleman are the inventors of the RSA cryptography algorithm. This algorithm is used in over one billion copies of secure software applications.[13]

Rivest, Shamir and Adleman met in the 1970s while working as assistant professors in Math at MIT. When Whitfield Diffie and Martin Hellman published their new theory of public-key cryptography in 1977, Rivest and Shamir tried to find a practical implementation. They enlisted Adleman to test out their ideas; he disproved over 40 of their designs until they finally found the mechanism that they published as "A Method for Obtaining Digital Signatures and Public-Key Cryptosystems" in *Communications of the ACM* in 1978.[14] Rivest, Shamir and Adleman obtained a patent for their algorithm and started the RSA Data Security company (now named RSA Security) in 1982.[15, 16]

Together they won the 2002 Turing Award for their development of the RSA code.[17]

The RSA Security company uses the RSA algorithm in security software including authentication mechanisms, smart cards, digital certificates and software development kits (SDKs) to facilitate the development of secure applications. RSA Security dominates the field of authentication software, controlling over 65 percent of the market.[18]

- a unique characteristic of the person (e.g., fingerprints, voiceprints, retina scans and signatures).
- ownership of an item (e.g., badges, identification cards, keys and smart cards).
- user knowledge (e.g., passwords, personal identification numbers (PINs) and lock combinations).

In the sections that follow, we discuss common authentication methods.

Self Review

1. Of the three identification methods mentioned in this section, which one is least likely to be compromised by eavesdroppers?
2. How might security be compromised in a system that requires only ownership of an item or only user knowledge for authentication?

Ans: **1)** A unique characteristic of a person. **2)** Under authentication by ownership of an item, the item may be stolen. Users tend to write down information such as passwords and PINs, so security could be compromised if an unauthorized user finds such a record.

19.3.1 Basic Authentication

The most common authentication scheme is simple **password protection**.[19] The user chooses a password, memorizes it and then enters it into the system to gain admission to a resource or system. Most systems suppress the display of a password on the screen by replacing password text with masking characters (which display "dummy" characters—often asterisks—for password characters entered) or by hiding password input.

Password protection introduces several weaknesses to a secure system.[20] Users tend to choose passwords that are easy to remember, such as the name of a spouse or pet. Someone who has obtained personal information about the user might try to log in several times using passwords that are characteristic of the user; several repeated attempts might result in a security breach. Some early systems limited users to short passwords; these systems were easily compromised by simply attempting all possible passwords—a technique known as **brute-force cracking**.

Most systems today require longer passwords that include both alphabetic and numeric characters to thwart such penetration attempts. Some systems even prohibit use of dictionary words as password values. However, long passwords do not necessarily improve the security of a system; if passwords are difficult to remember, users will be more inclined to make a note of them, making it easier for an intruder to obtain a password.

Penetration of an operating system's defenses need not necessarily result in a significant security compromise. For example, suppose an intruder manages to gain access to a system's master list of passwords. If the password file were stored in plaintext, such penetration would enable the intruder to access any information on the system by assuming the identity of any user. To reduce the effectiveness of a stolen password file, many operating systems encrypt the password file or store only hash values for each password. In this case, a copy of the password file is of little use unless the intruder can decrypt the passwords. To further thwart attempts at obtaining passwords, several systems employ **password salting**, which is a technique that inserts characters at various positions in the password before encryption (Fig. 19.5). Note how, in Fig. 19.5, a small amount of salting can significantly alter ciphertext, even when using a weak cipher such as a substitution cipher (base 64 encoding). Salting can prevent intruders from obtaining an encryption key based on patterns produced by common passwords after encryption.

Users are encouraged to change their passwords often; even if an intruder obtains a password, it may be changed before any real damage can be done. Some systems require that users choose new passwords on a regular basis. Unfortunately, some users will reuse two or three passwords cyclically, reducing overall security. In response, several authentication systems prohibit repeated use of a user's most recent password choices.

A simple defense against brute-force cracking and repeated password trials is to limit the number of login attempts that may be initiated in any period of time from a single terminal or workstation (or from a single account). Certainly, people make typing errors when attempting to log in, but it is unreasonable for someone who knows the correct password to require tens, hundreds or thousands of tries. Therefore, a system might allow three or four tries, then disconnect the terminal for several seconds or minutes. After a waiting period, the terminal may be reconnected.

Self Review

1. (T/F) Longer and more complicated passwords guarantee higher security.
2. How does salting improve password security?

Ans: **1)** False. Longer and more complicated passwords usually result in the user writing down the password, enabling intruders to steal it. **2)** Salting can prevent intruders from determining an encryption key based on patterns produced by common passwords after encryption.

19.3.2 Biometrics and Smart Cards

An innovation in security, once limited to the movies but becoming increasingly common in today's secure systems, is **biometrics**. Biometrics uses unique personal information—such as fingerprints, eyeball iris scans or face scans—to identify a user. The number of passwords an average user must remember has increased due to the prolif-

Plaintext	Ciphertext
password	cGFzc3dvcmQ=
psasaswlortd	cHNhc2Fzd2xvcnRk
newpassword	bmV3cGFzc3dvcmQ=
nsewaplatssewodrd	bnNld2FwbGF0c3Nld29kcmQ=

Figure 19.5 | Salting passwords (Base 64 encoding).

eration of sensitive data transmitted over unsecure channels. [*Note*: People in the security community prefer unsecure to insecure.] As a result, passwords have become an increasing burden to secure computing. This trend can be detrimental to security, as users record passwords on paper or employ the same password for several accounts. Consequently biometrics has become an attractive alternative to passwords, and the cost of biometric devices has dropped significantly.

Fingerprint-scanning, face-scanning and iris-scanning devices are replacing the use of passwords to log into systems, check e-mail or access secure information over a network. Each user's fingerprint, face scan or iris scan is stored in a secure database. Each time a user logs in, his or her scan is compared with the database. If a match is made, the login is successful. Two companies that specialize in biometric devices are IriScan (`www.iriscan.com`) and Keytronic (`www.keytronic.com`). For additional resources, see the Web Resources section at the end of the chapter.

Although passwords are currently the predominant means of authentication in computer systems and e-commerce, several platforms have embraced biometrics. In 2000, Microsoft announced its Biometric Application Programming Interface (BAPI), which is included in its Windows 2000 and Windows XP operating systems to simplify the integration of biometrics into personal and corporate systems.[21]

Keyware Inc. (`www.keyware.com`) has implemented a wireless biometrics system that stores user voiceprints on a central server. Keyware also created **layered biometric verification (LBV)**, which uses multiple physical measurements—face, finger and voice prints—simultaneously. The LBV feature enables a wireless biometrics system to combine biometrics with other authentication methods, such as personal identification numbers (PIN) and PKI (Public Key Infrastructure; see Section 19.9, Public-Key Infrastructure, Certificates and Certificate Authorities).[22]

Identix, Inc. (`www.identix.com`) also provides biometrics authentication technology for wireless transactions. The Identix fingerprint-scanning device is embedded in handheld devices. The Identix service offers transaction management and content protection services. Transaction management services prove that transactions took place, and content protection services control access to electronic documents, including limiting a user's ability to download or copy documents.[23]

A **smart card**, often designed to resemble a credit card, is typically used to perform authentication and store data. The most popular smart cards are memory cards and microprocessor cards. Memory cards can store and transfer data. Microprocessor cards contain computer components, managed by an operating system, that provide security and storage. Smart cards are also characterized by their interface to reading devices. One is a contact interface, whereby smart cards are inserted into a reading device, requiring physical contact between the device and the card for data transfer. Alternatively, a contactless interface allows data to be transferred without physical contact between the reader and the card, often accomplished with an embedded wireless device in the card.[24]

Smart cards can store private keys, digital certificates and other information necessary for implementing PKI. They may also store credit card numbers, personal contact information, and the like. Each smart card can be used in combination with a PIN. This feature provides two levels of security by requiring the user to possess a smart card and know the corresponding PIN to access information stored on the card. To further strengthen security, some microprocessor cards will delete or corrupt stored data in the event of malicious tampering with the card. Smart-card PKI allows users to access information from multiple devices using the same smart card.

Two-factor authentication employs two means to authenticate the user, such as biometrics or a smart card used in combination with a password. Though this system could potentially be compromised, using two methods of authentication typically provides better security than passwords alone.

Self Review

1. Why is it difficult for an unauthorized user to gain access in a system that uses biometrics for security?
2. Explain one disadvantage to storing unencrypted user information on a smart card.

Ans: **1)** It is difficult to replicate another user's physical features. **2)** If the smart card is stolen, another individual could access that user's potentially sensitive information.

19.3.3 Kerberos

Internal computer attacks (i.e., attacks that originate from a valid user) are common and can be extremely damaging. For example, disgruntled employees with network access can disable an organization's network or steal valuable proprietary information. It is estimated that 70–90 percent of attacks on corporate networks are internal.[25] A centralized, secure authentication system can facilitate a fast response to such security attacks. **Kerberos**, a freely available, open-source protocol developed at MIT, can provide protection against internal security attacks. It employs secret-key cryptography to authenticate users in a network and to maintain the integrity and privacy of network communications.[26, 27]

Authentication in Kerberos is handled by an authentication server and a secondary **Ticket Granting Service (TGS)**. This system is similar to the key distribution centers described in Section 19.2.1, Secret-Key Cryptography. The authentication server authenticates a client's identity to the TGS; the TGS authenticates the client's rights to access specific network services.

Each client in the network shares a secret key with the Kerberos system. This secret key may be stored by multiple TGSs in the Kerberos system. The Kerberos system works as follows:[28]

1. The client begins by submitting a username and password to the Kerberos authentication server.

2. The authentication server maintains a database of all clients in the network. If the username and password are valid, the authentication server returns a **Ticket-Granting Ticket (TGT)** encrypted with the client's secret key. Because the secret key is known only by the authentication server and

the client, only the client can decrypt the TGT, thus authenticating the client's identity.

3. The client sends the decrypted TGT to the Ticket Granting Service to request a **service ticket**. The service ticket authorizes the client's access to specific network services. Service tickets are assigned an expiration time and can be renewed or revoked by the TGS. If the TGT is valid, the TGS issues a service ticket encrypted with the client's session key.

4. The client then decrypts the service ticket, which it then presents to gain access to networked resources.

Self Review

1. In Kerberos authentication, why must the connection between clients and the authentication server be secure?
2. Why is it appropriate for tickets to expire?

Ans: **1)** If the connection is not secure, eavesdroppers could steal user names and passwords to gain access to secure resources. **2)** It is appropriate for tickets to expire because it forces users to reauthenticate often. For example, if an authorized user leaves a terminal while logged in, the ticket can expire before an unauthorized user can cause significant damage.

19.3.4 Single Sign-On

Single sign-on systems simplify the authentication process by allowing the user to log in once, using a single password. Users authenticated via a single sign-on system can then access multiple applications across multiple computers. Sign-on passwords should be closely guarded, because if a password becomes available to attackers, all applications protected by that password can be accessed and attacked.

Workstation login scripts are the simplest form of single sign-on. Users log in at their workstations, then choose applications from a menu. The workstation login script sends the user's password to the application servers to authenticate the user for future access to those applications. Many workstation login scripts do not provide a sufficient level of security, because user passwords are often stored on the client computer in plaintext. Even if the script uses simple password encryption, that algorithm must be present on the system, meaning that any intruder that gains access to the computer will be able to compromise the encryption.

Authentication server scripts authenticate users via a central server. The central server controls connections between the user and the applications the user wishes to access. Authentication server scripts are more secure than workstation login scripts because passwords are maintained on the server, which is generally more secure than the client computer. However, if the security of the server is compromised, the security of the entire system is also compromised.

The most advanced single sign-on systems employ **token-based authentication**. Once a user is authenticated, a unique **token** is issued to enable the user to access specific applications. The login that creates the token is secured by encryption or a single password. For example, Kerberos uses token-based authentication, in which the service ticket acts as the token. A key problem with token authentication is that applications must be modified to accept tokens, rather than traditional login passwords.[29]

Currently, the three leaders in development of single sign-on technology are the Liberty Alliance Project (www.projectliberty.org), Microsoft and Novell. The Liberty Alliance Project is a consortium of technology and security organizations working to create an open single sign-on solution. Microsoft's .NET Passport and Novell's SecureLogin are also viable solutions, though they are proprietary. To protect the privacy of information submitted to single sign-on and other applications, the **Platform for Privacy Preferences (P3P)** allows users to control the personal information that sites collect.[30, 31]

Self Review

1. Of the three single sign-on services, which is the most secure?
2. In what way are workstation login scripts more secure than authentication server scripts?

Ans: **1)** Token-based authentication is the most secure. However, it is also the most complicated scheme. **2)** Workstation login scripts are more secure in that the security for all of the other users in the system is not compromised if the security of a workstation login script is compromised.

19.4 Access Control

As a resource manager, the operating system must carefully guard against unintentional and malicious use of computer resources. Consequently, today's operating systems are designed to protect operating system services and sensitive information from users and/or software that have gained access to computer resources. Access rights protect system resources and services from potentially dangerous users by restricting or limiting the actions that can be performed on the resource. These rights are typically managed by access control lists or capability lists.

19.4.1 Access Rights and Protection Domains

The key to operating system security is to control access to internal data and resources. **Access rights** define how various subjects can access various objects. Subjects may be users, processes, programs or other entities. Objects are resources such as hardware, software and data; they may be physical objects that correspond to disks, processors or main memory. They may also be abstract objects that correspond to data structures, processes or services. Subjects can also be objects of the system; one subject may have rights to access another. Subjects are active entities; objects are passive. As a system runs, its population of subjects and objects tends to change. The manner in which a subject can access an object is called a **privilege** and can include reading, writing and printing.

Objects must be protected from subjects. If a process were allowed to access every resource on a system, a user could maliciously (or inadvertently) compromise system security or cause other programs to crash. To prevent such events from occurring, each subject must obtain authorization to access objects within a system.

A **protection domain** is a collection of access rights. Each access right in a protection domain is represented as an ordered pair with fields for the object name and its corresponding privileges. A protection domain is unique to a subject. For example, if a user can read and write the file `example.txt`, the corresponding ordered pair for this user's access right can be represented by `<example.txt, {read, write}>`.[32]

The most common access rights are read, write and execute. Some subjects may also grant access rights to other subjects. In most computing systems, the administrator possesses all access rights and is responsible for managing other users' rights.

Access rights may be copied, transferred or propagated from one domain to another. Copying an access right simply entails granting a right of one user to another user. When an access right is transferred from subject A to subject B, subject A's access right is revoked upon completion of the transfer. Propagating an access right is similar to copying an access right; however, in addition to sharing the original access right, both subjects can also copy the right to other subjects.

When a subject no longer needs access to an object, access rights can be revoked. Several issues arise—should revocation be immediate or delayed? Should revocation apply to all objects or a select few? Should revocation apply to specific subjects or an entire domain? Should revocation be permanent or temporary? Each implementation of access rights management addresses revocation differently; we discuss several implementations in Section 19.4.3.[33]

Self Review

1. (T/F) The term *subject* always refers to users in a system.
2. Explain the difference between copying access rights and propagating access rights.

Ans: **1)** False. The term *subject* can refer to users, processes, programs and other entities. **2)** If subject A copies a right to subject B, subject B will not be able to grant that right to other subjects. However, if subject A propagates a right to subject B, subject B will be able to grant that right to other subjects.

19.4.2 Access Control Models and Policies

Access control can be divided into three conceptual levels: models, policies and mechanisms. A **security model** defines a system's subjects, objects and privileges. A **security policy**, which is typically specified by the user and/or system administrator, defines which privileges to objects are assigned to subjects. The **security mechanism** is the method by which the system implements the security policy. In many systems, the policy changes over time as the system's set of resources and users change, but the security model and mechanisms that implement access control do not require modification, so the security policy is separated from the mechanism and model.

A popular security model organizes users into classes, as discussed in Section 13.8.2, Access Control by User Classes. A drawback is that access rights are stored in each file and specify a single owner and group, so at most one group can access a particular file. Further, the system might need to modify group permissions for several files when assigning new access rights to a group of users—an error-prone and time-consuming process.

In the **role-based access control (RBAC)** model, users are assigned **roles**, each typically representing a set of tasks assigned to a member of an organization. Each role is assigned a set of privileges, which define the objects that users in each role can access.[34] Users can belong to multiple roles; administrators need only modify permissions for a single role to change access rights for a group of users. The appeal of RBAC is that it assigns meaningful relationships between subjects and objects that are not limited by classes such as owners and groups.

For example, consider an academic computer system with the following roles: faculty members create and grade assignments, students submit completed assignments and staff members post grades to student transcripts. Under the RBAC model, this system consists of three roles (students, faculty and staff), two objects (assignments and grades) and three permissions (read, modify and create). In this example, faculty have permission to create, read and modify both assignments and grades; students have permission to read and modify copies of coursework and read grades; staff have permission to read and modify grades.

Although security policies vary to meet the needs of users in a system, most policies incorporate the principle of least privilege—a subject is granted access only to the objects it requires to perform its tasks. Policies can also implement discretionary or mandatory access control depending on the security needs of the environment. Most UNIX-based systems follow the **discretionary access control (DAC)** model, whereby the creator of an object controls the permissions for that object. On the contrary, **mandatory access control (MAC)** policies predefine a central permission scheme by which all subjects and objects are controlled. MAC is found in many high-security installations, such as classified government systems.[35]

Self Review

1. Why are access control policies and mechanisms typically separated?
2. How might MAC be more secure than DAC?

Ans: **1)** Policies often change without requiring modification to their underlying implementation; changing policies requires less work if the security policy is separated from the security mechanism. **2)** MAC prevents users from accidentally or intentionally assigning permissions that might compromise system security (e.g., the owner of a file assigning public access to sensitive information).

19.4.3 Access Control Mechanisms

In this section we discuss various techniques that an operating system can employ to manage access rights. Access control matrices match subjects and objects to the appropriate access rights. The concept behind the model is simple; however, most systems contain many subjects and objects, resulting in a large matrix that is an inefficient means for access control. Access control lists and capability lists are derived from the principle of least privilege and are often more efficient and flexible methods of managing access rights. Section 20.13.2, Access Control Methods, and Section 21.13.2, Authorization, discuss how Linux and Windows XP, respectively, use access control methods to secure their systems.

Access Control Matrices

One way to manage access rights is in an **access control matrix**. The various subjects are listed in the rows, and the objects to which they require access are listed in the columns. Each cell in the matrix specifies the actions that a subject (defined by the row) can perform on an object (defined by the column). Access rights in an access control matrix are granted on the basis of least privilege, so if an access right is not explicitly described in the matrix, the user has no access rights to the object.[36]

Because an access control matrix places all permission information in a central location, the matrix should be one of the most closely guarded entities in an operating system. If the matrix is compromised, any resources that were protected by the access rights defined in the matrix are susceptible to attack as well.

The access control matrix in Fig. 19.6 represents the access rights for the users (Alice, Bob, Chris, David and Guest) to the objects (File A, File B and Printer). The privileges that a user can obtain for an object are read, write and print. The read and write access rights apply only to files on the system, in this case, File A and File B. In some environments, not every user has access to the printer—a user must explicitly have the print privilege to send content to the printer. Any access right that is followed by an asterisk (*) can be copied from one user to another. In this access control matrix, Alice has all access rights as well as the ability to assign these rights to other users. David cannot access File A because there is no entry in the corresponding cell in the matrix. The Guest account contains no access rights by default. A Guest can access resources only when the right is explicitly granted by another user. Although generating and interpreting an access control matrix is straightforward, the matrix can become large and sparsely populated.

	File A	File B	Printer
Alice	Read* Write*	Read* Write*	Print*
Bob	Read* Write	Read* Write	Print
Chris	Read		Print
David		Read	
Guest			

Figure 19.6 | *Access control matrix for a small group of subjects and objects.*

Access Control Lists

An **access control list** stores the same data as an access control matrix, but it maintains a record of only those entries that specify an access right. The access control list for a system can be based on the rows of a matrix (the subjects) or the columns (the objects). For each object in an operating system, an access control list contains entries for each subject and the privileges associated with that subject for the object. When a subject attempts to access an object, the system searches the access control list for that object to find any privileges for the subject.[37]

A drawback to this method is the inefficiency with which the operating system determines user privileges for a particular object. The access control list for each object contains an entry for every subject with privileges for that object—a potentially large list. Each time an object is accessed, the system must search the list of subjects to find the proper privileges. It is difficult to determine which access rights belong to a certain protection domain when using access control lists; the access list for every object in the system must be searched for entries regarding that particular subject.

The access control list in Fig. 19.7 represents the set of access rights that were established in the access control matrix of Fig. 19.6. The implementation is smaller because empty entries in the matrix are not present. If an object does not contain an entry for a particular user, that user has no privileges for the object.

Capability Lists

A **capability** is a pointer or token that grants privileges to a subject that possesses it. It is analogous to a ticket used to gain access to a sporting event. Capabilities ordinarily are not modified, but they can be reproduced. Recall that a protection domain defines the set of privileges between subjects and objects. Alternatively, one can define the protection domain as the set of capabilities belonging to a subject.[38]

A capability is often implemented as a unique object identifier. Capabilities are granted to a subject, which presents the token for all subsequent accesses to the

```
1    File A:
2        <Alice, {read*, write*}>
3        <Bob, {read*, write}>
4        <Chris, {read}>
5    File B:
6        <Alice, {read*, write*}>
7        <Bob, {read*, write}>
8        <David, {read}>
9    Printer:
10        <Alice, {print*}>
11        <Bob, {print}>
12        <Chris, {print}>
```

Figure 19.7 | Access control list derived from the access control matrix.

object. Capabilities are created by carefully guarded operating system routines. A subject that possesses a capability may perform certain operations, including creating copies of the capability or passing it as a parameter.

Upon creation of an object, a capability for that object is created. This original capability includes full privileges for the new object. The subject that creates the object may pass copies of the capability to other subjects. Likewise, a subject receiving a capability may use it to access the object, or the subject may create additional copies and pass them to other subjects. When one subject passes a capability to another, it may reduce the associated privileges. Thus, as a capability propagates through the system, its privilege set can either remain the same or decrease in size.

Users must be prevented from creating capabilities arbitrarily. This can be accomplished by storing capabilities in segments that user processes cannot access.

The identifier in a capability may be implemented as a pointer to the desired object, or it may be a unique bit sequence (i.e., a token). Pointers simplify access to the address at which the object is stored, but all such pointers in the system must be updated if the object is moved, which can degrade performance. When using tokens, capabilities do not rely on the object's location in memory. However, because a token does not specify the location of its corresponding object, tokens require that the object's address be determined when the capability is first used. A hashing mechanism implements token-based capabilities efficiently; high-speed caches often reduce the overhead of repeated references to the same object.

Systems that employ capabilities can suffer from the "lost object" problem. If the last remaining capability for an object is destroyed, the associated object can no longer be accessed. To prevent this problem, many operating systems ensure that the system always maintains at least one capability for each object.

Controlling the propagation of capabilities is a difficult problem. Systems generally do not allow direct manipulation of capabilities by users; instead capability manipulation is performed by the operating system on behalf of the users. Keeping track of capabilities is an important task that becomes difficult in multiuser systems containing a large numbers of capabilities. Many systems employ a directory structure to manage their capabilities.[39]

Self Review

1. In what type of environment are access control lists more appropriate than access control matrices?
2. Discuss the advantages and disadvantages of token-based and pointer-based capabilities.

Ans: **1)** Access control lists are more appropriate than access control matrices when the matrices are sparse. In this case, access control lists require much less space than access control matrices. **2)** Pointers simplify access to the address at which the object is stored, but all such pointers in the system must be updated if the object is moved, which can degrade performance. When using tokens, capabilities are independent of the object's location in memory. However, because a token does not specify the location of its corresponding object, tokens require that an object's address be determined when the capability is first used.

19.5 Security Attacks

Recent cyber attacks on e-businesses have made the front pages of newspapers worldwide. Denial-of-service attacks (DoS), viruses and worms have cost companies billions of dollars and caused countless hours of frustration. Many of these attacks allow the perpetrator to penetrate a network or system, which can lead to data theft, data corruption and other attacks. In this section we discuss several types of attacks against computer systems. Section 19.6, Attack Prevention and Security Solutions, discusses possible solutions to protect a computer's information and integrity.

19.5.1 Cryptanalysis

A **cryptanalytic attack** attempts to decrypt ciphertext without possessing the decryption key. The most common form of cryptanalytic attacks are those in which the encryption algorithm is analyzed to find relations between bits of the encryption key and bits of the ciphertext. The goal of such an attack is to determine the key from the ciphertext.

Weak statistical trends between ciphertext and keys can be exploited to gain knowledge about the key. Proper key management and key expiration dates can reduce susceptibility to cryptanalytic attacks. The longer an encryption key is used, the more ciphertext an attacker can use to derive the key. If a key is covertly recovered by an attacker, it can be used to decrypt every message that uses the key.

Self Review

1. How do key expiration dates reduce the effectiveness of cryptanalytic attacks?

Ans: 1) The longer an encryption key is used, the more ciphertext an attacker can use to derive the key. Key expiration addresses this concern by limiting hour long each key is in use.

19.5.2 Viruses and Worms

A **virus** is executable code—often sent as an attachment to an e-mail message or hidden in files such as audio clips, video clips and games—that attaches to or overwrites other files to replicate itself. Viruses can corrupt files, control applications or even erase a hard drive. Today, viruses can be spread across a network simply by sharing "infected" files embedded in e-mail attachments, documents or programs.

A **worm** is executable code that spreads by infecting files over a network. Worms rarely require any user action to propagate, nor do they need to be attached to another program or file to spread. Once a virus or worm is released, it can spread rapidly, often infecting millions of computers worldwide within minutes or hours.

Viruses can be classified as follows:

1. **boot sector virus**—infects the boot sector of the computer's hard disk, allowing it to load with the operating system and potentially control the system.

2. **transient virus** — attaches itself to a particular computer program. The virus is activated when the program is run and deactivated when the program is terminated.

3. **resident virus** — once loaded into the memory of a computer, it operates until the computer is powered down.

4. **logic bomb** — executes its code, or **payload**, when a given condition is met. An example of a logic bomb is a **time bomb**, which is activated when the clock on the computer matches a certain time or date.

A **Trojan horse** is a malicious program that hides within a trusted program or simulates a legitimate program or feature, while actually causing damage to the computer or network when the program is executed. The name Trojan horse originates from the story of the Trojan War in Greek legend. [*Note*: In this story, Greek warriors hid inside a wooden horse, which the Trojans took within the walls of the city of Troy. When night fell and the Trojans were asleep, the Greek warriors came out of the horse and opened the gates to the city, letting the Greek army enter and destroy the city of Troy.] Trojan horse programs can be particularly difficult to detect, because they appear to be legitimate and operational applications.

Back-door programs are resident viruses that allow the sender complete, undetected access to the victim's computer resources. These types of viruses are especially threatening to the victim, as they can be programmed to log every keystroke (capturing all passwords, credit card numbers, etc.).

Widespread Viruses

Two viruses that attracted significant media attention are Melissa, which struck in March 1999, and the ILOVEYOU virus that hit in May 2000. Each caused billions of dollars of damage. The Melissa virus spread in Microsoft Word documents sent via e-mail. When the document was opened, the virus was triggered, at which point it accessed a user's Microsoft Outlook address book (i.e., a list of e-mail addresses) on that computer and sent the infected Word attachment by e-mail to a maximum of 50 people in the user's address book. Each time another user opened the attachment, the virus would send up to 50 additional messages. Once resident in a system, the virus also infected any files saved using Microsoft Word.

The ILOVEYOU virus was sent as an attachment to an e-mail posing as a love letter. The message in the e-mail said "Kindly check the attached love letter coming from me." Once opened, the virus accessed the Microsoft Outlook address book and sent messages to each address listed, enabling the virus to spread rapidly worldwide. The virus corrupted many types of files, including operating system files. Many networks were disabled for days due to the massive number of e-mails generated.

This virus exposed e-mail security inadequacies, such as a lack of software to scan file attachments for security threats before they are opened. It also taught users to be more aware of suspicious e-mails, even those from someone with whom they are familiar.

Sapphire/Slammer Worm: Analysis and Implications

Worms spread by exploiting weaknesses in communications channels established by software, either by applications or by the operating system. Once a weakness is discovered, a worm can produce network traffic sufficient to disable a single computer or a network of computers. Further, a worm can be designed to execute code on the computer it infects, potentially allowing the worm's creator to obtain or destroy sensitive information.

Worm attacks that have received media attention include Nimda, Code Red and Sapphire, also called Slammer. Slammer, which infected most vulnerable computers within 10 minutes of its release on January 25, 2003, doubled the number of computers it infected every 8.5 seconds. [*Note*: Vulnerable computers were those running Microsoft SQLServer 2000 to which a security patch, released by Microsoft in July 2002, was not applied.] The infection rate was two orders of magnitude faster than its notable predecessor, the Code Red worm. The latter, a 4KB worm, instantiated multiple threads to create TCP connections to infect new hosts. On the contrary, Slammer operated over UDP and its payload was contained in a single 404-byte UDP packet. The connectionless UDP protocol, coupled with a random-scanning algorithm to generate target IP addresses, made the Slammer worm particularly virulent. A **random-scanning algorithm** uses pseudorandom numbers to generate a broad distribution of IP addresses as targets to infect.

The Slammer worm caused system and network outages due to network saturation by its UDP packets. Interestingly, the worm included no malicious payload and attacked a vulnerability in an application of relatively limited worldwide use. The Slammer worm also contained what appeared to be a logic error in its random-scanning algorithm that significantly limited the number of IP addresses the worm could reach.[40]

Antivirus software can protect against viruses and some worms. Most antivirus software is reactive, meaning that it can attack known viruses, rather than protecting against unknown or future viruses. We discuss antivirus software in Section 19.6.3.

Self Review

1. How do worms differ from other viruses?

2. What weaknesses in computer systems did the Melissa and ILOVEYOU viruses expose?

Ans: **1)** Worms typically spread via network connections and do not require user interaction to spread. **2)** The viruses exposed insufficient file-scanning antivirus software for e-mail applications and demonstrated that users did not treat suspicious e-mails with appropriate care.

19.5.3 Denial-of-Service (DoS) Attacks

A **denial-of-service (DoS) attack** prevents a system from servicing legitimate requests. In many DoS attacks, unauthorized traffic saturates a network's resources, restricting access for legitimate users. Typically, the attack is performed by flooding servers with data packets. Denial-of-service attacks usually require a network of computers to work simultaneously, although some skillful attacks can be achieved with a single machine. Denial-of-service attacks can cause networked computers to crash or disconnect, disrupting service on a Web site or even disabling critical systems such as telecommunications or flight-control centers.

Another type of denial-of-service attack targets a network's routing tables. Recall that routing tables provide a view of the network topology and are used by a router to determine where to send data. This type of attack is accomplished by modifying the routing tables, thus maliciously redirecting network activity. For example, the routing tables can be changed to send all incoming data to one address in the network. A similar attack, called a **DNS (domain name system) attack**, can modify the address to which network traffic for a particular Web site is sent. Such attacks can be used to redirect users of a particular Web site to another, potentially malicious, Web site. These attacks are particularly dangerous if the illegitimate Web site poses as the real one, leading users to disclose sensitive information to the attacker.

In a **distributed denial-of-service attack**, packet flooding comes from multiple computers at once. Such attacks are typically initiated by an individual who has infected several computers with a virus to gain unauthorized access to them to carry out the attack. Distributed denial-of-service attacks can be difficult to stop, because it is not easy to determine which requests on a network are from legitimate users and which are part of the attack. It is also particularly difficult to identify the perpetrator of such attacks, because they are not carried out directly from the attacker's computer.

In February 2000, distributed denial-of-service attacks shut down a number of high-traffic Web sites, including Yahoo!, eBay, CNN Interactive and Amazon. In this case, a single user utilized a network of computers to flood the Web sites with traffic that overwhelmed the sites' computers. Although denial-of-service attacks merely shut off access to a Web site and do not affect the victim's data, they can be extremely costly. For example, when eBay's Web site went down for a 24-hour period on August 6, 1999, its stock value declined dramatically.[41]

Who is responsible for viruses and denial-of-service attacks? Most often the responsible parties are referred to as **hackers**, but really that is a misnomer. In the computer field, hacker refers to an experienced programmer, often one who programs as much for personal enjoyment as for the functionality of the application. The true term for such people is **cracker**, which is someone who uses a computer maliciously (and often illegally) to break into another system or cause another system to fail.

Self Review

1. How are DNS attacks harmful?
2. Why is it difficult to detect and stop distributed denial-of-service attacks?

Ans: **1)** Users unaware of malicious activity could submit sensitive information to a cracker. Legitimate Web sites may lose revenue because users are redirected to alternate sites. **2)** It may be difficult to distinguish between legitimate and malicious users.

19.5.4 Software Exploitation

Another problem plaguing e-businesses is software exploitation by crackers. Every program on a networked machine should be checked for vulnerabilities. However, with millions of software products available and vulnerabilities discovered daily, this becomes an overwhelming task. One common vulnerability exploitation method is a **buffer overflow**, in which a program receives input that is larger than its allocated space.

A buffer overflow occurs when an application sends more data to a buffer than it can hold. A buffer overflow attack can push the additional data into adjacent buffers, corrupting or overwriting existing data. A well-designed buffer overflow attack can replace executable code in an application's stack to alter its behavior. Buffer overflow attacks may contain malicious code that will then be able to execute with the same access rights as the application it attacked. Depending on the user and application, the attacker may gain access to the entire system. BugTraq (www.securityfocus.com) was created in 1993 to list vulnerabilities, how to exploit them and how to repair them.

Self Review

1. Why are buffer overflow attacks dangerous?
2. How can buffer overflow attacks be prevented?

Ans: 1) Buffer overflow attacks may modify an application's stack so that an attacker can execute code to gain access to the entire system. 2) An application can rigidly enforce buffer limits when accepting input. Also, the system can implement stack segments that are not executable.

19.5.5 System Penetration

The result of many security attacks is system or network penetration. According to a study by the Computer Security Institute (www.gocsi.com), 40 percent of the respondents reported that an outsider had successfully penetrated their systems.[42] After an attacker exploits an operating system or the software running on the computer, the system is vulnerable to a number of attacks—ranging from data theft and manipulation to a system crash. A **system penetration** is a successful breach of computer security by an unauthorized external user.[43] Every system penetration is potentially dangerous, although a quick response can usually thwart an intruder's attack before any significant damage is done. Many attacks, such as data theft and Web defacing, rely on a successful system penetration as a foundation.

Web defacing is a popular form of attack wherein the crackers illegally obtain access to modify an organization's Web site and change the contents. Web defacing has attracted significant media attention. A notable case occurred in 1996, when Swedish crackers changed the Central Intelligence Agency Web site to read "Central Stupidity Agency." The vandals placed obscenities, political messages, notes to system administrators and links to adult-content sites on the page. Many other popular and large Web sites have been defaced. Defacing Web sites has become overwhelmingly popular among crackers today, causing archives of attacked sites (with records of more than 15,000 vandalized sites) to close because of the volume of sites that were vandalized daily.[44]

System penetration often occurs as a result of a Trojan horse, back-door program or an exploited bug in software or the operating system. Allowing external users to access applications via the Web provides another channel for an attacker to penetrate a system.[45] Vulnerabilities in common Web server applications, such as Microsoft Internet Information Services (IIS) and Apache HTTP Server, give attackers a well-known route to penetrating a system if administrators fail to apply necessary patches. System penetration can also occur on personal computers through software connected to the Internet, such as Web browsers.

The CERT®/CC (Computer Emergency Response Team Coordination Center; www.cert.org) at Carnegie Mellon University's Software Engineering Institute is a federally funded research and development center. CERT/CC responds to reports of viruses and denial-of-service attacks and provides information on network security, including how to determine if a system has been compromised. The site provides detailed incident reports of viruses and denial of service attacks, including descriptions of the incidents, their impact and solutions. The site also reports the vulnerabilities in popular operating systems and software packages. The CERT Security Improvement Modules are excellent tutorials on network security. These modules describe the issues and technologies used to solve network security problems.

Self Review

1. List several techniques crackers use to penetrate systems.
2. Compare Web defacing to a DNS attack.

Ans: **1)** Crackers can issue a Trojan horse back-door program, place an exploited bug in software or the operating system or access applications via an organization's Web site. **2)** Web defacing occurs when crackers illegally obtain access to modify an organization's Web site and change its contents. DNS attacks modify the address to which network traffic for a particular Web site is sent, which can redirect users of a particular Web site to another.

19.6 Attack Prevention and Security Solutions

The previous section detailed several common attacks against computer security. Though the number of threats to computer security may seem overwhelming, in practice, common sense and diligence can prevent a large number of attacks. To further bolster security, additional hardware and software that specializes in thwarting a variety of attacks can be installed on computers and in networks. This section describes several common security solutions.

19.6.1 Firewalls

A **firewall** protects a local area network (LAN) from intruders outside the network. A firewall polices inbound and outbound traffic for the LAN. Firewalls can prohibit all data transmission that is not expressly allowed, or allow all data transmission that is not expressly prohibited. The choice between these two models can be determined by the network security administrator; the former provides a high level of security, but might prevent legitimate data transfer. The latter leaves the system more susceptible to attack, but generally does not restrict legitimate network transfer. Each LAN can be connected to the Internet through a gateway, which typically includes a firewall. For years, the most significant security threats originated from employees inside the firewall. Now that businesses rely heavily on access to the Internet, an increasing number of security threats originate outside the firewall—from the hundreds of millions of people connected to the company network via the Internet.[46]

There are two primary types of firewalls. A **packet-filtering firewall** examines all data sent from outside the LAN and rejects data packets based on predefined rules, such as reject packets that have local network addresses or reject packets from certain addresses or ports. For example, suppose that a hacker from outside the network obtains the address of a computer inside the network and attempts to pass a harmful data packet through the firewall by sending a packet indicating that it was sent from the computer inside the network. In this case, a packet-filtering firewall will reject the data packet because the return address of the inbound packet has clearly been modified. A limitation of packet-filtering firewalls is that they consider only the source of data packets; they do not examine the attached data. As a result, malicious viruses can be installed on an authorized user's computer, allowing an attacker access to the network without that user's knowledge. The goal of an **application-level gateway** is to protect the network against the data contained in packets. If the message contains a virus, the gateway can block it from being sent to the intended receiver.

Installing a firewall is one of the most effective and easiest ways to add security to a small network.[47] Often, small companies or home users who are connected to the Internet through permanent connections, such as cable modems, do not employ strong security measures. As a result, their computers are prime targets for crackers to exploit for denial-of-service attacks or information theft. However, it is important for all computers connected to the Internet to contain some degree of security for their systems. Many popular network products, such as routers, provide firewall capabilities and certain operating systems, such as Windows XP, provide software firewalls. In fact, the Windows XP Internet Connection Firewall (ICF) is enabled by default. Section 21.13.3, Internet Connection Firewall, discusses how Windows XP implements its firewall. Numerous other firewall software products are available; several are listed in the Web Resources section at the end of the chapter.

Air gap technology is a network security solution that complements the firewall. It secures private data from external traffic accessing the internal network. The air gap separates the internal network from the external network, and the organization decides which information will be made available to external users. Whale Communications created the e-Gap System, which is composed of two computer servers and a memory bank. The memory bank does not run an operating system; therefore hackers cannot take advantage of common operating system weaknesses to access network information.

Air gap technology does not allow outside users to view the network's structure, which prevents hackers from searching the network for weaknesses. The e-Gap Web Shuttle feature allows safe external access by restricting the system's "back office," where an organization's most sensitive information and IT-based business processes are controlled. Users who wish to access a network hide behind the air gap, where the authentication server is located. Authorized users gain access through a single sign-on capability, allowing them to use one login password to access authorized areas of the network.

The e-Gap Secure File Shuttle feature moves files in and out of the network. Each file is inspected behind the air gap. If the file is deemed safe, it is carried by the File Shuttle into the network.[48]

Air gap technology is used by e-commerce organizations to allow their clients and partners to access information with transparent security, thus reducing the cost of inventory management. Military, aerospace and government industries, which store highly sensitive information, employ air gap technology.

Self Review

1. Is a home user more likely to use a firewall to prohibit all data flow not expressly allowed or to allow all data that is not expressly prohibited?
2. Discuss the difference between packet-filtering firewalls and application gateways.

Ans: **1)** A home user would be more likely to allow all data that is not expressly prohibited, because the user will most likely want to access a large (and evolving) set of Web sites, located at different IP addresses. **2)** A packet-filtering firewall examines all data sent from outside the LAN and rejects data packets based on predefined rules, such as reject packets that have local network addresses or reject packets from certain addresses or ports. An application-level gateway protects the network against the data contained in packets. If the message contains a virus, the gateway can block it from being sent to the intended receiver.

19.6.2 Intrusion Detection Systems (IDSs)

Intrusion detection systems (IDSs) monitor networks and application **log files**, which record information about system behavior, such as the time at which operating system services are requested and the name of the process that requests them. IDSs examine log files to alert system administrators of suspicious application and/ or system behavior. If an application exhibits erratic or malicious behavior, an IDS can halt the execution of that process.[49]

Host-based intrusion detection systems monitor system and application log files, which is especially useful for detecting Trojan horses. **Network-based intrusion detection** software monitors traffic on a network for any unusual patterns that might indicate DoS attacks or access to a network by an unauthorized user. System administrators can then check their log files to determine if there was an intrusion and, if so, track the offender. Intrusion detection products are commercially available from companies such as Cisco (www.cisco.com/warp/public/cc/pd/sqsw/sqidsz), Hewlett-Packard (www.hp.com/security/home.html) and Symantec (www.symantec.com). There is also an open-source network intrusion detection system from Snort (www.snort.org).

Intrusion detection via **static analysis** attempts to detect when applications have been corrupted by a hacker. The static analysis technique assumes that hackers attempt to attack a system using system calls. Under this assumption, the first step in detecting intrusions is to build a model of an application's expected behavior (i.e., a pattern of system calls the application typically generates). The application's pattern of system calls is then monitored as it runs; an attack can be detected if this pattern differs from the static model.[50]

The **OCTAVE^{SM} (Operationally Critical Threat, Asset and Vulnerability Evaluation) method**, developed at the Software Engineering Institute at Carnegie Mellon University, evaluates a system's security threats. There are three phases in OCTAVE: building threat profiles, identifying vulnerabilities, and developing security solutions and plans. In the first stage, the organization identifies its important information and assets, then evaluates the levels of security required to protect them. In the second phase, the system is examined for weaknesses that could compromise the valuable data. The third phase is to develop a security strategy as advised by an analysis team of three to five security experts assigned by OCTAVE. This approach is one of the first of its kind, in which the owners of computer systems not only obtain professional analysis, but also participate in prioritizing the protection of crucial information.[51]

Self Review

1. Name a major drawback to IDSs.
2. Explain the difference between host-based and network-based IDSs.

Ans: **1)** IDSs cannot detect intrusion with perfect accuracy. Thus, an IDS may prevent an authorized user from performing a legitimate operation and may enable an intrusion to go undetected. **2)** Host-based IDSs monitor the current system's log files. Network-based IDSs monitor packets that travel over a network.

19.6.3 Antivirus Software

As discussed in Section 19.5.2, viruses and worms have become a menace to businesses and home users alike and have cost businesses billions of dollars.[52] The number of reported viruses has increased steadily since the mid-1990s.[53] In response, antivirus software has been developed and modified to meet the increasing number and variety of virus attacks on computer systems. **Antivirus software** attempts to protect a computer from a virus and/or identify and remove viruses on that computer. There are a variety of techniques antivirus software may use to detect and remove viruses from a system; however, none can offer complete protection.

Signature-scanning virus detection relies on knowledge about the structure of the computer virus's code. For example, many antivirus programs maintain a list of known viruses and their code. All viruses contain a region called the **virus signature** that does not change as the virus spreads. In practice, most known virus lists maintain a list of virus signatures. In this case, virus detection software scans the computer, comparing file data to virus code.

A weakness of known virus lists is that they could become prohibitively large as viruses proliferate. The virus list must be updated regularly to successfully identify emerging viruses. Perhaps the most serious weakness of known virus lists is that they can recognize only viruses that have been previously identified by the list provider. Thus, known virus lists generally do not protect against new and unidentified viruses.

A known virus list can be particularly ineffective against variants and polymorphic viruses. A **variant** is a virus whose code has been modified from its original form, yet still retains its malicious payload. A **polymorphic virus** changes its code (e.g., via encryption, substitution, insertion, and the like) as it spreads, to evade known virus lists (Fig. 19.8).

Although virus signatures improve a virus scanner's ability to detect viruses and their variants, they introduce the possibility of false positive and false negative virus detection. False positive virus alerts incorrectly indicate that a virus is resident in a file, whereas false negatives incorrectly determine that an infected file is clean. These incorrect results become more frequent as the size of a virus signature

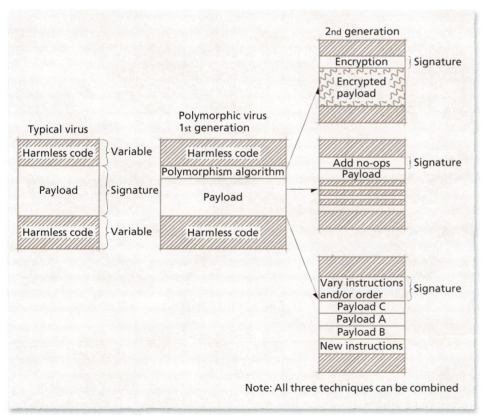

Figure 19.8 | *Polymorphic virus.*

becomes smaller. The problem of preventing false positive and false negative readings when scanning for viruses is a challenging one, as it has been demonstrated that virus signatures as small as two bytes can be created.[54, 55]

An alternative to signature scans is **heuristic scanning**. Viruses are characterized by replication, residence in memory and/or destructive code. Heuristic scans can prevent the spread of viruses by detecting and suspending any program exhibiting this behavior. The primary strength of heuristic scanning is that it can detect viruses that have not yet been identified. Similar to signature scanning, however, heuristic scanning is also susceptible to false reporting. Most antivirus software employs a combination of signature and heuristic scanning.

All viruses (with the exception of worms) must modify a file to infect a computer. Consequently, another antivirus technique is to monitor changes to files by checking file consistency. Most consistency checks are implemented as checksums of protected files. In a system that experiences a high volume of file I/O, maintaining a record of file consistency is not a viable option if users expect fast response times. Consequently, many antivirus programs ensure file consistency for a limited set of files (typically the operating system files). However, file consistency scans cannot protect against viruses resident on the computer before antivirus software installation. Some operating systems, such as Windows XP, perform consistency checks on vital system files and replace them if they are altered, to protect system integrity.[56]

In addition to scanning techniques, antivirus software can be characterized by its program behavior. For example, **real-time scanners** are resident in memory and actively prevent viruses, whereas other antivirus software must be loaded manually and serves only to identify viruses. Some antivirus software programs prompt the user for action when a virus is detected, whereas others remove viruses without user interaction.[57]

Self Review

1. Does signature scanning or heuristic scanning provide better protection against new and unidentified viruses?
2. Describe several weaknesses of known virus lists.

Ans: **1)** Heuristic scanning provides better protection against new and unidentified viruses because it can detect new virus behavior even when its signature is not available. **2)** A weakness of known virus lists is that they could become prohibitively large as viruses proliferate. The virus list must be updated regularly to successfully identify emerging viruses. Perhaps the most serious weakness of known virus lists is that they can recognize only viruses that have been previously identified by the list provider. Thus, known virus lists generally do not protect against new and unidentified viruses.

19.6.4 Security Patches

Operating systems and other software often contain security flaws that are not discovered until after many users have installed them. To address security flaws in a timely manner, the software developers must:

- discover previously unknown flaws,
- quickly release patches for the flaws and
- establish strong lines of communication with users.

To reduce the damage caused by security flaws, developers should address security flaws that have been exploited and actively search and fix those that have not. A code release that addresses a security flaw is often called a **security patch**.

Often, simply releasing a patch for a security flaw is insufficient to improve security. For example, the Slammer worm (Section 19.5.2, Viruses and Worms) exploited a security flaw for which a patch had been released six months earlier. Thus software developers should address security flaws by notifying their users quickly and providing software that facilitates the process of applying security patches.

OpenBSD is a BSD UNIX project whose primary goal is to create the most secure (UNIX-compatible) operating system (see the Mini Case Study, OpenBSD). The project includes an audit team that continuously searches for security flaws, a full-disclosure policy that describes each security flaw in a public forum and a team that releases security patches quickly. Users must subscribe to a mailing list or visit a Web page to learn of new security flaws and download patches.[58] Both the Open-BSD and Apple MacOS X operating systems close all ports and disable all network services by default to improve security (see the Mini Case Study, Macintosh).

Microsoft's Trustworthy Computing Initiative has resulted in a steady stream of security patches, called hotfixes, for the Windows line of operating systems. Microsoft offers free software called Automatic Updates that executes in the background of a Windows system to periodically determine if new hotfixes are available. If the Automatic Updates determines that a "critical update" such as a security patch is available, it will display a dialog to prompt the user to download and install the hotfix.[59] This software also enables critical updates to be installed without user interaction, which can improve system security.

Self Review

1. Why is it important to establish strong lines of communication between software developers and users when releasing security patches?
2. Why is it insufficient to address security flaws only after they are exploited?

Ans: **1)** Software developers should address security flaws by notifying their users quickly and providing software that facilitates the process of applying security patches, so that users can protect themselves against known security flaws. **2)** Some exploit actions of security flaws not detected by developers and could compromise system security and go undetected for days, months or even years.

19.6.5 Secure File Systems

Access to system resources, including data stored in a file system, can be regulated by the operating system's access control policy. However, such mechanisms do not necessarily prevent access to data stored on the hard drive when it is accessed by a different operating system. Consequently, several of today's operating systems support secure file systems that protect sensitive data regardless of how the data is accessed. Windows XP employs the New Technology File System (NTFS), which protects files via access control and encryption (see Section 21.8, File Systems Management).

The **Encrypting File System (EFS)** uses cryptography to protect files and folders in an NTFS file system. EFS uses secret-key and public-key encryption to secure files.[60] Each user is assigned a key pair and certificate that are used to ensure that only the user who encrypted the files can access them. File data is lost if the key is lost. EFS is often implemented in multiuser or mobile systems to ensure that protected files would not be accessible to somebody using a stolen or lost machine.

Mini Case Study

OpenBSD

Theo de Raadt, an original member of the NetBSD project, left NetBSD in 1995 to start the OpenBSD project using the open-source NetBSD source code as a base.[61, 62] OpenBSD is considered by many to be the most secure OS available.[63, 64, 65] It has been more than four years (as of the time this book was published) since OpenBSD has been cracked while running with default settings.[66, 67]

OpenBSD's extraordinary level of security has been achieved primarily by the core team's code-auditing process. Every source file in the system has been analyzed several times by various developers on the core project team—an ongoing process. These audits check for bugs such as classic security holes like buffer overflow opportunities.

Any found bugs are posted immediately to the OpenBSD project site and are generally fixed in less than a day.[68, 69, 70, 71]

OpenBSD includes several security features, such as built-in support for OpenSSH and OpenSSL (open-source implementations of the SSH and SSL security protocols).[72] OpenBSD was also the first operating system to implement IPsec, the IP Security protocol widely used in Virtual Private Networks (VPNs), discussed in Section 19.10.2. It also includes the network authentication protocol Kerberos version five.[73]

The OpenBSD group (www.openbsd.org) ensures that its operating system is secure upon installation by shipping OpenBSD with only minimal services enabled and all ports closed

(to prevent network attacks).[74, 75] It is interesting to note that Windows Server 2003 follows the same philosophy—a complete reversal from Microsoft's policy in Windows 2000—to enhance security in environments managed by inexperienced administrators.[76]

To maintain its secure core, OpenBSD provides a limited set of applications, though the OpenBSD team claims it can run programs written for any of the major UNIX-based systems.[77] There is no GUI, making this system an unlikely option for most desktop users but suitable for servers, which must be secure and generally have little direct interaction with users.[78]

Encryption can be applied to individual files or entire folders; in the latter case, every file inside the folder is encrypted. Applying encryption at the folder level often achieves a higher level of security by preventing programs from creating temporary files in plaintext. File encryption in Linux is discussed in Section 20.7, File Systems.

Mini Case Study

Macintosh

In the late 1970s, Apple Computer was working on two new computers: the Lisa, a high-end personal computer, and the **Macintosh**, a more affordable personal computer.[79, 80, 81] In 1979, Apple cofounder Steve Jobs (now CEO of Apple) visited Xerox's Palo Alto Research Center (PARC).[82] During his visit, Jobs saw a demo of the Alto—a personal computer that used a graphical user interface (GUI) and a computer mouse. The Alto, developed at PARC in the 1970s, was designed for personal use, however it was too large and expensive to be practical, therefore it was never sold.

Inspired by the Alto, Jobs incorporated GUIs and the computer mouse into both the Apple Lisa and Macintosh operating systems. The Apple GUIs included some features similar to those of the Alto, plus many original features including drag-and-drop file-icon movement, pull-down menus and windows that redraw automatically when uncovered—all of which worked using a mouse. The Lisa and Macintosh systems were the first personal computers on the market to include a mouse.[83] The Lisa debuted in 1983, but it cost ten thousand dollars and was not successful; Apple discontinued the model two years later.[84] The Macintosh was announced in 1984 with a famous commercial based on George Orwell's "1984,"[85] which debuted during the Super Bowl. The Macintosh, which was more space efficient and affordable than the Lisa (it sold for $2,495), became extraordinarily successful.[86, 87]

The first Macintosh operating system was System 1. Although it had GUI capabilities, it was a fairly rudimentary operating system—it had no virtual memory, did not support multiprogramming and had a single-level file system.[88] These features were updated in later versions; a hierarchical file structure was implemented in System 3, basic multiprogramming was added in System 4 and virtual memory was introduced in System 7 which was released in 1990.[89] In 1997, after numerous bug fixes and application upgrades, version 7.6 was released and the operating system was renamed **Mac OS**.[90, 91]

Mac OS was completely rebuilt in 2001 for Mac OS X, with the new Darwin kernel incorporating the Mach 3 microkernel and BSD UNIX.[92] Darwin is a complete UNIX environment including the X11 windows system as an option.[93] Apple also made Darwin an open-source project to make it more robust and stable.[94] Mac OS X has followed OpenBSD's (discussed in the OpenBSD mini case study) lead, improving security by shipping with all ports closed and all network services disabled.[95] Apple also made Mac OS X compatible with the Windows file formats and Windows Exchange mail servers, making it easy for Mac OS X users to integrate into a business environment.[96]

Self Review

1. When are access control mechanisms insufficient to protect file data?

2. What is the primary risk of implementing an encrypted file system?

Ans: **1)** Access control mechanisms are insufficient to protect file data when the storage device is removed from the computer, because it can be accessed by a system that bypasses the existing access control mechanisms. 2) File data is unrecoverable if the encryption key is lost.

19.6.6 Orange Book Security

To evaluate the security features of operating systems, the U.S. Department of Defense (DoD) published a document entitled "Department of Defense Trusted Computer System Evaluation Criteria," also called the **Orange Book**, in December 1985.[97, 98] This document is still used to define levles of security in operating systems. The Orange Book, originally designed for evaluating military systems, classifies systems into four levels of security protection—A, B, C and D. The lowest level of security is D and the highest is A. The requirements for each level follow.[99, 100]

- Level D: Any system that does not meet all the requirements in any other levels. Systems categorized as level D are generally unsecure.

- Level C: This level contains two sublevels. Level C1 requires the operating system to separate users and data, which means individuals or groups must log in a username or group name and password to use the system. Private information belonging to an individual or a group is secured to prevent other individuals and groups from reading or modifying it. Early versions of UNIX belong to this level. Level C2 supports only individual login with password, which means users cannot log in with a group name. Authorized individuals can access only certain files and programs. Both C1 and C2 allow individuals to control the access to their files and private information, which means they require only discretionary access control. Most operating systems, such as Windows NT, modern UNIX systems and IBM OS/400[101] fall into this category.

- Level B: In this level, mandatory access control is required, which means the operating system requires a predefined central permission scheme to determine the permissions assigned to subjects. The creator of an object does not control the permissions for that object. This level contains three sublevels. In addition to the requirements of C2, B1 requires the operating system to contain a predefined central permission scheme and apply sensitivity labels (e.g., "Confidential") on subjects and objects. The access control mechanism must use these sensitivity labels to determine permissions. Operating systems that satisfy B1 requirements include HP-UX BLS[102], SEVMS[103] and CS/SX[104]. B2 requires the communication line between the user and the operating system for authentication to be secure, in addition to the requirements from B1. Operating systems that satisfy B2 requirements include Multics[105] and VSLAN[106]. B3 requires all the features present in B2, in addition to implementing protection domains, providing secure recovery mechanisms (recovery without compromising protection after a system failure) and monitoring all access to subjects and objects for analysis. The XTS-300 operating system[107] satisfies B3 requirements.

- Level A: This level contains two sublevels. A1 requires all the features provided by B3, and it requires that the operating system's security is formally verified. An example of an operating system that satisfies the A1 requirements is the Boeing MLS LAN[108]. The requirements for A2 are reserved for future use.

Self Review

1. Does a system that belongs to category C2 need to satisfy the requirements for level B?
2. How does C2 differ from C1?

Ans: **1)** No. Level B is higher than level C2, hence level B has more features and requirements. **2)** C1 supports both individual and group logins while C2 supports only individual login.

19.7 Secure Communication

E-business has profited from the rapidly rising number of consumers that own computers with Internet connections. However, as the number of online transactions increases, so does the volume of sensitive data transmitted over the Internet. Applications that process transactions require secure connections through which sensitive data can be transmitted. Several methods for providing secure transactions have been developed in recent years. In the sections that follow, we describe some of these techniques.

There are five fundamental requirements for a successful, secure transaction:

- privacy
- integrity
- authentication
- authorization
- nonrepudiation

The **privacy** issue is: How do you ensure that the information you transmit over the Internet has not been captured or passed to a third party without your knowledge? The **integrity** issue is: How do you ensure that the information you send or receive has not been compromised or altered? The **authentication** issue is: How do the sender and receiver of a message verify their identities to each other? The **authorization** issue is: How do you manage access to protected resources on the basis of user **credentials**, which consists of user's identity (e.g., username) and proof of identify (e.g., password)? The **nonrepudiation** issue is: How do you legally prove that a message was sent or received? Network security must also address the issue of availability: How do we ensure that the network, and the computer systems to which it connects, will operate continuously? In the sections that follow, we discuss several implementations of secure communication that derive from encryption techniques discussed in Section 19.2.

Self Review

1. For which of the five fundamental requirements for a successful, secure transaction would encryption be useful?
2. Which of the five fundamental requirements deal with user login?

Ans: **1)** Encryption is useful for all five of the fundamental requirements for a successful, secure transaction. **2)** Authorization and authentication.

19.8 Key Agreement Protocols

Although public-key algorithms offer flexible and reliable security, they are not efficient for sending large amounts of data. Therefore, public-key algorithms should not be considered replacements for secret-key algorithms. Instead, public-key algorithms are most often employed to exchange secret keys securely. The process by which two parties can exchange keys over an unsecure medium is called a **key agreement protocol**.

The most common key agreement protocol is a **digital envelope** (Fig. 19.9). The message is encrypted using a secret key (Step 1), and the secret key is then encrypted using public-key encryption (Step 2). The sender attaches the encrypted secret key to the encrypted message and sends the receiver the entire package, or envelope. The sender could also digitally sign the envelope before sending it to prove the sender's identity to the receiver (covered in Section 19.8.2, Digital Signatures). To decrypt the envelope, the receiver first decrypts the secret key using the receiver's private key. Then, the receiver uses the secret key to decrypt the actual message. Because only the receiver can decrypt the encrypted secret key, the sender can be sure that only the intended receiver can read the message.

Self Review

1. Why are public-key algorithms employed to exchange secret keys?
2. In the digital envelope protocol, why is it inappropriate to encrypt the entire message using public-key encryption?

Ans: **1)** Public-key algorithms are efficient for sending small amounts of data, and they prevent attackers from obtaining the secret key while it is transmitted. **2)** Public-key encryption is not efficient for sending large amounts of data because it requires significant processing power.

19.8.1 Key Management

Maintaining the secrecy of private keys is essential to the maintenance of cryptographic system security. Most security breaches result from poor key management (e.g., the mishandling of private keys, resulting in key theft) rather than cryptanalytic attacks.[109]

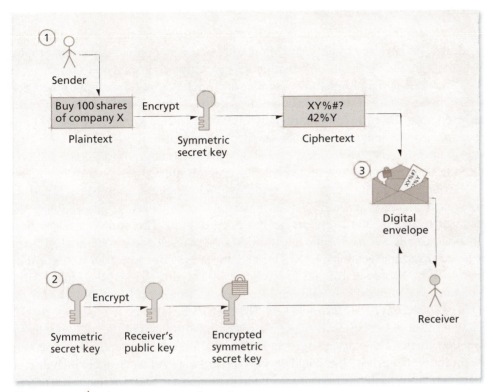

Figure 19.9 | *Creating a digital envelope.*

An important aspect of key management is **key generation**—the process by which keys are created. A malicious third party could try to decrypt a message by using every possible decryption key. Key-generation algorithms are sometimes unintentionally constructed to choose from only a small subset of possible keys. If the subset is too small, then the encrypted data is more susceptible to brute-force attacks. Therefore, it is important to use a key-generation program that can generate a large number of keys as randomly as possible. Key security is improved when key length is large enough that brute-force cracking is computationally infeasible.

Self Review

1. Why is it important to use a long key length?
2. Why are most security breaches due to poor key management rather than cryptanalytic attack?

Ans: **1)** If the total number of decryption keys is small, malicious third parties could generate all possible decryption keys quickly to break the encryption. **2)** When long key lengths are used, it is easier to take advantage of poor key management to steal private keys than it is to use a brute-force method such as a cryptanalytic attack.

19.8.2 Digital Signatures

Digital signatures, the electronic equivalents of written signatures, were developed to address the absence of authentication and integrity in public-key cryptography. A digital signature authenticates the sender's identity and is difficult to forge.

To create a digital signature, a sender first applies a hash function to the original plaintext message. Hash functions for secure applications are also typically designed such that it is computationally infeasible to compute a message from its hash value or to generate two messages with the same hash value. A secure hash algorithm is designed so that the probability that two different messages will produce the same message digest is statistically insignificant.

In digital signatures, the hash value uniquely identifies a message. If a malicious party changes the message, the hash value also changes, thus enabling the recipient to detect that the message has been altered. Two widely used hashing functions are the **Secure Hash Algorithm (SHA-1)**, developed by National Institute of Standards and Technology (NIST), and the **MD5 Message Digest Algorithm**, developed by Professor Ronald L. Rivest at MIT. Using SHA-1, the phrase "*Buy 100 shares of company X*" would produce the hash value *D8 A9 B6 9F 72 65 0B D5 6D 0C 47 00 95 0D FD 31 96 0A FD B5*. The hash value is called the **message digest**.

Next, the sender uses the sender's private key to encrypt the message digest. This step creates a digital signature and validates the sender's identity, because only the owner of that private key could encrypt the message. A message that includes the digital signature, hash function and the encrypted message is sent to the receiver. The receiver uses the sender's public key to decipher the digital signature (this establishes the message's authenticity) and reveal the message digest. The receiver then uses his or her own private key to decipher the original message. Finally, the receiver applies the hash function to the original message. If the hash value of the original message matches the message digest included in the signature, the **message integrity** is confirmed—the message has not been altered in transmission.

Digital signatures are significantly more secure than handwritten signatures. A digital signature is based upon the contents of the document, so a digital signature (contrary to a handwritten signature) is different for each document signed.

Digital signatures do not provide proof that a message has been sent. Consider the following situation: A contractor sends a company a digitally signed contract, which the contractor later would like to revoke. The contractor could do so by releasing the private key, then claiming that the digitally signed contract was generated by an intruder who stole the contractor's private key. **Time stamping**, which binds a time and date to a digital document, can help solve the problem of nonrepudiation. For example, suppose the company and the contractor are negotiating a contract. The company requires the contractor to sign the contract digitally and then have the document digitally time stamped by a third party, called a **time-stamping agency** or a **digital notary service**.

The contractor sends the digitally signed contract to the time-stamping agency. The privacy of the message is maintained, because the time-stamping agency sees only the encrypted, digitally signed message. The agency affixes the time and date of receipt to the encrypted, signed message and digitally signs the entire package with the time-stamping agency's private key. The time-stamp cannot be altered by anyone except the time-stamping agency, because no one else possesses the agency's private key. Unless the contractor reports that the private key was compromised before the document was time stamped, the contractor cannot legally prove that the document was signed by an unauthorized third party. The sender could also require the receiver to sign the message digitally and time stamp it as proof of receipt. To learn more about time-stamping, visit www.authentidate.com.

The U.S. government's digital authentication standard is called the **Digital Signature Algorithm (DSA)**. Legislation passed in June of 2000 allows digital signatures to be as legally binding as handwritten signatures, which has facilitated many e-business transactions. For the latest news about U.S. government legislation in information security, visit www.itaa.org/infosec.

Self Review

1. If digital signatures do not create a message digest, can a malicious third party modify a message's ciphertext?
2. When interpreting messages that are digitally signed, what is the difference between authenticating a message and verifying its integrity?

Ans: **1)** Although it is possible to modify the ciphertext, it is unlikely that the third party will be able to modify the message in any meaningful way without knowledge of the encryption key. **2)** To authenticate a message, the receiver uses the sender's public key to decipher the digital signature. To verify a message's integrity, the receiver checks the hash value of the original message with the message digest included in the signature.

19.9 Public-Key Infrastructure, Certificates and Certificate Authorities

A limitation of public-key cryptography is that multiple users might share the same set of keys, making it difficult to establish each party's identity. For example, suppose a customer wishes to place an order with an online merchant. How does the customer know that the Web site being viewed was created by that merchant and not by a third party masquerading as a merchant to steal credit card information? **Public Key Infrastructure (PKI)** provides a solution to such a problem by integrating public-key cryptography with digital certificates and certificate authorities to authenticate parties in a transaction.

A **digital certificate** is a digital document that identifies a user and is issued by a **certificate authority (CA)**. A digital certificate includes the name of the subject (the company or individual being certified), the subject's public key, a serial number (which uniquely identifies the certificate), an expiration date, the signature of the trusted certificate authority and any other relevant information. A CA can be a financial institution or any other trusted third party, such as VeriSign. Once issued, the CA makes the digital certificates publicly available in **certificate repositories**.

The CA signs the certificate by encrypting either the subject's public key or a hash value of the public key using the CA's own private key, so that a recipient can verify the certificate. The CA must verify every subject's public key. Thus, users must trust the public key of a CA. Usually, each CA is part of a **certificate authority hierarchy**. This hierarchy can be viewed as a tree structure in which each node relies on its parent for authentication information. The root of the certificate authority hierarchy is the Internet Policy Registration Authority (IPRA). The IPRA signs certificates using the **root key**, which signs certificates exclusively for **policy creation authorities**—organizations that set policies for obtaining digital certificates. In turn, policy creation authorities sign digital certificates for CAs. CAs then sign digital certificates for individuals and organizations.

The CA is responsible for authentication, so it must check user information carefully before issuing a digital certificate. In one case, human error caused Veri-Sign to issue two digital certificates to an imposter posing as a Microsoft employee.[110] Such an error can be significant; for example, the inappropriately issued certificates can cause users to download malicious code unknowingly onto their machines. VeriSign, Inc., is a leading certificate authority (`www.verisign.com`); other digital certificate vendors are listed in the Web Resources section at the end of the chapter.

Digital certificates are created with an expiration date to force users to refresh key pairs periodically. If a private key is compromised before its expiration date, the digital certificate can be cancelled, and the user can obtain a new key pair and digital certificate. Cancelled and revoked certificates are placed on a **certificate revocation list (CRL)**, which is maintained by the certificate authority that issued the certificates.

CRLs are analogous to the paper lists of revoked credit card numbers formerly used at the points of sale in retail stores.[111] This can substantially lengthen the process of determining the validity of a certificate. An alternative to CRLs is the **Online Certificate Status Protocol (OCSP)**, which validates certificates in real time.[112]

Many still consider e-commerce unsecure. However, transactions using PKI and digital certificates can be more secure than exchanging private information over public, unencrypted media such as voice phone lines, paying through the mail, or handing a credit card to a sales clerk. In contrast, the key algorithms used in most secure online transactions are nearly impossible to compromise. By some estimates, the key algorithms used in public-key cryptography are so secure that even millions of today's computers working in parallel could not break the codes after a century of dedicated computation. However, as computing power increases, key algorithms considered strong today could be easily compromised in the future.

Self Review

1. Describe how CAs ensure the security of their certificates.
2. Why are electronic transactions secured by PKI and digital certificates often more secure than those conducted over the phone or in person?

Ans: **1)** Each CA is part of a certificate authority hierarchy. This hierarchy can be viewed as a tree structure in which each node relies on its parent for authentication information. Its root is the Internet Policy Registration Authority (IPRA), which signs certificates for policy creation authorities. Policy creation authorities sign digital certificates for CAs. CAs then sign digital certificates for individuals and organizations. **2)** The reason is that it is computationally infeasible to compromise the key algorithms used in most secure online transactions. By some estimates, the key algorithms used in public-key cryptography are so secure that even millions of today's computers working in parallel could not break the codes after a century of dedicated computation. By comparison, it is far easier to tap a phone line or write down an individual's credit card number during an in-person transaction.

19.10 Secure Communication Protocols

Secure communication protocols have been developed for several layers of the traditional TCP/IP stack. In this section we discuss Secure Sockets Layer (SSL) and Internet Protocol Security (IPSec). We also discuss the protocols that are commonly used to implement secure wireless communication.

19.10.1 Secure Sockets Layer (SSL)

The **Secure Sockets Layer (SSL)** protocol, developed by Netscape Communications, is a nonproprietary protocol that secures communication between two computers on the Internet and the Web.[113] Many e-businesses use SSL for secure online transactions. Support for SSL is included in many Web browsers, such as Mozilla (a stand-alone browser that has been integrated into Netscape Navigator), Microsoft's Internet Explorer and other software products. It operates between the Internet's TCP/IP communications protocol and the application software.[114]

During typical Internet communication, a process sends and receives messages via a socket. Although TCP guarantees that messages are delivered, it does not determine whether packets have been maliciously altered during transmission. For example, an attacker can change a packet's source and destination addresses without being detected, so fraudulent packets can be disguised as valid ones.[115]

SSL implements public-key cryptography using the RSA algorithm and digital certificates to authenticate the server in a transaction and to protect private information as it passes over the Internet. SSL transactions do not require client authentication; many servers consider a valid credit card number to be sufficient for authentication in secure purchases. To begin, a client sends a message to a server to open a socket. The server responds and sends its digital certificate to the client for authentication. Using public-key cryptography to communicate securely, the client and server negotiate session keys to continue the transaction. Session keys are secret keys that are used for the duration of that transaction. Once the keys are established, the communication is secured and authenticated using the session keys and digital certificates.

Before sending a message over TCP/IP, the SSL protocol breaks the information into blocks, each of which is compressed and encrypted. When the receiver obtains the data through TCP/IP, SSL decrypts the packets, then decompresses and assembles the data. SSL is used primarily to secure point-to-point connections—interactions between exactly two computers.[116] SSL can authenticate the server, the client, both or neither. However, in most e-business SSL sessions, only the server is authenticated.

The Transport Layer Security (TLS) protocol, designed by the Internet Engineering Task Force (IETF), is the successor to SSL. Conceptually, SSL and TLS are nearly identical—they authenticate using symmetric keys and encrypt data with private keys. The difference between the two protocols is in the implementation of the algorithm and structure of TLS packets.[117]

Although SSL protects information as it is passed over the Internet, it does not protect private information, such as credit card numbers, once the information is stored on the merchant's server. Credit card information may be decrypted and stored in plaintext on the merchant's server until the order is placed. If the server's security is breached, an unauthorized party can access the information.

Self Review

1. Why do many transactions via SSL authenticate only the server?
2. Why is information compressed before encryption under SSL?

Ans: **1)** The reason is that many servers consider a valid credit card number to be sufficient for authentication in secure purchases. **2)** One reason is that compressed data consumes less space, thus requiring less time to transmit over the Internet. Another reason is that compression makes it more difficult for an attacker to interpret the unencrypted message, which provides greater protection against a cryptanalytic attack.

19.10.2 Virtual Private Networks (VPNs) and IP Security (IPSec)

Most home or office networks are private—computers in the network are connected via communication lines not intended for public use. Organizations can also use the existing infrastructure of the Internet to create **Virtual Private Networks (VPNs)**, which provide secure communication channels over public connections. Because VPNs use the existing Internet infrastructure, they are more economical than wide-area private networks.[118] Encryption enables VPNs to provide the same services and security as private networks.

A VPN is created by establishing a secure communication channel, called a tunnel, through which data passes over the Internet. **Internet Protocol Security (IPSec)** is commonly used to implement a secure tunnel by providing data privacy, integrity and authentication.[119] IPSec, developed by the IETF, uses public-key and symmetric-key cryptography to ensure data integrity, authentication and confidentiality.

The technology builds upon the Internet Protocol (IP) standard, whose primary security weakness is that IP packets can be intercepted, modified and retransmitted without detection. Unauthorized users can access the network by using a number of well-known techniques, such as **IP spoofing**—whereby an attacker simulates the IP address of an authorized user or host to obtain unauthorized access to resources. Unlike the SSL protocol, which enables secure, point-to-point connections between two applications, IPSec secures connections among all users of the network on which it is implemented.

The Diffie-Hellman and RSA algorithms are commonly used for key exchange in the IPSec protocol, and DES or 3DES are used for secret-key encryption, depending on the system and its encryption needs. [*Note*: The Diffie-Hellman encryption algorithm is a public-key algorithm.][120] IPSec encrypts packet data, called a payload, then places it in an unencrypted IP packet to establish the tunnel. The receiver discards the IP packet header, then decrypts the payload to access the packet's content.[121]

VPN security relies on three concepts—user authentication, data encryption and controlled access to the tunnel.[122] To address these three security issues, IPSec is composed of three components. The **authentication header (AH)** attaches information (such as a checksum) to each packet to verify the identity of the sender and prove that data was not modified in transit. The **encapsulating security payload (ESP)** encrypts the data using symmetric keys to protect it from eavesdroppers while the IP packet is transmitted across public communication lines. IPSec uses the **Internet Key Exchange (IKE)** protocol to perform key management, which allows secure key exchange.

VPNs are becoming increasingly popular in businesses, but remain difficult to manage. The network layer (i.e., IP) is typically managed by the operating system or hardware, not user applications. So, it can be difficult to establish a VPN because network users must install the proper software or hardware to support IPSec. For more information about IPSec, visit the IPSec Developers Forum at `www.ip-sec.com` and the IETF's IPSec Working Group at `www.ietf.org/html.charters/ipsec-charter.html`.

Self Review

1. Why do companies often choose VPNs over private WANs?
2. Why must the encrypted IP packet be sent inside an unencrypted IP packet?

Ans: **1)** Because VPNs use the existing infrastructure of the Internet, VPNs are much more economical than WANs. **2)** Existing routers must be able to forward the packet. If the entire IP packet were encrypted, routers could not determine its destination.

19.10.3 Wireless Security

As wireless devices become increasingly popular, transactions such as stock trading and online banking are commonly transmitted wirelessly. Unlike wired transmissions, which require a third party to physically tap into a network, wireless transmissions enable virtually anyone to access transmitted data. Because wireless devices exhibit limited bandwidth and processing power, high latency and unstable connections, establishing secure wireless communication can be challenging.[123]

The IEEE 802.11 standard, which defines specifications for wireless LANs, uses the **Wired Equivalent Privacy (WEP)** protocol to protect wireless communication. WEP provides security by encrypting transmitted data and preventing unauthorized access to the wireless network. To transmit a message, WEP first appends a checksum to the message to enable the receiver to verify message integrity. It then applies the RC4 encryption algorithm, which takes two arguments—a 40-bit secret key (shared between the sender and the receiver) and a random 24-bit value (called the initialization value)—and returns a keystream (a string of bytes). Finally, WEP encodes the message by XORing the keystream and the plain text. Each WEP packet contains the encrypted message and the unencrypted initialization value. Upon receiving a packet, the receiver extracts the initialization value. The receiver then uses the initialization value and the shared secret key to generate the keystream. Finally, it decodes the message by XORing the keystream and the encrypted message. To determine whether the contents of the packet have been modified, the receiver can calculate the checksum and compare it with the checksum appended to the message.[124]

The security provided by the WEP protocol is inadequate for many environments. For one, the 24-bit initialization value is small, causing WEP to use the same keystream to encode different messages, which can allow a third party to recover plaintext relatively easily. WEP also exhibits poor key management—the secret key can be cracked by brute-force attacks within hours using a personal computer. Most WEP-enabled wireless networks share a single secret key between every client on the network, and the secret key is often used for months and even years. Finally, the checksum computation uses simple arithmetic, enabling attackers to change both the message body and the checksum with relative ease.[125, 126]

To address these issues, the IEEE and the Wi-Fi Alliance (`www.weca.net/OpenSection/index.asp`) developed a specification called **Wi-Fi Protected Access (WPA)** in 2003. WPA is expected to replace WEP by providing improved data encryption and by enabling user authentication, a feature not supported by WEP. WPA also introduces dynamic key encryption, which generates a unique encryption key for each client. Authentication is achieved via an authentication server that stores user credentials.[127]

Both WEP and WAP are designed for communication using the 802.11 wireless standard. Other wireless technologies—such as Cellular Digital Packet Data (CDPD) for cell phones, PDAs and pagers, Third Generation Global System for Mobile Communications (3GSM) for 3GSM-enabled cell phones, PDAs and pagers, and Time Division Multiple Access (TDMA) for TDMA cell phones—define their own (often proprietary) wireless communication and security protocols.[128]

Self Review

1. What properties of wireless devices introduce challenges when implementing secure wireless communication?
2. How does WPA address the poor key management in WEP?

Ans: **1)** Limited bandwidth, limited processing power, high latency and unstable connections. **2)** WPA introduces dynamic key encryption, which generates a unique encryption key for each client.

19.11 Steganography

Steganography is the practice of hiding information within other information, derived from Greek roots meaning "covered writing." Like cryptography, steganography has been used since ancient times. Steganography can be used to hide a piece of information, such as a message or image, within another image, message or other form of multimedia.

Consider a simple textual example: Suppose a stock broker's client wishes to perform a transaction via communication over an unsecure channel. The client might send the message "BURIED UNDER YARD." If the client and broker agreed in advance that the message is contained in the first letters of each word, the stock broker extracts the message, "BUY."

An increasingly popular application of steganography is **digital watermarks** for intellectual property protection. Digital steganography exploits unused portions of files encoded using particular formats, such as in images or on removable disks. The insignificant space stores the hidden message, while the digital file maintains its intended semantics.[129] A digital watermark can be either visible or invisible. It is usually a company logo, copyright notification or other mark or message that indicates the owner of the document. The owner of a document could show the hidden watermark in a court of law, for example, to prove that the watermarked item was stolen.

Digital watermarking could have a substantial impact on e-commerce. Consider the music industry. Music and motion picture distributors are concerned that MP3 (compressed audio) and MPEG-4 (compressed video) technologies facilitate the illegal distribution of copyrighted material. Consequently, many publishers are hesitant to publish content online, as digital content is easy to copy. Also, because CD- and DVD-ROMs store digital information, users are able to copy multimedia files and share them via the Web. Using digital watermarks, music publishers can make indistinguishable changes to a part of a song at a frequency that is not audible to humans, to show that the song was, in fact, copied.

Blue Spike's Giovanni™ digital watermarking software uses cryptographic keys to generate and embed steganographic digital watermarks into digital music and images (`www.bluespike.com`). The watermarks are placed randomly and are undetectable without knowledge of the embedding scheme; thus, they are difficult to identify and remove.

Self Review

1. Compare and contrast steganography and cryptography.
2. In grayscale bitmap images, each pixel can be represented by a number between 0 and 255. The number represents a certain shade of gray between 0 (black) and 255 (white). Describe a possible steganography scheme, and explain why it works.

Ans: **1)** Steganography and cryptography are similar because they both involve sending a message privately. However, with steganography, third parties are unaware that a secret message has been sent, though the message is typically in plaintext. With cryptography, third parties are aware that a secret message is sent, but they cannot decipher the message easily. **2)** A secret message can be encoded by replacing each of the least significant bits of the picture with one bit of the message. This would not affect the picture much, because each pixel would become at most one shade lighter or darker. In fact, it would be undetectable by most third parties that the picture contained a hidden message.

19.12 Proprietary and Open-Source Security

When comparing the merits of open-source and proprietary software, security is an important concern. Supporters of open-source security claim that proprietary solutions rely on security through obscurity. Proprietary solutions assume that because attackers cannot analyze the source code for security flaws, fewer security attacks are possible.

Supporters of open-source security claim that proprietary security applications limit the number of collaborative users that can search for security flaws and contribute to the overall security of the application. If the public cannot review the software's source code, certain bugs that are overlooked by developers can be exploited. Developers of proprietary software argue that their software has been suitably tested by their security experts.

Open-source security supporters also warn that proprietary security developers are reluctant to publicly disclose security flaws, even when accompanied by appropriate patches, for fear that public disclosure would damage the company's reputation. This may discourage vendors from releasing security patches, thereby reducing their product's security.

A primary advantage to open-source applications is interoperability—open-source software tends to implement standards and protocols that many other developers can easily include in their products. Because users can modify the source, they can customize the level of security in their applications. Thus, an administrator can customize the operating system to include the most secure access control policy, file system, communication protocol and shell. By contrast, users of proprietary software often are limited to the features provided by the vendor, or must pay additional fees to integrate other features.

Another advantage to open-source security is that the application source code is available for extensive testing and debugging by the community at large. For example, the Apache Web server is an open-source application that survived four and half years without a serious vulnerability—an almost unrivaled feat in the field of computer security.[130, 131] Open-source solutions can provide code that is provably secure before deployment. Proprietary solutions rely on an impressive security track record or recommendations from a small panel of experts to vouch for their security.

The primary limitation of security in open-source applications is that open-source software is often distributed without standard default security settings, which can increase the likelihood that security will be compromised due to human error, such as inexperience or negligence. For example, several Linux distributions enable many network services by default, exposing the computer to external attacks. Such services require significant customization and modification to prevent skilled attackers from compromising the system. Proprietary systems, on the other hand, typically are installed with an appropriate security configuration by default. Unlike most UNIX-based distributions, the open-source OpenBSD operating system claims to install fully secured against external attacks by default. As any user will soon realize, however, significant configuration is required to enable all but the most basic of communication services.

It is important to note that proprietary systems can be as secure as open-source systems, despite opposition from the open-source community. Though each method offers relative merits and pitfalls, both require attention to security and timely releases of patches to fix any security flaws that are discovered.

Self Review

1. Why might a software development company be reluctant to admit security flaws?
2. How do open-source cryptography software solutions address the fact that the technique they use to generate keys is made public?

Ans: **1)** Acknowledgement of security flaws can damage a company's reputation. **2)** Such software must use a large set of decryption keys to prevent malicious third party brute-force attacks that attempt to compromise security by generating all possible decryption keys.

19.13 Case Study: UNIX Systems Security

UNIX systems are designed to encourage user interaction, which can make them more difficult to secure.[132, 133, 134, 135, 136, 137, 138] UNIX systems are intended to be open systems; their specifications and source code are widely available.

The UNIX password file is encrypted. When a user enters a password, it is encrypted and compared to the encrypted password file. Thus, passwords are unrecoverable even by the system administrator. UNIX systems use salting when encrypting passwords.[139] The salting is a two-character string randomly selected via a function of the time and the process ID. Twelve bits of the salting then modify the encryption algorithm. Thus, users who choose the same password (by coincidence or intentionally) will have different encrypted passwords (with high likelihood). Some installations modify the password program to prevent users from choosing weak passwords.

The password file must be readable by any user because it contains other crucial information (i.e., usernames, user IDs, and the like) that is required by many UNIX tools. For example, because directories employ user IDs to record file ownership, *ls* (the tool that lists directory contents and file ownership) needs to read the password file to determine usernames from user IDs. If crackers obtain the password file, they could potentially break the password encryption. To address this issue, UNIX protects the password file from crackers by storing information other than the encrypted passwords in the normal password file and storing the encrypted passwords in a **shadow password file** that can be accessed only by users with root privileges.[140]

With the UNIX *setuid* permission feature, a program may be executed by one user using the privileges of another user. This powerful feature has security flaws, particularly when the resulting privilege is that of the "superuser" (who has access to all files in a UNIX system).[141, 142] For example, if a regular user is able to execute a shell belonging to the superuser, and for which the *setuid* bit has been set, then the regular user essentially becomes the superuser.[143] Clearly, *setuid* should be employed carefully. Users, including those with superuser privileges, should periodically examine their directories to confirm the presence of *setuid* files and detect any that should not be *setuid*.

A relatively simple means of compromising security in UNIX systems (and other operating systems) is to install a program that prints out the login prompt, copies what the user then types, fakes an invalid login and lets the user try again. The user has unwittingly given away his or her password! One defense is that if you are confident you typed the password correctly the first time, you should log into a different terminal and choose a new password immediately.[144]

UNIX systems include the *crypt* command, which allows a user to enter a key and plaintext; ciphertext is output. The transformation can be reversed trivially with the same key. One problem with this is that users tend to use the same key repeatedly; once the key is discovered, all other files encrypted with this key can be read. Users sometimes forget to delete their plaintext files after producing encrypted versions. This makes discovering the key much easier.

Often, too many people are given superuser privileges. Restricting superuser privileges can reduce the risk of attackers gaining control of a system due to errors made by inexperienced users. UNIX systems provide a substitute user identity (*su*) command to enable users to execute shells with a different user's credentials. All *su* activity should be logged; this command lets any user who types a correct password of another user assume that user's identity, possibly even acquiring superuser privileges.

A popular Trojan horse technique is to install a fake *su* program, which obtains the user's password, e-mails it to the attacker and restores the regular *su* program.[145] Never allow others to have write permission for your files, especially for your directories; if you do, you're inviting someone to install a Trojan horse.

UNIX systems contain a feature called **password aging**, in which the administrator determines how long passwords are valid; when a password expires, the user receives a message and is asked to enter a new password.[146, 147] There are several problems with this feature:

1. Users often supply easy-to-crack passwords.

2. The system often prevents a user from resetting to the old (or any other) password for a week, so the user can not strengthen a weak password.

3. Users often switch between only two passwords.

Passwords should be changed frequently. A user can keep track of all login dates and times to determine whether an unauthorized user has logged in (which means that his or her password has been learned). Logs of unsuccessful login attempts often store passwords, because users sometimes accidentally type their password when they mean to type their username.

Some systems disable accounts after a small number of unsuccessful login attempts. This is a defense against the intruder who tries all possible passwords. An intruder who has penetrated the system can use this feature to disable the account or accounts of users, including the system administrator, who might attempt to detect the intrusion.[148]

The attacker who temporarily gains superuser privileges can install a trap-door program with undocumented features. For example, someone with access to source code could rewrite the login program to accept a particular login name and grant this user superuser privileges without even typing a password.[149]

It is possible for individual users to "grab" the system, thus preventing other users from gaining access. A user could accomplish this by spawning thousands of processes, each of which opens hundreds of files, thus filling all the slots in the open-file table.[150] Installations can guard against this by setting reasonable limits on the number of processes a parent can spawn and the number of files that a process can open at once, but this in turn could hinder legitimate users who need the additional resources.

Self Review

1. Why should the *setuid* feature be used with caution?
2. Discuss how UNIX systems protect against unauthorized logins and how attackers can circumvent and exploit these mechanisms.

Ans: **1)** When a user executes the program, the user's individual ID or group ID or both are changed to that of the program's owner only while the program executes. If a regular user is able to execute a shell belonging to the superuser, and for which the *setuid* bit has been set, then the regular user essentially becomes the superuser. **2)** To protect against unauthorized logins, UNIX systems use password aging to force users to change passwords frequently, track user logins and disable accounts after a small number of unsuccessful login attempts. Attackers can obtain user passwords using Trojan horses, exploiting the *su* command and *setuid* feature and disabling an account (e.g., the system administrator's account) to prevent that user from responding to an intrusion.

Web Resources

www.nsa.gov/selinux/index.html
Lists documents and resources for Security-Enhanced Linux.

www.microsoft.com/windowsxp/security
Provides links for maintaining security in Windows XP systems.

www.sun.com/software/solaris/trustedsolaris/index.html
Provides information about the trusted Solaris operating environment.

www.computerworld.com/securitytopics/security/story/0,10801,69976,00.html
Discusses two security flaws in Windows NT and 2000 and how they were fixed.

people.freebsd.org/~jkb/howto.html
Discusses how to improve FreeBSD system security.

www.deter.com/unix
Lists links for UNIX-related security papers.

www.alw.nih.gov/Security/Docs/network-security.html
Provides an architectural overview of UNIX network security.

www.newsfactor.com/perl/story/7907.html
Compares Linux and Windows security.

itmanagement.earthweb.com/secu/article.php/641211
Discusses the future of operating systems security.

www-106.ibm.com/developerworks/security/library/1-sec/index.html?dwzone=security

Provides links to Linux security issues and how to address these issues.

www.securemac.com/

Provides security news for Apple systems.

www.linuxjournal.com/article.php?sid=1204

Describes how to create a Linux firewall using the TIS Firewall Toolkit.

www.rsasecurity.com

Homepage of RSA security.

www.informit.com/isapi/guide~security/seq_id~13/guide/content.asp

Discusses operating system security overview, operating system security weakness.

www.ftponline.com/wss/

Homepage of the Windows Server System magazine, which contains various security articles.

www.networkcomputing.com/1202/1202f1d1.html

Provides a tutorial on wireless security.

www.cnn.com/SPECIALS/2003/wireless/interactive/wireless101/index.html

Provides a list of wireless security technologies for computers, PDAs, cell phones and other wireless devices.

www.securitysearch.com

This is a comprehensive resource for computer security, with thousands of links to products, security companies, tools and more. The site also offers a free weekly newsletter with information about vulnerabilities.

www.w3.org/Security/Overview.html

The *W3C Security Resources* site has FAQs, information about W3C security and e-commerce initiatives and links to other security-related Web sites.

www.rsasecurity.com/rsalabs/faq

This site is an excellent set of FAQs about cryptography from RSA Laboratories, one of the leading makers of public-key cryptosystems.

www.authentidate.com

Authentidate provides timestamping to verify the security of a file.

www.itaa.org/infosec

The Information Technology Association of America (ITAA) InfoSec site has information about the latest U.S. government legislation related to information security.

www.securitystats.com

This computer security site provides statistics on viruses, Web defacements and security spending.

www.ieee-security.org/cipher.html

Cipher is an electronic newsletter on security and privacy from the Institute of Electrical and Electronics Engineers (IEEE). You can view current and past issues online.

www.scmagazine.com

SC Magazine has news, product reviews and a conference schedule for security events.

www.cdt.org/crypto

Visit the Center for Democracy and Technology for U.S. cryptography legislation and policy news.

csrc.nist.gov/encryption/aes

The official site for the AES includes press releases and a discussion forum.

www.pkiforum.org/

The PKI Forum promotes the use of the Public Key Infrastructure.

www.verisign.com

VeriSign creates digital IDs for individuals, small businesses and large corporations. Check out its Web site for product information, news and downloads.

www.thawte.com

Thawte Digital Certificate Services offers SSL, developer and personal certificates.

www.belsign.be/

Belsign is the European authority for digital certificates.

www.interhack.net/pubs/fwfaq

This site provides an extensive list of FAQs on firewalls.

www.indentix.com

Identix specializes in fingerprinting systems for law enforcement, access control and network security. Using its fingerprint scanners, you can log on to your system, encrypt and decrypt files and lock applications.

www.keytronic.com

Key Tronic manufactures keyboards with fingerprint recognition systems.

www.ietf.org/html.charters/ipsec-charter.html

The IPSec Working Group of the Internet Engineering Task Force (IETF) is a resource for technical information related to the IPSec protocol.

www.vpnc.org

The Virtual Private Network Consortium has VPN standards, white papers, definitions and archives. VPNC also offers compatibility testing with current VPN standards.

www.outguess.org

Outguess is a freely available steganographic tool.

www.weca.net/OpenSection/index.asp

Wi-Fi alliance provides information about Wi-Fi and resources for setting up and securing a Wi-Fi network.

Summary

Computer security addresses the issue of preventing unauthorized access to resources and information maintained by computers. Computer security commonly encompasses guaranteeing the privacy and integrity of sensitive data, restricting the use of computer resources and providing resilience against malicious attempts to incapacitate the system. Protection entails mechanisms that shield resources such as hardware and operating system services from attack.

Cryptography focuses on encoding and decoding data so that it can be interpreted only by the intended recipients. Data is transformed by means of a cipher or cryptosystem. Modern cryptosystems rely on algorithms that operate on the individual bits or blocks (a group of bits) of data, rather than letters of the alphabet. Encryption and decryption keys are binary strings of a given length.

Symmetric cryptography, also known as secret-key cryptography, uses the same secret key to encrypt and decrypt a message. The sender encrypts a message using the secret key, then sends the encrypted message to the intended recipient, who decrypts the message using the same secret key. A limitation of secret-key cryptography is that before two parties can communicate securely, they must find a secure way to exchange the secret key.

Public-key cryptography solves the problem of securely exchanging symmetric keys. Public-key cryptography is asymmetric in that it employs two inversely related keys: a public key and a private key. The private key is kept secret by its owner, while the public key is freely distributed. If the public key encrypts a message, only the corresponding private key can decrypt it.

The most common authentication scheme is simple password protection. The user chooses a password, memorizes it and presents it to the system to gain admission to a resource or system. Password protection introduces several weaknesses to a secure system. Users tend to choose passwords that are easy to remember, such as the name of a spouse or pet. Someone who has obtained personal information about the user might try to log in several times using passwords that are characteristic of the user; several repeated attempts might result in a security breach.

Biometrics uses unique personal information—such as fingerprints, eyeball iris scans or face scans—to identify a user. A smart card is often designed to resemble a credit card and can serve many different functions, from authentication to data storage. The most popular smart cards are memory cards and microprocessor cards.

Single sign-on systems simplify the authentication process by allowing the user to log in once using a single password. Users authenticated via a single sign-on system can then access multiple applications across multiple computers. It is important to secure single sign-on passwords, because if a password becomes available to hackers, all applications protected by that password can be accessed and attacked. Single sign-on systems are available in forms of workstation login scripts, authentication server scripts and token-based authentication.

The key to operating system security is to control access to system resources. The most common access rights are read, write and execute. Techniques that an operating system employ to manage access rights include the access control matrices, access control lists and capability lists.

There are several types of security attacks against computer systems, including cryptanalytic attacks, viruses and worms (such as the ILOVEYOU virus and Sapphire/Slammer worm), denial-of-service attacks (such as a domain name system (DNS) attack), software exploitation (such as buffer overflow) and system penetration (such as Web defacing).

Several common security solutions include firewalls (including packet-filtering firewall and application-level gateways), intrusion detection systems (including host-based intrusion detection and network-based intrusion detection), antivirus software using signature scanning and heuristic scanning, security patches (such as hotfixes) and secure file systems (such as the Encrypting File System).

The five fundamental requirements for a successful, secure transaction are privacy, integrity, authentication, authorization and nonrepudiation. The privacy issue deals with ensuring that the information transmitted over the Internet has not been viewed by a third party. The integrity issue deals with ensuring that the information sent or received has not been altered. The authentication issue deals with verifying the identities of the sender and receiver. The authorization issue deals with managing access to protected resources on the basis of user credentials. The nonrepudiation issue deals with ensuring that the network will operate continuously.

Public-key algorithms are most often employed to exchange secret keys securely. The process by which two parties can exchange keys over an unsecure medium is called a key agreement protocol. Common key agreement protocols are the digital envelopes and digital signatures (using the SHA-1 and MD5 hash algorithms).

A limitation of public-key cryptography is that multiple users might share the same set of keys, making it difficult to establish each party's identity. Public Key Infrastructure (PKI) provides a solution by integrating public-key cryptography with digital certificates and certificate authorities to authenticate parties in a transaction.

The Secure Sockets Layer (SSL) protocol is a nonproprietary protocol that secures communication between two computers on the Internet. SSL implements public-key cryptography using the RSA algorithm and digital certificates to authenticate the server in a transaction and to protect private information as it passes over the Internet. SSL transactions do not require client authentication; many servers consider a valid credit card number to be sufficient for authentication in secure purchases.

Virtual Private Networks (VPNs) provide secure communications over public connections. Encryption enables VPNs to provide the same services and security as private networks. A VPN is created by establishing a secure communication channel over the Internet. IPSec (Internet Protocol Security), which uses public-key and symmetric-key cryptography to ensure data integrity, authentication and confidentiality, is commonly used to implement a secure tunnel.

Wireless devices have limited bandwidth and processing power, high latency and unstable connections, so establishing secure wireless communication can be challenging. The Wired Equivalent Privacy (WEP) protocol protects wireless communication by encrypting transmitted data and preventing unauthorized access to the wireless network. WEP has several drawbacks, which make it to be too weak for many environments. Wi-Fi Protected Access (WPA) addresses these issues by providing improved data encryption and by enabling user authentication, a feature not supported by WEP.

A primary advantage to open-source security applications is interoperability—open-source applications tend to implement standards and protocols that many developers include in their products. Another advantage to open-source security is that an application's source code is available for extensive testing and debugging by the community at large. The primary weaknesses of proprietary security are nondisclosure and the fact that the number of collaborative users that can search for security flaws and contribute to the overall security of the application is limited. Proprietary systems, however, can be equally as secure as open-source systems.

The UNIX password file is stored in encrypted form. When a user enters a password, it is encrypted and compared to the password file. Thus, passwords are unrecoverable even by the system administrator.

With the UNIX *setuid* permission feature, a program may be executed by one user using the privileges of another user. This powerful feature has security flaws, particularly when the resulting privilege is that of the "superuser" (who has access to all files in a UNIX system).

Key Terms

3DES—See Triple DES.

Advanced Encryption Standard (AES)—Standard for symmetric encryption that uses Rijndael as the encryption method. AES has replaced the Data Encryption Standard (DES) because AES provides enhanced security.

access control list—List that stores one entry for each access right granted to a subject for an object. An access control list consumes less space than an access control matrix.

access control matrix—Matrix that lists system's subjects in the rows and the objects to which they require access in the columns. Each cell in the matrix specifies the actions that a subject (defined by the row) can perform on an object (defined by the column). Access control matrices typically are not implemented because they are sparsely populated.

access right—Defines how various subjects can access various objects. Subjects may be users, processes, programs or other entities. Objects are information-holding entities; they may be physical objects that correspond to disks, processors or main memory or abstract objects that correspond to data structures, processes or services. Subjects are also considered to be objects of the system; one subject may have rights to access another.

air gap technology—Network security solution that complements a firewall. It secures private data from external users accessing the internal network.

antivirus software—Program that attempts to identify, remove and otherwise protect a system from viruses.

application-level gateway—Hardware or software that protects the network against the data contained in packets. If the message contains a virus, the gateway can block it from being sent to the intended receiver.

authentication (secure transaction)—One of the five fundamental requirements for a successful, secure transaction.

Authentication deals with how the sender and receiver of a message verify their identities to each other.

authentication header (AH) (IPSec)—Information that verifies the identity of a packet's sender and proves that a packet's data was not modified in transit.

authentication server scripts—Single sign-on implementation that authenticates users via a central server, which establishes connections between the user and the applications the user wishes to access.

authorization (secure transaction)—One of the five fundamental requirements for a successful, secure transaction. Authorization deals with how to manage access to protected resources on the basis of user credentials.

back-door program—Resident virus that allows an attacker complete, undetected access to the victim's computer resources.

biometrics—Technique that uses an individual's physical characteristics, such as fingerprints, eyeball iris scans or face scans, to identify the user.

block cipher—Encryption technique that divides a message into fixed-size groups of bits to which an encryption algorithm is applied.

boot sector virus—Virus that infects the boot sector of the computer's hard disk, allowing it to load with the operating system and take control of the system.

brute-force cracking—Technique to compromise a system simply by attempting all possible passwords or by using every possible decryption key to decrypt a message.

buffer overflow—Attack that sends input that is larger than the space allocated for it. If the input is properly coded and the system's stack is executable, buffer overflows can enable an attacker to execute malicious code.

capability (access control mechanism)—Token that grants a subject privileges for an object. It is analogous to a ticket the bearer may use to gain access to a sporting event.

certificate authority (CA)—Financial institution or other trusted third party, such as VeriSign, that issues digital certificates.

certificate authority hierarchy—Chain of certificate authorities, beginning with the root certificate authority, that authenticates certificates and CAs.

certificate repositories—Locations where digital certificates are stored.

certificate revocation list (CRL)—List of cancelled and revoked certificates. A certificate is cancelled/revoked if a private key is compromised before its expiration date.

cipher—Mathematical algorithm for encrypting messages. Also called cryptosystem.

ciphertext—Encrypted data.

cracker—Malicious individual that is usually interested in breaking into a system to disable services or steal data.

credential—Combination of user identity (e.g., username) and proof of identify (e.g., password).

cryptanalytic attack—Technique that attempts to decrypt ciphertext without possession of the decryption key. The most common such attacks are those in which the encryption algorithm is analyzed to find relations between bits of the encryption key and bits of the ciphertext.

cryptography—Study of encoding and decoding data so that it can be interpreted only by the intended recipients.

cryptosystem—Mathematical algorithm for encrypting messages. Also called a cipher.

Data Encryption Standard (DES)—Symmetric encryption algorithm that use a 56-bit key and encrypts data in 64-bit blocks. For many years, DES was the encryption standard set by the U.S. government and the American National Standards Institute (ANSI). However, due to advances in computing power, DES is no longer considered secure—in the late 1990s, specialized DES cracker machines were built that recovered DES keys after a period of several hours.

denial-of-service (DoS) attack—Attack that prevents a system from properly servicing legitimate requests. In many DoS attacks, unauthorized traffic saturates a network's resources, restricting access for legitimate users. Typically, the attack is performed by flooding servers with data packets.

digital certificate—Digital document that identifies a user or organization and is issued by a certificate authority. A digital certificate includes the name of the subject (the organization or individual being certified), the subject's public key, a serial number (to uniquely identify the certificate), an expiration date, the signature of the trusted certificate authority and any other relevant information.

digital envelope—Technique that protects message privacy by sending a package including a message encrypted using a secret key and the secret key encrypted using public-key encryption.

digital notary service—See time-stamping agency.

digital signature—Electronic equivalent of a written signature. To create a digital signature, a sender first applies a hash function to the original plaintext message. Next, the sender uses the sender's private key to encrypt the message digest (the hash value). This step creates a digital signature and validates the sender's identity, because only the owner of that private key could encrypt the message.

Digital Signature Algorithm (DSA)—U.S. government's digital authentication standard.

digital watermark—Popular application of steganography that hides information in unused (or rarely used) portions of a file.

discretionary access control (DAC)—Access control model in which the creator of an object controls the permissions for that object.

distributed denial-of-service attack—Attack that prevents a system from servicing requests properly by initiating packet flooding from separate computers sending traffic in concert.

DNS (domain name system) attack—Attack that modifies the address to which network traffic for a particular Web site is sent. Such attacks can be used to redirect users of a particular Web site to another, potentially malicious Web site.

encapsulating security payload (ESP) (IPSec)—Message data encrypted using symmetric-key ciphers to protect the data from eavesdroppers while the IP packet is transmitted across public communication lines.

Encrypting File System (EFS)—NTFS feature that uses cryptography to protect files and folders in Windows XP Professional and Windows 2000. EFS uses secret-key and public-key encryption to secure files. Each user is assigned a key pair and certificate that are used to ensure that only the user that encrypted the files can access them.

firewall—Software or hardware that protects a local area network from packets sent by malicious users from an external network.

hacker—Experienced programmer who often program as much for personal enjoyment as for the functionality of the application. This term is often used when the term cracker is more appropriate.

heuristic scanning—Antivirus technique that detects viruses by their program behavior.

host-based intrusion detection—IDS that monitors system and application log files.

integrity (secure transaction)—One of the five fundamental requirements for a successful, secure transaction. Integrity deals with how to ensure that the information you send or receive has not been compromised or altered.

Internet Key Exchange (IKE) (IPSec)—Key-exchange protocol used in IPSec to perform key management, which allows secure key exchange.

Internet Protocol Security (IPSec)—Transport-layer security protocol that provides data privacy, integrity and authentication.

intrusion detection system (IDS)—Application that monitors networks and application log files, which record information about system behavior, such as the time at which operating services are requested and the name of the process that requests it.

IP spoofing—Attack in which an attacker simulates the IP address of an authorized user or host to obtain unauthorized access to resources.

Kerberos—Freely available, open-source authentication and access control protocol developed at MIT that provides protection against internal security attacks. It employs secret-key cryptography to authenticate users in a network and to maintain the integrity and privacy of network communications.

key—Input to a cipher to encrypt data; keys are represented by a string of digits.

key agreement protocol—Rules that govern key exchange between two parties over an unsecure medium.

key distribution center (KDC)—Central authority that shares a different secret key with every user in the network.

key generation—Creation of encryption keys.

layered biometric verification (LBV)—Authentication technique that uses multiple measurements of human features (such as face, finger and voice prints) to verify a user's identity.

log file—Records information about system behavior, such as the time at which operating services are requested and the name of the process that requests them.

logic bomb—Virus that executes its code when a specified condition is met.

Lucifer algorithm—Encryption algorithm created by Horst Feistel of IBM, which was chosen as the DES by the United States government and the National Security Agency (NSA) in the 1970s.

Macintosh—Apple Computer's PC line that introduced the GUI and mouse to mainstream computer users.

Mac OS—Line of operating systems for Apple Macintosh computers first introduced in 1997.

mandatory access control (MAC)—Access control model in which policies predefine a central permission scheme by which all subjects and objects are controlled.

MD5 Message Digest Algorithm—Hash algorithm developed by Professor Ronald L. Rivest at MIT that is widely used to implement digital signatures.

message digest—Hash value produced by algorithms such as SHA-1 and MD5 when applied to a message.

message integrity—Property indicating whether message has been altered in transmission.

National Institute of Standards and Technology (NIST)—Organization that sets cryptographic (and other) standards for the U.S. government.

network-based intrusion detection—IDS that monitors traffic on a network for any unusual patterns that might indicate DoS attacks or attempted entry into a network by an unauthorized user.

nonrepudiation—Issue that deals with how to prove that a message was sent or received.

Online Certificate Status Protocol (OCSP)—Protocol that validates certificates in real time.

OpenBSD—BSD UNIX system whose primary goal is security.

Operationally Critical Threat, Asset and Vulnerability Evaluation (OCTAVE) method—Technique for evaluating security threats of a system developed at the Software Engineering Institute at Carnegie Mellon University.

Orange Book—Document published by U.S. Department of Defence (DoD) to establish guidelines for evaluating the security features of operating systems.

packet-filtering firewall—Hardware or software that examines all data sent from outside its LAN and rejects data packets based on predefined rules, such as reject packets that have local network addresses or reject packets from certain addresses or ports.

password aging—Technique that attempts to improve security by requiring users to change their passwords periodically.

password protection—Authentication technique that relies on a user's presenting a username and corresponding password to gain access to a resource or system.

password salting—Technique that inserts characters at various positions in the password before encryption to reduce vulnerability to brute-force attacks.

payload—Code inside a logic bomb that is executed when a specified condition is met.

plaintext—Unencrypted data.

Platform for Privacy Preferences (P3P)—Protects the privacy of information submitted to single sign-on and other applications by allowing users to control the personal information that sites collect.

policy creation authority—Organization that sets policies for obtaining digital certificates.

polymorphic virus—Virus that attempts to evade known virus lists by modifying its code (e.g., via encryption, substitution, insertion, and the like) as it spreads.

Pretty Good Privacy (PGP)—Public-key encryption system primarily used to encrypt e-mail messages and files, designed in 1991 by Phillip Zimmermann.

privacy (secure transaction)—One of the five fundamental requirements for a successful, secure transaction. Privacy deals with how to ensure that the information transmitted over the Internet has not been captured or passed to a third party without user knowledge.

private key—Key in public-key cryptography that should be known only by its owner. If its corresponding public key encrypts a message, only the private key should be able to decrypt it.

privilege (access right)—The manner in which a subject can access an object.

protection—Mechanism that prevents unauthorized use of resources such as hardware and operating system services.

protection domain—Collection of access rights. Each access right in a protection domain is represented as an ordered pair with fields for the object name and applicable privileges.

public key—Key in public cryptography that is available to all users that wish to communicate with its owner. If the public key encrypts a message, only the corresponding private key can decrypt it.

public-key cryptography—Asymmetric cryptography technique that employs two inversely related keys: a public key and a private key. To transmit a message securely, the sender uses the receiver's public key to encrypt the message. The receiver then decrypts the message using his or her unique private key.

Public Key Infrastructure (PKI)—Technique that integrates public-key cryptography with digital certificates and certificate authorities to authenticate parties in a transaction.

resident virus—Virus that, once loaded into memory, executes until the computer is powered down.

restricted algorithm—Algorithm that provides security by relying on the sender and receiver to use the same encryption algorithm and maintain its secrecy.

random-scanning algorithm—Algorithm that uses pseudorandom numbers to generate a broad distribution of IP addresses.

real-time scanner—Software that resides in memory and actively prevents viruses.

root key—Used by the Internet Policy Registration Authority (IPRA) to sign certificates exclusively for policy creation authorities.

Rijndael—Block cipher developed by Dr. Joan Daemen and Dr. Vincent Rijmen of Belgium. The algorithm can be implemented on a variety of processors.

role (RBAC)—Represents a set of tasks assigned to a member of an organization. Each role is assigned a set of privileges, which define the objects that users in each role can access.

role-based access control (RBAC)—Access control model in which users are assigned roles.

RSA—Popular public-key algorithm, which was developed in 1977 by MIT professors Ron Rivest, Adi Shamir and Leonard Adleman.

secret-key cryptography—Technique that performs encryption and decryption using the same secret key to encrypt and decrypt a message. The sender encrypts a message using the secret key, then sends the encrypted message to the intended recipient, who decrypts the message using the same secret key. Also called symmetric cryptography.

Secure Hash Algorithm (SHA-1)—Popular hash function used to create digital signatures; developed by NIST.

Secure Sockets Layer (SSL)—Nonproprietary protocol developed by Netscape Communications that secures communication between two computers on the Internet.

security mechanism—Method by which the system implements its security policy. In many systems, the policy changes over time, but the mechanism remains unchanged.

security model—Entity that defines a system's subjects, objects and privileges.

security patch—Code that addresses a security flaw.

security policy—Rules that govern access to system resources.

service ticket (Kerberos)—Ticket that authorizes the client's access to specific network services.

session key—Secret key that is used for the duration of a transaction (e.g., a customer's buying merchandise from an online store).

shadow password file (UNIX)—Protects the password file from crackers by storing information other than the encrypted passwords in the normal password file and storing the encrypted passwords in the shadow password file that can be accessed only by users with root privileges.

signature-scanning virus detection—Antivirus technique that relies on knowledge of virus code.

single sign-on—Simplifies the authentication process by allowing the user to log in once, using a single password.

smart card—Credit card size data store that serves many functions, including authentication and data storage.

steganography—Technique that hides information within other information, derived from Latin roots meaning "covered writing."

substitution cipher—Encryption technique whereby every occurrence of a given letter is replaced by a different letter. For example, if every "a" were replaced by a "b," every "b" by a "c," and so on the word "security" would encrypt to "tfdvsjuz."

static analysis—Intrusion detection method which attempts to detect when applications have been corrupted by a hacker.

system penetration—Successful breach of computer security by an unauthorized external user.

symmetric cryptography—See secret-key cryptography.

Ticket Granting Service (TGS) (Kerberos)—Server that authenticates client's rights to access specific network services.

Ticket-Granting Ticket (TGT) (Kerberos)—Ticket returned by Kerberos's authentication server. It is encrypted with the client's secret key that is shared with the authentication server. The client sends the decrypted TGT to the Ticket Granting Service to request a service ticket.

time bomb—Virus that is activated when the clock on the computer matches a certain time or date.

timestamping (nonrepudiation)—Technique that binds a time and date to a digital document, which helps solve the problem of nonrepudiation.

time-stamping agency—Organization that digitally time stamps a document that has been digitally signed.

token (in token-based authentication)—Unique identifier for authentication.

token-based authentication—Authentication technique that issues a token unique to each session, enabling users to access specific applications.

transient virus—Virus that attaches itself to a particular computer program. The virus is activated when the program is run and deactivated when the program is terminated.

transposition cipher—Encryption technique whereby the ordering of the letters is shifted. For example, if every other letter, starting with "s," in the word "security" creates the first word in the ciphertext and the remaining letters create the second word in the ciphertext, the word "security" would encrypt to "scrt euiy."

Triple DES—Variant of DES that can be thought of as three DES systems in series, each with a different secret key that operates on a block. Also called 3DES.

Trojan horse—Malicious program that hides within a trusted program or simulates the identity of a legitimate program or feature, while actually causing damage to the computer or network when the program is executed.

two-factor authentication—Authentication technique that employs two means to authenticate the user, such as biometrics or a smart card used in combination with a password.

variant—Virus whose code has been modified from its original form, yet still retains its malicious payload.

Virtual Private Network (VPN)—Technique that securely connects remote users to a private network using public communication lines. VPNs are often implemented using IPSec.

virus—Executable code (often sent as an attachment to an e-mail message or hidden in files such as audio clips, video clips and games) that attaches to or overwrites other files to replicate itself, often harming the system on which it resides.

virus signature—Segment of code that does not vary between virus generations.

Web defacing—Attack that maliciously modifies an organization's Web site.

Wi-Fi Protected Access (WPA)—Wireless security protocol intended to replace WEP by providing improved data encryption and by enabling user authentication.

Wired Equivalent Privacy (WEP)—Wireless security protocol that encrypts transmitted data and prevents unauthorized access to the wireless network.

workstation login scripts—Simple form of single sign-on in which users log in at their workstations, then choose applications from a menu.

worm—Executable code that spreads and infects files over a network. Worms rarely require any user action to propagate, nor do they need to be attached to another program or file to spread.

Exercises

19.1 Why is a precise statement of security requirements critical to the determination of whether a given system is secure?

19.2 Sharing and protection are conflicting goals. Give three significant examples of sharing supported by operating systems. For each, explain what protection mechanisms are necessary to control the sharing.

19.3 Give several reasons why simple password protection is the most common authentication scheme in use today. Discuss the weaknesses inherent in password protection schemes.

19.4 An operating systems security expert has proposed the following economical way to implement a reasonable level of security: Simply tell everyone who works at an installation that the operating system contains the latest and greatest in security mechanisms. Do not actually build the mechanisms, the expert says, just tell everyone that the mechanisms are in place. Who might such a scheme deter from attempting a security violation? Who would not likely be deterred? Discuss the advantages and disadvantages of the scheme. In what types of installations might this scheme be useful? Suggest a simple modification to the scheme that would make it far more effective, yet still far more economical than a comprehensive security program.

19.5 What is the principle of least privilege? Give several reasons why it makes sense. Why is it necessary to keep protection domains small to effect the least-privilege approach to security? Why are capabilities particularly useful in achieving small protection domains?

19.6 How does a capabilities list differ from an access control list?

19.7 Why is an understanding of cryptography important to operating systems designers? List several areas within operating systems in which the use of cryptography would greatly improve security. Why might a designer choose not to include encryption in all facets of the operating system?

19.8 Why is it desirable to incorporate certain operating systems security functions directly into hardware? Why is it useful to microprogram certain security functions?

19.9 Give brief definitions of each of the following terms.

    a. cryptography

    b. Data Encryption Standard (DES)

    c. privacy problem

    d. integrity problem

    e. problem of nonrepudiation

    f. plaintext

    g. ciphertext

    h. unsecure channel

    i. eavesdropper

    j. cryptanalysis

19.10 Give brief definitions of each of the following terms.

    a. public-key system

    b. public key

    c. private key

    d. digital signature

19.11 Why are denial-of-service attacks of such great concern to operating systems designers? List a few types of denial-of-service attacks. Why is it difficult to detect a distributed denial-of-service attack on a server?

19.12 What is a log file? What information might an operating system deposit in a log file? How does a log act as a deterrent to those who would commit a security violation?

19.13 Explain how public-key cryptography systems provide an effective means of implementing digital signatures.

Suggested Projects

19.18 At the moment, it appears that our computing systems are easy targets for penetration. Enumerate the kinds of weaknesses that are prevalent in today's systems. Suggest how to correct these weaknesses.

19.19 Design a penetration study for a large computer system with which you are familiar. Adhere to the following:

    a. Perform the study only with the full cooperation of the computer center administrators and personnel.

    b. Arrange to have ready access to all available system documentation and software source listings.

    c. Agree that any flaws you discover will not be made public until they have been corrected.

    d. Prepare a detailed report summarizing your findings and suggesting how to correct the flaws.

    e. Your primary goals are to achieve

        i. total system penetration

        ii. denial of access to legitimate system users

        iii. the crashing of the system.

Suggested Simulation

19.26 Create an application to encode and decode secret messages within bitmap pictures. When encoding, modify the least significant bit in each byte to store information about the mes-

19.14 Explain how cryptography is useful in each of the following.

    a. protecting a system's master list of passwords

    b. protecting stored files

    c. protecting vulnerable transmissions in computer networks

19.15 The UNIX systems administrator cannot determine the password of a user who has lost his or her password. Why? How can that user regain access to the computer?

19.16 How could a UNIX system user seize control of a system, thus locking out all other users? What defense may be employed against this technique?

19.17 Why do antivirus software companies and high-security installations hire convicted hackers?

    f. You may access the system only through conventional mechanisms available to nonprivileged users.

    g. Your attacks must be software and/or firmware oriented.

19.20 Prepare a research paper on the RSA algorithm. What mathematical principles aid the RSA algorithm in being difficult to crack?

19.21 Prepare a research paper on how antivirus software provides security while being minimally invasive.

19.22 Prepare a research paper on the implementation of PGP. Explain why the name "Pretty Good Privacy" is appropriate.

19.23 Prepare a research paper on the most costly viruses and worms. How did these worms or viruses spread? What flaws did they exploit?

19.24 Prepare a research paper on how IP spoofing is performed.

19.25 Discuss the ethical and legal issues surrounding the practice of hacking.

sage. To decode, just reassemble the message using the least significant bit of each byte.

Recommended Reading

Computer security has been researched extensively in academic and commercial environments. Most topics in the field are constantly evolving. Although the problems of cryptography and access control are well characterized, techniques that address security threats (such as software exploitation and network attacks) must continually evolve as new hardware, software and protocols with different vulnerabilities emerge.

A survey of cryptography and the related problem of computability is provided in Jörg Rothe's "Some Facets of Complexity Theory and Cryptography: A Five-Lecture Tutorial."[151] The problem of access control is actively discussed in the literature; a survey of access control can be found in Sandhu and Samarati's "Access Control: Principles and Practice."[152]

Due to the importance of security to e-business and the Internet revolution, a large number of security trade journals and publications have emerged since the 1990s. Commercial trade journals include *Information Security, SC (Secure Computing) Magazine* and *Access Control and Security Systems*. Academic security journals include the *Journal of Computer Security* and the *ACM Transactions on Information and System Security (TISSEC)*. Dieter Gollmann provides a thorough discussion of computer security theory.[153] The bibliography for this chapter is located on our Web site at `www.deitel.com/books/os3e/Bibliography.pdf`.

Works Cited

1. Gates, B., "Bill Gates: Trustworthy Computing," January 17, 2002, <`www.wired.com/news/business/0,1367,49826,00.html`>.

2. McFarland, M., "Ethical Issues of Computer Use," Syllabus for course Mc690, Boston College, Chestnut Hill, MA, Spring 1989.

3. Parnas, D. L., "Software Aspects of Strategic Defense Systems," *Communications of the ACM*, Vol. 28, No. 12, December 1985, pp. 1326–1335.

4. "Cryptography—Caesar Cipher," <`http://www.trincoll.edu/depts/cpsc/cryptography/caesar.html`>.

5. "Methods of Transposition," <`http://home.ecn.ab.ca/~jsavard/crypto/pp0102.htm`>.

6. RSA Laboratories, "RSA Laboratories' Frequently Asked Questions About Today's Cryptography," Version 4.1, 2000, RSA Security Inc., <`www.rsasecurity.com/rsalabs/faq`>.

7. Cherowitzo, B., "Math 5410 Data Encryption Standard (DES)," February 6, 2002, <`www-math.cudenver.edu/~wcherowi/courses/m5410/m5410des.html`>.

8. Dworkin, M., "Advanced Encryption Standard (AES) Fact Sheet," March 5, 2001, <`csrc.nist.gov/CryptoToolkit/aes/round2/aesfact.html`>.

9. Rijmen, V., "The Rijndael Page," May 20, 2003, <`www.esat.kuleuven.ac.be/~rijmen/rijndael`>.

10. McNett, D., "RC5-64 HAS BEEN SOLVED!" September 27, 2002, <`www.distributed.net/pressroom/news-20020926.html`>.

11. RSA Laboratories, "RSA-Based Cryptographic Schemes," 2003, <`www.rsasecurity.com/rsalabs/rsa_algorithm`>.

12. Ytteborg, S. S., "Overview of PGP," <`www.pgpi.org/doc/overview`>.

13. RSA Security Inc., "RSA Security at a Glance," 2003, <`www.rsasecurity.com/company/corporate.html`>.

14. Rivest, R. L.; A. Shamir and L. Adleman, "A Method for Obtaining Digital Signatures and Public-Key Cryptosystems," *Communications of the ACM*, Vol. 21, No. 2, February 1978, pp. 120–126.

15. Bass, T. A., "Gene Genie," *Wired*, August 1995, <`www.thomasbass.com/work12.htm`>.

16. Krieger, D., and W. E. Miles, "Innerview: Leonard Adleman," *Networker*, Vol. 7, No. 1, September 1996, <`www.usc.edu/isd/publications/networker/96-97/Sep_Oct_96/innerview-adleman.html`>.

17. ACM, "ACM: A. M. Turing Award," April 14, 2003, <`www.acm.org/announcements/turing_2002.html`>.

18. RSA Security Inc., "The Authentication Scorecard," 2003, <`www.rsasecurity.com/products/authentication/whitepapers/ASC_WP_0403.pdf`>.

19. Lamport, L., "Password Authentication with Insecure Communication," *Communications of the ACM*, Vol. 24, No. 11, November 1981, pp. 770–772.

20. National Infrastructure Protection Center, "Password Protection 101," May 9, 2002, <`www.nipc.gov/publications/nipcpub/password.htm`>.

21. Deckmyn, D., "Companies Push New Approaches to Authentication," *Computerworld*, May 15, 2000, p. 6.

22. Keyware, "Keyware Launches Its New Biometric and Centralized Authentication Products," January 2001, <`hwww.keyware.com/press/press.asp?pid=44&menu=4`>.

23. Vijayan, J., "Biometrics Meet Wireless Internet," *Computerworld*, July 17, 2000, p. 14.

24. Smart Card Forum, "What's So Smart About Smart Cards?" 2003, <`www.gemplus.com/basics/download/smartcardforum.pdf`>.

25. Gaudin, S., "The Enemy Within," *Network World*, May 8, 2000, pp. 122–126.

26. Needham, R. M. and M. D. Schroeder, "Using Encryption for Authentication in Large Networks of Computers," *Communications of the ACM*, Vol. 21, No. 12, December 1978, pp.993-- 999.

27. Steiner, J.; C. Neuman and J. Schiller, "Kerberos: An authentication service for open network systems," *In Proceedings of the Winter 1988 USENIX*, February 1988, pp. 191–202.

28. Steiner, J.; C. Neuman and J. Schiller, "Kerberos: An authentication service for open network systems," *In Proceedings of the Winter 1988 USENIX*, February 1988, pp. 191–202.

29. Trickey, F., "Secure Single Sign-On: Fantasy or Reality," Computer Security Institute, 1997.

30. Musthaler, L., "The Holy Grail of Single Sign-On," *Network World*, January 28, 2002, p. 47.

31. Press Release, "Novell Takes the Market Leader in Single Sign-On and Makes It Better," <www.novell.com/news/press/archive/2003/09/pr03059.html>.

32. "Protection and Security," <http://cs.nmu.edu/~randy/Classes/CS426/protection_and_security.html>.

33. Lampson, B., "Protection," *ACM Operating Systems Review 8*, January 1, 1974, pp. 18–24.

34. Sandhu, R., and E. Coyne, "Role-Based Access Control Models," *IEEE Computer*, February 1996, p. 39.

35. Sandhu, R., and E. Coyne, "Role-Based Access Control Models," *IEEE Computer*, February 1996, p. 40.

36. "Handbook of Information Security Management: Access Control," <www.cccure.org/Documents/HISM/094-099.html>.

37. Chander, A.; D Dean; and J. C. Mitchell, "A State-Transition Model of Trust Management and Access Control," *IEEE Computer, in Proceedings of the 14th Computer Security Foundations Workshop (CSFW)*, June 2001, pp. 27–43.

38. Lampson, B., "Protection," *Proceedings of the Fifth Princeton Symposium on Information Sciences and Systems*, 1971, pp. 437–443.

39. Linden, T. A., "Operating System Structures to Support Security and Reliable Software," *ACM Computing Surveys (CSUR)*, Vol. 8, No. 6, December 1976.

40. Moore, D., et al., "The Spread of the Sapphire/Slammer Worm," *CAIDA*, February 3, 2003, <www.caida.org/outreach/papers/2003/sapphire/>.

41. "Securing B2B," *Global Technology Business*, July 2000, pp. 50–51.

42. Computer Security Institute, "Cyber Crime Bleeds U.S. Corporations, Survey Shows; Financial Losses from Attacks Climb for Third Year in a Row," April 7, 2002, <www.gocsi.com/press/20020407.html>.

43. Connolly, P., "IT Outlook Appears Gloomy," *InfoWorld*, November 16, 2001, <www.infoworld.com/articles/tc/xml/01/11/19/011119tcstate.xml>.

44. Bridis, T., "U.S. Archive of Hacker Attacks to Close Because It Is Too Busy," *The Wall Street Journal*, May 24, 2001, p. B10.

45. Andress, M., "Securing the Back End," *InfoWorld*, April 5, 2002, <www.infoworld.com/articles/ne/xml/02/04/08/020408neappdetective.xml>.

46. Marshland, R., "Hidden Cost of Technology," *Financial Times*, June 2, 2000, p. 5.

47. Spangler, T., "Home Is Where the Hack Is," *Inter@ctive Week*, April 10, 2000, pp. 28–34.

48. Whale Communications, "Air Gap Architecture," 2003, <www.whalecommunications.com/site/Whale/Corporate/Whale.asp?pi=264>.

49. Azim, O., and P. Kolwalkar, "Network Intrusion Monitoring," *Business Security Advisor*, March/April 2001, pp. 16–19, <advisor.com/doc/07390>.

50. Wagner, D., and D. Dean, "Intrusion Detection via Static Analysis," *IEEE Symposium on Security and Privacy*, May 2001.

51. Alberts, C., and A. Dorofee, "OCTAVE Information Security Risk Evaluation," January 30, 2001, <www.cert.org/octave/methodintro.html>.

52. Delio, M., "Find the Cost of (Virus) Freedom," *Wired News*, January 14, 2002, <www.wired.com/news/infostructure/0,1377,49681,00.html>.

53. Bridwell, L. M., and P. Tippett, "ICSA Labs Seventh Annual Computer Virus Prevalence Survey 2001," *ICSA Labs*, 2001.

54. Helenius, M., "A System to Support the Analysis of Antivirus Products' Virus Detection Capabilities," *Academic dissertation, Dept. of Computer and Information Sciences, University of Tampere, Finland*, May 2002.

55. Solomon, A., and T. Kay, *Dr. Solomon's PC Anti-virus Book*, Butterworth-Heinemann, 1994, pp. 12–18.

56. University of Reading, "A Guide to Microsoft Windows XP," October 24, 2003, <www.rdg.ac.uk/ITS/info/training/notes/windows/guide/>.

57. Helenius, M., "A System to Support the Analysis of Antivirus Products' Virus Detection Capabilities," *Academic dissertation, Dept. of Computer and Information Sciences, University of Tampere, Finland*, May 2002.

58. OpenBSD Team, "OpenBSD Security," September 17, 2003, <www.openbsd.org/security.html>.

59. Microsoft Corporation, "Top 10 Reasons to Get Windows XP for Home PC Security," April 16, 2003, <www.microsoft.com/WindowsXP/security/top10.asp>.

60. Microsoft Corporation, "What's New in Security for Windows XP Professional and Windows XP Home Edition," July 2001, <www.microsoft.com/windowsxp/pro/techinfo/planning/security/whatsnew/WindowsXPSecurity.doc>.

61. *Security Electronics Magazine*, "OpenBSD: Secure by Default," January 2002, <www.semweb.com/jan02/itsecurityjan.htm>.

62. Howard, J., "Daemon News: The BSD Family Tree," April 2001, <www.daemonnews.org/200104/bsd_family.html>.

63. *Security Electronics Magazine*, "OpenBSD: Secure by Default," January 2002, <www.semweb.com/jan02/itsecurityjan.htm>.

64. Jorm, D., "An Overview of OpenBSD Security," August 8, 2000, <www.onlamp.com/pub/a/bsd/2000/08/08/OpenBSD.html>.

65. Howard, J., "Daemon News: The BSD Family Tree," April 2001, <www.daemonnews.org/200104/bsd_family.html>.

66. Howard, J., "Daemon News: The BSD Family Tree," April 2001, <www.daemonnews.org/200104/bsd_family.html>.

67. *Security Electronics Magazine*, "OpenBSD: Secure by Default," January 2002, <www.semweb.com/jan02/itsecurityjan.htm>.

68. OpenBSD Team, "OpenBSD Security," September 17, 2003, <www.openbsd.org/security.html>.

69. *Security Electronics Magazine*, "OpenBSD: Secure by Default," January 2002, <www.semweb.com/jan02/itsecurityjan.htm>.

70. Jorm, D., "An Overview of OpenBSD Security," August 8, 2000, <www.onlamp.com/pub/a/bsd/2000/08/08/OpenBSD.html>.

71. Howard, J., "Daemon News: The BSD Family Tree," April 2001, <www.daemonnews.org/200104/bsd_family.html>.

72. OpenBSD Team, "Cryptography in OpenBSD," September 25, 2003, <www.openbsd.org/crypto.html>.

73. OpenBSD Team, "OpenBSD Security," September 17, 2003, <www.openbsd.org/security.html>.

74. Howard, J., "Daemon News: The BSD Family Tree," April 2001, <www.daemonnews.org/200104/bsd_family.html>.

75. OpenBSD Team, "OpenBSD Security," September 17, 2003, <www.openbsd.org/security.html>.

76. Mullen, T., "Windows Server 2003—Secure by Default," April 27, 2003, <www.securityfocus.com/columnists/157>.

77. OpenBSD Team, "OpenBSD," September 27, 2003, <www.openbsd.org>.

78. *Security Electronics Magazine*, "OpenBSD: Secure by Default," January 2002, <www.semweb.com/jan02/itsecurityjan.htm>.

79. Sanford, G., "Lisa/Lisa 2/Mac XL," <www.apple-history.com/noframes/body.php? page=gallery&model=lisa>.

80. Sanford, G., "Macintosh 128k," <www.apple-history.com/noframes/body.php? page=gallery&model=128k>.

81. Trotot, J., "Mac™ OS History," <perso.club-internet.fr/jctrotot/Perso/History.html>.

82. Horn, B., "On Xerox, Apple, and Progress," <www.apple-history.com/noframes/body.php?page=gui_horn1>.

83. Horn, B., "On Xerox, Apple, and Progress," <www.apple-history.com/noframes/body.php?page=gui_horn1>.

84. Sanford, G., "Lisa/Lisa 2/Mac XL," <www.apple-history.com/noframes/body.php? page=gallery&model=lisa>.

85. Apple Computer, "1984 Commercial," <www.apple-history.com/noframes/body.php?page=gallery&model=1984>.

86. Sanford, G., "Macintosh 128k," <www.apple-history.com/noframes/body.php? page=gallery&model=128k>.

87. Sanford, G., "Company History: 1985–1993," <www.apple-history.com/noframes/body.php?page=history&section=h4>.

88. University of Utah, "Mac OS History," September 23, 2003, <www.macos.utah.edu/Documentation/MacOSXClasses/macosxone/macintosh.html>.

89. University of Utah, "Mac OS History," September 23, 2003, <www.macos.utah.edu/Documentation/MacOSXClasses/macosxone/macintosh.html>.

90. Trotot, J., "Mac™ OS History," <perso.club-internet.fr/jctrotot/Perso/History.html>.

91. University of Utah, "Mac OS History," September 23, 2003, <www.macos.utah.edu/Documentation/MacOSXClasses/macosxone/macintosh.html>.

92. Apple Computer, Inc., "The Evolution of Darwin," 2003, <developer.apple.com/darwin/history.html>.

93. Apple Computer, Inc., "Apple—Mac OS X—Features—UNIX," 2003, <www.apple.com/macosx/features/unix/>.

94. Apple Computer, Inc., "Apple—Mac OS X—Features—Darwin," 2003, <www.apple.com/macosx/features/darwin/>.

95. Apple Computer, Inc., "Apple—Mac OS X—Features—Security," 2003, <www.apple.com/macosx/features/security/>.

96. Apple Computer, Inc., "Apple—Mac OS X—Features—Windows," 2003, <www.apple.com/macosx/features/windows/>.

97. Dynamoo, "Orange Book FAQ," June 2002, <www.dynamoo.com/orange/faq.htm>.

98. The Jargon Dictionary, "Orange Book," <info.astrian.net/jargon/terms/o/Orange_Book.html>.

99. Dynamoo, "Orange Book Summary," March 2003, <www.dynamoo.com/orange/summary.htm>.

100. Dynamoo, "Orange Book—Full Text," June 2002, <www.dynamoo.com/orange/fulltext.htm>.

101. "EPL Entry CSC-EPL-95/006.D," January 2000, <www.radium.ncsc.mil/tpep/epl/entries/CSC-EPL-95-006-D.html>.

102. "EPL Entry CSC-EPL-93/008.A," July 1998, <www.radium.ncsc.mil/tpep/epl/entries/CSC-EPL-93-008-A.html>.

103. "EPL Entry CSC-EPL-93/003.A," July 1998, <www.radium.ncsc.mil/tpep/epl/entries/CSC-EPL-93-003-A.html>.

104. "EPL Entry CSC-EPL-93/006.A," July 1998, <www.radium.ncsc.mil/tpep/epl/entries/CSC-EPL-93-006-A.html>.

105. Corbató, F. J., and V. A. Vyssotsky, "Introduction and Overview of the Multics System," <www.multicians.org/fjcc1.html>.

106. "EPL Entry CSC-EPL-90/001.A," July 1998, <www.radium.ncsc.mil/tpep/epl/entries/CSC-EPL-90-001-A.html>.

107. "EPL Entry CSC-EPL-92/003.E," June 2000, <www.radium.ncsc.mil/tpep/epl/entries/CSC-EPL-92-003-E.html>.

108. "EPL Entry CSC-EPL-94/006," July 1998, <www.radium.ncsc.mil/tpep/epl/entries/CSC-EPL-94-006.html>.

109. RSA Laboratories, "4.1.3.14 How Are Certifying Authorities Susceptible to Attack?" April 16, 2003, <www.rsasecurity.com/rsalabs/faq/4-1-3-14.html>.

110. Hulme, G., "VeriSign Gave Microsoft Certificates to Imposter," *Information Week*, March 3, 2001.

111. Ellison, C., and B. Schneier, "Ten Risks of PKI: What You're Not Being Told about Public Key Infrastructure," *Computer Security Journal*, 2000.

112. "X.509 Internet Public Key Infrastructure Online Certificate Status Protocol—OCSP," RFC 2560, June 1999, <www.ietf.org/rfc/rfc2560.txt>.

113. Abbot, S., "The Debate for Secure E-Commerce," *Performance Computing*, February 1999, pp. 37–42.

114. Wilson, T., "E-Biz Bucks Lost Under the SSL Train," *Internet Week*, May 24, 1999, pp. 1, 3.

115. Gilbert, H., "Introduction to TCP/IP," February 2, 1995, <www.yale.edu/pclt/COMM/TCPIP.HTM>.

116. RSA Laboratories, "Security Protocols Overview," 1999, <www.rsasecurity.com/standards/protocols>.

117. "The TLS Protocol Version 1.0," RFC 2246, January 1999, <www.ietf.org/rfc/rfc2246.txt>.

118. Cisco Systems, Inc., "VPN Solutions," 2003, <www.cisco.com/warp/public/44/solutions/network/vpn.shtml>.

119. Burnett, S., and S. Paine, *RSA Security's Official Guide to Cryptography*, Berkeley: Osborne McGraw-Hill, 2001, p. 210.

120. RSA Laboratories, "3.6.1 What Is Diffie-Hellman?" April 16, 2003, <www.rsasecurity.com/rsalabs/faq/3-6-1.html>.

121. Naik, D., *Internet Standards and Protocols*, Microsoft Press, 1998, pp. 79–80.

122. Grayson, M., "End the PDA Security Dilemma," *Communication News*, February 2001, pp. 38–40.

123. Fratto, M., "Tutorial: Wireless Security," January 22, 2001, <www.networkcomputing.com/1202/1202f1d1.html>.

124. Westoby, K., "Security Issues Surrounding Wired Equivalent Privacy," March 26, 2002, <www.cas.mcmaster.ca/~wmfarmer/SE-4C03-02/projects/student_work/westobkj.html>.

125. Borisov, N.; I. Goldberg; and D. Wagner, "Security of the WEP algorithm," <www.isaac.cs.berkeley.edu/isaac/wep-faq.html>.

126. Geier, J., "802.11 WEP: Concepts and Vulnerability," June 20, 2002, <www.wi-fiplanet.com/tutorials/article.php/1368661>.

127. Geier, J., "WPA Plugs Holes in WEP," March 31, 2003, <www.nwfusion.com/research/2003/0331wpa.html>.

128. CNN Wireless Society, "Special Report: Wireless 101," 2003, <www.cnn.com/SPECIALS/2003/wireless/interactive/wireless101/index.html>.

129. Katzenbeisser, S., and F. Petitcolas, *Information Hiding: Techniques for Steganography and Digital Watermarking*, Norwood: Artech House, Inc., 2000, pp. 1–2.

130. Evers, J., "Worm Exploits Apache," *InfoWorld*, July 1, 2002, <www.infoworld.com/articles/hn/xml/02/07/01/020701hnapache.xml>.

131. Lasser, J., "Irresponsible Disclosure," *SecurityFocus Online*, June 26, 2002, <online.securityfocus.com/columnists/91>.

132. Grampp, F. T., and R. H. Morris, "UNIX Operating System Security," *AT&T Bell Laboratories Technical Journal*, Vol. 63, No. 8, October 1984, pp. 1649–1672.

133. Wood, P., and S. Kochan, *UNIX System Security*, Hasbrouck Heights, NJ: Hayden Book Co., 1985.

134. Farrow, R., "Security Issues and Strategies for Users," *UNIX World*, April 1986, pp. 65–71.

135. Farrow, R., "Security for Superusers, or How to Break the UNIX System," *UNIX World*, May 1986, pp. 65–70.

136. Filipski, A., and J. Hanko, "Making UNIX Secure," *Byte*, April 1986, pp. 113–128.

137. Coffin, S., *UNIX: The Complete Reference*, Berkeley, CA: Osborne McGraw-Hill, 1988.

138. Hecht, M. S.; A. Johri; R. Aditham; and T. J. Wei, "Experience Adding C2 Security Features to UNIX," *USENIX Conference Proceedings*, San Francisco, June 20–24, 1988, pp. 133–146.

139. Filipski, A., and J. Hanko, "Making UNIX Secure," *Byte*, April 1986, pp. 113–128.

140. Linux Password & Shadow File Formats, <www.tldp.org/LDP/lame/LAME/linux-admin-made-easy/shadow-file-formats.html>.

141. Coffin, S., *UNIX: The Complete Reference*, Berkeley, CA: Osborne McGraw-Hill, 1988.

142. Kramer, S. M., "Retaining SUID Programs in a Secure UNIX," *USENIX Conference Proceedings*, San Francisco, June 20–24, 1988, pp. 107–118.

143. Farrow, R., "Security Issues and Strategies for Users," *UNIX World*, April 1986, pp. 65–71.

144. Filipski, A., and J. Hanko, "Making UNIX Secure," *Byte*, April 1986, pp. 113–128.

145. Farrow, R., "Security Issues and Strategies for Users," *UNIX World*, April 1986, pp. 65–71.

146. Grampp, F. T., and R. H. Morris, "UNIX Operating System Security," *AT&T Bell Laboratories Technical Journal*, Vol. 63, No. 8, October 1984, pp. 1649–1672.

147. Coffin, S., *UNIX: The Complete Reference*, Berkeley, CA: Osborne McGraw-Hill, 1988.

148. Bauer, D. S., and M. E. Koblentz, "NIDX—A Real-Time Intrusion Detection Expert System," *USENIX Conference Proceedings*, San Francisco, June 20–24, 1988, pp. 261–274.

149. Farrow, R., "Security Issues and Strategies for Users," *UNIX World*, April 1986, pp. 65–71.

150. Filipski, A., and J. Hanko, "Making UNIX Secure," *Byte*, April 1986, pp. 113–128.

151. Rothe, J., "Some Facets of Complexity Theory and Cryptography: A Five-Lecture Tutorial," *ACM Computing Surveys (CSUR)*, Vol. 24, No. 4, December 2002.

152. Sandhu, R. S., and P. Samarati, "Access Control: Principles and Practice," *IEEE Communications*, Vol. 32, No. 9, 1994, pp. 40–48.

153. Gollmann, D., *Computer Security*, Hoboken, NJ: John Wiley & Sons Ltd. 1999.

Operating System Case Studies

Our children may learn about the heroes of the past.
Our task is to make ourselves architects of the future.
—Mzee Jomo Kenyatta—

Part 8

*T*he final two chapters present in-depth case studies of Linux and Microsoft Windows XP. These case studies reinforce the text's key concepts and demonstrate how operating system principles are applied in real-world operating systems. Chapter 20 examines the history and core components of Linux 2.6—the most popular open-source operating system— including kernel architecture, process management, memory management, file systems, I/O management, synchronization, IPC, networking, scalability and security. Chapter 21 explores the internals of Windows XP—the most popular proprietary operating system. The case study examines XP's history, design goals and core components, including system architecture, system management mechanisms, process and thread management, memory management, file systems management, input/output management, IPC, networking, scalability and security.

Freely ye have received, freely give.
—Matthew 10:8—

Freely ye have received, freely give.
—Matthew 10:8—

The world is moving so fast these days that the man who says it can't be done is generally interrupted by someone doing it.
—Elbert Hubbard—

When your Daemon is in charge, do not try to think consciously. Drift, wait and obey.
—Rudyard Kipling—

I long to accomplish a great and noble task, but it is my chief duty to accomplish small tasks as if they were great and noble.
—Helen Keller—

Our children may learn about heroes of the past. Our task is to make ourselves architects of the future.
—Jomo Mzee Kenyatta—

Chapter 20

Case Study: Linux

Objectives

After reading this chapter, you should understand:

- *Linux kernel architecture.*
- *the Linux implementation of operating system components such as process, memory and file management.*
- *the software layers that compose the Linux kernel.*
- *how Linux organizes and manages system devices.*
- *how Linux manages I/O operations.*
- *interprocess communication and synchronization mechanisms in Linux.*
- *how Linux scales to multiprocessor and embedded systems.*
- *Linux security features.*

Chapter Outline

Web Resources | Key Terms | Exercises | Recommended Reading | Works Cited

20.1 Introduction

The Linux kernel version 2.6 is the core of the most popular open-source, freely distributed, full-featured operating system. Unlike that of proprietary operating systems, Linux source code is available to the public for examination and modification and is free to download and install. As a result, users of the operating system benefit from a community of developers actively debugging and improving the kernel, an absence of licensing fees and restrictions and the ability to completely customize the operating system to meet specific needs. Though Linux is not centrally produced by a corporation, Linux users can receive technical support for a fee from Linux vendors or for free through a community of users.

The Linux operating system, which is developed by a loosely organized team of volunteers, is popular in high-end servers, desktop computers and embedded systems. Besides providing core operating system features, such as process scheduling, memory management, device management and file system management, Linux supports many advanced features such as symmetric multiprocessing (SMP), non-uniform memory access (NUMA), access to multiple file systems and support for a broad spectrum of hardware architectures. This case study offers the reader an opportunity to evaluate a real operating system in substantial detail in the context of the operating system concepts discussed throughout this book.

20.2 History

In 1991, Linus Torvalds, a 21-year-old student at the University of Helsinki, Finland, began developing the Linux (the name is derived from "Linus" and "UNIX") kernel as a hobby. Torvalds wished to improve upon the design of Minix, an educational operating system created by Professor Andrew S. Tanenbaum of the Vrije Universiteit in Amsterdam. The Minix source code, which served as a starting point for Torvalds's Linux project, was publicly available for professors to demonstrate basic operating system implementation concepts to their students.[1]

In the early stages of development, Torvalds sought advice about the shortcomings of Minix from those familiar with it: He designed Linux based on these suggestions and made further efforts to involve the operating systems community in his project. In September of 1991, Torvalds released the first version (0.01) of the Linux operating system, announcing the availability of his source code to a Minix newsgroup.[2]

The response led to the creation of a community that has continued to develop and support Linux. Developers downloaded, tested, and modified the Linux code, submitting bug fixes and feedback to Torvalds, who reviewed them and applied the improvements to the code. In October, 1991, Torvalds released version 0.02 of the Linux operating system.[3]

Although early Linux kernels lacked many features implemented in well-established operating systems such as UNIX, developers continued to support the concept of a new, freely available operating system. As Linux's popularity grew, developers worked to remedy its shortcomings, such as the absence of a login mechanism and its dependence on Minix to compile. Other missing features were floppy disk support and a virtual memory system.[4] Torvalds continued to maintain the Linux source code, applying changes as he saw fit.

As Linux evolved and drew more support from developers, Torvalds recognized its potential to become more than a hobby operating system. He decided that Linux should conform to the POSIX specification to enhance its interoperability with other UNIX-like systems. Recall that POSIX, the Portable Operating System Interface, defines standards for application interfaces to operating system services, as discussed in Section 2.7, Application Programming Interfaces (APIs).[5]

The 1994 release of Linux version 1.0 included many features commonly found in a mature operating system, such as multiprogramming, virtual memory, demand loading and TCP/IP networking.[6] It provided the functionality necessary for Linux to become a viable alternative to the licensed UNIX operating system.

Though it benefited from free licensing, Linux suffered from a complex installation and configuration process. To allow users unfamiliar with the details of Linux to conveniently install and use the operating system, academic institutions, such as the University of Manchester and Texas A&M University, and organizations such as Slackware Linux (www.slackware.org), created Linux **distributions**, which included software such as the Linux kernel, system applications (e.g., user account management, network management and security tools), user applications (e.g., GUIs, Web browsers, text editors, e-mail applications, databases, and games) and tools to simplify the installation process.[7]

As kernel development progressed, the project adopted a version numbering scheme. The first digit is the **major version number**, which is incremented at Torvalds's discretion for each kernel release that contains a feature set significantly different from that of the previous version. Kernels that are described by an even **minor version number** (the digit directly following the first decimal point), such as version 1.0.9, are considered to be stable releases, whereas an odd minor version number, such as 2.1.6, indicates a development version. The digit following the second decimal point is incremented for each minor update to the kernel.

Development kernels include new features that have not been extensively tested, so they are not sufficiently reliable for production use. Throughout the development process, developers create and test new features; then, once a development kernel becomes stable (i.e., the kernel does not contain any known bugs), Torvalds declares it a release kernel.

By the 1996 release of version 2.0, the Linux kernel had grown to over 400,000 lines of code.[1] Thousands of developers had contributed features and bug fixes, and more than 1.5 million users had installed the operating system.[9] Although this release was appealing to the server market, the vast majority of desktop users were

---

1   Red Hat version 6.2, which included version 2.0 of the Linux kernel, contained approximately 17 million lines of code. By comparison, Microsoft Windows 95 contained approximately 15 million lines of code and Sun Solaris approximately 8 million.[8]

still reluctant to use Linux as a client operating system. Version 2.0 provided enterprise features such as support for SMP, network traffic control and disk quotas. Another important feature allowed portions of the kernel to be modularized, so that users could add device drivers and other system components without rebuilding the kernel.

Version 2.2 of the kernel, which was released by Torvalds in 1999, improved the performance of existing 2.0 features, such as SMP, audio support and file systems, and added new features such as an extension to the kernel's networking subsystem that allowed system administrators to inspect and control network traffic at the packet level. This feature simplified firewall installation and network traffic forwarding, as requested by server administrators.[10]

Many new features in version 2.2, such as USB support, CD-RW support and advanced power management, targeted the desktop market. These features were labeled as experimental, because they were not sufficiently reliable for use in production systems. Although version 2.2 improved usability in desktop environments, Linux could not yet truly compete with popular desktop operating systems of the time, such as Microsoft's Windows 98. The desktop user was more concerned with the availability of applications and the "look and feel" of the user interface than with kernel functionality. However, as Linux kernel development continued, so did the development of Linux applications.

The next stable kernel, version 2.4, was released by Torvalds in January, 2001. In this release a number of kernel subsystems were modified and, in some cases, completely rewritten to support newer hardware and to use existing hardware more efficiently. In addition, Linux was modified to run on high-performance architectures including Intel's 64-bit Itanium, 64-bit MIPS and AMD's 64-bit Opteron, and handheld-device architectures such as SuperH.

Enterprise systems companies such as IBM and Oracle had become increasingly interested in Linux as it continued to stabilize and spread to new platforms. Viability in the enterprise systems market, however, required Linux to scale to both high-end and embedded systems, a need fulfilled by version 2.4.[11]

Version 2.4 addressed a critical scalability issue by improving performance on high-end multiprocessor systems. Although Linux had included SMP support since version 2.0, inefficient synchronization mechanisms and other issues limited performance on systems containing more than four processors. Improvements in version 2.4 enabled the kernel to scale to 8, 16 or more processors.[12]

Version 2.4 also addressed the needs of desktop users. Experimental features in the 2.2 kernel, such as USB support and power management, matured in the 2.4 kernel. This kernel supported a large set of desktop devices; however, a variety of issues, such as Microsoft's market power and the small number of user-friendly Linux applications, prevented widespread Linux use on desktop computers.

Development of the version 2.6 kernel focused on scalability, standards compliance and modifications to kernel subsystems to improve performance. Kernel developers focused on scalability by increasing SMP support, providing support for

NUMA systems and rewriting the process scheduler to increase the performance of scheduling operations. Other kernel enhancements included support for advanced disk scheduling algorithms, a new block I/O layer, improved POSIX compliance, an updated audio subsystem and support for large memories and disks.

20.3 Linux Overview

Linux has a distinct development process and benefits from a wealth of diverse (and free) system and user applications. In this section we summarize Linux kernel features, discuss the process of standardizing and developing the kernel, and introduce several user applications that improve Linux usability and productivity.

In addition to the kernel, Linux systems include user interfaces and applications. A user interface can be as simple as a text-based shell, though standard Linux distributions include a number of GUIs through which users can interact with the system. The Linux operating system borrows from the UNIX layered system approach. Users access applications via a user interface; these applications access resources via a system call interface, thereby invoking the kernel. The kernel may then access the system's hardware, as appropriate, on behalf of the requesting application. In addition to creating user processes, the system creates kernel threads that perform many kernel services. Kernel threads are implemented as **daemons**, which remain dormant until the scheduler or another component of the kernel wakes them.

Because Linux is a multiuser system, the kernel must provide mechanisms to manage user access rights and provide protection for system resources. Therefore, Linux restricts operations that may damage the kernel and/or the system's hardware to a user that has **superuser** (also called **root**) privileges. For example, the superuser privilege enables a user to manage passwords, specify access rights for other users and execute code that modifies system files.

20.3.1 Development and Community

The Linux project is maintained by Linus Torvalds, who is the final arbiter of any code submitted for the kernel. The community of developers constantly modifies the operating system and every two or three years releases a new stable version of the kernel. The community then shifts to the development of the next kernel, discussing new features via e-mail lists and online forums. Torvalds delegates maintenance of stable kernels to trusted developers and manages the development kernel. Bug fixes and performance enhancements for stable releases are applied to the source code and released as updates to the stable version. In parallel, development kernels are released at various stages of the coding process for public review, testing and feedback.

Torvalds and a team of approximately 20 members of his "inner circle"—a set of developers who have proven their competency by producing significant additions to the Linux kernel—are entrusted with enhancing current features and coding new ones. These primary developers submit code to Torvalds, who reviews and accepts or rejects it, depending on such factors as correctness, performance and style. When a development kernel has matured to a point at which Torvalds is satisfied with the content of its feature set, he will declare a **feature freeze**. Developers may continue to submit bug fixes, code that improves system performance and enhancements to features that are under development.[13] When the kernel is near completion, a **code freeze** occurs. During this phase only code that fixes bugs is accepted. When Torvalds decides that all important known bugs have been addressed, the kernel is declared stable and is released with a new, even kernel minor version number.

Though many Linux developers contribute to the kernel as individuals, corporations such as IBM have invested significant resources in improving the Linux kernel for use in large-scale systems. Such corporations typically charge for tools and support services. Free support is provided by other users and developers in the Linux community. Users may ask questions in user groups, electronic mailing lists (also called listservs) or forums, and may find answers to questions in FAQs (frequently asked questions) and HOWTOs (step-by-step guides). URLs for such resources can be found via the sites in the Web Resources section at the end of the chapter. Alternatively, dedicated support services can be purchased from vendors.

Linux is free for users to download, modify and distribute under the GNU General Public License (GPL). GNU (pronounced *guh-knew*) is a project created by the Free Software Foundation in 1984 that aims to provide free UNIX-like operating systems and software to the public.[14] The General Public License specifies that any distribution of the software under its license must be accompanied by the GPL, must clearly indicate that the original code has been modified and must include the complete source code. Although Linux is free software, it is copyrighted (many of the copyrights are held by Linus Torvalds); any software that borrows from Linux's copyrighted material must clearly credit its source and must also be distributed under the terms of the GPL.

20.3.2 Distributions

By the end of the 1990s, Linux had matured but was still largely ignored by desktop users. In a PC market dominated by Microsoft and Apple, Linux was considered too difficult to use. Those who wished to install Linux were required to download the source code, manually customize configuration files and compile the kernel. Users still needed to download and install applications to perform productive work. As Linux matured, developers realized a need for a friendly installation process, which led to the creation of distributions that included the kernel, applications and user interfaces as well as other tools and accessories.

Currently more than 300 distributions are available, each providing a variety of features. User-friendly and application-rich distributions are popular among users—they often include an intuitive GUI and productivity applications such as word processors, spreadsheets and Web browsers. Distributions are commonly divided into **packages**, each containing a single application or service. Users can customize a

Linux system by installing or removing packages, either during the installation process or at runtime. Examples of such distributions are Debian, Mandrake, Red Hat, Slackware and SuSE.[15] Mandrake, Red Hat and SuSE are commercial organizations that provide Linux distributions for markets such as high-end servers and desktop users.[16, 17, 18] Debian and Slackware are nonprofit organizations comprised of volunteer developers who update and maintain Linux distributions.[19, 20] Other distributions tailor to specific environments, such as handheld systems (e.g., OpenZaurus) and embedded systems (e.g., uClinux).[21, 22] All parts of distributions using GPL-licensed code can be freely modified and redistributed by end-users, but the GPL does not prohibit distributors from charging a fee for distribution costs (e.g., the cost of packaging materials) or technical support.[23, 24]

20.3.3 User Interface

In a Microsoft Windows XP or Macintosh OS X environment, the user is presented with a standard, customizable user interface composed of the GUI and an emulated terminal or shell (e.g., a window containing a command-line prompt). On the contrary, Linux is simply the kernel of an operating system and does not specify a "standard" user interface. Many console shells, such as *bash* (Bourne-again shell), *csh* (a shell providing C-like syntax, pronounced "seashell") and *esh* (easy shell) are commonly found on user systems.[25]

For users who prefer a graphical interface to console shells, there are several freely available GUIs, many of which are packaged as part of most Linux distributions. Those most commonly found in Linux systems are composed of several layers. In most Linux systems, the lowest layer is the X Window System (www.XFree86.org), a low-level graphical interface originally developed at MIT in 1984.[26] The X Window System provides to higher layers the mechanisms necessary to create and manipulate windows and other graphical components. The second layer of the GUI is the **window manager**, which builds on mechanisms in the X Window System interface to control the placement, appearance, size and other attributes of windows. An optional third layer is called the **desktop environment**. The most popular desktop environments are KDE (K Desktop Environment) and GNOME (GNU Network Object Model Environment). Desktop environments tend to provide a file management interface, tools to facilitate access to common applications and utilities, and a suite of software, typically including Web browsers, text editors and e-mail applications.[27]

20.3.4 Standards

A more recent goal of the Linux operating system has been to conform to a variety of widely recognized standards to improve compatibility between applications written for UNIX-like operating systems and Linux. The most prominent set of standards to which Linux developers strive to conform is POSIX (standards.ieee.org/regauth/posix/). Two other sets prominent in UNIX-like operating systems are the Single UNIX Specification (SUS) and the Linux Standards Base (LSB).

The **Single UNIX Specification** (www.unix.org/version3/) is a suite of standards that define user and application programming interfaces for UNIX operating systems, shells and utilities. Version 3 of the SUS combines several standards (including POSIX, ISO standards and previous versions of the SUS) into one.[28] The Open Group (www.unix.org), which holds the trademark rights and defines standards for the UNIX brand, maintains SUS. To bear the UNIX trademarked name, an operating system must conform to the SUS; The Open Group certifies SUS conformance for a fee.[29]

The **Linux Standard Base** (www.linuxbase.org) is a project that aims to standardize Linux so that applications written for one LSB-compliant distribution will compile and behave exactly the same on any other LSB-compliant distribution. The LSB maintains general standards that apply to elements of the operating system, including libraries, package format and installation, commands and utilities. For example, the LSB specifies a standard file system structure. The LSB also maintains architecture-specific standards that are required for LSB certification. Those who wish to test and certify a distribution for LSB compliance can obtain the tools and certification from the LSB organization for a fee.[30]

Until recently, standards compliance has been a low priority for the kernel, because most kernel developers are concerned with improving the feature set and reliability of Linux. Consequently, most kernel releases do not conform to any one set of standards. During the development of the version 2.6 Linux kernel, developers modified several interfaces to improve compliance with the POSIX, SUS and LSB standards.

20.4 Kernel Architecture

Although Linux is a monolithic kernel (see Section 1.13, Operating System Architectures), recent scalability enhancements have included modular capabilities similar to those supported by microkernel operating systems.[31] Linux is commonly referred to as a UNIX-like or a UNIX-based operating system because it provides many services that characterize UNIX systems, such as AT&T's UNIX System V and Berkeley's BSD. Linux is composed of six primary subsystems: process management, interprocess communication, memory management, file system management, I/O management and networking. These six subsystems are responsible for controlling access to system resources (Fig. 20.1). In the following sections, we examine these kernel subsystems and their interactions.

Process execution on a Linux system occurs in either user mode or kernel mode. User processes run in user mode and must therefore access kernel services via the system call interface. When a user process issues a valid system call (in user mode), the kernel executes the system call in kernel mode on behalf of the process. If the request is invalid (e.g., a process attempts to write to a file that is not open), the kernel returns an error.

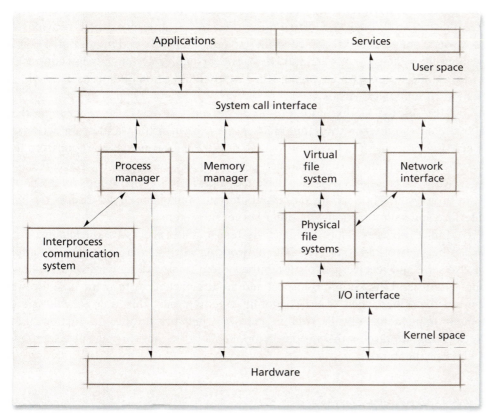

Figure 20.1 | *Linux architecture.*

The process manager is a fundamental Linux subsystem that is responsible for creating processes, providing access to the system's processor(s) and removing processes from the system upon completion (see Section 20.5, Process Management). The kernel's interprocess communication (IPC) subsystem allows processes to communicate with one another. This subsystem interacts with the process manager to permit information sharing and message passing using a variety of mechanisms, discussed in Section 20.10, Interprocess Communication.

The memory management subsystem provides processes with access to memory. Linux assigns each process a virtual memory address space, which is divided into the user address space and the kernel address space. Including the kernel address space within each execution context reduces the cost of context switching from user mode to kernel mode because the kernel can access its data from every user process's virtual address space. The algorithms to manage free (i.e., available) memory and select pages for replacement are discussed in Section 20.6, Memory Management.

Users access files and directories by navigating the directory tree. The root of the directory tree is called the root directory. From the root directory, users can navigate any available file systems. User processes access file system data through the system call interface. When system calls access a file or directory in the directory tree, they do so through the **virtual file system (VFS)** interface, which provides to processes a single interface to access files and directories stored in multiple heterogeneous file systems (e.g., ext2 and NFS). The virtual file system passes requests to particular file systems, which manage the layout and location of data, as discussed in Section 20.7, File Systems.

Based on the UNIX model, Linux treats most devices as files, meaning that they are accessed using the same mechanisms with which data files are accessed. When user processes read from or write to devices, the kernel passes requests to the virtual file system interface, which then passes requests to the I/O interface. The I/O interface passes requests to device drivers that perform I/O operations on the hardware in a system. In Section 20.8, Input/Output Management, we discuss the I/O interface and its interaction with other kernel subsystems.

Linux provides a networking subsystem to allow processes to exchange data with other networked computers. The networking subsystem accesses the I/O interface to send and receive packets using the system's networking hardware. It allows applications and the kernel to inspect and modify packets as they traverse the system's networking layers via the packet filtering interface. This interface allows systems to implement firewalls, routers and other network utilities. In Section 20.11, Networking, we discuss the various components of the networking subsystem and their implementations.

20.4.1 Hardware Platforms

Initially, Torvalds developed Linux for use on 32-bit Intel x86 platforms. As its popularity grew, developers implemented Linux on a variety of other architectures. The Linux kernel supports the following platforms: x86 (including Intel IA-32), HP/Compaq Alpha AXP, Sun SPARC, Sun UltraSPARC, Motorola 68000, PowerPC, PowerPC64, ARM, Hitachi SuperH, IBM S/390 and zSeries, MIPS, HP PA-RISC, Intel IA-64, AMD x86-64, H8/300, V850 and CRIS.[32]

Each architecture typically requires that the kernel use a different set of low-level instructions to perform operating system functions. For example, an Intel processor implements a different system call mechanism than a Motorola processor. The code that performs operations that are implemented differently across architectures is called **architecture-specific code**. The process of modifying the kernel to support new architecture is called **porting**. To facilitate the process of porting Linux to new platforms, architecture-specific code is separated from the rest of the kernel code into the /arch directory of the kernel source tree. The kernel **source tree** organizes each significant component of the kernel into different subdirectories. Each subdirectory in /arch contains code corresponding to a particular architecture (e.g., machine instructions for a particular processor). When the kernel must perform processor-specific operations, such as manipulating the contents of a processor cache, control passes to the architecture-specific code that was integrated into the kernel at compile time.[33] Although Linux relies on architecture-specific code to control computer hardware, Linux may also be executed on a set of virtual hardware devices. The Mini Case Study, User-Mode Linux (UML), describes one such Linux port.

For a system to execute properly on a particular architecture, the kernel must be ported to that architecture and compiled for a particular machine prior to execution. Likewise, applications may need to be compiled (and sometimes redesigned) to properly operate on a particular system. For many platforms, this work has already been accomplished—a variety of platform-specific distributions provide ports of common applications and system services.[34]

User-Mode Linux (UML)

Kernel development is a complicated and error-prone process that can result in numerous bugs. Unlike other software, the kernel may execute privileged instructions, meaning that a flaw in the kernel could damage a system's data and hardware. As a result, kernel development can be a tedious (and risky) endeavor. **User-Mode Linux (UML)** facilitates kernel development by allowing developers to test and debug the kernel without damaging the system on which it runs.

User-Mode Linux (UML) is a version of the Linux kernel that runs as a user application on a computer running Linux. Unlike most versions of Linux, which contain architecture-specific code to control devices, UML performs all architecture-specific operations using system calls to the Linux system on which it runs. As a result, UML is interestingly considered to be port of Linux to itself.[35]

The UML kernel runs in user mode, so it cannot execute privileged instructions available to the host kernel. Instead of controlling physical resources, the UML kernel creates virtual devices (represented as files on the host system) that simulate real devices. Because the UML kernel does not control any real hardware, it cannot damage the system.

Almost all kernel mechanisms, such as process scheduling and memory management, are handled in the UML kernel; the host kernel executes only when privileged access to hardware is required. When a UML process issues a system call, the UML kernel intercepts and handles it before it can be sent to the host system. Although this technique incurs significant overhead, UML's primary goal is to provide a safe (i.e., protected) environment in which to execute software, not to provide high performance.[36]

The UML kernel has been applied to more than just testing and debugging. For example, UML can be used to run multiple instances of Linux at once. It can also be used to port Linux such that it runs as an application in operating systems other than Linux. This could allow users to run Linux on top of a UNIX or a Windows system. The Web Resources section at the end of this chapter provides a link to a Web site that documents UML usage and development.

20.4.2 Loadable Kernel Modules

Adding functionality to the Linux kernel, such as support for a particular file system or a new device driver, can be tedious. Because the kernel is monolithic, drivers and file systems are implemented in kernel space. Consequently, to permanently add support for a device driver, users must patch the kernel source by adding the driver code, then recompiling the kernel. This can be a lengthy and error-prone process, so an alternative method has been developed for adding features to the kernel—**loadable kernel modules**.

A kernel module contains object code that, when loaded, is dynamically linked to a running kernel (see Section 2.8, Compiling, Linking and Loading). If a device driver or file system is implemented as a loadable kernel module, it can be loaded into the kernel on demand (i.e., when first accessed) without any additional kernel configuration or compilation. Also, because modules can be loaded on demand, moving code from the kernel into modules reduces the **memory footprint** of the kernel; hardware and file system drivers are not loaded into memory until needed. Modules execute in kernel mode (as opposed to user mode) so they can access kernel functions and data structures. Consequently, loading an improperly coded module can lead to disastrous effects in a system, such as data corruption.[37]

When a module is loaded, the module loader must resolve all references to kernel functions and data structures. Kernel code allows modules to access functions and data structures by exporting their names to a symbol table.[38] Each entry in the symbol table contains the name and address of a kernel function or data structure. The module loader uses the symbol table to resolve references to kernel code.[39]

Because modules execute in kernel mode, they require access to symbols in the kernel symbol table, which allows modules to access kernel functions. However, consider what can happen if a function is modified between kernel versions. If a module was written for a prior kernel version, the module may expect a particular, yet invalid, result from a current kernel function (e.g., an integer value instead of an unsigned long value), which may in turn lead to errors such as exceptions. To avoid this problem, the kernel prevents users from loading modules written for a version of the kernel other than the current one, unless explicitly overridden by the superuser.[40]

Modules must be loaded into the kernel before use. For convenience, the kernel supports dynamic module loading. When compiling the kernel, the user is given the option to enable or disable *kmod*—a kernel subsystem that manages modules without user intervention. The first time the kernel requires access to a module, it issues a request to *kmod* to load the module. *Kmod* determines any module dependencies, then loads the requested module. If a requested module depends on other modules that have not been loaded, *kmod* will load those modules on demand.[41]

20.5 Process Management

The process management subsystem is essential to providing efficient multiprogramming in Linux. Although responsible primarily for allocating processors to processes, the process management subsystem also delivers signals, loads kernel modules and receives interrupts. The process management subsystem contains the **process sched-uler**, which provides processes access to a processor in a reasonable amount of time.

20.5.1 Process and Thread Organization

In Linux systems, both processes and threads are called **tasks**; internally, they are represented by a single data structure. In this section, we distinguish processes from threads from tasks where appropriate. The process manager maintains a list of all tasks using two data structures. The first is a circular, doubly linked list in which each entry contains pointers to the previous and next tasks in the list. This structure is accessed when the kernel must examine all tasks in the system. The second is a hash table. When a task is created, it is assigned a unique **PID (process identifier)**. Process identifiers are passed to a hash function to determine their location in the process table. The hashing method provides quick access to a specific task's data structure when the kernel knows its PID.[42]

Each task in the process table is represented by a `task_struct` structure, which serves as the process descriptor (i.e., the PCB). The `task_struct` structure stores variables and nested structures containing information describing a process. For example, the variable `state` stores information about the current task state. [*Note*: The kernel is primarily written using the C programming language and makes extensive use of structures to represent software entities.]

A task transitions to the *running* state when it is dispatched to a processor (Fig. 20.2). A task enters the *sleeping* state when it blocks and the *stopped* state when it is suspended. The *zombie* state indicates that a task has been terminated but has not yet been removed from the system. For example, if a process contains several threads, it will enter the *zombie* state until its threads have been notified that it received a termination signal. A task in the *dead* state may be removed from the system. The states *active* and *expired* are process scheduling states (described in the next section), which are not stored in the variable `state`.

Other important task-specific variables permit the scheduler to determine when a task should run on a processor. These variables include the task's priority, whether the task is a real-time task and, if so, which real-time scheduling algorithm should be used (real-time scheduling is discussed in the next section).[43]

Nested structures within a `task_struct` store additional information about a task. One such structure, `mm_struct`, describes the memory allocated to a task (e.g., the location of its page table in memory and the number of tasks sharing its address space). Additional structures nested within a `task_struct` contain information such as register values that store a task's execution context, signal handlers and the task's access rights.[44] These structures are accessed by several kernel subsystems other than the process manager.

When the kernel is booted, it typically loads a process called *init*, which then uses the kernel to create all other tasks.[45] Tasks are created using the `clone` system call; any calls to `fork` or `vfork` are converted to clone system calls at compile

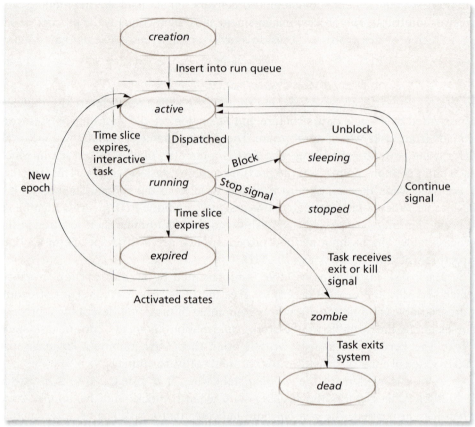

Figure 20.2 | Task state-transition diagram.

time. The purpose of fork is to create a child task whose virtual memory space is allocated using copy-on-write to improve performance (see Section 10.4.6, Sharing in a Paging System). When the child or the parent attempts to write to a page in memory, the writer is allocated its own copy of the page. As discussed in Section 10.4.6, copy-on-write can lead to poor performance if a process calls execve to load a new program immediately after the fork. For example, if the parent executes before its child, a copy-on-write will be performed for any page the parent modifies. Because the child will not use any of its parent's pages (if the child will immediately call execve when it executes), this operation is pure overhead. Therefore, Linux supports the vfork call, which improves performance when child processes will call execve. vfork suspends the parent process until the child calls execve or exit, to ensure that the child loads its new pages before the parent causes any wasteful copy-on-write operations. vfork further improves performance by not copying the parent's page tables to the child, because new page table entries will be created when the child calls execve.

Linux Threads and the clone *System Call*

Linux provides support for threads using the clone system call, which enables the calling process to specify whether the thread shares the process's virtual memory, file system information, file descriptors and/or signal handlers.[46] In Section 4.2, Definition of Thread, we mentioned that processor registers, the stack and other thread-specific data (TSD) are local to each thread, while the address space and open file handles are global to the process that contains the threads. Thus, depending on how many of the process's resources are shared with its thread, the resulting thread may be quite different from the threads described in Chapter 4.

Linux's implementation of threads has generated much discussion regarding the definition of a thread. Although clone creates threads, they do not precisely conform to the POSIX thread specification (see Section 4.8, POSIX and Pthreads). For example, two or more threads that were created using a clone call specifying maximum resource sharing still maintain several data structures that are not shared with all threads in the process, such as access rights.[47]

When clone is called from a kernel process (i.e., a process that executes kernel code), it creates a **kernel thread** that differs from other threads in that it directly accesses the kernel's address space. Several daemons within the kernel are implemented as kernel threads—these daemons are services that sleep until awakened by the kernel to perform tasks such as flushing pages to secondary storage and scheduling software interrupts (see Section 20.8.6, Interrupts).[48] These tasks are generally maintenance related and execute periodically.

There are several benefits to the Linux thread implementation. For example, Linux threads simplify kernel code and reduce overhead by requiring only a single copy of task management data structures.[49] Moreover, although Linux threads are less portable than POSIX threads, they allow programmers the flexibility to tightly control shared resources between tasks. A recent Linux project, Native POSIX Thread Library (NPTL), has achieved nearly complete POSIX conformance and is likely to become the default threading library in future Linux distributions.[50]

20.5.2 Process Scheduling

The goal of the Linux process scheduler is to run all tasks within a reasonable amount of time while respecting task priorities, maintaining high resource utilization and throughput, and reducing the overhead of scheduling operations. The process scheduler also addresses Linux's role in the high-end computer system market by scaling to SMP and NUMA architectures while providing high processor affinity. One of the more significant scalability enhancements in version 2.6 is that all scheduling functions are constant-time operations, meaning that the time required to execute scheduling functions does not depend on the number of tasks in the system.[51]

At each system timer interrupt (an architecture-specific number set to 1 millisecond by default for the IA-32 architecture[52]), the kernel updates various bookkeeping data structures (e.g., the amount of time a task has been executing) and performs scheduling operations as necessary. Because the scheduler is preemptive, each task runs until its quantum, or time slice, expires, a higher priority process becomes runnable or the process blocks. Each task's time slice is calculated as a function of the process's priority upon release of the processor (with the exception of real-time tasks, which are discussed later). To prevent time slices from being too small to allow productive work or so large as to diminish response times, the scheduler ensures that the time slice assigned to each task is between 10 and 200 timer intervals, corresponding to a range of 10 to 200 milliseconds on most systems (like most scheduler parameters, these default values have been chosen empirically). When a task is preempted, the scheduler saves the task state to its `task_struct` structure. If the process's time slice has expired, the scheduler recalculates the process's priority, determines the task's next time slice and dispatches the next process.

Run Queues

Once a task has been created using `clone`, it is placed in a processor's **run queue**, which contains references to all tasks competing for execution on that processor. Run queues, similar to multilevel feedback queues (Section 8.7.6, Multilevel Feedback Queues), assign tasks to priority levels. The **priority array** maintains pointers to each level of the run queue. Each entry in the priority array points to a list of tasks—a task of priority i is placed in the ith entry of a priority array in the run queue (Fig. 20.3).

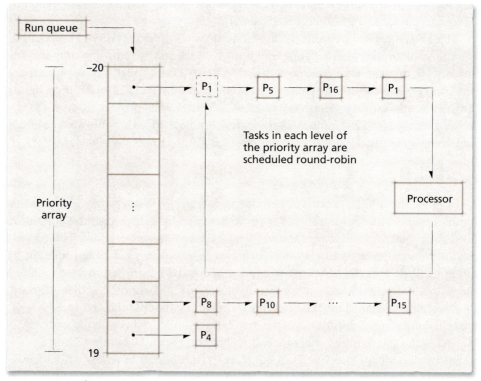

Figure 20.3 | Scheduler priority array.

The scheduler dispatches the task at the front of the list in the highest level of the priority array. If more than one task exists in a level of the priority array, tasks are dispatched from the priority array round-robin. When a task enters the *blocked* or *sleeping* (i.e., *waiting*) state, or is otherwise unable to execute, that task is removed from its run queue.

One goal of the scheduler is to prevent indefinite postponement by defining a period of time called an **epoch** during which each task in the run queue will execute at least once. To distinguish processes that are considered for processor time from those that must wait until the next epoch, the scheduler defines an *active* **state** and an *expired* **state**. The scheduler dispatches only processes in the *active* state.

The duration of an epoch is determined by the **starvation limit**—an empirically derived value that provides high-priority tasks with good response times while ensuring that low-priority tasks are dispatched often enough to perform productive work within a reasonable amount of time. By default, the starvation limit is set to $10n$ seconds, where n is the number of tasks in the run queue. When the current epoch has lasted longer than the starvation limit, the scheduler transitions each active task in the run queue to the *expired* state (the transition occurs after each active task's time slice expires). This temporarily suspends high-priority tasks (with the exception of real-time tasks), allowing low-priority tasks to execute. When all tasks in the run queue have executed at least once, all tasks in that run queue will be in the *expired* state. At this point, the scheduler transitions all tasks in the run queue to the *active* state and a new epoch begins.[53]

To simplify the transition from the *expired* state to the *active* state at the end of an epoch, the Linux scheduler maintains two priority arrays for each processor. The priority array that contains tasks in the active state is called the **active list**. The priority array that stores expired tasks (i.e., tasks that are not allowed to execute until the next epoch) is called the **inactive** (or **expired**) **list**. When a task transitions from the *active* state to the *expired* state, it is placed in the level of the expired list's priority array corresponding to its priority when it transitioned to the *expired* state. At the end of an epoch, all tasks are located in the *expired* state and must transition to the *active* state. The scheduler performs this operation quickly by simply swapping the pointers to the expired list and the active list. By maintaining two priority arrays per process, the scheduler can transition all tasks in a run queue using a single swap operation, a performance enhancement that generally outweighs the nominal memory overhead due.[54]

The Linux scheduler scales to multiprocessor systems by maintaining one run queue for each physical processor in the system. One reason for per-processor run queues is to assign tasks to execute on particular processors to exploit processor affinity. Recall from Chapter 15 that processes in some multiprocessor architectures, such as NUMA, achieve higher performance when a task's data is stored in a processor's local memory and in a processor's cache. Consequently, tasks can achieve higher performance if they are consistently assigned to a single processor (or node). However, per-processor run queues risk unbalancing processor loads, leading to reduced system performance and throughput (see Section 15.7, Process Migration). Later in this section, we discuss how Linux addresses this issue by dynamically balancing the number of tasks executing on each processor in the system.

Scheduling Priority

In the Linux scheduler, a task's priority affects the size of its time slice and the order in which it executes on a processor. Upon creation, tasks are assigned a **static priority**, also called the **nice value**. The scheduler recognizes 40 distinct priority levels, ranging from –20 to 19. Conforming to UNIX convention, smaller priority values denote higher priority in the scheduling algorithm (i.e., –20 is the highest priority a process can attain).

One goal of the Linux scheduler is to provide a high level of system interactivity. Because interactive tasks typically block to perform I/O or sleep (e.g., while waiting for a user response), the scheduler dynamically boosts the priority (by decrementing the static priority value) of a task that yields its processor before the task's time slice expires. This is acceptable because I/O-bound processes normally use the processor only briefly before generating an I/O request. Thus, giving I/O-bound tasks high priority has little effect on processor-bound tasks, which might use the processor for hours at a time if the system makes the processor available on a nonpreemptible basis. The modified priority level is called a task's **effective priority**, which is calculated when a task sleeps or consumes its time slice. A task's effective priority determines the level of the priority array in which a task is placed. Therefore, a task that receives a priority boost is placed in a lower level of the priority array, meaning it will execute before tasks of a higher effective priority value.

To further improve interactivity, the scheduler penalizes a processor-bound task by increasing its static priority value. This places a processor-bound task in a higher level of the priority array, meaning tasks of a smaller effective priority will be executed before it. Again, this ultimately has little effect on processor-bound tasks because the higher-priority interactive tasks execute only briefly before blocking.

To ensure that a task executes at or near the priority it was initially assigned, the task scheduler does not allow a task's effective priority to differ from its static priority by more than five units. In this sense, the scheduler honors the priority levels assigned to a task when it was created.

Scheduling Operations

The scheduler removes a task from a processor if the task is interrupted, preempted (e.g., if its time slice expires) or blocks. Each time a task is removed from a processor, the scheduler calculates a new time slice. If the task blocks, or is otherwise unable to execute, it is **deactivated**, meaning that it is removed from the run queue until it becomes ready to execute. Otherwise, the scheduler determines whether the task should be placed in the active list or the inactive list. The algorithm that determines this has been empirically derived to provide good performance; its primary factors are a task's static and effective priorities.

The result of the algorithm is depicted in Fig. 20.4. The *y*-axis of Fig. 20.4 indicates a task's static priority value and the *x*-axis represents a task's priority adjustment (i.e., boost or penalty) The shaded region indicates sets of static priority values and priority adjustments that cause a task to be rescheduled, meaning that it is placed at the end of its corresponding priority array in the active list. In general, if a task is of high priority and/or has received a significant bonus to its effective priority, it is rescheduled. This allows high-priority, I/O-bound and interactive tasks to execute more than once per epoch. In the unshaded region, tasks that are of low priority and/or have received priority penalties are placed in the expired list.

When a user process clones, it may seem reasonable to allocate each child its own time slice. However, if a task spawns a large number of new tasks, and all of its children are allocated their own time slices, other tasks in the system might experience unreasonably poor response times during that epoch. To improve fairness, Linux requires that each parent process initially share its time slice with its children when a user process clones. The scheduler enforces this requirement by assigning half of the parent's original time slice to both the parent process and its child the child is spawned. To prevent legitimate processes from suffering low levels of ser-

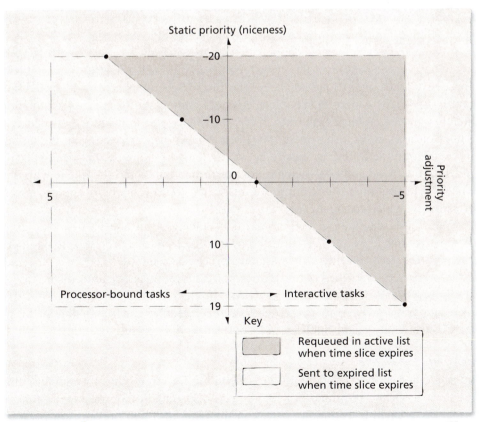

Figure 20.4 | *Priority values and their corresponding levels of interactivity.*[55]

vice due to spawning child processes, this reduced time slice applies only during the remainder of the epoch during which the child is spawned.

Multiprocessor Scheduling

Because the process scheduler maintains tasks in a per-processor run queue, tasks will generally exhibit high processor affinity. This means that a task will likely be dispatched to the same processor for each of its time slices, which can increase performance when a task's data and instructions are located in a processor's caches. However, such a scheme could allow one or several processors on an SMP system to lie idle even during a heavy system load. To avoid this, if the scheduler detects that a processor is idle, it performs **load balancing** to migrate tasks from one processor to another to improve resource utilization. If the system contains only one processor, load balancing routines are removed from the kernel when it is compiled.

The scheduler determines if it should perform load balancing routines after each timer interrupt, which is set to one millisecond on IA-32 systems. If the processor that issued the timer interrupt is idle (i.e., its run queue is empty), the scheduler attempts to migrate tasks from the processor with the heaviest load (i.e., the processor that contains the largest number of processes in its run queue) to the idle processor. To reduce load balancing overhead, if the processor that triggered the interrupt is not idle, the scheduler will attempt to move tasks to that processor every 200 timer interrupts instead of after every timer interrupt.[56]

The scheduler determines processor load by using the average length of each run queue over the past several timer interrupts, to minimize the effect of variations in processor loads on the load balancing algorithm. Because processor loads tend to change rapidly, the goal of load balancing is not to adjust the size of two run queues until they are of equal length; rather, it is to reduce the imbalance between the number of tasks in each run queue. As a result, tasks are removed from the larger run queue until the difference in size between the two run queues has been halved. To reduce overhead, load balancing is not performed unless the run queue with the heaviest load contains 25 percent more tasks than the run queue of the processor performing the load balancing.[57]

When the scheduler selects tasks for balancing, it attempts to choose tasks whose performance will be least affected by moving from one processor to another. In general, the least-recently active task on a processor will most likely be cache-cold on the processor—a **cache-cold** task does not contain much (or any) of the task's data in its processor's cache, whereas a **cache-hot** task contains most (or all) of the task's data in the processor cache. Therefore, the scheduler chooses to migrate tasks that are most likely cache-cold (i.e., tasks that have not executed recently).

Real-Time Scheduling

The scheduler supports soft real-time scheduling by attempting to minimize the time during which a real-time task waits to be dispatched to a processor. Unlike a normal task, which is eventually placed in the expired list to prevent low-priority tasks from being indefinitely postponed, a real-time task is always placed in the active list after its quantum expires. Further, real-time tasks always execute with higher priority than normal tasks. Because the scheduler always dispatches a task from the highest-priority queue in the active list (and real-time tasks are never removed from the active list), normal tasks cannot preempt real-time tasks.

The scheduler complies with the POSIX specification for real-time processes by allowing real-time tasks to be scheduled using the default scheduling algorithm described in the previous sections, or using the round-robin or FIFO scheduling algorithms. If a task specifies round-robin scheduling and its time slice has expired, the task is allocated a new time slice and is enqueued at the end of its priority array in the active list. If the task specifies FIFO scheduling, it is not assigned a time slice and therefore will execute on a processor until it exits, sleeps, blocks or is interrupted.[58] Clearly, real-time processes can indefinitely postpone other processes if coded improperly, resulting in poor response times. To prevent accidental or malicious misuse of real-time tasks, only users with root privileges can create them.

20.6 Memory Management

During the development of kernel versions 2.4 and 2.6, the memory manager was heavily modified to improve performance and scalability. The memory manager supports both 32- and 64-bit addresses as well as nonuniform memory access (NUMA) architectures to allow it to scale from desktop computers and workstations to servers and supercomputers.

20.6.1 Memory Organization

On most architectures, a system's physical memory is divided into fixed-size page frames. Generally, Linux allocates memory using a single page size (often 4KB or 8KB); on some architectures that support large pages (e.g., 4MB), kernel code may be placed in large pages. This can improve performance by minimizing the number of entries for kernel page frames in the translation lookaside buffer (TLB).[59] The kernel stores information about each page frame in a `page` structure. This structure contains variables that describe page usage, such as the number of processes sharing the page and flags indicating the state of the page (e.g., dirty, unused, etc).[60]

Virtual Memory Organization

On 32-bit systems, each process can address 2^{32} bytes, meaning that each virtual address space is 4GB. The kernel supports larger virtual address spaces on 64-bit systems—up to 2 petabytes (i.e., 2 million gigabytes) on Intel Itanium processors (the Itanium processor uses only 51 bits to address main memory, but the IA-64 architecture can support up to 64-bit physical addresses).[61] In this section, we focus on the 32-bit implementation of the virtual memory manager. Entries describing the virtual-to-physical address mappings are located in each process's page tables. The virtual memory system supports up to three levels of page tables to locate the mappings between virtual pages and page frames (see Fig. 20.5). The first level of the page table hierarchy, called the **page global directory**, stores addresses of sec-

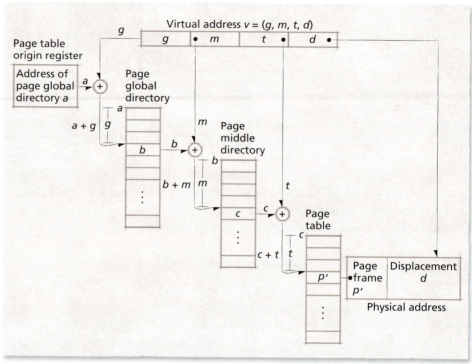

Figure 20.5 | *Page table organization.*

ond-level tables. Second-level tables, called **page middle directories**, store addresses of the third-level tables. The third level, simply called page tables, maps virtual pages to page frames.

The kernel partitions a virtual address into four fields to provide processors with multilevel page address translation information. The first three fields are indices into the process's page global directory, page middle directory and page table, respectively. These three fields allow the system to locate the page frame corresponding to a virtual page. The fourth field contains the displacement (also called offset) from the physical address of the beginning of the page frame.[62] Linux disables page middle directories when running on the IA-32 architecture, which supports only two levels of page tables when the Physical Address Extension (PAE) feature is disabled. Page middle directories are enabled for 64-bit architectures that support three or more levels of page tables (e.g., the x86-64 architecture, which supports four levels of page tables).

Virtual Memory Areas

Although a process's virtual address space is composed of individual pages, the kernel uses a higher-level mechanism, called **virtual memory areas**, to organize the virtual memory a process is using. A virtual memory area describes a contiguous set of pages in a process's virtual address space that are assigned the same protection (e.g., read-only, read/write, executable) and backing store. The kernel stores a process's executable code, heap, stack and each memory-mapped file (see Section 13.9, Data Access Techniques) in separate virtual memory areas.[63, 64]

When a process requests additional memory, the kernel attempts to satisfy that request by enlarging an existing virtual memory area. The virtual memory area the kernel selects depends on the type of memory the process is requesting (e.g., executable code, heap, stack, etc.). If the process requests memory that does not correspond to an existing virtual memory area, or if the kernel cannot allocate a contiguous address space of the requested size in an existing virtual memory area, the kernel creates a new virtual memory area.[65]

Virtual Memory Organization for the IA-32 Architecture

In Linux, virtual memory organization is architecture specific. In this section, we discuss how the kernel organizes virtual memory by default to optimize performance on the IA-32 architecture.

When the kernel performs a context switch, it must provide the processor with page address translation information for the process that is about to execute (see Section 10.4.1). Recall from Section 10.4.3 that an associative memory called the translation lookaside buffer (TLB) stores recently used page table entries (PTEs) so that the processor can quickly perform virtual-to-physical address translations for the process that is currently running. Because each process is allocated a different virtual address space, PTEs for one process are not valid for another. As a result, the PTEs in the TLB must be removed after a context switch. This is called flushing the TLB—the processor removes each PTE from the TLB and updates the PTEs in main memory to match any modified PTEs in the TLB. In particular, each time the value of the page table origin register changes, the TLB must be flushed. The overhead due to a TLB flush can be substantial because the processor must access main memory to update each PTE that is flushed. If the kernel changes the value of the page table origin register to execute each system call, the overhead due to TLB flushing can significantly reduce performance.

To reduce the number of expensive TLB flush operations, the kernel ensures that it can use any process's page table origin register to access the kernel's virtual address space. The kernel does this by dividing each process's virtual address space into user addresses and kernel addresses. The kernel allows each process to access up to 3GB of the process's virtual address space—the virtual addresses from zero to 3GB. Therefore, virtual-to-physical address translation information can vary between processes for the first 3GB of each 32-bit virtual address space. The kernel address space is the remaining 1GB of virtual addresses in each process's 32-bit virtual address space (addresses ranging from 3GB to 4GB), as shown in Fig. 20.6. The virtual-to-physical address translation information for this region of memory addresses does not vary from one process to another. Therefore, when a user process invokes the kernel, the processor does not need to flush the TLB, which improves performance by reducing the number of times the processor accesses main memory to update page table entries.[66]

Often, the kernel must access main memory on behalf of user processes (e.g., to perform I/O); therefore, it must be able to access every page frame in main memory. However, today's processors require that all memory references use virtual addresses to access memory (if virtual memory is enabled). As a result, the kernel generally must use virtual addresses to access page frames.

When using virtual addresses, the kernel must provide the processor with PTEs that map the kernel's virtual pages to the page frames it must access. The kernel could create these PTEs each time it accessed main memory; however, doing so would create significant overhead. Therefore, the kernel creates PTEs that map most of the pages in the kernel's virtual address space permanently to page frames in main memory. For example, the first page of the kernel's virtual address space always points to the first page frame in main memory; the 100th page of the kernel's virtual address space always points to the 100th page frame in main memory (Fig. 20.6).

Note that creating a PTE (i.e., mapping virtual page to a page frame) does not allocate a page frame to the kernel or a user process. For example, assume that page frame number 100 stores a process's virtual page p. When the kernel accesses virtual page number 100 in the kernel virtual address space, the processor maps the virtual page number to page frame number 100, which stores the contents of p. Thus, the kernel's virtual address space is used to access page frames that may be allocated to the kernel or user processes.

Ideally, the kernel would be able to create PTEs that permanently map to each page frame in memory. However, if a system contains more than 1GB of main memory, the kernel cannot create a permanent mapping to every page frame because it reserves only 1GB of each 4GB virtual address space for itself. For example, when the kernel performs I/O on behalf of a user process, it must be able to access the data using pages in its 1GB virtual address space. However, if a user pro-

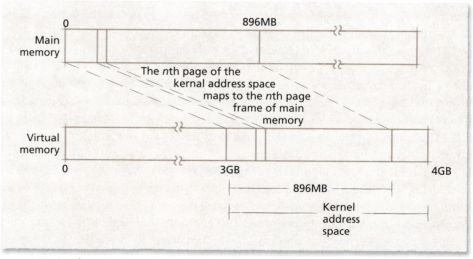

Figure 20.6 | *Kernel virtual address space mapping.*

cess requests I/O for a page that is stored at an address higher than 1GB, the kernel might not contain a mapping to that page. In this case, the kernel must be able to create a temporary mapping between a kernel virtual page and a user's physical page in main memory to perform the I/O. To address this problem, the kernel maps most of its virtual pages permanently to page frames and reserves several virtual pages to provide temporary mappings to the remaining page frames. In particular, the kernel creates PTEs that map the first 896MB of its virtual pages permanently to the first 896MB of main memory when the kernel boots. It reserves the remaining 128MB of its virtual address space for temporary buffers and caches that can be mapped to other regions of main memory. Therefore, if the kernel must access page frames beyond 896MB, it uses virtual addresses in this region to create a new PTE that temporarily maps a virtual page to a page frame.

Physical Memory Organization

The memory management system divides a system's physical address space into three **zones** (Fig. 20.7). The size of each zone is architecture dependent; in this section we present the configuration for the IA-32 architecture discussed in the previous section. The first zone, called **DMA memory**, includes the main memory locations from 0–16MB. The primary reason for creating a DMA memory zone is to ensure compatibility with legacy architectures. For example, some direct memory

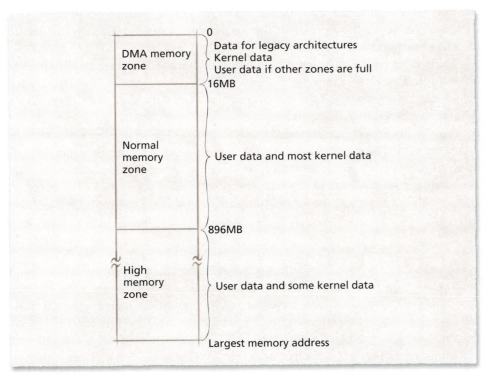

Figure 20.7 | Physical memory zones on the IA-32 Intel architecture.

access (DMA) devices can address only up to 16MB of memory, so Linux reserves memory in this zone for such devices. The DMA memory zone also contains kernel data and instructions (e.g., bootstrapping code) and might be allocated for user processes if free memory is scarce.

The second zone, called **normal memory**, includes the physical memory locations between 16MB and up to 896MB. The normal memory zone can be used to store user and kernel pages as well as data from devices that can access memory greater than 16MB using DMA. Note that because the kernel's virtual address space is mapped directly to the first 896MB of main memory, most kernel data structures are located in the low memory zones (i.e., the DMA or normal memory zones). If these data structures were not located in these memory zones, the kernel could not provide a permanent virtual-to-physical address mapping for kernel data and might cause a page fault while executing its code. Page faults not only reduce kernel performance but can be fatal when performing error-handling routines.

The third zone, called **high memory**, includes physical memory locations from 896MB to a maximum of 64GB on Pentium processors. (Intel's Page Address Extension feature enables 36-bit memory addresses, allowing the system to access 2^{36} bytes, or 64GB, of main memory.) High memory is allocated to user processes, any devices that can access memory in this zone and temporary kernel data structures.[67, 68]

Some devices, however, cannot access data in high memory because the number of physical addresses they can address is limited. In this case, the kernel copies such data to a buffer, called a **bounce buffer**, in DMA memory to perform I/O. After completing an I/O operation, the kernel copies any modified pages in the buffer to the page in high memory.[69, 70, 71]

Depending on the architecture, the first megabyte of main memory might contain data loaded into memory by initialization functions in the BIOS (see Section 2.3.1, Mainboards). To avoid overwriting such data, the Linux kernel code and data structures are loaded into a contiguous area of physical memory, typically beginning at the second megabyte of main memory. (The kernel reclaims most of the first megabyte of memory after loading.) Kernel pages are never swapped (i.e., paged) or relocated in physical memory. In addition to improving performance, the contiguous and static nature of kernel memory simplifies coding for kernel developers at a relatively low cost (the kernel footprint is approximately 2MB).[72]

20.6.2 Physical Memory Allocation and Deallocation

The kernel allocates page frames to processes using the **zone allocator**. The zone allocator attempts to allocate pages from the physical zone corresponding to each request. Recall that the kernel reserves as much of the DMA memory zone as possible for use by legacy architectures and kernel code. Also, performing I/O operations on high memory might require use of a bounce buffer, which is less efficient than using pages that are directly accessible by DMA hardware. Thus, although pages for user processes can be allocated from any zone, the kernel attempts to allocate them first from the high memory zone. If the high memory zone is full and pages in normal memory are available, then the zone allocator uses pages from normal memory. Only when free memory is scarce in both the normal and the high zone of memory does the zone allocator select pages in DMA memory.[73]

When deciding which page frames to allocate, the zone allocator searches for empty pages in each zone's `free_area` vector. The `free_area` vector contains references to a zone's free lists and bitmaps that identify contiguous blocks of memory. Blocks of page frames are allocated in groups of powers of two; each element in a zone's `free_area` vector contains a list of blocks that are the same size—the nth element in the vector references a list of blocks of size 2^n.[74] Figure 20.8 illustrates the first three entries of the `free_area` vector.

To locate blocks of the requested size, the memory manager uses the **binary buddy algorithm** to search the `free_area` vector. The buddy algorithm, described by Knowlton and Knuth, is a simple physical page allocation algorithm that provides good performance.[75, 76] If there are no blocks of the requested size, a block of the next-closest size in the `free_area` vector is halved repeatedly until the resulting block is of the correct size. When the memory manager finds a block of the correct size, it allocates it to the process that requested it and places any orphaned free blocks in the appropriate lists.[77]

When memory is deallocated, the buddy algorithm groups contiguous free pages as follows. When a process frees a block of memory, the memory manager checks the bitmap (in the `free_area` vector) that tracks blocks of that size. If the bitmap indicates that an adjacent block is free, the memory manager combines the two blocks (buddies) into a larger block. The memory manager repeats this process until there are no blocks with which to combine the resulting block. The memory manager then inserts the block into the proper list in `free_area`.[78]

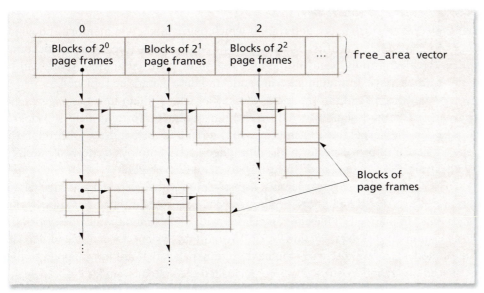

Figure 20.8 | *free_area vector.*

There are several kernel data structures (e.g., the structure that describes virtual memory areas) that consume much less than a page of memory (4KB is the smallest page size on most systems). Processes tend to allocate and release many such data structures during the course of execution. Requests to the zone allocator to allocate such small amounts of memory would result in substantial internal fragmentation because the smallest unit of memory the zone allocator can supply is a page. Instead, the kernel satisfies such requests via the **slab allocator**. The slab allocator allocates memory from any one of a number of available **slab caches**.[79] A slab cache is composed of a number of objects, called slabs, that span one or more pages and contain structures of the same type. Typically, a **slab** is one page of memory that serves as a container for multiple data structures smaller than a page. When the kernel requests memory for a new structure, the slab allocator returns a portion of a slab in the slab cache for that structure. If all of the slabs in a cache are occupied, the slab allocator increases the size of the cache to include more slabs. These new slabs contain pages allocated using the appropriate zone allocator.[80]

As previously discussed, serious or fatal system errors can occur if the kernel causes a page fault during interrupt- or error-handling code. Similarly, a request to allocate memory while executing such code must not fail if the system contains few free pages. To prevent such a situation, Linux allows kernel threads and device drivers to allocate memory pools. A **memory pool** is a region of memory that the kernel guarantees will be available to a kernel thread or device driver regardless of how much memory is currently occupied. Clearly, extensive use of memory pools limits the number of page frames available to user processes. However, because a system failure could result from a failed memory allocation, the trade-off is justified.[81]

20.6.3 Page Replacement

The Linux memory manager determines which pages to keep in memory and which pages to replace (known as "swapping" in Linux) when free memory becomes scarce. Recall that only pages in the user region of a virtual address space can be replaced; most pages containing kernel code and data cannot be replaced.

As pages are read into memory, the kernel inserts them into the **page cache**. The page cache is designed to reduce the time spent performing disk I/O operations. When the kernel must flush (i.e., write) a page to disk, it does so through the page cache. To improve performance, the page cache employs write-back caching (see Section 12.8, Caching and Buffering) to clean dirty pages.[82]

Each page in the page cache must be associated with a secondary storage device (e.g., a disk) so the kernel knows where to place pages when they are swapped out. Pages that are mapped to files are associated with a file's inode, which describes the file's location on disk (see Section 20.7.1, Virtual File System, for a detailed description of inodes). As we discuss in the next section, pages that are not mapped to files are placed on secondary storage in a region called the system swap file.[83]

When physical memory is full and a nonresident page is requested by processes or the kernel, a page frame must be freed to fill the request. The memory manager provides a simple, efficient page-replacement strategy. Figure 20.9 illustrates this strategy. In each memory zone, pages are divided into two groups: **active pages** and **inactive pages**. To be considered active, a page must have been referenced recently. One goal of the memory manager is to maintain the current working set inside the collection of active pages.[84]

Linux uses a variation of the clock page-replacement strategy (see Section 11.6.7). The memory manager uses two linked lists per zone to implement page replacement—the active list contains active pages, the inactive list contains inactive pages. The lists are organized such that the most-recently used pages are near the head of the active list, and the least-recently used pages are near the tail of the inactive list.[85]

When the memory manager allocates a page of memory to a process, the page's associated **page** structure is placed at the head of that zone's inactive list and

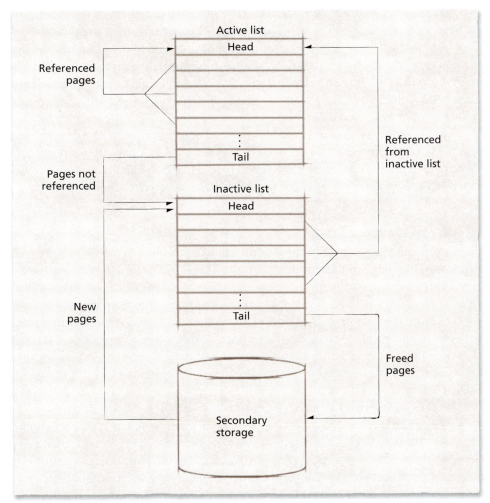

Figure 20.9 | *Page-replacement system overview.*

that page is marked as having been referenced by setting its referenced bit. The memory manager determines whether the page has been subsequently referenced at several points during kernel execution, such as when a PTE is flushed from the TLB. If the page has been referenced, the memory manager determines how to mark the page based on whether the page is active or inactive, and whether it has been referenced recently.

If the page is active or inactive and its referenced bit is off, the bit is turned on. Similar to the clock algorithm, this technique ensures that recently referenced pages are not selected for replacement. Otherwise, if the page is inactive and is being referenced for the second time (its referenced bit is already on), the memory manager moves the page to the head of the active list, then clears its referenced bit.[86] This allows the kernel to distinguish between referenced pages that have been accessed once and those that have been accessed more than once recently. The latter are placed in the active list so that they are not selected for replacement.

The memory manager updates the active list by transferring pages that have not been recently accessed to the inactive list. This is performed periodically and when available memory is low. The memory manager attempts to balance the lists such that approximately two-thirds of the total number of pages in the page cache are in the active list—an empirically derived value that achieves good performance in many environments.[87] The memory manager achieves this goal by periodically moving any unreferenced pages in the active list to the head of the inactive list.

This algorithm is repeated until the specified number of pages have been moved from the tail of the active list to the head of the inactive list. A page in the inactive list will remain in memory unless it is reclaimed (e.g., when free memory is low). While a page is in the active list, however, the page cannot be selected for replacement.[88]

20.6.4 Swapping

When available page frames become scarce, the kernel must decide which pages to swap out to free page frames for new requests. This is performed periodically by the kernel thread *kswapd* (the swap daemon), which reclaims pages by writing dirty pages to secondary storage. If the pages are mapped to a file in a particular file system (i.e., store file data in main memory), the system updates the file with any modifications to the page in memory. If the page corresponds to a process's data or procedure page, *kswapd* writes them to a region of data in secondary storage called the **system swap file**. *kswapd* selects pages to evict from entries at the tail of the inactive list.[89]

When swapping out a page, *kswapd* first determines whether it exists in the swap cache. The **swap cache** contains page table entries that describe whether a given page already exists in the system swap file on secondary storage. Under certain conditions, if the swap cache contains an entry for the page being swapped out, the page frame occupied by the page is freed immediately. By examining the swap cache, *kswapd* can avoid performing expensive I/O operations when an exact copy of the swapped page exists in the swap file.[90]

Before a page is replaced, the memory manager must determine whether to perform certain actions to ensure consistency (e.g., updating PTEs and writing data to disk). A page chosen for replacement cannot be immediately swapped under the following conditions:

- The page is shared (i.e., referenced by more than one process).
- The page has been modified.
- The page is **locked**—a process or device relies on its presence in main memory to perform an operation.[91]

If a page is being referenced by more than one process, *kswapd* must first **unmap** references to the page. The kernel unmaps a reference to a page by zeroing its PTE value. Linux uses **reverse mapping** to quickly find all page table entries pointing to a page, given a reference to a page frame. This is implemented in the page structure by a linked list of page table entries that reference the page. Without reverse mappings, the kernel would be required to search every page table in the system to find PTEs that map the page that is chosen for replacement. Although reverse mapping increases the size of each page object in the system, which in turn increases kernel memory usage, the performance improvement over searching page tables usually outweighs its cost.[92]

After the kernel unmaps all the page table entries that reference a page, it must determine if the page has been modified. Modified (i.e., dirty) pages must be flushed to disk before they can be freed. To improve performance and reduce data loss during system crashes, the kernel attempts to limit the number of dirty pages resident in memory. The kernel thread *pdflush* attempts to flush pages to disk (i.e., clean dirty pages) approximately every 5 seconds (depending on the system load) and defines an upper limit of 30 seconds during which pages can remain dirty. Once the disk flushing I/O is complete, *kswapd* can reclaim the page frame and allocate it to a new virtual page.[93, 94]

If a page is locked, *kswapd* cannot access the page to free it because a process or device relies on its presence in main memory to perform an operation. For example, a page of memory used to perform an I/O operation is typically locked. When the memory manager searches the inactive page list to choose pages for eviction, it does not consider locked pages. The page is freed on the next pass through the list if it is no longer locked and is still a member of the inactive list.[95]

20.7 File Systems

To meet the needs of users across multiple platforms, Linux must support a variety of file systems. When the kernel requires access to a specific file, it calls functions defined by the file system containing the file. Each particular file system determines how to store and access its data.

In Linux, a file refers to more than bits on secondary storage—files serve as access points to data, which can be found on a local disk, across a network, or even generated by the kernel itself. By abstracting the concept of a file, the kernel can access hardware devices, interprocess communication mechanisms, data stored on disk and a variety of other data sources using a single generic file system interface. Developers use this interface to quickly add support for new file systems as they become available. Linux kernel version 2.6 includes support for more than 40 file systems that can be integrated into the kernel or loaded as modules.[96] These include general-purpose file systems (e.g., ext2, FAT and UDF), network file systems (e.g., NFS, CIFS and Coda) and file systems that exist exclusively in memory (e.g., procfs, sysfs, ramfs and tmpfs). In the sections that follow, we discuss the ext2, procfs, sysfs, ramfs and tmpfs file systems.

20.7.1 Virtual File System

Linux supports multiple file systems by providing a virtual file system (VFS) layer. The VFS abstracts the details of file access, allowing users to view all the files and directories in the system under a single directory tree. Users can access any file in the directory tree without knowledge of where, and under which file system, the file data are stored. All file-related requests are initially sent to the VFS layer, which provides an interface to access file data on any available file system. The VFS provides only a basic definition of the objects that comprise a file system. Individual file systems expand that basic definition to include details of how objects are stored and accessed.[97] Figure 20.10 illustrates this layered file system approach. Processes issue

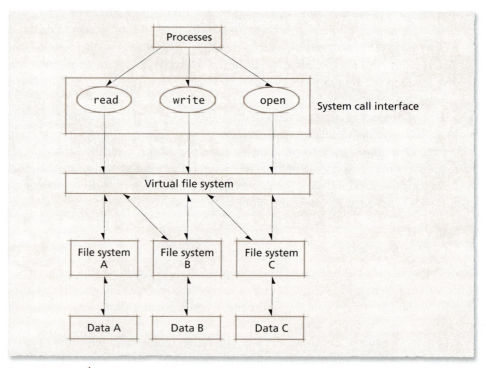

Figure 20.10 | Relationship between the VFS, file systems and data.

system calls such as `read`, `write` and `open`, which are passed to the virtual file system. The VFS determines the file system to which the request corresponds and calls the corresponding routines in the file system driver, which perform the requested operations. This layered approach simplifies application programming and enables developers to add support for new file systems quickly, at the cost of nominal execution-time overhead.

The VFS uses files to read and write data that are not necessarily stored as bits on secondary storage. The virtual file system layer defines a number of objects that locate and provide access to data. One such object, called an **inode**, describes the location of each file, directory or link within every available file system. VFS inodes do not contain the name of the file they represent; rather, inodes are uniquely identified by a tuple containing an inode number (which is unique to a particular file system) and a number identifying the file system that contains the inode.[98] The VFS enables several file names to map to a single inode. This allows users to create hard links—multiple file names that map to the same inode within a file system.

Linux uses files to represent many objects, including named sets of data, hardware devices and shared memory regions. The broad usage of files originates in UNIX systems, from which Linux borrows many concepts.

The VFS represents each file using a file descriptor, which contains information about the inode being accessed, the position in the file being accessed and flags describing how the data is being accessed (e.g. read/write, append-only).[99] For clarity, we refer to VFS file objects as "file descriptors" and use the term "file" to refer to named data within a particular file system.

To map file descriptors to inodes, the VFS uses a **dentry (directory entry)** object. A dentry contains the name of the file or directory an inode represents. A file descriptor points to a dentry, which points to the corresponding inode.[100] Figure 20.11 shows a possible dentry representation of the /home directory and its contents. Each dentry contains a name and pointers to the dentry of its parent, children and siblings. For example, the dentry corresponding to /home/chris contains pointers to its parent (/home), children (/home/chris/foo, /home/chris/bar and /home/chris/txt) and sibling (/home/jim) directory entries. Using this information, the virtual file system can quickly resolve pathname-to-inode conversions. Dentries are discussed further in Section 20.7.2, Virtual File System Caches.

The Linux directory tree is comprised of one or more file systems, each comprised of a tree of inodes. When a file system is **mounted**, its contents are attached to a specified part of the primary directory tree. This allows processes to access data located in different file systems transparently via a single directory tree. A **VFS superblock** contains information about a mounted file system, such as the type of file system, its root inode's location on disk and housekeeping information that protects the integrity of the file system (e.g., the number of free blocks and free inodes in the system).[101] The VFS superblock is created by the kernel and resides exclusively in memory. Each file system must provide the VFS with superblock data when it is mounted.

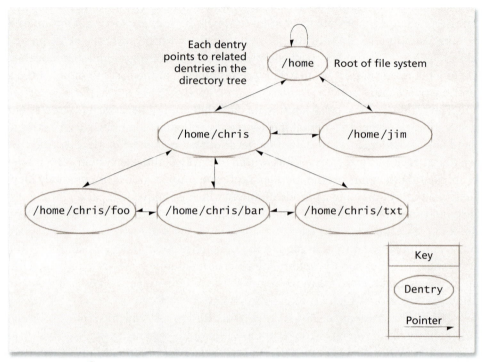

Figure 20.11 | Dentry organization for a particular /home directory.

The data stored in a file system's superblock is file-system dependent, but typically includes a pointer to the root inode (i.e., the inode that corresponds to the root of the file system) as well as information regarding the size and available space in the file system. Because a file system's superblock contains a pointer to the first inode in the file system, the operating system must load its superblock to access any other data in the file system. Most file systems place their superblock in one of the first blocks on secondary storage and maintain redundant copies of the superblock throughout their storage device to recover from damage.[102]

The virtual file system interprets data from the superblock, inodes, files and dentries to determine the contents of available file systems. The VFS defines generic file system operations and requires that each file system provide an implementation for each operation it supports. For example, the VFS defines a read function, but does not implement it. Example VFS file operations are listed in Fig. 20.12. Each file system driver must therefore implement a read function to allow processes to read its files. The virtual file system also provides generic file system primitives (e.g., files, superblocks and inodes). Each file system driver must assign file-system-specific information to these primitives.

VFS operation	Intended use
read	Copy data from a file to a location in memory.
write	Write data from a location in memory to a file.
open	Locate the inode corresponding to a file.
release	Release the inode associated with a file. This can be performed only when all open file descriptors for that inode are closed.
ioctl	Perform a device-specific operation on a device (represented by an inode and file).
lookup	Resolve a pathname to a file system inode and return a dentry corresponding to it.

Figure 20.12 | VFS file and inode operations.

20.7.2 Virtual File System Caches

The virtual file system maintains a single directory tree composed of one or more file systems. To improve performance for file and directory access, the virtual file system maintains two caches—the **directory entry cache (dcache)** and the **inode cache**. These caches contain information about recently used entries in the directory tree. The cache entries represent objects in any available mounted file system.[103, 104]

The dcache contains dentries corresponding to directories that have recently been accessed. This allows the kernel to quickly perform a pathname-to-inode translation if the file specified by the pathname is located in main memory. Because the amount of memory allocated to the dcache is limited, the VFS uses the dcache to store the most recently used dentries.[105] Although normally it cannot cache every file and directory in the system, the VFS ensures that if a dentry is in the dcache, its parent and other ancestors are also in the dcache. The only time this might not hold true is when file systems are accessed across a network (due to the fact that remote file system information can change without the local system being notified).[106]

Recall that when the VFS performs a pathname-to-inode translation, it uses dentries in the dcache to quickly locate inodes in the inode cache. The VFS then uses these inodes to locate a file's data when it is cached in main memory. Because the VFS relies on dentries to quickly locate inodes, each dentry's corresponding inode should be present in the inode cache. Therefore, the VFS ensures that each dentry in the dcache corresponds to an inode in the inode cache.

Conversely, if an inode is not referenced by a dentry, the VFS cannot access the inode. Therefore the VFS removes inodes that are no longer referenced by a dentry.[107, 108]

Locating the inode corresponding to a given pathname is a multistep process. The VFS must perform a directory-to-inode translation for each directory in the pathname. The translation begins at the root inode of the file system containing the pathname. The location of the file system's root inode is found in its superblock, which is loaded into memory when the file system is mounted. Beginning at the root inode, the VFS must resolve each directory entry in the pathname to its corresponding inode.[109]

When searching for the inode that represents a given directory, the VFS first checks the dcache for the directory. If the dentry is found in the dcache, the corresponding inode must exist in the inode cache. Note that in Fig. 20.13 the dentry corresponding to `foo.txt` exists in the dentry cache; that dentry then points to an inode, which points to data in a file system.

If the VFS cannot find the dentry in the dcache, it searches for the inode directly in the inode cache.[110] Figure 20.13 illustrates this case using `link.txt`, a hard link to the file `bar.txt`. In this case, a process has previously referenced `link.txt`, meaning that a dentry corresponding to `link.txt` exists in the dcache. Because `link.txt` is a hard link to `bar.txt`, `link.txt`'s dentry points to `bar.txt`'s inode. When `bar.txt` is referenced for the first time, its dentry does not exist in the dentry cache. However, because a process has referenced `bar.txt` using a hard link, the inode corresponding to `bar.txt` exists in the inode cache. When the VFS does not find an entry for `bar.txt` in the dcache, it searches the inode cache and locates the inode corresponding to `bar.txt`.

If the dentry is not in the dcache and its corresponding inode is not in the inode cache, the VFS locates the inode by calling its parent directory inode's lookup function (which is defined by the underlying file system).[111] Once the directory is located, its associated inode and corresponding dentry are loaded into memory. The new inode is added to the inode cache and the dentry is added to the dcache.[112]

The VFS repeats the process of searching the caches before calling the lookup function for each directory in the pathname. By utilizing the caches, the VFS can

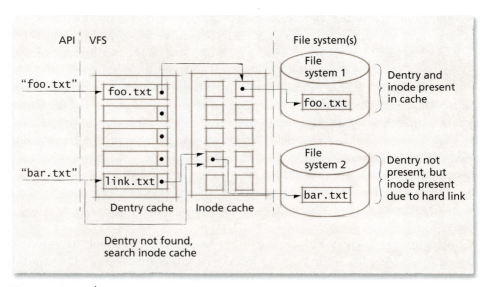

Figure 20.13 | *Dentry and inode caches.*

avoid lengthy delays due to a file system's accessing inodes on disk, across a network, or from other media.

The inode `lookup` function is one of several functions that file systems typically implement (see Fig. 20.12). The primary responsibilities of the VFS are to cache file system data and pass file access requests to the appropriate file systems. Most file systems provide the VFS with their own implementations of functions such as `lookup`, `read` and `write` to access files, directories and links. The VFS allows file systems a great deal of flexibility in choosing which functions to implement and how to implement them.

20.7.3 Second Extended File System (ext2fs)

After its 1993 release, the **second extended file system (ext2fs)** quickly became the most widely used Linux file system of its time. The primary goal of ext2fs is to provide a high-performance, robust file system with support for advanced features.[113] As required by the virtual file system, ext2fs supports basic objects such as the superblock, inodes and directories. The ext2fs implementation of these objects extends their definitions to include specific information about the location and layout of data on disk, as well as providing functions to retrieve and modify data.

When an ext2fs partition is formatted, its corresponding disk space is divided into fixed-size blocks of data. Typical block sizes are 1,024, 2,048, 4,096 or 8,192 bytes. The file system stores all file data and metadata in these blocks.[114] By default, five percent of the blocks are reserved exclusively for users with root privileges when the disk is formatted. This is a safety mechanism provided to allow root processes to continue to run if a malicious or errant user process consumes all other available blocks in the file system.[115] The remaining 95 percent of the blocks can be used by all users to organize and store file data.

An **ext2 inode** represents files and directories in an ext2 file system—each inode stores information relevant to a single file or directory, such as time stamps, permissions, the identity of the file's owner and pointers to data blocks (Fig. 20.14). A single block is rarely large enough to contain an entire file. Thus, there are 15 data block pointers (each 32 bits wide) in each ext2 inode. The first 12 pointers directly locate the first 12 data blocks. The 13th pointer is an **indirect pointer**. The indirect pointer locates a block that contains pointers to data blocks. The 14th pointer is a **doubly indirect pointer**. The doubly indirect pointer locates a block of indirect pointers. The 15th pointer is a **triply indirect pointer**—a pointer to a block of doubly indirect pointers.

Consider an ext2 file system that uses 32-bit block addresses and a block size of 4,096 bytes. If a file is less than 48KB in size (i.e., it consumes 12 blocks of data or fewer), the file system can locate the file's data using pointers directly from the file's inode. The block of singly indirect pointers locates up to 1,024 data blocks (4MB of file data). Thus, the file system need load only two blocks (the inode and the block of indirect pointers) to locate over 4MB of file data. Similarly, the doubly indirect block of pointers locates up to $1,024^2$, or 1,048,576, data blocks (4GB of file data).

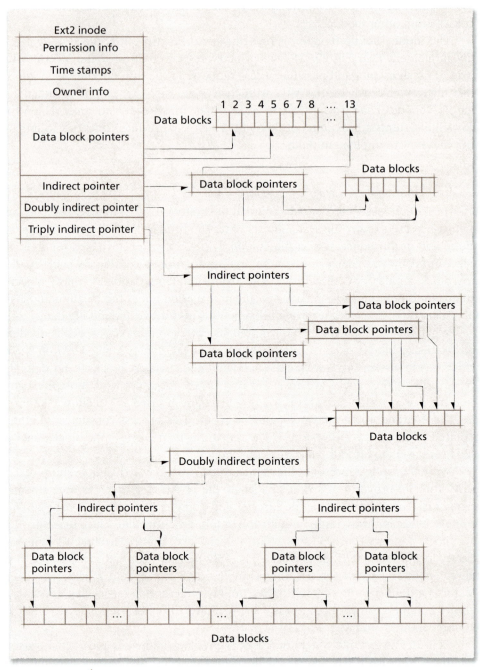

Figure 20.14 | **Ext2 inode contents.**

In this case, the file system must load one doubly indirect block, 1,025 singly indirect blocks and the file's inode (containing 12 direct pointers to data blocks) to access files of 4GB. Finally, the triply indirect block of pointers locates up to $1,024^3$, or 1,073,741,824, data blocks (4,096GB of file data). In this case, the file system must load one triply indirect block, 1,025 doubly indirect blocks, 1,149,601 singly indirect blocks and the file's inode (containing 12 direct pointers to data blocks) to access files of approximately 4,100GB. This design provides fast access to small files, while supporting larger files (maximum file sizes range from 16GB to 4,096GB, depending on the file system's block size).[116]

Block Groups

Blocks in an ext2fs partition are divided into clusters of contiguous blocks called **block groups**. The file system attempts to store related data in the same block group. This arrangement reduces the seek time for accessing large groups of related data (e.g., directory inodes, file inodes and file data) because blocks inside each block group are located in a contiguous region of disk. Figure 20.15 illustrates the structure of a block group. The first block is the superblock. The superblock contains critical information about the entire file system, not just a particular block group. This information includes the total number of blocks and inodes in the file system, the size of the block groups, the time at which the file system was mounted and other housekeeping data. Because the contents of the superblock are critical to the integrity of the file system, a redundant copy of the superblock is maintained in some block groups. As a result, if any copy is corrupted, the file system can be restored from one of the redundant copies.[117]

The block group contains several data structures to facilitate file operations on that group. One such structure is the **inode table**, which contains an entry for each inode in the block group. When the file system is formatted, it assigns a fixed number of ext2 inodes to each block group. The number of inodes in the system depends on the ratio of bytes to inodes in the file system, specified when the partition is formatted. Because the size of the inode table is fixed, the only way to increase the number of inodes in a formatted ext2 file system is to increase the size of the file system. The inodes in each group's inode table typically point to file and directory data located in that group, reducing the time necessary to load files from disk due to the phenomenon of locality.

The block group also maintains a block containing an **inode allocation bitmap** that tracks inode use within a block group. Each bit in the allocation bitmap corresponds to an entry in the group's inode table. When a file is allocated, an available

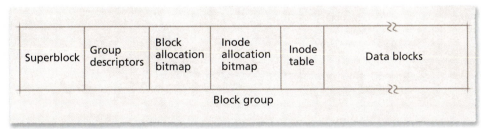

Figure 20.15 | Block group.

inode is selected from the inode table to represent the file. The bit in the allocation bitmap corresponding to the inode's index in the inode table is turned on to indicate that the inode is in use. For example, if inode table entry 45 is assigned to a file, the 45th bit in the inode allocation bitmap is turned on. When an inode is no longer needed, the corresponding bit in the inode allocation bitmap is cleared to indicate that the inode can be reused. This same strategy is employed to maintain the **block allocation bitmaps**, which track each group's block usage.[118]

Another element of metadata in each block group, called the **group descriptor**, contains the block numbers corresponding to the location of the inode allocation bitmap, block allocation bitmap and inode table (Fig. 20.16). It also contains accounting information, such as the number of free blocks and inodes in the group. Each block group contains a redundant copy of its group descriptor for recovery purposes.[119]

The remaining blocks in each block group store file and directory data. Directories are variable-length objects that associate file names with inode numbers using **directory entries**. Each directory entry is composed of an inode number, directory entry length, file name length, file type and file name (Fig. 20.17). Typical file types include data files, directories and symbolic links; however, ext2fs also can use files to represent other objects, such as devices and sockets.[120]

Ext2fs supports both hard and symbolic links (recall from Section 13.4.2, Metadata, that symbolic links specify a pathname, not an inode number). When the

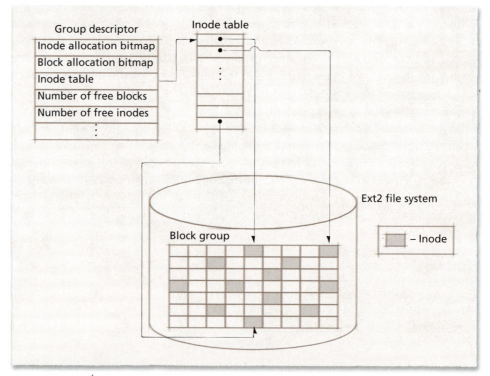

Figure 20.16 | *Group descriptor.*

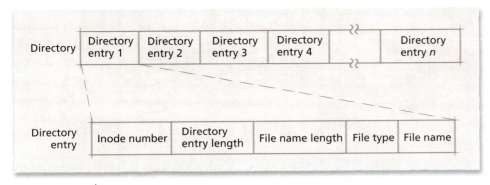

Figure 20.17 | *Directory structure.*

file system encounters a symbolic link while translating a pathname to an inode, the pathname being translated is replaced by the contents of the symbolic link, and the conversion is restarted. Because hard links specify an inode number, they do not require pathname-to-inode conversion. The file system maintains a count of the number of directory entries referencing an inode to ensure an inode is not deleted while it is still being referenced.[121]

File Security

Each file's inode stores information that the kernel uses to enforce its access control policies. In the ext2 file system, inodes contain two fields related to security: **file permissions** and **file attributes**. File permissions specify read, write and execute privileges for three categories of users: the owner of the file (initially the user that created the file), a group of users allowed to access the file (initially the group to which the user that created the file belongs), and all other users in the system.

File attributes control how file data can be modified. For example, the append-only file attribute specifies that users may append data to the file, but not modify data that already exists in the file. Ext2 file attributes can be extended to support other security features. For example, ext2 stores access control metadata in its extended file attributes to implement POSIX access control lists.[122]

Locating Data Using a Pathname

To locate a file in a file system, a pathname-to-inode conversion must be performed. Consider the example of finding the file given by the pathname /home/admin/pol-icydoc. The pathname is composed of a series of directory names separated by slashes (/home/admin) that specify the path to the file policydoc. The conversion begins by locating the inode representing the root directory of the file system. The inode number of the root directory (/) is stored in the file system superblock (and is always 2).[123] This inode number specifies the root directory inode in the appropriate block group. The data blocks referenced by the latter inode contain the directory entries for the root directory. Next, the file system searches these directory entries for the inode number of the home directory. This process is repeated until the inode representing the file `policydoc` is located. As each inode is accessed, the file system checks the permission information stored in it to ensure that the process performing the search is permitted to access the inode. The file's data can be directly accessed after the correct inode has been located and the file data (and metadata) have been cached by the system.[124]

20.7.4 Proc File System

One strength of the VFS is that it does not impose many restrictions on file system implementations. The VFS requires only that function calls to an underlying file system return valid data. This abstraction of a file system permits some intriguing file system implementations.

One such file system is **procfs (the proc file system)**. Procfs was created to provide real-time information about the status of the kernel and processes in a system. Similar to the VFS, the proc file system is created by the kernel at runtime.

The information provided by procfs can be found in the files and subdirectories within the /proc directory (Fig. 20.18). By examining the contents of /proc, users can obtain detailed information describing the system, from hardware status information to data describing network traffic.[125] For example, each number in Fig. 20.18 corresponds to a process in the system, identified by its process ID. By examining the contents of a process's directory in the proc file system, users can obtain information such as a process's memory usage or the location of its executable file. Other directories include `devices` (which contains information about devices in the system), `mounts` (which contains information regarding each mounted file system) and

```
root> ls /proc
1        20535   20656   751   978           interrupts   pci
10       20538   20657   792   acpi          iomem        self
137      20539   20658   8     asound        ioports      slabinfo
19902    20540   20696   811   buddyinfo     irq          stat
2        20572   20697   829   bus           kcore        swaps
20473    20576   20750   883   cmdline       kmsg         sys
20484    20577   3       9     cpuinfo       ksyms        sysvipc
20485    20578   4       919   crypto        loadavg      tty
20489    20579   469     940   devices       locks        uptime
20505    20581   5       960   dma           meminfo      version
20507    20583   536     961   dri           misc         vmstat
20522    20586   541     962   driver        modules
20525    20587   561     963   execdomains   mounts
20527    20591   589     964   filesystems   mtrr
20529    20621   6       965   fs            net
20534    20624   7       966   ide           partitions
root>
```

Figure 20.18 | *Sample contents of the /proc directory.*

uptime (which displays the amount of time the system has been running). Data provided by procfs is particularly useful for driver developers and system administrators who require detailed information about system usage. In this section, we limit our discussion to the implementation of procfs. A detailed explanation of the /proc directory's contents can be found in the Linux source code under Documentation/filesystems/proc.txt.

Procfs is a file system that exists only in main memory. The contents of files in the proc file system are not stored persistently on any physical medium—procfs files provide users an access point to kernel information, which is generated on demand. When a file or directory is registered with the proc file system, a proc directory entry is created. **Proc directory entries**, unlike VFS directory entries, allow each directory to implement its own read function. This enables a proc directory to generate its contents each time the directory entry is accessed. When a process accesses a particular procfs file, the kernel calls the corresponding file operation specified by the file. These functions allow each file to respond differently to read and write operations.[126] The kernel creates many procfs entries by default. Additional files and directories can be created using loadable kernel modules.

When a user attempts to read data from a procfs file, the VFS calls the procfs read function, which accesses a proc directory entry. To complete a read request, procfs calls the read function defined for the requested file. Procfs read functions typically gather status information from a resource, such as the amount of time the system has been running. Once information has been retrieved by a read function, procfs passes the output to the process that requested it.[127]

Procfs files can be used to send data to the kernel. Some system variables, such as the network host name of a machine, can be modified at runtime by writing to procfs files. When a process writes to a procfs file, the data provided by the process may be used to update the appropriate kernel data structures.[128]

20.8 Input/Output Management

This section explains how the kernel accesses system devices using the I/O interface. The kernel abstracts the details of the hardware in a system, providing a common interface for I/O system calls. The kernel groups devices into classes; members of each device class perform similar functions. This allows the kernel to address the performance needs of certain devices (or classes of devices) individually.

20.8.1 Device Drivers

Support for devices such as graphics cards, printers, keyboards and other such hardware is a necessary part of any operating system. A device driver is the software interface between system calls and a hardware device. Independent Linux developers, not device manufacturers, have written most of the drivers that operate devices commonly found in Linux systems. This generally limits the number of devices that are compatible with the Linux operating system. As the popularity of Linux increases, so does the number of vendors that ship Linux drivers with their devices.

Typically, device drivers are implemented as loadable kernel modules. Drivers implemented as modules can be loaded and unloaded as they are needed, avoiding the need to have them permanently loaded in the kernel.[129]

Most devices in a system are represented by **device special files**. A device special file is an entry in the /dev directory that provides access to a particular device. Each file in the /dev directory corresponds to a block device or a character device.[130] A list of block and character device drivers that are currently loaded on a particular system can be found in the file /proc/devices (Fig. 20.19).

Devices that perform similar functions are grouped into **device classes**. For example, each brand of mouse that connects to the computer may belong to the input device class. To uniquely identify devices in the system, the kernel assigns each device a 32-bit device identification number. Device drivers identify their devices using a **major identification number** and a **minor identification number**. Major and minor identification numbers for all devices supported by Linux are located in the Linux Device List, which is publicly available online.[131] Driver developers must use the numbers allocated to devices in the Linux Device List to ensure that devices in a system are properly identified.

Devices that are assigned the same major identification number are controlled by the same driver. Minor identification numbers allow the system to distinguish

```
root> cat /proc/devices
Character devices:
  1 mem       Physical memory access
  2 pty       BSD-style terminal (TTY) devices
  3 ttyp      BSD-style terminal (TTY) devices
  4 vc/%d     Virtual console
  5 ptmx      Multiplexor for AT&T-style terminal (TTY) devices
  6 lp        Parallel printer
  7 vcs       Virtual console capture devices
 10 misc      Non-serial mice, other devices
 13 input     Input core (typically contains a mouse)
 14 sound     Audio device
116 alsa      Advanced Linux Sound Driver
128 ptm       AT&T-style terminal (TTY) devices
136 pts       AT&T-style terminal (TTY) devices
180 usb       USB device
226 drm       Direct Rendering Manager (video card)

Block devices:
  2 fd        Floppy disk drive
  3 ide0      Primary IDE channel
 22 ide1      Secondary IDE channel
root>
```

Figure 20.19 | /proc/devices file contents.[132]

individual devices that are assigned the same major identification number (i.e., belong to the same device class).[133] For example, a hard disk is assigned a major identification number, and each partition on the hard disk is assigned a device minor number.

Device special files are accessed via the virtual file system. System calls pass to the VFS, which in turn issues calls to device drivers. Figure 20.20 illustrates the interaction between system calls, the VFS, device drivers and devices. Drivers implement generic virtual file system functions so that processes may access /dev files using standard library calls. For example, standard library calls for accessing files (such as printing to a file using the standard C library function fprintf) are implemented on top of lower-level system calls (such as read and write).[134] Individual device characteristics determine the drivers and their corresponding system calls necessary to support the device. Most devices that Linux supports belong to three primary categories: character devices, block devices and network devices.

Each class of device requires its corresponding device drivers to implement a set of functions common to the class. For example, a character device driver must implement a write function to transfer data to its device.[135] Further, if a device is attached to a kernel subsystem (e.g., the SCSI subsystem), the device's drivers must interface with the subsystem to control the device. For example, a SCSI device driver passes I/O requests to the SCSI subsystem, which then interacts directly with devices attached to the SCSI interface.[136] Subsystem interfaces exist to reduce redundant code; for example, each SCSI device driver need only provide access to a particular

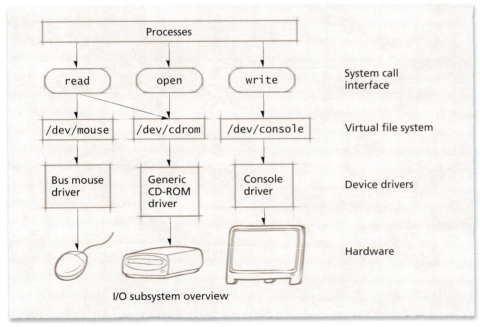

Figure 20.20 | *I/O interface layers.*

SCSI device, not to the SCSI controller to which it is attached. The SCSI subsystem provides access to common SCSI components, such as the SCSI controller.

Most drivers implement common file operations such as `read`, `write` and `seek`. These operations allow drivers to transfer data to and from devices, but do not allow them to issue hardware-specific commands. To support tasks such as ejecting a CD-ROM tray or retrieving status information from a printer, Linux provides the `ioctl` system call. `ioctl` allows developers to send control messages to any device in the /dev directory. The kernel defines several default control messages and allows a driver to implement its own messages for hardware-specific operations.[137] The set of messages supported by a device driver is dependent on the driver's device and implementation.

20.8.2 Character Device I/O

A **character device** transmits data as a stream of bytes. Devices that fall under this category include printers, consoles, mice, keyboards and modems. Because they transfer data as streams of bytes, most character devices support only sequential access to data.[138]

Most character device drivers implement basic operations such as opening, closing, reading from and writing to a character device. Each device in the system is represented by a **device_struct** structure that contains the driver name and a pointer to the driver's `file_operations` structure, which maintains the operations supported by the device driver. To initialize a character device, a device driver must register its operations with the virtual file system, which appends a `device_struct` structure to the array of registered drivers stored in **chrdevs**.[139] Figure 20.21

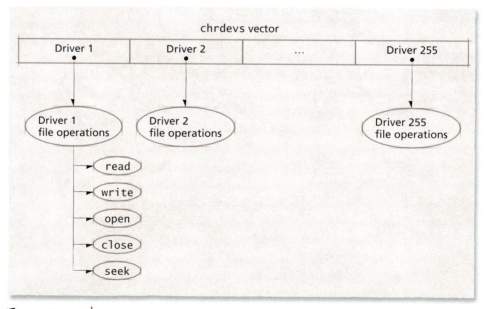

Figure 20.21 | *chrdevs vector.*

describes the contents of vector `chrdevs`. Each entry in `chrdevs` corresponds to a device driver major identification number. For example, the fifth entry in `chrdevs` is the `device_struct` for the driver with major number five.[140]

When a system call accesses a device special file, the VFS calls the appropriate function in the device's `file_operations` structure. This structure includes functions that perform read, write and other operations on the device. The inode representing the file stores a device special file's `file_operations` structure.[141]

After a device's file operations have been loaded into its inode, the VFS will use those operations whenever system calls access the device. The system can access this inode until a system call closes the device special file. However, once a system call closes the file, the inode must be recreated and initialized the next time the file is opened.[142]

20.8.3 Block Device I/O

Unlike character devices, block devices allow data stored in fixed-sized blocks of bytes to be accessed at any time, regardless of where those blocks are stored on the device. To facilitate nonsequential (i.e., random) access to a large amount of data (e.g., a file on a hard drive), the kernel must employ a more sophisticated system for handling block device I/O than it does for handling character device I/O. For example, the kernel provides algorithms that attempt to optimize moving-head storage (i.e., hard disks).

Like character devices, block devices are identified by major and minor numbers. The kernel's block I/O subsystem contains a number of layers to modularize block I/O operations by placing common code in each layer. Figure 20.22 depicts the layers through which block I/O requests pass. To minimize the amount of time spent accessing block devices, the kernel uses two primary strategies: caching data and clustering I/O operations.

Buffering and Caching

To reduce the number of block I/O operations for disk devices, the kernel buffers and caches I/O requests. When a process requests data from a block device (typically

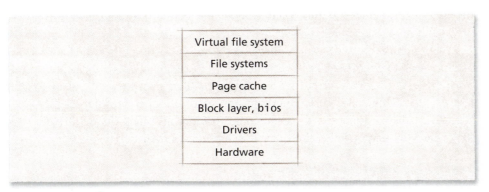

Figure 20.22 | *Block I/O subsystem layers.*

a hard disk), the kernel searches the page cache for the requested blocks. (Recall from Section 20.6.3, Page Replacement, that the page cache is a region of main memory that stores buffered and cached data from I/O requests.) If the page cache contains an entry for the requested block, the kernel will copy that page to the user's virtual space, provided there are no errors (e.g., improper permission). When a process attempts to write data to a block device, the request is typically placed on a list of pending requests that is sorted according to the kernel's disk scheduling strategy.

By performing **direct I/O**, a driver can bypass kernel caches when reading from (or writing to) devices. Some applications, such as high-end database applications, implement their own caching mechanisms; as a result, it would be wasteful for the kernel to maintain its own cache of the application's data.[143] When direct I/O is enabled, the kernel performs I/O directly between a process's user address space and the device, eliminating the overhead caused by copying data from a user address space to the kernel caches, then to the device.

Request Lists

If an I/O request corresponds to data that is not cached or data that must be written to secondary storage, the kernel must perform an I/O operation. Instead of submitting I/O requests to devices in the order in which they are received, the kernel adds a request to a **request list**. A request list, which contains pending I/O operations, is created for each block device in the system. The list allows the kernel to order requests to take into account factors such as the location of the disk head if the block device is a hard disk. As discussed in Chapter 12, the kernel can improve the performance of all block I/O operations by sorting requests for I/O on each block device.

To associate entries in the request list with page frames, each request contains a **bio structure**, which maps to a number of pages in memory corresponding to the request. The kernel maintains at least one request list per driver; each request corresponds to a read or write operation.[144, 145] Block drivers do not define read and write operations, but rather must implement a request function that the kernel calls, once it has queued requests.[146] This allows the kernel to improve I/O performance by sorting the list of requests according to its disk scheduling algorithm (discussed in the next section) before submitting requests to a block device. When the kernel calls a request function, the block device must perform all I/O operations in the list of I/O requests the kernel provides.

Although the kernel often reduces seek time by sorting block device requests, in some cases the request list is detrimental to performance. For example, certain device drivers, such as RAID drivers, implement their own methods for managing requests (see Section 12.10, Redundant Arrays of Independent Disks (RAID)). Such device drivers operate on `bio`s, unlike traditional block device drivers (e.g., IDE), which are passed a list of requests via a request function.[147]

Elevator Disk Scheduling Algorithm

Linux provides several disk scheduling algorithms to allow users to customize I/O performance to meet the individual needs of each system. The default disk scheduling algorithm is a variation of the elevator algorithm (i.e., the LOOK variation of the SCAN strategy presented in Section 12.5.6, LOOK and C-LOOK Disk Scheduling). To minimize disk seek time, the kernel arranges the entries in the list according to their location on disk. The request at the head of the list is closest to the disk head, which reduces the amount of time the disk spends seeking and increases I/O throughput. When an I/O request is submitted to a disk's request list, the kernel determines the location on disk corresponding to the request. The kernel then attempts to **merge** requests to adjacent locations on disk by combining two I/O requests into a single, larger request. Merging requests improves performance by reducing the number of I/O requests issued to a block device. If a request cannot be merged, the kernel attempts to insert that request in the sorted list in the position that maintains the list's least-seek-time-first ordering.[148]

Although the elevator algorithm provides high throughput by reducing disk seek latency, the algorithm allows requests at the end of the queue to be indefinitely postponed.[149] For example, consider two processes: process P_1 writes 200MB of data to a file and process P_2 recursively reads the contents of a directory on disk and prints the result to the terminal. Assume that the system is using an ext2 file system and the request list is initially empty. As P_1 executes, it may submit several write requests without blocking during its time slice—processes rarely block as result of write requests because they do not rely on the completion of write operations to execute subsequent instructions. P_1 is eventually preempted, at which point the request list contains several write requests. Many of the write requests will have been merged by the kernel because the ext2 file system attempts to locate file data within block groups, as discussed in Section 20.7.3, Second Extended File System (ext2fs). Process P_1's requests are then submitted to the block device, which moves the disk head to the location of the data blocks to be written.

When P_2 executes, it submits a request to read the contents of a directory. This request is a synchronous read operation because P_2 cannot print the directory contents until the read operation completes. Consequently, P_2 will submit a single I/O request and block. Unless the read request corresponds to a location adjacent to the disk head (which is now servicing P_1's write requests), the read request is placed after the pending write requests in the request list. Because P_2 has blocked, process P_1 may eventually regain control of the processor and submit additional write requests. Each subsequent write request will likely be merged with the previous requests at the front of the request list. As a result, process P_2's read request is pushed further back in the request list while P_2 remains blocked—meaning that P_2 cannot submit additional I/O requests. As long as process P_1 continues to submit write requests, process P_2's read request is indefinitely postponed.

Deadline and Anticipatory Disk Scheduling Algorithms

To eliminate indefinite postponement, the kernel provides two LOOK disk scheduling algorithms: deadline scheduling and anticipatory scheduling. The **deadline scheduler** prevents read requests from being indefinitely postponed by assigning each request a deadline—the scheduler attempts to service each request before its deadline passes. When the request has been waiting for the longest time permitted by the deadline, the request **expires**. The deadline scheduler processes requests from the head of the request list unless a request expires. At this point, the deadline scheduler services any requests that have expired and some that will soon expire. Servicing requests that will soon expire reduces the number of times the scheduler will be interrupted from servicing requests at the head of the list, which improves throughput. After all expired requests have been serviced, the scheduler continues by servicing requests from the front of the request list.[150]

To meet its deadlines, the scheduler must be able to quickly determine if any requests have expired. Using a single request list, the deadline scheduler would need to perform a linear search of requests to determine if any had expired. If the number of requests in the request list is large, this could require a significant amount of time, leading to poor performance and missed deadlines. Consequently, the deadline scheduler maintains two FIFO queues, one each for read and write requests. When a request is added to the request list, a reference to the request is added to the appropriate FIFO queue. Therefore, the request that has waited for the longest time is always located at the front of the FIFO queue. This means that the deadline I/O scheduler can quickly determine if a request is near its deadline by accessing the pointer to the front of each of the FIFO queues.[151, 152]

Because the deadline scheduler is designed to prevent read starvation, the deadline for read requests is shorter than the deadline for write requests. By default, read requests must be serviced 500ms after insertion into the request list, whereas write requests must be serviced after 5 seconds. These values were chosen because they provide good performance in general, but they can be modified by a system administrator at run time.[153]

Consider how the deadline scheduler performs given processes P_1 and P_2 from the previous section (process P_1 writes 200MB of data to a file and process P_2 recursively reads the contents of a directory on disk and prints the result to the screen). Recall from the previous section that process P_1's write requests are typically performed before read requests because its requests are merged. As a result, the disk will most likely be servicing a write request when P_2's read request's deadline expires. This means that the disk will likely perform a seek operation to perform the read request. Also, because synchronous read requests require process P_2 to block, the number of read requests in the request list is small. Consequently, the next request in the request list following the read operation will likely be a write operation that requires another seek operation. If several processes issue read requests while one or more processes submit write requests, several such pairs of seek operations (due to expired read requests) may occur within a short period of time. Thus, to reduce the number of seeks, the deadline I/O scheduler attempts to group several expired requests so that they will be serviced together before expired write requests are serviced, and vice versa.[154, 155]

The anticipatory scheduler eliminates read request starvation by preventing excessive seek activity and further improves performance by anticipating future requests. Recall that synchronous read requests often occur once per time slice because they require processes to block. However, similar to process P_2's requests for directory entries, many processes issue a series of synchronous read requests for contiguous data (or data on a single track). Consequently, if the disk scheduler paused briefly after completing a process's read request, that process may issue an additional read request that does not require a seek operation.[156] Even when there are several other requests in the request list, this read request would be placed at the head of request list and serviced without causing excessive seek activity.

By default, the amount of time during which the anticipatory I/O scheduler waits for a new request is 6ms—a pause that occurs only after completing a read request.[157] The 6ms pause (the value of the pause can be modified at run time) corresponds to the seek latency for many of today's hard disks, or roughly half the amount of time required to perform a request located on another track and return to the location of the previous read. If a read request is issued during the 6ms pause, the anticipatory scheduler can perform the request before seeking to another location on disk to perform requests for other processes. In this case, a traditional elevator scheduler would have performed two seek operations: one to perform the next request from another process and one to service the next read request. Therefore, the anticipatory I/O scheduler improves overall I/O throughput if it receives a read request within the 6ms pause more than 50 percent of the time.

The anticipatory scheduler has been shown to perform 5 to 100 times better than the traditional elevator algorithm when performing synchronous reads in the presence of write requests. However, the anticipatory I/O scheduler can introduce significant overhead due to its 6ms pause, leading to reduced I/O throughput. This occurs when the I/O scheduler does not receive a request for data near the disk's read/write head during the 6ms that it waits for a read request. To minimize this overhead, the scheduler maintains a history of process behavior that it uses to predict whether a process will benefit from the 6ms pause.[158]

20.8.4 Network Device I/O

The kernel's networking subsystem provides an interface for exchanging data with other hosts. This interface, however, cannot be accessed directly by user processes, which must send and receive data via the IPC subsystem's socket interface (discussed in Section 20.10.3, Sockets). When processes submit network data to the socket interface, they specify the network address of the destination, not the network device through which to deliver the data. The networking subsystem then determines which network device will deliver the packet. An important difference between network devices and block or character devices is that the kernel does not request data from a network device. Instead, network devices use interrupts to notify the kernel as they receive packets.

Because network traffic travels in packets, which can arrive at any time, the read and write operations of a device special file are not sufficient to access data from network devices. Instead, the kernel uses `net_device` structures to describe the network devices.[159] These objects are similar to the `device_struct` objects that represent block and character devices; however, because network devices are not represented as files, the `net_device` structure does not include a `file_operations` structure. Instead, it contains a number of functions defined by drivers that allow the kernel to perform actions such as starting a device, stopping a device and sending packets to a device.[160]

Once the kernel has prepared packets to transmit to another host, it passes them to the device driver for the appropriate network interface card (NIC). To determine which NIC will send the packet, the kernel examines an internal routing table that lists the destination addresses each network interface card can access. Once the kernel matches the packet's destination address to the appropriate interface in the routing table, the kernel passes the packet to the device driver. Each driver processes packets according to a queuing discipline, which specifies the order in which its device processes packets, such as the default FIFO policy, or other, more sophisticated, priority-based policies. By enabling priority queuing disciplines, the system can deliver higher-priority content, such as streaming media, more quickly than other network traffic.[161]

After passing packets to a network device's queue, the kernel wakes the device so that the driver may begin removing packets from the device's queue according to its queuing discipline. As packets are removed from the queue, they are passed to a packet transmission function specified by the device's driver.[162]

When a network interface receives a packet from an external source, it issues an interrupt. The interrupt causes processor control to pass to the appropriate interrupt handler for packet processing. The interrupt handler allocates memory for the packet, then passes the packet to the kernel's networking subsystem. In Section 20.11, Networking, we discuss the path taken by packets as they travel through the networking subsystem.

20.8.5 Unified Device Model

The **unified device model** is an attempt to simplify device management in the kernel. At the physical level, devices are attached to an interface (e.g., a PCI slot or a USB port) that is connected to the rest of the system via a bus. As discussed in the previous sections, Linux represents devices as members of device classes. For example, a mouse connected to a USB port and a keyboard connected to a PS/2 port both belong to the input device class, but each device connects to the computer via a different bus. Whereas a description of device interfaces and buses is a physical view of the system, a device class is a software (i.e., abstract) view of the system that simplifies device management by grouping devices of a similar type.

Before the unified device model, device classes were not related to system buses, meaning that it was difficult for the system to determine where in the system a device was physically located. This was not a problem when computers did not support **hot swappable devices** (i.e., devices that can be added and removed while the computer is running). In the absence of hot swappable devices, it is sufficient for the system to detect devices exactly once (at boot time). Once the kernel loads a driver corresponding to each device, the kernel rarely needs to access a device's physical location in the system. However, in the presence of hot swappable devices, the kernel must be aware of the physical layout of the system so it can detect when a device has been added or removed. Once it has located a new device, the kernel must be able to identify its class so the kernel can load the appropriate device driver.[163]

For example, devices are commonly added and removed from the USB bus. To detect such changes, the kernel must periodically poll the USB interface to determine which devices are attached to it.[164] If a new device is found, the kernel should identify it and load a device driver that supports it so that processes may use the device. If a device has been removed, the system should unregister the driver so that attempts to access the device are denied. Thus, the kernel must maintain a layout of the physical location of devices in the system so that it knows when the set of devices in the system changes. To support hot swappable devices, the kernel uses the unified device model to access the physical location of a device in addition to its device class representation.[165]

The unified device model defines data structures to represent devices, device drivers, buses, and device classes. The relationship between these structures is shown in Fig. 20.23. Each bus data structure represents a particular bus (e.g., PCI) and contains pointers to a list of devices attached to the bus and drivers that operate devices on the bus. Each class data structure represents a device class and contains pointers to a list of devices and device drivers that belong to that class. The unified device model associates each device and device driver with a bus and class. As a result, the kernel can access a bus, determine a list of devices and drivers on that bus and then determine the class to which each device and device driver belongs. Similarly, the kernel can access a device class, follow the pointers to its list of devices and device drivers and determine the bus to which each device is attached. As Fig. 20.23 demonstrates, the kernel requires a reference only to a single data structure to access all other data structures in the unified device model. This simplifies device management for the kernel as devices are added to and removed from the system.

When devices are registered with the system, these data structures are initialized and corresponding entries are placed in the **system file system, sysfs**. Sysfs provides an interface to devices described by the unified device model. Sysfs allows user applications to view the relationship between entities (devices, device drivers, buses and classes) in the unified device model.[166, 167, 168, 169]

Sysfs, typically mounted at /sys, organizes devices according to both the bus to which they are attached and the class to which they belong. The /sys/bus directory contains entries for each bus in the system (e.g., /sys/bus/pci). Within each bus subdirectory is a list of devices and device drivers that use the bus. Sysfs also organizes devices by class in the directory /sys/class. For example, the /sys/class/input contains input devices, such as a mouse or keyboard. Within each class subdirectory is a list of devices and device drivers that belong to that class.[170, 171]

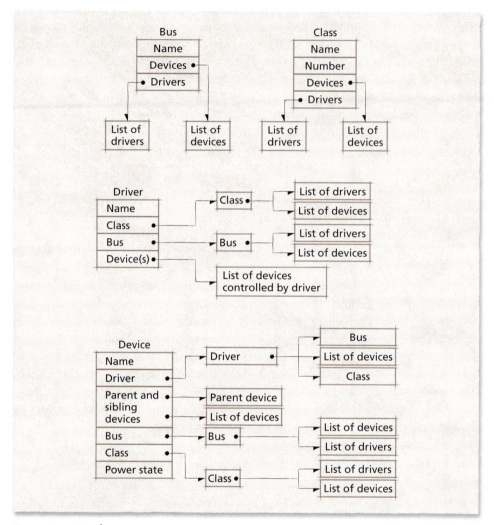

Figure 20.23 | Unified device model organization.

Power Management

The unified device model has also simplified how the kernel performs power management, an important consideration for battery-powered systems. As the number and power of mobile computers increases, a system's ability to manage power to increase battery life has become more important. Power management standards such as the Advanced Configuration and Power Interface (ACPI) specify several device power states, each of which results in different power consumption. For example, the ACPI defines four power states from fully on (D0) to fully off (D3). When a device transitions from fully on to fully off, the system does not provide any power to the device and any volatile data stored in the device, known as the device context, is lost.[172] The unified device model simplifies power management for the kernel by providing a data structure to store the context for each device when its power state changes.

There are several devices that provide powered connections to other devices. For example, a PCI card that contains USB ports may contain connections to USB devices. Because some USB devices are powered through the USB cable, if power is removed from the PCI card, then power is removed from each of its attached devices. Consequently, the PCI card should not enter the fully off state until each of its attached devices has entered the fully off state. The unified device model allows the kernel to detect such power dependencies by exposing the physical structure of devices in the system. As a result, the kernel can prevent a device from transitioning to a different power state if the transition will prevent other devices from properly functioning.[173]

20.8.6 Interrupts

The kernel requires that each device driver register interrupt handlers when the driver is loaded. As a result, when the kernel receives an interrupt from a particular device, the kernel passes control to its corresponding interrupt handler. Interrupt handlers do not belong to any single process context because they are not themselves programs. Because an interrupt handler is not identified as any `task_struct` object's executable code, the scheduler cannot place it in any run queues. This characteristic places some restrictions on interrupt handlers; lacking its own execution context, an interrupt handler cannot sleep or call the scheduler. If an interrupt handler were permitted to sleep or call the scheduler, it never would regain control of the processor.

Similarly, interrupt handlers cannot be preempted, as doing so would invoke the scheduler.[174] Any preemption requests received during interrupt handling are honored when the interrupt handler completes execution. Finally, interrupt handlers cannot cause exceptions or faults while executing. In many architectures, the system aborts when an exception is raised during an interrupt handler.[175]

To improve kernel performance, most drivers attempt to minimize the processor cycles required to handle hardware interrupts. This is another reason why kernel memory is never swapped to disk—loading a nonresident page while an interrupt handler is executing takes substantial time. In Linux, a driver handling one interrupt cannot be preempted by other interrupts that use the same interrupt line. If this were not the case, any device driver containing nonreentrant code might perform operations that leave a device in an inconsistent state. As a result, when one driver is processing an interrupt, the kernel queues or drops any other interrupts it receives that use the same interrupt line.[176] Therefore, driver developers are encouraged to write code that processes interrupts as quickly as possible.

The kernel helps improve interrupt-handling efficiency by dividing interrupt-handling routines into two parts—the **top half** and the **bottom half**. When the kernel receives an interrupt from a hardware device, it passes control to the top half of the driver's interrupt handler. The top half of an interrupt handler performs the minimum work required to acknowledge the interrupt. Other work (such as manipulating data structures)—which should be located in the bottom half of the interrupt handler—is scheduled to be performed later by a **software interrupt handler**. Top halves of interrupt routines cannot be interrupted by software interrupt handlers.

Two primary software interrupt-handler types are **softirqs** and **tasklets**. Softirqs can be executed concurrently on multiple processors (up to one per processor), making them ideal for SMP systems.[177] When a device driver allocates a softirq, it specifies the action to be performed each time the softirq is scheduled. Because multiple copies of a softirq can run simultaneously, softirq actions must be reentrant to perform reliably. Network devices on Web servers, which constantly receive packets of data from external sources, benefit from softirqs because multiple packets can be processed simultaneously on different processors.[178]

However, softirqs do not improve performance for several types of interrupt handlers. For example, a driver that requires exclusive access to data would need to enforce mutual exclusion if its code were executed simultaneously on multiple processors. In some cases, the overhead due to enforcing mutual exclusion can outweigh the benefits of multiprocessing. Other devices transfer data as a series of bits, requiring device drivers to sequentialize access to such data. Such devices cannot benefit from parallel processing and consequently use tasklets to perform bottom-half interrupt-handling routines.[179]

Tasklets are similar to softirqs but cannot run simultaneously on multiple processors and therefore cannot take advantage of parallel processing. As a result, most drivers use tasklets instead of softirqs to schedule bottom halves. Although multiple instances of a single tasklet cannot execute simultaneously, several different tasklets can execute simultaneously in SMP systems.[180]

Softirqs and tasklets normally are handled in interrupt context or in a process's context immediately after the top-half interrupt handler completes, executing with higher priority than user processes. If the system experiences a large number of softirqs that reschedule themselves, user processes might be indefinitely postponed. Thus, when user processes have not executed for a significant period of time, the kernel assigns softirqs and tasklets to be executed by the kernel thread ***ksoftirqd***, which executes with low-priority (+19). When the kernel is loaded, the Linux kernel creates an instance of the kernel thread *ksoftirqd* for each processor. These threads remain sleeping until the kernel wakes them. Once scheduled, *ksoftirqd* enters a loop in which it processes pending tasklets and softirqs sequentially. *ksoftirqd* continues processing tasklets and softirqs until the tasklets and/or softirqs have completed execution or until *ksoftirqd* is preempted by the scheduler.[181]

Partitioning interrupt handling into top and bottom halves minimizes the amount of time that hardware interrupts are disabled. Once a driver handles a hardware interrupt (the top half), the kernel can run the software interrupt handler (the bottom half), during which incoming interrupts can preempt the software interrupt handler.[182] This division of driver code improves the response time of a system by reducing the amount of time during which interrupts are disabled.

20.9 *Kernel Synchronization*

A process executing in user mode cannot directly access kernel data, hardware, or other critical system resources—such processes must rely on the kernel to execute privileged instructions on their behalf. These operations are called **kernel control paths**. If two kernel control paths were to access the same data concurrently, a race condition could result.[183] To prevent this, the kernel provides two basic mechanisms for providing mutually exclusive access to critical sections: locks and semaphores.

20.9.1 *Spin locks*

Spin locks allow the kernel to protect critical sections in kernel code executing on SMP-enabled systems. Before entering its critical section, a kernel control path acquires a spin lock. The region remains protected by the spin lock until the kernel control path releases the spin lock. If a second kernel control path attempts to acquire the same spin lock to enter its critical section, it will enter a loop in which it busy waits, or "spins," until the first kernel control path releases the spin lock. Once the spin lock becomes available, the second kernel control path can acquire it.[184]

Proper use of spin locks prevents race conditions among multiple kernel control paths executing concurrently in an SMP system, but serves no purpose in a uniprocessor system in which two kernel control paths cannot simultaneously execute. Consequently, kernels configured for uniprocessor systems exclude the locking portion of spin lock calls.[185] This improves performance by eliminating the costly instructions executed to acquire mutually exclusive access to a critical section in multiprocessor systems.

The kernel provides a set of spin lock functions for use in interrupt handlers. Because a hardware interrupt can preempt any execution context, any data shared between a hardware interrupt handler and a software interrupt handler must be protected using a spin lock. To address this issue, the kernel provides spin locks that disable interrupts on the local processor while still allowing concurrent execution on SMP systems. On uniprocessor systems, the spin lock code is removed when the kernel is compiled, but the code for enabling and disabling interrupts remains intact.[186] To protect data shared between user contexts and software interrupt handlers, the kernel uses **bottom-half spin locks**. These functions disable software interrupt handlers in addition to acquiring the requested spin lock.[187]

All spin lock variations disable preemption in both single and multiprocessor systems. Although disabling preemption could lead to indefinite postponement or even deadlock, allowing code protected by spin locks to be preempted introduces the same race conditions spin locks are designed to avoid. The kernel uses a preemption lock counter to determine if a kernel control path can be preempted. When a kernel control path acquires a spin lock, the preemption lock counter is incremented; the counter is decremented when the kernel control path releases the spin lock. Code executing in kernel mode can be preempted only when the preemption lock counter is reduced to zero. When a spin lock is released and its associated counter becomes zero, the kernel honors any pending preemption requests by invoking the scheduler.

Kernel developers must abide by certain rules to avoid deadlock when using any spin lock variant. First, if a kernel control path has already acquired a spin lock, the kernel control path must not attempt to acquire the spin lock again before releasing it. Attempting to acquire the spin lock a second time will cause the kernel control path to busy wait for the lock it controls to be released, causing deadlock. Similarly, a kernel control path must not sleep while holding a spin lock. If the next task that is scheduled attempts to acquire the spin lock, deadlock will occur.[188]

20.9.2 Reader/Writer Locks

In some cases, multiple kernel control paths need only to read (not write) the data accessed inside a critical section. When no kernel control path is modifying that data, there is no need to prevent concurrent read access to the data (see Section 6.2.4, Monitor Example: Readers and Writers). To optimize concurrency in such a situation, the kernel provides **reader/writer locks**. Reader/writer spin locks and kernel semaphores (Section 20.9.4, Kernel Semaphores) allow multiple kernel control paths to hold a read lock, but permit only one kernel control path to hold a write lock with no concurrent readers. A kernel control path that holds a read lock on a critical section must release its read lock and acquire a write lock if it wishes to modify data.[189] An attempt to acquire a write lock succeeds only if there are no other readers or writers concurrently executing inside their critical sections. Reader/writer locks effect a higher level of concurrency by limiting access to a critical section only when writes occur. Depending on the kernel control paths accessing the lock, this can lead to improved performance. If readers do not release their read locks, it is possible for writers to be indefinitely postponed. To prevent indefinite postponement and provide writers with fast access to critical sections, kernel control paths use the seqlock.

20.9.3 Seqlocks

In some situations, the kernel employs another locking mechanism designed to allow writers to access data immediately without waiting for readers to release the lock. This locking primitive, called a **seqlock**, represents the combination of a spin lock and a sequence counter. Writing to data protected by a seqlock is initiated by calling function `write_seqlock`. This function acquires the spin lock component of the seqlock (so that no other writers can enter their critical section) and it increments the sequence counter. After writing, function `write_sequnlock` is called, which once again increments the sequence counter, then releases the spin lock.[190]

To enable writers to access data protected by a seqlock immediately, the kernel does not allow readers to acquire mutually exclusive access to that data. Thus, a reader executing its critical section can be preempted, enabling a writer to modify the data protected by a seqlock. The reader can detect if a writer has modified the value of the data protected by the seqlock by examining the value of the seqlock's sequence counter as shown in the following pseudocode. The value of the seqlock's sequence counter is initialized to zero.

Do

    Store value of seqlock's sequence counter in local variable `seqTemp`
    Execute instructions that read the value of the data protected by the seqlock
While `seqTemp` *is odd or not equal to the value of the seqlock's sequence counter*

After entering its critical section, the reader stores the value of the seqlock's sequence counter. Let us assume that this value is stored in variable `seqTemp`. The reader then accesses the data protected by the sequence counter. Consider what occurs if the system preempts the reader and a writer enters its critical section to modify the protected data. Before modifying the protected data, the writer must acquire the seqlock, which increments the value of the sequence counter. When the reader next executes, it compares the value stored in `seqTemp` to the current value of the sequence counter. If the two values are not equal, a writer must have entered its critical section. In this case, the value read by the reader may not be valid. Therefore, the loop continuation condition in the preceding pseudocode determines if the value of the sequence counter has changed since the reader accessed the protected data. If so, the reader continues the loop until it has read a valid copy of the protected data. Because the value of the seqlock's sequence counter is initialized to zero, a write is being performed when that value is odd. Thus, if `seqTemp` is odd, the reader will read the protected data while a writer is in the process of modifying it. In this case, the loop continuation condition ensures that the reader continues the loop to ensure that it reads valid data. When no writers have attempted to modify the data while the reader executes inside its critical section, the reader exits the `do...while` loop.

Because writers need not wait for readers to release a lock, seqlocks are appropriate for interrupt handling and other instances when writers must execute quickly to improve performance. In most cases, readers successfully read data on the first try. However, it is possible for readers to be indefinitely postponed while multiple writers modify shared data, so seqlocks should be used in situations where protected data is read more often than it is written.[191]

20.9.4 Kernel Semaphores

Spin locks and seqlocks perform well when the critical sections they protect contain few instructions. However, as the size of the critical section increases, the amount of time spent busy waiting increases, leading to significant overhead and performance degradation. Also, spin locks can lead to deadlock if a process sleeps while holding the lock. When a critical section must be protected for a long time, **kernel semaphores** are a better choice for implementing mutual exclusion. For example, only one process at a time should be able to read an image from a scanner. Because scanners may take several seconds to scan an image, a scanner device driver typically enforces mutually exclusive access to its scanner using semaphores.

Kernel semaphores are counting semaphores (see Section 5.6.3, Counting Semaphores) represented by a wait queue and a counter. The wait queue stores processes that are waiting on the kernel semaphore. The value of the counter determines how many processes may simultaneously access their critical sections. When a kernel semaphore is created, the counter is initialized to the number of processes allowed to access the semaphore concurrently. For example, if a semaphore protects access to three identical resources, then the initial counter value would be set to 3.[192]

When a process attempts to execute its critical section, it calls function down on the kernel semaphore. Function down, which corresponds to the P operation (see Section 5.6, Semaphores), checks the current value of the counter and responds according to the following rules:

- If the value of the counter is greater than 0, down decrements the counter and allows the process to execute.
- If the value of the counter is less than or equal to 0, down decrements the counter, and the process is added to the wait queue and enters the *sleeping* state. By putting a process to sleep, the kernel reduces the overhead due to busy waiting because sleeping processes are not dispatched to a processor.

When a process exits its critical section, it releases the kernel semaphore by calling function up. This function inspects the value of the counter and responds according to the following rules:

- If the value of the counter is greater than or equal to 0, up increments the counter.
- If the value of the counter is less than 0, up increments the counter, and a process from the wait queue is awakened so that it can execute its critical section.[193]

Kernel semaphores cause processes to sleep if placed in the semaphore's wait queue, so they cannot be used in interrupt handlers or when a spin lock is held. However, the kernel provides an alternative solution that allows interrupt handlers to access semaphores using function down_trylock. If the interrupt handler cannot enter the critical section protected by the kernel semaphore, function down_trylock will return to the caller instead of causing the interrupt handler to sleep.[194] Kernel semaphores should be used only for process that need to sleep while holding the semaphore; processes that sleep while holding a spin lock can lead to deadlock.

20.10 Interprocess Communication

Many of the interprocess communication (IPC) mechanisms available in Linux are derived from traditional UNIX IPC mechanisms, and they all have a common goal: to allow processes to exchange information. Although all IPC mechanisms accomplish this goal, some are better suited for particular applications, such as those that communicate over a network or exchange short messages with other local applications. In this section, we discuss how IPC mechanisms are implemented in the Linux kernel and how they are employed in Linux systems.

20.10.1 Signals

Signals were one of the first interprocess communication mechanisms available in UNIX systems—the kernel uses them to notify processes when certain events occur. In contrast to the other Linux IPC mechanisms we discuss, signals do not allow processes to specify more than a word of data to exchange with other processes; signals are primarily intended to alert a process that an event has occurred.[195] The signals a Linux system supports depend on the processor architecture. Figure 20.24 lists the first 20 signals identified by the POSIX specification (all of today's architectures support these signals).[196]

Signals, which are created by the kernel in response to interrupts and exceptions, are sent to a process or thread either as a result of executing an instruction (such as a segmentation fault, SIGSEGV), from another process (such as when one process terminates another, SIGKILL) or from an asynchronous event (e.g., an I/O completion signal). The kernel delivers a signal to a process by pausing its execution

Signal	Type	Default Action	Description
1	SIGHUP	Abort	Hang-up detected on terminal or death of controlling process
2	SIGINT	Abort	Interrupt from keyboard
3	SIGQUIT	Dump	Quit from keyboard
4	SIGILL	Dump	Illegal instruction
5	SIGTRAP	Dump	Trace/breakpoint trap
6	SIGABRT	Dump	Abort signal from **abort** function
7	SIGBUS	Dump	Bus error
8	SIGFPE	Dump	Floating point exception
9	SIGKILL	Abort	Kill signal
10	SIGUSR1	Abort	User-defined signal 1
11	SIGSEGV	Dump	Invalid memory reference
12	SIGUSR2	Abort	User-defined signal 2
13	SIGPIPE	Abort	Broken pipe: write to pipe with no readers
14	SIGALRM	Abort	Timer signal from **alarm** function
15	SIGTERM	Abort	Termination signal
16	SIGSTKFLT	Abort	Stack fault on coprocessor
17	SIGCHLD	Ignore	Child stopped or terminated
18	SIGCONT	Continue	Continue if stopped
19	SIGSTOP	Stop	Stop process
20	SIGTSTP	Stop	Stop typed at terminal device

Figure 20.24 | POSIX signals.[197]

and invoking the process's corresponding signal handler. Once the signal handler completes execution, the process resumes execution.[198]

A process or thread can handle a signal in one of three ways. (1) Ignore the signal—processes can ignore all but the SIGSTOP and SIGKILL signals. (2) Catch the signal—when a process catches a signal, it invokes its signal handler to respond to the signal. (3) Execute the **default action** that the kernel defines for that signal—by default, the kernel defines one of five actions that is performed when a process receives a signal.[199]

The first default action is to abort, which causes the process to terminate immediately. The second is to perform a memory dump. A **memory dump** is similar to an abort; it causes a process to terminate, but before it does so, the process generates a **core file** that contains the process's execution context, which includes the process's stack, registers and other information useful for debugging. The third default action is simply to ignore the signal. The fourth is to stop (i.e., suspend) the process—often used to debug a process. The fifth is continue, which reverses the fourth by switching a process from the *suspended* state to the *ready* state.[200]

Processes can choose not to handle signals by **blocking** them. If a process blocks a specific signal type, the kernel does not deliver the signal until the process stops blocking it. Processes block a signal type by default while handling another signal of the same type. As a result, signal handlers need not be reentrant (unless the default behavior is not used), because multiple instances of the process's signal handler cannot be executed concurrently. It is, however, possible for a signal handler to interrupt a signal handler of a different type.[201]

Common signals, such as those shown in Fig. 20.24, are not queued by the kernel. If a signal is currently being handled by a process and a second signal of the same type is generated for that process, the kernel discards the latter signal. If two signals are generated simultaneously by an SMP system, the kernel simply drops one as a result of the race condition. In certain circumstances, dropped signals do not affect system behavior. For example, a single SIGKILL signal is sufficient for the system to terminate a process. In mission-critical systems, however, dropped signals could be disastrous. For example, a user-defined signal may be used to monitor safety systems that protect human life. If such signals were dropped, people's lives could be at risk. To ensure that such systems do not miss a signal, Linux supports **real-time signals**. These are queued by the kernel; therefore, multiple instances of the same signal can be generated simultaneously and not be discarded.[202, 203] By default the kernel queues up to 1,024 real-time signals of the same type; any further signals are dropped.

20.10.2 Pipes

Pipes enable two processes to communicate using the producer/consumer model. The producer process writes data to the pipe, after which the consumer process reads data from the pipe in first-in-first-out order.

When a pipe is created, an inode is allocated and assigned to the pipe. Similar to procfs inodes (see Section 20.7.4, Proc File System), pipe inodes do not point to disk blocks. Rather, they point to one page of data called a **pipe buffer** that the kernel uses as a circular buffer. Each pipe maintains a unique pipe buffer that stores data that is transferred between two processes.[204]

When pipes are created, the kernel allocates two file descriptors (see Section 20.7.1, Virtual File System) to allow access to the pipe: one for reading from the pipe and one for writing to the pipe. Pipes are represented by files and accessed via the virtual file system. To initiate communication using a pipe, one process must create the pipe, then fork a child process with which to communicate via the pipe. The fork system call enables pipe communication because it allows the child process to inherit the parent process's file descriptors. Alternatively, two processes can share a file descriptor using sockets, discuss in the section that follows. Although the kernel represents pipes as files, pipes cannot be accessed from the directory tree. This prevents a process from accessing a pipe unless it has obtained the pipe's file descriptor from the process that created it.[205]

One limitation of pipes is that they support communication only between processes that share file descriptors. Linux supports a variation of a pipe, called a **named pipe** or **FIFO**, that can be accessed via the directory tree. When a FIFO is created, its name is added to the directory tree. Processes can access the FIFO by pathname as they would any other file in the directory tree (the location and name of the file are typically known before the processes execute). Therefore, processes can communicate using a named pipe the same way they access data in a file system—by supplying the correct pathname and appropriate file permissions. However, unlike data files, FIFOs point to a buffer located in memory, not on disk. Therefore, FIFOs provide the simplicity of sharing data in files without the latency overhead created by disk access.[206] Another limitation of pipes that the fixed-size buffer can result in suboptimal performance if a producer and consumer work at different speeds, as discussed in Section 6.2.3, Monitor Example: Circular Buffer,

20.10.3 Sockets

The Linux **socket** IPC mechanism allows pairs of processes to exchange data by establishing direct bidirectional communication channels. Each process can use its socket to transfer data to and from another process. One limitation of pipes is that communication occurs in a single direction (from producer to consumer); however, many cooperating processes require bidirectional communication. In distributed systems, for example, processes may need to be able to send and receive remote procedure calls. In this case, pipes are insufficient, because they are limited to communication in one direction and are identified by file descriptors, which are not unique among multiple systems. To address this issue, sockets are designed allow communication between unrelated processes so that such processes can exchange information both locally and across a network. Because sockets allow such flexibility, they may perform worse than pipes in some situations. For example, if an application requires unidirectional communication between two processes in one system (i.e., sending the output of a decompression program to a file on disk), pipes should be used instead of sockets.

There are two primary socket types that processes can employ. **Stream sockets** transfer information as streams of bytes. **Datagram sockets** transfer information in independent units called datagrams, discussed in Section 16.6.2, User Datagram Protocol (UDP).[207]

Stream Sockets

Processes that communicate via stream sockets follow the traditional client/server model. The server process creates a stream socket and listens for connection requests. A client process can then connect to the server process and begin exchanging information. Because data is transferred as a stream of bytes, processes communicating with stream sockets can read or write variable amounts of data. One useful property of stream sockets is that, unlike datagram sockets, they use TCP to communicate, which guarantees that all data transmitted will eventually arrive and will be delivered in the correct order. Because stream sockets inherently provide data integrity, they are typically the better choice when communication must be reliable.[208]

Datagram Sockets

Although stream sockets provide powerful IPC features, they are not always necessary or practical. Enabling reliable stream sockets creates more overhead than some applications can afford. Faster, but less reliable communication can be accomplished using datagram sockets. For example, in some distributed systems, a server with many clients periodically broadcasts status information to all of its clients. In this case, datagram sockets are preferable to stream sockets, because they require only a single message to be sent from the server socket and do not require any responses from clients. Datagrams may also be sent periodically to update client information, such as for clock synchronization purposes. In this case, each subsequent datagram is intended to replace the information contained in previous datagrams. Therefore, the clients can afford not to receive certain datagram packets, provided that future datagram packets arrive eventually. In such situations, where data loss is either unlikely or unimportant, applications can use datagram sockets in lieu of stream sockets to increase performance.

Socketpairs

Although sockets are most often used for Internet communication, Linux enables bidirectional communication between multiple processes on the same system using sockets. When a process creates a socket in the local system, it specifies a file name that is used as the socket's address. Other sockets on that system can use the file name to communicate with that socket by reading from, and writing to, a buffer. Like many data structures in the Linux kernel, sockets are stored internally as files, and therefore can be accessed via the virtual file system using the `read` and `write` system calls.[209]

Linux provides another IPC mechanism that is implemented using sockets, called a **socketpair**. A socketpair is a pair of connected, unnamed sockets. When a process creates a socketpair, the kernel creates two sockets, connects them, and returns a file descriptor for each socket.[210] Similar to pipes, unnamed sockets are limited to use by processes that share file descriptors. Socketpairs are traditionally employed when related processes require bidirectional communication.

20.10.4 Message Queues

Messages are an IPC mechanism to allow processes to transmit information that is composed of a message type and a variable-length data area. Message types are not defined by the kernel; when processes exchange information, they specify their own message types to distinguish between messages.

Messages are stored in **message queues**, where they remain until a process is ready to receive them. Message queues, unlike pipes, can be shared by processes that are not parent and child. When the kernel creates a message queue, it assigns it a unique identifier. Related processes can search for a message queue identifier in a global array of **message queue descriptors**. Each descriptor contains a queue of pending messages, a queue of processes waiting for messages (message receivers), a queue of processes waiting to send messages (message senders), and data describing the size and contents of the message queue.[211]

When a process adds a message to a message queue, the kernel checks the queue's list of receivers for a process waiting for messages of that type. If it finds any such processes, the kernel delivers the message each of them. If no receiver is waiting for a message of the specified type and enough space is available in the message queue, the kernel adds the message to a queue of pending messages of that type. If insufficient space is available, the message sender adds itself to the queue of message senders. Senders wait in this queue until space becomes available (i.e., when a message is removed from the queue of pending messages).[212]

When a process attempts to receive a message, the kernel searches for messages of a specified type in the appropriate message queue. If it finds such a message, the kernel removes the message from the queue and copies it to a buffer located in the address space of the process receiving the message. If no messages of the requested type are found, the process is added to the queue of message receivers where it waits until the requested type of message becomes available.[213]

20.10.5 Shared Memory

The primary advantage of shared memory over other forms of IPC is that, once a region of shared memory is established, access to memory is processed in user space and does not require the kernel to access the shared data. Thus, because processes do not invoke the kernel for each access to shared data, this type of IPC improves performance for processes that frequently access shared data. Another advantage of shared memory is that processes can share as much data as they can address, potentially eliminating the time spent waiting when a producer and consumer work at different speeds using fixed-size buffers, as discussed in Section 6.2.3. Linux supports two standard interfaces to shared memory that are managed via tmpfs: System V and POSIX shared memory. [*Note*: Processes can also share memory using memory-mapped files.]

The Linux implementation of System V shared memory employs four standard system calls (Fig. 20.25). When a process has successfully allocated and attached a region of shared memory, it can reference data in that region as it would reference data using a pointer. The kernel maintains a unique identifier that describes the physical region of memory to which each shared memory segment belongs, deleting the shared memory region only when a process requests its deletion and when the number of processes to which it is attached is zero.[214]

POSIX shared memory requires the use of the system call `shm_open` to create a pointer to the region of shared memory and the system call `shm_unlink` to close the region. The shared memory region is stored as a file in the system's shared memory file system, which must be mounted at `/dev/shm`; in Linux, a tmpfs file system is typically mounted there (tmpfs is described in the next section). The `shm_open` call is analogous to opening a file, whereas the `shm_unlink` call is analogous to closing a link to a file. The file that represents the shared region is deleted when it is no longer attached to any processes.

Both System V and POSIX shared memory allow processes to share regions of memory and map that memory to each process's virtual address space. However, because POSIX shared memory does not allow processes to change privileges for shared segments, it is slightly less flexible than System V shared memory.[215] Neither POSIX nor System V shared memory provides any synchronization mechanisms to protect access to memory. If synchronization is required, processes typically employ semaphores.

Shared Memory Implementation

The goal of shared memory in an operating system is to provide access to shared data with low overhead while rigidly enforcing memory protection. Linux implements shared memory as a virtual memory area that is mapped to a region of physical memory. When a process attempts to access a shared memory region, the kernel

System V Shared Memory System Call	Purpose
shmget	Allocates a shared memory segment.
shmat	Attaches a shared memory segment to a process.
shmctl	Changes the shared memory segment's properties (e.g., permissions).
shmdt	Detaches (i.e., removes) a shared memory segment from a process.

Figure 20.25 | *System V shared memory system calls.*

first determines if the process has permission to access it. If so, the kernel allocates a virtual memory area that is mapped to the region of shared memory, then attaches the virtual memory area to the process's virtual address space. The process may then access shared memory as it would any other memory in its virtual address space.

The kernel keeps track of shared memory usage by treating the region as a file in **tmpfs**, the **temporary file system**. Tmpfs has been designed to simplify shared memory management while maintaining good performance for the POSIX and System V shared memory specifications. As its name suggests, tmpfs is temporary, meaning that shared memory pages are not persistent. When a file in tmpfs is deleted, its page frames are freed. Tmpfs is also swappable; that is, data stored in the tmpfs can be swapped to the backing store when available memory becomes scarce. The page(s) containing the file can then be loaded from the backing store when referenced. This allows the system to fairly allocate page frames to all processes in the system. Tmpfs also reduces shared memory overhead because it does not require mounting or formatting for use. Finally, the kernel can set permissions of tmpfs files, which enables the kernel to implement the shmctl system call in System V shared memory.[216]

When the kernel is loaded, an instance of tmpfs is created. If the user wishes to mount a tmpfs file system to the local directory tree (which, as previously discussed, is required for POSIX shared memory), the user can mount a new instance of the file system and access it immediately. To further improve shared memory performance, tmpfs interfaces directly with the memory manager—it has minimal interaction with the virtual file system. Although tmpfs creates dentries, inodes and file structures that represent shared memory regions, generic VFS file operations are ignored in favor of tmpfs-specific routines that bypass the VFS layer. This relieves tmpfs of certain constraints typically imposed by the VFS (e.g., the VFS does not allow a file system to grow and shrink while it is mounted).[217]

20.10.6 System V Semaphores

Linux implements two types of semaphores: kernel semaphores (discussed in Section 20.9.4, Kernel Semaphores) and **System V semaphores**. Kernel semaphores are synchronization mechanisms employed throughout the kernel to protect critical sections. System V semaphores also protect critical sections and are implemented using similar mechanisms; however, they are designed for user processes to access via the system call interface. For the remainder of this discussion, we refer to System V semaphores simply as semaphores.

Because processes often need to protect a number of related resources, the kernel stores semaphores in **semaphore arrays**. Each semaphore in an array protects a particular resource.[218, 219]

Before a process can access resources protected by a semaphore array, the kernel requires that there be sufficient available resources to satisfy the process's request. Thus, semaphore arrays can be implemented as a deadlock prevention mechanism by denying Havender's "wait-for" condition (see Section 7.7.1, Denying the "Wait-For" Condition). If a requested resource in semaphore array has been allocated to another process, the kernel blocks the requesting process and places its resource request in a queue of pending operations for that semaphore array. When a resource is returned to the semaphore array, the kernel examines the semaphore array's queue of pending operations for processes, and if a process can proceed, it is unblocked.[220]

To prevent deadlock from occurring if a process terminates prematurely while it holds resources controlled by a semaphore, the kernel tracks the operations each process performs on a semaphore. When a process exits, the kernel reverses all the semaphore operations it performed to allocate its resources. Finally, note that semaphore arrays offer no protection against indefinite postponement caused by poor programming in the user processes that access them.

20.11 Networking

The networking subsystem performs operations on network packets, each of which is stored in a contiguous physical memory area described by an sk_buff structure. As a packet traverses layers of the network subsystem, network protocols add and remove headers and trailers containing protocol-specific information (see Chapter 16, Introduction to Networking).[221]

20.11.1 Packet Processing

Figure 20.26 illustrates the path taken by network packets as they travel from a network interface card (NIC) through the kernel. When a NIC receives a packet, it issues an interrupt, which causes the NIC's interrupt handler to execute. The interrupt handler calls the network device's driver routine that allocates an sk_buff for the packet, then copies the packet from the network interface into the sk_buff and adds the packet to a queue of packets pending processing. A queue of pending packets is assigned to each processor; the interrupt handler assigns a packet to the queue belonging to the processor on which it executes.[222]

At this point, the packet resides in memory where it awaits further processing. Because interrupts are disabled while the top half of the interrupt handler executes, the kernel delays processing the packet. Instead, the interrupt handler raises a softirq to continue processing the packet. (Section 20.8.6, Interrupts, discussed softirqs.) After raising the softirq, the device driver routine returns and the interrupt handler exits.[223]

A single softirq processes all packets that the kernel receives on that processor. Because the kernel uses softirqs to process packets, network routines can execute concurrently on multiple processors in SMP systems, resulting in increased performance. When the scheduler dispatches the network softirq, the softirq processes packets in the processor's queue until either the queue is empty, a predefined maximum number of packets are processed or a time limit is reached. If one of the latter two conditions is met, the softirq is rescheduled and returns control of the processor to the scheduler.[224]

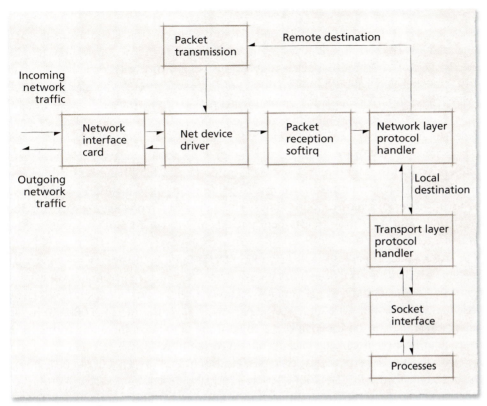

Figure 20.26 | *Path followed by network packets received by the networking subsystem.*

To process a packet, the network device softirq (called NET_RX_SOFTIRQ) removes the packet from the current processor's queue and passes it to the appropriate network layer protocol handler—typically the IP protocol handler. Although Linux supports other network layer protocols, they are rarely used. Therefore, we limit our discussion to the IP protocol handler.

When the IP protocol handler receives a packet, it first determines its destination. If the packet destination is another host, the handler forwards the packet to the appropriate host. If the packet is destined for the local machine, the IP protocol handler strips the IP protocol-specific header from the sk_buff and passes the packet to the appropriate transport layer packet handler. The transport layer packet handler supports the Transmission Control Protocol (TCP), User Datagram Protocol (UDP) and Internet Control Message Protocol (ICMP).[225]

The transport layer packet handler determines the port specified by the TCP header and delivers the packet data to the socket that is bound to that port. The packet data is then transmitted to the process via the socket interface.

20.11.2 Netfilter Framework and Hooks

As packets traverse the networking subsystem they encounter elements of the **netfilter** framework. Netfilter is a mechanism designed to allow kernel modules to directly inspect and modify packets. At various stages of the IP protocol handler, software constructs called **hooks** enable modules to register to examine, alter and/or discard packets. At each hook, modules can pass packets to user processes.[226]

Figure 20.27 lists the netfilter hooks and the packets that pass through each hook. The first hook packets encounter is NF_IP_PRE_ROUTING. All incoming packets pass it as they enter the IP protocol handler. One possible use for this hook is to enable a system that multiplexes network traffic (e.g., a load balancer). For example, a load balancer attempts to evenly distribute requests to a cluster of Web servers to improve average response times. Thus, the load balancer can register the NF_IP_PRE_ROUTING hook to intercept packets and reroute them according to the load on each Web server.

After a packet passes the NF_IP_PRE_ROUTING hook, the next hook it encounters depends on its destination. If the packet destination is the current network interface, it passes through the NF_IP_LOCAL_IN hook. Otherwise, if a packet needs to be passed to another network interface, it passes through the NF_IP_FORWARD hook. One possible use for these two hooks is to limit the amount of incoming traffic from a particular host by discarding packets once a certain threshold is reached.

All locally generated packets pass through the NF_IP_LOCAL_OUT hook, which, similar to the NF_IP_LOCAL_IN and NF_IP_FORWARD hooks, can be used to filter packets before they are sent across a network. Finally, immediately before leaving the system, all packets pass through the NF_IP_POST_ROUTING hook. A firewall can use this hook to modify the outgoing traffic to make it appear to have come from the firewall instead of from the original source.

20.12 Scalability

The early development of the Linux kernel focused on desktop systems and low-end servers. As additional features were implemented, Linux's popularity increased. This led to new interest in scaling Linux to larger systems (even mainframe computers) at large computer companies, such as IBM (www.ibm.com) and

Hook	Packets handled
NF_IP_PRE_ROUTING	All incoming packets.
NF_IP_LOCAL_IN	Packets sent to the local host.
NF_IP_LOCAL_OUT	Locally generated packets.
NF_IP_FORWARD	Packets forwarded to other hosts.
NF_IP_POST_ROUTING	All packets sent from the system.

Figure 20.27 | Netfilter hooks.

Hewlitt-Packard (www.hp.com), which cooperated with independent developers to scale Linux to be competitive in the high-end server market.

As Linux's scalability improves, designers must decide how far to enable the standard Linux kernel to scale. Increasing its scalability might negatively affect its performance on desktop systems and low-end servers. With this in mind, companies such as Red Hat (www.redhat.com), SuSE (www.suse.com) and Conectiva (www.conectiva.com) provide Linux distributions designed for high-performance servers and sell support services tailored to those distributions. By providing kernel modifications in a distribution, companies can tailor the Linux kernel to high-end servers without affecting users in other environments.

High-end servers are not the only reason to improve Linux's scalability—embedded-device manufacturers also use Linux to manage their systems. To satisfy the lesser needs of these limited-capability systems, software companies and independent developers create modified Linux kernels and applications designed for embedded devices. In addition to "home grown" embedded Linux kernels, companies such as Red Hat and projects such as uCLinux (www.uclinux.org) have developed Linux solutions for embedded systems. These modifications allow the kernel to execute in systems that do not support virtual memory, in addition to reducing resource consumption and enabling real-time execution. As developers continue to address these issues, Linux is becoming a viable choice for use in many embedded systems.

20.12.1 Symmetric Multiprocessing (SMP)

Much of the effort to increase Linux's performance on servers focuses on improved support for SMP systems. Version 2.0 was the first stable kernel release to support SMP systems.[227] Adding a global spin lock—called the **big kernel lock (BKL)**—was an early attempt at SMP support. When a process acquired the BKL in version 2.0, no process on any other processor could execute in kernel mode. Other processes were, however, free to execute in user mode.[228] The BKL enabled developers to serialize access to kernel data structures, which allowed the kernel to execute multiple processes concurrently in SMP systems. As one study showed, serializing access to the entire kernel meant that the system could not scale effectively to more than four processors per system.[229]

Locking the entire kernel is usually not required, because multiple processes can execute concurrently in kernel mode, provided they do not modify the same data structures. Linux kernel version 2.4 replaced most uses of the BKL with fine-grained locking mechanisms. This change allows SMP systems running Linux to scale effectively to 16 processors.[230]

Fine-grained locks, although a performance enhancement, tend to make developing and debugging the kernel more difficult. These locks force developers to carefully code the acquisition of the appropriate locks at the appropriate times to avoid causing deadlock (for example, by writing code that attempts to acquire the same spin lock twice). As a result, the use of fine-grained locks has slowed kernel development in many subsystems, as would be expected with the increased software complexity.[231]

Performance gains similar to those of large SMP systems have been achieved using alternative solutions, such as clustering (see Section 18.4, Clustering). Recall that a cluster of computer systems consists of several computers that cooperate to perform a common set of tasks. Such clusters of computers are typically connected by a dedicated, high-speed network. To perform work cooperatively using Linux systems, each system must run a modified kernel. Examples of features such a kernel might include are routines to balance workloads within the cluster and data structures to simplify remote interprocess communication, such as global process identifiers. If each machine in the Linux cluster contains a single processor, the complexity of fine-grained locks can be avoided, because only one kernel control path can execute at a time on each machine. Clusters can equal or outperform SMP systems, often at a lower cost of development and hardware.[232] For example, **Beowulf clusters**, a popular form of Linux clusters, have been used by NASA and the Department of Energy (DoE) to build high-performance systems at relatively low cost when compared to proprietary, multiprocessor supercomputer architectures.[233]

20.12.2 Nonuniform Memory Access (NUMA)

As the number of processors in high-end systems increases, buses that connect each processor to components such as memory become increasingly congested. Consequently, many system designers have implemented nonuniform memory access (NUMA) architectures to reduce the amount of bandwidth necessary to maintain high levels of performance in large multiprocessor systems. Recall from Section 15.4.2, Nonuniform Memory Access, that NUMA architectures divide a system into nodes, each of which provides high-performance interconnections between a set of processors, memory and/or I/O devices. The devices within a node are called local resources, while resources outside the node are called remote resources. Connections to remote resources are typically significantly slower than connections to local devices. To achieve high performance, the kernel must be aware of the layout of the NUMA system (i.e., the location and contents of each node) to reduce unnecessary internode access.

When the kernel detects a NUMA system, it must initially determine its layout (i.e., which devices correspond to which nodes) so that it can better allocate resources to processes. Most NUMA systems provide architecture-specific hardware that indicates the contents of each node. The kernel uses this information to assign each device an integer value indicating the node to which it belongs. Most NUMA systems partition a single physical memory address space into regions corresponding to each node. To support this feature, the kernel uses a data structure to associate a range of physical memory addresses with a particular node.[234]

To maximize performance, the kernel uses the layout of the NUMA system to allocate resources that are local to the node in which a process executes. For example, when a process is created on a particular processor, the kernel allocates the process local memory (i.e., memory that is assigned to the node containing the processor) using the data structure we mentioned. If a process were to subsequently execute on a processor on a different node, its data would be stored in remote memory, leading to poor performance due to high memory access latency. Recall from Section 20.5.2, Process Scheduling, that the process scheduler will dispatch a process to the same processor (to improve cache performance) unless the number of processes running on each processor becomes unbalanced. To support NUMA systems, the load balancing routines attempt to migrate a process only to processors within the process's current node. In the case that a processor in another node is idle; however, the process scheduler will migrate a process to another node. Although this results in high memory access latency for the migrated process, overall system throughput increases due to increased resource utilization.[235]

Several other kernel components support the NUMA architecture. For example, when a process requests memory and available local memory is low, the kernel should swap out pages only in local memory. As a result, the kernel creates a *kswapd* thread for each node to perform page replacement.[236]

Despite the kernel's broad support for the NUMA architecture, there are limitations to the current implementation. For example, if a process is migrated to a processor on a remote node, the kernel provides no mechanisms to migrate the process's pages to local memory (i.e., memory in the process's current node). Only when pages are swapped from disk does the kernel move the process's pages to its processor's local memory. Several development projects exist to improve kernel support for NUMA systems, and extensions are expected to be released in future versions of the kernel.

20.12.3 Other Scalability Features

Developers have increased the size of several fields to accommodate the growing demands of computer systems. For example, the maximum number of users in a system increased from 16-bit field (65,536 users) to a 32-bit field (over four billion users). This is necessary for institutions such as large universities that have more than 100,000 users. Similarly, the number of tasks a system can execute increased from 32,000 to 4 million, which was necessary to support mainframe and other high-end systems, which often execute tens or hundreds of thousands of threads.[237] Also, the variable that stores time, `jiffies`, has been increased from a 32-bit to a 64-bit value. This means that the value, which is incremented at every timer interrupt, will not overflow at the current timer frequency (1,000Hz) for over 2 billion billion years. Using a 32-bit number, jiffies would overflow after approximately 50 days with a timer frequency of 1,000Hz.[238, 239, 240]

Fields related to storage also increased in size to accommodate large memories. For example, Linux can reference disk blocks using a 64-bit number, allowing the system to access 16 quintillion disk blocks—corresponding to exabytes (billions of gigabytes) of data. Linux also supports Intel's Physical Address Extension (PAE) technology, which allows systems to access up to 64GB of data (corresponding to a 36-bit address) using a 32-bit processor.[241, 242]

Prior to version 2.6, the kernel could not be preempted by a user process. However, the 2.6 kernel is preemptible, meaning that the kernel will be preempted if an event causes a high-priority task to be *ready*, which improves response times for real-time processes. To ensure mutual exclusion and atomic operations, the kernel disables preemption while executing a critical section. Finally, Linux includes support for several high-performance architectures, such as 64-bit processors (both the Intel Itanium processors, `www.intel.com/products/server/processors/server/itanium2/`, and AMD Opteron processors, `www.amd.com/us-en/Processors/ProductInformation/0,,30_118_8825,00.html`) and Intel's HyperThreading technology (see `www.intel.com/info/hyperthreading/`).[243, 244]

20.12.4 Embedded Linux

Porting Linux to embedded devices introduces design challenges much different from those in SMP and NUMA systems. Embedded systems provide architectures with limited instruction sets, small memory and secondary storage sizes and devices that are not commonly found in desktops and workstations (e.g., touch-sensitive displays and device-specific input buttons). A variety of Linux distributions are tailored to meet the needs of embedded systems.

Often, providers of embedded Linux distributions must implement hard real-time process scheduling. Examples of systems requiring real-time embedded device management include cell phones, digital video recorders (e.g., TiVO; `www.tivo.com`) and network gateways.[245] To provide real-time execution in the Linux kernel, companies such as MontaVista Software (`www.mvista.com`) modify a few key components of the kernel. For example, developers must reduce scheduling overhead so that real-time process scheduling occurs quickly enough that the kernel meets real-time processes' timing constraints. The standard kernel's policy, although somewhat appropriate for real-time processes, is not sufficient for providing hard real-time guarantees (see Section 8.9, Real-Time Scheduling). This is because the Linux scheduler by default does not support deadlines. Embedded-device developers modify the scheduler to support additional priority levels, deadlines and lower scheduling latency.[246]

Other concerns specific to embedded systems also require modification to the Linux kernel. For example, some systems may include a relatively small amount of memory compared to desktop systems, so developers must reduce the size of the kernel footprint. Also, some embedded devices do not support virtual memory. As a result, the kernel must be modified to perform additional memory management operations (e.g., protection) in software.[247]

20.13 Security

The kernel provides a minimal set of security features, such as discretionary access control. Authentication is performed outside the kernel by user-level applications such as `login`. This simple security infrastructure has been designed to allow system administrators to redefine access control policies, customize the way Linux authenticates users and specify encryption algorithms that protect system resources.

20.13.1 Authentication

By default, Linux authenticates its users by requiring them to provide a username and password via the `login` process. Each username is linked to an integer user ID. Passwords are hashed using the MD5 or DES algorithms, then stored in entries corresponding to user IDs in either the `/etc/passwd` or `/etc/shadow` file. [*Note*: Although DES was originally developed as an encryption algorithm, it can be used as a hash algorithm.] The choice of encryption algorithm and location of the password file can be modified by a system administrator. Unlike encryption algorithms, which can reverse the encryption operation using a decryption key, hash algorithms are not reversible. Consequently, Linux verifies a password entered at the login prompt by passing it through the hash algorithm and comparing it to the entry that corresponds to the user's ID number in the `/etc/passwd` or `/etc/shadow` file.[248, 249]

As discussed in Section 19.3.1, Basic Authentication, username and password authentication is susceptible to brute-force cracking, such as dictionary attacks. Linux addresses such problems by allowing system administrators to load **pluggable authentication modules (PAMs)**. These modules can reconfigure the system at run time to include enhanced authentication techniques. For example, the password system can be strengthened to disallow terms found in a dictionary and require users to choose new passwords regularly. PAM also supports smart card, Kerberos and voice authentication systems.[250] System administrators can use PAMs to select an authentication system that is most suitable for their environment without modifying the kernel or utility programs such as `login`.[251]

20.13.2 Access Control Methods

Linux secures system resources by controlling access to files. As described in Section 20.3, Linux Overview, the root user is given access to all resources in the system. To control how other users access resources, each file in the system is assigned **access control attributes** that specify file permissions and file attributes, as discussed in Section 20.7.3. In Linux, file permissions consist of a combination of read, write and/or execute permissions specified for three categories: *user*, *group* and *other*. The *user* file permissions are granted to the owner of the file. By default, a Linux file's owner is initially the user that created the file. *Group* permissions are applied if the user requesting the file is not the owner of the file, but is a member of *group*. Finally, *other* permissions are applied to users that are members of *user* neither nor *group*.[252]

File attributes are an additional security mechanism that is supported by some file systems (e.g., the ext2 file system). File attributes allow users to specify constraints on file access beyond read, write and execute. For example, the **append-only** file attribute specifies that any changes to the file must be appended to the end of the file. The **immutable** file attribute specifies that a file cannot be modified (including renaming and deletion) or linked (i.e., referenced using symbolic or hard links).[253, 254]

Linux Security Modules (LSM) Framework

In many environments, security provided by the default access control policy (i.e., discretionary access control) is insufficient. Thus, the kernel supports the **Linux security modules (LSM) framework** to allow a system administrator to customize the access control policy for a particular system using loadable kernel modules. To choose a different access control mechanism, system administrators need only install the kernel module that implements that mechanism. The kernel uses hooks inside the access control verification code to allow an LSM to enforce its access control policy. As a result, an LSM is invoked only if a process has been granted access to a resource via the default access control policy. If a process is denied access by the default access control policy, the registered LSM does not execute, reducing the overhead caused by an LSM.[255]

One popular LSM is SELinux, developed by the National Security Agency (NSA). SELinux replaces Linux's default discretionary access control policy with a **mandatory access control** (MAC) policy (see Section 19.4.2, Access Control Models and Policies). Such a policy allows the system administrator to set the security rules for all files; these rules cannot be overridden by malicious or inexperienced users. The disadvantages of MAC policies result from the need for a greater number of complex rules. More information about the LSM framework and modules such as SELinux can be found at the official LSM Web site (`lsm.immunix.org`).[256]

Privilege Inheritance and Capabilities

When a process is launched by a user, normally it executes with the same privileges as the user who launched it. It is sometimes necessary for users to execute applications with privileges other than those defined by their username and group. For example, many systems allow users to change their passwords using the `passwd` program. This program modifies the `/etc/passwd` or `/etc/shadow` file, which can be read by everyone, but written only with root privileges. To allow users to execute such programs, Linux provides the `setuid` and `setgid` permission bits. If the `setuid` permission bit for an executable file is set, the process that executes that file is assigned the same privileges as the owner of the file. Similarly, if the `setgid` permission bit for an executable file is set, the process that executes that file is assigned the same privileges as the group specified in the file attributes. Thus, users can modify the `/etc/password` file if the passwd program is owned by a user with root privileges and its `setuid` permission bit is set.[257]

Poorly written programs that modify the `setuid` or `setgid` bits can allow users access to sensitive data and system resources. To reduce the possibility of such a situation occurring, Linux provides the LSM Capabilities module to implement capabilities (see Section 19.4.3, Access Control Mechanisms). This allows Linux administrators greater flexibility in assigning access control privileges, such as the ability to assign privileges to applications rather than to users, which promotes fine-grained security.[258]

20.13.3 Cryptography

Although PAM and the LSM framework allow system administrators to create secure authentication systems and customized access control policies, they cannot protect data that is not controlled by the Linux kernel (e.g., data transmitted over a network or stored on disk). To enable users to access several forms of encryption to protect their data, Linux provides the **Cryptographic API**. Using this interface, processes can encrypt information using powerful algorithms such as DES, AES and MD5 (see Section 19.2, Cryptography). The kernel uses the Cryptographic API to implement secure network protocols such as IPSec (see Section 19.10, Secure Communication Protocols).[259]

The Cryptographic API also allows users to create secure file systems without modifying the existing file system's code. To implement such a file system, encryption is implemented using a **loopback device** (Fig. 20.28), which is a layer between the virtual file system and the existing file system (e.g., ext2). When the virtual file system issues a read or write call, control passes to the loopback device. If the VFS issues a read call, the loopback device reads the requested (encrypted) data from the underlying file system. The loopback device then uses the Cryptographic API to decrypt the data and returns that data to the VFS. Similarly, the loopback device

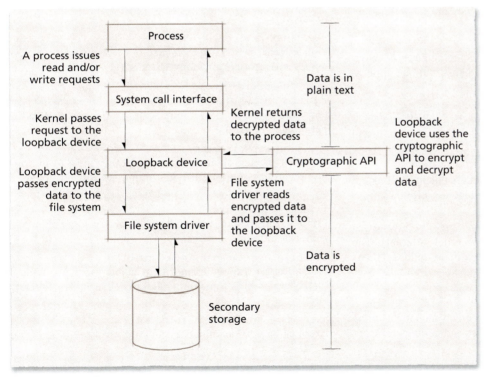

Figure 20.28 | *Loopback device providing an encrypted file system using the Cryptographic API.*

uses the Cryptographic API to encrypt data before transferring it to the file system. This technique can be applied to individual directories or the entire file system, so that data is protected even if an unauthorized user accesses the hard disk using another operating system.[260]

Web Resources

www.kernel.org/
Official site for hosting the latest Linux kernel releases. It also includes a brief description of Linux and contains links to Linux resources.

lxr.linux.no/
Contains a cross-reference to recent releases of the Linux source code. Users can navigate the source code specific to an architecture and version number, search the source for identifiers and other text, and compare two different versions of the source side by side. The /Documentation directory provides links to files referenced in the chapter.

loll.sourceforge.net/linux/links/
Provides an index of categorized links to a selection of online Linux resources. Categories include kernel, documentation, distributions, security and privacy, graphics and software applications.

www.linux.org/
Provides updated Linux information including news, development status and links to documentation, distributions, applications, source code and other resources.

www.kernelnewbies.org/
Provides information for people new to the Linux kernel. Features include a glossary, FAQ, articles, documentation, useful scripts and mailing lists.

www.spinics.net/linux/
Contains a large number of Linux resources, including links to information on kernels, security, embedded Linux and more.

www.tldp.org/LDP/lki/index.html
Part of the Linux Documentation Project hosted at www.tldp.org that discusses Linux kernel internals. The Linux Documentation Project provides many guides, HOW-TOs and FAQs for those interested in the kernel, and for users and administrators.

www.tldp.org/LDP/lkmpg/index.html
Focuses on programming for the Linux environment, including details on programming kernel modules and adding entries to the proc file system.

www.tldp.org/HOWTO/Module-HOWTO/
Describes how to program Linux loadable kernel modules (LKMs) and discusses the use and behavior of LKMs.

www.csn.ul.ie/~mel/projects/vm/
Provides documentation of the Linux version 2.4 virtual memory system, which remains largely intact in version 2.6. The documents include a comprehensive discussion of Linux virtual memory and a companion code commentary.

www.linuxjournal.com/search.php?query=&topic=4
The *Linux Journal* Web site provides numerous articles on Linux. Be sure to search the "Linux Kernel" category.

www.linuxsymposium.org/2003/
Provides information about the Linux Symposia, annual gatherings of the top Linux kernel developers from over 30 countries.

lse.sourceforge.net/
Home to the Linux Scalability Effort, an organization dedicated to porting Linux to larger and more complex computer systems.

www.linux-mag.com/
Online version of *Linux Magazine*, which provides articles, guides and tutorials for Linux systems.

www.linuxdevices.com/
Provides articles and resources on Linux for embedded systems and discusses how Linux scales to devices such as cell phones and PDAs.

www.linuxsecurity.com/
Contains articles, documentation and other links to information regarding Linux security for both users and developers.

kernelnewbies.org/documents/kdoc/kernel-locking/lklockingguide.html
Contains information written by a kernel developer about kernel locks and semaphores.

www.plig.org/xwinman/index.html
Describes the window managers available for the X Window Manager as well as some of the desktop environments that run on X.

user-mode-linux.sourceforge.net/
Explains how to download, install and use User-Mode Linux (UML).

lsm.immunix.org
Provides links to documentation, downloads and mailing lists for the Linux Security Modules project.

Key Terms

access control attribute (Linux)—Specifies the access rights for processes attempting to access a particular resource.

active list (Linux)—Scheduler structure that contains processes that will control the processor at least once during the current epoch.

active page (Linux)—Page of memory that will not be replaced the next time pages are selected for replacement.

active **state** (Linux)—Task state describing tasks that can compete for execution on a processor during the current epoch.

append-only file attribute (Linux)—File attribute that limits users to appending data to existing file contents.

architecture-specific code—Code that specifies instructions unique to a particular architecture.

Beowulf cluster (Linux)—High-performance parallel-processing system consisting of a cluster of computers each running the Beowulf modification to the Linux kernel.

big kernel lock (BKL) (Linux)—Global spin lock that served as an early implementation of SMP support in the Linux kernel.

binary buddy algorithm (Linux)—Algorithm that Linux uses to allocate physical page frames. The algorithm maintains a list of groups of contiguous pages; the number in each group is a power of two. This facilitates memory allocation for processes and devices that require access to contiguous physical memory.

bio structure (Linux)—Structure that simplifies block I/O operations by mapping I/O requests to pages.

block allocation bitmap (Linux)—Bitmap that tracks the usage of blocks in each block group.

block group (Linux)—Collection of contiguous blocks managed by groupwide data structures so that related data blocks, inodes and other file system metadata are contiguous on disk.

bottom half of an interrupt handler (Linux)—Portion of interrupt-handling code that can be preempted.

bounce buffer (Linux)—Region of memory that allows the kernel to map data from the high memory zone into memory that it can directly reference. This is necessary when the system's physical address space is larger than kernel's virtual address space.

cache-cold process—Process that contains little, if any, of its data or instructions in the cache of the processor to which it will be dispatched.

cache-hot process—Process that contains most, if not all, of its data and instructions in the cache of the processor to which it will be dispatched.

capability—Security mechanism that assigns access rights to a subject (e.g., a process) by granting it a token for an object (i.e., a resource). This enables administrators to specify and enforce fine-grained access control.

code freeze (Linux)—Point at which no new code should be added to the kernel unless the code fixes a known bug.

core file (Linux)—File that contains the execution state of a process, typically used for debugging purposes after a process encounters a fatal exception.

Cryptographic API (Linux)—Kernel interface through which applications and services (e.g., file systems) can encrypt and decrypt data.

datagram socket—Socket that uses the UDP protocol to transmit data.

deadline scheduler (Linux)—Disk scheduling algorithm that eliminates indefinite postponement by assigning deadlines by which I/O requests are serviced.

daemon (Linux)—Process that runs periodically to perform system services.

deactivated process (Linux)—Process that has been removed from the run queues and can therefore no longer contend for processor time.

dcache (directory entry cache) (Linux)—Cache that stores directory entries (dentries), which enables the kernel to quickly map file descriptors to their corresponding inodes.

default action for a signal handler (Linux)—Predefined signal handler that is executed in response to a signal when a process does not specify a corresponding signal handler.

dentry (directory entry) (Linux)—Structure that maps a file to an inode.

desktop environment—GUI layer above a window manager that provides tools, applications and other software to improve system usability.

device class—Group of devices that perform similar functions.

device special file (Linux)—Entry in the /dev directory that provides access to a particular device.

direct I/O—Technique that performs I/O without using the kernel's buffer cache. This leads to more efficient memory utilization in database applications, which typically maintain their own buffer cache.

discretionary access control—Access control policy that specifies the owner of a file as the user that can assign access rights to that file.

distribution (Linux)—Software package containing the Linux kernel, user applications and/or tools that simplify the installation process.

DMA memory (Linux)—Region of physical memory between zero and 16MB that is typically reserved for kernel bootstrapping code and legacy DMA devices.

doubly indirect pointer—Inode pointer that locates a block of (singly) indirect pointers.

effective priority (Linux)—Priority assigned to a process by adding its static priority to its priority boost or penalty.

epoch (Linux)—Time during which all processes move from the scheduler's active list to its expired list. This ensures that processes are not indefinitely postponed.

expired list (Linux)—Structure containing processes that cannot contend for the processor until the next epoch. Processes are placed in this list to prevent others from being indefinitely postponed. To quickly begin a new epoch, this list becomes the active list.

expired **state** (Linux)—Task state that prevents a task from being dispatched until the next epoch.

ext2 inode (Linux)—Structure that stores information such as file size, the location of a file's data blocks and permissions for a single file or directory in an ext2 file system.

ext2fs (Linux)—Popular inode-based Linux file system that enables fast access to small files and supports large file sizes.

feature freeze (Linux)—State of kernel development during which no new features should be added to the kernel, in preparation for a new kernel release.

FIFO (Linux)—Named pipe that enables two unrelated processes to communicate via the producer/consumer relationship using a page-size buffer.

file attribute—File metadata that implements access control information, such as whether a file is append-only or immutable, that cannot be specified using standard Linux file permissions.

file permission—Structure that determines whether a user may read, write and or execute a file.

group descriptor (Linux)—Structure that records information regarding a block group, such as the locations of the inode allocation bitmap, block allocation bitmap and inode table.

high memory (Linux)—Region of physical memory (which begins at 896MB on the IA-32 architecture) beginning at the largest physical address that is permanently mapped to the kernel's virtual address space and extending to the limit of physical memory (64GB on Intel Pentium 4 processors). Because the kernel must perform expensive operations to map pages in its virtual address space to page frames in high memory, most kernel data structures are not stored in high memory.

hot swappable device—Device that can be added to, or removed from, a computer while it is running.

hook—Software feature that enables developers to add features to an existing application without modifying its source file. An application uses a hook to call a procedure that can be defined by another application.

immutable attribute (Linux)—Attribute specifying that a file can be read and executed, but cannot be copied, modified or deleted.

inactive list (Linux)—See expired list.

inactive page (Linux)—Page in main memory that can be replaced by an incoming page.

indirect pointer—Inode pointer that points to a block of inode pointers.

inode (Linux)—Structure that describes the location of data blocks corresponding to a file, directory or link in a file system. In the VFS, this structure represents any file in the system. An ext2 inode represents a file in the ext2 file system.

inode allocation bitmap (Linux)—Bitmap that records a block group's inode usage.

inode cache (Linux)—Cache that improves inode lookup performance.

inode table (Linux)—Structure that contains an entry for each allocated inode in a block group.

kernel control path (Linux)—A kernel execution context that may perform operations requiring mutual exclusive access to kernel data structures.

kernel semaphore (Linux)—Semaphore implemented by the kernel to provide mutual exclusion.

kernel thread (Linux)—Thread that executes kernel code.

ksoftirqd (Linux)—Daemon that schedules software interrupt handlers when softirq load is high.

kswapd (Linux)—Daemon that swaps pages to disk.

Linux security modules (LSM) framework (Linux)—Framework that allows system administrators to specify the access control mechanism employed by the system.

Linux Standard Base (Linux)—Project that aims to specify a standard Linux interface to improve application portability between kernel versions (and distributions).

loadable kernel module (Linux)—Software that can be integrated into the kernel at runtime.

load balancing—Operation that attempts to evenly distribute system load between processors in the system.

loopback device (Linux)—Virtual device that enables operations to be performed on data between layers of a system service (e.g., the file system).

mandatory access control—Access control policy that relegates assignment of access rights to the system administrator.

major device identification number (Linux)—Value that uniquely identifies a device in a particular device class. The kernel uses this value to determine a device's driver.

major version number (Linux)—Value that uniquely identifies a significant Linux release.

memory dump (Linux)—Action that generates a core file before terminating a process.

memory footprint (Linux)—Size of unswappable memory consumed by the kernel.

memory pool (Linux)—Region of memory reserved by the kernel for a process to ensure that the process's future requests for memory are not denied.

merge I/O requests (Linux)—To combine two I/O requests to adjacent locations on disk into a single request.

message queue (Linux)—Structure that stores messages that have yet to be delivered to processes.

message queue descriptor (Linux)—Structure that stores data regarding a message queue.

message—IPC mechanism that allows data to be transmitted by specifying a message type and variable-length field of data.

minor device identification number (Linux)—Value that uniquely identifies devices that are assigned the same major number (e.g., a hard drive partition).

minor version number (Linux)—Value that identifies successive stable (even) and development (odd) versions of the Linux kernel.

mount—Insert a file system into a local directory structure.

named pipe (Linux)—Pipe that can be accessed via the directory tree, enabling processes that are not parent and child to communicate using pipes. See also pipe.

netfilter framework (Linux)—Mechanism that allows kernel modules to directly inspect and modify packets. This is useful for applications such as firewalls, which modify each packet's source address before the packet is transmitted.

nice value (Linux)—Measure of a process's scheduling priority. Processes with a low nice value receive a greater share of processor time than other processes in the system and are therefore "less nice" to other processes in the system.

normal memory (Linux)—Physical memory locations beyond 16MB that the kernel can directly map to its virtual address space. This region is used to store kernel data and user pages.

package (Linux)—Portion of a distribution containing an application or service. Users can customize their Linux systems by adding and removing packages.

page cache (Linux)—Cache storing pages of data from disk. When a process requests data from disk, the kernel first determines if it exists in the page cache, which can eliminate an expensive disk I/O operation.

page global directory (Linux)—Virtual memory structure that stores addresses of second-level page-mapping tables.

page middle directory (Linux)—Virtual memory structure that stores addresses of third-level page-mapping tables (also called page tables).

page table (Linux)—Virtual memory structure that contains direct mappings between virtual page numbers and physical page numbers.

PID (process identifier)—Integer that uniquely identifies a process.

pipe—Interprocess communication mechanism that uses a page of memory as a first-in-first-out buffer to transfer information between processes.

pipe buffer (Linux)—Page of data that is used to buffer data written to a pipe.

pluggable authentication module (PAM) (Linux)—Module that can be installed at runtime to incorporate enhanced authentication techniques in the Linux system.

port of Linux—Version of the Linux kernel that is modified to support execution in a different environment.

preemption lock counter (Linux)—Integer that is used to determine whether code executing in kernel mode may be preempted. The value of the counter is incremented each time a kernel control path enters a critical section during which it cannot be preempted.

priority array (Linux)—Structure within a run queue that stores processes of the same priority.

procfs (proc file system) (Linux)—File system built directly into the kernel that provides real-time information about the status of the kernel and processes, such as memory utilization and system execution time.

ramfs (Linux)—Region of main memory treated as a block device. The ramfs file system must be formatted before use.

reader/writer lock (Linux)—Lock that allows multiple threads to concurrently hold a lock when reading from a resource, but only one thread to hold a lock when writing to that resource.

real-time signal (Linux)—Signal implementation that helps to implement a real-time system by ensuring that no signals are dropped.

request list (Linux)—Structure that stores pending I/O requests. This list is sorted to improve throughput by reducing seek times.

reverse mapping (Linux)—Linked list of page table entries that reference a page of memory. This facilitates updating all PTEs corresponding to a shared page that is about to be replaced.

root user (Linux)—See superuser.

run queue (Linux)—List of processes waiting to execute on a particular processor.

second extended file system (ext2fs) (Linux)—See ext2fs.

semaphore array (Linux)—Linked list of semaphores that protect access to related resources.

seqlock (Linux)—Mutual exclusion structure that combines a spin lock with a sequence counter. Seqlocks are used by interrupt handlers, which require immediate exclusive access to data.

Single UNIX Specification—Specification (created by The Open Group) to which an operating system must conform to earn the right to display the UNIX trademark (see www.unix.org/version3/overview.html).

slab (Linux)—Page of memory that reduces internal fragmentation due to small structures by storing multiple structures smaller than one page.

slab allocator (Linux)—Kernel entity that allocates memory for objects placed in the slab cache.

slab cache (Linux)—Cache that stores recently used slabs.

socket—Interprocess communication mechanism that allows processes to exchange data by establishing direct communication channels. Enables processes to communicate over a network using read and write calls.

socketpair (Linux)—Pair of connected, unnamed sockets that can be used for bidirectional communication between processes on a single system.

socket address—Unique identifier for a socket.

software interrupt handler (Linux)—Interrupt-handling code that can be performed without masking interrupts and can therefore be preempted.

softirq (Linux)—Software interrupt handler that is reentrant and not serialized, so it can be executed on multiple processors simultaneously.

source tree (Linux)—Structure that contains source code files and directories. Provides a logical organization to the monolithic Linux kernel.

spin lock—Lock that provides mutually exclusive access to critical sections. When a process holding the lock is executing inside its critical section, any process concurrently executing on a different processor that attempts to acquire the lock before entering its critical section is made to busy wait.

starvation limit (Linux)—Time at which high-priority processes are placed in the expired list to prevent low-priority processes from being indefinitely postponed.

static priority level (Linux)—Integer value assigned to a process when it is created that determines its scheduling priority.

stream socket—Socket that transfers data using the TCP protocol.

superblock (Linux)—Block containing information regarding a mounted file system, such as the root inode and other information that protects the file system's integrity.

superuser (root user) (Linux)—User that may perform restricted operations (i.e., those that may damage the kernel and/or the system).

swap cache (Linux)—Cache of page table entries that describes whether a particular page exists in the system swap file on secondary storage. If a page table entry is present in the swap cache, then its corresponding page exists in the swap file and does not need to be written to the swap file.

system file system (sysfs) (Linux)—File system that allows processes to access structures defined by the unified device model.

task (Linux)—User execution context (i.e., process or thread) in Linux.

tasklet (Linux)—Software interrupt handler that cannot be executed simultaneously on multiple processors. Tasklets are used to execute nonreentrant bottom halves of interrupt handlers.

time slice (Linux)—Another term for quantum.

tmpfs (temporary file system) (Linux)—Similar to ramfs, but does not require formatting before use, meaning that the system can store files in the tmpfs without the organizational overhead typical of most file systems.

top half of an interrupt handler (Linux)—Nonpreemptible portion of interrupt-handling code that performs the minimum work required to acknowledge an interrupt before transferring execution to the preemptible bottom-half handler.

triply indirect pointer—Pointer in an inode that locates a block of doubly indirect pointers.

unified device model (Linux)—Internal device representation that relates devices to device drivers, device classes and system buses. The unified device model simplifies power management and hot swappable device management.

unmap a page (Linux)—To update page table entries to indicate that the corresponding page is no longer resident.

User-Mode Linux (UML) (Linux)—Linux kernel that executes as a user process within a host Linux system.

virtual file system (Linux)—Interface that provides users with a common view of files and directories stored across multiple heterogeneous file systems.

virtual memory area (Linux)—Structure that describes a contiguous region of a process's virtual address space so that the kernel can perform operations on this region as a unit.

window manager (Linux)—Application that controls the placement, appearance, size and other attributes of windows in a GUI.

zone (memory) (Linux)—Region of physical memory. Linux divides main memory in the low, normal and high zones to allocate memory according to the architectural limitations of a system.

zone allocator—Memory subsystem that allocates pages from the zone to which it is assigned.

Exercises

20.1 [*Section 20.4.1, Hardware Platforms*] Describe several applications of User-Mode Linux (UML).

20.2 [*Section 20.4.2, Loadable Kernel Modules*] Why is it generally unsafe to load a kernel module written for kernel versions other than the current one?

20.3 [*Section 20.5.1, Process and Thread Organization*] Which threading model (see Section 4.6, Threading Models) can threads created using the `clone` system call implement? How do Linux threads differ from traditional threads? Discuss the benefits and drawbacks of this implementation.

20.4 [*Section 20.5.2, Process Scheduling*] How are the Linux process scheduler's run queues similar to multilevel feedback queues (see Section 8.7.6, Multilevel Feedback Queues)? How are they different?

20.5 [*Section 20.5.2, Process Scheduling*] Why should the Linux process scheduler penalize processor-bound processes?

20.6 [*Section 20.5.2, Process Scheduling*] Why does Linux prevent users without root privileges from creating real-time processes?

20.7 [*Section 20.6.1, Memory Organization*] Why does the kernel allocate page frames to processes from normal and high memory before allocating pages from DMA memory?

20.8 [*Section 20.6.1, Memory Organization*] What are the benefits and drawbacks of embedding the kernel virtual address space in each process's virtual address space?

20.9 [*Section 20.6.1, Memory Organization*] The x86-64 architecture uses four levels of page tables; each level contains 512 entries (using 64-bit PTEs). However, the kernel provides only three levels of page tables. Assuming that each PTE points to a 4KB page, what is the largest address space the kernel can allocate to processes in this architecture?

20.10 [*Section 20.6.2, Physical Memory Allocation and Deallocation*] How does the kernel reduce the amount of internal fragmentation caused by allocating memory to structures that are much smaller than a page?

20.11 [*Section 20.6.3, Page Replacement*] When is the kernel unable to immediately free a page frame to make room for an incoming page?

20.12 [*Section 20.6.4, Swapping*] When nonresident pages are retrieved from the backing store in Linux, the memory manager retrieves not only the requested page but also up to eight pages contiguous to it in the *running* process's virtual address space. Identify the type of prepaging implemented and describe the benefits and disadvantages of such a policy.

20.13 [*Section 20.7.1, Virtual File System*] List at least four different objects a VFS file can represent and describe the usage of each object.

20.14 [*Section 20.7.1, Virtual File System*] What role does the dentry object serve in the Linux VFS?

20.15 [*Section 20.7.2, Virtual File System Caches*] Is it possible for a file's inode to exist in the inode cache if its dentry is not located in the dentry cache?

20.16 [*Section 20.7.3, Second Extended File System (ext2fs)*] Compare and contrast the VFS and ext2 representation of an inode.

20.17 [*Section 20.7.3, Second Extended File System (ext2fs)*] Why do most file systems maintain redundant copies of their superblock throughout the disk?

20.18 [*Section 20.7.3, Second Extended File System (ext2fs)*] What are the primary contents of a block group and what purpose do they serve?

20.19 [*Section 20.7.4, Proc File System*] In what ways does the proc file system differ from a file system such as ext2fs?

20.20 [*Section 20.8.1, Device Drivers*] Explain the concept and usage of device special files.

20.21 [*Section 20.8.3, Block Device I/O*] Identify two mechanisms employed by the Linux block I/O subsystem that improve performance. Discuss how they improve performance and how they may, if ever, degrade performance.

20.22 [*Section 20.8.4, Network Device I/O*] Compare and contrast networking I/O operations and block/character I/O operations.

20.23 [*Section 20.8.5, Unified Device Model*] How does the unified device model facilitate kernel support for hot swappable devices?

20.24 [*Section 20.8.6, Interrupts*] Why does the networking subsystem employ softirqs to process packets?

20.25 [*Section 20.9.1, Spin Locks*] What occurs if multiple kernel control paths concurrently attempt to acquire the same spin lock?

20.26 [*Section 20.10.1, Signals*] What problems can result from dropping a signal while a process handles a signal of the same type?

20.27 [*Section 20.10.4, Message Queues*] What could happen if a message's size is greater than a message queue's buffer?

20.28 [*Section 20.10.6, System V Semaphores*] Name a potential problem that occurs when processes are made to wait on a semaphore array.

20.29 [*Section 20.11.2, Netfilter Framework and Hooks*] What purpose does the netfilter framework serve?

20.30 [*Section 20.12.2, Nonuniform Memory Access (NUMA)*] Which kernel subsystems were modified to support NUMA?

20.31 [*Section 20.13.1, Authentication*] How does Linux protect user passwords from attackers, even if the attacker acquires the password file? How can this be circumvented?

20.32 [*Section 20.13.2, Access Control Methods*] Why might it be dangerous to set the setuid or setgid bits for an executable file?

Recommended Reading

Linux development is an ongoing process that includes contributions from developers worldwide. Because Torvalds frequently releases new kernel versions, some documentation can be outdated as soon as it is published. Hence, the most current information is usually found on the Web.

Useful resources include the magazines *Linux Journal* and *Linux Magazine*. Monthly issues cover a variety of Linux topics such as desktop and server applications, programming and, of course, the kernel. Selected articles and information about subscribing can be found at www.linuxjournal.com and www.linux-mag.com, respectively.

Readers looking to dig deeper into the Linux kernel should consider the book *Understanding the Linux Kernel*, 2nd ed., by Bovet and Cesati.[261] This book includes in-depth discussions of nearly all kernel subsystems. It explains kernel version 2.4—and, while some material has changed in kernel 2.6, much of the book's content is still relevant.

Another notable book is *Linux Device Drivers*, 2nd ed., by Rubini and Corbet.[262] The title can be misleading, as the book also explains a number of kernel subsystems of concern to device driver developers. It provides an in-depth explanation of the I/O subsystem as well as information about synchronization, memory management and networking. Like most Linux-related literature, the book is somewhat outdated compared to the most recent release of the kernel. The second edition discusses kernel version 2.4.

Works Cited

1. Kuwabara, K., "Linux: A Bazaar at the Edge of Chaos," *First Monday*, Vol. 5, No. 3, March 2000.

2. "Linux History," viewed July 8, 2003, <www.li.org/linuxhistory.php>.

3. "Linux History," viewed July 8, 2003, <www.li.org/linuxhistory.php>.

4. Torvalds, L., <www2.educ.umu.se/~bjorn/linux/misc/linuxhistory.html>.

5. Quinlan, D., "The Past and Future of Linux Standards," *Linux Journal*, Issue 62, June 1999.

6. Linux README, <lxr.linux.no/source/README? v=1.0.9>.

7. Wilburn, G., "Which Linux OS Is Best for You," *Computing Canada*, August 1999, p. 26.

8. Wheeler, D., "More Than a Gigabuck: Estimating GNU/Linux's Size," June 30, 2001 (updated July 29, 2002), version 1.07, <www.dwheeler.com/sloc/>.

9. McHugh, J., "Linux: The Making of a Global Hack," *Forbes Magazine*, August 1998.

10. Pranevich, J., "The Wonderful World of Linux 2.2," January 26, 1999, <linuxtoday.com/news_story.php3?ltsn=1999-01-26-015-05-NW-SM>.

11. McCarty, B., and P. McCarty, "Linux 2.4," January 2001, <www.linux-mag.com/2001-01/linux24_01.html>.

12. McCarty, B., and P. McCarty, "Linux 2.4," January 2001, <www.linux-mag.com/2001-01/linux24_01.html>.

13. "Whatever Happened to the Feature Freeze?" December 18, 2002, <lwn.net/Articles/18454/>.

14. Index, <www.gnu.org>.

15. "LWN Distributions List," updated May 2003, <old.lwn.net/Distributions>.

16. <www.linux-mandrake.com>.

17. <www.redhat.com>.

18. <www.suse.com>.

19. <www.debian.org>.

20. <www.slackware.org>.

21. <www.uclinux.org>.

22. <www.zauruszone.com/wiki/index.php?OpenZaurus.org>.

23. <www.tldp.org/LDP/lfs/LFS/>.

24. slashdot.org/askslashdot/99/03/07/1357235.shtml.

25. Casha, R., "The Linux Terminal—A Beginners' Bash," November 8, 2001, <linux.org.mt/article/terminal>.

26. "CG252-502 X Windows: History of X," modified June 19, 1996, <nestroy.wi-inf.uni-essen.de/Lv/gui/cg252/course/lect4c1.html>.

27. Manrique, D., "X Window System Architecture Overview HOWTO," 2001, <www.linux.org/docs/ldp/howto/XWindow-Overview-HOWTO/>.

28. "The Single UNIX Specification, Version 3—Overview," modified January 27, 2002, <www.unix.org/version3/overview.html>.

29. "The Unix System Specification," <unix.org/what_is_unix/single_unix_specification.html>.

30. Linux Standard Base Specification 1.3, (c) 2000-2002 Free Standards Group, October 27, 2002.

31. Liedtke, J., "Toward Real Microkernels," *Communications of the ACM*, Vol. 39, No. 9, September 1996, p. 75.

32. "The Linux Kernel Archives," <www.kernel.org>.

33. Linux kernel source code, version 2.5.56, <www.kernel.org>.

34. "LinuxHQ: Distribution Links," <www.linuxhq.com/dist.html>.

35. "The User-Mode Linux Kernel Home Page," July 23, 2003, <user-mode-linux.sourceforge.net>.

36. Dike, J., "A User-Mode Port of the Linux Kernel," August 25, 2000, <user-mode-linux.sourceforge.net/als2000/index.html>.

37. Rusling, D., "The Linux Kernel," 1999, <www.tldp.org/LDP/tlk/tlk.html>.

38. Welsh, M., "Implementing Loadable Kernel Modules for Linux," *Dr. Dobb's Journal*, May 1995, <www.ddj.com/articles/1995/9505/>.

39. Henderson, B., "Linux Loadable Kernel Module HOWTO," May 2002, <www.tldp.org/HOWTO/Module-HOWTO/>.

40. Henderson, B., "Linux Loadable Kernel Module HOWTO," May 2002, <www.tldp.org/HOWTO/Module-HOWTO/>.

41. Petersen, K., "Kmod: The Kernel Module Loader," Linux kernel source file, Linux/Documentation/kmod.txt <www.kernel.org>.

42. Aivazian, T., "Linux Kernel 2.4 Internals," August 23, 2001, <www.tldp.org/LDP/lki/lki.html>.

43. Rusling, D., "The Linux Kernel," 1999, <www.tldp.org/LDP/tlk/tlk.html>.

44. SchlapBach, A., "Linux Process Scheduling," May 2, 2000, <iamexwiwww.unibe.ch/studenten/schlpbch/linuxScheduling/LinuxScheduling.htm>.

45. Aivazian, T., "Linux Kernel 2.4 Internals," August 23, 2001, <www.tldp.org/LDP/lki/lki.html>.

46. Walton, S., "Linux Threads Frequently Asked Questions," January 21, 1997, <www.tldp.org/FAQ/Threads-FAQ/>.

47. McCracken, D., "POSIX threads and the Linux Kernel," *Proceedings of the Ottawa Linux Symposium*, 2002, p. 332.

48. Arcomano, R., "KernelAnalysis-HOWTO," June 2, 2002, <www.tldp.org/HOWTO/KernelAnalysis-HOWTO.html>.

49. Walton, S., "Linux Threads Frequently Asked Questions" <linas.org/linux/threads-faq.html>.

50. Drepper, U., and I. Molnar, "The Native POSIX Thread Library for Linux," January 30, 2003, <people.redhat.com/drepper/nptl-design.pdf>.

51. Molnar, I., Announcement to Linux mailing list, <lwn.net/2002/0110/a/scheduler.php3>.

52. Cross-Referencing Linux, <lxr.linux.no/source/include/asm-i386/param.h?v=2.6.0-test7#L5> and <lxr.linux.no/source/kernel/sched.c?v=2.6.0-test7#L1336>.

53. Cross-Referencing Linux, <lxr.linux.no/source/kernel/sched.c?v=2.5.56>.

54. Cross-Referencing Linux, <lxr.linux.no/source/kernel/sched.c?v=2.5.56>.

55. Linux kernel source code, version 2.6.0-test2, /kernel/sched.c, lines 80–106, <lxr.linux.no/source/kernel/sched.c?v=2.6.0-test2>.

56. Linux kernel source code, version 2.5.75, <lxr.linux.no/source/kernel/sched.c?v=2.5.75>.

57. Linux kernel source code, version 2.5.75, <lxr.linux.no/source/kernel/sched.c?v=2.5.75>.

58. Linux kernel source code, version 2.5.75, <lxr.linux.no/source/kernel/sched.c?v=2.5.75>.

59. Linux kernel source code, version 2.6.0-test2, <lxr.linux.no/source/arch/i386/mm/pageattr.c?v=2.6.0-test2>.

60. Linux kernel source code, version 2.5.75, <miller.cs.wm.edu/lxr3.linux/http/source/include/linux/mm.h?v= 2.5.75>.

61. Eranian, S., and David Mosberger, "Virtual Memory in the IA-64 Linux Kernel," *informIT.com*, November 8, 2002, <www.informit.com/isapi/product_id~%7B79EC75E3-7AE9-4596-AF39-283490FAFCBD%7D/element_id~%7BCE3A6550-B6B6-44BA-B496-673E8337B5F4%7D/st~%7BBAC7BB78-22CD-4E1E-9387-19EEB5B71759%7D/session_id~%7B9E8FCA0D-31BA-42DD-AEBB-EC1617DE0EC7%7D/content/articlex.asp>.

62. Rusling, D., "The Linux Kernel," 1999, <www.tldp.org/LDP/tlk/tlk.html>.

63. Gorman, M., "Understanding the Linux Virtual Memory Manager," <www.csn.ul.ie/~mel/projects/vm/guide/html/understand/>.

64. Linux kernel source code, version 2.5.75, <miller.cs.wm.edu/lxr3.linux/http/source/mm/page_alloc.c?v=2.5.75>.

65. Linux kernel source code, version 2.6.0-test2, `<miller.cs.wm.edu/lxr3.linux/http/source/include/linux/mm.h?v=2.6.0-test2>`.

66. Linux source code, `<lxr.linux.no/source/include/asm-i386/page.h?v=2.5.56>`.

67. Van Riel, R., "Page Replacement in Linux 2.4 Memory Management" `<www.surriel.com/lectures/linux24-vm.html>`.

68. Gorman, M., "Understanding the Linux Virtual Memory Manager," `<www.csn.ul.ie/~mel/projects/vm/guide/html/understand/>`.

69. Van Riel, R., "Page Replacement in Linux 2.4 Memory Management" `<www.surriel.com/lectures/linux24-vm.html>`.

70. Linux kernel source code, version 2.5.56, `<lxr.linux.no/source/include/linux/mmzone.h?v=2.5.56>`.

71. Linux kernel source code, version 2.5.75, `/Documentation/block/biodoc.txt`.

72. Bovet, D., and M. Cesati, *Understanding the Linux Kernel*, O'Reilly, 2001.

73. Gorman, M., "Understanding the Linux Virtual Memory Manager," `<www.csn.ul.ie/~mel/projects/vm/guide/html/understand/>`.

74. Rusling, D., "The Linux Kernel," 1999 `<www.tldp.org/LDP/tlk/tlk.html>`.

75. Knowlton, K. C., "A Fast Storage Allocator," *Communications of the ACM*, Vol. 8, No. 10, October 1965, pp. 623–625.

76. Knuth, D. E., *The Art of Computer Programming*, Vol. 1, *Fundamental Algorithms*, Addison-Wesley, Reading, MA, 1968, pp. 435-455.

77. Rusling, D., "The Linux Kernel," 1999, `<www.tldp.org/LDP/tlk/tlk.html>`.

78. Rusling, D., "The Linux Kernel," 1999, `<www.tldp.org/LDP/tlk/tlk.html>`.

79. Nayani, A.; M. Gorman; and R. S. de Castro, "Memory Management in Linux: Desktop Companion to the Linux Source Code," May 25, 2002, `<www.symonds.net/~abhi/files/mm/index.html>`.

80. Gorman, M., "Slab Allocator," `<www.csn.ul.ie/~mel/projects/vm/docs/slab.html>`.

81. "Driver Porting: Low-Level Memory Allocation," LWN.net, February 2003, `<lwn.net/Articles/22909/>`.

82. Knapka, J., "Outline of the Linux Memory Management System," `<home.earthlink.net/~jknapka/linux-mm/vmoutline.html>`.

83. Knapka, J., "Outline of the Linux Memory Management System," `<home.earthlink.net/~jknapka/linux-mm/vmoutline.html>`.

84. Arcangeli, A., "Le novita' nel Kernel Linux," December 7, 2001, `<old.lwn.net/2001/1213/aa-vm-talk/mgp00001.html>`.

85. Arcangeli, A., "Le novita' nel Kernel Linux," December 7, 2001, `<old.lwn.net/2001/1213/aa-vm-talk/mgp00001.html>`.

86. Linux kernel source code, version 2.5.75, `<www.kernel.org>`.

87. Arcangeli, A., "Le novita' nel Kernel Linux," December 7, 2001, `<old.lwn.net/2001/1213/aa-vm-talk/mgp00001.html>`.

88. Linux kernel source code, version 2.5.75, `<www.kernel.org>`.

89. Arcangeli, A., "Le novita' nel Kernel Linux," December 7, 2001, `<old.lwn.net/2001/1213/aa-vm-talk/mgp00001.html>`.

90. Rusling, D., "The Linux Kernel," 1999, `<www.tldp.org/LDP/tlk/tlk.html>`.

91. Arcangeli, A., "Le novita' nel Kernel Linux," December 7, 2001, `<old.lwn.net/2001/1213/aa-vm-talk/mgp00001.html>`.

92. Corbet, J., "What Rik van Riel Is Up To," *Linux Weekly News*, January 24, 2002, `<http//php.lwn.net/2002/0124/kernel.php3>`.

93. Arcangeli, A., "Le novita' nel Kernel Linux," December 7, 2001, `<old.lwn.net/2001/1213/aa-vm-talk/mgp00001.html>`.

94. Linux source code, version 2.5.75, `<miller.cs.wm.edu/lxr3.linux/http/source/mm/page-writeback.c?v=2.5.75>`.

95. Arcangeli, A., "Le novita' nel Kernel Linux," December 7, 2001, `<old.lwn.net/2001/1213/aa-vm-talk/mgp00001.html>`.

96. Linux kernel source code, version 2.5.56, `<www.kernel.org>`.

97. Rusling, D., "The Linux Kernel," 1999, `<www.tldp.org/LDP/tlk/tlk.html>`.

98. Brown, N., "The Linux Virtual File-System Layer," December 29, 1999, `<www.cse.unsw.edu.au/~neilb/oss/linux-commentary/vfs.html>`.

99. Rubini, A., "The Virtual File System in Linux," *Linux Journal*, May 1997, `<www.linuxjournal.com/print.php?side=2108>`.

100. Brown, N., "The Linux Virtual File-System Layer," December 29, 1999, `<www.cse.unsw.edu.au/~neilb/oss/linux-commentary/vfs.html>`.

101. Rusling, D., "The Linux Kernel," 1999, `<www.tldp.org/LDP/tlk/tlk.html>`.

102. Linux source code, version 2.5.75, `<miller.cs.wm.edu/lxr3.linux/http/source/include/linux/fs.h?v=2.5.75>`.

103. Rusling, D., "The Linux Kernel," 1999, `<www.tldp.org/LDP/tlk/tlk.html>`.

104. Linux kernel source code, version 2.5.75, `<miller.cs.wm.edu/lxr3.linux/http/source/fs/dcache.c?v=2.5.75>`.

105. Gooch, R., "Overview of the Virtual File System," July 1999, `<www.atnf.csiro.au/people/rgooch/linux/vfs.txt>`.

106. Linux kernel source code, version 2.5.56, `<www.kernel.org>`.

107. Brown, N., "The Linux Virtual File-System Layer," December 29, 1999, `<www.cse.unsw.edu.au/~neilb/oss/linux-commentary/vfs.html>`.

108. Linux kernel source code, version 2.5.75, `<miller.cs.wm.edu/lxr3.linux/http/source/fs/dcache.c?v=2.5.75>`.

109. Rusling, D., "The Linux Kernel," 1999, `<www.tldp.org/LDP/tlk/tlk.html>`.

110. Linux kernel source code, version 2.5.75, `<miller.cs.wm.edu/lxr3.linux/http/source/fs/namei.c?v=2.5.75>`.

111. Brown, N., "The Linux Virtual File-System Layer," December 29, 1999, `<www.cse.unsw.edu.au/~neilb/oss/linux-commentary/vfs.html>`.

112. Linux kernel source code, version 2.5.75, `<miller.cs.wm.edu/lxr3.linux/http/source/fs/namei.c?v=2.5.75>`.

113. Card, R.; T. Ts'O; and S. Tweedie, "Design and Implementation of the Second Extended Filesystem," <e2fsprogs.source-forge.net/ext2intro.html>.

114. /Linux/Documentation/filesystems/ext2.txt, Linux kernel source, version 2.4.18, <www.kernel.org>.

115. Card, R.; T. Ts'O; and S. Tweedie, "Design and Implementation of the Second Extended Filesystem," <e2fsprogs.source-forge.net/ext2intro.html>.

116. /Linux/Documentation/filesystems/ext2.txt, Linux kernel source, version 2.5.75, <www.kernel.org>.

117. Card, R.; T. Ts'O; and S. Tweedie, "Design and Implementation of the Second Extended Filesystem," <e2fsprogs.source-forge.net/ext2intro.html>.

118. Appleton, R., "A Non-Technical Look Inside the Ext2 File System," *Linux Journal,* August 1997, <www.linuxjournal.com/print.php?sid=2151>.

119. Rusling, D., "The Linux Kernel," 1999, <www.tldp.org/LDP/tlk/tlk.html>.

120. Linux kernel source code, version 2.5.75, <www.kernel.org>.

121. Card, R.; T. Ts'O; and S. Tweedie, "Design and Implementation of the Second Extended Filesystem," <e2fsprogs.source-forge.net/ext2intro.html>.

122. Pranevich, J., "The Wonderful World of Linux 2.6," July 13, 2003, <www.kniggit.net/wwol26.html>.

123. Linux kernel source code, version 2.6.0-test2, /include/linux/ext2_fs.h, line 60, <lxr.linux.no/source/include/linux/ext2_fs.h?v=2.6.0-test2>.

124. Appleton, R., "A Non-Technical Look Inside the Ext2 File System," *Linux Journal,* August 1997, <www.linuxjournal.com/print.php?sid=2151>.

125. Bowden, T.; B. Bauer; and J. Nerin, "The /proc Filesystem," Linux kernel source file, Linux/Documentation/filesystems/proc.txt <www.kernel.org>.

126. Rubini, A., "The Virtual File System in Linux," *Linux Journal,* May 1997, <www.linuxjournal.com/print.php?side=2108>.

127. Linux kernel source code, version 2.5.75, <www.kernel.org>.

128. Mouw, E., "Linux Kernel Procfs Guide," June 2001, <www.kernelnewbies.org/documents/kdoc/procfs-guide/lkprocfs-guide.html>.

129. Rusling, D., "The Linux Kernel," 1999, <www.tldp.org/LDP/tlk/tlk.html>.

130. Rusling, D., "The Linux Kernel," 1999, <www.tldp.org/LDP/tlk/tlk.html>.

131. "Linux Allocated Devices," <www.lanana.org/docs/device-list/devices.txt>.

132. <www.lanana.org/docs/device-list/devices.txt>.

133. Rubini, A., and J. Corbet, *Linux Device Drivers,* O'Reilly, 2001, pp. 55–57.

134. Matia, F., "Kernel Korner: Writing a Linux Driver," *Linux Journal,* April 1998, <www.linuxjournal.com/print.php?sid=2476>.

135. "The HyperNews Linux KHG Discussion Pages, Device Driver Basics," December 30, 1997, <users.evtek.fi/~tk/rt_html/ASICS.HTM>.

136. Rusling, D., "The Linux Kernel," 1999, <www.tldp.org/LDP/tlk/tlk.html>.

137. Zezschwitz, G., and A. Rubini, "Kernel Korner: The Devil's in the Details," *Linux Journal,* May 1996, <www.linuxjournal.com/article.php?sid=1221>.

138. Rusling, D., "The Linux Kernel," 1999, <www.tldp.org/LDP/tlk/tlk.html>.

139. Linux kernel source code, version 2.5.75, <miller.cs.wm.edu/lxr3.linux/http/source/fs/char_dev.c?v=2.5.7>.

140. Rusling, D., "The Linux Kernel," 1999, <www.tldp.org/LDP/tlk/tlk.html>.

141. Linux kernel source code, version 2.5.75, <www.kernel.org>.

142. Linux kernel source code, version 2.5.75, <www.kernel.org>.

143. Kalev, D., "Raw Disk I/O," October 2001, <www.itworld.com/nl/lnx_tip/10122001/pf_index.html>.

144. Rubini, A., and J. Corbet, *Linux Device Drivers,* O'Reilly, 2001, 323–328, 334–338.

145. Linux kernel source code, version 2.5.75, <miller.cs.wm.edu/lxr3.linux/http/source/include/linux/bio.h?v=2.5.75>.

146. Linux kernel source code, version 2.5.75, <miller.cs.wm.edu/lxr3.linux/http/source/include/linux/bio.h?v=2.5.75>.

147. Linux kernel source code, version 2.5.75, <www.kernel.org>.

148. Gopinath, K.; N. Muppalaneni; N. Suresh Kumar; and P. Risbood, "A 3-Tier RAID Storage System with RAID1, RAID5 and Compressed RAID5 for Linux," *Proceedings of the FREENIX Track: 2000 USENIX Annual Technical Conference,* June 2000, pp. 18–23.

149. Love, R., "Interactive Kernel Performance," *Proceedings of the Linux Symposium,* 2003, pp. 306–307.

150. Linux kernel source code, version 2.5.75, <miller.cs.wm.edu/lxr3.linux/http/source/drivers/block/deadline-iosched.c?v=2.5.75>.

151. Linux kernel source code, version 2.5.75, <miller.cs.wm.edu/lxr3.linux/http/source/drivers/block/deadline-iosched.c?v=2.5.75>.

152. Axboe, J., "[PATCH] block/elevator updates + deadline i/o scheduler," Linux kernel mailing list, July 26, 2002.

153. Linux kernel source code, version 2.5.75, <miller.cs.wm.edu/lxr3.linux/http/source/drivers/block/deadline-iosched.c?v=2.5.75>.

154. Linux kernel source code, version 2.5.75, <miller.cs.wm.edu/lxr3.linux/http/source/drivers/block/deadline-iosched.c?v=2.5.75>.

155. Love, R., "Interactive Kernel Performance," *Proceedings of the Linux Symposium,* 2003, p. 308.

156. Iyer, S., and P. Druschel, "Anticipatory Scheduling: A Disk Scheduling Framework to Overcome Deceptive Idleness in Synchronous I/O," *ACM SIGOPS Operating Systems Review, Proceedings of the Eighteenth ACM Symposium on Operating Systems Principles,* Vol. 35, No. 5, October 2001.

157. Linux kernel source code, version 2.5.75, <miller.cs.wm.edu/lxr3.linux/http/source/drivers/block/as-iosched.c>.

158. Morton, A., "IO Scheduler Benchmarking," Linux kernel mailing list, February 20, 2003.

159. Rubini, A., and J. Corbet, *Linux Device Drivers,* O'Reilly, 2001, pp. 430–433.

160. Linux kernel source code, version 2.5.75, <miller.cs.wm.edu/lxr3.linux/http/source/include/linux/netdevice.h?v=2.5.75>.

161. Adel, A., "Differentiated Services on Linux," <user.cs.tu-berlin.de/~adelhazm/study/diffserv.pdf>

162. Rubini, A., and J. Corbet, *Linux Device Drivers,* O'Reilly, 2001, pp. 445–448.

163. Corbet, J., "Porting Drivers to the 2.5 Kernel," *Proceedings of the Linux Symposium,* 2003, p. 149.

164. "Universal Serial Bus Specification," Compaq, Hewlitt-Packard, Intel, Lucent, Microsoft, NEC, Phillips, rev. 2.0, April 27, 2002, p. 18.

165. Corbet, J., "Driver Porting: Device Model Overview," <lwn.net/Articles/31185/>, May 2003.

166. Corbet, J., "Driver Porting: Device Model Overview," <lwn.net/Articles/31185/>, May 2003.

167. Mochel, P., "Sysfs—The Filesystem for Exporting Kernel Objects," Linux kernel source code, version 2.5.75, Documentation/filesystems/sysfs.txt, January 10, 2003.

168. Linux kernel source code, version 2.5.75, Documentation/driver-model/overview.txt.

169. Linux kernel source code, version 2.5.75, <miller.cs.wm.edu/lxr3.linux/http/source/include/linux/device.h>.

170. Linux kernel source code, version 2.5.75, Documentation/driver-model/bus.txt.

171. Linux kernel source code, version 2.5.75, Documentation/driver-model/class.txt.

172. Compaq Computer Corporation, Intel Corporation, Microsoft Corporation, Phoenix Technologies Ltd., Toshiba Corporation, "Advanced Configuration and Power Management," rev. 2.0b, October 11, 2002, <www.acpi.info/spec.htm> p. 26.

173. Mochel, P., "Linux Kernel Power Management," *Proceedings of the Linux Symposium,* 2003, <archive.linuxsymposium.org/ols2003/Proceedings/All-Reprints/Reprint-Mochel-OLS2003.pdf>, pp. 344, 347.

174. Russell, P., "Unreliable Guide to Hacking the Linux Kernel," 2000, <www.netfilter.org/unreliable-guides/kernel-hacking/lk-hacking-guide.html>.

175. Intel Corporation, *IA-32 Intel Architecture Software Developer's Manual,* Vol. 3, *System Programmer's Guide,* 2002, pp. 5–32

176. Russell, P., "Unreliable Guide to Hacking the Linux Kernel," 2000, <www.netfilter.org/unreliable-guides/kernel-hacking/lk-hacking-guide.html>.

177. Gatliff, W., "The Linux Kernel's Interrupt Controller API," 2001, <billgatliff.com/articles/emb-linux/interrupts.pdf>.

178. Linux kernel source code, version 2.5.75, <miller.cs.wm.edu/lxr3.linux/http/source/include/linux/interrupt.h?v=2.5.75>.

179. Linux kernel source code, version 2.5.75, <miller.cs.wm.edu/lxr3.linux/http/source/include/linux/interrupt.h?v=2.5.75>.

180. Gatliff, W., "The Linux Kernel's Interrupt Controller API," 2001, <billgatliff.com/articles/emb-linux/interrupts.pdf>.

181. Linux kernel source code, version 2.5.75, <miller.cs.wm.edu/lxr3.linux/http/source/kernel/softirq.c?v=2.5.75>.

182. Rubini, A., and J. Corbet, *Linux Device Drivers,* O'Reilly, 2001, p. 19.

183. Bovet, D., and M. Cesati, *Understanding the Linux Kernel,* O'Reilly, 2001, pp. 300–301, 305–306, 523–532, 545.

184. Love, R., "Kernel Korner: Kernel Locking Techniques," *Linux Journal,* August 2002, <www.linuxjournal.com/article.php?sid=5833>.

185. Love, R., "Kernel Korner: Kernel Locking Techniques," *Linux Journal,* August 2002, <www.linuxjournal.com/article.php?sid=5833>.

186. Torvalds, L., "/Documentation/spinlocks.txt," Linux kernel source code, version 2.5.75, <www.kernel.org>.

187. Russell, P., "Unreliable Guide to Locking," 2000, <www.kernel-newbies.org/documents/kdoc/kernel-locking/lklocking-guide.html>.

188. Russell, P., "Unreliable Guide to Locking," 2000, <www.kernel-newbies.org/documents/kdoc/kernel-locking/lklocking-guide.html>.

189. Torvalds, L., "/Documentation/spinlocks.txt," Linux kernel source code, version 2.5.75, <www.kernel.org>.

190. "Driver Porting: Mutual Exclusion with Seqlocks," <lwn.net/Articles/22818/>.

191. "Driver Porting: Mutual Exclusion with Seqlocks," <lwn.net/Articles/22818/>.

192. Bovet, D., and M. Cesati, *Understanding the Linux Kernel,* O'Reilly, 2001, pp. 305–306.

193. Love, R., "Kernel Korner: Kernel Locking Techniques," *Linux Journal,* August 2002, <www.linuxjournal.com/article.php?sid=5833>.

194. Love, R., "Kernel Korner: Kernel Locking Techniques," *Linux Journal,* August 2002, <www.linuxjournal.com/article.php?sid=5833>.

195. Bar, M., "Kernel Korner: The Linux Signals Handling Model," *Linux Journal,* May 2000, <www.linuxjournal.com/article.php?sid=3985>.

196. Linux kernel source code, version 2.5.75, <miller.cs.wm.edu/lxr3.linux/http/source/kernel/signal.c?v=2.5.75>.

197. Linux kernel source code, version 2.5.75, <miller.cs.wm.edu/lxr3.linux/http/source/kernel/signal.c?v=2.5.75>

198. Troan, E., "A Look at the Signal API," *Linux Magazine,* January 2000, <www.linux-mag.com/2000-01/compile_01.html>.

199. Bovet, D., and M. Cesati, *Understanding the Linux Kernel,* O'Reilly, 2001, p. 253.

200. Bar, M., "Kernel Korner: The Linux Signals Handling Model," *Linux Journal,* May 2000, <www.linuxjournal.com/article.php?sid=3985>.

201. Rusling, D., "The Linux Kernel," 1999, <www.tldp.org/LDP/tlk/tlk.html>.

202. Bovet, D., and M. Cesati, *Understanding the Linux Kernel,* O'Reilly, 2001, p. 253.

203. Linux kernel source code, version 2.6.0-test2, signal.c, line 38 <lxr.linux.no/source/kernel/signal.c?v=2.6.0-test2>

204. Bovet, D., and M. Cesati, *Understanding the Linux Kernel,* O'Reilly, 2001, pp. 524–532.

205. Chelf, B., "Pipes and FIFOs," *Linux Magazine,* January 2001, <www.linux-mag.com/2001-01/compile_01.html>.

206. Chelf, B., "Pipes and FIFOs," *Linux Magazine,* January 2001, <www.linux-mag.com/2001-01/compile_01.html>.

207. Free Software Foundation, "The GNU C Library," 1998, <www.gnu.org/manual/glibc-2.2.5/index.html>.

208. Sechrest, S., "An Introductory 4.4BSD Interprocess Communication Tutorial," <docs.freebsd.org/44doc/psd/20.ipctut/paper.html>.

209. Free Software Foundation, "The GNU C Library," 1998, <www.gnu.org/manual/glibc-2.2.5/index.html>.

210. Sechrest, S., "An Introductory 4.4BSD Interprocess Communication Tutorial," <docs.freebsd.org/44doc/psd/20.ipctut/paper.html>.

211. Aivazian, T., "Linux Kernel 2.4 Internals," August 23, 2001, <www.tldp.org/LDP/lki/lki.html>.

212. Bovet, D., and M. Cesati, *Understanding the Linux Kernel,* O'Reilly, 2001, p. 545.

213. Aivazian, T., "Linux Kernel 2.4 Internals," August 23, 2001 <www.tldp.org/LDP/lki/lki.html>.

214. Goldt, S., et al., "Shared Memory," *The Linux Programmer's Guide,* <en.tldp.org/LDP/lpg/node65.html>, version 0.4, March 1995, and Linux source 2.5.56.

215. Linux man page: shm_open, <www.cwi.nl/~aeb/linux/man2html/man3/shm_open.3.html>.

216. Linux source, <lxr.linux.no/source/Documentation/filesystems/tmpfs.txt?v=2.5.56> and <lxr.linux.no/source/mm/shmem.c?v=2.5.56>

217. Linux source, <lxr.linux.no/source/Documentation/filesystems/tmpfs.txt? v=2.5.56> and <lxr.linux.no/source/mm/shmem.c?v=2.5.56>.

218. Aivazian, T., "Linux Kernel 2.4 Internals," August 23, 2001, <www.tldp.org/LDP/lki/lki.html>.

219. Linux kernel source code, version 2.5.75, <miller.cs.wm.edu/lxr3.linux/http/source/ipc/sem.c?v=2.5.75>.

220. Aivazian, T., "Linux Kernel 2.4 Internals," August 23, 2001, <www.tldp.org/LDP/lki/lki.html>.

221. Cox, A., "Network Buffers," <www.linux.org.uk/Documents/buffers.html>.

222. Linux kernel source code, version 2.5.75, <miller.cs.wm.edu/lxr3.linux/http/source/net/core/dev.c?v=2.5.75>.

223. Welte, H., "The Journey of a Packet Through the Linux 2.4 Network Stack," October 14, 2000, <www.gnumonks.org/ftp/pub/doc/packet-journey-2.4.html>.

224. Linux kernel source code, version 2.5.75, <miller.cs.wm.edu/lxr3.linux/http/source/net/core/dev.c?v=2.5.75>.

225. Dobbelaere, J., "Linux Kernel Internals: IP Network Layer," 2001, <www.cs.wm.edu/~jdobbela/papers/ip.pdf>.

226. Welte, H., "The Netfilter Framework in Linux 2.4," September 24, 2000, <www.gnumonks.org/papers/netfilter-lk2000/presentation.html>.

227. Schmidt, J., "Symmetrical Multiprocessing with Linux," 1999, <www.heise.de/ct/english/98/13/140/>.

228. Tumenbayer, E., et al., "Linux SMP HOWTO," July 9, 2002, <www.ibiblio.org/pub/Linux/docs/HOWTO/other-formats/pdf/SMP-HOWTO.pdf>.

229. Intel Corporation, "Linux Scalability: The Enterprise Question," 2000, <www.intel.com/internetservices/intelsolution-services/downloads/linux_scalability.pdf>.

230. Bergmann, K., "Linux for z/Series Performance Overview," April 3, 2002, <www.linuxvm.org/present/SHARE98/S2561kba.pdf>.

231. McVoy, L., "SMP Scaling Considered Harmful," July 22, 1999, <www.bitmover.com/llnl/smp.pdf>.

232. McVoy, L., "SMP Scaling Considered Harmful," July 22, 1999, <www.bitmover.com/llnl/smp.pdf>.

233. Merkey, P., "Beowulf History," <www.beowulf.org/beowulf/history.html>, viewed July 21, 2003.

234. Linux kernel source code, version 2.5.75, <miller.cs.wm.edu/lxr3.linux/http/source/include/linux/mmzone.h>.

235. Dobson, M.; P. Gaughen; M. Hohnbaum; and E. Focht, "Linux Support for NUMA Hardware," *Proceedings of the Linux Symposium,* 2003, pp. 181–195.

236. Dobson, M.; P. Gaughen; M. Hohnbaum; and E. Focht, "Linux Support for NUMA Hardware," *Proceedings of the Linux Symposium,* 2003, pp. 181–195.

237. Linux kernel source code, version 2.6.0-test7, <lxr.linux.no/source/include/linux/threads.h?v=2.6.0-test7#L33>.

238. Pranevich, J., "The Wonderful World of Linux 2.6," July 13, 2003, <www.kniggit.net/wwol26.html>.

239. Linux kernel source code, version 2.5.75, <www.kernel.org>.

240. Corbet, J., "Driver Porting: Timekeeping Changes," February 2003, <lwn.net/Articles/22808/>.

241. Pranevich, J., "The Wonderful World of Linux 2.6," July 13, 2003, <www.kniggit.net/wwol26.html>.

242. Linux source kernel version 2.5.75 <www.kernel.org>.

243. J. Pranevich, "The Wonderful World of Linux 2.6," July 13, 2003, <www.kniggit.net/wwol26.html>.

244. Linux kernel source code, version 2.5.75, <www.kernel.org>.

245. "The Embedded Linux 'Cool Devices' Quick Reference Guide," modified March 21, 2002, <www.linuxdevices.com/articles/AT4936596231.html>.

246. "MontaVista Linux—Real-time Performance," May 2002, MontaVista Software, <www.mvista.com/dswp/realtime.pdf>.

247. Lehrbaum, R., "Using Linux in Embedded Systems and Smart Devices," viewed July 21, 2003, <www.linuxdevices.com/articles/AT3155773172.html>.

248. Hatch, B., and J. Lee, *Hacking Linux Exposed*, McGraw-Hill: Osborne, 2003, pp. 384–386.

249. Toxen, B., *Real World Linux Security*, 2nd ed., Prentice Hall PTR, 2002.

250. "Modules/Applications Available or in Progress," modified May 31, 2003, <www.kernel.org/pub/linux/libs/pam/modules.html>.

251. Morgan, A., "The Linux-PAM Module Writers' Guide," May 9, 2002, <www.kernel.org/pub/linux/libs/pam/Linux-PAM-html/pam_modules.html>.

252. Hatch, B., and J. Lee, *Hacking Linux Exposed*, McGraw-Hill: Osborne, 2003, pp. 15–19.

253. Linux man pages, "CHATTR(1), change file attributes on a Linux second extended file system," <nodevice.com/cgi-bin/searchman?topic=chattr>.

254. Hatch, B., and J. Lee, *Hacking Linux Exposed*, McGraw-Hill: Osborne, 2003, p. 24.

255. Smalley, S.; T. Fraser; and C. Vance, "Linux Security Modules: General Security Hooks for Linux," <lsm.immunix.org/docs/overview/linuxsecuritymodule.html>.

256. Jaeger, T.; D. Safford; and H. Franke, "Security Requirements for the Deployment of the Linux Kernel in Enterprise Systems," <oss.software.ibm.com/linux/papers/security/les_whitepaper.pdf>.

257. Wheeler, D., "Secure Programming for Linux HOWTO," February 9, 2000, <www.theorygroup.com/Theory/FAQ/Secure-Programs-HOWTO.html>.

258. Wright, C., et al., "Linux Security Modules: General Security Support for the Linux Kernel," 2002, <lsm.immunix.org/docs/lsm-usenix-2002/html/>.

259. Bryson, D., "The Linux CryptoAPI: A User's Perspective," May 31, 2002, <www.kerneli.org/howto/index.php>.

260. Bryson, D., "Using CryptoAPI," May 31, 2002, <www.kerneli.org/howto/node3.php>.

261. Bovet, D., and M. Cesati, *Understanding the Linux Kernel,* O'Reilly, 2001.

262. Rubini, A., and J. Corbet, *Linux Device Drivers,* O'Reilly, 2001.

But, soft! what light through yonder window breaks?
It is the east, and Juliet is the sun!
—William Shakespeare—

An actor entering through the door, you've got nothing. But if he enters through the window, you've got a situation.
—Billy Wilder—

Chapter 21

Case Study: Windows XP

Objectives

After reading this chapter, you should understand:

- *the history of DOS and Windows operating systems.*

- *the Windows XP architecture.*

- *the various Windows XP subsystems.*

- *asynchronous and deferred procedure calls.*

- *how user processes, the executive and the kernel interact.*

- *how Windows XP performs process, thread, memory and file management.*

- *the Windows XP I/O subsystem.*

- *how Windows XP performs interprocess communication.*

- *networking and multiprocessing in Windows XP.*

- *the Windows XP security model.*

Chapter Outline

21.1 Introduction

Windows XP, released by the Microsoft Corporation in 2001, combines Microsoft's corporate and consumer operating system lines. By early 2003, over one-third of all Internet users ran Windows XP, making it the most widely used operating system.[1]

Windows XP ships in five editions. *Windows XP Home Edition* is the desktop edition, and the other editions provide additional features. *Windows XP Professional* includes extra security and privacy features, more data recovery support and broader networking capabilities. *Windows XP Tablet PC Edition* is built for notebooks and laptops that need enhanced support for wireless networking and digital pens. *Windows XP Media Center Edition* provides enhanced multimedia support.[2] *Windows XP 64-Bit Edition* is designed for applications that manipulate large amounts of data, such as programs that perform scientific computing or render 3D graphics. At the time of this writing, Microsoft plans to release a sixth edition, *Windows XP 64-Bit Edition for 64-Bit Extended Systems*, which is designed specifically to support AMD Opteron and Athlon 64 processors.[3] Windows XP 64-Bit Edition currently executes on Intel Itanium II processors.

Despite their differences, all Windows XP editions are built on the same core architecture, and the following case study applies to all editions (except when we explicitly differentiate between editions). This case study investigates how a popular operating system implements the components and strategies we have discussed throughout the book.

21.2 History

In 1975, a Harvard University junior and a young programmer at Honeywell showed up at Micro Instrumentation and Telemetry Systems (MITS) headquarters with a BASIC compiler. The two men had written the compiler in just eight weeks and had never tested it on the computer for which it was intended. It worked on the first run. This auspicious beginning inspired the student, Bill Gates, and the programmer, Paul Allen, to drop everything they were doing and move to Albuquerque, New Mexico, to found Microsoft (see the Biographical Note, Bill Gates).[4,5] By 2003, the two-man company had become a global corporation, employing over 50,000 people and grossing a yearly revenue of over $28 billion.[6] Microsoft is the second most valuable and the sixth most profitable company in the world. *Forbes Magazine* in 2003 listed Bill Gates as the richest man on Earth, worth over $40.7 billion, and Paul Allen as the fourth richest man, worth $20.1 billion.[7]

Microsoft released the Microsoft Disk Operating System—MS-DOS 1.0—in 1981. MS-DOS 1.0 was a 16-bit operating system that supported 1MB of main memory (1MB was enormous by the standards of the time). The system ran one process at a time in response to user input from a command line. All programs executed in **real mode**, which provided them direct access to all of main memory, including the portion storing the operating system.[8] MS-DOS 2.0, released two years later, supported a 10MB hard drive and 360KB floppy disks.[9] Subsequent

Microsoft operating systems continued the trend of increasing disk space and supporting an ever-growing number of peripheral devices.

Microsoft released Windows 1.0, its graphical-user-interface (GUI)-based operating system, in 1985. The GUI foundation had been developed by Xerox in the 1970s and popularized by Apple's Macintosh computers. The Windows GUI

Biographical Note

Bill Gates

William H. Gates III was born in Seattle, Washington, in 1955.[10] His first experience with computers was in high school.[11,12] He befriended Paul Allen, a fellow computer enthusiast, and with two other students formed the Lakeside Programming Group. The group obtained computer time from nearby companies by arranging deals to find bugs in the companies' systems. They also earned money by forming a small and short-lived company named Traf-O-Data, writing software to process traffic flow data.[13, 14]

Gates went on to Harvard University, but in 1974 Intel announced the 8080 chip, and Gates and Paul Allen realized that the future of computing was microprocessing.[15, 16, 17] When the MITS Altair 8800 was announced only months later—the world's first microcomputer—Gates and Allen quickly contacted MITS to say they had a implementation of BASIC (Beginner's All-purpose Symbolic Instruction Code) for the Altair.[18, 19] In fact they had no such thing, but Altair was interested; Gates took a leave of absence from Harvard (he never returned) and he and Allen ported BASIC to the Altair in just over one month, based only on Intel's manual for the 8080.[20, 21, 22] Early personal computers did not have operating systems, so all that was needed was a language interpreter built for the specific system to run programs. Gates' and Allen's implementation of BASIC was, in effect, the first operating system for the Altair. It was also the beginning of Microsoft.[23, 24]

Over the next several years, Microsoft continued to develop their BASIC language and licensed it to other new microcomputer companies including Apple and Commodore.[25] Microsoft also implemented other languages for microcomputers and, because they had a jump-start on other microcomputer software compa-nies, began to take over the field.[26] In 1980, Gates hired his Harvard classmate, Steve Ballmer, to help with the business side of the growing company (Ballmer is the current CEO of Microsoft.)[27, 28] Only two years later, Microsoft developed MS-DOS based on Seattle Computing Product's 86-DOS; it was offered as the cheapest operating system option for IBM's new line of personal computers and was a great success. In 1984 they broke into the office applications market with Word and Excel for the Apple Macintosh. The following year they released Windows 1.0, one of the first GUI operating systems for IBM-compatibles.[29] Microsoft's commercial success has continued to mount with progressive versions of Windows and their Microsoft Office software. Gates is currently the Chairman and Chief Software Architect of Microsoft.[30] He is also the richest person in the world.[31]

improved with each version. The window frames in Windows 1.0 could not overlap; Microsoft fixed this problem in Windows 2.0. The most important feature in Windows 2.0 was its support for **protected mode** for DOS programs. Although protected mode was slower than real mode, it prevented a program from overwriting the memory space of another program, including the operating system, which improved system stability. Even in protected mode, however, programs addressed memory directly. In 1990, Microsoft released Windows 3.0, quickly followed by Windows 3.1. This version of the operating system completely eliminated the unsafe real mode. Windows 3.1 introduced an enhanced mode, which allowed Windows applications to use more memory than DOS programs. Microsoft also released Windows for Workgroups 3.1, an upgrade to Windows 3.1 that included network support, especially for local area networks (LANs), which, at the time, were starting to become popular. Microsoft attempted to increase system stability in Windows by tightening parameter checking during API system calls; these changes broke many older programs that exploited "hidden" features in the API.[32, 33]

Emboldened by the success of its home-user-oriented operating systems, Microsoft ventured into the business market. Microsoft hired Dave Cutler, an experienced operating systems designer who helped develop Digital Equipment Corporation's VMS operating system, to create an operating system specifically for the business environment (see the Biographical Note, David Cutler). Developing the new operating system took five years, but in 1993, Microsoft released Windows NT 3.1, a New Technology operating system. In so doing, Microsoft created its corporate line of operating systems, which was built from a separate code base than its consumer line. The two lines were not to merge until the release of Windows XP in 2001, although operating systems from one line used features and ideas from the other. For example, Windows NT 3.1 and Windows 95 included different implementations of the same API. In addition, the business and consumer GUI interfaces were always similar, although the business version tended to lag behind.[34]

Because Windows NT 3.1 was developed for business users, its chief focus was security and stability. Windows NT introduced the New Technology File System (NTFS), which is more secure and more efficient than the then-popular Windows 3.1 FAT and IBM OS/2 HPFS file systems (see the Mini Case Study, OS/2). In addition, the 32-bit operating system protects its memory from direct access by user applications. The NT kernel runs in its own protected memory space. This extra layer of security came at a price; many existing graphics-intensive games could not run on Windows NT because they need to access memory directly to optimize performance. Windows NT 3.1 also lacks much of the multimedia support that made Windows 3.1 popular with home users.[35]

Microsoft released Windows NT 4.0 in 1996. The upgraded operating system provides additional security and networking support and includes the popular Windows 95 user-interface.[36] Windows 2000 (whose kernel is NT 5.0), released in 2000, introduced the Active Directory. This database of users, computers and devices makes it easy for users to find information about resources spread across a network.

In addition, system administrators can configure user accounts and computer settings remotely. Windows 2000 supports secure Kerberos single sign-on authentication and authorization (see Section 19.3.3, Kerberos). In general, Windows 2000 is more secure and has better networking support than previous Windows operating systems. It is Microsoft's last purely business-oriented desktop operating system.[37]

Microsoft continued developing consumer operating systems. It released Windows 95 in 1995 to replace Windows 3.1 for home users. Like Windows NT 3.1, Windows 95 makes the jump to 32-bit addressing, although it supports 16-bit applications for backward compatibility. Windows 95 permits applications to access

Biographical Note

David Cutler

David Cutler graduated from Olivet College in Michigan in 1965[38] with a degree in Mathematics.[39] He first became interested in computers when he worked on a software simulation project at DuPont.[40, 41] Cutler moved to its engineering department, where he was involved in various programming projects, became interested in operating systems and worked on the development of several small, real-time operating systems.[42]

In 1971 Cutler moved to Digital Equipment Corporation (DEC),[43, 44] where he led the team developing the RSX-11M operating system. This operating system was difficult to design for two reasons—there were severe memory limitations due to the PDP-11's 16-bit addressing, and it had to be compatible with all of the popular PDP-11 models. A few years later,

DEC began work on the VAX 32-bit architecture, because increasing application sizes made the memory space accessible by a 16-bit address insufficient.[45]

Cutler managed what was probably DEC's most important OS project ever—**VMS** for the VAX systems.[46, 47] Because the PDP-11 was so widely used, VMS needed to be backward compatible with the PDP-11 system and it had to be scalable to VAX systems of varying power.[48, 49] Cutler also led the MicroVAX project, DEC's microprocessor version of the VAX.[50]

In 1988, Cutler accepted an offer from Bill Gates to be one of the leaders on Microsoft's successor to OS/2—OS/2 New Technology, or OS/2 NT, which would use the OS/2 API.[51, 52] Cutler insisted on bringing 20 of his developers from DEC to form the core of this

new team. Meanwhile, Microsoft released Windows 3.0, and its popularity led to a change in plans for Cutler's project. His operating system would now be Windows NT and would primarily support the Win32 interface. However, it needed to support parts of the DOS, POSIX and OS/2 APIs in addition to running Windows 3.0 programs.[53] Inspired by the Mach microkernel operating system, Cutler's team designed Windows NT to have a fairly small kernel with layers of separate modules to handle the various interfaces. Windows NT, originally intended for Microsoft's professional line of operating systems, eventually was used for the consumer line in version 5.1, more popularly known as Windows XP. Cutler remains a lead operating systems architect at Microsoft.

main memory directly. However, Microsoft introduced DirectX, which simulates direct hardware access while providing a layer of protection. Microsoft hoped that DirectX, combined with faster hardware, would give game developers a viable alternative to accessing the hardware directly. Windows 95 introduced multithreading, an improvement on the multitasking support provided by Windows 3.1. Microsoft released Windows 98 in 1998, although most of the changes were minor (primarily increased multimedia and networking support). The biggest innovation was combining Internet Explorer (IE) with the operating system. Bundling IE made Windows easier to use when accessing the Internet and the Web. Windows Millennium Edition (Windows Me), released in 2000, is the last version in the consumer line. Windows Me has even more device drivers and multimedia and networking support than previous versions of Windows. It is also the first consumer version of Windows that cannot boot in DOS mode.[54]

Mini Case Study

OS/2

OS/2 was first released in 1987. The operating system was a joint project between Microsoft and IBM designed to run on IBM's new PS/2 line of personal computers.[55] OS/2 was based on DOS, the most popular operating system at the time of OS/2's release, and was similar to DOS in many ways (e.g., they had similar commands and command prompts). OS/2 also made significant improvements over DOS. OS/2 was the first PC operating system to allow multitasking (however, only one application could be on the screen at a time). OS/2 also supported multithreading, interprocess communication (IPC), dynamic linking and many other features that were not supported by DOS.[56]

OS/2 1.1, released in 1988, was its first version with a graphical user interface. The interface was similar to early versions of Windows. However, unlike Windows and many of today's interfaces, the coordinate (0,0) referred to the lower-left corner of the screen as opposed to the upper-left corner.[57] This made transferring programs from OS/2 to other operating systems difficult.

OS/2 version 2.0, released in 1992, was the first 32-bit operating system for personal computers. OS/2 2 contained the Integrating Platform, designed to run OS/2 2, OS/2 1, DOS and Windows applications. This benefitted OS/2, because there were few applications writ-ten for OS/2 2 at the time. As a result, many developers wrote programs specifically for Windows, since they would work on both platforms.[58]

IBM and Microsoft disagreed on the progress and direction of OS/2 because Microsoft wanted to devote more resources to Windows than to OS/2, whereas IBM wished to further develop OS/2 1. In 1990, IBM and Microsoft agreed to work independently on upcoming OS/2 projects: IBM took control of all future versions of OS/2 1 and OS/2 2, while Microsoft developed OS/2 3. Soon after this agreement, Microsoft renamed OS/2 3 to Windows NT.[59]

Microsoft released Windows XP in 2001 (whose kernel is NT 5.1). Windows XP unified the consumer and commercial code bases. Windows XP comes in several editions, each of which is built from the same code base but is tailored to fit the needs of a specific group of users. Every edition of Windows XP combines the stability, security and network support of the corporate line with the multimedia and device support of the consumer line.

21.3 Design Goals

Microsoft's main design goal for Windows XP was reintegrating the code bases from its consumer and business operating system lines. In addition, Microsoft attempted to better meet the traditional goals of each individual line. For example, the corporate line has often focused on providing security and stability, whereas the consumer line provides enhanced multimedia support for games.

When Microsoft created the NT line for business users, its chief focuses were stability, security and scalability.[60] Businesses often employ computers to execute critical applications and store essential information. It is important for the system to be reliable and run continuously without error. The internal architecture described in this case study was developed over many years to enhance the stability of Microsoft operating systems.

Corporate computers need to protect sensitive data while being connected to multiple networks and the Internet. For this reason, Microsoft devoted a great deal of effort to developing an all-encompassing security system. Windows XP uses modern security technologies such as Kerberos, access control lists and packet filtering firewalls to protect the system. The Windows XP security system is built on the codebase of Windows 2000, to which the government gave C2 level certification (the C2 certification applies only to Windows 2000 machines unconnected to a network).[61] At the time of this writing, Microsoft is in the process of gaining the same certification for Windows XP Professional.

Computers must be scalable to meet the needs of different users. Microsoft developed Windows XP 64-Bit Edition to support high-performance desktop computers and Windows XP Embedded to support devices such as routers. Windows XP Professional supports symmetric multiprocessing (see Chapter 15, Multiprocessor Management).

Windows XP incorporates many of the features that made the consumer line popular. The system contains an improved GUI and more multimedia support than previous versions of Windows. For the first time, both business and home users can take advantage of these innovations.

Besides incorporating the strengths of its two lines of operating systems, Microsoft added another goal specifically for Windows XP. Customers had often complained that Windows started too slowly. As a result, Microsoft aimed at dramatically decreasing boot time. Windows XP must be usable in 30 seconds after a user turns on the power, 20 seconds after waking from hibernation (on a laptop) and 5 seconds after resuming from standby. Later in the chapter, we describe how Windows XP meets these goals by prefetching files necessary to load the operating system.[62]

21.4 System Architecture

Windows XP is modeled on a microkernel architecture—often called a modified microkernel architecture. On the one hand, Windows XP is a modular operating system with a compact kernel that provides base services for other operating system components. However, unlike a pure microkernel operating system, these components (e.g., the file system and memory manager) execute in kernel mode rather than user mode. Windows XP is also a layered operating system, composed of discrete layers with lower layers providing functionality for higher layers.[63] However, unlike a pure layered operating system, there are times when non-adjacent layers communicate. For a description of microkernel and layered operating system designs, see Section 1.13, Operating System Architectures.

Figure 21.1 illustrates Windows XP's system architecture. The **Hardware Abstraction Layer (HAL)** interacts directly with the hardware, abstracting hardware specifics to the rest of the system. The HAL handles device components on the mainboard such as the cache and system timers. The HAL abstracts hardware specifics that might differ between systems of the same architecture, such as the exact layout of the mainboard. In many cases, kernel-mode components do not access the hardware directly, but instead call functions exposed by the HAL. Therefore, kernel-mode components can be constructed with little regard for architecture-specific details such as cache sizes and the number of processors included. The HAL interacts with device drivers to support access to peripheral devices.[64]

The HAL also interacts with the microkernel. The microkernel provides basic system mechanisms, such as thread scheduling, to support other kernel-mode components. [*Note*: The Windows XP microkernel should not be confused with the microkernel design philosophy discussed in Section 1.13, Operating System Architectures.] The microkernel also handles thread synchronization, dispatches interrupts and handles exceptions.[65] Additionally, the microkernel abstracts architecture-specific features—features that differ between two different architectures, such as the number of interrupts. The microkernel and the HAL combine to make Windows XP portable, allowing it to run in many different hardware environments.[66]

The microkernel forms only a small part of kernel space. Kernel space describes an execution environment in which components can access all system memory and services. Components that reside in kernel space execute in kernel mode. The microkernel provides the base services for the other components residing in kernel space.[67]

Layered on top of the microkernel are the kernel-mode components responsible for administering the operating system subsystems (e.g., the I/O manager and virtual memory manager). Collectively, these components are known as the **executive**. Figure 21.1 displays the key executive components. The rest of this chapter is devoted to describing these subsystems and the executive components which man-

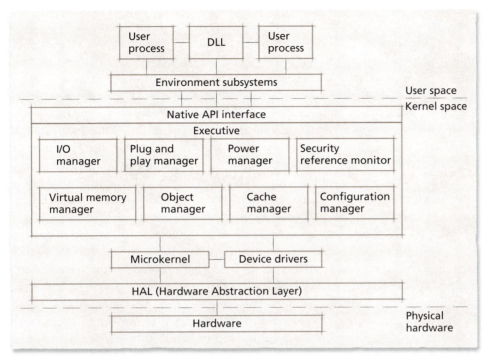

Figure 21.1 | *Windows XP system architecture.*

age the subsystems. The executive exposes services through an application programming interface (API) to user processes.[68] This API is called the **native API**.

However, most user processes do not call native API functions directly; rather, they call API functions exposed by user-mode system components called **environment subsystems**. Environment subsystems are user-mode processes interposed between the executive and the rest of user space that export an API for a specific computing environment. For example, the **Win32 environment subsystem** provides a typical 32-bit Windows environment. Win32 processes call functions defined in the Windows API; the Win32 subsystem translates these function calls to system calls in the native API (although, in some cases, the Win32 subsystem process itself can fulfill an API request without calling the native API).[69] Although Windows XP allows user-mode processes to call native API functions, Microsoft urges developers to use an environment subsystem's interface.[70]

By default, 32-bit Windows XP includes only the Win32 subsystem, but users can install a POSIX subsystem. Microsoft replaced the POSIX subsystem in older versions of Windows with a more robust UNIX environment, called Service For UNIX (SFU) 3.0. Running SFU 3.0, users can port code written for a UNIX environment to Windows XP. To run 16-bit DOS applications, Windows XP provides a Virtual DOS Machine (VDM), which is a Win32 process that provides a DOS environment for DOS applications.[71]

On Windows XP 64-Bit Edition, the default subsystem supports 64-bit applications. However, Windows XP 64-Bit Edition provides a subsystem called the Windows on Windows 64 (WOW64) subsystem, which allows users to execute 32-bit Windows applications. Windows XP 64-Bit Edition does not support 16-bit applications.[72]

The top layer of the Windows XP architecture consists of user-mode processes. These are typical applications (e.g., word processors, computer games and Web browsers) as well as **dynamic link libraries (DLLs)**. DLLs are modules that provide data and functions to processes. As shown in Fig. 21.1, the environment subsystems' APIs are simply DLLs that processes dynamically link when calling a function in a subsystem's API. Because DLLs are dynamically linked, applications can be more modular. If the implementation of a DLL function changes, only the DLL must be recompiled and not the applications that use it.[73]

Windows XP also includes special user-mode processes called **system services** (or **Win32 services**), which are similar to Linux daemons (see Section 20.3, Linux Overview). These processes usually execute in the background whether or not a user is logged onto the computer and typically execute the server side of client/server applications.[74] Examples of system services are the Task Scheduler (which allows users to schedule tasks to be executed at specific times), IPSec (which manages Internet security usually during data transfer operations) and Computer Browser (which maintains a list of computers connected on the local network).[75] [*Note*: Sometimes, authors also use the term "system services" to refer to native API functions.]

21.5 System Management Mechanisms

Before we investigate each component in the Windows XP operating system, it is important to understand the environment in which these components execute. This section describes how components and user processes store and access configuration data in the system. We also consider how Windows XP implements objects, how these objects are managed and how user- and kernel-mode threads can manipulate these objects. Finally, we describe how Windows XP prioritizes interrupts and how the system employs software interrupts to dispatch processing.

21.5.1 Registry

The **registry** is a database, accessible to all processes and kernel-mode components, that stores configuration information[76] specific to users, applications and hardware. For example, user information might include desktop settings and printer settings. Application configuration includes such settings as recently used menus, user preferences and application defaults. Hardware information includes which devices are currently connected to the computer, which drivers serve each device and which resources (e.g., hardware ports) are assigned to each device. The registry also stores system information such as file associations (e.g., .doc files are associated with

Microsoft Word). Applications, device drivers and the Windows XP system use the registry to store and access data in a centralized manner. For example, when a user installs a hardware device, device drivers place configuration information into the registry. When Windows XP allocates resources to various devices, it accesses the registry to determine what devices are installed in the system and distributes resources accordingly.[77]

Windows XP organizes the registry as a tree, and each node in the tree represents a registry key. A key stores subkeys and values; values consist of a value name and value data.[78] The system provides several predefined keys. For example, HKEY_LOCAL_MACHINE is a predefined key which forms the root of all configuration data for the local computer. Values in the HKEY_LOCAL_MACHINE key or its subkeys store such information as the hardware devices connected to the computer, system memory and network information (e.g., server names). Predefined keys act as roots for a single type of data, such as application-specific data or user preferences.[79]

Threads can access subkeys by navigating the tree structure. Beginning with any key that is open, a thread can enumerate that key's subkeys and open any of them. The system's predefined keys remain open at all times. Once a key is open, values and subkeys can be read, modified, added or deleted (assuming the thread has access rights for the key to accomplish all these actions).[80, 81]

Windows XP stores the registry in a collection of hives, which are portions of the registry tree. Most hives are stored as files and flushed to disk periodically to protect the data against crashes, whereas other hives remain solely in memory (e.g., HKEY_LOCAL_MACHINE\HARDWARE, which stores hardware information that the system collects at boot time and updates as it runs).[82] The **configuration manager** is the executive component responsible for managing the registry. Device drivers, system components and user applications communicate with the configuration manager to modify or obtain data from the registry. The configuration manager is also responsible for managing registry storage in system memory and in the hives.[83]

21.5.2 Object Manager

Windows XP represents physical resources (e.g., peripheral devices) and logical resources (e.g., processes and threads) with objects. Note that these objects do not refer to objects in any object-oriented programming language, but rather constructs that Windows XP uses to represent resources. Windows XP represents objects with a data structure in memory; this data structure stores the object's attributes and procedures.[84] Each object in Windows XP is defined by an object type; the object type is also stored as a data structure. Object types are created by executive components; for example, the I/O manager creates the file object type. The object type specifies the types of attributes an instance of this type possesses and the object's standard procedures. Examples of standard procedures include the open procedure, close procedure and delete procedure.[85] Object types in Windows XP include files, devices, processes, threads, pipes, semaphores and many others. Each Windows XP object is an instance of an object type.[86]

User-mode processes and kernel components can access objects through **object handles**. An object handle is a data structure that allows processes to manipulate the object. Using an object handle, a thread can call one of the object's procedures or manipulate the object's attributes. A kernel-mode component or user-mode process with sufficient access rights can obtain a handle to an object by specifying the object's name in a call to the object's open method or by receiving a handle from another process.[87] Once a process obtains a handle to an object, this process can duplicate the handle; this can be used by a process that wishes to pass a handle to another process and also retain a handle to the object.[88] Processes can use a handle in similar way as pointers, but a handle gives the system extra control over the actions of a user process (e.g., by restricting what the process can do with the handle, such as not allowing the process to duplicate it).

Kernel-mode components can use handles when interacting with user-mode processes, but otherwise can access objects directly through pointers. In addition, kernel-mode components can create **kernel handles**, which are handles accessible from any process's address space, but only from kernel mode. In this way, a device driver can create a kernel handle to an object and be guaranteed access to that object, regardless of the context in which the driver executes.[89] Objects can be named or unnamed, although only kernel-mode components can open a handle to an unnamed object. A user-mode thread can obtain a handle to an unnamed object only by receiving it from a kernel-mode component. [90]

The **object manager** is the executive component that manages objects for a Windows XP system. The object manager is responsible for creating and deleting objects and maintaining information about each object type, such as how many objects of a certain type exist.[91] The object manager organizes all named objects into a hierarchal directory structure. For example, all device objects are stored in the \Device directory or one of its subdirectories. This directory structure composes the **object manager namespace** (i.e., group of object names in which each name is unique in the group).[92]

To create an object, a process passes a request to the object manager; the object manager initializes the object and returns a handle (or pointer if a kernel-mode component called the appropriate function) to it. If the object is named, the object manager enters it into the object manager namespace.[93] For each object, the object manager maintains a count of how many existing handles refer to it and a count of how many existing references (both handles and pointers) refer to it. When the number of handles reaches zero, the object manager removes the object from the object manager namespace. When the number of references to the object reaches zero, the object manager deletes the object.[94]

21.5.3 Interrupt Request Levels (IRQLs)

Interrupt definition and handling are crucial to Windows XP. Because some interrupts, such as hardware failure interrupts, are more important than others, Windows XP defines **interrupt request levels (IRQLs)**. IRQLs are a measure of interrupt priority; a processor always executes at some IRQL, and different processors in a multiprocessor system can be executing at different IRQLs. An interrupt that executes at an IRQL higher than the current one can interrupt the current execution and obtain the processor. The system masks (i.e., delays processing) interrupts that execute at an IRQL equal to or lower than the current one.[95]

Windows XP defines several IRQLs (Fig. 21.2). User- and kernel-mode threads normally execute at the **passive IRQL**, which is the lowest-priority IRQL. Unless user-mode threads are executing asynchronous procedure calls (APCs), which we describe in Section 21.5.4, Asynchronous Procedure Calls (APCs), these threads always execute at the passive IRQL. In some instances, kernel-mode threads execute at a higher IRQL to mask certain interrupts, but typically, the system executes threads at the passive level so that incoming interrupts can be serviced promptly. Executing at the passive IRQL implies that no interrupt is currently being processed and no interrupts are masked. APCs, which are procedure calls that threads or the system can queue for execution by a specific thread, execute at the **APC IRQL**. Above the APC level is the **DPC/dispatch IRQL** at which deferred procedure calls (i.e., software interrupts that can be executed in any thread's context) and various other important kernel functions execute, including thread scheduling.[96] We describe DPCs in Section 21.5.5, Deferred Procedure Calls (DPCs). All software interrupts execute at the APC level or DPC/dispatch level.[97]

Hardware interrupts execute at the remaining higher IRQLs. Windows XP provides multiple **device IRQLs (DIRQLs)** at which interrupts from devices execute.[98] The number of DIRQLs varies, depending on how many interrupts a given architecture supports, but the assignment of these levels to devices is arbitrary; it is dependent on the specific interrupt request line at which a device interrupts. Therefore, Windows XP maps device interrupts to DIRQLs without priority; still, if a processor is executing at a certain DIRQL, interrupts that occur at DIRQLs less than or equal to the current one are masked.[99]

The system reserves the highest five IRQLs for critical system interrupts. The first level above DIRQL is the **profile IRQL**, which is used when kernel profiling is enabled (see Section 14.5.1, Tracing and Profiling). The system clock, which issues interrupts at periodic intervals, interrupts at the **clock IRQL**. Interprocessor requests (i.e., interrupts sent by one processor to another such as when shutting down the system) execute at the **request IRQL**. The **power IRQL** is reserved for power failure notification interrupts, although this level has never been used in any NT-based operating system. Interrupts issued at the **high IRQL** (which is the highest IRQL) include hardware failure interrupts and bus errors.[100]

For each processor, the HAL masks all interrupts with IRQLs less than or equal to the IRQL at which that processor is currently executing. This allows the system to prioritize interrupts and execute critical interrupts as quickly as possible. For example, executing at the DPC/dispatch level masks all other DPC/dispatch level interrupts and APC level interrupts. Interrupts that execute at an IRQL that is currently masked are not discarded (i.e., removed from the system). When the

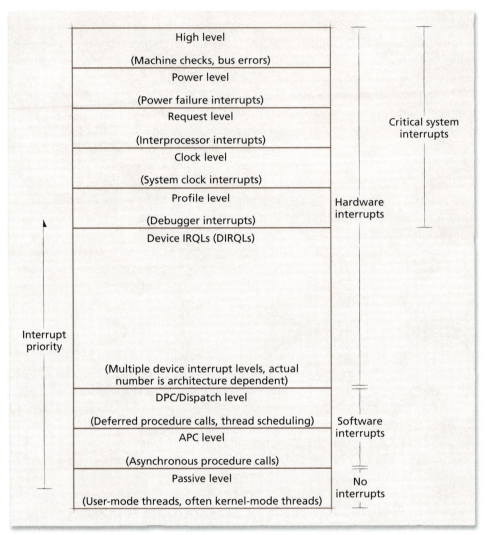

Figure 21.2 | *Interrupt request levels (IRQLs)*

IRQL drops low enough, the processor processes the waiting interrupts. Kernel-mode threads can raise the IRQL, and a thread that does so is responsible for subsequently lowering the IRQL to its previous level; user-mode threads cannot change the IRQL. Windows XP attempts to do as much processing as possible at the passive level, at which no interrupts are masked, so that all incoming interrupts can be serviced immediately.[101]

21.5.4 Asynchronous Procedure Calls (APCs)

Asynchronous procedure calls (APCs) are procedure calls that threads or the system can queue for execution by a specific thread; the system uses APCs to complete various functions that must be done in a specific thread's context. For example, APCs facilitate asynchronous I/O. After initiating an I/O request, a thread can perform other work. When the I/O request completes, the system sends an APC to that thread, which the thread executes to complete the I/O processing. Windows XP uses APCs to accomplish a variety of system operations. For example, APCs are used by the SFU to send signals to POSIX threads and by the executive to notify a thread of an I/O completion or direct a thread to perform an operation.[102]

Each thread maintains two APC queues: one for **kernel-mode APCs** and one for **user-mode APCs**.[103] Kernel-mode APCs are software interrupts that are generated by kernel-mode components, and a thread must process all pending kernel-mode APCs as soon as it obtains a processor. A user-mode thread can create a user-mode APC and request to queue this APC to another thread; the system queues the APC to the target thread if the queuing thread has sufficient access rights. A thread executes user-mode APCs when the thread enters an **alertable** *wait* **state**.[104] In an alertable *wait* state, a thread awakens either when it has a pending APC or when the object or objects on which the thread is waiting become available. A thread can specify that it enters an alertable *wait* state when it waits on an object, or a thread can simply enter an alertable *wait* state without waiting on any object.[105]

Windows XP also differentiates between normal kernel APCs and special kernel APCs. A thread executes kernel APCs in FIFO order, except that the thread executes all special kernel APCs before all normal kernel APCs.[106] When the system queues a kernel APC, the target thread does not execute the APC until the thread gains the processor. However, once the thread begins executing at the passive level, it begins executing kernel APCs until it drains (i.e., empties) its queue.

Unlike kernel APCs, threads can choose when to execute user-mode APCs. A thread drains its user-mode APC queue when the thread enters an alertable *wait* state. If the thread never enters such a state, its pending user-mode APCs are discarded when it terminates.[107]

A thread executing an APC is not restricted, except that it cannot receive new APCs. It can be preempted by another higher-priority thread. Because scheduling is not masked at the APC level (this occurs at the DPC/dispatch level), a thread executing an APC can block or access pageable data (which might cause a page fault and hence cause Windows XP to execute scheduling code at the DPC/dispatch IRQL). APCs can also cause the currently executing thread to be preempted. If a thread queues an APC to a thread of higher priority that is in an alertable *wait* state, the waiting thread awakens, preempts the queuing thread and executes the APC.[108]

21.5.5 Deferred Procedure Calls (DPCs)

Most of Windows XP's hardware interrupt processing occurs in **deferred procedure calls (DPCs)**. DPCs are software interrupts that execute at the DPC/dispatch IRQL[109] and which run in the context of the currently executing thread. In other words, the routine that creates the DPC does not know the context in which the DPC will execute. Therefore, DPCs are meant for system processing, such as interrupt processing, that does not need a specific thread context in which to execute.[110] These procedure calls are called "deferred" because Windows XP processes most hardware interrupts by calling the associated interrupt service routine, which is responsible for quickly acknowledging the interrupt and queuing a DPC for later execution. This strategy increases the system's responsiveness to incoming device interrupts.

Windows XP attempts to minimize the time it spends at DIRQLs to maintain high responsiveness to all device interrupts. Recall that the system maps device interrupts arbitrarily to DIRQLs. Still, device interrupts mapped to a high DIRQL can interrupt the processing of a device interrupt mapped to a lower DIRQL. By using DPCs, the system returns to an IRQL below all DIRQLs and therefore can minimize this difference in the level of interrupt servicing.[111]

Device interrupt handlers can schedule DPCs, and Windows XP executes some kernel functions, such as thread scheduling, at the DPC/dispatch IRQL.[112] When an event that prompts scheduling occurs—such as when a thread enters the *ready* state, when a thread enters the *wait* state, when a thread's quantum expires or when a thread's priority changes—the system executes scheduling code at the DPC/dispatch IRQL.[113]

As we noted above, DPCs are restricted because the routine that creates a DPC does not specify the context in which the DPC executes (this context is simply the currently executing thread). DPCs are further restricted because they mask thread scheduling. Therefore, a DPC cannot cause the thread within whose context it is executing to block, because this would cause the system to attempt to execute scheduling code. In this case no thread would execute because the executing thread blocks, but the scheduler does not schedule a new thread because scheduling is masked (in reality, Windows XP halts the system and displays an error message).[114] As a result, DPCs cannot access pageable data because if a page fault occurs, the executing thread blocks to wait for the completion of the data access. DPCs, however, can be preempted by hardware interrupts.[115, 116]

When a device driver generates a DPC, the system places the DPC in a queue associated with a specific processor. The driver routine can request a processor to which the DPC should be queued (e.g., to ensure that the DPC routine is executed on the processor with relevant cached data); if no processor is specified, the processor queues the DPC to itself.[117] The routine can also specify the DPC's priority. Low- and medium-priority DPCs are placed at the end of the processor's DPC queue; high-priority DPCs enter at the front of the queue. In most cases, when the IRQL drops to the DPC/dispatch level, the processor drains the DPC queue. However, when a low-priority DPC has been waiting for only a short time and the DPC queue is short, the processor does not immediately execute the DPC. The next time the processor drains the DPC queue, it processes this DPC. This policy allows the system to return to the passive level faster to unmask all interrupts and resume normal thread processing.[118]

21.5.6 System Threads

When a kernel-mode component, such as a device driver or executive component, performs some processing on behalf of a user thread, the component's functions often execute in the context of the requesting thread. However, in some cases, kernel-mode components must accomplish a task that is not in response to a particular thread request. For example, the cache manager must periodically flush dirty cache pages to disk. Also, a device driver servicing an interrupt might not be able to accomplish all necessary processing at an elevated IRQL (i.e., the device's DIRQL when it interrupts or the DPC/dispatch level when executing a DPC). For example, the driver might need to accomplish some work at the passive IRQL, because it must access pageable data.[119]

Developers of kernel-mode components have two options to perform this processing. A component can create a kernel thread, which is a thread that executes in kernel mode and typically belongs to the System process—a kernel-mode process to which most kernel-mode threads belong. Aside from executing in kernel mode, kernel threads behave and are scheduled the same as user threads.[120] Kernel threads normally execute at the passive IRQL, but can raise and lower the IRQL.[121]

A second option is to use a **system worker thread**—a thread, which is created at system initialization time or dynamically in response to a high volume of requests, that sleeps until a work item is received. A work item consists of a function to execute and a parameter describing the context in which to execute that function. System worker threads also belong to the System process. Windows XP includes three types of worker threads: delayed, critical and hypercritical. The distinction arises from the scheduling priority given to each type. Delayed threads have the lowest priority of the three types; critical threads have a relatively high priority; and the hypercritical thread (there is only one), which is reserved for system use (e.g., device drivers cannot queue work items to this thread), has the highest priority of the three types.[122, 123]

21.6 Process and Thread Management

In Windows XP, a process consists of program code, an execution context, resources (e.g., object handles) and one or more associated threads. The execution context includes such items as the process's virtual address space and various attributes (e.g., security attributes and working set size limitations). Threads are the actual unit of execution; threads execute a piece of a process's code in the process's context, using the process's resources. A thread also contains its own execution context which includes its runtime stack, the state of the machine registers and several attributes (e.g., scheduling priority).[124] Both processes and threads are objects, so other processes can obtain handles for processes and threads, and other threads can wait on process and thread events just as with other object types.[125, 126]

21.6.1 Process and Thread Organization

Windows XP stores process and thread context information in several data structures. An **executive process block (EPROCESS block)** is the main data structure that describes a process. The EPROCESS block stores information that executive components use when manipulating a process object; this information includes the process's ID, a pointer to the process's handle table, a pointer to the process's access token and working set information (e.g., the process's minimum and maximum working set size, page fault history and the current working set). The system stores EPROCESS blocks in a linked list.[127, 128]

Each EPROCESS block also contains a **kernel process block (KPROCESS block)**. A KPROCESS block stores process information used by the microkernel. Recall that the microkernel manages thread scheduling and thread synchronization. Therefore, the KPROCESS block stores such information as the process's base priority class, the default quantum for each of its threads and its spin lock.[129, 130]

The EPROCESS and KPROCESS blocks exist in kernel space and store information for kernel-mode components to access while manipulating a process. The system also stores process information in a **process environment block (PEB)**, which is stored in the process's address space. A process's EPROCESS block points to the process's PEB. The PEB stores information useful for user processes, such as a list of DLLs linked to the process and information about the process's heap.[131, 132]

Windows XP stores thread data in a similar manner. An **executive thread block (ETHREAD block)** is the main data structure describing a thread. It stores information that executive components use when manipulating a thread object. This information includes the ID of the thread's process, its start address, its access token and a list of its pending I/O requests. The ETHREAD block for a thread also points to the EPROCESS block of its process.[133, 134]

Each ETHREAD block stores a **kernel thread block (KTHREAD block)**. The microkernel uses information in the KTHREAD block for thread scheduling and synchronization. For example, the KTHREAD block stores information such as the thread's base and current priority (later in this section we see how a thread's priority can change), its current state (e.g., *ready*, *waiting*) and any synchronization objects for which it is waiting.[135, 136]

The ETHREAD and KTHREAD blocks exist in kernel space and therefore are not accessible to users. A **thread environment block (TEB)** stores information about a thread in the thread's process's address space. Each KTHREAD block points to a TEB. A thread's TEB stores information such as the critical sections owned by the thread, its ID and information about its stack. A TEB also points to the PEB of the thread's process.[137, 138]

All threads belonging to the same process share a virtual address space. Although most of this memory is global, threads can maintain their own data in **thread local storage (TLS)**. A thread within a process can allocate a TLS index for the process; the thread stores a pointer to local data in a specified location (called a **TLS slot**) in this index. Each thread using the index receives one TLS slot in the index in which it can store a data item. A common use for a TLS index is to store data associated with a DLL that a process links. Processes often contain many TLS indexes to accommodate multiple purposes, such as for DLL and environment subsystem data. When threads no longer need a TLS index (e.g., the DLL completes execution), the process can discard the index.[139] A thread also possesses its own runtime stack on which it can also store local data.

Creating and Terminating Processes

A process can create another process using API functions. For Windows processes, the parent (i.e., creating) process and child (i.e., created) process are completely independent. For example, the child process receives a completely new address space.[140] This differs from the `fork` command in Linux, in which the child receives a copy of its parent's address space. The parent process can specify certain attributes that the child process **inherits** (i.e., the child acquires a duplicate from the parent), such as most types of handles, environment variables—i.e., variables that define an aspect of the current settings, such as the operating system version number—and the current directory.[141] When the system initializes a process, the process creates a **primary thread**. The primary thread acts as any other thread, and any thread can create other threads belonging to that thread's process.[142]

A process can terminate execution for a variety of reasons. If all of its threads terminate, a process terminates, and any of a process's threads can explicitly terminate the process at any time. Additionally, when a user logs off, all the processes running in the user's context are terminated. Because parent and child processes are independent of one another, terminating a parent process has no affect on its children and vice versa.[143]

Jobs

Sometimes, it is preferable to group several processes together into a unit, called a job. A **job object** allows developers to define rules and set limits on a number of processes. For example, a single application might consist of a group of processes. A developer might want to restrict the number of processor cycles and amount of memory that the application consumes (e.g., so that an application executing on behalf of a client does not monopolize all of a server's resources). Also, the developer might want to terminate all the processes of a group at once, which is difficult because all processes are normally independent of one another.[144] A process can be a member of at most one job object. The job object specifies such attributes as a base priority class, a security context, a working set minimum and maximum size, a virtual memory size limit and both a per-process and jobwide processor time limit. Just as a thread inherits these attributes from the process to which it belongs, a process inherits these attributes from its associated job (if the process belongs to a job).[145, 146] The system can terminate all processes in a job by terminating the job.[147]

Systems executing batch processes, such as data mining, benefit from jobs. Developers can limit the amount of processor time and memory a computationally intensive job consumes to free more resources for interactive processes. Sometimes it is useful to create a job for a single process, because a job allows the developer to specify tighter restrictions than a process allows. For example, with a job object, a developer can limit the process's total processor time; a developer cannot use the process object to do this.[148]

Fibers

Threads can create **fibers**, which are similar to threads, except that a fiber is scheduled for execution by the thread that creates it, rather than the microkernel. Windows XP includes fibers to permit the porting of code written for other operating systems to Windows XP. Some operating systems, such as many UNIX varieties, schedule processes and require them to schedule their own threads. Developers can use fibers to port code to and from these operating systems. A fiber executes in the context of the thread that creates the fiber.[149]

Creating fibers generates additional units of execution within a single thread. Each fiber must maintain state information, such as the next instruction to execute and the values in a processor's registers. The thread stores this state information for each fiber. The thread itself is also a unit of execution, and thus must convert itself into a fiber to separate its own state information from other fibers executing in its context. In fact, the Windows API forces a thread to convert itself into a fiber before creating or scheduling other fibers. Although the thread becomes a fiber, the thread's context remains, and all fibers associated with that thread execute in that context.[150]

Whenever the kernel schedules a thread that has been converted to a fiber for execution, the converted fiber or another fiber belonging to that thread runs. Once a fiber obtains the processor, it executes until the thread in whose context the fiber executes is preempted, or the fiber switches execution to another fiber (either within the same thread or a fiber created by a separate thread). Just as threads possess their own thread local storage (TLS), fibers possess their own **fiber local storage (FLS)**, which functions for fibers exactly as TLS functions for a thread. A fiber can also access its thread's TLS. If a fiber deletes itself (i.e., terminates), its thread terminates.[151]

Fibers permit Windows XP applications to write code executed using the many-to-many mapping; typical Windows XP threads are implemented with a one-to-one mapping (see Section 4.6.2, Kernel-Level Threads). Fibers are user-level units of execution and invisible to the kernel. This makes context switching between fibers of the same thread fast because it is done in user mode. Therefore, a single-threaded process with many fibers can simulate a multithreaded process. However, the Windows XP microkernel only recognizes one thread, and because Windows XP schedules threads, not processes, the single-threaded process receives less execution time (all else being equal).[152,153]

Thread Pools

Windows XP also provides each process with a **thread pool** that consists of a number of **worker threads**, which execute functions queued by user threads. The worker threads sleep until a request is queued to the pool.[154] The thread that queues the request must specify the function to execute and must provide context information.[155] When a process is created, it receives an empty thread pool; the system allocates space for worker threads when the process queues its first request.[156]

Thread pools have many purposes. Developers can use them to handle client requests. Instead of incurring the costly overhead of creating and destroying a thread for each request, the developer simply queues the request to the thread pool. Also, several threads that spend most of their time sleeping (e.g., waiting for events to occur) can be replaced by a single worker thread that awakens each time one of these events occurs. Furthermore, applications can use the thread pool to accomplish asynchronous I/O by queuing a worker thread to execute the I/O completion routines. Using thread pools can make an application more efficient and simpler because developers do not have to create and delete as many threads. However, thread pools transfer some control from the programmer to the system, which can introduce inefficiency. For example, the system grows and shrinks the size of a process's thread pool in response to request volume; in some cases, the programmer can better guess how many threads are needed. Thread pools also require memory overhead, because the system grows a process's (initially empty) thread pool as the process's threads queue work items.[157]

21.6.2 Thread Scheduling

Windows XP does not contain a specific "thread scheduler" module—the scheduling code is dispersed throughout the microkernel. The scheduling code collectively is referred to as the **dispatcher**.[158] Windows XP supports preemptive scheduling among multiple threads. The dispatcher schedules each thread without regard to the process to which the thread belongs. This means that, all else being equal, the same process implemented with more threads will get more execution time.[159] The scheduling algorithm used by Windows XP is based on a thread's priority. Before describing the scheduling algorithm in detail, we investigate the lifecycle of a Windows XP thread.

Thread States

In Windows XP, threads can be in any one of eight states (Fig. 21.3). A thread begins in the *initialized* **state** during thread creation. Once initialization concludes, the thread enters the *ready* **state**. Threads in the ready state are waiting to use a processor. A thread that the dispatcher has decided will execute on a particular processor next enters the *standby* **state** as it awaits its turn for that processor. A thread is in the standby state, for example, during the context switch from the previously executing thread to that thread. Once the thread obtains a processor, it enters the *running* **state**. A thread transitions out of the *running* state if it terminates execution, exhausts its quantum, is preempted, is suspended or waits on an object. If a thread terminates, it enters the *terminated* **state**. The system does not necessarily delete a *terminated* thread; the object manager deletes a thread only when the thread object's

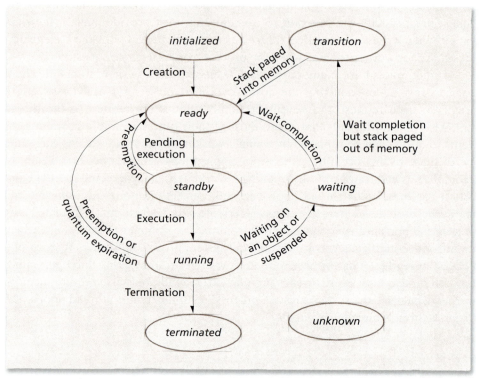

Figure 21.3 | *Thread state-transition diagram.*

reference count becomes zero. If a *running* thread is preempted or exhausts its quantum, it returns to the *ready* state. If a *running* thread begins to wait on an object handle, it enters the ***waiting* state**. Also, another thread (with sufficient access rights) or the system can suspend a thread, forcing it into the *waiting* state until the thread is resumed. When the thread completes its wait, it either returns to the *ready* state or enters the ***transition* state**. A thread in the *transition* state has had its kernel stack paged out of memory (e.g., because it has not executed in a while and the system needed the memory for other purposes), but the thread is otherwise ready to execute. The thread enters the *ready* state once the system pages the thread's kernel stack back into memory. The system places a thread in the ***unknown* state** when the system is unsure of the thread's state (usually because of an error).[160, 161]

Thread Scheduling Algorithm

The dispatcher schedules threads based on priority—the next subsection describes how thread priorities are determined. When a thread enters the *ready* state, the kernel places it into the ready queue that corresponds to its priority. Windows XP has 32 priority levels, denoted by integers from 0 through 31, where 31 is the highest priority and 0 is the lowest. The dispatcher begins with the highest-priority ready queue and schedules the threads in this queue in a round-robin fashion. A thread remains in a ready queue as long as the thread is in either the *ready* state or the *running* state. Once the queue empties, the dispatcher proceeds to the next queue; it continues in this manner until either all queues are empty or a thread with a higher priority than the currently executing thread enters its *ready* state. In the latter case, the dispatcher preempts execution of the lower-priority thread and executes the new thread.[162] The dispatcher then executes the first thread in the highest-priority nonempty ready queue and resumes its normal scheduling procedure.[163]

Each thread executes for at most one quantum. In the case of preemption, real-time threads have their quantum reset, whereas all other threads finish their quantum when they reacquire a processor. Giving real-time threads fresh quanta after preemption allows Windows XP to favor real-time threads, which require a high level of responsiveness. The system returns preempted threads to the front of the appropriate ready queue.[164] Note that user-mode threads can preempt kernel-mode threads in many cases. However, kernel-mode threads can prevent this by masking certain interrupts. Events such as a thread entering the *ready* state, a thread exiting the *running* state or a change in a thread's priority trigger the system to execute dispatcher routines—routines that execute at DPC/dispatch level. By raising the IRQL to the DPC/dispatch IRQL, kernel-mode threads can mask scheduling and avoid being preempted. However, user-mode threads can still block the execution of system threads if they have a higher priority than the system threads.[165]

Determining Thread Priority

Windows XP divides its 32 priority levels (0–31) into two categories. Real-time threads (i.e., threads that must maintain a high level of responsiveness to user requests) occupy the upper 16 priority levels (16–31), and dynamic threads occupy the lower 16 priority levels (0–15). Only the zero-page thread has priority level 0. This thread uses spare processor cycles to zero free memory pages so they are ready for use.

Each thread has a **base priority**, which defines the lower limit that its actual priority may occupy. A user-mode thread's base priority is determined by its process's base priority class and the thread's priority level. A process's **base priority class** specifies a narrow range that the base priority of each of a process's threads can have. There are six base priority classes: idle, below normal, normal, above normal, high and real-time. The first five of these priority classes (called the **dynamic priority classes**) encompass priority levels 0 through 15; these are called dynamic priority classes, because threads belonging to processes in these classes can have their priorities dynamically altered by the operating system. The threads belonging to processes in the **real-time priority class** have a priority between 16 and 31; real-time threads have a static priority. Within each priority class, there are several **base priority levels**: idle, lowest, below normal, normal, above normal, highest and time critical. Each combination of base priority class and base priority level maps to a specific base priority (e.g., a thread with a normal base priority level and a normal priority class has a base priority of 7).[166]

A dynamic-priority thread's priority can change. A thread receives a priority boost when the thread exits the *waiting* state, such as after the completion of an I/O or after the thread gains a handle to a resource for which the thread is waiting. Similarly, a window that receives input (such as from the keyboard, mouse or timer) gets a priority boost. The system also can reduce a thread's priority. When a thread executes until its quantum expires, its priority is reduced one unit. However, a thread's dynamic priority can never dip below its base priority or rise into the real-time range.[167]

Finally, to reduce the likelihood of threads being indefinitely postponed, the dispatcher periodically (every few seconds) scans the lists of ready threads and boosts the priority of dynamic threads that have been waiting for a long time. This scheme also helps solve the problem of **priority inversion**. Priority inversion occurs when a high-priority thread is prevented from gaining the processor by a lower-priority thread. For example, a high-priority thread might wait for a resource held by a low-priority thread. A third, medium-priority thread obtains the processor, preventing the low-priority thread from running. In this way, the medium-priority thread is also preventing the high-priority thread from executing—hence, priority inversion. The dispatcher will eventually boost the priority of the low-priority thread so it can execute and, hopefully, finish using the resource.[168]

Scheduling on Multiprocessors

Multiprocessor thread scheduling extends the preceding uniprocessor scheduling algorithm. All editions of Windows XP, except the Home Edition, provide support for multiple processors. However, even Home Edition provides support for symmetric multiprocessing (SMP) using Intel's hyper-threading (HT) technology. Recall from Section 15.2.1 that HT technology allows the operating system to view one physical processor as two virtual processors. Scheduling in an SMP system is similar to that in a uniprocessor system. Generally, when a processor becomes available, the dispatcher tries to schedule the thread at the front of the highest-priority nonempty ready queue. However, the system also attempts to keep threads on the same processors to maximize the amount of relevant data stored in L1 caches (see Section 15.4, Memory Access Architectures).

Processes and threads can specify the processors on which they prefer to execute. A process can specify an **affinity mask**, which is a set of processors on which its threads are allowed to execute. A thread can also specify an affinity mask, which must be a subset of its process's affinity mask.[169] Similarly, a job also can have an affinity mask, which each of its associated processes must set as its own affinity mask. One use of affinity masks is restricting computationally intensive processes to a few processors so these processes do not interfere with more time-critical interactive processes.

In addition to affinity masks, each thread stores its **ideal processor** and **last processor**. Manipulating the value of a thread's ideal processor allows developers to influence whether related threads should execute in parallel (by setting related threads' ideal processors to different processors) or on the same processor to share cached data (by setting the threads' ideal processors to the same processor). By default, Windows XP attempts to assign threads of the same process different ideal processors. The dispatcher uses the last processor in an effort to schedule a thread on the same processor on which the thread last executed. This strategy increases the likelihood that data cached by the thread during an execution can be accessed during the next execution of that thread.[170, 171]

When a processor becomes available, the dispatcher schedules threads by considering each thread's priority, ideal processor, last processor and how long a thread has been waiting. Consequently, the thread at the front of the highest-priority non-empty ready queue might not be scheduled to the next available processor (even if the processor is in the thread's affinity mask). If this thread has not been waiting long and the available processor is not its ideal or last processor, the dispatcher might choose another thread from that ready queue which meets one or more of these other criteria.[172]

21.6.3 *Thread Synchronization*

Windows XP provides a rich variety of synchronization objects and techniques, designed for various purposes. For example, some synchronization objects execute at the DPC/dispatch level. These objects provide certain guarantees—a thread holding one of these objects will not be preempted—but restrict functionality (e.g., a thread holding one of these objects cannot access pageable data). Some synchronization objects are designed specifically for kernel-mode threads, whereas others are designed for all threads. In the following subsections, we introduce some synchronization mechanisms provided in Windows XP, how they are used and their benefits and drawbacks.

Dispatcher Objects

Windows XP provides a number of **dispatcher objects** that kernel- and user-mode threads can use for synchronization purposes. Dispatcher objects provide synchronization for resources such as shared data structures or files. These objects include many familiar synchronization constructs such as mutexes, semaphores, events and timers. Kernel threads use kernel dispatcher objects; synchronization objects available to user processes encapsulate these kernel dispatcher objects (i.e., synchronization objects translate many API calls made by user-mode threads into function calls for kernel dispatcher objects). A thread holding a dispatcher object executes at the passive IRQL.[173] A developer can use these objects to synchronize the actions of threads of the same process or different processes.[174]

Dispatcher objects can be in either a *signaled* **state** or *unsignaled* **state** (some dispatcher objects also have states relating to error conditions). The object remains in the *unsignaled* state while the resource for which the dispatcher object provides synchronization is unavailable. Once the resource becomes available, the object enters its *signaled* state. If a thread wishes to access a protected resource, the thread can call a **wait function** to wait for one or more dispatcher objects to enter a *sig-*

naled state. When calling a wait function for a single object, the thread specifies the object on which it is waiting (by passing the object's handle) and a maximum wait time for the object. Multiple-object wait functions can be used when a thread must wait on more than one object. The thread can specify whether it is waiting for all the objects or any one of them. Windows XP supplies numerous variations to these generic wait functions; e.g., a thread can specify that it enters an alertable *wait* state, allowing it to process any APCs queued to it while waiting. After calling a wait function, a thread blocks and enters its *wait* state. When the required object enters its *signaled* state, one or more threads can access the resource (later in this section, we describe how a dispatcher object enters its *signaled* state).[175] In many cases, the kernel maintains FIFO queues for waiting resources, but kernel APCs can disrupt this ordering. Threads process kernel APCs immediately, and when a thread resumes its wait, it is placed at the end of the queue.[176]

Event Objects

Threads often synchronize with an event, such as user input or I/O completion, by using an **event object**. When the event occurs, the object manager sets the event object to the *signaled* state. The event object returns to the *unsignaled* state by one of two methods (specified by the object's creator). In the first method, the object manager sets the event object to the *unsignaled* state when one thread is released from waiting. This method can be used when only one thread should awaken (e.g., to process the completion of an I/O operation). In the other method, the event object remains in the *signaled* state until a thread specifically sets the event to its *unsignaled* state; this allows multiple threads to awaken. This option can be used, for example, when multiple threads are waiting to read data. When a writing thread completes its operation, the writer can use an event object to signal all the waiting threads to awaken. The next time a thread begins writing, the thread can reset the event object to the *unsignaled* state.[177]

Mutex Objects

Mutex objects provide mutual exclusion for shared resources; they are essentially binary semaphores (see Section 5.6, Semaphores). Only one thread can own a mutex at a time, and only that thread can access the resource associated with the mutex. When a thread finishes using the resource protected by the mutex, it must release the mutex to transition it into its *signaled* state. If a thread terminates before releasing a mutex object, the mutex is considered **abandoned**. In this case the mutex enters an *abandoned* state. A waiting thread can acquire this abandoned mutex. However, the system cannot guarantee that the resource protected by the mutex is in a consistent state. To be safe, a thread should assume an error has occurred if it acquires an abandoned mutex.[178]

Semaphore Objects

Semaphore objects extend the functionality of mutex objects; they allow the creating thread to specify the maximum number of threads that can access a shared resource.[179] For example, a process might have a small number of preallocated buffers; the process can use a semaphore to synchronize access to these buffers.[180] Semaphore objects in Windows XP are counting semaphores (see Section 5.6.3, Counting Semaphores). A semaphore object maintains a count, which is initialized to the maximum number of threads that can simultaneously access the pool of resources. The count is decremented every time a thread acquires access to the pool of resources protected by the semaphore and incremented when a thread releases the semaphore. The semaphore remains in its *signaled* state while its count is greater than zero; it enters the *unsignaled* state when the count drops to zero.

A single thread can decrement the count by more than one by specifying the semaphore object in multiple wait functions. For example, a thread might use several of the process's buffers in separate asynchronous I/O operations. Each time the thread issues a buffered I/O request, the thread reacquires the semaphore (i.e., by specifying the semaphore object in a wait function), which decrements the semaphore's count. The thread must release the semaphore, which increments the semaphore's count, each time a request completes.[181]

Waitable Timer Objects

Threads might need to perform operations at regular intervals (e.g., autosave a user's document) or at specific times (e.g., display a calendar item). For this type of synchronization, Windows XP provides **waitable timer objects**. These objects become *signaled* after a specified amount of time elapses. **Manual-reset timer objects** remain *signaled* until a thread specifically resets the timer. **Auto-reset timer objects** remain *signaled* only until one thread finishes waiting on the object. Waitable timer objects can be **single use**, after which they become deactivated, or they can be **periodic**. In the latter case, the timer object reactivates after a specified interval and becomes *signaled* once the specified time expires. Figure 21.4 lists Windows XP's dispatcher objects. [182]

Several other Windows XP objects, such as console input, jobs and processes, can function as dispatcher objects as well. For example, jobs, processes and threads are set to the *signaled* state when they terminate, and a console input object is set to the *signaled* state when the console's input buffer contains unread data. In these cases, threads use wait functions and treat these objects just like other dispatcher objects.[183]

Dispatcher Object	Transitions from Unsignaled to Signaled State When
Event	Associated event occurs.
Mutex	Owner of the mutex releases the mutex.
Semaphore	Semaphore's count rises above zero.
Waitable timer	Specified amount of time elapses.

Figure 21.4 | *Dispatcher objects in Windows XP.*

Kernel Mode Locks

Windows XP provides several mechanisms for synchronizing access to kernel data structures. If a thread is interrupted while accessing a shared data structure, it might leave the data structure in an inconsistent state. Unsynchronized access to a data structure can result in erroneous results. If the thread belongs to a user process, an application might malfunction; if the thread belongs to a kernel process, the system might crash. In a uniprocessor system, one solution to the synchronization problem is to raise the IRQL level above the one at which any component that might preempt the thread executes and access the data structure. The thread lowers the IRQL level when it completes executing the critical code.[184]

Raising and lowering the IRQL level is inadequate in a multiprocessor system—two threads, executing concurrently on separate processors, can attempt to access the same data structure simultaneously. Windows XP provides spin locks to address this problem. Threads holding spin locks execute at the DPC/dispatch level or DIRQL, ensuring that the holder of the spin lock is not preempted by another thread. Threads should execute the fewest instructions possible while holding a spin lock to reduce wasteful spinning by other threads.

When a thread attempts to access a resource protected by a spin lock, it requests ownership of the associated spin lock. If the resource is available, the thread acquires the lock, accesses the resource, then releases the spin lock. If the resource is not available, the thread keeps trying to acquire the spin lock until successful. Because threads holding spin locks execute at the DPC/dispatch level or DIRQL, developers should restrict the actions these threads perform. Threads holding spin locks should never access pageable memory (because a page fault might occur), cause a hardware or software exception, attempt any action that could cause deadlock (e.g., attempt to reacquire that spin lock or attempt to acquire another spin lock unless the thread knows that this will not cause deadlock) or call any function that performs any of these actions.[185]

Windows XP provides generic spin locks and **queued spin locks**. A queued spin lock enforces FIFO ordering of requests and is more efficient than a normal spin lock,[186] because it reduces the processor-to-memory bus traffic associated with the spin lock. With a normal spin lock, a thread continually attempts to acquire the lock by executing a test-and-set instruction (see Section 5.5.2, Test-and-Set Instruction) on the memory line associated with the spin lock. This creates bus traffic on the processor-to-memory bus. With a queued spin lock, a thread that releases the lock notifies the next thread waiting for it. Threads waiting for queued spin locks do not create unnecessary bus traffic by repeating test-and-set. Queued spin locks also increase fairness by guaranteeing FIFO ordering of requests, because the releasing thread uses a queue associated with the spin lock to notify the appropriate waiting thread.[187] Windows XP supports both spin locks (for legacy compatibility) and queued spin locks, but Microsoft recommends the use of the latter.[188]

Alternatively, kernel-mode threads can use **fast mutexes**, a more efficient variant of mutexes that operate at the APC level. Although they require less overhead than mutexes, fast mutexes somewhat restrict the actions of the thread owning the lock. For example, threads cannot specify a maximum wait time to wait for a fast mutex—they can either wait indefinitely or not wait at all for an unavailable fast mutex. Also, if a thread attempts to acquire a fast mutex that it already owns, it creates a deadlock (dispatcher mutexes allow a thread to reacquire a mutex the thread already owns as long as it releases the mutex for each acquisition of the mutex).[189] Fast mutexes operate at the APC IRQL, which masks APCs that might require the thread to attempt to acquire a fast mutex it already owns.[190] However, some threads might need to receive APCs. For example, a thread might need to process the result of an asynchronous I/O operation; the system often uses APCs to notify threads that an asynchronous I/O request has been processed. For this purpose, Windows XP provides a variant of fast mutexes that execute at the passive IRQL.[191]

Another synchronization resource available only to kernel-mode threads is the **executive resource lock**. Executive resource locks have two modes: shared and exclusive. Any number of threads can simultaneously hold an executive resource lock in shared mode, or one thread can hold an executive resource lock in exclusive mode. This lock is useful for solving the readers-and-writers problem (see Section 6.2.4, Monitor Example: Readers and Writers). A reading thread can gain shared access to a resource if no other thread currently holds or is waiting for exclusive (i.e., write) access to the resource. A writing thread can gain exclusive access to a resource as long as no other thread holds either shared (i.e., read) or exclusive (i.e., write) access to it.[192]

Other Available Synchronization Tools

Aside from dispatcher objects and kernel-mode locks, Windows XP provides to threads several other synchronization tools. Kernel-mode locks are not applicable in all situations—they cannot be used by user-mode threads, and many of them operate at an elevated IRQL, restricting what threads can do while holding them. Dispatcher objects facilitate general synchronization but are not optimized for specific cases. For example, dispatcher objects can be used by threads of different processes but are not optimized for use among threads of the same process.

Critical section objects provide services similar to mutex objects but can be employed only by threads within a single process. Moreover, critical section objects do not allow threads to specify a maximum wait time (it is possible to wait indefinitely for a critical section object), and there is no way to determine if a critical section object is abandoned. However, critical section objects are more efficient than mutex objects because critical section objects do not transition to kernel mode if there is no contention. This optimization requires that critical section objects be employed only to synchronize threads of the same process. Also, critical section objects are implemented with a processor-specific test-and-set instruction, further increasing efficiency.[193,194]

A **timer-queue timer** is an alternate method for using waitable timer objects that allows threads to wait on timer events while executing other pieces of code. When a thread wishes to wait on a timer, it can place a timer in a timer queue and specify a function to perform when the timer becomes *signaled*. At that time, a worker thread from a thread pool performs the specified function. In cases where the thread waits on both a timer and another object, the thread should use a wait-able timer object with a wait function.[195]

For variables shared among multiple threads, Windows XP provides **inter-locked variable access** through certain functions. These functions provide atomic read and write access to variables, but they do not ensure the order in which accesses are made. For example, the `InterlockedIncrement` function combines incrementing a variable and returning the result into a single atomic operation. This can be useful, for example, when providing unique ids. Each time a thread needs to obtain a unique id, it can call `InterlockedIncrement`. This avoids a situation in which one thread increments the value of the id variable but is interrupted before checking the result. The interrupting thread might then access the id variable, caus-ing two items to have the same id. Because `InterlockedIncrement` both incre-ments the variable and returns the result in an atomic operation, this situation will not occur.[196] Windows XP also provides **interlocked singly linked lists (SLists)**, which provide atomic insertion and deletion operations.[197]

This section provided a broad survey of Windows XP's synchronization tools. However, Windows XP provides other tools; readers interested in more informa-tion should visit the MSDN Library at `msdn.microsoft.com/library`. In addition to these synchronization tools, threads can synchronize by communicating through various IPC mechanisms (described in Section 21.10, Interprocess Communication) or by queuing APCs to other threads.

21.7 Memory Management

The Windows XP **virtual memory manager (VMM)** creates the illusion that each process has a 4GB contiguous memory space. Because the system allocates more virtual memory to processes than can fit into main memory, the VMM stores some of the data on disk in files called **pagefiles**. Windows XP divides virtual memory into fixed-size pages which it stores either in page frames in main memory or files on disk. The VMM uses a two-level hierarchical addressing system.

Windows XP has two strategies for optimizing main memory usage and reduc-ing disk I/O. The VMM uses copy-on-write pages (see Section 10.4.6, Sharing in a Paging System) and employs **lazy allocation**, which is a policy of postponing allocat-ing pages and page table entries in main memory until absolutely necessary. How-ever, when the VMM is forced to perform disk I/O, it prefetches pages from disk and places pages into main memory before they are needed (see Section 11.4, Anticipatory Paging). Heuristics ensure that the gain in the rate of disk I/O out-weighs the cost of filling main memory with potentially unused pages. When main memory fills, Windows XP performs a modified version of the LRU page-replace-ment algorithm. The following sections describe the internals of the Windows XP memory management system.

21.7.1 *Memory Organization*

Windows XP systems provide either a 32-bit or a 64-bit address space, depending on the processor and the edition of Windows XP. We limit our discussion to memory operations using the Intel IA-32 architecture (e.g., Intel Pentium and AMD Athlon systems), because the vast majority of today's Windows systems are built for that platform. See the MSDN Library for more information on Windows XP 64-Bit Edition.[198]

Windows XP allocates a unique 4GB virtual address space to each process. By default, a process can access only the first 2GB of its virtual address space. The system reserves the other two gigabytes for kernel-mode components—this space is called system space. [199]

Physical memory is divided into fixed-size page frames, which are 4KB on a 32-bit system (except in the case when the system uses large pages as described later in this section). The VMM maintains a two-level memory map in the system portion of each process's virtual address space that stores the location of pages in main memory and on disk.[200] The VMM assigns each process one **page directory table**. When a processor switches contexts, it loads the location of the new process's page directory table into the **page directory register**. The page directory table is composed of page directory entries (PDEs); each PDE points to a **page table**. Page tables contain page table entries (PTEs); each PTE points to a page frame in main memory or a location on disk. The VMM uses the virtual address in conjunction with the memory map to translate virtual addresses into physical addresses. A virtual address is composed of three portions; the offset in a page directory table, the offset in a page table and the offset on a page in physical memory.[201]

Windows XP translates a virtual address in three stages, as shown in Fig. 21.5. In the first stage of address translation, the system calculates the sum $a + d$, which is the value in the page directory register plus the first portion of the virtual address, to determine the location of the page directory entry (PDE) in the page directory table. In the second stage, the system calculates the sum $b + t$, which is the value in the PDE plus the second portion of the virtual address, to find the page table entry (PTE) in the page table. This entry contains c, the page frame number corresponding to the virtual page's location in main memory. Finally, in the last stage, the system concatenates c and the page offset, o, to form the physical address (see Section 10.4.4, Multilevel Page Tables). The system performs all of these operations quickly; the delay occurs when the system must read the PDE and PTE from main memory.[202] Address translation is often accelerated by the Translation Look-aside Buffer (TLB) as discussed in Section 10.4.3, Paging Address Translation with Direct/Associative Mapping.

The PTE is structured differently depending on whether it points to a page in memory or a page in a pagefile. Five of the PTE's 32 bits are for protection—they indicate whether a process may read the page, write to the page and execute code on the page. These protection bits also tell the system whether the page is a copy-on-write page and whether the system should raise an exception when a process

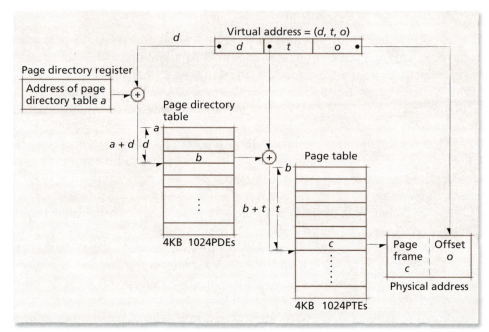

Figure 21.5 | Virtual address translation.

accesses the page.[203] Twenty bits index a frame in memory or offset in a pagefile on disk; this is enough to address 1,048,576 virtual pages. If the page is stored on disk, a designated four bits indicate in which of 16 possible pagefiles the page is located. If the page is in memory, a different set of three bits indicate the state of the page. Figure 21.6 lists these three bits and their meaning.

Windows XP allows applications to allocate **large pages**. A large page is a set of contiguous pages that the operating system treats as one page. Large pages are useful when the system knows it will repeatedly need the same large chunk of code or data. The system needs to store only one entry in the TLB. Because the page is bigger, it is more likely to be accessed, and less likely to be deleted from the TLB. Page access is accelerated because the VMM can look up address translations in the TLB rather than consulting page tables.[204] Windows XP stores information that cannot be swapped to disk (i.e., the nonpaged pool) and memory maps on large pages.[205]

Page state bit	Definition
Valid	PTE is valid—it points to a page of data.
Modified	Page in memory is no longer consistent with the version on disk.
Transition	VMM is in the process of moving the page to or from disk. Pages in transition are always invalid.

Figure 21.6 | Page states.[206]

Windows XP imposes several restrictions on the use of large pages:

- Each type of processor has a minimum size for large pages, usually 2MB or greater. The size of every large page must be a multiple of that minimum large page size.[207]

- Large pages always allow read and write access. This means that read-only data, such as program code and system DLLs, cannot be stored in large pages.[208]

- The pages that compose a large page must be contiguous in both virtual and physical memory.[209, 210]

Windows XP uses copy-on-write pages (see Section 10.4.6, Sharing in a Paging System) as one of its lazy allocation mechanisms. The system manages copy-on-write pages using **prototype page tables**. The system also uses prototype page tables to manage file mappings. A file mapping is a portion of main memory that multiple processes may access simultaneously to communicate with one another (this is discussed further in Section 21.10.3, Shared Memory). The PTE of a copy-on-write page does not point directly to the frame in which the page is stored. Instead, it points to a **Prototype Page Table Entry (PPTE)**, a 32-bit record that points to the location of the shared page.

When a process modifies a page whose PTE protection bits indicate that it is a copy-on-write page, the VMM copies the page to a new frame and sets the process's PPTE to reference the new location. All of the other processes's PPTE's continue pointing to the original frame. Using copy-on-write pages conserves memory, because processes share main memory page frames. As a result, each process can store more of its pages in main memory. This causes fewer page faults, because there is more space in main memory, and once the VMM fetches a page from disk, it is less likely to move the page back to disk. However, PPTEs add a level of indirection; it takes four memory references instead of three to translate an address. Therefore, translating an address that is not in the TLB is more expensive for copy-on-write pages than for normal pages.[211]

21.7.2 Memory Allocation

Windows XP performs memory allocation in three stages (Fig. 21.7). A process must first **reserve** space in its virtual address space. Processes can either specify what virtual addresses to reserve or allow the VMM to decide. A process may not access space it has reserved until it **commits** the space. When a process commits a page, the VMM creates a PTE and ensures that there is enough space in either main memory or a pagefile for the page. A process usually commits a page only when it is ready to write to the page; however, the Windows API supports single-step reserve and commit. Separating memory allocation into two steps allows a process to reserve a large contiguous virtual memory region and sparsely commit portions of it.[212, 213] Finally, when a process is ready to use its committed memory, it accesses the committed virtual memory. At that point, the VMM writes the data to a zeroed

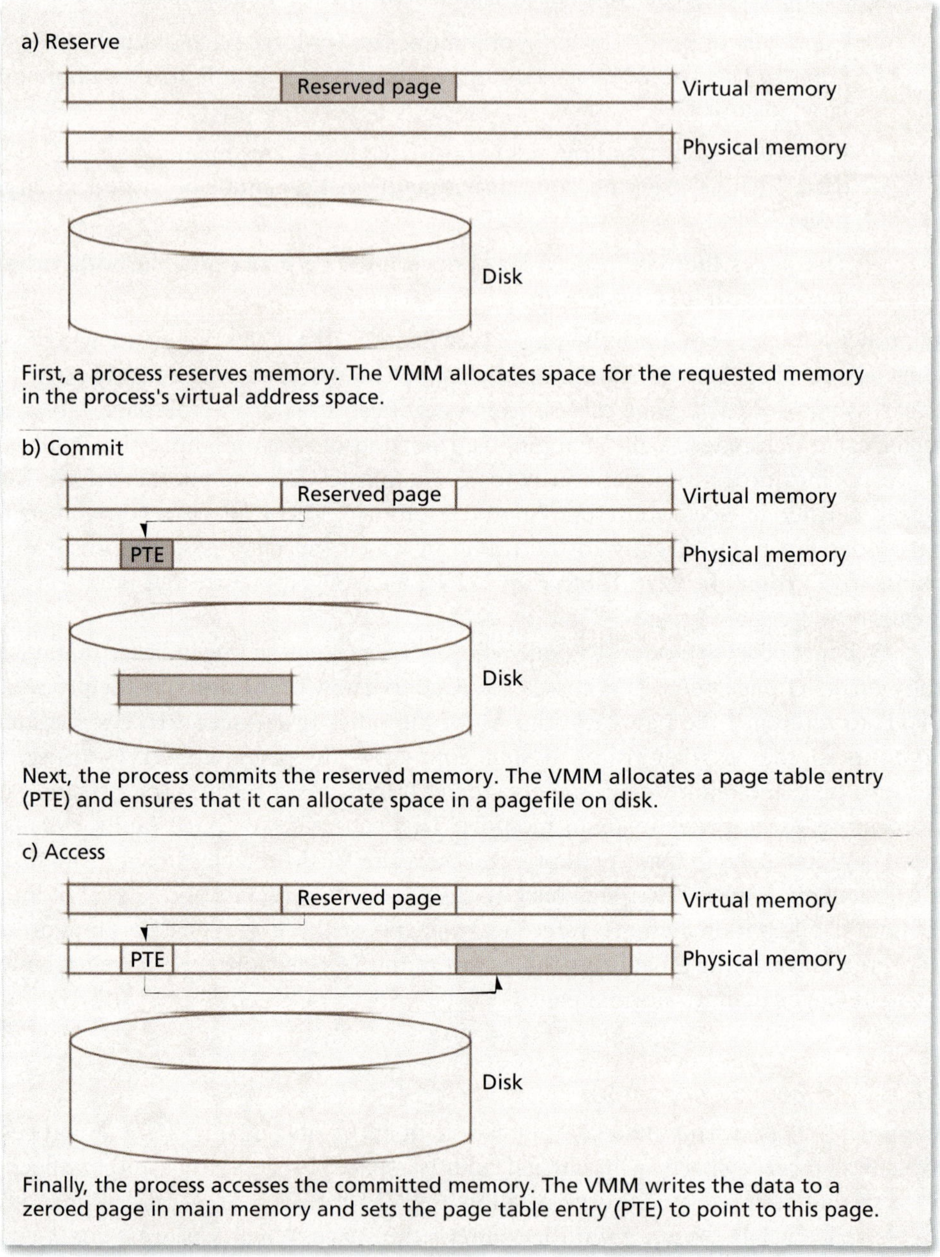

a) Reserve

Reserved page | Virtual memory

Physical memory

Disk

First, a process reserves memory. The VMM allocates space for the requested memory in the process's virtual address space.

b) Commit

Reserved page | Virtual memory

PTE | Physical memory

Disk

Next, the process commits the reserved memory. The VMM allocates a page table entry (PTE) and ensures that it can allocate space in a pagefile on disk.

c) Access

Reserved page | Virtual memory

PTE | Physical memory

Disk

Finally, the process accesses the committed memory. The VMM writes the data to a zeroed page in main memory and sets the page table entry (PTE) to point to this page.

Figure 21.7 | Memory allocation stages.

page in main memory. This three-stage process ensures that processes use only as much space in main memory as they need, rather than the amount they reserve.[214]

A system rarely has enough main memory to satisfy all processes. Previous versions of Windows allowed an application that required more main memory to function properly to issue **must-succeed requests**. Device drivers often issued these requests, and the VMM always fulfilled a must-succeed request. This led to system crashes when the VMM was forced to allocate main memory when none was available. Windows XP does not suffer from this problem; it denies all must-succeed requests. The system expects components to handle a denied memory allocation request without crashing.[215, 216]

Windows XP has a special mechanism for handling low-memory conditions when all or most of main memory is allocated. Under normal circumstances, Windows XP optimizes performance by handling multiple memory allocation requests simultaneously. When there are few page frames in main memory to allocate, the system runs into the same scarce-resource problem faced by all multiprogramming systems. Windows XP solves this problem via a process called **I/O throttling**; when the system detects that it has only a few available page frames, it begins to manage memory one page at a time. I/O throttling slows the system, because the VMM ceases to manage multiple requests in parallel but instead retrieves pages from disk only one at a time. However, it does make the system more robust and helps prevent crashes.[217]

To track main memory, Windows XP uses a **page frame database**, which lists the state of each frame, ordered by page frame number. There are eight possible states, as shown in Fig. 21.8.

The system tracks page frames by state. It has a singly linked list, called a **page list**, for each of the eight states. A page list is referred to by the state of its pages; for example, the Free Page List contains all free pages, the Zeroed Page List contains all zeroed pages and so on. The page lists permit the VMM to swap pages and allocate memory quickly. For example, to allocate two new pages, the VMM

Frame State	Definition
Valid	Page belongs to a process's working set and its PTE is set to valid.
Transition	Page is in the process of being transferred to or from disk.
Standby	Page has just been removed from a process's working set; its PTE is set to invalid and in transition.
Modified	Page has just been removed from a process's working set; it is not consistent with the on-disk version. The VMM must write this page to disk before freeing this page. The PTE of this page is set to invalid and in transition.
Modified No-Write	Page has just been removed from a process's working set; it is not consistent with the on-disk version. The VMM must write an entry to the log file before freeing this page. The PTE of this page is set to invalid and in transition.
Free	Page frame does not contain a valid page; however it might contain an invalid page that has no PTE and is not part of any working set.

Figure 21.8 | Page frame states.[218] (Part 1 of 2.)

Frame State	Definition
Zeroed	Page frame is not part of any working set and all of its bits have been set to zero. For security reasons, only zeroed page frames are allocated to processes.
Bad	Page frame has generated a hardware error and should not be used.

Figure 21.8 | *Page frame states.[218] (Part 2 of 2.)*

needs to access only the first two frames in the Zeroed Page List. If the Zeroed Page List is empty, the VMM takes a page from another list, using the algorithm described in Section 21.7.3, Page Replacement.[219]

The system uses **Virtual Address Descriptors (VADs)** to manage the virtual address space of each process. Each VAD describes a range of virtual addresses allocated to the process.[220]

Windows XP attempts to anticipate requests for pages on disk and move pages to main memory to prevent page faults. A process can invoke API functions to tell the system the process's future memory requirements.[221] In general, the system employs a policy of demand paging, loading pages into memory only when a process requests them. It also loads several nearby pages—spatial locality implies that these pages are likely to be referenced soon. The Windows file systems divide disk space into **clusters** of bytes; pages in the same cluster are, by definition, part of the same file. Windows XP takes advantage of spatial locality by loading all pages in the same cluster at once, a paging policy referred to as **clustered demand paging**. These two mechanisms reduce disk seek time because only one disk seek is needed to fetch the entire cluster. Prefetching, however, potentially places some unneeded pages into main memory, leaving less space for needed pages and increasing the number of page faults. It might also decrease efficiency during periods of heavy disk I/O by forcing the system to page out pages that are needed right away for pages that are not needed yet.[222]

Windows XP reduces the time needed to load (i.e., start) applications, including the operating system itself, by prefetching files. The system records what pages are accessed and in what order during the last eight application loads. Before loading an application, the system asks for all of the pages it will need in one asynchronous request, thus decreasing disk seek time.[223, 224]

The system decreases the time it takes to load Windows by simultaneously prefetching pages and initializing devices. When Windows XP starts, it must direct numerous peripheral hardware devices to initialize—the system cannot continue loading until they are done. This is the ideal time to perform prefetching, because the system is otherwise idle.[225]

Windows XP uses the **Logical Prefetcher** to perform prefetching. The user can set a special registry key to tell Windows XP for which scenarios, such as all application loads or Windows start-up, the user wants the system to run the Logical

Prefetcher.[226] When an application loads, Windows XP stores a trace of memory accesses in a scenario file. Each application, including the Windows operating system, has its own scenario file. The system updates scenario files ten seconds after a successful application load. Storing scenario files has a price: recording each memory access uses processor cycles and occupies space on the disk. However, the reduced disk I/O offsets the extra time it takes to store the memory trace, and most users are willing to give up some disk space in return for significantly faster load time for all applications, including for Windows itself.[227]

The Logical Prefetcher accesses pages based on their location on disk rather than waiting for a process to explicitly request them. As a result, Windows XP can load applications faster and more efficiently. However, the pages and files indicated in scenario files could be scattered throughout the disk. To further optimize application load time, the Logical Prefetcher periodically reorganizes portions of the hard drive to ensure that all files that the system has previously prefetched are contiguous on disk. Every few days, when the system is idle, the Logical Prefetcher updates a layout file which contains the ideal disk layout and uses this layout to rearrange pages on disk.[228]

21.7.3 Page Replacement

Windows XP bases its page-replacement policy on the working set model. Recall from Section 11.7, Working Set Model, that a process's working set is the set of pages that a process is currently using. Because this is difficult to determine, Windows XP simply considers a process's **working set** to be all of its pages in main memory. Pages not in the process's working set, but mapped to its virtual address space, are stored on disks in pagefiles.[229, 230] Storing pagefiles on different physical disks accelerates swapping because it enables the system to read and write multiple pages concurrently.[231]

When memory becomes scarce, the **balance set manager** moves parts of different processes' working sets to pagefiles. Windows XP employs a **localized least-recently used** (LRU) policy to determine which pages to move to disk. The policy is localized by process. When the system needs to free a frame to meet a process's request, it removes a page belonging to the process which the process has not recently accessed. The VMM assigns each process a **working set maximum** and a **working set minimum** that denote an acceptable range for the size of the process's working set. Whenever a process whose working set size is equal to its working set maximum requests an additional page, the balance set manager moves one of the process's pages to secondary storage, then fulfills the request. A process using less than its working set minimum is not in danger of losing pages unless available memory drops below a certain threshold. The balance set manager checks the amount of free space in memory once per second and adjusts the working set maximums accordingly. If the number of available bytes exceeds a certain threshold, the working set maximums of processes working at their working set maximum shift upward; if it drops below a certain threshold, all working set maximums shift downward.[232]

Windows XP does not wait until main memory is full to move pages to disk. It regularly tests each process to ensure that only the pages the process needs are in main memory. Windows XP uses **page trimming** to remove pages from memory. Periodically, the balance set manager moves all of a process's pages above the working set minimum from the Valid Page List to the Standby Page List, Modified Page List, or Modified No-Write Page List, as appropriate. Collectively, these are called the **transitional page list**, although there is no such actual list in memory.[233]

The VMM chooses which pages to trim, using the localized LRU policy, as illustrated in Fig. 21.9. The system sets the status bits of the PTEs of trimmed pages to invalid, meaning the PTEs no longer point to a valid frame, but the system does not modify the PTEs in any other way. The state in the page frame database of trimmed pages is set to transition, standby, modified or modified no-write.[234] If the process requests a page that is in one of these transitional page lists, the MMU issues a **transitional fault**. In this situation, the VMM removes the page from the transitional list and puts it back on the Valid Page List. Otherwise, the page is reclaimed. A system thread writes pages in the Modified Page List to disk. Components, such as file systems, use the Modified No-Write Page List to ensure that the VMM does not write a dirty page to disk without first making an entry in a log file. The application notifies the VMM when it is safe to write the page.[235] Once a modi-

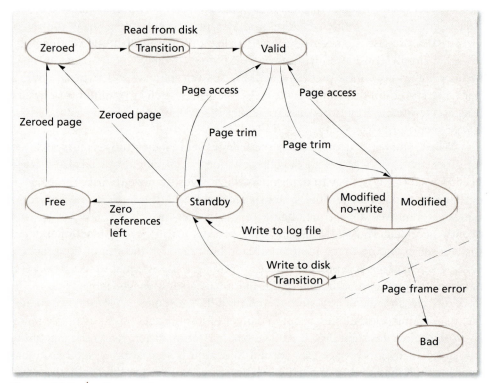

Figure 21.9 | *Page-replacement process.*

fied or modified no-write page becomes consistent with the data on disk, the VMM moves the page to the Standby Page List. After a waiting period, the VMM moves pages on the Standby Page List to the Free Page List. Later, another low-priority thread zeroes the bits of pages on the Free Page List and moves the pages to the Zeroed Page List. Windows XP zeroes pages to prevent a process that is allocated a page from reading the (potentially sensitive) information that another process previously stored on that page. When the system needs to allocate a new page to a process, it claims a page from the Zeroed Page List.[236]

The localized LRU algorithm requires certain hardware features not available on all systems. Because portability between different platforms is an important design criterion for all Windows operating systems, many early Windows systems avoided using hardware-specific features to ensure that the same operating system could be used on multiple platforms. Operating systems commonly simulate LRU page replacement with the clock algorithm (see Section 11.6.7, Modifications to FIFO: Second-Chance and Clock Page Replacement). Doing so requires an accessed bit which the system sets on for each page that has been accessed within a certain time interval. Many early computers did not have an accessed bit. As a result, early versions of Windows NT used the FIFO page-replacement policy (see Section 11.6.2, First-In-First-Out (FIFO) Page Replacement) or even an effectively random page replacement. Microsoft later developed versions of Windows specifically for Intel IA-32 and other platforms that support the accessed bit, allowing Windows XP to employ the more effective LRU algorithm.[237]

Some data cannot be paged out of memory. For example, code that handles interrupts must stay in main memory, because processing a page fault during an interrupt would cause an unacceptable delay and might even crash the system. Paging passwords presents a security risk if the system crashes, because an unencrypted copy of secret data would be stored on disk. All such data is stored in a designated area of system space called the **nonpaged pool**. Data that can be sent to disk is stored in the **paged pool**.[238] Portions of device drivers and VMM code are stored in the nonpaged pool.[239]

A device driver developer must consider several trade-offs when deciding what portions of the code to place in the nonpaged pool. Space in the nonpaged pool is limited. In addition, code in the nonpaged pool may not access paged pool code or data because the VMM might be forced to access the disk, which defeats the purpose of nonpaged pool code.[240]

21.8 File Systems Management

Windows XP file systems consist of three layers of drivers. At the very bottom are various volume drivers that control a specific hardware device, such as the hard disk. File system drivers, which compose the next level, implement a particular file system format, such as New Technology File System (NTFS) or File Allocation Table (FAT). These drivers implement what a typical user views as the file system: a hierarchical organization of files and the related functions to manipulate these files. Finally, file system filter drivers accomplish high-level tasks such as virus protection, compression and encryption.[241,242] NTFS is the native Windows XP file system (and the one described in depth in this case study), but FAT16 and FAT32 are also supported (see Section 13.6.3, Tabular Noncontiguous File Allocation) and typically used for floppy disks. Windows XP also supports Compact Disc File System (CDFS) for CDs and Universal Disk Format (UDF) for CDs and DVDs. The following subsections introduce Windows XP file system drivers and describe the NTFS file system.[243]

21.8.1 File System Drivers

File system drivers cooperate with the I/O manager to fulfill file I/O requests. File system drivers provide a link between the logical representation of the file system exposed to applications and its corresponding physical representation on a storage volume. The I/O manager interface enables Windows XP to support multiple file systems. Windows XP divides each data storage device into one or more volumes, and associates each volume with a file system.

To understand how file system drivers and the I/O manger interact, consider the flow of a typical file I/O request. A user-mode thread that wishes to read data from a file sends an I/O request via a subsystem API call. The I/O manager translates the thread's file handle into a pointer to the file object and passes the pointer to the appropriate file system driver. The file system driver uses the pointer to locate the file object and determine the location of the file on disk. Next, the file system driver passes the read request through the layers of drivers and eventually the request reaches the disk. The disk processes the read request and returns the requested data.[244]

A file system driver can be either a local file system driver or a remote file system driver. Local file system drivers process I/O for hardware devices such as hard disk drives or DVD drives. The preceding paragraph described the role of a local file system driver in fulfilling a disk I/O request. Remote file system drivers transfer files to and from remote file servers via network protocols. Remote file system drivers cooperate with the I/O manager, but instead of interacting with volume drivers, remote file system drivers interact with remote file system drivers on other computers.[245]

In general, a file system driver can act as a black box; it provides support for a particular file system, such as NTFS, independent of the underlying storage volume on which the files reside. File system drivers provide the link between the user's view of a file system and the data's actual representation on a storage volume.

21.8.2 NTFS

NTFS is the default file system for Windows XP. When creating the NT line of operating systems, Microsoft decided to construct a new file system to address the limitations of the FAT file system used in DOS and older versions of Windows. FAT, which uses a tabular noncontiguous allocation scheme (see Section 13.6.3, Tabular Noncontiguous File Allocation), does not scale well to large disk drives. For example, a file allocation table for FAT32 (the file system included in Windows ME) on a 32GB hard drive using 2KB clusters consumes 64MB of memory. Furthermore, FAT32 can address no more than 2^{32} data blocks. FAT's addressing limitation was a problem for FAT12 (12-bit FAT) and FAT16 (16-bit FAT) and undoubtedly will be a problem in the future for FAT32. To avoid these shortcomings, NTFS uses an indexed approach (see Section 13.6.4, Indexed Noncontiguous File Allocation) with 64-bit pointers. This allows NTFS to address up to 16 exabytes (i.e., 16 billion gigabytes) of storage. Furthermore, NTFS includes additional features that make a file system more robust. These features include file compression, file encryption, support for multiple data streams and user-level enhancements (e.g., support for hard links and easy file system and directory browsing).

Master File Table

The most important file on an NTFS volume is the **Master File Table (MFT)**. The MFT stores information about all files on the volume, including file metadata (e.g., time of creation, the filename and whether the file is read-only, archive, etc.). The MFT is divided into fixed-size records, usually 1KB long. Each file has an entry in the MFT, which consists of at least one record, plus additional ones if necessary.[246]

NTFS stores all information about a file in attributes, each consisting of a header and data. The header contains the attribute's type (e.g., `file_name`), name (necessary for files with more than one attribute of the same type) and flags. If any of a file's attributes do not fit into the file's first MFT record, NTFS creates a special attribute that stores pointers to the headers of all attributes located on different records. An attribute's data can be of variable length. Attribute data that fits in an MFT entry is stored in the entry for quick access; attributes whose data reside in the MFT entry are called **resident attributes**. Because the actual file data is an attribute, the system stores small files entirely within their MFT entry. NTFS stores **nonresident attributes**, the attributes whose data does not fit inside the MFT entry, elsewhere on disk.[247]

The system records the location of nonresident attributes using three numbers. The logical cluster number (LCN) tells the system on which cluster on disk the attribute is located. The run length indicates how many clusters the attribute spans. Because a file attribute might be split into multiple fragments, the virtual cluster number (VCN) tells the system to which cluster in the attribute the LCN points. The first VCN is zero.[248]

Figure 21.10 shows a sample multirecord MFT entry that contains both resident and nonresident attributes. Attribute 3 is a nonresident attribute. The data portion of attribute 3 contains a list of pointers to the file on disk. The first 10 clusters are stored on disk clusters (i.e., LCNs) 1023–1032. The eleventh cluster, VCN 10, is stored on disk cluster 624. Attributes 1 and 2 are resident attributes, so they stored on the first MFT record; attributes 3 and 4 are nonresident attributes stored on the second MFT record.

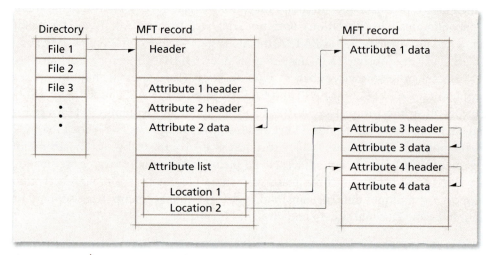

Figure 21.10 | *Master File Table (MFT) entry for a sample file.*

NTFS stores directories as files. Each directory file contains an attribute called `index` that stores the list of files inside the directory. Each file's directory entry contains the file's name and standard file information, such as the time of the most recent modification to the file and the file's access (e.g., read-only). If the `index` attribute is too large to be a resident attribute, NTFS creates index buffers to contain the additional entries. An additional attribute, the `index_root`, describes where on disk any index buffers are stored.

For easy directory searching, NTFS sorts directory entries alphabetically. NTFS structures a large directory (one that is not a resident attribute) in a two-level B-tree. Figure 21.11 shows a sample directory. Suppose the system directs NTFS to find the file `e.txt`. NTFS begins searching in the `index` attribute, where it finds `a.txt`. The file `a.txt` comes before `e.txt`, so NTFS scans to the next file, `j.txt`. Because `j.txt` comes after `e.txt`, NTFS proceeds to the appropriate child node of `a.txt`. NTFS searches in the first index buffer, obtaining its location on the volume from information in the `index_root` attribute. This index buffer begins with `b.txt`; NTFS scans the first index buffer until it finds `e.txt`.[249]

Windows XP allows multiple directory entries (either in the same directory or in different directories) to point to the same physical file. The system can create a new path (i.e., a new directory entry) to an already existing file, i.e., a hard link (see Section 13.4.2, Metadata). It first updates the existing file's MFT entry by adding a new `file_name` attribute and incrementing the value of the `hard_link` attribute. Next, it creates the new directory entry to point to the MFT entry of the existing file. NTFS treats each newly created hard link to a file exactly as it treats the original file name. If a user "moves" the file, the value of a `file_name` attribute is changed from the old to the new path name. NTFS does not delete the file until all hard links to the file are removed. It does not permit hard links to directory files,

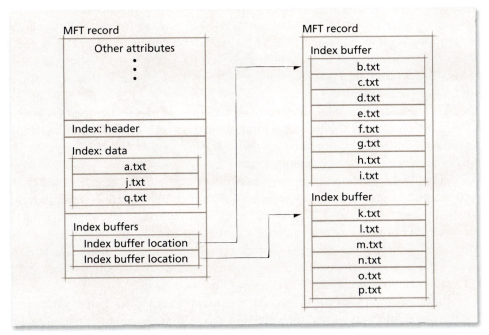

Figure 21.11 | *Directory contents are stored in B-trees.*

and because hard links point directly to MFT entries, a hard link must point to a file residing on the same physical volume.[250, 251]

Data Streams

The contents (i.e., the actual file data) of an NTFS file are stored in one or more **data streams**. A data stream is simply an attribute in an NTFS file that contains file data. Unlike many other file systems, including FAT, NTFS allows users to place multiple data streams into one file. The unnamed **default data stream** is what most people consider to be the "contents" of a file. NTFS files can have multiple **alternate data streams**. These streams can store metadata about a file, such as author, summary or version number. They also can be a form of supplemental data, such as a small preview image associated with a large bitmap or a backup of a text file.

NTFS considers each data stream of a file to be an attribute of type `Data`. Recall that header information for an attribute stores both the attribute type (in this case `Data`) and the attribute's name. NTFS differentiates between different alternate data streams using the attribute's name; the default data stream is unnamed. Using separate attributes for each data stream enables the system to access any data stream without scanning through the rest of the file.[252]

File Compression

NTFS permits users to compress files and folders through the GUI interface or via system calls. When a user compresses a folder, the system compresses any file or folder that is added to the compressed folder. Compression is transparent; applications can open, manipulate and save compressed files using the same API calls as they would with uncompressed files. This capability exists because NTFS decompresses and recompresses files at the system level; i.e., the system reads the compressed file and decompresses it in memory, and then recompresses when the file is saved.[253]

NTFS uses the **Lempel-Ziv algorithm** to compress files.[254] Lempel-Ziv is one of the most commonly used compression algorithms. For example, the Windows application *WinZip* and the application *gzip*, which is popular on UNIX-compatible systems, both use Lempel-Ziv compression.[255]

NTFS uses segmented compression, dividing files into **compression units** and compressing one unit at a time. A compression unit consists of 16 clusters; on most systems the cluster size is 2KB or 4KB, but clusters can range anywhere from 512 bytes to 64KB. Sometimes compressing a portion of the file does not significantly reduce its size. In that case, compression and decompression add unnecessary overhead. If the compressed version of a compression unit still occupies 16 clusters, NTFS stores the compression unit in its uncompressed state.[256]

Although larger files (or sections of files) tend to compress better than small files, this segmented approach decreases file access time. Segmented compression enables applications to perform random file I/O without decompressing the entire file. Segmented compression also enables NTFS to compress a file while an application modifies it. Modified portions of the file are cached in memory. Because a portion of the file that has been modified once is likely to be modified again, constantly recompressing the file while it is open is inefficient. A low-priority lazy-writer thread is responsible for compressing the modified data and writing it to disk.[257]

File Encryption

NTFS performs file encryption, like file compression, by dividing the file into units of 16 clusters and encrypting each unit separately. Applications can specify that a file should be encrypted on disk when created, or if the user has sufficient access rights, an application executing on the user's behalf can encrypt an existing file. The system will encrypt any file or folder for a user-mode thread, except system files, system folders and root directories. Because these files and folders are shared among all users, no user-mode thread can encrypt them (and therefore not allow other users access to them).[258]

NTFS uses a public/private key pair (see Section 19.2, Cryptography) to encrypt files. NTFS creates **recovery keys** that administrators can use to decrypt any file. This prevents files from being permanently lost when users forget their private keys or change jobs.[259]

NTFS stores encryption keys in the nonpaged pool in system memory. This is done for security reasons to ensure that the encryption keys are never written to disk. Storing keys on disk would compromise the security of the storage volume, because malicious users could first access the encryption keys, then use them to decrypt the data.[260] Instead of storing the actual keys, NTFS encrypts private keys using a randomly generated "master key" for each user; the master key is a symmetric key (i.e., it does both encryption and decryption). The private key is stored on disk in this encrypted form. The master key itself is encrypted by a key generated from the user's password and stored on disk. The administrator's recovery key is stored on disk in a similar manner.[261]

When NTFS encrypts a file, it encrypts all data streams of that file. NTFS's encryption and decryption of files is transparent to applications. Note that NTFS encryption ensures that files residing on a secondary storage volume are stored in an encrypted form. If data is stored on a remote server, the user must take extra precautions to protect it during network transfer, such as using a Secure Sockets Layer (SSL) connection.[262]

Sparse Files

A file in which most of the data is unused (i.e., set to zero), such as an image file that is mostly white space, is referred to as a **sparse file**. Sparse files can also appear in databases and scientific data with sparse matrices. A 4MB sparse file might contain only 1MB of nonzero data; storing the 3MB of zeroes on disk is wasteful. Compression, although an option, degrades performance, owing to the need to decompress and compress the files when they are used. Therefore, NTFS provides support for sparse files.[263]

A thread explicitly specifies that a file is sparse. If a thread converts a normal file to a sparse file, it is responsible for indicating areas of the file that contain large runs of zeroes. NTFS does not store these zeroes on disk but keeps track of them in a zero block list for the file. Each entry in the list contains the start and end position of a run of zeroes in the file. The used portion of the file is stored in the usual manner on disk. Applications can access just the used file segments or the entire file, in which case NTFS generates streams of zeroes where necessary.[264]

When an application writes new data to a sparse file, the writing thread is responsible for indicating areas of the data that should not be stored on disk but rather in the zero block list. If a write contains an entire compression unit of zeroes (i.e., 16 clusters of zeroes), NTFS recognizes this and records the empty block in the zero block list instead of writing the compression unit full of zeroes to disk. (The write operation must be done using a special API call that notifies NTFS that the written data consists exclusively of zeroes.) As a result, while an application can specify exact ranges of zeroes for better memory management, the system also performs some memory optimizations on its own.[265]

Reparse Points and Mounted Volumes

Recall our earlier discussion of NTFS hard links from the Master File Table subsection. We noted that they are limited because they cannot point to directories, and the data to which they point must reside on the same volume as the hard link. NTFS includes a file attribute, called a **reparse point**, to address these limitations. A reparse point contains a 32-bit tag and can contain up to 16KB of attribute data. When the system accesses a file with a reparse point, the system first processes the information in the reparse point. NTFS uses the tag to determine which file system filter driver should handle the data in the reparse point. The appropriate filter driver reads the attribute data and performs some function, such as scanning for viruses, decrypting a file or locating the file's data.[266]

Reparse points permit applications to establish links to files on another volume. For example, little-used hard disk data is sometimes moved to a tertiary storage device such as a tape drive. Although NTFS might delete the file's data after it is copied to the tertiary storage (to save space on the hard disk), it retains the file's MFT record. NTFS also adds a reparse point specifying from where to retrieve the data. When an application accesses the data, NTFS encounters the reparse point and uses its tag to call the appropriate file system driver, which retrieves the data from tertiary storage and copies it back to disk. This operation is transparent to the application.[267]

Additionally, reparse points are used to mount volumes. The reparse point data specifies the root directory of the volume to mount and how to find the volume, and the file system driver uses this information to mount that volume. In this way, a user can browse a single directory structure that includes multiple volumes. A reparse point can associate any directory within an NTFS volume with the root directory of any volume; this directory is called a mounting directory. NTFS redirects all access to the mounting directory to the mounted volume.[268]

A reparse point can be used to create a **directory junction**—a directory referring to another directory, similar to a symbolic directory link in Linux. The reparse point specifies the pathname of the directory to which the directory junction refers. This is similar to mounting volumes, except that both directories must be within the same volume. The referring directory must be empty; a user must remove the directory junction before inserting files or folders into the referring directory.[269]

21.9 Input/Output Management

Managing input/output (I/O) in Windows XP involves many operating system components (Fig. 21.12). User-mode processes interact with an environment subsystem (such as the Win32 subsystem) and not directly with kernel-mode components. The environment subsystems pass I/O requests to the **I/O manager**, which interacts with device drivers to handle such requests. Often, several device drivers, organized into a driver stack, cooperate to fulfill an I/O request.[270] The **Plug and Play (PnP) manager** dynamically recognizes when new devices are added to the system (as long as these devices support PnP) and allocates and deallocates resources, such as I/O ports or DMA channels, to them. Most recently developed devices support PnP. The **power manager** administers the operating system's power management policy. The power policy determines whether to power down devices to conserve energy or keep them fully powered for high responsiveness.[271] We describe the PnP manager and power manager in more detail later in this section. First, we describe how these components and device drivers cooperate to manage I/O in Windows XP.

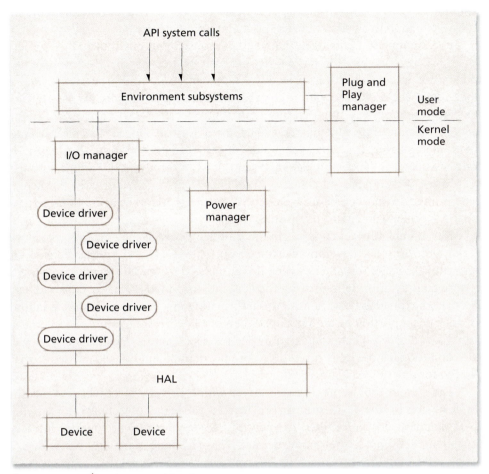

Figure 21.12 | Windows XP I/O support components.

21.9.1 Device Drivers

Windows XP stores information about each device in one or more **device objects**. A device object stores device-specific information (e.g., the type of device and the current I/O request being processed) and is used for processing the device's I/O requests. Often, a particular device has several device objects associated with it, because several drivers, organized into a **driver stack**, handle I/O requests for that device. Each driver creates a device object for that device.[272]

The driver stack consists of several drivers that perform different tasks for I/O management. A **low-level driver**—a driver that interacts most closely with the HAL—controls a peripheral device and does not depend on any lower-level drivers; a bus driver is a low-level driver. A **high-level driver** abstracts hardware specifics and passes I/O requests to low-level drivers. An NTFS driver is a high-level driver that abstracts how data is stored on disk. An **intermediate driver** can be interposed between high- and low-level drivers to filter or process I/O requests and export an interface for a specific device; a class driver (i.e., a driver that implements services common to a class of devices) is an intermediate driver.

For example, a driver stack that handles mouse input might include a PCI bus driver, a USB controller driver, a USB hub driver, a driver that performs mouse acceleration and a driver that provides the user interface and processes incoming mouse data. The drivers cooperate to process mouse input. The drivers for the various hardware buses (i.e., the PCI bus, USB controller and USB hub) process interrupts and handle PnP and power management for the mouse; the intermediate driver manipulates the data, providing mouse acceleration; and the high-level driver translates the incoming data and sends it to a user-level GUI application.[273]

These driver types all refer to **kernel-mode drivers**. Other drivers, such as some printer drivers, can be **user-mode drivers**; these drivers execute in user space and are specific to an environment subsystem.[274]

Kernel-mode drivers operate in the thread context of the currently executing thread, implying that developers cannot assume that a driver will execute in the context of the same thread each time driver code executes. However, drivers need to store context information such as device state information, driver data and handles to kernel objects. Drivers store this information in a **device extension**. Windows XP allocates a portion of the nonpaged memory for drivers to store device extensions. Each device object points to a device extension, and a driver uses the device extension for each device it serves to store information and objects needed to process I/O for that device.[275]

The system represents a device driver with a **driver object** which stores the device objects for the devices the driver services. The driver object also stores pointers to standard driver routines.[276] Many of the standard driver routines must be implemented by all kernel-mode drivers. These include functions for adding a device, unloading the driver and certain routines for processing I/O requests (such as read and write). Other standard driver routines are implemented only by certain classes of drivers. For example, only low-level drivers need to implement the standard routine for handling interrupts. In this way, all drivers expose a uniform interface to the system by implementing a subset of the standard driver routines.[277]

Plug and Play (PnP)

Plug and Play (PnP), introduced in Section 2.4.4, describes the ability of a system to dynamically add or remove hardware components and redistribute resources (e.g., I/O ports or DMA channels) appropriately. A combination of hardware and software support enables this functionality. Hardware support involves recognizing when a user adds or removes components from a system and easily identifying these components. Both the operating system and third-party drivers must cooperate to provide software support for PnP. Windows XP support for PnP involves utilizing information provided by hardware devices, the ability to dynamically allocate resources to devices and a programming interface for device drivers to interact with the PnP system.[278]

Windows XP implements PnP with the **PnP manager**, which is divided into two components, one in user space and the other in kernel space. The kernel-mode PnP manager configures and manages devices and allocates system resources. The user-mode PnP manager interacts with device setup programs and notifies user-mode processes when some device event has occurred for which the process has registered a listener. The PnP manager automates most device maintenance tasks and adapts to hardware and resource changes dynamically.[279]

Driver manufacturers must adhere to certain guidelines to support PnP for Windows XP. The PnP manager collects information from drivers by sending driver queries. These queries are called **PnP I/O requests**, because they are sent in the form of I/O request packets (IRPs). IRPs are described in Section 21.9.2, Input/Output Processing. PnP drivers must implement functions that respond to these PnP I/O requests. The PnP manager uses information from the requests to allocate resources to hardware devices. PnP drivers must also refrain from searching for hardware or allocating resources, because the PnP manager handles these tasks.[280] Microsoft urges all driver vendors to support PnP, but Windows XP supports non-PnP drivers for legacy compatibility.[281]

Power Management

The **power manager** is the executive component that administers the system's **power policy**.[282] The power policy dictates how the power manager administers system and device power consumption. For example, when the power policy emphasizes conservation, the power manager attempts to shut down devices that are not in use. When the power policy emphasizes performance, the power manager leaves these devices on for quick response times.[283] Drivers that support power management must be able to respond to queries or directives made by the power manager.[284] The power manager queries a driver to determine whether a change in the power state of a device is feasible or will disrupt the device's work. The power manager also can direct a driver to change the power state of a device.[285]

Devices have power states D0, D1, D2 and D3. A device in state D0 is fully powered, and a device in D3 is off.[286] In states D1 and D2, the device is in a sleep (i.e., low-powered) state, and when the device returns to the D0 state, the system will need to reinitialize some of its context. A device in D1 retains more of its context and is in a higher-powered state than a device in D2.[287] In addition to controlling devices' power states, the power manager controls the overall system's power state, which is denoted by values S0–S5. State S0 is the fully powered working state, and S5 denotes that the computer is off. States S1–S4 represent states in which the computer is on, but in a sleeping state; a system in S1 is closest to fully powered, and in S4 is closest to off.[288]

Windows Driver Model (WDM)

Microsoft has defined a standard driver model—the **Windows Driver Model (WDM)**—to promote source-code compatibility across all Windows platforms.

Windows XP supports non-WDM drivers to maintain compatibility with legacy drivers, but Microsoft recommends that all new drivers be WDM drivers. This section briefly outlines the WDM guidelines.[289]

WDM defines three types of device drivers. **Bus drivers** interface with a hardware bus, such as a SCSI or PCI bus, provide some generic functions for the devices on the bus, enumerate these devices and handle PnP I/O requests. Each bus must have a bus driver, and Microsoft provides bus drivers for most buses.[290]

Filter drivers are optional and serve a variety of purposes. They can modify the behavior of hardware (e.g., provide mouse acceleration or enable a joystick to emulate a mouse) or add additional features to a device (e.g., implement security checks or merge audio data from two different applications for simultaneous playback). Additionally, filter drivers can sort I/O requests among several devices. For example, a filter driver might serve multiple storage devices and sort read and write requests between the devices. Filter drivers can be placed in numerous locations in the device stack—a filter driver that modifies hardware behavior is placed near the bus driver, whereas one that provides some high-level feature is placed near the user interface.[291]

A **function driver** implements a device's main function. A device's function driver does most of the I/O processing and provides the device's interface. Windows XP groups devices that perform similar functions into a device class (such as the printer device class).[292] A function driver can be implemented as a **class/miniclass driver pair**.[293] A class driver provides generic processing for a particular device class (e.g., a printer); a miniclass driver provides the functionality specific to a particular device (e.g., a particular printer model). Typically, Microsoft provides class drivers, and software vendors provide the miniclass drivers.[294]

All WDM drivers must be designed as either a bus driver, filter driver or function driver.[295] Additionally, WDM drivers must support PnP, power management and **Windows Management Instrumentation (WMI)**.[296] Drivers that support WMI provide users with measurement and instrumentation data. This data includes configuration data, diagnostic data and custom data. Also, WMI drivers permit user applications to register for WMI driver-defined events. The main purpose of WMI is to provide hardware and system information to user processes and allow user processes greater control in configuring devices.[297]

21.9.2 Input/Output Processing

Windows XP describes I/O requests with **I/O request packets (IRPs)**. IRPs contain all the information necessary to process an I/O request. An IRP (Fig. 21.13) consists of a header block and an I/O stack. Most header block information does not change during request processing. The header block records such information as the requestor's mode (either kernel or user), flags (e.g., whether to use caching) and information about the requestor's data buffer.[298] The header block also contains the **I/O status block**, which indicates whether an I/O request completed successfully or, if not, the request's error code.[299]

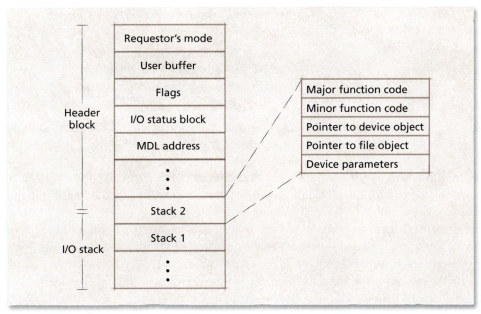

Figure 21.13 | I/O request packet (IRP).

The I/O stack portion of an IRP contains at least one different stack location for each driver in the device stack of the target device. Each I/O stack location contains specific information that each driver needs in order to process the IRP, in particular the IRP's **major function code** and the **minor function code**. Figure 21.14 lists several major function codes. The major function code specifies the general IRP function such as read (IRP_MJ_READ) or write (IRP_MJ_WRITE). In some cases, it designates a class of IRPs, such as IRP_MJ_PNP, which specifies that the IRP is a PnP

Major function code	Typical reason to send an IRP with this major function code
IRP_MJ_READ	User-mode process requests to read from a file.
IRP_MJ_WRITE	User-mode process requests to write to a file.
IRP_MJ_CREATE	User-mode process requests a handle to a file object.
IRP_MJ_CLOSE	All handles to a file object have been released and all outstanding I/O requests have been completed.
IRP_MJ_POWER	Power manager queries a driver or directs a driver to change the power state of a device.

Figure 21.14 | Major function code examples in Windows XP. (Part 1 of 2.)

Major function code	Typical reason to send an IRP with this major function code
IRP_MJ_PNP	PnP manager queries a driver, allocates resources to a device or directs a driver to perform some operation.
IRP_MJ_DEVICE_CONTROL	User-mode process calls a device I/O control function to retrieve information about a device or direct a device to perform some operation (e.g., format a disk).

Figure 21.14 | *Major function code examples in Windows XP. (Part 2 of 2.)*

I/O request. The minor function code then indicates the particular I/O function to perform.[300] For example, the PnP manager starts a device by specifying the major function code IRP_MJ_PNP and the minor function code IRP_MN_START_DEVICE. Each I/O stack location contains several other fields, including a pointer to the target device object and some driver-specific parameters.[301] Each driver accesses one location in the stack, and before passing the IRP to the next driver, the currently executing driver initializes the stack location of the next driver by assigning each field in the stack a value.[302]

Processing an I/O Request

The I/O manager and device drivers cooperate to fulfill an I/O request. Figure 21.15 describes the path an IRP travels as the system fulfills a read I/O request from a user-mode process. First, a thread passes the I/O request to the thread's associated environment subsystem (1). The environment subsystem passes this request to the I/O manager (2). The I/O manager interprets the request and builds an IRP (3). Each driver in the stack accesses its I/O stack location, processes the IRP, initializes the stack location for the next driver and passes the IRP to the next driver in the stack (4 and 5). Additionally, a high-level or intermediate driver can divide a single I/O request into smaller requests by creating more IRPs. For example, in the case of a read to a RAID subsystem, the file system driver might construct several IRPs, enabling different parts of the data transfer to proceed in parallel.[303] Any driver, except a low-level driver, can register an **I/O completion routine** with the I/O manager. Low-level drivers complete the I/O request and, therefore, do not need I/O completion routines. When processing of an IRP completes, the I/O manager proceeds up the stack, calling all registered I/O completion. A driver can specify that its completion routine be invoked if an IRP completes successfully, produces an error and/or is canceled. An I/O completion routine can be used to retry an IRP that fails.[304] Also, drivers that create new IRPs are responsible for disposing of them when processing completes; they accomplish task by using an I/O completion routine.[305]

Once the IRP reaches the lowest-level driver, this driver checks that the input parameters are valid, then notifies the I/O manager that an IRP is pending for a particular device (6). The I/O manager determines whether the target device is available.[306] If it is, the I/O manager calls the driver routine that handles the I/O operation (7). The driver routine cooperates with the HAL to direct the device to

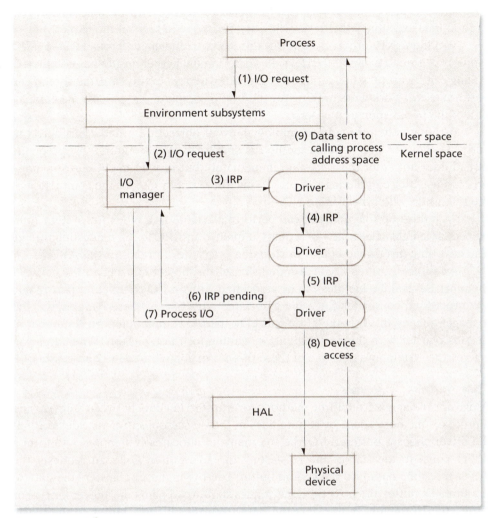

Figure 21.15 | *Servicing an IRP.*

perform an action on behalf of the requesting thread (8). Finally, the data is sent to the calling process's address space (9). The different methods for transferring I/O are described later in this section. If the device is not available, the I/O manager queues the IRP for later processing.[307] Section 21.9.3, Interrupt Handling, describes how Windows XP completes I/O processing.

Synchronous and Asynchronous I/O

Windows XP supports both synchronous and asynchronous I/O requests. Microsoft uses the term **overlapped I/O** to mean asynchronous I/O. If a thread issues a synchronous I/O request, the thread enters its *wait* state. Once the device services the I/O request, the thread enters its *ready* state, and when it obtains the processor, it completes I/O processing. However, a thread that issues an asynchronous I/O request can continue executing other tasks while the target device services the request.[308]

Windows XP provides several options for managing asynchronous I/O requests. A thread can poll the device to determine whether an I/O has completed. Polling can be useful when a thread is executing a loop. In this case, the thread can perform useful work while waiting for the I/O to complete and process the completion of the I/O as soon as it occurs.

Alternatively, a thread can employ an event object and wait for this object to enter its *signaled* state.[309] This method is similar to synchronous I/O, except the thread does not enter the *wait* state immediately, but instead might perform some processing. After completing this processing, the thread waits for the completion of the I/O just as with synchronous I/O.

As a third option, a thread can perform **alertable I/O**. When the system completes servicing an alertable I/O request, it queues an APC to the requesting thread. The next time this thread enters an alertable *wait* state, it processes this APC.[310]

Additionally, threads can accomplish asynchronous I/O using an **I/O completion port**. Several file handles can be associated with an I/O completion port. When I/O processing completes for a file associated with one of these handles, the I/O manager queues an I/O completion packet to the I/O completion port. A number of threads register with the port and block, waiting for these packets. When a packet arrives, the system awakens one of these threads to complete the I/O processing.[311]

Data Transfer Techniques

A driver can choose from three methods for transferring data between a device and a process's memory space by setting flags in the device object for that device.[312] If the driver chooses buffered I/O, the I/O manager allocates system pages to form a buffer equal to the size of the requesting thread's buffer. On read requests, the driver reads the data into the system buffer. The I/O manager transfers the data to the thread's buffer the next time the requesting thread gains the processor.[313] For writes, the I/O manager transfers the data from the thread's buffer to the newly allocated system buffer before passing the IRP to the top-level driver.[314] The system buffer does not act as a cache; it is reclaimed after I/O processing completes.

Buffered I/O is useful for small transfers, such as mouse and keyboard input, because the system does not need to lock physical memory pages due to the fact that the system transfers the data first between the device and nonpaged pool. When the VMM locks a memory page, the page cannot be paged out of memory. However, for large transfers (i.e., more than one memory page), the overhead of first copying the data into the system buffer and then making a second copy to the process buffer reduces I/O performance. Also, because system memory becomes fragmented as the system executes, the buffer for a large transfer likely will not be contiguous, further degrading performance.[315]

As an alternative, drivers can employ **direct I/O**, with which the device transfers data directly to the process's buffer. Before passing the IRP to the first driver, the I/O manager creates a **memory descriptor list (MDL)**, which maps the applicable range of the requesting process's virtual addresses to physical memory addresses. The VMM then locks the physical pages listed in the MDL and constructs the IRP with a pointer to the MDL. Once the device completes transferring data (using the MDL to access the process's buffer), the I/O manager unlocks the memory pages.[316]

Drivers can choose not to use buffered I/O or direct I/O and, instead, use a technique called **neither I/O**. In this technique, the I/O manager passes IRPs that describe the data's destination (for a read) or origin (for a write) using the virtual addresses of the calling thread. Because a driver performing neither I/O needs access to the calling thread's virtual address space, the driver must execute in the calling thread's context. For each IRP, the driver can decide to set up a buffered I/O transfer by creating the two buffers and passing a buffered I/O IRP to the next lowest driver (recall that the I/O manager handles this when the buffered I/O flag is set). The driver can also choose to create an MDL and set up a direct I/O IRP. Alternatively, the driver can perform all the necessary transfer operations in the context of the calling thread. In any of these cases, the driver must handle all exceptions that might occur and ensure that the calling thread has sufficient access rights. The I/O manager handles these issues when direct I/O or buffered I/O is used.[317]

Because a driver employing neither I/O must execute in the context of the calling thread, only high-level drivers can use neither I/O. High-level drivers can guarantee that they will be entered in the context of the calling thread; on the other hand, an intermediate or low-level driver is called by another driver and cannot assume that the other driver will execute in the context of the calling thread.[318] All drivers in a device stack must use the same transfer technique for that device—otherwise the transfer would fail due to device drivers' executing conflicting operations—except that the highest-level driver can use neither I/O instead. [319]

21.9.3 Interrupt Handling

Once a device completes processing an I/O request, it notifies the system with an interrupt. The interrupt handler calls the **interrupt service routine (ISR)** associated with that device's interrupt.[320] An ISR is a standard driver routine used to process interrupts. It returns false if the device with which it is associated is not interrupting; this can occur because more than one device can interrupt at the same DIRQL. If the associated device is interrupting, the ISR processes the interrupt and returns true.[321] When a device that generates interrupts is installed on a Windows XP system, a driver for that device must register an ISR with the I/O manager. Typically, low-level drivers are responsible for providing ISRs for the devices they serve.

When a driver registers an ISR, the system creates an **interrupt object**.[322] An interrupt object stores interrupt-related information, such as the specific DIRQL at which the interrupt executes, the interrupt vector of the interrupt and the address of the ISR.[323] The I/O manager uses the interrupt object to associate an interrupt vector in the kernel's **Interrupt Dispatch Table (IDT)** with the ISR. The IDT maps hardware interrupts to interrupt vectors.[324]

When an interrupt occurs, the kernel maps a hardware-specific interrupt request into an entry in its IDT to access the correct interrupt vector.[325] Often, there are more devices than entries in the IDT, so the processor must determine which ISR to use. It does this by executing, in succession, each ISR associated with the applicable vector. When an ISR returns false, the processor calls the next ISR.[326]

An ISR for a Windows XP system should execute as quickly as possible, then queue a DPC to finish processing the interrupt. While a processor is executing an ISR, it executes at the device's DIRQL. This masks interrupts from devices with lower DIRQLs. Quickly returning from an ISR, therefore, increases a system's responsiveness to all device interrupts. Also, executing at a DIRQL restricts the support routines that can be called (because some of these routines must run at some IRQL below DIRQL). Additionally, executing an ISR can prevent other processors from executing the ISR—and some other pieces of the driver's code—because the kernel interrupt handler holds the driver's spin lock while processing the ISR. Therefore, an ISR should determine if the device with which it is associated is interrupting. If it is not interrupting, the ISR should return false immediately; otherwise, it should clear the interrupt, gather the requisite information for interrupt processing, queue a DPC with this information and return true. The driver can use the device extension to store the information needed for the DPC. Typically, the DPC will be processed the next time the IRQL drops below DPC/dispatch level.[327]

21.9.4 File Cache Management

Not all I/O operations require the process outlined in the previous sections. When requested data resides in the system's file cache, Windows XP can fulfill an I/O request without a costly device access and without executing device driver code. The **cache manager** is the executive component that manages Windows XP's file cache, which consists of main memory that caches file data.[328] Windows XP does not implement separate caches for each mounted file system, but instead maintains a single systemwide cache.[329]

Windows XP does not reserve a specific portion of RAM to act as the file cache, but instead allows the file cache to grow or shrink dynamically, depending on system needs. If the system is running many I/O-intensive routines, the file cache grows to facilitate fast data transfer. If the system is executing large programs that consume lots of system memory, the file cache shrinks to reduce page faults. Furthermore, the cache manager never knows how much cached data currently resides in physical memory. This is because the cache manager caches by mapping files into the system's virtual address space, rather than managing the cache from physical memory. The memory manager is responsible for paging the data in these views into or out of physical memory. This caching method allows easy integration of Windows XP's two data access methods: memory-mapped files (see Section 13.9, Data Access Techniques) and traditional read/write access. The same file can be accessed via both methods (i.e., as a memory-mapped file through the memory manager and as a traditional file through the file system), because the cache manager maps file data into virtual memory. The cache manager bridges the gap between these two file representations, ensuring consistency in file data between the two views.[330]

　　When a file is read from a disk, its contents are stored in the system cache, which is a portion of the system address space. Then, a user-mode process copies the data from the cache into its own address space. A thread can set a flag that overrides this default behavior; in this case, the transfer occurs directly between the disk and the process's address space. Similarly, instead of writing directly to the disk, a process writes new data to the cache entry (unless a flag is set).[331] Fulfilling an I/O request without generating an IRP or accessing a device is called **fast I/O**.[332]

　　Dirty cache entries can be written to disk in several ways. The memory manager might need to page a dirty cache page out of memory to make room for another memory page. When this occurs, the contents of the cache page are queued to be written to disk. If a dirty cache page is not paged out of memory by the memory manager, the cache manager must flush the page back to disk. It accomplishes this by using a lazy writer thread. The lazy writer is responsible for, once per second, choosing one-eighth of the dirty pages to be flushed to disk. It constantly reevaluates how often dirty pages are being created and adjusts the amount of pages it queues to be flushed accordingly. The lazy writer chooses pages based on how long a page has been dirty and the last time the data on that page was accessed for a read operation. Additionally, threads can force a specific file to be flushed. Threads can also specify write-through caching (see Section 12.8, Caching and Buffering) by setting a flag when creating the file object.[333]

21.10 *Interprocess Communication*

Windows XP provides many interprocess communication (IPC) mechanisms to allow processes to exchange data and cooperate to complete tasks. It implements many traditional UNIX IPC mechanisms, such as pipes, message queues (called mailslots by Windows XP)[334] and shared memory. In addition to these "data-oriented" IPCs, Windows XP allows processes to communicate through "procedure-oriented" or "object-oriented" techniques, using such tools as remote procedure calls or Microsoft's Component Object Model. Users on a Windows XP system also can initiate IPC with familiar features such as the clipboard and drag-and-drop capabilities. In each of Windows XP's IPC mechanisms, a server process makes some communication object available. A client process can contact the server process via this communication object to place a request. The request might be for the server to execute a function or to return data or objects. The remainder of this section describes these IPC tools. Section 21.11, Networking, introduces techniques and tools, such as sockets, that processes can use to communicate across a network.

21.10.1 *Pipes*

Windows XP provides pipes for direct communication between two processes.[335] If communicating processes have access to the same memory bank, pipes use shared memory. Thread can manipulate pipes using standard file system routines (e.g., read, write and open). A process that creates the pipe is called the **pipe server**; processes that connect to a pipe are referred to as **pipe clients**.[336] Each pipe client communicates solely with the pipe server (i.e., not with other clients using the same pipe) because the pipe server uses a unique instance of the pipe for each client process.[337] The pipe server specifies a mode (read, write or duplex) when the pipe is created. In read mode, the pipe server receives data from clients; in write mode, it sends data to pipe clients; in duplex mode, it can both send and receive data via the pipe.[338] Windows XP provides two types of pipes: **anonymous pipes** and **named pipes**.

Anonymous Pipes

Anonymous pipes are used for unidirectional communication (i.e., duplex mode is not allowed) and can be used only among local processes. Local processes are processes that can communicate with each other without sending messages over a network.[339] A process that creates an anonymous pipe receives both a read handle and a write handle for the pipe. A process can read from the pipe by passing the read handle as an argument in a read function call, and a process can write to the pipe by passing the write handle as an argument in a write function call (for more information on handles see Section 21.5.2, Object Manager). To communicate with another process, the pipe server must pass one of these handles to another process. Typically, this is accomplished through inheritance (i.e., the parent process allows the child process to inherit one of the pipe handles). Alternatively, the pipe server can send a handle for the pipe to another, unrelated process via some IPC mechanism.[340]

Anonymous pipes support only synchronous communication. When a thread attempts to read from the pipe, it waits until the requested amount of data has been read from the pipe. If there is no data in the pipe, the thread waits until the writing process places the data in the pipe. Similarly, if a thread attempts to write to a pipe containing a full buffer (the buffer size is specified at creation time), it waits until the reading process removes enough data from the pipe to make room for the new data. A thread that is waiting to read data via a pipe can stop waiting if all write handles to the pipe are closed or if some error occurs. Similarly, a thread waiting to write data to a pipe can stop waiting if all read handles to the pipe are closed or if some error occurs.[341]

Named Pipes

Named pipes support several features absent in anonymous pipes. Named pipes can be bidirectional, be shared between remote processes[342] and support asynchronous communication. However, named pipes introduce additional overhead. When the pipe server creates a pipe, the pipe server specifies its mode, its name and the maximum number of instances of the pipe. A pipe client can obtain a handle for the pipe by specifying the pipe's name when attempting to connect to the pipe. If the number of pipe instances is less than the maximum, the client process connects to a new instance of the pipe. If there are no available instances, the pipe client can wait for an instance to become available. [343]

Named pipes permit two pipe writing formats. The system can transmit data either as a stream of bytes or as a series of messages. All instances of a pipe must use the same write format (recall that a single pipe server can communicate with multiple clients by creating a unique instance of the pipe for each client). Although sending data as a series of bytes is faster, messages are simpler for the receiver to process because they package related data. [344]

Windows XP permits a process to enable **write-through mode**. When the write-through flag is set, write operations do not complete until the data reaches the receiving process's buffer. In the default mode, once the data enters the writer's buffer, the write method returns. Write-through mode increases fault tolerance and permits greater synchronization between communicating processes because the sender knows whether a message successfully reaches its destination. However, write-through mode degrades performance, because the writing process must wait for the data to be transferred across a network from the writer's end of the pipe to the reader's end.[345] The system always performs writes using the write-through method when a process is using messages to ensure that each message remains a discrete unit.[346]

Asynchronous I/O capability increases named pipes' flexibility. Threads can accomplish asynchronous communication via named pipes in several ways. A thread can use an event object to perform an asynchronous read or write request. In this case, when the function completes, the event object enters its *signaled* state (see Section 21.6.3, Thread Synchronization). The thread can continue processing, then wait for one or more of these event objects to enter *signaled* states to complete a communication request. Alternatively, a thread can specify an I/O completion routine. The system queues this routine as an APC when the function completes, and the thread executes the routine the next time the thread enters an alertable *wait* state.[347] In addition, a pipe can be associated with an I/O completion port because pipes are manipulated like files.

21.10.2 Mailslots

Windows XP provides **mailslots** for unidirectional communication between a server and clients.[348] The process that creates the mailslot is the **mailslot server**, whereas the processes that send messages to the mailslot are **mailslot clients**. Mailslots act as repositories for messages sent by mailslot clients to a mailslot server. Mailslot clients can send messages to either local or remote mailslots; in either case, there is no confirmation of receipt. Windows XP implements mailslots as files in the sense that a mailslot resides in memory and can be manipulated with standard file functions (e.g., read, write and open). Mailslots are temporary files (the Windows XP documentation refers to them as "pseudofiles"); the object manager deletes a mailslot when no process holds a handle to it.[349]

Mailslot messages can be transmitted in two forms. Small messages are sent as datagrams, which are discussed in Section 16.6.2, User Datagram Protocol (UDP). Datagram messages can be broadcast to several mailslots within a particular **domain**. A domain is a set of computers that share common resources such as printers.[350, 351] Larger messages are sent via a Server Message Block (SMB) connection.[352] SMB is a network file sharing protocol used in Windows operating systems.[353] Both SMB and datagram messages can be sent from a mailslot client to a mailslot server by specifying the server name in a write operation.[354]

21.10.3 Shared Memory

Processes can communicate by mapping the same file to their respective address spaces, a technique known as shared memory. The Windows XP documentation calls this mechanism **file mapping**. A process can create a **file mapping object** that maps any file, including a pagefile, to memory. The process passes a handle for the file mapping object to other processes, either by name or through inheritance. The process communicates by writing data into these shared memory regions, which other processes can access.

A process can use the handle to create a **file view** that maps all or part of the file to the process's virtual address space. A process may own multiple file views of the same file. This allows a process to access the beginning and end of a large file without mapping all of the file to memory, which would reduce its available virtual address space. Because identical file views map to the same memory frames, all processes see a consistent view of a memory-mapped file. If one process writes to its file view, the change will be reflected in all file views of that portion of the file.[355, 356]

File mapping objects accelerate data access. The system maps file views independently to each process's virtual address space, but the data is located in the same frames in main memory. This minimizes the necessity of reading data from the disk. The VMM treats file mappings the same way it treats copy-on-write pages (see Section 21.7.1, Memory Organization). Because the VMM has been optimized to deal with paging, file access is efficient. Due to its efficient implementation, file mapping has uses beyond communication. Processes can use file mapping to perform random and sequential I/O quickly. File mapping is also helpful for databases that need to overwrite small sections of large files.[357, 358]

File mapping objects do not provide synchronization mechanisms to protect the files they map. Two processes can overwrite the same portion of the same file simultaneously. To prevent race conditions, processes must use synchronization mechanisms, such as mutexes and semaphores, that are provided by Windows XP and described in Section 21.6.3, Thread Synchronization.[359]

21.10.4 Local and Remote Procedure Calls

Many IPC mechanisms facilitate data exchange between two processes. **Local procedure calls (LPCs)** and remote procedure calls (RPCs), which we described in Section 17.3.2, provide a more procedural form of IPC and largely hide the underlying network programming. LPCs and RPCs allow a process to communicate with another process by calling functions executed by the other process.[360] The process that calls the function is the client process, and the one that executes the function is the server process.

When client and server processes reside on the same physical machine, processes execute LPCs; when they reside on separate machines, processes execute RPCs.[361] A designer employs LPCs and RPCs the same as procedure calls within a process. However, in some cases, the programmer takes a few extra steps to establish a connection (these are described shortly).

Note that Microsoft does not publicly document the LPC interface, and user-mode threads cannot expose LPCs. The system reserves LPCs for use by the Windows XP kernel. For example, when a user thread calls a function in an environment subsystem's API, the kernel might convert the call into an LPC. Also, Windows XP converts RPCs between two processes on the same machine (called **local remote procedure calls** or **LRPCs**) into LPCs, because LPCs are more efficient.[362] LPCs have less overhead than RPCs, because all data transfers using LPCs involve direct memory copying rather than network transport.[363] Although the name "local remote procedure call" might sound like an oxymoron, it is simply a descriptive name for a procedure call made with the RPC interface between local processes.

Figure 21.16 describes the path through which data travels during an LPC or RPC call. In both an RPC and an LPC, the client process calls a procedure that maps to a stub (1). This stub marshals the necessary function arguments (i.e., gathers the function arguments into a message to send to the server) and converts them to **Network Data Representation (NDR)**, which is a standard network data format, described in The Open Group's Distributed Computing Environment (DCE) standard (2).[364, 365] Next, the stub calls the appropriate functions from a runtime library to send the request to the server process. The request traverses the network (in the case of an RPC) to reach the server-side runtime library (3), which passes the request to

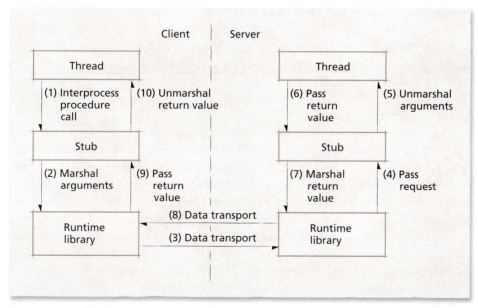

Figure 21.16 | Flow of an LPC or RPC call.

the server stub (4). The server stub unmarshals the data (i.e., converts the client's message into a call to the intended procedure) for the server function (5). The server process executes the requested function and sends any return values to the client via the reverse path (6 through 10).[366] Developers can employ RPCs using many different transport and network protocols such as TCP/IP and Novell Netware's Internetworking Packet eXchange/Sequenced Packet eXchange (IPX/SPX).[367] Both client processes and server processes can execute RPCs either synchronously or asynchronously, and the communicating processes need not use the same method.[368]

Client and Server Communication in an RPC

To expose a procedure as an RPC, the server process must create an **Interface Definition Language (IDL) file**. This file specifies the interfaces that the RPC server presents to other processes.[369] The developer writes the interface in **Microsoft IDL (MIDL)**, which is Microsoft's extension of IDL—The Open Group's Distributed Computing Environment (DCE) standard for RPC interoperability.[370] The IDL file consists of a header and an interface body. The header describes information global to all interfaces defined in the body such as the **universally unique identifier (UUID)** for the interface and an RPC version number.[371] The body contains all variable and function prototype declarations. The MIDL compiler builds the client and server stubs from the IDL file.[372] The server and client also can create **application configuration files (ACFs)**, which specify platform-specific attributes, such as the manner in which data should be marshalled or unmarshalled.[373]

The physical communication in an RPC is accomplished through an endpoint that specifies the network-specific address of the server process and is typically a hardware port or named pipe. The server creates an endpoint before exposing the RPC to other processes.[374] Client-side runtime library functions are responsible for establishing a **binding** to this endpoint, so that a client can send a request to the server. A binding is a connection between the client and the server. To create a binding, the client process must obtain a **binding handle**, which is a data structure that stores the connection information.[375] The binding handle stores such information as the name of the server, address of the endpoint and the **protocol sequence**.[376] The protocol sequence specifies the RPC protocol (e.g., connection-oriented, LRPC), the transport protocol (e.g., TCP) and the network protocol (e.g., IP).[377]

Windows XP supports three types of binding handles: **automatic**, **implicit** and **explicit handles**. Using an automatic handle, the client process calls the remote function, and the stub manages all the communication tasks. Implicit handles permit the client process to specify the particular server to use with an RPC, but once the client process passes the handle to the runtime library functions, it no longer needs to manage the handle. With explicit handles, the client process must specify the binding information as well as create and manage the handle.[378] This extra control permits client processes using explicit handles to connect to more than one server process and simultaneously execute multiple RPCs.[379]

Communication via an LPC is similar to an RPC, although some steps are omitted. The server must still create an IDL file, which is compiled by a MIDL compiler. The client process must include the client-side runtime library with the file that calls the LPC. The stub handles the communication, and the client and server processes communicate over a port for procedure calls that involve small data transfers. Procedure calls in which processes transfer a large amount of data must use shared memory. In this case, the sender and receiver place message data into a section of shared memory.[380]

21.10.5 Component Object Model (COM)

Microsoft's **Component Object Model (COM)** provides a software architecture allowing interoperability between diverse software components. In the COM architecture, the relative location of two communicating components is transparent to the programmer and can be in process, cross process or cross network. COM is not a programming language, but a standard designed to promote interoperability between components written in different programming languages. COM also is implemented on some flavors of UNIX and Apple Macintosh operating systems. Developers use COM to facilitate cooperation and communication between separate components in large applications.[381]

COM objects (a COM object is the same as a COM component) interact indirectly and exclusively through interfaces.[382] A COM interface, which is written in MIDL, is similar to a Java interface; it contains function prototypes that describe function arguments and return values, but does not include the actual implementation of the functions. As with Java, a COM object must implement all of the methods described in the interface and can implement other methods as well.[383] Once created, a COM interface is immutable (i.e., it cannot change). A COM object can have more than one interface; developers augment COM objects by adding a new interface to the object. This permits clients dependent on the old features of a COM object to continue functioning smoothly when the object is upgraded. Each interface and object class possesses a **globally unique ID (GUID)**, which is a 128-bit integer that is, for all practical purposes, guaranteed to be unique in the world. **Interface IDs (IIDs)** are GUIDs for interfaces, and **class IDs (CLSIDs)** are GUIDs for object classes. Clients refer to interfaces using the IID, and because the interface is immutable and the IID is globally unique, the client is guaranteed to access the same interface each time.[384]

COM promotes interoperability between components written in diverse languages by specifying a binary standard (i.e., a standard representation of the object after it has been translated into machine code) for calling functions. Specifically, COM defines a standard format for storing pointers to functions and a standard method for accessing the functions using these pointers.[385] Windows XP, and other operating systems with COM support, provide APIs for allocating and deallocating memory using this standard. The COM library in Windows XP provides a rich variety of support functions that hide most of the COM implementations.[386]

COM servers can register their objects with the Windows XP registry. Clients can query the registry using the COM object's CLSID to obtain a pointer to the

COM object.[387] A client can also obtain a pointer to a COM object's interface from another COM object or by creating the object. A client can use a pointer to any interface for a COM object to find a pointer to any other interface that the COM object exposes.[388]

Once the client obtains a pointer to the desired interface, the client can execute a function call to any procedure exposed by this interface (assuming the client has appropriate access rights). For in-process procedure calls, COM executes the function directly, adding essentially no overhead. For cross-process procedure calls in which both processes reside on the same computer, COM uses LRPCs (see Section 21.10.4, Local and Remote Procedure Calls), and Distributed COM (DCOM) supports cross-network function calls.[389] COM marshals and unmarshals all data, creates the stubs and proxies (proxies are client-side stubs) and transports the data (via direct execution, LRPCs or DCOM).[390]

COM supports several threading models a process can employ to maintain its COM objects. In the **apartment model**, only one thread acts as a server for each COM object. In the **free thread model**, many threads can act as the server for a single COM object (each thread operates on one or more instances of the object). A process can also use the **mixed model** in which some of its COM objects reside in single apartments and others can be accessed by free threads. In an apartment model, COM provides synchronization by placing function calls in the thread's window message queue. COM objects that can be accessed by free threads must maintain their own synchronization (see Section 21.6.3, Thread Synchronization, for information on thread synchronization).[391]

Microsoft has built several technologies on top of COM to further facilitate cooperation in component software design. **COM+** extends COM to handle advanced resource management tasks; e.g., it provides support for transaction processing and uses thread pools and object pools, which move some of the responsibility for resource management from the component developer to the system.[392] COM+ also adds support for Web services and optimizes COM scalability.[393] Distributed COM (DCOM) provides a transparent extension to basic COM services for cross-network interactions and includes protocols for finding DCOM objects on remote services.[394] Object Linking and Embedding (OLE), discussed in the next section, builds on COM to provide standard interfaces for applications to share data and objects. **ActiveX Controls** are self-registering COM objects (i.e., they insert entries in the registry upon creation). Typically, ActiveX Controls support many of the same embedding interfaces as OLE objects; however, ActiveX Controls do not need to support all of them. This makes ActiveX Controls ideal for embedding in Web pages because they have less overhead.[395]

21.10.6 Drag-and-Drop and Compound Documents

Windows XP provides several techniques that enable users to initiate IPC. A familiar example is permitting users to select text from a Web page, copy this text and paste it into a text editor. Users can also embed one document inside another; e.g., a user could place a picture created in a graphical design program into a word processing document. In both of these cases, the two applications represent different processes that exchange information. Windows XP provides two primary techniques for this type of data transport: the **clipboard** and **Object Linking and Embedding (OLE)**.

The clipboard is a central repository of data, accessible to all processes.[396] A process can add data to the clipboard when the user invokes either the copy or the cut command. The selected data is stored in the clipboard along with the data's format.[397] Windows XP defines several standard data formats, including text, bitmap and wave. Processes can register new clipboard formats, create private clipboard formats and synthesize one or more of the existing formats.[398] Any process can retrieve data from the clipboard when the user invokes the paste command.[399] Conceptually, the clipboard acts as a small area of globally shared memory.

OLE builds on COM technology by defining a standard method for processes to exchange data. All OLE objects implement several standard interfaces that describe how to store and retrieve data for an OLE object, how to access the object and how to manipulate the object. Users can create compound documents—documents with objects from more than one application—either by linking outside objects or embedding them. When a document links an object from another source, it does not maintain the object inside its document container (the document container provides storage for the document's objects and methods for manipulating and viewing these objects). Rather, the document maintains a reference to the original object. The linked object reflects updates made by the server process to the object. Embedding an object places it, along with the interfaces for manipulating the object, inside the client document. The linked or embedded object is a COM component complete with a set of interfaces that the client can use to manipulate the object.[400]

21.11 Networking

Windows XP supports many networking protocols and services. Developers employ networking services to accomplish IPC with remote clients and make services and information available to users. Users exploit networks to retrieve information and access resources available on remote computers. This section investigates various aspects of Windows XP's networking model. We examine network I/O and the driver architecture employed by Windows XP. We consider the network, transport and application protocols supported by Windows XP. Finally, we describe the network services that Windows XP provides, such as the Active Directory and .NET.

21.11.1 Network Input/Output

Windows XP provides a transparent I/O programming interface. In particular, programmers use the same functions regardless of where the data reside. However, the Windows XP system must handle network I/O differently than local I/O.[401]

Figure 21.17 illustrates how Windows XP handles a network I/O request. The client contains a driver called a **redirector** (or **network redirector**).[402] A redirector is a file system driver that directs network I/O requests to appropriate devices over a network.[403] First, the client process passes an I/O request to an environment subsystem (1). The environment subsystem then sends this request to the I/O manager (2), which packages the request as an IRP, specifying the file's location in **Uniform Naming Convention (UNC) format**. UNC format specifies the file's pathname, including on which server and in which directory on that server the file is located. The I/O manager sends the IRP to the **Multiple UNC Provider (MUP)**, which is a file system driver that determines the appropriate redirector to which to send the request (3). Later in this section we see that Windows XP ships with two file sharing protocol, CIFS and WebDAV, which use different redirectors. After the redirector receives the IRP (4), the redirector sends the request over the network to the appropriate server file system driver (5). The server driver determines whether the client has sufficient access rights for the file, then communicates the request to the target device's driver stack via an IRP (6). The server driver receives the result of the I/O request (7). If there is an error processing the request, the server driver informs the client. Otherwise, the server driver passes the data back to the redirector (8), and this data is passed to the client process (9).[404,405]

The **Common Internet File System (CIFS)** is Windows XP's native file sharing protocol. CIFS is used for the application layer of the TCP/IP stack (see Section 16.4,

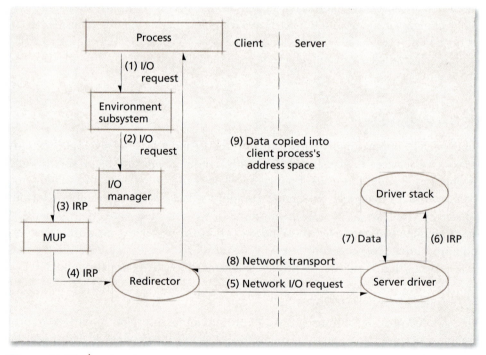

Figure 21.17 | *Handling a network I/O request.*

TCP/IP Protocol Stack). VMS and several varieties of UNIX also support CIFS. Developers often pair CIFS with NetBIOS (discussed later in this section) over TCP/IP for the network and transport layers, but CIFS can use other network and transport protocols as well.[406] CIFS is meant to complement HTTP and replace older file sharing protocols such as FTP.[407] Windows XP also supports other network file sharing protocols such as **Web-based Distributed Authoring and Versioning (WebDAV)**. WebDAV allows users to write data directly to HTTP servers and is designed to support collaborative authoring between groups in remote locations.[408]

To share files using CIFS, the client and server must first establish a connection. Before a client can access a file, the client and server connect, and the server authenticates the client (see Section 19.3, Authentication) by evaluating the username and password sent by the client. The redirectors interact to set up the session and transfer data.[409] CIFS provides several types of **opportunistic locks (oplocks)** to enhance I/O performance. A client uses an oplock to secure exclusive access to a remote file. Without one of these oplocks, a client cannot cache network data locally, because other clients also might be accessing the data. If two clients both cache data locally and write to this data, their caches will not be coherent (see Section 15.5, Multiprocessor Memory Sharing). Therefore, a client obtains an oplock to ensure that it is the only client accessing the data.[410] When a second client attempts to gain access to the locked file (by attempting to open it), the server may break (i.e., invalidate) the first client's oplock. The server allows the client enough time to flush its cache before granting access to the second client.[411]

21.11.2 Network Driver Architecture

Windows XP uses a driver stack to communicate network requests and transmit network data. This driver stack is divided into several layers, which promotes modularity and facilitates support for multiple network protocols. This subsection describes the low-level driver architecture employed in Windows XP.

Microsoft and 3Com developed the **Network Driver Interface Specification (NDIS)**, which specifies a standard interface between lower-level drivers in the network driver stack. NDIS drivers provide the functionality of the link layer and some functionality of the network layer of the TCP/IP protocol stack (see Section 16.4, TCP/IP Protocol Stack).[412] NDIS drivers communicate through functions provided in Windows XP's NDIS library. The NDIS library functions translate one driver's function call into a call to a function exposed by another driver. This standard interface increases the portability of NDIS drivers.[413] NDIS allows the same programming interface (e.g., Windows sockets, see Section 21.11.3, Network Protocols) to establish connections using different network protocols, such as IP and Internet Packet eXchange (IPX).[414]

Figure 21.18 illustrates the architecture that Windows XP employs to process network data. Windows XP divides the network architecture into three layers that map to layers of the TCP/IP protocol stack. The physical network hardware, such as the network interface card (NIC) and the network cables, form the physical layer.

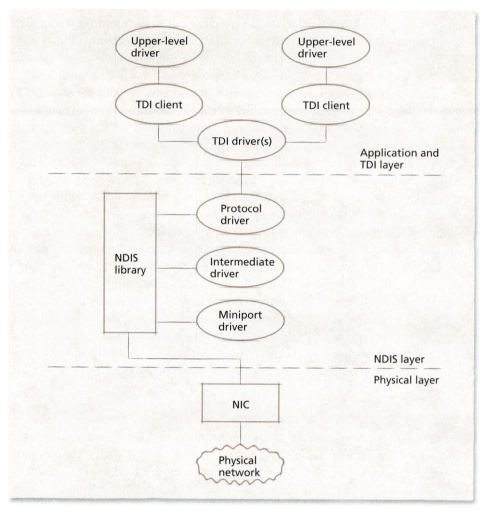

Figure 21.18 | Network driver architecture.

NDIS drivers (described in the following paragraphs) manage the data link and net-work layers. **Transport Driver Interface (TDI) drivers** and TDI clients compose the top layer. The TDI drivers provide a transport interface between NDIS drivers and TDI clients. TDI clients are low-level application drivers and might interact with other application-layer drivers.

Designers implement the NDIS layer with several drivers. An **NDIS miniport driver** manages the NIC and transmits data between the NIC and higher-level driv-ers. The miniport driver interfaces with the drivers above it in the driver stack to transmit outgoing network data to the NIC. An upper-level driver invokes an NDIS function that passes the packet to the miniport driver, and the miniport driver passes the data to the NIC. The miniport driver also processes the NIC's interrupts and passes data that the NIC receives up the driver stack.[415]

NDIS intermediate drivers are optional drivers that reside between a miniport driver and a higher-level driver. Intermediate drivers translate packets between different communication media, filter packets or provide load balancing across several NICs.[416]

NDIS protocol drivers are the highest-level NDIS drivers. Protocol drivers place data into packets and pass these packets to lower-level drivers (such as intermediate drivers or miniport drivers). Protocol drivers provide an interface between the transport drivers and other NDIS drivers and can be used as the lowest layer in the implementation of a transport protocol stack (such as TCP/IP).[417]

The NDIS protocol driver interacts with TDI drivers. A TDI driver exports a network interface to upper-level kernel-mode clients. The redirectors described in the previous subsection are TDI clients. Winsock applications (described in the next subsection) also are TDI clients. TDI drivers implement transport protocols such as UDP and TCP; NDIS protocol drivers often implement the network protocol (e.g., IP). Alternatively, a TDI transport driver can implement both the network and transport protocols. Upper-level kernel-mode drivers send network requests to TDI drivers.[418] These drivers implement the application layer of the TCP/IP protocol stack. The next subsections describe the various protocols and network services available to Windows XP applications.

21.11.3 Network Protocols

Windows XP supports several different protocols for the network, transport and application layers of the TCP/IP stack. Windows XP supports some of these protocols to provide compatibility with popular legacy programs or other network clients.

Network and Transport Protocols

IP is installed by default on Windows XP systems; IP provides routing for packets traversing a network and is the Internet's network protocol. Users can install other network protocols, such as the **Internetwork Packet eXchange (IPX)** protocol, which is used by Novell's Netware.[419] IPX provides services similar to IP; IPX routes packets between different locations in a network, but is designed for LANs.[420] Because the NDIS library supports a standard interface between protocol drivers and NICs, Windows XP can use the same NIC to operate both protocols.[421]

Windows XP also supports several transport protocols. TCP, by far the most commonly used transport protocol, is installed by default. TCP provides a connection-oriented transport; i.e., the participants of a network communication must create a session before communicating.[422] For connectionless transport, Windows XP supports UDP.[423] Users can also install support for **Sequenced Packet eXchange (SPX)**, which offers connection-oriented services for IPX packets. Windows XP provides SPX for interoperability with clients and servers using IPX/SPX protocols, such as Netware.[424]

Before the explosion of interest in the Internet and World Wide Web, the DOS and Windows operating systems supported **NetBIOS Extended User Inter-**

face (NetBEUI) as the native network and transport protocols. **Network Basic Input/Output System (NetBIOS)** is the programming API that supports NetBEUI. NetBEUI is a fairly primitive protocol most applicable for small networks. It has several limitations; for example, it does not provide for network connection routing outside a LAN.[425] Windows XP does not provide support for NetBEUI, although support can be manually installed by a user.

However, **NetBIOS over TCP/IP (NBT)** is still supported by Windows XP to provide compatibility with old applications that employ the NetBIOS API.[426] NetBIOS layered over TCP and IP provides connection-oriented communication using NBT. Alternatively, developers can layer NetBIOS over UDP and IP for connectionless communication using NBT. CIFS is commonly used with NBT as the underlying network and transport protocols. However, in Windows XP, CIFS can execute over TCP/IP without NetBIOS encapsulation.[427]

Application Layer Protocols

At the application layer, Windows XP supports HTTP for Web browsing and CIFS for file and print sharing. For HTTP support, Windows XP provides **WinHTTP** and **WinINet**. WinHTTP supports communication between clients and servers over an HTTP session. It provides SSL security and is integrated with Microsoft Passport (see Section 19.3.4, Single Sign-On). WinHTTP also provides other HTTP services, such as tracing and Kerberos authentication (see Section 19.3.3, Kerberos) and allows synchronous and asynchronous communication.[428] WinINet is an older API that allows applications to interact with the FTP, HTTP and Gopher protocols to access resources over the Internet.[429] WinINET is designed for client applications, whereas WinHTTP is ideal for servers.[430]

CIFS, described in the previous section, is an extension of the **Server Message Block (SMB)** file sharing protocol. SMB is the native file sharing protocol of older Windows operating systems such as Windows NT and Windows 95. SMB uses NetBIOS to communicate with other computers in a virtual LAN. A virtual LAN consists of computers that share the same NetBIOS namespace; the computers can be anywhere in the world. To share files with SMB, two computers on the same virtual LAN set up an SMB session; this includes acknowledging the connection, authenticating the identity of both parties and determining the access rights of the client. CIFS extends SMB, adding a suite of protocols that improve access control and handle announcing and naming of network resources. The familiar My Network Places program included with Windows XP allows users to share files through CIFS.[431]

Winsock

Windows XP supports network communication through sockets. **Windows sockets 2 (Winsock 2)** is an application of BSD sockets (see Section 20.10.3, Sockets) to the Windows environment. Sockets create communication endpoints that a process can use to send and receive data over a network.[432] Sockets are not a transport protocol; consequently, they need not be used at both ends of a communication connection. Developers can layer Winsock 2 on top of any transport and network protocols (e.g,

TCP/IP or IPX/SPX). Users can port code written for UNIX-style sockets to Winsock applications with minimal changes. However, Winsock 2 includes extended functionality that might make porting an application from Windows XP to a UNIX-based operating system implementing Berkeley sockets difficult.[433, 434]

The Winsock specification implements many of the same functions that Berkeley sockets implement to provide compatibility with Berkeley socket applications. As with Berkeley sockets, a Windows socket can be either a stream socket or a datagram socket. Recall that stream sockets provide reliability and packet ordering guarantees.[435] Winsock adds extra functionality to sockets, such as asynchronous I/O, protocol transparency (i.e., developers can choose the network and transport protocols to use with each socket) and quality-of-service (QoS) capabilities.[436] The latter provide to processes information about network conditions and the success or failure of socket communication attempts.[437]

21.11.4 Network Services

Windows XP includes various network services that allow users to share information, resources and objects across a network. **Active Directory** provides directory services for shared objects (e.g., files, printers, services, users, etc.) on a network.[438] Its features include location transparency (i.e., users do not know the address of an object), hierarchical storage of object data, rich and flexible security infrastructure and the ability to locate objects based on different object properties.[439]

Lightweight Directory Access Protocol (LDAP) is a protocol for accessing, searching and modifying Internet directories. An Internet directory contains a listing of computers or resources accessible over the Internet. LDAP employs a client/server model.[440] LDAP clients can access an Active Directory.[441]

Windows XP provides **Remote Access Service (RAS)**, which allows users to remotely connect to a LAN. The user must be connected to the network through a WAN or a VPN. Once the user connects to the LAN through RAS, the user operates as though directly on the LAN.[442]

Support for distributed computing on Windows XP is provided through the Distributed Component Object Model (DCOM) and .NET. DCOM is an extension of COM, which we described in Section 21.10.5, Component Object Model (COM), for processes that share objects across a network. Constructing and accessing DCOM objects is done just as with COM objects, but the underlying communication protocols support network transport. For information on using DCOM for distributed computing see Section 17.3.5, DCOM (Distributed Component Object Model).[443] The next section introduces .NET.

21.11.5 .NET

Microsoft has developed a technology called **.NET**, which supplants DCOM for distributed computing in newer applications. .NET is aimed at transforming computing from an environment where users simply execute applications on a single computer to a fully distributed environment. In this computing model, local applications communicate with remote applications to execute user requests. This contrasts with the traditional view of a computer as merely fulfilling a single user's requests. .NET is a middleware technology, which provides a platform- and language-neutral development environment for components that can easily interoperate.[444, 445]

Web services are the foundation of .NET; they encompass a set of XML-based standards that define how data should be transported between applications over HTTP. Because of XML's large presence in this technology, .NET Web services are often called XML Web services. Developers use Web services to build applications that can be accessed over the Internet. Web service components can be exposed over the Internet and used in many different applications (i.e., Web services are modular). Because XML messages (which are sent and retrieved by Web services) are simply text messages, any application can retrieve and read XML messages. Web services make .NET interoperable and portable between different platforms and languages.[446]

The .NET programming model is called the **.NET framework**. This framework provides an API which expands on the Windows API to include support for Web services. The .NET framework supports many languages, including Visual Basic .NET, Visual C++ .NET and C#. The .NET framework facilitates development of .NET Web services.[447]

.NET server components include Web sites and .NET enterprise servers, such as Windows Server 2003. Many Web service components that home users access are exposed on these two platforms. Although desktop operating systems, such as Windows XP, or server systems running Windows XP can expose Web services, Windows XP systems are mainly consumers (i.e., clients) of .NET services.[448, 449]

21.12 Scalability

To increase Windows XP's flexibility, Microsoft developed several editions. For example, Windows XP Home Edition is tailored for home users, whereas Windows XP Professional is more applicable in a corporate environment. Microsoft has also produced editions of Windows XP to address scalability concerns. Although all editions of Windows XP support symmetric multiprocessing (SMP), Windows XP 64-Bit Edition is specifically designed for high-performance desktop systems, which are often constructed as SMP systems (see Section 15.4.1, Uniform Memory Access). Additionally, Microsoft has developed an embedded operating system derived from Windows XP, called Windows XP Embedded. An embedded system consists of tightly coupled hardware and software designed for a specific electronic device, such as a cellular phone or an assembly-line machine. This section describes the features included in Windows XP to facilitate scaling up to SMP systems and down to embedded systems.

21.12.1 Symmetric Multiprocessing (SMP)

Windows XP scales to symmetric multiprocessor (SMP) systems. Windows XP supports multiprocessor thread scheduling, locking the kernel, a 64-bit address space (in Windows XP 64-Bit Edition) and API features that support programming server applications.

Windows XP can schedule threads efficiently on multiprocessor systems, as described in Section 21.6.2, Thread Scheduling. Windows XP attempts to schedule a thread on the same processor on which it recently executed to exploit data cached on a processor's private cache. The system also uses the ideal processor attribute to increase the likelihood that a process's threads execute concurrently, thus increasing performance. Alternatively, developers can override this default and use the ideal processor attribute to increase the likelihood that a process's threads execute on the same processor to share cached data.[450]

Windows XP implements spin locks (described in Section 21.6.3, Thread Synchronization), which are kernel locks designed for multiprocessor systems. Specifically, the queued spin lock decreases traffic on the processor-to-memory bus, increasing Windows XP's scalability.[451] In addition, as the original NT kernel has evolved (recall that Windows XP is NT 5.1), designers have reduced the size of critical sections, which reduces the amount of time a processor is busy waiting to obtain a lock. Sometimes, a processor cannot perform other work when waiting for a spin lock, such as when a processor needs to execute thread scheduling code. Reducing the size of this critical section increases Windows XP's scalability.[452] Additionally, Windows XP provides a number of other fine-grained locks (e.g., dispatcher objects and executive resource locks), so that developers need only lock specific sections of the kernel, allowing other components to execute without disruption.[453]

Memory support for large SMP systems emanates from Windows XP 64-Bit Edition. 64-bit addressing provides 2^{64} bytes (or 16 exabytes) of virtual address space; this contrasts with 2^{32} bytes (or 4 gigabytes) for 32-bit versions of Windows XP. In practice, Windows XP 64-Bit Edition provides processes with 7152GB of virtual memory address range.[454] Windows XP 64-Bit Edition currently supports up to 1 terabyte of cache memory, 128 gigabytes of paged system memory and 128 gigabytes of nonpaged pool. Windows XP 64-Bit Edition has been ported to Intel Itanium II processors, which are described in Section 14.8.4, Explicitly Parallel Instruction Computing (EPIC)[455]. Soon (as of this writing), Microsoft plans to release Windows XP 64-Bit Edition for Extended Systems to support AMD Opteron and Athlon 64 processors.[456] The 64-bit editions of Windows also offer greater performance and precision when manipulating floating point numbers, because these systems store floating point numbers using 64 bits.[457]

Finally, Windows XP has added several programming features tailored for high-performance systems, which is an environment in which many SMP systems are employed. The job object (described in Section 21.6.1, Process and Thread Organization) allows servers to handle resource allocation to a group of processes. In this way, a server can manage the resources it commits to a client request.[458] Also, I/O completion ports (described in Section 21.9.2, Input/Output Processing) facilitate the processing of large numbers of asynchronous I/O requests. In a large server program, many threads might issue asynchronous I/O requests; I/O completion ports provide a central area where dedicated threads can wait and process incoming I/O completion notifications.[459] Additionally, thread pools (described in Section 21.6.1, Process and Thread Organization) permit server processes to handle incoming client requests without the costly overhead of creating and deleting threads for each new request. Instead, these requests can be queued to the thread pool.[460]

21.12.2 *Windows XP Embedded*

Microsoft has created an operating system called **Windows XP Embedded**, which scales Windows XP for embedded devices. Microsoft divides Windows XP into clearly defined functional units called **components**. Components range from user-mode applications such as Notepad to portions of kernel space such as the CD-ROM interface and power management tools. The designer of a Windows XP Embedded system chooses from over 10,000 components to customize a system for a particular device.[461] Components for Windows XP Embedded contain the same code as Windows XP Professional, providing full compatibility with Windows XP. Windows XP Embedded also contains the core Windows XP microkernel.[462]

Windows XP Embedded is designed for more robust embedded devices such as printers, routers, point-of-sale systems and digital set-top boxes. Microsoft provides a different operating system, Windows CE, for lighter devices such as cellular phones and PDAs. The goal of Windows XP Embedded is to allow devices with limited resources to take advantage of the Windows XP computing environment.[463]

Devices such as medical devices, communication equipment and manufacturing equipment would benefit from Windows XP Embedded, but require hard real-time guarantees. Recall from Section 8.9, Real-Time Scheduling, the difference between soft real-time scheduling (like that provided by Windows XP) and hard real-time scheduling. Soft real-time scheduling assigns higher priority to real-time threads, whereas hard real-time scheduling provides guarantees that, given a start time, a thread will finish by a certain deadline. Venturcom[464] has designed a Real-Time Extension (RTX) for Windows XP Embedded and Windows XP. RTX includes a new threading model (implemented as a device driver), a collection of libraries and an extended HAL. Venturcom's RTX achieves hard real-time goals by masking all non-real-time interrupts when real-time threads execute, never masking real-time interrupts (recall that interrupt masking is accomplished through the HAL) and enforcing strict thread priorities. For example, threads waiting for synchronization objects, such as mutexes and semaphores, are placed in the *ready* state in priority order (as opposed to FIFO order). RTX implements 128 priority levels to increase scheduling flexibility.

21.13 *Security*

Any operating system aimed at the corporate market must offer substantial security capabilities. Windows XP Professional provides a wide variety of security services to its users, whereas Windows XP Home Edition has a slightly more limited range and is targeted at consumers with simple security needs. The following subsections describe security in Windows XP Professional. Much of the information, especially non-networking related material, applies to Windows XP Home Edition as well.

Windows XP provides users with a range of authentication and authorization options that permit access a physical terminal, a local network or the Internet. A database of users' credentials helps provide users with single sign-on; once a user logs onto Windows XP, the system takes care of authenticating the user to other domains and networks without prompting for credentials. The operating system includes a built-in firewall (see Section 19.6.1, Firewalls) that protects the system from malicious access.

21.13.1 Authentication

Windows XP has a flexible authentication policy. Users provide the system with credentials which consists of their identity (e.g. username) and proof of identity (e.g. password). For local access, the system authenticates a user's credentials against the **Security Account Manager (SAM)** database. A designated computer, called the **domain controller,** handles remote authentication. The native authentication system for network access is Kerberos V5 (see Section 19.3.3, Kerberos). Windows XP also supports the NT LanMan (NTLM) authentication protocol for backward compatibility with domain controllers running NT 4.0.[465]

Authentication begins at a logon screen; this can be either the standard logon program (called MSGINA) or a third-party **Graphical Identification and Authentication (GINA)** DLL.[466] GINA passes the user's username and password to the Winlogon program, which passes the credentials to the Local Security Authority (LSA). The LSA is responsible for handling all authentication and authorization for users physically accessing that particular machine.[467]

If the user is logging on only to the local machine, the LSA verifies the user's credentials with the local SAM database. Otherwise, the LSA passes the credentials over the network to the domain controller (the computer responsible for handling authentication) via the **Security Support Provider Interface (SSPI)**. This is a standard interface for obtaining security services for authentication that is compatible with both Kerberos V5 and NTLM. The domain controller first attempts to authenticate using Kerberos, which verifies credentials using the Active Directory. If Kerberos fails, GINA resends the username and password. This time the domain controller attempts to authenticate via the NTLM protocol, which relies on a SAM database stored on the domain controller. If both Kerberos and NTLM fail, GINA prompts the user to reenter the username and password.[468, 469] Figure 21.19 illustrates the authentication process.

Computers, especially mobile ones such as laptops, often use different credentials to connect to different domains. This is done for security reasons; if one domain is compromised, accounts on the other domains remain secure. Windows XP lets users store domain-specific credentials in Stored User Names and Passwords. Upon an authentication error, the LSA first attempts to authenticate using a saved credential for that domain. Upon failure, the LSA activates the GINA screen

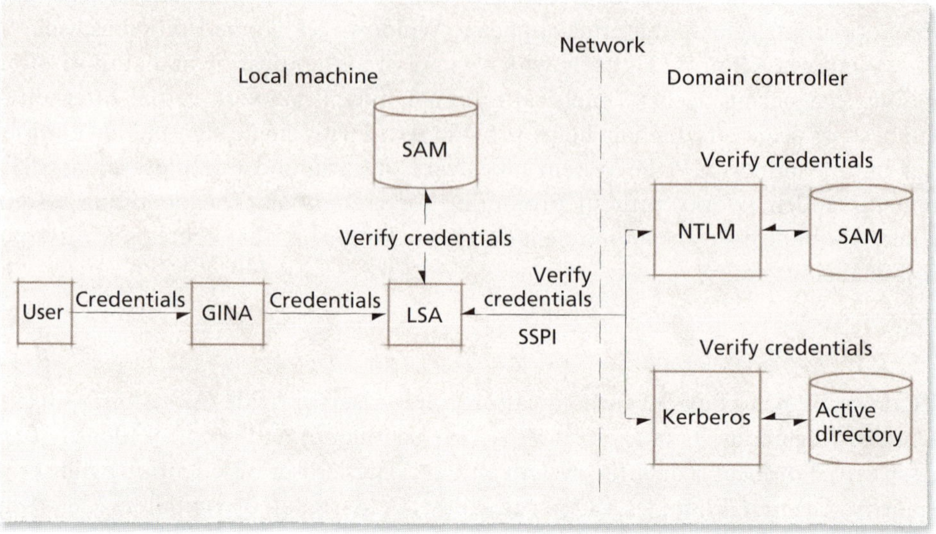

Figure 21.19 | *Authentication process in a Windows XP network.*

to prompt the user for a credential. The screen lets the user select a stored credential from a drop-down menu. The system records every credential that a user enters to a GINA (as long as the user selects a box giving the system permission to do so). In addition, users may use a special GUI to add, edit and remove credentials.[470]

21.13.2 Authorization

Any user, group, service or computer that performs an action in a Windows XP system is considered a **security principal**. A user can set security permissions for any security principal.[471] It is often advantageous to place users with the same security privileges into a security group, then set security permissions based on the security group. Security groups can be nested and grouped to form larger security groups. Using security groups simplifies managing the security policy for a large system.[472]

The system assigns each security principal a unique **security identifier (SID)**. When a security principal logs on, the system uses the security principal's SID to assign an **access token**. The access token stores security information about the security principal, including its SID, the SID of all groups to which the security principal belongs and the default access control list (see Section 19.4.3, Access Control Mechanisms) to assign to all objects the security principal creates. The system attaches a copy of the access token to every process and thread that the security principal runs. The system uses a thread's access token to verify that the thread is authorized to perform a desired action.[473]

Windows XP uses access tokens to implement **fast user switching**—enabling a new user to log on without logging off the current user. (Fast user switching works only on computers that are not members of a domain). Often, especially in home environments, a user may start a long-running process, then leave the computer to execute unattended. Fast user switching permits another person to log on, run programs, check e-mail, play a game, and so on. The first user's processes continue executing in the background; however, this is transparent to the new user. An access token stores a session ID that is unique to each logon session. The system uses the access token attached to each thread and process to determine to which user a process or thread belongs.[474, 475]

Every resource, such as a file, folder or device, has a **security descriptor** that contains the resource's security information. A descriptor contains the resource owner's SID and a **discretionary access control list (DACL)** that determines which security principals may access the resource. The DACL is an ordered list of **access control entries (ACEs)**; each ACE contains the SID of a security principal and the type of access (if any) the security principal has to that particular resource.[476]

When a thread attempts to access a resource, Windows XP uses the thread's access token and the resource's security descriptor to determine whether to permit access. The system traverses the DACL and stops when it finds an ACE with a SID that matches one of the SIDs in the access token. The thread is permitted to perform the requested operation only if the first matching ACE authorizes the action. If the security descriptor has no DACL, access is granted; if the DACL has no matching ACE, access is denied.[477]

Windows XP offers users flexibility in specifying the security policy of their system. The main role of the operating system is to enforce the policy that its users set. However, with so many options to choose from, an administrator might inadvertently create an insecure security policy. To prevent this, Windows XP includes many useful features to help administrators maintain system security.

Recall the notion of security groups mentioned at the start of the section. Windows XP defines three basic security groups: Everyone (all authenticated security principals), Anonymous (all unauthenticated security principals) and Guest (a general-purpose account). System administrators can use these three security groups as the building blocks of their security policy. In addition, Windows XP includes several default security policies that administrators can employ as a starting point for creating their own policy. In general, each default policy uses the highest level of security, and system administrators are responsible for increasing user privileges. For example, by default, users who log on from a remote machine are forced to use Guest privileges. Although this might be an annoyance, this policy is preferable to inadvertently overlooking a security hole.[478]

21.13.3 Internet Connection Firewall

Windows XP has a built-in packet filtering firewall (see 18.6.1, Firewalls) called the **Internet Connection Firewall (ICF)**. This firewall can be used to protect either an entire network or a single computer.[479] ICF filters out all unsolicited inbound traffic, with the exception of packets sent to ports explicitly designated as open. The firewall stores information about all outgoing packets in a flow table. It permits an incoming packet to enter the system only if there is an entry in the flow table corresponding to an outgoing packet sent to the home address of the incoming packet.[480] ICF does not filter outgoing packets; it assumes that only legitimate processes would send an outgoing packet. (This can cause problems if a Trojan Horse program gains access to the system.)[481]

ICF supports common Internet communication protocols such as FTP and LDAP. To permit applications to communicate with a Windows XP system via these protocols, ICF leaves certain ports open for all incoming traffic. Also, many applications such as MSN Messenger and online games require an open port to run successfully. Users and applications with administrative privileges can designate a particular port open for all incoming traffic; this process is called **port mapping**.[482, 483]

21.13.4 Other Features

Windows XP comes with many features that help keep the system secure. For example, users can encrypt files and folders using the Encrypting File System (see Section 21.8.2, NTFS, for more information). Users can control which Web sites may store cookies (small temporary files used by a server to store user-specific information) on their computer. Administrators can limit which applications may execute on the system; each application can be identified by its file hash, so that moving or renaming it would not bypass the restriction. Windows XP can also check whether the application is signed with a trusted certificate (i.e., a signature from an entity that the user specified as trustworthy) or comes from a trusted Internet Zone (i.e., an Internet domain that the user specified as safe).[484] Users can use Automatic Update to get notification, or even installation, of the latest security patches.[485]

Web Resources

`msdn.microsoft.com/library`
The MSDN Library provides information about Microsoft products and services, including the most recent platform Software Development Kit (SDK) and Driver Development Kit (DDK). Go to the menu on the left side of the screen and click on Windows Development, followed by Windows Base Services, to research the Windows XP SDK. To research the DDK, click on Windows Development, followed by Driver Development Kit. Particularly useful information can be found by next clicking Kernel-Mode Driver Architecture, followed by Design Guide. The MSDN Library also provides networking information (click Networking and Directory Services) and COM information (click Component Development).

`www.microsoft.com/windowsxp/default.asp`
Microsoft's homepage for Windows XP. From here, the reader can find XP overviews, support information and gateways to other areas of Microsoft with more technical information on Windows XP.

`www.microsoft.com/technet/prodtechnol/winxppro`
Microsoft TechNet provides technical information on Microsoft products. This section is devoted to Windows XP Professional; particularly useful is the Resource Kit (click Resource Kits).

`www.winnetmag.com`
Publishes technical articles about Windows & .NET ranging from introductions for novice users to in-depth internals descriptions for advanced developers.

`www.osronline.com`
Features technical articles and tutorials about the internals of Windows operating systems. It offers online articles, as well as a free subscription to *NT Insider*, a technical magazine about the NT line of operating systems.

`www.extremetech.com/category2/0,3971,23445,00.asp`
ExtremeTech's page for operating systems. It includes news articles, some technical insight and a forum to discuss operating systems.

www.theeldergeek.com/index.htm

Describes Windows XP from the user's perspective, including excellent information about the registry, system services and networking.

www.windowsitlibrary.com

Provides free articles and sells books and articles about Windows operating systems. Some of these articles and books provide technical internals information.

www.sysinternals.com

Dedicated to providing internals information about Windows operating systems, especially the NT line.

msdn.microsoft.com/msdnmag/default.aspx

The *MSDN Magazine* (formerly know as *Microsoft Systems Journal*) contains articles about Microsoft's products, targeted for developers.

www.winsupersite.com

Provides updated information about Windows products. It evaluates them from both technical and user perspectives.

developer.intel.com

Provides technical documentation regarding Intel products, including Pentium and Itanium processors. Their system programmer guides (e.g., for the Pentium 4 processor, developer.intel.com/design/Pentium4/manuals/) provide information about how Intel processors interact with the operating system.

developer.amd.com

Provides technical documentation regarding AMD products, including Athlon and Opteron processors. Their system programmer guides (e.g., for the Opteron processor, www.amd.com/us-en/Processors/DevelopWithAMD/0,,30_2252_739_7044,00.html) provide information about how AMD processors interact with the operating system.

Key Terms

.NET—Microsoft initiative aimed at transforming computing from an environment in which users simply execute applications on a single computer to a fully distributed environment; .NET provides a platform- and language-neutral development environment for components that can easily interoperate.

.NET framework—Programming model for creating XML-based Web services and applications. The .NET framework supports over 20 programming languages and facilitates application programming by providing libraries to perform common operations (e.g., input/output, string manipulation and network communication) and access data via multiple database interfaces (e.g., Oracle and SQL Server).

abandoned mutex (Windows XP)—Mutex that was not released before the termination of the thread that held it.

access control entry (ACE) (Windows XP)—Entry in a discretionary access control list (DACL) for a specific resource that contain the security identifier (SID) of a security principal and the type of access (if any) the security principal has to that particular resource.

access token (Windows XP)—Data structure that stores security information, such as the security identifier (SID) and group memberships, about a security principal.

Active Directory (Windows XP)—Network service that provides directory services for shared objects (e.g., files, printers, services, etc.) on a network.

ActiveX Controls—Self-registering COM objects useful for embedding in Web pages.

affinity mask (Windows XP)—List of processors on which a process's threads are allowed to execute.

alertable I/O (Windows XP)—Type of asynchronous I/O in which the system notifies the requesting thread of the completion of the I/O with an APC.

alertable *wait* state (Windows XP)—State in which a thread cannot execute until it is awakened either by an APC entering the thread's APC queue or by receiving a handle to the object (or objects) for which the thread is waiting.

alternate data stream—File attribute that stores the contents of an NTFS file that are not in the default data stream. NTFS files may have multiple alternate data streams.

anonymous pipe (Windows XP)—Unnamed pipe that can be used only for synchronous one-way communication between local processes.

apartment model—COM object threading model in which only one thread acts as a server for each COM object.

APC IRQL (Windows XP)—IRQL at which APCs execute and incoming asynchronous procedure calls (APCs) are masked.

application configuration file (ACF) (Windows XP)—File that specifies platform-specific attributes (e.g., how data should be formatted) for an RPC function call.

asynchronous procedure call (APC) (Windows XP)—Procedure calls that threads or the system can queue for execution by a specific thread.

automatic binding handle (Windows XP)—RPC binding handle in which the client process simply calls a remote function, and the stub manages all communication tasks.

auto-reset timer object (Windows XP)—Timer object that remains *signaled* only until one thread finishes waiting on the object.

Bad Page List (Windows XP)—List of page frames that have generated hardware errors; the system does not store pages on these page frames.

balance set manager (Windows XP)—Executive component responsible for adjusting working set minimums and maximums and trimming working sets.

base priority class (Windows XP)—Process attribute that determines a narrow range of base priorities the process's threads can have.

base priority level (Windows XP)—Thread attribute that describes the thread's base priority within a base priority class.

binding (Windows XP)—Connection between the client and the server used for network communication (e.g., for an RPC).

binding handle (Windows XP)—Data structure that stores the connection information associated with a binding between a client and a server.

bus driver—WDM (Windows Driver Model) driver that provides some generic functions for devices on a bus, enumerates those devices and handles Plug and Play I/O requests.

cache manager (Windows XP)—Executive component that handles file cache management.

class ID (CLSID)—Globally unique ID given to a COM object class.

class/miniclass driver pair (Windows XP)—Pair of device drivers that act as a function driver for a device; the class driver provides generic processing for the device's particular device class, and the miniclass driver provides processing for the specific device.

clipboard (Windows XP)—Central repository of data that is accessible to all processes, typically used with copy, cut and paste commands.

clock IRQL (Windows XP)—IRQL at which clock interrupts occur and at which APC, DPC/dispatch, DIRQL and profile-level interrupts are masked.

cluster (NTFS)—Basic unit of disk storage in an NTFS volume, consisting of a number of contiguous sectors; a system's cluster size can range from 512 bytes to 64KB, but is typically 2KB, 4KB or 8KB.

COM+—Extension of COM (Microsoft's Common Object Model) that handles advanced resource management tasks, such as providing support for transaction processing and using thread and object pools.

commit memory (Windows XP)—Necessary stage before a process can access memory. The VMM ensures that there is enough space in a pagefile for the memory and creates page table entries (PTEs) in main memory for the committed pages.

Common Internet File System (CIFS)—Native file sharing protocol of Windows XP.

Component Object Model (COM)—Microsoft-developed software architecture that allows interoperability between diverse components through the standard manipulation of object interfaces.

component (Windows XP)—Functional unit of Windows XP. Components range from user-mode applications such as Notepad to portions of kernel space such as the CD-ROM interface and power management tools. Dividing Windows XP into components facilitates operating system development for embedded systems.

compression unit (NTFS)—Sixteen clusters. Windows XP compresses and encrypts files one compression unit at a time.

configuration manager (Windows XP)—Executive component that manages the registry.

critical section object (Windows XP)—Synchronization object, which can be employed only by threads within a single process, that allows only one thread to own a resource at a time.

data stream (NTFS)—File attribute that stores the file's content or metadata; a file can have multiple data streams.

default data stream (NTFS)—File attribute that stores the primary contents of an NTFS file. When an NTFS file is copied to a file system that does not support multiple data streams, only the default data stream is preserved.

deferred procedure call (DPC) (Windows XP)—Software interrupt that executes at the DPC/dispatch IRQL and executes in the context of the currently executing thread.

device extension (Windows XP)—Portion of the nonpaged pool that stores information a driver needs to process I/O requests for a particular device.

device IRQL (DIRQL) (Windows XP)—IRQL at which devices interrupt and at which APC, DPC/dispatch and lower DIRQLs are masked; the number of DIRQLs is architecture dependent.

device object (Windows XP)—Object that a device driver uses to store information about a physical or logical device.

direct I/O—I/O transfer method whereby data is transferred between a device and a process's address space without using a system buffer.

directory junction (Windows XP)—Directory that refers to another directory within the same volume, used to make navigating the file system easier.

discretionary access control list (DACL) (Windows XP)—Ordered list that tells Windows XP which security principals may access a particular resource and what actions those principals may perform on the resource.

dispatcher (Windows XP)—Thread scheduling code dispersed throughout the microkernel.

dispatcher object (Windows XP)—Object, such as a mutex, semaphore, event or waitable timer, that kernel and user threads can use for synchronization purposes.

domain (Windows XP)—Set of computers that share common resources.

domain controller (Windows XP)—Computer responsible for security on a network.

DPC/dispatch IRQL (Windows XP)—IRQL at which DPCs and the thread scheduler execute and at which APC and incoming DPC/dispatch level interrupts are masked.

driver object (Windows XP)—Object used to describe device drivers; it stores pointers to standard driver routines and to the device objects for the devices that the driver services.

driver stack—Group of related device drivers that cooperate to handle the I/O requests for a particular device.

dynamic-linked library (DLL) (Windows XP)—Module that provides data or functions to which processes or other DLLs link at execution time.

dynamic priority class (Windows XP)—Priority class that encompasses the five base priority classes within which a thread's priority can change during system execution; these classes are idle, below normal, normal, above normal and high.

environment subsystem (Windows XP)—User-mode component that provides a computing environment for other user-mode processes; in most cases, only environment subsystems interact directly with kernel-mode components in Windows XP.

event object (Windows XP)—Synchronization object that becomes *signaled* when a particular event occurs.

executive (Windows XP)—Portion of the Windows XP operating system that is responsible for managing the operating system's subsystems (e.g., I/O subsystem, memory subsystem and file system).

executive resource lock (Windows XP)—Synchronization lock available only to kernel-mode threads and that may be held either in shared mode by many threads or in exclusive mode by one thread.

executive process (EPROCESS) block (Windows XP)—Executive data structure that stores information about a process, such as that process's object handles and the process's ID; an EPROCESS block also stores the process's KPROCESS block.

executive thread (ETHREAD) block (Windows XP)—Executive data structure that stores information about a thread, such as the thread's pending I/O requests and the thread's start address; an ETHREAD block also stores the thread's KTHREAD block.

explicit handle (Windows XP)—Binding handle in which the client must specify all binding information and create and manage the handle.

fast mutex (Windows XP)—Efficient mutex variant that operates at the APC level with some restrictions (e.g., a thread cannot specify a maximum wait time to wait for a fast mutex).

fast user switching (Windows XP)—Ability of a new user to logon to a Windows XP machine without logging off the previous user.

fiber (Windows XP)—Unit of execution created by a thread and scheduled by that thread.

fiber local storage (FLS) (Windows XP)—Area of a process's address space where a fiber can store data that only the fiber can access.

file mapping (Windows XP)—Interprocess communication mechanism in which multiple processes access the same file by placing it in their virtual memory space. The different virtual addresses correspond to the same main memory addresses.

file mapping object (Windows XP)—Object used by processes to map any file into memory.

file view (Windows XP)—Portion of a file specified by a file mapping object that a process maps into its memory.

filter driver—WDM (Windows Driver Model) driver that modifies the behavior of a hardware device (e.g., providing mouse acceleration) or adds some extra services (e.g., security checks).

free model—COM (Microsoft's Component Object Model) object threading model in which many threads can act as the server for a COM object.

Free Page List (Windows XP)—List of page frames that are available for reclaiming; although these page frames do not contain any valid data, they may not be used until the zero-page thread sets all of their bits to zero.

function driver—WDM (Windows Driver Model) device driver that implements a device's main functions; it does most of the I/O processing and provides the device's interface.

globally unique ID (GUID)—128-bit integer that is, for all practical purposes, guaranteed to be unique in the world. COM (Microsoft's Component Object Model) uses GUIDs to uniquely identify interfaces and object classes.

Graphical Identification and Authentication (GINA) (Windows XP)—Graphical user interface used that prompts users for credentials, usually in the form of a username and password. Windows XP ships with its own implementation of GINA called MSGINA, but it accepts third-party DLLs.

Hardware Abstraction Layer (HAL) (Windows XP)—Operating system component that interacts directly with the hardware and abstracts hardware details for other system components.

high IRQL (Windows XP)—Highest-priority IRQL, at which machine check and bus error interrupts execute and all other interrupts are masked.

high-level driver (Windows XP)—Device driver that abstracts hardware specifics and passes I/O requests to low-level drivers.

ideal processor (Windows XP)—Thread attribute that specifies a processor on which the system should attempt to schedule the thread for execution.

inheritance (Windows XP)—Technique by which a child process obtains attributes (e.g., most types of handles and the current directory) from its parent process upon creation.

initialized state (Windows XP)—State in which a thread is created.

I/O completion port (Windows XP)—Port at which threads register and block, waiting to be awakened when processing completes on an I/O request.

I/O completion routine (Windows XP)—Function registered by a device driver with the I/O manager in reference to an IRP; the I/O manager calls this function when processing of the IRP completes.

I/O request packet (IRP) (Windows XP)—Data structure that describes an I/O request.

I/O manager (Windows XP)—Executive component that interacts with device drivers to handle I/O requests.

I/O throttling (Windows XP)—Technique that increases stability when available memory is low; the VMM manages memory one page at a time during I/O throttling.

I/O status block (Windows XP)—Field in an IRP that indicates whether an I/O request completed successfully or, if not, the request's error code.

Interface Definition Language (IDL) file (Windows XP)—File that specifies the interfaces that an RPC server exposes.

interface ID (IID)—Globally unique ID for a COM interface.

interlocked singly linked list (SList) (Windows XP)—Singly linked list in which insertions and deletions are performed as atomic operations.

interlocked variable access (Windows XP)—Method of accessing variables that ensures atomic reads and writes to shared variables.

intermediate driver (Windows XP)—Device driver that can be interposed between high- and low-level drivers to filter or process I/O requests for a device.

Internet Connection Firewall (ICF)—Windows XP's packet filtering firewall.

Internetwork Packet eXchange (IPX)—Novell Netware's network protocol designed specifically for LANs.

Interrupt Dispatch Table (IDT)—Kernel data structure that maps hardware interrupts to interrupt vectors.

interrupt request level (IRQL) (Windows XP)—Measure of interrupt priority; an interrupt that occurs at an IRQL equal to or lower than the current IRQL is masked.

interrupt service routine (ISR) (Windows XP)—Function, registered by a device driver, that processes interrupts issued by the device that the driver services.

job object (Windows XP)—Object that groups several processes and allows developers to manipulate and set limits on these processes as a group.

kernel handle (Windows XP)—Object handle accessible from any process's address space, but only in kernel mode.

kernel-mode APC (Windows XP)—APC generated by a kernel-mode thread and queued to a specified user-mode thread; the user-mode thread must process the APC as soon as the user-mode thread obtains the processor.

kernel-mode driver—Device driver that executes in kernel mode.

kernel process (KPROCESS) block (Windows XP)—Kernel data structure that stores information about a process, such as that process's base priority class.

kernel thread (KTHREAD) block (Windows XP)—Kernel data structure that stores information about a thread, such as the objects on which that thread is waiting and the location in memory of the thread's kernel stack.

large page (Windows XP)—Set of pages contiguous in memory that the VMM treats as a single page.

last processor (Windows XP)—Thread attribute equal to the processor that most recently executed the thread.

lazy allocation—Policy of waiting to allocate resources, such as pages in virtual memory and page frames in main memory, until absolutely necessary.

Lempel-Ziv compression algorithm—Data compression algorithm that NTFS uses to compress files.

Lightweight Directory Access Protocol (LDAP) (Windows XP)—Protocol for accessing, searching and modifying Internet directories (e.g., Active Directory).

localized least-recently used page replacement (Windows XP)—Policy of moving to disk the least-recently used page of a process at its working set maximum when that process requests a page in main memory. The policy is localized by process, because Windows XP moves only the requesting process's pages; Windows XP approximates this policy using the clock algorithm.

local procedure call (LPC) (Windows XP)—Procedure call made by a thread in one process to a procedure exposed by another process in the same domain (i.e., set of computers that share common resources); LPCs can be created only by system components.

local remote procedure call (LRPCs) (Windows XP)—RPCs between two processes on the same machine.

low-level driver (Windows XP)—Device driver that controls a peripheral device and does not depend on any lower-level drivers.

mailslot (Windows XP)—Message queue, which a process can employ to receive messages from other processes.

mailslot client (Windows XP)—Process that sends mailslot messages to mailslot servers.

mailslot server (Windows XP)—Process that creates a mailslot and receives messages in it from mailslot clients.

major function code (Windows XP)—Field in an IRP that describes the general function (e.g., read or write) that should be performed to fulfill an I/O request.

manual-reset timer object (Windows XP)—Timer object that remains *signaled* until a thread specifically resets the timer.

Master File Table (MFT) (NTFS)—File which is structured as a table in which NTFS stores information (e.g. name, time stamp, and location) about all files in the volume.

memory descriptor list (MDL) (Windows XP)—Data structure used in an I/O transfer that maps a process's virtual addresses to be accessed in the transfer to physical memory addresses.

memory map—Data structure that stores the correspondence between a process's virtual address space and main memory locations.

Microsoft IDL (MIDL)—Microsoft's extension of Interface Definition Language (IDL)—The Open Group's Distributed Computing Environment (DCE) standard for RPC interoperability.

minor function code (Windows XP)—Field in an IRP that, together with the major function code, describes the specific function that should be performed to fulfill an I/O request (e.g., to start a device, a PnP major function code is used with a start device minor function code).

mixed model—COM threading model, in which some COM objects reside in single apartments and others can be accessed by free threads.

Modified No-write Page List (Windows XP)—List of page frames for which the VMM must write an entry to a log file before freeing.

Modified Page List (Windows XP)—List of page frames that the VMM must write to the pagefile before freeing.

Multiple UNC Provider (MUP) (Windows XP)—File system driver that determines the appropriate redirector to which to send a network I/O request.

must-succeed request (Windows XP)—Request for space in main memory that a process issues when it requires more main memory to continue functioning properly. Windows XP always denies must-succeed requests; previous versions of Windows always fulfilled them.

mutex object (Windows XP)—Synchronization object that allows at most one thread access to a protected resource at any time; it is essentially a binary semaphore.

named pipe (Windows XP)—Type of pipe that can provide bidirectional communication between two processes on local or remote machines and that supports both synchronous and asynchronous communication.

native API (Windows XP)—Programming interface exposed by the executive, which environment subsystems employ to make system calls.

NDIS intermediate driver (Windows XP)—NDIS driver that can be interposed between a miniport driver and a higher-level driver and adds extra functionality, such as translating packets between different communication media, filtering packets or providing load balancing across several NICs.

NDIS miniport driver (Windows XP)—NDIS driver that manages a NIC and sends and receives data to and from the NIC.

NDIS protocol driver (Windows XP)—NDIS driver that places data into packets and passes these packets to lower-level drivers. NDIS protocol drivers provide an interface between the transport drivers and other NDIS drivers and can be used as the lowest layer in the implementation of a transport protocol stack such as TCP/IP.

neither I/O (Windows XP)—I/O transfer technique in which a high-level driver executes in the context of the calling thread to set up a buffered I/O transfer or direct I/O transfer or to directly perform the transfer in the process's address space.

NetBIOS Extended User Interface (NetBEUI) (Windows XP)—Native network and transport protocol for DOS and older Windows operating systems.

NetBIOS over TCP/IP (NBT) (Windows XP)—Replacement protocol for NetBEUI that provides backward compatibility with older applications (by keeping the NetBIOS interface) and takes advantage of TCP/IP protocols.

Network Basic Input/Output System (NetBIOS) (Windows XP)—API used to support NetBEUI and now used with NBT.

Network Data Representation (NDR)—Standard format for network data described in the The Open Group's Distributed Computing Environment (DCE) standard.

Network Driver Interface Specification (NDIS) (Windows XP)—Specification that describes a standard interface between lower-level layered drivers in the network driver stack; NDIS drivers provide the functionality of the link layer in the TCP/IP stack and are used on Windows XP systems.

network redirector—*See* redirector (Windows XP).

nonpaged pool—Area of main memory that stores pages that are never moved to disk.

nonresident attribute—NTFS file attribute whose data does not fit inside the MFT entry and is stored elsewhere.

object handle (Windows XP)—Data structure that allows threads to manipulate an object.

Object Linking and Embedding (OLE)—Microsoft technology built on COM that defines a standard method for processes to exchange data by linking or embedding COM objects.

object manager (Windows XP)—Executive component that manages objects.

object manager namespace (Windows XP)—Group of object names in which each name is unique in the group.

opportunistic lock (oplock) (Windows XP)—Lock used by a CIFS client to secure exclusive access to a remote file, ensuring that the client can cache data locally and keep its cache coherent.

overlapped I/O (Windows XP)—Microsoft synonym for asynchronous I/O.

page directory register—Hardware register that stores a pointer to the current process's page directory table.

page directory table (Windows XP)—4KB page that contains 1024 entries that point to frames in memory.

paged pool (Windows XP)—Pages in memory that may be moved to the pagefile on disk.

pagefile (Windows XP)—File on disk that stores all pages that are mapped to a process's virtual address space but do not currently reside in main memory.

page frame database (Windows XP)—Array that contains the state of each page frame in main memory.

page list (Windows XP)—List of page frames that are in the same state. The eight state lists are: the Valid Page List, the Standby Page List, the Modified Page List, the Modified No-write Page List, the Transitional Page List, the Free Page List, the Zeroed Page List, and the Bad Page List.

page trimming (Windows XP)—Technique in which Windows XP takes a page belonging to a process and sets the page's PTE to invalid to determine whether the process actually needs the page. If the process does not request the page within a certain time period, the system removes it from main memory.

passive IRQL (Windows XP)—IRQL at which user- and kernel-mode normally execute and no interrupts are masked. Passive IRQL is the lowest-priority IRQL.

periodic timer (Windows XP)—Waitable timer object that reactivates after a specified interval.

pipe client (Windows XP)—Process that connects to an existing pipe to communicate with that pipe's server.

pipe server (Windows XP)—Process that creates a pipe and communicates with pipe clients that connect to the pipe.

PnP I/O requests (Windows XP)—IRPs generated by the PnP manager to query a driver for information about a device, to assign resources to a device or to direct a device to perform some action.

Plug and Play (PnP) manager (Windows XP)—Executive component (which also exists partly in user space) that dynamically recognizes when new devices are added to the system (as long as these devices support PnP), allocates and deallocates resources to devices and interacts with device setup programs.

port mapping (Windows XP)—Process of explicitly allowing the Internet Connection Firewall (ICF) to accept all incoming packets to a particular port.

power IRQL (Windows XP)—IRQL at which power failure interrupts execute and at which all interrupts except high-IRQL interrupts are masked.

power manager (Windows XP)—Executive component that administers the operating system's power management policy.

power policy (Windows XP)—Policy of a system with regard to balancing power consumption and responsiveness of devices.

primary thread (Windows XP)—Thread created when a process is created.

priority inversion—Situation which occurs when a high-priority thread is waiting for a resource held by a low-priority thread, and the low-priority thread cannot obtain the processor because of a medium-priority thread; hence, the high-priority thread is blocked from execution by the medium-priority thread.

process environment block (PEB) (Windows XP)—User-space data structure that stores information about a process, such as a list of DLLs linked to the process and information about the process's heap.

profile IRQL (Windows XP)—IRQL at which debugger interrupts execute and at which APC, DPC/dispatch, DIRQL and incoming debugger interrupts are masked.

protocol sequence (Windows XP)—String used by a client in an RPC call that specifies the RPC protocol, transport protocol and network protocol for that RPC.

Prototype Page Table Entry (PPTE) (Windows XP)—32-bit record that points to a frame in memory that contains either a copy-on-write page or a page that is part of a process's view of a mapped file.

queued spin lock (Windows XP)—Spin lock in which a thread releasing the lock notifies the next thread in the queue of waiting threads.

***ready* state** (Windows XP)—State in which a thread is waiting to use a processor.

real-time priority class (Windows XP)—Base priority class encompassing the upper 16 priority levels; threads of this class have static priorities.

recovery key (NTFS)—Key that NTFS stores that can decrypt an encrypted file; administrators can use recovery keys when a user has forgotten the private key needed to decrypt the file.

redirector (Windows XP)—File system driver that interacts with a remote server driver to facilitate network I/O operations.

registry (Windows XP)—Central database in which user, system and application configuration information is stored.

Remote Access Service (RAS) (Windows XP)—Network service, which allows users to remotely connect to a LAN.

reparse point (NTFS)—File attribute containing a tag and a block of up to 16KB of data that a user associates with a file or directory; when an application accesses a reparse point, the system executes the file system filter driver specified by the reparse point's tag.

request IRQL (Windows XP)—IRQL at which interprocess interrupts execute and all interrupts except power-level and high-level interrupts are masked.

reserve memory (Windows XP)—To indicate to the VMM that a process intends to use an area of virtual memory; the VMM allocates memory in the process's virtual address space but does not allocate any page frames in main memory.

resident attribute (NTFS)—File attribute whose data is stored within the MFT entry.

***running* state** (Windows XP)—State in which a thread is currently in execution.

Security Accounts Manager (SAM) (Windows XP)—Database that administers information about all security principals in the system. It provides services such as account creation, account modification and authentication.

security descriptor (Windows XP)—Data structure that stores information about which security principals may access a resource and what actions they may perform on that resource. The most important element of a security descriptor is its discretionary access control list (DACL).

security identifier (SID) (Windows XP)—Unique identification number assigned to each security principal in the system.

security principal (Windows XP)—Any user, process, service or computer that can perform an action in a Windows XP system.

Security Support Provider Interface (SSPI) (Windows XP)—Microsoft's standardized protocol for authentication and authorization recognized by both the Kerberos and NTLM authentication services.

semaphore object (Windows XP)—Synchronization object that allows a resource to be owned by up to a specified number of threads; it is essentially a counting semaphore.

Sequenced Packet eXchange (SPX)—Novell Netware's transport protocol, which offers connection-oriented services for IPX packets.

Server Message Block (SMB)—Network file-sharing protocol used in Windows operating systems on top of which CIFS (Common Internet File System) is built.

single-use timer (Windows XP)—Waitable timer object that is used once and then discarded.

signaled state (Windows XP)—State in which a synchronization object can be placed, allowing one or more threads *waiting* on this object to awaken.

sparse file (NTFS)—File with large blocks of regions filled with zeroes that NTFS tracks using a list of empty regions rather than explicitly recording each zero bit.

Standby Page List (Windows XP)—List of page frames that are consistent with their on-disk version and can be freed.

standby state (Windows XP)—Thread state denoting a thread that has been selected for execution.

system service (Windows XP)—Process that executes in the background whether or not a user is logged into the computer and typically executes the server side of a client/server application; a system service for Windows XP is similar to a daemon for Linux.

system worker thread (Windows XP)—Thread controlled by the system that sleeps until a kernel-mode component queues a work item for processing.

terminated state (Windows XP)—Thread state that denotes a thread is no longer available for execution.

thread local storage (TLS) (Windows XP)—Area of a thread's process's address space where the thread can store private data, inaccessible to other threads.

thread environment block (TEB) (Windows XP)—User-space data structure that stores information about a thread, such as the critical sections owned by a thread and exception-handling information.

thread pool (Windows XP)—Collection of worker threads that sleep until a request is queued to them, at which time one of the threads awakens and executes the queued function.

timer-queue timer (Windows XP)—Timer that signals a worker thread to perform a specified function at a specified time.

transitional fault (Windows XP)—Fault issued by the MMU when it tries to access a page that is in main memory, but whose page frame's status is set to standby, modified, or modified no-write.

Transitional Page List (Windows XP)—List of page frames whose data is in the process of being moved to or from disk.

transition state (Windows XP)—Thread state denoting a thread that has completed a wait but is not yet ready to run because its kernel stack has been paged out of memory.

Transport Driver Interface (TDI) driver (Windows XP)—Network driver that exports a network interface to upper-level kernel-mode clients and interacts with low-level NDIS drivers.

universally unique identifier (UUID)—ID that is guaranteed, for all practical purposes, to be unique in the world. UUIDs uniquely identify an RPC interface.

Uniform Naming Convention (UNC) format (Windows XP)—Format that specifies a file's pathname, including on which server and in which directory on that server the file is located.

unknown state (Windows XP)—Thread state denoting that the some error has occurred and the system does not know the state of the thread.

unsignaled state (Windows XP)—State in which a synchronization object can be; threads *waiting* on this object do not awaken until the object transitions to the *signaled* state.

user-mode APC (Windows XP)—APC queued by user-mode thread and executed by the target thread when the target thread enters an alertable *wait* state.

user-mode driver (Windows XP)—Device driver that executes in user space.

Valid Page List (Windows XP)—List of page frames that are currently in a process's working set.

Virtual Address Descriptor (VAD) (Windows XP)—Structure in memory that contains a range of virtual addresses that a process may access.

virtual memory manager (VMM) (Windows XP)—Executive component that manages virtual memory.

VMS—Operating system for the DEC VAX computers, designed by David Cutler's team.

waitable timer object (Windows XP)—Synchronization object that becomes *signaled* after a specified amount of time elapses.

wait function (Windows XP)—Function called by a thread to wait for one or more dispatcher objects to enter a *signaled* state; calling this function places a thread in the *waiting* state.

waiting state (Windows XP)—Thread state denoting that a thread is not ready for execution until it is awakened (e.g., by obtaining a handle to the object on which it is waiting).

Web-based Distributed Authoring and Versioning (WebDAV) (Windows XP)—Network file-sharing protocol that allows users to write data directly to HTTP servers and is designed to support collaborative authoring between groups in remote locations.

Win32 environment subsystem (Windows XP)—User-mode process interposed between the executive and the rest of user space that provides a typical 32-bit Windows environment.

Win32 service (Windows XP)—*See* system service (Windows XP).

Windows Driver Model (WDM) (Windows XP)—Standard driver model that enables source-code compatibility across all Windows platforms; each WDM driver must be written as a bus driver, function driver or filter driver and support PnP, power management and WMI.

Windows Management Instrumentation (WMI) (Windows XP)—Standard that describes how drivers provide measurement and instrumentation data to users (e.g., configuration data, diagnostic data or custom data) and allow user applications to register for WMI driver-defined events.

Windows XP Embedded—Embedded operating system, which uses the same binary files as Windows XP but allows designers to choose only those components applicable for a particular device.

WinINet (Windows XP)—API that allows applications to interact with FTP, HTTP and Gopher protocols to access resources over the Internet.

WinHTTP (Windows XP)—API that supports communication between clients and servers over an HTTP session.

Windows sockets version 2 (Winsock 2)—Adaptation and extension of BSD sockets for the Windows environment.

worker thread (Windows XP)—Kernel-mode thread that the system uses to execute functions queued by user-mode or other kernel-mode threads.

working set (Windows XP)—All of the pages in main memory that belong to a specific process.

working set maximum (Windows XP)—Upper limit on the number of pages a process may have simultaneously in main memory.

working set minimum (Windows XP)—Number of pages in main memory the working set manager leaves a process when it executes the page-trimming algorithm.

write-through mode (Windows XP)—Method of writing to a pipe whereby write operations do not complete until the data being written is confirmed to be in the buffer of the receiving process.

Zeroed Page List (Windows XP)—List of page frames whose bits are all set to zero.

Exercises

21.1 [*Section 21.4, System Architecture*] What aspects of the Windows XP architecture make the system modular and portable to different hardware? In what ways has Microsoft sacrificed modularity and portability for performance?

21.2 [*Section 21.5.2, Object Manager*] What are the benefits of managing all objects in a centralized object manager?

21.3 [*Section 21.5.5, Deferred Procedure Calls (DPCs)*] Why might a routine that generates a DPC specify the processor (in a multiprocessor system) on which the DPC executes?

21.4 [*Section 21.5.5, Deferred Procedure Calls (DPCs)*] How do DPCs increase the system's responsiveness to incoming device interrupts?

21.5 [*Section 21.5.5, Deferred Procedure Calls (DPCs)*] Why is it that DPCs cannot access pageable data?

21.6 [*Section 21.6.1, Process and Thread Organization*] Give an example of why it may be useful to create a job for a single process.

21.7 [*Section 21.6.1, Process and Thread Organization*] What entity schedules fibers?

21.8 [*Section 21.6.1, Process and Thread Organization*] How might thread pools introduce inefficiency?

21.9 [*Section 21.6.2, Thread Scheduling*] The dispatcher schedules each thread without regard to the process to which the thread belongs, meaning that, all else being equal, the same process implemented with more threads receives a greater share of execution time. Name a disadvantage of this strategy.

21.10 [*Section 21.6.2, Thread Scheduling*] Why does the system reset a real-time thread's quantum after preemption?

21.11 [*Section 21.6.2, Thread Scheduling*] Under what circumstances would Windows XP increase a dynamic-priority thread's priority? Under what circumstances would Windows XP decrease it?

21.12 [*Section 21.6.2, Thread Scheduling*] How can policies implemented in Windows XP lead to priority inversion? How does Windows XP handle priority inversion? In what ways is this a good policy? What are its drawbacks?

21.13 [*Section 21.6.2, Thread Scheduling*] Why might a developer manipulate the value of a thread's ideal processor?

21.14 [*Section 21.6.3, Thread Synchronization*] Windows XP does not explicitly detect deadlock situations for threads using dispatcher objects. How might threads using dispatcher objects create a deadlock? What mechanisms does Windows XP include to help avoid these situations?

21.15 [*Section 21.6.3, Thread Synchronization*] In what ways are threads executing at an IRQL equal to or greater than DPC/dispatch level restricted? Why is this so?

21.16 [*Section 21.6.3, Thread Synchronization*] Why use a queued spin lock in preference to a generic spin lock?

21.17 [*Section 21.6.3, Thread Synchronization*] Explain how an executive resource can be used to solve the readers-and-writers problem.

21.18 [*Section 21.7.1, Memory Organization*] Suppose an enterprising programmer modifies the Windows XP virtual memory manager so that it allocates space for all page table entries that a process may need as soon as the process is created. Assume that page table entries cannot be moved to secondary storage and that no page table entries are shared.

   a. How much space would be needed to store all the page table entries for one process (on a 32-bit system)?

   b. Windows XP stores each process's page table entries in system space, which is shared between all processes. If a system devoted all of its system space to page table entries, what is the maximum number of processes that could be active simultaneously?

21.19 [*Section 21.7.1, Memory Organization*] Large pages need to be stored contiguously in main memory. There are several ways to do this: a system can designate a portion of main memory exclusively for large pages, a system can rearrange pages in main memory whenever a process requests a large page, or a system can do nothing and deny large-page memory allocation requests whenever necessary. Discuss the pros and cons of each of these three policies.

21.20 [*Section 21.7.1, Memory Organization*] A Windows XP TLB entry contains the full 32-bit virtual address and the 32-bit physical address to which it corresponds. Associative memory is very expensive. Suggest a space-saving optimization for the TLB.

21.21 [*Section 21.7.2, Memory Allocation*] When a process opens a file, Windows XP does not move the entire file into main memory. Instead, the system waits to see which portions of the file the process will access. The VMM moves only the accessed pages into main memory and creates PTEs for them.

This creates extra overhead whenever the process accesses a new portion of an open file. What would happen if the operating system tried to save time by creating all PTEs at once?

21.22 [*Section 21.7.2, Memory Allocation*] Windows XP eliminated must-succeed requests to make the system more stable. Suppose an enterprising programmer rewrote the operating system to accept must-succeed requests, but only when the system had enough main memory to fulfill the requests. What are the pitfalls of this policy?

21.23 [*Section 21.7.3, Page Replacement*] Why does Windows XP enable pagefiles to be stored on separate disks?

21.24 [*Section 21.7.3, Page Replacement*] Why does Windows XP zero pages?

21.25 [*Section 21.7.3, Page Replacement*] Suppose process A requests a new page from disk. However, the Zeroed Page List and the Free Page List are empty. One page frame originally belonging to process B is in the Standby Page List, and one page frame belonging to process A is in the Modified Page List. Which page frame will the system take and what will happen to that page frame? What are the pros and cons of taking the other page frame?

21.26 [*Section 21.8.1, File System Drivers*] The operating system uses different local file system drivers to access different storage devices. Would it make sense to develop a remote block file system driver and remote character file system driver to access different types of storage devices on remote computers?

21.27 [*Section 21.8.2, NTFS*] In Windows XP, shortcuts (the icons that users put on their desktop) are implemented as soft links—if the file or program to which they are connected is moved, the shortcuts point to nothing. What are the advantages and disadvantages of replacing shortcuts with hard links?

21.28 [*Section 21.8.2, NTFS*] A user wants to compress a 256KB file stored on an NTFS volume with 4KB clusters. Lempel-Ziv compression reduces the four 64KB compression units to 32KB, 31KB, 62KB, and 48KB. How much space does the compressed file take on the disk?

21.29 [*Section 21.8.2, NTFS*] Windows XP performs file encryption using reparse points. The file is piped through the Encrypting File System filter, which does all of the encryption and decryption. Windows XP allows an application to ignore a reparse point and access the file directly. Does this compromise the security of encrypted data? Why or why not?

21.30 [*Section 21.9.1, Device Drivers*] What are the advantages of servicing device I/O requests with a clearly defined driver stack rather than a single device driver?

21.31 [*Section 21.9.1, Device Drivers*] What are some of the benefits that systems and users realize from Plug and Play?

21.32 [*Section 21.9.2, Input/Output Processing*] We discussed four types of asynchronous I/O: polling, waiting on an event object that signals the completion of the I/O, alertable I/O and using I/O completion ports. For each technique, describe a situation for which it is useful; also, state a drawback for each technique.

21.33 [*Section 21.9.3, Interrupt Handling*] Why should an ISR do as little processing as necessary and return quickly, saving most of the interrupt processing for a DPC?

21.34 [*Section 21.11.2, Network Driver Architecture*] Suppose a new set of protocols were to replace TCP and IP as standard network protocols. How difficult would it be to incorporate support for these new protocols into Windows XP?

21.35 [*Section 21.11.3, Network Protocols*] Winsock adds new functionality on top of BSD sockets, extending sockets' functionality, but hindering portability. Do you think this was a good design decision? Support your answer.

21.36 [*Section 21.12.1, Symmetric Multiprocessing (SMP)*] Why does Windows XP attempt to schedule a thread on the same processor on which it recently executed?

21.37 [*Section 21.13.1, Authentication*] Suppose a company network has only Windows XP machines. What are the advantages of allowing both NTLM and Kerberos authentication? What are the disadvantages?

21.38 [*Section 21.13.2, Authorization*] When Windows XP compares an access token to a DACL (discretionary access control list), it scans the ACEs (access control entries) one by one and stops when it finds the first ACE whose SID (security identifier) matches an SID in the access token. Consider an administrator that wants to permit all authenticated users except interns to use a printer. The first ACE in the printer's DACL would deny the security group Interns and the second ACE would permit the security group Everyone. Assume that an intern's access token lists the security group Everyone first and the security group Interns second. What would happen if instead the system scanned the access token and stopped when it found an SID in the DACL?

21.39 [*Section 21.13.3, Internet Connection Firewall*] The Windows XP ICF filters only inbound packets. What are the advantages of not checking outgoing packets? What are the disadvantages?

Recommended Reading

A superb exposition of Windows NT-line internals can be found in *Inside Windows 2000*, 3d ed., by Mark Russinovich and David Solomon and published by Microsoft Press. These authors also discuss kernel enhancements from Windows 2000 to Windows XP in their article "Windows XP: Kernel Improvements Create a More Robust, Powerful, and Scalable OS," published in the December 2001 edition of *MSDN Magazine*. Helen Custer's *Inside Windows NT*, published by Microsoft Press, introduces many NT concepts still applicable for Windows XP. For the most updated reference on Windows XP, see the platform Software Development Kit (SDK) and Driver Development Kit (DDK) for Windows XP. Both are available from the *MSDN Library* at msdn.microsoft.com/library. Also, *Microsoft Windows XP Professional Resource Kit Documentation* by the Microsoft Corporation and published by Microsoft Press provides useful documentation about Windows XP. Some of the chapters of this book are available on *Microsoft Technet* at www.microsoft.com/technet/ prodtechnol/winxppro/Default.asp. The *NT Insider* and *Windows & .NET Magazine* both provide excellent articles on Windows internals. Both of these magazines have archives of old editions. The *NT Insider* archives are available at www.osronline.com, and the *Windows & .NET Magazine* archives are available at www.winntmag.com.

Works Cited

1. "Windows XP Captures More Than One-Third of O/S Market on Web," *StatMarket* 13, May 2003, <www.statmarket.com/cgi-bin/sm.cgi?sm&feature&week_stat>.

2. "Windows XP Product Information," Microsoft Corporation, July 29, 2003, <www.microsoft.com/windowsxp/evaluation/default.asp>.

3. Connolly, C., "First Look: Windows XP 64-Bit Edition for AMD64," *Game PC* September 5, 2003 <www.gamepc.com/labs/view_content.asp?id=amd64xp&page=1>.

4. Mirick, John, "William H. Gates III," Department of Computer Science at Virginia Tech, September 29, 1996, <ei.cs.vt.edu/~history/Gates.Mirick.html>.

5. Corrigan, Louis, "Paul Allen's Wide Wild Wired World," *The Motley Fool,* June 17, 1999 <www.fool.com/specials/1999/sp990617allen.htm>.

6. *Forbes,* "*Forbes'* World's Richest People 2003," 2003, <www.forbes.com/finance/lists/10/2003/LIR.jhtml?passListId=10&passYear=2003&passListType=Person&uniqueId=BH69&datatype=Person>.

7. "Bill Gates," *Microsoft,* September 2002, <www.microsoft.com/billgates/bio.asp>.

8. Krol, Louisa, and Leo Goldman, "Survival of the Richest," *Forbes.com,* March 17, 2003, <www.forbes.com/free_forbes/2003/0317/087.html>.

9. "MS-DOS," *Computer Knowledge,* 2001, <www.cknow.com/ckinfo/acro_m/msdos_1.shtml>.

10. Microsoft Corporation, "Bill Gates' Web Site," September 2003, <www.microsoft.com/billgates/bio.asp>.

11. Microsoft Corporation, "Bill Gates' Web Site," September 2003, <www.microsoft.com/billgates/bio.asp>.

12. Allison, D., "Interview with Bill Gates," 1993, <www.americanhistory.si.edu/csr/comphist/gates.htm>.

13. Allison, D., "Interview with Bill Gates," 1993, <www.americanhistory.si.edu/csr/comphist/gates.htm>.

14. Gates, W., *The Road Ahead,* New York: Viking Penguin, 1995, pp. 1, 12, 14–17, 48, 54.

15. Microsoft Corporation, "Bill Gates' Web Site," September 2003, <www.microsoft.com/billgates/bio.asp>.

16. Allison, D., "Interview with Bill Gates," 1993, <www.americanhistory.si.edu/csr/comphist/gates.htm>.

17. Gates, W., *The Road Ahead,* New York: Viking Penguin, 1995, pp. 1, 12, 14–17, 48, 54.

18. Allison, D., "Interview with Bill Gates," 1993, <www.americanhistory.si.edu/csr/comphist/gates.htm>.

19. Gates, W., *The Road Ahead,* New York: Viking Penguin, 1995, pp. 1, 12, 14–17, 48, 54.

20. Microsoft Corporation, "Bill Gates' Web Site," September 2003, <www.microsoft.com/billgates/bio.asp>.

21. Allison, D., "Interview with Bill Gates," 1993, <www.americanhistory.si.edu/csr/comphist/gates.htm>.

22. Gates, W., *The Road Ahead,* New York: Viking Penguin, 1995, pp. 1, 12, 14–17, 48, 54.

23. Allison, D., "Interview with Bill Gates," 1993, <www.americanhistory.si.edu/csr/comphist/gates.htm>.

24. Gates, W., *The Road Ahead,* New York: Viking Penguin, 1995, pp. 1, 12, 14–17, 48, 54.

25. Allison, D., "Interview with Bill Gates," 1993, <www.americanhistory.si.edu/csr/comphist/gates.htm>.

26. Allison, D., "Interview with Bill Gates," 1993, <www.americanhistory.si.edu/csr/comphist/gates.htm>.

27. Gates, W., *The Road Ahead,* New York: Viking Penguin, 1995, pp. 1, 12, 14–17, 48, 54.

28. Microsoft Corporation, "PressPass—Steve Ballmer," <www.microsoft.com/presspass/exec/steve/default.asp>.

29. Gates, W., *The Road Ahead,* New York: Viking Penguin, 1995, pp. 1, 12, 14–17, 48, 54.

30. Microsoft Corporation, "Bill Gates' Web Site," September 2003, <www.microsoft.com/billgates/bio.asp>.

31. "Microsoft DOS Version Features," *EMS,* <www.emsps.com/oldtools/msdosv.htm>.

32. "History of Microsoft Windows," *Wikipedia,* <www.wikipedia.org/wiki/History_of_Microsoft_Windows>.

33. "Windows Desktop Products History," Microsoft Corporation, 2003, <www.microsoft.com/windows/WinHistoryDesktop.mspx>.

34. "History of Microsoft Windows," *Wikipedia,* <www.wikipedia.org/wiki/History_of_Microsoft_Windows>.

35. Munro, Jay, "Windows XP Kernel Enhancements," *ExtremeTech,* June 8, 2001, <www.extremetech.com/print_article/0,3998,a=2473,00.asp>.

36. "The Foundations of Microsoft Windows NT System Architecture," *MSDN Library,* Microsoft Corporation, September 1997, <msdn.microsoft.com/ARCHIVE/en-us/dnarwbgen/html/msdn_ntfound.asp>.

37. "Microsoft Windows 2000 Overview," *Dytech Solutions,* Microsoft Corporation, 1999, <www.dytech.com.au/technologies/Win2000/Features/Features.asp>.

38. Russinovich, M., "Windows NT and VMS: The Rest of the Story," December 1998, <www.winnetmag.com/Articles/Index.cfm?ArticleID=4494>.

39. Custer, H., *Inside Windows NT,* Microsoft Press, 1992. Foreword by David Cutler.

40. Russinovich, M., "Windows NT and VMS: The Rest of the Story," December 1998, <www.winnetmag.com/Articles/Index.cfm?ArticleID=4494>.

41. Custer, H., *Inside Windows NT,* Microsoft Press, 1992. Foreword by David Cutler.

42. Custer, H., *Inside Windows NT,* Microsoft Press, 1992. Foreword by David Cutler.

43. Russinovich, M., "Windows NT and VMS: The Rest of the Story," December 1998, <www.winnetmag.com/Articles/Index.cfm?ArticleID=4494>.

44. Custer, H., *Inside Windows NT,* Microsoft Press, 1992. Foreword by David Cutler.

45. Custer, H., *Inside Windows NT,* Microsoft Press, 1992. Foreword by David Cutler.

46. Russinovich, M., "Windows NT and VMS: The Rest of the Story," December 1998, <www.winnetmag.com/Articles/Index.cfm?ArticleID=4494>.

47. Custer, H., *Inside Windows NT,* Microsoft Press, 1992. Foreword by David Cutler.

48. Russinovich, M., "Windows NT and VMS: The Rest of the Story," December 1998, <www.winnetmag.com/Articles/Index.cfm?ArticleID=4494>.

49. Custer, H., *Inside Windows NT,* Microsoft Press, 1992. Foreword by David Cutler.

50. Custer, H., *Inside Windows NT*, Microsoft Press, 1992. Foreword by David Cutler.

51. Russinovich, M., "Windows NT and VMS: The Rest of the Story," December 1998, `<www.winnetmag.com/Articles/Index.cfm?ArticleID=4494>`.

52. Custer, H., *Inside Windows NT*, Microsoft Press, 1992. Foreword by David Cutler.

53. Russinovich, M., "Windows NT and VMS: The Rest of the Story," December 1998, `<www.winnetmag.com/Articles/Index.cfm?ArticleID=4494>`.

54. J. Munro. "Windows XP Kernel Enhancements," *ExtremeTech*, June 8, 2001, `<www.extremetech.com/print_article/0,3998,a=2473,00.asp>`.

55. IBM, "Year 1987," `<www-1.ibm.com/ibm/history/history/year_1987.html>`.

56. Both, D., "A Short History of OS/2," December 18, 2002, `<www.millennium-technology.com/HistoryOfOS2.html>`.

57. Necasek, M., "OS/2 1," `<pages.prodigy.net/michaln/history/os210/index.html>`.

58. Necasek, M., "OS/2 2," `<pages.prodigy.net/michaln/history/os220/index.html>`.

59. Both, D., "A Short History of OS/2," December 18, 2002, `<www.millennium-technology.com/HistoryOfOS2.html>`.

60. "The Foundations of Microsoft Windows NT System Architecture," *MSDN Library*, Microsoft Corporation, September 1997, `<msdn.microsoft.com/ARCHIVE/en-us/dnarwbgen/html/msdn_ntfound.asp>`.

61. "Windows NT C2 Evaluations," *Microsoft TechNet*, Microsoft Corporation, December 2, 1999, `<www.microsoft.com/technet/treeview/default.asp?url=/technet/security/news/c2summ.asp>`.

62. "Fast Boot/Fast Resume Design," Microsoft Corporation, June 12, 2002, `<www.microsoft.com/whdc/hwdev/platform/performance/fastboot/default.mspx>`.

63. "MS Windows NT Kernel-Mode User and GDI White Paper," *Microsoft TechNet*, viewed July 22, 2003, `<www.microsoft.com/technet/prodtechnol/ntwrkstn/evaluate/featfunc/kernelwp.asp>`.

64. "DDK Glossary—Hardware Abstraction Layer (HAL)," *MSDN Library*, June 6, 2003, `<msdn.microsoft.com/library/en-us/gloss/hh/gloss/glossary_01ix.asp>`.

65. Walla, M., and R. Williams, "Windows .NET Structure and Architecture," *Windows IT Library*, April 2003, `<www.windowsitlibrary.com/Content/717/02/1.html>`.

66. Solomon, D., and M. Russinovich, *Inside Windows 2000*, 3rd ed., Redmond: Microsoft Press, 2000.

67. "MS Windows NT Kernel-Mode User and GDI White Paper," *Microsoft TechNet*, viewed July 22, 2003, `<www.microsoft.com/technet/prodtechnol/ntwrkstn/evaluate/featfunc/kernelwp.asp>`.

68. "Windows 2000 Architectural Tutorial," FindTutorials, viewed July 10, 2003, `<tutorials.findtutorials.com/read/category/97/id/379>`.

69. Walla, M., and R. Williams, "Windows .NET Structure and Architecture," *Windows IT Library*, April 2003, `<www.windowsitlibrary.com/Content/717/02/1.html>`.

70. S. Schreiber, *Undocumented Windows 2000 Secrets*, Boston: Addison-Wesley, 2001.

71. Walla, M., and R. Williams, "Windows .NET Structure and Architecture," *Windows IT Library*, April 2003, `<www.windowsitlibrary.com/Content/717/02/1.html>`.

72. "Windows XP 64-Bit Frequently Asked Questions," March 28, 2003, `<www.microsoft.com/windowsxp/64bit/evaluation/faq.asp>`.

73. "Dynamic-Link Libraries," *MSDN Library*, February 2003, `<msdn.microsoft.com/library/en-us/dllproc/base/dynamic_link_libraries.asp>`.

74. "System Services Overview," *Microsoft TechNet*, viewed July 25, 2003, `<www.microsoft.com/TechNet/prodtechnol/winxppro/proddocs/sys_srv_overview_01.asp>`.

75. Foley, J., "Services Guide for Windows XP," *The Elder Geek*, viewed July 25, 2003 `<www.theeldergeek.com/services_guide.htm#Services>`.

76. "Registry," *MSDN Library*, February 2003, `<msdn.microsoft.com/library/en-us/sysinfo/base/registry.asp>`.

77. "Chapter 23—Overview of the Windows NT Registry," *Microsoft TechNet*, viewed July 21, 2003, `<www.microsoft.com/technet/prodtechnol/ntwrkstn/reskit/23_regov.asp>`.

78. "Structure of the Registry," *MSDN Library*, February 2003, `<msdn.microsoft.com/library/en-us/sysinfo/base/structure_of_the_registry.asp>`.

79. "Predefined Keys," *MSDN Library*, February 2003, `<msdn.microsoft.com/en-us/sysinfo/base/predefined_keys.asp>`.

80. "Predefined Keys," *MSDN Library*, February 2003, `<msdn.microsoft.com/en-us/sysinfo/base/predefined_keys.asp>`.

81. "Opening, Creating, and Closing Keys," *MSDN Library*, February 2003, `<msdn.microsoft.com/library/en-us/sysinfo/base/opening_creating_and_closing_keys.asp>`.

82. "Registry Hives," *MSDN Library*, February 2003, `<msdn.microsoft.com/library/en-us/sysinfo/base/registry_hives.asp>`.

83. Russinovich, M., "Inside the Registry," *Windows & .NET Magazine*, May 1999 `<www.win2000mag.com/Articles/Index.cfm?ArticleID=5195>`.

84. "Object Management," *MSDN Library*, June 6, 2003, `<msdn.microsoft.com/library/en-us/kmarch/hh/kmarch/objects_033b.asp>`.

85. Russinovich, M., "Inside NT's Object Manager," *Windows & .NET Magazine*, October 1997, `<www.winnetmag.com/Articles/Index.cfm?IssueID=24&ArticleID=299>`.

86. "Object Categories," *MSDN Library*, February 2003, `<msdn.microsoft.com/library/en-us/sysinfo/base/object_categories.asp>`.

87. "Object Handles," *MSDN Library,* June 6, 2003, <msdn.microsoft.com/library/en-us/kmarch/hh/kmarch/objects_5btz.asp>.

88. "Handle Inheritance," *MSDN Library,* February 2003, <msdn.microsoft.com/library/en-us/sysinfo/base/handle_inheritance.asp>.

89. "Object Handles," *MSDN Library,* June 6, 2003 <msdn.microsoft.com/library/en-us/kmarch/hh/kmarch/objects_5btz.asp>.

90. "Object Names," *MSDN Library,* June 6, 2003, <msdn.microsoft.com/library/en-us/kmarch/hh/kmarch/objects_9k13.asp>.

91. "Object Manager," *MSDN Library,* February 2003, <msdn.microsoft.com/library/en-us/sysinfo/base/object_manager.asp>.

92. Russinovich, M., "Inside NT's Object Manager," *Windows & .NET Magazine,* October 1997, <www.winnetmag.com/Articles/Index.cfm?IssueID=24&ArticleID=299>.

93. "Object Manager," *MSDN Library,* February 2003, <msdn.microsoft.com/library/en-us/sysinfo/base/object_manager.asp>.

94. "Life Cycle of an Object," *MSDN Library,* June 6, 2003, <msdn.microsoft.com/library/en-us/kmarch/hh/kmarch/objects_16av.asp>.

95. "IRQL," *MSDN Library,* June 6, 2003, <msdn.microsoft.com/library/en-us/kmarch/hh/kmarch/k101_62b6.asp>.

96. "Managing Hardware Priorities," *MSDN Library,* June 6, 2003, <msdn.microsoft.com/library/en-us/kmarch/hh/kmarch/intrupts_0kh3.asp>.

97. "Key Benefits of the I/O APIC," *Windows Hardware and Driver Central,* <www.microsoft.com/whdc/hwdev/platform/proc/IO-APIC.mspx>.

98. "Managing Hardware Priorities," *MSDN Library,* June 6, 2003, <msdn.microsoft.com/library/en-us/kmarch/hh/kmarch/intrupts_0kh3.asp>.

99. "Windows DDK Glossary—Interrupt Dispatch Table (IDT)," *MSDN Library,* June 6, 2003, <msdn.microsoft.com/library/en-us/gloss/hh/gloss/glossary_1qbd.asp>.

100. "Windows DDK Glossary—Interrupt Dispatch Table (IDT)," *MSDN Library,* June 6, 2003, <msdn.microsoft.com/library/en-us/gloss/hh/gloss/glossary_1qbd.asp>.

101. "Managing Hardware Priorities," *MSDN Library,* June 6, 2003, <msdn.microsoft.com/library/en-us/kmarch/hh/kmarch/intrupts_0kh3.asp>.

102. "Asynchronous Procedure Calls," *NT Insider,* Vol. 5, No. 1, January 1998, <www.osr.com/ntinsider/1998/apc.htm>.

103. "Asynchronous Procedure Calls," *NT Insider,* Vol. 5, No. 1, January 1998, <www.osr.com/ntinsider/1998/apc.htm>.

104. "QueueUserAPC," *MSDN Library,* February 2003, <msdn.microsoft.com/library/en-us/dllproc/base/queueuserapc.asp>.

105. "Alterable I/O," *MSDN Library,* February 2003, <msdn.microsoft.com/library/en-us/fileio/base/alertable_i_o.asp>.

106. "Asynchronous Procedure Calls," *MSDN Library,* February 2003, <msdn.microsoft.com/library/en-us/dllproc/base/asynchronous_procedure_calls.asp>.

107. Hadjidoukas, P. E., "A Device Driver for W2K Signals," *Windows Developer Network,* September 7, 2003, <www.windevnet.com/documents/s=7637/wdj0108a/0108a.htm?temp=evgyijptOa>.

108. "Asynchronous Procedure Calls," *NT Insider,* Vol. 5, No. 1, January 1998, <www.osr.com/ntinsider/1998/apc.htm>.

109. "Introduction to DPCs," *MSDN Library,* June 6, 2003, <msdn.microsoft.com/library/en-us/kmarch/hh/kmarch/intrupts_2zzb.asp>.

110. "Managing Hardware Priorities," *MSDN Library,* June 6, 2003, <msdn.microsoft.com/library/en-us/kmarch/hh/kmarch/intrupts_0kh3.asp>.

111. "Writing an ISR," *MSDN Library,* June 6, 2003, <msdn.microsoft.com/library/en-us/kmarch/hh/kmarch/intrupts_4ron.asp>.

112. "Introduction to DPC Objects," *MSDN Library,* June 6, 2003, <msdn.microsoft.com/library/en-us/kmarch/hh/kmarch/intrupts_0m1z.asp>.

113. Russinovich, M., "Inside NT's Interrupt Handling," *Windows & .NET Magazine,* November 1997, <www.winntmag.com/Articles/Print.cfm?ArticleID=298>.

114. "Stop 0x0000000A or IRQL_NOT_LESS_OR_EQUAL," *Microsoft TechNet,* viewed July 17, 2003, <www.microsoft.com/technet/prodtechnol/winxppro/reskit/prmd_stp_hwpg.asp>.

115. "Guidelines for Writing DPC Routines," *MSDN Library,* <msdn.microsoft.com/library/en-us/kmarch/hh/kmarch/intrupts_6zon.asp>.

116. Russinovich, M., "Inside NT's Interrupt Handling," *Windows & .NET Magazine,* November 1997, <www.winntmag.com/Articles/Print.cfm?ArticleID=298>.

117. "KeSetTargetProcessorDPC," *MSDN Library,* June 6, 2003, <msdn.microsoft.com/library/en-us/kmarch/hh/kmarch/k105_9ovm.asp>.

118. "KeSetImportanceDPC," *MSDN Library,* June 6, 2003, <msdn.microsoft.com/library/en-us/kmarch/hh/kmarch/k105_2pf6.asp>.

119. "I've Got Work To Do—Worker Threads and Work Queues," *NT Insider,* Vol. 5, No. 5, October 1998 (updated August 20, 2002) <www.osronline.com/article.cfm?id=65>.

120. "Device-Dedicated Threads," *MSDN Library,* June 6, 2003, <msdn.microsoft.com/library/en-us/kmarch/hh/kmarch/synchro_9b1j.asp>.

121. "Managing Hardware Priorities," *MSDN Library,* June 6, 2003, <msdn.microsoft.com/library/en-us/kmarch/hh/kmarch/intrupts_0kh3.asp>.

122. "I've Got Work To Do—Worker Threads and Work Queues," *NT Insider,* Vol. 5, No. 5, October 1998 (updated August 20, 2002) <www.osronline.com/article.cfm?id=65>.

123. "System Worker Threads," *MSDN Library,* June 6, 2003, <msdn.microsoft.com/en-us/kmarch/hh/kmarch/synchro_9y1z.asp>.

124. "Processes and Threads," *MSDN Library,* <msdn.microsoft.com/library/en-us/dllproc/base/about_processes_and_threads.asp>.

125. "Creating Processes," *MSDN Library,* <msdn.microsoft.com/library/en-us/dllproc/base/creating_processes.asp>.

126. "Event Objects," *MSDN Library,* <msdn.microsoft.com/library/en-us/dllproc/base/event_objects.asp>.

127. Solomon, D., and M. Russinovich, *Inside Windows 2000,* 3rd ed., Redmond: Microsoft Press, 2000.

128. Schreiber, S., *Undocumented Windows 2000 Secrets,* Boston: Addison-Wesley, 2001.

129. Schreiber, S., *Undocumented Windows 2000 Secrets,* Boston: Addison-Wesley, 2001, p. 416.

130. Solomon, D., and M. Russinovich, *Inside Windows 2000,* 3rd ed, Redmond: Microsoft Press, 2000, p. 291.

131. Schreiber, S., *Undocumented Windows 2000 Secrets,* Boston: Addison-Wesley, 2001, p. 429.

132. Solomon, D., and M. Russinovich, *Inside Windows 2000,* 3rd ed, Redmond: Microsoft Press, 2000, p. 291.

133. Schreiber, S., *Undocumented Windows 2000 Secrets,* Boston: Addison-Wesley, 2001, p. 416.

134. Solomon, D., and M. Russinovich, *Inside Windows 2000,* 3rd ed, Redmond: Microsoft Press, 2000, p. 319.

135. Schreiber, S., *Undocumented Windows 2000 Secrets,* Boston: Addison-Wesley, 2001, p. 419.

136. Solomon, D., and M. Russinovich, *Inside Windows 2000,* 3rd ed, Redmond: Microsoft Press, 2000, pp. 320–321.

137. Schreiber, S., *Undocumented Windows 2000 Secrets,* Boston: Addison-Wesley, 2001, p. 429.

138. Solomon, D., and M. Russinovich, *Inside Windows 2000,* 3rd ed, Redmond: Microsoft Press, 2000, p. 328.

139. "Thread Local Storage," *MSDN Library,* February 2003, <msdn.microsoft.com/library/en-us/dllproc/base/thread_local_storage.asp>.

140. "Creating Processes," *MSDN Library,* February 2003, <msdn.microsoft.com/library/en-us/dllproc/base/creating_processes.asp>.

141. "Inheritance," *MSDN Library,* February 2003, <msdn.microsoft.com/library/en-us/dllproc/base/inheritance.asp>.

142. "About Processes and Threads," *MSDN Library,* February 2003, <msdn.microsoft.com/library/en-us/dllproc/base/about_processes_and_threads.asp>.

143. "Terminating a Process," *MSDN Library,* February 2003, <msdn.microsoft.com/library/en-us/dllproc/base/terminating_a_process.asp>.

144. Richter, J., "Make Your Windows 2000 Processes Play Nice Together with Job Kernel Objects," *Microsoft Systems Journal,* March 1999, <www.microsoft.com/msj/0399/jobkernelobj/jobkernelobj.aspx>.

145. "JobObject_Basic_Limit_Information," *MSDN Library,* February 2003, <msdn.microsoft.com/library/en-us/dllproc/base/jobobject_basic_limit_information_str.asp>.

146. "SetInformationJobObject," *MSDN Library,* February 2003, <msdn.microsoft.com/library/en-us/dllproc/base/setinformationjobobject.asp>.

147. "Job Objects," *MSDN Library,* February 2003, <msdn.microsoft.com/library/en-us/dllproc/base/job_objects.asp>.

148. Richter, J., "Make Your Windows 2000 Processes Play Nice Together with Job Kernel Objects," *Microsoft Systems Journal,* March 1999, <www.microsoft.com/msj/0399/jobkernelobj/jobkernelobj.aspx>.

149. "Fibers," *MSDN Library,* February 2003, <msdn.microsoft.com/library/en-us/dllproc/base/fibers.asp>.

150. "Convert Thread to Fiber," *MSDN Library,* February 2003, <msdn.microsoft.com/library/en-us/dllproc/base/convertthreadtofiber.asp>.

151. "Fibers," *MSDN Library,* February 2003, <msdn.microsoft.com/library/en-us/dllproc/base/fibers.asp>.

152. Zabatta, F., and K. Ying, "A Thread Performance Comparison: Windows NT and Solaris on a Symmetric Multiprocessor," *Proceedings of the Second USENIX Windows NT Symposium,* August 5, 1998, pp. 57–66.

153. Benjamin, C., "The Fibers of Threads," *Compile Time (Linux Magazine),* May 2001, <www.linux-mag.com/2001-05/compile_06.html>.

154. "Thread Pooling," *MSDN Library,* February 2003, <msdn.microsoft.com/library/en-us/dllproc/base/thread_pooling.asp>.

155. "Queue User Worker Item," *MSDN Library,* February 2003, <msdn.microsoft.com/library/en-us/dllproc/base/queueuserworkitem.asp>.

156. Richter, J., "New Windows 2000 Pooling Functions Greatly Simplify Thread Management," *Microsoft Systems Journal,* April 1999, <www.microsoft.com/msj/0499/pooling/pooling.aspx>.

157. Richter, J., "New Windows 2000 Pooling Functions Greatly Simplify Thread Management," *Microsoft Systems Journal,* April 1999, <www.microsoft.com/msj/0499/pooling/pooling.aspx>.

158. Solomon, D., and M. Russinovich, *Inside Windows 2000,* 3rd ed, Redmond: Microsoft Press, 2000.

159. "Scheduling Priorities," *MSDN Library,* February 2003, <msdn.microsoft.com/library/en-us/dllproc/base/scheduling_priorities.asp>.

160. "Win_32 Thread," *MSDN Library*, July 2003, <msdn.microsoft.com/library/en-us/wmisdk/wmi/win32_thread.asp>.

161. Solomon, D., and M. Russinovich, *Inside Windows, 2000*, 3rd ed, Redmond: Microsoft Press, 2000, pp. 348–349.

162. "Scheduling Priorities," *MSDN Library*, February 2003, <msdn.microsoft.com/library/en-us/dllproc/base/scheduling_priorities.asp>.

163. "Scheduling Priorities," *MSDN Library*, February 2003, <msdn.microsoft.com/library/en-us/dllproc/base/scheduling_priorities.asp>.

164. Solomon, D., and M. Russinovich, *Inside Windows 2000*, 3rd ed, Redmond: Microsoft Press, 2000, pp. 356–358.

165. Solomon, D., and M. Russinovich, *Inside Windows 2000*, 3rd ed, Redmond: Microsoft Press, 2000, pp. 338, 347.

166. "Scheduling Priorities," *MSDN Library*, <msdn.microsoft.com/library/en-us/dllproc/base/scheduling_priorities.asp>.

167. "Priority Boosts," *MSDN Library*, <msdn.microsoft.com/library/en-us/dllproc/base/priority_boosts.asp>.

168. "Priority Inversion," *MSDN Library*, <msdn.microsoft.com/library/en-us/dllproc/base/priority_inversion.asp>.

169. "Multiple Processors," *MSDN Library*, <msdn.microsoft.com/library/en-us/dllproc/base/multiple_processors.asp>.

170. Solomon, D., and M. Russinovich, *Inside Windows 2000*, 3rd ed, Redmond: Microsoft Press, 2000, p. 371.

171. "Multiple Processors," *MSDN Library*, <msdn.microsoft.com/library/en-us/dllproc/base/multiple_processors.asp>.

172. Solomon, D., and M. Russinovich, *Inside Windows 2000*, 3rd ed, Redmond: Microsoft Press, 2000, pp. 371–373.

173. "Introduction to Kernel Dispatcher Objects," *MSDN Library*, June 6, 2003, <msdn.microsoft.com/library/en-us/kmarch/hh/kmarch/synchro_7kfb.asp>.

174. "Interprocess Synchronization," *MSDN Library*, February 2003, <msdn.microsoft.com/library/en-us/dllproc/base/interprocess_synchronization.asp>.

175. "Wait Functions," *MSDN Library*, February 2003, <msdn.microsoft.com/library/en-us/dllproc/base/wait_functions.asp>.

176. "Mutex Objects," *MSDN Library*, February 2003, <msdn.microsoft.com/library/en-us/dllproc/base/mutex_objects.asp>.

177. "Event Objects," *MSDN Library*, February 2003, <msdn.microsoft.com/library/en-us/dllproc/base/event_objects.asp>.

178. "Mutex Objects," *MSDN Library*, February 2003, <msdn.microsoft.com/library/en-us/dllproc/base/mutex_objects.asp>.

179. "Semaphore Objects," *MSDN Library*, February 2003, <msdn.microsoft.com/library/en-us/dllproc/base/semaphore_objects.asp>.

180. "Synchronicity: A Review of Synchronization Primitives," *NT Insider*, Vol. 9, No. 1, January 1, 2002, <www.osr.com/ntinsider/2002/synchronicity/synchronicity.htm>.

181. "Semaphore Objects," *MSDN Library*, February 2003, <msdn.microsoft.com/library/en-us/dllproc/base/semaphore_objects.asp>.

182. "Waitable Timer Objects," *MSDN Library*, February 2003, <msdn.microsoft.com/library/en-us/dllproc/base/waitable_timer_objects.asp>.

183. "Synchronization Objects," *MSDN Library*, February 2003, <msdn.microsoft.com/library/en-us/dllproc/base/synchronization_objects.asp>.

184. "Synchronizing Access to Device Data," *MSDN Library*, June 6, 2003, <msdn.microsoft.com/library/en-us/kmarch/hh/kmarch/intrupts_9sfb.asp>.

185. "Introduction to Spin Locks," *MSDN Library*, June 6, 2003, <msdn.microsoft.com/library/en-us/kmarch/hh/kmarch/synchro_8qsn.asp>.

186. "Queued Spin Locks," *MSDN Library*, June 6, 2003, <msdn.microsoft.com/library/en-us/kmarch/hh/kmarch/synchro_8ftz.asp>.

187. Friedman, M., and O. Pentakola, "Chapter 5: Multiprocessing," *Windows 2000 Performance Guide*, January 2002, <www.oreilly.com/catalog/w2kperf/chapter/ch05.html>.

188. "Queued Spin Locks," *MSDN Library*, June 6, 2003, <msdn.microsoft.com/library/en-us/kmarch/hh/kmarch/synchro_8ftz.asp>.

189. "Fast Mutexes," *MSDN Library*, June 6, 2003, <msdn.microsoft.com/library/en-us/kmarch/hh/kmarch/synchro_3zmv.asp>.

190. "Synchronicity: A Review of Synchronization Primitives," *NT Insider*, Vol. 9, No. 1, January 2002, <www.osr.com/ntinsider/2002/synchronicity/synchronicity.htm>.

191. "Fast Mutexes," *MSDN Library*, June 6, 2003, <msdn.microsoft.com/library/en-us/kmarch/hh/kmarch/synchro_3zmv.asp>.

192. "Synchronicity: A Review of Synchronization Primitives," *NT Insider*, Vol. 9, No. 1, January 2002, <www.osr.com/ntinsider/2002/synchronicity/synchronicity.htm>.

193. "Critical Section Objects," *MSDN Library*, February 2003, <msdn.microsoft.com/library/en-us/dllproc/base/critical_section_objects.asp>.

194. Prasad, S., "Windows NT Threads," *BYTE*, November 1995, <www.byte.com/art/9511/sec11/art3.htm>.

195. "Time Queues," *MSDN Library*, February 2003, <msdn.microsoft.com/library/en-us/dllproc/base/timer_queues.asp>.

196. "Interlocked Variable Access," *MSDN Library*, February 2003, <msdn.microsoft.com/library/en-us/dllproc/base/interlocked_variable_access.asp>.

197. "Interlocking Singly Linked Lists," *MSDN Library*, February 2003, <msdn.microsoft.com/library/en-us/dllproc/base/interlocked_singly_linked_lists.asp>.

198. "Introducing 64-Bit Windows," *MSDN Library*, February 2003, `<msdn.microsoft.com/library/en-us/win64/win64/intro ducing_64_bit_windows.asp>`.

199. "Memory Support and Windows Operating Systems," Microsoft Windows Platform Development, Microsoft Corporation, December 4, 2001, `<www.microsoft.com/hwdev/platform/ server/PAE/PAEmem.asp>`.

200. "NT Memory, Storage, Design, and More," `<www.windowsitli- brary.com/Content/113/01/1.html>`.

201. R. Kath, "The Virtual-Memory Manager in Windows NT," *MSDN Library*, December 21, 1992, `<msdn.microsoft.com/ library/en-us/dngenlib/html/ msdn_ntvmm.asp?frame=true>`.

202. R. Kath, "The Virtual-Memory Manager in Windows NT," *MSDN Library*, December 21, 1992, `<msdn.microsoft.com/ library/en-us/dngenlib/html/ msdn_ntvmm.asp?frame=true>`.

203. "Memory Protection," *MSDN Library*, February 2003, `<msdn.microsoft.com/library/default.asp?url=/library/ en-us/memory/base/memory_protection.asp>`.

204. "Large Page Support," *MSDN Library*, February 2001, `<msdn.microsoft.com/library/en-us/memory/base/ large_page_support.asp?frame=true>`.

205. Russinovich, M., and D. Solomon, "Windows XP: Kernel Improvements Create a More Robust, Powerful, and Scalable OS," *MSDN Magazine*, December 2001, `<msdn.microsoft.com/ msdnmag/issues/01/12/XPKernel/print.asp>`.

206. R. Kath, "The Virtual-Memory Manager in Windows NT," *MSDN Library*, December 21, 1992, `<msdn.microsoft.com/ library/en-us/dngenlib/html/ msdn_ntvmm.asp?frame=true>`.

207. "GetLargePageMinimum," *MSDN Library*, February 2003, `<msdn.microsoft.com/library/en-us/memory/base/get- largepageminimum.asp>`.

208. "Large Page Support," *MSDN Library*, February 2001, `<msdn.microsoft.com/library/en-us/memory/base/ large_page_support.asp?frame=true>`.

209. GetLargePageMinimum," *MSDN Library*, February 2003, `<msdn.microsoft.com/library/en-us/memory/base/get- largepageminimum.asp>`.

210. "Large Page Support in the Linux Kernel," *LWN.net. 2002*, `<lwn.net/Articles/6969/>`.

211. Kath, R., "The Virtual-Memory Manager in Windows NT," *MSDN Library*, December 21, 1992, `<msdn.microsoft.com/ library/en-us/dngenlib/html/msdn_ntvmm.asp>`.

212. Friedman, M. B., "Windows NT Page Replacement Policies," *Computer Measurement Group*, 1999, `<www.demandtech.com/ Resources/Papers/WinMemMgmt.pdf>`.

213. "Allocating Virtual Memory," *MSDN Library*, February 2003, `<msdn.microsoft.com/library/en-us/memory/base/ allocating_virtual_memory.asp?frame=true>`.

214. "Memory Management Enhancements," *MSDN Library*, February 13, 2003, `<msdn.microsoft.com/library/en-us/appen- dix/hh/appendix/enhancements5_3oc3.asp?frame=true>`.

215. "Bug Check 0x41: Must_Succeed_Pool_Empty," *MSDN Library*, June 6, 2003, `<msdn.microsoft.com/library/en-us/ddtools/ hh/ddtools/bccodes_0bon.asp?frame=true>`.

216. Munro, J., "Windows XP Kernel Enhancements," *ExtremeTech*, June 8, 2001, `<www.extremetech.com/print_article/ 0,3998,a=2473,00.asp>`.

217. Munro, J., "Windows XP Kernel Enhancements," *ExtremeTech*, June 8, 2001, `<www.extremetech.com/print_article/ 0,3998,a=2473,00.asp>`.

218. Russinovich, M., "Inside Memory Management, Part 2," *Windows & .NET Magazine*, September 1998, `<www.winnet- mag.com/Articles/Print.cfm?ArticleID=3774>`.

219. Kath, R., "The Virtual-Memory Manager in Windows NT," *MSDN Library*, December 21, 1998, `<msdn.microsoft.com/ library/en-us/dngenlib/html/msdn_ntvmm.asp? frame=true>`.

220. "Windows NT Virtual Memory (Part II)," *OSR Open Systems Resources, Inc.*, 1999, `<www.osr.com/ntinsider/1999/ virtualmem2/virtualmem2.htm>`.

221. Friedman, M., "Windows NT Page Replacement Policies," *Computer Measurement Group CMG,* 1999, `<www.demandtech.com/ Resources/Papers/WinMemMgmt.pdf>`.

222. "How Windows NT Provides 4 Gigabytes of Memory," *Microsoft Knowledge Base Article—99707*, February 20, 2002, `<www.itpa- pers.com/cgi/PSummaryIT.pl?paperid= 23661&scid=273>`.

223. Munro, J., "Windows XP Kernel Enhancements," June 8, 2001, `<www.extremetech.com/print_article/ 0,3998,a=2473,00.asp>`.

224. LaBorde, D., "TWEAKS for Windows XP for Video Editing (v. 1.0)," *SlashCAM*.com, 2001, `<www.slashcam.de/artikel/Tips/ TWEAKS_for_Windows_XP_for_Video_ Editing__v_1_0_.html>`.

225. "Memory Management Enhancements," *MSDN Library*, `<msdn.microsoft.com/library/en-us/appendix/hh/appen- dix/enhancements5_3oc3.asp>`.

226. "Memory Management Enhancements," *MSDN Library*, `<msdn.microsoft.com/library/en-us/appendix/hh/appen- dix/enhancements5_3oc3.asp>`.

227. LaBorde, D., "Windows XP Tweaks/Optimizations for Windows XP for Video Editing Systems–Part II," *SlashCAM*, 2002, `<www.slashcam.de/artikel/Tips/Windows _XP_TWEAKS___Optimization_for_Video_Editing_Systems__ _PART_II.html>`.

228. "Fast System Startup for PCs Running Windows XP," *Windows Platform Design Notes: Designing Hardware for the Microsoft® Windows® Family of Operating Systems*, Microsoft Corporation, January 31, 2002, `<www.microsoft.com/hwdev/platform/per- formance/fastboot/fastboot-winxp.asp>`.

229. Kath, R., "Managing Virtual Memory in Win23," *MSDN Library*, January 20, 1993, <msdn.microsoft.com/library/en-us/dngenlib/html/msdn_virtmm.asp?frame=true>.

230. Kath, R., "The Virtual-Memory Manager in Windows NT," *MSDN Library*, December 21, 1992, <msdn.microsfot.com/library/en-us/dngenlib/html/msdn_ntvmm.asp?frame=true>.

231. LaBorde, D., "TWEAKS for Windows XP for Video Editing (v. 1.0)," *Slashcam.com*, 2001, <www.slashcam.de/artikel/Tips/TWEAKS_for_Windows_XP_for_Video_Editing__v_1_0_.html>.

232. Friedman, M. B., "Windows NT Page Replacement Policies," *Computer Measurement Group CMG*, 1999, <www.demand-tech.com/Resources/Papers/WinMemMgmt.pdf>.

233. Friedman, M. B., "Windows NT Page Replacement Policies," *Computer Measurement Group CMG*, 1999, <www.demand-tech.com/Resources/Papers/WinMemMgmt.pdf>.

234. Kath, R., "The Virtual-Memory Manager in Windows NT," *MSDN Library*, December 21, 1992, <msdn.microsoft.com/library/en-us/dngenlib/html/msdn_ntvmm.asp?frame=true>.

235. Russinovich, M., "Inside Memory Management, Part 2," *Windows & .NET Magazine*, September 1998, <www.winnetmag.com/Articles/Index.cfm?ArticleID=3774&pg=2>.

236. Friedman, M. B., "Windows NT Page Replacement Policies," *Computer Measurement Group CMG*, 1999, <www.demand-tech.com/Resources/Papers/WinMemMgmt.pdf>.

237. Friedman, M. B., "Windows NT Page Replacement Policies," *Computer Measurement Group CMG*, 1999, <www.demand-tech.com/Resources/Papers/WinMemMgmt.pdf>.

238. Anderson, C., "Windows NT Paging Fundamentals," *Windows & .NET Magazine*, November 1997, <www.winnetmag.com/Articles/Print.cfm?ArticleID=595>.

239. Munro, J., "Windows XP Kernel Enhancements," *ExtremeTech*, June 8, 2001, <www.extremetech.com/print_article/0,3998,a=2473,00.asp>.

240. "When Should Code and Data Be Pageable?" *MSDN Library*, <msdn.microsoft.com/library/en-us/kmarch/hh/kmarch/memmgmt_7vhj.asp?frame=true>.

241. "Device Drivers and File System Drivers Defined," *MSDN Library*, February 13, 2003, <msdn.microsoft.com/library/en-us/gstart/hh/gstart/gs_basics_4w6f.asp>.

242. Custer, H., *Inside the Windows NT File System,* Redmond: Microsoft Press, 1994.

243. "File Systems," *Microsoft TechNet*, September 10, 2003, <www.microsoft.com/technet/prodtechnol/winxppro/reskit/prkc_fil_buvl.asp>.

244. Custer, H., *Inside the Windows NT File System,* Redmond: Microsoft Press, 1994, p. 17.

245. Solomon, D., and M. Russinovich, *Inside Windows 2000,* 3rd ed., Redmond: Microsoft Press, 2000.

246. Richter, J., and L. F. Cabrera. "A File System for the 21st Century: Previewing the Windows NT 5.0 File System," *Microsoft Systems Journal*, November 1998, <www.microsoft.com/msj/1998/ntfs/ntfs.aspx>.

247. Russinovich, M., "Inside NTFS," *Windows & .NET Magazine*, January 1998, <www.win2000mag.com/Articles/Print.cfm?ArticleID=3455>.

248. Custer, H., *Inside the Windows NT File System,* Redmond: Microsoft Press, 1994, pp. 24–28.

249. Russinovich, M., "Inside NTFS," *Windows & .NET Magazine*, January 1998. <www.win200mag.com/Articles/Print.cfm?ArticleID=3455>.

250. Esposito, D., "A Programmer's Perspective on NTFS 2000, Part 1: Stream and Hard Link," *MSDN Library*, March 2000, <msdn.microsoft.com/library/en-us/dnfiles/html/ntfs5.asp>.

251. Richter, J., and L. F. Cabrera, "A File System for the 21st Century: Previewing the Windows NT 5.0 File System," *Microsoft Systems Journal*, November 1998, <www.microsoft.com/msj/1198/ntfs/ntfs.aspx>.

252. Richter, J., and L. F. Cabrera, "A File System for the 21st Century: Previewing the Windows NT 5.0 File System," *Microsoft Systems Journal*, November 1998, <www.microsoft.com/msj/1198/ntfs/ntfs.aspx>.

253. Esposito, D., "A Programmer's Perspective on NTFS 2000, Part 2: Encryption, Sparseness, and Reparse Points," *MSDN Library*, May 2000, <msdn.microsoft.com/library/en-us/dnfiles/html/ntfs2.asp>.

254. "NTFS," *MSDN Library*, February 2003, <msdn.microsoft.com/library/en-us/fileio/base/ntfs.asp>.

255. Phamdo, N., "Lossless Data Compression," *Data-Compression.com*, 2001, <www.data-compression.com/lossless.html>.

256. Richter, J., and L. F. Cabrera, "A File System for the 21st Century: Previewing the Windows NT 5.0 File System," *Microsoft Systems Journal*, November 1998, <www.microsoft.com/msj/1198/ntfs/ntfs.aspx>.

257. Richter, J., and L. F. Cabrera, "A File System for the 21st Century: Previewing the Windows NT 5.0 File System," *Microsoft Systems Journal*, November 1998, <www.microsoft.com/msj/1198/ntfs/ntfs.aspx>.

258. Esposito, D., "A Programmer's Perspective on NTFS 2000, Part 2: Encryption, Sparseness, and Reparse Points," *MSDN Library*, May 2000, <msdn.microsoft.com/library/en-us/dnfiles/html/ntfs2.asp>.

259. Richter, J., and L. F. Cabrera, "A File System for the 21st Century: Previewing the Windows NT 5.0 File System," *Microsoft Systems Journal*, November 1998, <www.microsoft.com/msj/1198/ntfs/ntfs.aspx>.

260. Richter, J., and L. F. Cabrera, "A File System for the 21st Century: Previewing the Windows NT 5.0 File System," *Microsoft Systems Journal*, November 1998, <www.microsoft.com/msj/1198/ntfs/ntfs.aspx>.

261. "Microsoft Windows XP: What's New in Security for Windows XP Professional and Windows XP Home," *Microsoft Corpora-

tion, July 2001, <www.microsoft.com/windowsxp/pro/techinfo/planning/security/whatsnew/WindowsXPSecurity.doc>.

262. Richter, J., and L. F. Cabrera, "A File System for the 21st Century: Previewing the Windows NT 5.0 File System," *Microsoft Systems Journal*, November 1998, <www.microsoft.com/msj/1198/ntfs/ntfs.aspx>.

263. Esposito, D., "A Programmer's Perspective on NTFS 2000, Part 1: Stream and Hard Link," *MSDN Library*, March 2000, <msdn.microsoft.com/library/en-us/dnfiles/html/ntfs5.asp>.

264. Esposito, D., "A Programmer's Perspective on NTFS 2000, Part 2: Encryption, Sparseness, and Reparse Points," *MSDN Library*, May 2000, <msdn.microsoft.com/library/en-us/dnfiles/html/ntfs2.asp>.

265. Richter, J., and L. F. Cabrera, "A File System for the 21st Century: Previewing the Windows NT 5.0 File System," *Microsoft Systems Journal*, November 1998, <www.microsoft.com/msj/1198/ntfs/ntfs.aspx>.

266. Richter, J., and L. F. Cabrera, "A File System for the 21st Century: Previewing the Windows NT 5.0 File System," *Microsoft Systems Journal*, November 1998, <www.microsoft.com/msj/1198/ntfs/ntfs.aspx>.

267. Esposito, D., "A Programmer's Perspective on NTFS 2000, Part 2: Encryption, Sparseness, and Reparse Points," *MSDN Library*, May 2000, <msdn.microsoft.com/library/en-us/dnfiles/html/ntfs2.asp>.

268. Esposito, D., "A Programmer's Perspective on NTFS 2000, Part 2: Encryption, Sparseness, and Reparse Points," *MSDN Library*, May 2000, <msdn.microsoft.com/library/en-us/dnfiles/html/ntfs2.asp>.

269. Richter, J., and L. F. Cabrera, "A File System for the 21st Century: Previewing the Windows NT 5.0 File System," *Microsoft Systems Journal*, November 1998, <www.microsoft.com/msj/1198/ntfs/ntfs.aspx>.

270. "Overview of the Windows I/O Model," *MSDN Library*, June 6, 2003, <msdn.microsoft.com/library/en-us/kmarch/hh/kmarch/irps_0rhj.asp>.

271. "Plug and Play for Windows 2000 and Windows XP," *Windows Hardware and Driver Central*, December 4, 2001, <www.microsoft.com/whdc/hwdev/tech/pnp/pnpnt5_2.mspx>.

272. "Introduction to Device Objects," *MSDN Library*, June 6, 2003, <msdn.microsoft.com/library/en-us/kmarch/hh/kmarch/devobjts_4fqf.asp>.

273. "WDM Driver Layers: An Example," *MSDN Library*, June 6, 2003, <msdn.microsoft.com/library/en-us/kmarch/hh/kmarch/wdmintro_4uuf.asp>.

274. "Types of Drivers," *MSDN Library*, June 6, 2003, <msdn.microsoft.com/library/en-us/kmarch/hh/kmarch/intro_8r6v.asp>.

275. "Device Extensions," *MSDN Library*, June 6, 2003, <msdn.microsoft.com/library/en-us/kmarch/hh/kmarch/devobjts_1gdj.asp>.

276. "Introduction to Driver Objects," *MSDN Library*, June 6, 2003, <msdn.microsoft.com/library/en-us/kmarch/hh/kmarch/drvcomps_6js7.asp>.

277. "Introduction to Standard Driver Routines," *MSDN Library*, June 6, 2003, <msdn.microsoft.com/library/en-us/kmarch/hh/kmarch/drvcomps_24kn.asp>.

278. "Introduction to Plug and Play," *MSDN Library*, June 6, 2003, <msdn.microsoft.com/library/en-us/kmarch/hh/kmarch/plugplay_2tyf.asp>.

279. "PnP Components," *MSDN Library*, June 6, 2003, <msdn.microsoft.com/library/en-us/kmarch/hh/kmarch/plugplay_4bs7.asp>.

280. "PnP Driver Design Guidelines," *MSDN Library*, June 6, 2003, <msdn.microsoft.com/library/en-us/kmarch/hh/kmarch/plugplay_890n.asp>.

281. "Levels of Support for PnP," *MSDN Library*, June 6, 2003, <msdn.microsoft.com/library/en-us/kmarch/hh/kmarch/plugplay_78o7.asp>.

282. "Power Manager," *MSDN Library*, June 6, 2003, <msdn.microsoft.com/library/en-us/kmarch/hh/kmarch/pwrmgmt_30vb.asp>.

283. "System Power Policy," *MSDN Library*, June 6, 2003, <msdn.microsoft.com/library/en-us/kmarch/hh/kmarch/pwrmgmt_8baf.asp>.

284. "Driver Role in Power Management," *MSDN Library*, June 6, 2003, <msdn.microsoft.com/library/en-us/kmarch/hh/kmarch/pwrmgmt_47jb.asp>.

285. "Power IRPs for Individual Devices," *MSDN Library*, June 6, 2003, <msdn.microsoft.com/library/en-us/kmarch/hh/kmarch/pwrmgmt_6azr.asp>.

286. "Device Power States," *MSDN Library*, June 6, 2003, <msdn.microsoft.com/library/en-us/kmarch/hh/kmarch/pwrmgmt_20fb.asp>.

287. "Device Sleeping States," *MSDN Library*, June 6, 2003, <msdn.microsoft.com/library/en-us/kmarch/hh/kmarch/pwrmgmt_2ip3.asp>.

288. "System Power States," *MSDN Library*, June 6, 2003, <msdn.microsoft.com/library/en-us/kmarch/hh/kmarch/pwrmgmt_919j.asp>.

289. "Introduction to WDM," *MSDN Library*, <msdn.microsoft.com/library/en-us/kmarch/hh/kmarch/wdmintro_1ep3.asp>.

290. "Bus Drivers," *MSDN Library*, June 6, 2003, <msdn.microsoft.com/library/en-us/kmarch/hh/kmarch/wdmintro_8nfr.asp>.

291. "Filter Drivers," *MSDN Library*, June 6, 2003, <msdn.microsoft.com/library/en-us/kmarch/hh/kmarch/wdmintro_7dpj.asp>.

292. "Introduction to Device Interface," *MSDN Library,* June 6, 2003, <msdn.microsoft.com/library/en-us/install/hh/install/setup-cls_8vs7.asp>.

293. "Function Drivers," *MSDN Library,* June 6, 2003. <msdn.microsoft.com/library/en-us/kmarch/hh/kmarch/wdmintro_27fr.asp>.

294. "Types of Drivers," *MSDN Library,* June 6, 2003, <msdn.microsoft.com/library/en-us/kmarch/hh/kmarch/intro_8r6v.asp>.

295. "Types of WDM Drivers," *MSDN Library,* June 6, 2003, <msdn.microsoft.com/library/en-us/kmarch/hh/kmarch/wdmintro_3ep3.asp>.

296. "Introduction to WDM," *MSDN Library,* <msdn.microsoft.com/library/en-us/kmarch/hh/kmarch/wdmintro_1ep3.asp>.

297. "Introduction to WMI," *MSDN Library,* June 6, 2003, <msdn.microsoft.com/library/en-us/kmarch/hh/kmarch/wmi_5a1z.asp>.

298. "How NT Describes I/O Requests," *NT Insider,* Vol. 5, No. 1, January 1998, <www.osr.com/ntinsider/1998/Requests/requests.htm>.

299. "I/O Status Blocks," *MSDN Library,* June 6, 2003, <msdn.microsoft.com/library/en-us/kmarch/hh/kmarch/irps_0ofb.asp>.

300. "I/O Stack Locations," *MSDN Library,* June 6, 2003, <msdn.microsoft.com/library/en-us/kmarch/hh/kmarch/irps_8lgn.asp>.

301. "Starting a Device," *MSDN Library,* June 6, 2003, <msdn.microsoft.com/library/en-us/kmarch/hh/kmarch/plugplay_4otj.asp>.

302. "I/O Stack Locations," *MSDN Library,* June 6, 2003, <msdn.microsoft.com/library/en-us/kmarch/hh/kmarch/irps_8lgn.asp>.

303. "Example I/O Request—The Details," *MSDN Library,* June 6, 2003, <msdn.microsoft.com/library/en-us/kmarch/hh/kmarch/irps_1e3r.asp>.

304. "Registering an I/O Completion Routine," *MSDN Library,* June 6, 2003, <msdn.microsoft.com/library/en-us/kmarch/hh/kmarch/irps_6dd3.asp>.

305. "Example I/O Request—The Details," *MSDN Library,* June 6, 2003, <msdn.microsoft.com/library/en-us/kmarch/hh/kmarch/irps_1e3r.asp>.

306. "Example I/O Request—The Details," *MSDN Library,* June 6, 2003, <msdn.microsoft.com/library/en-us/kmarch/hh/kmarch/irps_1e3r.asp>.

307. "Queuing and Dequeuing IRPs," *MSDN Library,* June 6, 2003, <msdn.microsoft.com/library/en-us/kmarch/hh/kmarch/irps_4mqv.asp>.

308. "Synchronous and Asynchronous I/O," *MSDN Library,* February 2003 <msdn.microsoft.com/library/en-us/fileio/base/synchronous_and_asynchronous_i_o.asp>.

309. "Synchronization and Overlapped Input and Output," *MSDN Library,* February 2003, <msdn.microsoft.com/library/en-us/dllproc/base/synchronization_and_overlapped_input_and_output.asp>.

310. "Alertable I/O," *MSDN Library,* February 2003, <msdn.microsoft.com/library/en-us/fileio/base/alertable_i_o.asp>.

311. "I/O Completion Ports," *MSDN Library,* February 2003, <msdn.microsoft.com/library/en-us/fileio/base/i_o_completion_ports.asp>.

312. "Methods for Accessing Data Buffers," *MSDN Library,* June 6, 2003, <msdn.microsoft.com/library/en-us/kmarch/hh/kmarch/iputoput_3m07.asp>.

313. "Using Buffered I/O," *MSDN Library,* June 6, 2003, <msdn.microsoft.com/library/en-us/kmarch/hh/kmarch/iputoput_1ulj.asp>.

314. "Methods for Accessing Data Buffers," *MSDN Library,* June 6, 2003, <msdn.microsoft.com/library/en-us/kmarch/hh/kmarch/iputoput_3m07.asp>.

315. "Using Buffered I/O," *MSDN Library,* June 6, 2003, <msdn.microsoft.com/library/en-us/kmarch/hh/kmarch/iputoput_1ulj.asp>.

316. "Using Direct I/O with DMA," *MSDN Library,* June 6, 2003, <msdn.microsoft.com/library/en-us/kmarch/hh/kmarch/iputoput_0gx3.asp>.

317. "Using Neither Buffered nor Direct I/O," *MSDN Library,* June 6, 2003, <msdn.microsoft.com/library/en-us/kmarch/hh/kmarch/iputoput_3cbr.asp>.

318. "How NT Describes I/O Requests," *NT Insider,* Vol. 5, No. 1, January 1998, <www.osr.com/ntinsider/1998/Requests/requests.htm>.

319. "Methods for Accessing Data Buffers," *MSDN Library,* June 6, 2003, <msdn.microsoft.com/library/en-us/kmarch/hh/kmarch/iputoput_3m07.asp>.

320. "Example I/O Request—The Details," *MSDN Library,* June 6, 2003, <msdn.microsoft.com/library/en-us/kmarch/hh/kmarch/irps_1e3r.asp>.

321. "InterruptService," *MSDN Library,* June 6, 2003, <msdn.microsoft.com/library/en-us/kmarch/hh/kmarch/drvrrtns_29ma.asp>.

322. "Registering an ISR," *MSDN Library,* June 6, 2003, <msdn.microsoft.com/library/en-us/kmarch/hh/kmarch/intrupts_87qf.asp>.

323. "Introduction to Interrupt Objects," *MSDN Library,* June 6, 2003, <msdn.microsoft.com/library/en-us/kmarch/hh/kmarch/intrupts_417r.asp>.

324. "Registering an ISR," *MSDN Library,* June 6, 2003, <msdn.microsoft.com/library/en-us/kmarch/hh/kmarch/intrupts_87qf.asp>.

325. "Solomon, D., and M. Russinovich, *Inside Windows 2000,* 3rd ed, Redmond: Microsoft Press, 2000, p. 92.

326. "Key Benefits of the I/O APIC," *Windows Hardware and Driver Central,* <www.microsoft.com/whdc/hwdev/platform/proc/IO-APIC.mspx>.

327. "Writing an ISR," *MSDN Library,* June 6, 2003, <msdn.microsoft.com/library/en-us/kmarch/hh/kmarch/intrupts_4ron.asp>.

328. "File Caching," *MSDN Library,* February 2003, <msdn.microsoft.com/library/en-us/fileio/base/file_caching.asp>.

329. "The NT Cache Manager," *NT Insider*, Vol. 3, No. 2, April 1996, <www.osr.com/ntinsider/1996/cacheman.htm>.

330. "The NT Cache Manager," *NT Insider*, Vol. 3, No. 2, April 1996, <www.osr.com/ntinsider/1996/cacheman.htm>.

331. "File Caching," *MSDN Library,* February 2003, <msdn.microsoft.com/library/en-us/fileio/base/file_caching.asp>.

332. "Life in the Fast I/O Lane," *NT Insider*, Vol. 3, No. 1, February 15, 1996, updated October 31, 2002, <www.osronline.com/article.cfm?id=166>.

333. "File Caching," *MSDN Library,* February 2003, <msdn.microsoft.com/library/en-us/fileio/base/file_caching.asp>.

334. "Mailslots," *MSDN Library,* February 2003, <msdn.microsoft.com/library/en-us/ipc/base/mailslots.asp>.

335. "About Pipes," *MSDN Library,* February 2003, <msdn.microsoft.com/library/en-us/ipc/base/about_pipes.asp>.

336. "Pipes," *MSDN Library,* February 2003, <msdn.microsoft.com/library/en-us/ipc/base/pipes.asp>.

337. "Named Pipes," *MSDN Library,* February 2003, <msdn.microsoft.com/library/en-us/ipc/base/named_pipes.asp>.

338. "Named Pipes Open Modes," *MSDN Library,* February 2003, <msdn.microsoft.com/library/en-us/ipc/base/named_pipe_open_modes.asp>.

339. "Anonymous Pipes," *MSDN Library,* February 2003, <msdn.microsoft.com/library/en-us/ipc/base/anonymous_pipes.asp>.

340. "Anonymous Pipe Operations," *MSDN Library,* February 2003, <msdn.microsoft.com/library/en-us/ipc/base/anonymous_pipe_operations.asp>.

341. "Anonymous Pipe Operations," *MSDN Library,* February 2003, <msdn.microsoft.com/library/en-us/ipc/base/anonymous_pipe_operations.asp>.

342. "Named Pipes," *MSDN Library,* February 2003, <msdn.microsoft.com/library/en-us/ipc/base/named_pipes.asp>.

343. "CreateNamedPipe," *MSDN Library,* February 2003, <msdn.microsoft.com/library/en-us/ipc/base/create-namedpipe.asp>.

344. "Named Pipe Type, Read, and Wait Modes," *MSDN Library,* February 2003, <msdn.microsoft.com/library/en-us/ipc/base/named_pipe_type_read_and_wait_modes.asp>.

345. "Named Pipes Open Modes," *MSDN Library,* February 2003, <msdn.microsoft.com/library/en-us/ipc/base/named_pipe_open_modes.asp>.

346. "Named Pipe Type, Read, and Wait Modes," *MSDN Library,* February 2003, <msdn.microsoft.com/library/en-us/ipc/base/named_pipe_type_read_and_wait_modes.asp>.

347. "Synchronous and Overlapped Input and Output," *MSDN Library,* February 2003, <msdn.microsoft.com/library/en-us/ipc/base/synchronous_and_overlapped_input_and_output.asp>.

348. "Mailslots," *MSDN Library,* February 2003, <msdn.microsoft.com/library/en-us/ipc/base/mailslots.asp>.

349. "About Mailslots," *MSDN Library,* February 2003, <msdn.microsoft.com/library/en-us/ipc/base/about_mailslots.asp>.

350. "About Mailslots," *MSDN Library,* February 2003, <msdn.microsoft.com/library/en-us/ipc/base/about_mailslots.asp>.

351. "Common Windows Term Glossary," *Stanford Windows Infrastructure,* viewed July 10, 2003, <windows.stanford.edu/docs/glossary.htm>.

352. "About Mailslots," *MSDN Library,* February 2003, <msdn.microsoft.com/library/en-us/ipc/base/about_mailslots.asp>.

353. "CIFS/SMB Protocol Overview," *MSDN Library,* February 2003, <msdn.microsoft.com/library/en-us/fileio/base/cifs_smb_protocol_overview.asp>.

354. "Server and Client Functions," *MSDN Library,* February 2003, <msdn.microsoft.com/library/en-us/ipc/base/server_and_client_functions.asp>.

355. "File Mapping," *MSDN Library,* February 2003, <msdn.microsoft.com/library/en-us/fileio/base/file_mapping.asp?frame=true>.

356. "Sharing Files and Memory," *MSDN Library,* February 2003, <msdn.microsoft.com/library/en-us/fileio/base/sharing_files_and_memory.asp?frame=true>.

357. "File Mapping," *MSDN Library,* February 2003, <msdn.microsoft.com/library/en-us/fileio/base/file_mapping.asp?frame=true>.

358. Kath, R., "Managing Memory-Mapped Files in Win32," *MSDN Library,* February 9, 1993, <msdn.microsoft.com/library/en-us/dngenlib/html/msdn_manamemo.asp? frame=true>.

359. "Sharing Files and Memory," *MSDN Library,* February 2003, <msdn.microsoft.com/library/en-us/fileio/base/sharing_files_and_memory.asp?frame=true>.

360. Dabak, P.; M. Borate; and S. Phadke, "Local Procedure Call," *Windows IT Library,* October 1999, <www.windowsitlibrary.com/Content/356/08/1.html>.

361. Dabak, P.; M. Borate; and S. Phadke, "Local Procedure Call," *Windows IT Library,* October 1999, <www.windowsitlibrary.com/Content/356/08/1.html>.

362. Solomon, D., and M. Russinovich, *Inside Windows 2000,* 3rd ed, Redmond: Microsoft Press, 2000, p. 171.

363. Dabak, P.; M. Borate; and S. Phadke, "Local Procedure Call," *Windows IT Library,* October 1999, <www.windowsitlibrary.com/Content/356/08/1.html>.

364. "How RPC Works," *MSDN Library,* February 2003, <msdn.microsoft.com/library/en-us/rpc/rpc/how_rpc_works.asp>.

365. "DCE Glossary of Technical Terms," *Open Group,* 1996, <www.opengroup.org/dce/info/papers/dce-glossary.htm>.

366. "How RPC Works," *MSDN Library,* February 2003, <msdn.microsoft.com/library/en-us/rpc/rpc/how_rpc_works.asp>.

367. "Protocol Sequence Constants," *MSDN Library,* February 2003, <msdn.microsoft.com/library/en-us/rpc/rpc/protocol_sequence_constants.asp>.

368. "Asynchronous RPC," *MSDN Library,* February 2003, <msdn.microsoft.com/library/en-us/rpc/rpc/asynchronous_rpc.asp>.

369. "The IDL and ACF Files," *MSDN Library,* February 2003, <msdn.microsoft.com/library/en-us/rpc/rpc/the_idl_and_acf_files.asp>.

370. "Microsoft Interface Definition Language SDK Documentation," *MSDN Library,* February 2003, <msdn.microsoft.com/library/en-us/midl/midl/midl_start_page.asp>.

371. "The IDL Interface Header," *MSDN Library,* February 2003, <msdn.microsoft.com/library/en-us/rpc/rpc/the_idl_interface_header.asp>.

372. "The IDL Interface Body," *MSDN Library,* February 2003, <msdn.microsoft.com/library/en-us/rpc/rpc/the_idl_interface_body.asp>.

373. "Application Configuration File (ACF)," *MSDN Library,* February 2003, <msdn.microsoft.com/library/en-us/midl/midl/application_configuration_file_acf_.asp>.

374. "Registering Endpoints," *MSDN Library,* February 2003, <msdn.microsoft.com/library/en-us/rpc/rpc/registering_endpoints.asp>.

375. "Binding Handles," *MSDN Library,* February 2003, <msdn.microsoft.com/library/en-us/rpc/rpc/binding_handles.asp>.

376. "Client-Side Binding," *MSDN Library,* February 2003, <msdn.microsoft.com/library/en-us/rpc/rpc/client_side_binding.asp>.

377. "Selecting a Protocol Sequence," *MSDN Library,* February 2003, <msdn.microsoft.com/library/en-us/rpc/rpc/selecting_a_protocol_sequence.asp>.

378. "Types of Binding Handles," *MSDN Library,* February 2003, <msdn.microsoft.com/library/en-us/rpc/rpc/types_of_binding_handles.asp>.

379. "Explicit Binding Handles," *MSDN Library,* February 2003, <msdn.microsoft.com/library/en-us/rpc/rpc/explicit_binding_handles.asp>.

380. Dabak, P.; M. Borate; and S. Phadke, "Local Procedure Call," *Windows IT Library,* October 1999, <www.windowsitlibrary.com/Content/356/08/1.html>.

381. Williams, S., and C. Kindel, "The Component Object Model," October 1994, <msdn.microsoft.com/library/en-us/dncomg/html/msdn_comppr.asp>.

382. Williams, S., and C. Kindel, "The Component Object Model," October 1994, <msdn.microsoft.com/library/en-us/dncomg/html/msdn_comppr.asp>.

383. "COM Objects and Interfaces," *MSDN Library,* February 2003, <msdn.microsoft.com/library/en-us/com/htm/com_0alv.asp>.

384. S. Williams and C. Kindel, "The Component Object Model," October 1994, <msdn.microsoft.com/library/en-us/dncomg/html/msdn_comppr.asp>.

385. S. Williams and C. Kindel, "The Component Object Model," October 1994, <msdn.microsoft.com/library/en-us/dncomg/html/msdn_comppr.asp>.

386. "The COM Library," *MSDN Library,* February 2003, <msdn.microsoft.com/library/en-us/com/htm/com_1fuh.asp>.

387. "Registering COM Servers," *MSDN Library,* February 2003, <msdn.microsoft.com/library/en-us/com/htm/comext_05pv.asp>.

388. "QueryInterface: Navigating an Object," *MSDN Library,* February 2003, <msdn.microsoft.com/library/en-us/com/htm/com_02b8.asp>.

389. Williams, S., and C. Kindel, "The Component Object Model," October 1994, <msdn.microsoft.com/library/en-us/dncomg/html/msdn_comppr.asp>.

390. "DCOM Technical Overview," Microsoft Corporation, 1996, <msdn.microsoft.com/library/en-us/dndcom/html/msdn_dcomtec.asp>.

391. "Processes, Threads and Apartments," *MSDN Library,* February 2003, <msdn.microsoft.com/library/en-us/com/htm/aptnthrd_8po3.asp>.

392. "Introducing COM+," *MSDN Library,* February 2003, <msdn.microsoft.com/library/en-us/cossdk/htm/betaintr_6d5r.asp>.

393. "What's New in COM+ 1.5," *MSDN Library* February 2003, <msdn.microsoft.com/library/en-us/cossdk/htm/whatsnewcomplus_350z.asp>.

394. "DCOM Technical Overview," Microsoft Corporation, 1996, <msdn.microsoft.com/library/en-us/dndcom/html/msdn_dcomtec.asp>.

395. "Introduction to ActiveX Controls," *MSDN Library,* July 9, 2003, <msdn.microsoft.com/workshop/components/activex/intro.asp>.

396. "Clipboard," *MSDN Library,* 2003, <msdn.microsoft.com/library/en-us/winui/winui/windowsuserinterface/dataexchange/clipboard.asp>.

397. "About the Clipboard," *MDSN Library,* 2003, <msdn.microsoft.com/library/en-us/winui/winui/windowsuserinterface/dataexchange/clipboard/abouttheclipboard.asp>.

398. "Clipboard Formats," *MSDN Library,* 2003, <msdn.microsoft.com/library/en-us/winui/winui/windowsuserinterface/dataexchange/clipboard/clipboardformats.asp>.

399. "About the Clipboard," *MSDN Library,* 2003, <msdn.microsoft.com/library/en-us/winui/winui/windowsuserinterface/dataexchange/clipboard/abouttheclipboard.asp>.

400. Brockschmidt, K., "OLE Integration Technologies: A Technical Overview," Microsoft Corporation, October 1994, <msdn.microsoft.com/library/en-us/dnolegen/html/msdn_ddjole.asp>.

401. "Network Redirectors," *MSDN Library,* February 2003, <msdn.microsoft.com/library/en-us/fileio/base/network_redirectors.asp>.

402. "Description of a Network I/O Operation," *MSDN Library,* February 2003, <msdn.microsoft.com/library/en-us/fileio/base/description_of_a_network_i_o_operation.asp>.

403. "Network Redirectors," *MSDN Library,* February 2003, <msdn.microsoft.com/library/en-us/fileio/base/network_redirectors.asp>.

404. "Description of a Network I/O Operation," *MSDN Library,* February 2003, <msdn.microsoft.com/library/en-us/fileio/base/description_of_a_network_i_o_operation.asp>.

405. Zacker, C., "Multiple UNC Provider: NT's Traffic Cop," *Windows & .NET Magazine,* May 1998, <www.winnetmag.com/Articles/Index.cfm?ArticleID=3127>.

406. "CIFS/SMB Protocol Overview," *MSDN Library,* February 2003, <msdn.microsoft.com/library/en-us/fileio/base/cifs_smb_protocol_overview.asp>.

407. Leach, P., and D. Perry, "CIFS: A Common Internet File System," *Microsoft.com,* November 1996, <www.microsoft.com/mind/1196/cifs.asp>.

408. Munro, J., "Windows XP Kernel Enhancements," *ExtremeTech,* June 8, 2001, <www.extremetech.com/print_article/0,3998,a=2473,00.asp>.

409. "CIF Packet Exchange Scenario," *MSDN Library,* June 6, 2003, <msdn.microsoft.com/library/en-us/fileio/base/cif_packet_exchange_scenario.asp>.

410. "Opportunistic Locks," *MSDN Library,* February 2003, <msdn.microsoft.com/library/en-us/fileio/base/opportunistic_locks.asp>.

411. "Breaking Opportunistic Locks," *MSDN Library,* February 2003, <msdn.microsoft.com/library/en-us/fileio/base/breaking_opportunistic_locks.asp>.

412. "NDIS Drivers," *MSDN Library,* June 6, 2003, <msdn.microsoft.com/library/en-us/network/hh/network/102gen_0w2v.asp>.

413. "Benefits of Remote NDIS," *MSDN Library,* June 6, 2003, <msdn.microsoft.com/library/en-us/network/hh/network/rndisover_44mf.asp>.

414. "Introduction to Intermediate Drivers," *MSDN Library,* June 6, 2003, <msdn.microsoft.com/library/en-us/network/hh/network/301int_78mf.asp>.

415. "NDIS Miniport Drivers," *MSDN Library,* June 6, 2003, <msdn.microsoft.com/library/en-us/network/hh/network/102gen_1v5d.asp>.

416. "NDIS Intermediate Drivers," *MSDN Library,* June 6, 2003, <msdn.microsoft.com/library/en-us/network/hh/network/102gen_4mw7.asp>.

417. "NDIS Protocol Drivers," *MSDN Library,* June 6, 2003, <msdn.microsoft.com/library/en-us/network/hh/network/102gen_67hj.asp>.

418. "TDI Drivers," *MSDN Library,* June 6, 2003, <msdn.microsoft.com/library/en-us/network/hh/network/102gen_4y93.asp>.

419. "TCP/IP and Other Network Protocols," *Windows XP Professional Resource Kit,* viewed July 7, 2003, <www.microsoft.com/technetprodtechnol/winxppro/reskit/prcf_omn_gzcg.asp>.

420. "Network Protocols," *Windows XP Resource Kit,* viewed July 7, 2003, <www.microsoft.com/technet/prodtechnol/winxppro/reskit/prch_cnn_lafg.asp>.

421. "Introduction to Intermediate Drivers," *MSDN Library,* June 6, 2003, <msdn.microsoft.com/library/en-us/network/hh/network/301int_78mf.asp>.

422. "TCP/IP and Other Network Protocols," *Windows XP Professional Resource Kit,* viewed July 7, 2003, <www.microsoft.com/technet/prodtechnol/winxppro/reskit/prcc_tcp_tuoz.asp>.

423. "Defining TCP/IP," *Windows XP Professional Resource Kit,* viewed July 7, 2003, <www.microsoft.com/technet/treeview/default.asp?url=/technet/prodtechnol/winxppro/reskit/prcc_tcp_utip.asp>.

424. "Network Protocols," *Windows XP Resource Kit,* viewed July 7, 2003, <www.microsoft.com/technet/prodtechnol/winxppro/reskit/prch_cnn_actp.asp>.

425. Hertel, C., "Understanding the Network Neighborhood," *Linux Magazine,* May 2001, <www.linux-mag.com/2001-05/smb_01.html>.

426. "Network Protocol Support in Windows," *MSDN Library*, February 2003, <msdn.microsoft.com/library/en-us/winsock/winsock/network_protocol_support_in_windows.asp>.

427. Hertel, C., "Understanding the Network Neighborhood," *Linux Magazine*, May 2001, <www.linux-mag.com/2001-05/smb_01.html>.

428. "About WinHTTP," *MSDN Library*, July 2003, <msdn.microsoft.com/library/en-us/winhttp/http/about_winhttp.asp>.

429. "About WinINet," *MSDN Library*, February 2003, <msdn.microsoft.com/library/en-us/wininet/wininet/about_wininet.asp>.

430. "Porting WinINET applications to WinHTTP," *MSDN Library*, February 2003, <msdn.microsoft.com/library/en-us/winhttp/http/wininet.asp>.

431. Hertel, C., "Understanding the Network Neighborhood," *Linux Magazine*, May 2001, <www.linux-mag.com/2001-05/smb_01.html>.

432. "Windows Sockets Background," *MSDN Library*, February 2003, <msdn.microsoft.com/library/en-us/vccore/html/_core_Windows_Sockets.3a_.Background.asp>.

433. "Windows Sockets 2 API," *MSDN Library*, February 2003, <msdn.microsoft.com/library/en-us/winsock/winsock/windows_sockets_2_api_2.asp>.

434. Lewandowski, S., "Interprocess Communication in UNIX and Windows NT," 1997, <www.cs.brown.edu/people/scl/files/IPCWinNTUNIX.pdf>.

435. "Windows Sockets Background," *MSDN Library*, February 2003, <msdn.microsoft.com/library/en-us/vccore/html/_core_Windows_Sockets.3a_.Background.asp>.

436. "Windows Sockets 2 API," *MSDN Library* February 2003, <msdn.microsoft.com/library/en-us/winsock/winsock/windows_sockets_2_api_2.asp>.

437. "Windows Sockets Functions," *MSDN Library*, February 2003, <msdn.microsoft.com/library/en-us/winsock/winsock/windows_sockets_functions_2.asp>.

438. "Active Directory," *MSDN Library*, July 2003, <msdn.microsoft.com/library/en-us/netdir/ad/active_directory.asp>.

439. "About Active Directory," *MSDN Library*, July 2003, <msdn.microsoft.com/library/en-us/netdir/ad/about_active_directory.asp>.

440. "Lightweight Directory Access Protocol," *MSDN Library*, July 2003, <msdn.microsoft.com/library/en-us/netdir/ldap/lightweight_directory_access_protocol_ldap_api.asp>.

441. "Active Directory Services Interface (ADSI): Frequently Asked Questions," *MSDN Library*, viewed July 7, 2003, <msdn.microsoft.com/library/en-us/dnactdir/html/msdn_adsifaq.asp>.

442. "Remote Access Service," *MSDN Library*, February 2003, <msdn.microsoft.com/library/en-us/rras/rras/ras_start_page.asp>.

443. "DCOM Technical Overview," Microsoft Corporation, 1996, <msdn.microsoft.com/library/en-us/dndcom/html/msdn_dcomtec.asp>.

444. Kaiser, J., "Windows XP and .NET: An Overview," *Microsoft TechNet*, July 2001, <www.microsoft.com/technet/prodtechnol/winxppro/evaluate/xpdotnet.asp>.

445. Ricciuti, M., "Strategy: Blueprint Shrouded in Mystery," *CNET News.com*, October 18, 2001, <news.com.com/2009-1001-274344.html>.

446. M. Ricciuti, "Strategy: Blueprint Shrouded in Mystery," *CNET News.com*, October 18, 2001, <news.com.com/2009-1001-274344.html>.

447. Ricciuti, M., "Strategy: Blueprint Shrouded in Mystery," *CNET News.com*, October 18, 2001, <news.com.com/2009-1001-274344.html>.

448. J. Kaiser, "Windows XP and .NET: An Overview," *Microsoft TechNet*, July 2001, <www.microsoft.com/technet/prodtechnol/winxppro/evaluate/xpdotnet.asp>.

449. M. Ricciuti, "Strategy: Blueprint Shrouded in Mystery," *CNET News.com*, October 18, 2001, <news.com.com/2009-1001-274344.html>.

450. "Multiple Processors," *MSDN Library*, February 2003, <msdn.microsoft.com/library/en-us/dllproc/base/multiple_processors.asp>.

451. "Queued Spin Locks," *MSDN Library*, June 6, 2003, <msdn.microsoft.com/library/en-us/kmarch/hh/kmarch/synchro_8ftz.asp>.

452. Russinovich, M., and D. Solomon, "Windows XP: Kernel Improvements Create a More Robust, Powerful, and Scalable OS," *MSDN Magazine*, December 2001, <msdn.microsoft.com/msdnmag/issues/01/12/XPKernel/print.asp>.

453. "Introduction to Kernel Dispatcher Objects," *MSDN Library*, June 6, 2003, <msdn.microsoft.com/library/en-us/kmarch/hh/kmarch/synchro_7kfb.asp>.

454. Russinovich, M., and D. Solomon, "Windows XP: Kernel Improvements Create a More Robust, Powerful, and Scalable OS," *MSDN Magazine*, December 2001, <msdn.microsoft.com/msdnmag/issues/01/12/XPKernel/print.asp>.

455. "Overview of Windows XP 64-Bit Edition," *Microsoft TechNet*, viewed July 24, 2003, <www.microsoft.com/technet/prodtechnol/winxppro/reskit/prka_fea_ayuw.asp>.

456. Connolly, C., "First Look: Windows XP 64-Bit Edition for AMD64," *Game PC* September 5, 2003 <www.gamepc.com/labs/view_content.asp?id=amd64xp&page=1>.

457. "Overview of Windows XP 64-Bit Edition," *Microsoft TechNet*, viewed July 24, 2003, <www.microsoft.com/technet/prodtechnol/winxppro/reskit/prka_fea_ayuw.asp>.

458. "Job Objects," *MSDN Library*, February 2003, <msdn.microsoft.com/library/en-us/dllproc/base/job_objects.asp>.

459. "I/O Completion Ports," *MSDN Library*, February 2003, <msdn.microsoft.com/library/en-us/fileio/base/i_o_completion_ports.asp>.

460. "Thread Pooling," *MSDN Library,* February 2003, <msdn.microsoft.com/library/en-us/dllproc/base/thread_pooling.asp>.

461. Fincher, J., "Getting to Know Windows NT Embedded and Windows XP Embedded," *MSDN Library,* November 20, 2001, <msdn.microsoft.com/library/en-us/dnembedded/html/embedded11202001.asp>.

462. "About Windows XP Embedded," *MSDN Library,* June 2, 2003, <msdn.microsoft.com/library/en-us/xpehelp/html/xecon-AboutWindowsXPEmbeddedTop.asp>.

463. Fincher, J., "Getting to Know Windows NT Embedded and Windows XP Embedded," *MSDN Library,* November 20, 2001, <msdn.microsoft.com/library/en-us/dnembedded/html/embedded11202001.asp>.

464. Cherepov, M., et al., "Hard Real-Time with Venturcom RTX on Microsoft Windows XP and Windows XP Embedded," *MSDN Library,* June 2002, <msdn.microsoft.com/library/en-us/dnxpembed/html/hardrealtime.asp>.

465. "Components Used in Interactive Logon," *Microsoft TechNet,* 2003, <www.microsoft.com/technet/prodtechnol/winxppro/reskit/prdp_log_axsg.asp>.

466. "Interactive Logons Using Kerberos Authentication," *Microsoft TechNet,* 2003, <www.microsoft.com/technet/prodtechnol/winxppro/reskig/prdp_log_brso.asp>.

467. "Components Used in Interactive Logon," *Microsoft TechNet,* 2003, <www.microsoft.com/technet/prodtechnol/winxppro/reskit/prdp_log_axsg.asp>.

468. "Protocol Selection," *Microsoft TechNet,* 2003, <www.microsoft.com/technet/prodtechnol/winxppro/reskit/prdp_log_axsg.asp>

469. "Components Used in Interactive Logon," *Microsoft TechNet,* 2003, <www.microsoft.com/technet/prodtechnol/winxppro/reskit/prdp_log_axsg.asp>.

470. "What's New in Security for Windows XP Professional and Windows XP Home Edition," *Microsoft Corporation,* July 2001, <www.microsoft.com/windowsxp/pro/techinfo/planning/security/whatsnew/WindowsXPSecurity.doc>.

471. "Security Principals," *Microsoft TechNet,* 2003, <www.microsoft.com/technet/prodtechnol/winxppro/reskit/prdp_log_jrut.asp>.

472. "Security Groups," *Microsoft TechNet,* 2003, <www.microsoft.com/technet/treeview/default.asp?url=/technet/prodtechnol/winxppro/reskit/prdp_log_jrut.asp>.

473. "Security Identifiers," *Microsoft TechNet,* 2003, <www.microsoft.com/technet/prodtechnol/winxppro/reskit/prdp_log_zhiu.asp>.

474. "Security Identifiers," *Microsoft TechNet,* 2003, <www.microsoft.com/technet/prodtechnol/winxppro/reskit/prdp_log_zhiu.asp>.

475. "What's New in Security for Windows XP Professional and Windows XP Home Edition," Microsoft Corporation, July 2001, <www.microsoft.com/windowsxp/pro/techinfo/planning/security/whatsnew/WindowsXPSecurity.doc>.

476. "Important Terms," *Microsoft TechNet,* 2003, <www.microsoft.com/technet/prodtechnol/winxppro/reskit/prdd_sec_zrve.asp>.

477. "User-Based Authorization," *Microsoft TechNet,* 2003, <www.microsoft.com/technet/prodtechnol/winxppro/reskit/prdd_sec_qjin.asp>.

478. "New in Windows XP Professional," *Microsoft TechNet,* 2003, <www.microsoft.com/technet/prodtechnol/winxppro/reskit/prdp_log_oeec.asp>.

479. "Internet Connection Firewalls," *MSDN Library,* 2003, <www.microsoft.com/technet/prodtechnol/winxppro/reskit/prcg_cnd_brph.asp>.

480. "What's New in Security for Windows XP Professional and Windows XP Home Edition," Microsoft Corporation, July 2001, <www.microsoft.com/windowsxp/pro/techinfo/planning/security/whatsnew/WindowsXPSecurity.doc>.

481. Wong, D., "Windows ICF: Can't Live With It, Can't Live Without It," *SecurityFocus,* August 22, 2002, <www.securityfocus.com/infocus/1620>.

482. Wong, D., "Windows ICF: Can't Live With It, Can't Live Without It," *SecurityFocus,* August 22, 2002, <www.securityfocus.com/infocus/1620>.

483. "What's New in Security for Windows XP Professional and Windows XP Home Edition," Microsoft Corporation, July 2001, <www.microsoft.com/windowsxp/pro/techinfo/planning/security/whatsnew/WindowsXPSecurity.doc>.

484. "What's New in Security for Windows XP Professional and Windows XP Home Edition," Microsoft Corporation, July 2001. <www.microsoft.com/windowsxp/pro/techinfo/planning/security/whatsnew/WindowsXPSecurity.doc>.

485. "Top 10 Reasons to Get Windows XP for Home PC Security," Microsoft Corporation, 2003, <www.microsoft.com/WindowsXP/security/top10.asp>.

Glossary

Numerics

2-D mesh network—Multiprocessor interconnection scheme that arranges nodes in an $m \times n$ rectangle.

3DES—See Triple DES.

4-connected 2-D mesh network—2-D mesh network in which nodes are connected with the nodes directly to the north, south, east and west.

A

abandoned mutex (Windows XP)—Mutex that was not released before the termination of the thread that held it.

abort—Action that terminates a process prematurely. Also, in the IA-32 specification, an error from which a process cannot recover.

absolute loading—Loading technique in which the loader places the program in memory at the address specified by the programmer or compiler.

absolute path—Path beginning at the root directory.

absolute performance measure—Measure of the efficiency with which a computer system meets its goals, described by an absolute quantity such as the amount of time in which a system executes a certain benchmark. This contrasts with relative performance measures such as ease of use, which only can be used to make comparisons between systems.

Accelerated Graphics Port (AGP)—Popular bus architecture used for connecting graphics devices; AGPs typically provide 260MB/s of bandwidth.

access control attribute (Linux)—Specifies the access rights for processes attempting to access a particular resource.

access control entry (ACE) (Windows XP)—Entry in a discretionary access control list (DACL) for a specific resource that contains the security identifier (SID) of a security principal and the type of access (if any) the security principal has to that particular resource.

access control list—List that stores one entry for each access right granted to a subject for an object. An access control list consumes less space than an access control matrix.

Access Control List (ACL) (Multics)—Multics' discretionary access control implementation.

access control matrix—Matrix that lists system's subjects in the rows and the objects to which they require access in the columns. Each cell in the matrix specifies the actions that a subject (defined by the row) can perform on an object (defined by the column). Access control matrices typically are not implemented because they are sparsely populated.

access control mode—Set of privileges (e.g., read, write, execute and/or append) that determine how a page or segment of memory can be accessed.

Access Isolation Mechanism (AIM) (Multics)—Multics' mandatory access control implementation.

access method—Technique a file system uses to access file data. See also queued access methods and basic access methods.

access right—Defines how various subjects can access various objects. Subjects may be users, processes, programs or other entities. Objects are information-holding entities; they may be physical objects that correspond to disks, processors or main memory or abstract objects that correspond to data structures, processes or services. Subjects are also considered to be objects of the system; one subject may have rights to access another.

access token (Windows XP)—Data structure that stores security information, such as the security identifier (SID) and group memberships, about a security principal.

access transparency—Hides the details of networking protocols that enable communication between computers in a distributed system.

accessed bit—See referenced bit.

accessibility (file)—File property that places restrictions on which users can access file data.

acknowledgement segment (ACK)—In TCP, a segment that is sent to the source host to indicate that the destination host has received a segment. If a source host does not receive and ACK for a segment, it will retransmit that segment. This guarantees that each transmitted segment is received.

acquire operation—In several coherence strategies, an operation indicating that a process is about to access shared memory.

Active Directory (Windows XP)—Network service that provides directory services for shared objects (e.g., files, printers, services, etc.) on a network.

active list (Linux)—Scheduler structure that contains processes that will control the processor at least once during the current epoch.

active page (Linux)—Page of memory that will not be replaced the next time pages are selected for replacement.

active state (Linux)—Task state describing tasks that can compete for execution on a processor during the current epoch.

ActiveX Controls—Self-registering COM objects useful for embedding in Web pages.

activity (file)—Percentage of a file's records accessed during a given period of time.

actuator—See disk arm.

ad hoc network—Network characterized as being spontaneous—any number of wireless or wired devices may be connected to it at any time.

Ada—Concurrent, procedural programming language developed by the DoD during the 1970s and 1980s.

adaptive lock—Mutual exclusion lock that allows processes to switch between using a spin lock or a blocking lock, depending on the current condition of the system.

adaptive mechanism—Control entity that adjusts a system in response to its changing behavior.

add-on card—Device that extends the functionality of a computer (e.g., sound and video cards).

address binding—Assignment of memory addresses to program data and instructions.

address bus—Part of a bus that specifies the memory location from or to which data is to be transferred.

address space—Set of memory locations a process can reference.

address translation map—Table that assists in the mapping of virtual addresses to their corresponding real memory addresses.

admission scheduling—See high-level scheduling.

Advanced Configuration and Power Interface (ACPI)—Power management specification supported by many operating systems that allows a system to turn off some or all of its devices without loss of work.

Advanced Encryption Standard (AES)—Standard for symmetric encryption that uses Rijndael as the encryption method. AES has replaced the Data Encryption Standard (DES) because AES provides enhanced security.

Advanced Research Projects Agency (ARPA)—Government agency under the Department of Defense that laid the groundwork for the Internet; it is now called the Defense Advanced Research Projects Agency (DARPA).

advertisement (in JXTA)—XML document formatted according to JXTA specifications that is used by a peer to advertise itself and notify others of its existence.

advisable process lock (APL)—Locking mechanism in which an acquirer estimates how long it will hold the lock; other processes can use this estimate to determine whether to block or spin when waiting for the lock.

affinity mask (Windows XP)—List of processors on which a process's threads are allowed to execute.

agent level (in JMX)—JMX level that provides services for exposing the managed resources.

aging of priorities—Method of preventing indefinite postponement by increasing a process's priority gradually as it waits.

air gap technology—Network security solution that complements a firewall. It secures private data from external users accessing the internal network.

alertable I/O (Windows XP)—Type of asynchronous I/O in which the system notifies the requesting thread of the completion of the I/O with an APC.

alertable *wait* state (Windows XP)—State in which a thread cannot execute until it is awakened either by an APC entering the thread's APC queue or by receiving a handle to the object (or objects) for which the thread is waiting.

alternate data stream—File attribute that stores the contents of an NTFS file that are not in the default data stream. NTFS files may have multiple alternate data streams.

analytic model—Mathematical representation of a computer system or component of a computer system for the purpose of estimating its performances quickly and relatively accurately.

Andrew File System (AFS)—Scalable distributed file system that would grow to support a large community while being secure. AFS is a global file system that appears as a branch of a traditional UNIX file system at each workstation. AFS is completely location transparent and provides a high degree of availability.

anonymous pipe (Windows XP)—Unnamed pipe that can be used only for synchronous one-way communication between local processes.

anticipatory buffering—Technique that allows processing and I/O operations to be overlapped by buffering more than one record at a time in main memory.

anticipatory movement—Movement of the disk arm during disk arm anticipation.

anticipatory paging—Technique that preloads a process's nonresident pages that are likely to be referenced in the near future. Such strategies attempt to reduce the number of page faults a process experiences.

antivirus software—Program that attempts to identify, remove and otherwise protect a system from viruses.

anycast—Type of IPv6 address that enables a datagram to be sent to any host within a group of hosts.

Apache Software Foundation—Provides open-source software, such as Tomcat, the official reference implementation of JSP and servlet specifications.

apartment model—COM object threading model in which only one thread acts as a server for each COM object.

APC IRQL (Windows XP)—IRQL at which APCs execute and incoming asynchronous procedure calls (APCs) are masked.

append access—Access right that enables a process to write additional information at the end of a segment but not to modify its existing contents; see also execute access, read access and write access.

append-only file attribute (Linux)—File attribute that limits users to appending data to existing file contents.

application base—Combination of the hardware and the operating system environment in which applications are developed. It is difficult for users and application developers to convert from an established application base to another.

application configuration file (ACF) (Windows XP)—File that specifies platform-specific attributes (e.g., how data should be formatted) for an RPC function call.

application layer (in grid computing)—Contains applications that use lower-level layers to access the distributed resources.

application layer (in OSI)—Interacts with the applications and provides various network services, such as file transfer and e-mail.

application layer (in TCP/IP)—Protocols in this layer allow applications on remote hosts to communicate with each other. The application layer in TCP/IP performs the functionality of the top three layers of OSI—the application, presentation and session layers.

application-level gateway—Hardware or software that protects the network against the data contained in packets. If the message contains a virus, the gateway can block it from being sent to the intended receiver.

application programming—Software development that entails writing code that requests services and resources from the operating system to perform tasks (e.g., text editing, loading Web pages or payroll processing).

application programming interface (API)—Set of functions that allows an application to request services from a lower level of the system (e.g., the operating system or a library module).

application vector—Vector that contains the relative demand on operating system primitives by a particular application, used in an application-specific performance evaluation.

architecture-specific code—Code that specifies instructions unique to a particular architecture.

Arithmetic and Logic Unit (ALU)—Component of a processor that performs basic arithmetic and logic operations.

ARPAnet—Predecessor to the Internet that enabled researchers to network their computers. ARPAnet's chief benefit proved to be quick and easy communication via what came to be known as electronic mail (e-mail).

array processor—SIMD (single-instruction-stream, multiple-data-stream) system consisting of many (possibly tens of thousands) simple processing units, each executing the same instruction in parallel on many data elements.

arrival rate—Rate at which new requests are made for a resource.

artificial contiguity—Technique employed by virtual memory systems to provide the illusion that a program's instructions and data are stored contiguously when pieces of them may be spread throughout main memory; this simplifies programming.

ASCII (American Standard Code for Information Interchange)—Character set, popular in personal computers and in data communication systems, that stores characters as 8-bit bytes.

assembler—Translator program that converts assembly-language programs to machine language.

assembly language—Low-level language that represents basic computer operations as English-like abbreviations.

associative mapping—Content-addressed associative memory that assists in the mapping of virtual addresses to their corresponding real memory addresses; all entries of the associative memory are searched simultaneously.

associative memory—Memory that is searched by content, not by location; fast associative memories can help implement high-speed dynamic address translation mechanisms.

asynchronous cancellation (POSIX)—Cancellation mode in which a thread is terminated immediately upon receiving the cancellation signal.

asynchronous concurrent threads—Threads that exist simultaneously but operate independently of one another and that occasionally communicate and synchronize to perform cooperative tasks.

asynchronous procedure call (APC) (Windows XP)—Procedure calls that threads or the system can queue for execution by a specific thread.

asynchronous real-time process—Real-time process that executes in response to events.

asynchronous signal—Signal generated for reasons unrelated to the current instruction of the running thread.

asynchronous transmission—Transferring data from one device to another that operates independently via a buffer to eliminate the need for blocking; the sender can perform other work once the data arrives in the buffer, even if the receiver has not yet read the data.

atomic broadcast—Guarantees that all messages in a system are received in the same order at each process. Also known as totally ordered or agreed broadcast.

atomic operation—Operation performed without interruption.

atomic transaction—Group of operations that have no effect on the state of the system unless they complete in their entirety.

attenuation—Deterioration of a signal due to physical characteristics of the medium.

attraction memory (AM)—Main memory in a COMA (cache-only memory architecture) multiprocessor, which is organized as a cache.

attribute (of an object)—See property.

authentication (secure transaction)—One of the five fundamental requirements for a successful, secure transaction. Authentication deals with how the sender and receiver of a message verify their identities to each other.

authentication header (AH) (IPSec)—Information that verifies the identity of a packet's sender and proves that a packet's data was not modified in transit.

authentication server scripts—Single sign-on implementation that authenticates users via a central server, which establishes connections between the user and the applications the user wishes to access.

authorization (secure transaction)—One of the five fundamental requirements for a successful, secure transaction. Authorization deals with how to manage access to protected resources on the basis of user credentials.

auto-reset timer object (Windows XP)—Timer object that remains *signaled* only until one thread finishes waiting on the object.

automatic binding handle (Windows XP)—RPC binding handle in which the client process simply calls a remote function, and the stub manages all communication tasks.

auxiliary storage—See secondary storage.

auxiliary storage management—Component of file systems concerned with allocating space for files on secondary storage devices.

available volume storage group (AVSG) (in Coda)—Members of the VSG with which the client can communicate.

B

back-door program—Resident virus that allows an attacker complete, undetected access to the victim's computer resources.

backup—Creation of redundant copies of information.

Bad Page List (Windows XP)—List of page frames that have generated hardware errors; the system does not store pages on these page frames.

balance set manager (Windows XP)—Executive component responsible for adjusting working set minimums and maximums and trimming working sets.

bandwidth—Information-carrying capacity of a communications line. Also, the amount of data transferred over a unit of time.

base priority class (Windows XP)—Process attribute that determines a narrow range of base priorities the process's threads can have.

base priority level (Windows XP)—Thread attribute that describes the thread's base priority within a base priority class.

base register—Register containing the lowest memory address a process may reference.

baseline network—Type of multistage network.

basic access method—File access method in which the operating system responds immediately to user I/O demands. It is used when the sequence in which records are to be processed cannot be anticipated, particularly with direct accessing.

basic input/output system (BIOS)—Low-level software instructions that control basic hardware initialization and management.

batch process—Process that executes without user interaction.

behavior (of an object)—See method.

Belady's anomaly—See FIFO anomaly.

benchmark—Real program that an evaluator executes on the system being evaluated to determine how efficiently the system executes that program; benchmarks are used to compare systems.

Beowulf cluster—Linux clustering solution, which is a high-performance cluster. A Beowulf cluster may contain several nodes or several hundred. Theoretically, all nodes have Linux installed as their operating system and are interconnected with high-speed Ethernet. Usually, all the nodes in the cluster are connected within a single room to form a supercomputer.

Berkeley Software Distribution (BSD) UNIX—UNIX version modified and released by a team led by Bill Joy at the University of California at Berkeley. BSD UNIX is the parent of several UNIX variations.

best-fit memory placement strategy—Memory placement strategy that places an incoming job in the smallest hole in memory that can hold the job.

bidding algorithm—Dynamic load balancing algorithm in which processors with smaller loads "bid" for jobs on overloaded processors; the bid value depends on the load of the bidding processor and the distance between the underloaded and overloaded processors.

big kernel lock (BKL) (Linux)—Global spin lock that served as an early implementation of SMP support in the Linux kernel.

binary buddy algorithm (Linux)—Algorithm that Linux uses to allocate physical page frames. The algorithm maintains a list of groups of contiguous pages; the number in each group is a power of two. This facilitates memory allocation for processes and devices that require access to contiguous physical memory.

binary relation—Relation (in a relational database) of degree 2.

binary semaphore—Semaphore whose value can be no greater than one, typically used to allocate a single resource.

binding (Windows XP)—Connection between the client and the server used for network communication (e.g., for an RPC).

binding handle (Windows XP)—Data structure that stores the connection information associated with a binding between a client and a server.

bio structure (Linux)—Structure that simplifies block I/O operations by mapping I/O requests to pages.

biometrics—Technique that uses an individual's physical characteristics, such as fingerprints, eyeball iris scans or face scans, to identify the user.

BIPS (billion instructions per second)—Unit commonly used to categorize the performance of a particular computer; a rating of one BIPS means a processor can execute one billion instructions per second.

bisection width—Minimum number of links that need to be severed to divide a network into two unconnected halves.

bit pattern—Lowest level of the data hierarchy. A bit pattern is a group of bits that represent virtually all data items of interest in computer systems.

bitmap—Free space management technique that maintains one bit for each block in memory, where the ith bit corresponds to the ith block in memory. Bitmaps enable a file system to more easily allocate contiguous blocks but can require substantial execution time to locate a free block.

block—Fixed-size unit of contiguous data, typically much larger than a byte. Placing contiguous data records in blocks enables the system to reduce the number of I/O operations required to retrieve them.

block allocation—Technique that enables the file system to manage secondary storage more efficiently and reduce file traversal overhead by allocating extents (blocks of contiguous sectors) to files.

block allocation bitmap (Linux)—Bitmap that tracks the usage of blocks in each block group.

block cipher—Encryption technique that divides a message into fixed-size groups of bits to which an encryption algorithm is applied.

block device—Device such as a disk that transfers data in fixed-size groups of bytes, as opposed to a character device, which transfers data one byte at a time.

block group (Linux)—Collection of contiguous blocks managed by group-wide data structures so that related data blocks, inodes and other file system metadata are contiguous on disk.

block map table—Table containing entries that map each of a process's virtual blocks to a corresponding block in main memory (if there is one). Blocks in a virtual memory system are either segments or pages.

block map table origin register—Register that stores the address in main memory of a process's block map table; this high-speed register facilitates rapid virtual address translation.

block mapping—Mechanism that, a virtual memory system, reduces the number of mappings between virtual memory addresses and real memory addresses by mapping blocks in virtual memory to blocks in main memory.

blocked list—Kernel data structure that contains pointers to all *blocked* processes. This list is not maintained in any particular priority order.

blocked record—Record that may contain several logical records for each physical record.

blocked state—Process (or thread) state in which the process (or thread) is waiting for the completion of some event, such as an I/O completion, and cannot use a processor even if one is available.

blocking—Grouping of contiguous records into larger blocks that can be read using a single I/O operation. This technique reduces access times by retrieving many records with a single I/O operation.

boom—See disk arm.

boot sector—Specified location on a disk in which the initial operating system instructions are stored; the BIOS instructs the hardware to load these initial instructions when the computer is turned on.

boot sector virus—Virus that infects the boot sector of the computer's hard disk, allowing it to load with the operating system and take control of the system.

bootstrapping—Process of loading initial operating system components into system memory so that they can load the rest of the operating system.

born state—Thread state in which a new thread begins its life cycle.

bottleneck—Condition that occurs when a resource receives requests faster than it can process them, which can slow process execution and reduce resource utilization. Hard disks are a bottleneck in most systems.

bottom half of an interrupt handler (Linux)—Portion of interrupt-handling code that can be preempted.

bounce buffer (Linux)—Region of memory that allows the kernel to map data from the high memory zone into memory that it can directly reference. This is necessary when the system's physical address space is larger than kernel's virtual address space.

boundary register—Register for single-user operating systems that was used for memory protection by separating user memory space from kernel memory space.

bounded buffer—See circular buffer.

bounds register—Register that stores information regarding the range of memory addresses accessible to a process.

branch penalty—Performance loss in pipelined architectures associated with a branch instruction; this occurs when a processor cannot begin processing the instruction after the branch until the processor knows the outcome of the branch. The branch penalty can be reduced by using delayed branching, branch prediction or branch predication.

branch predication—Technique used in EPIC processors whereby a processor executes all possible instructions that could follow a branch in parallel and uses only the result of the correct branch once the predicate (i.e., the branch comparison) is resolved.

branch prediction—Technique whereby a processor uses heuristics to determine the most probable result of a branch in code; when the processor predicts correctly, performance increases, because the processor can continue to execute instructions immediately after the branch.

brute-force cracking—Technique to compromise a system simply by attempting all possible passwords or by using every possible decryption key to decrypt a message.

buffer—Temporary storage area that holds data during I/O between devices operating at different speeds. Buffers enable a faster device to produce data at its full speed (until the buffer fills) while waiting for the slower device to consume the data.

buffer overflow—Attack that sends input that is larger than the space allocated for it. If the input is properly coded and the system's stack is executable, buffer overflows can enable an attacker to execute malicious code.

bullet server—Standard file server used in the Amoeba file system.

burping the memory—See memory compaction.

bus—Collection of traces that form a high-speed communication channel for transporting information between different devices on a mainboard.

bus driver—WDM (Windows Driver Model) driver that provides some generic functions for devices on a bus, enumerates those devices and handles Plug and Play I/O requests.

bus mastering—DMA transfer in which a device assumes control of the bus (preventing others from accessing the bus simultaneously) to access memory.

bus network—Network in which the nodes are connected by a single bus link (also known as a linear network).

bus snooping—Coherence protocol in which processors "snoop" the shared bus to determine whether a requested write is to a data item in that processor's cache or, if applicable, local memory.

Business Application Performance Corporation (BAPCo) — Organization that develops standard benchmarks, such as the popular SYSMark for processors.

business-critical system — System that must function properly, but whose failure of which leads to reduced productivity and profitability; not as crucial as a mission-critical system, where failure could put human lives could be at risk.

busy waiting — Form of waiting where a thread continuously tests a condition that will let the thread proceed eventually; while busy waiting, a thread uses processor time.

byte — Second-lowest level in the data hierarchy. A byte is typically 8 bits.

bytecode — Intermediate code that is intended for virtual machines (e.g., Java bytecode runs on the Java Virtual Machine).

C

C — Procedural programming language developed by Dennis Ritchie that was used to create UNIX.

C-threads — Threads supported natively in the Mach micro-kernel (on which Macintosh OS X is built).

C# — Object-oriented programming language developed by Microsoft that provides access to .NET libraries.

C++ — Object-oriented extension of C developed by Bjarne Stroustup.

cache coherence — Property of a system in which any data item read from a cache has the value equal to the last write to that data item.

cache-coherent NUMA (CC-NUMA) — NUMA multiprocessor that maintains cache coherence, usually through a home-based approach.

cache-cold process — Process that contains little, if any, of its data or instructions in the cache of the processor to which it will be dispatched.

cache hit — Request for data that is present in the cache.

cache-hot process — Process that contains most, if not all, of its data and instructions in the cache of the processor to which it will be dispatched.

cache line — Entry in a cache.

cache manager (Windows XP) — Executive component that handles file cache management.

cache memory — Small, expensive, high-speed memory that holds copies of programs and data to decrease memory access times.

cache miss — Request for data that is not present in the cache.

cache miss latency — Extra time required to access data that does not reside in the cache.

cache-only memory architecture (COMA) multiprocessor — Multiprocessor architecture in which nodes consist of a processor, cache and memory module; main memory is organized as a large cache.

cache snooping — Bus snooping used to ensure cache coherency.

callback (in AFS) — Sent by the server to notify the client that the cached file is modified.

cancellation of a thread — Thread operation that terminates the target thread. Three modes of cancellation are disabled, deferred and asynchronous cancellation.

capability — Security mechanism that assigns access rights to a subject (e.g., a process) by granting it a token for an object (i.e., a resource). This enables administrators to specify and enforce fine-grained access control. The token is analogous to a ticket the bearer may use to gain access to a sporting event.

capacity — Measure of the maximum throughput a system can attain, assuming that whenever the system is ready to accept more jobs, another job is immediately available.

Carrier Sense Multiple Access with Collision Avoidance (CSMA/CA) — Protocol used in 802.11 wireless communication. Devices must send a Request To Send (RTS) and receive a Clear To Send (CTS) from the destination host before transmitting.

Carrier Sense Multiple Access with Collision Detection (CSMA/CD) — Protocol used in Ethernet that enables transceivers to test a shared medium to see if it is available before transmitting data. If a collision is detected, transceivers continue transmitting data for a period of time to ensure that all transceivers recognize the collision.

causal broadcast — Ensures that when a message is sent from one process to all other processes, any given process will receive the message before it receives a response to the message from a different process.

causal ordering — Ensures that all processes recognize that a causally dependent event must occur only after the event on which it is dependent.

causally dependent — Event B is causally dependent on event A if event B may occur only if event A occurs.

cell (in AFS-3) — Unit in AFS-3, which preserves namespace continuity while allowing different systems administrators to oversee each cell.

central deadlock detection — A strategy in distributed deadlock detection, in which one site is dedicated to monitoring the TWFG of the entire system. Whenever a process requests or releases a resource, it informs the central site. The site continuously checks the global TWFG for cycles.

central migration server — Workstation in a Sprite distributed operating system that keeps information about idle workstations.

central processing unit (CPU) — Processor responsible for the general computations in a computer.

centralized P2P application — Uses a server that connects to each peer.

certificate authority (CA) — Financial institution or other trusted third party, such as VeriSign, that issues digital certificates.

certificate authority hierarchy — Chain of certificate authorities, beginning with the root certificate authority, that authenticates certificates and CAs.

certificate repositories — Locations where digital certificates are stored.

certificate revocation list (CRL) — List of cancelled and revoked certificates. A certificate is cancelled/revoked if a private key is compromised before its expiration date.

chaining—Indexed noncontiguous allocation technique that reserves the last few entries of an index block to store pointers to more index blocks, which in turn point to data blocks. Chaining enables index blocks to reference large files by storing references to its data across several blocks.

chaining (hash tables)—Technique that resolves collisions in a hash table by placing each unique item in a data structure (typically a linked list). The position in the hash table at which the collision occurred contains a pointer to that data structure.

character—In the data hierarchy, a fixed-length pattern of bits, typically 8, 16 or 32 bits.

character device—Device such as a keyboard or mouse that transfers data one byte at a time, as opposed to a block device, which transfers data in fixed-size groups of bytes.

character set—Collection of characters. Popular character sets include ASCII, EBCDIC and Unicode.

checkpoint (transaction logging)—Marker indicating which transactions in a log have been transferred to permanent storage. The system need only reapply the transactions from the latest checkpoint to determine the state of the file system, which is faster than reapplying all transactions starting at the beginning of the log.

checkpoint (deadlock recovery)—Record of a state of a system so that it can be restored later if a process must be prematurely terminated (e.g., to perform deadlock recovery).

checkpoint/rollback—Method of deadlock and system recovery that undoes every action (or transaction) of a terminated process since the process's last checkpoint.

checksum—Result of a calculation on the bits of a message. The checksum calculated at the receiver is compared to the checksum calculated by the sender (which is embedded in the control information). If the checksums do not match, the message has been corrupted.

child process—Process that has been spawned from a parent process. A child process is one level lower in the process hierarchy than its parent process. In UNIX systems, child processes are created using the fork system call.

chipset—Collection of controllers, coprocessors, buses and other hardware specific to the mainboard that determine the hardware capabilities of a system.

cipher—Mathematical algorithm for encrypting messages. Also called cryptosystem.

ciphertext—Encrypted data.

circular buffer—In the producer/consumer relationship, a fixed-size region of shared memory that stores multiple values produced by a producer. If the producer occasionally produces values faster than the consumer, a circular buffer reduces the time the producer spends waiting for a consumer to consume the values, when compared to a buffer that stores a single value. If the consumer temporarily consumes values faster than the producer, a circular buffer can similarly reduce the time a consumer spends waiting for the producer to produce values.

circular LOOK (C-LOOK) disk scheduling—Disk scheduling strategy that moves the arm in one direction, servicing requests on a short-

est-seek basis. When there are no more requests on a current sweep, the read-write head moves to the request closest to the cylinder opposite its current location (without servicing requests in between) and begins the next sweep. The C-LOOK policy is characterized by potentially lower variance of response times compared to LOOK; it offers high throughput (although lower than that of LOOK).

circular SCAN (C-SCAN) disk scheduling—Disk scheduling strategy that moves the arm in one direction, servicing requests on a shortest-seek basis. When the arm has completed its sweep, it jumps (without servicing requests) to the cylinder opposite its current location, then resumes its inward sweep, processing requests. C-SCAN maintains high levels of throughput while further limiting variance of response times by avoiding the discrimination against the innermost and outermost cylinders.

circular wait—Condition for deadlock that occurs when two or more processes are locked in a "circular chain," in which each process in the chain is waiting for one or more resources that the next process in the chain is holding.

circular-wait necessary condition for deadlock—One of the four necessary conditions for deadlock; states that if a deadlock exists, there will be two or more processes in a circular chain such that each process is waiting for a resource held by the next process in the chain.

class—Type of an object. Determines an object's methods and attributes.

class ID (CLSID)—Globally unique ID given to a COM object class.

class/miniclass driver pair (Windows XP)—Pair of device drivers that act as a function driver for a device; the class driver provides generic processing for the device's particular device class, and the miniclass driver provides processing for the specific device.

Clear to Send (CTS)—Message that a receiver broadcasts in the CSMA/CA protocol to indicate that the medium is free. A CTS message is sent in response to a Request to Send (RTS).

client—Process that requests a service from another process (a server). The machine on which the client process runs is also called a client.

client caching—Clients keep local copies of files and flush them to the server after having modified the files.

client modification log (CML) (in Coda)—Log which is updated to reflect file changes on disk.

client stub—Stub at the client side that prepares outbound data for transmission and translates incoming data so that it may be correctly interpreted.

client/server model—Popular networking paradigm in which processes that need various services performed (clients) transmit their requests to processes that provide these services (servers). The server processes the request and returns the result to the client. The client and the server are typically on different machines on the network.

clipboard (Windows XP)—Central repository of data that is accessible to all processes, typically used with copy, cut and paste commands.

clock IRQL (Windows XP)—IRQL at which clock interrupts occur and at which APC, DPC/dispatch, DIRQL and profile-level interrupts are masked.

clock page-replacement strategy—Variation of the second-chance page-replacement strategy that arranges the pages in a circular list instead of a linear list. A list pointer moves around the circular list, much as the hand of a clock rotates, and replaces the page nearest the pointer (in circular order) that has its referenced bit turned off.

clocktick—See cycle.

close (file)—Operation that prevents further reference to a file until it is reopened.

cluster—Set of nodes that forms what appears to be a single parallel machine.

cluster (NTFS)—Basic unit of disk storage in an NTFS volume, consisting of a number of contiguous sectors; a system's cluster size can range from 512 bytes to 64KB, but is typically 2KB, 4KB or 8KB.

clustering—Interconnection of nodes within a high-speed LAN so that they function as a single parallel computer.

CMS Batch Facility (VM)—VM Component that allows the user to run longer jobs in a separate virtual machine so that the user can continue interactive work.

coalescing memory holes—Process of merging adjacent holes in memory in variable-partition multiprogramming systems. This helps create the largest possible holes available for incoming programs and data.

coarse-grained strip (RAID)—Strip size that enables average files to be stored in a small number of strips. In this case, some requests can be serviced by only a portion of the disks in the array, so it is more likely that multiple requests can be serviced simultaneously. If requests are small, they are serviced by one disk at a time, which reduces their average transfer rates.

Coda Optimistic Protocol—Protocol used by Coda clients to write a copy of the file to each of the members of the AVSG, which provides a consistent view of a file within an AVSG.

code freeze (Linux)—Point at which no new code should be added to the kernel unless the code fixes a known bug.

code generator—Part of a compiler responsible for producing object code from a higher-level language.

collective layer (in grid computing)—Layer responsible for coordinating distributed resources, such as scheduling a task to analyze data received from a scientific device.

collision (CSMA/CD protocol)—Simultaneous transmission in CSMA/CD protocol.

collision (hash tables)—Event that occurs when a hash function maps two different items to the same position in a hash table. Some hash tables use chaining to resolve collisions.

COM+—Extension of COM (Microsoft's Common Object Model) that handles advanced resource management tasks, such as providing support for transaction processing and using thread and object pools.

commit memory (Windows XP)—Necessary stage before a process can access memory. The VMM ensures that there is enough space in a pagefile for the memory and creates page table entries (PTEs) in main memory for the committed pages.

committed transaction—Transaction that has completed successfully.

COmmon Business Oriented Language (COBOL)—Procedural programming language developed in the late 1950s that was designed for writing business software that manipulates large volumes of data.

Common Internet File System (CIFS)—Native file sharing protocol of Windows XP.

Common Object Request Broker Architecture (CORBA)—Conceived in the early 1990s by the Object Management Group (OMG), CORBA is a standard specification of distributed systems architecture that has gained wide acceptance.

communication deadlock—One of the two types of distributed deadlock, which is a circular waiting for communication signals.

compact disk (CD)—Digital storage medium in which data is stored as a series of microscopic pits on a flat surface.

compile—Translate high-level-language source code into machine code.

compiler—Application that translates high-level-language source code into machine code.

complex instruction set computing (CISC)—Processor-design philosophy, emphasizing expanded instruction sets that incorporate single instructions that perform several operations.

component (Windows XP)—Functional unit of Windows XP. Components range from user-mode applications such as Notepad to portions of kernel space such as the CD-ROM interface and power management tools. Dividing Windows XP into components facilitates operating system development for embedded systems.

Component Object Model (COM)—Microsoft-developed software architecture that allows interoperability between diverse components through the standard manipulation of object interfaces.

compression unit (NTFS)—Sixteen clusters. Windows XP compresses and encrypts files one compression unit at a time.

compute-bound—See processor-bound.

concurrent—The description of a process or thread that exists in a system simultaneously with other processes and/or threads.

concurrent (happens-before relation)—Two events are concurrent if it cannot be determined which occurred earlier by following the happens-before relation.

concurrent program execution—Technique whereby processor time is shared among multiple active processes. On a uniprocessor system, concurrent processes cannot execute simultaneously; on a multiprocessor system, they can.

concurrent write sharing—Occurs when two clients modify cached copies of the same file.

condition variable—Variable that contains a value and an associated queue. When a thread waits on a condition variable inside a monitor, it exits the monitor and is placed in the condition variable's queue. Threads wait in the queue until signaled by another thread.

configurable lock—See adaptive lock

configuration manager (Windows XP)—Executive component that manages the registry.

congestion control—Means by which TCP restricts the number of segments sent by a single host in response to network congestion.

connection-oriented transport—Method of implementing the transport layer in which hosts send control information to govern the session. Handshaking is used to set up the connection. The connection guarantees that all data will arrive and in the correct order.

connectionless transport—Method of implementing the transport layer in which there is no guarantee that data will arrive in order or at all.

connectivity layer (in grid computing)—Layer that carries out reliable and secure transactions between distributed resources.

consumer thread—Thread whose purpose is to read and process data from a shared object.

contention—In multiprocessing, a situation in which several processors compete for the use of a shared resource.

context switching—Action performed by the operating system to remove a process from a processor and replace it with another. The operating system must save the state of the process that it replaces. Similarly, it must restore the state of the process being dispatched to the processor.

contiguous memory allocation—Method of assigning memory such that all of the addresses in the process's entire address space are adjacent to one another.

control information—Data in the form of headers and/or trailers that allows protocols of the same layer on different machines to communicate. Control information might include the addresses of the source and destination hosts and the type of data or size of the data that is being sent.

Control Program (CP) (VM)—Component of VM that runs the physical machine and creates the environment for the virtual machine.

controller—Hardware component that manages access to a bus by devices.

Conversational Monitor System (CMS) (VM)—Component of VM that is an interactive application development environment.

cooperative multitasking—Process scheduling technique in which processes execute on a processor until they voluntarily relinquish control of it.

coprocessor—Processor, such as a graphics or digital signal processor, designed to efficiently execute a limited set of special-purpose instructions (e.g., 3D transformations).

copy (file)—Operation that creates another version of a file with a new name.

copy-on-reference migration—Process migration technique in which only a process's dirty pages are migrated with the process, and the process can request clean pages either from the sending node or from secondary storage.

copy-on-write—Mechanism that improves process creation efficiency by sharing mapping information between parent and child until a process modifies a page, at which point a new copy of the page is created and allocated to that process. This can incur substantial overhead if the parent or child modifies many of the shared pages.

core file (Linux)—File that contains the execution state of a process, typically used for debugging purposes after a process encounters a fatal exception.

coscheduling—Job-aware process scheduling algorithm that attempts to execute processes from the same job concurrently by placing them in adjacent global-run-queue locations.

cost of an interconnection scheme—Total number of links in a network.

counting semaphore—Semaphore whose value may be greater than one, typically used to allocate resources from a pool of identical resources.

CP/CMS—Timesharing operating system developed by IBM in the 1960s.

cracker—Malicious individual that is usually interested in breaking into a system to disable services or steal data.

create (file)—Operation that builds a new file.

credential—Combination of user identity (e.g., username) and proof of identify (e.g., password).

critical region—See critical section.

critical section—Section of code that performs operations on a shared resource (e.g., writing data to a shared variable). To ensure program correctness, at most one thread can simultaneously execute in its critical section.

critical section object (Windows XP)—Synchronization object, which can be employed only by threads within a single process, that allows only one thread to own a resource at a time.

crossbar-switch matrix—Processor interconnection scheme that maintains a separate path from every sender node to every receiver node.

cryptanalytic attack—Technique that attempts to decrypt ciphertext without possession of the decryption key. The most common such attacks are those in which the encryption algorithm is analyzed to find relations between bits of the encryption key and bits of the ciphertext.

Cryptographic API (Linux)—Kernel interface through which applications and services (e.g., file systems) can encrypt and decrypt data.

cryptography—Study of encoding and decoding data so that it can be interpreted only by the intended recipients.

cryptosystem—Mathematical algorithm for encrypting messages. Also called a cipher.

CTSS—Timesharing operating system developed at MIT in the 1960s.

cycle (clock)—One complete oscillation of an electrical signal. The number of cycles that occur per second determines a device's frequency (e.g., processors, memory and buses) and can be used by the system to measure time.

cycle stealing—Method that gives channels priority over a processor when accessing the bus to prevent signals from channels and processors from colliding.

cylinder—Set of tracks that can be accessed by the read/write heads for a specific position of the disk arm.

D

daemon (Linux)—Process that runs periodically to perform system services.

data bus—Bus that transfers data to or from locations in memory that are specified by the address bus.

data compression—Technique that decreases the size of a data record by replacing repetitive patterns with shorter bit strings. This can reduce seeks, and transmission times, but may require substantial processor time to compress the data for storage on the disk, and to decompress the data to make it available to applications.

data definition language (DDL)—Type of language that specifies the organization of data in a database.

data-dependent application—Application that relies on a particular file system's organization and access techniques.

Data Encryption Standard (DES)—Symmetric encryption algorithm that uses a 56-bit key and encrypts data in 64-bit blocks. For many years, DES was the encryption standard set by the U.S. government and the American National Standards Institute (ANSI). However, due to advances in computing power, DES is no longer considered secure—in the late 1990s, specialized DES cracker machines were built that recovered DES keys after a period of several hours.

data hierarchy—Classification that groups different numbers of bits to extract meaningful data. Bit patterns, bytes and words contain small numbers of bits that are interpreted by hardware and low-level software. Fields, records and files may contain large numbers of bits that are interpreted by operating systems and user applications.

data independence—Property of applications that do not rely on a particular file organization technique or access technique.

data link layer (in OSI)—At the sender, converts the data representation from the network layer into bits to be transmitted over the physical layer. At the receiver, converts the bits into the data representation for the network layer.

data manipulation language (DML)—Type of language that enables data modification.

data regeneration (RAID)—Reconstruction of lost data (due to disk errors or failures) in RAID systems.

data region—Section of a process's address space that contains data (as opposed to instructions). This region is modifiable.

data stream (NTFS)—File attribute that stores the file's content or metadata; a file can have multiple data streams.

data striping (RAID)—Technique in RAID systems that divides contiguous data into fixed-size strips that can be placed on different disks. This enables multiple disks to service requests for data.

database—Centrally controlled collection of data that is stored in a standardized format and can be searched based on logical relations between data. Databases organize data according to content

as opposed to pathname, which tends to reduce or eliminate redundant information.

database language—Language that provides for organizing, modifying and querying of structured data.

database management system (DBMS)—Software that controls database organization and operations.

database system—A particular set of data, the storage devices on which it resides and the software that controls its storage and retrieval (called a database management system or DBMS).

datagram—Piece of data transferred using UDP or IP.

datagram socket—Socket that uses the UDP protocol to transmit data.

dcache (directory entry cache) (Linux)—Cache that stores directory entries (dentries), which enables the kernel to quickly map file descriptors to their corresponding inodes.

deactivated process (Linux)—Process that has been removed from the run queues and can therefore no longer contend for processor time.

dead state—Thread state entered after a thread completes its task or otherwise terminates.

deadline rate-monotonic scheduling—Scheduling policy in real-time systems that meets a periodic process's deadline that does not equal its period.

deadline scheduler (Linux)—Disk scheduling algorithm that eliminates indefinite postponement by assigning deadlines by which I/O requests are serviced.

deadline scheduling—Scheduling a process or thread to complete by a definite time; the priority of the process or thread may need to be increased as its completion deadline approaches.

deadlock—Situation in which a process or thread is waiting for an event that will never occur and therefore cannot continue execution.

deadlock avoidance—Strategy that eliminates deadlock by allowing a system to approach deadlock, but ensuring that deadlock never occurs. Avoidance algorithms can achieve higher performance than deadlock prevention algorithms. (See also Dijktra's Banker's Algorithm.)

deadlock detection—Process of determining whether or not a system is deadlocked. Once detected, a deadlock can be removed from a system, typically resulting in loss of work.

deadlock prevention—Process of disallowing deadlock by eliminating one of the four necessary conditions for deadlock.

deadlock recovery—Process of removing a deadlock from a system. This can involve suspending a process temporarily (and preserving its work) or sometimes killing a process (thereby losing its work) and restarting it.

deadly embrace—See deadlock.

decentralized peer-to-peer application—Also called a pure peer-to-peer application. It does not have a server and therefore does not suffer from the same deficiencies as applications that depend on servers.

decryption—Technique that reverses data encryption so that data can be read in its original form.

dedicated resource — Resource that may be used by only one process at a time. Also known as a serially reusable resource.

default action for a signal handler (Linux) — Predefined signal handler that is executed in response to a signal when a process does not specify a corresponding signal handler.

default data stream (NTFS) — File attribute that stores the primary contents of an NTFS file. When an NTFS file is copied to a file system that does not support multiple data streams, only the default data stream is preserved.

deferred cancellation (POSIX) — Cancellation mode in which a thread is terminated only after explicitly checking that it has received a cancellation signal.

deferred procedure call (DPC) (Windows XP) — Software interrupt that executes at the DPC/dispatch IRQL and executes in the context of the currently executing thread.

defragmentation — Moving parts of files so that they are located in contiguous blocks on disk. This can reduce access times when reading from or writing to files sequentially.

degree — Number of attributes in a relation in a relational database.

degree of a node — Number of other nodes with which a node is directly connected.

degree of multiprogramming — Total number of processes in main memory at a given time.

Dekker's Algorithm — Algorithm that ensures mutual exclusion between two threads and prevents both indefinite postponement and deadlock.

delayed blocking — Technique whereby a process spins on a lock for a fixed amount of time before it blocks; the rationale is that if the process does not obtain the lock quickly, it will probably have to wait a long time, so it should block.

delayed branching — Optimization technique for pipelined processors in which a compiler places directly after a branch an instruction that must be executed whether or not the branch is taken; the processor begins executing this instruction while determining the outcome of the branch.

delayed consistency — Memory coherence strategy in which processors send update information after a release, but a receiving node does not apply this information until it performs an acquire operation on the memory.

delegation (in NFS) — Allows the server to temporarily transfer the control of a file to a client. When the server grants a read delegation of a particular file, then no other clients can write to that file, but they can read it. When the server grants a write delegation of a particular file to the client, then no other clients can read or write that file.

delete (file) — Operation that removes a data item from a file.

demand fetch strategy — Method of bringing program parts or data into main memory as they are requested by a process.

demand paging — Technique that loads a process's nonresident pages into memory only when the process explicitly references the pages.

denial-of-service (DoS) attack — Attack that prevents a system from properly servicing legitimate requests. In many DoS attacks, unauthorized traffic saturates a network's resources, restricting access for legitimate users. Typically, the attack is performed by flooding servers with data packets.

dentry (directory entry) (Linux) — Structure that maps a file to an inode.

derived speed — Actual speed of a device as determined by the front-side bus speed and clock multipliers or dividers.

desktop environment — GUI layer above a window manager that provides tools, applications and other software to improve system usability.

destroy (file) — Operation that removes a file from the file system.

device class — Group of devices that perform similar functions.

device driver — Software through which the kernel interacts with hardware devices. Device drivers are intimately familiar with the specifics of the devices they manage — such as the arrangement of data on those devices — and they deal with device-specific operations such as reading data, writing data and opening and closing a DVD drive's tray. Drivers are modular, so they can be added and removed as a system's hardware changes, enabling users to add new types of devices easily; in this way they contribute to a system's extensibility.

device extension (Windows XP) — Portion of the nonpaged pool that stores information a driver needs to process I/O requests for a particular device.

device independence — Property of files that can be referenced by an application using a symbolic name instead of a name indicating the device on which it resides.

device IRQL (DIRQL) (Windows XP) — IRQL at which devices interrupt and at which APC, DPC/dispatch and lower DIRQLs are masked; the number of DIRQLs is architecture dependent.

device object (Windows XP) — Object that a device driver uses to store information about a physical or logical device.

device special file (Linux) — Entry in the /dev directory that provides access to a particular device.

Dhrystone — Classic synthetic program that measures how effectively an architecture runs systems programs.

digital certificate — Digital document that identifies a user or organization and is issued by a certificate authority. A digital certificate includes the name of the subject (the organization or individual being certified), the subject's public key, a serial number (to uniquely identify the certificate), an expiration date, the signature of the trusted certificate authority and any other relevant information.

digital envelope — Technique that protects message privacy by sending a package including a message encrypted using a secret key and the secret key encrypted using public-key encryption.

digital notary service — See time-stamping agency.

digital signature — Electronic equivalent of a written signature. To create a digital signature, a sender first applies a hash function to the original plaintext message. Next, the sender uses the sender's private key to encrypt the message digest (the hash value). This step creates a digital signature and validates the sender's identity, because only the owner of that private key could encrypt the message.

Digital Signature Algorithm (DSA) — U.S. government's digital authentication standard.

digital watermark — Popular application of steganography that hides information in unused (or rarely used) portions of a file.

Dijkstra's algorithm — Efficient algorithm to find the shortest paths in a weighted graph.

Dijkstra's Banker's Algorithm — Deadlock avoidance algorithm that controls resource allocation based on the amount of resources owned by the system, the amount of resources owned by each process and the maximum amount of resources that the process will request during execution. Allows resources to be assigned to processes only when the allocation results in a safe state. (See also safe state and unsafe state.)

Dining Philosophers — Classic problem introduced by Dijkstra that illustrates the problems inherent in concurrent programming, including deadlock and indefinite postponement. The problem requires the programmer to ensure that a set of n philosophers at a table containing n forks, who alternate between eating and thinking, do not starve while attempting to acquire the two adjacent forks necessary to eat.

direct file organization — File organization technique in which a record is directly (randomly) accessed by its physical address on a direct access storage device (DASD).

direct I/O — Technique that performs I/O without using the kernel's buffer cache. This leads to more efficient memory utilization in database applications, which typically maintain their own buffer cache.

direct mapping — Address translation mechanism that assists in the mapping of virtual addresses to their corresponding real addresses, using an index into a table stored in location-addressed memory.

direct memory access (DMA) — Method of transferring data from a device to main memory via a controller that requires interrupting the processor only when the transfer completes. I/O transfer via DMA is more efficient than programmed I/O or interrupt-driven I/O because the processor does not need to supervise the transfer of each byte or word of data.

directory — File storing references to other files. Directory entries often include a file's name, type, and size.

directory junction (Windows XP) — Directory that refers to another directory within the same volume, used to make navigating the file system easier.

dirty bit — Page table entry bit that specifies whether the page has been modified (also known as the modified bit).

dirty eager migration — Process migration method in which only a process's dirty pages are migrated with the process; clean pages must be accessed from secondary storage.

disable (mask) interrupts — When a type of interrupt is disabled (masked), interrupts of that type are not delivered to the process that has disabled (masked) the interrupts. The interrupts are either queued to be delivered later or dropped by the processor. This technique can be used to temporarily ignore interrupts, allowing a thread on a uniprocessor system to execute its critical section atomically.

disabled cancellation (POSIX) — Cancellation mode in which a thread does not receive pending cancellation signals.

discovery (in Jini) — Process of finding the lookup services and obtaining references to them.

discretionary access control (DAC) — Access control model in which the creator of an object controls the permissions for that object.

discretionary access control list (DACL) (Windows XP) — Ordered list that tells Windows XP which security principals may access a particular resource and what actions those principals may perform on the resource.

disk arm — Moving-head disk component that moves read/write heads linearly, parallel to disk surfaces.

disk arm anticipation — Moving the disk arm to a location that will minimize the next seek. Disk arm anticipation can be useful in environments where process disk-request patterns exhibit locality and when the load is light enough that there is sufficient time to move the disk arm between disk requests without degrading performance.

disk cache buffer — A region of main memory that the operating system reserves for disk data. In one context, the reserved memory acts as a cache, allowing processes quick access to data that would otherwise need to be fetched from disk. The reserved memory also acts as a buffer, allowing the operating system to delay writing the data to improve I/O performance by batching multiple writes into a small number of requests.

disk mirroring (RAID) — Data redundancy technique in RAID that maintains a copy of each disk's contents on a separate disk. This technique provides high reliability and simplifies data regeneration but incurs substantial storage overhead, which increases cost.

disk reorganization — Technique that moves file data on disk to improve its access time. One such technique is defragmentation, which attempts to place sequential file data contiguously on disk. Another technique attempts to place frequently requested data on tracks that result in low average seek times.

disk scheduler — Operating system component that determines the order in which disk I/O requests are serviced to improve performance.

disk scheduling — Technique that orders disk requests to maximize throughput and minimize response times and the variance of response times. Disk scheduling strategies improve performance by reducing seek times and rotational latencies.

dispatcher — Operating system component that assigns the first process on the ready list to a processor.

dispatcher (Windows XP) — Thread scheduling code dispersed throughout the microkernel.

dispatcher object (Windows XP) — Object, such as a mutex, semaphore, event or waitable timer, that kernel and user threads can use for synchronization purposes.

dispatching — Act of assigning a processor to a process.

dispersion—Measure of the variance of a random variable.

displacement—Distance of an address from the start of a block, page or segment, also called offset.

Distributed Component Object Model (DCOM)—Distributed systems extension of Microsoft's COM.

distributed computing—Using multiple independent computers to perform a common task.

distributed database—Database that is spread throughout the computer systems of a network.

distributed deadlock—Similar to deadlock in a uniprocessor system, except that the processes concerned are spread over different computers.

distributed deadlock detection strategy—Technique used to find deadlock in a distributed system.

distributed denial-of-service attack—Attack that prevents a system from servicing requests properly by initiating packet flooding from separate computers sending traffic in concert.

distributed file system—File system that is spread throughout the computer systems of a network.

distributed operating system—Provides all of the same services as a traditional operating system, but must provide adequate transparency such that objects in the system are unaware of the computers that provide the service.

distributed search—Searching technology used in peer-to-peer applications to make networks more robust by removing single points of failure, such as servers. In a distributed search, if a peer cannot answer the client's request, the peer forwards the request to its directly connected peers, and the search is distributed to the entire peer-to-peer network.

distributed system—Collection of remote computers that cooperate via a network to perform a common task.

distribution (Linux)—Software package containing the Linux kernel, user applications and/or tools that simplify the installation process.

distribution of response times—Set of values describing the response times for jobs in a system and the relative frequencies with which those values occur.

DMA memory (Linux)—Region of physical memory between zero and 16MB that is typically reserved for kernel bootstrapping code and legacy DMA devices.

DNS (domain name system) attack—Attack that modifies the address to which network traffic for a particular Web site is sent. Such attacks can be used to redirect users of a particular Web site to another, potentially malicious Web site.

domain—Set of possible values for attributes in a relational database system.

domain (in Sprite file system)—Unit that represents a portion of the global file hierarchy and is stored at one server.

domain (Windows XP)—Set of computers that share common resources.

domain controller (Windows XP)—Computer responsible for security on a network.

Domain Name System (DNS)—System on the Internet used to translate a machine's name to an IP address.

double data rate (DDR)—Chipset feature that enables a frontside bus to effectively operate at twice its clock speed by performing two memory transfers per clock cycle. This feature must be supported by the system's chipset and RAM.

doubly indirect pointer—Inode pointer that locates a block of (singly) indirect pointers.

DPC/dispatch IRQL (Windows XP)—IRQL at which DPCs and the thread scheduler execute and at which APC and incoming DPC/dispatch level interrupts are masked.

drafting algorithm—Dynamic load balancing algorithm that classifies each processor's load as low, normal or high; each processor maintains a table of the other processors' loads, and the system uses a receiver-initiated policy to exchange processes.

driver object (Windows XP)—Object used to describe device drivers; it stores pointers to standard driver routines and to the device objects for the devices that the driver services.

driver stack—Group of related device drivers that cooperate to handle the I/O requests for a particular device.

dynamic address translation (DAT)—Mechanism that converts virtual addresses to physical addresses during execution; this is done at extremely high speed to avoid slowing execution.

dynamic-linked library (DLL) (Windows XP)—Module that provides data or functions to which processes or other DLLs link at execution time.

dynamic linking—Linking mechanism that resolves references to external functions when the process first makes a call to the function. This can reduce linking overhead because external functions that are never called while the process executes are not linked.

dynamic load balancing—Technique that attempts to distribute processing responsibility equally by changing the number of processors assigned to a job throughout the job's life.

dynamic loading—Method for loading that specifies memory addresses at runtime.

dynamic partitioning—Job-aware process scheduling algorithm that divides processors in the system evenly among jobs, except that no single job can be allocated more processors than runnable processes; this algorithm maximizes processor affinity.

dynamic priority class (Windows XP)—Priority class that encompasses the five base priority classes within which a thread's priority can change during system execution; these classes are idle, below normal, normal, above normal and high.

dynamic RAM (DRAM)—RAM that must be continuously read by a refresh circuit to keep the contents in memory.

dynamic real-time scheduling algorithm—Scheduling algorithm that uses deadlines to assign priorities to processes throughout execution.

 E

eager migration—Process migration strategy that transfers the entire address space of a process during the initial phases of migration to eliminate a migrated process's residual dependencies on its original node.

earliest-deadline-first (EDF)—Scheduling policy that gives a processor to the process with the closest deadline.

ease of use—Measure of the comfort and convenience associated with system use.

EBCDIC (Extended Binary-Coded Decimal Interchange Code)—Eight-bit character set for representing data in mainframe computer systems, particularly systems developed by IBM.

effective priority (Linux)—Priority assigned to a process by adding its static priority to its priority boost or penalty.

efficient operating system—Operating system that exhibits high throughput and small turnaround time.

elevator algorithm—See SCAN disk scheduling.

embedded system—Small computer containing limited resources and specialized hardware to run devices such as PDAs or cellular phones.

emulation stage—When a Coda client becomes disconnected, it is said to enter the emulation stage. During this stage all file read requests are satisfied from cache. Write requests during the emulation stage occur in two steps. First, the file is updated on disk. Second, a log called the client modification log (CML) is updated to reflect file changes.

encapsulating security payload (ESP) (IPSec)—Message data encrypted using symmetric-key ciphers to protect the data from eavesdroppers while the IP packet is transmitted across public communication lines.

Encrypting File System (EFS)—NTFS feature that uses cryptography to protect files and folders in Windows XP Professional and Windows 2000. EFS uses secret-key and public-key encryption to secure files. Each user is assigned a key pair and certificate that are used to ensure that only the user that encrypted the files can access them.

encryption—Technique that transforms data to prevent it from being interpreted by unauthorized users.

entry queue—See entry set.

entry set—In Java, a queue of threads waiting to enter a monitor after calling a `synchronized` method.

environment subsystem (Windows XP)—User-mode component that provides a computing environment for other user-mode processes; in most cases, only environment subsystems interact directly with kernel-mode components in Windows XP.

epoch (Linux)—Time during which all processes move from the scheduler's active list to its expired list. This ensures that processes are not indefinitely postponed.

Ethernet (IEEE 802.3)—Network that supports many speeds over a variety of cables. Ethernet uses the Carrier Sense Multiple Access with Collision Detection (CSMA/CD) protocol. Ethernet is the most popular type of LAN.

event-driven simulator—Simulator controlled by events that are made to occur according to probability distributions.

event object (Windows XP)—Synchronization object that becomes *signaled* when a particular event occurs.

exception—Error caused by a process. Processor exceptions invoke the operating system, which determines how to respond. Processes can register exception handlers that are executed when the operating system receives the corresponding exception.

exception (Intel IA-32 specification)—Hardware signal generated by an error. In the Intel IA-32 specification, exceptions are classified as traps, faults and aborts.

execute access (virtual memory)—Access right that enables a process to execute instructions from a page or segment; see also read access, write access and append access.

execute access (file)—Permission that enables a user to execute a file.

execution mode—Operating system execution mode (e.g., user mode or kernel mode) that determines which instructions can be executed by a process.

executive (Windows XP)—Portion of the Windows XP operating system that is responsible for managing the operating system's subsystems (e.g., I/O subsystem, memory subsystem and file system).

executive mode—Protected mode in which a processor can execute operating system instructions on behalf of a user (also called kernel mode).

executive process (EPROCESS) block (Windows XP)—Executive data structure that stores information about a process, such as that process's object handles and ID; an EPROCESS block also stores the process's KPROCESS block.

executive resource lock (Windows XP)—Synchronization lock available only to kernel-mode threads and that may be held either in shared mode by many threads or in exclusive mode by one thread.

executive thread (ETHREAD) block (Windows XP)—Executive data structure that stores information about a thread, such as the thread's pending I/O requests and the thread's start address; an ETHREAD block also stores the thread's KTHREAD block.

expected value—Sum of a series of values each multiplied by its respective probability of occurrence.

expired list (Linux)—Structure containing processes that cannot contend for the processor until the next epoch. Processes are placed in this list to prevent others from being indefinitely postponed. To quickly begin a new epoch, this list becomes the active list.

expired state (Linux)—Task state that prevents a task from being dispatched until the next epoch.

explicit acknowledgement—The client sends an acknowledgement to the server in an additional packet when the client receives the response from the server.

explicit handle (Windows XP)—Binding handle in which the client must specify all binding information and create and manage the handle.

Explicitly Parallel Instruction Computing (EPIC)—Processor-design philosophy whose goals are to provide a high degree of instruction-level parallelism, reduce processor hardware complexity and improve performance.

exponential backoff—Method employed by Ethernet to calculate the interval before retransmission after a collision; this reduces the chance of subsequent collisions on the same transmission, thus increasing throughput.

export local file—Performed by an NFS server to make the local directory of files available to the remote client via the mount protocol.

ext2 inode (Linux)—Structure that stores information such as file size, the location of a file's data blocks and permissions for a single file or directory in an ext2 file system.

ext2fs (Linux)—Popular inode-based Linux file system that enables fast access to small files and supports large file sizes.

Extensible Firmware Interface (EFI)—Interface designed by Intel that improves upon a traditional BIOS by supporting device drivers and providing a shell interface at boot time.

Extensible Markup Language (XML)—Language for marking up data so that information can be exchanged between applications and platforms.

extensible operating system—An operating system that can incorporate new features easily.

extent—Block of contiguous sectors.

external fragmentation—Phenomenon in variable-partition memory systems in which there are holes distributed throughout memory that are too small to hold a process.

external name—Symbol defined in a module that can be referenced by other modules.

external reference—Reference from one module to an external name in a different module.

F

fabric layer (in grid computing)—Layer that accesses physical resources, such as disks.

failure transparency—Method by which a distributed system provides fault tolerance so that the client is unaware of the failure of a computer.

fair share group—Group of processes that receives a percentage of the processor time under a fair share scheduling (FSS) policy.

fair share scheduling (FSS)—Scheduling policy developed for AT&T's UNIX system that places processes in groups and assigns these groups a percentage of processor time.

fairness—Property of a scheduling algorithm that treats all processes equally.

false sharing—Situation that occurs when processes on separate processors are forced to share a page because they are each accessing a data item on that page, although not the same data item.

family of computers—Series of computers that are compatible in that they can run the same programs.

far page-replacement strategy—Graph-based page-replacement strategy that analyzes a program's reference patterns to determine which page to replace. This strategy replaces the page that is further

thest from any referenced page in the graph and that has not been referenced recently.

fast instruction set computing (FISC)—Term describing the processor-design philosophy resulting from the convergence of RISC and CISC design philosophies. The FISC design philosophy stresses inclusion of any construct that improves performance.

fast mutex (Windows XP)—Efficient mutex variant that operates at the APC level with some restrictions (e.g., a thread cannot specify a maximum wait time to wait for a fast mutex).

fast mutual exclusion algorithm—Implementation of mutual exclusion that avoids the overhead of a thread performing multiple tests when no other thread is contending for its critical section. This first fast mutual exclusion algorithm was proposed by Lamport.

fast user switching (Windows XP)—Ability of a new user to log onto a Windows XP machine without logging off the previous user.

FAT file system—An implementation of tabular noncontiguous file allocation developed by Microsoft.

fault—In the Intel IA-32 specification, an exception as the result of an error such as division by zero or illegal access to memory. Some faults can be corrected by appropriate operating system exception handlers.

fault tolerance—Operating system's ability to handle software or hardware errors.

feature freeze (Linux)—State of kernel development during which no new features should be added to the kernel, in preparation for a new kernel release.

feedback loop—Technique in which information about the current state of the system can influence the number of requests arriving at a resource (e.g., positive and negative feedback loops).

fetch strategy—Method of determining when to obtain the next piece of program or data for transfer from secondary storage to main memory.

fiber (Windows XP)—Unit of execution in Windows XP created by a thread and scheduled by that thread. Fibers facilitate portability for applications that schedule their own threads.

Fiber Distributed Data Interface (FDDI)—Protocol that shares many properties of a Token Ring, but operates over fiber-optic cable, allowing the transfer of more information at greater speeds. In FDDI, a token circulates around the optical fiber ring; stations cannot transmit until they obtain the token by receiving it from a preceding station. FDDI uses a second Token Ring as backup or to circulate tokens in the reverse direction of the primary Token Ring.

fiber local storage (FLS) (Windows XP)—Area of a process's address space where a fiber can store data that only the fiber can access.

field—In the data hierarchy, a group of characters (e.g., a person's name, street address or telephone number).

FIFO (Linux)—Named pipe that enables two unrelated processes to communicate via the producer/consumer relationship using a page-size buffer.

FIFO anomaly—Phenomenon in FIFO page-replacement strategy whereby increasing a process's page frame allocation increases the number of page faults it experiences; normally, page faults should decrease as more page frames become available.

FIFO broadcast—Guarantees that when two messages are sent from one process to another, the message that was sent first will arrive first.

file—Named collection of data that may be manipulated as a unit by operations such as open, close, create, destroy, copy, rename and list. Individual data items within a file may be manipulated by operations like read, write, update, insert and delete. File characteristics include location, accessibility, type, volatility and activity. Files can consist of one or more records.

file allocation table (FAT)—Table storing pointers to file data blocks in Microsoft's FAT file system.

file attribute (Linux)—File metadata that implements access control information, such as whether a file is append-only or immutable, that cannot be specified using standard Linux file permissions.

file control block—Metadata containing information the system needs to manage a file, such as access control information.

file descriptor—Non-negative integer that indexes into an opened-file table. A process references a file descriptor instead of a pathname to access file data without incurring the overhead of a directory structure traversal.

file handle—Identifies a file on the file server with file type, location and access permissions.

file identifiers (fids) (in AFS)—Entity that specifies a volume, an index within a volume and an identifier to guarantee object uniqueness within a volume.

file integrity mechanism—Mechanism that ensures that the information in a file is uncorrupted. When file integrity is assured, files contain only the information they are intended to have.

file management—Component of a file system concerned with providing the mechanisms for files to be stored, referenced, shared and secured.

file mapping (Windows XP)—Interprocess communication mechanism in which multiple processes access the same file by placing it in their virtual memory space. The different virtual addresses correspond to the same main memory addresses.

file mapping object (Windows XP)—Object used by processes to map any file into memory.

file organization—Manner in which the records of a file are arranged on secondary storage (e.g., sequential, direct, indexed sequential and partitioned).

file permission—Structure that determines whether a user may read, write and or execute a file.

file server—System dedicated to provide remote processes access to its files.

file system—Component of an operating system that organizes files and manages access to data. File systems are concerned with organizing files logically (using pathnames) and physically (using metadata). They also manage their storage device's free space, enforce security policies, maintain data integrity and so on.

file system identifier—Value that uniquely identifies the file system a storage device is using.

file system manager—Operating system component that organizes named collections of data on storage devices and provides an interface for accessing data on those devices.

File Transfer Protocol (FTP)—Application layer protocol that moves files between different hosts on a network. FTP specifies connections between two pairs of ports: one pair sends control information that governs the session, the other sends the actual data.

file view (Windows XP)—Portion of a file specified by a file mapping object that a process maps into its memory.

filter driver—WDM (Windows Driver Model) driver that modifies the behavior of a hardware device (e.g., providing mouse acceleration) or adds some extra services (e.g., security checks).

fine-grained strip (RAID)—Strip size that causes average files to be stored in multiple stripes. Fine-grained strips can reduce each request's access time and increase transfer rates because multiple disks simultaneously retrieve portions of the requested data.

firewall—Software or hardware that protects a local area network from packets sent by malicious users from an external network.

firmware—Microcode that specifies simple, fundamental instructions necessary to implement machine-language instructions.

first-come-first-served (FCFS) disk scheduling—Disk scheduling strategy in which the earliest arriving request is serviced first. FCFS is a fair method of allocating service, but when the request rate (i.e., the load) becomes heavy, FCFS can result in long waiting times. FCFS exhibits a random seek pattern in which successive requests can cause time-consuming seeks from the innermost to the outermost cylinders.

first-come-first-served (FCFS) process scheduling—Job-blind multiprocessor scheduling algorithm that places arriving processes in a queue; the process at the head of the queue executes until it freely relinquishes the processor.

first-fit memory placement strategy—Memory placement strategy that places an incoming process in the first hole that is large enough to hold it.

first-in-first-out (FIFO)—Nonpreemptive scheduling policy that dispatches processes according to their arrival time in the ready queue.

first-in-first-out (FIFO) page replacement—Page-replacement strategy that replaces the page that has been in memory longest. FIFO incurs low overhead but generally does not predict future page usage accurately.

fixed-partition multiprogramming—Memory organization that divides main memory into a number of fixed-size partitions, each holding a single job.

flat directory structure—File system organization containing only one directory.

flow control—Means by which TCP regulates the number of segments sent by a host to avoid overwhelming the receiver.

flushing—Process migration strategy in which the sending node writes all of the process's memory pages to a shared disk at the start of migration; the process then accesses the pages from the shared disk as needed on the receiving node.

flushing a page—Copying the contents of a modified page in main memory to secondary storage so another page can be placed in its frame. When this occurs, the page's dirty bit is cleared, which enables the operating system to quickly determine that the page can be overwritten by an incoming page, which can reduce page-wait times.

format a storage device—To prepare a device for a file system by performing operations such as inspecting its contents and writing storage management metadata.

Fortran—Procedural programming language developed by IBM in the mid-1950s for scientific applications that require complex mathematical computations.

fragmentation (of main memory)—Phenomenon wherein a system is unable to make use of certain areas of available main memory.

fragmented disk—Disk that stores files in discontinuous blocks as the result of file creation and deletion. Such disks exhibit high seek times when reading files sequentially. Disk defragmentation can reduce or eliminate the problem.

frame—Piece of data in the link layer. Contains both the message and the control information.

free list—Linked list of blocks that contain the addresses of free blocks.

free memory list—Operating system data structure that points to available holes in memory.

free model—COM (Microsoft's Component Object Model) object threading model in which many threads can act as the server for a COM object.

Free Page List (Windows XP)—List of page frames that are available for reclaiming; although these page frames do not contain any valid data, they may not be used until the zero-page thread sets all of their bits to zero.

frontside bus (FSB)—Bus that connects a processor to main memory.

FSCAN disk scheduling—Disk scheduling strategy that uses SCAN to service only those requests waiting when a particular sweep begins (the "F" stands for "freezing" the request queue at a certain time). Requests arriving during a sweep are grouped together and ordered for optimum service during the return sweep.

fully-connected mesh network—Mesh network in which each node is directly connected to every other node. These networks are faster and more fault tolerant than other networks, but also unrealizable on all but the smallest of networks because of the cost of the potentially enormous number of connections.

function driver—WDM (Windows Driver Model) device driver that implements a device's main functions; it does most of the I/O processing and provides the device's interface.

gang scheduling—Another name for coscheduling.

garbage collection—See memory compaction.

general protection fault (GPF) (IA-32 Intel architecture)—Occurs when a process references a segment to which it does not have appropriate access rights or references an address outside of the segment.

General Public License (GPL)—Open-source software license which specifies that software distributed under it must contain the complete source code, must clearly indicate any modifications to the original code and must be accompanied by the GPL. End users are free to modify and redistribute any software under the GPL.

general-purpose register—Register that can be used by processes to store data and pointer values. Special-purpose registers cannot be accessed by user processes.

general semaphore—See counting semaphore.

global descriptor table (GDT) (IA-32 Intel architecture)—Segment map table that contains mapping information for process segments or local descriptor table (LDT) segments, which contain mapping information for process segments.

global least-recently-used (gLRU) page replacement—Global page-replacement strategy that replaces the page that has not been referenced for the longest time in the entire system. LRU can perform poorly because variants of round-robin scheduling cause the system to exhibit a large-scale looping reference pattern. The SEQ variant of gLRU page replacement attempts to improve performance by replacing the most-recently-used page when it detects a looping reference pattern.

global run queue—Process scheduling queue used in some multiprocessor scheduling algorithms, which is independent of the processors in a system and into which every process or job in the system is placed.

globally unique ID (GUID)—128-bit integer that is, for all practical purposes, guaranteed to be unique in the world. COM (Microsoft's Component Object Model) uses GUIDs to uniquely identify interfaces and object classes.

GNU—Project initiated by Stallman in the 1980s aimed at producing an open-source operating system with the features and utilities of UNIX.

granularity bit (IA-32 Intel architecture)—Bit that determines how the processor interprets the size of each segment, specified by the 20-bit segment limit. When the bit is off, segments range in size from 1 byte to 1MB, in 1-byte increments. When the bit is on, segments range in size from 4KB to 4GB, in 4KB increments.

graph reduction—Altering a resource-allocation graph by removing a process if that process can complete. This also involves removing any arrows leading to the process (from the resources allocated to the process) or away from the process (to resources the process is requesting). A resource-allocation graph can be reduced by a process if all of that process's resource requests can be granted, enabling that process to run to completion and free its resources.

Graphical Identification and Authentication (GINA) (Windows XP)—Graphical user interface that prompts users for credentials, usually in the form of a username and password. Windows XP ships with its own implementation of GINA called MSGINA, but it accepts third-party DLLs.

graphical user interface (GUI)—User-friendly point of access to an operating system that uses graphical symbols such as windows, icons and menus to facilitate program and file manipulation.

grid computing—Links computational resources that are distributed over the wide area network (such as computers, data storages and scientific devices) to solve complex problems.

group (file access control)—Set of users with the same file access rights (e.g., members of a group that is working on a particular project).

group descriptor (Linux)—Structure that records information regarding a block group, such as the locations of the inode allocation bitmap, block allocation bitmap and inode table.

H

hacker—Experienced programmer who often program as much for personal enjoyment as for the functionality of the application. This term is often used when the term cracker is more appropriate.

Hamming error-correcting codes (Hamming ECCs)—Technique of generating parity bits that enables systems to detect and correct errors in data transmission.

handshaking—Mechanism in a connection-oriented transport layer in which hosts send control information to create a logical connection between the hosts.

happens before relation—A happens before B if A and B belong to the same process and A occurred before B; or A is the sending of a message and B is the receiving of that message.

hard affinity—Type of processor affinity in which the scheduling algorithm guarantees that a process only executes on a single node throughout its life cycle.

hard disk drive—Magnetic, rotational secondary storage device that provides persistent storage for, and random access to, data.

hard link—Directory entry specifying the location of a file on its storage device.

hard real-time scheduling—Scheduling policy that ensures processes meet their deadlines.

Hardware Abstraction Layer (HAL) (Windows XP)—Operating system component that interacts directly with the hardware and abstracts hardware details for other system components.

Hartstone—Popular synthetic benchmark used to evaluate real-time systems.

hash anchor table—Hash table that points to entries in an inverted page table. Increasing the size of the hash anchor table decreases the number of collisions, which improves the speed of address translation, at the cost of the increased memory overhead required to store the table.

hash function—Function that takes a number as input and returns a number, called a hash value, within a specified range. Hash functions facilitate rapidly storing and retrieving information from hash tables.

hash table—Data structure that indexes items according to their hash values; used with hash functions to rapidly store and retrieve information.

hash value—Value returned by a hash function that corresponds to a position in a hash table.

Havender's linear ordering—See linear ordering.

hbench microbenchmark suite—Popular microbenchmark suite, which enables evaluators to effectively analyze the relationship between operating system primitives and hardware components.

head node (in a Beowulf cluster)—Node, also called master node, that acts as a server to distribute the workload, control access to the cluster and handle the shared resources.

header—Control information placed in front of a data message.

heavyweight process (HWP)—A traditional process, which may contain one or more threads. The process is "heavyweight" because it is allocated its own address space upon creation.

heuristic scanning—Antivirus technique that detects viruses by their program behavior.

heuristics—Technique that solves complex problems using rules of thumb or other approximations that incur low execution overhead and generally provide good results.

hierarchical deadlock detection—A strategy in distributed deadlock, which arranges each site in the system as a node in a tree. Each node, except the leaf nodes, collects the resource allocation information of all dependent nodes.

hierarchical process structure—Organization of processes when parent processes spawn child processes and, in particular, only one parent creates a child.

hierarchically structured file system—File system organization in which each directory can contain multiple subdirectories but exactly one parent.

high-availability cluster—Cluster in which only some of the nodes are working while other nodes act as backups. The goal of a high-availability cluster is to stay up all the time.

high IRQL (Windows XP)—Highest-priority IRQL, at which machine check and bus error interrupts execute and all other interrupts are masked.

high-level driver (Windows XP)—Device driver that abstracts hardware specifics and passes I/O requests to low-level drivers.

high-level language—Programming language that uses English-like identifiers and common mathematical notation to represent programs using fewer statements than assembly-language programming.

high-level scheduling—Determining which jobs a system allows to compete actively for system resources.

high memory (Linux)—Region of physical memory (which begins at 896MB on the IA-32 architecture) beginning at the largest physical address that is permanently mapped to the kernel's virtual address space and extending to the limit of physical memory (64GB on Intel Pentium 4 processors). Because the kernel must perform expensive operations to map pages in its virtual address space to page frames in high memory, most kernel data structures are not stored in high memory.

high-performance cluster—Cluster in which all the nodes work to achieve maximum performance.

highest-response-ratio-next (HRRN) — Scheduling policy that assigns priority based on a process's service time and the amount of time the process has been waiting.

hoarding stage (in Coda) — Stage that clients enter when they are connected to Coda. In this stage, clients prepare for a possible disconnection from the system by caching any requested file.

hole — An unused area of memory in a variable-partition multiprogramming system.

home-based consistency — Memory-coherence strategy in which processors send coherence information to a home node associated with the page being written; the home node forwards update information to other nodes that subsequently access the page.

home computer (in process migration) — Computer on which the process originates.

home node — Node that is the "home" for a physical memory address or page and is responsible for maintaining the data's coherence.

hook — Software feature that enables developers to add features to an existing application without modifying its source file. An application uses a hook to call a procedure that can be defined by another application.

host — Entity, such as a computer or Internet-enabled cellular phone, that receives and/or provides services over a network. Also called a node.

host-based intrusion detection — IDS that monitors system and application log files.

hot spare disk (RAID) — Disk in a RAID system that is not used until a disk fails. Once the system regenerates the failed disk's data, the hot spare disk replaces the failed disk.

hot spot — Disk cylinder that contains frequently requested data. Some disk arm anticipation techniques move the disk head to hot spots to reduce average seek times.

hot swappable device — Device that can be added to, or removed from, a computer while it is running.

HTTP request — Resource request from an HTTP client to an HTTP server.

HTTP response — Reply message from an HTTP server to an HTTP client, consisting of a status, header and data.

hub — Central node (such as in a star network) responsible for relaying messages between nodes.

hybrid methodology — Performance evaluation technique that combines the vector-based methodology with trace data to measure performance for applications whose behavior depends strongly on user input.

hypercube — Multiprocessor interconnection scheme that consists of $2n$ nodes (where n is an integer); each node is linked with n neighbor nodes.

HyperText Markup Language (HTML) — Language that specifies the content and arrangement of information on a Web page and provides hyperlinks to access other pages.

Hypertext Transfer Protocol (HTTP) — Application layer protocol used for transferring HTML documents and other data formats between a client and a server. This is the key protocol of the World Wide Web.

I

I/O-bound — Process (or job) that tends to use a processor for a short time before generating an I/O request and relinquishing the processor.

I/O channel — Component responsible for handling device I/O independently of a main processor.

I/O completion interrupt — Message issued by a device when it finishes servicing an I/O request.

I/O completion port (Windows XP) — Port at which threads register and block, waiting to be awakened when processing completes on an I/O request.

I/O completion routine (Windows XP) — Function registered by a device driver with the I/O manager in reference to an IRP; the I/O manager calls this function when processing of the IRP completes.

I/O manager — Operating system component that receives, interprets and performs I/O requests.

I/O manager (Windows XP) — Executive component that interacts with device drivers to handle I/O requests.

I/O request packet (IRP) (Windows XP) — Data structure that describes an I/O request.

I/O status block (Windows XP) — Field in an IRP that indicates whether an I/O request completed successfully or, if not, the request's error code.

I/O throttling (Windows XP) — Technique that increases stability when available memory is low; the VMM manages memory one page at a time during I/O throttling.

IBSYS — Operating system for the IBM 7090 mainframe.

ideal processor (Windows XP) — Thread attribute that specifies a processor on which the system should attempt to schedule the thread for execution.

idempotent request — A requested operation that if performed several times will return the same result, so it is acceptable to perform the same operation twice.

IEEE 1394 port — Commonly used serial port that provides transfer speeds of up to 800MB per second, sometimes supplies power to devices and allows devices to be hot swappable; these ports are commonly referred to as FireWire (from Apple) or iLink (from Sony).

IEEE 802.11 — One of the standards that governs wireless communication. It dictates that hosts follow the CSMA/CA protocol.

immutable attribute (Linux) — Attribute specifying that a file can be read and executed, but cannot be copied, modified or deleted.

immutable file — A file that cannot be modified after it is created.

implicit acknowledgement — The response message implies the acknowledgement for the request message.

inactive list (Linux) — See expired list.

inactive page (Linux)—Page in main memory that can be replaced by an incoming page.

incremental backup—Backup technique that copies only data in the file system that has changed since the last backup.

indefinite postponement—Situation in which a thread waits for an event that might never occur.

independent software vendor (ISV)—Organization that develops and sells software. ISVs prospered after the release of the IBM PC.

index block—Block that contains a list of pointers to file data blocks.

indexed sequential file organization—File organization that arranges records in a logical sequence according to a key contained in each record.

indirect block—Index block containing pointers to data blocks in inode-based file systems.

indirect pointer—Inode pointer that points to a block of inode pointers.

indivisible operation—See atomic operation.

information hiding—Software architectural technique that facilitates the development of more reliable software systems by preventing direct access to data within an object by outside objects.

inheritance (Windows XP)—Technique by which a child process obtains attributes (e.g., most types of handles and the current directory) from its parent process upon creation.

initialized **state** (Windows XP)—Thread state in which the thread is created by the operating system.

inode—Index block in a UNIX-based system that contains the file control block and pointers to singly, doubly and triply indirect blocks of pointers to file data.

inode (Linux)—Structure that describes the location of data blocks corresponding to a file, directory or link in a file system. In the VFS, this structure represents any file in the system. An ext2 inode represents a file in the ext2 file system.

inode allocation bitmap (Linux)—Bitmap that records a block group's inode usage.

inode cache (Linux)—Cache that improves inode lookup performance.

inode map—Block of metadata written to the log of a log-structured file system that indicates the location of the file system's inodes. Inode maps improve LFS performance by reducing the time required to determine file locations in the LFS.

inode table (Linux)—Structure that contains an entry for each allocated inode in a block group.

input/output control system (IOCS)—Precursor to modern operating systems that provided programmers with a basic set of functions to perform I/O.

insert (file)—Operation that adds a new data item to a file.

instruction decode unit—Component of a processor that interprets instructions and generates appropriate control signals that cause the processor to perform each instruction.

instruction fetch unit—Component of a processor that loads instructions from the instruction cache so they can be decoded and executed.

instruction length—Number of bits that comprise an instruction in a given architecture. Some architectures support variable-length instructions; instruction lengths also vary among different architectures.

instruction-level parallelism (ILP)—Parallelism that permits two machine instructions to be executed at once. Two instructions exhibit ILP if the execution of one does not affect the outcome of the other (i.e., the two instructions do not depend on each other).

instruction set—Set of machine instructions a processor can perform.

instruction set architecture (ISA)—Interface exposed by a processor that describes the processor, including its instruction set, number of registers and memory size.

instrumentation level (in JMX)—Makes any Java-based object manageable so that the management application can access and operate these objects.

integrity (secure transaction)—One of the five fundamental requirements for a successful, secure transaction. Integrity deals with how to ensure that the information you send or receive has not been compromised or altered.

intensive resource management—Notion of devoting substantial resources to managing other resources to improve overall utilization.

interactive operating system—Operating system that allows applications to respond quickly to user input.

Interactive Problem Control System (IPCS) (VM)—VM component that provides online analysis and correction of VM software problems.

interactive process—Process that requires user input as it executes.

interactive users—Users that are present when the system processes their jobs. Interactive users communicate with their jobs during execution.

interconnection scheme—Design that describes how a multiprocessor system physically connects its components, such as processors and memory modules.

Interface Definition Language (IDL)—A language used to specify the details of the RPCs, which provides a language-independent representation of interfaces and allows distributed applications to transparently call procedures on remote computers.

Interface Definition Language (IDL) file (Windows XP)—File that specifies the interfaces that an RPC server exposes.

interface ID (IID)—Globally unique ID for a COM interface.

interfault time—Time between a process's page faults. This is used in the page-fault-frequency page-replacement strategy to determine when to increase or decrease a program's page frame allocation.

interlocked singly linked list (SList) (Windows XP)—Singly linked list in which insertions and deletions are performed as atomic operations.

interlocked variable access (Windows XP)—Method of accessing variables that ensures atomic reads and writes to shared variables.

intermediate code generator—Stage of the compilation process that receives input from the parser and outputs a stream of instructions to the optimizer.

intermediate driver (Windows XP)—Device driver that can be interposed between high- and low-level drivers to filter or process I/O requests for a device.

intermediate-level scheduling—Determining which processes may enter the low-level scheduler to compete for a processor.

internal fragmentation—Phenomenon in fixed-partition multiprogramming systems in which holes occur when the size of a process's memory and data is smaller than the partition in which the process executes.

Internet—Network of communication channels that provides the backbone for telecommunication and the World Wide Web. Each computer on the Internet determines which services it uses and which it makes available to other computers connected to the Internet.

Internet Connection Firewall (ICF)—Windows XP's packet filtering firewall.

Internet Key Exchange (IKE) (IPSec)—Key-exchange protocol used in IPSec to perform key management, which allows secure key exchange.

Internet Protocol (IP)—Primary protocol for directing information over a network. Destinations on the Internet are specified by 32-bit numbers called IP addresses.

Internet Protocol Security (IPSec)—Transport-layer security protocol that provides data privacy, integrity and authentication.

Internet Protocol version 6 (IPv6)—New version of the Internet Protocol that uses 128-bit addresses and specifies three types of addresses: unicast, anycast and multicast.

Internetwork Packet eXchange (IPX)—Novell Netware's network protocol designed specifically for LANs.

interoperability—Permits software components to interact among different hardware and software platforms, programming languages and communication protocols.

interpreter—Application that can execute code other than machine code (e.g., high-level-language instructions).

interprocess communication (IPC) manager—Operating system component that governs communication between processes.

interrupt—Hardware signal indicating that an event has occurred. Interrupts cause the processor to invoke a set of software instructions called an interrupt handler.

Interrupt Dispatch Table (IDT)—Kernel data structure that maps hardware interrupts to interrupt vectors.

interrupt handler—Kernel code that is executed in response to an interrupt.

interrupt request level (IRQL) (Windows XP)—Measure of interrupt priority; an interrupt that occurs at an IRQL equal to or lower than the current IRQL is masked.

interrupt service routine (ISR) (Windows XP)—Function, registered by a device driver, that processes interrupts issued by the device that the driver services.

interrupt vector—Array in protected memory containing pointers to the locations of interrupt handlers.

interrupting clock—Hardware device that issues an interrupt after a certain amount of time (called a quantum), e.g., to prevent a process from monopolizing a processor. This can ensure that a processor will not be monopolized by a malicious or malfunctioning process.

interval timer—See interrupting clock.

intrusion detection system (IDS)—Application that monitors networks and application log files, which record information about system behavior, such as the time at which operating services are requested and the name of the process that requests them.

invalidate—To invalidate a file, the client checks the time stamp of the copy of the file on the server. If this copy has been updated since the client last copied the file, then the client must download the latest version. If the server copy has not been updated since the client copied it, then the client can work on its cached copy.

invalidation—Memory-coherence protocol in which a process first invalidates—i.e., voids—all other copies of a page before writing to the page.

inverted page table—Page table containing one entry for each page frame in main memory. Inverted page tables incur less table fragmentation than traditional page tables, which typically maintain in memory a greater number of page table entries than page frames. Hash functions map virtual page numbers to an index in the inverted page table.

IOStone—Popular synthetic benchmark that evaluates file systems.

IP address—Address of a particular host on the Internet.

IP spoofing—Attack in which an attacker simulates the IP address of an authorized user or host to obtain unauthorized access to resources.

J

Jakarta project—Provides commercial-quality server solutions based on the Java platform that are developed in an open and cooperative fashion.

Java—Object-oriented programming language developed by Sun Microsystems that promotes portability by running on a virtual machine.

Java Community Process—Open organization that focuses on developing Java technology specifications, including servlet and JavaServer Pages.

Java Management Extensions (JMX)—Developed by Sun and network management industry leaders, which defines a component framework that enables developers to build automated, intelligent and dynamic network management solutions.

Java Virtual Machine (JVM)—Virtual machine that enables Java programs to execute on many different architectures without recompiling Java programs into the native machine language of the computer on which they execute. The JVM promotes application portability and simplifies programming by freeing the programmer from architecture-specific considerations.

JavaServer Pages (JSP)—Allows Web-page programmers to create pages that use encapsulated Java functionality and even to write scriptlets of actual Java code directly in the page.

JavaSpaces—Jini service that implements a simple, high-level architecture for building distributed systems. The JavaSpaces service provides distributed, shared storage (and shared memory) for Java objects and enables Java objects to communicate, share objects and coordinate tasks using the storage.

Jini—Framework for building reliable and fault-tolerant distributed systems with existing Java technologies. Jini extends the idea of providing services beyond industry-based computer networks and into home-based networks.

job—Set of work to be done by a computer.

job-aware scheduling—Multiprocessor scheduling algorithms that account for job properties when making scheduling decisions; these algorithms typically attempt to maximize parallelism or processor affinity.

job-blind scheduling—Multiprocessor scheduling algorithms that ignore job properties when making scheduling decisions; these algorithms are typically simple to implement.

job control language—Commands interpreted by a job stream processor that define and facilitate the setup of the next job in a single-stream batch-processing system.

job object (Windows XP)—Object that groups several processes and allows developers to manipulate and set limits on these processes as a group.

job scheduling—See high-level scheduling.

job stream processor—Entity in single-stream batch-processing systems that controls the transition between jobs.

job-to-job transition—Time during which jobs cannot execute in single-stream batch-processing systems while one job is purged from the system and the next job is loaded and prepared for execution.

join—Thread operation that causes the calling thread to block until the thread it joins terminates. A primary thread often joins each of threads it creates so that its corresponding process does not exit until all of its threads have terminated.

join (database)—Operation that combines relations.

journaling file system—See log-structured file system (LFS).

JXTA—Project created at Sun Microsystems, Inc., which creates a standard, low-level, platform- and language-independent protocol that promotes interoperability among peer-to-peer applications.

K

Kerberos—Freely available, open-source authentication and access control protocol developed at MIT that provides protection against internal security attacks. It employs secret-key cryptography to authenticate users in a network and to maintain the integrity and privacy of network communications.

kernel—Software that contains the core components of an operating system.

kernel control path (Linux)—A kernel execution context that may perform operations requiring mutual exclusive access to kernel data structures.

kernel handle (Windows XP)—Object handle accessible from any process's address space, but only in kernel mode.

kernel-level thread—Thread created by an operating system (also called kernel thread).

kernel mode—Execution mode of a processor that allows processes to execute privileged instructions.

kernel-mode APC (Windows XP)—APC generated by a kernel-mode thread and queued to a specified user-mode thread; the user-mode thread must process the APC as soon as the user-mode thread obtains the processor.

kernel-mode driver—Device driver that executes in kernel mode.

kernel process (KPROCESS) block (Windows XP)—Kernel data structure that stores information about a process, such as that process's base priority class.

kernel program—Typical program that might be run at an installation; it is executed "on paper" using manufacturers' instruction timings and used for application-specific performance evaluation.

kernel semaphore (Linux)—Semaphore implemented by the kernel to provide mutual exclusion.

kernel thread (Linux)—Thread that executes kernel code.

kernel thread (KTHREAD) block (Windows XP)—Kernel data structure that stores information about a thread, such as the objects on which that thread is waiting and the location in memory of the thread's kernel stack.

key—Input to a cipher to encrypt data; keys are represented by a string of digits.

key agreement protocol—Rules that govern key exchange between two parties over an insecure medium.

key distribution center (KDC)—Central authority that shares a different secret key with every user in the network.

key generation—Creation of encryption keys.

ksoftirqd (Linux)—Daemon that schedules software interrupt handlers when softirq load is high.

kswapd (Linux)—Daemon that swaps pages to disk.

L

Lamport's bakery algorithm—N-thread mutual exclusion algorithm based on a "take a ticket" system.

lane—Route between two points in a PCI Express bus. PCI Express devices are connected by a link that may contain up to 32 lanes.

large page (Windows XP)—Set of pages contiguous in memory that the VMM treats as a single page.

last processor (Windows XP)—Thread attribute equal to the processor that most recently executed the thread.

latency (process scheduling)—Time a task spends in a system before it is serviced.

laxity—Value determined by subtracting the sum of the current time and a process's remaining execution time from the process's deadline. This value decreases as a process nears its deadline.

layer—Level of abstraction in the TCP/IP protocol stack associated with certain conceptual functions. These layers are the application layer, transport layer, network layer and link layer.

layered biometric verification (LBV)—Authentication technique that uses multiple measurements of human features (such as face, finger and voice prints) to verify a user's identity.

layered operating system—Modular operating system that places similar components in isolated layers. Each layer accesses the services of the layer below and returns results to the layer above.

lazy allocation—Policy of waiting to allocate resources, such as pages in virtual memory and page frames in main memory, until absolutely necessary.

lazy copying—Process migration strategy that transfers pages from the sender only when the process at the receiving node references these pages.

lazy data propagation—Technique in which writing processors send coherence information after a release, but not the data; a processor retrieves the data when it accesses a page that it knows is not coherent.

lazy migration—Process migration strategy in multiprocessor systems that does not transfer all pages during initial migration. This increases residual dependency but reduces initial migration time.

lazy release consistency—Memory-coherence strategy in which a processor does not send coherence information after writing to a page until a new processor attempts an acquire operation on that memory page.

lease—Agreement between the client and server for controlling file locks.

least-frequently-used (LFU) page replacement—Page-replacement strategy that replaces the page that is least frequently used or least intensively referenced. LFU is easy to implement, but generally does not predict future page usage well.

least-recently-used (LRU) page replacement—Page-replacement strategy that replaces the page that has not been referenced for the longest time. LRU generally predicts future page usage well but incurs significant overhead.

Lempel-Ziv compression algorithm—Data compression algorithm that NTFS uses to compress files.

level (RAID)—A particular organization of a RAID system, such as level 1 (mirroring) or level 2 (Hamming ECC parity). See also RAID level 0, RAID level 1, RAID level 2, RAID level 3, RAID level 4 and RAID level 5.

level of multiprogramming—See degree of multiprogramming.

lexer—See lexical analyzer.

lexical analyzer—Part of a compiler that separates the source code into tokens.

library module—Precompiled module that performs common computer routines, such as I/O routines or mathematical functions.

Lightweight Directory Access Protocol (LDAP) (Windows XP)—Protocol for accessing, searching and modifying Internet directories (e.g., Active Directory).

lightweight process (LWP)—A single thread of program instructions (also called a thread of execution or thread of control). Threads are "lightweight" because they share their address space with other threads in the same process.

limit register—Register used in fixed-partition multiprogramming systems to mark where a process's memory partition ends.

linear address space (IA-32 Intel architecture)—32-bit (4GB) virtual address space. Under pure segmentation, this address space is mapped directly to main memory. Under segmentation/paging, this address space is divided into page frames that are mapped to main memory.

linear ordering (Havender)—Logical arrangement of resources that requires that processes request resources in a linear order. This method denies the circular-wait necessary condition for deadlock.

link (file system)—Directory entry that references an existing file. Hard links reference the location of the file on its storage device; soft links store the file's pathname.

link (network)—Medium over which services are physically transmitted in a network.

link layer (in TCP/IP)—Responsible for interfacing with and controlling the physical medium over which data is sent.

linking—Process of integrating a program's object modules into a single executable file.

linking loader—Application that performs both linking and loading.

Linux security modules (LSM) framework (Linux)—Framework that allows system administrators to specify the access control mechanism employed by the system.

Linux Standard Base (Linux)—Project that aims to specify a standard Linux interface to improve application portability between kernel versions (and distributions).

list (file)—Operation that prints or displays a file's contents.

lmbench microbenchmark—Microbenchmark suite that enables evaluators to measure and compare system performance on a variety of UNIX platforms.

load—See request rate.

load balancer—Node in a load balancing cluster that distributes the workload (such as thousands of requests from the clients) to a set of nodes so that all hardware is efficiently utilized.

load balancing—Operation that attempts to evenly distribute system load between processors in the system.

load balancing cluster—Cluster in which one particular node works as a load balancer to distribute the load to a set of nodes, so that all hardware is efficiently utilized.

load module—Integrated module produced by a linker that consists of object code and relative addresses.

loadable kernel module (Linux)—Software that can be integrated into the kernel at runtime.

loader—Application that loads linked executable modules into memory.

local area network (LAN)—Type of network used to interconnect resources using high-speed communication paths optimized for local area environments, such as office buildings or college campuses.

local descriptor table (LDT) (IA-32 Intel architecture)—Segment map table that contains mapping information for process segments. The system may contain up to 8,191 LDTs, each containing 8,192 entries.

local procedure call (LPC) (Windows XP)—Procedure call made by a thread in one process to a procedure exposed by another process in the same domain (i.e., set of computers that share common resources); LPCs can be created only by system components.

local remote procedure call (LRPCs) (Windows XP)—RPCs between two processes on the same machine.

locality—Empirical phenomenon describing events that are closely related in space or time. When applied to memory access patterns, spatial locality states that when a process references a particular address, it is also likely to access nearby addresses; temporal locality states that when a process references a particular address, it is likely to reference it again soon.

localized least-recently used page replacement (Windows XP)—Policy of moving to disk the least-recently used page of a process at its working set maximum when that process requests a page in main memory. The policy is localized by process, because Windows XP moves only the requesting process's pages; Windows XP approximates this policy using the clock algorithm.

location (file)—Address of a file on a storage device or in the system's logical file organization.

location-dependent call—System call that depends on the workstation (in Sprite) on which the call is executed. Location-dependent calls produce different results for different workstations.

location-independent call—System call that does not depend on the workstation (in Sprite) on which the call is executed. Location-independent calls produce the same result for all workstations.

location transparency—Builds on access transparency to hide the location of resources in a distributed system from those attempting to access them.

lockstep synchronization—Situation where asynchronous threads execute code in strict alternation.

log file—Records information about system behavior, such as the time at which operating services are requested and the name of the process that requests them.

log-structured file system (LFS)—File system that performs all file operations as transactions to ensure that file system data and metadata is always in a consistent state. An LFS generally exhibits good write performance because data is also appended to the end of a system-wide log file. To improve read performance, an LFS typically distributes metadata throughout the log and employs large caches to store that metadata so that the locations of file data can be found quickly.

logic bomb—Virus that executes its code when a specified condition is met.

logical address space (IA-32 Intel architecture)—Set of addresses contained in a segment.

logical backup—Backup technique that stores file data and the file system's directory structure, often in a common, compressed format.

logical block—See logical record.

logical clock—Assigns a timestamp to each event that happens in a system in order to create a total ordering of events.

logical record—Collection of data treated as a unit by software.

logical topology—Map of a network that depicts which nodes are directly connected.

logical view—View of files that hides the devices that store them, their format and the system's physical access techniques.

long-term scheduling—See high-level scheduling.

LOOK disk scheduling—Variation of the SCAN disk scheduling strategy that "looks" ahead to the end of the current sweep to determine the next request to service. If there are no more requests in the current direction, LOOK changes the preferred direction and begins the next sweep, stopping when passing a cylinder that corresponds to a request in the queue. This strategy eliminates unnecessary seek operations experienced by other variations of SCAN by preventing the read/write head from moving to the innermost or outermost cylinder unless it needs to service a request at those cylinders.

lookup service—Heart of the Jini architecture, which maintains information about available Jini services and enables clients to discover and use them.

loopback device (Linux)—Virtual device that enables operations to be performed on data between layers of a system service (e.g., the file system).

loosely coupled system—System in which processors do not share most resources; these systems are flexible and fault tolerant but perform worse than tightly coupled systems.

low-level driver (Windows XP)—Device driver that controls a peripheral device and does not depend on any lower-level drivers.

low-level scheduling—Determining which process will gain control of a processor.

Lucifer algorithm—Encryption algorithm created by Horst Feistel of IBM, which was chosen as the DES by the United States government and the National Security Agency (NSA) in the 1970s.

M

Mac OS—Line of operating systems for Apple Macintosh computers first introduced in 1997.

Mach—Early microkernel operating system, designed at Carnegie-Mellon University by a team led by Richard Rashid. Mach has influenced the design of Windows NT and has been used to implement Mac OS X.

machine language—Language that is defined by a computer's hardware design and can be natively understood by the computer.

Macintosh—Apple Computer's PC line that introduced the GUI and mouse to mainstream computer users.

magnetic tape storage—Rewritable magnetic storage medium that accesses data sequentially. Its sequential nature makes it unsuitable for direct access applications.

mailslot (Windows XP)—Message queue, which a process can employ to receive messages from other processes.

mailslot client (Windows XP)—Process that sends mailslot messages to mailslot servers.

mailslot server (Windows XP)—Process that creates a mailslot and receives messages in it from mailslot clients.

main memory—Volatile memory that stores instructions and data; it is the lowest level of the memory hierarchy that can be directly referenced by a processor.

main thread of execution—Thread created upon process creation (also called primary thread).

mainboard—Printed circuit board that provides electrical connections between computer components such as processor, memory and peripheral devices.

major device identification number (Linux)—Value that uniquely identifies a device in a particular device class. The kernel uses this value to determine a device's driver.

major function code (Windows XP)—Field in an IRP that describes the general function (e.g., read or write) that should be performed to fulfill an I/O request.

major version number (Linux)—Value that uniquely identifies a significant Linux release.

manager level (in JMX)—Level that gives a management application access to managed resources (created in the instrumentation level) and operates these resources via the JMX agents.

mandatory access control (MAC)—Access control model in which policies predefine a central permission scheme by which all subjects and objects are controlled.

manual-reset timer object (Windows XP)—Timer object that remains *signaled* until a thread specifically resets the timer.

many-to-many (*m*-to-*n*) thread mapping—Threading model in which a set of user threads is assigned to a set of kernel threads so that applications can benefit both from kernel-level threads and user-level features such as scheduler activations. In practice the number of user threads is greater than or equal to the number of kernel threads in the system to minimize memory consumption.

many-to-one thread mapping—Threading model in which all user-level threads in a process are assigned to one kernel thread.

marshaling of data—A routine for the client stub to package procedure arguments and return values for transmission over a network.

mask a signal—Prevent a signal from being delivered. Signal masking enables a multithreaded process to specify which of its threads will handle signals of a particular type.

massive parallelism—Property of a system containing large numbers of processors so that many parts of computations can be performed in parallel.

massively parallel processor—Processor that performs a large number of instructions on large data sets at once; array processors are often called massively parallel processors.

Master File Table (MFT) (NTFS)—File which is structured as a table in which NTFS stores information (e.g. name, time stamp, and location) about all files in the volume.

master node (in a Beowulf cluster)—Node, also known as the head node, that acts as a server to distribute the workload, control the access to the cluster and handle the shared resources.

master/slave multiprocessor organization—Scheme for delegating operating system responsibilities in which only one processor (the "master") can execute the operating system, and the other processors (the "slaves") can execute only user processes.

maximum need (Dijkstra's banker's algorithm)—Characteristic of a process in Dijkstra's banker's algorithm that describes the largest number of resources (of a particular type) the process will need during execution.

MD5 Message Digest Algorithm—Hash algorithm developed by Professor Ronald L. Rivest at MIT that is widely used to implement digital signatures.

mean—Average of a set of values.

mean response time (disk scheduling)—Average time a system spends waiting for a disk request to be serviced.

mean-time-to-failure (MTTF) (RAID)—Average time before a single-disk failure.

member—Sequential subfile of a partitioned file.

memory coherence—State of a system in which the value obtained from reading a memory address is always the same as the most-recently written value at that address.

memory compaction—Relocating all partitions in a variable-partition multiprogramming system to one end of main memory to create the largest possible memory hole.

memory descriptor list (MDL) (Windows XP)—Data structure used in an I/O transfer that maps a process's virtual addresses to be accessed in the transfer to physical memory addresses.

memory dump (Linux)—Action that generates a core file before terminating a process.

memory footprint (Linux)—Size of unswappable memory consumed by the kernel.

memory hierarchy—Classification of memory from fastest, lowest-capacity, most expensive memory to slowest, highest-capacity, least expensive memory.

memory line—Entry in memory that stores one machine word of data, which is typically four or eight bytes.

memory management strategy—Specification of how a particular memory organization performs operations such as fetching, placing and replacing memory.

Memory Management Unit (MMU)—Special-purpose hardware that performs virtual-to-physical address translation.

memory manager—Component of an operating system that implements the system's memory organization and memory management strategies.

memory map—Data structure that stores the correspondence between a process's virtual address space and main memory locations.

memory-mapped file—File whose data is mapped to a process's virtual address space, enabling a process to reference file data as it would other data. Memory-mapped files are useful for programs that frequently access file data.

memory organization—Manner in which the system views main memory, addressing concerns such as how many processes exist in memory, where to place programs and data in memory and when to replace those pieces with other pieces.

memory pool (Linux)—Region of memory reserved by the kernel for a process to ensure that the process's future requests for memory are not denied.

memory protection—Mechanism that prevents processes from accessing memory used by other processes or the operating system.

merge I/O requests (Linux)—To combine two I/O requests to adjacent locations on disk into a single request.

mesh network—Network in which at least two nodes have more than one path connecting them. Faster and more fault tolerant than all but fully-connected mesh networks.

message—IPC mechanism that allows data to be transmitted by specifying a message type and variable-length field of data.

message digest—Hash value produced by algorithms such as SHA-1 and MD5 when applied to a message.

message integrity—Property indicating whether message has been altered in transmission.

message passing—Mechanism to allow unrelated processes to communicate by exchanging data.

message queue (Linux)—Structure that stores messages that have yet to be delivered to processes.

message queue descriptor (Linux)—Structure that stores data regarding a message queue.

metadata—Data that a file system uses to manage files and that is inaccessible to users directly. Inodes and superblocks are examples of metadata.

method (of an object)—Part of an object that manipulates object attributes or performs a service.

micro-op—Simple, RISC-like instruction that is the only type of instruction processed by a Pentium processor; the Pentium's instruction decoder converts complex instructions into a series of micro-ops.

microbenchmark—Performance evaluation tool that measures the speed of a single operating system operation (e.g., process creation).

microbenchmark suite—Program that consists of a number of microbenchmarks, typically used to evaluate many important operating system operations.

microcode—Microprogramming instructions.

microkernel operating system—Scalable operating system that puts a minimal number of services in the kernel and requires user-level programs to implement services generally delegated to the kernel in other types of operating systems.

microprogramming—Layer of programming below a computer's machine language that includes instructions necessary to implement machine-language operations. This enables processors to divide large, complex instructions into simpler ones that are performed by its execution unit.

Microsoft IDL (MIDL)—Microsoft's extension of Interface Definition Language (IDL)—The Open Group's Distributed Computing Environment (DCE) standard for RPC interoperability.

middleware—Layer of software that enables communication between different applications. Middleware simplifies application programming by performing work such as network communication and translation between different data formats.

migration transparency—Masks the movement of an object from one location to another in the system, such as the movement of a file from one server to another.

minimum-laxity-first—Scheduling policy that assigns higher priority to processes that will finish with minimal processor usage.

minor device identification number (Linux)—Value that uniquely identifies devices that are assigned the same major number (e.g., a hard drive partition).

minor function code (Windows XP)—Field in an IRP that, together with the major function code, describes the specific function that should be performed to fulfill an I/O request (e.g., to start a device, a PnP major function code is used with a start device minor function code).

minor version number (Linux)—Value that identifies successive stable (even) and development (odd) versions of the Linux kernel.

MIPS (million instructions per second)—Unit commonly used to categorize the performance of a particular computer; a rating of one MIPS means a processor can execute one million instructions per second.

mirroring (RAID)—See disk mirroring.

missing-segment fault—Fault that occurs when a process references a segment that is not currently in main memory. The operating system responds by loading the segment from secondary storage into main memory when space is available.

mission-critical system—System that must function properly; its failure could lead to loss of property, money or even human life.

mixed model—COM threading model, in which some COM objects reside in single apartments and others can be accessed by free threads.

MobileMark—Popular benchmark for evaluating systems installed on mobile devices developed by Business Application Performance Corporation (BAPCo).

modified bit—Page table entry bit that indicates whether a page has been modified and hence must be copied to secondary storage before being replaced (also known as the dirty bit).

Modified No-write Page List (Windows XP)—List of page frames for which the VMM must write an entry to a log file before freeing.

Modified Page List (Windows XP)—List of page frames that the VMM must write to the pagefile before freeing.

module—Independently developed subprogram that can be combined with other subprograms to create a larger, more complex program; programmers often use precompiled library modules to perform common computer functions such as I/O manipulations or random number generation.

monitor—Concurrency construct that contains both the data and procedures needed to provide mutual exclusion while allocating a serially reusable shared resource or group of serially reusable shared resources.

monitor entry routine—Monitor routine that can be called by any thread, but that can be executed by only one thread at a time. Unlike private monitor routines, which can be called only by threads executing inside the monitor, monitor entry routines enforce mutual exclusion.

monolithic operating system—Operating system whose kernel contains every component of the operating system. The kernel typically operates with unrestricted access to the computer system.

Moore's law—Prediction regarding the evolution of processor design that asserts the number of transistors in a processor will double approximately every 18 months.

most trusted user status—See kernel mode.

motherboard—See mainboard.

mount—Insert a file system into a local directory structure.

mount operation—Operation that combines disparate file systems into a single namespace so they can be accessed by a single root directory.

mount point—User-specified directory within the native file system hierarchy where the mount command places the root of a mounted file system.

mount tables—Tables that store the locations of mount points and their corresponding devices.

moving-arm assembly—See disk arm.

MS-DOS—Popular operating system for the first IBM Personal Computer and compatible microcomputers.

multi-op instruction—Instruction word used by an EPIC system in which the compiler packages a number of smaller instructions for the processor to execute in parallel.

multicast—Type of IPv6 address used to send packets to all hosts in a group of related hosts.

multicomputer system—System in which processors do not share a common memory or bus. Each processor has access to its own resources. These independent processors are connected in a network to operate cooperatively to form a multicomputer system.

Multics—One of the first operating systems to implement virtual memory. Developed by MIT, GE and Bell Laboratories as the successor to MIT's CTSS.

Multics Relational Data Store (MRDS)—First commercial relational database system, included in Multics.

multilevel feedback queue—Process scheduling structure that groups processes of the same priority in the same round-robin queue. Processor-bound processes are placed in lower-priority queues because they are typically batch processes that do not require fast response times. I/O-bound processes, which exit the system quickly due to I/O, remain in high-priority queues. These processes often correspond to interactive processes that should experience fast response times.

multilevel paging system—Technique that enables the system to store portions of a process's page table in discontiguous locations in main memory and store only those portions that a process is actively using. Multilevel page tables are implemented by creating a hierarchy of page tables, each level containing a table that stores pointers to tables in the level below. The bottom-most level is comprised of tables containing the page-to-page-frame mappings. This reduces memory waste compared to single-level page tables, but incurs greater overhead due to the increased number of memory accesses required to perform address translation when corresponding mappings are not contained in the TLB.

multiple-instruction-stream, multiple-data-stream (MIMD) computer—Computer architecture consisting of multiple processing units, which execute independent instructions and manipulate independent data streams; this design describes multiprocessors.

multiple-instruction-stream, single-data-stream (MISD) computer—Computer architecture consisting of several processing units, which execute independent instruction streams on a single stream of data; these architectures have no commercial application.

multiple shared bus architecture—Interconnection scheme that employs several shared buses connecting processors and memory. This reduces contention, but increases cost compared to a single shared bus.

Multiple UNC Provider (MUP) (Windows XP)—File system driver that determines the appropriate redirector to which to send a network I/O request.

Multiple Virtual Spaces (MVS)—IBM operating system for System/370 mainframes allowing any number of 16MB virtual address spaces.

multiprocessing system—Computing system that employs more than one processor.

multiprogramming—Ability to store multiple programs in memory at once so that they can be executed concurrently.

Multipurpose Internet Mail Extensions (MIME)—Electronic mail standard defining five content types: text, image, audio, video and application.

multistage network—Multiprocessor interconnection scheme that uses switch nodes as hubs for communication between processor nodes that each have their own local memory.

multithreading—Technique that incorporates multiple threads of execution within a process to perform parallel activities, possibly simultaneously.

must-succeed request (Windows XP)—Request for space in main memory that a process issues when it requires more main memory to continue functioning properly. Windows XP always denies must-succeed requests; previous versions of Windows always fulfilled them.

mutex object (Windows XP)—Synchronization object that allows at most one thread access to a protected resource at any time; it is essentially a binary semaphore.

mutual exclusion—Restriction whereby execution by a thread of its critical section precludes execution by other threads of their critical sections. Mutual exclusion is crucial to correct execution when multiple threads access shared writable data.

mutual exclusion lock—Variable that indicates if a thread is executing its critical section; if the lock indicates that a thread is in its critical section, other threads are locked out of their own critical sections.

mutual exclusion necessary condition for deadlock—One of the four necessary conditions for deadlock; states that deadlock can occur only if processes cannot claim exclusive use of their resources.

mutual exclusion primitives—Fundamental operations that are needed to implement mutual exclusion: `enterMutualExclusion()` and `exitMutualExclusion()`.

N

n-ary relation—Relation of degree *n*.

N-Step SCAN disk scheduling—Disk scheduling strategy that services the first *n* requests in the queue using the SCAN strategy. When the sweep is complete, the next *n* requests are serviced. Arriving requests are placed at the end of the request queue. *N*-Step SCAN offers good performance due to high throughput, low mean response times and a lower variance of response times than SSTF and SCAN.

n-tier system—Architecture for network-based applications. The three-tier system, for example, has a client tier, an application logic tier and a data tier.

named pipe (Linux)—Pipe that can be accessed via the directory tree, enabling processes that are not parent and child to communicate using pipes. See also pipe.

named pipe (Windows XP)—Type of pipe that can provide bidirectional communication between two processes on local or remote machines and that supports both synchronous and asynchronous communication.

namespace—Set of files that can be identified by a file system.

National Institute of Standards and Technology (NIST)—Organization that sets cryptographic (and other) standards for the U.S. government.

native API (Windows XP)—Programming interface exposed by the executive, which environment subsystems employ to make system calls.

NDIS intermediate driver (Windows XP)—NDIS driver that can be interposed between a miniport driver and a higher-level driver and adds extra functionality, such as translating packets between different communication media, filtering packets or providing load balancing across several NICs.

NDIS miniport driver (Windows XP)—NDIS driver that manages a NIC and sends and receives data to and from the NIC.

NDIS protocol driver (Windows XP)—NDIS driver that places data into packets and passes these packets to lower-level drivers. NDIS protocol drivers provide an interface between the transport drivers and other NDIS drivers and can be used as the lowest layer in the implementation of a transport protocol stack such as TCP/IP.

necessary condition for deadlock—Condition that must be true for deadlock to occur. The four necessary conditions are the mutual exclusion condition, no-preemption condition, wait-for condition and circular-wait condition.

negative feedback—Data informing the system that a resource is having difficulty servicing all requests and the processor should decrease the arrival rate for requests at that resource.

neither I/O (Windows XP)—I/O transfer technique in which a high-level driver executes in the context of the calling thread to set up a buffered I/O transfer or direct I/O transfer or to directly perform the transfer in the process's address space.

.NET—Microsoft initiative aimed at transforming computing from an environment in which users simply execute applications on a single computer to a fully distributed environment; .NET provides a platform- and language-neutral development environment for components that can easily interoperate.

.NET framework—Programming model for creating XML-based Web services and applications. The .NET framework supports over 20 programming languages and facilitates application programming by providing libraries to perform common operations (e.g., input/output, string manipulation and network communication) and access data via multiple database interfaces (e.g., Oracle and SQL Server).

NetBIOS Extended User Interface (NetBEUI) (Windows XP)—Native network and transport protocol for DOS and older Windows operating systems.

NetBIOS over TCP/IP (NBT) (Windows XP)—Replacement protocol for NetBEUI that provides backward compatibility with older applications (by keeping the NetBIOS interface) and takes advantage of TCP/IP protocols.

netfilter framework (Linux)—Mechanism that allows kernel modules to directly inspect and modify packets. This is useful for applications such as firewalls, which modify each packet's source address before the packet is transmitted.

network-based intrusion detection—IDS that monitors traffic on a network for any unusual patterns that might indicate DoS attacks or attempted entry into a network by an unauthorized user.

Network Basic Input/Output System (NetBIOS) (Windows XP)—API used to support NetBEUI and now used with NBT.

Network Data Representation (NDR)—Standard format for network data described in the The Open Group's Distributed Computing Environment (DCE) standard.

network diameter—Shortest path between the two most remote nodes in a system.

Network Driver Interface Specification (NDIS) (Windows XP)—Specification that describes a standard interface between lower-level layered drivers in the network driver stack; NDIS drivers provide the functionality of the link layer in the TCP/IP stack and are used on Windows XP systems.

network file system—System that allows clients to access files on remote computers. Network file systems do not provide location transparency as distributed file systems do.

Network File System (NFS)—Current de facto standard created by Sun Microsystems for network file sharing, natively supported in most varieties of UNIX (and many other operating systems) with client and server software available for other common platforms.

network layer—Protocols responsible for sending data to the next host toward the destination. This layer exists in both the TCP/IP model and the OSI model of network communication.

network link—Connection between two nodes.

network operating system—Operating system that can manipulate resources at remote locations but does not hide the location of these resources from applications (as distributed systems can).

network redirector—See redirector (Windows XP).

network topology—Representation of the relationships of nodes in a network. Some examples are bus networks, ring networks, star networks, tree networks and mesh networks.

next-fit memory placement strategy—Variation of the first-fit memory placement strategy that begins each search for an available hole at the point where the previous search ended.

nice value (Linux)—Measure of a process's scheduling priority. Processes with a low nice value receive a greater share of processor time than other processes in the system and are therefore "less nice" to other processes in the system.

no-preemption necessary condition for deadlock—One of the four necessary conditions for deadlock; states that deadlock can occur only if resources cannot be forcibly removed from processes.

no-remote-memory-access (NORMA) multiprocessor—Multiprocessor architecture that does not provide global shared memory. Each processor maintains its own local memory. NORMA multiprocessors implement a common shared virtual memory.

node—System component, such as a processor, memory module or switch, attached to a network; sometimes a group of components might be viewed as a single node.

noncontiguous memory allocation—Method of memory allocation that divides a program into several, possibly nonadjacent, pieces that the system places throughout main memory.

nonpaged pool—Area of main memory that stores pages that are never moved to disk.

nonpreemptible resource—Resource that cannot be forcibly removed from a process, e.g., a tape drive. Such resources are the kind that can become involved in deadlock.

nonpreemptive scheduling—Scheduling policy that does not allow the system to remove a processor from a process until that process voluntarily relinquishes its processor or runs to completion.

nonrepudiation—Issue that deals with how to prove that a message was sent or received.

nonresident attribute—NTFS file attribute whose data does not fit inside the MFT entry and is stored elsewhere.

nonuniform-memory-access (NUMA) multiprocessor—Multiprocessor architecture in which each node consists of a processor, cache and memory module. Access to a processor's associated memory module (called local memory) is faster than access to other memory modules in the system.

nonuniform request distribution—Set of disk requests that are not uniformly distributed across disk surfaces. This occurs because processes exhibit spatial locality, leading to localized request patterns.

nonvolatile storage—The contents of nonvolatile storage are not lost when the machine loses power or is powered off.

normal memory (Linux)—Physical memory locations beyond 16MB that the kernel can directly map to its virtual address space. This region is used to store kernel data and user pages.

not-used-recently (NUR) page replacement—Low-overhead approximation to the LRU page-replacement strategy; uses referenced bits and dirty bits to replace a page. NUR first attempts to replace a page that has not been referenced recently and that has not been modified. If no such page is available, the strategy replaces a dirty page that has not been referenced recently, a clean page that has been referenced recently or a referenced page that has been referenced recently, in that order.

notify—Thread operation that transitions its target thread from the *waiting* to the *ready* state.

notify (Java)—Java method that wakes one thread in a monitor's wait set. The thread that is awakened depends on the JVM implementation.

notifyAll—Java method that awakens all threads in a monitor's wait and entry sets. Method `notifyAll` ensures that waiting threads are not indefinitely postponed, but incurs more overhead than `notify`.

O

object—Reusable software component that can model real-world items through properties and actions.

object code—Code generated by a compiler that contains machine-language instructions that must be linked and loaded before execution.

object handle (Windows XP)—Data structure that allows threads to manipulate an object.

Object Linking and Embedding (OLE)—Microsoft technology built on COM that defines a standard method for processes to exchange data by linking or embedding COM objects.

object manager (Windows XP)—Executive component that manages objects.

object manager namespace (Windows XP)—Group of object names in which each name is unique in the group.

object-oriented operating system (OOOS)—Operating system in which components and resources are represented as objects. Object-oriented concepts such as inheritance and interfaces help create modular operating systems that are easier to maintain and extend than operating systems built with previous techniques. Many operating systems use objects, but few are written entirely using object-oriented languages.

object-oriented programming (OOP) — Style of programming that allows programmers to quickly build complex software systems by reusing components called objects, built from "blueprints" called classes.

Object Request Broker (ORB) — Component residing on both CORBA client and server, which is responsible for initiating communication between systems.

object serialization — Allows objects to be encoded into byte streams and transmitted from one address space to another.

offset — See displacement.

on-board device — Device that is physically connected to a computer's mainboard.

on-demand migration — Another name for lazy process migration.

one-to-one mapping — Threading model in which each user-level thread is assigned to a kernel-level thread.

online — State describing a computer that is turned on (i.e., active) and directly connected to a network.

Online Certificate Status Protocol (OCSP) — Protocol that validates certificates in real time.

online spare — See hot spare disk.

online transaction processing (OLTP) — Type of system that typically receives many disk requests to randomly distributed locations containing small amounts of data (e.g., databases and Web servers). Such systems significantly improve performance using disk scheduling algorithms.

open (file) — Operation that prepares a file to be referenced.

Open DataBase Connectivity (ODBC) — Protocol for middleware that permits applications to access a variety of databases that use different interfaces. The ODBC driver handles connections to the database and retrieves information requested by applications. This frees the application programmer from writing code to specify database-specific commands.

Open Software Foundation (OSF) — Coalition of UNIX developers that built the OSF/1 UNIX clone to compete with AT&T's and Sun's Solaris. The OSF and the AT&T/Sun partnership were the participants in the UNIX Wars.

open-source initiative (OSI) — Group that supports and promotes open-source software (see www.opensource.com).

open-source software — Software that includes the application's source code and is often distributed under the General Public License (GPL) or a similar license. Open-source software is typically developed by teams of independent programmers worldwide.

OpenBSD — BSD UNIX system whose primary goal is security.

operating system — Software that manages system resources to provide services that allow applications to execute properly. An operating system may manage both hardware and software resources. Operating systems provide an application programming interface to facilitate application development. They also help make system resources conveniently available to users while providing a reliable, secure and responsive environment to applications and users.

Operationally Critical Threat, Asset and Vulnerability Evaluation (OCTAVE) method — Technique for evaluating security threats of a system developed at the Software Engineering Institute at Carnegie Mellon University.

opportunistic lock (oplock) (Windows XP) — Lock used by a CIFS client to secure exclusive access to a remote file, ensuring that the client can cache data locally and keep its cache coherent.

optimal (OPT) page replacement — Unrealizable page-replacement strategy that replaces the page that will not be used until furthest in the future. This strategy has been shown to be optimal.

optimizer — Part of the compiler that attempts to improve the execution efficiency and reduce the space requirement of a program.

Orange Book — Document published by U.S. Department of Defence (DoD) to establish guidelines for evaluating the security features of operating systems.

OS/360 — Operating system for the IBM System/360 mainframes. OS/360 had two major options, MFT and MVT, which stood for "Multiprogramming with a Fixed number of Tasks" and "Multiprogramming with a Variable number of Tasks." OS/360-MVT evolved into MVS, the ancestor of the current IBM mainframe operating system z/OS.

OSF/1 — UNIX clone built by the Open Software Foundation to compete with Solaris.

out-of-order execution (OOO) — Technique in which a processor analyzes a stream of instructions and dynamically reorders instructions to isolate groups of independent instructions for parallel execution.

overlapped I/O (Windows XP) — Microsoft synonym for asynchronous I/O.

overlay — Concept created to enable programs larger than main memory to run. Programs are broken into pieces that do not need to exist simultaneously in memory. An overlay contains one such piece of a program.

owner (file access control) — User who created the file.

P

P operation — Operation on a semaphore. If the variable in the semaphore is 0, then the *P* operation blocks the calling thread. If the variable is greater than 0, the operation will decrement the variable by one and allow the calling thread to proceed.

package (Linux) — Portion of a distribution containing an application or service. Users can customize their Linux systems by adding and removing packages.

packet-filtering firewall — Hardware or software that examines all data sent from outside its LAN and rejects data packets based on predefined rules, such as reject packets that have local network addresses or reject packets from certain addresses or ports.

page—Fixed-size set of contiguous addresses in a process's virtual address space that is managed as one unit. A page contains portions of a process's data and/or instructions and can be placed in any available page frame in main memory.

page cache (Linux)—Cache storing pages of data from disk. When a process requests data from disk, the kernel first determines if it exists in the page cache, which can eliminate an expensive disk I/O operation.

page directory entry (IA-32 Intel architecture)—Entry in a page directory that maps to the base address of a page table, which stores page table entries.

page directory register—Hardware register that stores a pointer to the current process's page directory table.

page directory table (Windows XP)—4KB page that contains 1,024 entries that point to frames in memory.

page fault—Fault that occurs as the result of an error when a process attempts to access a nonresident page, in which case the operating system can load it from disk.

page-fault-frequency (PFF) page replacement—Algorithm that adjusts a process's resident page set based on the frequency with which the process is faulting. If a process is switching to a larger working set, then it will fault frequently, and PFF will allocate more page frames. Once the process has accumulated its new working set, the page fault rate will stabilize, and PFF will either maintain the resident page set or reduce it. The key to the proper and efficient operation of PFF is maintaining the thresholds at appropriate values.

page frame—Block of main memory that can store a virtual page. In systems with a single page size, any page can be placed in any available page frame.

page frame database (Windows XP)—Array that contains the state of each page frame in main memory.

page global directory—In a two-tiered multilevel page table, the page global directory is a table of pointers to portions of a process's page table. Page global directories are the top level of a multilevel page table hierarchy.

page global directory (Linux)—Virtual memory structure that stores addresses of second-level page-mapping tables.

page list (Windows XP)—List of page frames that are in the same state. The eight state lists are: the Valid Page List, the Standby Page List, the Modified Page List, the Modified No-write Page List, the Transitional Page List, the Free Page List, the Zeroed Page List, and the Bad Page List.

page map table—See page table.

page middle directory (Linux)—Virtual memory structure that stores addresses of third-level page-mapping tables (also called page tables).

page migration—Technique in which the system transfers pages to the processor (or processors when used with page replication) that accesses the pages most.

page-replacement strategy—Strategy that determines which page to replace to provide space for an incoming page. Page replacement

strategies attempt to optimize performance by predicting future page usage.

page replication—Technique in which the system maintains multiple copies of a page at different nodes so that it can be accessed quickly by multiple processors.

page table—Table that stores entries that map page numbers to page frames. A page table contains an entry for each of a process's virtual pages.

page table entry (PTE)—Entry in a page table that maps a virtual page number to a page frame number. Page table entries store other information about a page, such as how the page may be accessed and whether the page is resident.

page table origin register—Register that holds the location of a process's page table in main memory; having this information accessible in a high-speed register facilitates rapid virtual-to-physical address translation.

page trimming (Windows XP)—Technique in which Windows XP takes a page belonging to a process and sets the page's PTE to invalid to determine whether the process actually needs the page. If the process does not request the page within a certain time period, the system removes it from main memory.

paged pool (Windows XP)—Pages in memory that may be moved to the pagefile on disk.

pagefile (Windows XP)—File on disk that stores all pages that are mapped to a process's virtual address space but do not currently reside in main memory.

paging—Virtual memory organization technique that divides an address space into fixed-size blocks of contiguous addresses. When applied to a process's virtual address space, the blocks are called pages, which store process data and instructions. When applied to main memory, the blocks are called page frames. A page is stored on secondary storage and loaded into a page frame if one is available. Paging trivializes the memory placement decision and does not incur external fragmentation (for systems that contain a single page size); paging does incur internal fragmentation.

parallel port—Interface to a parallel I/O device such as a printer.

parent directory—In hierarchically structured file systems, the directory that points to the current directory.

parent process—Process that has spawned one or more child processes. In UNIX, this is accomplished by issuing a `fork` system call.

parity—Technique that detects an even number of errors in data transmission. Parity information is generated by determining whether the data contains an even (or odd) number of 1's (or 0's). This parity information is generated after transmission and compared to the value generated before transmission. Error-correction codes (ECCs), such as Hamming or XOR, use the parity of a string of bits to detect and correct errors. Parity enables RAID systems to provide fault tolerance with lower storage overhead than mirrored systems.

parity logging (RAID)—Technique that increases write performance in RAID systems using parity by postponing writes to the parity disk while the system is busy. Because parity logging stores information in volatile memory, parity information could be lost if the system loses power.

parser—Part of the compiler that receives a stream of tokens from the lexical analyzer and groups the tokens so they can be processed by the intermediate code generator.

partial ordering—An ordering of events that follows the happens-before relation. Some events cannot be ordered using this system which is why it is only a partial ordering.

partition (file system)—Area of a disk whose boundaries cannot be crossed by file data. Partitions can reduce disk fragmentation.

partition (real memory organization)—Portion of main memory allocated to a process in fixed- and variable-partition multiprogramming. Programs are placed into partitions so that the operating system can protect itself from user processes and so that processes are protected from each other.

partitioned file—File composed of sequential subfiles.

Pascal—Structured programming language developed in 1971 by Wirth that became popular for teaching introductory programming courses.

passive IRQL (Windows XP)—IRQL at which user- and kernel-mode normally execute and no interrupts are masked. Passive IRQL is the lowest-priority IRQL.

password aging—Technique that attempts to improve security by requiring users to change their passwords periodically.

password protection—Authentication technique that relies on a user's presenting a username and corresponding password to gain access to a resource or system.

password salting—Technique that inserts characters at various positions in the password before encryption to reduce vulnerability to brute-force attacks.

pathname—String identifying a file or directory by its logical name, separating directories using a delimiter (e.g., "/" or "\"). An absolute pathname specifies the location of a file or directory starting at the root directory; a relative pathname specifies the location of a file or directory beginning at the current working directory.

payload—Code inside a logic bomb that is executed when a specified condition is met.

peer—Single computer in a peer-to-peer system.

peer discovery—Finding peers in a peer-to-peer application.

peer group—Logical construct that represents a set of peers. A peer group is one of the basic types of entities in a network built with the JXTA protocols.

peer-to-peer (P2P) application—Distributes processing responsibilities and information to many computers, thus reclaiming otherwise wasted computing power and storage space and eliminating central points of failure. In a peer-to-peer system, each peer performs both client and server functions.

pending signal—Signal that has not been delivered to a thread because the thread is not *running* and/or because the thread has masked signals of that type.

per-node run queue—Process scheduling queue associated with a group of processors; processes entering the queue are scheduled on the associated node's processors independently of the scheduling decisions made in rest of the system.

per-processor run queue—Process scheduling queue associated with a specific processor; processes entering the queue are scheduled on the associated processor independently of the scheduling decisions made in rest of the system.

performance monitoring—Collection and analysis of system performance information for existing systems; the information includes a system's throughput, response times, predictability, bottlenecks, etc.

performance projection—Estimate of the performance of a system that does not exist, useful for deciding whether to build that system or to modify an existing system's design.

periodic real-time process—Real-time process that performs computation at a regular time interval.

periodic timer (Windows XP)—Waitable timer object that reactivates after a specified interval.

Peripheral Components Interconnect (PCI) bus—Popular bus used to connect peripheral devices, such as network and sound cards, to the rest of the system. PCI provides a 32-bit or 64-bit bus interface and supports transfer rates of up to 533MB per second.

persistence transparency—Hides the information about where the resource is stored—memory or disk.

persistent storage—See secondary storage.

phantom deadlock—Situation due to communications delay associated with distributed computing, when a deadlock detection algorithm (DDA) might detect a deadlock that does not exist.

physical address—See real address.

Physical Address Extension (PAE) (IA-32 Intel architecture)—Mechanism that enables IA-32 processors to address up to 64GB of main memory.

physical address space—Range of physical addresses corresponding to the size of main memory in a given computer. The physical address space may be (and is often) smaller than each process's virtual address space.

physical backup—Copy of each bit of the storage device; no attempt is made to interpret the contents of its file system.

physical block—See physical record.

physical device name—Name given to a file that is specific to a particular device.

physical layer (in OSI)—Transmits bits over physical media, such as cables. The data link layer and physical layer in OSI correspond to the link layer in TCP/IP.

physical memory—See main memory.

physical record—Unit of information actually read from or written to disk.

physical view—View of file data concerned with the particular devices on which data is stored, the form the data takes on those devices, and the physical means of transferring data to and from those devices.

PID (process identifier)—Integer that uniquely identifies a process.

pipe—Interprocess communication mechanism that uses a page of memory as a first-in-first-out buffer to transfer information between processes.

pipe (in JXTA)—Virtual communication channel that connects two or more peers for sending and receiving messages among peers.

pipe buffer (Linux)—Page of data that is used to buffer data written to a pipe.

pipe client (Windows XP)—Process that connects to an existing pipe to communicate with that pipe's server.

pipe server (Windows XP)—Process that creates a pipe and communicates with pipe clients that connect to the pipe.

placement strategy (main memory)—Strategy that determines where in the main memory to place incoming programs and data.

plaintext—Unencrypted data.

Platform for Privacy Preferences (P3P)—Protects the privacy of information submitted to single sign-on and other applications by allowing users to control the personal information that sites collect.

platter—Magnetic disk medium that stores bits on its surfaces.

plug-and-play—Technology that facilitates driver installation and hardware configuration performed by the operating system.

Plug and Play (PnP) manager (Windows XP)—Executive component (which also exists partly in user space) that dynamically recognizes when new devices are added to the system (as long as these devices support PnP), allocates and deallocates resources to devices and interacts with device setup programs.

pluggable authentication module (PAM) (Linux)—Module that can be installed at runtime to incorporate enhanced authentication techniques in the Linux system.

PnP I/O requests (Windows XP)—IRPs generated by the PnP manager to query a driver for information about a device, to assign resources to a device or to direct a device to perform some action.

policy creation authority—Organization that sets policies for obtaining digital certificates.

polling—Technique to discover hardware status by repeatedly testing each device. Polling can be implemented in lieu of interrupts but typically reduces performance due to increased overhead.

polymorphic virus—Virus that attempts to evade known virus lists by modifying its code (e.g., via encryption, substitution, insertion, and the like) as it spreads.

port (hardware interface)—Bus that connects two devices.

port (networking)—Identifies the specific socket on a machine to which to send data. For example, HTTP communicates by default on port 80.

port mapping (Windows XP)—Process of explicitly allowing the Internet Connection Firewall (ICF) to accept all incoming packets to a particular port.

port of Linux—Version of the Linux kernel that is modified to support execution in a different environment.

portability—Property of software that can run on different platforms.

portable operating system—Operating system that is designed to operate on many hardware configurations.

Portable Operating Systems Interface (POSIX)—API based on early UNIX operating systems.

positioning time—Access time plus latency. Positioning time is used by the SPTF strategy to order requests.

positive feedback—Data informing the system that a resource has excess capacity, so the processor can increase the arrival rate for requests at that resource.

power IRQL (Windows XP)—IRQL at which power failure interrupts execute and at which all interrupts except high-IRQL interrupts are masked.

power manager (Windows XP)—Executive component that administers the operating system's power management policy.

power policy (Windows XP)—Policy of a system with regard to balancing power consumption and responsiveness of devices.

precopy—Process migration strategy in which the sender begins transferring dirty pages before the original process is suspended; once the number of untransferred dirty pages at the sender reaches some threshold, the process migrates.

predicate—Logical decision made on a subject (e.g., a branch comparison).

predictability—Measure of the variance of an entity, such as response time. Predictability is particularly important for interactive systems, where users expect predictable (and short) response times.

preemptible resource—Resource that may be removed from a process such as a processor or memory. Such resources cannot be involved in deadlock.

preemption lock counter (Linux)—Integer that is used to determine whether code executing in kernel mode may be preempted. The value of the counter is incremented each time a kernel control path enters a critical section during which it cannot be preempted.

preemptive scheduling—Scheduling policy that allows the system to remove a processor from a process.

preferred direction—Direction in which the disk head is moving in SCAN-based scheduling algorithms.

preferred server (PS) (in Coda)—Member of the AVSG that provides copies of files for Venus.

prefetching—See anticipatory paging.

prefix table (in Sprite)—Table that stores domain information to aid in file lookups. Each entry in the table represents a separate domain and consists of the absolute path to the root directory within the domain, the server which houses the domain and a token that identifies the domain.

prepaging—See anticipatory paging.

presentation layer (in OSI)—Solves compatibility problems by translating the application data into a standard format that can be understood by other layers.

Pretty Good Privacy (PGP)—Public-key encryption system primarily used to encrypt e-mail messages and files, designed in 1991 by Phillip Zimmermann.

primary key—In a relational database, a combination of attributes whose value uniquely identifies a tuple.

primary thread—Thread created upon process creation (also called main thread of execution). When the primary thread returns, its process terminates.

primary thread (Windows XP)—Thread created when a process is created.

principle of least privilege—Resource access policy that states that a user should only be granted the amount of privilege and access that the user needs to accomplish its designated task.

printed circuit board (PCB)—Piece of hardware that provides electrical connections to devices that can be placed at various locations throughout the board.

priority—Measure of a process's or thread's importance used to determine the order and duration of execution.

priority array (Linux)—Structure within a run queue that stores processes of the same priority.

priority inversion—Situation which occurs when a high-priority thread is waiting for a resource held by a low-priority thread, and the low-priority thread cannot obtain the processor because of a medium-priority thread; hence, the high-priority thread is blocked from execution by the medium-priority thread.

priority of a process—Importance or urgency of a process relative to other processes.

privacy (secure transaction)—One of the five fundamental requirements for a successful, secure transaction. Privacy deals with how to ensure that the information transmitted over the Internet has not been captured or passed to a third party without user knowledge.

private key—Key in public-key cryptography that should be known only by its owner. If its corresponding public key encrypts a message, only the private key should be able to decrypt it.

privilege (access right)—The manner in which a subject can access an object.

privileged instruction—Instruction that can be executed only from kernel mode. Privileged instructions perform operations that access protected hardware and software resources (e.g., switching the processor between processes or issuing a command to a hard disk).

problem state—See user mode.

procedural programming language—Programming language that is based on functions rather than objects.

process—Entity that represents a program in execution.

process cloning—Creates a copy of a process on a remote machine.

process control block (PCB)—Data structure containing information that characterizes a process (e.g., PID, address space and state); also called a process descriptor.

process descriptor—See process control block (PCB).

process environment block (PEB) (Windows XP)—User-space data structure that stores information about a process, such as a list of DLLs linked to the process and information about the process's heap.

process identification number (PID)—Value that uniquely identifies a process.

process migration—Transferring a process and its associated state between two processors.

process priority—Value that determines the importance of a process relative to other processes. It is often used to determine how a process should be scheduled for execution on a processor relative to other processes.

process scheduler—Operating system component that determines which process can gain access to a processor and for how long.

process state—Status of a process (e.g., *running*, *ready*, *blocked*, etc.).

process table—Table of known processes. In a segmentation/paging system, each entry points to a process's virtual address space, among other items.

processor—Hardware component that executes machine-language instructions and enforces protection for system resources such as main memory.

processor affinity—Relationship of a process to a particular processor and a corresponding memory bank.

processor-bound—Process (or job) that consumes its quantum when executing. These processes (or jobs) tend to be calculation intensive and issue few, if any, I/O requests.

processor pool—Component in Amoeba system, which contains a collection of processors, each having its own memory and Ethernet connection.

processor scheduling discipline—See processor scheduling policy.

processor scheduling policy—Strategy used by a system to determine when and for how long to assign processors to processes.

procfs (proc file system) (Linux)—File system built directly into the kernel that provides real-time information about the status of the kernel and processes, such as memory utilization and system execution time.

producer—Thread or process that creates and places data into a shared object.

producer thread—Thread that creates and places data into a shared object.

producer/consumer relationship—Interaction between threads that produce data (called producers) and threads that consume produced data (called consumers) that illustrates many of the intricacies of asynchronous concurrent execution.

production program—Program that is run regularly at an installation.

profile—Record of kernel activity taken during a real session, which indicates the operating system functions that are used most often and should therefore be optimized.

profile IRQL (Windows XP)—IRQL at which debugger interrupts execute and at which APC, DPC/dispatch, DIRQL and incoming debugger interrupts are masked.

program counter—Pointer to the instruction a processor is executing for a running process. After the processor completes the instruction, the program counter is adjusted to point to the next instruction the processor should execute.

programmed I/O (PIO)—Implementation of I/O for devices that do not support interrupts in which the transfer of every word from memory must be supervised by the processor.

projection (database)—Operation that creates a subset of attributes.

property (of an object)—Part of an object that stores data about the object.

protected variable (semaphores)—Integer variable storing the state of a semaphore that can be accessed and altered only by calling *P* or *V* on that semaphore.

protection—Mechanism that implements a system's security policy by preventing applications from accessing resources and services without authorization.

protection domain—Collection of access rights. Each access right in a protection domain is represented as an ordered pair with fields for the object name and applicable privileges.

protocol—Set of rules that govern how two entities should interact. Common examples include Transmission Control Protocol (TCP), Internet Protocol (IP) and Hypertext Transfer Protocol (HTTP).

protocol sequence (Windows XP)—String used by a client in an RPC call that specifies the RPC protocol, transport protocol and network protocol for that RPC.

Prototype Page Table Entry (PPTE) (Windows XP)—32-bit record that points to a frame in memory that contains either a copy-on-write page or a page that is part of a process's view of a mapped file.

proxy—In DCOM, the client-side stub that is responsible for marshaling and unmarshaling messages.

Pthread (POSIX 1003.1c thread)—Thread that conforms to the POSIX 1003.1c standard.

public (file access control)—File that may be accessed by any member of the system's user community.

public key—Key in public cryptography that is available to all users that wish to communicate with its owner. If the public key encrypts a message, only the corresponding private key can decrypt it.

public-key cryptography—Asymmetric cryptography technique that employs two inversely related keys: a public key and a private key. To transmit a message securely, the sender uses the receiver's public key to encrypt the message. The receiver then decrypts the message using his or her unique private key.

Public Key Infrastructure (PKI)—Technique that integrates public-key cryptography with digital certificates and certificate authorities to authenticate parties in a transaction.

purchase priority—To pay to receive higher priority in a system.

pure paging—Memory organization technique that employs paging only, not segmentation.

pure peer-to-peer application—Also called a decentralized peer-to-peer application. It does not have a server and therefore does not suffer from the same deficiencies as applications that depend on servers.

Q

quad pumping—Technique for increasing processor performance by performing four memory transfers per clock cycle.

quantum—Unit of time during which a process can execute before it is removed from the processor. Helps prevent processes from monopolizing processors.

query language—Language that allows users to search a database for data that meets certain criteria.

queued access method—File access method that does not immediately service user I/O demands. This can improve performance when the sequence in which records are to be processed can be anticipated and requests can be ordered to minimize access times.

queued spin lock (Windows XP)—Spin lock in which a thread releasing the lock notifies the next thread in the queue of waiting threads.

R

race condition—Occurs when multiple threads simultaneously compete for the same serially reusable resource, and that resource is allocated to these threads in an indeterminate order. This can cause subtle program errors when the order in which threads access a resource is important.

RAID (Redundant Array of Independent Disks)—Family of techniques that use an array of disks to improve disk transfer rates while providing fault tolerance.

RAID controller—Special-purpose hardware that efficiently performs operations such as dividing files into strips, forming files from strips, determining the locations of strips in the array and implementing the array's fault-tolerance mechanism.

RAID level 0—RAID system that uses a striped disk array with no redundancy. Level 0 arrays are not fault tolerant; if one disk fails, all the data in the array that depend on the failed disk are lost. Depending on the array's strip size, all data stored in the array could become unusable with the loss of a single disk. Although RAID 0 is not fault tolerant, it is simple to implement, yields high transfer rates and does not incur any storage overhead. Level 0 arrays are implemented in systems where performance is more important than fault tolerance, such as supercomputers.

RAID level 1—RAID system that employs disk mirroring (also called shadowing) to provide redundancy, so that each disk in the array is duplicated. Stripes are not implemented in level 1, reducing both hardware complexity and system performance. While this results in the highest degree of fault tolerance of any RAID level, only half of the array's capacity can be used to store unique data, which increases cost. Level 1 arrays are implemented in systems where high availability is more important than cost, such as database systems.

RAID level 2—RAID system that is striped at the bit level (i.e., each strip stores one bit). Level 2 arrays are designed to reduce the storage overhead incurred by implementing fault tolerance using mirroring. Instead of maintaining redundant copies of each data item, RAID level 2 uses a version of Hamming error-correcting codes (Hamming ECCs) to store parity information that allows the system to detect up to two errors, correct up to one error and determine the location of the error in a stripe. The size of Hamming ECC codes, and thus the number of parity disks, increases according to the logarithm (base 2) of the number of data disks. Thus, level 2 arrays containing a large number of disks incur significantly less storage overhead than level 1 arrays.

RAID level 3—RAID system that stripes data at the bit or byte level. RAID 3 uses XOR (exclusive-or) error-correcting codes (XOR ECCs), which use the logical XOR operation to generate parity information. XOR ECC uses only one disk to hold parity information, regardless of the size of the array. The system can use the parity bits to recover from any single disk failure. Due to parity checking, RAID level 3 reads and writes require access to the entire array. Similar to RAID level 2, this yields high transfer rates when reading and writing large files, but only one request can be serviced at a time.

RAID level 4—RAID system that is striped using fixed-size blocks (typically larger than a byte) and uses XOR ECC to generate parity data that is stored on a single parity disk. Because level 4 arrays enable coarse-grained striping, the system can potentially service multiple read requests simultaneously, if parity is not determined for each read. When servicing a write request, however, the system must update parity information to ensure that no data is lost in the event of a disk failure. This means that write requests must be performed one at a time, creating a write bottleneck.

RAID level 5—RAID system that is striped at the block level and uses XOR ECC for parity, but distributes parity blocks throughout the array of disks. Because parity blocks are distributed across many disks, multiple parity strips can be accessed simultaneously, removing the write bottleneck for many requests. Although RAID level 5 increases performance relative to RAID levels 2–4, it is complex to implement and more costly. Level 5 arrays are considered general-purpose arrays and are often found in file and application servers, enterprise resource planning (ERP) and other business systems.

RAMAC (Random Access Method of Accounting and Control)—First commercial hard drive produced by IBM.

ramfs (Linux)—Region of main memory treated as a block device. The ramfs file system must be formatted before use.

random access memory (RAM)—Memory whose contents can be accessed in any order.

random delay—Interval of time calculated by the exponential backoff method of CSMA/CD before a transceiver can retransmit a frame after a collision.

random (RAND) page replacement—Page-replacement strategy in which each page in main memory has an equal likelihood of being selected for replacement. Although this strategy is fair and incurs little overhead, it does not attempt to predict future page usage.

random policy—Dynamic load balancing policy in which the system arbitrarily chooses a processor to receive a migrated process.

random-scanning algorithm—Algorithm that uses pseudorandom numbers to generate a broad distribution of IP addresses.

random seek pattern—Series of requests to cylinders randomly distributed across disk surfaces. FCFS causes random seek patterns that result in high response times and low throughput.

random variable—Variable that can assume a certain range of values, where each value has an associated probability.

rate-monotonic (RM) scheduling—Real-time scheduling policy that sets priority to a value that is proportional to the rate at which the process must be dispatched.

read (file)—Operation that inputs a data item from a file to a process.

read access (virtual memory)—Access right that enables a process to read data from a page or segment; see also execute access, write access and append access.

read access (file)—Permission to access a file for reading.

read–modify–write cycle (RAID)—Operation that reads a stripe, modifies its contents and parity, then writes the stripe to the array. It is performed for each write request in RAID systems that use parity. Some systems reduce the cost of read–modify–write cycles by caching strips or by updating parity information only periodically.

read–modify–write (RMW) memory operation—Operation that atomically reads the contents of a variable, changes the contents (possibly based on what it has read) and writes the new value to memory. These operations simplify mutual exclusion algorithms by providing atomic operations.

read operation (in JavaSpaces)—Operation that is similar to the take operation, but does not remove the object from the JavaSpaces service so that other clients can still find it.

read/write head—Moving-head disk component that hovers over a disk surface, reading and writing bits as the disk moves.

read/write lock—Lock that allows a single writer process or multiple reading processes (i.e., processes that will not alter shared variables) to enter a critical section.

reader/writer lock (Linux)—Lock that allows multiple threads to concurrently hold a lock when reading from a resource, but only one thread to hold a lock when writing to that resource.

ready (or *runnable*) *state*—Thread state from which a thread can transition to the *running* state and execute on a processor. In Windows XP, a *ready* thread transitions to the *standby* state, from which it transitions to the *running* state.

ready list—Kernel data structure that organizes all *ready* processes in the system. The ready list is typically ordered by process scheduling priority.

ready **state**—Process (or thread) state from which a process (or thread) may be dispatched to the processor.

real address—Address in main memory.

real memory—See main memory.

real-time priority class (Windows XP)—Base priority class encompassing the upper 16 priority levels; threads of this class have static priorities.

real-time scanner—Software that resides in memory and actively prevents viruses.

real-time scheduling—Scheduling policy that bases priority on timing constraints.

real-time signal (Linux)—Signal implementation that helps to implement a real-time system by ensuring that no signals are dropped.

real-time system—System that attempts to service requests within a specified (usually short) time period. In mission-critical real-time systems (e.g., air traffic control and petroleum refinery monitors), money, property or even human life could be lost if requests are not serviced on time.

receiver-initiated policy—Dynamic load balancing policy in which processors with low utilization attempt to find overloaded processors from which to receive a migrated process.

record—In the data hierarchy, a group of fields (e.g., for storing several related fields containing information about a student or a customer).

recovery—Restoration of the system's data after a failure.

recovery key (NTFS)—Key that NTFS stores that can decrypt an encrypted file; administrators can use recovery keys when a user has forgotten the private key needed to decrypt the file.

redirector (Windows XP)—File system driver that interacts with a remote server driver to facilitate network I/O operations.

reduced instruction set computing (RISC)—Processor-design philosophy that emphasizes small, simple instruction sets and optimization of the most-frequently used instructions.

redundancy—Technique that maintains multiple identical resources to enable recovery upon failure.

Redundant Array of Independent Disks (RAID)—See RAID.

reentrant code—Code that cannot be changed while in use and therefore can be shared among processes and threads.

referenced bit—Page table entry bit indicating whether a page has been referenced recently. Several strategies reset this bit to more accurately determine how recently a page has been referenced.

register—High-speed memory located on a processor that holds data for immediate use by the processor.

registry (Windows XP)—Central database in which user, system and application configuration information is stored.

reintegration stage (in Coda)—Stage right after the client reconnects to the system during which Venus asynchronously updates the server using the CML.

relation—A set of tuples in the relational model.

relational model—A model of data proposed by Codd that is the basis for most modern database systems.

relative address—Address that is specified based on its location in relation to the beginning of a module.

relative path—Path that specifies the location of a file relative to the current working directory.

relaxed consistency—Category of memory-coherence strategies that permit the system to be in an incoherent state for a few seconds after a write, but improve performance over strict consistency.

release consistency—Memory-coherence strategy in which multiple accesses to shared memory are considered a single access; these accesses begin with an acquire and end with a release, after which coherence is enforced throughout the system.

release operation—In several coherence strategies, this operation indicates that a process is done accessing shared memory.

reliability—Measure of fault tolerance. The more reliable a resource, the less likely it is to fail.

reliable network—Network which does not damage or lose packets.

relocatable loading—Method of loading that translates relative addresses in a load module to absolute addresses based on the location of a requested block of memory.

relocating—Process of adjusting the addresses of program code and data.

relocation transparency—Masks the relocation of an object from other objects that communicate with it.

Remote Access Service (RAS) (Windows XP)—Network service, which allows users to remotely connect to a LAN.

remote method invocation (RMI)—Allows Java programmers to implement distributed systems without having to explicitly program sockets.

remote procedure call (RPC)—Allows a process executing on one computer to invoke a procedure (or function) in a process executing on another computer.

remote reference layer (RRL)—Works with the transport layer to send marshaled messages between the client and server in RMI.

Remote Spooling Communications Subsystem (RSCS) (VM)—Component of VM that provides the capability to send and receive files in a distributed system.

rename (file)—Operation that changes a file's name.

reparse point (NTFS)—File attribute containing a tag and a block of up to 16KB of data that a user associates with a file or directory; when an application accesses a reparse point, the system executes the file system filter driver specified by the reparse point's tag.

replacement strategy (main memory)—Method that a system uses to determine which piece of program or data to displace to accommodate incoming programs or data.

replication—Provides multiple resources that perform the same function in a system.

replication transparency—Hides the fact that multiple copies of a resource are available in the system. All access to a group of replicated resources occurs as if there were one such resource available.

request IRQL (Windows XP)—IRQL at which interprocess interrupts execute and all interrupts except power-level and high-level interrupts are masked.

request list (Linux)—Structure that stores pending I/O requests. This list is sorted to improve throughput by reducing seek times.

request rate—Measure of request frequency. The higher the request rate, the greater the system load. Systems experiencing a high disk request rate tend to benefit from disk scheduling.

Request to Send (RTS)—Message sent from a wireless device in the CSMA/CA protocol that indicates a desire to transmit data, the length of the transmission, the sender address and the receiver address. If the medium is available, the receiver will send a Clear To Send (CTS) message.

reserve memory (Windows XP)—To indicate to the VMM that a process intends to use an area of virtual memory; the VMM allocates memory in the process's virtual address space but does not allocate any page frames in main memory.

resident attribute (NTFS)—File attribute whose data is stored within the MFT entry.

resident page set—Set of a process's pages that are currently in memory; these pages may be referenced without generating a page fault. The resident page set might differ in size from a process's working set, which is the set of pages that must be in memory for a process to execute efficiently.

resident virus—Virus that, once loaded into memory, executes until the computer is powered down.

residual dependency—Dependency of a migrated process on its original node after process migration because some of the process's state remains on the original node.

resource-allocation graph—Graph that shows processes and resources in a system. An arrow pointing from a process to a resource indicates that the process is requesting the resource. An arrow pointing from a resource to a process indicates that the resource is allocated to the process. Such a graph helps determine if a deadlock exists and, if so, helps identify the processes and resources involved in the deadlock.

resource type—Grouping of resources that perform a common task.

resources layer (in grid computing)—Layer that enables applications to query and share a resource.

response time—In an interactive system, the time from when a user presses an *Enter* key or clicks a mouse until the system delivers a final response.

restricted algorithm—Algorithm that provides security by relying on the sender and receiver to use the same encryption algorithm and maintain its secrecy.

resume—Remove a process from a suspended state.

reverse mapping (Linux)—Linked list of page table entries that reference a page of memory. This facilitates updating all PTEs corresponding to a shared page that is about to be replaced.

Rijndael—Block cipher developed by Dr. Joan Daemen and Dr. Vincent Rijmen of Belgium. The algorithm can be implemented on a variety of processors.

ring network—Network consisting of a set of nodes, each maintaining exactly two connections to other nodes in that network. These networks have a low fault tolerance since the failure of any single node can cause the whole network to fail.

robust operating system—Operating system that is fault tolerant and reliable—the system will not fail due to unexpected application or hardware errors (but if it must fail, it does so gracefully). Such an operating system will provide services to each application unless the hardware those services requires fails to function.

role (RBAC)—Represents a set of tasks assigned to a member of an organization. Each role is assigned a set of privileges, which define the objects that users in each role can access.

role-based access control (RBAC)—Access control model in which users are assigned roles.

roll—See swap.

roll back a transaction—To return the system to the state that existed before the transaction was processed.

root—Beginning of a file system's organizational structure.

root directory—Directory that points to the various user directories.

root key—Used by the Internet Policy Registration Authority (IPRA) to sign certificates exclusively for policy creation authorities.

root user (Linux)—See superuser.

rotational latency—Time required for a disk to rotate a requested data item from its current position to a position adjacent to the read/write head.

rotational optimization—Disk scheduling technique that reduces access times by next servicing the request to the nearest sector in the read/write head's current cylinder.

round-robin (RR) scheduling—Scheduling policy that permits each *ready* process to execute for at most one quantum per round. After the last process in the queue has executed once, the scheduler begins a new round by scheduling the first process in the queue,

round-robin job (RRJob) scheduling—Job-aware process scheduling algorithm employing a global run queue in which jobs are dispatched to processors in a round-robin fashion.

round-robin process (RRprocess) scheduling—Job-blind multiprocessor scheduling algorithm that places each process in a global run queue and schedules these process in a round-robin manner.

router—Computer that is an intermediate destination between the sending host and the receiving host. The router is responsible for determining where to send a datagram next in order for it to eventually reach its destination.

routing—Determining the best route between two points and sending packets along this route.

Routing Information Protocol (RIP)—Protocol that defines how routing information is propagated throughout networks. RIP requires routers to share their entire routing table with other routers; this limits its use to small networks.

routing table—Representation of a network used to determine where routers should send datagrams next on their path to their destination.

RSA—Popular public-key algorithm, which was developed in 1977 by MIT professors Ron Rivest, Adi Shamir and Leonard Adleman.

run queue (Linux)—List of processes waiting to execute on a particular processor.

running state—Process (or thread) state in which a process (or thread) is executing on a processor.

S

safe asynchronous write (in NFS-3)—Allows a server to return before a write has been completed.

safe state—State of a system in Dijkstra's banker's algorithm in which there exists a sequence of actions that will allow every process in the system to finish without the system becoming deadlocked.

saturation—Condition of a resource that has no excess capacity to fulfill new requests.

saturation threshold—A level of resource utilization above which the resource will refuse access. Designed to reduce deadlock, it also reduces throughput.

scalability (scheduler)—Characteristic of a scheduler that ensures system performance degrades gracefully under heavy loads.

scalable operating system—Operating system that is able to employ resources as they are added to the system. It can readily adapt its degree of multiprogramming to meet the needs of its users.

SCAN disk scheduling—Disk scheduling strategy that reduces unfairness and variance of response times as compared to SSTF by servicing the request that requires the shortest seek distance in a preferred direction. SCAN behaves much like SSTF in terms of high throughput and good mean response times. However, because SCAN ensures that all requests in a given direction will be serviced before the requests in the opposite direction, it offers a lower variance of response times than SSTF. Also called the elevator algorithm.

scanner—See lexical analyzer.

scheduler activation—Mechanism that allows a user-level library to schedule kernel threads.

script-driven simulator—Simulator controlled by data carefully designed to reflect the anticipated environment of the simulated system; evaluators derive this data from empirical observations.

scriptlet—Java code embedded in a JSP.

second-chance page-replacement strategy—Variation of FIFO page replacement that uses the referenced bit and a FIFO queue to determine which page to replace. If the oldest page's referenced bit is off, second chance replaces the page; otherwise it turns off the referenced bit on the oldest page and moves it to the tail of the FIFO queue. If its referenced bit is on, the strategy turns off the bit and examines the next page or pages until it locates a page with its referenced bit turned off.

second extended file system (ext2fs) (Linux)—See ext2fs.

secret-key cryptography—Technique that performs encryption and decryption using the same secret key to encrypt and decrypt a message. The sender encrypts a message using the secret key, then sends the encrypted message to the intended recipient, who decrypts the message using the same secret key. Also called symmetric cryptography.

secondary storage—Memory that typically stores large quantities of data persistently. Secondary storage is one level lower than main memory in the memory hierarchy. After a computer is powered on, information is shuttled between secondary storage and main memory so that program instructions and data can be accessed by a processor. Hard disks are the most common form of secondary storage.

sector—Smallest portion of a track that can be accessed by an I/O request.

sector queuing—See rotational optimization.

Secure Hash Algorithm (SHA-1)—Popular hash function used to create digital signatures; developed by NIST.

secure operating system—Operating system that prevents users and software from gaining unauthorized access to services and data.

Secure Sockets Layer (SSL)—Nonproprietary protocol developed by Netscape Communications that secures communication between two computers on the Internet.

Security Accounts Manager (SAM) (Windows XP)—Database that administers information about all security principals in the system. It provides services such as account creation, account modification and authentication.

security descriptor (Windows XP)—Data structure that stores information about which security principals may access a resource and what actions they may perform on that resource. The most important element of a security descriptor is its discretionary access control list (DACL).

security identifier (SID) (Windows XP)—Unique identification number assigned to each security principal in the system.

security mechanism—Method by which the system implements its security policy. In many systems, the policy changes over time, but the mechanism remains unchanged.

security model—Entity that defines a system's subjects, objects and privileges.

security patch—Code that addresses a security flaw.

security policy—Rules that govern access to system resources.

security principal (Windows XP)—Any user, process, service or computer that can perform an action in a Windows XP system.

Security Support Provider Interface (SSPI) (Windows XP)—Microsoft's standardized protocol for authentication and authorization recognized by both the Kerberos and NTLM authentication services.

seek operation—Operation that moves the disk head to a different cylinder.

seek optimization—Disk scheduling technique that reduces seek times by generally servicing requests to the cylinder near the read/write head.

seek time—Time it takes for the read/write head to move from its current cylinder to the cylinder containing the requested data record.

segment (TCP)—Piece of data sent by TCP. It includes the message and the TCP header.

segment (virtual memory)—Variable-size set of contiguous addresses in a process's virtual address space that is managed as one unit. A segment is typically the size of an entire set of similar items, such as a set of instructions in a procedure or the contents of an array, which enables the system to protect such items with fine granularity using appropriate access rights. For example, a data segment typically is assigned read-only or read/write access, but not execute access. Similarly, a segment containing executable instructions typically is assigned read/execute access, but not write access. Segments tend to create external fragmentation in main memory but do not suffer from internal fragmentation.

segment descriptor (IA-32 Intel architecture)—Segment map table entry that stores a segment's base address, present bit, limit address and protection bits.

segment map table origin register—Register that holds the location of a process's segment map table in main memory; having this information accessible in a high-speed register facilitates rapid virtual-to-physical address translation.

segment-overflow exception—Exception that occurs when a process attempts to access an address that is outside a segment.

segment-protection exception—Exception that occurs when a process attempts to access a segment in ways other than those specified by its access control mode (e.g., attempting to write to a read-only segment).

segment selector (IA-32 Intel architecture)—16-bit value indicating the offset into the segment map table at which the corresponding segment descriptor (i.e., segment map table entry) is located.

selection evaluation—Analysis regarding whether obtaining a computer system or application from a particular vendor is appropriate.

selfish round-robin (SRR) scheduling—Variant of round-robin scheduling in which processes age at different rates. Processes that enter the system are placed in a holding queue, where they wait until their priority is high enough for them to be placed in the active queue, in which processes compete for processor time.

semaphore—Mutual exclusion abstraction that uses two atomic operations (P and V) to access a protected integer variable that determines if threads may enter their critical sections.

semaphore array (Linux)—Linked list of semaphores that protect access to related resources.

semaphore object (Windows XP)—Synchronization object that allows a resource to be owned by up to a specified number of threads; it is essentially a counting semaphore.

sender-initiated policy—Dynamic load balancing policy in which overloaded processors attempt to find underloaded processors to which to migrate a process.

separate kernels multiprocessor organization—Scheme for delegating operating system responsibilities in which each processor executes its own operating system, but the processors share some global system information.

seqlock (Linux)—Mutual exclusion structure that combines a spin lock with a sequence counter. Seqlocks are used by interrupt handlers, which require immediate exclusive access to data.

Sequenced Packet eXchange (SPX)—Novell Netware's transport protocol, which offers connection-oriented services for IPX packets.

sequential consistency—Category of memory-coherence strategies in which coherence protocols are enforced immediately after a write to a shared memory location.

sequential file organization—File organization technique in which records are placed in sequential physical order. The "next" record is the one that physically follows the previous record.

sequential write sharing—Occurs when one client modifies a file, then another client tries to read or write its own cached copy of the file. Sequential write sharing introduces cache inconsistency.

serial port—Interface to a device that transfers one bit at a time (e.g, keyboards and mice).

serialize—To control access to a shared variable such that only one thread can access the variable at a time; another thread can access the variable only after the first has finished.

serially reusable code—Code that can be modified but is reinitialized each time it is used. Such code can be used by only one process or thread at a time.

serially reusable resource—See dedicated resource.

serially reusable shared resource—Resource that can be used by only one thread at a time.

server—Process that provides services to other processes (called clients). The machine on which these processes run is also called a server.

Server Message Block (SMB)—Network file sharing protocol used in Windows operating systems on top of which CIFS (Common Internet File System) is built.

server stub—A stub at the server side in RPC that prepares outbound data for transmission and translates incoming data so that it may be correctly interpreted.

service rate—Rate at which requests are completed by a resource.

service ticket (Kerberos)—Ticket that authorizes the client's access to specific network services.

servlet—Enhances the functionality of Web servers to provide capabilities such as secure access to Web sites, interacting with databases on behalf of a client, dynamically generating custom documents to be displayed by browsers and maintaining unique session information for each client.

servlet container—Server that executes a servlet. Also known as servlet engine.

session key—Secret key that is used for the duration of a transaction (e.g., a customer's buying merchandise from an online store).

session layer (in OSI)—Establishes, manages and terminates the communication between two end users.

setup time—Time required by a system operator and the operating system to prepare the next job to be executed.

shadow page—Block of data whose modified contents are written to a new block. Shadow pages are one way to implement transactions.

shadow paging—Transaction implementation that writes modified blocks to a new block. The copy of the block that is unmodified is released as free space when the transaction has been committed.

shadow password file (UNIX)—Protects the password file from crackers by storing information other than the encrypted passwords in the normal password file and storing the encrypted passwords in the shadow password file that can be accessed only by users with root privileges.

shadowing (RAID)—See mirroring.

shared bus—Multiprocessor interconnection scheme that uses a single communication path to connect all processors and memory modules.

shared library—Collection of functions shared between several programs.

shared resource—Resource that can be accessed by more than one process.

shared virtual memory (SVM)—An extension of virtual memory concepts to multiprocessor systems; SVM presents the illusion of shared physical memory between processors and ensures coherence for pages accessed by separate processors.

shell—Application (typically GUI or text based) that enables a user to interact with an operating system

shortest-access-time-first (SATF) disk scheduling—Disk scheduling strategy that next services the request that requires the shortest access time (i.e., positioning time plus transmission time). SATF exhibits higher throughput than SPTF, but large requests can be indefinitely postponed by a series of smaller requests, and requests to the innermost or outermost cylinders can be indefinitely postponed by requests to intermediate cylinders.

shortest-latency-time-first (SLTF) disk scheduling—Disk scheduling strategy that examines all of the waiting requests and services the one with the shortest rotational delay first. This strategy has been shown to be close to the theoretical optimum and is relatively easy to implement.

shortest-positioning-time-first (SPTF) disk scheduling—Disk scheduling strategy that next services the request that requires the shortest positioning time. SPTF results in high throughput and a low mean response time, similar to SSTF, and can also indefinitely postpone requests to the innermost and outermost cylinders.

shortest-process-first (SPF) scheduling (multiprocessor)—Job-blind multiprocessor scheduling algorithm, employing a global run queue, that selects the process with the smallest processor time requirement to execute on an available processor.

shortest-process-first (SPF) scheduling (uniprocessor)—Nonpreemptive scheduling algorithm in which the scheduler selects a process with the smallest estimated runtime-to-completion and runs the process to completion.

shortest-remaining-time (SRT) scheduling—Preemptive version of SPF in which the scheduler selects a process with the smallest estimated remaining runtime-to-completion.

shortest-seek-time-first (SSTF) disk scheduling—Disk scheduling strategy that next services the request that is closest to the read/write

head's current cylinder (and thus incurs the shortest seek time), even if that is not the first one in the queue. By reducing average seek times, SSTF achieves higher throughput rates than FCFS, and mean response times tend to be lower for moderate loads. One significant drawback is that higher variances occur on response times because of the discrimination against the outermost and innermost tracks; in the extreme, starvation of requests far from the read/write heads could occur.

signal—Message sent by software to indicate that an event or error has occurred. Signals cannot pass data to their recipients.

signal (semaphores)—Operation on a semaphore that increments the value of the semaphore's variable. If threads are sleeping on the semaphore, the signal wakes one and decrements the semaphore's value by 1.

signal-and-continue monitor—Monitor that allows a thread to signal that the monitor is available, but does not require the thread to release the lock until it exits the monitor, at which point a signaled thread may enter the monitor.

signal-and-exit monitor—Monitor that requires a thread to release the lock on the monitor as soon as the thread signals another thread.

signal handler—Code that is executed in response to a particular signal type.

signal mask—Data structure that specifies which signals are not delivered to a thread. Depending on the signal type and default action, masked signals are either queued or dropped.

signaled state (Windows XP)—State in which a synchronization object can be placed, allowing one or more threads *waiting* on this object to awaken.

signature-scanning virus detection—Antivirus technique that relies on knowledge of virus code.

Simple Object Access Protocol (SOAP)—Messaging protocol for transporting information and instructions between Web services, using XML as a foundation for the protocol.

simulation—Performance evaluation technique in which an evaluator develops a computerized model of a system being evaluated. The model is then run to reflect the behavior of the system being evaluated.

single-instruction-stream, multiple-data-stream (SIMD) computer—Computer architecture consisting of one or more processing elements that execute instructions from a single instruction stream that act on multiple data items.

single-instruction-stream, single-data-stream (SISD) computer—Computer architecture in which one processor fetches instructions from a single instruction stream and manipulates a single data stream; this architecture describes traditional uniprocessors.

single-level directory structure—See flat directory structure.

single sign-on—Simplifies the authentication process by allowing the user to log in once, using a single password.

single-stream batch-processing system—Batch-processing system that places ready jobs in available partitions from one queue of pending jobs.

Single UNIX Specification—Specification (created by The Open Group) to which an operating system must conform to earn the right to display the UNIX trademark (see `www.unix.org/version3/overview.html`).

single-use timer (Windows XP)—Waitable timer object that is used once and then discarded.

single-user contiguous memory allocation system—System in which programs are placed in adjacent memory addresses and the system services only one program at a time.

size (file)—Amount of information stored in a file.

skeleton—Server-side stub.

slab (Linux)—Page of memory that reduces internal fragmentation due to small structures by storing multiple structures smaller than one page.

slab allocator (Linux)—Kernel entity that allocates memory for objects placed in the slab cache.

slab cache (Linux)—Cache that stores recently used slabs.

slave node (in a Beowulf cluster)—Beowulf cluster node that is not a head node.

sleep interval—Period of time (specified by the thread that is about to enter the *sleeping* state) during which a thread remains in the *sleeping* state.

sleep/wakeup lock—Mutual exclusion lock in which waiting processes block, and a releasing process wakes the highest-priority waiting process and gives it the lock.

sleeping state—Thread state in which a thread cannot execute until being returned to the *ready* state after the sleep interval expires.

Small Computer Systems Interface (SCSI)—Interface designed to support multiple devices and high-speed connections. The SCSI interface supports a larger number of devices than the less inexpensive IDE interface and is popular in Apple systems and computers containing large numbers of peripheral devices.

smallest-number-of-processes-first (SNPF) scheduling—Job-aware process scheduling algorithm, employing a global job-priority queue, where job priority is inversely proportional to the number of processes in a job.

smart card—Credit card size data store that serves many functions, including authentication and data storage.

socket—Interprocess communication mechanism that allows processes to exchange data by establishing direct communication channels. Enables processes to communicate over a network using `read` and `write` calls.

socket (network)—Software construct that represents one endpoint of a connection.

socket address—Unique identifier for a socket.

socketpair (Linux)—Pair of connected, unnamed sockets that can be used for bidirectional communication between processes on a single system.

soft affinity—Type of processor affinity in which the scheduling algorithm tries, but does not guarantee, to schedule a process only on a single node throughout its life cycle.

soft link—File that specifies the pathname corresponding to the file to which it is linked.

soft real-time scheduling—Scheduling policy that guarantees that real-time processes are scheduled with higher priority than non-real-time processes.

softirq (Linux)—Software interrupt handler that is reentrant and not serialized, so it can be executed on multiple processors simultaneously.

software interrupt handler (Linux)—Interrupt-handling code that can be performed without masking interrupts and can therefore be preempted.

Solaris—UNIX version based on both System V Release 4 and SunOS, designed by AT&T and Sun collaboratively.

Solo—Small operating system created by Per Brinch Hansen to demonstrate fail-safe concurrent programming.

source code—Program code typically written in a high-level language or assembly language that must be compiled or interpreted before it can be understood by a computer.

source tree (Linux)—Structure that contains source-code files and directories. Provides a logical organization to the monolithic Linux kernel.

space-partitioning scheduling—Multiprocessor scheduling strategy that attempts to maximize processor affinity by scheduling collaborative processes on a single processor (or single set of processors); the underlying assumption is that these processes will access the same shared data.

space-time product—Value that measures the product of a process's execution time (i.e., the duration for which a process occupies memory) and the amount of real-memory space the process occupies. Ideally, memory management strategies should reduce this quantity to increase a system's degree of multiprogramming.

sparse file (NTFS)—File with large blocks of regions filled with zeroes that NTFS tracks using a list of empty regions rather than explicitly recording each zero bit.

spatial locality—Empirical property that, in paging systems, states that processes tend to favor certain subsets of their pages, and that these pages tend to be near one another in a process's virtual address space. A process accessing sequential indices of an array exhibits spatial locality.

spawning a process—A parent process creating a child process.

specified user (file access control)—Identity of an individual user (other than the owner) that may use a file.

SPECmark—Standard benchmark for testing systems; SPECmarks are published by the **Standard Performance Evaluation Corporation (SPEC)**.

speculative loading—Technique whereby a processor retrieves from memory data specified by an instruction that has yet to be executed; when the instruction is executed, the processor performs a verifying load to ensure the data's consistency.

spin lock—Lock that provides mutually exclusive access to critical sections. When a process holding the lock is executing inside its critical section, any process concurrently executing on a different processor that attempts to acquire the lock before entering its critical section is made to busy wait.

spindle — Moving-head disk component that spins platters at high speeds.

spool (simultaneous peripheral operations online) — Method of I/O in which processes write data to secondary storage where it is buffered before being transferred to a low-speed device.

Sprite — Distributed operating system whose goal is transparency and complete consistency.

stability — Condition of a system that functions without error or significant performance degradation.

stack region — Section of process's address space that contains instructions and values for open procedure calls. The contents of the stack grow as a process issues nested procedure calls and shrink as called procedures return.

Standard Application (SAP) benchmarks — Popular benchmarks used to evaluate a system's scalability.

Standard Performance Evaluation Corporation (SPEC) — Organization that develops standard, relevant benchmarks (called SPECmarks), which are used to evaluate a variety of systems; SPEC publishes the results of tests with these benchmarks on real systems.

standardized interface — Allows each client/server pair to communicate using a single, common interface that is understood by both sides.

Standby Page List (Windows XP) — List of page frames that are consistent with their on-disk version and can be freed.

standby state (Windows XP) — Thread state denoting a thread that has been selected for execution.

star network — Network containing a hub that is directly connected to all other nodes in the network. The hub is responsible for relaying messages between nodes.

starvation — Situation in which a thread waits for an event that might never occur, also called indefinite postponement.

starvation limit (Linux) — Time at which high-priority processes are placed in the expired list to prevent low-priority processes from being indefinitely postponed.

state information — Data that describes the status of one or more resources.

state transition — Change of a process from one state to another.

stateful server — Keeps state information of the client requests — such as the file name, a pointer to the file and the current position in the file — so that the subsequent access to the file is easier and faster.

stateless server — The server does not keep state information of the client requests, so the client must specify which file to access in each request.

static analysis — Intrusion detection method which attempts to detect when applications have been corrupted by a hacker.

static load balancing — Category of load balancing algorithms that assign a fixed number of processors to a job when it is first scheduled.

static priority level (Linux) — Integer value assigned to a process when it is created that determines its scheduling priority.

static RAM (SRAM) — RAM that does not need to be refreshed and will hold data as long as it receives power.

static real-time scheduling algorithm — Scheduling algorithm that uses timing constraints to assign fixed priorities to processes before execution.

steganography — Technique that hides information within other information, derived from Latin roots meaning "covered writing."

stream — Sequence of objects fed to the processor.

STREAM — Popular synthetic benchmark which tests the memory subsystem.

stream socket — Socket that transfers data using the TCP protocol.

strip (RAID) — Smallest unit of data operated on by a RAID system. The set of strips at the same location on each disk is called a stripe.

stripe (RAID) — Set of strips at the same location on each disk in a RAID system. Striping enables RAID systems to access files using multiple disks at once, which improves transfer times.

structured programming — Disciplined approach to creating programs that are clear, correct and easy to modify.

Structured Query Language (SQL) — Database language that allows users to find data items that have certain properties, and also to create tables, specify integrity constraints, manage consistency and enforce security.

stub — prepares outbound data for transmission and translates incoming data so that it may be correctly interpreted

stub/skeleton layer in RMI — Contains parameter-marshaling structures analogous to the client and server stubs of RPC.

substitution cipher — Encryption technique whereby every occurrence of a given letter is replaced by a different letter. For example, if every "a" were replaced by a "b," every "b" by a "c," and so on the word "security" would encrypt to "tfdvsjuz."

sufficient conditions for deadlock — The four conditions — mutual exclusion, no-preemption, wait-for and circular-wait — which are necessary and sufficient for deadlock.

Sun Open Net Environment (Sun ONE) — Consists of three components — a vision, an architecture and a conceptual model for developing standards-based software.

superblock — Block containing information critical to the integrity of the file system (e.g., the location of the file system's free block list or bitmap, the file system identifier and the location of the file system root).

superscalar architecture — Technique in which a processor contains multiple execution units so that it can execute more than one instruction in parallel per clock cycle.

superuser (root user) (Linux) — User that may perform restricted operations (i.e., those that may damage the kernel and/or the system).

supervisor call — Request by a user process to the operating system to perform an operation on its behalf (also called a system call).

supervisor state — See kernel mode.

suspend/resume—Method of halting a process, saving its state, releasing its resources to other processes, then restoring its resources after the other processes have released them.

suspended state—Process state (either *suspendedblocked* or *suspended-ready*) in which a process is indefinitely removed from contention for time on a processor without being destroyed. Historically, this operation allowed a system operator to manually adjust the system load and/or respond to threats of system failure.

suspendedblocked state—Process state resulting from the process being suspended while in the *blocked* state. Resuming such a process places it into the *blocked* state.

suspendedready state—Process state resulting from the process being suspended while in the *ready* state. Resuming such a process places it into the *ready* state.

swap—Method of copying a process's memory contents to secondary storage, removing the process from memory and allocating the freed memory to a new process.

swap cache (Linux)—Cache of page table entries that describes whether a particular page exists in the system swap file on secondary storage. If a page table entry is present in the swap cache, then its corresponding page exists in the swap file and does not need to be written to the swap file.

swap instruction—Operation that exchanges the values of two variables atomically. This instruction simplifies mutual exclusion implementations by eliminating the possibility that a thread will be preempted while performing a read–modify–write memory operation.

switch—Node that routes messages between component nodes.

Symbian OS—Small operating system for smart phones (mobile phones with the functionality of a PDA).

symbol resolution—Procedure performed by a linker that matches external references in one module to external names in another.

symbol table—Part of an object module that lists an entry for each external name and each external reference found in the module.

symbolic name—Device-independent name (e.g., a pathname).

symmetric cryptography—See secret-key cryptography.

symmetric multiprocessor (SMP)—Multiprocessor system in which processors share all resources equally, including memory, I/O devices and processes.

symmetric policy—Dynamic load balancing policy that combines the sender-initiated policy and the receiver-initiated policy to provide maximum versatility to adapt to environmental conditions.

symmetrical multiprocessor organization—Scheme for delegating operating system responsibilities in which each processor can execute the single operating system.

synchronization—Coordination between asynchronous concurrent threads to sequentialize their access to shared resources.

synchronization segment (SYN)—In TCP, the first handshaking segment sent; contains the sequence number of the source host.

synchronization/acknowledgement segment (SYN/ACK)—In TCP, the second handshaking segment sent; acknowledges that the SYN segment was received and contains the sequence number of the destination host.

synchronized—Java keyword that imposes mutual exclusive access to code inside an object.

synchronous signal—Signal generated due to execution of the currently *running* thread's instructions.

syntax analyzer—See parser.

synthetic benchmark—Another name for a synthetic program.

synthetic program—Artificial program used to evaluate a specific component of a system or constructed to mirror the characteristics of a large set of programs.

SYSmark benchmark—Popular benchmark for desktop systems developed by Business Application Performance Corporation (BAPCo).

system call—Procedure call that requests a service from an operating system. When a process issues a system call, the processor execution mode changes from user mode to kernel mode to execute operating system instructions that respond to the call.

system file system (sysfs) (Linux)—File system that allows processes to access structures defined by the unified device model.

system penetration—Successful breach of computer security by an unauthorized external user.

system reaction time—Time from when a job is submitted to a system until the first time slice of service is given to that job.

system service (Windows XP)—Process that executes in the background whether or not a user is logged into the computer and typically executes the server side of a client/server application; a system service for Windows XP is similar to a daemon for Linux.

system tuning—Process of making fine adjustments to a system based on performance monitoring to optimize the system's execution for a specific operating environment.

system vector—Vector containing the results of microbenchmarks for a number of operating system primitives for a specific system, used in an application-specific evaluation.

system worker thread (Windows XP)—Thread controlled by the system that sleeps until a kernel-mode component queues a work item for processing.

systems programming—Development of software to manage a system's devices and applications.

T

table fragmentation—Wasted memory consumed by block mapping tables; small blocks tend to increase the number of blocks in the system, which increases table fragmentation.

take operation (in JavaSpaces)—Removes from the JavaSpaces service an object that matches the given criteria. Take operations, together with write and read operations, allow distributed applications to dynamically exchange objects within JavaSpaces services.

target computer (in process migration)—Computer to which the process is migrated.

task (Linux)—User execution context (i.e., process or thread) in Linux.

tasklet (Linux)—Software interrupt handler that cannot be executed simultaneously on multiple processors. Tasklets are used to execute nonreentrant bottom halves of interrupt handlers.

TCP window—Flow-control and congestion-control mechanism in which only a certain amount of data can be sent by the network layer without the receiver explicitly authorizing the sender to send more.

TCP/IP Protocol Stack—Hierarchical decomposition of computer communications functions into four levels of abstraction called layers. These layers are the application layer, transport layer, network layer and link layer.

teardown time—Time required by a system operator and the operating system to remove a job from a system after the job has completed.

temporal locality—Property of events that are closely related over time. In memory references, temporal locality occurs when processes reference the same memory locations repeatedly within a short period.

terminated state (Windows XP)—Thread state that denotes a thread has finished executing.

termination housekeeping—In the case of mutual exclusion algorithms, task performed by the operating system to ensure that mutual exclusion is not violated and that threads can continue to execute if a thread terminates while executing its critical section.

ternary relations—Relation of degree 3.

test-and-set—Instruction implemented in hardware that atomically tests the value of a variable and sets the value of the variable to true. This instruction simplifies mutual exclusion implementations by eliminating the possibility that a thread will be preempted while performing a read–modify–write memory operation.

text region—Section of a process's address space that contains instructions that are executed by a processor.

THE Multiprogramming System—First layered operating system architecture, created by Edsger Dijkstra.

thin client—Application that requires minimal client-side support.

thrashing—Excessive paging activity causing low processor utilization that occurs when a process's memory allocation is smaller than its working set. This results in poor performance, as the process spends most of its time waiting as pages are transferred between secondary storage and main memory.

thread—Entity that describes an independently executable stream of program instructions (also called a thread of execution or thread of control). Threads facilitate parallel execution of concurrent activities within a process.

thread environment block (TEB) (Windows XP)—User-space data structure that stores information about a thread, such as the critical sections owned by a thread and exception-handling information.

thread local storage (TLS) (Windows XP)—Area of a thread's process's address space where the thread can store private data, inaccessible to other threads.

thread pool (Windows XP)—Collection of worker threads that sleep until a request is queued to them, at which time one of the threads awakens and executes the queued function.

thread pooling—Threading technique that employs a number of kernel threads that exist for the duration of the process that creates them. This technique can improve performance by reducing the number of costly thread creation and termination operations.

thread state—Status of a thread (e.g., *running, ready, blocked,* and so on).

three-tier system—System which offers a separation of the application logic, the user interface and the data. The user interface tier (also called the client tier) communicates with the user. The application logic tier is responsible for the logic associated with the system's function. The data tier stores the information that the user wishes to access.

throughput—Amount of work performed per unit time. Throughput can be measured as the number of processes that complete per unit time.

thundering herd—Phenomenon that occurs when many processes awaken when a resource becomes available; only one process acquires the resource, and the others test the lock's availability and reblock, wasting processor cycles.

Ticket Granting Service (TGS) (Kerberos)—Server that authenticates client's rights to access specific network services.

Ticket-Granting Ticket (TGT) (Kerberos)—Ticket returned by Kerberos's authentication server. It is encrypted with the client's secret key that is shared with the authentication server. The client sends the decrypted TGT to the Ticket Granting Service to request a service ticket.

tightly coupled system—System in which processors share most resources; these systems provide higher performance but are less fault tolerant and flexible than loosely coupled systems.

time bomb—Virus that is activated when the clock on the computer matches a certain time or date.

time-of-day clock—Clock that measures time as perceived outside of a computer system, typically accurate to thousandths or millionths of a second.

time slice—See quantum.

time slicing—Scheduling each process to execute for at most one quantum before preemption.

time stamp—Records the local time at which the message was sent.

time stamping (nonrepudiation)—Technique that binds a time and date to a digital document, which helps solve the problem of nonrepudiation.

time-stamping agency—Organization that digitally time stamps a document that has been digitally signed.

timer-queue timer (Windows XP)—Timer that signals a worker thread to perform a specified function at a specified time.

timesharing scheduling—Multiprocessor scheduling technique that attempts to maximize parallelism by scheduling collaborative processes concurrently on different processors.

timesharing system—Operating system that enables multiple simultaneous interactive users.

timing—Raw measure of an isolated hardware performance metric, such as a BIPS rating, used for quick comparisons between systems.

timing constraint—Time period during which a process (or subset of a process's instructions) must complete.

TIPS (trillion instructions per second)—Unit used to categorize the performance of a particular computer; a rating of one TIPS means a processor can execute one trillion instructions per second.

tmpfs (temporary file system) (Linux)—Similar to ramfs, but does not require formatting before use, meaning that the system can store files in the tmpfs without the organizational overhead typical of most file systems.

token—Empty frame used to ensure that only one host is transmitting data at a time in the Token Ring and FDDI protocols.

token (in compiling)—Characters in a program, separated by the lexical analyzer, that generally represent keywords, identifiers, operators or punctuation.

token (in token-based authentication)—Unique identifier for authentication.

token-based authentication—Authentication technique that issues a token unique to each session, enabling users to access specific applications.

Token Ring—Protocol in which a token is circulated around a ring network. Only one host can own the token at a time, and only its owner can transmit data.

Tomcat—Official reference implementation of the JSP and servlet standards.

top half of an interrupt handler (Linux)—Nonpreemptible portion of interrupt-handling code that performs the minimum work required to acknowledge an interrupt before transferring execution to the preemptible bottom-half handler.

total ordering—Ensures that all events are observed in the same order by all processes.

trace—Tiny electrically conducting line that forms part of a bus.

trace (performance evaluation)—Record of real system activity, which is executed on systems to test how the system handles a sample workload.

track—Circular region of data on a platter. Sequential file data is typically placed contiguously on one track to improve access time by reducing seeking activity.

trailer—Control information appended to the end of a data message.

transaction—Atomic, mutually exclusive operation that either completes or is rolled back. Modifications to database entries are often performed as transactions to enable high performance and reduce the cost of deadlock recovery.

Transaction Processing Performance Council (TPC) benchmarks—Popular benchmarks which target database systems.

transaction transparency—Allows a system to achieve consistency by masking the coordination among a set of resources.

transaction wait-for graph (TWFG)—Graph that represents processes as nodes and dependencies as directed edges, which is used for distributed deadlock detection algorithms.

transceiver—Hardware device that attaches an Ethernet node to the network transmission medium. Transceivers test a shared medium to see if it is available before transmitting data, and monitor the medium to detect a simultaneous transmission called a collision.

transient virus—Virus that attaches itself to a particular computer program. The virus is activated when the program is run and deactivated when the program is terminated.

transistor—Miniature switch that either allows or prevents current from passing to enable processors to perform operations on bits.

***transition* state** (Windows XP)—Thread state denoting a thread that has completed a wait but is not yet ready to run because its kernel stack has been paged out of memory.

transitional fault (Windows XP)—Fault issued by the MMU when it tries to access a page that is in main memory, but whose page frame's status is set to standby, modified, or modified no-write.

Transitional Page List (Windows XP)—List of page frames whose data is in the process of being moved to or from disk.

translation lookaside buffer (TLB)—High-speed associative memory map that holds a small number of mappings between virtual page numbers and their corresponding page frame numbers. The TLB typically stores recently used page table entries, which improves performance for processes exhibiting locality.

Transmission Control Protocol (TCP)—Connection-oriented transmission protocol designed to provide reliable communication over unreliable networks.

Transmission Control Protocol/Internet Protocol (TCP/IP)—Family of protocols that provide a framework for networking on the Internet.

transmission medium—Material used to propagate a signal (e.g., optical fiber or copper wire).

transmission time—Time required for a data record to pass by the read/write head.

transparency—Hides the distribution aspects from users of a distributed system.

Transport Driver Interface (TDI) driver (Windows XP)—Network driver that exports a network interface to upper-level kernel-mode clients and interacts with low-level NDIS drivers.

transport layer—Set of protocols responsible for end-to-end communication of data in a network. This layer exists in both the TCP/IP model and the OSI model of network communication.

transport layer (in RMI)—Works with the RRL to send marshaled messages between the client and server in RMI.

transposition cipher—Encryption technique whereby the ordering of the letters is shifted. For example, if every other letter, starting with "s," in the word "security" creates the first word in the ciphertext and the remaining letters create the second word in the ciphertext, the word "security" encrypts to "scrt euiy."

trap—In the IA-32 specification, an exception generated by an error such as overflow (when the value stored by a register exceeds the capacity of the register). Also generated when program control reaches a breakpoint in code.

tree network—Hierarchical network that consists of multiple star networks. The hub of the first star network is the root of the tree.

Each node that this hub connects serves as a hub for another star network and is a root of a subtree.

Triple DES — Variant of DES that can be thought of as three DES systems in series, each with a different secret key that operates on a block. Also called 3DES.

triply indirect pointer — Pointer in an inode that locates a block of doubly indirect pointers.

Trojan horse — Malicious program that hides within a trusted program or simulates the identity of a legitimate program or feature, while actually causing damage to the computer or network when the program is executed.

TSS — Operating system designed by IBM in the 1960s that offered timesharing and virtual memory capabilities. Although it was never released commercially, many of its capabilities appeared in later IBM systems.

tunneling — Process of placing IPv6 datagrams in the body of IPv4 datagrams when communicating with routers that do not support IPv6.

tuple — Particular element of a relation.

turnaround time — Time from when a request is submitted until the system completes servicing it.

two-factor authentication — Authentication technique that employs two means to authenticate the user, such as biometrics or a smart card used in combination with a password.

two-tier system — A system in which the user interface resides on the client, the data resides on the server and the application logic lies on one or both of these components.

type (file) — Description of a file's purpose (e.g., an executable program, data or directory).

U

unblock — Remove a process from the *blocked* state after the event on which it was waiting has completed.

unblocked record — Record containing exactly one logical record for each physical record.

undivided coscheduling algorithm — Job-aware process scheduling algorithm in which processes of the same job are placed in adjacent locations in the global run queue, and processes are scheduled round-robin.

unicast address — IP address used to deliver data to a single host.

Unicode — Character set that supports international languages and is popular in Internet and multilingual applications.

unified device model (Linux) — Internal device representation that relates devices to device drivers, device classes and system buses. The unified device model simplifies power management and hot swappable device management.

uniform-memory-access (UMA) multiprocessor — Multiprocessor architecture that requires all processors to share all of main memory; in general, memory-access time is constant, regardless of which processor requests data, except when the data is stored in a processor's cache.

Uniform Naming Convention (UNC) format (Windows XP) — Format that specifies a file's pathname, including on which server and in which directory on that server the file is located.

Uniform Resource Identifier (URI) — Name that references a specific resource on the Internet.

Uniform Resource Locator (URL) — A URI used to access a resource in a common protocol such as HTTP and FTP. Consists of the protocol, host name, port and path of the resource.

UNIVAC 1 (UNIVersal Automatic Computer) — First computer to introduce a magnetic storage tape.

Universal Description, Discovery and Integration (UDDI) — Defines XML-based rules for building directories in which companies advertise themselves and their Web services.

universal serial bus (USB) — Serial bus interface that transfers data up to 480Mbits per second, can supply power to its devices and supports hot swappable devices.

universally unique identifier (UUID) — ID that is guaranteed, for all practical purposes, to be unique in the world. UUIDs uniquely identify an RPC interface.

UNIX — Operating system developed at Bell Laboratories that was written using the C high-level programming language.

unknown state (Windows XP) — Thread state denoting that the some error has occurred and the system does not know the state of the thread.

unmap a page (Linux) — To update page table entries to indicate that the corresponding page is no longer resident.

unreliable network — Network that may damage or lose packets.

unsafe state — State of a system in Dijkstra's banker's algorithm that might eventually lead to deadlock because there might not be enough resources to allow any process to finish.

unsignaled state (Windows XP) — State in which a synchronization object can be; threads *waiting* on this object do not awaken until the object transitions to the *signaled* state.

update (file) — Operation that modifies an existing data item in a file.

update image (RAID) — Method to reduce parity computation time by storing the difference between new and old parities in memory instead of performing a read–modify–write cycle.

update set (in Coda) — Specifies, to each member of the AVSG, the members of the AVSG that have successfully performed the write.

usable operating system — Operating system that has the potential to serve a significant user base by providing an easy-to-use interface and supporting a large set of user-oriented applications.

user classes — Classification scheme that specifies individual users or groups of users that can access a file.

User Datagram Protocol (UDP) — Connectionless transmission protocol which allows datagrams to arrive out of order, duplicated or not at all.

user directory — Directory that contains an entry for each of a user's files; each entry points to where the corresponding file is stored on its storage device.

user-level threads—Threading model in which all threads in a process are assigned to one execution context.

user mode—Mode of operation that does not allow processes to directly access system resources.

user-mode APC (Windows XP)—APC queued by user-mode thread and executed by the target thread when the target thread enters an alertable *wait* state.

user-mode driver (Windows XP)—Device driver that executes in user space.

User-Mode Linux (UML) (Linux)—Linux kernel that executes as a user process within a host Linux system.

user state—See user mode.

utilization—Fraction of time that a resource is in use.

V

V operation—Operation on a semaphore that increments the value of the semaphore's variable if there are no threads waiting on the semaphore. If threads are waiting, the *V* operation wakes one of these.

Valid Page List (Windows XP)—List of page frames that are currently in a process's working set.

validate a model—To demonstrate that a computer model is an accurate representation of the real system the model is simulating.

variable-partition multiprogramming—Method of assigning partitions that are the exact size of the job entering the system.

variance in response times—Measure of how much individual response times deviate from the mean response time.

variant—Virus whose code has been modified from its original form, yet still retains its malicious payload.

vector-based methodology—Method of calculating an application-specific evaluation of a system based on the weighted average of the microbenchmark results for the target system's primitives; the weights are determined by the target application's relative demand for each primitive.

vector processor—Type of SIMD computer containing one processing unit that executes instructions that operate on multiple data items.

Venus (in AFS)—User-level process that interacts with the Vice processes run on distributed file servers to govern distributed file access.

very long instruction word (VLIW)—Technique in which a compiler chooses which instructions a processor should execute in parallel and packages them into a single (very long) instruction word; the compiler guarantees that there are no dependencies between instructions that the processor executes at the same time.

Vice (in AFS)—Entity that governs distributed file access in AFS.

virtual address—Address that a process accesses in a virtual memory system; virtual addresses are translated to real addresses dynamically at execution time.

Virtual Address Descriptor (VAD) (Windows XP)—Structure in memory that contains a range of virtual addresses that a process may access.

virtual address space—Set of memory addresses that a process can reference. A virtual address space may allow a process to reference more memory than is physically available in the system.

virtual file system (Linux)—Interface that provides users with a common view of files and directories stored across multiple heterogeneous file systems.

virtual file system (VFS) (in distributed systems)—Provides the abstraction of a common file system at each client and is responsible for all distributed file operations.

virtual machine—Application that emulates the functionality of a computer system. A virtual machine can execute applications that are not directly compatible with the physical system that runs the virtual machine. The user "sees" the computer not as the virtual machine, but as the underlying physical machine.

virtual machine operating system—Software that creates the virtual machine.

virtual memory—Capability of operating systems that enables programs to address more memory locations than are actually provided in main memory. Virtual memory systems help remove much of the burden of memory management from programmers, freeing them to concentrate on application development.

virtual memory area (Linux)—Structure that describes a contiguous region of a process's virtual address space so that the kernel can perform operations on this region as a unit.

virtual memory manager (VMM) (Windows XP)—Executive component that manages virtual memory.

Virtual Private Network (VPN)—Technique that securely connects remote users to a private network using public communication lines. VPNs are often implemented using IPSec.

virus—Executable code (often sent as an attachment to an e-mail message or hidden in files such as audio clips, video clips and games) that attaches to or overwrites other files to replicate itself, often harming the system on which it resides.

virus signature—Segment of code that does not vary between virus generations.

VM operating system—One of the first virtual machine operating systems; developed at IBM in the 1960s and still used widely today; its latest version is the z/VM.

VMS—Operating system for the DEC VAX computers, designed by David Cutler's team.

volatile storage—Storage medium that loses data in the absence of power.

volatility (file)—Frequency with which additions and deletions are made to a file.

volume—Unit of storage that may hold multiple files.

volume (in AFS-2)—Introduced in AFS-2 to manage subtrees. Volumes are primarily of administrative value, allowing replication and isolation of certain subtrees, and are therefore transparent to users.

volume storage group (VSG) (in Coda)—Volumes are logical pieces of the file system and are replicated physically across multiple file servers. Servers that hold the same volume are known as a volume storage group (VSG).

voluntary page release—Occurrence when a process explicitly releases a page frame that it no longer needs. This can improve performance by reducing the number of unused page frames allocated to a process, leaving more memory available.

W

wait (semaphores)—If the variable in the semaphore is 0, then the operation blocks the calling thread. If the variable is greater than 0, the operation will decrement the variable by one and allow the calling thread to proceed. Wait is also called the *P* operation.

wait-die deadlock prevention strategy—Prevents deadlock by denying the wait-for condition. Assigns individual processes unique priorities based on when they were created. A process will wait if it was created after the process it is waiting on. A process will die if it was created before the process it is waiting on.

wait-for condition—One of the four necessary conditions for deadlock; states that deadlock can occur only if a process is allowed to wait for a resource while it holds another.

wait function (Windows XP)—Function called by a thread to wait for one or more dispatcher objects to enter a *signaled* state; calling this function places a thread in the *waiting* state.

wait queue—See wait set.

wait set—In Java, a set of threads waiting to reacquire the lock on a monitor.

waitable timer object (Windows XP)—Synchronization object that becomes *signaled* after a specified amount of time elapses.

waiting state—Thread state from which a thread cannot execute until transitioning to the *ready* state via a wake or notify operation.

wake—Thread operation that transitions its target from the *waiting* state to the *ready* state.

wall clock time—Measure of time as perceived by a user.

Web-based Distributed Authoring and Versioning (WebDAV) (Windows XP)—Network file sharing protocol that allows users to write data directly to HTTP servers and is designed to support collaborative authoring between groups in remote locations.

Web defacing—Attack that maliciously modifies an organization's Web site.

Web service methods (in .NET)—Methods contained in a .NET Web service class.

Web services—Set of services and related standards that can allow any two computer applications to communicate and exchange data over the Internet. Web services operate using open, text-based standards that enable components written in different languages and on different platforms to communicate. They are ready-to-use pieces of software on the Internet.

Web Services Description Language (WSDL)—Provides a standard method of describing Web services and their specific capabilities.

WebMark—Popular benchmark for Internet performance developed by Business Application Performance Corporation (BAPCo).

WebNFS—Allows NFS clients to access WebNFS-enabled servers with a minimum of protocol overhead. Marketed as the file system for the Web, WebNFS is designed to improve NFS functionality and performance over wide area Internet and intranets.

Whetstone—Classic synthetic program which measures how well systems handle floating point calculations, and has thus been helpful in evaluating scientific programs.

wide area network (WAN)—Type of network connecting two or more local area networks, usually operating over great geographical distances. WANs are generally implemented with a mesh topology and high-capacity connections. The largest WAN is the Internet.

Wi-Fi Protected Access (WPA)—Wireless security protocol intended to replace WEP by providing improved data encryption and by enabling user authentication.

Win32 environment subsystem (Windows XP)—User-mode process interposed between the executive and the rest of user space that provides a typical 32-bit Windows environment.

Win32 service (Windows XP)—See system service (Windows XP).

Win32 thread—Threads natively supported in the Microsoft 32-bit Windows line of operating systems.

WinBench 99—Popular synthetic program used extensively today in testing a system's graphics, disk and video subsystems in a Microsoft Windows environment.

window manager (Linux)—Application that controls the placement, appearance, size and other attributes of windows in a GUI.

Windows API—Microsoft's interface for applications that execute in a Windows environment. The API enables programmers to request operating system services, which free the application programmer from writing the code to perform these operations and enables the operating system to protect its resources.

Windows Driver Model (WDM) (Windows XP)—Standard driver model that enables source-code compatibility across all Windows platforms; each WDM driver must be written as a bus driver, function driver or filter driver and support PnP, power management and WMI.

Windows Management Instrumentation (WMI) (Windows XP)—Standard that describes how drivers provide measurement and instrumentation data to users (e.g., configuration data, diagnostic data or custom data) and allow user applications to register for WMI driver-defined events.

Windows sockets version 2 (Winsock 2)—Adaptation and extension of BSD sockets for the Windows environment.

Windows XP Embedded—Embedded operating system, which uses the same binary files as Windows XP but allows designers to choose only those components applicable for a particular device.

WinHTTP (Windows XP)—API that supports communication between clients and servers over an HTTP session.

WinINet (Windows XP)—API that allows applications to interact with FTP, HTTP and Gopher protocols to access resources over the Internet.

Wired Equivalent Privacy (WEP)—Wireless security protocol that encrypts transmitted data and prevents unauthorized access to the wireless network.

word—Number of bits a system's processor(s) can process at once. In the data hierarchy, words are one level above bytes.

worker thread—Kernel thread that is a member of a thread pool. Worker threads may be mapped to any user thread in the process that created its thread pool.

working directory—Directory that contains files that a user can access directly.

working set—A program's favored subset of pages in main memory. Given a working set window, w, the process's working set of pages $W(t, w)$, is defined as the set of pages it references during the process-time interval $t - w$ to t.

working set (Windows XP)—All of the pages in main memory that belong to a specific process.

working set maximum (Windows XP)—Upper limit on the number of pages a process may have simultaneously in main memory.

working set minimum (Windows XP)—Number of pages in main memory the working set manager leaves a process when it executes the page-trimming algorithm.

working set theory of program behavior—Theory presented by Denning, which asserts that for a program to run efficiently, the system must maintain that program's favored subset (i.e., its working set) of pages in main memory. Given a working set window, w, the process's working set of pages $W(t, w)$, is defined as the set of pages referenced by the process during the process-time interval $t - w$ to t. Choosing the window size, w, is a crucial aspect of implementing working set memory management.

working set window size—Value that determines how far into the past the system should consider to determine what pages are in the process's working set.

workload—Measure of the amount of work that has been submitted to a system; evaluators determine typical workloads for a system and evaluate the system using these workloads.

workstation login scripts—Simple form of single sign-on in which users log in at their workstations, then choose applications from a menu.

World Wide Web (WWW)—Collection of hyperlinked documents accessible via the Internet using the Hypertext Transfer Protocol (HTTP). Web documents are typically written in languages such as HyperText Markup Language (HTML) and Extensible Markup Language (XML).

worm—Executable code that spreads and infects files over a network. Worms rarely require any user action to propagate, nor do they need to be attached to another program or file to spread.

worst-fit strategy—Memory placement strategy that places an incoming job in the largest hole in memory.

wound—When a process is wounded by another process, it will be rolled back.

wound-wait deadlock prevention strategy—Prevents deadlock by denying the no-preemption condition. Assigns individual processes unique priorities based on when they were created. A process requesting a resource held by another process will wound that process if the first one was created before the other. A process will wait if it was created after the process it is waiting on.

write (file)—Operation that outputs a data item from a process to a file.

write access (virtual memory)—Access right that enables a process to modify the contents of a page or segment; see also execute access, read access and append access.

write access (file)—Permission to access a file for writing.

write-back caching—Technique that writes buffered data to disk periodically, enabling the operating system to batch multiple I/Os that are serviced using a single request, which can improve system performance.

write broadcast—Technique for maintaining memory coherence in which the processor that performs a write broadcasts the write throughout the system.

Write-Once, Read-Many (WORM) medium—Storage medium that can be modified only once, but whose contents can be accessed repeatedly.

write operation (in JavaSpaces)—Operation that adds an object into the JavaSpaces service.\

write-through caching—Technique that writes data both to the disk cache buffer and to disk each time cached data is modified. This technique prevents the system from batching requests, but reduces the possibility of inconsistent data in the event of a system crash.

write-through mode (Windows XP)—Method of writing to a pipe whereby write operations do not complete until the data being written is confirmed to be in the buffer of the receiving process.

X

XOR (exclusive-or) operation—Operation on two bits that returns 1 if the two bits are not the same, 0 otherwise. RAID levels 3–5 use the XOR operation to generate parity bits.

Z

z/OS—IBM operating system for zSeries mainframes and the latest version of MVS.

Zeroed Page List (Windows XP)—List of page frames whose bits are all set to zero.

zone (memory) (Linux)—Region of physical memory. Linux divides main memory in the low, normal and high zones to allocate memory according to the architectural limitations of a system.

zone allocator—Memory subsystem that allocates pages from the zone to which it is assigned.

Index

X

Z